DEFENSE ACQUISITION GUIDEBOOK (DAG

The Defense Acquisition System exists to manage the Nation's in
and product support necessary to achieve the National Security S.
Armed Forces. In that context, our objective is to acquire quality products that satisfy user needs with
measurable improvements to mission capability at a fair and reasonable price. The fundamental
principles and procedures that the Department follows in achieving those objectives are described in DoD
Directive 5000.01 and DoD Instruction 5000.02.

The Defense Acquisition Guidebook is designed to complement those policy documents by providing the
acquisition workforce with discretionary best practice that should be tailored to the needs of each
program. The Guidebook is not a rule book or a checklist and does not require specific compliance with
the business practice it describes. It is intended to inform thoughtful program planning and facilitate
effective program management.

The DAG includes the following chapter content:

Chapter 1, Program Management, provides the principal concepts and business practice needed to
thoughtfully organize, plan, and execute a DoD acquisition program regardless of acquisition category,
program model, or program type. **Page 1.**

Chapter 2, Analysis of Alternatives, Cost Estimating and Reporting, addresses resource estimation and
program life-cycle costs, as well as the processes for conducting Analysis of Alternatives. **Page 155.**

Chapter 3, Systems Engineering, describes standard systems engineering processes and how they apply
to the DoD acquisition system. **Page 170.**

Chapter 4, Life-Cycle Sustainment, provides guidance for program managers and program support
managers to develop and execute successful sustainment strategies. **Page 380.**

Chapter 5, Manpower Planning and Human Systems Integration explains the total-systems approach to
HSI, including documenting manpower, personnel and training elements, and the use of program
manager tools that appropriately incorporate HSI considerations into the acquisition process. **Page 431.**

Chapter 6, Acquiring Information Technology and Business Systems, describes policy and procedure
applicable to the development of DoD Information Technology (IT). **Page 449.**

Chapter 7, Intelligence Support to Acquisition, provides information to enable the program manager to
use intelligence information and data to ensure maximum war-fighting capability at minimum risk to cost
and schedule. **Page 501.**

Chapter 8, Test and Evaluation, supplements direction and instruction in DoD Directive 5000.01 and DoD
Instruction 5000.02 with processes and procedures for planning and executing an effective and affordable
T&E program. **Page 518.**

Chapter 9, Program Protection, explains the actions needed to ensure effective program protection
planning throughout the acquisition life cycle. **Page 626.**

Chapter 10, Acquisition of Services, describes the principles of successful services acquisition based on
the Seven Steps to the Service Acquisition Process included in DoD Instruction 5000.74, Defense
Acquisition of Services. **Page 669.**

CH 1-1. Purpose

The Defense Acquisition Guidebook (DAG), Chapter 1, is intended to provide the information needed to thoughtfully organize, plan, and execute a DoD acquisition program regardless of acquisition category, program model, or program type.

CH 1–2. Background

This Chapter describes the principal concepts and business practice that support the development and management of defense acquisition programs. The objective is to provide the program management team with a primer--- in one readily accessible on line location. The Chapter describes the larger management framework in which DoD acquisition is conducted while providing the information and the management tools needed to thoughtfully design and effectively execute an acquisition strategy tailored to the capability to be acquired.

CH 1–3. Business Practice

This section describes the Departments operating context and the information needed to organize and plan a successful acquisition program. The unifying concept for this Section is the great value derived from attending to the fundamentals of program management.

CH 1–3.1 The External and Internal Acquisition Environment

Planning an acquisition requires an understanding of the external and internal environments: the three DoD decision support systems and the organization, staffing, and operation of a Program Management Office (PMO).

The external environment, DoD decision support systems (aka "BIG A"), consists of the Joint Capabilities Integration and Development System (JCIDS); Planning, Programming, Budgeting, and Execution (PPBE); and the Defense Acquisition System (DAS). In combination the three systems provide an integrated approach to strategic planning, identification of needs for military capabilities, program and budget development, and systems acquisition. Effective Program Managers (PMs) achieve synchronization among requirements, budgeting, and execution by maintaining a keen awareness of the status of their program relative to each of the decision support systems.

An overview of the interaction and relationships among the three DoD decision support systems is presented in CH 1–3.2. "Big A". For detailed discussions on each of the three DoD decision support systems, refer to CH 1-3.2.1 (JCIDS), CH 1–3.2.2 (PPBE), and CH 1-3.2.3 (DAS).

The internal environment is the program office, with supporting organizations that function as an Integrated Product Team (IPT) for the duration of the program. As the program is executed, the Leads for various disciplines such as Systems Engineering (SE), Test and Evaluation (T&E), Sustainment, Financial Management, etc., develop and implement specific plans for their areas of responsibility. They also actively participate in the development of an event-based PMO IMP. The PMO IMP includes detailed criteria for events at a level of detail to effectively manage the program from prior to initiation to fielding and life-cycle support. That is not to say that at initiation all events can or should be planned to an execution level of detail with specified accomplishments and criteria. A PMO IMS is developed from the IMP so that both a top-down and bottoms-up approach are in place to manage program development and execution.

Further discussion on the PMO IMP and related IMS is provided in CH 1–3.4.2 PMO IMP/IMS.

CH 1–3.2 "BIG A"

Commonly called DoD's decision support systems, "BIG A" acquisition consists of the JCIDS, PPBE, and the DAS (of phases and milestones), sometimes called "Little A."

- **Joint Capabilities Integration and Development System (JCIDS)**. The systematic method to support the Joint Requirements Oversight Council (JROC) and Chairman of the Joint Chiefs of Staff (CJCS) responsibilities in identifying, assessing, validating, and prioritizing Joint military capability requirements. JCIDS provides a transparent process that allows the JROC to balance Joint equities and make informed decisions on validation and prioritization of capability requirements. CJCS Instruction 5123.01 describes the roles and responsibilities of the JROC, while CJCS Instruction 3170.01, Joint Capabilities Integration and Development System, and Manual for the Operation of the Joint Capabilities Integration and Development System (commonly referred to as the JCIDS Manual describe the policies and procedures for the requirements process.
- **Planning, Programming, Budgeting, and Execution (PPBE) Process.** The Department's strategic planning, program development, and resource determination process. The PPBE process is used to craft plans and programs that satisfy the demands of the National Security Strategy (NSS) within resource constraints. Per DoDD 7045.14, The Planning, Programming, Budgeting, and Execution (PPBE) process serves as the annual resource allocation process for DoD within a quadrennial planning cycle. The National Military Strategy (NMS), force development guidance, program guidance, and budget guidance are the principal guides used in this process. Programs and budgets are formulated annually. The budget covers 1 year, and the program encompasses an additional 4 years.
- **Defense Acquisition System (DAS).** The management process by which the Department acquires weapon systems, automated information systems, and services. See DoDI 5000.02. Although the system is based on centralized policies and principles, it allows for decentralized and streamlined execution of acquisition activities. This approach provides flexibility and encourages innovation, while maintaining strict emphasis on discipline and accountability.

While this Chapter focuses on the DAS, it is important to remember that the acquisition system interacts with other systems that control the finances and requirements for items being acquired. Moreover, all three of these systems are driven by broader policies and strategies created and evolved to meet the missions given to the Department by the nation. Figure 1 illustrates the three principal systems that affect acquisition of defense capability.

Figure 1: DoD Decision Support Systems

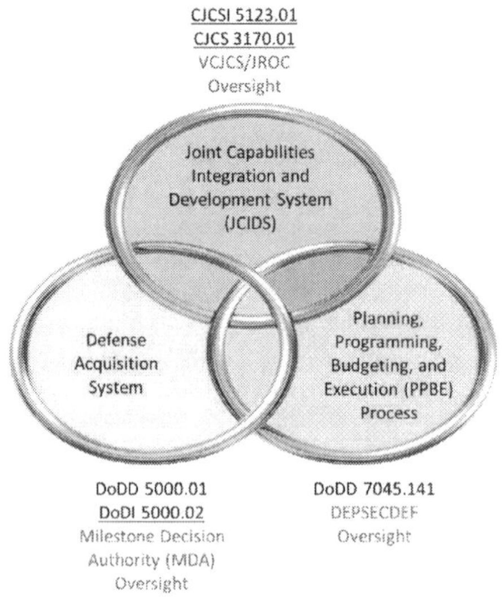

CJCSI 5123.01
CJCS 3170.01
VCJCS/JROC
Oversight

Joint Capabilities Integration and Development System (JCIDS)

Defense Acquisition System

Planning, Programming, Budgeting, and Execution (PPBE) Process

DoDD 5000.01
DoDI 5000.02
Milestone Decision Authority (MDA)
Oversight

DoDD 7045.141
DEPSECDEF
Oversight

The three systems provide an integrated approach to strategic planning, identification of needs for military capabilities, systems acquisition, and program and budget development.

Effective interaction of the processes is essential in order to ensure the Department's development and delivery of Doctrine, Organization, Training, materiel, Leadership and Education, Personnel, Facilities–Policy (DOTmLPF-P) solutions to meet current and future warfighter requirements. Together, the three processes provide a means to determine, validate, and prioritize capability requirements and associated capability gaps and risks, and then fund, develop, and field non-materiel and materiel capability solutions for the warfighter in a timely manner. The three systems impact a program differently. The requirements process is a capability gap process, the PPBE is a fiscal- and time-based process, and the acquisition system is an event-based process. Therefore, PMs need to ensure their programs are continuously synchronized with the realities and imperatives of the BIG A three decision support systems.

Requirements (JCIDS), resources (PPBE), and acquisition (DAS) are closely aligned and operate simultaneously with full cooperation and in close coordination. Throughout the product's life cycle, adjustments are made to keep the three processes aligned. Requirements (either Key Performance Parameters [KPPs] or Key System Attributes [KSAs]) may have to be adjusted to conform to technical and fiscal realities. Acquisition programs may have to adjust to changing requirements and funding availability. Budgeted funds may have to be adjusted to make programs executable or to adapt to evolving validated requirements and priorities. Those responsible for the three processes at the DoD level, and within the DoD Components, work closely together to adapt to changing circumstances, and to identify and resolve issues as early as possible.

The intent of Figure 1 is to emphasize that acquisition requires the synchronization of requirements (JCIDS), resources (PPBE), and the acquisition system (DAS) across the program's acquisition life cycle. A more expansive view of the DAS, which includes the Contracting process, is shown in Figure 2. This takes into account other major sources of regulatory direction (for contracts), through which most acquisition is accomplished, and includes the Federal Acquisition Regulation (FAR), Defense FAR Supplement (DFARS), and Service-specific contracting regulations.

Figure 2: Five Dimensions of DoD Decision Support Systems

JCIDS	Defense Acquisition System		PPBE
Requirements Management	Program Management	Contract Management	Resource Management

	JCIDS Requirements Management	Defense Acquisition System Program Management	Defense Acquisition System Contract Management	PPBE Resource Management
Rules	CJCSI 3170.01 series JCIDS Manual	DOD 5000 Series	FAR DFARS	DPG/POM/Budget DoD 7000 Series
Players	User/Service Chief VCJCS/JROC	PEO/CAE/DAE	PCO/HCA/SPE DCMA	PEO/Service HQ/OSD OMB/Congress
Reviews	JROC	Milestones	Business Clearance	DMAG
Decisions	Capability Need	Next Phase	Contracts	Funding/Resources
Focus	Threat/Capability	System Life Cycle R&D/Proc/O&S	Contractor Performance	Annual Funding & FYDP

CJCS: Chairman, Joint Chiefs of Staff
CJCSI: Chairman, Joint Chiefs of Staff Instruction
CAE: Component Acquisition Executive
DAB: Defense Acquisition Board
DMAG: Deputy's Management Advisory Group
DFARS: Defense FAR Supplement

DCMA: Defense Contract Mgmt Agency
DPG: Defense Planning Guidance
FAR: Federal Acquisition Regulation
FYDP: Future Years' Defense Program
HCA: Head of Contracting Activity
JROC: Joint Requirements Oversight Council
OMB: Office of Management & Budget

OSD: Office of the Secretary of Defense
PCO: Procuring Contracting Officer
PEO: Program Executive Officer
POM: Program Objectives Memorandum
SPE: Senior Procurement Executive
VCJS: Vice Chairman, Joint Chiefs of Staff

Figure 2 compares the DoD decision support systems in five dimensions: Rules, Players, Reviews, Decisions, and Focus.

The next three subsections provide brief descriptions of the PPBE, JCIDS, and DAS processes.

CH 1–3.2.1 Capability Requirements

JCIDS plays a key role in identifying the capabilities needed by warfighters to support the National Security Strategy (NSS), the National Defense Strategy (NDS), and the National Military Strategy (NMS). Successful delivery of those capabilities relies on the JCIDS working in concert with the resourcing and acquisition decision support systems. JCIDS supports the Chairman and JROC in advising the Secretary of Defense (SECDEF) on identifying, assessing, and prioritizing joint military capability needs. JCIDS is a Joint Concepts-centric capabilities identification and requirements development process that enables joint forces to meet short-, mid-, and long-term future military challenges. The JCIDS process assesses existing and proposed capabilities in light of their contribution to future joint concepts and warfighting needs. The DoD created the JCIDS to support the statutory JROC responsibility of validating joint warfighting requirements.

The primary objective of the JCIDS process is to ensure the capabilities needed by joint warfighters to successfully execute their missions are consistent with their associated operational performance attributes. This is accomplished through an open process that provides the JROC with the information needed to make decisions on needed capabilities. The requirements development process then provides validated capability needs and associated performance attributes used by the materiel provider as the basis for acquiring the appropriate weapon systems. Additionally, the PPBE process informs the JCIDS with affordability information and goals through the Capabilities-Based Assessment (CBA), which identifies needed capabilities, capability gaps, and potential non-materiel (DOTmLPF-P) and materiel solution options.

JCIDS is reciprocal to the DoDD 5000.01 direction for early and continuous collaboration throughout the DoD. The system uses a capabilities-based approach that leverages the expertise of government agencies, industry, and academia by encouraging collaboration between operators and materiel providers early in the process. It is imperative that the Combat Developer and the Materiel Developer collaborate throughout the JCIDS process to ensure development of a requirement document that is stable, technologically feasible, and affordable. JCIDS defines interoperable, joint capabilities that should best meet future needs. The DoD acquisition community then delivers a technologically sound, sustainable, affordable "materiel solution" of militarily useful capability to the Joint warfighters.

JCIDS policy is described in CJCS Instruction 3170.01 while the role of the JROC is described in CJCSI 5123.01. The JCIDS Manual provides the details necessary for identifying, describing, and justifying joint warfighting capabilities. The manual also includes the formats that describe the content required for each JCIDS document.

For Major Defense Acquisition Programs (MDAPs) or Major Automated Information Systems (MAIS) subject to OSD oversight, the products of the JCIDS process directly support the Defense Acquisition Board (DAB) in advising the Milestone Decision Authority (MDA) for Acquisition Category (ACAT) ID programs (and ACAT IAM programs that have not been delegated). JCIDS also provides similar support to all other acquisition programs, regardless of the MDA.

Figure 3: JCIDS and Defense Acquisition

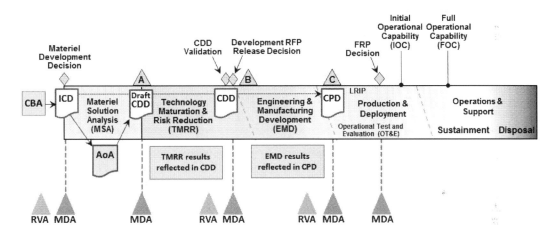

Figure 3 depicts the following key points:

- JCIDS uses a variety of approaches to determine capability requirements. The JCIDS Manual identifies some of these approaches, to include the conduct of a Capabilities-Based Assessment or other study. The key JCIDS intent is to identify the high-level operational capability requirements, establish quantifiable attributes and metrics, and articulate the traceability from those capability requirements to the tasks, conditions, standards, missions, threats, and overall strategic guidance.

- JCIDS analysis compares capability requirements to current and programmed force capabilities to determine if there are any capability gaps that present an unacceptable level of risk and warrant development of capability solutions to mitigate or eliminate the gaps in capability. The DoD may then address these gaps using a combination of materiel and/or non-materiel solutions (non-materiel solutions would be changes to DOTmLPF-P).
- The Initial Capabilities Document (ICD) documents the results JCIDS analysis (commonly a CBA or other study) that the appropriate authority validates prior to the Materiel Development Decision (MDD). The operational attributes identified in the ICD are mission, not system specific, and also inform the Analysis of Alternatives (AoA) conducted during the MSA phase.
- The results of the AoA then inform the development of a draft Capabilities Development Document (CDD) to support Milestone A and inform the RFP for the TMRR phase contract. This draft CDD contains performance attributes, to include KPPs, KSAs and APAs that reflect the capability requirements for the solution selected at Milestone A. Toward the end of the TMRR phase, the prototyping and other activities (to include an AoA update, when appropriate) provide information to update the draft CDD that ultimately results in a validated CDD prior to the Development RFP Release Decision. This validated CDD in-turn informs the RFP for the EMD phase. Also, the KPPs from this validated CDD are inserted verbatim into the APB approved by the MDA at Milestone B.
- The validated CDD then drives EMD phase activities. After the system-level critical design review (CDR), this CDD is updated and designated a Capabilities Production Document (CPD), which is then validated prior to Milestone C. For an incremental acquisition program, the CDD may contain performance attributes for more than one increment while the CPD may contain only those attributes for the first production increment.

Fundamental to a successful program acquisition is the ability of the Requirements Manager (RM) to identify and clearly communicate warfighter capability needs and gaps and to team with the Materiel Developer on defining what is expected, both in terms of explicit and implicit requirements. Of significance when planning a program is realism in terms of understanding not only KPPs, KSAs, and APAs, but also those requirements resulting from sound engineering and manufacturing practice, with the ultimate goal of maturing and producing a design in the necessary quantities needed by the warfighter. This teaming arrangement also requires understanding further infrastructure requirements to utilize and sustain the new capability. Failure to recognize those latter imperatives leads to rework and cost/schedule growth.

Further information on CBA, as well as the nature and role of the Initial Capabilities Document (ICD), Capability Development Document (CDD), and Capability Production Document (CPD) can be found in the JCIDS Manual.

CH 1–3.2.1.1 Joint Requirements Oversight Council

10 USC 181 (para (b)), establishes JROC responsibilities. The Vice Chairman of the Joint Chiefs of Staff chairs the JROC and is also a member of the DAB. The Vice Chiefs of each military service are statutory members of the JROC. Also, unless directed by the JROC Chairman, the various Combatant Commanders (or Deputy Commanders) are highly encouraged to participate as appropriate when matters of that command will be under consideration by the JROC. For ACAT I and IA programs, and other programs designated as high-interest, the Joint Requirements Oversight Council (JROC) reviews and validates all JCIDS documents under its purview. For Acquisition Category ID and IAM programs, the JROC also makes recommendations to the DAB, based on such reviews. For all other ACAT level programs (ACAT II and III) the Service's respective Army Requirements Oversight Council (AROC), Marine Corps Requirements Oversight Council (MROC), and Air Force Capability Development Council (AFCDC) address the capability gaps and validate the requirements documents.

10 USC 181 (para (d)), mandates key stakeholder advisors from across the Department and inter-DoD Agencies, when appropriate, to shape decisions in support of the Joint warfighter. This same Act specifically designated the following officials of the DoD as civilian advisors to the JROC:

- The Under Secretary of Defense (Acquisition, Technology, and Logistics)
- The Under Secretary of Defense (Comptroller)
- The Under Secretary of Defense (Policy)
- The Director of Cost Assessment and Program Evaluation
- The Director of Operational Test and Evaluation

Other civilian officials of the DoD may be designated by the SECDEF in accordance with the statute.

CH 1–3.2.2 Planning, Programming, Budgeting, and Execution

The purpose of the Planning, Programming, Budgeting, and Execution (PPBE) process is to allocate resources within the DoD. It is important for PMs and their staffs to be aware of the nature and timing of each of the events in the PPBE process since they may be called upon to provide critical information that could be important to program funding and success. The primary output of the PPBE process is the DoD funding proposed to be included in the President's Budget (PB) that is submitted to Congress.

In the PPBE process, the SECDEF establishes policies, strategy, and prioritized goals for the Department, which are subsequently used to guide resource allocation decisions that balance the guidance with fiscal constraints. The PPBE process consists of three phases: Planning, Programming, and Budgeting.

CH 1–3.2.2.1 Planning

The Planning Phase of PPBE is a collaborative effort by the Office of the Secretary of Defense and the Joint Staff, with participation of the Services and Combatant Commands (COCOMs). It begins with issuance of the NSS (which defines national-level strategic outcomes that are to be achieved and are further refined in the SECDEF's Defense Strategic Guidance [DSG] and the CJCS's National Military Strategy [NMS]). It culminates with the Defense Planning Guidance (DPG). The DPG depicts a strategic view of the security environment and helps shape the investment blueprint for the Future Years Defense Plan (FYDP) (five years), informing the "programmers" on what to include in their Program Objectives Memorandum (POM) submission.

CH 1–3.2.2.2 Programming

The purpose of the Programming Phase is to allocate resources consistent with the DPG to support the roles and missions of the Military Services (i.e., Army, Air Force, Navy, and Marines) and Defense Agencies. During the Programming Phase, planning guidance contained in the DPG and other documents, OSD programming guidance, and congressional guidance are translated into detailed allocations of time-phased resource requirements that include forces, personnel, and funds. This is accomplished through systematic review and approval processes that "cost out" force objectives and personnel resources in financial terms for 5 years into the future. This process gives the SECDEF and the President an idea of the impact that present-day decisions have on the future defense posture. The OSD Director, Cost Assessment and Program Evaluation (D/CAPE) is responsible for overall coordination of the Programming Phase and is considered the *official Lead* for this phase of PPBE.

CH 1–3.2.2.3 Budgeting

The Budgeting phase of the PPBE process includes formulation, justification, execution, and control of the budget. The primary purpose is to scrutinize the first 1 or 2 years of a program's budget to ensure efficient use of resources. The Under Secretary of Defense (Comptroller) (USD(C)) is responsible for overall coordination and is the Lead for the Budgeting phase of PPBE. While DoD Components submit their POMs to D/CAPE in mid-July and the Secretary of Defense/Deputy Secretary of Defense

(SECDEF/DEPSECDEF) is likely to sign the Program Decision Memorandum (PDM) in early November, the DoD Components submit their Budget Estimate Submission (BES), to the USD(C) in the fall, and SECDEF/DEPSECDEF signs Program Budget Decisions (PBDs) in November and December. The USD(C) and budget examiners from Office of Management and Budget (OMB) conduct a review of the DoD Components' BES submission. Per agreement between OSD and OMB, senior budget examiners from OMB participate in the DoD budget review process at this point to preclude the necessity of OSD submitting the Defense Budget to OMB for a separate review as is required for all other federal agencies. The USD(C) and OMB emphasis during this review is on proper budget justification and ability to execute the proposed budget. OSD decisions pertaining to budget issues are reflected in PBDs (November/December) and incorporate all OSD decisions made during the Budgeting Phase. Four of the areas examined by the USD(C) budget analysts during the review and "scrub" of the Services' and Agencies' budget submissions include:

- Program Pricing
- Program Phasing
- Funding Policies
- Budget Execution

CH 1–3.2.2.4 Execution

The final activity in the PPBE process is the Execution Review, which occurs concurrently with the Program and Budget reviews. The purpose of the Program Review is to prioritize the programs that best meet military strategy needs, whereas the purpose of the Budget Review is to decide how much to spend on each of these programs. The purpose of the Execution Review, therefore, is to assess what is received for the money spent (e.g., actual performance versus planned performance). Performance metrics are developed and used to measure program achievements and attainment of performance goals. These metrics are analyzed to determine whether resources have been appropriately allocated.

The decisions associated with all phases of the PPBE process are reflected in the FYDP.

CH 1–3.2.2.5 Funding Realism

Based on the processes and reviews discussed previously, it is important that PMs recognize funding realism in terms of resources required to execute the program strategy—including personnel, funding, and facilities—that ought to be carefully planned, budgeted, and executed by the program. Further, it is well to recognize that the cycle for establishing and gaining funding is quite different and separate from the cycle for planning and executing an acquisition program.

CH 1–3.2.3 Defense Acquisition System

The Defense Acquisition System (DAS) is the management process for all DoD acquisition programs. DoDD 5000.01, Defense Acquisition System, provides the overarching management principles and mandatory policies that govern the DAS. DoDI 5000.02, Operation of the Defense Acquisition System, provides detailed procedures that guide the operation of the system through statutory and regulatory requirements that govern defense acquisition programs. One key principle of the DAS is the use of acquisition categories (ACATs). Programs are categorized by definitions and dollar thresholds. DoDI 5000.02 (Encl. 1, Table 1) prescribes the assignment of the cognizant Milestone Decision Authority (MDA) depending upon ACAT.

This results in a tiered acquisition category designation based on statutory requirements of increasing dollar value and management interest that are subject to increasing levels of oversight and reporting. While the category into which a program falls impacts acquisition procedures, documentation, and oversight criteria, the structure of a DoD acquisition program and the procedures employed should be tailored to the characteristics of the materiel solution being acquired, and consistent with the circumstances associated with the program, including operational urgency, risk factors, and affordability.

Statutory requirements are complied with, unless waived in accordance with relevant provisions. Figure 4 illustrates the interaction between the Capability Requirements Process of the JCIDS and the DAS.

Figure 4: Interaction between JCIDS and Defense Acquisition System

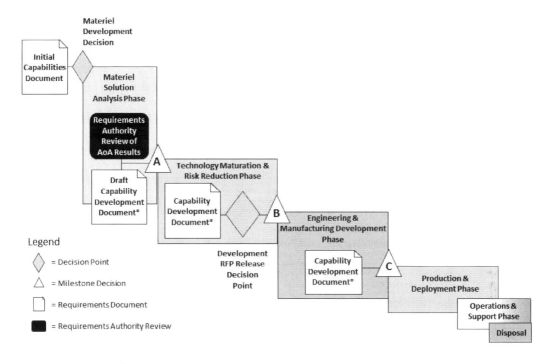

* Or equivalent Approved/Validated Requirements Document.

Note. AoA = Analysis of Alternatives; RFP = Request for Proposal.

All acquisition programs respond to validated capabilities requirements that require the acquisition of a materiel solution.

CH 1–3.2.3.1 Acquisition Category Definition Criteria, Thresholds, and Reporting

The programs requiring the highest level of investment are known as Major Defense Acquisition Programs (MDAPs) or Major Automated Information System (MAIS) programs. MDAPs and MAIS programs have the most extensive statutory and regulatory reporting requirements. Refer to DoDI 5000.02 (Encl. 1, Table 1) for a description and categorization criteria for ACAT I through ACAT III.

Acquisition programs are divided into categories to facilitate decentralized decision-making, execution, and compliance with statutorily imposed requirements. The categories determine the level of review, decision authority, and applicable procedures. Figure 5 provides an overview of the Acquisition Categories, Decision Authority, and Reviews.

Figure 5: Acquisition Categories, Decision Authority, and Reviews

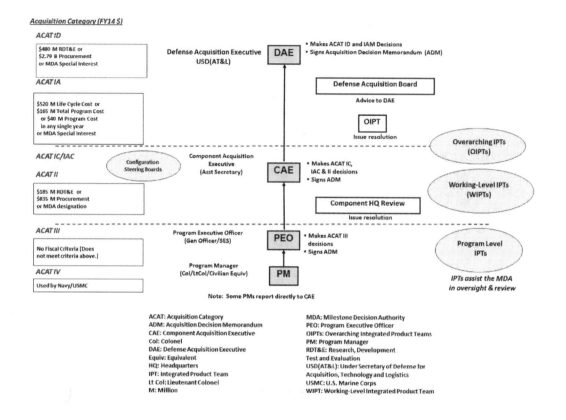

Acquisition Category (FY14 $)

ACAT ID
$480 M RDT&E or
$2.79 B Procurement
or MDA Special Interest

ACAT IA
$520 M Life Cycle Cost or
$165 M Total Program Cost
or $40 M Program Cost
in any single year
or MDA Special Interest

ACAT IC/IAC
ACAT II
$185 M RDT&E or
$835 M Procurement
or MDA designation

ACAT III
No Fiscal Criteria [Does
not meet criteria above.]

ACAT IV
Used by Navy/USMC

Defense Acquisition Executive
USD(AT&L) **DAE**
• Makes ACAT ID and IAM Decisions
• Signs Acquisition Decision Memorandum (ADM)

Defense Acquisition Board
Advice to DAE

OIPT
Issue resolution

Overarching IPTs
(OIPTs)

Configuration
Steering Boards

Component Acquisition
Executive
(Asst Secretary) **CAE**
• Makes ACAT IC,
IAC & II decisions
• Signs ADM

Working-Level IPTs
(WIPTs)

Component HQ Review
Issue resolution

Program Executive Officer
(Gen Officer/SES) **PEO**
• Makes ACAT III
decisions
• Signs ADM

Program Level
IPTs

Program Manager
(Col/LtCol/Civilian Equiv) **PM**

IPTs assist the MDA
in oversight & review

Note: Some PMs report directly to CAE

ACAT: Acquisition Category
ADM: Acquisition Decision Memorandum
CAE: Component Acquisition Executive
Col: Colonel
DAE: Defense Acquisition Executive
Equiv: Equivalent
HQ: Headquarters
IPT: Integrated Product Team
Lt Col: Lieutenant Colonel
M: Million

MDA: Milestone Decision Authority
PEO: Program Executive Officer
OIPTs: Overarching Integrated Product Teams
PM: Program Manager
RDT&E: Research, Development
Test and Evaluation
USD(AT&L): Under Secretary of Defense for
Acquisition, Technology and Logistics
USMC: U.S. Marine Corps
WIPT: Working-Level Integrated Product Team

For acquisition programs, the chain of command runs upward from the PM, through the PEO to the CAE; and for ACAT I, IA, and other programs so designated, to the DAE, refer to DoDI 5000.02 (Encl. 2, para 2).

CH 1–3.2.3.1.1 ACAT I

Acquisition Category (ACAT) I programs are MDAPs by statute when they meet either of the following criteria:

- The dollar value for all increments of the program is estimated by the DAE to require eventual expenditure for Research, Development, Test, and Evaluation (RDT&E) of more than $480 million (Fiscal Year [FY] 2014 constant dollars) or procurement, including all planned increments, of more than $2.79 billion (FY 2014 constant dollars).
- Programs can also be designated by the MDA as ACAT I programs based on a "special interest" designation. This designation is based on one or more of the following factors: technology complexity, congressional interest, a large commitment of resources, or the program is critical to achievement of a capability or set of capabilities, part of a system-of-systems, or a Joint program. Programs that already meet the MDAP and MAIS thresholds cannot be designated as Special Interest.

The USD(AT&L) designates programs as **ACAT ID or ACAT IC**:

- *ACAT ID* for which the MDA is the USD(AT&L).
- *ACAT IC* for which the MDA is the DoD Component head or, if delegated, the DoD CAE.

CH 1–3.2.3.1.2 ACAT IA

A *Major Automated Information System (MAIS)* program is a DoD acquisition program for an Automated Information System (AIS). It becomes an ACAT IA program when it is either designated by the MDA as a MAIS, or by statute when it is estimated to exceed:

- $40 million (FY 2014 constant dollars) for all increments, regardless of appropriation or fund source, directly related to the AIS definition, design, development, and deployment, and incurred in any single FY; or
- $165 million (FY 2014 constant dollars) for all expenditures, for all increments, regardless of appropriation or fund source, directly related to the AIS definition, design, development, and deployment, and incurred from the beginning of the Materiel Solution Analysis (MSA) phase through deployment at all sites; or
- $520 million (FY 2014 constant dollars) for all expenditures, for all increments, regardless of appropriation or fund source, directly related to the AIS definition, design, development, deployment, Operation and Maintenance (O&M), and incurred from the beginning of the MSA phase through sustainment for the estimated useful life of the system; or
- Programs can also be designated by the MDA as ACAT I programs based on a "Special Interest" designation. This designation is based on one or more of the following factors: technology complexity, congressional interest, a large commitment of resources or the program is critical to achievement of a capability or set of capabilities, part of a system-of-systems, or a Joint program. Programs that already meet the MDAP and MAIS thresholds cannot be designated as Special Interest.

Note: AISs do not include computer resources, neither hardware nor software, that: are an integral part of a weapon or weapon system; are used for highly sensitive classified programs (as determined by the SECDEF); are used for other highly sensitive Information Technology (IT) programs (as determined by the DoD Chief Information Officer [DoD CIO]); or are determined by the USD(AT&L) or designee to be better overseen as a non-AIS program.

The USD(AT&L) designates programs as **ACAT IAM** or **ACAT IAC**:

- *ACAT IAM* for which the MDA is the USD(AT&L) or as designated by the USD(AT&L). The "M" (in ACAT IAM) refers to MAIS.
- *ACAT IAC* for which the USD(AT&L) has delegated to the head of the DoD Component—the CAE. The "C" (in ACAT IAC) refers to Component.

CH 1–3.2.3.1.3 ACAT II

Programs are defined as those acquisition programs that do not meet the criteria for an ACAT I program, *but do meet the criteria for a major system*. A *major system is defined* as a program estimated by the DoD Component head to require eventual expenditure for RDT&E of more than $185 million in FY 2014 constant dollars, or for procurement of more than $835 million in FY 2014 constant dollars, or those designated by the DoD Component head to be ACAT II. The MDA is the DoD CAE.

CH 1–3.2.3.1.4 ACAT III

Programs are defined as those acquisition programs that do not meet the criteria for ACAT II. The MDA is designated by the CAE. This category includes less-than-major AISs.

CH 1–3.2.3.1.5 ACAT IV (Navy and Marine Corps Only)

Programs in the Navy and Marine Corps not otherwise designated as ACAT III are designated ACAT IV. ACAT IV programs fall into two categories: IVT (Test) and IVM (Monitor). ACAT IVT programs require Operational Test and Evaluation (OT&E), while ACAT IVM programs do not.

CH 1–3.2.3.1.6 ACAT and Non-ACAT programs in the Operations and Support Phase

Programs operating in this phase will require modifications and upgrades to remain viable and relevant to their operating environments. These efforts may or may not reach an ACAT level in dollar terms but it is likely some portion of the DoDI 5000.02 guidance and document set will require completion. Tailoring of guidance and documentation should be consistent with the programs environment including operational urgency, risk factors, and affordability. Guidance and documentation should also account for sustainment elements that are not directly present in the acquisition process of new systems--organic labor and capital, existing sustainment contracts, Service O&M budgets.

CH 1–3.2.3.2 Defense Acquisition Program Models

As a starting point in structuring an acquisition program, an acquisition PM can use one of the program models described below and then tailor it to fit a specific acquisition program. DoDI 5000.02 (para 5) provides a description of the four basic examples and two hybrid models.

- Model 1: Hardware-Intensive Program
- Model 2: Defense-Unique Software-Intensive Program
- Model 3: Incrementally Deployed Software-Intensive Program
- Model 4: Accelerated Acquisition Program
- Model 5: Hybrid Program A (Hardware-Dominant)
- Model 6: Hybrid Program B (Software-Dominant)

CH 1-4.2.7 through CH 1-4.2.10 provide detailed information on specific types of programs including Information Technology (IT), International Acquisition and Exportability (IA&E), and Joint and Urgent Capability Acquisition.

CH 1–3.3 Organizing an Acquisition Program

The fundamental responsibility of the defense acquisition workforce is to ensure that high-quality, affordable, supportable, and effective defense systems are delivered as quickly as possible—all while balancing the many factors that influence cost, schedule, and technical performance. In order to achieve maximum program effectiveness and delivery success, the tailoring of acquisition process requirements is encouraged. (See Tailoring and Critical Thinking: Key Principles for Acquisition Success, *Defense AT&L Magazine*, September-October 2015, pages 7-11.)

The Department's extensive use of high-value, complex systems guides the need for a world-class, highly competent program management workforce. The following Section describes key personnel and infrastructure concepts for defense acquisition programs.

CH 1–3.3.1 Program Executive Officer

A Program Executive Officer (PEO) is a senior acquisition manager and is typically responsible for a specific program, or for an entire portfolio of similar programs. The PEO normally only reports to, and receives guidance and direction from, the DoD Component Acquisition Executive (CAE). PEO assignment of acquisition program responsibilities is made by the CAE based on the criteria contained in (Encl. 2, para 3).

The PEO's mission is to provide executive-level management of all assigned acquisition programs. The PEO has oversight responsibility for cost, schedule, and performance in a DoD acquisition program and/or portfolio. PEOs exercise executive-level authority and responsibility for program management, including: optimizing interoperability and standardization; technical and quality management; logistics support; and readiness management activities for assigned programs. PEOs are responsible for programmatic processes and the various aspects of planning and budgeting required to oversee their assigned program(s) through the applicable decision points and milestones. In this capacity, the PEO provides overall direction and integration of assigned programs and assures effective interface with Defense-level headquarters and Departments, as well as other Services, combat system developers, and supporting commands and activities.

Program responsibilities for programs not assigned to a PEO or to a direct reporting PM may be assigned to a commander of a systems, logistics, or materiel command in accordance with DoDI 5000.02 (Encl. 2, para 3).

CH 1–3.3.2 Program Manager

The Program Manager (PM) is the designated individual with the responsibility *and* authority to accomplish program objectives for development, production, and sustainment of a capability that satisfies validated user requirements.

CH 1–3.3.2.1 Roles, Actions, and Activities

An effective PM has the "big picture" perspective of the program, including in-depth knowledge of the interrelationships among its elements. DoDI 5000.02 (Encl. 2, para 6) describes program management responsibilities.

PM's have key responsibilities in four principal areas: Acquisition Management, Technical Management, Business Management, and Executive Leadership. Additional information regarding PM responsibilities is available in Introduction to Defense Acquisition Management (CH 3).

CH 1–3.3.2.2 PM Assignment

The CAE selects a PM and establishes a PMO to complete the necessary actions associated with planning the acquisition program with emphasis on the next phase. DoDI 5000.02 (Encl. 2, para 4) addresses PM selection criteria and assignment duration by program type. To reach the requisite level of confidence essential within the acquisition chain of command, successful PMs possess the specialized skills, tools, certifications, and experience standards that establish their credentials. They also possess skill in managing resources and sustaining an environment that enables the successful acquisition and management of the program.

The PM is identified as early as possible, and it is the PM's responsibility, working with the PEO and CAE, to organize and staff a program management office commensurate with the scope and complexity of the program. See DoDI 5000.02 (Encl. 2, para 5) for more information.

CH 1–3.3.3 Program Management Office Key Leadership Positions

Designation of key program staff is critical to the operations of the PMO. Program staff is tailored to program size and complexity and comprised of individuals and groups who are required to perform program management functions, as well as support program management activities. They maintain certifications, standards, and sound business practice, as well as possess the knowledge and practical expertise necessary to successfully execute a program. USD(AT&L) memorandum, "Key Leadership Positions (KLP) and Qualification Criteria," designates certain MDAP and MAIS program office positions as KLPs and prescribes qualification requirements essential for selection to these positions. Additional functional-specific requirements and preferences for KLPs are located at the DAU Certification & Core Plus Development Guides. These requirements are updated by the functional leader for the individual career field.

CH 1–3.3.3.1 Cross-Functional Competencies

As stated in the USD(AT&L) memorandum, "Key Leadership Positions (KLP) and Qualification Criteria," listed positions are required to be assigned to each MDAP and MAIS program, and filled by properly qualified members of the armed forces or full-time employees of the DoD. Five factors are identified as requirements essential for KLP selection. Attachment 1 of the memorandum, Common Cross-Functional

KLP Requirements, lists the requirements for KLP selection. KLPs benefit from broad experience within the following cross-functional competencies:

- **Executive Leadership**. Demonstrated competencies in leading change, leading people, managing results, building coalitions, business acumen, and an enterprise-wide perspective. The DoD leader competency framework provides the governing model. Refer to DoDI 1430.16, Growing Civilian Leaders (Encl. 3, Table 1).
- **Program Execution.** The leadership and management of a defense acquisition program covering every aspect of the acquisition process, such as integration, engineering, program control, test and evaluation, deployment, configuration management, production and manufacturing, quality assurance, and logistics support.
- **Technical Management.** The organization, governance, and effective application of current technology, acquisition practice, design, and security considerations in building/acquiring and maintaining large complex systems.
- **Business Management.** The oversight of controlling, leading, monitoring, organizing, and planning for the business success of a program. This includes achieving best value to the government.

KLPs require a significant level of authority commensurate with the responsibility and accountability for acquisition program success. In accordance with the USD(AT&L) key leadership memorandum, the following positions are designated as mandatory KLPs for ACAT I and International Acquisition (IA) programs, and are designated in the position category associated with the lead function.

- The following KLPs are dedicated to a single ACAT Program:
  - Program Manager (PM) (additionally, ACAT II)
  - Deputy Program Manager (DPM)
  - Chief Engineer/Lead Systems Engineer
  - Product Support Manager (Program Lead Logistician)
  - Chief Developmental Tester (see 10 USC 139b)
  - Program Lead, Business Financial Manager

The following lead positions on MDAP/MAIS programs are necessary when the function is required based on the phase or type of acquisition program. These lead positions may be associated exclusively with a single program or be shared across multiple programs:

- Program Lead, Contracting Officer
- Program Lead, Cost Estimator
- Program Lead, Production, Quality, and Manufacturing
- Program Lead, Information Technology
- Program Lead, International Acquisition

Key Program Management staff strive to improve critical thinking skills as a strong contributing factor for increasing personal and team program effectiveness and competitiveness in a resource-constrained environment. Additional functional-specific requirements and preferences for KLPs are located at the Defense Acquisition University (DAU) Certification & Core Plus Development Guides. These requirements are updated by the functional leader for the individual career field.

CH 1–3.3.4 Key Stakeholders

Program Managers (PMs) develop a program-specific stakeholder management strategy for their programs. Who are my stakeholders? Where does my communication plan fit in my Integrated Master Plan (IMP)/Integrated Master Schedule (IMS)? They can be individuals or groups that are both inside and outside the organization. These stakeholders can be positively or negatively impacted by the program. Stakeholders can positively or negatively influence program outcomes.

CH 1–3.3.4.1 Stakeholder Engagement Process

To increase the probability that the program or project succeeds, use the 6-stage (refer to Figure 6) "Stakeholder Engagement Process."

Figure 6: Stakeholder Engagement Process

Succeed!

6) Evaluate (Plan for Success)

5) Plan Engagement Actions (What, When, Who)

4) Focus Engagements (Involvement Matrix)

3) Analyze Stakeholders (Interests, Expectations *Requirements

2) Prioritize Stakeholders (Power Grid)

1) Identify Stakeholders (Stakeholder Map)

This is a proven process that includes analysis, planning and execution, with an outcome that enhances the probability of success. While the first four stages are important, the Stage 5 engagement of the key stakeholders is the most crucial activity.

Step 1: Identify your stakeholders using a **stakeholder map** (refer to Figure 7).

Figure 7: Stakeholder Map

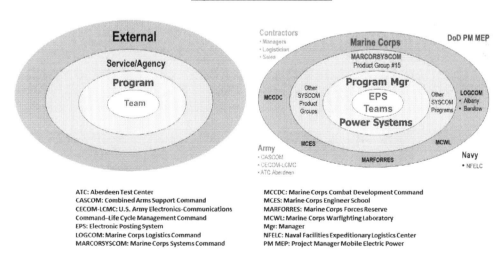

ATC: Aberdeen Test Center
CASCOM: Combined Arms Support Command
CECOM-LCMC: U.S. Army Electronics-Communications
Command–Life Cycle Management Command
EPS: Electronic Posting System
LOGCOM: Marine Corps Logistics Command
MARCORSYSCOM: Marine Corps Systems Command

MCCDC: Marine Corps Combat Development Command
MCES: Marine Corps Engineer School
MARFORRES: Marine Corps Forces Reserve
MCWL: Marine Corps Warfighting Laboratory
Mgr: Manager
NFELC: Naval Facilities Expeditionary Logistics Center
PM MEP: Project Manager Mobile Electric Power

Step 2: Prioritize stakeholders (primary, secondary, and other) by rating their influence and importance on the **power grid** (refer to Figure 8).

Figure 8: Stakeholder Power Grid

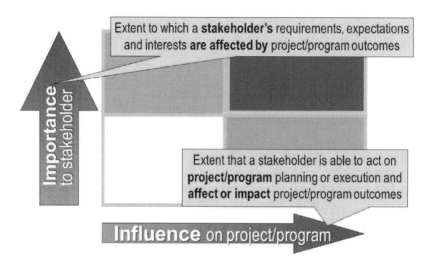

Step 3: Analyze the Interests, Expectations, and Requirements (IERs) for each key stakeholder. What are the stakeholder's interests? What does the stakeholder like or desire? Perhaps the stakeholder desires cost control. Next, what are the stakeholder's expectations? What does the stakeholder **want** from others? Perhaps the stakeholder has expectations of communication to avoid surprises. Finally, what are the stakeholder's requirements? **"What was agreed to?"** Both the government and the stakeholder now have a contract and have agreed to a cost (refer to Table 1).

Table 1: Stakeholder Interests, Expectations, and Requirements

Stakeholder	Requirements	Expectations	Interests
Customers			
Supervisor			
Subordinates			
Contractors			
Peers			

Step 4: Focus on engagement by assessing each stakeholder in an Involvement matrix to examine their current state (refer to Figure 9).

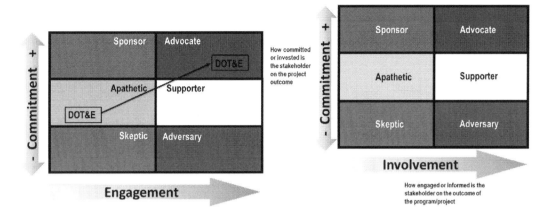

Figure 9: Stakeholder Involvement Matrix

Step 5: Plan stakeholder engagement on where the government and stakeholders envision their future state as compared to the Involvement matrix, e.g., perhaps moving a stakeholder from being apathetic to being an advocate. How is the action going to be done (inform, consult, monitor, or partner). Who is responsible for carrying out the action, and when will that action be accomplished? This means a plan of what needs to be accomplished.

Step 6: Finally, engage and evaluate how stakeholder involvement is progressing. Strategy adjustments may be necessary to optimize success in stakeholder engagements.

CH 1–3.3.5 Integrated Product and Process Development/Integrated Product Team

Defense acquisition works best when all of DoD works together. Cooperation and empowerment are essential. Per DoDD 5000.01 (Encl. 1, para E1.1.2 – page 5), the Department's acquisition, financial, and capability needs communities use Integrated Product Teams (IPTs) to maintain continuous and effective communications with one another.

Integrated Product and Process Development (IPPD) is the management technique used in DoD to simultaneously integrate all essential acquisition activities through the use of multidisciplinary teams to optimize design, manufacturing, and supportability processes. One key tenet of program management is the use of multidisciplinary teamwork through IPTs.

IPTs are an integral part of the defense acquisition process and support to the PMO. For ACAT ID and ACAT IAM programs, there are generally two levels of IPTs: the Working-Level Integrated Product Team (WIPT) and the Overarching Integrated Product Team (OIPT). Figure 10 illustrates the Defense Acquisition IPT structure.

Figure 10: Defense Acquisition IPT Structure

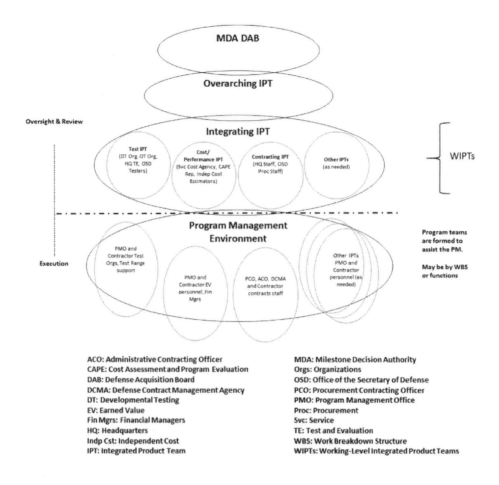

ACO: Administrative Contracting Officer
CAPE: Cost Assessment and Program Evaluation
DAB: Defense Acquisition Board
DCMA: Defense Contract Management Agency
DT: Developmental Testing
EV: Earned Value
Fin Mgrs: Financial Managers
HQ: Headquarters
Indp Cst: Independent Cost
IPT: Integrated Product Team

MDA: Milestone Decision Authority
Orgs: Organizations
OSD: Office of the Secretary of Defense
PCO: Procurement Contracting Officer
PMO: Program Management Office
Proc: Procurement
Svc: Service
TE: Test and Evaluation
WBS: Work Breakdown Structure
WIPTs: Working-Level Integrated Product Teams

CH 1–3.3.5.1 Integrated Product and Process Development

Within the PMO under the PM leadership the IPPD integrates all acquisition activities starting with requirements definition through production, fielding/deployment, and operational support in order to optimize the design, manufacturing, business, and supportability processes. *One of the key IPPD tenets is multidisciplinary teamwork through Integrated Product Teams (IPTs).*

CH 1–3.3.5.1.1 IPPD Key Tenets

Integrated Product and Process Development (IPPD) stresses cross-functional communication throughout the acquisition process and includes the following key tenets:

- **Customer-focused.** Meet the customer's needs better, faster, and cheaper.
- **Concurrent development of products and processes.** Processes used during all phases are considered throughout product design and development.
- **Early and continuous life-cycle planning.** This begins with science and technology efforts and extends throughout the entire acquisition life cycle.
- **Maximize flexibility for optimization and use of various contractor approaches.** Contracts are designed to allow contractors to apply IPPD principles and make use of effective commercial standards, practice, and processes.

- **Encourage robust design and process improvement capability.** Techniques are used that achieve quality through design, focus on process capability, and stress continuous process improvement.
- **Event-driven scheduling.** Scheduling relates program events to their respective accomplishments and accomplishment criteria.
- **Multidisciplinary teamwork.** Decision-making is based on input from the entire team to reduce risk and create a work environment that is more likely to result in successful suggestions.
- **Empowerment.** Team members have the authority to make decisions at the lowest possible level commensurate with risk.
- **Seamless management tools.** A management framework is established that helps show the interrelationship of all products and processes.
- **Proactive identification and management of risk.** Risk analyses and user needs are evaluated to identify critical cost, schedule, and technical parameters.

CH 1–3.3.5.1.2 IPPD Pitfalls

Integrated Product and Process Development (IPPD) pitfalls can arise that impact the quality, effectiveness, and timeliness of the overall process. Some of these barriers include:

- **Lack of commitment from top management**, which can hurt team member motivation and impact their ability to achieve results.
- **Need for significant cultural change** due to the inherent hierarchical structure of the military, which contrasts with the philosophy set forth in the IPPD process.
- **Lack of adaptation to the IPPD process by functional organizations**, thereby reducing everyone's performance.
- **Lack of planning**, which causes teams to rush to catch up, thus impacting quality
- **Poor or non-existent education/training** in the IPPD process.
- **No effort to identify and/or share best practice** in IPPD implementation.
- **A "not invented here" mentality** that can arise due to the many functional areas involved in the IPPD process, which leads to a lack of information sharing.
- **Contractually imposed practice** that hinder a contractor's flexibility.
- **Use of IPPD by the contractor, but not by DoD**, resulting in morale problems and less effective working relationships.
- **Awarding of contracts to traditional approach contractors** who are not familiar with the IPPD process, even if it is specified in the Request for Proposal (RFP).
- **Unrealistic promises** by contractor to implement IPPD.
- **Poor contract award fees or incentives** that don't encourage IPPD.
- **Poorly run meetings or reviews**, resulting in over-emphasis of a particular topic or functional area to the exclusion of others.

CH 1–3.3.5.2 Integrated Product Teams

Program oversight and IPPD processes are implemented through Integrated Product Team (IPT) members who represent technical, business, and support functions. The following guiding principles improve the productivity of any IPT:

- **Chartering, launch, and initiation.** To get the team off to a good start, prepare a charter documenting the mission, timeframe, and membership of the IPT; train participants in IPT principles and the role of each team member; and prepare a Plan of Actions and Milestones (POA&M).
- **Goal alignment.** Team leaders ensure that the goals and objectives of each team member are consistent with the goals of the project. Effective feedback mechanisms can be put in place to facilitate this.

- **Open discussions with no secrets.** Due to the unique design of IPTs in which each member has expertise in a specific area, free and open communication among all members is essential.
- **Empowered, qualified team members.** Team members have the authority to represent their superiors in the decision-making process. They remain in close communication with their bosses to ensure their advice is sound and not subject to change later, barring unforeseen circumstances.
- **Dedicated/Committed, Proactive Participation.** Because team success hinges on participation by members with institutional knowledge of functional areas, IPTs are organized so that all key stakeholders can contribute effectively. In many cases, this means minimizing membership to enhance communication and trust.
- **Issues Raised and Resolved Early.** All issues are raised openly and discussed at the earliest possible opportunity, and solved through team consensus and discussion, not isolated conversations "offline."

CH 1–3.3.5.2.1 IPT Procedures, Roles, and Responsibilities

Each program has an Overarching Integrated Product Team (OIPT) and at least one Working-Level Integrated Product Team (WIPT). WIPTs focus on a particular topic such as cost/performance, program baseline, Acquisition Strategy, test and evaluation, or contracting. An Integrating Integrated Product Team (IIPT), which is itself a WIPT, coordinates WIPT efforts and covers all program topics, including those not otherwise assigned to another IPT. IPT participation is the primary way for any organization to participate in an acquisition program. IIPTs are essential for ACAT ID and ACAT IAM programs to facilitate the PM's engagement with Office of the Secretary of Defense (OSD) and Joint Staff-level stakeholders. IIPTs also provide the requisite input to the OIPT. Table 2 provides a summary of DoD IPT types, focus, and responsibilities.

Table 2: Summary of DoD IPT Types, Focus, and Responsibilities

Org.	Type	Focus	Responsibilities
OSD and Components	OIPT (applies to MDAPs)	• Strategic Guidance • Tailoring • Program Assessment • Resolve Issues Elevated by WIPTs	• Program Success • Functional Area Leadership • Independent Assessment • Issue Resolution
	WIPTs	• Planning for Program Success • Opportunities for Acquisition Reform (e.g., innovation, streamlining) • Identify/Resolve Program Issues • Program Status	• Functional Knowledge & Experience • Empowered Contribution • Recommendations for Program Success • Communicate Status & Unresolved Issues
Program Teams & System Contractors	Program IPTs	• Program Execution • Identify & Implement • Acquisition Reform	• Manage the Complete Scope of Program, Resources & Risk • Integrate Government & Contractor Efforts for Program Success • Report Program Status & Issues

The PM, or designee, in collaboration with OSD staff specialists from the offices of the OIPT Leader and other key stakeholders for the program, forms an Integrating IPT (IIPT) and WIPTs, *as necessary*. There is no "one size fits all" WIPT structure. IIPT/WIPTs *may*, but *are not required* to, be formed to support the development of strategies for acquisition and contracts, cost estimates, evaluation of alternatives, logistics management, test and evaluation, and other areas, *as appropriate* for that program. If formed, the IIPT assists the PM in the development of a WIPT structure to propose to the OIPT. The IIPT also coordinates the activities of the remaining WIPTs and ensures that issues not formally addressed by other WIPTs are reviewed. (Refer to Figure 10, which depicts a complete OIPT, IIPT, and WIPT structure.)

The membership of a particular WIPT depends on its purpose and includes relevant stakeholders, such as members of program oversight, user, testing, logistics, contracting, and systems engineering communities, as appropriate. Contractors, although not formal members, are not precluded from WIPT participation; however, since WIPTs have an oversight function that may require discussion of competition-sensitive and/or government information, contractor participation is considered on a case-by-case basis. WIPTs meet on an *as required* basis to help the PM plan the program's structure and documentation, and resolve issues. While there is no one-size-fits-all WIPT approach, there are three basic tenets to which any approach adheres:

- The PM is in charge of the program.
- WIPTs are advisory bodies to the PM.
- Direct communication between the program office and all levels in the acquisition oversight and review process is expected as a means of exchanging information and building trust.

The leader of each WIPT is normally the PM or the PM's representative, but the OSD action officer may co-chair WIPT meetings at the invitation of the PM. The following roles and responsibilities apply to all WIPTs:

- Assist the PM in developing strategies and in program planning, as requested by the PM.
- Establish WIPT Plan of Actions and Milestones (POA&M).
- Propose tailored documentation and milestone requirements.
- Review and provide early input to documents.
- Coordinate WIPT activities with the OIPT members.
- Resolve or elevate issues in a timely manner.
- Assume responsibility to obtain principals' concurrence on issues, applicable documents, or portions of documents.

CH 1–3.3.6 Program Leadership and Battle Rhythm

Key to being a successful PM is integration of leadership with the program battle rhythm.

CH 1–3.3.6.1 Program Leadership

Program Managers need to think about the distribution of time to the challenges most important to program success. So how does one select where to spend their time? The key is to understand a PM's role in establishing, managing, as well as leading an acquisition team. The PMs leadership roles are varied:

- The first is to set direction and establish goals. The establishment of goals contains emotional and logical elements. The emotional side of goal setting is for motivating and inspiring the team members to perform their best—not because they are directed to do so, but because they want to do it. The logical part of goal setting is tangible, measurable, and time-phased. Key management tools are the IMP/IMS.

- The second is establishing the culture of the team. Culture is the values, rituals, and symbols the team accepts, which are passed along by imitation from one generation to the next. How a team brands itself is critical to its performance. Key for program management is to have a disciplined culture that uses the program tools to accomplish the mission. The PM needs to lead this disciplined culture.
- The third is to provide a winning environment. Often, PMs too narrowly focus their efforts in this area on just resources. Does the team have the right people, enough money, a workable schedule, the proper materials, and access to information? But part of creating a winning environment entails building spheres of influence, which then allows team members to have sway with key stakeholders and their own chain of command. Finally, part of building a winning environment means an acquisition leader creates an environment for the team to evaluate and learn as it performs. In the book *Clear Leadership,* Gervase Bushe says the rapidness of change in the world today often means internal mental models for addressing challenges no longer apply. This is perhaps what the USD(AT&L) had in mind in the memorandum dated January 7, 2015, issuing the new DoDI 5000.02, by writing:

  > Successful defense acquisition depends on careful thinking and sound professional judgments about the best Acquisition Strategy to use for a given product. Even more than previous versions, this DoDI 5000.02 emphasizes tailoring of program structures, content, and decision points to the product being acquired.

- To move a program forward, the team is constantly aware of new opportunities in a changing environment. After meetings, reviews, and decisions, a leader holds timely discussions on what worked and what could be improved. What needs to change in the plan—the IMP/IMS? Don't hold onto a plan that needs to change. Change the plan—the IMP/IMS. Leaders are not assigned to maintain the status quo.
- The fourth is to provide mentorship—that is, to grow the team. The previous bullet was about improving the synergy amongst team members. This is about the performance of individuals on the team. All leaders claim to care about their team. What separates the leaders of teams is that they go beyond saying they care to developing plans and strategies for demonstrating their concern for their employees' growth and well-being. It is on their calendar.
- The fifth and final role is that leaders set and enforce standards of performance that drive command performance. Everyone on the team is responsible for cost, schedule, and performance. If performance expectations are not set down to the team level, there can be no expectation for teams to meet a standard of performance.

CH 1–3.3.6.2 Program Battle Rhythm

As for setting a battle rhythm, the key is to remember PMs are what they do—what is on the calendar. To set a good battle rhythm, routinely review the calendar to see where time is being spent. The tyranny of today's challenges can easily distract a PM's focus from fulfilling leadership responsibilities/roles. Every PM can commit to a daily routine of reviewing their calendar and recognizing how much of their time is committed to Leadership 101. An example battle rhythm is depicted in Table 3.

Table 3: Battle Rhythm Example

Daily	Weekly	Monthly	Quarterly
• Walk the office • Be positive • Communicate your purpose (Why & How) today	• Weekly activity report • Feedback to Senior Leaders • Engage top-tier stakeholders	• Update on status to your direct reports • Feedback – formal (SBI)	• All hands update • Update org succession plan and review individual development plans

Daily	Weekly	Monthly	Quarterly
• Say hello, thank you, and thanks for correction • Live & maintain a climate of integrity, dignity, profession-alism, & open com-munications • Respect people's time • Lead from the front....personal example & appearance • Keep commitments • Appreciative Inquiry • Give informal SBI (situation, impact, behavior) feedback • Stress relief activity • Take the job, not yourself, seriously • Do not pass up the teachable moment	• Highlight WINS • Delegate and monitor • Reflect on week completed • Reward positive behavior/correct negative behavior • Always learning • Celebrate the successes • Alignment with stakeholders (user, industry, sponsor)	• Develop workforce (DAWIA, education, professional training, etc.) • Get to know your people • Hold second tier supervisors accountable to know their people, reward, feedback, etc. • Hole exit interviews • Review calendar for holidays, Service anniversaries, heritage months, etc.	• All hands team building (chili cook-off, costume party, etc.) • Formally update PEO/Senior Leadership • Review latest program information (CRS, GAO, testimony, industry annual reports)

As the program leader, the PM, along with the other key leaders on the program, sets a rhythm along with a culture that empowers the PMO team. One thing the PM may want to consider is how the battle rhythm addresses or compensates for real or perceived personal or PMO challenges. As appropriate, given IPT dynamics, daily and weekly assessments help maintain an overall program execution status. This information flows into part of the overall daily, weekly, monthly, and quarterly program reporting process cycle.

Most PMO work activity is event-driven and outlined as tasks in the IMS to be accomplished in a sequence. Some work activity, especially management efforts such as cost, schedule, and risk management are cyclical. The event-driven and cyclical activiites are planned into a battle rhythm that aligns with the major events for management of the program as outlined in the program IMP. It is critical that both technical and management tasks are tracked within the IMS. PMO team activities such as contracting actions and budget execution activities are tracked in the same schedule as the technical work, thus allowing for a complete picture for the program team on work that needs to be accomplished.

Establishing a realistic and executable battle rhythm enables the PM and PMO team to manage the work detailed in the program schedule (IMS) and to identify changes to the IMS when appropriate. The Acquisition Program Baseline (APB) may not change, but the details to reach that baseline will likely need to be adjusted as the program progresses.

Leading that effort with a realistic battle rhythm that allows for adjustments gives the team confidence to meet program execution challenges and grow in skill and ability. The PM-established and -led battle rhythm provides a higher probability of delivering a system that meets requirements within established cost and schedule.

CH 1–3.4 Integrated Acquisition Planning and Execution

As a solid understanding of requirements, both explicit and implicit, and realistic funding profile are necessary at the initiation of an acquisition, so also is a reasonable and realistic plan and schedule of work. Sound schedules merge with cost and technical data to influence program management decisions and actions. Robust schedules used in a disciplined manner help stakeholders make key go-ahead decisions, track and assess past performance, and predict future performance and costs. Proven and effective tools for planning, scheduling, and execution of work are the Integrated Master Plan (IMP) and Integrated Master Schedule (IMS). **PMO realization of an IMP/IMS at the program level depends upon the development and integration of IMP and IMS inputs from all functional areas.** This development and integration cannot happen on its own. Leadership example and active use of the tools are required. The IMP and IMS:

- Are management tools that enhance the management of acquisition, modification, and sustainment programs?
- Provide a systematic approach to program planning, scheduling, and execution.
- Are equally applicable to competitive and sole-source procurements with industry, as well as to government in-house efforts.
- Improve day-to day program execution and facilitate ongoing insight into program status by both government PMO personnel and contractor personnel.
- Help develop and support "what if" exercises, and identify and assess candidate problem workarounds.

The IMP documents the significant criteria necessary to complete the accomplishments, and ties each to a key program event. The IMS expands on the IMP with an integrated network of tasks, sub-tasks, activities, schedule for deliverables, and milestones with sufficient logic and duration. It answers the question, "How will we do this and when will we be done?" The IMS also serves as a tool for time-phasing work and assessing technical performance. IMS activities are thus traceable to the IMP and the Work Breakdown Structure (WBS), and allow integrated assessments of cost, schedule, technical performance, and associated risks.

To assist the PM and the PMO team, refer to the IMS "Cheat Sheet" for additional information.

CH 1–3.4.1 Program Schedule

The PM working with the PMO team should develop a high-level Program Schedule in conjunction with the IMP development activities. This high-level Schedule along with the IMP will drive, and be driven by, the development of the program Acquisition Strategy. Additionally, this high-level Program Schedule is not the same as the IMS, but they must be fully aligned. The high-level Program Schedule maybe referred to as a "Program Roadmap" The high-level Program Schedule would provide a detailed graphic illustrating program milestones, phases, and events; it is usually a Power Point chart format. Depicted events and milestones will vary by program, but will minimally include key acquisition decision points; principal systems engineering and logistics activities such as technical reviews and assessments; planned contracting actions such as request for proposal (RFP) release, source selection activity, and contract awards; production events and deliveries; and key test activities. (Figure 11 is a notional depiction of the expected level of detail. For example, contract details will vary with the contracting approach and the plan for competition and multiple suppliers; the use of options, re-competes, and/or new negotiated sole source; etc.)

Figure 11: Notional Depiction of the Program Schedule

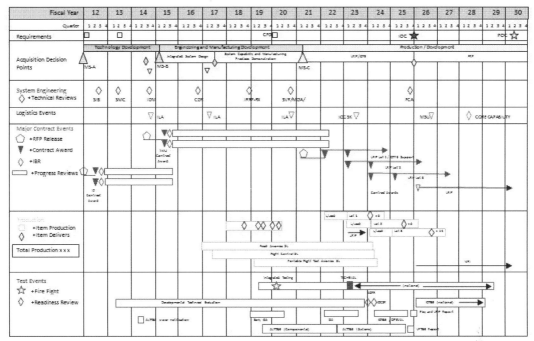

AOFR: Assessment of Operational Field Readiness	IOT&E: Initial Operational Test & Evaluation	PDR: Preliminary Design Review
ALPT&E: Alternative Live Pro Test & Evaluation	LPT&E: Live Pro Test & Evaluation	PRR: Production Readiness Review
CDR: Critical Design Review	LRIP: Low-Rate Initial Production	SFR: System Functional Review
EMD: Engineering & Manufacturing Development	MDA: Milestone Decision Authority	SIB: System Integration Lab
FCA: Functional Certification Audit	MSD: Material Support Date	SRR: System Requirements Review
FOT&E: Follow-On Operational Test & Evaluation	OA: Operational Assessment	SVR: System Verification Review
FRP: Full Rate Production	OASD(SE): Office of the Assistant Secretary of Defense	TD: Technology Development
FRR: Flight Readiness Review	(Systems Engineering)	TECHEVAL: Technical Evaluation
GTV: Ground Test Vehicle	OPEVAL: Operational Evaluation	TRR: Test Readiness Review
ILA: Integrated Logistics Analysis	OTRR: Operational Test Readiness Review	
IOCSR: Initial Operation Capability Supportability Review	PCA: Physical Configuration Audit	

CH 1–3.4.2 Program Management Office IMP/IMS

Each program has a high-level Program Schedule along with an Integrated Master Plan (IMP) and Integrated Master Schedule (IMS), and requires the same from its contractor(s). The IMP and IMS communicate the program execution expectations of the program team and provide traceability to the management and execution of the program by IPTs. The government program schedule should incorporate the contractor(s) schedule in the same manner the program WBS incorporates the contractor(s) WBS. This will also provide traceability to the program WBS, the Contract WBS (CWBS), the Statement of Work (SOW), and risk management, which together define the products and key processes associated with program execution. A best practice may be to provide the government IMP, along with other government planning documents (Program WBS, Systems Engineering Plan [SEP], Program Protection Plan [PPP], etc.) as a part of the RFP.

The IMP is an event-based plan consisting of a hierarchy of program events tailored and scaled according to the size, content, maturity, and risk of the program. It consists of three main elements: Program Events, Significant Accomplishments, and Accomplishment Criteria.

- *Program Events* are decision and/or assessment points that occur at the culmination of significant program activities. Typical examples might be major milestone reviews (such as a Milestone B), technical reviews (System Requirements Review [SRR], Preliminary Design

Review [PDR], Critical Design Review [CDR], etc.), and program reviews (such as an Integrated Baseline Review [IBR]).

- *Significant Accomplishments* are typically entry and/or exit criteria relative to the program event. For example, want/desire requirements analysis to be "completed"—among other things—in order to claim credit for a successful PDR.
- *Accomplishment Criteria* describe the specific conditions necessary to claim full credit for a significant accomplishment. In this case, requirements analysis is "completed" at this PDR when the requirements analysis for element A, element B, and element C are all completed.

Construction in this fashion enables the IMP to reflect how program leaders characterize and make decisions about their programs. In addition, accomplishment criteria can be directly associated with specific WBS elements, IPT leader, SOW paragraphs, Contract Data Requirements Lists (CDRLs), or Risks and Opportunities. This facilitates very robust traceability as depicted in Table 4. The government PMO and contractor can each employ IMPs.

Table 4: Example IMP Numbering System

Activity Number	Activities		
A	IMP Event		
A01		IMP Accomplishment	
A01a			IMP Criteria
A01a01-n			IMS Task
A	PDR Complete		
A01		Requirements Analysis Completed	
A01a			Avionics Requirements Analysis Complete
A01a01			Perform Avionics Requirements Analysis
A01a02			Develop Avionics Draft Specification
A01a03			Coordinate Avionics Draft Specification for Review
A01a04			Publish Avionics Specification

The IMP and the program WBS then are used to develop the program IMS.

The PM and the PMO team determine an appropriate level of detail for the IMS. For the IMS, what level of detail is needed? In general, the IMS should go at least one level lower than the detail outlined in the WBS. Over time that detail is expanded as the program is further defined.

- **Proposal.** Include enough detail to allow for program documentation, such as cost estimates, SEP, TEMP, etc., can be linked together through the Integrated Master Schedule (IMS). Provide enough detail to convince the reviewers that the problem is understood and an executable solution is in place that takes anticipated risk and opportunities into consideration. Conduct a macro-level program schedule risk analysis with input from the overall IMS, thus allowing the program team to understand the impacts risk/opportunities will have on the schedule.
- **Execution.** Include lower level detail for all tasks as the required details for execution. This can be done in a "rolling wave" manner; thus, later tasks become more detailed and clearer through execution of early tasks. The program execution schedule should be supplemented by the contractor's schedule. The two schedules are linked together through the program WBS, as the contract WBS is a subset of the program WBS.

Ultimately, the IMP and IMS represent the plan and schedules for satisfying the capability need. The IMP and IMS then allow for continuous program assessments of the program status. Therefore, the PMO team can greatly enable future program execution through the effective layout of the program IMP and IMS. The IMP and IMS help the PM and PMO team:

- Identify a baseline for program monitoring, reporting, and control.
- Plan, execute, and track risk and opportunity efforts.
- Support resource analysis and leveling, exploration of alternatives, and cost/schedule trade-off studies.
- Provide a roadmap for stakeholders.
- Enable effective communication within the government team and with the developer(s).

CH 1–3.4.2.1 IMP/IMS Development

The Key Leaders provide inputs to the program Integrated Master Plan/Integrated Master schedule (IMP/IMS). The team can use the IMP/IMS to integrate processes and products, and provide an auditable sequence of tasks and events that can be used to measure technical progress. A resource-loaded schedule can also be used to measure cost performance, as is done within Earned Value. Program Managers can consider how cost and technical performance tracking are integrated with the schedule. The riskier the program, the more value an integrated performance measurement approach will be. The development and analysis of program IMP/IMS data:

- Permit assessments of the developer's activities, efforts, and products.
- Contribute to a better understanding of the technical basis of cost and schedule variances.
- Provide a framework for developing corrective actions.

The PMO IMP is an event-driven government document that provides a framework against which all work is measured. It includes functional, focused activities necessary to successfully deliver the desired capability. It aids in defining and documenting tasks required to define, develop, and deliver a system, and facilitates operation and support of that system throughout its life cycle. The format usually reflects an Event-Accomplishment-Criteria hierarchical structure for program tracking and execution.

The IMS is an integrated, networked model containing all the detailed discrete tasks necessary to realize the IMP accomplishment criteria. The IMS is directly traceable to the IMP and the program WBS, and includes all the elements associated with development, production, modification, and delivery of the total product or program level plan. The result is a fully networked dynamic model that supports engaged leadership decision-making. There are two types of schedules:

- **Government Integrated Master Schedule (IMS).** This IMS is used to manage the program on a daily basis from the Materiel Development Decision (MDD) through disposal. This IMS tracks all government activities at a level appropriate for both management of the tasks as well as leadership decision-making. Note that the government work is scheduled to the same level as the contractors' work, thus allowing for a common approach across all IPTs. The government IMS draws status and forecasting information from contractor IMS, as required to maintain program situational awareness.
- **Contractor IMS**. This IMS is used to manage the contract on a daily basis from contract award through contract completion. This IMS tracks all contractor activities at a level appropriate for leadership decision-making, but also in a manner that accounts for *all* contract scope. This typically results in a "tiered" and linked IMS structure from program level down to detailed level. This IMS is typically anchored in the WBS and is resource-loaded. A best practice is to update the IMS on a regular basis as part of a monthly Contractor CDRL.

The IMS focuses on the product and relationship of the tasks/efforts required to execute the program. It is resource-loaded and includes margin for risk mitigation. The IMS supplements the IMP, but it can be

WBS-based or event-based. Either way, all of the tasks are mapped to a WBS element. When the IMP (Events-Accomplishments-Criteria) dictate the structure of the IMS, then the CWBS is integrated into this framework as a referenced substructure. When the CWBS dictates the structure on the IMS, then the IMP Criteria are integrated into this framework as a referenced substructure. It is important to keep this in mind when defining these items in order to arrive at a product that clearly articulates the PM's intentions and is useable as a tool for managing the program.

The IMS describes the work required to complete the effort in sufficient detail to fully demonstrate understanding of the scope and flow of the work. It enables the PM to better understand the links and relationships among the various activities and the resources supporting them.

The first, best opportunity to explore in detail the relationship among cost, schedule, and technical risk is through close-up assessment of the IMP and IMS at an Integrated Baseline Review (IBR). IBRs examine the baseline as a means to assess risk and opportunity, and thus do not require Earned Value Management (EVM). They are simply a best practice approach. To assist the PM and the PMO team, refer to the IBR "Cheat Sheet" for additional information.

The PM and PMO team monitor development of the IMS by the contractor/developer to ensure that activity durations and resources are reasonable. However, monitoring is not management. The analysis and predictions include the impacts of the risk. If any mitigation works, the schedule moves left. The IMS also includes opportunities and the actions associated with their pursuit. This oversight aids risk and opportunity analysis, and the development of mitigation/pursuit plans.

Early identification of, and adherence to, critical path tasks are essential to ensure that the program remains on track toward achieving schedule and cost goals. The IMS provides linkages between tasks to capture the relationship of predecessor and successor tasks required to initiate or complete major tasks.

Lastly, remember the IMS is a living document that is continuously updated to reflect the progress of the program or project.

Three sources of comprehensive information on developing and using IMPs and IMSs are:

- Integrated Master Plan and Integrated Master Schedule Preparation and Use Guide
- NDIA, Planning & Scheduling Excellence Guide (PASEG)
- GAO Scheduling Assessment Guide
- PM CoP

CH 1–3.4.3 Functional Integrated Master Plan/Integrated Master Schedule Inputs

Accepting that detailed planning is a requirement for an acquisition program by both government and industry, the Integrated Master Plan/Integrated Master Schedule (IMP/IMS) construct should be used not just by the contractor, but also by the government PMO. Thorough planning in accordance with statutory, regulatory, and policy requirements at both the functional and program level is an ongoing necessity. As changes related to external and internal factors occur, they need to be accommodated in an integrated program plan, which is also represented in the program IMS. The use of a PMO IMP and IMS for daily, weekly, and monthly management of the acquisition at all levels, not just the prime Contractor(s), is both appropriate and effective.

The following seven figures (Figures 12 through 18) depict typical, but definitely not all-inclusive samples of Activities, Documentation, and Reviews by acquisition functional area and acquisition phase that, as applicable to the program, are considered in functional inputs to the PMO IMP/IMS. The graphics present higher level activities and events for which accomplishments and criteria would need to be agreed upon as the IMP is developed. IMPs for other ACAT and/or Acquisition Model programs would have similar activities and events tailored to the size and type of the acquisition being planned. The functional IMP inputs are also supported by functional IMS inputs, as the PMO IMP is implemented by a PMO IMS.

Development and utilization of IMPs and IMSs are intensive activities, but they provide PMs and functional leaders with necessary visibility into program execution to manage the acquisition.

CH 1–3.4.3.1 Systems Engineering

DoDI 5000.02 (Encl. 3, para 2) and CH 3–2.2, set requirements and expectations for Systems Engineering (SE) planning for any program, of any type or model, that is to be documented in the Acquisition Strategy (AS), Systems Engineering Plan (SEP), Program Protection Plan (PPP) and other documents. The plan is expected to the most effective and efficient path to deliver a capability, from identifying user needs and concepts through delivery and sustainment.

Figure 12 provides a starting point for SE activities, reviews, and documentation by acquisition phase from Materiel Solution Analysis to Operations and Support. It serves only as an example—every IMP is tailored to the specific program being planned and executed.

Figure 12: System Engineering Considerations

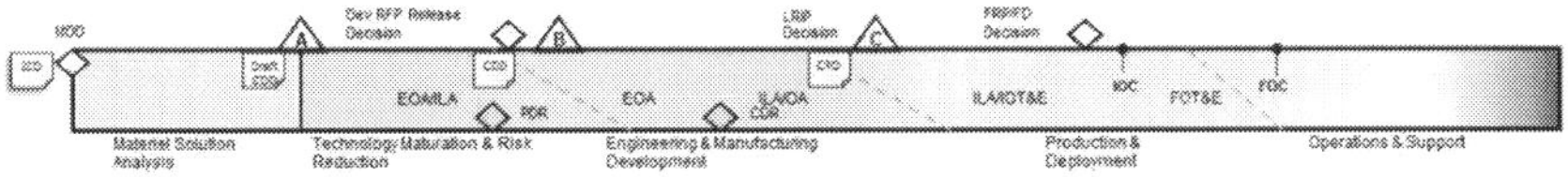

DAG Chapter 3 Systems Engineering, and DAG Chapter 9 Program Protection can be used as guides to developing the SE input to the program IMP.

CH 1–3.4.3.2 Product Support

DoDI 5000.02 (Encl. 6) and CH 4–2.2 both address expectations for sustainment planning. DoDI 5000.02 (Encl. 6, paras 2 and 3) and Figure 13 list specific activities that should be considered in sustainment planning and content for the LCSP that is a deliverable at Milestone A.

DAG Chapter 4 provides best practice and guidance for executing a weapon system's sustainment planning and states that sustainment planning should begin as early as initial capability reviews as a best practice to ensure sustainment can be effectively executed when first production quantities are fielded.

Figure 13 has activities by phase that are in two Sections: Considerations and Documentation and Reviews. Developing a Sustainment IMP to be supported by an IMS can be a collection of parallel IMPs, the results of which would be documented in the LCSP. One or more sustainment IMPs would be initiated for later consolidation by Logistics Trade Studies and other activities listed in the Materiel Solution Analysis phase as for Risk, Issues and Opportunities; another for fielding strategy; or another for CORE, 50/50/ and DSOR/SOR evaluation. The separate IMPs would feed a Product Support IMP initiated in the Materiel Solution Analysis phase leading to development of a draft LCSP that would be updated throughout the remaining acquisition phases.

Figure 13: Product Support

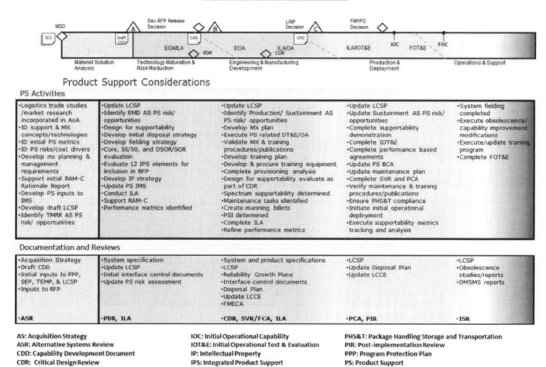

AS: Acquisition Strategy
ASR: Alternative Systems Review
CDD: Capability Development Document
CDR: Critical Design Review
CPD: Capability Production Document
CONOPs: Concept of Operations
DSOR: Depot Source of Repair
EOA: Early Operational Assessment
FMECA: Failure Modes Effects Criticality Analysis
FOC: Final Operational Capability
FOT&E: Follow-on Test & Evaluation
ICD: Initial Capabilities Document
ID: Identify
ILA: Independent Logistics Assessment
IMS: Integrated Master Schedule

IOC: Initial Operational Capability
IOT&E: Initial Operational Test & Evaluation
IP: Intellectual Property
IPS: Integrated Product Support
ISR: In Service Review
LCCE: Life Cycle Cost Estimate
LCSP: Life-Cycle Sustainment Plan
MDD: Materiel Development Decision
MX: Maintenance
OA: Operational assessment
OMS/MP: Operational Mode Summary/Mission Profile
OTRR: Operational Test Readiness Review
PCA: Physical Configuration Audit
PDR: Preliminary Design Review

PHS&T: Package Handling Storage and Transportation
PIR: Post-implementation Review
PPP: Program Protection Plan
PS: Product Support
RAM-C: Reliability, Availability, & Maintainability – Cost
SVR: System Verification Review
SEP: System Engineering Plan
SFR: System Functional Review
SOR: Source of Repair
SVR/FCA: System Verification Review/ Functional Configuration Audit
TEMP: Test and Evaluation Master Plan
TRA: Technology Readiness Assessment
TRR: Test Readiness Review
TSFD: Technology Security & Foreign Disclosure

CH 1–3.4.3.3 Contracts

Figure 14 identifies Considerations and Documentation and Reviews for defense acquisition, most of which are associated with developing and executing the Acquisition Plan (AP), which may be a separate document or the required AP elements may be included in the AS. Whether planning a separate AP or incorporating required elements in the program AS development of a Contracts IMP that identifies key events, developing AP content with supporting IMS enables visibility and tracking throughout the acquisition. For more information on PM interactions with contracting activities refer to CH 1–4.2.11.

Figure 14: Contracts

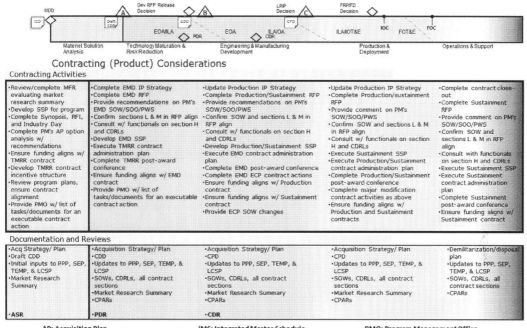

Contracting (Product) Considerations

Contracting Activities

•Review/complete MFR evaluating market research summary •Develop SSP for program •Complete Synopsis, RFI, and Industry Day •Complete PM's AP option analysis w/ recommendations •Ensure funding aligns w/ TMRR contract •Develop TMRR contract incentive structure •Review program plans, ensure contract alignment •Provide PMO w/ list of tasks/documents for an executable contract action	•Complete EMD IP Strategy •Complete EMD RFP •Provide recommendations on PM's EMD SOW/SOO/PWS •Confirm sections L & M in RFP align •Consult w/ functionals on section H and CDRLs •Develop EMD SSP •Execute TMRR contract administration plan •Complete TMRR post-award conference •Ensure funding aligns w/ EMD contract •Provide PMO w/ list of tasks/documents for an executable contract action	•Update Production IP Strategy •Complete Production/Sustainment RFP •Provide recommendations on PM's SOW/SOO/PWS •Confirm SOW and sections L & M in RFP align •Consult w/ functionals on section H and CDRLs •Develop Production/Sustainment SSP •Execute EMD contract administration plan •Complete EMD post-award conference •Complete EMD ECP contract actions •Ensure funding aligns w/ Production contract •Ensure funding aligns w/ Sustainment contract •Provide ECP SOW changes	•Update Production IP Strategy •Complete Production/sustainment RFP •Provide comment on PM's SOW/SOO/PWS •Confirm SOW and sections L & M in RFP align •Consult w/ functionals on section H and CDRLs •Execute Sustainment SSP •Execute Production/Sustainment contract administration plan •Complete Production/Sustainment post-award conference •Complete major modification contract activities as above •Ensure funding aligns w/ Production and Sustainment contracts	•Complete contract close-out •Complete Sustainment RFP •Provide comment on PM's SOW/SOO/PWS •Confirm SOW and sections L & M in RFP align •Consult with functionals on section H and CDRLs •Execute Sustainment SSP •Execute Sustainment contract administration plan •Complete Sustainment post-award conference •Ensure funding aligns w/ Sustainment contract

Documentation and Reviews

•Acq Strategy/ Plan •Draft CDD •Initial inputs to PPP, SEP, TEMP, & LCSP •Market Research Summary •ASR	•Acquisition Strategy/ Plan •CDD •Updates to PPP, SEP, TEMP, & LCSP •SOWs, CDRLs, all contract sections •Market Research Summary •CPARs •PDR	•Acquisition Strategy/ Plan •CPD •Updates to PPP, SEP, TEMP, & LCSP •SOWs, CDRLs, all contract sections •Market Research Summary •CPARs •CDR	•Acquisition Strategy/ Plan •CPD •Updates to PPP, SEP, TEMP, & LCSP •SOWs, CDRLs, all contract sections •Market Research Summary •CPARs	•Demilitarization/disposal plan •Updates to PPP, SEP, TEMP, & LCSP •SOWs, CDRLs, all contract sections •CPARs

AP: Acquisition Plan	IMS: Integrated Master Schedule	PMO: Program Management Office
AS: Acquisition Strategy	IOC: Initial Operational Capability	PPP: Program Protection Plan
ASR: Alternative Systems Review	IOT&E: Initial Operational Test & Evaluation	PS: Product Support
CDD: Capability Development Document	IP: Intellectual Property	PWS: Performance Work Statement
CDR: Critical Design Review	IPS: Integrated Product Support	RFI: Request for Information
CDRLs: Contract Data Requirements Lists	LCCE: Life Cycle Cost Estimate	RFP: Request fro Proposal
CPARs: Contractor Performance Assessment Reports	LCSP: Life-Cycle Sustainment Plan	SEP: System Engineering Plan
	LRIP: Low-Rate Initial Production	SOW: Statement of Work
CPD: Capability Production Document	MDD: Materiel development Decision	SOO: Statement of Objectives
ECP: Engineering Change Proposals	MFR: Memorandum for Record	SSP: Source Selection Plan
EOA: Early Operational Assessment	MX: Maintenance	SVR: System Verification Review
FOC: Final Operational Capability	OA: Operational Assessment	TEMP: Test and Evaluation Master Plan
FOT&E: Follow-on Test & Evaluation	OTRR: Operational Test Readiness Review	
ICD: Initial Capabilities Document	PCA: Physical Configuration Audit	
ILA: Independent Logistics Assessment	PDR: Preliminary Design Review	

CH 1–3.4.3.4 Test and Evaluation

DoDI 5000.02 (Encl. 4 and 5) detail Test and Evaluation (T&E) expectations to provide engineers and decision-makers with knowledge to assist in managing risks, to measure technical progress, and to characterize operational effectiveness, suitability, and survivability. Accomplishing those goals requires planning, resourcing, and executing a robust and rigorous T&E program. A T&E program begins early in the life cycle and continues through the life of the system, with major events at every phase of the acquisition. Planning, resourcing, and executing the T&E is a program management responsibility that is documented in the Test and Evaluation Master Plan (TEMP).

DoDI 5000.02 (Encl. 4 and 5) provide extensive expectations for program office involvement with test activities, including field activities. Figure 15 includes some, but hardly all, Considerations, Documentation and Reviews, by phase, for T&E. The information outlined in Figure 14, along with DoDI 5000.02 (Encl. 4 and Encl. 5), clearly indicates that in any defense system acquisition program, regardless of scope or cost, management needs a roadmap of T&E events. Those T&E events identify specified accomplishments and criteria to create an IMP that enables development of a T&E IMS to identify resources required and to track T&E progress. Refer to CH 8–3 for additional T&E guidance.

Figure 15: Test and Evaluation

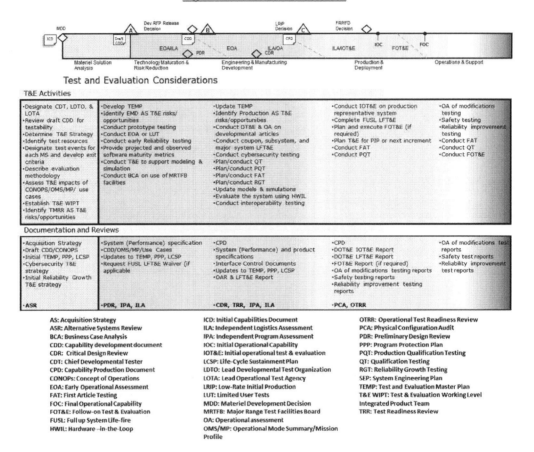

CH 1–3.4.3.5 Budget, Cost Estimating, and Financial Management
CH 1–3.4.3.5 Budget, Cost Estimating, and Financial Management

Figure 16 is intended as a starting point for the input of a Business and Financial Manager (BFM) to the program Integrated Master Plan (IMP), to which events may be added or deleted depending on the program and its status. The following graphic includes both DAS and PPBE events in the sequential acquisition phases from which the PMO BFM can develop an IMP input with accomplishments and criteria in order to develop and deliver documentation for DAS and/or PPBE activities.

Figure 16: Budget, Cost Estimating, and Financial Management

MDD		Dev RFP Release Decision				LRIP Decision		FRP/FD Decision		
ICD	A	Draft CDD	B	CDD		C	CPD			
		EOA/ILA	PDR	EOA	ILA/OA CDR			ILA/IOT&E	IOC FOT&E FOC	
Materiel Solution Analysis	Technology Maturation & Risk Reduction		Engineering & Manufacturing Development			Production & Deployment		Operations & Support		

Business, Cost Estimating & Financial Management Considerations

BCEFM Activities

•Receive AoA guidance from CAPE •Participate in AoA •Create affordability assessment for MS A •Justify full funding in FYDP by MS A •Complete 2366A determination (MDAP only) •Budget request vetted in PPBE process •Budget request vetted in Congressional enactment process •Establish TMRR RDT&E PE	•Prepare CARD •Prepare Service cost position •Prepare ICE or sufficiency review or EA (IS systems) •Update affordability assessment for MS B •Full funding in FYDP by MS B •2366B certification by MS B (MDAP only) •Establish EMD RDT&E PE •Develop/update program funding reports •Update budget documents (e.g., R forms) •Develop Spend Plan (O&E Forecast) •Complete LCCE	•Update cost estimate •Execute should cost program •Full funding in FYDP •Establish procurement budget line item •Establish sustainment funding line item •Update affordability assessment •Develop/update program funding reports •Update budget documents (e.g., P&R forms) •Develop Spend Plan (O&E Forecast) •Update LCCE	•Update cost estimate •Execute should cost program •Full funding in FYDP •Update procurement budget line item •Update sustainment funding line item •Develop/update program funding reports •Update budget documents (e.g., P&O forms) •Develop Spend Plan (O&E Forecast) •Update LCCE	•Develop/update program funding reports •Update budget documents (e.g., P&O forms) •Develop Spend Plan (O&E Forecast) •Update LCCE

Documentation and Reviews

•Acquisition Strategy •Draft CDD •Inital inputs to PPP, SEP, TEMP, & LCSP •Inputs to RFP •Mid-year Review •Year-End Close-Out	•Acquisition Strategy •CDD •Update PPP, SEP, TEMP, LCSP •Mid-year Review •Year-End Close-Out •SAR/MAR (as appropriate) •RAM-C Report	•Acquisition Strategy •CPD •Update PPP, SEP, TEMP, LCSP •Mid-year Review •Year-End Close-Out •SAR/MAR (as appropriate)	•Acquisition Strategy •CPD •Update PPP, SEP, TEMP, LCSP •Mid-year Review •Year-End Close-Out •SAR/MAR (as appropriate)	•Acquisition Strategy •CPD •Update PPP, SEP, TEMP, LCSP •Mid-year Review •Year-End Close-Out •SAR/MAR (as appropriate)
•PDR, ILA, IPA	•PDR, ILA, IPA	•CDR, ILA, IPA	•ISR	•PIR

AoA: Analysis of Alternatives
CAPE: Cost Analysis & Program Evaluation
CARD: Cost Analysis Requirements Description
CDD: Capability Development Document
CDR: Critical Design Review
CPD: Capability Production Document
DFF: Defense Exportability Features
EA: Economic Analysis
EOA: Early Operational Assessment
FOC: Final Operational Capability
FOT&E: Follow-on Test & Evaluation
FRP: Full Rate Production
FYDP: Future Years Defense Program
ICD: Initial Capabilities Document

ILA: Independent Logistics Assessment
IOC: Initial Operational Capability
IOT&E: Initial Operational Test & Evaluation
ICE: Independent Cost Estimate
IPS: Integrated Product Support
LCCE: Life Cycle Cost Estimate
LCSP: Life-Cycle Sustainment Plan
MAIS: Major Automated Information System
MAR: MAIS Annual Report
MDAP: Major Defense Acquisition Program
MDD: Materiel Development Decision
O&E: Obligations and Expenditures
OA: Operational Assessment
PDR: Preliminary Design Review

PE: Program Element
PIR: Post-implementation Review
PPBE: Planning, Programming, Budgeting, & Execution
PPP: Program Protection Plan
RDT&E: Research, Development, Test & Evaluation
RAM-C: Reliability, Availability, Maintenance-Cost
RFP: Request for Proposal
SAR: Selected Acquisition Report
SEP: System Engineering Plan
TEMP: Test and Evaluation Master Plan

CH 1–3.4.3.6 Production

Figure 17 represents typical, but not necessarily a complete or universal, set of Considerations, Documentation, and Reviews associated with weapon systems production to ensure integration of manufacturing readiness and risk as part of design activities. (Refer to CH 3–3.3.7 for additional information on production planning and manufacturing readiness activities.) Figure 17 indicates that as with other PMO processes, it is expected that planning for production should begin as early as the Materiel Solution Phase and continue through intervening phases until key events as the Production Readiness Review (PRR) CH 3–3.3.7, Physical Configuration Audit (PCA) CH 3–3.3.8 and Factory Acceptance Test (FAT) CH 8–4.4.1 are accomplished with achievement of previously established exit criteria.

Figure 17: Production

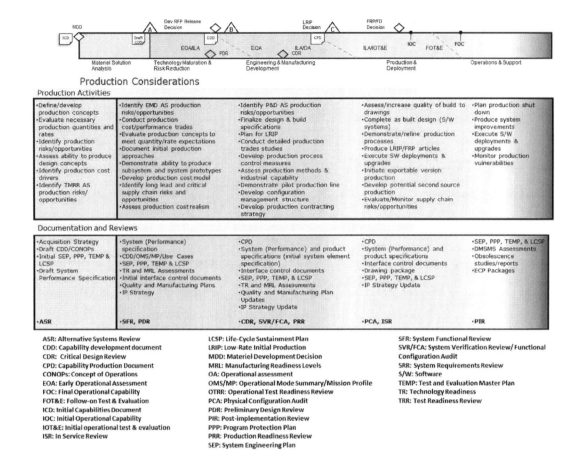

Production Considerations

Production Activities

•Define/develop production concepts •Evaluate necessary production quantities and rates •Identify production risks/opportunities •Assess ability to produce design concepts •Identify production cost drivers •Identify TMRR AS production risks/ opportunities	•Identify EMD AS production risks/opportunities •Conduct production cost/performance trades •Evaluate production concepts to meet quantity/rate expectations •Document initial production approaches •Demonstrate ability to produce subsystem and system prototypes •Develop production cost model •Identify long lead and critical supply chain risks and opportunities •Assess production cost realism	•Identify P&D AS production risks/opportunities •Finalize design & build specifications •Plan for LRIP •Conduct detailed production trades studies •Develop production process control measures •Assess production methods & industrial capability •Demonstrate pilot production line •Develop configuration management structure •Develop production contracting strategy	•Assess/increase quality of build to drawings •Complete as built design (S/W systems) •Demonstrate/refine production processes •Produce LRIP/FRP articles •Execute SW deployments & upgrades •Initiate exportable version production •Develop potential second source production •Evaluate/Monitor supply chain risks/opportunities	•Plan production shut down •Produce system improvements •Execute S/W deployments & upgrades •Monitor production vulnerabilities

Documentation and Reviews

•Acquisition Strategy •Draft CDD/CONOPs •Initial SEP, PPP, TEMP & LCSP •Draft System Performance Specification	•System (Performance) specification •CDD/OMS/MP/Use Cases •SEP, PPP, TEMP & LCSP •TR and MRL Assessments •Initial interface control documents •Quality and Manufacturing Plans •IP Strategy	•CPD •System (Performance) and product specifications (initial system element specification) •Interface control documents •SEP, PPP, TEMP, & LCSP •TR and MRL Assessments •Quality and Manufacturing Plan Updates •IP Strategy Update	•CPD •System (Performance) and product specifications •Interface control documents •Drawing package •SEP, PPP, TEMP, & LCSP •IP Strategy Update	•SEP, PPP, TEMP, & LCSP •DMSMS Assessments •Obsolescence studies/reports •ECP Packages
•ASR	•SFR, PDR	•CDR, SVR/FCA, PRR	•PCA, ISR	•PIR

ASR: Alternative Systems Review	LCSP: Life-Cycle Sustainment Plan	SFR: System Functional Review
CDD: Capability development document	LRIP: Low-Rate Initial Production	SVR/FCA: System Verification Review/ Functional
CDR: Critical Design Review	MDD: Materiel Development Decision	Configuration Audit
CPD: Capability Production Document	MRL: Manufacturing Readiness Levels	SRR: System Requirements Review
CONOPs: Concept of Operations	OA: Operational assessment	S/W: Software
EOA: Early Operational Assessment	OMS/MP: Operational Mode Summary/Mission Profile	TEMP: Test and Evaluation Master Plan
FOC: Final Operational Capability	OTRR: Operational Test Readiness Review	TR: Technology Readiness
FOT&E: Follow-on Test & Evaluation	PCA: Physical Configuration Audit	TRR: Test Readiness Review
ICD: Initial Capabilities Document	PDR: Preliminary Design Review	
IOC: Initial Operational Capability	PIR: Post-implementation Review	
IOT&E: Initial operational test & evaluation	PPP: Program Protection Plan	
ISR: In Service Review	PRR: Production Readiness Review	
	SEP: System Engineering Plan	

A Production IMP and supporting Production IMS that are populated with events and supporting activities enable program management not only to track progress toward those key events, but also to ensure that resources are in place at the right time.

CH 1–3.4.3.7 International Acquisition and Exportability

DoD instructions governing early consideration of International Acquisition and Exportability (IA&E) include DoDI 5000.02 (Encl. 2, para 7.a.(1)), require program management to consider the potential for cooperative development or production, and/or foreign sales or transfers early in the acquisition planning process, and throughout the acquisition life cycle. See CH 1–4.2.8 and Chapter 1, Supplement 1 International Acquisition and Exportability (IA&E) for details on IA&E actions during the acquisition phases. A top-level summary of IA&E considerations across the acquisition phases and related activities, documentation, and programs are illustrated in Figure 18.

Figure 18: International Acquisition & Exportability

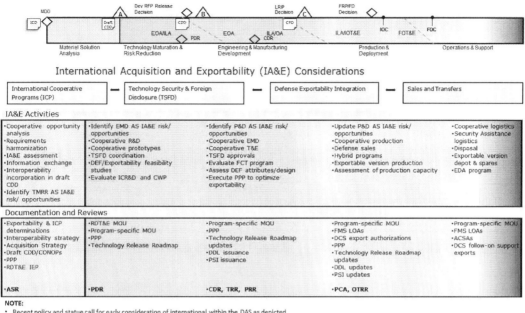

International Acquisition and Exportability (IA&E) Considerations

| International Cooperative Programs (ICP) | — | Technology Security & Foreign Disclosure (TSFD) | — | Defense Exportability Integration | — | Sales and Transfers |

IA&E Activities

•Cooperative opportunity analysis •Requirements harmonization •IA&E assessment •Information exchange •Interoperability incorporation in draft CDD •Identify TMRR AS IA&E risk/ opportunities	•Identify EMD AS IA&E risk/ opportunities •Cooperative R&D •Cooperative prototypes •TSFD coordination •DEF/Exportability feasibility studies •Evaluate ICR&D and CWP	•Identify P&D AS IA&E risk/ opportunities •Cooperative EMD •Cooperative T&E •TSFD approvals •Evaluate FCT program •Assess DEF attributes/design •Execute PPP to optimize exportability	•Update P&D AS IA&E risk/ opportunities •Cooperative production •Defense sales •Hybrid programs •Exportable version production •Assessment of production capacity	•Cooperative logistics •Security Assistance logistics •Disposal •Exportable version depot & spares •EDA program

Documentation and Reviews

•Exportability & ICP determinations •Interoperability strategy •Acquisition Strategy •Draft CDD/CONOPs •PPP •RDT&E IEP	•RDT&E MOU •Program-specific MOU •PPP •Technology Release Roadmap	•Program-specific MOU •PPP •Technology Release Roadmap updates •DDL issuance •PSI issuance	•Program-specific MOU •FMS LOAs •DCS export authorizations •PPP •Technology Release Roadmap updates •DDL updates •PSI updates	•Program-specific MOU •FMS LOAs •ACSAs •DCS follow-on support exports
•ASR	•PDR	•CDR, TRR, PRR	•PCA, OTRR	

NOTE:
* Recent policy and statue call for early consideration of international within the DAS as depicted.
* Historically many of these activities/decisions have occurred later in the DAS process.

ACSA: Acquisition and Cross-Servicing Arrangement	FCT: Foreign Comparative Testing	OTRR: Operational Test Reediness Review
ASR: Alternative Systems Review	FMS: Foreign Military Sales	PCA: Physical Configuration Audit
CDD: Capability development document	FOT&E: Follow-on Test & Evaluation	P&D: Production and Deployment
CDR: Critical Design Review	ICP: International Cooperative Programs	PDR: Preliminary Design Review
CWP: Coalition Warfare Program	ICR&D: International Cooperative R&D	PPP: Program Protection Plan
DEF: Defense exportability features	IA&E: International Acquisition and Exportability	PRR: Production Readiness Review
DDL: Delegation of Disclosure Letter	IEP: Information Exchange Program	PSI: Program Security Instruction
DCS: Direct Commercial Sales	IOT&E: Initial operational test & evaluation	R&D: Research & development
EDA: Excess Defense Articles	LOA: Letter of Offer and Acceptance	TRR: Teat Readiness Review
EOA: Early Operational Assessment	MOU: Memorandum of Understanding	TSFD: Technology Security & Foreign Disclosure
	OA: Operational assessment	

CH 1–3.4.4 Organizing and Planning Pitfalls

When it comes to program management, and the integration and orchestration of program activities, including working with stakeholders and enabling sound decisions, there are a variety of pitfalls. The following is a list of concerns for PMs to consider.

- Starting to write before thinking through and understanding the risks and opportunities associated with the desired program outcomes.
- Flawed framing assumption(s) (refer to CH 1–4.2.4).
- Overly optimistic or incomplete acquisition planning (IMP/IMS) (refer to CH 1–3.4.2).
- Taking the easy road to generating the necessary program documentation by using "Fluff" and "Cut and Paste" approach.
- No margin—no ability to cope with unidentified risks.
  - Lack of substantive business planning:
  - Artificially limited scope
  - Contract type and contract incentive not aligned with program risks and opportunities
  - "Red" funding numbers in the near years
  - And the Biggy—following policy without knowing the **why.**
  - Poor integration within documents and with the other key documents.
- Linking high-technology dependency with a moderate-low technical risk assessment.

- Ignoring stakeholder concerns (refer to CH 1–3.3.4.1).
- Program lacks formal documented risk mitigation plans for all medium/high risks.
- Program fails to track execution progress toward mitigation plans, e.g., mitigation tasks do not have resources assigned, due dates, or the status of the task.
- Lack of off-ramps for major program risks.
- Programs underestimate the power of opportunity management and limit use of *Should Cost* techniques/thinking (refer to CH 1–4.2.17.1).
- Program performance baseline not well understood by the government PM.
- Risks and their mitigations are disconnected from Earned Value Management/Work Breakdown Structure/Integrated Master Schedule/Integrated Master Plan (EVM/WBS/IMS/IMP) planning and processes.
- Earned value management not effectively utilized as a program execution management tool (refer to CH 1–4.2.16).
- Program planning/execution does not link Technical Performance Measures with EVM/Risk Management/WBS/IMS/IMP.
- Program management fails to have a portfolio view of risk and opportunity management.
- Lack of internal training process.
- Failure to plan for international acquisition involvement—including program protection and exportability aspects—early enough.

Certainly, this is not an all-inclusive list, but it represents a good sanity check for PMs to walk through and reflect on whether their team has fallen into one or more of these pitfalls. The next question is: What other pitfalls do PMs need to be mindful of regarding successful delivery of the capability required?

CH 1–3.4.5 Organizing and Planning Expected Benefits

The expected benefit of planning and organizing an acquisition initially and throughout its life cycle is a higher probability of delivering a system that meets requirements within established cost and schedule. The JCIDS, PPBE, and DAS each have detailed expectations for program management that are not met in the absence of a sound understanding of those enterprises and their expectations. This requires the PMO, operating as an IPT, executing or overseeing the execution of many detailed plans that are captured in both a government and a contractor Integrated Master Plan and Integrated Master Schedule (IMP/IMS). These tools can be used to status program execution on a daily, weekly, and monthly basis. Clearly, the IMP and IMS are not the only tools in the tool box—but they enable the PMO to maintain visibility into all aspects of the program during the very complicated process of taking a capability requirement to a fielded system. Thoughtful and detailed planning that is documented in an IMP and IMS can enable the resourcing and timely execution of events documented in program acquisition documents such as the Acquisition Strategy, Systems Engineering Plan, Life Cycle Sustainment Plan, and Test and Evaluation Master Plan.

CH 1–4. Additional Planning Considerations

Section 4 presents more than 20 key considerations for program management consideration during development of an acquisition program, an Acquisition Strategy, and other documentation. While every acquisition program does not have to be concerned with each of the topics, most will. The level of detail is meant to be far more than an introduction to a subject. Enough significant detail is included to create a roadmap (IMP view) for program management. Checklists are omitted; most of the topics reference other resources for additional guidance and/or more details for addressing the topic as it pertains to an acquisition program or Acquisition Strategy.

CH 1–4.1 Acquisition Strategy

The Acquisition Strategy (AS) is the primary means that a PM uses to define the approach for an acquisition program. An Acquisition Strategy is a statutory requirement for Major Defense Programs (IAW 10 USC 2431a) at Milestone A, the Pre-RFP Milestone, and updates at Milestone C and Full Rate Production Fielding Decision. Acquisition strategies are required for all major system acquisition programs by FAR 34.004, which states, the PM, as specified in agency procedures, shall develop an Acquisition Strategy tailored to the particular major system acquisition program. This strategy is the PM's overall plan for satisfying the mission need in the most effective, economical, and timely manner. The strategy shall be in writing and prepared in accordance with the requirements of Subpart 7.1, except where inconsistent with this part, and shall qualify as the acquisition plan for the major system acquisition, as required by that subpart. The use and purpose of the Acquisition Strategy are further defined in DoDI 5000.02 (Encl2, para 6). The statutory topics required in an Acquisition Strategy (see DoDI 5000.02, Encl. 1, Table 2) include:

- Benefit Analysis and Determination
- Consideration of Technology Issues
- Contract Type Determination
- Cooperative Opportunities
- General Equipment Valuation
- Industrial Base Capabilities Considerations
- Intellectual Property (IP) Strategy
- Market Research
- Small Business Innovation Research
- Termination Liability Estimate
- Federal Acquisition Regulation 34.004, Acquisition Strategy, establishes broader requirements for the Acquisition Strategy (Acquisition Plan)

This Section provides a discussion on planning an acquisition strategy as well as related topics, including the capability being developed, budgeting, and listing of acquisition models from which to choose that best fit the performance, schedule, and cost of the acquisition being planned. Program Managers can use one of the following models as a starting point in structuring an acquisition program to acquire and tailor it to fit their specific acquisition program. DoDI 5000.02 (para 5) provides a description of the four basic examples and two hybrid models.

- Model 1: Hardware Intensive Program
- Model 2: Defense-Unique Software Intensive Program
- Model 3: Incrementally Fielded Software Intensive Program
- Model 4: Accelerated Acquisition Program
- Model 5: Hybrid Program A (Hardware Dominant)
- Model 6: Hybrid Program B (Software Dominant)

After determining which of the models best fits the planned acquisition, PMs can consider how to address the statutory and regulatory requirements in the Acquisition Strategy. Additional considerations for developing a program strategy are found in CH 1–4.2.

For the PM and the PMO team, the Acquisition Strategy provides a comprehensive, integrated plan that identifies the acquisition approach and describes the business, technical, and support strategies that the PM plans to employ to manage program risks/opportunities and meet program objectives. It communicates the relationship between the acquisition phases and work efforts, and key program events as outlined in the Integrated Master Plan (IMP) referred to in CH 1–3.4.2 such as decision points, reviews, contract awards, test activities, production lot/delivery quantities, and operational deployment objectives.

The primary authors of the Acquisition Strategy are the PM and acquisition team (PMO). To assist in the development of the Acquisition Strategy, a template — the Milestone Document Information Tool (MDID) — has been developed to outline the required sections and key questions. Final approval of the Acquisition Strategy is made by the Milestone Decision Authority (MDA).

In addition to the statutorily required topics, the Acquisition Strategy addresses key elements such as requirements satisfaction, concept of operations/use cases, technical risks, resources requirements, and funding requirements. For each of these broad topics, there are other program documents, such as the SEP, ICD, CDD, and TEMP, which provide the foundation for critical thinking that is summarized in the Acquisition Strategy. As such, the goal of the Acquisition Strategy is not to provide all the foundational information, but sufficient information and data with references to demonstrate validity of the specific approach and planning for the acquisition.

Once approved by the MDA, the PM will execute the Acquisition Strategy to complete the program. A significant caution in developing a program Acquisition Strategy is the framing assumptions that underlie the overall strategy. If they are not identified and taken into consideration, or prove to be incorrect (see CH 1–4.2.4 for a discussion on Framing Assumptions), there will be, at some point in the acquisition, realization that the Acquisition Strategy is flawed. Frequently, the failure of a framing assumption is a precursor to a restructuring of the program.

Revisions/updates to the Acquisition Strategy are required at major milestones (by statute), prior to the release of an RFP (if independent of a milestone), and after a Nunn-McCurdy determination. These updates can range from a minor update to a major rewrite with change pages for the MDA's approval.

10 USC 2305, Contracts: Planning, Solicitation, Evaluation, and Award Procedures establishes a requirement for acquisition planning. According to 10 USC 2305 (a)(1)(A), in preparing for the procurement of property or services, the head of an agency shall— (ii) use advance procurement planning and market research.

In addition to the Acquisition Strategy, the PM is also responsible for developing another document—the Acquisition Plan. According to the Defense Federal Acquisition Regulation Supplement (DFARS 207.103(g), "the PM or other official responsible for the program has overall responsibility for acquisition planning." FAR 7.104(c)) states that, "The planner [read as PM] shall coordinate with and secure the concurrence of the Contracting Officer in all acquisition planning."

From a regulatory perspective, FAR 34.004 – Acquisition Strategy, states, "The strategy shall be in writing and prepared in accordance with the requirements of FAR Subpart 7.1, except where inconsistent with this part, and shall qualify as the acquisition plan for the major system acquisition, as required by that subpart." Those requirements are divided into two main Sections (i.e., Acquisition Background and Objectives, and Plan of Action) as depicted in FAR Subpart 7.105. A summary is provided below:

- Acquisition Background and Objectives
  - Statement of Need and applicable conditions, including:
    - Cost (life-cycle cost; design-to-cost; and application of should-cost)
    - Capability or performance
    - Delivery or performance-period requirements
    - Tradeoffs; risks; acquisition streamlining
- Plan of Action
  - Sources
  - Competition
  - Contract type selection
  - Source-selection procedures
  - Acquisition considerations
  - Budgeting and funding
  - Product or service descriptions
  - Priorities, allocations, and allotments
  - Contractor versus government performance
  - Inherently governmental functions
  - Management information requirements
  - Make or buy
  - Test and evaluation
  - Logistics considerations

- ○ Government-furnished property
- ○ Government-furnished information
- ○ Environmental and energy conservation objective
- ○ Security considerations
- ○ Contract administration
- ○ Other considerations
- ○ Milestones for the acquisition cycle
- ○ Identification of participants in acquisition plan preparation
- ○ Considerations in Developing a Program Strategy

CH 1–4.2 Considerations in Developing a Program Strategy

The following subsections present potentially significant subjects for PM consideration in developing the program plan and acquisition strategy.

CH 1–4.2.1. Improving Acquisition Outcomes

Improving acquisition outcomes is a perennial goal, and every acquisition professional has a role. From early materiel solution analysis onward, requirements and acquisition professionals can team to find efficient solution alternatives to minimize the need for customized or DoD-unique solutions to capability gaps. As solutions are acquired, the drive to capture opportunities to reduce life-cycle cost is the focus of many initiatives (aka "Should Cost"—see CH 1–4.2.17.1) on a program or across a portfolio. And finally, throughout operations and support, program teams continue to capture opportunities that increase net buying power through cost-effective enhancements to fill emerging capability gaps, or to more efficiently support existing capabilities. These efforts help our warfighting customers make efficient use of precious discretionary funds to meet portfolio-wide capability needs.

During program planning and execution, including well into sustainment, the following key areas warrant consideration to improve acquisition outcomes:

CH 1–4.2.1.1 Program Affordability

At its core, affordability requires teamwork. OSD and Service decision authorities (requirements, programming, and acquisition communities) ensure a system can be afforded in future budgets by conducting an affordability analysis at the portfolio level, to establish both production and sustainment affordability caps before a program is initiated. This customer-defined affordability goal, reviewed at each major milestone, enables a PM to focus the acquisition team on program cost drivers, and to offer requirements tradeoffs if needed, across the planned life cycle. See CH 1–4.2.15 for more information.

CH 1–4.2.1.2 Achieving Dominant Capabilities While Controlling Life Cycle Costs

- **Agility vs. Responsive and Emerging Threats.** Most capability areas face responsive threats; moreover, new threats mature with shorter lead times than in past decades. Being adaptive warrants a very strong Acquisition, Intelligence, and Requirements (AIR) community triad to inform portfolio planning, technology development, system design, product improvement, and technical refresh.
  - ○ *Critical Intelligence Parameters (CIP).* Use of CIPs focuses the program management team on the importance of integrating with the requirements and intelligence communities on key threat performance levels that could impact the viability of the materiel solution being acquired. PEOs and PMs work with requirements sponsors to identify threshold values for CIPs to enable the intelligence community to alert them when an adversary's capability substantially changes or seems likely to change. Timely notification of threat changes relative to a CIP enables a conversation on whether to change operational requirements and make a design change, or to take other appropriate actions. CIPs are continuously monitored by the Intelligence Community (IC), and should be discussed at the program's annual Configuration Steering Boards

(CSBs). If a CIP is breached, the CAE can convene an out-of-cycle CSB to deal with the threat change.

- ○ *Integration of Intel at Major Milestones.* Program Managers can factor in planning and resourcing for operational intelligence mission data (IMD) requirements across the life cycle. The acquisition strategy and systems engineering approach can also factor in the latest threat projections including review of program CIPs.
- **Cybersecurity.** Program teams address cybersecurity planning and execution across the program life cycle. Protection is also critical for classified and unclassified program information as well as potential access to DoD products in the field and through the supply chain. The DoD Chief Information Officer (CIO) published guidance to go beyond information assurance (IA) and focus on overall cybersecurity. The guidance replaced the former DOD-unique process (called "DIACAP") with the Risk Management Framework (RMF) for implementing and certifying cybersecurity. The USD(AT&L) and the DoD CIO jointly published a DoD Program Manager's Guidebook for Integrating the Cybersecurity Risk Management (RMF) Framework into the System Acquisition Lifecycle. The T&E community also published a DoD Cybersecurity Test and Evaluation Guidebook that is useful for program planning.

CH 1–4.2.1.3 Incentivizing Productivity and Cost Savings

Business strategies can increase buying power based on a variety of considerations:

- Careful selection of contract type. The use of incentive-type contracts (Cost Plus Incentive Fee [CPIF] and Fixed Price Incentive [Firm Target] [FPIF]) has been highly correlated with better cost and schedule performance. Although not mandated for use, OSD guidance reinforces a preference for these types of contracts when appropriate. [*Note:* The title of this paragraph is linked to a convenient table on contract type considerations.]
- **Effective use of Performance-Based Logistics (PBL) Arrangements**: PBL arrangements can balance cost and performance, whether industry or the government is the provider. PBL provides explicit productivity incentives that drive increased DoD buying power, particularly for service contracts such as maintenance and support contracts. For more details on best practice, consult the DoD PBL Guidebook: A Guide to Developing Performance-Based Arrangements.
- **Removing Barriers to Commercial Technology Use.** Military products are developed and fielded on longer time scales than pure commercial products, particularly electronics and information technology. Cycle time could be reduced through more effective use of commercial technologies. This initiative can be accelerated by small business research and development initiatives and the use of Modular Open Systems Architectures (MOSA) where practical, to foster shorter update cycles and to ease commercial tech insertion.

CH 1–4.2.1.4 Incentivizing Industry and Government Innovation

Acquisition outcomes can often be increased by fostering innovation and more timely technology insertion for the products DoD uses. Use of commercial technology is a way to boost productivity and reduce cycle times.

- **System architecture considerations to stimulate innovation.** Since many defense systems have long life cycles, incremental enhancements are commonplace; this expectation drives initial design and sustainment planning. The selection of MOSA (see CH 3–2.4.1 and CH 6–3.7.1.1) is one way to enable agility to more rapidly insert new capabilities, or to enhance cybersecurity, both of which provide needed military advantage throughout the life cycle. OSD has published a guidebook of best practice on Contracting for MOSA (DoD Open Systems Architecture Contract Guidebook for Program Managers). Architecture considerations are central to the program's systems engineering planning; likewise, the

Intellectual Property Strategy (CH 1–4.2.18.1) can enable the program to leverage the MOSA throughout the product life cycle.

- **Emphasize technology insertion and refresh in program planning.** Early focus on "developmental planning" efforts enables program offices to understand refresh/replacement cycle timelines for various technologies. This enables life-cycle opportunities for technology insertion to be part of program plans. The PM leads life-cycle forecasting with the user, and Science and Technology (S&T) communities. Opportunities can include commercial technologies, S&T transitioning from government laboratories, and military technologies being matured through rapid prototyping, including industry Independent Research and Development (IRAD)-funded efforts.
- **Engage industry early and often**. Much of the Defense acquisition community's program results are attained in relationship with industry, be it firms focused on defense-related products and services, commercial products, or firms that provide DoD a wide spectrum of support services. The following specific efforts to improve acquisition outcomes are focused on leveraging a strong and open relationship with industry:
  - *Provide draft technical requirements to industry early, and iteratively if necessary.*
    - Program teams that do not communicate with suppliers about requirements may be operating under misconceptions.
    - A typical Request for Proposal (RFP) will give industry 30-60 days to provide a proposal, even for large-scale systems developments. Short timelines are beneficial only if RFPs and industry proposals have had the benefit of previous sharing of thinking on issues such as risks, cost drivers, performance drivers, and technology opportunities.
    - A spectrum of interaction can be very advantageous—using broad industry days to share business opportunities across a portfolio, and focused engagements like RFIs, Program Industry Days with one-on-one meetings, and draft RFPs.
  - *Involve industry in funded concept definition.* Beyond early communications, consider funding competitive concept definition studies (e.g., early design trade studies and operations research) to inform decisions about requirements and as inputs to the formal Analyses of Alternatives (AoAs). Although this is an up-front expense, it can boost net buying power by fueling industry innovations, which can enable better user requirements that enable more responsive capability solutions.
  - *Provide industry clear definitions of "best value."* The customer funding a solution is the best judge of the value they place on increased capabilities. Therefore, in RFPs, program teams capture customer value, in monetary terms, of higher levels of performance than minimally acceptable or threshold levels. OSD has published updated DoD Source Selection Procedures with more details on these practices.

CH 1–4.2.1.5 Eliminate Unproductive Processes to Reduce Cycle Time and Cost

PEOs and PMs are positioned to influence a drive for leaner processes at the Service/Agency and OSD levels. Moreover, PEOs and PMs can, through their actions, drive the factors that can create a lean culture in their program teams—a culture that pervades the processes they govern. Some suggestions:

- **Create a Lean culture.** The use of incentives is one way to overtly demonstrate an interest in driving more lean business practice. Command- or Agency-sponsored internal suggestion or "IDEA" programs can provide financial rewards and more importantly, peer recognition of innovative ideas.
- **Leverage Value Engineering.** Value Engineering is a DoD-wide program that focuses on creating more value—it can recognize ideas from government or contractor employees or teams. On contracts, the Value Engineering Clause can be used to incentivize Value Engineering Change Proposals from contractors (and their subcontractors, through the prime) that ultimately increase the government's buying power.
- **Reduce Cycle Times**. Eliminating non-valued added staffing of numerous program documents can certainly help reduce cycle times. It is incumbent on PEOs and PMs to

advocate program tailoring to the maximum extent in program planning, leveraging early reviews of program strategy outlines and in-process reviews of tailored program plans.

CH 1–4.2.1.6 Promote Competition through Market Research to Increase Small Business Participation

Market research is the cornerstone of determining supplier capabilities in DoD acquisition and can reveal sweet spots for small business utilization. In addition, program offices and PEO teams can work with their Service Small Business Office to plan and participate in at least one small business-focused outreach event each year. Such events can inform the Small Business industrial base on policy updates and enable Small Business matchmaking with program offices and S&T organizations.

CH 1–4.2.1.7 Improve Tradecraft in Acquisition of Services

- **Improve requirements definition for services.** Defining requirements well is a challenging, but essential prerequisite to achieving desired services acquisition outcomes. As most services are integrated into the performance of a mission, it is critical for the program office (the acquirer) to get the mission owner (often an operational commander) involved in the requirement definition, as well as the acquisition and execution phases. Clearer, more focused requirements will help prevent clarifications that lead to protracted source selections and/or contract modifications to correct vagueness. For more specific program management actions for planning services acquisition, see CH 10–2.1.1.
- **Improve the effectiveness and productivity of contracted engineering and technical services.** DoD relies extensively on contracted services for technical management, systems engineering, and engineering services. CAEs and PEOs are expected to pursue enterprise approaches for acquiring these Engineering and Technical Services (ETS). PMs can leverage such enterprise contracts to reduce acquisition lead times and reduce costs for acquiring such support services.

CH 1–4.2.1.8 Continuously Improve Acquisition Workforce Skills and Qualifications

PMs and PEOs can have a great impact on their team, especially in terms of creating a culture of continuous learning. There are many skills that can offer significant leverage, if cultivated carefully and continuously:

- **Cultivate organic program office engineering and critical thinking capabilities.** PEOs and PMs can strengthen organic engineering capabilities by equipping the technical workforce with essential education, training, and job experiences, along with the right physics-based tools, models, data, and engineering facilities. These organic engineering capabilities posture the program team to better understand and manage requirements and technical risks. Moreover, program office and staff members with non-technical backgrounds can hone *systems thinking* skills, as well as more skilled *critical thinking,* through training and mentoring. Program Managers can proactively manage their organic workforce and elevate to the PEO any specific organic skill gaps that add risk in managing their projects.
- **Improve ability to perceive and mitigate technical risk and capture cost-saving opportunities.** Successful product development requires understanding and actively managing risks, beginning with requirements formulation, through planning and conducting a risk-reduction phase, if needed, and in structuring and executing development and test activities. PMs recognize that often net buying power is increased by *spending* money up front on active risk management or to capture opportunities that will have the greatest net impact on program performance. Anticipating possible adverse events, evaluating probabilities, understanding potential consequences and secondary cost/schedule impacts, and taking timely action to limit their impact if they occur is the essence of risk management. Likewise, opportunity management requires astute perception of favorable events that, if

cultivated, could result in net cost savings and therefore improve acquisition outcomes. Capturing cost-saving opportunities is the essence of "Should Cost." PMs lead risk management activities throughout the program life cycle. The DoD Risk, Issue, and Opportunity Management Guide for Defense Acquisition Programs is a reliable, up-to-date reference and team training tool.

The goal of improving acquisition outcomes is an overriding focus that permeates program management. There are specific actions acquisition professionals can take to be effective in this quest for efficiency in the midst of rapidly changing threats and technologies. Innovation comes from many sources, and increasingly, it comes from the commercial sector, including small businesses, and from both the United States and allied nations.

CH 1–4.2.2 Program Structure

Every program is different and should be individually structured. Determining the best structure for a program starts with an understanding of the product to be acquired. The program Acquisition Strategy should be based on tailoring one of the six models, but program content and decision points can be influenced by the following, among other considerations:

- Technology maturity
- Level of risk
- Design maturity and complexity
- DoD's experiences with similar designs or products
- Integration aspects
- Manufacturing technology and capabilities
- Life-cycle sustainment
- International or Joint program intent

While all programs will have a Materiel Development Decision Milestone, these considerations and others inform the decision of whether a Technology Maturation and Risk Reduction phase is needed, and the required duration prior to the start of Engineering and Manufacturing Development (EMD). Similar processes guide the structure beyond the EMD through Production and Deployment, and into Operations and Support.

In addition to a thorough understanding of the product itself and the risk inherent in developing and producing it, a range of other considerations that might influence program structure can be considered:

- Urgency of product delivery
- Industry capability to design and produce the product
- Uncertainty or imbalance of cost and capability
- Customer's priorities for performance
- Resource constraint effects on program risks

Each program is structured in a way that optimizes the chances of success. Evidence leading to a strong probability of a successful acquisition program is reflected in the program Acquisition Strategy. The thought process and the supporting data that led to the specific, unique Acquisition Strategy are well documented and clearly communicated to senior leadership during program reviews and when presenting program plans.

Additional program structure considerations are described in CH 1–4.2.2, CH 3–3.1.1, CH 6–3.2, CH 9–3.2.5 and CH 9–3.3.1.

Also refer to "The Optimal Program Structure," an article by Frank Kendall, Under Secretary of Defense (AT&L), and *Defense AT&L* magazine: July–August 2012

CH 1–4.2.2.1 Relevant Documents and Data Research and Analyses

Most, if not all, defense acquisition system programs share characteristics with other already developed and fielded systems. In developing a program plan and other documentation for a new acquisition, it is worth the effort for the PMO to seek out and understand the planning, strategies, and experiences of those similar programs during development, production, testing, fielding, and support. Comparing the planned strategy with the executed strategy—as well as planned and achieved capabilities, resources utilized, and schedule—can provide valuable insight into issues encountered and how, at what impact to the program, they were addressed and mitigated. The Services and Department have a wealth of historical, relevant data on the development and execution of Defense acquisition programs. CH 1–5.4 provides an overview of relevant databases to which reporting is required for most programs. Access can be requested to review documentation and data for a PM's own program, as well as documentation and data from other related programs. In addition, market research to gather information about potential solutions and sources is critical.

CH 1–4.2.3 Tailoring

A PM has the opportunity to use tailoring of regulatory requirements and acquisition procedures to more efficiently and effectively achieve program objectives consistent with statutory intent, sound business practice, and the specific risks associated with the product or service being acquired. It is unlikely that all DoD programs require the complete spectrum of the regulatory process; therefore, an individual acquisition program and the associated procedures used should be tailored as much as possible to the unique characteristics of the product/service being acquired. Such tailoring should also consider the circumstances associated with the program, including operational urgency, complexity, and risk factors. Program Managers work with their staffs and MDA to tailor program strategies and oversight, including program information, acquisition phase content, the timing and scope of decision reviews, and decision levels to the minimum required to satisfy validated capability requirements. Program Managers and their staffs maintain focus on the basics of sound acquisition planning, management, and decision-making as their primary responsibility.

Tailoring is not a one-time event, but rather a continuous review of the program's maturity and circumstances (costs, risks, technical progress, etc.). Tailoring is always based upon the logical progression of development, deployment, and fielded usage of the product/service. Tailoring is always appropriate when it will produce a more efficient and effective acquisition approach for the specific product. Also refer to CH 6–3.1 and CH 1–4.2.10.1. for additional information on tailoring for Information Technology and Urgent Capability Acquisition/Quick Reaction Capability programs.

CH 1–4.2.3.1 Program Tailoring

As discussed in DoDI 5000.02 (Encl. 2, paragraph 2), the Acquisition chain of command has the responsibility and authority for all aspects of program planning and execution to achieve maximum efficiencies and effectiveness from the Defense Acquisition System. The policy and procedures in DoDI 5000.02 authorize and strongly encourage MDAs to tailor regulatory requirements and procedures, including:

- Strategies
- Oversight
- Program information
- Phase content
- Timing and scope of decision reviews
- Decision levels based on specifics of the product being acquired

When there is a strong threat-based or operationally driven need to field a capability in the shortest time, MDAs are authorized to implement additional procedures designed to accelerate acquisition system responsiveness as long as adequate oversight of the program is maintained and all statutory requirements are met. See DoDI 5000.02 (Encl. 13).

In consultation with the appropriate stakeholders, PMs may propose, for MDA approval, tailoring of regulatory program information. MDAs will document all information tailoring decisions. While the DoD encourages tailoring, acquisition managers ensure that programs comply with the mandated requirements of DoDI 5000.02 (Encl. 1). As the program progresses through the acquisition phases and decision points, program tailoring continues, based on the outcomes and performance results determined by executive-level decision forums, and the tenets and processes of Integrated Product Teams (IPTs), program assessments, and periodic reporting. Non-MDAP and non-MAIS programs will use analogous DoD Component processes.

Additional or modified procedures and tailoring considerations applicable to IT programs and Defense Business Systems (DBS) are described in CH 6–3.1.

Urgent Capability Acquisition (UCA) tailoring procedures are described in DoDI 5000.02 (Encl. 13) and summarized in CH 1–4.2.10. Additional information regarding Tailoring is available at:

- DoDI 5000.02 (5.c.(3).(e))
- DoDI 5000.02 (Encl. 13, para 3)

CH 1–4.2.3.2 Documentation Tailoring

DoDI 5000.02 (Encl. 1, para 3 and following tables) describe Acquisition Program Information Requirements at Milestones and Other Decision Points. Program management assesses these information requirements early to allow sufficient time to collect the information, coordinate with participating DoD Components, and provide for timely routing. A significant number of documents with appropriate information and data are required to support Milestone Reviews and other critical program decision points. A determination of how these issues are addressed and the specific supporting documentation required are the result of a tailoring process between the PM and MDA.

DoDI 5000.02 (Encl. 1) identifies the specific Information Requirements (Statutory and Regulatory) for each milestone and decision point by:

- Program Type – Table 2
- Recurring Program Reports – Table 5
- Waivers, and Alternative Management and Reporting Requirements – Table 6
- Reporting Requirements - CH 1–5.1.

Information Requirements unique to the Urgent Capability Acquisition/Quick Reaction Capability Process are included in Encl. 13.

Information listed in the Tables required by statute is addressed and cannot be waived unless the statute specifically provides for waiver of the stated requirement. Information listed in the Tables required by regulation may be tailored at the MDA's discretion.

DoD maintains the Milestone Document Identification (MDID) tool that presents a collection of information requirements based on user selected filtering of program acquisition category (and subcategory type if applicable), life-cycle event, and the source of the information requirement (Statutory or Regulatory). Each information requirement is linked to an information card containing pertinent content and linked sources (Description/Definition, Notes, Approval Authority, and DAG Topic Discussions). A capability is provided for ad-hoc filtering by keyword. Note that DoDI 5000.02 policy takes precedence over the MDID tool. The MDID Tool is discussed in CH 1–5.3.1.

CH 1–4.2.4 Framing Assumptions

Framing assumptions are any explicit or implicit assumptions that are central in shaping the cost, schedule, and/or performance expectations for a program. Their purpose is to inform acquisition leadership of key program assumptions, stimulate discussion of their validity, and establish context for program assessments. Framing assumptions are critical, without work-arounds, foundational, and program-specific.

- **Critical**. An invalid framing assumption significantly affects the program's cost, schedule, or performance.
- **Without Work-arounds**. The consequences of an incorrect framing assumption cannot be easily mitigated. The effects are generally outside the project team's control.
- **Foundational**. A framing assumption represents some central feature of the program. It is not subordinate, derivative, or linked to other assumptions.
- **Program-Specific**. A framing assumption reflects some specific aspect of the program rather than presenting a general statement that could describe many programs.

Framing assumptions are required to be presented at the Milestone A, Development RFP Release, and Milestone B reviews; and are documented in the Acquisition Strategy. They may change and evolve as a program progresses through the acquisition life cycle. The following subsections discuss the steps and considerations when identifying and tracking framing assumptions.

CH 1–4.2.4.1 Framing Assumptions Development

Framing assumptions are created by the program office, owned by the PM, reviewed and approved by acquisition leadership, and documented in the Acquisition Strategy. Identifying and tracking framing assumptions is a multi-step process that includes representatives from the different functional and technical areas. The following subsections contain the steps that are followed when identifying and tracking framing assumptions.

CH 1–4.2.4.1.1 Brainstorm Candidate Framing Assumptions

This phase is one of idea generation, where no candidate framing assumption is immediately dismissed. The goal is to obtain a robust list that will be pared down using eligibility criteria. For an assumption to be central to a program's cost, schedule, or performance expectations, it is considered and assumed true (explicitly or implicitly) during development of the program's requirements, cost and schedule estimates, and Acquisition Program Baseline (APB). Whether a framing assumption is applicable to a specific program depends on whether it is inherent to the program's Acquisition Strategy and procurement environment.

Sources of candidate framing assumptions include technological and engineering challenges; cost, schedule, and requirements tradeoffs; effectiveness of program-specific managerial or organizational structures; suitability of contractual terms and incentives to deliver specific expected outcomes; interdependencies with other programs; and industrial base, market, or political considerations. While brainstorming, the following questions can be asked:

- What is essential to believe about this system?
- If it doesn't happen, does it change the nature of the program?

The resultant or final list of candidate framing assumptions only includes those suppositions that have grave consequences if not true. One potential pitfall is to focus solely on risks. While risks are important, "sure bets" are equally as important. If failure of a "sure bet" will significantly impact the program, then the "sure bet" is included as a candidate framing assumption. An example of a "sure bet" that could be a framing assumption is "Significant commercial demand for this class of product will reduce unit cost."

CH 1–4.2.4.1.2 Validate Candidate Framing Assumptions

Determine the eligibility of each candidate framing assumption by asking the following three questions:

- Is it critical?
- Is it foundational?

- Is it program-specific?
- Is it without work-arounds?

Eliminate or rework those candidate framing assumptions that do not meet all three criteria. Candidate framing assumptions that are determined not to be foundational may be grouped to form a foundational framing assumption. Validated candidate framing assumptions become potential framing assumptions. Examples of framing assumptions that meet these criteria are:

- Commonality of variants will be at least x percent.
- Open systems architecture and available technical data rights allow for competition.
- Legacy performance requirements are adequate for this system.
- Re-use of legacy components or subsystems will meet requirements and reduce cost.

CH 1–4.2.4.1.3 Prioritize and Limit Potential Framing Assumptions

Once framing assumptions are validated, evaluate how critical each framing assumption is to the success of the program and order the framing assumptions by criticality. The top three to five items become the framing assumptions.

CH 1–4.2.4.1.4 Identify Benefits/Consequences and Metrics

Since framing assumptions are central to the system, if a framing assumption is true, then a number of benefits will follow. If it is not true, then a number of logical consequences will follow. The benefits and consequences are used as input to metric definition, as it is often easier to measure the consequences than the actual framing assumptions. Determine the benefits and consequences of each framing assumption, and then decompose the framing assumptions into metrics that will be used to confirm or negate the framing assumptions as the program is executed.

CH 1–4.2.4.1.5 Track and Report on the Metrics

Once framing assumptions have been developed and metrics identified, it is imperative the metrics are tracked, as failure to meet a metric is an early indicator that a framing assumption is invalid and provides warning of future program consequences. Since by definition framing assumptions are critical to a program's success, further analysis is then completed to determine the root cause of the problem. Metrics are reported in the Defense Acquisition Executive Summary (DAES) reports and at program reviews.

CH 1–4.2.5 Risk, Issue, and Opportunity Management

The PM is charged with directing the development, production, and deployment of a new defense system within the cost, schedule, and performance parameters specified in the Acquisition Program Baseline (APB). A Risk and Opportunity Management process helps achieve this objective by supporting the PM's responsibilities for prioritizing planning and work effort.

The PM integrates risk and opportunity management with other program processes during all phases of the program. The program uses the WBS and IMS to identify risks and opportunities during periodic reviews of work packages, and then pursues appropriate activities and tracks mitigation/effectiveness. Mitigation and pursuit activities are linked to the associated work packages in the IMS to track progress. The IMP includes major program-level risks or opportunities.

Two sources of information and lessons learned can be found at:

- The Risk and Opportunity Community of Practice (CoP)
- The DoD Risk, Issue, and Opportunity Management Guide for Defense Acquisition Programs.

CH 1–4.2.5.1 Setting the Stage

When all is said and done, attention to risks, issues, and opportunities is probably one of the PM's—and the PMO's—most important jobs as they have the potential to significantly positively or negatively impact approved cost, schedule, and performance baselines. Moreover, the PMO and contractors' dynamic, visible, and positive attention to risk, issues, and opportunities is an indication of active program management that seeks to influence outcomes vice waiting for events to occur.

Senior acquisition leaders agree that the most important decisions to control risk and issues or to pursue opportunities are made in the planning activities of a program. Development of a PMO IMP and supporting IMS as early as possible from functional IMP and IMS inputs provides the basic structure of a program. With a plan available, the PMO leadership can actually identify risks, issues, and opportunities associated with accomplishing IMP events. The PMO can game multiple "what if" alternative events toward developing an achievable Acquisition Strategy. That strategy includes an understanding of, and plans to address, identified risks and opportunities toward planning for a realistic (defendable) program entry point, as well as cost and schedule to complete the program and deliver required performance. If re-planning a program that includes possibly changing requirements, seeking relief on cost and schedule expectations or entry at an earlier acquisition stage to address risks that are already issues is a sound consideration. One rule of thumb for program planning is "to do the hard things first." A realistic IMP with accomplishments and criteria for events and accompanying IMS will enable program management to address that rule of thumb.

Figure19 illustrates a simple portrayal of technical, programmatic, and business events that may lead to risks, issues, and opportunities, each with cost, schedule, or performance consequences, both positive and negative. When scoping Risk and Opportunity Management Plans, PMs consider whether "the cost of a risk mitigation or opportunity pursuit is less than the cost of the realized risk or provides greater gain than not pursuing the opportunity."

Figure 19: Technical, Programmatic, and Business Events Considerations

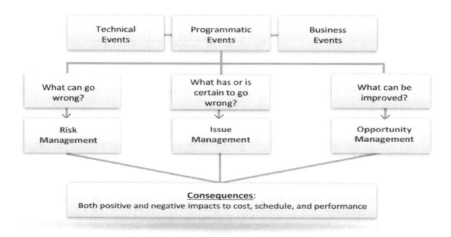

As mentioned previously, continuous positive attention to risk, issues, and opportunities by program management fosters an environment in the PMO and with industry, that the organization is strong enough, experienced enough, competent enough, to handle emergent situations—which is characteristic of high-performing organizations. Notably, is every new risk viewed as a crisis requiring "all hands on deck" to address? Or is there a PMO-wide awareness of the need for constant attention to the internal and external environment, geared toward establishing a positive attitude of identifying risks as early as possible in the planning process? Is program management cognizant of other risks that may be identified as the program progresses, and are required plans being developed to address both "original' and "emergent" risks, issues, and opportunities? The task of program management, as is the task of any leadership group, is to establish an environment that positively rewards careful planning, including identification of risks early in the planning cycle, but also does not "kill the messenger" when new risks are identified as the program progresses through the acquisition phases. In the best of all worlds, proactive leadership is continuously seeking program risks, issues, and opportunities. Such leadership is analogous to the captain of a ship, squadron commander, or battalion commander who has a plan, but recognizes the primary function once the battle is engaged is to look across the whole engagement to identify what could go wrong, what could be done better, and to take steps to address either or both.

Program management is all about proactively shaping and controlling risks, issues, and opportunities, not just observing progress and reacting as events unfold. Anticipating possible adverse or positive events, evaluating probabilities of occurrence, understanding cost and schedule impacts, and deciding to take cost-effective steps ahead of time are the essence of effective risk, issues, and opportunity management. Concepts and processes for risk and issue management are well documented; opportunity management follows the same processes, but does not always enjoy the same urgency as risk and issue management, perhaps because while acting on the latter is seen as necessary, acting on the former, while potentially beneficial, introduces new risk to the program. That said, program management ought to be as focused, or possibly more focused, on seeking opportunities to reduce cost and schedule without affecting performance, particularly where there is a significant Return on Investment (ROI) in production and/or life-cycle support. Alternately, there may be an opportunity for an acceptable modification to performance requirements that can have a positive effect on the program's likelihood of successful execution. Opportunity management and Should Cost management are closely aligned—both seek to identify different ways to execute a program that reduces cost and schedule without negatively affecting warfighter satisfaction.

Successful program management not only includes continuous proactive attention to the possibility of changing circumstances, but also a disciplined process of identification and tracking program risks, issues, and opportunities. That includes establishing rational, executable, and resourced mitigation or pursuit plans, which are tracked to completion within PMO and/or Contractor IMP and IMS. Top program risks and opportunities, and respective risk and pursuit plans are detailed in the program Acquisition Strategy and presented at all relevant decision points and milestones.

CH 1–4.2.5.2 Risk, Issue, and Opportunity Management Process

All PMO functional disciplines retain a role in planning and execution of risk, issue, and opportunity management. Risk, issue, and opportunity management can be managed similarly—the basic risk management framework can be adapted to issue and opportunity management. The process encompasses **identification, analysis, handling, and monitoring** risks. [Note that issues and opportunities are discussed in CH 3–4.1.5 and the DoD Risk, Issue, and Opportunity (R, I, & O) Management Guide for Defense Acquisition Programs.]

Without duplicating the information in either CH 3 or the Guide, the following paragraphs briefly overview the process toward ensuring a full view of this key program management function.

CH 1–4.2.5.2.1 Risk Identification

The single most important question is, "What can go wrong?" Program Managers are encouraged to ask the question, "What is hard or difficult?" CH 3–4.1.5 and the DoD Risk, Issue, and Opportunity (R, I, & O) Management Guide for Defense Acquisition Programs provide a list of potential approaches to creatively identifying risk. As a baseline, the program management team considers risk in the technical, programmatic, and business areas. One subject that deserves significant consideration is Framing Assumptions used in program planning. Program leadership can consider and document program Framing Assumptions because of the risks they may introduce should the assumptions prove invalid. See Framing Assumptions CH 1–4.2.4. In addition, the PM documents key risk management ground rules to be used across the risk management program. Typical ground rules for risk management relevant to programs include time frame, time of risk event, and WBS level.

Programs can fall into the trap of identifying ongoing baseline program activities as risk handling activities, without the requisite changes to the planning, requirements, or program budget/resource allocation. This approach is typically insufficient. In most situations, reliance on previously planned program activities results in the program's de facto acceptance of the risk.

CH 1–4.2.5.2.2 Opportunity Identification

Opportunities may be realized in Research, Development, Test, and Evaluation (RDT&E), production, and Operations and Maintenance (O&M). Opportunity management measures potential program improvement in terms of likelihood and benefits.

Through the opportunity management process, the PM identifies potential enhancements to cost, schedule, and/or performance. Opportunities may be identified continuously during program planning and execution, and across the program life cycle. Important sources of opportunities include system and program changes that yield reductions in total ownership cost. For example, a modular open systems approach or securing appropriate government rights to a technical data package can offer opportunities for competition in sparing and later modifications. During production, the PM continuously seeks opportunities for design and manufacturing changes that yield reductions in production costs. Design changes to production configurations (and the product baseline) may take the form of a Value Engineering Proposal and Value Engineering Change Proposals within the context of ongoing production contracts. These may change the system performance, but could yield production or support cost reductions.

During the Operations and Support (O&S) phase, opportunities often may arise from the observation and analysis of actual in-service performance. In addition, the emergence of more efficient production practice or better performing components can provide opportunities for improved reliability, more efficient fuel consumption, improved maintenance practice, other reduced support costs, or economic capability enhancements.

CH 1–4.2.5.3 Risk Analysis

The risk analysis process answers the questions, what is the likelihood and consequence of the risk? For PMs to more effectively make decisions regarding handling of risks commensurate with available resources, PMs compare cost-burdened risk and handling strategies. There are a variety of techniques for estimating cost exposure from realization of a given risk. However, multiple factors, including Return on Investment (ROI) as well as potential schedule and performance impacts, are considered when determining a risk mitigation strategy. Figure 20 shows a sample excerpt of a risk analysis register for use at a Risk Management Board, Program Management Review, or other type review.

Figure 20: Sample Risk Analysis Register

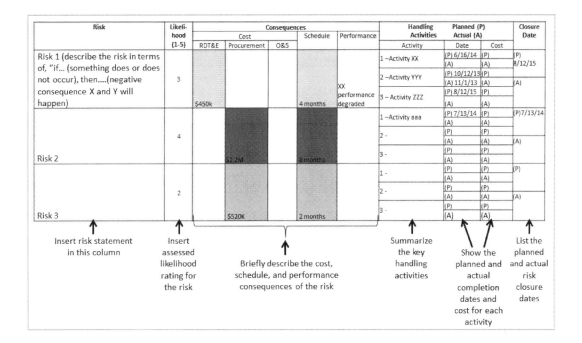

Risk	Likeli-hood (1-5)	Consequences					Handling Activities	Planned (P) Actual (A)		Closure Date
		Cost			Schedule	Performance	Activity	Date	Cost	
		RDT&E	Procurement	O&S						
Risk 1 (describe the risk in terms of, "if... (something does or does not occur), then....(negative consequence X and Y will happen)	3					XX performance degraded	1 –Activity XX	(P) 6/16/14 (A)	(P) (A)	(P) 8/12/15
							2 –Activity YYY	(P) 10/12/13 (A) 11/1/13	(P) (A)	(A)
							3 – Activity ZZZ	(P) 8/12/15 (A)	(P) (A)	
		$450k			4 months					
Risk 2	4						1 –Activity aaa	(P) 7/13/14 (A)	(P) (A)	(P)7/13/14
							2 -	(P) (A)	(P) (A)	(A)
							3 -	(P) (A)	(P) (A)	
		$2.2M			8 months					
Risk 3	2						1 -	(P) (A)	(P) (A)	(P)
							2 -	(P) (A)	(P) (A)	(A)
		$520k			2 months		3 -	(P) (A)	(P) (A)	

Insert risk statement in this column — Insert assessed likelihood rating for the risk — Briefly describe the cost, schedule, and performance consequences of the risk — Summarize the key handling activities — Show the planned and actual completion dates and cost for each activity — List the planned and actual risk closure dates

CH 1–4.2.5.3.1 Opportunity Analysis

As with risk, after identification the next step is to perform a cost, schedule, and performance benefit analysis for each approved opportunity and document the results. Opportunities with sufficient potential are then evaluated relative to potential handling options.

Opportunities are evaluated for both advantages and disadvantages. This is important because potential benefits associated with an opportunity may be overstated and corresponding risks may be understated. In addition, all candidate opportunities are thoroughly screened for potential risks before they are approved, and handling plans are developed and implemented as appropriate. Figure 21 shows a sample of an Opportunity Analysis Register for use at Opportunity Management Boards, Program Management Reviews, or other type reviews.

Figure 21: Opportunity Analysis Register

Opportunity	Likeli-hood	Cost to Implement	Benefit					Oppor-tunity Level	Handling Strategy	Expected Closure
			Cost			Schedule	Performance			
			RDT&E	Procurement	O&M					
Opportunity 1: Procure Smith rotor blades instead of Jones rotor blades.	Mod	$3.2M			$4M	3 month margin	4% greater lift	Moder-ate	Reevaluate - Summarize the handling plan	March 2017
Opportunity 2: Summarize the opportunity activity.	Mod	$350K	$25K		$375K			Low	Reject	May 2017
Opportunity 3: Summarize the opportunity activity.	High	$211K		$0.4M	$3.6M	4 months less long-lead time needed		High	Summarize the handling plan to realize the opportunity	January 2017

Insert opportunity statement in this column

Insert assessed likelihood rating for the opportunity

Show the planned pursue cost for each activity

Briefly describe the cost, schedule, and performance benefit of the opportunity

Summarize the key handling activities

List the planned opportunity pursue closure dates

CH 1–4.2.6 Market Research – Understanding Industry

Better understanding of the defense industry, specifically the companies involved with a particular program, is important for DoD PMs. With understanding provided by market research and business knowledge, they can provide best taxpayer value to the government on defense products while providing defense companies a fair and reasonable profit. Whether systems or services companies, a wide range of PM market research and business knowledge increases a program's chance of success. Understanding industry is important for other key acquisition workforce positions such as senior program engineer, product support manager, senior business finance manager, Contracting Officer, and senior-level IPT Leads who interface with Defense contractors.

Increasing market intelligence starts with a good general view of current defense industry markets. Follow that with a closer look at how and why the companies competing in a given market segment develop and execute strategies to grow, compete, propose, and provide customer solutions. Many powerful market intelligence tools are available online—some for a cost, some for free. The company's own annual (10K) and quarterly (10Q) reports are a good place to start.

In generally assessing an overall company's market position, some specific areas are important for PMs to consider. These include, but are not limited to:

- How is a company of interest organized?
- What is its financial health?
- What investments is it making for the future, both in capital and research and development?
- What business strategy does it advertise—and follow?
- What are its core products—or new products?
- Who are its competitors and what other market segments?
- Who are its Tier 1 and 2 suppliers?
- What risks tied to potential incentives/strategies is it willing and capable of handling?

Defense companies are generally focused on the long term—to earn profits that exceed the cost of capital, attract investors by demonstrating profitability, and attract and retain world-class employees. The company's financial pipeline is kept afloat by sales, orders, cash flow, and profit. Business development personnel work the corporate strategy into a nominal 5-year operating plan where picking the right program priorities is paramount based on the marketing funnel, market intelligence, and capture plans. The Wall Street factor is always in play because the shareholders own the company—unless it's not public.

Company financial health is measurable, but not always clear. The language of finance—when better mastered and in sync between government and business—improves a program's and company's probability of success. Company incentives, motivations, and rewards lead to best-value negotiating strategies for the company to get the right contract consistent with accepted risk.

Considering some important business areas would help in understanding:

- Key financial ratios are used to show how companies and stakeholders measure financial performance trends and investment potential to achieve the revenues and profit margins needed to keep companies in business. While not all-inclusive, some general considerations are shown below on financial performance areas important at different company levels. Government PMs can consider what these ratios represent in terms of how changes in the areas represented in the numerators and denominators may impact key performance measures, which may in turn affect different levels of decision-making within the company:

   A **contractor general manager** motivated by:

   $$Return\ on\ Assets\ (ROA) = \frac{Profit}{Sales} \ x\ \frac{Sales}{Total\ Assets} + Cash\ Generated$$

   A **chief operating officer** motivated by:

   $$Return\ on\ Equity = \frac{Profit}{Sales}\ x\ \frac{Sales}{Assets}\ x\ \frac{Assets}{Shareholder\ Equity}$$

   A **chief executive officer** measured and motivated by:

   $$EPS = \frac{Profit}{Sales}\ x\ \frac{Sales}{Assets}\ x\ \frac{Assets}{Shareholder\ Equity}\ x\ \frac{Shareholder\ Equity}{Shares\ Outstanding}$$

- Find additional company information on its view of financial health in its quarterly (10Q) and annual (10K) financial reports. These reports can be quickly reviewed for financial and risk data provided directly from the company to help understand financial, operational, and strategic considerations. The reports on each public company are readily available at The Securities and Exchange Commission website.
- Understand operating plan cost components leading to profit margins that all companies use to make their numbers (financial reporting via financial statements and ratios that are used by customers, investors, and competitors to compare a company's efficiency and progress as a business).
- Understand the financial health of companies when making program decisions. These revenues and profit margins are outlined in companies' operating plans. Profitable and Predictable are best.
- Look at impacts of company cost, prices, and rates to margins; time value of money; and resourcing projects compared to competitors in that market segment.

- Consider supplier management issues which are important both for pre- and post-contract award, through the production and sustainment phases. Outsourcing, international, and make-buy decisions are all important in supplier and subcontractor management when considering desired business outcomes.

Business communications and understanding requirements are critical, especially leading to the RFP development phase. Business acumen and the language of finance are critical to a company's financial success across its supply chain. All companies are not the same, so understanding each company will help with better incentives, motivations, and rewards as they pursue "making their numbers"—competing in their market space to deliver DoD customers best-taxpayer-value, quality products on cost, schedule, and performance.

CH 1–4.2.7 Defense Acquisition Information Technology (IT) Programs

The following subsections provide an overview of the different types of Information Technology (IT) programs that can be based on acquisition program models 2, 3, or 6 (or a combination of those models). In amplification of the following, if planning an IT acquisition program, DoDI 5000.02 (Encl. 11) for Information Technology and/or DoDI 5000.02 (Encl. 12) for Defense Business Systems, as appropriate, and CH 6–2.1 should be consulted.

CH 1–4.2.7.1 Information Technology

Information Technology (IT) is any equipment or interconnected system or subsystem of equipment used in the automatic acquisition, storage, analysis, evaluation, manipulation, management, movement, control, display, switching, interchange, transmission, or reception of data or information by the executive agency. IT equipment constitutes the equipment used by the executive agency directly, or used by a contractor under a contract with the executive agency that requires:

- IT equipment be used by DoD directly or used by a contractor under a contract with the DoD that requires use of that equipment.
- IT equipment be used to a significant extent in the performance of a service or the furnishing of a product.

IT equipment includes computers, ancillary equipment (including imaging peripherals, input, output, and storage devices necessary for security and surveillance), peripheral equipment designed to be controlled by the central processing unit of a computer, software, firmware, and similar procedures, services (including support services), and related resources. For additional information, refer to 40 USC 11101.

Note: IT equipment does not include any equipment acquired by a federal contractor incidental to a federal contract. IT includes both National Security Systems and Defense Business Systems. Refer to CH 6–2.1 for a more complete discussion regarding IT Systems acquisition.

CH 1–4.2.7.2 JCIDS Information Technology (IT) Box Model

The JCIDS IT Box model applies to Information Systems (IS) involving software development only, integration onto Commercial Off-The-Shelf (COTS) hardware, and IS programs with costs exceeding $15 million. Refer CH 6–3.5.1 and the JCIDS Manual (Encl. D) for additional information.

CH 1–4.2.7.3 National Security Systems

A National Security System (NSS) is any information system (including any telecommunications system) used or operated by an agency or a contractor of an agency, or other organization on behalf of an agency. The function, operation, or use of NSS involves intelligence activities; cryptologic activities related to national security; the command and control of military forces; equipment that is an integral part of a weapon or weapons system; or equipment that is critical to the direct fulfillment of military or intelligence missions. The last item (direct fulfillment of military or intelligence mission) *does not* include systems to be used for routine administrative and business applications (including payroll, finance, logistics, and personnel management applications). Net Ready Key Performance Parameter (KPP) requirements for NSS are documented in the JCIDS Manual (page D-E-1, Appendix E to Encl. D) and acquired under the acquisition process defined in DoDI 5000.02 (Encl. 11, para 1 and para 2.b). Refer to the National Institute of Standards and Technology (NIST) Standard SP-800-59 for additional information.

CH 1–4.2.7.4 Defense Business Systems

Defense Business Systems (DBS) are information systems *other than a National Security System (NSS)*, operated by, for, or on behalf of DoD, including financial systems, management information systems, financial data feeder systems, and the Information Technology (IT) infrastructure used to support business activities. Business activities may include contracting, pay and personnel management systems, some logistics systems, financial planning and budgeting, installations management, and human resource management. DBS generally do not fall under JCIDS for the development and validation of capability requirements documents; instead, they employ a Problem Statement (see below). Refer to the JCIDS Manual for additional discussion on JCIDS and DBS. DBS are governed by DoDI 5000.02 (Encl. 12); the JCIDS Information Technology (IT) Box model does not apply to DBS.

A Problem Statement is applicable to DBS and is a stand-alone document to support the Materiel Development Decision (MDD) and later key decision events and milestones. The Problem Statement documents DBS requirements and is approved by the Investment Review Board (IRB) chair. It documents business and supporting analyses and evolves over time as those needs are refined. The Joint Staff (JS) (J-8) reviews the initial Problem Statement to determine if there is JS interest.

An Annual Investment Decision Certification is also required for all DBS per 10 USC 2222 and as described in DoDI 5000.02 (Encl.12). The obligation of DoD funds for a covered DBS program that has not been certified is a violation of 31 USC 1341(a)(1)(A).

CH 1–4.2.7.5 Information Systems

Information systems are a discrete set of information resources organized for the collection, processing, maintenance, use, sharing, dissemination, or disposition of information.

CH 1–4.2.8 International Acquisition and Exportability Considerations

Many DoD acquisition programs include allied and friendly nation participation either as a cooperative partner on an International Cooperative Program (ICP), or as a customer through Foreign Military Sales (FMS) programs, Building Partner Capacity (BPC) programs, or though industry Direct Commercial Sales (DCS). These programs not only contribute to DoD and U.S. Government (USG) security cooperation objectives but also provide opportunities to enhance DoD acquisition outcomes. In these international acquisition programs, the PM is responsible for delivering a capability to an international partner or customer that may be involved in future coalition operations with the DoD.

CH 1–4.2.8.1 Identifying International Acquisition Programs

DoDD 5000.01 (Encl. 1, para E.1.1.18) and DoDI 5000.02 (Encl. 2, para 7.a.) requires the acquisition managers consider international cooperation and exportability, develop systems that are interoperable with coalition partners, and identify potential technologies from both domestic and foreign sources. DoDI 2010.06, Materiel Interoperability and Standardization with Allies and Coalition Partners (para 3.a), addresses design efforts to enhance coalition interoperability. See also 10 USC 2431a (c)(2)(G), Section 2350a regarding international involvement, including FMS and cooperative opportunities.

CH 1–4.2.8.2 International Acquisition Management

The term International Acquisition and Exportability (IA&E) encompasses all of the elements of international involvement in a DoD program—Foreign Solutions, ICPs, Exportability Design, Technology Security and Foreign Disclosure (TSFD), and Foreign Sales or Transfers. Consult the Chapter 1, Supplement 1 International Acquisition and Exportability (IA&E) for more details on foreign solutions, foreign sales and transfers, defense exportability integration, the Defense Exportability Features (DEF) Pilot Program, and other related topics. The DAU Acquisition Community Connection International Acquisition Management Community of Practice website contains best practice Job Support Tools that address key aspects of these various IA&E functional areas.

To comply with Congressional and DoD policies, and gain the benefits of IA&E activities, the PM should address the following international considerations at the beginning of the acquisition planning process:

- Are there existing foreign systems or foreign systems under development that DoD can use or modify to meet DoD's requirements?
- Are there coalition interoperability requirements for the system?
- What is the potential for developing the system cooperatively?
- Does the likelihood of future foreign sales warrant designing in exportability?
- What DoD/U.S. Government TSFD and export control approvals will be required?

CH 1–4.2.8.2.1 Advantages

The potential benefits of including IA&E activities in acquisition program planning and execution include some of the following:

- Reducing overall life-cycle costs by designing exportability and interoperability capabilities into systems or equipment during early development phases;
- Leveraging foreign government investments in research and development, production, and logistics support, thereby reducing DoD costs, markedly enhancing U.S. and partner nation affordability throughout the life cycle; and,
- Delivering interoperable and exportable systems that are coalition-ready, thereby reducing costly requirements for upgrades later in the life cycle and increasing overall coalition operational effectiveness.

CH 1–4.2.8.2.2 Challenges

International cooperation and exportability initiatives to facilitate foreign military sales require program management understanding of, and compliance with, the statutory and policy requirements associated with international cooperative programs and technology security and foreign disclosure approvals. Navigating these issues can be challenging and the Department has a number of resources available to assist program offices prepare for and execute international cooperative development programs and plan for foreign sales of U.S. defense articles. The Chapter 1, Supplement 1 International Acquisition and Exportability (IA&E) provides a number of reference documents and organizations that can assist program office staff in developing international aspects for their programs.

CH 1–4.2.8.3 Planning and Execution

Planning IA&E efforts should be documented in the International Involvement Section of the program's Acquisition Strategy as required by 10 USC 2431a and 10 USC 2350a, as amended. Updates to the International Involvement Section of the Acquisition Strategy at each respective Milestone include an analysis of IA&E requirements and foreign sales potential. For a detailed description of the International Involvement Section, refer to CH1-S–3. Table 5 outlines the IA&E planning actions that occur during each acquisition phase and may be considered for incorporation into the program IMP/IMS CH 1–3.4.2 and, if applicable, an International Business Plan.

Table 5: IA&E Actions during the Acquisition Phases

Acquisition Phase	IA&E Actions
Pre-Materiel Solution Analysis	• Conduct an initial IA&E assessment to identify potential existing foreign solutions, ICP opportunities, foreign technology, or potential for future foreign sales. • Review Initial Capabilities Document (ICD) to identify potential coalition requirements, and potential foreign market to gain an understanding of coalition interoperability and exportability requirements.
Materiel Solution Analysis	• Assess procurement or modifications of existing U.S. or foreign solutions as part of the OSD CAPE Analysis of Alternatives prior to starting a new development program. • Assess program's potential for international cooperative research, development, production, logistics support, interoperability, and defense exportability. • Update the program's IA&E assessment to identify specific existing or projected international agreements(s), Joint Requirements Oversight Council (JROC)-validated coalition interoperability requirements, international markets, and potential program protection issues and requirements. • Use the program's Acquisition Strategy at Milestone A to advise the Milestone Decision Authority if the program should address international involvement (e.g., foreign solutions, coalition interoperability, ICP participation, future foreign sales, and design for exportability) during TMRR.
Technology Maturity and Risk Reduction	• Consider establishing one or more mutually beneficial system development ICPs. • Consider establishing cooperative RDT&E projects under the terms of existing RDT&E MOUs with allied and friendly nations. • Continue TSFD planning and approval activities. • Conduct defense exportability feasibility study and design efforts. • Conduct initial FMS planning efforts. • Use the program's Acquisition Strategy at Milestone B to advise the Milestone Decision Authority which international involvement efforts should be planned and implemented during EMD.
Engineering and Manufacturing Development	• Continue TSFD and export control efforts in support of existing ICPs, as appropriate. • Complete defense exportability design efforts. • Establish initial FMS arrangements in the latter stages of EMD and Low Rate Initial Production (LRIP), as appropriate. • Use the program's Acquisition Strategy at Milestone C to advise the Milestone Decision Authority which international involvement efforts should be planned and implemented during Production & Deployment phase. • For programs with substantial international involvement, develop an initial International Business Plan (IBP).
Production and Deployment	• Use the updated IBP to achieve synergies and economies of scale through a combination of DoD and foreign recurring production procurement requirements or non-recurring product improvement investment. • Pursue appropriate type(s) of ICPs and foreign sales/transfer arrangements throughout the program's life-cycle.
Operations and Support	• Use the updated IBP to achieve synergies and economies of scale affordability benefits through a combination or coordination of DoD and foreign Operations and Support (O&S) non-recurring investment and recurring O&S phase procurement requirements. • Enhance logistics support for foreign operators of U.S. systems through logistics support ICPs, FMS/DCS, or Acquisition and Cross-Servicing Agreements (ACSAs) throughout the program's lifecycle.

Defense exportability integration is a critical tool to help program management achieve the range of successful IA&E actions discussed above. Defense exportability integration refers to DoD activities within the Defense Acquisition System to incorporate technology protection measures (i.e. "defense exportability features" (DEF)) in initial designs – including the design and development of anti-tamper and differential capabilities - leading to production of exportable system configurations for ICPs or foreign sales. Incorporating DEF in initial designs facilitates timely, efficient implementation of future DoD cooperative programs or foreign sales and transfers.

Program management may pursue differential capability initiatives either under the sponsorship of the Office of the Under Secretary of Defense for Acquisition, Technology and Logistics OUSD (AT&L) DEF Pilot Program, or outside of the pilot using other sources of budgeted and authorized funding (i.e., DSCA Special Defense Acquisition Fund (SDAF), or FMS funding). Consistent with MDA decisions at each Milestone, these DEF efforts may include investigating the feasibility of differential capability and enhanced program protection measures for exportable configurations in the early phases of the acquisition process. Consult IA&E CH1-S–4 for more details on DEF planning and integration.

CH 1–4.2.8.4 International Cooperative Programs

An ICP is any acquisition program or technology project that includes participation (e.g., cooperative development, cooperative production, and research and development) by the United States and one or more foreign nations through an international agreement during any phase of a system's life cycle.

Program management should assess the system's ICP prospects based on known and projected allied/friendly nation capability requirements, plans for development of similar systems in the global defense market, previous foreign purchases of similar U.S. systems undergoing major upgrades, and other indicators of prospective foreign demand for the new system. If the system is not restricted as a U.S.-only system, the program manager must plan for export to safeguard CPI and any other controlled or classified information. DoDI 5000.02 (Encl. 2, para 7.b.) establishes overall ICP program management requirements.

CH 1–4.2.8.4.1 ICP Management

In deciding whether to pursue an ICP, the PM consults with their respective DoD Component International Programs Organization (IPO) (i.e., Deputy Assistant Secretary of the Army for Defense Exports and Cooperation [DASA-DE&C], Navy International Programs Office [Navy IPO], or Deputy Under Secretary of the Air Force for International Affairs [SAF-IA]), and consider the following criteria:

- Ability of the partner nation(s) to participate in an ICP, taking into account TSFD considerations, where there are clear DoD benefits (e.g. interoperability, cost savings, operational burden-sharing, and political-military benefits);
- Ability to establish an ICP management structure in the international agreement where the designated PM (U.S. or foreign) is fully responsible and accountable for the cost, schedule, and performance of the resulting system; and
- Demonstrated DoD Component and partner nation(s') willingness to fully fund their share of the ICP.

Program Managers, working closely with their DoD Component's IPO, are encouraged to follow the procedures outlined in IA&E CH1-S–6 to establish international agreements for ICPs with allied and friendly nations, the procedures in IA&E CH1-S–9 for TSFD considerations, and the guidance in IA&E CH1-S–4 regarding designing in exportability as part of ICP efforts. Once an ICP is established via a signed international agreement, the DoD Component remains responsible for approval of most statutory, regulatory, and contracting reports and milestone requirements, as listed in DoDI 5000.02, Enclosure 1, Table 2.

CH 1–4.2.8.4.2 Developing an ICP

As outlined in IA&E CH1-S–2.2, several mechanisms are available to identify potential international cooperative program opportunities. Some key examples include:

- International Fora
- International exchanges of information and personnel
- Exploratory discussions
- Science and Technology cooperation
- Coalition Warfare Program (CWP) cooperative projects

While most funding for cooperative RDT&E activities may need to be provided from program funding, program management should explore additional parallel funding for these efforts through the OUSD(AT&L)/International Cooperation CWP and/or the Military Department's International Cooperative Research and Development (ICR&D) programs. See IA&E CH1-S–5.5 for more on CWP.

CH 1–4.2.8.4.3 International Agreement Procedures

U.S. law requires an International Agreement (IA) for all ICPs. DoDD 5530.3, "International Agreements," defines IAs, along with the authorities and processes to establish them. For AT&L-related IAs only, DoDI 5000.02 (Encl. 2, para 7.b.(1)) encourages the use of separate, streamlined agreement procedures to establish IAs for ICPs.

- Programs staff members should refer to IA&E Supplement Section 6 and the IC in AT&L Handbook for a detailed description of these procedures.

CH 1–4.2.9 Joint Acquisition Programs

When a defense acquisition program involves the satisfaction of validated capability requirements from multiple DoD Components and/or international partners, and is funded by more than one DoD Component or partner during any phase of the acquisition process, a Joint Program Office is established in accordance with DoDI 5000.02 (Encl. 2, paragraph 5.b).

CH 1–4.2.9.1 Identifying Joint Capabilities

As part of CJCS Instruction 3170.01, Joint Capabilities Integration and Development System (JCIDS), the Joint Staff J-8, with the assistance of the DoD Components, evaluates all JCIDS documents, regardless of Acquisition Category or previous delegation decisions, to determine whether the proposal has Joint Force implications. The Joint Staff documents—CJCS Instruction 5123.01, Charter of the Joint Requirements Oversight Council (JROC), CJCS Instruction 3170.01, and the JCIDS Manual—provide full detail and direction on this topic.

CH 1–4.2.9.2 Joint Acquisition Management

Reasons for initiating a Joint acquisition effort are many and varied, but are generally based on an anticipated operational or economic advantage to the Department. One or more of the following factors is typically considered:

- **Improvement of Core Mission Area Capabilities**. An improvement to or elimination of a gap within a Core Mission Area Capability. DoD's core mission areas are: homeland defense and civilian support; deterrence operations; major combat operations; irregular warfare; military support to stabilization, security, transition, and reconstruction operations; and military contribution to cooperative security.
- **Coordination of Efforts.** Reduces fragmentation, duplication, and overlap to enhance productivity, achieve cost savings, and facilitate individual Service efforts into a mutually coordinated, single effort.

- **Interoperability.** Ability of systems, units, or forces to provide data, information, materiel, and services to, and accept the same from, other systems, units, or forces and to use the data, information, materiel, and services so exchanged to enable them to operate effectively together.
- **Reduction in Development Cost**. Joint funding of one program based on solution component compatibility, and that program consolidation does not unduly increase risk, minimize alternatives, or reduce performance to an unacceptable level.
- **Reduction in Production Costs**. Consolidated production requirements result in lower unit price through savings in set-up costs, learning curve impacts, and quantity production.
- **Reduction in Logistics Requirements**. Standardization offers potential for reduction in support (spares, storage, transportation, and training) costs while improving support to operating forces.
- **Affordability.** Joint funding of one program to improve the program potential (over individual Service programs) to be produced and supported within reasonable expectations for future budgets.

These factors, as well as other influences are for the establishment of a Joint Program Office to plan and execute a Joint acquisition program. Few programs become Joint without some initiative by the Joint Staff, USD(AT&L), or Congress.

CH 1–4.2.9.2.1 Challenges

Joint programs face challenges to successfully balance competing requirements, priorities, and budgets. Program costs, strategic importance and urgency, as well as other factors influence the program's visibility and certainly affect how the Joint program operates and reports. Furthermore, since Joint programs have the continuing interest of each participating DoD Component or international partner, the Department, and Congress, additional requirements for coordination and documentation should be expected. There is no doubt that Joint programs require considerably more planning, coordination, and time-consuming effort than do single-Service programs.

CH 1–4.2.9.2.2 Advantages

Acquisition programs that contribute to Joint capabilities or provide a budgetary/financial advantage may be managed as Joint acquisition programs. A "Joint acquisition" is any acquisition system, subsystem, component, or technology program with a strategy that includes funding by more than one DoD Component or partner during any acquisition phase. DoDI 5000.02 (Encl. 2, paragraph 5.b.(2)) addresses DoD Component fiscal responsibilities associated with participation in programs under Joint acquisition management.

CH 1–4.2.9.2.3 Designation

Considering the recommendation of the Joint Staff and the Heads of the DoD Components, the Milestone Decision Authority decides whether to place the program under Joint acquisition management. The Milestone Decision Authority makes this decision and, if appropriate, designates the Lead Executive DoD Component as early as possible in the acquisition process.

The DoD Components periodically review their programs to determine the potential for Joint cooperation. The DoD Components can structure program strategies to encourage, and to provide an opportunity for, multi-DoD Component participation.

CH 1–4.2.9.2.4 Execution

The designated Lead Executive DoD Component for a Joint acquisition acts on behalf of all DoD Components involved in the acquisition. A Memorandum of Agreement (MOA) should specify the relationship and respective responsibilities of the Lead Executive DoD Component and the other participating components. The MOA addresses system capabilities and the development of capabilities documents, funding, manpower, and the approval process for other program documentation.

The following additional considerations have proven effective in managing Joint programs:

- The assignment of a Lead Executive DoD Component considers the demonstrated best business practice of the DoD Components, including plans for effective, economical, and efficient management of the Joint program; and the demonstrated willingness of the DoD Component to fund the core program—essential to meeting Joint program needs.
- The Milestone Decision Authority and DoD Components can consolidate and co-locate the supporting efforts of the Joint program at the Lead Executive DoD Component's program office to the maximum extent practicable.
- The Component Acquisition Executive of the Lead Executive DoD Component can optimally use the acquisition organizations, test organizations, and other facilities of all Military Departments.
- The designated Lead Executive DoD Component selects the qualified PM for the designated program under Joint acquisition. The single PM can then be fully responsible and accountable for the cost, schedule, and performance of the development system.
- If the Joint program results from a consolidation of several different DoD Component programs, each with a separate PM, the selected Joint Program Manager can have the necessary responsibility and authority to effectively manage the overall system development and integration.
- A designated program under Joint acquisition can have one quality assurance program, one program change control program, one integrated test program, and one set of documentation and reports (specifically: one set of capabilities documents, with Service-unique capability requirements identified), one Information Support Plan, one Test and Evaluation Master Plan, one Acquisition Program Baseline, etc.).
- The Milestone Decision Authority designates the lead Operational Test Agency to coordinate all operational test and evaluation. The lead Operational Test Agency produces a single operational effectiveness and suitability report for the program.
- Documentation for decision points and periodic reporting flow only through the Lead Executive DoD Component acquisition chain, supported by the participating DoD Components.
- The program can use inter-DoD Component logistics support to the maximum extent practicable, consistent with effective support to the operational forces and efficient use of DoD resources.
- Unless statute, the Milestone Decision Authority, or an MOA signed by all DoD Components direct otherwise, the Lead Executive DoD Component can budget for and manage the common RDT&E funds for the assigned Joint programs.
- Individual DoD Components can budget for their unique requirements.

The MOA signatories can conduct periodic reviews, as necessary, to ensure MOA accuracy and relevancy for the successful acquisition and management of the Joint program.

Acquisition managers of a Joint program having the potential for international partner participation can refer to CH 1–4.2.8 regarding the IA&E programs.

CH 1–4.2.9.2.5 Joint Program Manager Perspectives

At the outset of a Joint program, the Joint PM conducts a detailed technical requirements review that examines mission requirements, operational concepts and environments, and performance parameters. The PM ensures that requirements are well understood, conflicts are resolved, and that there is ample latitude to make tradeoffs critical to a program's success. The PM's review accomplishes:

- Identifying similarities and differences in DoD Components' or partners' requirements and in the operational environments.
- Determining a clear distinction between the "would like to have" and the "must have" requirements.
- Identifying principal areas of technical risk or uncertainty.
- Identifying similarities and differences in the DoD Component or partner logistics concepts, requirements, or processes, including their approach to implementation of the life-cycle cost concepts.
- Determining the most effective program structure and tailoring criteria to effectively achieve requisite capabilities.

Some Joint programs may be considered successful only if they develop identical or near identical acquisition solutions for use by all participants. Trying to develop identical or near identical solutions for all participating DoD Components or partners may frustrate the program and, ultimately, lead to its failure. Solution variations are based on requirements and operational environments in relationship to cost, schedule, and performance considerations. The approaches for long-term sustainment of the Joint program's solution are not made within narrow organizational boundaries. Consideration of the full range of capabilities in the enterprise identifies a more cost-effective option. Such a consideration would help determine whether the enterprise has the capability to sustain such a solution and, if not, whether it would be beneficial to develop the capability.

The preparation for each Milestone and Decision Point review includes a re-examination of the same items reviewed at the initiation of the Joint program. This re-examination determines not only that the participating DoD Components' or partners' perceptions of the requirements have not changed, but also that the threat or other basis for acquiring the capability remains consistent with the initial requirements(s).

CH 1–4.2.10 Urgent Capability Acquisition

DoDI 5000.02 (Encl.13) provides policy and procedure for acquisition programs that provide capabilities to fulfill urgent operational needs and other quick-reaction capabilities that can be fielded in less than 2 years and are below the cost thresholds of Acquisition Category (ACAT) I and IA programs. The following paragraphs are an overview of Urgent Capability Acquisition as a point of reference for program management. Encl. 13 has significant additional content about the execution of an Urgent Capability Acquisition, specifically amplification of the activities in the phases depicted in Figure 22, including reporting requirements.

<u>Figure 22: Urgent Capability Acquisition</u>

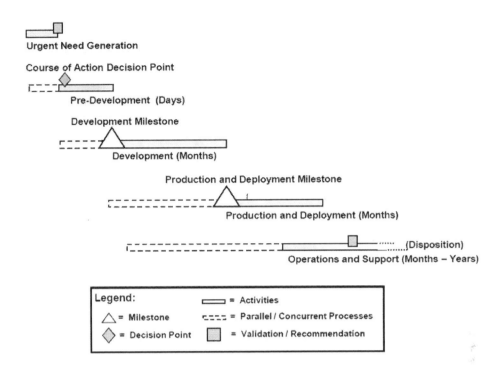

Urgent Need Generation

Course of Action Decision Point

Pre-Development (Days)

Development Milestone

Development (Months)

Production and Deployment Milestone

Production and Deployment (Months)

(Disposition)

Operations and Support (Months – Years)

Legend:
- ▭ = Activities
- △ = Milestone
- ◇ = Decision Point
- ╒╕ = Parallel / Concurrent Processes
- ▨ = Validation / Recommendation

CH 1–4.2.10.1 Urgent Operational Needs and Other Quick-Reaction Capabilities

DoD's highest priority is to provide warfighters involved in conflict or preparing for imminent contingency operations with the capabilities urgently needed to overcome unforeseen threats, achieve mission success, and reduce risk of casualties, as described in DoD Directive 5000.71, Rapid Fulfillment of Combatant Commander Urgent Operational Needs. The objective is to deliver capability quickly, within days or months. DoD Components use all available authorities to expeditiously fund, develop, assess, produce, deploy, and sustain these capabilities for the duration of the urgent need, as determined by the requesting DoD Component.

- **Application**. DoDI 5000.02 (Encl. 13) policies and procedures apply to acquisition programs for the following types of Quick-Reaction capabilities:
  - Validated Urgent Operational Need (UON). UONs include:
    - Joint Urgent Operational Needs (JUONs) and Joint Emergent Operational Needs (JEONs). These are either an urgent need (JUON) or an emergent need (JEON) identified by competent authority.
    - Warfighter Senior Integration Group (SIG)-Identified Urgent Issue. This is a critical warfighter issue identified by the co-chairs of the Warfighter SIG in accordance with DoD Directive 5000.71. They approve a critical warfighter issue statement and provide instructions to the DoD Component.
    - Secretary of Defense/Deputy Secretary of Defense Rapid Acquisition Authority (RAA) Determination. Such a determination is made in response to a documented deficiency following consultation with the Joint Staff. RAA is considered when a waiver of a law, policy, directive, or regulation will greatly accelerate delivery of effective capability to the warfighter.
- **Procedures**

- o **Tailoring and Streamlining**. MDAs and PMs tailor and streamline program strategies and oversight. A risk area for urgent acquisition programs is the potential to compromise product support.
- o **Parallel Processes**. DoD Components employ parallel rather than sequential processes to identify and refine capability requirements, resources, and execution to expedite delivery of solutions.
- o **Support**. DoD Components ensure that all support organizations and contractors are fully aware of the urgency of the need and of expedited action.
- o **Funding**. Generally, funds are reprioritized and/or reprogrammed to expedite the acquisition process.
- o **Fielding**. If the desired capability cannot be delivered within 2 years, the MDA assesses the suitability of partial or interim capabilities that can be fielded more rapidly. In those cases, the actions necessary to develop the desired solution may be initiated concurrent with the fielding of the interim solution.
- o **Documentation and Reviews.** Expected activities are a highly tailored version and are intended to expedite the fielding of capability by tailoring the documentation and reviews normally required. Figure 22 depicts a representative acquisition.

CH 1–4.2.11 Contracting

This Section addresses the relationship between the PM and the Contracting Officer as well as key program management concerns in the development of RFPs and executing the contract.

CH 1–4.2.11.1 Roles

Acquisition is a team responsibility. The FAR states the "Acquisition Team": Consists of all participants in government acquisition, including not only representatives of the technical, supply, and procurement communities, but also the customers they serve, and the contractors who provide the products and services. Some members of the team are called out more often in law, regulation, policy, and guidance. Chief among those are the Program Manager, Contracting Officer, and Contracting Officer's Representative.

Program Manager. Designated individual with responsibility for and authority to accomplish program objectives for development, production, and sustainment to meet the user's operational needs. The PM shall be accountable for credible cost, schedule, and performance reporting to the MDA. (DoDD 5000.01)

Contracting Officer. Person with the authority to enter into, administer, and/or terminate contracts and make related determinations and findings. The term includes certain authorized representatives of the Contracting Officer acting within the limits of their authority as delegated by the Contracting Officer. Administrative Contracting Officer (ACO) refers to a Contracting Officer who is administering contracts. Termination Contracting Officer (TCO) refers to a Contracting Officer who is settling terminated contracts. A single Contracting Officer may be responsible for duties in any or all of these areas.

Contracting Officer's Representative. An individual, including a Contracting Officer's Technical Representative (COTR), designated and authorized in writing by the Contracting Officer to perform specific technical or administrative functions. (FAR 2.101)

A Contracting Officer's Representative (COR) may be called by various titles (e.g., Contracting Officer's Technical Representative [COTR], Quality Assurance Evaluator [QAE], and Quality Assurance Representative [QAR]). Whatever the title, the COR must be designated and authorized, in writing, by the Contracting Officer. Recommendation of the COR most likely comes from the program office. [*Note:* More than one COR may be appointed, but, to avoid confusion in such cases, roles and responsibilities must be clearly distinguished.]

CH 1–4.2.11.2 Responsibilities

The responsibilities of PMs and Contracting Officers, and their authorized representatives are predominantly governed in different ways.

The responsibilities of PMs are governed by the "5000 series" (e.g., DoDD 5000.01, DoDI 5000.02, and DoDI 5000.74). The 5000 series is comprised of policy and guidance for use internal to the DoD. The documents in the 5000 series are not regulations.

The responsibilities of Contracting Officers and their authorized representatives are governed by title 48 Code of Federal Regulations (CFR) Chapters 1 and 2 (i.e., Federal Acquisition Regulation [FAR] and Defense Federal Acquisition Regulation Supplement [DFARS]). "The FAR and DFARS are issued under statutory authority and published in conformance with required statutory and regulatory procedures. FAR § 1.301(b). Accordingly, those regulations have the force and effect of law." (Davies Precision Machining, Inc. v. U.S., 35 Fed. Cl. 651 [1995]).

The FAR and the DFARS are applicable to all members of the PMO Team, including specific responsibilities for PMs (e.g., conducting acquisition planning; developing an Acquisition Strategy; promoting full and open competition and sustaining effective competition between alternative major system concepts and sources; executing certification of non-personal services; assigning technical representation in contractor facilities to perform non-Contract Administration Service [CAS] technical duties; and providing liaison, guidance, and assistance on systems and programs).

Similarly, the 5000 series includes responsibilities for the Contracting Officer and authorized representatives (e.g., preparing an acquisition plan, seeking small business opportunities, solicitation content preparation, formally validating and accepting the contractor's EVM system, negotiating contract funds status reporting, and conducting quality assurance inspections).

The COR assists the Contracting Officer in the technical monitoring or administration of the contract. The COR is the "eyes and ears," but not necessarily the "mouth" of the Contracting Officer. As the eyes and ears of the Contracting Officer, the knowledge of the COR is imputed to the Contracting Officer for purposes of contract management and contract administration, including any litigation.

The COR serves as the on-site technical manager responsible for assessing actual contractor performance against contract performance standards. The COR shares with the acquisition team personal field experience in surveillance of the contract. The COR performs the actual surveillance of the contractor's work. However, the COR may not be delegated responsibility to perform functions that have been delegated to a Contract Administration Office (CAO) (e.g., Defense Contract Management Agency). The Contracting Officer may retain almost any of these functions, and delegate them to a COR. Some functions are, however, retained exclusively for the CAO.

CH 1–4.2.11.3 Relationships

A fundamental question (or issue) often discussed between PMs and Contracting Officers is, "Whose contract is it, the PM's or the Contracting Officer's?" The answer is, "Neither." A glance at the cover page of a contract (e.g., Standard Form [SF] 26, Award/Contract, Block 20B, or SF 33, Solicitation, Offer and Award, Block 27) reveals the answer, which is "United States of America."

Program Managers and Contracting Officers, and their authorized representatives function in what should be a beneficial symbiotic relationship—a relationship that should benefit the nation's warfighters and the United States of America. In doing so, they fulfill the vision for the Federal Acquisition System addressed in the statement of guiding principles for the Federal Acquisition System, ". . . to deliver on a timely basis the best value product or service to the customer, while maintaining the public's trust and fulfilling public policy objectives." (FAR 1.102(a)).

To make those relationships operate more smoothly, consider the following:

- A meeting between the PM and Contracting Officer is appropriate and advantageous—together up front, and early on and often.
  - The best time is before the PMO Team begins to write documentation that may otherwise need to be rewritten.
  - It is best to establish a working relationship when things are going well rather than trying to establish one in a period of program problems or crisis management.
  - An invitation to the Contracting Officer as a regular attendee to program office staff meetings is appropriate and advantageous.
  - If appropriate and feasible, co-locate the Contracting Officer within the program office, thereby shortening the lines of communication and allowing for greater flow of information.
- Acquisition is a document-driven process. The PM and the Contracting Officer jointly establish a Standard Operating Procedure (SOP) that addresses what constitutes a complete acquisition package to kick off a contract action. The SOP addresses all the items in a contract file that require program office input (e.g., requirements document, funding, new start validation, market research, acquisition plan, organizational conflict of interest, advisory and assistance service determinations, and make-or-buy program decisions). The SOP also contains a set of standard, reasonable timelines for various kinds of contract actions.
- The PM and Contracting Officer may need to address special or unique contracting actions. Although the Standard Operating Procedures (SOP) have a set of standard timelines, each contract action is unique, including: developing and agreeing to each piece of documentation required for the contract file; identifying the final approval authority, if any; assigning responsibility for the contract's development and coordination; and stating a date by which the contract is required to be produced. In this case, the PM and Contracting Officer may find it beneficial to establish a signed agreement for any modifications to the SOP. Both parties need to sign the agreement.

CH 1–4.2.11.4 Contract Types

"Contract types are grouped into two broad categories: fixed-price contracts (see FAR Subpart 16.2) and cost-reimbursement contracts (see FAR Subpart 16.3). The specific contract types range from firm-fixed-price, in which the contractor has full responsibility for the performance costs and resulting profit (or loss), to cost-plus-fixed-fee, in which the contractor has minimal responsibility for the performance costs, and the negotiated fee (profit) is fixed. In between are the various incentive contracts (see FAR Subpart 16.4), in which the contractor's responsibility for the performance costs and the profit or fee incentives offered are tailored to the uncertainties involved in contract performance" (FAR 16.101(b)). In addition to those two broad categories, there are also Time-and-Materials (T&M) and Labor-Hour (LH) contracts, under which the government pays the contractor a fixed hourly rate for labor. Under a T&M contract, the government typically reimburses materials at actual cost.

Fixed-price and cost-reimbursement contracts may also be divided into Completion and Term forms. The Completion form normally requires the contractor to complete and deliver the specified end product within the estimated cost, if possible. However, in the event the work cannot be completed within the estimated cost, the government may require more effort without increase in fee, provided the government increases the estimated cost. The Term form describes the scope of work in general terms and obligates the contractor to devote a specified level of effort for a stated time period (see FAR 16.306). Fixed-price type contracts are generally of the Completion form, except for firm-fixed-price, level-of-effort term contracts, which require the contractor to provide a specified level of effort, over a stated period of time, on work that can be stated only in general terms (see FAR 16.207-1).

There is a preference in contract type for fixed-price contracts over cost-reimbursement contracts. Firm-fixed-price contracts, which best utilize the basic profit motive of business enterprises, are to be used when the risk involved is minimal or can be predicted with an acceptable degree of certainty. When that is not the case, other contract types may be more suitable. T&M and LH contracts are the least preferred of contract types, only to be used when no other contract type is suitable. There is a preference in the FAR for the Completion form of contract types over the Term form.

Under a fixed-price contract, the contractor commits to delivering a quality "acceptable" product at a fixed price regardless of actual cost. Thus, under a fixed-price type contract, the possibility exists that the contractor could ultimately end up losing money on the effort.

Under a cost-reimbursement type contract, the government agrees to pay all of a contractor's allowable costs up to the amount of funding obligated under the contract. Above that limit, the contractor is not obligated to expend funds in performance of the contract, but may do so at its own risk. Costs are required to meet certain requirements to be allowable under a contract (i.e., Reasonableness; Allocability; Standards promulgated by the CAS Board, if applicable – otherwise, generally accepted accounting principles and practice appropriate to the circumstances; terms of the contract; and any limitations set forth in FAR 31.2). With the government reimbursing all allowable cost up to the specified limit, that means that the risk to the government is high, with no guarantee that a usable product will be delivered. The contractor only ". . . agrees to use its best efforts to perform the work specified in the Schedule and all obligations under this contract within the estimated cost . . . ." The risk to the contractor is low because all of its allowable costs are reimbursed by the government. Refer to Figure 23 which compares Risk to Contract Types.

Figure 23: Risk to Contract Types

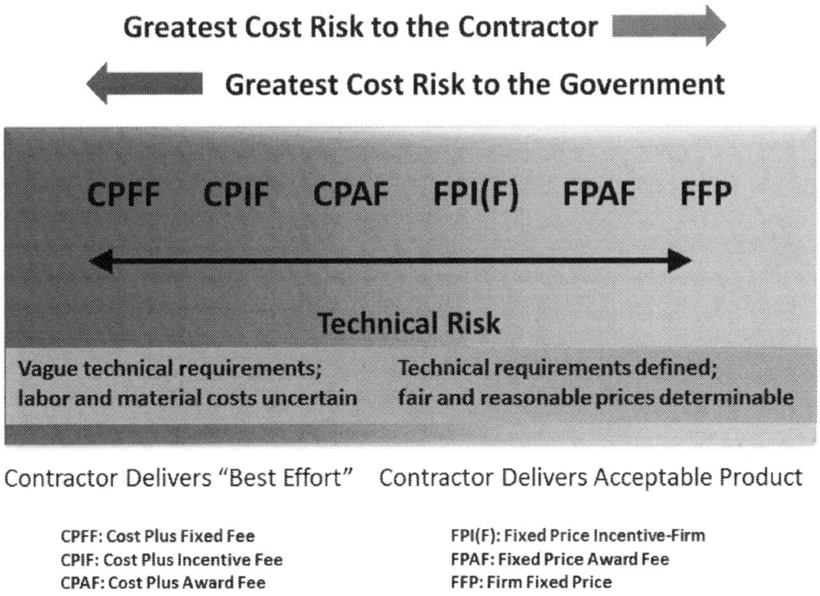

Greatest Cost Risk to the Contractor ▶

◀ **Greatest Cost Risk to the Government**

CPFF   CPIF   CPAF   FPI(F)   FPAF   FFP

◀――――――――――――――――――▶

Technical Risk

Vague technical requirements; labor and material costs uncertain   Technical requirements defined; fair and reasonable prices determinable

Contractor Delivers "Best Effort"   Contractor Delivers Acceptable Product

CPFF: Cost Plus Fixed Fee
CPIF: Cost Plus Incentive Fee
CPAF: Cost Plus Award Fee

FPI(F): Fixed Price Incentive-Firm
FPAF: Fixed Price Award Fee
FFP: Firm Fixed Price

For supplemental information regarding contract types and incentives go to: Contract Pricing Reference Guides or Guidance on Using Incentive and Other Contract Types.

Selecting the contract type is generally a matter for negotiation and requires the exercise of sound judgment. Negotiating the contract type and negotiating prices are closely related and are to be considered together. The objective is to negotiate a contract type and price (or estimated cost and fee) that results in reasonable contractor risk and provide the contractor with the greatest incentive for efficient and economical performance (FAR 16.103 (a)). Use market research, industry days, and other pre-solicitation communication with industry to help determine the risk to all parties and the right contract type for a given situation.

Although the Contracting Officer ultimately determines the selection of contract type, it is a topic that is best carefully discussed between the PM and the Contracting Officer. Any contract type or combination of contract types described in the FAR may be used in an acquisition. The cost-plus-a-percentage-of-cost system of contracting is prohibited by law. In addition, there are some limitations on contract type based on method of contracting used (e.g., commercial item acquisition and sealed bidding).

Program Managers and Contracting Officers ensure the selection of contract type and contracting approach is a "best fit" business solution to achieving their program goals. The Contracting Officer manages these business solutions in a manner that optimizes the program's ability to achieve successful results. Source selection evaluation factors and contract incentives reflect the principal goals and risks of the program. Once the contracting approach and contracting type are established, the PM can see where risks and special objectives have been addressed in the selected business solution(s).

During the Defense Acquisition Life Cycle, different contract types are more appropriate for each phase. Figure 24 illustrates "typical" contract types by phase, keeping in mind that the best contract type is one that appropriately shares the risk between government and contractor.

Figure 24: Typical Contract Types by Acquisition Phase

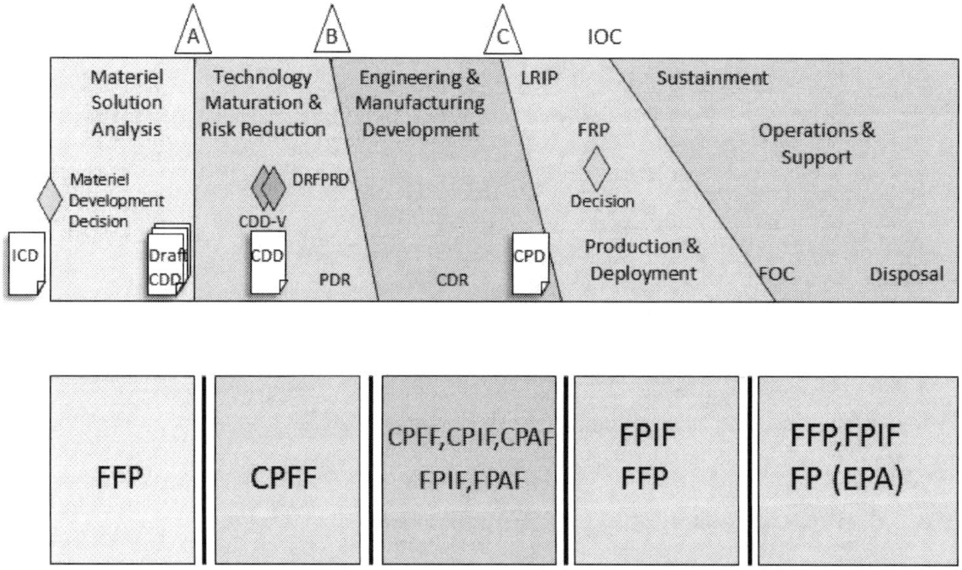

CDD: Capability Development Document
CDD-V: Capability Development Document-Validation
CDR: Critical Design Review
CPAF: Cost Plus Award Fee
CPD: Capability Production Document
CPFF: Cost Plus Fixed Fee
CPIF: Cost Plus Incentive Fee
DRFPRD: Development Request for Proposal Release Decision
FFP: Firm Fixed Price

FOC: Full Operational Capability
FP (EPA): Fixed Price Economic Price Adjustment
FPIF: Fixed Price Incentive Firm
FRP: Full Rate Production
ICD: Initial Capabilities Document
IOC: Initial Operational Capability
LRIP: Low-Rate Initial Production
PDR: Preliminary Design Review

Although the specified types may be "typical," selection is based on the following 12 factors (FAR 16.104):

- Price competition
- Price analysis
- Cost analysis
- Type and complexity of the requirement
- Combining contract types
- Urgency of the requirement
- Period of performance or length of production run
- Contractor's technical capability and financial responsibility
- Adequacy of the contractor's accounting system
- Concurrent contracts
- Extent and nature of proposed subcontracting
- Acquisition history

In the Materiel Solution Analysis phase, programs contract for analytical studies, usually using Firm-Fixed-Price (FFP) contracts. In Technology Maturation and Risk Reduction, programs contract with multiple contractors for competitive prototyping of critical program technologies. This creates a competitive situation that provides built-in incentives for contractors to perform well, so specific incentives are generally unnecessary. Cost Plus Fixed Fee (CPFF) contracts frequently make the most sense in this situation. In Engineering and Manufacturing Development, programs contract for completion of the system design and preparation for production. Although Fixed Price Incentive-Firm (FPI-F) contracts are preferred in EMD, the Milestone Decision Authority may approve a different contract type, consistent with the level of program risk. In Production and Deployment, programs contract for low-rate and full-rate production as well as initial sustainment. At this point in the program, requirements are well known and stable, and the design has been proven in testing. Therefore, the program risk is now low enough to use fixed-price type contracts from Milestone C forward.

CH 1–4.2.11.5 Specifications

10 USC 2305, Contracts: Planning, Solicitation, Evaluation, and Award Procedures, establishes the requirements for specifying requirements in DoD acquisition. The PM and the Contracting Officer need to describe agency needs in contractual requirements and specifications in such a fashion as to promote full and open competition. Restrictive provisions or conditions are included only to the extent necessary to satisfy the needs of the agency or as authorized by law.

The type of specification included in a solicitation depends on the nature of the needs of the program and market availability of solutions to meet those needs. To the maximum extent practicable, requirements are stated in terms of:

- Function to be performed so that a variety of products or services may qualify.
- Performance required, including specifications of the range of acceptable characteristics or of the minimum acceptable standards.
- Essential physical characteristics or design requirements (FAR 11.002).

Some or all of a requirement's performance levels or performance specifications may be identified in a solicitation (e.g., RFP) as targets rather than as fixed or minimum requirements. Some performance levels may include threshold and objective values.

The PM may select from existing requirements documents, modify or combine existing requirements documents, or create new requirements documents to meet program needs. In doing so, the PM follows the following order of precedence:

- Documents mandated for use by law.

- Performance-oriented documents (e.g., a Performance Work Statement [PWS] or Statement of Objectives [SOO]).
- Detailed design-oriented documents.
- Standards, specifications, and related publications issued by the government outside the Defense or Federal series for the non-repetitive acquisition of items (FAR 11.101).

Note: See FAR Part 11 and DFARS Part 211 for specific guidance on Describing Agency Needs.

When an RFP cites a requirements document listed in the General Services Administration (GSA) Index of Federal Specifications, Standards and Commercial Item Descriptions, the DoD Acquisition Streamlining and Standardization Information System (ASSIST – Account and CAC required) or other agency index identifies each document's approval date, and the dates of any applicable amendments and revisions. General identification references are discouraged, such as "the issue in effect on the date of the solicitation" (FAR 11.201(a)). Unless changed after contract award, this is the specific document that establishes the contract requirement. If the document is updated in the contract, an equitable adjustment may be appropriate.

Part of the purpose of conducting market research and discussing requirements with industry is to determine the availability of commercial items and non-developmental items. The government has a preference for the acquisition of commercial items, including providing special, less cumbersome methods for acquiring commercial items. The PM defines requirements in terms that enable and encourage offerors to supply commercial items or, if commercial items are unsuitable or unavailable, non-developmental items (FAR 11.002(a)(2)(ii)). These provide offerors of commercial items and non-developmental items an opportunity to compete in any acquisition to fulfill program requirements. If no commercial or non-developmental items can meet the government's requirement, the PM considers whether the requirement can be modified.

The PM and the Contracting Officer engage industry as early as possible in the acquisition process, beginning with the establishment of the requirement. These engagements improve the understanding of government requirements and industry capabilities. Exchange of information helps the government shape requirements, which enhances the ability of the government to get the supplies and services it needs. Exchange of information allows potential offerors to decide whether or how they can satisfy the government's requirements, make bid/no-bid decisions, and consider partnering arrangements with subcontractors or teaming arrangements with other contractors. There are numerous ways that a PM can engage industry, but particularly useful are Requests for Information (RFIs) and one-on-one meetings with potential offerors.

To the extent practicable and consistent with organizational conflict of interest issues, potential offerors are given an opportunity to comment on agency requirements or to recommend application and tailoring of requirements documents and alternative approaches. Release of a draft RFP can be useful in providing that opportunity. The PM applies specifications, standards, and related documents initially for guidance only, making final decisions on the application and tailoring of these documents as a product of the design and development process. The government refrains from dictating detailed design solutions prematurely.

Before releasing the final RFP, the program office needs to allow enough time to develop and mature the performance and functional specifications that are included in the RFP. When carefully prepared, the RFP and supporting technical documentation clearly define the government's expectations in terms of the performance and functional specifications, program planning, program process, risks, and assumptions. The RFP also directs potential offerors to integrate their approach to reflect the government's expectations. See CH 3–2.7 for additional information on the Systems Engineering role in contracting.

There are certain things a PM and Contracting Officer typically avoid, or use carefully, in establishing contract requirements and specifications:

- **Use of brand name or equal purchase descriptions**. The use of performance specifications is preferred to encourage offerors to propose innovative solutions. However, the use of brand name or equal purchase descriptions may be advantageous under certain circumstances. To further competition, brand name or equal purchase descriptions include, in addition to the brand name, a general description of those salient physical, functional, or performance characteristics of the brand name item that an "equal" item is required to meet to be acceptable for award. Use brand name or equal descriptions when the salient characteristics are firm requirements. A brand name or equal description, without a discussion of what constitutes "equal," may prove to be problematic in the event of a protest.
- **Items peculiar to one manufacturer.** Requirements are not written to require a particular brand name, product, or a feature of a product peculiar to one manufacturer, thereby precluding consideration of a product manufactured by another company, unless the particular brand name, product, or feature is essential to the government's requirements, and market research indicates other companies' similar products, or products lacking the particular feature, do not meet, or cannot be modified to meet, the agency's needs.
- **Inherently governmental functions**. In drafting purchase descriptions for service contracts, the government avoids requiring contractors to perform inherently governmental functions. [*Note*: A list of inherently governmental functions may be found at FAR 7.503.] In addition, there are functions that are generally not considered to be inherently governmental functions, but are closely related or may approach being in that category. This may be as a result of nature of the function, the manner in which the contractor performs the contract, or the manner in which the government administers contractor performance. If these latter requirements are to be included in a contract, careful consideration is given to the writing of the requirement.

CH 1–4.2.11.6 Work Statements

The PM pays particular attention to work statements, as they drive to what standards offerors are to write their proposals and, ultimately, the contract requirements that drive contractor performance. These are key documents as they serve as a baseline for stating what the contractor is to accomplish and for determining the success of their performance.

The PM works with the Contracting Officer early in the development process of the work statement to ensure delivery of a quality product to the Contracting Officer, consistent with any "contract" they have established. The PM ensures alignment between the work statement and the Program Work Breakdown Structure (PWBS), and the work statement and the Contract Work Breakdown Structure (CWBS). The work statement, also described in CH 1–4.2.11.6.1 and CH 3–4.1.1.1 are aligned with the acquisition milestones and phases.

There are different types of work statements (i.e., Statement of Work [SOW], Performance Work Statement [PWS], and Statement of Objectives [SOO]).

CH 1–4.2.11.6.1 Statement of Work

Statement of Work (SOW) is the portion of a contract that establishes and defines all non-specification requirements for contractor's efforts either directly or with the use of specific cited documents. This document describes the actual work that is to be performed by the contractor and often uses references to such documents as specifications and documents incorporated into the SOW as compliance documents or reference documents. Some documents can be presented in full text while others may be incorporated by reference. The SOW specifies in clear, understandable terms the work to be done in developing or producing the supplies to be delivered or services to be performed by a contractor. Preparation of an effective SOW requires both an understanding of the supplies or services that are needed to satisfy a particular requirement and an ability to define what is required in specific, performance-based, quantitative, or qualitative terms. A SOW prepared in explicit terms enables offerors to clearly understand the government's requirements, including international acquisition documents (International Agreements, Foreign Military Sales Letters of Offer and Acceptance), as applicable. This understanding facilitates the preparation of responsive proposals and delivery of the required supplies or services. A well-written SOW also aids the government in selecting the source for contract award, and for contract management and contract administration after award. A Data Requirements Review Board (DRRB), Solicitation Review Panel (SRP), "Murder Board," or other such group may review each SOW to ensure compliance with the policy, guidance, and procedures contained in MIL-HDBK-245D, Department of Defense Handbook for Preparation of Statement of Work (SOW).

CH 1–4.2.11.6.2 Performance Work Statement

Performance Work Statement (PWS) is a statement of work for performance-based acquisition that describes the required results in clear, specific, and objective terms with measurable outcomes. These are often used in services, but can also be used in supply contracts when describing outcomes. The PWS states requirements in general terms of what is to be done (result), rather than how it is done (method). The PWS gives the contractor maximum flexibility to devise the best *method* to accomplish the required *result*. The PWS is written to ensure that offerors compete fairly based on their capabilities. The government can remove PWS requirements that unfairly restrict competition. However, the PWS is descriptive and specific enough to protect the interests of the government, including international acquisition documents (International Agreements and Foreign Military Sales Letters of Offer and Acceptance, as applicable), and promote competition unless otherwise specified by the FMS customer nation. The clarity and explicitness of the requirements in the PWS invariably enhance the quality of the proposals submitted. A definitive PWS is likely to produce definitive proposals, thus reducing the time needed for proposal evaluation.

- Preparing a PWS begins with an analytical process, often referred to as a "job analysis." It involves a close examination of the agency's requirements and tends to be a "bottom up" assessment with "re-engineering" potential. This analysis is the basis for establishing performance requirements, developing performance standards, writing the PWS, and producing the quality assurance plan. Those responsible for the mission or program are essential to the performance of the job analysis.
- A different approach to the analytical process is described in the Guidebook for the Acquisition of Services. It describes the Requirements Roadmap Process and the availability of a database PWS and Quality Assurance Surveillance Plan (QASP) authoring tool known as the Acquisition Requirements Roadmap Tool (ARRT). The ARRT provides authoring question-and-answer "wizards" to guide users through the requirements roadmap process. The ARRT allows an author to use standardized PWS and QASP templates to create a PWS and QASP tailored to a specific requirement. The requirements roadmap process includes two specific tasks: (1) Define the desired outcomes—what must be accomplished to satisfy the requirement? and (2) Conduct an outcome analysis—what tasks must be accomplished to arrive at the desired outcomes?

CH 1–4.2.11.6.3 Statement of Objectives

The Statement of Objectives (SOO) is an alternative to a SOW or PWS. It is a summary of key agency goals, outcomes, or both, that is incorporated into a performance-based acquisition so that competitors may have maximum flexibility in proposing their own specific solutions. Solutions may include a technical approach, performance standards, and a quality assurance surveillance plan, which may be based on commercial business practice. SOO content depends both on the type of supplies or services and on the program phase. It is possible that a "mature" program, such as a software product, which is the maintenance phase, could require slightly more detail in the SOO to properly integrate with other software programs under development or operation. The key is to keep the document short and concise. The SOO does not specifically address each Work Breakdown Structure (WBS) element, but each WBS element is traceable to the SOO. For example, a SOO may instruct the offerors to address an engineering approach. That is not a particular WBS element, but several WBS elements might be created to break out the engineering tasks. Try not to group all WBS elements in the same objective. In so doing, end users get the best supplies or services, and competition is enhanced if dissimilar solutions are submitted in response to the solicitation. There is no predetermined length for the SOO document. Ideally, it is a concise, cogent document of appropriate length.

The following actions provide the conceptual process for developing the SOO:

- Conduct market research to determine whether commercial items or non-developmental items are available to meet program requirements.
- Review the requirements documents that authorize the program, various DoD, Military Departments, Joint Services requirements documents, and applicable international acquisition documents (International Agreements, Foreign Military Sales Letters of Offer and Acceptance) for program management and acquisition management impact to the program.
- Prepare a bibliography citing the specific portions of all applicable governing directives, instructions, specifications, and standards with which the program is required to comply. Keep these requirements to the absolute minimum.
- Develop the program objectives by completing a risk assessment that highlights the high and moderate risks in the areas of business, programmatic, and technical identified in the program based on the requirements and users' high-level objectives.

Access more information on creating a SOW, PWS, or SOO on the Acquisition Community Connection website (e.g., MIL-HDBK-245D).

CH 1–4.2.11.7 Request for Proposal Sections L & M

When the government seeks to acquire supplies or services, including major systems, it does so through "Solicitation" (i.e., FAR 2.101). Solicitation means any request to submit offers or quotations to the government. Solicitations under sealed bid procedures are called "invitations for bids." Solicitations under negotiated procedures are called "Requests for Proposal." Solicitations under simplified acquisition procedures may require submission of either a quotation or an offer. Other than for simplified acquisition, the solicitation is likely to be a Request for Proposal (RFP).

The RFP is structured using a Uniform Contract Format (UCF) so that solicitations and contracts have a common structure (see Figure 25). The common structure makes it easier for the government and contractors to work together.

Figure 25: Uniform Contract Format (Table 15-1 of the FAR)

Section	Title
	Part I—The Schedule
A	Solicitation/contract form
B	Supplies or services and prices/costs
C	Description/specifications/statement of work
D	Packaging and marking
E	Inspection and acceptance
F	Deliveries or performance
G	Contract administration data
H	Special contract requirements
	Part II—Contract Clauses
I	Contract clauses
	Part III—List of Documents, Exhibits, and Other Attachments
J	List of attachments
	Part IV—Representations and Instructions
K	Representations, certifications, and other statements of offerors or respondents
L	Instructions, conditions, and notices to offerors or respondents
M	Evaluation factors for award

The UCF provides the structure for the RFP, including how offerors are to structure offers and proposals (i.e., Section L Instructions, conditions, and notices to offerors or respondents) and how the government evaluates those offers and proposals (i.e., Section M Evaluation factors for award). Sections A through K constitute the "Model Contract"—what the government anticipates the final contract to look like. When Sections A through K have been filled in by the offeror, and signed by both parties, the resultant document becomes the contract between the government and the contractor. Section K representations, certifications, and other statements of offerors or respondents are not present in the contract document; however, the representations and certifications are incorporated by reference in the contract by using a contract clause.

Although the Contracting Officer signs the contract on behalf of the United States of America, most of the input for the solicitation and contract comes from the PM and the PM's other functional experts. Section I, Contract Clauses, is probably the one section where the Contracting Officer has the most responsibility, but even then many of the contract clauses selected are driven by the needs of the program.

Figure 26 shows the documents that are provided in the solicitation, are provided in an offeror's proposal, and will be in the final contract. From a source selection perspective, Sections L and M may be the most important, and require particular attention of the PM and the Contracting Officer. Section M is the PM's statement of what looks like success in the eyes of the government, and how offers and proposals will be differentiated or distinguished from one another. Having established what is important in Section M, Section L is written to assure that the government has all the information that is needed to make an assessment.

Figure 26: Contract Document Linkages

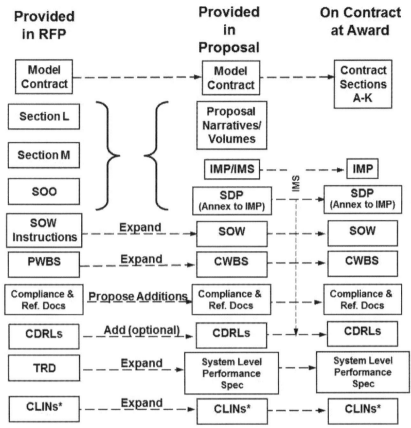

Provided in RFP

- Model Contract
- Section L
- Section M
- SOO
- SOW Instructions
- PWBS
- Compliance & Ref. Docs
- CDRLs
- TRD
- CLINs*

Provided in Proposal

- Model Contract
- Proposal Narratives/ Volumes
- IMP/IMS
- SDP (Annex to IMP)
- SOW
- CWBS
- Compliance & Ref. Docs
- CDRLs
- System Level Performance Spec
- CLINs*

On Contract at Award

- Contract Sections A-K
- IMP
- SDP (Annex to IMP)
- SOW
- CWBS
- Compliance & Ref. Docs
- CDRLs
- System Level Performance Spec
- CLINs*

Expand (SOW Instructions → SOW)
Expand (PWBS → CWBS)
Propose Additions (Compliance & Ref. Docs)
Add (optional) (CDRLs)
Expand (TRD → System Level Performance Spec)
Expand (CLINs*)

* The contract line items (CLINs) will be reflected in the structure of Sections B Supplies or services and prices/costs, D Packaging and marking, E Inspection and acceptance, and Deliveries or performance of the Model Contract and Contract.

CDRLs: Contract Data Requirements Lists
CLINS: Contract Line Item Numbers
CWBS: Contract Work Breakdown Structure
IMP/IMS: Integrated Master Plan/Integrated Master Schedule
PWBS: Program Work Breakdown Structure
Ref. Docs: Reference Documents

RFP: Request for Proposal
SDP: Software Development Plan
SOO: Statement of Objectives
SOW: Statement of Work
Spec: Specification
TRD: Technical Requirements Document

The government does not generally request any information from offers under Section L that is not to be evaluated under Section M. Similarly, the government does not generally evaluate anything under Section M where offeror information has not been requested under Section L. In addition, there should be alignment between Sections L and M, and the remainder of the solicitation. The PM and the Contracting Officer are following a best practice by completing a compliance matrix (refer to Table 6) to ensure this alignment. It might prove beneficial to offerors to include the matrix in the RFP. Many, if not most, offerors will develop a matrix as part of the proposal development process if the government does not provide one. Such a matrix ensures a compliant offer and proposal.

Table 6: Sample Compliance Matrix

Sample Compliance Matrix					
DESCRIPTION	**CLIN / SECTION B**	**CDRL/ SECTION J**	**SOW/PWS/ SECTION C**	**SECTION L**	**SECTION M**
Administrative Support	0001	004A2	1.1	4.3	3.1
Records Management	0002	010A2	1.1.1	4.3.1	3.1.1
Forms and Publications	0003	020A2	1.1.2	4.3.2	3.1.2
Operations & Maintenance	0004	021A2	1.2	4.4	3.2
Equipment Records	0005	053A2	1.2.1.1	4.4.2	3.2.1
Maintenance Analysis	0006	054A2	1.2.2	4.4.3	3.2.2
Price	Section B			1.5.3	4.0
Past Performance				6.0	5.0

CH 1–4.2.11.7.1 Section L

The PM and Contracting Officer explain in Section L of the RFP (Instructions, Conditions, and Notices to Offerors or Respondents) the structure, format, and content of an offeror's offer and proposal. The PM and Contracting Officer ensure the instructions for submission of proposals are complete and thorough, but not overly long, complex, or restrictive. Submission instructions vary, but most agencies have a standard or preferred format that is familiar to Contracting Officers and evaluators. For example, proposals may be submitted via disks, electronic media, orally, or in paper-based form. The most common content items to be prescribed in the instructions include the following: volumes, page limits, font, spacing, and other layout instructions. Reference the DoD Source Selection Procedures for additional informational instructions.

Some solicitations include a requirement for oral presentations. Oral presentations may be of two different kinds. The first kind is where information provided orally is a substitute for information that would normally be provided in written form. The second kind is a "test" in which the information is used to determine an offeror's understanding of the requirements, capability to perform, or other purpose. When using oral presentations, have the presenter be the proposed PM or other person assigned to the program, not a professional speaker.

CH 1–4.2.11.7.2 Section M

The key to successful use of any evaluation factor is to establish a clear relationship between the work to be performed under the contract, Section L of the solicitation, and Section M (Evaluation Factors for Award) of the solicitation. The evaluation factors selected should link clearly with the Statement of Work (SOW) or Performance Work Statement (PWS), and represent those areas that are important to stakeholders or have been identified as high risk during risk analysis. Refer to DFARS 215.300, which incorporates DoD Source Selection Procedures by reference.

Section M is uniquely tailored for each contract and is intended to give offerors guidance concerning the basis of award. All the evaluation factors and significant subfactors that will be considered in making the source selection, along with their relative order of importance, are explained (see FAR 15.304).

Although evaluation factors and significant subfactors are at the broad discretion of the government, some factors are required by law. An evaluation of cost or price to the government is required, and the Government Accountability Office has ruled that this evaluation is a "significant" factor. Unless waived by the Contracting Officer, past performance is also a required evaluation factor. Quality of the product service shall be a consideration, but it need not be a stand-alone evaluation factor. A statement is also required in Section M as to whether all evaluation factors other than cost or price, when combined, are significantly more important than, approximately equal to, or significantly less important than cost or price.

One of the main challenges in determining best value is assessing performance risk. This is challenging because the offerors may be proposing different approaches that can be difficult to compare (an apples-to-oranges comparison). While Section M of a solicitation provides the basis for evaluation, there is no precise science to assessing dissimilar approaches toward fulfilling a Performance-Based Acquisition (PBA) requirement.

Evaluation Factors/Subfactors. Be sure that Section M is clear and complete in describing the evaluation factors and significant sub-factors to be used. Factors/subfactors are to be fully explained and their relationship to one another (relative importance) clearly stated. The goal here is to make the offerors fully aware of how the source selection will be made.

CH 1–4.2.12 Industrial Base

The development and implementation of acquisition plans for each Major Defense Acquisition Program requires, by law (10 USC 2440, Technology and Industrial Base Plans) consideration of the national technology and industrial base. These considerations are enumerated in law (10 USC 2501, National Security Strategy for National Technology and Industrial Base) and include, among other things: reconstituting industrial capabilities; providing for the development, manufacture, and supply of items and technologies; providing for the generation of services; maintaining critical design skills; ensuring reliable sources of materials; and reducing the presence of counterfeit parts.

CH 1–4.2.12.1 Strategic Perspective

Industrial capability, in the context of Title 10, generally refers to entire industrial sectors and their underlying infrastructure and processes. Industrial sectors are usually thought of broadly such as aircraft, ground vehicles, electronics, etc. These sectors consist of a variety of discrete capabilities found in a work breakdown structure such as control surface actuators, diesel engines, microprocessors, etc. In many cases, industrial capabilities support both military and civilian customers. It is often, but not always, the case that industrial base issues arise with capabilities that are defense-specific such as tactical aircraft propulsion, tank armor, or trusted electronics. The degree and timing of industrial capability issues in any of these areas can exceed the ability of any individual program, Service, or Agency to address, and sometimes are elevated and addressed at the DoD level. Sometimes coordination across programs and across Services is necessary to address risk. In other cases, there may be no existing programs and in order to ensure future availability of specific industrial capabilities, the Department makes its own direct investments. To address industrial base considerations at a strategic level, the Department has an executive-level Industrial Base Council, with Service and Agency representatives, a senior-level working group, multiple cross-program and cross-Service working groups, and multiple sector-wide risk remediation tools.

CH 1–4.2.12.2 Industrial Base Consideration in Program Planning

10 USC 2440 requires consideration of the national technology and industrial base in acquisition plans for each MDAP. DoD has implemented these requirements through DoDI 5000.02 (Encl. 2, para 8), DoDI 5000.60, Defense Industrial Base Assessment, and DoD 5000.60-H, Assessing Defense Industrial Capabilities. These policies and handbook incorporate the statutory requirement for industrial base analysis into acquisition planning and execution, and the importance of documenting industrial base considerations in acquisition strategies.

Because of this broad, strategic focus, it may not be necessary, or even desirable, for each PM to perform an independent analysis of all industrial base considerations when developing a program's Acquisition Strategy. At the beginning of Acquisition Strategy development, it is highly recommended that PMs consult with their Service's industrial base assessment activity and the OSD Office of Manufacturing and Industrial Base Policy to determine what work has already been done, what risks are known, what risks are considered relevant, and what knowledge gaps remain to be addressed. These organizations will later be reviewers of the Acquisition Strategy. A proactive approach reaching out to the reviewers prior to developing the strategy can result in a very efficient, cost-effective, and highly tailored consideration of industrial base factors.

Addressing Industrial base considerations should not be confused with market research, another important part of effective acquisition. Market research tends to be focused on identifying the full range of capabilities, opportunities, and alternatives that are available in the market at the top tier of the supply chain for a complete end product or weapon system. There is an emphasis on identifying commercial products and services that may be applied to military requirements, and an expectation that most such information will be relatively easy to discover. On the other hand, industrial base assessment focuses much more on the risks that certain discrete capabilities—frequently defense-unique, often at lower tiers of the supply chain—won't be available. It also looks at the difficulty of constituting or reconstituting at-risk capabilities and what can be done to address those risks. Supply chain risks tend to be carefully guarded as trade secrets and quite difficult, if not impossible, to identify with public information. Once an at-risk capability is identified though, market research can be quite valuable to identify alternatives. Review more information on Market Research at the Defense Acquisition University Continuous Learning Module CLC 004 – Market Research.

To minimize the expenditure of program resources, avoid repeating complex assessments. To quickly tap into DoD corporate knowledge of essential industrial base issues and to efficiently tailor industrial base considerations in program acquisition strategies, it is highly recommended that PMs consult with the Office of Manufacturing and Industrial Base Policy (MIBP) and other appropriate members of the Joint Industrial Base Working Group at the beginning of Acquisition Strategy development.

CH 1–4.2.12.3 Industrial Base Analysis Program Process

The Industrial Base Analysis Program process is simply to focus attention on specific industry sectors, identify relevant information, assess capability and risk, act, and start over refocusing attention. Sustained efforts and continuous learning maintain and strengthen the process over time. The reservoir of knowledge accumulated in the process contributes to Acquisition Strategy decisions, helps ensure realistic program objectives, reduces programming swings that disrupt companies' investments and operations, and contributes to the Department's merger, acquisition, and divestiture reviews and other industrial base policies. Review the Industrial Base Analysis Program for more information regarding Objectives and Assessment Methodology.

CH 1–4.2.12.4 Fragility and Criticality Assessment

Fragility and Criticality (FaC) Assessment are designed to systematically evaluate the need for program adjustments or investments to sustain specific niches in the defense industrial base. This common framework allows DoD leadership to compare industrial capabilities across all the sectors and tiers of the industrial base and combine scores for industrial capabilities that contribute to multiple programs, allowing portfolio analysis as part of DoD's normal budget process.

Industrial base issues are usually thought of in terms of risk. What is the risk that the defense department will not be able to get what it needs when it needs it? Specialized terms and criteria have been developed for industrial base risk assessment. Criticality is the difficulty of constituting or reconstituting a capability if disrupted. Fragility is the likelihood that a capability will be disrupted.

Fragility and Criticality (FaC) is similar to the familiar risk model of probability and consequence although the methodology is not the same. Industrial base FaC assessment results make a valid comparison of industrial base risks to each other within a sector but only a Program Manager (PM) can make the determination of how important a particular capability is to their particular program. Given a rigorous FaC assessment of a sector, a PM can make a separate determination of how identified industrial base risks fit into their overall program risk framework of probability and consequence. Figure 27 illustrates then process assessment activities, actions and outcomes.

Figure 27: FAC Assessment Activities, Actions and Outcomes

Process Activity	Action	Outcome
Select Sector/SubSector	Scope the problem (existing risk assessments; program shutdowns)	Sector Taxonomy
Search Available Data	Identify IB-related risks & related capabilities/products Identify suppliers and market	Potential IB Risks/Issues
FaC Screening/Filtering	Focused set of IB-related risks for further assessment	Screened IB/Issues Capability-Supplier Pairs
Conduct FaC Matrix Assessment	Facilitated scoring, based on standardized criteria, by SMEs	FaC Risk Matrix
Validate & Mitigate High Risk IB Issues	SME "deep dive" into IB risk areas; facility visits	Solutions to High Risk IB Issues

Process Activity Steps are as follows:

CH 1–4.2.12.4.1 FaC First Activity

The first activity in the FaC assessment process is to **select** the assessment subject and scope. The assessment generally begins by choosing an industrial base sector or subsector within that sector. However, as additional insight is acquired, future iterations may focus on more limited technology or commodity areas. Selection of a program or sector for a FaC assessment is based on leadership priorities, industrial base analysis, and the results of prior industrial base assessments.

CH 1–4.2.12.4.2 FaC Second Activity

The second activity in the process is to **search** for data and filter out non-industrial base issues to support industrial base assessment. In a resource constrained environment, the analyst cannot afford to conduct an open, unbounded search for information. Once the assessment scope is selected, industrial base analysts will evaluate available data sources for potential inclusion in the FaC assessment. Specific program or sector and supplier information included in existing databases, tools, programs, etc. is identified through the FaC criteria lens. Care is taken to ensure a transparent link to all data sources, and to share data sources among the FaC assessments. When the analyst finds deficiencies in the available information, they may contact subject matter experts (SMEs) knowledgeable in relevant technologies or the acquisition supply chain to augment the knowledge base.

A DoD platform can have thousands of parts and associated vendors and an industrial base sector has even more – so many that it would be impractical to evaluate all of them in any single assessment. Accordingly, before conducting a FaC assessment, the IPT applies a set of filters to arrive at the target set of capabilities and vendors. The filtering activity is essential to the FaC process: filtering rids the assessment of non- industrial base issues, and it protects against data overload by focusing the efforts of the IPT on areas of higher probability of risk.

CH 1–4.2.12.4.3 FaC Third Activity

The third activity is to **conduct** the FaC assessment. The heart of the assessment process is the set of criticality and fragility criteria that serves as indicators of potential industrial base-related risk. Criticality, from an industrial base perspective, consists of indicators to identify when a capability would be difficult to replace if it was lost or disrupted. Fragility indicators focus on the robustness of current suppliers of a capability and the availability of potential firms in the current marketplace. Go to Fragility and Criticality factors for a complete listing of characteristics.

The information required to assess FaC criteria in combination with demographic and economic data of the commercial organizations permits industrial base analysts to sort risks based on whether a given risk is rooted in broad industrial base issues or is unique to a particular capability. Armed with the filtered list of target capabilities to assess, SMEs evaluate the criticality and fragility factors for each capability. This assessment process leads to a FaC Assessment Risk Matrix, identifying the most critical capabilities and fragile suppliers. The high-risk capabilities become the subject for further investigation and validation. SME recommendations for areas that require further investigation, along with any risk mitigation suggestions, are some of the workshop results and a basis for follow-up actions.

Figure 28: Fragility & Criticality Risk Matrix Assessments

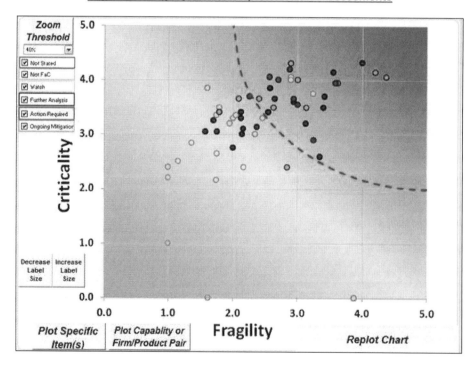

CH 1–4.2.12.4.4 FaC Fourth Activity

The fourth activity is to **validate** high-risk industrial issues and develop mitigation strategies. Figure 28 presents a visual example of a final FaC Assessment Risk Matrix generated by the pilots. The dots representing capability/supplier pairs in the upper right quadrant of the chart are capabilities that represent potential risks to the DoD in the industrial base. The scoring allows analysts to focus on the highest risk (red-orange) items as the most critical and fragile elements, which are also mapped back onto the taxonomy to reveal whether specific subcomponents contain multiple risks.

The scores from a FaC assessment should not be taken at face value but verified with follow-up to specific vendors. As much information as possible should gathered by phone calls, interviews, site assessments and other means confirm that an issue has been accurately identified and appropriately

CH 1–4.2.12.4.5 FaC Fifth Activity

The fifth activity is to *document* results in the acquisition strategy. Fragility and Criticality assessment results and risk mitigation plans should be documented in the industrial capabilities section. Industrial base risks comparable in magnitude to other program risks should also be documented in the risk section.

The scores from a FaC assessment should not be taken at face value but verified with follow-up to specific vendors. The collection of as much information (phone calls, interviews, site assessments, etc.) is warranted to ensure that an issue has been accurately identified and appropriately mitigated. Very often, industrial base considerations for a program are pervasive in an industrial sector or technology group, and are not specific to a program or weapons system. In the industrial base portion of an acquisition strategy, this can present an opportunity for collaboration and considerable reuse of existing work with a resultant savings in resources as well as better results.

CH 1–4.2.12.4.6 Resulting Risks

Given that industrial base considerations are generally pervasive in an industrial sector or technology group, identified risks very often cross program, Service and Agency boundaries. From the perspective of a program, there exists shared industrial base or sector common risks. Figure 29 illustrates the set of potential causes of risk. In an economic concept known as the "tragedy of the commons," individual users acting independently according to their own self-interest may sometimes behave contrary to the common good by depleting that resource or adding to its risks. In the closely related "free-rider" phenomenon, an individual program may be very reluctant to address a risk in the industrial commons out of concern that other programs or Services will pay less than their fair share and ride free one program's risk reduction investments.

Figure 29: Industrial Base Risk Causes

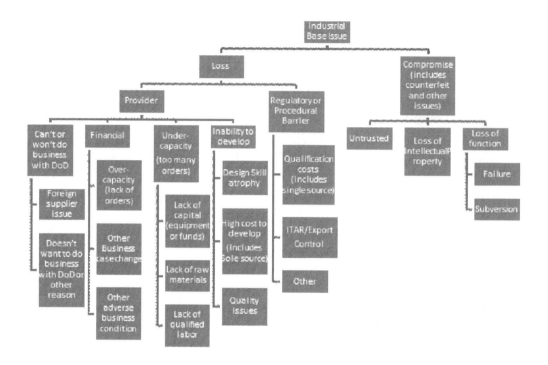

CH 1–4.2.12.5 Cross Program Working Groups

Cross program working groups, the Joint Industrial Base Working Group, the Industrial Base Council, Sector Working Groups, and strategic portfolio reviews may all be entry points to collaborative efforts ensuring that costs of industrial base risk reduction are shared equitably. While there are thousands of possible industrial base risks, they are generally only a few types of causes.

Assessing Defense Industrial Capabilities, A DoD Guide to 5000.60 provides the framework and guidelines for evaluating, on a case-by-case basis, the need for Government action to preserve industrial capabilities vital to national security. There are a wide variety of methods to address industrial base risk, depending upon the nature and severity of the risk.

CH 1–4.2.12.5.1 Joint Industrial Base Working Group

The Joint Industrial Base Working Group (JIBWG) is an action officer level forum with membership that parallels the industrial base council. In general, the JIBWG includes nearly all of the people in the DoD engaged full time in industrial base assessment and embodies the Department's corporate knowledge in this field. The JIBWG shares industrial base insights and, when applicable, performs the staff work and implements the decisions of the IBC.

CH 1–4.2.12.5.2 The Industrial Base Council

The Industrial Base Council (IBC) is an executive level forum for senior DoD leaders to review and discuss key defense industrial base trends and issues to:

- Inform DoD investment decisions
- Foster innovation and collaboration between government and industry
- Encourage relationships with new commercial partners.

The IBC includes representatives from all the Services and from Agencies with major acquisition responsibilities.

- The IBC receives insights and analyses on:
- Global market trends
- Foreign direct investments
- Innovative technology suppliers
- Fragile and critical capabilities in the industrial base

It also reviews opportunities available to address related concerns. It acts to:

- Inform and facilitate enterprise-wide program investment decisions
- Develop policies, programs and business incentives to mitigate industrial base vulnerabilities and attract innovative technology suppliers
- Seek ways to diversify investments to attract new and innovative technology suppliers.

IBC outcomes include:

- Forward-looking view of the IB enterprise from the strategic to operational levels
- Alignment of industrial base efforts to DoD's strategic priorities
- More timely and effective consideration of industrial base issues across the DoD enterprise
- Ability to facilitate the best business decisions to acquire the latest-state of the art industrial capabilities and sustain the current ones

CH 1–4.2.12.5.3 Sector Working Groups

There are a variety of inter-Service, inter-Agency working groups that address industrial base issues. Examples include the Space Industrial Base Working Group (SIBWG), the Critical Energetic Materials Working Group (CEMWG), the Fuze Integrated Product Team (IPT), and the Joint Army, Navy, NASA, Air Force (JANNAF) interagency propulsion committee. These working groups are excellent sources of information about known industrial base issues and industrial base assessments that could save a program a considerable amount of effort addressing industrial base concerns to meet acquisition strategy requirements.

CH 1–4.2.13 Small Business Participation

Small business considerations are important and relevant to every Acquisition Strategy because they affect cost, schedule, performance, vendor lock, supply chain diversity, and flexibility of approach. The following subsections provide information on program management activities with the small business community, including:

- What Small Businesses Offer to DoD
- Small Business Programs
- Program Management Expectations for Small Business Professionals
- Program Management Engagement with Small Business Community

CH 1–4.2.13.1 What Small Businesses Offer to DoD

Small businesses are typically more innovative, agile, and willing to take greater risks than larger firms with entrenched and rigid corporate strategies and profitability structures. Small businesses often have the flexibility to quickly adapt to changing requirements or to adopt high-risk ventures or technologies that larger companies will not be willing to engage. Due to lower indirect costs and overhead costs, small companies often offer lower prices for services. These characteristics of small business can lead to lower prices, faster delivery, and greater performance for the program if the small businesses are intelligently integrated into the Acquisition Strategy.

CH 1–4.2.13.2 Small Business Programs

Small business participation is not limited to traditional small businesses or socioeconomic subcategories, such as Service-Disabled, Veteran-Owned Small Business or Historically Underutilized Business Zones (HUB Zones). In fact, many small business programs are specifically designed to integrate cutting-edge, high-risk, and high-reward technology into existing and future major programs. The Small Business Innovation Research (SBIR) and Small Business Technology Transfer (STTR) provide cutting-edge research firms the seed capital to conduct research and development that will be useful to the DoD. SBIR contracts are intended to reach commercialization after demonstrating feasibility and creating a working prototype. Commercialization includes insertion into major programs of record, as well as private sector applications. The Rapid Innovation Fund (RIF) program inserts promising and mature technologies with immediate application potential, including SBIR, into programs of record.

CH 1–4.2.13.3 Program Management Expectations for Small Business Professionals

Program Managers can expect small business specialists to provide intelligent analysis and suggestions regarding the possibility of small business participation in the Acquisition Strategy. They can also expect small business specialists to justify any recommendations for the use of small business in terms of how it benefits the program and the defense industrial base, not simply in terms of meeting small business annual goals.

Small business specialists understand the mission and important goals of the program, and are able to provide suggestions to avoid vendor lock and to diversify the supply chain with vendors. They provide recommendations that use the advantages of small businesses to directly increase the strategic strength, effectiveness, or efficiency of the program. This comes in the form of (a) identifying work or requirements that can be performed by small business, and (b) identifying and providing background information and capabilities of specific small businesses that can perform the work or complete the requirements.

Early Acquisition Strategy decisions that do not include small business considerations can force the program into vendor lock (i.e., reliance on only one source, creating poor negotiation and pricing conditions). Diversity of the supply chain strengthens the defense industrial base, lowers pricing, and creates better conditions for optimal performance and schedule metrics.

Program Managers and their teams can expect the small business specialists to provide suggestions for the insertion of any beneficial and relevant SBIR, STTR, or RIF technologies into the program. The small business specialists can explain technologies and the vendors who developed them in terms of how the technologies may strengthen the overall program. For the more traditional small business programs, the small business specialists are able to suggest vendors and small business or socioeconomic subcategories that can perform the work, as well as identify work that is appropriate to set-aside for small businesses.

Program Managers and their teams can expect their Small Business Office specialists to provide the following:

- An overview of Small Business Programs, such as SBIR or the Mentor-Protégé Program (MPP), which may be relevant to the program.
- Near-expert insights on the providers of products and services on the part of the industrial base associated with the program.
- Screening of small businesses that desire to meet with government small business representatives.
- Market Research to support Acquisition Strategies and to stay abreast of the industrial base in general, particularly the small business industrial base.

- Insights on how prime contractors are using small businesses as subcontractors.
- Small business goals for the PMOs and clear expression of each program's contribution to achieving small business goals.
- Answers to any process questions associated with an Acquisition Strategy such as subcontracting considerations.
- Answers to any process questions associated with Contracting such as the responsibilities associated with completing the Small Business Coordination Review (DD 2579).
- Advice regarding contract bundling or consolidation.

CH 1–4.2.13.4 Program Management Engagements for Small Business

The following subsections address engaging with small business specialists as well as small and large contractors regarding developing small business involvement in an acquisition program

CH 1–4.2.13.4.1 Engaging with Small Businesses

Program Managers can expect Small Businesses to work through the small business specialist for PMO access. To make the first meeting between a PM and a small business specialist mutually beneficial, the small business specialist informs small businesses about the program. When successfully accomplished, the small business can then effectively present how its capabilities are relevant to the program, along with the rationale for its relevancy. It also enables small businesses to ask questions that are relevant to solving challenges faced by the program. One topic of concern is how small business addresses cybersecurity expectations. Program Managers can review Defense Cybersecurity Requirements: What Small Businesses Need to Know and discuss cybersecurity issues further with small business participants. The PM can expect small businesses to provide a one-page capabilities document that outlines the work they do, their North American Industry Classification System (NAICS) and Data Universal Numbering System (DUNS), past performance, certifications, and characteristics that differentiate them from others in their industry such as SBIR experience.

CH 1–4.2.13.4.2 Engaging with Prime Contractors (Not Small Businesses)

If the prime contractor is other than a small business, it is important the program management team develop challenging SB subcontracting goals. Once on contract, it is also important to hold the prime contractors accountable for meeting their small business subcontracting goals. This means ensuring that the Contracting Officer reviews and accepts subcontracting reports uploaded to the electronic Subcontracting Reporting System (eSRS). Program Managers can expect other than small business prime contractors to provide the following:

- How they will subcontract.
- Possible SBIR Phase III activities.
- Possible Mentor-Protégé program activities.
- An overview of their capabilities, such as a Small Business Liaison Office, to engage with small businesses in their supply chain.
- Updates on their performance in meeting small business subcontracting goals.

Program Managers, as they develop and refine the program Acquisition Strategy, are likely to find great benefit in the engagement of their local small business specialist and the small businesses that can bring innovation and competition to their program strategies.

CH 1–4.2.14 Intelligence Dependencies

Threat analysis and intelligence supportability assessments are increasingly critical to DoD acquisition programs. Early identification of the threat and Intelligence Mission Data (IMD) needs will also inform a program's technical risk assessment and can optimize system performance and warfighting capability, while minimizing costs to the government across both the intelligence support and acquisition processes. Support to the acquisition community from the intelligence community involves a number of staff organizations and support activities that may be unfamiliar to members of the requirements and acquisition communities. CH 7–3.1, Intelligence and Requirements describes the importance of the dedicated supporting intelligence subject matter expert to the requirements developer and PM (requirements and acquisition communities).

Early and consistent involvement and collaboration with the DoD Intelligence Community (DoD IC) helps reduce program risks to schedule, cost, and performance. Early collaboration also increases the likelihood that the delivered system will be fully capable and more survivable against relevant adversary threats through the following categories of reduced risk to schedule, cost, and performance:

- Reduced risk to schedule is derived from the early identification of work to be performed by the DoD IC, tasking of the DoD IC through production and collection requirements, identification of capability gaps, costing, and negotiated delivery dates for products.
- Reduced risk to cost is derived from the earliest identification of the costs and resource strategies to realize the full scope of intelligence support needed to close capability gaps throughout the acquisition life cycle. Collaboration with the DoD IC assists both the DoD IC and the acquisition communities in determining the costs to be borne by the DoD IC and/or the program.
- Reduced risk to performance is driven by obtaining and incorporating threat analysis information and intelligence support requirements from Materiel Solution Analysis through Full-Rate Production phases.

Supportability refers to the availability, suitability, and sufficiency of intelligence support required by a program or capability. Assessing supportability requires a comparison of the sponsor's stated operational/capability requirements with the derived intelligence support requirements and the intelligence support capabilities, as expected throughout a program or capability's life cycle. For a discussion of the relationship between the requirements and intelligence communities, refer to CH 7–3.1 and CH 7–3.2, also see CH 7–4.1.3, Life-cycle Mission Data Plan (LMDP).

For Program Protection, Security, and Counterintelligence support to acquisition programs, refer to CH 7–4.3 and CH 9–4.4.

CH 1–4.2.15 Program Affordability

Affordability has long been an overarching mandate in DoDD 5000.01 that until recently was not clearly specified in policy. The January 2015 release of DoDI 5000.02 (Encl. 8) clarifies affordability through two specific overarching processes that ensure affordability (refer to Figure 30).

Figure 30: Elements of Affordability at Component Level

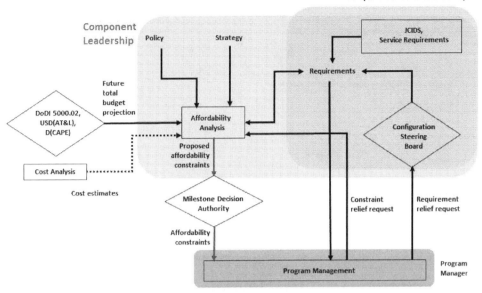

The first process is *Affordability Analysis*, which—like the PPBS and JCIDS process—is a DoD Component leadership responsibility **outside the PM's responsibility and purview**. The PM provides information into this process, but does **not** conduct the analysis or make the decisions.

The second process is the management of the program to stay within *Affordability Constraints* (goals or caps), which are assigned to the program by the Milestone Decision Authority (MDA) and are based on the DoD Component's affordability analysis. Program affordability management involves various aspects across this guidebook, such as program management, strategies, systems engineering, and design elements of life-cycle sustainment. Those functions that relate to affordability management are centralized in this Chapter to help clarify for the PM how they interrelate.

A useful overview of key elements of the affordability processes can be found in the *Defense AT&L* magazine article, "Dispelling the Myths of DoD's Affordability Policy" (Ohlandt, 2013).

The DoD Component determines when updates are needed to its affordability analysis, including recommendations to the MDA to adjust a program's affordability constraints when a program can no longer stay within the assigned constraints. Any such adjustments need to meet the basic criteria specified in the DoDI 5000.02 (Encl. 8, para 2) and may entail program cancellations, curtailments, and other negative effects on the program in question or other programs.

CH 1–4.2.15.1 Component Decisions and Tradeoffs

Affordability analysis involves DoD Component leadership decision-making and tradeoffs reflecting policy, strategy, and requirements, as defined in DoDI 5000.02 (Encl. 8, para 2). The objective is to determine how many dollars the DoD Component can afford to provide the program. Requirements tradeoffs may be needed to reflect technical, industrial, and other programmatic realities from the PM so that the program is viable. The dollars afforded are summarized in the affordability constraints that DoD Component leadership proposes to the MDA.

When affordable, margins in the constraints are highly recommended so that the program is more likely to be executable and manageable from its beginning. Generally, programs in early stages have high risk if their constraints are set without a margin for such uncertainties, leaving the programs little room for engineering problems and threat-based adjustments on developmental programs. Of course, if the constraint is all the DoD Component can afford, then the program will need to live within that constraint, making engineering tradeoffs and potentially seeking relief from Key Performance Parameters (KPPs) and Key System Attributes (KSAs). If the constraint is below the current cost estimate, then by definition the program is not currently affordable as configured.

There is not (and should not be) a predefined "textbook" margin recommended for affordability constraints. If a DoD Component can afford a margin, the size of that margin is based on the availability of resources in the affordability analysis, the relative importance of the program in question, and the magnitude of the uncertainties in the program. Flexibility and professional judgement are applied.

CH 1–4.2.15.1.1 Program Manager and Cost Analysis Inputs

While affordability analysis is the responsibility of DoD Component leadership, the acquisition community (including the PM) plays a role in informing those decision makers of the practical implications (e.g., risks and realities from cost, schedule, technology, engineering, and interoperability perspectives) as tradeoffs are considered and made. This includes the magnitude of uncertainties and the associated implications of setting affordability constraints at or near current cost estimates.

Fundamentally, however, it is important to remember that affordability analysis and constraints are not synonymous with cost estimation, but rather are a top-down process by which the resources a DoD Component has available are projected for allocation to a system, given inventory objectives and all other fiscal demands on the DoD Component. Cost estimates are generated in a bottom-up or parametric manner, and provide a forecast of what a product will cost for budgeting purposes. The difference between the affordability constraints and the cost estimates indicates whether actions are in order to further reduce cost and thereby remain within affordability constraints.

CH 1–4.2.15.1.2 Component Portfolio Analysis

DoDI 5000.02 (Encl. 8, para 3.a(6)) allows the DoD Components to determine the portfolios used in their affordability analysis. Currently, the portfolios used by the three Military Departments serve as the basis for illustrating how a program will fit in the DoD Component's long-range plans. The PM uses this information to provide the analysis from the DoD Component at major program reviews.

CH 1–4.2.15.1.3 Configuration Steering Boards – Requirements Management

During program execution, fact-of-life events (e.g., unforeseen technical difficulties, threat evolution, industrial-base issues, and budgetary reductions) may cause the PM to conclude that, despite efforts to control costs and reduce engineering requirements, an affordability constraint may be exceeded unless external help is obtained. In that case, the PM can seek KPP or KSA requirements relief to stay within the constraints. The Configuration Steering Board (CSB) is used for discussing changes in major requirements and significant technical configuration changes to optimize cost, schedule or performance. In either case, the CSB allows a discussion that may involve requirements relief from KPPs or quantity adjustments. Any decision affecting user requirements still requires a subsequent discussion with the operational requirement decision authority.

CH 1–4.2.15.2 Component-Level Affordability Analysis

While PMs do not conduct the affordability analysis, the PM reaches out to the DoD Component Resource Manager contact who is responsible for conducting the analysis. After the analysis is completed, the PM provides the results of that analysis as part of the information at program decision points (except for the CDD Validation decision point).

CH 1–4.2.15.2.1 Data Analysis

For major milestone reviews, the PM is responsible for providing a summary of the portfolio analysis and the DoD Component's constraint recommendations for MDA approval. A supporting spreadsheet is also provided by the PM listing the allocations by year for each program and portfolio in the DoD Component's analysis—including all programs in all of the DoD Component's portfolios—against the future total budget projection.

CH 1–4.2.15.3 Program Manager Responsibilities for Affordability Management

The 2015 release of DoDI 5000.02 (Encl. 8) clarifies affordability through two specific overarching processes that ensure affordability (see Figure 31). Affordability analysis, which is briefly discussed in CH 1–4.2.1.1 is *not* the responsibility of the PM.

Figure 31: Elements of Affordability and Responsible Parties

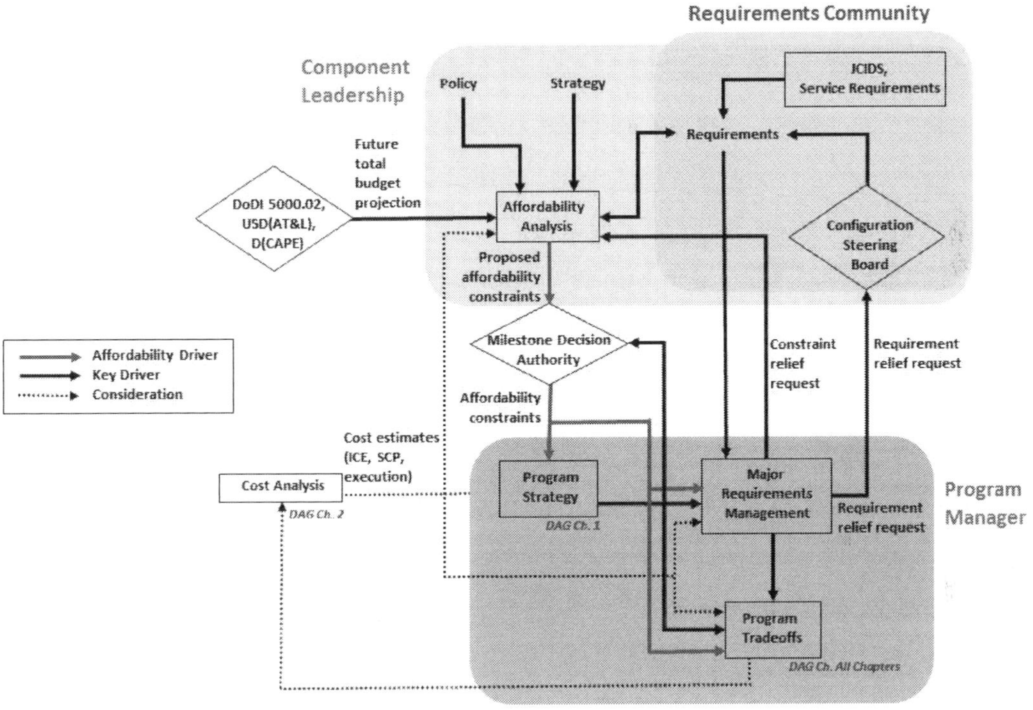

However, executing the program to stay within the affordability constraints (i.e., goals or caps) is a major responsibility of the PM. These constraints are assigned to the program by the Milestone Decision Authority (MDA) and are based on the DoD Component's affordability analysis. As with KPPs, PMs view affordability constraints as givens that must be met. Moreover, past the Development RFP Release Decision Point, affordability constraints must be met—even if that involves obtaining relief from KPPs.

Assigned affordability constraints, therefore, affect broadly the major elements of program management. The PM reflects the effects and implications of those constraints in the program's Acquisition Strategy. Like technical requirements, they need to be managed through tradeoffs and engineering decisions to ensure that they are met or beaten.

Of note, the affordability constraints are not defined by cost estimates, but rather by what the DoD Component determines it can afford. Thus, cost estimates impose fiscal reality on the program and require a strategy for meeting those affordability constraints.

CH 1–4.2.15.3.1 Strategizing How to Stay within Affordability Constraints

The PM considers whether the affordability constraints approved and assigned by the MDA require an explicit strategy that is described in the Acquisition Strategy document. For example, if the cost estimate (usually the 50 percent probability point) equals the constraint, then by definition there is a 50 percent probability that the program is unaffordable as currently structured. Thus, the PM needs a strategy for dealing with this likely event. This undesirable situation puts the program at risk and leaves no reserve for the PM to deal with unforeseen problems. It also imposes a very different strategic concern that should be addressed in the Acquisition Strategy than if the cost estimate is well below the constraint at the start of the program.

While the PM cannot change the constraints, it is important to make sure the DoD Component knows during its affordability analysis of the practical implications of tight constraints on the viability of the program, as configured, and the risks to meeting the requirements. Of course, if the cost estimate is above the constraint, then the program is not viable as configured from the beginning.

CH 1–4.2.15.3.2 Managing Requirements to Stay Affordable

Given assigned constraints, the PM needs to reduce requirements to stay within the constraints—either through the Configuration Steering Board (for major requirements) or engineering trades (for lower level requirements and specifications, see CH 3–4.3.2).

CH 1–4.2.15.4 Operations and Support Affordability

The objective of the affordability process is to control total life-cycle costs. Thus, in addition to a constraint on unit procurement, programs are given a constraint on sustainment costs. This requires special consideration and management given that such costs are only estimates during the acquisition phase and early sustainment phase. Meanwhile, external factors outside the PM's control (e.g., Operations and Support [O&S] labor rates, healthcare costs, and fuel prices) may affect total O&S costs. While this introduces additional challenges, PMs have some insights into these costs (e.g., through historical data on analog systems (CH 1–5.4), modeling, and early testing) and can affect system reliability, maintainability, and efficiency. CH 2–2.1, Life-cycle Cost Estimating and CH 5–3.1, Manpower Planning, respectively, provide details on how to estimate and manage life-cycle costs. But note here, however, that the intent of the sustainment constraint is to drive early PM decisions to lower sustainment costs where major technology and design decisions have their largest effects.

CH 1–4.2.16 Earned Value Management

The PM obtains integrated cost, schedule, performance, and risk information at an appropriate level of summarization to monitor program execution. The PM requires contractors and government organizations to use internal performance management processes that allow for the following:

- Plan and assign all work scope to the applicable areas in the product-oriented Work Breakdown Structure (WBS).
- Objectively assess accomplishment where work is being performed.
- Assess variances, implement corrective actions, and provide forecasts of cost and schedule.
- Use performance information for decision-making and Joint situational awareness.

Cost-control and cost-reduction approaches are central to maximizing the buying power of the Department and are considered in all phases and aspects of program management as ways to meet or beat affordability constraints. Cost need never be addressed in isolation. It is always viewed within the context of schedule, technical performance, and risk.

The PM uses Earned Value Management (EVM) as an integrated program management tool to provide Joint situational awareness of contract status and to assess the cost, schedule, and technical performance of contracts for proactive decision-making. EVM is an integrated program management technique for measuring contract performance and progress in an objective manner. To be useful as a program management tool, PMs incorporate EVM into their acquisition decision-making processes, with actionable data provided by EVM.

The underlying management control systems used to plan and control contract performance complies with Electronic Industries Alliance Standard 748, Earned Value Management Systems (EIA-748) also see DoDI 5000.02, (Encl. 2 para 6.c). The PM does not impose a specific system or method of management control or require a contractor to change its system, provided it complies with EIA-748.

EIA-748 provides guidelines for an acceptable Earned Value Management System (EVMS) and certification authorities. The essence of that guidance is that the government expects contractors to:

- Plan all work scope.
- Assign all work scope.
- Integrate scope, schedule, and cost for measuring performance.
- Record actual costs incurred.
- Objectively assess accomplishment where work is being performed.
- Assess variances, implement corrective actions, and periodically forecast.
- Use performance information for decision-making.

But this is not unique to EVM. While EVM demands a high level of discipline associated with these activities, the list reflects best program management practice for development and delivery of both products and services. This means the government PMO receives performance information that:

- Is exactly the same as what the contractor uses.
- Is timely, accurate, reliable, and auditable.
- Relates time-phased budget to scope of work.
- Measures progress as objectively as practicable.
- Enables independent government predictions of future cost and schedule conditions.
- Contributes to Acquisition Program Baseline (APB) trade-space decisions.

The characteristics of EVM are the foundation of disciplined program management and performance measurement. For DoD, the Performance Assessments and Root Cause Analyses (PARCA) Office in AT&L is the policy owner for EVM. For more information on EVM, refer to the OSD PARCA EVM website or the EVM Community of Practice website on the Defense Acquisition University's Acquisition Community Connection knowledge sharing system.

CH 1–4.2.16.1 Earned Value Management System

An Earned Value Management System (EVMS) is the management control system that integrates the contract's work scope, schedule, risk, and cost parameters via highly disciplined program planning and control processes. All contracts under that system are expected to operate in a manner consistent with those processes, and helps ensure that contract performance data generated are consistently timely, accurate, reliable, and verifiable.

PARCA developed and maintains the EVMS Interpretation Guide (EVMSIG) as the DoD's official interpretation of the application of the 32 Guidelines to DoD contracts. The EVMSIG is used as the basis for EVMS compliance reviews by the Defense Contract Management Agency (DCMA), the organization responsible for determining EVMS compliance when DoD is the cognizant federal agency.

Government PMs determine the applicability of EVM to their respective programs and whether or not a waiver is required in accordance with DoDI 5000.02 (Encl. 1, Table 8). Program Managers require EVM, in cost- and/or incentive-type contracts and subcontracts valued at or above $20 million, unless its use is waived by the DoD CAE.

Regardless of whether or not EVM is required, PMs require disciplined scheduling practice that enable accurate status reporting, including reasonable and actionable forecasting. To ensure such practices are demonstrated by contractors, the Integrated Program Management Report (IPMR) Data Item Description (DID) DI-MGMT-81861A ought to be applied to such contracts, tailored such that the IPMR "format 6" is the only section of the DID that is applied.

CH 1–4.2.16.1.1 DoD Organization Roles

The following organizations can provide the program management team with significant insights into specific areas the team needs to consider as they develop plans, consider contract strategies, and execute their approved plan.

Department of Defense (DoD). *Performance Assessment and Root Cause Analyses (PARCA):* The Office of PARCA is the single voice accountable for EVM policy, oversight, and governance across the DoD. The EVM division of PARCA is responsible for the EVM Central Repository and EVM Interpretation and Communication to facilitate timely, accurate, and equitable EVM implementation across the DoD.

Services and Agencies. The DoD Services and Agencies have the following EVM focal points:

- *Assistant Secretary of the Army for Acquisition, Logistics, and Technology* develops, acquires, fields, and sustains Army equipment and services through efficient leveraging of technologies and capabilities to meet current and future needs.
- *Assistant Secretary of the Navy for Research, Development, and Acqui*sition has authority, responsibility, and accountability for all acquisition functions and programs, and for enforcement of Under Secretary of Defense for Acquisition, Technology and Logistics procedures.
- *Assistant Secretary of the Air Force for Acquisition* is responsible for research, development, and non-space acquisition activities.
- *Missile Defense Agency's (MDA)* mission is to develop, test, and field an integrated, layered Ballistic Missile Defense System (BMDS).

Intelligence Community (IC). The IC Agencies also have EVM focal points, including the following organizations.

- *National Reconnaissance Office (NRO):* NRO is in charge of designing, building, launching, and maintaining America's intelligence satellites.
- *National Geospatial-Intelligence Agency (NGA):* NGA provides timely, relevant, and accurate geospatial intelligence in support of national security.
- *National Security Agency (NSA):* NSA leads the U.S. Government in cryptology and enables Computer Network Operations (CNO) in order to gain a decision advantage.

Compliance Agencies. The Compliance Agencies have the following focal points:

- *Defense Contract Management Agency (DCMA):* As a DoD Combat Support Agency, DCMA helps to ensure the integrity of the contracting process, and provides a broad range of contract-procurement management services. DCMA works directly with the defense contractors to help ensure that DoD, federal, and allied government supplies and services are delivered on time, at projected cost, and meet all performance requirements.
- *Defense Contract Audit Agency (DCAA):* DCAA provides audit and financial advisory services to DoD and other federal entities responsible for acquisition and contract administration.

CH 1–4.2.16.1.2 Earned Value Management Applicability

EVM is required to be applied to cost-reimbursable or incentive contracts, inclusive of options, where the nature of the work scope lends itself to the use of EVM (as prescribed in DoDI 5000.02 and Defense Federal Acquisition Regulation Supplement (DFARS) Subpart 234.2).

The EVM time and dollar application thresholds for EVMS compliance (total contract value, including planned options in then-year dollars) are summarized below:

- With 18 months or greater period of performance.
- $20 million, but less than $100 million—EVM implementation compliant with EIA-748 is required. The government reserves the right to review a contractor's EVMS to verify compliance.
- $100 million or greater—the contractor is required to have an EVMS that has been approved by the Contracting Officer.

EVM applies to discrete work scope, which is defined as tasks related to the completion of specific end products or services that can be directly planned and measured. PARCA reviews and approves EVM applicability for ACAT I programs in coordination with the applicable Service/Agency EVM focal point. For all other ACAT levels, the Service/Agency EVM focal point will determine EVM applicability. This determination of application of EVM is provided to the PM.

The DoD PM uses DFARS clauses 252.234-7001 and 252.234-7002 to place the EVMS requirement in solicitations (7001) and contracts (7002). The program's Acquisition Strategy reflects the PM's approach to satisfying the EVM requirement for applicable contracts. The contract language and Contract Data Requirements Lists (CDRLs) provided to the contractor for a given contract then also mirror and describe the approach.

A contract does not, either at the time of award or in subsequent modifications, specify requirements in special contract requirements and/or statements of work that are not consistent with the EVM policy and EVMS guidelines (required by DFARS 252.234-7002), or which may conflict with offerors' or contractors' approved EVM system descriptions. Consult DCMA for guidance on EVMS contractor compliance.

CH 1–4.2.16.1.3 Earned Value Management Applicability Determination

EVM applies to discrete work scope defined as tasks related to the completion of specific end products or services, and can be directly planned and measured. Program Managers employ EVM, when applicable, unless waived by the CAE. The PM utilizes the determination of EVM applicability provided by PARCA or the EVM focal point for their Service or Agency.

When considering EVM applicability, the dollar threshold for the purpose of applicability is the final anticipated dollar value of the action, including the dollar value of all options. If the action establishes a maximum quantity of supplies or services to be acquired or establishes a ceiling price or establishes the final price to be based on future events, the final anticipated dollar value is the highest final priced alternative to the government. Note that the final anticipated dollar value includes the dollar value of all options. This means that if the value of a contract is expected to grow to $20 million or more, the PM can impose an EVM requirement at contract award in anticipation of meeting the threshold. In some cases, a contract modification not known at time of award can cause a contract value to cross the thresholds for EVM requirements. The application of EVM in those cases is required, and the PM works with the contractor to implement EVM in a manner that best meets the need for decision-making and Joint situational awareness. In no case should there be an attempt to circumvent EVM policy by excluding known work from contract award and including it later as a contract modification.

The decision to implement EVM on contracts outside the criteria prescribed in DoDI 5000.02 (Encl. 2 para 6e – page 77) and DFARS Subpart 234.2) is a risk-based decision at the discretion of the PM. The PM conducts a cost-benefit analysis before deciding to implement EVM on these contracts and then receives

MDA approval. The purpose of the cost-benefit analysis is to explain the rationale for the decision to require cost/schedule visibility into the contract and to substantiate that the benefits to the government outweigh the associated costs. Factors to consider when making a risk-based decision to apply EVM are as follows:

- Type of work and level of reporting—for example, developmental or integration work is inherently more risky to the government, and reporting reflects how programs are managing that risk basis.
- Schedule criticality of the contracted effort to a program's mission—items required to support another program or schedule event may warrant EVM requirements.

The application of EVM to contracts that may be categorized as non-schedule-based, i.e., those that do not ordinarily contain work efforts that are discrete in nature, are considered on a case-by-case basis. Non-schedule-based contracts may include:

- Contracts compensated on the basis of "time and materials" used, such as in Time and Material (T&M) contracts.
- "Services" contracts, including those for maintenance, repair, sustainment, and other services that are provided on an as needed basis.
- Any contracts composed primarily of Level of Effort (LOE) activity, such as program management support contracts.

Non-schedule-based contracts might not permit objective work measurement due to the nature of the work, most of which cannot be divided into segments that produce tangible, measurable product(s). The nature of the work associated with the contract is the key factor in determining whether there is any appreciable value in obtaining EVM information. Every effort is made to identify, separate, and measure any discrete work from any work that is typically identified as LOE in nature. In cases where the nature of the work does not lend itself to meaningful EVM information, it may be appropriate to not apply the EVM requirement. If the EVM requirement is not placed on a contract due to the nature of the work, the PM implements an alternative method of management control to provide advanced warning of potential performance problems.

The EVM requirements are placed on the base Indefinite Delivery/Indefinite Quantity (ID/IQ) contract (i.e., definite quantity contract, requirements contract, or indefinite quantity contract) and applied to the task/deliver orders, or group(s) of related task/delivery orders. "Related" refers to dependent efforts that can be measured and scheduled across task/delivery orders. In some cases, a contract modification not known at the time of award can cause a contract value to cross the thresholds for EVM requirements. The application of EVM in those cases is required, and the PM works with the contractor to implement EVM in a manner that best meets the needs for decision-making and Joint situational awareness. In no case should there be an attempt to circumvent EVM policy by excluding known work from contract award and including it later as a contract modification.

Due to the nature of Foreign Military Sales (FMS) contracts, special considerations are given to ensure EVM can be effectively implemented. A case-by-case analysis of the contractual structure, expectations, as well as the EVM application requirements described above—all factor into the determination to apply EVM.

CH 1–4.2.16.1.4 Earned Value Management Reporting

Although the PM uses EVM reporting to collect data for decision-making and Joint situational awareness, the benefits of EVM and EVM analysis are not limited to reporting. The PM and the PMO staff develop relationships with their contractor counterparts to facilitate discussions regarding performance towards completion of the contractual scope of work. EVM reporting encourages dialogue with actionable, trustworthy data and generally does not contain "surprises."

The Contract Data Requirements List (CDRL) is used by the PM to document the data needs of the contract utilizing the appropriate Data Item Descriptions (DIDs). The CDRL provides contractual direction for preparation and submission of reports, including reporting frequency, distribution, and tailoring instructions. DD Form 1423-1 is used to specify the data item requirements and contains any tailoring requirements. Guidance on tailoring the IPMR is found in the Integrated Program Management Report (IPMR) Implementation Guide.

- *Integrated Program Management Report (IPMR).* Data Item Description (DID) DI-MGMT-81861A: The IPMR contains the instructions for a contractor to provide cost and schedule performance on DoD acquisition contracts. Seven formats comprise the structure of the IPMR, which contain the content and relationships required for electronic submission of cost and schedule performance data from the performing contractors. Program Managers use the IPMR whenever they choose to receive cost or schedule performance information, even when EVM is not required on contract. The IPMR provides performance data, which are used to identify problems early in the contract and forecast future contract performance. Requirements for the IPMR follow:
    - o For contracts, task orders, and delivery orders between $20 million and $50 million, the IPMR is required to be delivered monthly; Formats 2, 3, and 4 may be excluded from the CDRL at the PM's discretion based on risk.
    - o For contracts, task orders, and delivery orders greater than $50 million, the IPMR is required monthly; all Formats are included in the CDRL.
    - o For contracts, task orders, and delivery orders less than $20 million, the IPMR is not required; however, it can be used if cost and/or schedule reporting is wanted by the PMO.
    - o For subcontracts, flow-down of the IPMR DID is determined by the prime contractor; the prime contractor obtains the information and data necessary to meet the contractual requirements to the government.
- *The Contract Funds Status Report (CFSR).* The CFSR supplies funding data about defense contracts to PMs for updating and forecasting contract funding requirements, planning and decision-making on funding changes to contracts, and developing funding requirements and budget estimates in support of approved programs. CFSR funding data also inform PMs on determining funds in excess of contract needs and available for de-obligation, and obtaining rough estimates of termination costs. The CFSR is required for contracts over 6 months in duration. No specific application thresholds are established, but application to contracts of less than $1,000,000 is evaluated carefully to ensure only the minimum information necessary for effective management control.

It is important that government program offices know how to compare CFSR and IPMR information. Both reports reflect current and predicted performance and estimates. The IPMR reflects program execution dollars without fee, whereas the CFSR reflects price information, including fee. Hence the two documents show consistent, though not identical, values when reflecting the same contractual scope of work.

A product-oriented Work Breakdown Structure (WBS) is required for EVM systems and reporting. Suggested structures for EVM are found in the DoD Work Breakdown Structure Standard (MIL-STD-881C) (current version at time of award). Note that the 881C structures are required for the Contractor Cost Data Report (CCDR). For EVM reporting purposes, the WBS reflects 881C unless the contractor can demonstrate the need to use a different product-oriented structure to manage the contract. Similarly, the government PM ensures that the Program Work Breakdown Structure (PWBS) is likewise aligned to how the program is managed.

In situations when EVM does not apply, such as in Firm Fixed Price (FFP) contracts, PMs can require disciplined scheduling practice that enable accurate status reporting, including reasonable and reliable forecasting. To ensure such practices are demonstrated by contractors, the Integrated Program Management Report (IPMR) Data Item Description (DID) DI-MGMT-81861A is to be applied to such contracts, tailored such that the IPMR Formats 5 and 6 are the only sections of the DID applied.

CH 1–4.2.16.2 Earned Value Management for Program Performance Measurement

During the planning phase of a contract, an integrated baseline (refer to Figure 32) is developed by time-phasing resources for the defined contractual scope of work. As work is performed, completion is measured against the baseline, and the corresponding budget value is "earned." From this earned value metric, cost and schedule variances can be determined and analyzed. Using these basic variance measurements, the PM can identify significant drivers, forecast future cost and schedule performance, and construct corrective action plans to get the program back on track. If significant deviation occurs, then updated risk assessment activities may need to be performed, resulting in new/changed risk handling activities. Usually, cost or schedule deviations are indications of a technical problem so it is essential that any analysis determines the root cause of the cost or schedule deviation. EVM encompasses both performance measurement (i.e., What is the program status?) and performance management (i.e., What we can do about it?). Additionally, and most critically, EVM deals in forecasting of future conditions.

Figure 32: Earned Value Management Baseline and Metrics Graph

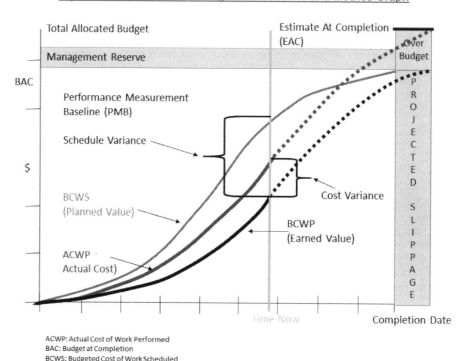

ACWP: Actual Cost of Work Performed
BAC: Budget at Completion
BCWS: Budgeted Cost of Work Scheduled
BCWP: Budgeted Cost of Work Preformed

CH 1–4.2.16.2.1 Integrated Baseline Reviews

An IBR is a Joint assessment of the Performance Measurement Baseline (PMB) conducted by the government PM and the contractor. The IBR allows the PM to assess the risk to execution in the contractor's plan for completing the contractual scope of work. The IBR is not a one-time event, but is a process culminating in a review event. It is not a compliance review. The PMB is continually evaluated as changes to the baseline are made (modifications, restructuring, etc.) and is not limited to review during the IBR process.

IBRs are required with the clause in DFARS 252.234-7002 and DoDI 5000.02 on all contracts that require the implementation of EVM. The IBR is not dependent on the contractor's EVMS being formally validated as complying with the guidelines in EIA-748. As a best practice, IBRs are recommended for subcontracts, intra-government work agreements, and other agreements. The scope of the IBRs can be tailored to the nature of the work effort.

IBRs are scheduled as early as practicable, and the timing of the IBRs takes into consideration the contract period of performance. The process is conducted not later than 180 calendar days (6 months) after a significant program event or contract change including, but not limited to: (1) contract award, (2) the exercise of large contract options, and (3) the incorporation of major modifications. IBRs are also performed at the discretion of the PM at any time, even without the occurrence of a major event in the life of a program.

Events that may trigger an IBR include completion of the Preliminary Design Review, completion of the Critical Design Review, a significant shift in the content and/or time phasing of the PMB, or when a major milestone such as the start of the production option of a development contract is reached. Continuous assessment of the PMB helps identify when a new IBR should be conducted.

In situations where the entire work scope is not known within the 180 days, the IBR can be conducted in stages, such as with an undefinitized contract action. A review of the known work scope can be conducted within the 180-day window, with follow-up IBRs scheduled at a later time for the work not yet completed in the context of the entire PMB. As a rule of thumb, this initial IBR runs through the first major milestone for the program. Any IBR event increment is not to be driven by definitization, but should represent the best time to hold the IBR to assess the plan for the work and risks to execution. An IBR is always conducted within 180 days after award, even if it does not cover the entire scope of an unpriced contract action. A letter from the Contracting Officer to the contractor may be needed to clarify initial IBR requirements.

Policy allows for the use of IBRs prior to contract award in situations where they may be appropriate and beneficial. If a PM elects to conduct a pre-award IBR on a DoD contract, that requirement can be included in the Statement of Work.

CH 1–4.2.16.2.2 Over-Target Baseline or Over-Target Schedule

When performance measurement against available budgets and/or contractual milestones becomes unrealistic, the contractor may want to initiate an Over-Target Baseline or Over-Target Schedule (OTB/OTS). To implement an OTB or OTS, the contractor submits a request for approval to the government. At a minimum, the request includes a top-level projection of cost and/or schedule growth, a determination of whether or not a single point adjustment to remove performance variances occurs, and a schedule of implementation for the process. The ensuing actions can only be implemented after government PM formal approval and conducted in accordance with the contractor's EVMS processes. Additionally, the government can direct initiation of an OTB/OTS.

CH 1–4.2.16.2.3 Earned Value Management Concepts

It is important for the PM to keep in mind that measurement and forecasting of EVM data are of little value unless the contractor can perform the fundamental tasks (reflective of EIA-748). The basic premise of EVM is that the value of a piece of work is equal to the amount of funds budgeted to complete it. As part of EVM, program management uses the following information to assess schedule and cost performance throughout the life of a contract.

Contract Work Breakdown Structure (CWBS). It is important that the contractor can clearly articulate in a product-oriented structure the contractual scope for which it is responsible in a manner that reflects the way the efforts are planned to be completed. The CWBS is the outline that forms the basis for contractor program management and EVM reporting. The CWBS also supports correct financial accounting treatments required to support the Chief Financial Officers Act of 1990.

Budgeted Cost for Work Scheduled (BCWS). The EVM guidelines require the contractor to plan work into resourced and time-phased control accounts, which may be further subdivided into work packages. Activities are scheduled within the work packages and form the basis for the Integrated Master Schedule. Resources are then time-phased against the work packages, forming the BCWS, also known as "Planned Value." All work packages sum to control account level and all control accounts sum to the PMB, against which performance is measured. At the close of each reporting period, the contractor reports the BCWS planned during each reporting period and the cumulative total to date.

Another way of thinking about BCWS is that it is a dollarized interpretation of planned work. The derivation of BCWS is no trivial manner, because the work progress ought to be measured in a way that makes sense and supports leadership decision-making. It is in the development of BCWS that government PMs see some of the first reflections of contractor discipline in program planning, as they translate the assigned CWBS scope into a time-phased view of accomplishment.

Performance Measurement Baseline (PMB). All work packages sum to control account level and all control accounts sum to the PMB. The PMB is the time-phased budget plan against which performance is measured. Therefore, it is critical that PMB changes are made in a disciplined fashion. In gauging the reasonableness of a baseline, a pictorial view often provides a useful input for PMs. More often than not, a PMB forms an "S" type curve, and PMs ought to pay attention to the slope of that curve at every point, especially where there is a significant change.

Budget at Completion (BAC). The cumulative sum of all BCWS at completion is known as BAC. Note that the value of BAC can be stated at any level, e.g., work package, control account, and higher levels; however, the term usually refers to the value of cumulative BCWS at completion for the PMB. Note that since the BCWS is a translation of work into dollars or hours, the BAC is likewise a translation.

Management Reserve (MR). MR is dollarized work (e.g., BCWS) set-aside in anticipation of unplanned, but in-scope work that usually arises in normal execution of a contract. Thus, MR is a reflection of anticipated risk-handling actions, mitigation in particular. Program Managers ought to inquire as to how contractor MR was created and from which parts of the program. There ought to be some discernible relationship between the amount set aside for MR and the relative risk of the program. However, MR is owned and managed by the contractor and is not a government-controlled item. During the life of the contract, PMs are cognizant of the rate at which MR is being "burned" because high rates of MR burn typically indicate a lack of discipline in program planning. Above all, it is important to recognize that the amount and allocation of MR on a contract is entirely the province of the contractor PM, not the government.

Budgeted Cost for Work Performed (BCWP). In addition to the BCWS, the EVM guidelines require the contractor to report the budgeted dollar value of work completed during each reporting period and the cumulative total. This is the BCWP, also known as Earned Value. This value represents the budgeted value of work completed, not the actual cost. Similar to the BCWS, BCWP is a translation of work into a dollarized figure. The BCWP can be based on an objective assessment of work actually performed. This objective method is established during the baseline process. Here it is very important to pay attention to how work progress is measured, as the rate at which BCWP is credited significantly impacts an evaluation of program performance and possible forecasted end states. Program Managers are encouraged to take a second look at BCWP that significantly outstrips the BCWS.

Level of Effort (LOE). When BCWP consistently equals BCWS in successive reporting periods, it may mean the work is measured using a technique called "level of effort" or LOE. LOE has a very specific meaning in EVM, and is not applied to any type of work that warrants precise, discrete measurement. Program Managers can ask contractors to measure the amount of LOE measurement technique planned as a percentage of the PMB in dollars. As the percentage of LOE measurement in the PMB climbs beyond 10 percent, PMs need to query how work is being measured. When LOE exceeds 15 percent, PMs may be justifiably concerned as the result tends to distort measurements of progress.

Actual Cost of Work Performed (ACWP). The EVM guidelines require the contractor to accumulate the ACWP, which flows directly from the general books of accounting during each reporting period. These are the actual costs (ACWP) for work performed (BCWP) in that reporting period. These include all contract direct and indirect costs. Unlike BCWS, BCWP, and BAC, ACWP reflects actual expenditures. Note that there might be some instances where estimated actuals are utilized due to various timing issues with materials and/or subcontractors.

Schedule Variance (SV). The difference between the BCWP and BCWS is the dollar value of work the contractor is ahead of or behind schedule, called schedule variance (SV). Significant variances are analyzed to determine the cause, impact, and corrective action required. It is important to note that SV is not a reflection of the performance against the Integrated Master Schedule; it is a measurement of performance against the PMB. Although there is a time-phased aspect of SV (because BCWS is a component), actual schedule performance is contained in the IMS. All explanations relative to SV ought to include specific references to the schedule. As an example, a task that has an unfavorable SV may have enough float/slack in the IMS to complete within the plan. If the contractor cannot convincingly align SV discussions with IMS discussions, then the EVM performance information is suspect.

Cost Variance (CV). The difference between the BCWP and ACWP is the CV. Again, significant variances are analyzed to determine the cause, impact, and corrective action required. Negative cost variance almost always appears in the months following a recovery in schedule variance.

Estimate at Completion (EAC). The contractor has a means for estimating costs at completion of the contract. EACs are generated at control account (lowest level of integrated management control) and then integrated upwards into a program-level EAC. It is important to verify that a contractor EAC reasonably reflects known and anticipated risks and opportunities. Thus contractors ought to derive realistic "best" and "worst" case EACs that reasonably reflect the nature of risk on the contract. For an EAC to equal the BAC, it suggests the contract has to integrate all conceivable risks into the baseline. All programs contain known and unknown risks; consequently, there is always some variation between work scope budgeted and downstream estimate of cost at completion. Similarly, the government program management office EAC varies from that of the contractor's because each is an estimate derived from different assumptions.

Variance at Completion (VAC). The difference between the BAC and EAC is the VAC. This represents the projected amount of overrun or underrun against a contractual scope of work. Significant variances are analyzed to determine the cause, impact, and corrective action required. The government, through the CDRL, determines the significant variance thresholds for reporting.

Cost Performance Index (CPI). CPI is a measurement of cost efficiency in the management of the program. While a CPI of at least 1.0 is desirable, a PM incorporates trends in the measurements rather than single "snapshots." It is important to note that PMBs containing significant levels of LOE measurement will, more often than not, have artificially high CPIs, including CPIs measured above 1.0. Also, as a summarized measurement at the program level, CPIs include "bad actors" as well as "good actors," and it is possible that the "trouble spots" in the program will be "washed out" by the areas with exceptionally positive performance. Program Managers need to ask the contractor for CPI based exclusively on discretely measured (e.g., non-LOE) tasks in the program to gauge actual performance and help ensure reasonably predictive forecasting.

Schedule Performance Index (SPI). SPI is a measurement of work accomplishment efficiency in the management of the program. While an SPI of at least 1.0 is favorable, a PM can review the trend of SPI and be able to forecast future performance. Also, similar to SV, SPI is reviewed in conjunction with the IMS to assess actual schedule performance. As noted with CPI, a summarized top-level WBS SPI measurement can mask trouble areas in lower level WBS elements due to the inclusion of WBSs with positive performance. While an SPI of at least 1.0 is desirable, a PM can incorporate trends in the measurements rather than single "snapshots." It is important to note that PMBs containing significant levels of LOE measurement will, more often than not, have artificially high SPIs near or at 1.0. Also, as a summarized measurement at the program level, SPIs include "bad actors" as well as "good actors," and it is possible that the "trouble spots" in the program will be "washed out" by the areas with exceptionally positive performance. Program Managers can ask the contractor for SPI based exclusively on discretely measured (e.g., non-LOE) tasks at or near the program critical path to gauge actual performance and help ensure reasonably predictive forecasting.

To-Complete Performance Index (TCPI). Sometimes termed "run-out efficiency," TCPI is a calculated value that depicts the CPI required from a given point forward in order to theoretically reach the contractor's reported BAC or EAC. Thus, TCPI is best used as a comparative index to CPI. If for any given reporting period the TCPI (measured with respect to achieving the EAC) is 5 percent greater than the cumulative CPI, a PM ought to investigate the reasonableness of the EAC. If the TCPI exceeds the CPI by 10 percent or greater, it is reasonable to assume that the reported EAC is not achievable.

Integrated Master Plan (IMP). The IMP is a direct reflection of leadership decision-making approaches and as such offers key insights into true EVM performance and simultaneously serves as the foundation of the IMS. The IMP is an event-driven plan for executing the program. The IMP defines all the events, accomplishments, and completion criteria necessary to successfully execute the program and is contractually binding. The IMS correlates directly to the events, accomplishments, and criteria contained in the IMP and is traceable to the Contractor WBS, Statement of Work, and other contractual documentation to ensure an accurate and consistent status of program execution. Refer to CH 1–3.4.2 for detailed information.

There are three fundamental components to an IMP:

- **Program Events** (PE)—PEs are the key decision points in a program. Typical examples might be major milestone reviews (such as a Milestone B), technical reviews (SRR, PDR, CDR, etc.), and program reviews (such as an IBR).
- **Significant Accomplishments** (SA) – SAs are what need to happen to realize success/completion of a given decision point. For example, requirements in order to claim credit for a successful PDR.
- **Accomplishment Criteria** (AC). AC are those conditions that explain how a given SA can be achieved.

Integrated Master Schedule (IMS). The IMS is an integrated schedule developed by logically networking detailed program activities. In its simplest form, a schedule is a listing of activities and events, organized by time. In its more complex form, the IMS defines all program activities and their relationships to one another in terms of realistic constraints of time, funding, and people (e.g., resources). The IMS is a planning, control, and communications tool that, when properly executed, supports time and cost estimates, opens communications among personnel involved in program activities, and establishes a commitment to program activities by all interested parties. The desired and/or required traits of the contractor IMS are typically represented by the IPMR Format 6 and relate to the CWBS. If the government PM uses an internal IMS, it ought to relate to, and utilize the contractor-provided IMS for status and planning.

The IMS reflects the tasks required to realize the desired conditions as outlined in the IMP—if an IMP is not used, then the IMS traces to the planning documentation the contractor uses to turn the contractual scope into actionable tasks. The IMS is the set of networked tasks required to meet the AC, which, in turn, contributes to the SA and then to the PE.

CH 1–4.2.16.3 Earned Value Management Special Topics

The following four topics are areas of frequent concern to the program management teams in the area of Earned Value Management.

CH 1–4.2.16.3.1 Harvesting Underruns

The DoD Earned Value Management System Interpretation Guide (EVMSIG) offers flexibility for a variety of program execution and development methodologies. An important principle of EVMS outlined in the EVMSIG is a disciplined approach to maintaining EVM baselines. "To ensure the ongoing integrity of the Contract Budget Base (CBB), budget traceability throughout the life cycle of a program must be maintained. Current budgets are reconciled to prior budgets in terms of changes to work scope, resources, schedule, and rates so that the contract changes and internal re-planning on overall program growth is visible to all stakeholders."

Situations occur where contractors are asked to move budget from control accounts that have cost underruns and apply the remaining budget to new work—an activity sometimes known as "harvesting underruns." However, to maintain EVM and EVMS integrity, EVM budget amounts ought to remain with the scope for which they were budgeted, even where that scope is completed with favorable cost performance. In no cases should underrunning budget in the baseline serve as a means to develop new baseline activities.

An underrun to the budget in the CBB does not automatically mean excess funds have become available. Practitioners may erroneously treat EVM budget and contract funding in the same ways. The application of budgets and funding are distinct and follow separate rules; budget follows EVM rules, while use of funding follows contracting and fiscal rules:

- The term "budget" has a very specific meaning for EVM and refers to the resources estimated to be required to complete the contracted scope of work.
- "Funding" refers to the actual government dollars obligated on the contract and available for payment for work being accomplished on the contract.
- The amount of obligated funding does not always equal the contract price. There is no rule that requires the CBB to equal either the amount of obligated funding or the contract price.

When the contract scope has been completed for less than the amount funded, there may exist an opportunity for using that funding for new scope. The ability to use any underrun for new scope becomes a contracting action, not an EVM action, and follows prescribed contracting, and fiscal laws and regulations. When funds are available due to an underrun, and are then used to acquire new work scope using proper contracting policies and procedures, budget for the new scope is added to the CBB.

CH 1–4.2.16.3.2 Level of Detail in Earned Value Management

The level of detail in the EVM reporting, which is placed on contract through a CDRL referencing the IPMR, is based on scope, complexity, and risk. The IPMR's primary value to the government is its utility in reflecting current contract status and projecting future contract performance. It is used by the DoD Component staff, including PMs, engineers, cost estimators, and financial management personnel as a basis for communicating performance status with the contractor. The IPMR DID states that the reporting level is defined through tailoring the WBS from the applicable MIL-STD-881 appendix and does not prescribe a required level of detail. In their oversight role, PMOs should require EVM data to a level that matches the risks on the program. EVM data can be reported at different levels on different WBSs based on the risk and management needs. The level of reporting discussed at the IBRs can and should be adjusted if necessary for effective management.

In particular, collection of data for cost analysis purposes ought not drive the level of detail for EVM reporting. EVM data are for management of project execution, not cost estimating for which the government has other dedicated means to obtain data.

CH 1–4.2.16.3.3 Metrics in Award Fee

EVM information is used for program management, Joint situational awareness, and decision-making. Award fee criteria reflect the quality and utility of the EVM data for those purposes. EVM and the associated metrics can be used to underpin the understanding of technical accomplishment, but the metrics themselves are not directly used as award fee criteria.

CH 1–4.2.16.3.4 Agile and Earned Value Management

Agile philosophies promote rapid incremental product deliveries, provide flexibility to respond to changing requirements, and advocate close customer collaboration. A major aspect of Agile is that changes to requirements, design details, or functional capabilities can be incorporated based on customer value, at any stage of the development cycle. While Agile is primarily used on software development projects, Agile methods are being used for complex system and hardware developments as well.

Agile for software development in the DoD is still an emerging product development approach. To be effective, the adoption of Agile methodologies is integrated with existing DoD program management and systems engineering processes. EVM is not tied to any specific development methodology. While there may be additional metrics and data sources in the implementation of Agile, the government PMO still receives performance information that:

- Is accurate and is drawn from the contractor's Agile and EVM systems.
- Is timely, accurate, reliable, and auditable.
- Relates time-phased budget to scope of work.
- Measures progress as objectively as practicable.
- Enables independent government predictions of future cost and schedule conditions.
- Contributes to APB trade-space decisions.

Agile and EVM are complementary when properly implemented together, and help enable a robust overall management process. In order to be effective, Agile is always evaluated for its applicability on a program-specific basis and tailored to best align with programmatic and contractual requirements. See the PARCA-maintained Agile and Earned Value Management: A Program Manager's Desk Guide for more information.

CH 1–4.2.16.4 Earned Value Management Information and Resources

The following references provide additional information and resources on Cost Control (Earned Value Management [EVM] and Should Cost Management [SCM]):

- OSD Performance Assessment and Root Cause Analysis, Earned Value Management
- Department of Defense Earned Value Management System Interpretation Guide
- Earned Value Management Policies and Guidance
- DFARS Subpart 234.2 — Earned Value Management System
- DAU EVM Gold Card
- GAO Schedule Assessment Guide: Best Practice for Project Schedules
- DI-MGMT-81861 — Integrated Program Management Report (IPMR)
- GAO Cost Estimating and Assessment Guide: Best Practice for Developing and Managing Capital Program Costs
- EIA-748-C Earned Value Management Systems ANSI/EIA-748-C Intent Guide

CH 1–4.2.17 Improving Cost Performance – Should Cost Management

As a matter of opportunity management, PMs are expected to proactively seek out and eliminate low-value-added or unnecessary elements of program cost; to motivate better cost performance wherever possible; and to reward those that succeed in achieving those goals. Should Cost is a powerful opportunity management construct PMs can use to actively target cost reduction and drive productivity improvement into programs. Should Cost Management challenges PMs to identify and achieve savings below budgeted most-likely costs. Should Cost analysis can be used during contract negotiations (particularly for sole-source procurements), and throughout program execution, including sustainment.

Program management can develop, own, track, and report against Should Cost targets. Estimates and results are provided at milestone reviews and at specified decision points. For MDAPs and MAIS programs, PMs report progress against Should Cost goals at Defense Acquisition Executive Summary (DAES) reviews. Subject to the approval of the MDA via the Acquisition Strategy, the PM may recommend that the Contracting Officer consider contractual incentives that can be used to incentivize disciplined cost control by contractors.

CH 1–4.2.17.1 Should Cost Management

Should Cost Management (SCM) is fundamental to proactive cost control throughout the acquisition life cycle. *Will Cost* estimates (Cost Assessment and Program Evaluation [CAPE] Independent Cost Estimates for ACAT I programs or the Service Cost Position, whichever is directed in the Acquisition Decision Memorandum) remain the basis for President's Budget positions; however, program management need not accept these estimates as the only reality. The goal is to identify opportunities to do better than Will Cost and to manage toward that goal. Managers scrutinize each element of cost under their control and assess how it can be reduced without unacceptable reductions in value received.

Should Cost encourages programs to actively manage costs through the careful assessment of the contributing drivers of cost across a program, identification of goals for cost reduction (Should Cost Goals), and implementation of specific efforts designed to achieve those cost reductions.

Should Cost applies to all acquisition activities, and includes both product and services acquisition. The PM needs to understand "how" products and services are being acquired to ensure that the appropriate guidance for Should Cost is considered or applied.

There are differences between *the levels of rigor* for Should Cost depending on whether the acquisition is under DoDI 5000.02, Operation of the Defense Acquisition System, or DoDI 5000.74, Acquisition of Services. Additionally CH 1–4.2.17.1 to CH 1–4.2.17.3 provide Should Cost guidance for ACAT I, IA, II, and III programs. For services being acquired, refer to CH 10–3.3.2.2.1 for Should Cost-related guidance.

The key to Should Cost is to seek out and eliminate, through discrete actions, low-value-added ingredients of program cost and to appropriately reward those who succeed in doing this, both in government and in industry. For government managers, this could mean additional resources to enhance their programs (for example, by freeing up funds to buy more warfighting capability) and professional recognition (raters of acquisition managers ought to consider effective cost control when evaluating performance). For each DoD Component, this could free up funds for other pressing needs. For industry, it is a matter of tying financial incentives to overall cost reduction.

CH 1–4.2.17.2 Developing Should Cost Management Targets

Should Cost Management (SCM) applies to programs in all ACATs, in all phases of the product's life cycle, and to all elements of program cost. A program's MDA (Defense Acquisition Executive [DAE], Component Acquisition Executives [CAE], or Program Executive Officer [PEO]) reviews and approves Should Cost targets, monitors progress, and directs or recommends allocation of realized cost savings, as appropriate.

Program Managers routinely analyze all cost elements and consider reasonable measures to reduce them, with prudent, cost-benefit-based considerations of associated risks. Program Managers determine specific, discrete, and measurable items or initiatives that can achieve savings against the Will Cost estimate. These actionable items are to be tracked and managed as part of Should Cost estimate progress reporting. Arbitrary reductions and unsubstantiated high-risk goals against the Will Cost estimate are not acceptable. Should Cost estimates need to be consistent with the defined program of record and have actionable content. Immediate short-term savings ought not come at the expense of long-term degradation of effectiveness or suitability; investments that result in long-term returns in production or sustainment efficiency ought to be, and are appropriate uses of Should Cost-related savings. Managers also apprise their leadership of opportunities for life-cycle cost savings that are outside their span of control.

CH 1–4.2.17.3 Ingredients of Should Cost Management

The following Should Cost Management (SCM) aspects can be used to identify potential cost reductions, develop cost targets, and manage investment costs throughout the acquisition life cycle:

- Scrutinize each contributing ingredient of program cost and justify it. Why is it as reported or negotiated? What reasonable measures might reduce it?
- Particularly challenge the basis for indirect costs in contractor proposals.
- Track recent program cost, schedule, and performance trends and identify ways to reverse negative trend(s).
- Benchmark against similar DoD programs and commercial analogues (where possible), and against other programs performed by the same contractor or in the same facilities.
- Promote Supply Chain Management to encourage competition and incentivize cost performance at lower tiers.
- Reconstruct the program (government and contractor) team to be more streamlined and efficient.
- Identify opportunities to break out components as Government-Furnished versus Prime Contractor-provided items.
- Identify items or services contracted through a second or third party vehicle. Eliminate unnecessary pass-through costs by considering other contracting options.
- In the area of test:
  - Take full advantage of integrated Developmental Testing/Operational Testing (DT/OT) to reduce overall cost of testing.
  - Integrate Modeling and Simulation into the test construct to reduce overall costs and ensure optimal use of national test facilities and ranges.
- Identify an alternative technology/material that can potentially reduce development or life-cycle costs for a program. Ensure the prime product contract includes the development of this technology/material at the right time.
- Consider value engineering change proposals to incentivize the contractor to reduce contract costs (refer to CH 3–2.4.4 for Value Engineering-related guidance).
- Consider government value engineering proposals to reduce program cost.
- Focus areas:
  - System specifications
  - Design for affordability
  - Build strategy
  - Contracting strategy
  - Schedule reduction
  - Facility/production enhancements
  - Reduction of contractor scrap rates
  - Reduction of contractor rework
  - Changing to lower cost material options (e.g., composite to steel)
- Programs operating under Firm-Fixed Price (FFP) contracts use common sense in adopting Should Cost initiatives—only reopen FFPs if there is a clear benefit.
- Consider international acquisition-related affordability impacts.

CH 1–4.2.17.4 How Should Cost Management and Affordability Differ

Should Cost Management (SCM) establishes Should Cost Initiatives (SCIs), which are stretch goals that identify discrete and measurable initiatives to achieve savings against a Will Cost estimate (WCE). SCM is one method to meet affordability constraints; however, it is not relevant to setting those constraints.

The USD(AT&L) defines affordability as "conducting a program at a cost constrained by the maximum resources the Department can allocate for that capability [...]," per a Better Buying Power: Mandate for Restoring Affordability and Productivity in Defense Spending memorandum, June 28, 2010. Affordability trades are budget-constrained, and program scope may be altered or removed.

CH 1–4.2.17.5 Use of Should Cost Management Savings

DoD Components continue to baseline acquisition budgets using Will Cost estimates and CAPE Independent Cost Estimates, when available, or DoD Component Cost Positions. However, successful Should Cost Management (SCM) initiatives can drive down future program budgets once the savings have been demonstrated and realized. DoD Components have the latitude to apply savings to their most pressing unfunded requirements, or may reinvest this funding within the same programs to accelerate the acquisition, fund cost-reduction initiatives, or cover critical unfunded requirements.

CH 1–4.2.17.6 Should Cost Management Reporting

Component Acquisition Executives determine their own Should Cost Management (SCM) reporting requirements for effective SCM oversight. PMs and PEOs of Major Defense Acquisition Programs and Major Automated Information System programs, however, report Should Cost targets, and progress in achieving them at Defense Acquisition Executive Summary (DAES) and Defense Acquisition Board (DAB) reviews. Program Manager presentations include Plans of Action and Milestones (POA&M) for major Should Cost initiatives, along with annual savings projected and realized. PEOs provide—via the DAES briefings—quantitative metrics addressing how Should Cost has been implemented within their portfolios, incentive and recognition mechanisms that are in place, and lessons learned. Should Cost Templates may be found embedded in the DAB and DAES Slide Templates (User Registration and CAC required). In addition, Should Cost implementation and performance are reviewed by the DAE and Better Buying Power Senior Integration Group on a quarterly basis.

CH 1–4.2.17.7 Should Cost Management Assistance and Lessons Learned

The Defense Contract Management Agency (DCMA) Cost and Pricing Center is available to assist program offices and PEO organizations with developing Should Cost Management (SCM) targets for indirect contract costs in particular. DCMA solicits information from the Component Acquisition Executives on an annual basis to identify specific contractor divisions where overhead Should Cost analyses would be beneficial. Integrated Cost Analysis Teams (ICATs), presently co-located with at least 12 major defense contractor sites, focus on all elements of proposal pricing engagement. Such focus includes performing continuous evaluation of a contractor's entire pricing system, including cost models, cost estimating relationships, labor hour estimating, contractor and supplier proposal analysis, historical data maintenance and analysis, profit analysis and weighted guidelines, and interaction with Divisional Administrative Contracting Officer teams.

The Defense Acquisition University (DAU) works with the DAE and CAEs to collect successful Should Cost case studies and lessons learned to make available to the broader Defense Acquisition Workforce. They can be found in the Should Cost Repository for best practice as well as Rapid Deployment Training for the acquisition workforce. The Should Cost Repository is a restricted-access site—restricted to government Defense Acquisition Workforce members. The Should Cost Repository requires a Common Access Card (CAC) or login-password sign-on to access. See also the AT&L Implementation Directive for BBP 3.0 and the *Defense Acquisition Research Journal* (April 2014) article, Applications of Should Cost to Achieve Cost Reductions.

CH 1–4.2.18 Intellectual Property, Technical Data, Computer Software Documentation, and Computer Software

Intellectual Property (IP) is an expression of a useful concept that is legally protected such that the originator (e.g., inventor, author) is granted certain exclusive rights. The most commonly known forms of IP protection are patents, copyrights, trade secrets, and trademarks. Any or all of these may arise in DoD programs. DoD programs use the term "data rights" as a short-hand way to refer to the license rights that

DoD acquires in copyrights and trade secrets relating to data deliverables—usually technical data and computer software. This approach allows DoD to use a single set of license rights to address what would otherwise be two separate forms of IP protection.

CH 1–4.2.18.1 Intellectual Property (IP) Strategy

The Program Manager establishes and maintains an IP Strategy to identify and manage the full spectrum of IP and related issues including technical data, computer software deliverables, patented technologies, and appropriate license rights associated with these forms of IP, from the inception of a program through the complete life cycle.

The IP Strategy is the PM's approach to managing the IP needs that will affect the program's cost, schedule, and performance. The strategy needs to be captured as part of the program documentation. There are at least five questions PMs ought to consider regarding development of an IP Strategy:

- What data do I need to support my short- and long-term production, and the operations and sustainment strategy?
- What data do I already have (and what rights/licenses do I have to such data)?
- When do I need the data?
- What are the risks and opportunities associated with the lack of, or availability of, data?
- What will it cost (on the existing contract and to the total life-cycle cost)?

Specific contracting mechanisms (e.g., evaluation during source selection, priced options, or delivery requirements) are available to PMs to implement the IP Strategy and achieve the business objectives of the program. There are two key considerations for PMs regarding "data rights":

- Data rights clauses do not specify the type, quantity, or quality of data that is to be delivered, but only the respective rights of the government and the contractor regarding the use, disclosure, or reproduction of the data. Accordingly, the contract shall specify the data to be delivered (including computer software). (DFARS 227.7103-1(b)(1), DFARS 227.72203-1(b)(1))
- The government cannot exercise its rights in data that have not been contracted. Mere access to data is not delivery and does not allow the government to exercise its data rights. Listing data as items in a Contract Data Requirements List (CDRL) makes those data required deliverables. Alternatively, rights in data may be established as a future option for some or all data. Only data to be delivered under the contract are subject to the DFARS Part 227 clauses requiring assertions as well as formal and justified markings. Therefore, DoD cannot assume it has any useable rights in data that are informally provided unless such rights are explicitly granted by the contractor. PMs work with contracting and legal staff to ensure that any data requirements in the contract are structured so as to ensure they are flowed down to subcontractors, who often generate large amounts of data that the government may require.

The PM, working with the Contracting Officer, establishes IP and Acquisition Strategies (or acquisition plan, as appropriate) that provide for the technical data deliverables and associated license rights needed to sustain program systems and subsystems over their life cycles. The IP Strategy will describe how program management will assess program needs for the IP deliverables and associated license rights needed for competitive and affordable acquisition and sustainment over the entire product life cycle. It is recommended that the PM and Contracting Officer coordinate with an attorney advisor, particularly one well versed in IP issues to better understand IP.

Starting at Milestone A, the IP Strategy applies to all program types covered by DoDI 5000.02 (Encl. 1, Table 2), including MDAPs, MAIS, and all other acquisition categories. Further information can be found in the <u>Milestone Document Identification (MDID)</u> tool as well as in the <u>Intellectual Property (IP) Strategy</u> guidance. However, the IP Strategy is best considered and developed well before Milestone A as Figure 33 indicates. It is subsequently updated, as appropriate, throughout the remainder of the entire program life cycle.

<u>Figure 33: IP Strategy</u>

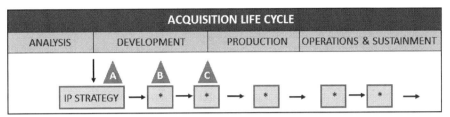

*Revisions as needed over the life cycle

Initially, the IP Strategy is summarized in the Acquisition Strategy. During the Operations and Sustainment phase, it is presented with the Life Cycle Sustainment Plan.

There are 5 basic levels of rights that can be applied to non-commercial items or other negotiable IP:

- **Unlimited Rights**. The government may "use, modify, reproduce, perform, display, release, or disclose" the data to anyone and for any purpose.
- **Government Purpose Rights.** The government may "use, modify, reproduce, perform, display, release, or disclose" the data within the government or may release or disclose such data to another outside the government so long as the recipient uses the data for government purposes.
- **Limited Rights.** The government may "use, modify, reproduce, perform, display, release, or disclose" the data only within the government except that the government may release to another if "necessary for emergency repair and overhaul.")
- **Restricted Rights.** The government may use the software on one computer/CPU/terminal at a time within the government and make the minimum number of archival copies needed, but cannot reverse engineer the software or release the software outside the government except unless the release is "necessary for emergency repair and overhaul"; or the release is to a service contractor for the purpose of diagnosing and correcting deficiencies in the software or combining, adapting, or merging the software with other computer programs, or when needed to respond to urgent tactical situations.
- **Specifically Negotiated Rights**. The government and the contractor may modify these predetermined levels of rights so long as the government receives no less than limited rights in technical data related to noncommercial items and restricted rights in noncommercial computer software.

Some IP, like commercial items, comes with pre-existing rights approaches, which cannot be or are not normally negotiable:

- **License Rights in Technical Data Related to Commercial Items.** DoD may use, modify, reproduce, release, perform, display, or disclose technical data only within the government. The data may not be used to manufacture additional quantities of the commercial items and, except for emergency repair or overhaul and for covered government support contractors, may not be released or disclosed to, or used by, third parties without the contractor's written permission.

- **Commercial Computer Software License** (Applicable to the acquisition of commercial computer software and its documentation). DoD may use the software and documentation only in accordance with the terms of the license customarily provided to the public. If that license is inconsistent with Federal procurement law or does not otherwise satisfy user needs, the government negotiates with the contractor to determine if acceptable terms can be reached. The terms of any license for commercial computer software are enumerated in the contract or in an addendum to the contract.
- **SBIR/STTR Data Rights** For a limited period (the Small Business Innovative Research/Small Business Technology Transfer [SBIR/STTR] Data Rights Period), the government acquires Limited Rights in technical data related to noncommerci9al items generated under an SBIR/STTR award; and Restricted Rights in noncommercial computer software generated under an SBIR/STTR award. Unless extended by delivery of the technical data/computer software under a subsequent SBIR/STTR award, the SBIR/STTR Data Rights Period extends five (5) years after completion of the program from which the data were generated. After the expiration of the SBIR/STTR Data Rights Period, the government acquires Unlimited Rights. All questions regarding whether SBIR/STRR Data Rights have expired should be referred to an attorney well-versed in IP issues.

Note: The definitions in FAR and the DFARS differ from one another, and the DoD is to follow the DFARS implementation. The definitions above are derived from the definitions in the DFARS, which are more detailed.

IP associated with items of foreign sale or international development are subject to additional considerations. During contract award and contract administration, the Contracting Officer takes certain actions to maintain the government's rights on behalf of DoD, International Cooperative Program (ICP) partner nations, and Foreign Military Sales (FMS) customer nations, as applicable, based on signed ICP International Agreements and FMS Letters of Offer and Acceptance (LOAs). International Trade and Arms Regulations (ITAR) considerations must also be taken into account.

During the contract award process for a non-commercial acquisition, the contractor (IAW the RFP) develops and provides the Contracting Officer with a data assertions list identifying any data where the government will not receive unlimited rights. Upon contract award, the data list identifies any noncommercial computer software or technical data related to a noncommercial item for which the government has less than Unlimited Rights (e.g., Government Purpose Rights, Limited Rights, SBIR/STTR Data Rights, and Specifically Negotiated Rights). *The basic rule (barring any other information) is that the government will have Unlimited Rights to any technical data related to noncommercial items or noncommercial computer software not on that list. One notable exception is that an SBIR contract does not need to include assertions for SBIR data rights in technical data or computer software developed under that contract.*

During contract management and administration, due to change proposals, the contractor may propose bringing more data onto the program. If the contractor desires to provide the government less than Unlimited Rights, it would need to propose that. If the government agrees with any restrictions, the Contracting Officer would add the data to the data accession list contained in the contract.

During contract performance, contractors often must provide proprietary data to the government. When the contractor does this, it must mark each piece of data with any restrictions by a marking or legend indicating the level of rights it believes the government has in the data. This is a required action for a contractor to maintain its rights to the data.

If the Contracting Officer notifies the contractor that restrictive markings are not in the format authorized by the contract, e.g., use language not authorized by the data rights clauses, the contractor has sixty (60) days to remove or correct the markings. Other format inconsistencies noted by the Contracting Officer may include:

- Data restrictive markings that do not conform to the marking instructions of the data rights clauses.
- Data restrictive markings that are applied to technical data related to a noncommercial item, a noncommercial computer software, or its documentation.
- Restrictive markings that are inconsistent with the contractor's data rights assertions.

If the contractor fails to act, the government can ignore, remove, or correct the marking.

Restrictive markings that are in the appropriate format, but are not justified (i.e., restrictive markings that purport to provide lesser rights than the government is entitled to under the contract), must be challenged in order to protect the government's rights. There is a specific process that the Contracting Officer must follow to protect government rights. Any contract that entails delivery of technical data or computer software will include the "Validation of Restrictive Markings on Technical Data" clause. Under this clause:

- If the Contracting Officer disagrees with a restrictive marking, a written notice is provided to the contractor challenging the marking.
- If the contractor fails to respond within 60 days or responds, but does not justify the asserted marking, the Contracting Officer issues a final decision indicating whether the marking is justified.
- The government must abide by the marking for ninety (90) days after final decision, or one year after the final decision if, within the ninety (90) days, the contractor provides notice that it will appeal the final decision to the Armed Services Board of Contract Appeals (ASBCA) or file suit in an appropriate court. If an appeal or suit is filed in an appropriate court, the government must still abide by the marking until final disposition by the ASBCA or the court. [*Note*: The timeline for the Court of Federal Claims is twelve (12) months.]

The PM and Contracting Officer work together to ensure that the government's rights are protected. This is a methodical process that is carefully followed. If it is not followed, the government may lose its rights to vital intellectual property. Again, the PM and Contracting Officer are diligent in protecting the government's rights to needed data.

The following IP Strategy references provide additional information, guiding principles, and resources:

- Intellectual Property Strategy
- Understanding and Leveraging Data Rights in DoD Acquisitions

CH 1–4.2.19 Encouraging a Quality Focus

Applying best practice as described throughout this Chapter may not be sufficient to manage and mitigate process-based risks that may start a chain of events leading to undesirable outcomes. PMOs can stress the importance of effective quality management to industry. By encouraging a quality focus, PMOs can help avoid mismatches among value, beliefs, and behaviors. Delivery of systems that prevent or avoid problems are the goal. PMOs can also use advanced quality management systems (such as ISO 9000, Quality Management; AS 9100, Quality Systems – Aerospace: Model for Quality Assurance in Design, Development, Production, Installation and Servicing; and the Malcolm Baldrich Quality Award criteria) to develop their quality strategy and approach. PMOs can also conduct quality control using acceptance sampling procedures. MIL-STD-1916, DoD Preferred Methods for Acceptance of Product, provides standardized acceptance sampling systems, which are consistent with the contract requirements for submission of all conforming products or services. These sampling systems allow PMs to influence continuous improvement through corrective action while still allowing a maximum degree of flexibility to contractors.

International Quality Standard ISO 21247, Combined Accept-Zero Sampling Systems and Process Control Procedures for Product Acceptance, is an acceptable alternative to MIL-STD-1916.

CH 1–4.2.19.1 Quality Implementation

Other effective practice for program management to consider in order to achieve a Quality Focus throughout each of the acquisition life-cycle phases are listed in Table 7.

Table 7: Acquisition Management Effective Quality Focus Practice

Where quality responsibility is placed in the program:
• Role in the general risk identification, classification, and mitigation process;   • Involvement in the design change control and release process;   • Role in processing waivers, deviations, and engineering change proposals;   • Representation on Integrated Process Teams and boards (e.g., change control board, risk) for all product and process development activities;   • Involvement in test plans, material reviews, design reviews, build/buy/support to packages;   • Participation in the integration of inspection points into processing and test documentation; and   • Role in the supplier management, development, incentivization, and control process.
How quality skills have been assigned to the project:
• The process to identify the need for quality management, quality engineering (hardware and software), quality planning, supplier quality, and product verification skills across the life cycle;   • The process to identify quality skills and any associated certifications and qualifications; and   • The process for addressing quality staffing ratios and skill shortfalls.

CH 1–4.2.19.2 Contractor Performance Appraisal System

A Contractor Performance Appraisal System (CPARS) report is an annual requirement on contracts valued over the simplified acquisition threshold for most acquisition. CPARS is an objective report of the contractor's performance against the contract cost, schedule, and performance standards during a given period of time. The CPARS report goes into the Past Performance Information Retrieval System (PPIRS) database, which collects Past Performance Information (PPI). PPI is one of the tools used to communicate contractor strengths and weaknesses to source selection officials and Contracting Officers. Communication between the government and contractor during the performance period is essential. The contractor performance evaluation contained in the PPIRS is a method of *recording* contractor performance and does not represent the sole method for reporting it to the contractor.

Regular performance reviews with contractors ensure there are no surprises at the end of the performance period about the rating a contractor will receive. These ratings are very important to a contractor; they can affect future business opportunities.

Consult A Guide to Collection and Use of Past Performance Information for more information.

CH 1–4.2.20 Dependencies and Interdependencies

The acquisition of systems, subsystems, and/or major components often involves a series of dependencies and interdependencies. For the purpose of this discussion, in DoD acquisition and project planning dependencies generally refer to the vertical and horizontal integration of the system, subsystems, or components with other systems. This integration is either as part of a larger system/system-of-systems, or as a predecessor or successor in the sequence of system development, production, operations, and/or maintenance and support. Interdependencies generally refer to resources, technology, funding, requirements, or other factors that apply to more than one program. However, these terms are frequently used in an interchangeable manner.

Program Managers can identify and address risk of external dependencies in order to ensure timely design, development, deployment, and sustainment of the system. They document interface requirements and interface products to track interdependent program touch points.

In compliance with DoDI 5000.02 (Encl. 3, para 2.a), PMs will document program dependencies and interdependencies in the Systems Engineering Plan (SEP) to ensure timely design, development, deployment, and sustainment of the system. Refer to CH 3–2.2 and CH 3–4.3.13 for guidance related to the SEP; and Interoperability and Dependencies, respectively.

Finally, program risks associated with dependencies and interdependencies are identified and managed as part of the program risk assessment.

CH 1–4.2.20.1 System-Level Dependencies

In preparation for the Analysis of Alternatives (AoA), DoD Components conduct early analysis and assessments of how the proposed candidate materiel solution approaches have the potential to effectively address capability gaps, desired operational attributes, and associated external dependencies.

Analysis of dependencies includes the impact to or from other systems, as well as the interoperability dependencies with Joint and potential foreign systems. The following examples illustrate this principle:

- Analysis of ship dimensions, infrastructure, and support capabilities for a new aircraft design planned to land and take off from U.S. and allied ships.
- Analysis of a new weapon designed to be aircraft-launched on the dimensions, aerodynamic limitations, and interfaces (mechanical, electrical, hydraulic) of current and future aircraft planning to use it.
- Analysis of a new vehicle design to determine its ability to be transported by current and planned vehicles (i.e., rail, ship, or aircraft).

CH 1–4.2.20.2 Interdependencies

Acquisition PMs specify programmatic interdependencies with other programs and discuss the relationship of the interdependencies with other program activity personnel on the critical path. If any Memorandums of Agreement are required to formalize these relationships, the following actions are beneficial:

- Identify the interface (i.e., the system this product interfaces with).
- Identify the agency that owns the other system.
- Identify the authority (e.g., CAE, PEO, delegated PM) responsible for controlling the interface (i.e., the individual who can set the requirements).
- Direct the solution to the interface issue and direct who provides the funding for the solution.
- Identify the "required by" date.
- Identify the impact if not completed.

The following examples illustrate this principle:

- Analysis of a new weapon or weapon system design requiring the use of global positioning system data in order to properly function.
- Analysis of an unmanned air vehicle design that leverages advanced development in low observable technology in order to achieve required survivability and mission effectiveness objectives.
- Analysis of a cargo transport aircraft design that requires use of an advanced detection and countermeasures system developed as a separate Joint program.

More information is available on the Defense Acquisition University Acquisition Community Connection "Interoperability and Dependencies" website.

CH 1–4.2.21 Program Information Protection

Program Managers are responsible for ensuring adequate protection of DoD information. This includes information about the system, such as the key technologies, applications, processes, capabilities, suppliers, and end items, as well as information processed by, or transiting through, a system. In addition to classified information, this also includes information that, alone, may not be damaging and may be unclassified, but in combination with other information, could allow an adversary to compromise, counter, clone, or defeat warfighting capability. Protection of information is achieved through the implementation of a number of activities and analyses across a system's life cycle. One set of activities focuses on identifying, classifying, and marking program information to ensure properly controlled dissemination and adequate protection are applied. Other sets of activities aim to ensure the confidentiality, integrity, and availability of information to preserve the assurance of the system being acquired.

Program information protection includes implementation of some of the activities discussed in CH 1–4.2.21.3, Data Protection, including:

- Safeguarding controlled unclassified technical information resident on, or transiting through, contractor unclassified information systems in accordance with DFARS Subpart 204.73.
- Ensuring compliance with 22 CFR 120-130, International Traffic in Arms Regulations (ITAR) and 15 CFR Chapter VII, subchapter C, Export Administration Regulations (EAR) By DoD Contractors.

Program Information Protection is a key element of program protection—the Department's integrating process for mitigating and managing risks of advanced technology and mission-critical system functionality from foreign collection, design vulnerability, supply chain exploitation/insertion, battlefield loss, and unauthorized or inadvertent disclosure throughout the acquisition life cycle.

DAG Chapter 9 discusses in detail the requirements, processes, and resulting artifacts employed to protect program information. CH 9–3.1.1.1, Foundational Activities, contains further information on the activities related to classification, marking, and protecting program information as part of Program Information Protection.

Per DoDI 5000.02 (Encl. 2, para 9), PMs will ensure that all program documents and records, regardless of media or security classification, are created, maintained, used, and disposed of or preserved effectively and efficiently in accordance with statutory and regulatory requirements discussed in the following paragraphs

CH 1–4.2.21.1 Program Documents and Records

Program Managers ensure that prior to acquisition and implementation, a records retention schedule is identified in contracts and Service-Level Agreements (SLAs) that includes, but is not limited to, secure storage, retrievability, and proper disposition of all federal records. Proper storage, retrievability, and disposition of all federal records is prescribed in the Federal Records Act, National Archives and Records Administration (NARA) Bulletin 2010-05, and DoDI 5015.02, DoD Records Management Program.

DoD 5015.02-STD, Electronic Records Management Software Applications Design Criteria Standard, establishes the functional requirements for records management software.

CH 1–4.2.21.2 Personally Identifiable Information

Personally Identifiable Identification (PII) is information about an individual that identifies, links, relates, or is unique to, or describes him or her (e.g., a social security number; age; military rank; civilian grade; marital status; race; salary; home or office phone numbers; other demographic, biometric, personnel, medical, and financial information). Such information also is known as personally identifiable information (e.g., information that can be used to distinguish or trace an individual's identity, such as his or her name; social security number; date and place of birth; mother's maiden name; and biometric records, including any other personal information which is linked or linkable to a specified individual).

Program Managers of systems that collect, maintain, use, or disseminate PII comply with the policies and instructions established in DoDD 5400.11, DoD Privacy Program, and DoDI 5400.16, DoD Privacy Impact Assessment (PIA) Guidance. Program Managers also prepare a Privacy Impact Assessment (PIA) using DD Form 2930 and coordinate with the DoD Component Privacy Officer.

CH 1–4.2.21.3 Data Protection

Program Managers of DoD IT systems (including those supported through contracts with external sources) that collect, maintain, use, or disseminate data are to protect against disclosure to non-approved sources. Program Managers ensure that DoD data:

- Are protected in transit using an approved Federal Information Processing Standard Publication (FIPS) PUB 140-2, Security Requirements for Cryptographic Modules.
- Are protected in accordance with the DoDI 2000.03, International Interchange of Patent Rights and Technical Information.
- Conform to the standards established to protect DoD personal health information (PHI) in DoD 8580.02-R, Security of Individually Identifiable Health Information in DoD Health Care Programs.
- Adhere to 22 CFR 120-130, International Traffic in Arms Regulations (ITAR).
- Are protected in accordance with DoDI 3200.12, DoD Scientific and Technical Information Program (STIP), e.g., scientific and technical information that is managed to make scientific knowledge and technological innovations fully accessible to the research community, industry, the military operational community, and the general public within the boundaries of law, regulation, other directives, and executive requirements.
- Are safeguarded by adequate security measures that will be implemented to safeguard controlled unclassified technical information resident on, or transiting through, contractor unclassified information systems in accordance with DFARS Subpart 204.73 and DoDI 8582.01, Security of Unclassified DoD Information on Non-DoD Information Systems.
- Adhere to DoD 5015.02-STD Electronic Records Management Software Application Design Criteria Standards.
- Are subject to enduring, holistic, global forensic capability that supports the full range of military operations according to DoDD 5205.15E, DoD Forensic Enterprise (DFE).
- Are made available for legal discovery by allowing all data to be located, preserved, collected, processed, reviewed, and produced (e-discovery) as required by Federal Rules of Civil Procedure.
- Adhere to the policies and procedures listed in DoDI 8410.01, Internet Domain Name and Internet Protocol Address Space Use and Approval, to ensure correct approval and use of internet domain names.
- Adhere to the Freedom of Information Act (FOIA) program policies and procedures listed in DoDD 5400.07, DoD Freedom of Information Act (FOIA) Program, to ensure that all DoD data and information stored in an external service provider's environment will be available for

appropriate handling. Implementing guidelines are available in the DoDM 5400.07, DoD Freedom of Information Act Program.

- Implement the appropriate FAR Subpart 27.4, Rights in Data and Copyrights, and applicable DFARS clauses in contracts, as appropriate.

CH 1–4.2.21.4 Enterprise Infrastructure

Increasingly, DoD mission success depends on the ability of military commanders and civilian leaders to act quickly and effectively based on the most accurate and timely data available. In today's national security environment, it is imperative that DoD resolve barriers to trusted information sharing and collaboration, within the Department and with DoD's mission partners, to provide better access to information and to enhance the nation's effectiveness to defend against cyber threats and vulnerabilities. DoD can achieve this in a fiscal environment that demands reduced Information Technology (IT) infrastructure costs.

DoD, through the Chief Information Officer (CIO)'s The Department of Defense Strategy for Implementing the Joint Information Environment or JIE, is transitioning to a single, Joint, secure, reliable, and agile Command, Control, Communications, and Computers (C4) enterprise information environment.

The JIE is a construct that facilitates the convergence of the DoD's multiple networks into one common and shared global network. Primary objectives behind this transition are increased operational efficiency, enhanced network security, and cost savings through reduced infrastructure and manpower.CH 6–3.9.1, Joint Information Environment, provides detailed information regarding Enterprise infrastructure considerations for program planning and execution.

CH 1–4.2.22 Cybersecurity in Program Acquisition

The nature of today's globalized and interconnected world combined with the extensive reliance on technology, computer systems, and internet connectivity means that non-state actors, whether individuals or groups of some kind, or actors sanctioned by a state, can have a significant impact through cyber activity. DoD program and system information and systems are continually at risk of being attacked by these actors.

Program Managers play a key role in assessing all aspects of their programs, with particular attention on the elements that these malicious actors are likely to target.

- **Government Program Office**. Untrained personnel, malicious insiders, insufficient classification and handling of information, inadequate network security.
- **Contractor organizations and environments.** Design, development, and production environments, networks, supply chains, and personnel.
- **Software and hardware.** Components that are deliberately compromised while in the supply chain or inherently vulnerable to attack.
- **System interfaces.** Interfaces to networks, other systems, and operators,
- **Enabling and support equipment, systems, and facilities**. Test, certification, maintenance, design, development, manufacturing, training systems, equipment, and facilities.
- **Fielded systems.** Systems in operation exposed to changing threat environments.

Program Managers rely on program protection processes, techniques, and methodologies to help prioritize and address cybersecurity risks. Program protection also helps the PM to identify those technologies, components, and information worth protecting, and to determine the most appropriate mix of measures to protect them (given cost, schedule, performance, and all other constraints). Protection measures may include information security, Operations Security (OPSEC), personnel security, physical security, industrial security, designed-in system protections, Supply Chain Risk Management (SCRM), software assurance, hardware assurance, anti-counterfeit practice, and Anti-Tamper (AT). These protections may impact the development of the system being acquired, the operations of the program office, and the means by which the items are acquired.

Systems engineering trade-off analyses can inform the PM's tough choices among competing system requirements within cost, schedule, and performance constraints. Sufficiently mitigating cybersecurity risks is more successful and cost-effective if security is a thoughtful consideration early and throughout the design process. Program Managers can consider the size and complexity of the program as these can impact the time it takes to conduct protection analyses and the cost to mitigate vulnerabilities.

It is the responsibility of the PM to ensure that program protection efforts are initiated early in the program, are conducted throughout all phases of the acquisition life cycle, and are continued throughout sustainment of the system as attacks may occur at any time. Within each phase of the life cycle, program protection analyses are iteratively updated to reflect the maturity of the system. CH 9–3.4.2 details the activities in the Acquisition Life Cycle Phases.

The PM can use the Program Protection Plan (PPP) to guide and focus program efforts for managing the cybersecurity risks. This milestone acquisition document captures and helps the program to communicate what in the program and what systems associated with the program will be protected, and how they are or will be protected. The PPP captures the risk decisions and activities that inform future contracts. After deployment, the responsibilities of the PPP transition to the appropriate life-cycle manager.

CH 1–4.2.22.1 Key Challenges for Program Managers

The following factors represent some key challenges to consider and actions PMs can take when planning cybersecurity and program security:

- **Integrating the Risk Management Framework (RMF) for DoD IT into acquisition**. Strive to meet the objectives of the RMF for DoD IT within the performance, cost, and schedule constraints of their programs. This includes development of a shared understanding for cybersecurity implementation among the program office, RMF for DoD IT Authorizing Official, and the operational user, in accordance with the DoD Component implementing guidance. Ensure effective reuse of information to meet RMF for DoD IT documentation requirements in accordance with their DoD Component implementing instructions and guidance.
- **Cloud implementation**. Understand their program's need for cloud implementation and use the DoD Cloud Computing Security Requirements Guide (SRG) and/or appropriate Defense Federal Acquisition Regulation Supplement (DFARS) contracting clauses.
- **Technical dependencies on other systems**. Understand all system interfaces, and associated risks and vulnerabilities, including those to information networks and support equipment (e.g., training or maintenance systems).
- **Dependencies on other organizations**. Understand organizational dependencies, including the program offices using the same or similar equipment and information, intelligence/CI organizations providing information to enable program security decisions, and organizations with responsibilities related to certain aspects of cybersecurity (e.g., National Security Agency [NSA], DoD Component Offices of Primary Responsibility for Anti-Tamper, RMF for DoD IT Authorizing Official).
- **Exportability and Sales**. Understand the impacts of international acquisition and exportability on program and system protections, and consider these early in the protection planning process. Program Managers can consider historical sales of their capability to facilitate assessment of future foreign sales. Platform PMs can also consider contacting the Government Furnished Equipment providers to understand if the capability is exportable for the platform.
- **Test and Evaluation**. Ensure the cybersecurity measures identified in the Test and Evaluation Master Plan (TEMP) are measurable and testable.
- **Rapid Fielding and Urgent Operational Needs.** For PMs of programs fulfilling urgent operational needs and other quick reaction capabilities, understand the impact of protection

decisions on the system being deployed, as well as on other DoD systems providing similar capabilities.

CH 1–4.2.23 Property

"Government Property" means all property owned or leased by the government. Government property includes both government-furnished property and contractor-acquired property. Government property includes material, equipment, special tooling, special test equipment, and real property. Government property does not include intellectual property and software (FAR 45.101). An area not covered by the FAR is software, especially Internal Use Software (IUS). IUS is addressed through intellectual property and information technology. IUS has management rules similar to those placed upon other types of government property.

DoDI 4161.02, Accountability and Management of Government Contract Property provides instructions and guidance, assigns responsibilities, and prescribes procedures in accordance with FAR Part 45, DFARS Part 245, and DFARS Procedures, Guidance, and Information (PGI) for the accountability and management of government contract property in the custody of defense contractors. The PGI directs the performance of the business case analysis that covers the circumstances of when to provide government property. DoDI 5000.64, Accountability and Management of DoD Equipment and Other Accountable Property, outlines requirements that reflect the accountability perspective of property management, which supports the life-cycle management of items, including the documentation of life-cycle events and transactions.

In the normal course of doing business, contractors are expected to provide all property necessary for performing government contracts. The government only provides property to contractors under certain circumstances (i.e., when it is clearly demonstrated in the government's best interest; the overall benefit to the acquisition significantly outweighs the increased cost of administration, including ultimate property disposal; providing the property does not substantially increase the government's assumption of risk; and government requirements cannot otherwise be met). Providing property is not done just because a contractor is unable or unwilling to provide the property itself, or because property "has always been furnished." Program Managers and Contracting Officers prevent the unnecessary furnishing of government property, including reviewing the program and contracts periodically to validate property is still required.

The PM assigns management authority within the program office and identifies needed actions, reviews, and reports. This may be accomplished by assigning an Accountable Property Officer (defined in DoDI 5000.64) or other knowledgeable personnel. Decisions about acquisition, retention, disposition, and delivery requirements are well informed and timely. The Contracting Officer may appoint a Property Administrator as an authorized representative of the Contracting Officer to administer the contract requirements and obligations relating to Government Contract Property (defined in DoDI 4161.02).

Program Managers and their staffs need to determine how property will be considered and utilized throughout the acquisition life cycle. Three areas of property include: Government Property in the Possession of a Contractor (GPPC); Contractor-Acquired Property; and Government Furnished Property. Each of these areas has its own advantages and disadvantages that PMs factor into how they will manage their programs, including how these areas will be considered in source selections conducted under competitive negotiations.

CH 1–4.2.23.1 Government Property in the Possession of a Contractor

All PMs and Contracting Officers need to prevent the unnecessary furnishing of Government Contract Property. The PM assigns property management authority within the program office and identifies needed actions, reviews, and reports. Decisions about acquisition, retention, disposition, and delivery requirements need to be well informed and timely. Government Contract Property no longer needed for current contract performance or future needs is promptly disposed of or reutilized in accordance with applicable laws and regulations; or stored under a funded storage agreement. The PM and Contracting Officer then document decisions regarding Government Contract Property in the contract file.

Government Contract Property is not "owned" by the PM, but is "used" on the program, with the PM having accountability responsibilities. Government property may only be furnished to contractors under the criteria, restrictions, and documentation requirements addressed in FAR 45.102 and FAR 45.105, as supplemented in the DFARS and the DFARS Procedures, Guidance, and Information (PGI). Government contract property is divided into two categories: Government-Furnished Property and Contractor-Acquired Property.

CH 1–4.2.23.2 Government Furnished Property

"Government Furnished Property" means property in the possession of, or directly acquired by, the government and subsequently furnished to the contractor for performance of a contract. Government-Furnished Property includes, but is not limited to, spares and property furnished for repair, maintenance, overhaul, or modification. Government-Furnished Property also includes Contractor-Acquired Property if the Contractor-Acquired Property is a deliverable under a cost contract when accepted by the government for continued use under the contract (FAR 45.101).

Although the DoD may not have physical custody of property furnished to a contractor, to maintain effective property accountability and control and for financial reporting purposes, DoD Components establish accountable property records (defined in DoDI 5000.64) and maintain accountability for property furnished to contractors as Government Furnished Property. Accountable property records are maintained in an Accountable Property System of Record (APSR). The APSR is approved by the DoD Component sponsoring the program; Joint programs can use the lead DoD Component's system.

CH 1–4.2.23.3 Contractor-Acquired Property

Contractor-Acquired Property (CAP) means property acquired, fabricated, or otherwise provided by the contractor for performing a contract and property to which the government has title (FAR 45.101).

DoD policies, processes, and practices are structured on delivery, receipt, and acceptance of property. This aligns and is consistent with other DoD processes and practices (e.g., Wide-Area Work Flow and Unique Item identification). [Note: The Wide-Area Flow site access is conditional based on registration and identification of user roles.] Although the DoD may have title to CAP, such property has not yet been delivered.

Upon delivery to the government, CAP is recorded in the appropriate Accountable Property System of Record (APSR). If this property is subsequently provided to a contractor for use on contracts, it will be managed as Government Furnished Property. Consistent with DoDI 5000.64, there is no requirement for property accountability by DoD Components for such property prior to delivery to the government. Contractors have stewardship responsibility, including creating and maintaining records of all government property accountable to the contract, consistent with the terms and conditions of the contract, for the government property in their care.

CH 1–4.2.23.4 Government Property

During the life of the program, property items may be developed as Contractor-Acquired Property (CAP) that support the deliverable item. This property may be test equipment, ground support equipment, or other equipment items. The PM and Contracting Officer remain aware of any CAP that meets or exceeds the DoD Component capitalization threshold (see DoD 7000.14-R, Financial Management Regulation). Per the guidance in PGI 245.402-70, the Contracting Officer enables delivery of these capital items so accountable property records can be established in the Accountable Property System of Record (APSR). This allows the DoD Component to correctly report the property on the financial statement. The delivered CAP is then managed as Government Furnished Property while used on the contract.

CH 1–4.2.23.5 Accountable Property System of Record

The PM knows which Accountable Property Systems of Record (APSRs) will be used within the program. An APSR is approved by the DoD Component, and there may be multiple APSRs depending on the types of property (e.g., equipment, real property, operating materials and supplies, inventory, internal use software) and the complexity of the program. The APSR is also part of the Life Cycle Sustainment Plan. The assigned property manager within the program uses the APSRs to perform the required management tasks and keep the PM informed. A contractor's property system is not an APSR and cannot be used instead of a DoD Component's system.

CH 1–4.2.23.6 Item Unique Identification

Item Unique Identification (IUID) requires budgeting and planning early in the acquisition process. The PM identifies components and subcomponents that will need item-level traceability. IUID is applied within the structure of DoDI 8320.04, Item Unique Identification Standards for Tangible Personal Property, and contracts contain the required clause (DFARS).

CH 1–4.2.24 Acquisition Program Transition Workshops

A best practice in recent years for PMs of all Acquisition Category (ACAT) ID, ACAT IAM, and special interest programs is to conduct an Acquisition Program Transition Workshop (APTW) with their industry PM counterparts within the first few weeks following contract award or significant program redirection. These workshops are focused on aligning government/contractor teams with the contract for contract execution success.

An APTW is a significant risk mitigation tool for both the government and contractor PMs and PMOs as they jumpstart a program to go in a new direction. In a contract award situation, the executing teams have either been focused on source selection or contract proposal activities. Setting the stage for the first area of success is careful planning for government program management in the RFP. Baselining contract execution processes early is *essential*. [*Note*: Workshop preparation and conduct are tailored to each program event to make the best use of the approximate 3 days of the workshop.] The following lessons learned/re-learned become important when contract requirements and/or people change:

- Responsibility Assignment Matrix—Thorough knowledge of counterpart organization/ individuals and individual contract roles.
- Joint team charters—Purpose, responsibilities, authority, accountability, leadership, membership, interfaces and interdependencies, team risks, issue resolution process.
- Common understanding of IMP and IMS and a proactive understanding of team contract execution responsibilities, usually weekly for high-performing teams to understand what the real workload is.
- Common understanding of contract requirements, interpretations, and assumptions.
- Team plans for 60/90/120 days, including communications and metrics.

Program Managers are encouraged to contact the Defense Acquisition University in a timely manner to facilitate the following acquisition planning and execution activities in Table 8. Supplemental information regarding APTWs may be obtained by e-mailing MissionAssistance@dau.mil for more information on *WSM 011 (Acquisition Program Transition Workshop)*.

Table 8: Acquisition Events and Activities

Acquisition Events	Activities
Draft Request for Proposal (RFP)	Include an Acquisition Program Transition Workshop (APTW) requirement in the RFP and Statement of Work and address in Draft RFP briefings to possible respondents.
Pre-Contract Award	Engage in APTW government team training and/or process development for contract execution.

Post-Contract Award	An APTW within five weeks following contract award is optimum to set contract execution expectations and processes for contract execution.

CH 1–4.3 Milestone Decision Authority Decision Reviews

Milestone Decision Authority Decision Reviews are applicable to all ACAT I, II, III, or IV programs. Program Managers are encouraged to consider the following key elements as part of any discussion with the Milestone Decision Authority, or for consideration as the decision-maker. Other focus areas contain a rundown of best practice and lessons learned regarding milestone decisions at every level.

- **Ensure the audience understands program context**. Key considerations for the decision being requested are first, then present appropriate program information so advisors and the MDA understand the program. Some examples include:
  - Mission and key requirements—usually KPPs, KSAs, and APAs.
  - Context regarding how the system fits into its mission area, and perhaps an operational architecture view (OV-1)—how this new capability compares with legacy systems being replaced (if applicable).
  - Results of market research (especially if relevant to a competition strategy).
  - Expected sustainment environment (likelihood of changes, enhancements, and expected obsolescence).
  - Any critical dependencies—internal or external to the program.
- **Refine the message**. Following are additional considerations for structuring a decision brief :
  - Leverage critical thinking to outline/develop answers to questions relevant to the program, and especially to topics in the brief. Review current Acquisition Decision Memorandum (ADM); review the status of requirements, budget/funding, and contractor performance; review how the system fits into the Joint and Service visions.
  - Outline key focus areas for the decision brief, including a summary of how prior work supports exit from current phase and satisfaction of entry criteria into next phase. Use exit and entry criteria from prior ADM as a guide.
  - Decide on your key messages. Some examples: What was learned from the completed phase and readiness for next phase? Tradeoffs user made in terms of changes to Additional Performance Attributes (APAs), Key System Attributes (KSAs), or Key Performance Parameters (KPPs) based on insights gained during critical design, software coding/manufacturing design for the hardware, and/or developmental /operational testing. Risks and opportunities that remain and why they are manageable.
  - Use data to support the message.
  - Establish a logical flow in the briefing to help the MDA. Consider presenting the requested decision and recommendations up front along with prior work, including previous ADM direction to underpin arguments and rationale for proceeding that are in the remainder of the brief.

The bottom line is to clearly articulate the decision(s) requested; present rationale/data that support the decision(s) being requested in a logical sequence; be prepared to answer questions relevant to the decision and/or any aspect of the program.

CH 1–4.3.1 General Considerations for All Milestone Decision Briefs

The follow paragraphs provide recommendations in preparation for any milestone or acquisition decision meeting.

CH 1–4.3.1.1 Considerations for All Milestone Decision Meetings

- What is the purpose of the program and its fit in the larger portfolio (background)?

- What are key outcomes and lessons the program team learned in the phase?
- What insight was gleaned from the phase just completed that influences the Acquisition Strategy?
- Was exit criteria for the phase met?
- Were any criteria/goals added based on how the work unfolded, and were the criteria/goals met?
- Is expected system performance responsive to the latest threat provided by the intelligence community?
- What are the key risks and opportunities in the program up to this point? (Show risks retired/opportunities captured.)
- If one or more of the phase exit criteria was not achieved, or only partially achieved, why is it still appropriate to seek approval to enter the next phase?
- If implementing an incremental strategy, is there reason to shift requirements to a later stage? If so, is user in agreement, and if so, why (e.g., why will a less capable first increment still be worth operational testing and release into the field)?
- How does the competition approach address risks and pursue opportunities?
- Were there any issues surfaced, but not resolved during discussion or staffing of phase-relevant documentation?

Note. For ACAT I/IAs, sometimes the open issues are briefed by the Overarching Integrated Product Team (OIPT) lead before the PM briefing starts at a Defense Acquisition Board (DAB)—be sure to synchronize this.

- Review the MDID tool to scope/tailor documentation effort.
- What is the scope of the work to be done in the coming phase?
- What questions are addressed through this phase? What data will be acquired to address these questions?
- What are the knowledge points to gain insight during the phase? What data will be acquired to address those knowledge points—either metrics data or other Contract Data Requirements List (CDRL) items?
- How do predicted product support needs drive architecture? The Acquisition Strategy, including IP strategy? The Systems Engineering approach?
- Did user requirements evolve in the prior phase, and what are the key requirements for the coming phase? What is the plan to address any requirements challenges that are unresolved at the start of this coming phase?
- What are the program risks? How have they been reduced in the prior phase? What is the plan to continue to manage/mitigate risks in the coming phase?
- What opportunities have been captured? What opportunities are planned for pursuit/capture in the coming phase? *Should Cost* versus *Will Cost* progress?
- What are the latest time-phased cost estimates (Service Cost Position [SCP] and Cost Assessment and Program Evaluation [CAPE]'s Independent Cost Estimate [ICE]), and what are the key assumptions or techniques leading to differences between them? What are the major cost drivers? [Perhaps in back-up: How/why has the estimate changed since the prior phase?]
- How does the "recommended" estimate (CAPE, ICE, or SCP) compare with the current Future Years Defense Program (FYDP) budget? What is the Service's/Agency's plan to close on any deltas?
- What are the user's affordability goals/caps for acquisition cost and Life Cycle Cost?
- Develop desired Acquisition Decision Memorandum draft key points. If the program is an MDAP or MAIS, then share it with the OIPT Lead for use in the OIPT portion of the brief. Otherwise, include it in the PM portion of the brief. The key points include, but are not limited to:
  - Approval to proceed with or without caveats/restrictions/comebacks, if appropriate.
  - Exit criteria for next phase.
  - Funding issues to be resolved, if present.

CH 1–4.3.1.2 Specific Consideration by Milestone Decision and Phase

The following paragraphs, briefly summarized and paraphrased from DoDI 5000.02 (para 5d), are included to provide program management with a view toward developing decision briefs that address expectations for the milestone meeting. There is additional information in paragraph 5d that program management can use to frame that brief.

CH 1–4.3.1.2.1 Materiel Development Decision/Materiel Solution Analysis Phase

- **Decision.** The Materiel Development Decision is based on a validated initial requirements document (an ICD or equivalent requirements document) and the completion of the Analysis of Alternatives (AoA) Study Guidance and the AoA Study Plan. This decision directs execution of the AoA and authorizes the DoD Component to conduct the Materiel Solution Analysis Phase.
- **Purpose of the MSA Phase.** Conduct the analysis and other activities needed to choose the concept for the product that will be acquired, to begin translating validated capability gaps into system-specific requirements, including the Key Performance Parameters (KPPs) and Key System Attributes (KSAs). Also conduct planning to support a decision on the Acquisition Strategy for the product. AoA solutions; key trades among cost, schedule, and performance; affordability analysis; risk analysis; and planning for risk mitigation are key activities in this phase.

CH 1–4.3.1.2.2 Milestone A Decision/Technology Maturation and Risk Reduction Phase

- **Decision.** The Milestone A decision approves program entry into the Technology Maturation and Risk Reduction (TMRR) phase and release of final RFPs for TMRR activities. The responsible DoD Component may decide to perform TMRR work in-house and/or award contracts associated with the conduct of this phase. Competitive prototypes are part of this phase unless specifically waived by the MDA. Key considerations are:
  - ○ The justification for the preferred materiel solution.
  - ○ The affordability and feasibility of the planned materiel solution.
  - ○ The scope of the capability requirements' trade space and understanding of the priorities within that trade space.
  - ○ The understanding of the technical, cost, and schedule risks of acquiring the materiel solution, and the adequacy of the plans and programmed funding to mitigate those risks prior to Milestone B.
- **Purpose of the TMRR Phase.** Reduce technology, engineering, integration, and life-cycle cost risk to the point that a decision to contract for Engineering and Manufacturing Development (EMD) can be made with confidence in successful program execution for development, production, and sustainment.

CH 1–4.3.1.2.3 Development RFP Release Decision Point

- **Decision.** This decision point authorizes the release of RFPs for EMD and often for Low-Rate Initial Production (LRIP) or Limited Deployment options. This review is the critical decision point in an acquisition program. The program will either successfully lead to a fielded capability or fail, based on the soundness of the capability requirements, the affordability of the program, and the executability of the Acquisition Strategy. The Acquisition Strategy is put into execution at this decision point by asking industry for bids that comply with the strategy. Release of the RFP for EMD sets in motion all that will follow. This is the last point at which significant changes can be made without a major disruption.
- **Purpose of the Development RFP Release Decision.** Ensure, prior to the release of the solicitation for EMD, that an executable and affordable program has been planned using a sound business and technical approach. One goal at this point is to avoid any major program delays at Milestone B, when source selection is already complete and award is

imminent. Therefore, prior to release of final RFPs, there needs to be confidence that the program requirements to be bid against are firm and clearly stated; the risk of committing to development and presumably production has been or will be adequately reduced prior to contract award and/or option exercise; the program structure, content, schedule, and funding are executable; and the business approach and incentives are structured to both provide maximum value to the government and treat industry fairly and reasonably.

CH 1–4.3.1.2.4 Milestone B Decision/Engineering and Manufacturing Development Phase

- **Decision**. This milestone provides authorization to enter into the EMD Phase and for the DoD Components to award contracts for EMD. It also commits the required investment resources to the program. Most requirements for this milestone can be satisfied at the Development RFP Release Decision Point; however, if any significant changes have occurred, or if additional information not available at the Development RFP Release Decision Point could impact this decision, its provision is required at Milestone B. Milestone B requires final demonstration that all sources of risk have been adequately mitigated to support a commitment to design for production. This includes technology, engineering, integration, manufacturing, sustainment, and cost risks. Validated capability requirements, full funding in the Future Years Defense Program (FYDP), and compliance with affordability goals for production and sustainment, as demonstrated through an Independent Cost Estimate (ICE), are required. The framing assumptions central to shaping the program's cost, schedule, and performance expectations are also required. Milestone B is normally the formal initiation of an acquisition program with the MDA's approval of the Acquisition Program Baseline (APB).
- **Purpose of the EMD Phase**. To develop, build, and test a product to verify that all operational and derived requirements have been met, and to support production or deployment decisions.

CH 1–4.3.1.2.5 Milestone C/Limited Deployment Decision

- **Decision**. The point at which a program or increment of capability is reviewed for entrance into the Production and Deployment (P&D) Phase or for Limited Deployment. Approval depends in part on specific criteria defined at Milestone B and included in the Milestone B ADM. The following general criteria will normally be applied: demonstration that the production/deployment design is stable and will meet stated and derived requirements based on acceptable performance in developmental test events; an operational assessment; mature software capability consistent with the software development schedule; no significant manufacturing risks; a validated Capability Production Document (CPD) or equivalent requirements document; demonstrated interoperability; demonstrated operational supportability; costs within affordability caps; full funding in the FYDP; properly phased production ramp-up; and deployment support. [**Note:** For a MAIS program, the two most important items to discuss are (1) whether the system is secure, and (2) what is the fallback plan should problems occur?]
- **Purpose**. Produce and deliver requirements-compliant products to receiving military organizations.

CH 1–4.3.1.2.6 Post-Milestone C Decision/Full-Rate Production Decision or Full Deployment Decision

- **Decision.** This decision assesses the results of initial Operational Test and Evaluation (OT&E), initial manufacturing and limited deployment, and determines whether or not to approve proceeding to Full-Rate Production (FRP) or Full Deployment (FD).
- **Purpose.** Confirm control of the manufacturing process, acceptable performance and reliability, and the establishment of adequate sustainment and support systems. Consider any new validated threat environments that might affect operational effectiveness, and consult with the requirements validation authority as part of the decision-making process to

ensure that capability requirements are current. Critical deficiencies identified in testing will be resolved prior to proceeding beyond Low-Rate Initial Production (LRIP) or limited deployment. Remedial action will be verified in follow-on test and evaluation. Normally the FRP/FD review and decision completes the Post-Implementation Review (PIR), which verifies the Measures of Effectiveness (MOEs) of the ICD or the benefits of a business plan. A PIR answers the question, "Did the Service/Agency get what it needed, per the ICD/Business Plan, and if not, what should be done? A PIR is required for all acquisition program increments at the Full-Rate Decision Review (FRDR).

CH 1–4.3.1.2.7 Post-Milestone C Decision/Operations and Support Phase

- **Decision.** Execute the product support strategy, satisfy materiel readiness and operational support performance requirements, and sustain the system over its life cycle (including disposal). The Operations and Support (O&S) Phase begins after the production or deployment decision and is based on an MDA-approved LCSP.
- **Purpose:** Over the system life cycle, operational needs, technology advances, evolving threats, process improvements, fiscal constraints, plans for follow-on systems, or a combination of these influences and others may warrant revisions to the product support strategies. The PM revalidates the supportability analyses and reviews the most current product support requirements, senior leader guidance, and fiscal assumptions to evaluate product support changes or alternatives, and determines best-value acquisition strategies.

CH 1–5. Business Practice/Additional Management Considerations

This Section provides descriptions of document and data repositories (e.g., AIR [Acquisition Information Repository], DAMIR [Defense Acquisition Management Information Retrieval]) of which program management ought to be aware, as discussed in Section 4.2.2.1. Also included is an explanation of the Defense Acquisition Executive Summary (DAES) and where it applies (Major Defense Acquisition Program [MDAP], Major Automated Information System [MAIS]). DAES, with tailoring, also lends itself to Milestone Decision Authority (MDA) review of other than MDAP and MAIS programs. An overview of the Milestone Document Identification (MDID) Tool is also provided as a resource for program management.

CH 1–5.1 Reporting Requirements

DoDI 5000.02 (Encl. 1), identifies the specific Information Requirements (Statutory and Regulatory) for each milestone and decision point by Program Type, as well as Recurring Program Reports (Encl. 1, Table 5); Exceptions, Waivers, and Alternative Management and Reporting Requirements (Encl. 1, Table 6). Information requirements unique to the Urgent Needs Rapid Acquisition Process (Encl. 13, Table 10) are also identified.

Information listed in the three Tables linked in the above paragraph and required by statute is addressed as dictated by law and cannot be waived unless the statute specifically provides for waiver of the stated requirement. These Information Requirements (Statutory and Regulatory) may also be tailored at the MDA's discretion.

In addition to reporting requirements in DoDI 5000.02 (Encl. 1), Service reviews and reporting requirements are detailed in each Service's Acquisition Instructions.

The DAES Assessment process that follows is mandatory for MDAPs quarterly, only after the initial Selected Acquisition Report (SAR) is submitted. Likewise, the process is mandatory for MAIS quarterly, only after the program is baselined. The DAES process, however, is potentially useful for the Program Manager (PM) and Program Executive Officer (PEO) review of any program, regardless of Acquisition Category (ACAT), Model, or Type.

CH 1–5.1.1 Program Assessments (Defense Acquisition Executive Summary)

The Defense Acquisition Executive Summary (DAES) process provides senior leadership with current situational awareness of the execution status of Major Defense Acquisition Programs (MDAPs), Major Automated Information Systems (MAIS), and designated "special interest" programs. The DAES Assessment serves as a common reference to achieve shared stakeholder insight regarding a program's current status and planned approach. It provides a documented understanding of how the program will accommodate cost, schedule, performance, and sustainment trades, and how these products will contribute to program decision-making. The purpose of the assessments is twofold:

- Provide awareness of the execution status of all reporting programs, including those that are performing well, by evaluating them at regular intervals.
- Enable identification of emerging execution issues that warrant the attention of senior leadership.

Program Managers provide assessments on their respective programs via the quarterly DAES submission. The assessments are conducted on 11 categories. Eight working days after a DAES report is submitted, Office of the Secretary of Defense (OSD) staff specialists will also assess program performance. The categories evaluated by OSD are identical to the categories evaluated by the PMs. The OSD assessments provide an independent assessment of program execution status and are used when selecting programs to be briefed at the monthly DAES Review meeting. Additionally, the OSD ratings support various Significant Acquisition Watchlist (SAW) displays within the Defense Acquisition Management Information Retrieval (DAMIR).

CH 1–5.1.1.1 Quick View of Overall Acquisition Status

A color code rating system for DAES assessments is used as a subjective means of evaluating a program's status in a given assessment category. The color ratings provide a quick view of overall acquisition status and are used to screen programs during the program selection process. Assessors will provide the status color that best reflects their concerns with the program.

On-Track (GREEN). The program is progressing satisfactorily in the given assessment area. Some minor problems may exist, but appropriate solutions to those problems are available; none of the problems are expected to affect overall program cost, schedule, interdependency risk, and performance requirements; and none are expected to require managerial attention or action.

Potential or Actual Problem (YELLOW). Some event, action, or delay has occurred that may impair progress against major objectives in one or more segments of the program, and may affect the program's ability to meet overall cost schedule and performance requirements or other major program objective, or may eventually result in a breach of Nunn-McCurdy unit cost targets.

Critical (RED). An event, action, or delay has occurred that, if not corrected, poses a serious risk to the program's ability to meet overall cost, schedule, and performance requirements, or other major program objective; would require significant funding changes; or may result in a breach of Nunn-McCurdy unit cost thresholds or a Chapter 144A Significant or Critical Change.

CH 1–5.1.1.2 Assessment Area and Criteria

The following paragraphs amplify the topic of overall program status with further discussion of key program attributes.

Program Cost. Assess the program's progress toward meeting its overall program cost objectives and measure performance against the unit costs and total costs found in the current Acquisition Program Baseline (APB). Such assessment incorporates all sources of program acquisition cost, such as large active contracts, small contracts, government costs, future contracts, completed contracts, and management reserve. This assessment may incorporate analyses of individual contracts, such as those performed in the Contract Performance assessment, but take a broader, more cumulative view of program costs. Also, various cost estimates such as Service Cost Positions or the Cost Assessment and Program Evaluation Independent Cost Estimate (CAPE ICE) are considered, when possible. Specific assessment methods vary by program, but may include examining the realism of projected unit costs given trends in actual costs, comparisons of spending profiles to previous plans, or a determination of whether outlined in the Better Buying Power initiatives are also evaluated, including updates on the progress of initiatives that would drive costs to should-cost levels. For programs that are early in the acquisition life cycle, and that therefore do not have data to support cost evaluations, the assessment considers the program's key assumptions, or Framing Assumptions.

Program Schedule. Assess how the program is progressing towards meeting schedule objectives, including meeting the schedule requirements of interdependent programs. The primary standards for measuring schedule performance are the APB's milestone dates. More detailed information is required to evaluate progress toward these milestones, including the contract schedule analysis. Tools that can be applied to a schedule assessment include traditional analysis of variances and critical path for a program-level Integrated Master Schedule (IMS) or equivalent, as well as a review of the program's history.

System Performance. Assess whether the program is on track to meet the required system performance objectives, thresholds, and other important performance requirements. This includes evaluation of current performance estimates and trends against program Key Performance Parameters (KPPs), Key System Attributes (KSAs), and the requirements allocated from these standards. Select critical elements that are most important to program success, that contain the largest elements of perceived risk, or have historically been problematic on other programs and evaluate progress against plans and requirements. The evaluation includes progress toward design goals as well as developmental and operational test results as they become available. The analysis evaluates reported performance regarding the planned Reliability Growth Curve and compares assessment and/or performance results to reliability growth expectations.

Contract Performance. Assess the cost and schedule performance of the program's individual contracts. Include analysis of the government's exposure to cost, schedule, and technical risk in each contract. Earned value tools and Integrated Master Schedule (IMS) analyses are the primary tools for evaluating contract performance, but are supplemented by other data and analyses. Evaluate a contract's current cost and schedule performance, effort remaining, and estimates to complete, while also observing trends that may imply changes in future performance. Key metrics used to determine current contract health include Cost Performance Index (CPI), Schedule Performance Index (SPI), variances, Baseline Execution Index (BEI), and Critical Path Length Index (CPLI). Assessments evaluate the realism of various Estimates at Completion (EAC) based on To Complete Performance Index (TCPI) analysis and conclusions reached through the performance and trend analyses. Monitor non-Earned Value Management (EVM) data such as staffing levels, labor rates, achievement of milestones and technical goals, and other project-specific metrics, as appropriate. Where contract costs exceed ceiling prices, estimate the overruns and their implications for future contract costs.

Management. Assess the extent to which the program has adequate management structure and resources, appropriate contractual mechanisms and progress, appropriate processes, and current data documentation.

Funding. Evaluate the extent to which the program is funded in the Future Years Defense Program (FYDP) to meet the funding requirements of the entire program, including all contracts, procurement of Government Furnished Equipment, and program office staffing and agreements with other government agencies for support, given current efficiencies and funding priorities.

Test and Evaluation. Assess the planning, execution, and results of developmental and operational Test and Evaluation (T&E) activities, and describe the implications of T&E outcomes on overall program performance.

Sustainment. Assess the adequacy of the logistics and personnel systems to support the program throughout its life cycle. Sustainment assessments include evaluation of system characteristics such as availability and reliability, as well as manpower, personnel, and training.

Interoperability/Information Security (IS). Assess issues that may affect the program's ability to integrate functions and capabilities with other interdependent systems, or affect its ability to maintain appropriate information security.

Threat. Assess changes in the current operation threat based on the most recent intelligence community information.

Production. Assess the extent to which the program is capable of meeting the required production goals, taking into account demonstrated performance, emerging issues, and the health of the industrial base.

International Program Aspects. The international aspects of a program are a key consideration in the Defense Acquisition Management Framework and may be present at any point in time (pre-systems acquisition, systems acquisition, and sustainment) and include capability determination, technology development, system development, production, and operations and support. The assessor derives and employs relevant information from literature and enabling government, commercial, and academic services, and determines its influence on DoD budgets and programs. The assessor also analyzes and evaluates the impacts of policies on managing international programs.

For additional information, see the DAES Assessment Guidance and accompanying DAES Desk Book, which are available for download from the DAMIR website, under the Guidance link/DAES Guidance/Assessment Guidance.

CH 1–5.2 Compliance Considerations

DoDI 5000.02 and its enclosures contain programmatic expectations established by statute, regulation, and acquisition policy that are to guide program management planning in functional areas across the life cycle of the acquired system.

CH 1–5.3 Acquisition Documentation Development Tools

The following subsections provide resources for PMs and acquisition leadership in the development and use of documentation, including content required and timing.

CH 1–5.3.1 Milestone Document Identification Tool

To assist program management and acquisition professionals in filtering through statutory and regulatory information requirements, DoD maintains the Milestone Document Identification (MDID) tool that allows for a collection of information requirement results based on user-selected filtering of program acquisition category (and subcategory type, if applicable), life-cycle event, and the source of the information requirement (Statutory or Regulatory). Each resulting information requirement is linked to an information card containing pertinent content and linked sources (Description/ Definition, Notes, Approval Authority, and DAG Topic Discussions). A capability is provided for ad-hoc filtering by keyword. DoDI 5000.02 policy takes precedence over the MDID tool.

The MDID tool allows the filtering of Statutory and Regulatory information requirements, at specific milestones or decision points, and for specific ACAT levels or subcategory type (i.e., Defense Business System [DBS], Urgent Operational Needs Statement [UONS]) for the information requirements identified in DoDI 5000.02 (Encl. 1, Tables 2, 5, 6; Encl. 13, Table 10). When this source Instruction is updated or re-issued, or an applicable Directive-Type Memorandum (DTM) or policy memorandum is issued, the MDID tool is updated. The MDID capability is a content evolving tool and is critiqued by the Acquisition Community through a built-in feedback function.

The filtered results of the MDID tool indicate the potential Statutory and Regulatory information requirements that are considered "as probable information requirements" for the program. After this initial determination of Statutory and Regulatory requirements, a determination needs to be made by the Acquisition chain of command on the applicability of the statutory requirements, and if applicable, how they would be addressed or documented.

CH 1–5.4 Defense Acquisition Documentation and Data Repositories

The following subsections describe repositories of information and data, as well as analysis capabilities for awareness of, and use by, the PM and acquisition leadership.

CH 1–5.4.1 Defense Acquisition Visibility Environment

The Defense Acquisition Visibility Environment (DAVE) is the DoD's authoritative source of enterprise-wide acquisition data and capabilities for program oversight, analysis, and decision-making, as well as data integration and longitudinal analysis across and among programs.

The key capabilities DAVE currently provides are listed in the following sections. Access for authorized users is available at DAVE [CAC Required, Restricted Access]. Contact osd.dave@mail.mil for access information.

CH 1–5.4.1.1 Acquisition Data Management

The following paragraphs present acquisition data sets and how they can be used.

CH 1–5.4.1.1.1 Acquisition Visibility Data Framework

As DoD moves more and more to a data-focused approach to acquisition decision-making, program offices and analysts throughout the Department need a reference to clarify and explain the authoritative data used in that process. The Acquisition Visibility Data Framework (AVDF) is that resource.

The AVDF enables the Department to understand the data and how it should be used, which is the foundation for reporting, analysis, and decision-making. The AVDF provides the foundation for DAVE and establishes the data standard for DoD, integrating and providing context for all existing AV data components. The AVDF has two sections: the Acquisition Visibility Data Matrix (AVDM) and Use Cases, which are described below. The AVDF is accessible to authorized DAVE users.

CH 1–5.4.1.1.2 Acquisition Visibility Data Matrix

The Acquisition Visibility Data Matrix (AVDM) is the core of acquisition data management for the Department. It answers questions such as, "What data is available?" and "How is the data defined?" It documents data definitions; data owners; and associated laws, regulations, policies, guidance, and other information that enables PMO personnel and acquisition analysts to understand the 500+ data elements under the Office of the Under Secretary of Defense for Acquisition, Technology, and Logistics (OUSD(AT&L)) governance. Additional data may be added, as needed, through the Acquisition Visibility Steering Group (AVSG). The governed data support Defense acquisition decision-making on major programs. The AVDM is accessible to authorized DAVE users.

CH 1–5.4.1.1.3 Acquisition Visibility Data Framework Use Cases

In the AVDF, Use Cases are closely tied to the AVDM information. They answer the question, "Where is the AVDM data used?"—documenting the context within which the data are provided or used. The AVDF includes the following Use Cases. Additional Use Cases may be added as needed.

- Acquisition Program Baseline (APB)
- Budget Estimate Submission (BES)
- Defense Acquisition Board (DAB)

- Defense Acquisition Executive Summary (DAES)
- Major Automated Information System (MAIS) Annual Report (MAR)
- Obligations and Expenditures
- President's Budget (PB)
- Program Objectives Memorandum (POM)
- Selected Acquisition Report (SAR)
- Selected Acquisition Report (SAR) Baseline

The Use Cases [CAC Required, Restricted Access] are accessible to authorized DAVE users.

CH 1–5.4.1.1.4 Data Opportunities Visualization Capability

Acquisition Visibility Data Opportunities Visualization capability provides information about data used in the Defense Acquisition process. The searchable table view lists 80+ data sources that can answer questions about acquisition data for the Department. Additional acquisition data sources may be added as identified. It provides details about each data source, including the capability it offers, where to access it, the data it offers, who owns it, who can access it, and who is the point of contact for access. For a subset of the data sources, additional information is provided, including issues associated with accessing the information, whether it is an authoritative source, and the composition of users. AV Data Opportunities Visualization also offers a tree view, which allows for a more visual exploration of acquisition data sources. Data Opportunities Visualization [CAC Required, Restricted Access] is accessible to authorized DAVE users.

CH 1–5.4.2 Defense Acquisition Reporting Capabilities

The Department provides capabilities to support PMOs in reporting program status and plans to the DoD Components and OSD, and to support the USD(AT&L) in reporting program status to Congress.

CH 1–5.4.2.1 Defense Acquisition Management Information Retrieval

Defense Acquisition Management Information Retrieval (DAMIR) is the reporting mechanism and authoritative source for data associated with the following reports: the Defense Acquisition Executive Summary (DAES) and associated Program Office and OSD assessments, Selected Acquisition Reports (SAR), SAR Baseline, Acquisition Program Baselines (APBs), MAIS Annual Reports (MAR), and MAIS Original Estimates. DAMIR [CAC Required, Restricted Access] is only accessible to authorized users.

To request an account, please contact the Organizational Point of Contact. If the organization POC is unknown, e-mail DAMIR Support at osd.pentagon.ousd-atl.mbx.damir-support@mail.mil and provide name and organization. For technical issues, send questions to osd.damir@mail.mil, or call 703-679-5345.

CH 1–5.4.2.2 Affordability Capability

The Affordability capability is the authoritative source for Program Current Estimates, which PMs report based on Program Objectives Memorandum (POM) or President's Budget (PB) reports in the Defense Acquisition Management Information Retrieval (DAMIR). In addition, it is also the repository for Acquisition and Sustainment Goals or CAPS, which are initially recorded in Acquisition Decision Memoranda. Affordability is accessible to authorized DAMIR users at AFFORDABILITY [CAC Required, Restricted Access]. For questions about access, contact osd.damir@mail.mil, or call 703-679-5345.

CH 1–5.4.2.3 Earned Value Management Central Repository

The Integrated Program Management Reports (IPMRs) for all Acquisition Category (ACAT) I programs are submitted directly to the Earned Value Management Central Repository (EVM-CR) by the reporting contractors. The EVM-CR, which is managed by the PARCA Deputy Director for EVM, is the sole addressee on the Contract Data Requirements Lists for these reports.

The EVM-CR provides:

- Centralized reporting, collection, and distribution of Key Acquisition EVM data for ACAT IC & ID (MDAP) and ACAT IAM (MAIS) programs.
- A reliable source of authoritative EVM data and access for OSD, the Services, and the DoD Components
- Housing for the IPMR and Contract Funds Status Report (CFSR) as well as the Contract Performance Reports (CPRs) and the Integrated Master Schedules (IMS) for legacy contracts. Contractor-submitted reports are reviewed and approved by Program Management Offices prior to publication.
- Approximately 110 active ACAT IA, IC, and ID programs comprised of close to 700 contracts/efforts are currently reporting. The EVM-CR also houses over 40 historical programs with approximately 500 contracts/efforts

EVM-CR [CAC Required, Restricted Access] is accessible to authorized users.

For questions about access, contact the Cost Assessment Data Enterprise (CADE) help desk at CADESupport@Tecolote.com or 253-564-1979 Ext. 1.

CH 1–5.4.2.4 Defense Acquisition Information Repository (AIR)

Acquisition Information Repository (AIR) is the Department of Defense authoritative repository for final, approved milestone information and other decision documents for pre-Major Defense Acquisition Programs, un-baselined Major Automated Information Systems, Acquisition Category (ACAT) ID, ACAT IAM, and Special Interest Programs. AIR also supports document storage and retrieval for ACAT IC and IAC, ACAT II, and ACAT III programs. AIR is available on both the Non-Secure Internet Protocol Router Network (NIPRnet) and Secret Internet Protocol Router Network (SIPRNet). AIR facilitates timely access to accurate, authoritative, and reliable information, and supports acquisition oversight, accountability, and decision-making throughout the DoD for effective and efficient delivery of warfighter capabilities.

The implementation of AIR requires that milestone documents be uploaded to the system within 5 business days of their approval. Offices of Primary Responsibility (OPRs) are responsible for loading documents, appropriately marking documents, setting document permissions, and managing access to their documents. It is important that OPRs load documents in a timely fashion and with appropriate accessibility.

All AIR users are able to view the entire list of documents uploaded to AIR for all programs through the AIR Structured Metadata Search function. Access to view/download specific documents is dependent on the view permissions set by the document uploader. The system provides the capability for every user to request access to a document that has been uploaded with restricted view permissions.

AIR is available to registered users. AIR registration is available to DoD and DoD Contractors.

CH 1–5.4.3 Analytical Capabilities

This Section provides an overview of information and data analytics.

CH 1–5.4.3.1 Affordability Capability

The Affordability capability supports both reporting and analysis, and contains the following data:

- Acquisition and Sustainment Goals or Caps, which are initially recorded in Acquisition Decision Memoranda.
- Current estimates recorded in Affordability by the PMs for Major Defense Acquisition Programs (MDAPs) and Major Automated Information System (MAIS) programs

Affordability information can help Milestone Decision Authorities (MDAs) and their staffs compare program current estimates with their caps or goals, and assist DoD Components and OSD in planning and budgeting. Refer to CH 1–5.4.2.3., Earned Value Management Central Repository (EVM-CR), for current information on MDAP and MAIS programs with earned value reporting.

CH 1–5.4.3.2 Standard Data Queries

DAMIR provides 80+ Standard Data Queries—views of the data reported in DAMIR. These queries are grouped in the following categories and provide support for cross-program analysis:

- Constant Year
- Strategic Planning
- Contracts
- Data Quality
- DAES Reports
- Funding and Appropriations
- Breaches
- Program Information
- MAIS Unique Reports
- Affordability

Standard Data Queries are available to authorized DAMIR users from the home page of DAMIR.

All users have access to queries related to SARs. For questions about access, please contact osd.damir@mail.mil, or call 703-679-5345.

Users may request a one-time report or a query of the DAMIR database by sending the request to osd.damir@mail.mil. Results from queries are delivered in an Excel spreadsheet.

CH 1–5.4.3.3 Portfolio Views

The Portfolio View section of DAMIR provides dashboards, which are graphical representations of the Selected Acquisition Report (SAR) and Defense Acquisition Executive Summary (DAES) data for a selected portfolio of programs. Users can select from standard portfolios or create their own.

Portfolio Views are accessible to authorized DAMIR users from the home page of DAMIR [CAC Required, Restricted Access].

CH 1–5.4.4 Dashboards

The following Sections describe the available dashboards:

CH 1–5.4.4.1 Significant Acquisition Watchlist (SAW) Dashboards

The Significant Acquisition Watchlist (SAW) dashboards present views of Defense Acquisition Executive Summary (DAES) data for Major Defense Acquisition Programs (MDAPs), Major Automated Information System (MAIS) programs, and Special Interest programs to support acquisition analysis and decision-making. The SAW provides information regarding DAES Assessment ratings, Earned Value (EV) data, and performance against Acquisition Program Baseline (APB) thresholds to better facilitate analysis. Additionally, the SAW provides the capability to click through to supporting program data in DAMIR.

SAW provides the following data views:

- **Program Assessments.** Program office, DoD Component personnel, and DAB members and advisors who participate in the DAES have a consolidated view of Program Management Office and OSD assessment ratings, contract information, and milestone information, which provides a helpful starting point for discussion of program status.
- **Contractor Performance.** Program Management Office, DoD Component personnel, and DAB members and advisors who participate in the DAES can see a quick snapshot of earned value information, by contract.
- **Assessment Change Indicator and Status**. Program Management Office, DoD Component personnel, and DAB members and advisors who participate in the DAES can see an overview of the status of the programs in the portfolio, including differences and changes that may be indicators that deeper analysis and explanation are needed.

CH 1–5.4.4.2 Contract Dashboard

The Contract Dashboard has three views:

- **Contract Location.** OSD and DoD Component analysts can understand what state economies are supported by programs and contracts, which may be useful in communicating with Congress
- **Contract Performance.** OSD and DoD Component analysts can understand the performance of high-priority contracts, which may provide insight useful in managing vendors.
- **Contractors.** OSD and DoD Component analysts can understand what contractors support what programs, and what DoD Component owns each contract, which may help identify potential economies of scale or partnership opportunities.

The top-level Contract Dashboard provides all three individual dashboards in one screen.

CH 1–5.4.4.3 Cost Dashboard

The Cost Dashboard provides the following:

- **Cost Variance Total Current Change.** OSD and DoD Component analysts can see a graphical representation of Cost Variance changes for their portfolios, by category, which may highlight issues that need to be addressed or factors that need to be considered in management and planning.
- **Current Estimate Analysis.** OSD and DoD Component analysts can understand programs' portion of total estimated costs, by appropriation category, which may provide insight for planning.
- **Unit Cost by % Change.** OSD and DoD Component analysts can understand the extent to which programs' unit cost has changed in comparison to their baselines, which may highlight issues that need to be addressed or factors that need to be considered in management and planning.

CH 1–5.4.4.4 Funding Dashboard

The Funding Dashboard provides the following:

- **Acquisition Funding Projection.** OSD and DoD Component analysts can see how funding for programs is expected to change over time, which may provide insight about programs' life cycles and OSD priorities.
- **Sunk Funding.** OSD and DoD Component analysts can see what funding has been used and what funding remains on programs, which provides insight for planning.

CH 1–5.4.4.5 Schedule Dashboard

The Schedule Dashboard provides:

- Major Schedule Milestones. OSD and DoD Components have a quick reference and graphic depiction of major milestones for a portfolio, which provides a high-level understanding of program history and plans.

CH 1–5.4.5 Earned Value Analysis

Earned Value Analysis (EVA) is a suite of earned value charts and graphs designed to visually illustrate a contract's cost and schedule performance. It also serves as a decision support tool that displays Earned Value trends and highlights ranges of Estimates at Completion (EACs) used to inform leadership of the contract's overall health and risk. EVA [CAC Required, Restricted Access] is accessible to authorized DAMIR users.

CH 1–5.4.6 Minimum/Maximum/Economical Production Rate

The Minimum/Maximum/ Economical Production Rate (MME) capability provides analysts quick production efficiency assessments of equipment procurements projected in the President's Budget. MME [CAC Required, Restricted Access] is accessible to authorized DAVE users.

CH 1–5.4.7 Obligations and Expenditures

The Obligations and Expenditures (O&E) capability provides analysts with insight into financial execution performance of Major Defense Acquisition Programs (MDAPs) and Major Automated Information System (MAIS) programs. The capability also offers the ability to analyze by budget line item. O&E [CAC Required, Restricted Access] is accessible to authorized DAVE users.

CH 1–5.4.8 Cost and Software Data Reporting System

The Cost Assessment Data Enterprise (CADE) is a secure web-based information management system that hosts Contractor Cost Data Reporting (CCDR) and Software Resources Data Reporting (SRDR) repositories for all acquisition programs with Cost and Software Data Reporting System (CSDR) contract requirements. The CSDR-Submit Review (SR) provides a collaborative data requirements planning feature, centralized reporting, collection, and distribution of key CSDR data, and supporting CSDR materials for current MDAP and MAIS programs.

CAPE's Defense Cost and Resource Center (DCARC) is the team that plans, validates, and manages the CSDR requirements for the DoD while working with many different stakeholders, including the Service Cost Centers, Program Management Offices (PMOs) and Systems Commands (SYSCOMs). The CAPE Deputy Director of Cost Analysis is the approval authority for CSDRs.

DACIMS (Defense Automated Cost Information Management System) is an application within CADE that hosts scanned images of historical contractor cost data reports for legacy MDAPs and MAIS, dating back to 1966. DACIMS also contains supporting CSDR materials such as CWBS (Contractor Work Breakdown Structure) dictionaries and CSDR validation memos. DACIMS can be accessed via the CADE Portal.

CH 1–5.4.8.1 Cost Assessment Data Enterprise

The Cost Assessment Data Enterprise (CADE) is an OSD CAPE initiative with the goal of increasing analyst productivity and effectiveness by collecting, organizing, and displaying data in an integrated single web-based application. CADE provides government analysts with a command and control website housing seamless integration of authoritative source data, which are easily searchable and retrievable. CADE increases analyst productivity and effectiveness while improving data quality, reporting compliance, and source data transparency.

Another CADE goal is to provide common data visualization methods to help depict each program's unique story; a task which previously took months to create. CADE offers the analyst a reduction in the time spent on ad hoc data collection and validation, allowing more time for in-depth, meaningful analysis in support of the DoD's mission.

Full access is available for government analysts. Support contractors may access those data for which they have a valid Non-Disclosure Agreement (NDA) with the weapons contractor. Further information may be found at the CADE Portal.

CH 1–5.4.9 DoD Resources Data Warehouse

The DoD Resources Data Warehouse (DRDW) is OSD CAPE's authoritative web-based solution for accessing and analyzing reports and data associated with the DoD Future Years Defense Program (FYDP), DoD Budget, Selected Acquisition Reports (SAR), and Defense Acquisition Executive Summary (DAES) reports from the 1960s to the present.

Using the Business Intelligence tools available at the DRDW, DoD analysts can conduct ad hoc analyses regarding Program/Budget dollar, manpower, and forces data across a variety of areas, including major headquarters' activities, space, intelligence, and the IT budget. Besides researching Comptroller's Procurement dollars and quantities, analysts can also conduct ad hoc analysis on MDAP data, including Funding, Baseline, and Unit Cost.

OSD CAPE conducts a 1-day course regarding the use of the Business Intelligence tools needed to build queries, tables, pivots, charts, and reports from DRDW data. The course includes a detailed explanation of the DoD resource data structure and the processes used to develop a variety of Title X resource documents. This is an 8-hour block of instruction, accredited in the DoD Financial Management Certification Program.

DRDW can be accessed via the Secret Internet Protocol Router Network (SIPRnet) at OSD CAPE's portal. Once there, as part of creating an OSD CAPE EXPRESSO account, request DRDW access.

Chapter 1 Supplement—International Acquisition and Exportability
CH 1-S–1. Purpose

The purpose of this Supplement is to provide detailed information regarding the International Acquisition & Exportability (IA&E) concepts summarized in the Defense Acquisition Guidebook (DAG) Chapter 1 – Program Management. The term "IA&E" in DoDI 5000.02 is used to encompass all of the elements of international involvement in a Department of Defense (DoD) program – exploring foreign solutions, international cooperative programs (ICPs), foreign sales or transfers, defense exportability design and development, and Technology Security and Foreign Disclosure (TSFD).

CH 1-S–2. Background

Program management should strive to identify and address IA&E considerations during each phase of the acquisition life cycle. Program management decisions on the extent of potential allied and friendly nation participation in systems development—as well as efforts to incorporate Defense Exportability Features (DEF) in DoD systems to facilitate future sales and transfers—should be addressed as early as possible. Given the wide array of U.S. laws, regulations, and policies governing these IA&E areas, and the multiple DoD and U.S. Government organizations that oversee them, achieving successful IA&E outcomes requires a comprehensive, integrated approach to international acquisition activities by program management during each phase of the Defense Acquisition System.

Within this Supplement, program management can find further information on the following key aspects of IA&E:

- Types of international acquisition involvement.
- Tools available to identify and develop international acquisition programs.
- Incorporation of international acquisition considerations into program acquisition strategies.
- Procedures used to establish international agreements.
- Details on Security Assistance/Foreign Military Sales policies

- International logistics agreements and related cooperative logistics activities
- Technology Security and Foreign Disclosure processes.
- Program protection documentation requirements.

CH 1-S–2.1 International Acquisition Involvement

International involvement in a DoD acquisition program include various forms of international acquisition activity such as exploring foreign solutions (often through international contracting activities); ICPs; and Foreign Sales or Transfers, as outlined in CH 1–4.2.8.

Statutory requirements and DoD Guidance requires that program management consider international acquisition involvement across the acquisition life cycle, in order to meet U.S. national security objectives to enhance coalition interoperability, decrease costs to the DoD and taxpayer through greater economies of scale, and improve the international competitiveness of U.S. defense systems. In particular, DoDD 5000.01 (Encl. 1, para E.1.1.18) and DoDI 5000.02 (Encl. 2, para 7.a. (1)) require acquisition managers to consider international cooperation and exportability, develop systems that are interoperable with coalition partners, and identify potential technologies from both domestic and foreign sources. DoDI 2010.06 (para 3.a), addresses design efforts to enhance coalition interoperability. Statutory requirements in 10 USC 2431a (para (c)(2)(G)) and 10 USC 2350a (para (e)), require an IA&E assessment of a program's international involvement before the first milestone or decision point and at subsequent milestones.

A key goal of international acquisition is to reduce weapons system acquisition costs through cooperative development, production and support ICPs, Foreign Military Sales (FMS), and/or Direct Commercial Sales (DCS). Program managers should consider international acquisition involvement to the maximum extent feasible consistent with core business practices and with the overall political, economic, technological, and national security goals of the United States.

CH 1-S–2.2 Exploring Foreign Solutions

A potential viable alternative business approach to development of a U.S. item is the acquisition of foreign defense equipment to meet DoD capability requirements established through DoD's Joint Capabilities Integration and Development System (JCIDS) process. Per DoDD 5000.01 (Encl. 1, para E1.1.18), program managers first consider the procurement or modification of commercially available products, services, and technologies from domestic or international sources, or the development of dual-use technologies, before proceeding with other acquisition options. Prior to the Materiel Development Decision (MDD), program management conducts an initial IA&E assessment to determine whether there are potential foreign solutions that would meet U.S. capability requirements:

- Are there allied or friendly nation systems that may potentially meet the U.S. requirements, either as-is or with modifications?
- Are there allied and friendly nations with similar operational requirements that either have or are actively considering initiation of a program with similar objectives, providing a basis for potential ICP participation?
- Are there leading-edge capabilities or technologies in other countries that should be evaluated for incorporation into the program through either ICP participation or international contracting? (See CH1-S-2.2 and CH1-S-5 for further details on ICPs.)

While individual acquisition program offices can conduct evaluations of potential foreign solutions with their own resources, the Office of the Secretary of Defense (OSD) Foreign Comparative Testing (FCT) program offers a structured and funded means for evaluating the suitability of purchasing foreign non-developmental items to fulfill DoD capability requirements, in lieu of developing a similar U.S. item. See the OSD Comparative Technology Office Portal for additional details on the FCT program.

CH 1-S–2.3 International Cooperative Programs

An ICP is any acquisition program or technology project that includes participation (e.g., cooperative development, cooperative production, coalition interoperability, and research and development) by the United States and one or more foreign nations through an international agreement during any phase of a system's life cycle.

The key objectives of ICPs are to reduce weapon systems acquisition costs through cooperative development, production, product improvement and support, and to enhance interoperability with allied and friendly nations. Program management efforts to identify ICP opportunities before entering into a formal acquisition program may be challenging, but such activities can provide DoD with potentially high payoffs in future cost savings, increased interoperability, operational burden-sharing, and more affordable life-cycle costs.

Program management should assess the system's ICP prospects based on known and projected allied/friendly nation capability requirements, plans for development of similar systems in the global defense market, previous foreign purchases of similar U.S. systems undergoing major upgrades, and other indicators of prospective foreign demand for the new system. If the system is not restricted as a U.S.-only system, the program manager must plan for export to safeguard critical program information (CPI) and any other controlled or classified information. DoDI 5000.02 (Encl. 2, para 7.b.) establishes overall ICP program management requirements.

In deciding whether to pursue an ICP, the program manager consults with their respective DoD Component International Programs Organization (IPO) (i.e., Deputy Assistant Secretary of the Army for Defense Exports and Cooperation, Navy International Programs Office, Deputy Under Secretary of the Air Force for International Affairs), and consider the following criteria:

- Ability of the partner nation(s) to participate in an ICP, taking into account TSFD considerations, where there are clear DoD benefits (e.g. interoperability, cost savings, operational burden-sharing, and political-military benefits);
- Ability to establish an ICP management structure in the international agreement where the designated program manager (U.S. or foreign) is fully responsible and accountable for the cost, schedule, and performance of the resulting system; and
- Demonstrated DoD Component and partner nation(s') willingness to fully fund their share of the ICP.

Formulation of ICPs normally requires harmonization of U.S. and coalition requirements, cost and work sharing, intellectual property rights, and technology transfer (including TSFD and exportability design considerations), among others. Program managers, working closely with their DoD Component's IPO, are encouraged to follow the procedures outlined in CH1-S-6.1 to establish international agreements for ICPs with allied and friendly nations, the procedures in CH1-S-9 for TSFD considerations, and the guidance in CH1-S-4 regarding designing in exportability as part of ICP program efforts. Once an ICP is established through a signed international agreement, the DoD Component remains responsible for preparation and approval of most statutory, regulatory, and contracting reports and milestone requirements, as listed in DoDI 5000.02 (Encl. 1, Table 2) for system-related ICP international agreements. Prior to terminating or substantially reducing U.S. participation in Major Defense Acquisition Program ICPs with signed International Agreements (IAs), DoDI 5000.02 (Encl. 2, para 7.b(2)) requires DoD Components to notify and obtain the approval of the Defense Acquisition Executive.

While most of the funding for cooperative Research, Development, Test and Evaluation (RDT&E) activities may need to be provided from program funding, program management should explore the availability of additional parallel funding for these efforts through the Office of the Under Secretary of Defense for Acquisition, Technology and Logistics/International Cooperation Coalition Warfare Program (CWP) and/or the Military Department's International Cooperative Research and Development (ICR&D) programs. See CH1-S-5.5 for details about the CWP.

Additional information on ICP planning and execution considerations may be found on Defense Acquisition University's International Acquisition Management Community of Practice (ICoP) website.

CH 1-S–2.4 Foreign Sales and Transfers

Sales and transfers refer to the transfer of U.S.-origin defense articles and services to allies, friendly countries, and authorized international organizations under a variety of authorized programs. The following subsections provide guidance on pursuing the various activities.

Per 10 USC 2431a (c)(2)(G) and 10 USC 2350a(e), program managers should assess the system's prospects for foreign sales and transfers of the system based on a worldwide inventory of similar systems, U.S. share of the market, previous foreign purchases of similar U.S. systems, and prospective foreign demand for the new system. If this assessment indicates that there is a reasonable potential for future foreign sales and transfers, program managers also assess whether to explore designing in exportability. Types of foreign sales that may be considered include FMS, DCS, Hybrid FMS/DCS/ICP programs, and Building Partner Capacity (BPC) programs. Decisions about designing in defense exportability made during the Materiel Solution Analysis (MSA) and Technology Maturation and Risk Reduction (TMRR) phases generally define the nature of the entire program. Once the program enters the Engineering and Manufacturing Development (EMD) phase, it is difficult to adopt major IA&E-related programmatic changes without significant schedule or cost adjustments.

DoD policy states that the U.S. Government should agree to sell through FMS or DCS only those major defense equipment systems that have satisfactorily completed U.S. Operational Test and Evaluation (OT&E) required prior to approval of full rate production. An exception to the policy requires a Yockey Waiver, described further in CH1-S-7.4 on Yockey Waivers.

CH 1-S–3. Documenting International Acquisition and Exportability in the Acquisition Strategy

As described in CH 1–4.2.8, program management should document their planned IA&E efforts in the International Involvement section of the program's Acquisition Strategy as required by 10 USC 2431a(para (c)(2)(G)) and 10 USC 2350a (para (e)), as amended. As part of this process, program management should update the International Involvement section with an analysis of IA&E requirements and foreign sales potential at each respective Milestone. A summary of requirements for each Milestone is illustrated in DoDI 5000.02 (Encl. 1, Table 2). Table 1 shows the IA&E planning actions that occur during each acquisition phase and may be considered for incorporation into the program IMP/IMS.

Table S-1: IA&E Actions during the Acquisition Phases

Acquisition Phase	IA&E Actions
Pre-Materiel Solution Analysis	• Conduct an initial IA&E assessment to identify potential existing foreign solutions, ICP opportunities, foreign technology, or potential for future foreign sales. • Review Initial Capabilities Document (ICD) to identify potential coalition requirements, and potential foreign market to gain an understanding of coalition interoperability and exportability requirements.
Materiel Solution Analysis	• Assess procurement or modifications of existing U.S. or foreign solutions as part of the OSD CAPE Analysis of Alternatives prior to starting a new development program. • Assess program's potential for international cooperative research, development, production, logistics support, interoperability, and defense exportability.

Acquisition Phase	IA&E Actions
	• Update the program's IA&E assessment to identify specific existing or projected international agreements(s), Joint Requirements Oversight Council (JROC)-validated coalition interoperability requirements, international markets, and potential program protection issues and requirements. • Use the program's Acquisition Strategy at Milestone A to advise the Milestone Decision Authority if the program should address international involvement (e.g., foreign solutions, coalition interoperability, ICP participation, future foreign sales, and design for exportability) during TMRR.
Technology Maturity and Risk Reduction	• Consider establishing one or more mutually beneficial system development ICPs. • Consider establishing cooperative RDT&E projects under the terms of existing RDT&E MOUs with allied and friendly nations. • Continue TSFD planning and approval activities. • Conduct defense exportability feasibility study and design efforts. • Conduct initial FMS planning efforts. • Use the program's Acquisition Strategy at Milestone B to advise the Milestone Decision Authority which international involvement efforts should be planned and implemented during EMD.
Engineering and Manufacturing Development	• Continue TSFD and export control efforts in support of existing ICPs, as appropriate. • Complete defense exportability design efforts. • Establish initial FMS arrangements in the latter stages of EMD and Low Rate Initial Production (LRIP), as appropriate. • Use the program's Acquisition Strategy at Milestone C to advise the Milestone Decision Authority which international involvement efforts should be planned and implemented during Production & Deployment phase. • For programs with substantial international involvement, develop an initial International Business Plan (IBP).
Production and Deployment	• Use the updated IBP to achieve synergies and economies of scale through a combination of DoD and foreign recurring production procurement requirements or non-recurring product improvement investment. • Pursue appropriate type(s) of ICPs and foreign sales/transfer arrangements throughout the program's life-cycle.
Operations and Support	• Use the updated IBP to achieve synergies and economies of scale affordability benefits through a combination or coordination of DoD and foreign Operations and Support (O&S) non-recurring investment and recurring O&S phase procurement requirements. • Enhance logistics support for foreign operators of U.S. systems through logistics support ICPs, FMS/DCS, or Acquisition and Cross-Servicing Agreements throughout the program's lifecycle.

CH 1-S–3.1 Acquisition Strategy International Involvement

The following information (at a minimum) is expected in the Acquisition Strategy International Involvement section:

- Any limitations on foreign contractors being allowed to participate at the prime contractor level.
- International Cooperation
  - Summary of any plans for cooperative programs.

- o Summary or listing of any existing and/or projected international agreements (e.g. Treaties, cooperative programs, MOUs, project arrangements, etc.).
  - o Cooperative Opportunities Document required elements from 10 USC 2350a (para (e)), as amended:
    - Identify whether there is a requirement for the system or subsystems to be interoperable with friendly nations, partners, or organizations.
    - Summarize whether projects similar to the one under consideration by DoD are in development or production by one or more friendly nations, partners, or organizations.
    - Advantages and disadvantages of seeking a cooperative development program with regard to program timing, developmental and life cycle costs, and technology sharing.
    - Recommendation on whether DoD should pursue a cooperative development program for the system.
- Defense Exportability
  - o Describe whether the program is planning or conducting an OUSD (AT&L)-funded or acquisition program-funded DEF feasibility study of the foreign market, technical feasibility, and costs associated with designing in defense exportability.
  - o Summarize the interim or final results of any such study and plans to incorporate DEF into final designs.
- Sales and Transfers
  - o Specify the potential or plans for foreign sales and transfers, the likelihood of these sales (High, Medium, or Low), and the countries involved.
  - o Include whether previous generations of the system have been sold and to which countries they were sold.
  - o For those programs with existing or potential foreign sales and transfers, specify the projected impact (risk and benefits) to the program's cost, schedule, and performance of these foreign sales.

To implement their Acquisition Strategy, DoD acquisition programs with substantial international involvement should also consider developing an International Business Plan (IBP) prior to Milestone C to ensure effective integration of domestic and international acquisition efforts throughout the program's life-cycle.

CH 1-S–4. Defense Exportability Integration

Defense Exportability Integration refers to DoD design and development activities pursued within the Defense Acquisition System to incorporate technology protection measures (also referred to as DEF) in initial designs—including the design and development of anti-tamper and differential capabilities—leading to production of one or more exportable system configurations for ICPs or foreign sales. Developing and incorporating defense exportability in initial designs facilitates timely and efficient implementation of future DoD cooperative programs or foreign sales and transfers. The primary objectives and benefits of designing and incorporating DEF in DoD systems include:

- Enhances interoperability with allied and friendly nations.
- Enables more timely and efficient ICPs and/or sales and transfers that leverage partner nations' defense investments to improve overall DoD system production and sustainment affordability through economies of scale savings.
- Provides flexibility for U.S. production and sustainment by extending active production and sustainment capability through ICPs and/or sales and transfers.
- Enables the capability to be available to allies and friendly countries earlier in production, thereby building partner capacity for operational burden-sharing sooner.

When considering whether to pursue defense exportability in a program, program managers may pursue DEF initiatives either under the sponsorship of the OUSD(AT&L) DEF Pilot Program, or outside of the pilot program using other sources of budgeted and authorized funding (e.g., program funding, DSCA Special Defense Acquisition Fund [SDAF], or ICP/FMS/BPC funding). Consistent with Milestone Decision Authority decisions at each milestone, these DEF efforts may include investigating the feasibility (from potential international market, cost, engineering, and exportability perspectives) of designing and developing differential capability and program protection measures for exportable configurations. These efforts would be conducted in the early phases of the acquisition process and continue throughout the program's life cycle. See the DEF Policy Implementation Memorandum and Guidelines (USD(AT&L)), April 9, 2015, for overarching DEF policy guidance and procedures.

CH 1-S–4.1 Defense Exportability Features (DEF) Pilot Program

Authorized by the Fiscal Year 2011 National Defense Authorization Act (Section 243, as amended), the DEF Pilot Program expanded the Department's authority to conduct defense exportability efforts by enabling selected programs to develop and incorporate technology protection features into designated systems during their research and development phases.

The DEF Pilot Program is administered by the Director, International Cooperation (IC), OUSD(AT&L). On an annual basis, DoD Components nominate systems to participate in the pilot program, which are reviewed and selected by OUSD(AT&L)/IC in coordination with the Assistant Secretary of Defense for Acquisition. Once selected as a DEF Pilot project, Program Offices may request funding from OUSD (AT&L)/IC to support an agreed industry cost-sharing contract to conduct feasibility or design studies to determine: the potential international market; technical feasibility; non-recurring engineering (NRE) costs; and return on investment of designing and implementing DEF in one or more future export variant(s).

AT&L DEF policy guidance for the pilot program can be found in the USD (AT&L) DEF Policy Implementation Memorandum and Guidelines (April 9, 2015). Amplifying Guidance on adjusted industry cost-sharing requests can be found in Supplemental Guidance for Reviewing and Submitting Industry Requests for an Adjusted Cost-Sharing Portion (February 23, 2016).

AT&L's Better Buying Power (BBP) 2.0 and 3.0 capitalized and expanded upon the DEF Pilot Program by including program consideration of "incorporation of DEF in initial designs" under its "Control Costs throughout the Product Life Cycle" section. Bringing greater attention to the benefits of considering exportability throughout the acquisition lifecycle, BBP 2.0 and 3.0 have helped to incentivize DoD program management to assess the feasibility of designing and developing technology protection features into systems early in their acquisition life cycle.

CH 1-S–4.2 Defense Exportability Implementation

The Milestone Decision Authority decision on whether to proceed with development of one or more exportable system versions may be influenced by the results of DEF feasibility studies and/or design efforts, and several factors that may include:

- Total NRE costs to design and develop exportability features.
- Availability of funding to pay the NRE costs (e.g., program funds, DSCA SDAF, ICP or foreign sales funding).
- A signed ICP international agreement.
- One or more signed FMS Letter(s) of Offer and Acceptance (LOA).
- A U.S. Government-approved export of proposed U.S. industry DCS transactions.

The Defense Acquisition University's International Community of Practice website provides best practice advice on planning and implementing Defense Exportability Integration efforts.

CH 1-S–5. Developing an International Program

As noted in CH 1–4.2.8.1, several mechanisms are available to program management to help identify potential ICP opportunities. The following subsections, as well as the International Cooperation in

Acquisition, Technology and Logistics (IC in AT&L) Handbook and the Defense Acquisition University's International Community of Practice website, provide additional information on DoD International Armaments Cooperation activities.

CH 1-S–5.1 International Fora

There are many international fora dedicated to discussing mutual armaments needs and early technology cooperative projects available to program management to gain information about potential ICP partners. NATO has a number of fora that may be useful to program management in identifying support for cooperative programs. In particular, the subsidiary "Main Armaments Groups" to NATO's Conference of National Armaments Directors are:

- NATO Army Armaments Group
- NATO Navy Armaments Group
- NATO Air Force Armaments Group

Program management may also explore cooperative opportunities through the NATO Science and Technology Organization, which conducts and promotes cooperative research and information exchange in NATO, and The Technical Cooperation Program with Australia, Canada, New Zealand, and the United Kingdom, which is dedicated to cooperation in conventional military technology development. In addition there are about 30 bilateral fora, such as the U.S.-Japan Systems and Technology Forum and the U.S./Canadian Armaments Cooperation Management Committee, that have a similar purpose. For the full list of international fora, see the IC in AT&L Handbook, Chapter 11.

Many Combatant Commands hold Science and Technology conferences to engage DoD, industry, and allied/friendly nations to discuss challenges and priorities in research and development. In addition, the MILDEP R&D offices (i.e. Office of Naval Research – Global; Army International Technology Centers; and Air Force Research Lab/Office of Scientific Research) also hold workshops with foreign partners to encourage science and technology information exchanges to assess potential cooperative programs.

CH 1-S–5.2 International Exchanges of Information and Personnel

Another useful source for identifying and formulating cooperative program opportunities that has proven useful to program management is the DoD RDT&E Information Exchange Program (IEP), which provides a standardized way of conducting bilateral science and technology information exchange (formerly called data exchange). The exchange of RDT&E information on a reciprocal basis with other countries is governed by DoDI 2015.4 (paras 4 - 5), "Defense RDT&E Information Exchange Program (IEP)."

Another source for identifying cooperative opportunities is the Defense Personnel Exchange Program, which includes the Engineer and Scientist Exchange Program (ESEP). Under the ESEP, an engineer or scientist is sent from the U.S. to a foreign lab or from a foreign defense organization or lab to a U.S. lab for a specific time period (typically 1-2 years) to be part of that national team.

Other exchanges that support ICPs are exchanges of personnel as Foreign Liaison Officers (FLOs). Under a FLO assignment, the military personnel continue to report to their nation while conducting information exchanges with the host nation to support understanding of common areas of interest and to support national defense planning.

CH 1-S–5.3 Exploratory Discussions

Before entering into an ICP, program management should pursue dialogue with potential partners. Such dialogue may be conducted through informal discussions; a forum (e.g., working group or steering committee) established under an existing international agreement; or as a stand-alone forum, all of which require appropriate disclosure guidance. In addition to disclosure guidance, these fora typically have a Terms of Reference. When the intent of a dialogue is to discuss the potential establishment of an international agreement, they are usually called "exploratory" or "technical" discussions. They are not "negotiations," since the provision or negotiation of international agreement text must first be formally authorized. See CH1-S-6 for further details regarding AT&L ICP international agreement procedures.

Exploratory discussions are characterized by the avoidance of any binding commitments and are focused on laying out details for a proposed project plan. Program management should seek and obtain any required TSFD release authority from their DoD Component Foreign Disclosure Office (FDO) prior to engaging in exploratory discussions involving sensitive or classified DoD information or technology. DoD contractors supporting program management in exploratory discussions should also ensure they seek and obtain any required U.S. Government export control approvals prior to participation (see CH1-S-9 and CH1-S-10 for further details regarding TSFD and export control).

CH 1-S–5.4 Science and Technology Cooperation

Typically, DoD programs and potential partner nations pursue Science and Technology (S&T) cooperative projects or conduct ICP feasibility studies before entering into an ICP systems acquisition.

- Program management may use S&T cooperative projects with allied and friendly nations in basic research or early technology development to develop, mature, or demonstrate defense technology. S&T cooperative projects typically focus on technology maturation or demonstration efforts that may or may not relate to a future acquisition program.
- ICP feasibility studies are used to explore the potential for future bilateral or multilateral ICPs. These studies provide nations considering participation in a future ICP with a programmatic and technical appraisal of the nations' ability to successfully develop and produce equipment for their operational forces.

Both S&T cooperative projects and feasibility studies are established and implemented through international agreements. See CH1-S-6 for details on international agreements related to ICPs.

CH 1-S–5.5 Coalition Warfare Program

The Coalition Warfare Program (CWP) is an Office of the Under Secretary of Defense, Acquisition, Technology and Logistics/International Cooperation (OUSD (AT&L)/IC program that funds cooperative research and development projects between the DoD and foreign partners that meet strategic, Combatant Command, and "coalition warfighter" needs. The CWP pursues projects that enhance and increase U.S. and coalition defense capabilities in support of the following DoD technological or political objectives:

- Collaboratively addressing strategic technology gaps for current and future missions.
- Developing interoperability solutions for coalition operations.
- Strengthening current defense partnerships and developing new relationships.

CWP projects take new technology and mature it into the next stage of development or prepare it for transition to operational forces. These projects may also form the basis for future cooperation with our international partners.

CH 1-S–6. International Agreement Procedures

U.S. law requires an International Agreement (IA) for all ICPs. An IA is any agreement concluded with one or more foreign governments including their agencies, instrumentalities, or political subdivisions, or with an international organization. The IA delineates the respective responsibilities of the U.S. and partner nation(s) and is considered binding under international law. CH1-S-6 discusses "streamlined agreement procedures" and resources.

Per DoDI 5000.02, (Encl. 2, para 7.b.(1)), DoD Components are encouraged to use the OUSD(AT&L) "streamlined agreement procedures" for all AT&L-related IAs to comply with the more extensive IA documentation and coordination requirements described in DoDD 5530.3 (para 5.1), "International

Agreements." MILDEPS and other DoD Components using these agreement procedures should obtain authority through this process from the Director, International Cooperation, OUSD (AT&L), prior to initiating negotiations on or concluding such IAs. Refer to the IC in AT&L Handbook for further guidance on International agreement procedures.

CH 1-S–6.1 Preparation, Documentation, Coordination, and Approval

The following procedures apply to DoD Components seeking to develop an IA:

Request for Authority to Develop and Negotiate (RAD) for all AT&L-related IAs:

- **Pre-RAD Actions.** As they plan and develop IAs, program staff members should consult with the cognizant DoD Component's International Programs Organization (i.e., Deputy Assistant Secretary of the Army for Defense Exports and Cooperation, Navy International Programs Office, Deputy Under Secretary of the Air Force for International Affairs), as well as its foreign disclosure, legal, contracting, comptroller, and other relevant offices, and follow the provisions of the most recent version of DoD IA Generator (DoD IA Generator) products (i.e., document templates, formats, and guidance). The supporting IPO should consult with OUSD (AT&L)/IC prior to the development of an IA to ensure the latest DoD IAG template or guidance is being applied. Programs should contact their responsible IPO for specific details about how to obtain and use the DoD IAG.
- **RAD Initiation.** Prior to providing a proposed IA text to the foreign partner (i.e., initiating formal IA negotiations), the DoD Component should prepare and obtain OUSD (AT&L)/IC approval of a RAD package. This package will be comprised of a cover memo signed by senior-level management requesting such authority, a Summary Statement of Intent (SSOI) that describes the DoD Component's "business case" for the proposed project, and the draft IA text.
    - All DoD Components should prepare a complete RAD package for Memoranda of Agreement/ Understanding (MOAs/MOUs), including Master Information/Data Exchange Agreements/Arrangements (MIEAs/MDEAs), and forward the RAD package under a senior-level management cover memo to OUSD (AT&L)/IC for approval.
    - The three MILDEPS and the Missile Defense Agency have delegated authority, in accordance with strict guidelines from OUSD (AT&L)/IC, to develop and negotiate, but not conclude, Project Arrangements/Agreements (PAs) under a master/framework agreement/arrangement, Equipment and Material Transfer Arrangements/Agreements (E&MTAs), and 22 USC 2796d (Arms Export Control Act (AECA) Section 65) Loan Agreements (LAs). (Note: This delegated RAD approval process is further described in CH1-S–6.1.1). All other DoD Components are required to provide a RAD package to OUSD (AT&L)/IC for such approval.
    - The three MILDEPS have authority to develop, negotiate, and conclude Information/Data Exchange Annexes (IEAs/DEAs) under MIEAs/MDEAs after obtaining the concurrence of its own legal, foreign disclosure, and other relevant officials as part of its internal approval procedures. All other DoD Components should provide a RAD (and RFA) package to OUSD (AT&L)/IC for approval. In all cases, these IEAs/DEAs should be developed in accordance with DoDI 2015.4 (further guidance is detailed in the IC in AT&L Handbook, Chapter 13).
    - Per DoDI 5000.02, (Encl. 2, para 7.b.(1)), ICPs containing classified information require a Delegation of Disclosure Authority Letter (DDL) or other written authorization issued by the DoD Component's cognizant FDO prior to entering into discussions with potential foreign partners. The DoD Component is not required to submit the DDL with the RAD package; however, the SSOI should include a statement confirming such authorization exists, including for controlled unclassified information, as applicable.
- **RAD Coordination/Approval.** OUSD (AT&L)/IC reviews the RAD package for completeness and quality, resolves any issues with the DoD Component, and then conducts

DoD/interagency coordination, as appropriate. The standard coordination period for MOAs/MOUs is 21 working days; for PAs, E&MTAs, and LAs it is 15 working days. This period may be expedited upon senior-level request at OUSD (AT&L)/IC's discretion. OUSD (AT&L)/IC then adjudicates any staffing comments prior to granting authority to develop and negotiate the IA via a formal memo.

- **IA Negotiation**. Typically, within 6-18 months of receipt of RAD authority, the DoD Component will complete negotiation of an IA in accordance with the provisions of the most recent version of the DoD IAG. OUSD (AT&L)/IC may also assist the DoD Components as needed, answering questions or providing guidance during negotiations, especially for any significant deviations to established procedures in the DoD IAG or other IA policy and guidance.

Request for Final Authority to Conclude (RFA) for all AT&L-related IAs:

- **RFA Initiation**. The DoD Component prepares the RFA package, which is comprised of a cover memo signed by senior-level leadership requesting such authority, an updated SSOI, and the negotiated IA text. For those IAs for which OUSD (AT&L)/IC provided RAD authority, the RFA package should also include a track change version of the IA text that clearly indicates the changes made to the RAD-approved text, as well as a brief comment indicating the reason for each change. Additional Congressional notification document requirements include:
  - o RFA for an IA using 22 USC 2767 of the Arms Export Control Act (AECA Section 27) as the legal authority should also include a Project Certification for Congressional notification.
  - o RFA for an IA using 10 USC 2350a as the legal authority with partners designated a "friendly foreign country" (i.e., countries that are not NATO members or major non-NATO allies) should also include a Project Report for Congressional notification.
- **RFA Coordination/Approval**. OUSD (AT&L)/IC next reviews the package for completeness and quality, resolves any issues with the DoD Component, and then conducts DoD/interagency coordination, as appropriate. The standard coordination period for MOAs/MOUs is 21 working days; for PAs, E&MTAs, and LAs it is 15 working days. This period may be expedited upon senior-level request at OUSD (AT&L)/IC's discretion. OUSD (AT&L)/IC then adjudicates any staffing comments prior to granting authority to conclude the IA via a formal memo. Note that the RFA coordination process regularly results in IA text changes that require re-engagement with the partner nation(s). Upon completion of RFA package staffing, but before OUSD (AT&L)/IC provides RFA approval, the following actions are applicable:
  - o For IAs using 10 USC 2350a legal authority, OUSD (AT&L)/IC requests a determination from USD (AT&L), or designee, in accordance with 10 USC 2350a(b) that the project will improve, through the application of emerging technology, the conventional defense capabilities of NATO or common conventional defense capabilities of the United States and the partner nation.
  - o For IAs using 10 US 2350a legal authority with those partners designated a "friendly foreign country," OUSD (AT&L)/IC submits to Congress a Project Report for a required period of 30 calendar days.
  - o For IAs using 22 USC 2767 legal authority, OUSD (AT&L)/IC requests coordination from the Department of State (DoS) within 21 working days and then submits to Congress a Project Certification for a required period of 30 calendar days.

CH 1-S–6.1.1 Delegated RAD Approval Process

An additional element of the "streamlined agreement procedures" referenced in DoDI 5000.02 is the IA delegated RAD approval process (also known as "Streamlining I" authority), which is an accredited IA coordination process applicable only to PAs, E&MTAs, and LAs. As stated earlier, all three MILDEPS and the Missile Defense Agency currently have this authority from OUSD (AT&L)/IC to develop and negotiate, but not conclude, these types of IAs. DoD Components interested in this delegated authority should formally apply to OUSD (AT&L)/IC to obtain it. A separate delegated authority, known as "Streamlining II" and authorized only for the Department of the Navy, is no longer in use and is not described here. The following procedures apply to DoD Components who have been delegated RAD approval authority:

- **RAD Initiation/Coordination/Approval.** The DoD Component prepares a RAD package, as described previously, and obtains the concurrence of its own legal, financial management, foreign disclosure, and other relevant officials as part of its internal, DoD Component RAD approval procedures. Upon completion of coordination, the RAD package should be approved at the DoD Component's senior management level. The DoD Component should forward any coordination disputes to OUSD (AT&L)/IC for resolution.
- **RFA Initiation/Coordination/Approval.** Upon conclusion of IA negotiations, the DoD Component should follow the standard procedures in CH1-S-6 to obtain RFA approval.

CH 1-S–6.1.2 Nuclear, Chemical, and Biological Fields Coordination

OUSD (AT&L)/IC coordinates all IAs (including MOAs/MOUs, PAs, E&MTAs, and LAs) and IEAs/DEAs relating to nuclear, chemical, and biological (NCB) weapons technologies (including defenses against such technologies) with the Office of the Assistant Secretary of Defense for Nuclear, Chemical and Biological Defense Programs prior to approving the IA for negotiations or conclusion. DoD policy also requires such coordination as part of a DoD Component's delegated RAD approval processes for NCB-related IAs.

CH 1-S–6.2 AT&L IA Services and Responsibilities

OUSD (AT&L)/IC oversees, develops and maintains the following policy, guidance, and tools in support of DoD Component IA development, negotiation, and conclusion:

- RAD/RFA package requirements and coordination processes
- SSOI format requirements and drafting guidance
- DoD IAG products, including MOA/MOU, MIEA/MDEA, PA, E&MTA, and LA templates, models, and guidance
- IEA/DEA format requirements and drafting guidance
- 22 USC 2767 Project Certification format requirements and drafting guidance
- 10 USC 2350a "Friendly Foreign Country" designation congressional notification format requirements and drafting guidance
- IC in AT&L Handbook (Chapter 12)
- End-User Certificate Waivers, when required
- Review and approval of DoD Component requests for DoD IAG text deviations or waivers in RAD/RFA package submissions or during negotiations

OUSD (AT&L)IC supports fulfilment of statutory requirements as follows:

- Obtains USD (AT&L) determination under 10 USC 2350a(b) ("Cooperative research and development agreements: NATO organizations; allied and friendly foreign countries") that a project will improve, through the application of emerging technology, the conventional defense capabilities of NATO or common conventional defense capabilities of the United States and the partner nation.
- Notifies Congress of those IAs that use 22 USC 2767 (Authority of President to enter into cooperative projects with friendly foreign countries) as their legal authority prior to authorizing IA signature.
- Notifies Congress of DoD designation of certain IA partners as "friendly foreign countries" (i.e., countries that are not NATO members or major non-NATO allies) as required by 10 USC 2350a(a)(3).
- Conducts interagency coordination with the DoS and the Department of Commerce (DoC) (see 22 USC 2767 and DoDD 5530.3) during RFA process.

provides IA formulation and negotiation best practice advice. DAU also offers courses that provide specific training in this area that should be taken by defense acquisition workforce personnel who will be directly involved in ICP IA efforts.

CH 1-S–7. Security Assistance/Foreign Military Sales

The U.S. Government's security cooperation efforts include planning and implementation of Security Assistance program transfers of military articles and services to friendly foreign governments and specified international organizations through sales, grants, or leases. The Secretary of State is responsible for continuous supervision and general direction of the Security Assistance program. Within the DoD, Security Assistance efforts are conducted under the oversight of the Under Secretary of Defense for Policy (USD (P)), and are administered by the Defense Security Cooperation Agency (DSCA). While Foreign Military Sales (FMS) is the primary mechanism used to implement Security Assistance efforts, it is not the only mechanism. The Security Assistance Management Manual (SAMM) issued by DSCA defines policies and procedures for FMS and other Security Assistance programs.

The purchasing government is responsible for all costs associated with Security Assistance program sales. There is a signed Government-to-Government agreement, normally documented in a FMS Letter of Offer and Acceptance (LOA) between the U.S. Government and a foreign government. Each LOA is commonly referred to as an FMS case and is assigned a unique case identifier for accounting purposes. Under FMS, military articles and services, including logistics support and training, may be provided from DoD stocks or from new procurement. If the source of supply is new procurement, on the basis of having an LOA that has been accepted by the foreign government, the U.S. Government agency or MILDEP assigned as the Implementing Agency for the case is authorized to enter into contractual arrangements with U.S. industry to provide the articles or services requested.

The FMS process begins when the foreign government starts to develop requirements for a U.S. defense article or service. As the customer defines their requirements, that government may submit a Letter of Request (LOR) for either Price and Availability (P&A) data (rough order of magnitude pricing data provided for planning purposes) or a formal sales offer in the form of an LOA. On a major system sale, program management should take actions to ensure that the customer's LOR is complete and addresses all elements required to provide an operational capability. This can be accomplished by developing and providing LOR checklists, working with the in-country Security Cooperation Organization (SCO), or through direct engagement with the country.

The SAMM provides that acquisition in support of FMS cases be conducted in the same manner as it is for U.S. requirements, thus affording the customer the same benefits and protections that apply to DoD procurements. Many FMS system sales involve modifications to existing DoD systems than can entail significant development or integration efforts. Program management should ensure these efforts are managed with the same rigor used on comparable efforts for the DoD.

Contracting for FMS mirrors the process DoD uses for its own contracting actions. There are a few peculiarities associated with FMS contracts that are addressed in "Acquisitions for Foreign Military Sales," DFARS (Subpart 225.7300). FMS procurement requirements may be consolidated on a single contract with U.S. requirements or may be placed on a separate contract, whichever is most expedient and cost effective. DAU's International Acquisition Management website also provides advice on planning and implementing program management FMS-Acquisition best practices.

CH 1-S–7.1 Direct Commercial Sales

A Direct Commercial Sale (DCS) involves the commercial export by U.S. defense industry directly to a foreign entity of defense articles, services, training, or dual use items. Unlike the procedures employed for ICPs and FMS, DCS transactions are not administered by DoD and do not involve a Government-to-Government agreement. Rather, the U.S. Government control procedure is accomplished through license approvals by either the DoS or the DoC. The license approval authority is based on whether an item or technology is identified on the U.S. Munitions List (USML) and is governed by the International Traffic in Arms Regulations (ITAR) or is governed by the Export Administration Regulations (EAR) through the Commerce Control List (CCL). If the item or technology is governed by the USML, DoS is the licensing authority in accordance with the ITAR. If the item or technology is governed by the CCL, then DoC is the licensing authority in accordance with the EAR.

DoD's role in the export license approval process is to review proposed defense-related commercial sales or transfers for national security concerns. DoD's recommendation is provided by the Defense Technology Security Agency (DTSA) to the cognizant licensing agency during the U.S. Government interagency coordination process. DTSA, as DoD's lead agency for export license reviews, conducts in-depth national security reviews of export license requests for transfers of defense-related items referred from both DoS and DoC. DTSA also works closely with industry and international counterparts before licenses are requested to identify potential technology security or foreign disclosure issues. DoS and DoC consider all U.S. Government interagency positions when determining whether to approve export license requests.

The U.S. Government is not a participant in the ensuing DCS contract between the U.S. company and the foreign entity. However, it is common that some DoD support may be required for the effort. FAR (Subpart 245.302) provides that a contractor may use U.S. Government property for work with foreign governments and international organizations when approved in writing by the DoD. DSCA's SAMM CH 4 (para C4.3.6) provides additional guidance on DCS.

CH 1-S–7.2 Hybrid Foreign Sales

The most frequent forms of "hybrid" foreign sales programs are FMS/DCS programs. DCS efforts involving major systems will typically have companion FMS -only efforts for sensitive components or equipment in support of the DCS case, resulting in a hybrid program. Program management should work with their industry partner to maintain an awareness of U.S. industry marketing of their system to ensure timely initiation of any required companion FMS cases.

Hybrid programs can also be constructed using a variety of ICP, FMS, and DCS program forms. These include programs where foreign nations have purchased a U.S. system through either FMS or DCS with the development of system upgrades or logistics sustainment conducted as an ICP in partnership with the DoD under the terms of an MOU.

Another hybrid program model provides production articles to foreign nations that participated in the cooperative development of the system under the terms of an ICP MOU, while the system is sold via FMS to those nations that did not participate in the ICP. In structuring these cooperative/sales hybrid programs, program management should ensure that ICP activities and FMS activities are segregated as the pricing principles and OSD oversight responsibilities for these programs are different. This can be achieved by using different program forms for different phases or with different foreign nations. Defense Acquisition University's International Acquisition Management Community of Practice (ICoP) website provides advice on FMS-Acquisition best practices in this area.

CH 1-S–7.3 Building Partner Capacity Programs

BPC programs resemble FMS but have significant differences that program management should understand. Since 2004 Congress has authorized and funded a variety of BPC programs, such as the Iraq Security Forces Fund the Afghanistan Security Forces Fund, and the Global Train and Equip program. Enacted in December 2014, 10 U.S.C § 2282 provides DoD permanent authority to build the capacity of foreign security forces. These BPC programs are funded with U.S. Government appropriations rather than foreign funding or the State Department's Foreign Military Financing program. BPC programs may provide defense articles and/or services to other U.S. Government departments and agencies under the authority of the Economy Act or other transfer authorities for the purpose of building the capacity of partner nation security forces and enhancing their capability to conduct counterterrorism, counter drug, and counterinsurgency operations, or to support U.S. military and stability operations, multilateral peace operations, and other programs. DSCA policies and procedures are specified in DSCA's SAMM CH 15.

While BPC programs may look like FMS programs, program management should ensure their contracting officers are aware of the key differences between BPC and FMS transactions. Unlike the funding for FMS programs, which does not have an obligation period, the U.S. Government funding used for BPC programs retains the period of obligation associated with the appropriation of the funds as indicated in the pseudo LOA. In addition, in awarding contracts pursuant to a pseudo LOA, the provisions of the Federal Acquisition Regulation (FAR) applicable to FMS procurements do not apply to BPC programs.

Additional information on program management FMS-Acquisition Planning and Execution Considerations, may be found in the Defense Security Cooperation Agency (DSCA) SAMM (Chapter 4) and on the Defense Acquisition University's International Acquisition Management Community of Practice (ICoP) website.

CH 1-S–7.4 Yockey Waivers

DoD policy states that the U.S. Government should agree to sell through FMS or DCS only those major defense equipment systems that have satisfactorily completed U.S. Operational Test and Evaluation (OT&E) required prior to approval of full rate production. Therefore before offering FMS Price and Availability (P&A) data or a Letter of Offer and Acceptance (LOA) -- or approving an export approval for a DoD system that has not yet completed OT&E, the Component IPO should forward a request to DSCA for an OUSD(AT&L) "Yockey Waiver." The Yockey Waiver authorizes the release of P&A data and/or an LOA (or a DCS offer) to a foreign customer, and directs the IPO to include precautionary language identifying the risks to the foreign customer should problems be discovered in OT&E that may require retrofit or redesign of components, support equipment, and/or other hardware or software; or if the U.S. Government decides not to place the system into production after it completes OT&E. The Yockey Waiver highlights that a foreign customer risks the potential of higher costs, nonstandard support to sustain the system, or reduced interoperability with U.S. forces. If DSCA concurs with the request, they forward the package to OUSD (AT&L)/IC for review and final approval.

The reason for the Yockey Waiver policy is that, prior to a DoD full rate production decision at Milestone C, there is the risk that the United States may decide not to produce the system based on the results of OT&E. This would present an undesirable situation if the United States has provided unrepresentative P&A data or committed under an LOA to deliver a system to an FMS customer – or approved a DCS or hybrid U.S. Government export approval for sale and delivery of the system -- but decided not to deliver this same system to U.S. forces. The foreign customer would be faced with nonstandard support to sustain the system, potentially higher costs than the FMS, DCS or hybrid offer for sale reflected, and might not achieve the desired level of interoperability with U.S. forces.

Details of this requirement and the steps to follow in submitting a Yockey Waiver request are found in DoDI 5000.02 (Encl. 2, para 7.c.) and DSCA's SAMM (para C5.1.8.3).

CH 1-S–8. International Logistics Agreements

DoD cooperative logistics standardization activities in support of acquisition programs include:

- International Standardization Agreements developed in conjunction with member nations of the North Atlantic Treaty Organization and other allies and coalition partners, as described in DoDM 4120.24 (Encl. 7, para 1.a.). Defense Acquisition University's International Acquisition Management Community of Practice (ICoP) website also provides best practice advice (including related websites) on international standardization activities.

Benefits of cooperative logistics support agreements may be tangible, such as the U.S. receiving support for its naval vessels when in a foreign port; or intangible, such as the foreign nation receiving the implied benefit of a visible U.S. naval presence in the region. DoD cooperative logistics support activities include:

- Acquisition and Cross-Servicing Agreements (ACSAs)
- Logistics Cooperation IAs, used to improve sharing of logistics support information and standards, and to monitor accomplishment of specific cooperative logistics programs
- Host Nation Support Agreements
- Cooperative Logistics Supply Support Arrangements
- Cooperative Military Airlift Agreements
- War Reserve Stocks for Allies
- Agreements for acceptance and use of real property or services

The following sections provide more detailed discussion on the two types of acquisition-related agreements.

CH 1-S–8.1 Acquisition and Cross-Servicing Agreements

10 USC 2342 (para (a)(1)), "Acquisition Cross-Servicing Agreements (ACSAs)," authorizes the DoD, upon consultation with the Secretary of State, to conclude reciprocal agreements with foreign countries and regional and international organizations for the provision of logistics, support, supplies and services (LSSS). In an ACSA, each party may acquire or transfer LSSS to the other party on a reimbursable basis. Beyond the obvious material benefits, such agreements can lead to opening dialogue and creating relationships between the parties, which may serve to strengthen political-military relationships. ACSA authority is exercised by the Unified Combatant Commands. See the International Cooperation in Acquisition, and Logistics Handbook, Chapter 5 and the Defense Acquisition University's International Acquisition Management Community of Practice (ICoP) website for additional information on ACSAs.

ACSAs allow for the provision of cooperative logistics support under the authority granted in 10 USC 2341-2350 (10 USC 2341, 10 USC 2342, 10 USC 2343, 10 USC 2344, 10 USC 2345, 10 USC 2346, 10 USC 2347, 10 USC 2348, 10 USC 2349, 10 USC 2349a, and 10 USC 2350). They are governed by DoDD 2010.9 and implemented by CJCSI 2120.01B. These documents are intended to provide an alternative acquisition option for logistics support in support of exercises or exigencies.

A current listing of ACSAs and countries and organizations eligible to negotiate them is maintained by the Director for Logistics, the Joint Staff (J-4). DoDD 2010.9 (para 5.1.2) provides the official process for nominating countries for eligibility for such agreements as well as for concluding them.

- **Permitted and Prohibited Uses.** An ACSA is for the transfer of LSSS only. General purpose vehicles and other items of non-lethal military equipment not designated as Significant Military Equipment on the USML promulgated pursuant to 22 USC 2778 (Sections 38 and 47(7)), may be leased or loaned for temporary use. Specific questions on the applicability of certain items should be referred to the Combatant Command's legal office for review and approval. Per DoDD 2010.9 (para 4.5.1), items that may not be acquired or transferred under ACSA authority include:
  - Weapon systems, specifically:
    - Guided missiles; naval mines and torpedoes; nuclear ammunition, and included items such as warheads, warhead sections, projectiles, and demolition munitions;
    - Guidance kits for bombs or other ammunition; and
    - Chemical ammunition (other than riot control agents)
  - Initial quantities of replacement and spare parts for major end items of equipment covered by tables of organization and equipment, tables of allowances and distribution, or equivalent documents; and
  - Major end items of equipment.
- **Repayment of Obligations.** In addition to the use of cash and subject to the agreement of the parties, ACSA obligations may be reconciled by either Replacement-in-Kind (RIK) or Equal Value Exchange (EVE). ACSA obligations not repaid by RIK or EVE automatically convert to cash obligations after one year.

- o An RIK repayment allows the party receiving supplies or services under the ACSA to reconcile their obligation via the provision or supplies and services of an identical or substantially identical nature to the ones received. As an example, a country may provide extra water to the United States during a training exercise with the proviso that the United States will provide the same amount of water during a future exercise.
  - o An EVE repayment enables the party receiving supplies or services under the ACSA to reconcile their obligation via the provision of supplies or services that are considered to by both parties to be of an equal value to those received. As an example, a country may provide extra water to the United States during a training exercise in exchange for the United States providing extra ammunition.
- **Implementation.** DoDD 2010.9 and CJCSI 2120.01B provide management guidance on initiating ACSA orders, receiving support, reconciling bills, and maintaining records. As this is a Combatant Command-managed program, organizations interested in acquiring logistics, support, supplies and services should work through the applicable logistics branch to receive further guidance on this topic.

CH 1-S–8.2 Acquisition-Only Authority Agreements

10 USC 2341 authorizes elements of the U.S. Armed Forces, when deployed outside the United States, to acquire logistic support, supplies, and services from eligible foreign entities on a reimbursable basis. The authority is not reciprocal and does not require the existence of a cross-servicing agreement or implementing arrangement. The Acquisition-only authority is a very limited authority that has been mainly supplanted by the use of broader authorities in ACSAs. Acquisition-only authority may be used with the governments of NATO members, NATO and its subsidiary bodies, the United Nations Organization, any regional organization, and any other country that meets one or more of the following criteria:

- Has a defense alliance with the United States.
- Permits the stationing of members of the U.S. armed forces in such country or the home porting of naval vessels of the United States in such country.
- Has agreed to preposition materiel of the United States in such country.
- Serves as the host country to military exercises, which include elements of the U.S. armed forces, or permits other military operations by the U.S. armed forces in such country.

CH 1-S–9. Technology Security and Foreign Disclosure Processes

Technology Security and Foreign Disclosure (TSFD) requires planning and implementation of several U.S. Government and DoD processes, both within and outside the span of control of the DoD acquisition process. The following paragraphs describe key TSFD processes that normally require program management integration efforts to ensure successful IA&E outcomes.

Before embarking on an international acquisition effort, program management consults appropriate TSFD authorities (e.g., a Principal Disclosure Authority or Designated Disclosure Authority) in order to determine whether the classified or controlled unclassified information can be disclosed to other governments or international organization participants. Foreign assurances to protect the information are normally in the form of bilateral security agreements or security requirements detailed in a program-specific agreement. Failure to consider security requirements prior to obtaining foreign commitments on involvement can result in program delays at critical stages of the program.

Program management should also consult with TSFD experts in their DoD Component or the Principal Staff Assistant, as appropriate, as early as possible to enhance their awareness of the TSFD processes and their linkage (or not) to the program's security documentation. The DoD Components – especially the MILDEPS – typically rely on their IPOs, where the TSFD function is usually located. Figure 1 depicts the specific DoD TSFD processes (or "pipes"), DoD Leads, reference documents, and whether the processes are Primary or Specialized, and DoD only or Interagency. (Note: "Primary Process" refers to the processes for which there is documentation and multiple participants. "Specialized Process" refers to the processes for which there is little or no documentation and a limited number of organizational participants).

Figure S-1: Technology Security and Foreign Disclosure Processes

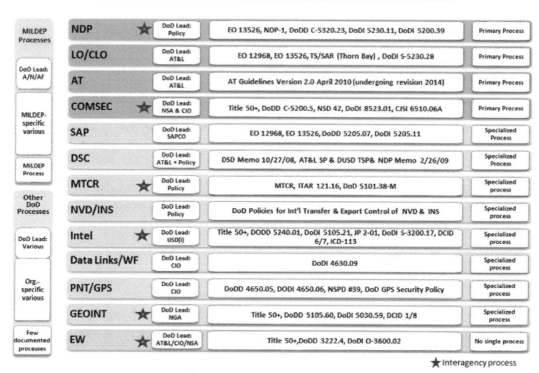

MILDEP Processes	**NDP** ★	DoD Lead: Policy	EO 13526, NDP-1, DoDD C-5320.23, DoDI 5230.11, DoDI 5200.39	Primary Process
DoD Lead: A/N/AF	**LO/CLO**	DoD Lead: AT&L	EO 12968, EO 13526, TS/SAR (Thorn Bay) , DoDI S-5230.28	Primary Process
	AT	DoD Lead: AT&L	AT Guidelines Version 2.0 April 2010 (undergoing revision 2014)	Primary Process
MILDEP-specific various	**COMSEC** ★	DoD Lead: NSA & CIO	Title 50+, DoDD C-5200.5, NSD 42, DoDI 8523.01, CJSI 6510.06A	Primary Process
	SAP	DoD Lead: SAPCO	EO 12968, EO 13526, DoDD 5205.07, DoDI 5205.11	Specialized Process
MILDEP Process	**DSC**	DoD Lead: AT&L + Policy	DSD Memo 10/27/08, AT&L SP & DUSD TSP& NDP Memo 2/26/09	Specialized Process
Other DoD Processes	**MTCR** ★	DoD Lead: Policy	MTCR, ITAR 121.16, DoD 5101.38-M	Specialized process
	NVD/INS	DoD Lead: Policy	DoD Policies for Int'l Transfer & Export Control of NVD & INS	Specialized process
DoD Lead: Various	**Intel** ★	DoD Lead: USD(I)	Title 50+, DODD 5240.01, DoDI 5105.21, JP 2-01, DoDI S-3200.17, DCID 6/7, ICD-113	Specialized process
	Data Links/WF	DoD Lead: CIO	DoDI 4630.09	Specialized process
Org.-specific various	**PNT/GPS**	DoD Lead: CIO	DoDD 4650.05, DODI 4650.06, NSPD #39, DoD GPS Security Policy	Specialized process
	GEOINT ★	DoD Lead: NGA	Title 50+, DoDD 5105.60, DoDI 5030.59, DCID 1/8	Specialized process
Few documented processes	**EW** ★	DoD Lead: AT&L/CIO/NSA	Title 50+,DoDD 3222.4, DoDI O-3600.02	No single process

★ Interagency process

A: Army
AF: Air Force
AT: Anti Tamper
AT&L: Acquisition Technology & Logistics
AT&L SP: AT&L Special Programs
CIO: Chief Information Officer
CJSI: Chairman Joint Chiefs of Staff Instruction
CLO: Counter Low Observable
COMSEC: Communication Security
DCID: Director Central Intelligence Directive
DoDD: Department of Defense Directive
DoDI: Department of Defense Instruction
DSC: Defensive Systems Committee

DSD: Deputy Secretary of Defense
DUSD TSP: Deputy Under Secretary of Defense Technology Security Policy
EO: Executive Order
EW: Electronic Warfare
GPS: Global Positioning System
GEOINT: Geospatial Intelligence
ICD: Intelligence Community Directive
INS: Inertial Navigation System
Intel: Intelligence
ITAR: International Traffic in Arms Regulation
JP: Joint Publication
LO: Low Observable
MILDEP: Military Deputy

MTCR: Missile Technology Control Regime
N: Navy
NDP: National Disclosure Policy
NGA: National Geospatial-Intelligence Agency
NSA: National Security Agency
NSPD: National Security Policy Directive
NVD: Night Vision Device
PNT: Precision Navigation & Timing
SAP: Special Access Program
SAPCO: SAP Coordinating Office
TS/SAR: Top Secret/Special Access Required
USD(I): Under Secretary of Defense (Intelligence)
WF: Waveform

The DoD Technology Security and Foreign Disclosure Office (TSFDO), located within the Defense Technology Security Administration (DTSA), was established to improve the processing of high-priority TSFD issues on a DoD-wide basis and to serve as the Executive Secretariat to the DoD Arms Transfer and Technology Release Senior Steering Group (ATTR SSG). The ATTR SSG, which is co-chaired by the Under Secretary of Defense for Acquisition, Technology and Logistics (USD (AT&L)) and the Under Secretary of Defense for Policy (USD (P)), is a senior DoD coordination body that provides guidance and direction to DoD TSFD processes involved in the transfer of defense articles and/or the release of classified or sensitive technology to international partners in support of U.S. policy and national security objectives (see DoDD 5111.21 (Encl. 2) for additional details about the ATTR SSG and TSFDO).

The TSFDO, in coordination with the Office of the Under Secretary of Defense for International Cooperation (USD(AT&L)/IC), supports the ATTR SSG by working in concert with DoD Components to facilitate high-level TSFD policy issues related to international programs. To do this, TSFDO screens, prepares, and tracks DoD Priority TSFD Reviews (PTRs) to ensure they are identified in a timely fashion and appropriately routed to, and addressed by, all relevant DoD TSFD processes and subject matter experts. A PTR is related to an offer for cooperation, sale, or other transfer that is deemed by a DoD Component or ATTR SSG member to have real or high potential for senior leader (e.g., Secretary, Deputy Secretary, Under Secretary, or 4-Star General Officer) direction, interest, and/or involvement. Program management can work with their DoD Component International Program Office (IPO) and TSFD organizations and, if necessary, the DoD TSFDO to help in identifying or processing PTRs related to the international aspects of their programs.

Program management should also consult with TSFD experts in their DoD Component or the appropriate Principal Staff Assistant, as appropriate, as early as possible to enhance their awareness of the TSFD processes and their linkage (or not) to the program's security documentation. The DoD Components – especially the MILDEPS – typically rely on their IPOs, where the TSFD function is usually located. Figure 1 depicts the specific DoD TSFD processes (or "pipes"), DoD Leads, reference documents, and whether the processes are Primary or Specialized, and DoD only or Interagency. (Note: "Primary Process" refers to the processes for which there is documentation and multiple participants. "Specialized Process" refers to the processes for which there is little or no documentation and a limited number of organizational participants).

See the IC in AT&L Handbook, CH 7, and Defense Acquisition University's International Acquisition Management Community of Practice (ICoP) website for additional guidance on TSFD policy and procedural guidance.

CH 1-S–10. Program Protection Documentation

In addition to the guidance provided in DAG Chapter 9 on Program Protection, the following subsections describe IA&E program protection documentation requirements that support Program Protection Plan (PPP) development and other international security program activities.

CH 1-S–10.1 Technology Assessment/Control Plan

Per DoDI 5530.03 (para 9.3.4), TA/CP information should be developed by defense acquisition workforce personnel involved in IA&E activities. Much of the information needed to develop TA/CP information for acquisition programs can be obtained from the AoA, Acquisition Strategy, and supporting documentation. If a program is required to draft a PPP, then program management should include TA/CP information in its acquisition program PPP. If the program's PPP addresses all of the information required in the Technology Assessment/Control Plan (TA/CP), then the requirement for a separate TA/CP may be met by referencing to the completed PPP. When incorporating TA/CP information into an acquisition program PPP, program management should use the PPP Outline and Template (see CH 9–2.3).

If no PPP is required, then a stand-alone TA/CP should be prepared after completing the identification of CPI and development of a Security Classification Guide (SCG) that addresses applicable IA&E activities. See CH1-S-10.4 for additional details on the SCG. Preparation should commence concurrently with the decision that could lead to IA&E activity. Stand-alone TA/CPs should include the following four sections:

- Program Concept
- Nature and Scope of the Effort and Objectives
- Technology Assessment
- Control Plan

TA/CP information (in PPPs or stand-alone TA/CPs) should address the following (per DoDI 5530.03 (Encl. 7):

- Assessment of the feasibility of U.S. participation in joint programs from a foreign disclosure and technical security perspective.
- Preparation of guidance for negotiating the transfer of sensitive or classified DoD information and critical technologies involved in the envisioned IA&E activities.
- Identification of security arrangements for the envisioned IA&E activities.
- Preparation of a DDL that contains specific guidance on proposed disclosures.
- Support of the acquisition or cooperative S&T project decision review process.
- Support of decisions on foreign sales, co-production, or licensed production, commercial sales of the system, or international cooperative agreements involving U.S. technology or processes.
- Support of TSFD and export control decisions on the extent and timing of IA&E involvement and related access to DoD information by allied and friendly nations.

CH 1-S–10.2 Program Protection Plan (PPP)

DoDI 5000.02 (Encl. 1, Table 2 and Encl. 3, para 13) IA&E program protection requirements. Program protection efforts should assess and, where applicable, implement U.S. Government and DoD TSFD process decisions, as well as overall DoD program protection policy guidance. CH 9–2.3 provides additional program protection direction. Based on a number of U.S. Government and DoD policies, program managers can take measures to identify and protect program information, system information, CPI, as well as mission-critical functions and components from inadvertent disclosure and unauthorized entities, whether there are ongoing or projected IA&E activities or not. Additionally, programs with potential and actual international involvement can address foreign disclosure, foreign sales, co-production, import/export licenses, or other export authorization requirements in the PPP. For ICPs where non-U.S. entities are involved in co-development and/or co-production, program protection measures will be accordance with relevant international agreements and in compliance with national laws and regulations.

The following key foreign involvement requirements should be included in the PPP (see CH 9–2.2).

- Summary of any potential, plans for, or existing foreign cooperative development or foreign sales of the system.
- Identity of the subsystems, components, and/or information involving CPI and/or critical components that are not included or shared in any end item sale of the system.
- Whether previous generations of the system have been sold to foreign partners.
- How export requirements will be addressed if foreign customer is identified.
- Whether program is participating in the current OUSD (AT&L) DEF Pilot Program, is a viable future candidate for the DEF Pilot Program, and the results of any completed DEF studies.

If the program adds new foreign activity involving CPI, the PPP should be updated accordingly.

Program management can conduct an early review of anticipated TSFD and export approval requirements for the capability. As discussed in Section 9, the acronym "TSFD" refers to DoD and U.S. Government processes that review and approve proposed release, sale, or other transfers of defense articles and classified or sensitive technology/information to other nations. Early PM consideration of DoD/U.S. Government TSFD and U.S. Government export control requirements enables DoD acquisition programs to achieve maximum benefit from international participation while minimizing negative impacts on program cost, schedule, and performance (see CH1-S-9 for details on TSFD processes.)

CH 1-S–10.3 Technology Release Road Map

Program management should prepare an initial Technology Release Roadmap (TRR) during the MSA or TMRR phases if a substantial amount of IA&E activity is envisioned. The TRR should also be included in the program's PPP. The TRR should describe when the critical milestones regarding TSFD planning and implementation should be addressed and provide a projection of when U.S. industry export approvals (e.g., export licenses, Technology Assistance Agreements, ITAR exemptions, etc.) may be required to support initial IA&E efforts. The TRR should be consistent with the program's PPP or TA/CP, SCG, DDL, and any other TFSD guidance. Prior to the EMD phase of an acquisition program with substantial IA&E involvement by foreign industry, the program manager should update the TRR or (if not previously prepared) develop a TRR that addresses the U.S. industry export approvals needed to implement EMD program efforts.

The TRR should take the following actions to address the program's acquisition phase-specific IA&E activities:

1. Provide early DoD Component planning for the program management's proposed sensitive or classified information technology releases to foreign industry.
2. Establish a detailed export authorization approval planning process for U.S.-foreign industry cooperation arrangements to meet critical program and contract timelines.

The TRR should contain three sections:

1. A timeline mapping key projected export approvals against the program acquisition schedule;
2. A definition of the technologies involved in each export approval; and
3. A list of U.S. contractors (export) as well as foreign contractors (end users) for each export approval.

CH 1-S–10.4 Security Classification Guide

In addition to the PPP (or TA/CP if there is no PPP) required to support other DoD IA&E activities, DoDM 5200.01 (para 18.f.(2) – Page 31) requires international programs to develop a Security Classification Guide (SCG) for all programs containing classified information of the nations involved. The SCG, as prescribed in DoDD 5230.11 (Encl. 6), identifies the items or information to be protected in the program, and indicates the specific classification to be assigned to each item.

CH 1-S–10.5 Delegation of Disclosure Authority Letter

The authorization for release of classified or controlled unclassified information (developed or used during any part of the life cycle of the program) to any potential or actual foreign involvement in the IA&E activity should be in the form of a DDL, as prescribed in DoDD 5230.11 (Encl. 4), or other written authorization issued by the DoD Component FDO. In accordance with DoDI 5000.02 (Encl. 2, para 7.b.(1)), a written authorization to disclose any classified or controlled unclassified information must be obtained prior to engaging in IA&E activities with allied and friendly nations. The authorization for release of classified or controlled unclassified information must comply with DoD Component policies for release of such information.

CH 1-S–10.6 Program Security Instruction

A Program Security Instruction (PSI) details security arrangements for the program and harmonizes the requirements of the participants' national laws and regulations. Program management should consult with their DoD Component IPO on PSI requirements and should use the DoD IA Generator (described in CH1-S–6.1) to address whether a PSI needs to be developed. If all security arrangements to be used in an IA&E activity are in accordance with existing industrial security arrangements between the U.S. and the allied/friendly nations involved, a separate PSI may not be required. Additional information about the PSI is found in the IC in AT&L Handbook, Chapter 7, Section 7.6.

Chapter 1 - Version and Revision History

Use the table below to provide the version number, the date that the particular version was approved and a brief description of the reason for and content changes contained in the revised version.

Version #	Revision Date	Reason
Rev. 0	02-02-17	Initial Launch
Rev. 1	06-07-17	Update of embedded links from DAU

CH 2-1. Purpose

This chapter addresses Analysis of Alternatives (AoAs) and cost estimation. It provides explanations of the Office of the Secretary of Defense's Office of Cost Assessment and Program Evaluation's (CAPE's) policies and procedures found in DoDI 5000.73, *Cost Analysis Guidance and Procedures* and the Operating and Support Cost Estimating Guidebook as well as information required by DoDI 5000.02, *Operation of the Defense Acquisition System*.

CH 2–2. Background

CH 2–2.1 Life-Cycle Cost Estimating

Independent and sound cost estimates are vital for effective acquisition decision-making and oversight. Cost estimates also support efficient and effective resource allocation decisions throughout the Planning, Programming, Budgeting, and Execution process. Life-cycle cost estimates cover the entire life cycle of the program and include the development, production, operations and support (including both sustainment and disposal) phases, regardless of funding source.

CH 2–2.1.1 Major Defense Acquisition Programs

DoDI 5000.02, Enc 10, sec. 2 requires that a DoD Component Cost Estimate (CCE) and DoD Component Cost Position (CCP) be submitted prior to an MDAP receiving Milestone A or B approval or entering low-rate initial production or full- rate production.

The CCE documents the cost analysis conducted by the Service Cost Agency (SCA) in cases where the SCA is not developing an independent cost estimate (ICE). This cost analysis may range from an SCA non-advocate estimate, independent SCA assessment of another government estimate, or other SCA cost analysis, as determined by the SCA and reflected in DoD Component policy.

The CCP is the cost position established by the DoD Component. It is derived from the CCE and program office estimate per DoD Component policy. The CCP must be signed by the DoD Component Deputy Assistant Secretary for Cost and Economics (or Defense Agency equivalent) and include a date of record.

Additionally, 10 USC 2334 requires that the Office of Cost Assessment and Program Evaluation (CAPE) conduct or approve ICEs for MDAPs and major subprograms at the following times:

    1) prior to certification at Milestone A and certification at Milestone B;
    2) before any decision to enter into low-rate initial production or full-rate production;
    3) in advance of certification following critical cost growth; and
    4) at any time considered appropriate by DCAPE or upon the request of the USD(AT&L) or the milestone decision authority.

If DCAPE does not conduct the ICE for an MDAP or major subprogram, the appropriate Service Cost Agency or Defense Agency equivalent conducts the ICE for DCAPE's review and approval.

CH 2–2.1.2 Major Automated Information System Programs

DoDI 5000.02, Enc 10, sec. 2 requires that a CCE and CCP be submitted prior to a MAIS program receiving Milestone A, B, or C approval or a full deployment decision.

Additionally, DoDI 5000.02, Enc 10, sec. 2 and DoDI 5000.73 (Encl. 2, para 3.a.(1)(b)) provide that DCAPE may prepare an ICE for ACAT IAC programs at any time considered appropriate by the DCAPE or upon the request of the USD(AT&L) or the MDA.

CH 2–2.1.3 Acquisition Category II and III Programs

Cost estimates for ACAT II and III programs are conducted in accordance with each Service's policy. While OSD does not play an active role in the preparation of these estimates, the guidelines set forth in CH 2–3.3. and CH 2–3.4. should be followed to the greatest degree possible.

CH 2–2.1.4 Operating and Support

DoDI 5000.73 (Encl. 2, para 2.d.(6)) provides that post-initial operational capability (IOC) DoD Components must continue to track operating and support (O&S) costs and update O&S cost estimates yearly throughout a program's life cycle to determine whether preliminary information and assumptions remain relevant and accurate and to identify and record reasons for variances.

O&S cost estimates are independently reviewed at post-IOC reviews. Each O&S cost estimate must be compared to earlier estimates and the program's O&S affordability caps, and, as appropriate, used to update the life-cycle affordability analysis provided to the MDA and requirements validation authority. This comparison must identify the reasons for significant changes and categorize those reasons into external and internal ones.

CAPE provides guidance on O&S cost estimating in its Operating and Support Cost Estimating Guidebook.

CH 2–2.2 Cost and Software Data Reporting

Systematic and institutionalized cost data collection by each DoD Component is important to support credible cost estimates of current and future programs. The cost data collection systems subject to CAPE oversight are the Cost and Software Data Reporting system and the Visibility and Management of Operating and Support Costs system. CAPE also provides technical oversight to the central repository for earned value management (EVM) data.

DoDI 5000.02, Enc 1 (Table 7) requires cost reporting for all contracts over $50 million for MDAPs and MAIS programs and may be required for special interest contracts or those requested by the Services or CAPE. When it is determined that cost reporting is required for a contract, the cost working group integrated product team (CWIPT) meets to develop an appropriate cost reporting plan. Figure1 sets forth the CWIPT participants and each participant's role.

Figure 1: CWIPT Participants and Roles

Participants	Role
SYSCOM	Initiate CSDR process at Program Office; Assist in identifying all RFPs going out
Program Office	Help develop initial plans; work directly with contractors; identify RFPs
OSD CAPE	Provide input to plan to ensure cost needs are being met; provide final approval of plans
Service Cost Center	Help develop initial plan; provide input to plan to ensure cost needs are being met; provide initial approval
Service EV Center/Lead	Provide input to plan to ensure EV needs are being met; provide initial review & approval [as needed - coordinated w/Syscom & PM]
DCARC	Manage the entire CSDR planning process; ensure all rules and regulations are being followed; identify RFPs
Industry	If sole source, provide input and help government understand processes and procedures
PARCA	Provide input to ensure cost reporting structure and WBS are consistent where needed
L&MR (Sustainment Only)	Provide input to ensure sustainment data reporting supports PSM analysis

The CWIPT follows the timeline found in DoD 5000.04-M-1 (Encl. 2, Fig 1) when developing the cost reporting plan.

The CWIPT remains active with the validation of cost reports as the reports are submitted. The timeline found in DoD 5000.04-M-1 (Encl. 2, Fig 2) is followed for the submission and validation of cost reports.

Additional forms, templates, requirements, and contact information for cost and data reporting are set forth on the Cost Assessment Data Enterprise (CADE) website, http://cade.osd.mil/. CADE provides the users in the cost community with single-point access to the complete range of authoritative acquisition, cost, EVM, and technical data. Access to CADE is made available to government analysts throughout the cost and acquisition communities.

CH 2–2.3 Analysis of Alternatives

The Analysis of Alternatives (AoA) is an important element of the defense acquisition process. An AoA is an analytical comparison of the operational effectiveness, suitability, and life-cycle cost of alternatives that satisfy established capability needs. After the Materiel Development Decision, the AoA is initiated to examine potential materiel solutions with the goal of identifying the most promising option, thereby guiding the Materiel Solution Analysis phase. Subsequently, an update to the AoA is initiated when necessary or mandated by the DAE at the start of the Technology Maturation and Risk Reduction phase and is reviewed at Milestone B (which usually represents the first major funding commitment to the acquisition program). The update to the AoA is used to refine the proposed materiel solution, as well as to reaffirm the rationale, in terms of cost-effectiveness, for initiation of the program into the formal systems acquisition process. For Major Defense Acquisition Programs at Milestone A, the Milestone Decision Authority (MDA) must certify in writing to the Congress that the Department has completed an AoA consistent with the study guidance developed by the Director, Cost Assessment and Program Evaluation (DCAPE), in addition to meeting other certification criteria. For Major Defense Acquisition Programs at Milestone B, the MDA must certify in writing to Congress that the Department has completed an AoA with respect to the program, in addition to meeting other certification criteria. Pursuant to DoDI 5000.02, the AoA is updated as needed at Milestone C.

CH 2–2.3.1   Role of the Analysis of Alternatives as Part of the Materiel Solution Analysis

The AoA process plays a key role in support of the Materiel Solution Analysis Phase. After a program has an approved Materiel Development Decision, the AoA process is necessary to better define the trade space across cost, schedule, and performance to enable the DAE and Service Sponsor to select a preferred materiel solution that addresses the capability gaps documented in the approved Initial Capabilities Document (ICD).

The DCAPE develops and approves study guidance for MDAP AoAs. The guidance is developed in consultation with other DoD organizations, as necessary. Prior to the MDD review, DCAPE provides the AoA study guidance to the DoD Component designated by the MDA. Following receipt of the AoA study guidance, the DoD Component prepares an AoA study plan that describes the intended methodology for the management and execution of the AoA. The AoA study plan is coordinated with the MDA and approved by DCAPE prior to the MDD review. A suggested template for the AoA study plan is provided in Section 2.3.2.

The study guidance requires, at minimum, full consideration of possible trade-offs among cost, schedule, and performance objectives for each alternative considered. The study guidance also requires an assessment of whether or not the joint military requirement can be met in a manner consistent with the cost and schedule objectives recommended by the JROC. The AoA study guidance and resulting AoA study plan should build on the prior analyses conducted as part of the Joint Capabilities Integration and Development System (JCIDS). The JCIDS process is described in CJCS Instruction 3170.01. The JCIDS analysis process that leads to an approved Initial Capabilities Document (ICD) is built upon the analysis known as the Capabilities-Based Assessment (CBA). The CBA provides recommendations (documented in the ICD) to pursue a materiel solution to address an identified capability gap. The CBA does not provide specific recommendations as to a particular materiel solution, but rather provides a more general recommendation as to the type of materiel solution (such as Information Technology system, incremental improvement to an existing capability, or an entirely new "breakout" or other transformational capability). In this way, the ICD can be used to establish boundary conditions for the scope of alternatives to be considered in the subsequent AoA. The AoA study guidance should be crafted to ensure that the AoA considers a sufficiently robust set of alternatives, given program cost, schedule, and performance constraints.

CH 2–2.3.2. Analysis of Alternatives Study Plan

The first major step leading to a successful AoA is the creation and coordination of a well-considered analysis plan. The study plan establishes a road map of how the analysis will proceed, and who is responsible for doing what. At a minimum, the study plan facilitates full consideration of possible trade-offs among cost, schedule, and performance objectives for each alternative considered, as well as an assessment of whether or not the joint military requirement can be met in a manner consistent with the cost and schedule objectives recommended by the JROC.

A recommended outline for the AoA study plan may resemble the following (but note that the study plan specifics will depend on the scope of the analysis and the criteria outline in the study guidance):

- Introduction
    - Background
    - Purpose
    - Scope

- Ground Rules
  - Scenarios
  - Threats
  - Environment
  - Constraints, Limitations, and Assumptions
  - Timeframe
  - Excursions
- Alternatives
  - Description of Alternatives
  - Nonviable Alternatives
  - Operations Concepts
  - Sustainment Concepts
- Determination of Effectiveness Measures
  - Mission Tasks
  - Measures of Effectiveness
  - Measures of Performance
- Effectiveness Analysis
  - Effectiveness Methodology
  - Models, Simulations, and Data
  - Effectiveness Sensitivity Analysis
- Cost Analysis
  - Life-Cycle Cost Methodology
  - Additional Total Ownership Cost Considerations (if applicable)
  - Fully Burdened Cost of Delivered Energy (if applicable)
  - Models and Data
  - Cost Sensitivity and/or Risk Analysis
- Cost-Effectiveness Comparisons
  - Cost-Effectiveness Methodology
  - Displays or Presentation Formats
  - Criteria for Screening Alternatives
- Organization and Management
  - Study Team/Organization
  - AoA Review Process
  - Schedule

As every AoA is unique, the above outline should be tailored to support the analytic scope outlined in the respective study guidance. Each point in the above outline is discussed further in the next several sections.

CH 2–2.3.2.1. Analysis of Alternatives Study Plan-Introduction

The introduction to the AoA plan describes the developments that led to the AoA, including prior relevant analyses (such as the Capabilities-Based Assessment). It should reference the applicable capability-needs document(s) and other pertinent documents, and highlight the capability gaps being addressed through the applicable capability needs. The introduction should describe the applicable AoA study guidance and any other terms of reference. It also should provide a broad overview of the planned AoA, which describes in general terms the level of detail of the study and the scope (breadth and depth) of the analysis necessary to support the specific milestone decision.

CH 2–2.3.2.2. Analysis of Alternatives Study Plan-Ground Rules

The ground rules described in the analysis plan include the scenarios and threats, as well as the assumed physical environment and any constraints or additional assumptions. The scenarios are typically derived from defense-planning scenarios and associated joint operational plans, augmented by more detailed intelligence products such as target information and enemy and friendly orders of battle. Environmental factors that impact operations (e.g., climate, weather, or terrain) are important as well. In addition, environment, safety, and occupational health factors associated with the use of chemical and/or biological weapons may need to be considered as excursions to the baseline scenario(s).

The study plan should describe what future timeframe, or timeframes, will be considered in the analysis. Often, the time period(s) selected will be determined by the time period(s) assumed in the DoD-approved planning scenario. However, there is some flexibility on this point, especially if something significant -- such as the deployment of a new capability, or the retirement of a legacy system -- is projected to occur one or two years after one of the time periods in the scenario. A common and desirable practice is to consider two time periods of interest, say "near-term" and "far-term," separated by a decade or so.

The AoA study plan should describe the planned analytic excursions to the baseline scenarios and other major ground rules. Such excursions are strongly encouraged in order to explore any impact of changing threat levels, warning times, involvement of allied forces, and political constraints on basing or overflights, just to name a few issues. These excursions can be used to see if any major issues are critical to the relative cost-effectiveness of the alternatives considered in the AoA.

CH 2–2.3.2.3. Analysis of Alternatives Study Plan-Range of Alternatives
The analysis plan also should document the range of alternatives to be addressed in the analysis. In many cases, there will be a minimum set of alternatives required by the initial analysis guidance. Additional direction during subsequent AoA reviews may insert yet other alternatives. Practically, the range of alternatives should be kept manageable to ensure that the acquisition trade space is sufficiently well analyzed, while keeping the study schedule within a reasonable allotment. The number of alternatives can be controlled by avoiding similar but slightly different alternatives and by early elimination of alternatives (due to factors such as unacceptable life-cycle cost or inability to meet Key Performance Parameters). In many studies, the first alternative (base case) is to retain one or more existing systems, representing a benchmark of current capabilities. An additional alternative based on major upgrades and/or service-life extensions to existing systems also may be considered.

For each alternative, evaluation of system performance, unit effectiveness, and estimation of its life-cycle cost (or total ownership cost, if applicable) requires a significant level of understanding of its operations and support concepts. The operations concept describes the details of the peacetime, contingency, and wartime employment of the alternative within projected military units or organizations. It also may be necessary to describe the planned basing and deployment concepts (contingency and wartime) for each alternative. The sustainment concept for each alternative describes the plans and resources for system training, maintenance, and other logistics support.

It is important that the alternatives considered in the AoA should address alternative concepts for maintenance, training, supply chain management, and other major sustainment elements. In this way, the AoA can identify the preferred materiel solution not only in terms of traditional performance and design criteria (e.g., speed, range, lethality), but also support strategy and sustainment performance as well. In other words, the AoA should describe and include the results of the supportability analyses and trade-offs conducted to determine the most cost-effective support concept as part of the proposed system concept.

CH 2–2.3.2.4. Analysis of Alternatives Study Plan-Effectiveness Measures
The analysis plan should describe how the AoA will establish metrics associated with the military worth of each alternative. Military worth often is portrayed in AoAs as a hierarchy of mission tasks, measures of effectiveness, and measures of performance. Military worth is fundamentally the ability to perform mission tasks, which are derived from the identified capability needs. Mission tasks are usually expressed in terms of general tasks to be performed to correct the gaps in needed capabilities (e.g., hold targets at risk or communicate in a jamming environment). Mission tasks should not be stated in solution-specific language. Measures of effectiveness are more refined and provide the details that allow the proficiency of each alternative in performing the mission tasks to be quantified. Each mission task should have at least one measure of effectiveness supporting it, and each measure of effectiveness should support at least one mission task. Typically, a measure of performance is a quantitative measure of a system characteristic (e.g., range, weapon load-out, logistics footprint, etc.) chosen to enable calculation of one or more measures of effectiveness. Measures of performance are often linked to Key Performance

Parameters or other parameters contained in the approved capability needs document(s). Also, measures of performance are usually the measures most directly related to test and evaluation criteria.

CH 2–2.3.2.5. Analysis of Alternatives Study Plan-Effectiveness Analysis

The analysis plan spells out the analytic approach to the effectiveness analysis, which is built upon the hierarchy of military worth, the assumed scenarios and threats, and the nature of the selected alternatives. The analytic approach describes the level of detail at various points of the effectiveness analysis. In many AoAs involving combat operations, the levels of effectiveness analysis can be characterized by the numbers and types of alternative and threat elements being modeled. A typical classification would consist of four levels: (1) system performance, based on analyses of individual components of each alternative or threat system; (2) engagement, based on analyses of the interaction of a single alternative and a single threat system, and possibly the interactions of a few alternative systems with a few threat systems; (3) mission, based on assessments of how well alternative systems perform military missions in the context of many-on-many engagements; and (4) campaign, based on how well alternative systems contribute to the overall military campaign, often in a joint context. For AoAs involving combat support operations, the characterization would need to be modified according to the nature of the support. Nevertheless, most AoAs involve analyses at different levels of detail, where the outputs of the more specialized analysis are used as inputs to more aggregate analyses. At each level, establishing the effectiveness methodology often involves the identification of suitable models (simulation or otherwise), other analytic techniques, and data. This identification primarily should be based on the earlier selection of measures of effectiveness. The modeling effort should be focused on the computation of the specific measures of effectiveness established for the purpose of the particular study. Models are seldom good or bad per se; rather, models are either suitable or not suitable for a particular purpose.

It also is important to address excursions and other sensitivity analyses in the overall effectiveness analysis. Typically, there are a few critical assumptions that often drive the results of the analysis, and it is important to understand and point out how variations in these assumptions affect the results. As one example, in many cases the assumed performance of a future system is based on engineering estimates that have not been tested or validated. In such cases, the effectiveness analysis should describe how sensitive the mission or campaign outcomes are to the assumed performance estimates.

CH 2–2.3.2.6. Analysis of Alternatives Study Plan-Cost Analysis

The AoA plan also describes the approach to the life-cycle cost estimate. The cost analysis normally is performed in parallel with the operational effectiveness analysis. It is equal in importance as part of the overall AoA process. The cost analysis estimates the total life-cycle cost of each alternative, and its results are later combined with the operational effectiveness analysis to portray cost-effectiveness comparisons. It is important to emphasize that the cost analysis will be a major effort that will demand the attention of experienced, professional cost analysts.

The principles of economic analysis apply to the cost analysis in an AoA. Although the cost estimates used in an AoA originally are presented in constant dollars, they should be adjusted for discounting (time value of money), accounting for the distribution of the costs over the study time period of interest. In addition, the cost estimates should account for any residual values associated with capital assets that have remaining useful value at the end of the period of analysis. Further guidance on economic analysis is provided in DoDI 7041.3, "Economic Analysis for Decisionmaking."

The cost analysis should also describe the planned approach for addressing the Fully Burdened Cost of Energy for those AoAs where this issue is applicable.

CH 2–2.3.2.7. Analysis of Alternatives Study Plan-Cost-Effectiveness Comparisons

Typically, the next analytical section of the AoA plan deals with the planned approach for the cost-effectiveness comparisons of the study alternatives. In most AoAs, these comparisons involve alternatives that have both different levels of effectiveness and cost, which leads to the question of how to judge when additional effectiveness is worth additional cost. Cost-effectiveness comparisons in theory would be best if the analysis structured the alternatives so that all the alternatives have equal effectiveness (the best alternative is the one with lowest cost) or equal cost (the best alternative is the one with the greatest effectiveness). Either case would be preferred; however, in actual practice, in many cases the ideal of equal effectiveness or equal cost alternatives is difficult or impossible to achieve due to the complexity of AoA issues. A common method for dealing with such situations is to provide a scatter plot of effectiveness versus cost. Figure 2 presents a notional example of such a plot.

Note that the notional sample display shown in Figure 2 does not make use of ratios (of effectiveness to cost) for comparing alternatives. Usually, ratios are regarded as potentially misleading because they mask important information. The advantage to the approach in the figure above is that it reduces the original set of alternatives to a small set of viable alternatives for decision makers to consider.

<u>Figure 2: Sample Scatter Plot of Effectiveness versus Cost</u>

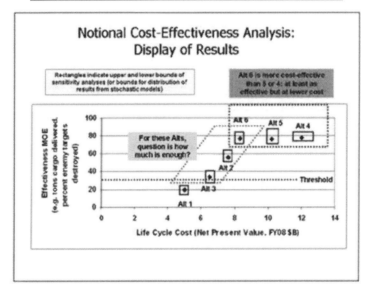

CH 2–2.3.2.8. Analysis of Alternatives Study Plan-Organization and Management

Finally, the AoA plan should address the AoA study organization and management. Often, the AoA is conducted by a working group (study team) led by a study director and staffed appropriately with a diverse mix of military, civilian, and contractor personnel. Program offices or similar organizations may provide assistance or data to the AoA study team, but the responsibility for the AoA may not be assigned to a program manager, and the study team members should not reside in a program office. In some cases, the AoA may be assigned to an in-house analytic organization, a federally funded research and development center, or a similar organization.

The AoA study team is usually organized into panels along functional lines, with a chair for each panel. Typical functional areas for the panels could be threats and scenarios, technology and alternatives (responsible for defining the alternatives), operations and support concepts (for each alternative), effectiveness analysis, and cost analysis. In many cases, the effectiveness panel occupies the central position and integrates the work of the other panels. The study plan also should describe the planned oversight and review process for the AoA. It is important to obtain guidance and direction from senior reviewers with a variety of perspectives (operational, technical, and cost) throughout the entire AoA process.

The analysis plan is fundamentally important because it defines what will be accomplished, and how and when it will be accomplished. However, the plan should be treated as a living document, and updated as needed throughout the AoA to reflect new information and changing study direction. New directions are inevitably part of the AoA process, so the analysis should be structured so as to be flexible. Frequently, AoAs turn out to be more difficult than originally envisioned, and the collaborative analytical process associated with AoAs is inherently slow. There are often delays in obtaining proper input data, and there may be disagreements among the study participants concerning ground rules or alternatives that lead to an increase in excursions or cases to be considered. Experience has shown that delays for analyses dealing with Special Access materials can be especially problematic, due to issues of clearances, access to data, storage, modeling, etc. It is often common for the study director to scale back the planned analysis (or at least consider doing so) to maintain the study schedule.

CH 2–2.3.3. Analysis of Alternatives Final Results
CH 2–2.3.3.1. Analysis of Alternatives Final Results and Assessment
Normally, the final results of the AoA initially are presented as a series of briefings. For potential and designated major defense acquisition programs (Acquisition Category (ACAT) I) and major automated information systems (ACAT IA), the final AoA results are provided to the Office of the Director, Cost Assessment and Program Evaluation (CAPE), no later than 60 days prior to the milestone decision meeting (Defense Acquisition Board or Information Technology Acquisition Board review). Providing emerging results to CAPE prior to the final briefing is wise to ensure that there are no unexpected problems or issues. For other programs, the AoA results should be provided to the DoD Component entity equivalent to CAPE, if applicable. In any case, the AoA final results should follow all of the important aspects of the study plan, and support the AoA findings with the presentation. In particular, all of the stated AoA conclusions and findings should follow logically from the supporting analysis.

Having received the final AoA briefing(s), the CAPE evaluates the AoA and provides an independent assessment to the Head of the DoD Component (or the Principal Staff Assistant) and to the Milestone Decision Authority. CAPE, in collaboration with the OSD and Joint Staff, shall assess the extent to which the AoA:

1. Illuminated capability advantages and disadvantages
2. Considered joint operational plans
3. Examined sufficient feasible alternatives
4. Discussed key assumptions and variables and sensitivity to changes in them;
5. Calculated costs
6. Assessed the following:
   - Technology risk and maturity
   - Alternative ways to improve the energy efficiency of DoD tactical systems with end items that create a demand for energy consistent with mission requirements and cost effectiveness
   - Appropriate system training to ensure that effective and efficient training is provided with the system

CH 2–2.3.3.2. Analysis of Alternatives Final Report
Usually, in addition to a final briefing, the AoA process and results are documented in a written final report. The report typically is not published formally by the time of the program milestone decision review, due to schedule constraints. However, the report nevertheless may be important to the historical record of the program, since the report serves as the principal supporting documentation for the AoA. The report also may serve as a reference source for analysts conducting future AoAs. The final report can follow the same format as the study plan, with the addition of these sections:

- Effectiveness Analysis
  - Effectiveness Results
- Cost Analysis
  - Life-Cycle Cost Results
- Cost-Effectiveness Comparisons
  - Cost-Effectiveness Results

By following the same format, much of the material from the (updated) study plan can be used in the final report.

CH 2–2.3.4. Analysis of Alternatives Considerations for Major Automated Information Systems

DoDI 5000.02, Enc 1 requires an AoA for MAIS programs at milestone decisions. Much of the discussion on AoAs provided in the earlier sections of the Guidebook is more applicable to weapon systems, and needs to be modified somewhat for MAIS programs. This section discusses AoA issues for MAIS programs. The AoA should include a discussion of whether the proposed program: (1) supports a core/priority mission or function performed by the DoD Component; (2) needs to be undertaken because no alternative private sector or governmental source can better support the function; and (3) supports improved work processes that have been simplified or otherwise redesigned to reduce costs, improve effectiveness, and make maximum use of commercial off-the-shelf technology. The analysis should be tied to benchmarking and business process reengineering studies (such as analyses of simplified or streamlined work processes, or outsourcing of non-core functions).

For all MAIS program AoAs, one alternative should be the status quo alternative as used in the Economic Analysis, and one alternative should be associated with the proposed MAIS program. Other possible alternatives could be a different system, network, and/or data architectures, or they might involve different options for the purchase and integration of commercial off-the-shelf products, modifications, and upgrades of existing assets or major in-house development.

Most likely, the effectiveness analysis in a MAIS program AoA will not involve scenario-based analysis as is common for the weapon system AoAs. The effectiveness analysis for an MAIS program should be tied to the organizational missions, functions, and objectives directly supported by the implementation of the system being considered. The results of the AoA should provide insight into how well the various alternatives support the business outcomes that have been identified as the business goals or capabilities sought. In some cases, it may be possible to express the assessment of effectiveness across the alternatives in monetary terms, so effectiveness could be assessed as benefits in the framework for the Economic Analysis. In other cases, the effectiveness might be related to measurable improvements to business capabilities or better or timelier management information (leading to improved decision-making, where it can be difficult or impossible to quantify the benefits). In these cases, a common approach is to portray effectiveness by the use of one or more surrogate metrics. Examples of such metrics might be report generation timeliness, customer satisfaction, or supplier responsiveness. In addition to management information, the effectiveness analysis also should consider information assurance and interoperability issues.

The cost analysis supporting the AoA should follow the framework of the Economic Analysis. The life-cycle cost estimates of the alternatives considered in the AoA should be consistent with and clearly linked to the alternatives addressed in the Economic Analysis. Both the effectiveness analysis and the cost analysis should address the risks and uncertainties for the alternatives, and present appropriate sensitivity analysis that describes how such uncertainties can influence the cost-effectiveness comparison of the alternatives.

The appropriate sponsor or domain owner should lead the development of the AoA for a MAIS program. Experience has shown that the MAIS programs for which the sponsor or domain owner engages with CAPE early in the process are much more likely to be successful than those that select a preferred alternative before contacting CAPE or completing the AoA.

The DoD Component performing the AoA should develop a study plan that addresses the AoA study guidance, as applicable. At a minimum, the study plan should address the following topics:

AoA Study Plan Outline

    a. Introduction (Background, Purpose and Scope)
    b. Ground Rules: Constraints and Assumptions
    c. Description of Alternatives
    d. Determination of Effectiveness Measures

1. Measures of Effectiveness (MOEs) operationally relevant and measurable
2. Measures of Performance technical characteristics required to satisfy MOEs, which are measurable and employed as an operational test criterion
   e. Effectiveness Analysis Methodology
   f. Cost Analysis
   g. Cost-Effectiveness Comparisons
   h. Risk & Sensitivity Analysis
      1. Mission
      2. Technology
      3. Programmatic, to include funding
   i. Study Organization and Management
   j. Schedule, with associated deliverables

CH 2–3. Business Practice

CH 2–3.1 Acquisition Category ID Cost Estimate Timeline

Figure 3 sets forth the typical timeline of events and deadlines to support the timely completion of an ICE for ACAT ID programs. This timeline may be tailored, as needed, depending on the program and the information needed to best support the decision-maker. The key events are as follows:

- At least 210 days before the planned overarching integrated product team (OIPT) meeting, the SCA will notify CA of a program's upcoming milestone or acquisition event requiring an ICE.
- A kick-off meeting is held no later than 180 days before the OIPT meeting. Before the kick-off meeting, the SCA and CA will develop an agenda of information to discuss; the agenda will include requirements for the cost estimates, alternatives to consider, and the assumptions on which the cost estimates will be based. A CA representative and SCA representative will co-chair the kick-off meeting.
- The Program Management Office (PMO) will prepare and deliver the draft Cost Analysis Requirements Description (CARD) to CA no later than 180 days before the planned OIPT meeting. For joint programs, the CARD will include the common program agreed to by all participating DoD Components, as well as any unique program requirements of the participating DoD Components. Templates and instructions for preparing the CARD are available at http://cade.osd.mil/policy/card.
- No later than 45 days after receipt of the draft CARD (usually at least 135 days before the planned OIPT meeting), CA will provide feedback to the PMO on the draft CARD.
- No later than 45 days after receipt of the draft CARD (usually at least 135 days before a planned OIPT meeting), if the CARD is insufficient, CA and the SCA will sign a memorandum to the PMO informing the PMO that the CARD is insufficiently developed to continue with the preparation of the cost estimates. In this scenario, the planned OIPT meeting and defense acquisition board (DAB) meeting may be delayed.
- Following the kick-off meeting and continuing until the OIPT meeting, the CA analyst and representatives from the SCA and PMO will conduct site visits and collect and review program data. During this time, the CA analyst and SCA and PMO representatives will have ongoing discussions concerning the cost estimating strategies and methodologies used to develop all relevant cost estimates, including the ICE, CCE, program office estimate (POE), and CCP.
- At least 45 days before the OIPT meeting, the PMO and SCA representatives will brief CA on the working level drafts of the POE, CCE, CCP, and any other relevant estimates available at the time. Following this briefing, the PMO and SCA representatives will provide CA with any updates to the working level drafts of the estimates as appropriate or on request.
- A final copy of the CARD, signed by the program executive officer and program manager, must be provided to CA by the PMO at least 45 days before the scheduled OIPT meeting and placed into the electronic CA Library.
- At CA's discretion, approximately 28 days before the OIPT meeting, the CA, PMO, and SCA representatives may meet to compare and discuss the results of the ICE and the CCP.

- The SCA must deliver the final, signed CCP and full funding certification memorandum to CA at least 10 days before the planned OIPT meeting. Copies of these documents will be submitted to the CA Library. If the program concept evolves after a milestone review, the SCA may update the CCP, and the DoD Component may fully fund the program in the Future Years Defense Program (FYDP) to the updated CCP. A copy of the updated CCP must be submitted to the CA Library.
- A CA representative will brief a summary of the ICE at the OIPT.
- Before the DAB review, CA will issue its ICE report, a copy of which will be placed in the CA Library.

Figure 3: Timeline for Preparation of ACAT ID ICEs

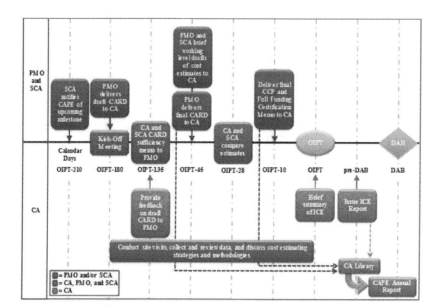

CH 2–3.2 Acquisition Category IC Cost Estimate Timeline

The DCAPE typically reviews the ICE prepared by the DoD Component for ACAT IC programs. In certain cases, the DCAPE will prepare the ICE for ACAT IC milestone reviews. The timeline in Figure 4 is followed when determining whether CA or the DoD Component will prepare the ICE and, if the DoD Component is preparing the ICE, the timeline for CA review.

- At least 210 days before the planned cost review board (CRB) meeting, the SCA will notify CA of an ACAT IC program's upcoming milestone that requires either a DoD Component ICE or a CA ICE.
- No later than 180 days before the planned CRB meeting, the PMO and SCA will brief the appropriate CA division director on the program, to include available data and methodologies. At or before the briefing, the PMO must deliver a draft CARD to CA. Templates and instructions for preparing the CARD are available at http://cade.osd.mil/policy/card.
- At least 165 days before the planned CRB meeting, CA will make a decision whether to review the DoD Component ICE or prepare a CA ICE. CA will issue a memorandum, a copy of which will be placed into the CA Library, documenting its decision. If CA decides to prepare the ICE, the program will follow a tailored version of the timeline and procedures described in paragraph 2b(1) of this enclosure for ACAT ID programs.

- If CA decides to review the DoD Component ICE, the CA analyst will continue to meet with technical and cost analysts from the PMO and SCA from 165 to 30 days before the CRB meeting. If, during this time, CA determines that there are significant changes to the program or increased cost or schedule risk, CA may decide to perform a CA ICE of the program.
- The PMO will deliver the final draft CARD to CA at least 45 days before the CRB meeting. The final draft CARD should be in near complete form, with only minor changes occurring between its delivery and the delivery of the final signed CARD at least 21 days before the CRB meeting.
- At least 30 days before the CRB meeting, PMO and SCA representatives will brief CA on working level drafts of the POE, DoD Component ICE, CCP, and any other relevant estimates available at the time.
- During the 30 days before the CRB meeting, CA will review the DoD Component ICE and provide feedback to the SCA. Based on the feedback, SCA will revise the DoD Component ICE as needed.
- At the CRB, the SCA will deliver the final DoD Component ICE to CA. CA will review and assess the adequacy of the ICE and document its assessment in a memorandum, copies of which will be delivered to the DoD Component Acquisition Executive (CAE) and placed in the CA Library.
- Following the CAE decision, the SCA will deliver to CA a signed CCP and full funding certification memorandum, copies of which will be placed into the CA Library.

Figure 4: Timeline for ACAT IC Cost Estimate Review

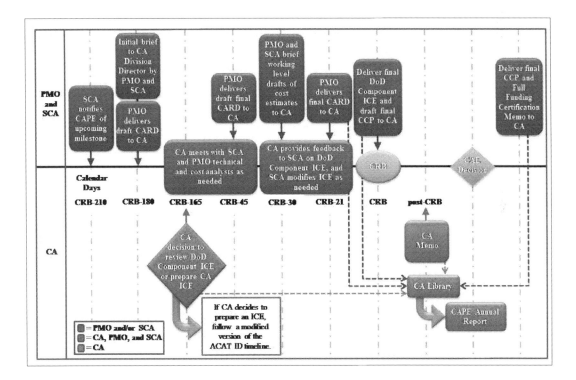

CH 2–3.3 How to Conduct a Cost Estimate

Conduct of a cost estimate is a multistep process involving planning, gathering data, conducting the estimate, risk and uncertainty analysis, and presenting the estimate. Depending on the program and data available, the methodology for the conduct of the estimate may vary. The BCF 131 presentations set forth guidance for each stage of the estimating process.

CH 2–3.4 Milestone-Specific Analysis

At each milestone or decision point, the analyst should provide a holistic view of the program and not just an estimate of the proposed solution. The cost analyst should provide analysis to the decision maker which provides insight enabling the decision maker to answer two main questions:

- Has the DoD fully funded the program of record within the Future Years Defense Program (FYDP)?
- Is the program of record an affordable solution for the DoD's needs?

Determining the answer to the first question is straightforward: namely, is there funding in the budget and the FYDP that corresponds to the amount of funding forecasted to be necessary to carry out the program? The answer to the second question is more complex, and the analysis will vary at each milestone. Specific strategic questions for analysis at each milestone are described below.

At all milestones, when presenting analysis that will help the decision maker determine whether the program of record is one that fulfills the DoD's needs and that the DoD can afford, the analyst should provide insight into:

- The cost of the solution
- Time needed to achieve the solution
- Whether the solution pushes the envelope on performance
- Any potential cost in extending the life of the current materiel solution until the new proposed solution is operational
- Whether the solution impacts the DoD Component's portfolio by affecting other programs that are valuable to the DoD.

The key strategic questions the analyst should consider while conducting the Milestone A cost estimate are:

- What is the cost and performance trade space for the conceptual materiel solution and other potential solutions?
- Is the program affordable to both buy and operate in the long term?
- Are CA's insights into the program consistent with the preferred solution of the AoA?

When conducting the Milestone B cost estimate, the key strategic questions the analyst should consider are:

- What is the cost and performance trade space for the detailed materiel solution and other potential solutions?
- Is the program affordable to both acquire and operate in the long term?
- Are there alternative acquisition or programmatic strategies that can result in a more affordable and efficient program?
  - What is the nature and duration of competition for both prime and major subcontractors? What is the appropriate time to down select to one contractor?
  - Are there ways to invest in manufacturing efficiencies?
- What technologies or strategies can be pursued to lower the overall sustainment cost?
  - What investments can be made in sustainability?
  - Have alternative sustainment strategies been considered in the BCA?
  - Is there a way to introduce competition into planned contractor logistics support for a system?

When conducting the cost estimate for the low-rate initial production decision, the analyst should answer key strategic questions, including:

- What is the most efficient and affordable way to procure the system when considering rate of procurement, programmatics, recompeting the contract, and use of government furnished equipment?

- What is the most efficient and affordable way to transition to low-rate initial production and full-rate production?
  - What is the timing of initial procurement relative to operational testing results and demonstrated manufacturing capabilities?
  - How many operational systems should be purchased before testing is complete?
- What technologies or strategies can be pursued to lower the sustainment costs?
- Do the results of the cost analysis support the product support strategy BCA results?
- Is the system affordable when compared to the annual O&S costs of the legacy system being replaced?
- Is contractor logistics support or organic support more efficient and affordable?
- Is the system cost effective, balancing the risks associated with the estimate of its O&S costs and related parameters such as reliability with higher system readiness and better mission availability?

When conducting the cost estimate for the full-rate production decision, the analyst should consider key strategic questions, including:

- Are there alternative procurement profiles that result in a more affordable and efficient program?
- Could substantial savings be achieved through the use of a multiyear procurement contract for the program?
- What changes should be made to the sustainment strategy in the BCA?

CH 2–3.5 Cost Analysis Requirements Description

The Cost Analysis Requirements Description (CARD) is a complete, detailed description of a DoD program for use in preparing an ICE, POE, CCE, CCP, or other cost estimate, as required. The CARD is completed by the program office staff as they should have the most in-depth knowledge and understanding of the program details.

The foundation of a sound cost estimate is a well-defined program, and the CARD is used to articulate details about the program. The primary objective of the CARD is to succinctly describe the key technical, programmatic, operational, and sustainment characteristics of a program, along with supporting data sources, and to provide all of the program information necessary to develop a cost estimate. By using the CARD, different organizations preparing cost estimates can develop their estimates based on the same understanding of program requirements. As a program evolves and its costs and funding needs change, the CARD, as a living document, evolves with it.

The secondary objective of the CARD is to collect in-depth technical data to allow for validation or updating of cost estimating relationships (CERs) and the development of new CERs. Though not required for completion of estimates, this information, particularly for systems whose designs have matured to the point of deployment, is of great value to the entire acquisition community in ensuring high quality estimates in the future.

The CARD is composed of a narrative and a workbook. Requirements for the narrative, as well as template workbooks for each commodity, are available electronically at http://cade.osd.mil/policy/card.

CH 2–Version and Revision History

The table below tracks chapter changes. It indicates the current version number and date published, and provides a brief description of the content.

Version #	Revision Date	Reason
0	1/31/17	Chapter 2 initial upload
1	4/10/17	Updated link and text in paragraph 3.3

CH 3–1. Purpose

The Defense Acquisition Guidebook (DAG), Chapter 3 provides overarching guidance on the systems engineering discipline, its activities and processes and its practice in defense acquisition programs. The Program Manager (PM) and the Systems Engineer should use this chapter to effectively plan and execute program activities across the system life cycle.

CH 3–2. Background

Systems engineering (SE) establishes the technical framework for delivering materiel capabilities to the warfighter. SE provides the foundation upon which everything else is built and supports program success. SE ensures the effective development and delivery of capability through the implementation of a balanced approach with respect to cost, schedule, performance and risk, using integrated, disciplined and consistent SE activities and processes regardless of when a program enters the acquisition life cycle. SE also enables the development of resilient systems that are trusted, assured and easily modified. The value of systems engineering is supported by the GAO Report 17-77, which indicates that, "Systems engineering is the primary means for determining whether and how the challenge posed by a program's requirements can be met with available resources. It is a disciplined learning process that translates capability requirements into specific design features and thus identifies key risks to be resolved. Our prior best practices work has indicated that if detailed systems engineering is done before the start of product development, the program can resolve these risks through trade-offs and additional investments, ensuring that risks have been sufficiently retired or that they are clearly understood and adequately resourced if they are being carried forward."

SE planning, as documented in the Systems Engineering Plan (SEP), identifies the most effective and efficient path to deliver a capability, from identifying user needs and concepts through delivery and sustainment. SE event-driven technical reviews and audits assess program maturity and determine the status of the technical risks associated with cost, schedule and performance goals.

"Positive acquisition outcomes require the use of a knowledge-based approach to product development that demonstrates high levels of knowledge before significant commitments are made. In essence, knowledge supplants risk over time." (Source: GAO Report 12-400SP)

Additional SE benefits are that it:

- Supports development of realistic and achievable program performance, schedule and cost goals as documented in the Joint Capabilities Integration and Development System (JCIDS) documents, Acquisition Program Baseline (APB) and Acquisition Strategy (AS).
- Provides the end-to-end, integrated perspective of the technical activities and processes across the system life cycle, including how the system fits into a larger system of systems (SoS) construct.
- Emphasizes the use of integrated, consistent and repeatable processes to reduce risk while maturing and managing the technical baseline. The final product baseline forms the basis for production, sustainment, future changes and upgrades.
- Provides insight into system life-cycle resource requirements and impacts on human health and the environment.

This chapter uses the following terms:

- The "Systems Engineer" refers to the Program Lead Systems Engineer, the Chief Engineer or Lead Engineer with SE responsibility and the SE staff responsible for SE processes and who plan, conduct and/or manage SE activities in the program.
- The "end user" includes the warfighter and other operational users, including support personnel, maintainers and trainers who use or support the system
- The "developer" refers to the system prime contractor (including associated subcontractors) or the Government agency responsible for designing and building the system.

Definition of Systems Engineering

1

Systems engineering (SE) is a methodical and disciplined approach for the specification, design, development, realization, technical management, operations and retirement of a system. As illustrated in Figure 1, a system is an aggregation of system elements and enabling system elements to achieve a given purpose or provide a needed capability. The enabling system elements provide the means for delivering a capability into service, keeping it in service or ending its service, and may include those processes or products necessary for developing, producing, testing, deploying and sustaining the system.

Figure 1: The System

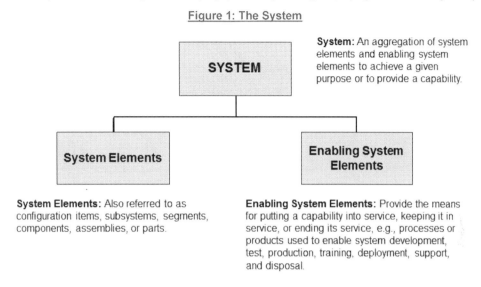

System: An aggregation of system elements and enabling system elements to achieve a given purpose or to provide a capability.

System Elements: Also referred to as configuration items, subsystems, segments, components, assemblies, or parts.

Enabling System Elements: Provide the means for putting a capability into service, keeping it in service, or ending its service, e.g., processes or products used to enable system development, test, production, training, deployment, support, and disposal.

Each **system element or enabling system element** may include, but is not limited to, hardware, software, people, data, processes, facilities, and tools.

SE applies critical thinking to the acquisition of a capability. It is a holistic, integrative discipline, whereby the contributions across engineering disciplines, such as structural engineers, electrical engineers, mechanical designers, software engineers, human factors engineers and reliability engineers, are evaluated and balanced to produce a coherent capability -- the system.

The Systems Engineer balances the conflicting design constraints of cost, schedule, and performance while maintaining an acceptable level of risk. SE solves systems acquisition problems using a multi-disciplined approach. The Systems Engineer should possess the skills, instincts and critical thinking ability to identify and focus efforts on the activities needed to enhance the overall system effectiveness, suitability, survivability and sustainability.

SE activities begin before a program is officially established and are applied throughout the acquisition life cycle. Any effective SE approach should support and be integrated with sound program management. Prior to program initiation, the Program Manager (PM), or Service lead if no PM has been assigned, should perform development planning to lay the technical foundation for successful acquisition. Development planning encompasses the engineering analyses and technical planning activities that provide the foundation for informed investment decisions on which path a materiel development decision takes. Development planning effectively addresses the capability gap(s), desired operational attributes and associated dependencies of the desired capability. In addition, development planning ensures that there exists a range of technically feasible solutions generated from across the entire solution space and that consideration has been given to near-term opportunities to provide a more rapid interim response to the capability need. Development planning is initiated prior to the Materiel Development Decision review,

2

continues throughout the Materiel Solution Analysis phase, and transitions the knowledge (documents, tools and related data) to the designated program.

Affordability

The Systems Engineer contributes to defining, establishing and achieving affordability goals and caps throughout the life cycle of the system. Affordability goals are set early in the program to inform capability requirements and major design trade-offs to define the product being acquired. Likewise, affordability caps are fixed cost requirements set prior to Milestone B that are equivalent to Key Performance Parameters (KPP). Affordability goals and caps are based on future estimates of what the Department can afford to spend for the capability, including program procurement and sustainment costs. Affordability goals and caps are used as design constraints in the development, procurement and sustainment of an affordable system. See CH 3–4.3.2. Affordability - Systems Engineering Trade-Off Analyses, for more information on how affordability drives design decisions.

The PM controls requirements growth and should use affordability goals early to guide design trades and program decisions. The Systems Engineer assists in managing affordability by working closely with the program cost estimator/analyst team when developing common cost and technical models and aligning baselines. See CH 1–4.2.1.1. for more information on affordability.

Throughout the acquisition life cycle, the PM and Systems Engineer should monitor the system affordability, seek out cost saving opportunities and identify any associated cost, schedule and performance risks. The PM's emphasis prior to Milestone B should be on defining and achieving affordability goals and caps and desired capabilities. During the Technology Maturation and Risk Reduction (TMRR) phase, the PM and Systems Engineer work to reduce technical risk and develop a sufficient understanding of the materiel solution development to validate design approaches and cost estimates, to refine requirements, and to ensure affordability is designed in to the desired capability. After Milestone B, the affordability emphasis shifts to defining and achieving should-cost estimates.

Should-cost management is a deliberate strategy to drive cost efficiencies and productivity growth into programs. The will-cost estimate is the likely life-cycle cost of the system based on historical data and represents the program's independent cost estimate, e.g., as generated by the Cost Assessment and Program Evaluation (CAPE) office or Service equivalent. As the program identifies inefficiencies, the should-cost estimate is developed based on specific actions and opportunities to mitigate, eliminate or reduce those inefficiencies that allow the program to come in below the expected will-cost estimates. The PM, with support from the Systems Engineer, develops program office cost estimates reflecting should-cost opportunities and plans. The PM and Systems Engineer use the should-cost estimate as a tool to:

- Influence design trades and choices when analyzing and setting contract/production execution targets
- Manage all costs throughout the product's life cycle
- Manage the product's final unit and sustainment cost
- Provide incentives for both of the parties (Government and industry) to execute efficiently: Government managers, who seek more value for the warfighter and taxpayer; and industry managers, who develop, build and sustain the systems and provide needed services

Should-cost management focuses on controlling the cost of both current and planned work. To have an impact, these activities should inform contract negotiations leading up to Engineering and Manufacturing Development (EMD) and Production and Deployment (P&D) phases. Should-cost management does not mean trading away the long-term value of sound design practices and disciplined SE activities for short-term gain; it does mean eliminating low-value-added activities and reports that are not required and that are deemed unessential. The Under Secretary of Defense for Acquisition, Technology, and Logistics (USD(AT&L)) Memorandum, "Should Cost Management in Defense Acquisition" describes that should-cost management is a core initiative of Better Buying Power and is an important tool to control costs in the short term and throughout the product life cycle. For guidance on implementing should-cost management, see the Better Buying Power website.

3

PMs address affordability requirements and begin to apply should-cost management early in the acquisition life cycle. This includes applying SE to define an affordable system design while also working to eliminate inefficiencies and duplication where applicable and to drive productivity improvements into their programs. Throughout the life cycle, PMs and Systems Engineers should consider Value Engineering as a key tool for meeting or beating affordability constraints and should-cost targets (See CH 3–2.4.4. Value Engineering).

Systems Engineering Processes

The practice of SE is composed of 16 processes: eight technical processes and eight technical management processes as listed in Figure 2 and described in CH 3–4. Additional Planning Considerations. These 16 processes provide a structured approach to increasing the technical maturity of a system and increasing the likelihood that the capability being developed balances mission performance with cost, schedule, risk, and design constraints.

The eight technical management processes are implemented across the acquisition life cycle and provide insight and control to assist the PM and Systems Engineer to meet performance, schedule and cost goals. The eight technical processes closely align with the acquisition life-cycle phases and include the top-down design processes and bottom-up realization processes that support transformation of operational needs into operational capabilities.

The purpose of the SE processes is to provide a framework that allows the program to structure and conduct its technical efforts to efficiently and effectively deliver a capability to satisfy a validated operational need. To fulfill that purpose, a program implements the SE technical processes in an integrated and overlapping manner to support the iterative maturation of the system solution. Implementation of the SE processes begins with the identification of a validated operational need as shown in the top left corner of the V-diagram (see Figure 2). The technical processes enable the SE team to ensure that the delivered capability accurately reflects the operational needs of the stakeholders. The key activities accomplished by the execution of the technical processes are described below:

- During the Stakeholder Requirements Definition process, the operational requirements and inputs from relevant stakeholders are translated into a set of top-level technical requirements. These requirements are decomposed and elaborated during the Requirements Analysis process to produce a complete set of system functional and performance requirements.
- During the Architecture Design process, the Systems Engineer, often through system modeling, trade-offs, and decision analyses, captures the functional requirements and interdependencies in the system architecture. Trade-offs and analyses are also used to mature and realize the design of the system and system elements during the Implementation process, generating the product baseline.
- During the Integration process, the program assembles the system elements together to provide the system for testing in the Verification process (developmental tests verifying the functional requirements) and Validation process (operational tests validating the system meets the operational need), resulting in a validated solution.
- During the Transition process, the program formally delivers the system capability to the end users, including all enabling system elements to support operational use and sustainment activities.

The technical management processes, listed at the bottom of Figure 2, provide a consistent approach to managing the program's technical activities and controlling information and events that are critical to the success of the program. Taken together, these 16 processes are a systematic approach focused on providing operational capability to the warfighter while reducing technical and programmatic risk.

Figure 2: Systems Engineering Processes

4

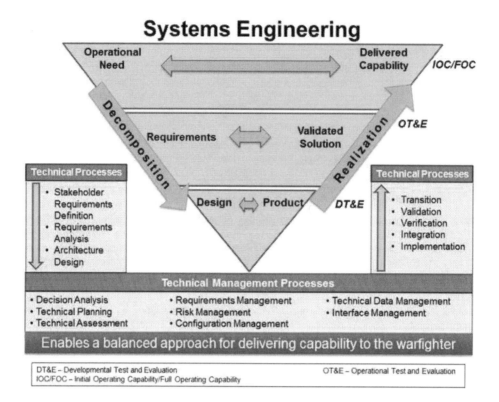

Systems Engineering

Operational Need — Delivered Capability / IOC/FOC

Decomposition

Requirements — Validated Solution — OT&E

Realization

Technical Processes
- Stakeholder Requirements Definition
- Requirements Analysis
- Architecture Design

Design — Product / DT&E

Technical Processes
- Transition
- Validation
- Verification
- Integration
- Implementation

Technical Management Processes

• Decision Analysis	• Requirements Management	• Technical Data Management
• Technical Planning	• Risk Management	• Interface Management
• Technical Assessment	• Configuration Management	

Enables a balanced approach for delivering capability to the warfighter

DT&E – Developmental Test and Evaluation   OT&E – Operational Test and Evaluation
IOC/FOC – Initial Operating Capability/Full Operating Capability

All organizations performing SE should scale their application and use of the processes in CH 3–4. Additional Planning Considerations on to reflect the unique needs of the program and the type of product or system being developed. This scaling should reflect the system's maturity and complexity, size and scope, life-cycle phase and other relevant considerations. For example, lower-risk, less-complex programs may scale the processes to ensure key activities are effective but not overly cumbersome (e.g., simpler and less-expensive tools, less-frequent reporting and activities adjusted to fit smaller organizations with fewer personnel). In CH 3–4., Figure 30 provides a representation of how much effort is typically focused on each of the SE processes throughout the acquisition life cycle.

CH 3–2.1 Systems Engineering Policy and Guidance

Policy and guidance related to systems engineering (SE) are intended to minimize the burden and cost on programs while maintaining technical integrity through the planning and execution of SE activities across the acquisition life cycle. Program Managers (PMs) and Systems Engineers should know and understand the statutory and regulatory SE mandates. Table 1 identifies top-level SE-related policy.

Table 1: Systems Engineering-Related Policy

SE Policy
DoDD 5000.01, The Defense Acquisition System
DoDI 5000.02, Operation of the Defense Acquisition System

5

DoDI 5134.16, Deputy Assistant Secretary of Defense for Systems Engineering (DASD(SE))
USD(AT&L) Memorandum, "Implementation of Will-Cost and Should-Cost Management"
USD(AT&L) Memorandum, "Better Buying Power: Mandate for Restoring Affordability and Productivity in Defense Spending"
USD(AT&L) Memorandum, "Better Buying Power 2.0: Continuing the Pursuit for Greater Efficiency and Productivity in Defense Spending"
USD(AT&L) Memorandum, "Implementation Directive for Better Buying Power 2.0 – Achieving Greater Efficiency and Productivity in Defense Spending"
USD(AT&L) Memorandum, "Implementation Directive for BBP 3.0 - Achieving Dominant Capabilities through Technical Excellence and Innovation"

Additional SE-related policy and guidance is provided on the Deputy Assistant Secretary of Defense for Systems Engineering (DASD (SE)) website.

SE-related policy, guidance, specifications and standards are intended to successfully guide the technical planning and execution of a program across the acquisition life cycle. Understanding the use and value of SE specifications and standards is fundamental to establishing, executing and maintaining disciplined SE processes. The Acquisition Streamlining and Standardization Information System (ASSIST) database is the official source for current Department of Defense (DoD) specifications and standards.

Compliance with DoD SE policy is required for program approval and completion of successful milestone decisions. DoD policy and guidance provide a framework for structuring the program and help define the areas available for tailoring to effectively and efficiently deliver capability to the warfighter.

Within this policy and guidance framework, tailoring the acquisition effort to meet program cost, schedule and performance goals is not only desired but mandated in accordance with DoD Directive (DoDD) 5000.01, para 4.3.1 and DoD Instruction (DoDI) 5000.02, para 5. In July 2012, USD(AT&L) emphasized there is no one-size-fits-all optimal program structure. Every program has its own optimal structure, and that structure is dependent on many variables that contribute to program success or failure. In accordance with applicable laws and regulations, program tailoring should be based on the specifics of the product being acquired, including complexity, acquisition category, risk factors and required timelines to satisfy validated capability requirements. Areas that should be considered for tailoring include:

- Documentation of program information
- Execution of the acquisition phases
- Type of acquisition strategy
- Timing and scope of decision reviews
- Decision approval levels

The requirements of DoD SE policy that are identified for tailoring by the PM are submitted to the Milestone Decision Authority (MDA) for approval.

Program structuring should start with a deep understanding of the nature of the capability intended to be acquired and the effort needed to realize that capability. Critical thinking during early program formulation is important to clearly identify the internal and external stakeholders, system interdependencies, technological opportunities, contractual and budgetary constraints and policy mandates. The optimal program structure includes the set of technical activities, events and management mechanisms that best address the unique circumstances and risks of the program. DoDI 5000.02, para 5.c.3 describes several acquisition models that serve as examples of defense program structures tailored to the type of product being acquired or to the need for accelerated acquisition. (See CH 3–3.1.1. Systems Engineering in

6

Defense Acquisition Program Models for more information on these models and the expected application for each model, highlighting the relevant SE activities.)

All program strategy and planning documents depend on SE activities to define and balance requirements against cost, schedule and risks; identify potential solutions; assess the maturity and feasibility of available technologies; develop a realistic schedule; and allow for multiple other considerations affecting the final cost and delivery of capability to the warfighter. Therefore, the PM should build a program office structure that ensures the Systems Engineer is an integrated part of the program planning and execution activities.

The Systems Engineer leads or is a key enabler in the planning and execution of the program's technical approach. To aid this planning, the Systems Engineer should proactively seek experience from similar past and current programs and map this learning as applicable into the SE planning of the program (see CH 3–2.4.5. Lessons Learned, Best Practices, Case Studies).

CH 3–2.2 Systems Engineering Plan

The purpose of the Systems Engineering Plan (SEP) is to help Program Managers (PMs) develop, communicate and manage the overall systems engineering (SE) approach that guides all technical activities of the program. The SEP documents key technical risks, processes, resources, metrics, SE products, organizations, design considerations and completed and scheduled SE activities. The SEP is a living document that should be updated as needed to reflect the program's evolving SE approach and/or plans and current status. DoDI 5000.02, Enc 3, sec. 2 requires PMs to prepare a SEP to guide the systems engineering activities on the program. PMs should use the SEP Outline to guide preparation of the plan. The SEP Outline identifies the minimum expected content to be addressed. The SEP should be consistent with and complementary to the Acquisition Program Baseline (APB), Acquisition Strategy (AS), Test and Evaluation Master Plan (TEMP), Program Protection Plan (PPP), Life-Cycle Sustainment Plan (LCSP) and other program plans as appropriate. The SEP should be written in plain language to clearly communicate plans for each phase of the acquisition life cycle, and should be written to avoid redundancy and maintain consistency with other planning documents (see DoDI 5025.13, DoD Plain Language Program for additional information).

In an effort to promote a higher probability of mission success, Major Defense Acquisition Programs (MDAPs) should review, tailor and implement applicable mission assurance concepts and principles when developing their SEP. MDAPs should use resources provided by their service (for example, the Aerospace/Air Force Mission Assurance Guide TOR-2007(8546)-6018).

For MDAPs and Major Automated Information Systems (MAIS), the PM should formally charter a SE Working-Level Integrated Product Team (WIPT), led by the Systems Engineer, to assist in developing and monitoring SE activities as documented in the program SEP. DoDI 5000.02, Enc 3, sec. 2 requires a formal SEP to be approved by the Milestone Decision Authority (MDA) before Milestone A, B, and C and program restructures. DoDI 5000.02, Enc 3, sec. 2 and 10 USC 139b (para (b)) requires the Deputy Assistant Secretary of Defense (Systems Engineering) (DASD(SE)) to review the SEP for all MDAPs and MAIS programs. DoD Components are required to submit the SEP to the DASD(SE) 45 calendar days prior to the scheduled Defense Acquisition Board Milestone review for all MDAPs and MAIS programs. Additionally, a draft SEP (as defined in DoDI 5000.02, Enc 1, sec. 3) is due to the MDA at the Development RFP Release Decision Point. For MDAP and MAIS, this draft SEP will be provided to DASD(SE) 45 calendar days prior to the Development RFP Release Decision Point. As a best practice, SEP updates should be approved by the Program Executive Office (PEO) prior to each technical review and when the program changes in a way that has an impact on the technical strategy. The PM may approve other periodic updates to the SEP.

The SEP describes the integration of SE activities with other program management and control efforts, including the Integrated Master Plan (IMP), Work Breakdown Structure (WBS), Integrated Master Schedule (IMS), Risk Management Plan (RMP), Technical Performance Measures (TPMs) and other documentation fundamental to successful program execution. The SEP also describes the program's technical requirements, engineering resources and management and technical activities and products as well as the planning, timing, conduct and success criteria of event-driven SE technical reviews throughout the acquisition life cycle. Consistent with the DoDI 5000.02, Enc 3, sec. 2, PMs should include the SEP (either an approved or a draft SEP) in the Request for Proposal (RFP) to the offerors as either guidance or as a compliance document depending on the maturity of the plan and the acquisition strategy.

Before providing the SEP to the offerors, the PM and Systems Engineer should determine if the document contains sensitive information and, if so, remove this sensitive information from the SEP before attaching it to the RFP. The developer's Systems Engineering Management Plan (SEMP), which is the contractor-developed plan for the conduct, management and control of the integrated engineering effort, should be consistent with the Government SEP to ensure that Government and contractor technical plans are aligned. The SEMP should define the contractor technical planning and how it is accomplished from the contractor perspective, and articulates details of their processes, tools and organization.

As the program's blueprint for the conduct, management and control of all technical activities, the SEP captures decisions made during the technical planning process and communicates objectives and guidance to program personnel and other stakeholders. The SEP should define the "who, what, when, why, and how" of the SE approach, for example:

- The program organization with roles and responsibilities, authority, accountability and staffing resources. This includes the coordination of the program's integrated product teams (IPTs) and their products, resources, staffing, management metrics and integration mechanisms.
- The key activities, resources, tools and events that support execution of the SE technical processes and technical management processes (see CH 3–4. Additional Planning Considerations) to deliver a balanced solution to meet the warfighter's needs. It should identify unique processes, tools and/or tailoring of organizational and Government standards, how these processes and tools are integrated and how products are developed and managed. For instance, the description of the program's risk management approach and the status of top-level technical risk, issues and opportunities (RIOs), including the mitigation and handling activities, should be documented in the SEP or summarized and referenced in separate planning documentation. As a best practice, the RIOs should be collected monthly and reported to senior leadership stakeholders at least quarterly (see CH 3–4.1.5. Risk Management Process).
- The event-driven technical review approach based on successful completion of key activities as opposed to calendar-based deadlines. Document the plans for conducting each technical review with particular emphasis on the entry/exit criteria and details of the systems engineering technical reviews planned in the program's next acquisition phase. The SEP should identify the timing of SE events in relation to other program events and key knowledge points, and it should describe how technical activities are integrated in the program's overall plan and schedule. The SEP should include the assumptions made in developing the schedule and the process for conducting schedule risk assessments and updates. SEPs submitted to the approval authority should include a current schedule, with all appropriate technical reviews, no more than three months old.
- The prototyping strategy that ensures the system requirements (including Key Performance Parameters (KPPs) and Key System Attributes (KSAs)) are achievable within cost and schedule constraints.
- The description of the architecture products that will be developed to better describe and understand the system, to include internal and external interfaces. As a best practice, to ensure architectures are properly formulated, the SEP should include a description of mission thread analysis completed to support material development and the mapping between interoperability/interface specifications.
- The approach for how requirements and technical performance trade-offs are balanced within the larger program scope to deliver operationally effective, suitable and affordable systems. Key design considerations and criteria (see CH 3–4.3.) should be listed in the mandatory table as applicable, with all the associated documentation submitted with each SEP submission.
- The program's strategy for identifying, prioritizing and selecting the set of technical performance measures and metrics (TPMM) should provide sufficient insight into the technical progress and program risks. Each measure or metric should have threshold, margin and contingency values. The values should measure achievement over time and be reported at every major program event. The measures and metrics should be specific, measurable, achievable, relevant and time-

bound. As a best practice, the measures and metrics should be collected monthly and reported to senior leadership stakeholders at least quarterly, and at least 15 TPMMs should be selected and reported to adequately identify, measure, track and manage technical and programmatic risks. The following TPMMs should be considered for inclusion: Risk Management, Schedule Risk, Net Ready KPP, Number of Class 1 Engineering Change Proposals (ECPs) and Number of Class 2 ECPs. Additionally, the program should ensure that each Critical Technical Parameter (CTP) has a corresponding TPM (see CH 3–4.1.3.1. Technical Performance Measures).

- The plan and description should be documented for how the system design enables technology insertion and refresh.
- The SE tools and other enablers integrated and used to support SE processes, technical design initiatives and activities.

CH 3–2.3 Systems Level Considerations

A system should not be acquired in isolation from other systems with which it associates in the operational environment. The Program Manager (PM) and Systems Engineer should understand how their system fills the needs for which it was designed and the enterprise context within which it operates. When the system functions as part of a Family of Systems/ System of Systems (FoS/SoS), systems engineers should examine the Concept of Operations (CONOPS)/Operational Mode Summary/Mission Profile (OMS/MP) and Initial Capability Document (ICD) for dependencies/interfaces. These documents should adequately describe the interactions between the proposed system and the associated FoS/SoS dependencies/interfaces. This includes understanding the diverse or dissimilar mix of other systems (hardware, software and human) with which the system needs to exchange information. To that end, the PM and Systems Engineer should define intersystem interfaces using a systems engineering (SE) document, i.e., the interface control document(s). In addition to interface control documents, the PM and Systems Engineer should also actively pursue Memoranda of Agreement or Memoranda of Understanding (MOA/MOU) with companion programs regarding interfaces, data exchanges, and advance notices of changes interdependencies and schedule (timing) that may affect either program. These agreements are a professional courtesy and a means of mitigating the inherent risk in planning to deliver a capability to an anticipated future technical baseline when there is uncertainty that the other programs are able to maintain schedule and have adequate resources to deploy the capabilities as planned. The agreements should indicate responsible organizations for all interactions requiring cost allocation, (e.g., training, facilities and staffing).

SE is increasingly recognized as key to addressing the evolution of complex systems of systems. SE principles and tools can be used to apply systems thinking and engineering to the enterprise levels. An enterprise in this usage is understood to be the organization or cross-organizational entity supporting a defined business scope and mission, and includes the interdependent resources (people, organizations and technology) to coordinate functions and share information in support of a common mission or set of related missions, (see "Federal Enterprise Architecture Framework (FEAF)," January 2013).

This application of SE to address enterprises as complex systems builds on traditional SE activities and expands them to address enterprise challenges. The Systems Engineer can also assist with enterprise strategic planning and enterprise investment analysis. These two additional roles for Systems Engineers at the enterprise level are "shared with the organization's senior line management, and tend to be more entrepreneurial, business-driven, and economic in nature in comparison to the more technical nature of classical systems engineering," (Source: Charlock, P.G., and R.E. Fenton, "System-of-Systems (SoS) Enterprise Systems for Information-Intensive Organizations," Systems Engineering, Vol. 4, No. 4 (2001), pages 242-261).

Each DoD Service and Agency, and the Department itself, are examples of enterprises as systems. Such organizations have the challenge of integrating and evolving multiple portfolios of systems often with conflicting sets of objectives, constraints, stakeholders and demands for resources.

The Systems Engineer should be cognizant of the enterprise context and constraints for the system in development and should factor these enterprise considerations into acquisition technical decisions from the outset. Mission areas, for example, can be viewed as cross-organizational enterprises and also

9

provide critical context for system acquisition. Controlled interfaces with enabling systems in the SoS architecture drive system design. In some cases, enterprise considerations have been articulated as standards and certification requirements. In other cases, system decisions need to be made in the context of the larger Service portfolio of systems and mission area needs.

Most DoD capabilities today are provided by an aggregation of systems often referred to as systems of systems (SoS). An SoS is described as a set or arrangement of systems that results when independent and useful systems are integrated into a larger system that delivers unique capabilities. For complex SoS, the interdependencies that exist or are developed between and/or among the individual systems being integrated are significantly important and need to be tracked. Each SoS may consist of varying technologies that matured decades apart, designed for different purposes but now used to meet new objectives that may not have been defined at the time the systems were deployed.

Both individual systems and SoS conform to the accepted definition of a system in that each consists of parts, relationships and a whole that is greater than the sum of its parts; however, not all systems are SoS. There are distinct differences between systems and SoS that should be taken into account in the application of SE to SoS (see Table 2, adapted from DoD Systems Engineering Guide for Systems of Systems and SoS Systems Engineering and Test & Evaluation: Final Report of the NDIA SE Division SoS SE and T&E Committees).

Table 2: Comparing Systems and Systems of Systems

	System	System of Systems (SoS)
Management & Oversight		
Stakeholder Involvement	Clearer set of stakeholders	Two or more levels of stakeholders with mixed, possibly competing interests. The stakeholders represent: 1. the independent and useful systems 2. the aggregation of the independent and useful systems
Governance	Aligned PM and funding. Higher levels of governance such as PEO and AT&L (internal and external governance)	Added levels of complexity due to management and funding for both SoS and systems; No single manager controls all constituent systems in the SoS
Operational Environment		
Operational Focus	Designed and developed to meet operational objectives	Called upon to provide integrated capabilities using systems whose objectives have not been directly derived from current SoS system's objectives
Implementation		
Acquisition	Aligned to established acquisition process	Multiple system life cycles across acquisition programs, involving legacy systems, systems under development, new developments and technology insertion; Stated capability objectives but may not have formal requirements
Test & Evaluation	Test and evaluation (T&E) of the system is possible	Testing more challenging due to systems' asynchronous life cycles, independence of constituent systems, and the complexity of all the moving parts; Given these challenges, the T&E approach may need to focus on system or

10

	System	System of Systems (SoS)
		subsystem testing in risk areas of the capability and evaluate evidence from SoS level activities or roll-ups of system-level activities
Engineering & Design Considerations		
Boundaries & Interfaces	Focuses on boundaries and interfaces	Focus on identifying systems contributing to SoS objectives and enabling flow of data, control and functionality across and/or between the SoS while balancing needs of systems. The boundaries and interfaces between systems become very important, since they serve as a conduit for data transfer
Performance & Behavior	Ability of the system to meet performance objectives	Performance across the SoS that satisfies SoS user capability needs while balancing needs of the systems

Application of Systems Engineering to Systems of Systems

Systems of systems (SoS) systems engineering (SE) deals with planning, analyzing, organizing and integrating the capabilities of new and existing systems into a SoS capability greater than the sum of the capabilities of its constituent parts. Consistent with the DoD transformation vision and enabling net-centric operations, SoS may deliver capabilities by combining multiple collaborative and independent-yet-interacting systems. The mix of systems may include existing, partially developed and yet-to-be-designed independent systems.

The DoD Guide to Systems Engineering for Systems of Systems and International Organization for Standards / International Electrotechnical Commission / Institute of Electrical and Electronics Engineers (ISO/IEC/IEEE) 15288, Appendix G addresses the application of SE to SoS. The DoD guide defines four types of SoS (see Table 3). When a SoS is recognized as a "directed," "acknowledged," or "collaborative" SoS, SE is applied across the constituent systems and is tailored to the characteristics and context of the SoS. Due to increased efforts to network systems to facilitate information-sharing across the battlespace, most DoD systems also may be viewed as components of a "virtual" SoS. For virtual SoS, DoD net-centric policies and strategies, such as, Department of Defense Net-Centric Services Strategy, provide SE guidance regarding SoS contexts where there is an absence of explicit shared objectives or central management.

Table 3: Four Types of Systems of Systems

Type	Definition
Directed	Directed SoS are those in which the SoS is engineered and managed to fulfill specific purposes. It is centrally managed during long-term operation to continue to fulfill those purposes as well as any new ones the system owners might wish to address. The component systems maintain an ability to operate independently, but their normal operational mode is subordinated to the centrally managed purpose
Acknowledged	Acknowledged SoS have recognized objectives, a designated manager, and resources for the SoS; however, the constituent systems retain their independent ownership, objectives, funding, development, and sustainment approaches. Changes in the systems are based on cooperative agreements between the SoS and the system

11

Type	Definition
Collaborative	In collaborative SoS, the component systems interact more or less voluntarily to fulfill agreed-upon central purposes
Virtual	Virtual SoS lacks a central management authority and a centrally agreed-upon purpose for the system of systems. Large-scale behavior emerges-and may be desirable-but this type of SoS relies upon relatively invisible, self-organizing mechanisms to maintain it

CH 3–2.3.1 Software

Software (SW) is critical to advanced warfighting capability and virtually all DoD systems: weapon systems; Command, Control, Communications, Computers, Intelligence, Surveillance, and Reconnaissance (C4ISR); logistics; enterprise networks; defense business systems; and National Security Systems. SW is a key driver of system complexity and performance and is critical to battlefield dominance and maintaining operational advantage in an environment of change. Accordingly, SW development and sustainment frequently contributes a major portion of total system life-cycle cost, schedule and risk and should be considered throughout the acquisition and Systems Engineering (SE) life cycle.

Key SW Engineering Enablers. Given the challenge and importance of SW acquisition, the Program Manager (PM) should understand and emphasize the following key Software Engineering (SWE) principles that enable efficient capability delivery to the warfighter:

- Integrate SWE into the SE Process:
  - Plan for and integrate SWE activities within SE processes and acquisition documents, particularly for system-level technical reviews and technical baselines.
  - Integrate SWE design analysis, test and demonstrations within SE processes.
- Commit to Measurement: use predictive SW metrics and quantitative analysis techniques to support data-driven decisions at every level (e.g. IPT Lead, Chief SE, PM, PEO, SAE).
- Continuously Evaluate and Update SW Schedule Estimates:
  - Substantiate SW schedule realism with a rigorous basis of estimate.
  - Continuously evaluate the viability and degree of optimism in SW schedules.
- Measure and Project SW Maturity & Readiness for T&E / User: (e.g., defects, stability).
- Rigorously Manage SW Requirements:
  - Integrate SW considerations into system requirements and design.
  - Ensure SW requirements are stable, traceable, allocated to iterations and assessed for dependencies to meet iteration goals for capability and test.
  - Manage cascading/deferred requirements and mitigate development concurrency.
- Adopt Continuous Integration/Delivery and Automated Testing:
  - Measure and incrementally deliver end-to-end performance and capabilities.
  - Verify and validate capabilities (to include prototypes) through early, incremental user demonstrations and tests in high-fidelity environments.
  - Use SW development environments that enable continuous builds and automated test.
- Continuously Assess Sufficiency of SW Staffing: quantity/experience within The Program Management Office/Contractor Program Office (PMO/KTR).

Software Engineering Competencies. In addition to the key enablers above, successful SWE requires unique expertise to address a wide range of SW knowledge areas (e.g., acquisition, development and maintenance) and SW activities and competencies (e.g., contracting, planning, requirements engineering, architecture, design, integration, build planning, measurement, technical data rights, quality assurance, verification and validation (V&V), interoperability, security, development environments, etc.). Critical competencies for SW acquisition professionals include:

- **SW Development Methodology Selection:** Plan for software acquisition by selecting appropriate software life-cycle models (e.g., incremental, spiral, iterative, evolutionary).
- **SW Build Planning and Management:** Manage an iterative SW development approach using testable and/or deployable builds (integrated subsets of overall capability); establish a build plan that addresses: (1) dependencies, synchronization and integration; (2) prototype- or target-hardware (HW) availability to enable developmental and operational testing of builds; and, (3) detailed SW staffing plans (derived from SW effort and schedule estimates).
- **SW Trade Studies:** Conduct trade-offs of SW technologies (e.g., government off-the-shelf (GOTS); commercial off-the-shelf (COTS) / non-developmental items (NDI); reuse; open source software (OSS); modular open systems approach (MOSA); service-oriented architecture (SOA); cloud, high performance and mobile computing).
- **SW Risk Management:** Evaluate/track SW risks as part of related component/system risks.
- **SW Measurement:** Identify, track and report metrics for SW technical performance (with respect to product performance, process, development progress and quality).

SWE knowledge should cut across the acquirer and developer/supplier teams. PMs should understand SW development principles and best practices (see CH 3–2.4.5. Lessons Learned, Best Practices and Case Studies), terms, tools, development methods (e.g., Agile software), challenges and risks. Developers should have knowledge and demonstrated experience with SW development of similar scale and complexity. Chief System Engineers and SW Engineers should be well versed in the technical and management activities of SW acquisition and SWE. SW Engineers should engage early in the life cycle to ensure that all requirements, cost/schedule estimates and risk identification/mitigation efforts (including uncertainties in estimates) address SW considerations. SW engineers are also needed to evaluate the developer's artifacts, SW architecture; functional- , allocated-, and product-baselines; monthly SW metrics reports, SW documentation, plans, estimates, modeling and simulation capabilities and facilities/environments. Program-independent SW engineers should support validation activities.

Software Considerations in the Acquisition Strategy. As part of the program's Acquisition Strategy, the PM and Systems Engineer should establish a SW acquisition strategy aligned with the program's Acquisition Strategy, as early as possible. The strategy should address function and component allocation to determine the SW to be (1) newly developed; (2) provided as GOTS, COTS, or OSS; and (3) acquired from a combination of sources. The strategy should incorporate plans for associated data and intellectual property rights for all acquired SW. In general, DoDI DoDI 5000.02, para 5.c.3 emphasizes tailoring and offers several example acquisition models intended to serve as a starting point in structuring a program, including guidance for software-dominant programs (see CH 3–3.1.1. SE in Defense Acquisition Program Models for a summary of the tailored models).

Software Risk Management. SW acquisition is a critical high-risk area for most programs. As such, the PM should maintain consistent awareness of its contribution to overall program and system risk, and should manage those aspects of the program. Effective SE and SWE principles and practices should help anticipate, plan for and mitigate SW development and system integration challenges and risks. Risk and opportunity management processes should address SW considerations, particularly with respect to schedule, maturity, integration, interfaces and interoperability.

Quantitative SWE and SW Measurement. Quantitative insight is crucial for program success. Commitment to a quantitative (i.e. data-driven) SWE and SE approach is vital to shape program plans; monitor execution; and inform leadership of technical risks throughout the life cycle, particularly in support of major decisions. The lack of effective SW measurement plans and practice– addressing acquirer, supplier and developer needs – exposes the program to high risk.

The PM and SE/SWE should plan and use predictive metrics on a frequent, periodic basis to rigorously: (1) measure and control SW product performance; and, (2) assess SW schedule realism and maturity/readiness of SW for test and delivery to user. Leading indicators provide "early warning" to enable timely risk mitigation. The program's measurement process and its associated goals, metrics and

13

reports should be planned/contracted for early in the life cycle to ensure maximum insight across the prime and subcontractor suppliers/developers. The plan should consider both knowledge points (and associated decision makers) and inflection points (changes in metric values/trends that alert decision makers to emerging problems).

Planning Artifacts. A SEP with insufficient SW Technical Performance Measures (TPMs) is inadequate to track, assess and mitigate risks related to complex SW development and maturity. Beyond the TPMs documented in the SEP, a SW Measurement Plan is recommended (for acquirer and developer) to further elaborate the quantitative management approach and to capture finer-grain SW metrics. An example of a template for a SW Measurement Plan is available from Naval Air Systems Command (NAVAIR), as Standard Work Package SWP4140-024, Software Measurement Plan Template, AIR-4.1.4, Version 3.0, dated 25 June, 2015.

Best Practices for SW Acquisition. Table 4 identifies several vital practices, and briefly describes essential elements and approaches for their implementation. Less-than-rigorous implementation of these practices has often contributed to program failure.

Table 4: SWE Best Practices: Essential Elements & Implementation Approaches

Practice	Essential Elements and Implementation Approaches
Establish high-confidence cost, effort and schedule estimates For additional guidance on software cost estimation for different system types and operating environments, see the Software Cost Estimation Metrics Manual for Defense Systems	• Estimate the cost, effort and schedule (planning) as a yardstick for measuring progress and performance (executing) • Use at least two methods: the methods include, e.g. Wideband Delphi, Analogy, Parametric, Bottoms-Up; SW parametric statistical analysis is a best practice • Reconcile multiple estimate methods and derive the estimate confidence level • Frequently monitor, reassess and update initial SW estimates and schedules given the uncertainty with initial assumptions (e.g., sizing and staffing estimates) • Benchmark estimates against similar DoD projects, industry norms, and most importantly with the developer's historical performance (e.g., productivity) • Update estimates and confidence based on SW metrics collected during execution • Present updated estimates-to-complete at every major program review to identify deviations from the original effort/schedule baselines and risk likelihood.
Establish and manage to a core set of predictive quantitative metrics	• Establish predictive metrics within the SEP, SDP and SW Measurement Plan • Key areas to monitor include: Requirements development progress and volatility, Design progress, Code development progress (e.g., effective software lines of code (eSLOC), Story Points) eSLOC growth; SW staffing, Build delivery progress; Capability delivery; SW test progress; Defects discovered/ fixed/ deferred /backlog, Defect aging/density, SW maturity/quality (e.g. stability) • The PM and developer should select metrics relevant to the development methodology in use. (e.g., Agile metrics – such as Team & Aggregate Velocity) • Ensure that the RFP requires the collecting and reporting of SW metrics • Establish time-based plans (monthly, key knowledge points) with thresholds and control bounds to mitigate metrics that are off track from the goal • Regularly (e.g., monthly) review metrics; understand how they serve as "leading indicators," provide early warning, and use this information to make informed decisions • Establish benchmarks based on actual performance to inform future planning
Ensure the developer establishes and utilizes effective SW development processes,	• The SDP provides details below the level of the SEP and the contractor's SE Management Plan (SEMP) for managing SW development and integration • The SDP Data Item Description (DID) DI-IPSC-81427 is a tailorable template and a useful starting point in defining the format for an SDP

14

Practice	Essential Elements and Implementation Approaches
according to a Software Development Plan	• The SDP provides the SE with insight into, and a tool for monitoring, the processes being followed by the developer for each activity, the project schedules, the developer's SW organization and resource allocations • Compare software development processes and tools to assumptions used in the effort and schedule estimates • Refer to IEEE 12207 and/or ISO/IEC 15288 for SW processes and activities

Establish and manage to quality targets and conduct SW maturity and defect analyses	• The PMO should assess SW maturity/readiness and conduct defect analysis that:
	   o Establishes realistic defect discovery and burn-down plans by severity and life cycle phase which enable delivery of mature SW to test and the user
	   o Evaluates adequacy of resources and capacity for defect resolution
	   o Assesses maturity for each increment/release
	   o Establishes triggers for reviewing breaches in SW maturity predictions
	• Clearly and unambiguously define quality goals for delivered products at project inception; quality targets and projections should consider the expected number of defects by priority and estimated fix rate, as well as the expected defect density (goals will vary with application types and domains).
	• Projected maturity at delivery should consider capabilities met (e.g., Use Cases delivered, features accepted); trend toward meeting end-to-end and critical mission thread-related TPMs; and key quality attributes (e.g. stability)
	• Defects should be measured during all phases of the life cycle, from requirements through post-deployment, and analyzed in a defect phase containment matrix.

Post-Deployment Software Support (PDSS) -- establish plans and budgets for life cycle software support	• Address SW supportability, the SW test environment, and other equipment, material and documentation, including data rights that are required to provide PDSS for those end users identified in the SDP or documents similar to the Computer Resources Life Cycle Management Plan and LCSP • DoDI 5000.02, para 5.d.9, requires SW sustainment processes in place by end of EMD Phase • Estimate costs of development and run-time licenses over the system's life cycle • Consider product line practices for leveraging resources across related programs

Expectations for System-Level SE Technical Reviews and Technical Baselines Given Incremental SW Development. Development of several software builds using an incremental, spiral, iterative, evolutionary software development approach enables the developers to deliver capability in a series of manageable releases or builds, to gain user acceptance and feedback for the next build or increment and reduce the overall level of risk. Frequent requirements and design validation activities involving the end users can help the program define viable increments of capabilities that have operational value for limited deployment before complete system/capability delivery.

Some programs implementing incremental software development approaches (and specifically those using an Agile software development methodology or an Information Technology (IT) Box approach to requirements) may have multiple build-level reviews and evolving lower-level requirements and design maturity that in turn can impact delivery of fully established technical baselines. In these cases, incremental approaches (particularly Agile) by acquirer and developer can confuse stakeholder expectations at system-level reviews. It is therefore critical to use the SEP to communicate tailoring/expectations for SE technical reviews, exit success criteria and when technical baselines will be fully established -- all without compromising SE rigor. (For additional considerations, see Agile & Incremental SW Development in the Defense Acquisition System.)

For example, the requirements at an initial Preliminary Design Review (PDR) may be fully defined for an initial set of capabilities, with future builds or increments fully defining low-level requirements for additional capabilities and the complete system allocated baseline. Figure 3 shows a single system-level PDR and multiple build-level PDRs for multiple, successive builds. System and software architectures should

15

support both the current build and future builds in accordance with the approved program/system requirements and constraints. PMs and SEs should consider the following practices for incremental development approaches:

- Develop the minimum viable requirements: high-level system (e.g., system requirements specification, functional requirements document) and architecturally significant requirements (non-functional requirements) covering the full scope of effort.
- Define configuration item level requirements for the build(s) or increment under review and those requirements to meet critical functions and key quality attributes.
- Develop a minimum viable architecture that consists of an initial software architecture and design with artifacts to show evidence of SW architectural evaluation and system-level architectural trade-offs (e.g., COTS software candidates to meet requirements).
- Document expectations for lower-level component artifacts and a minimum set of characteristics that defines the level of tailoring and acceptance criteria for these artifacts.
- Conduct a risk assessment that covers the full scope of the system; for design decisions not defined at PDR; track technical debt and architectural dependencies as system-level risks.
- Define progress and product metrics for iterations/builds and total system development.

Figure 3: Example Implementation of PDR for Incremental SW Development

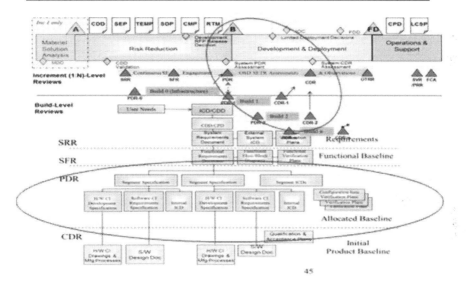

Other reviews (e.g., System Requirements Review (SRR), Software Specification Review (SSR) and Critical Design Review (CDR)) should follow similar practices. See CH 3–3.3. and DoDI 5000.02, Enc 3, sec. 7 for additional information about Technical Reviews.

This type of incremental approach – with expectations for limited deployments – should identify interdependencies and associated technical risks as part of determining the content for each increment or build. It should include a clear understanding of the final end state of supporting physical hardware elements when functionality or capability is added over time, the synchronization of SW and HW requirements and schedules, continuous integration and end-to-end demonstration of the total system, and the ability to release working software on an agreed-to integrated plan and schedule. Memory, processor overhead, and input/output capacity designs should support growth in capability; this includes emerging technologies such as Cloud and Infrastructure-as-a-Service (IaaS).

16

While DoDI 5000.02, para 5.c.3 supports tailoring for incremental development, limited deployments may not be viable when the end system is not usable until the entire set of essential capabilities is integrated and tested. For example, most weapon systems depend on SW for real-time controls that can affect life and safety; these systems require security, safety and interoperability qualification/certification before release for operational use. (Life-cycle approaches that incrementally deploy SW products or releases that include intermediate builds (e.g., DoDI 5000.02 Models 3 or 6) should also consider such qualification and certification.) In addition, safety/security assurance certifications and approvals require a predetermined objective level of rigor in verification, validation, and accreditation (VV&A) of these SW releases. This VV&A is based on risk, not on the complexity or size of each release. The Joint Software Systems Safety Handbook provides guidance for implementing safety-critical software designs with the reasonable assurance that the software executes at an acceptable level of safety risk. The Handbook includes discussion of MIL-STD-882 (DoD Standard Practice for System Safety), which is required for implementation of software safety.

SEP Considerations. In addition to identifying SW considerations as an essential element of all SE activities in the SEP, the PM and SE/SWE should ensure that the SEP addresses:

- Software-unique risks, issues and opportunities
- Inclusion of software in technical reviews, with the addition of the SSR as a precursor to the PDR for software-intensive systems
- SW technical performance, process, progress and quality metrics (importantly, those associated with End-to-End performance and capability delivery (see CH 3–4.1.3.1. Technical Performance Measures)
- SW safety, security and protection, including associated SW processes, architecture and interfacing systems
- Configuration Management (CM) for SW integration facilities/laboratories, verification/validation and development tools
- SW technology/infrastructure such as Cloud, common operating environments (COE) and MOSA; associated data rights; and sustainment considerations
- Independent verification and validation (IV&V), especially for contractor-proprietary SW
- Verification of documentation, configuration management, test relevancy and other considerations for reuse of legacy SW as well as new SW

The Services provide additional guidance to assist PMs, Systems Engineers and Software Engineers on software aspects of acquisition programs for all types of systems:

- Air Force: Weapon Systems Software Management Guidebook
- Army: DA-PAM-70-3, Army Acquisition Procedures and DA-PAM-73-1, Test and Evaluation in Support of Systems Acquisition (software metrics recommendations)
- Navy: Guidebook for Acquisition of Naval Software-Intensive Systems

Software Architecture. Architecture is the bridge between mission drivers and system design, focused on planning, analyzing, organizing and integrating current and emerging operational and system capabilities to achieve desired warfighting mission effects. These outcomes are documented in quality attributes (ranging from "-ilities" to system performance), which are then evolved to system requirements and lower-level design. Architecture should consider external interface definition, support growing scale and functionality and accommodate technology insertion opportunities. SW architecture balances trade-offs (e.g., system modularity with very high performance), by frequently using techniques such as system modeling and mission simulation to evaluate solution alternatives. Implementing MOSA as part of the SW design and development can increase design flexibility, support incremental deliveries, allow for opportunities to use COTS SW and OSS, facilitate future upgrades and modifications and support technology insertion (see CH 3–4.3.4. Commercial-Off-the-Shelf and CH 3–2.4.1. Modular Open Systems Approach).

17

COTS/GOTS SW. Weapon system acquisitions often contain a mix of GOTS SW with complete technical data and software rights, other SW items (e.g., COTS) with restricted Government purpose rights and SW with virtually no rights other than the commercial license to use or access the SW (see FAR (Subpart 27.4)). The PM should be aware of the implications of these differences regarding acquisition and sustainment costs, performance and the consequences on change control and sustainment of deployed systems; this is also particularly relevant in the areas of security and SW assurance. The Systems Engineer should understand the system concept of operations /operational mode summary / mission profile, any maintenance plans and the expected users of COTS/GOTS SW applications including their level of training. This understanding is necessary to effectively balance cost, scheduling and potential risks in maintenance, training and documentation.

Software Services. In programs for which software capability is procured as a service, the service-level agreement(s) (SLA) should reflect operational or fielded performance requirements, including all path constraints, such as satellite time delays, low data rate access, and intermittent service, as part of the operational environmental constraints and potential security requirements. SLA provisions are important because service providers may not be willing to disclose details of their operations and staffing (such as overseas data centers or help desks).

Software Data Management and Technical Data Rights: Rights associated with commercial products are defined in licenses that may impose limits on product use, such as restricting the buyer's ability to alter the product or the number of copies the buyer can make. In many cases, commercial vendors offer their products on a completely "as-is" basis, making no assurance of suitability for intended purposes and offering the buyer no recourse in the event of problems. Open-source software, sometimes referred to as "freeware," may not actually be free; it may also have restrictions or carry embedded modules that are more restrictive than the overall package. The PM, Systems Engineer, software engineer, and contracting officer should be familiar with the restrictions placed on each software item used in the contract or deliverable to the Government. The Program Office should ensure that necessary intellectual property rights to software are determined in advance of the RFP and contract award, and that they are acquired as needed; these rights can include such things as:

- All requirements tools and data sets
- All test software and supporting information necessary to build and execute the tests
- All other software test tools such as interface simulators and test data analyzers whether custom-developed or not
- All information for defects remaining in the software upon delivery to the Government

Software Reuse: Any reuse of any system, hardware, firmware or software throughout the acquisition life cycle should be addressed in multiple plans and processes, including the SEP, Software Development Plan (SDP), firmware development plan, configuration management plan, Test and Evaluation Master Plan (TEMP), Software Test Plan (STP), Independent Verification and Validation (IV&V) Plan) and quality assurance plans (system and software). (**Note:** Software reuse has traditionally been overestimated in the beginning of programs. PMs and Systems Engineers should monitor software reuse as a potential risk.) For more discussion of software reuse, see CH 3–2.4.1. Modular Open Systems Approach.

Software System Safety: Software system safety is applicable to most DoD systems; this reflects the ubiquitous nature of software-driven functions, network connectivity and systems of systems (SoS). Specific mandatory certifications such as safety, security, cybersecurity and airworthiness require attention early in the development cycle to ensure documentation and testing are planned and executed to meet certification criteria. Systems Engineers are encouraged to check with certification authorities frequently, as rules can change during development.

Software Integrated within Acquisition Life Cycles Table 5 through Table 9 identify software considerations and specific activities associated with each phase of the acquisition life cycle. Table entries identify whether the considerations are unique to a particular DoDI 5000.02, para 5.c.3 acquisition

18

life cycle model (hardware dominant Models 1, 2 and 5; software dominant Models 3 and 6; and accelerated acquisition Model 4) or common to all models. Common to all acquisition models, the PMO should consider the integration of hardware/software and plan/resource appropriate software acquisition and risk management. In "SW dominant" acquisition models, hardware may be a commodity (e.g., server racks in MAIS programs) or may have been established in an earlier increment (e.g., SW upgrades to established platform hardware), and software development and integration may then comprise the bulk of the effort, requiring even greater focus on software issues. In an 'Accelerated Acquisition' model, the programs can be integration-intensive, and may require rapidly developing and assembling many software components to deliver capability or services. This may involve limited deployments leading up to full capability/deployment (e.g., IT Box), and may also involve consideration of adopting mature architectures that enable rapid insertion of technology and services (e.g., UAS with evolving CPU and sensor requirements; SOA with orchestrated services in a MAIS). Concerns here can include 'glue' code required for integration, and integration and interface concerns that can complicate integration and testing.

Table 5: Software Considerations During the MSA Phase

LIFE-CYCLE PHASE	ACQUISITION MODEL	SOFTWARE ENGINEERING CONSIDERATIONS
Materiel Solution Analysis (MSA)	Common	Identify system requirements that map directly to software requirements to facilitate trade-offs and studies to optimize design and reduce vulnerabilities, risks and life-cycle cost
	SW dominant	Mission-driven capability analysis is key to informing sequencing of software capabilities. An incremental approach will focus on specific content in a first build or increment, followed by additional builds that add or refine capability. The PM, Systems Engineer, and Software Engineer should emphasize mission understanding to set the stage for good systems/software architecture and capability-based releases/increments
	Accelerated Acquisition	For an integration-intensive system that relies substantially if not completely on NDI/COTS/GOTS software, trade-space analysis can provide important information to understand the feasibility of capability and mission requirements. Consider software and system alternatives to refine the system concept and prevent vendor "lock-in." To discover and mitigate risks, consider materiel solutions opportunities for early software development prototyping, integration, and reuse of NDI/COTS/GOTS software. To the extent possible at this early stage, ensure MSA contracts reduce technical and programmatic risk related to software, particularly for high-risk components. MSA phase should factor software sustainment considerations to inform cost and acquisition strategy, to include government technical data rights

Table 6: Software Considerations During the TMRR Phase

LIFE CYCLE PHASE	ACQUISITION MODEL	SOFTWARE ENGINEERING CONSIDERATIONS
Technology Maturation and Risk Reduction (TMRR)	Common	Competitive prototyping helps identify and mitigate technical risks. System prototypes may be physical or math models and simulations that emulate expected performance. High-risk concepts may require scaled models to reduce uncertainty too difficult to resolve purely by mathematical emulation. SW prototypes that reflect the results of key trade-off analyses

19

LIFE CYCLE PHASE	ACQUISITION MODEL	SOFTWARE ENGINEERING CONSIDERATIONS
		should be demonstrated during the TMRR phase. These demonstrations will provide SW performance data (e.g., latency, security architecture, integration of legacy services and scalability) to inform decisions as to maturity; further, EMD estimates (schedule and life-cycle cost) often depend on reuse of SW components developed in TMRR.
	HW dominant	Hardware-dominant programs may conduct a separate SSR to assess requirements and interface specifications for computer software configuration items (CSCI) in support of the system PDR.
	SW dominant	Software programs typically conduct an SSR to assess the software requirements and interface specifications for CSCIs in support of the PDR. The program focused on a given build/release/increment may only produce artifacts for that limited scope, but the chief engineer may need a more comprehensive system-level architecture or design in order to handle capabilities across multiple releases. A PDR or its equivalent needs to maintain this system-level and longer-term, end-state perspective, as one of its functions is to provide data for the Milestone Decision Authority to assess prior to Milestone B.
	Accelerated Acquisition	In an integration-intensive environment, software and system models may be difficult to develop and fully explore if many software or system components come from proprietary sources or commercial vendors with restrictions on data rights. Validating end-to-end system and internal software performance assumptions may be difficult or even impossible. Proactive work with commercial vendors to support model development is important. To the extent possible at this early stage, ensure TMRR contracts reduce technical and programmatic risk related to software, particularly for high-risk components. As is feasible, TMRR phase should factor software sustainment considerations to inform cost and acquisition strategy, to include government technical data rights. The PM, Systems Engineer, and Software Engineer should carefully establish and manage criteria for such reviews in order to properly focus the scope and purpose of the reviews. Increasing knowledge/definition of elements of the integrated system design should include details of support and data rights. Initial SLAs with the user community and vendor community are an important tool for understanding and managing the details of support requirements in a diverse system environment.

Table 7: Software Considerations During the Engineering and Manufacturing Development Phase

LIFE CYCLE PHASE	ACQUISITION MODEL	SOFTWARE ENGINEERING CONSIDERATIONS
Engineering and Manufacturing Development (EMD)	Common	CDR software documentation should represent the design, performance, and test requirements, along with development and software/systems integration facilities for coding and integrating the deliverable software. Software and systems used for CSCI development (e.g., simulations and emulations) should be validated, verified, and ready to begin coding upon completion of the CDR. Problem report metadata should be selected so that the reports are relevant in development, test, and in operation to tracking and assessments. Legacy problem report tracking information can be used to generally profile and predict which types of software functions may accrue what levels of problem reports. Assessments of patterns of

20

LIFE CYCLE PHASE	ACQUISITION MODEL	SOFTWARE ENGINEERING CONSIDERATIONS
		problem reports among software components of the system can provide valuable information to support program progress decisions.
	SW dominant	For a program using an incremental SW development approach, technical debt may accrue within a given build/increment, or across multiple builds/increments. Technical reviews, both at the system and build/increment levels, should have a minimum viable requirements and architecture baseline at the system level, as well as ensuring fulfillment of a build/increment-centric set of review criteria and requirements. For build/increment content that may truly need to evolve across builds/increments, the PM and the Systems Engineer should ensure that system-level risks are recorded and mitigated to ensure any related development or risk reduction activities occur in a timely manner. Configuration management and associated change control/review boards can facilitate the recording and management of build/increment information
	Accelerated Acquisition	The emphasis in an integration-intensive system environment may be less on development and more on implementation and test. System components should be installed in a System Integration Lab (SIL) and evaluated continuously through EMD. Details of the use of system interfaces should be exposed and validated to ensure their scalability and suitability for use. Progressive levels of integration, composition, and use should be obtained in order to evaluate ever higher levels of system performance, ultimately encompassing end-to-end testing based on user requirements and expectations. Where needed, the Software Engineer may pursue the use of "glue" code and other extensions to the system environment to provide capability. Such glue code should be handled in as rigorous a manner as any developed software: i.e., kept under configuration management, reviewed, and inspected; updates should be properly regression-tested and progressively integrated/tested.

Table 8: Software Considerations During the P&D Phase

LIFE CYCLE PHASE	ACQUISITION MODEL	SOFTWARE ENGINEERING CONSIDERATIONS
Production and Deployment (P&D)	Common	Software may be refined as needed in response to Operational Test and Evaluation (OT&E) activities, and in support of the Full-Rate Production and/or Full Deployment Decision and Initial Operational Capability (IOC).
	SW dominant	For a program using an incremental SW development approach, these activities may occur in phases or steps associated with a given build or increment. In an Agile-based software process, collaboration between the test community and the development community increases understanding of system performance and verification requirements. Development and Operational Test may occur in phases or continuously as the system is updated.
	Accelerated Acquisition	Progressive deployment of an integration-intensive system provides infrastructure and services and higher-level capabilities as each release is validated and verified. A rigorous release process includes configuration management and the use of regression test suites. The PM, Systems Engineer, and Software Engineer should ensure user involvement in

21

LIFE CYCLE PHASE	ACQUISITION MODEL	SOFTWARE ENGINEERING CONSIDERATIONS
		gaining understanding and approval of changes to form, fit, and/or functions. As much as possible, builds should be rationally time-blocked and synchronized to avoid forced upgrades or other problems at end-user sites, and should be tested and supported as a unit. End-user sites that perform their own customization or tailoring of the system installation should ensure that knowledge of their actions is sent back to the integrator/developer so that problem reporting and resolution activities fully understand operational and performance implications of site-specific changes. Such customizations may also serve as leading indicators of user community preferences or needs when considering future system upgrades and enhancements.

Table 9: Software Considerations During the Operations and Support Phase

LIFE-CYCLE PHASE	ACQUISITION MODEL	SOFTWARE ENGINEERING CONSIDERATIONS
Operations and Support (O&S)	Common	A defined block change or follow-on incremental development delivers new or evolved capability, maintenance, safety, or urgent builds and upgrades to the field in a controlled manner. Procedures for updating and maintaining software on fielded systems often require individual user action, and may require specific training. Procedures should be in place to facilitate/ensure effective configuration management and control. There are inherent risks involved in modifying software on fielded weapon systems in use in frontline activities; software updates to business and IT systems can also pose risks to operational availability. PMs and systems and software engineers should maintain vigilance as part of supply chain risk management (see CH 4–3.5. and CH 9–3.2.6.), since maliciously altered devices or inserted software can infect the supply chain, creating unexpected changes to systems.
	Accelerated Acquisition	In an integration-intensive environment, security upgrades, technical refreshes and maintenance releases can proliferate, causing confusion and problems at end-user sites. System upgrades/updates should be timed to limit the proliferation of releases and therefore conserve maintenance and support resources. Problem reporting and associated severity should track impacts on other system elements to help establish the true priority of upgrades and updates. Configuration management and regression testing should be used to ensure system coherence.

CH 3–2.4 Tools, Techniques and Lessons Learned

Systems engineering (SE) tools and techniques support the performance of activities, the development of products and the completion of specific tasks. SE tools and techniques support the Program Manager (PM) and Systems Engineer in performing and managing the SE activities and processes to improve productivity and system cost, schedule, capabilities and adaptability. The PM and Systems Engineer should begin applying SE tools, techniques and lessons learned during the early stages of program definition to improve efficiency and traceability and to provide a technical framework for managing the weapon system development.

22

Collaboration tools allow the program office and developer to exchange data and analyses easily. Analytical tools and techniques also can assist in the development and validation of system designs. It is critical that the Systems Engineer understand the constraints and limitations of any particular analysis tool or technique, and apply this understanding when making assessments or recommendations based on its output.

Before selecting and implementing a SE tool or technique, the Systems Engineer should consider:

- Needs and constraints of the program (e.g., complexity, size and funding)
- Applicability to required tasks and desired products
- Computer system requirements, including peripheral equipment
- Licensing and maintenance costs
- Technical data management (see CH 3–4.1.7.)
- Integration with other SE tools in use within the program, by the developer, and by externally interfacing programs
- Cost to train the user to apply the tool or technique
- Number and level of expertise of Government and contractor staff (both users of the tool and users of the tool outputs)
- Feasibility of implementing the tool or technique throughout the acquisition life cycle

Major Defense Acquisition Programs (MDAPs) and Major Automated Information System (MAIS) programs should clearly identify tools in use, define tool interfaces when the Government and developer select different tools to use for the same purpose and describe how the tools support the program's SE approach. This information is documented in the program's Systems Engineering Plan (SEP) Table 4.7-1 Engineering Tools.

Table 10 lists general capabilities and features of SE tools and the SE processes they might support.

Table 10: SE Process-Related Tools

SE Process	Tool Capabilities / Features
Technical Planning	<ul><li>Assists in planning and scheduling activities</li><li>Assists in resource planning, tracking and allocation</li><li>Facilitates cost estimation</li></ul>
Decision Analysis	<ul><li>Assists in trade-off analysis</li><li>Provides optimization and sensitivity analysis capability</li><li>Assists in recording, tracking, evaluating and reporting decision outcomes</li></ul>
Technical Assessment	<ul><li>Assists in tracking, measuring and assessing metrics</li><li>Assists in metric collection</li></ul>
Requirements Management	<ul><li>Provides requirements bi-directional traceability capability</li><li>Provides requirements flow-down capability</li><li>Tracks requirements changes</li></ul>
Risk Management	<ul><li>Assists in risk, issue, opportunity planning, identification, analysis, mitigation/management and monitoring</li></ul>
Configuration Management	<ul><li>Assists in the identification of configuration items</li><li>Assists in baseline/version control of all configuration items</li><li>Assists in ensuring configuration baselines and changes are identified, recorded, evaluated, approved, incorporated and verified</li></ul>

23

SE Process	Tool Capabilities / Features
Technical Data Management	• Assists in identification of data requirements • Assists in recording and managing data rights • Assists in storage, maintenance, control, use and exchange of data • Assists in document preparation, update, and analysis
Interface Management	• Assists in capturing system internal and external interfaces and their requirement specifications • Assists in assessing compliance of interfaces among system elements of the system or systems of systems • Produces a view of interface connectivity
Stakeholder Requirements Definition	• Assists in capturing and identifying stakeholder requirements • Assists in analyzing and maintaining stakeholder requirements
Requirements Analysis	• Assists in requirements definition and decomposition • Interfaces with architecting tools • Supports Requirements Validation
Architecture Design	• Assists in development of functional and physical architectures • Provides traceability among system elements • Supports multiple views
Implementation	• Assists in development of the system design, prototypes and alternate solutions • Assists in realization of the system, system elements and enabling system elements
Integration	• Assists in integration-planning activities • Assists in assembling lower-level system elements into successively higher-level system elements • Provides analysis and simulation capability
Verification	• Assists in determining the system and system elements performance as designed through demonstration, examination, analysis and test
Validation	• Assists in determining, the effectiveness, suitability and survivability of the system in meeting end-user needs
Transition	• Assists in planning and executing delivery and deploying of the system to the end user for use in operational environment

CH 3–2.4.1 Modular Open Systems Approach

A modular open systems approach (MOSA) is defined as an acquisition and design strategy consisting of a technical architecture that adopts open standards and supports a modular, loosely coupled and highly cohesive system structure. This modular open architecture includes publishing of key interfaces within the system and relevant design disclosure. The key enabler for MOSA is the adoption of an open business model that requires doing business in a transparent way that leverages the collaborative innovation of numerous participants across the enterprise, permitting shared risk, maximized reuse of assets and reduced total ownership costs. The combination of open systems architecture and an open business model permits the acquisition of systems that are modular and interoperable, allowing for system elements to be added, modified, replaced, removed and/or supported by different vendors throughout the life cycle in order to afford opportunities for enhanced competition and innovation. MOSA is not an end result sought by the warfighter or end-item user; it is an approach to system design that can enable additional characteristics in the end item.

DoD identifies the primary benefits of MOSA as:

24

- Increased interoperability
- Enhanced competition
- Facilitation of technology refresh
- Increased innovation
- Potential cost savings or cost avoidance

MOSA benefits Program Managers (PMs) by using a general set of principles to help manage system complexity by breaking up complex systems into discrete pieces, which can then communicate with one another through well-defined interfaces. In this way, MOSA is broadly defined and inclusive of a variety of tools and practices.

Acquisition programs adopting MOSA may benefit from:

- Reduced life-cycle costs without sacrificing capability
- Reduced reliance on single-source vendors ("Vendor Lock")
- Shortened program acquisition timeline
- Enhanced rapid and agile development
- Accelerated transition from science and technology into acquisition due to modular insertion
- Increased ability and flexibility to retrofit/upgrade system elements for new/evolving capability
- Enhanced incremental approach to capabilities
- Increased competition and innovation
- Enhanced ability to create security structures within a design to reduce security risk

MOSA may also benefit warfighters by:

- Reducing operator learning curves by using systems that have similar functions and are operated in similar ways, thereby reducing costs
- Increasing interchangeability
- Reducing support and sustainment costs

Although a PM may employ MOSA to achieve some or all of these benefits, the methods the PM's staff uses, and the associated business implications, can vary widely and may drive different techniques and additional responsibilities into programs. The implementation strategy chosen should consider both impacts to the program and to the system's performance (e.g., its effectiveness and feasibility). These factors underpin the Department's policy for MOSA in acquisition.

DoDI 5000.02, Enc 2, sec. 6a and DoDI 5000.02, Enc 3, sec. 14 direct PMs to evaluate and implement MOSA where feasible and cost-effective. The USD(AT&L) memorandum, "Better Buying Power 2.0: Continuing the Pursuit for Greater Efficiency and Productivity in Defense Spending," November 13, 2012, raises the relevance of MOSA along with the acquisition of data rights for appropriate system elements. The overarching business case for DoD is increasing the level of competition by enabling small and large businesses to participate in competition for new or upgraded capabilities. Programs should develop a business model, documenting the strategy for use of MOSA and associated data rights.

The DoD Open Systems Architecture Contract Guidebook for Program Managers contains guidance regarding contract language programs should use to acquire data rights in support of a program's MOSA strategy. Additional information and supporting details amplifying each aspect of MOSA are available on the DASD(SE) website.

The PM should:

- Establish supportive requirements; business practices; and technology development, acquisition, test and evaluation and product support strategies for effective development of open systems
- Ensure data deliverables support the Intellectual Property (IP) Strategy (see Acquisition Strategy template) and secure the necessary data rights to support and sustain the system.

25

- Map modular open systems strategy and functional architecture to Statement of Work (SOW) requirements, Data Item Descriptions (DID) and Contract Data Requirements List (CDRL) items consistently across the enterprise.
- Ensure compliance.
- Consider including MOSA as one of the evaluation criteria for contract proposals.
- Determine the appropriateness of MOSA by considering software constraints, security requirements and procedures, availability and cost of data rights, life-cycle affordability and reliability of open standards, as well as other relevant factors such as environmental constraints (e.g., temperature, humidity) and environment, safety and occupational health (ESOH) considerations

The Systems Engineer should:

- Employ an overall plan for MOSA that supports the system functional architecture and uses prescribed USD(AT&L) business case analyses
- Ensure the system functional architecture is structured to accommodate Open Systems Architecture (OSA) where feasible, due to the high potential for reduced risk and cost
- Assess performance
- Balance current implementation of MOSA with performance and evolving technology at the physical level; MOSA establishes a technical baseline that may support modular architecture, but formally constrains the interfaces between modules, where interfaces close to current performance limits may quickly become obsolete
- Evaluate the technical appropriateness of MOSA by considering software constraints, security requirements and procedures, availability and cost of data rights, life-cycle affordability and reliability of open standards, as well as other relevant factors, such as environmental constraints (e.g., temperature, humidity) and ESOH considerations

Open systems benefits may not be realized without deliberate planning and guidance at the Program Executive Office (PEO) level. Re-use may be challenging if open systems and software on other systems (even other open systems) are not developed and modularized in a common fashion. As an example, an aviation platform may develop an Automatic Dependent Surveillance-Broadcast (ADS-B) software application that is MOSA conformant, but that application may never be re-used by a sister platform that may have its ADS-B and Tactical air navigation software combined in a single module.

Modular open system designs, developed from the system architecture, should be analyzed at each design review because there is a link between MOSA and the level and type of technical data, computer software and data rights the Government needs for life-cycle support. In many cases weapon systems using MOSA system elements can have increased opportunities for competitive sourcing during the life-cycle sustainment, and a correspondingly lesser need for detailed design data and associated data rights. This benefit enables an incremental approach to capability adaptation in MOSA-enabled systems and is a benefit of the modularity originally specified in the functional architecture.

The engineering trade analyses conducted prior to Milestone B help determine which system elements can be adapted to MOSA in order to reduce program cost and development time lines. Correct application of MOSA principles and practices results in modular system elements having well-defined functions and open standards-based interfaces. Threat analyses, functional criticality analyses, technology opportunities and evolved capability assessments are examples of assessments against the functional architecture to determine which system elements should be MOSA-enabled. When these system elements require an upgrade, replacement should be competitive, faster and cheaper because the MOSA-enabled system elements are modular. Because system functional architecture maps from the higher-level enterprise architecture, engineering trade analyses and assessments supporting MOSA should be completed and MOSA-enabled system elements specified, before contracts are let for technology development of those system elements. Successful implementation of MOSA approaches requires the synchronized acquisition of data rights for modular open systems and interfacing architecture elements. These data rights are initially structured to support acquisition of modular open system designs but also should address life-cycle support.

26

Figure 4: Sample MOSA and Data Rights Analysis

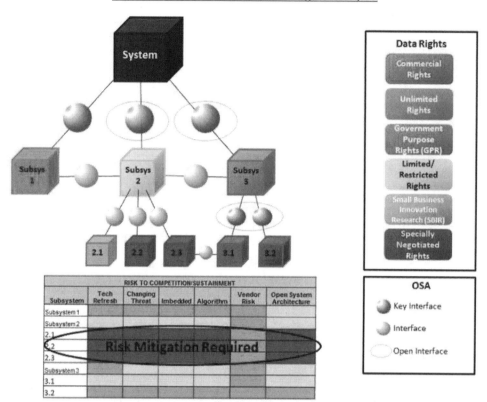

Figure 4 depicts an example architectural approach for mapping and assessing which system element interfaces can be open, how associated risk is ascertained and how to visualize the impact to interfaces with other system elements. The figure presents a top-level system view of the MOSA characteristics of system elements. Not all interfaces need to be open at any one level of the design, only those that are required to meet anticipated incremental capability updates, changes in threat or technology insertion. A system view such as this includes a record of the data rights that are required to enable the planned MOSA design. The levels of data rights that need to be required for each MOSA-enabled system element are determined in order to assert the requisite contract requirements to obtain them. The data rights strategy ensures that enterprise-level data rights flow to system elements and that they support the system architecture. Levels of data rights are described in Chapter (CH) 1 and in Appendix 9 of the OSA Contract Guidebook.

Successfully implementing a MOSA strategy results in the identification of required technical data and software deliverables necessary to field and maintain weapon systems and their logistics support. The Acquisition Strategy should be updated throughout the system's life cycle to reflect changes in the MOSA approach resulting from technology and software evolutionary developments. The Systems Engineering Plan (SEP) is also updated to reflect the MOSA-related updates and modifications employed throughout the system and its system elements.

Specific MOSA-related data deliverables that should be considered include:

- Software Development Plans (DI-IPSC-81427)
- Software Development Status Reports (DI-MCCR-80459)

27

- Software Development Summary Reports (DI-MCCR-80902)
- Software Design Descriptions (DI-IPSC-81435)
- Hardware development plans and Hardware Design Descriptions

In addition, the PM should maintain an open systems management plan. The plan describes the offeror's approach for:

- OSA, modularity and open design
- Inter-system element dependencies
- Design information documentation
- Technology insertion
- Life-cycle sustainability
- Interface design and management
- Treatment of proprietary or vendor-unique elements
- Reuse of preexisting items, including all commercial-off-the-shelf/non-developmental item (COTS/NDI) system elements, their functionality and proposed function in the system
- Copies of license agreements related to the use of COTS/NDI system elements for Government approval

The open system management plan should also include a statement explaining why each COTS/NDI system element was selected for use.

Program products typically used in making decisions regarding MOSA include:

- System Requirements
- Acquisition Strategy (AS)
- Program Protection Plan (PPP)
- Analysis of Alternatives (AoA)
- Enterprise Architecture

Modular open systems approaches and requirements should be addressed at design reviews, e.g., System Requirements Review (SRR), Preliminary Design Review (PDR and Critical Design Review (CDR).

See DoD Acquisition Streamlining and Standardization Information System (ASSIST) homepage for more data item deliverables that may be appropriate for each specific program and DoD 5010.12-M for data deliverables.

CH 3–2.4.2 Modeling and Simulation

Models and simulations are SE tools used by multiple functional area disciplines during all system life-cycle phases. Models, simulations, data and artifacts should be developed in a well-defined and controlled engineering environment to support the program's reuse of the information across the acquisition life cycle or for reuse and repurposing in support of other acquisition efforts. DoDI 5000.02, Enc 3, sec. 9 requires all models, simulations, data and artifacts to be integrated, managed and controlled to ensure that the products maintain consistency with the system and external program dependencies, provide a comprehensive view of the program and increase efficiency and confidence throughout the program's life cycle. Models are essential to aid in understanding complex systems and system interdependencies, and to communicate among team members and stakeholders. Simulation provides a means to explore concepts, system characteristics and alternatives; open up the trade space; facilitate informed decisions and assess overall system performance.

Models and simulations provide:

- Understanding of capabilities and the requirements set
- Data to inform program and technical decisions

28

- Efficient communication and shared understanding among stakeholders about relationships between system requirements and the system being developed, through precise engineering artifacts and traceability of designs to requirements
- Exploration of system alternatives to support the early identification of viable system solutions and any necessary doctrine change requests
- An alternative solution for building prototypes and enabling cost savings
- Better analysis and understanding of system designs, including system elements and enabling system elements
- Improved capability to address defects and failures at all levels through a greater understanding of the system.
- Support to engineering and design trade-off analysis studies
- Support for early interface and interoperability testing
- Greater efficiencies in design and manufacturing by reducing the time and cost of iterative build/test/fix cycles
- Timely understanding of program impacts of proposed changes
- Insight into program cost, schedule, performance and supportability risk

The Systems Engineering Digital Engineering Fundamentals recommends that all programs identify and maintain a system model, representing all necessary viewpoints on the design and capturing all relevant system interactions. The system model should include, but not be limited to, parametric descriptions, structure, definitions of behaviors, design assumptions, internal and external interfaces, cost inputs and traces from operational capabilities to requirements and design constructs.

The system model should be captured digitally to create an integrated set of authoritative technical data, information and knowledge, generated and used by all stakeholders throughout the system life cycle. Use of a digital system model can help drive consistency and integration among SE and analytical tools, and provide the program with a capability to assess potential design changes, as well as system upgrades, throughout the life cycle. The Program Manager (PM) and Systems Engineer should consider establishing and using a digital system model when planning for the development, incorporation and application of models, simulations and analyses on their program. Figure 5 shows some benefits of using models and simulation throughout the acquisition life cycle. This figure is adapted from a 2010 National Defense Industrial Association (NDIA) Systems Engineering Division "Model-Based Engineering (MBE)" study and is used with permission.

Figure 5: Benefits of Using Models and Simulation throughout the Acquisition Life Cycle

29

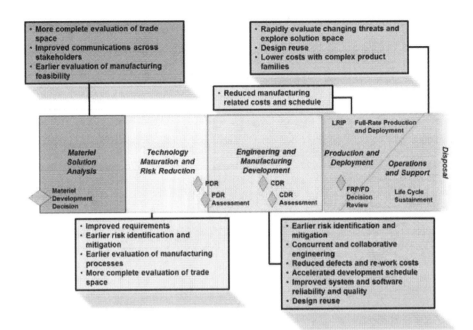

Models and simulations should take advantage of opportunities for reuse (see DoD Modeling and Simulation Catalog [requires Common Access Card (CAC) to access website]). Models and simulations developed in early acquisition phases may be repurposed for other activities during later phases (e.g., engineering models can be used in training simulations). SE should use models and simulations from many disciplines and across a hierarchy of perspectives that range from an engineering/technical level up to the campaign/strategic level in order to effectively analyze requirements, design, cost, schedule, performance and risk. These models and simulations often exist, but sometimes need to be newly developed, which can be costly. An option for new development is to consider federating existing models and simulations, using any of various interoperability standards in order to create needed capability. PMs and Systems Engineers should consider how to leverage models, simulations, and their interoperability as they plan for their use throughout a program's life cycle. Modeling and simulation is also used to support developmental test and evaluation (DT&E) and operational test and evaluation (OT&E).

Roles, Responsibilities, and Activities

To make effective and appropriate use of models and simulations, the PM and Systems Engineer should ensure that planned modeling and simulation activities are:

- Complete, comprehensive and trusted, including all efforts anticipated throughout the life cycle, to include planning, development and acceptance as well as verification, validation, and accreditation (VV&A) (see CH 8–3.7.7.)
- Integrated into the program's technical planning (Work Breakdown Structure (WBS), schedules, budgets, Systems Engineering Plan (SEP) and other program documentation; see CH 3–4.1.1. Technical Planning Process)
- Appropriately resourced, including a properly skilled workforce

The PM and Systems Engineer should establish, manage, control, and maintain integrated sources of all relevant models, simulations, data and other artifacts that describe what the system is and does. These data sources also should contain descriptive system information that could be used to feed other models, simulations and acquisition efforts.

Figure 6 provides examples of models, simulations and analyses throughout the life cycle.

30

Figure 6: Applications of Models and Simulation in the DoD Acquisition Life Cycle

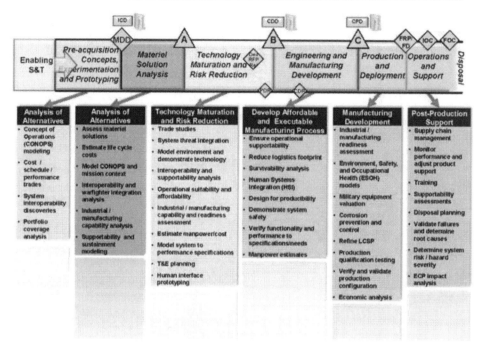

The PM and Systems Engineer should ensure that the program's modeling and simulation activities are coordinated, managed and controlled such that products are consistent with the system and architecture design at all levels. Plans to use models and simulations should be integrated with the overall program plan. The program may choose to integrate the modeling and simulation planning details into the program plan or create a separate modeling and simulation planning document. If the documents are separate, the program ensures the modeling and simulation planning is kept up to date as the program plan adjusts. PMs should follow their organization's standards for planning, managing and controlling such activities.

Models and simulations should be:

- Developed and matured through the life of the program
- Developed and documented, to include metadata and open standards, to maximize opportunity for reuse and repurposing (both within the program and in support of other acquisition efforts)
- Properly managed and controlled as part of the program's technical baseline.
- Included as part of the technical data package to be transitioned into the next phase of the life cycle or into other efforts

Models, data and artifacts should be evident in the contents of the required program technical reviews and in the baselined technical data needed to support major program reviews and program decisions.

CH 3–2.4.3 Sustainability Analysis

The sustainability analysis, using a Life Cycle Assessment (LCA) method, is a tool to assist the Systems Engineer in designing more sustainable systems -- those that use fewer resources over the life cycle, have fewer impacts on human health and the environment and thus have a lower total ownership cost (TOC). The Program Manager (PM) should make sustainability considerations an integral part of both a robust trade space analysis and a comprehensive supportability analysis. These sustainability analyses can help reduce system TOC by uncovering previously hidden or ignored life-cycle costs, leading to more

31

informed decisions earlier in the acquisition life cycle. They can also help make systems more affordable and improve the accuracy of life-cycle cost estimates.

Large military systems and platforms can have a life cycle of 30 years or more. To meet evolving mission needs far into the future, the system design should incorporate long-term sustainability considerations in order to reduce life-cycle costs. Without a full understanding of life-cycle impacts, significant costs may be unintentionally inserted during development or procurement and later exposed by the logistics and operational communities.

"Sustainability" differs from "sustainment" in that it relates to the use of resources, and the associated impacts and costs over the system's life cycle. In contrast, sustainment is more concerned with the end user's ability to operate and maintain a system once it is in inventory and deployed. Both aspects need to be addressed in the design process.

Executive Order (E.O.) 13693, "Planning for Federal Sustainability in the Next Decade," dated March 25, 2015, establishes an integrated Federal Government strategy for sustainability. As required by the E.O., DoD generated a Strategic Sustainability Performance Plan (SSPP), which is updated annually. The SSPP identifies DoD goals for efficiency and reductions in energy, water, solid waste and use of hazardous chemicals and materials.

A sustainability analysis compares alternative designs or sustainment activities regarding their use of energy, water, chemicals and land. Outputs include impacts on resource availability, human health and the environment and the total life-cycle costs of the alternatives that meet the minimum performance requirements. The life-cycle costs can include both internal (to DoD) and external (to society) by monetizing the impacts.

A sustainability analysis can support numerous acquisition activities, including:

- Analysis of Alternatives to compare conceptual alternatives
- Trade-space analysis to compare how sustainability attributes (e.g., chemical or material choices, water or solid waste) affect life-cycle cost, TOC, performance, human health and the environment
- Business Case Analysis using the LCA method to include sustainability as one of the elements in the analysis
- Preliminary design to select the most sustainable system that meets performance requirements and end-user needs
- Supportability analysis to help ensure the use of resources throughout the life cycle is considered
- Detailed design to select the most sustainable components

The Streamlined Life Cycle Assessment Process for Sustainability in DoD Acquisitions is specifically for use in the DoD acquisition process. It combines LCA with multi-attribute analysis; it integrates a number of trade-space and design considerations and provides a procedure to compare conceptual or detailed design alternatives. It is intended to ensure consideration of important downstream impacts and costs in trade-off and design decisions. The method is consistent, without duplication, with other considerations, such as operational energy, supportability and environment, safety and occupational health (ESOH).

CH 3–2.4.4 Value Engineering

Program Managers (PMs) use Value Engineering (VE) across the life cycle for supplies and services, including those for major systems, and construction. VE is one of many tools used for increasing value to the warfighter; it focuses on functions (purpose or use of a "program, project, system," etc.) to achieve best value, ensuring that a "program, project, system," etc., consistently performs the required basic function at the lowest life-cycle cost while maintaining acceptable levels of performance and quality. VE maximizes the buying power of the DoD and should be considered throughout the life cycle as a way to meet or beat affordability constraints and should-cost targets. The Components implement VE to improve military worth or reduce acquisition and ownership costs wherever it is advantageous. VE policy is provided through DoDI 4245.14, "Value Engineering (VE) Program" which implements 41 U.S.C. 1711 and Office of Management and Budget (OMB) Circular No. A-131, "Value Engineering."

SD-24, "Value Engineering: A Guidebook of Best Practices and Tools" provides details on the key VE activities, the two parts of VE and the application, including examples, of VE.

PMs perform VE by:

- Scoping the issue, improvement targets, and evaluation factors
- Identifying specific areas/functions for evaluation
- Collecting and analyzing data
- Exploring alternative approaches
- Developing and presenting specific recommendations
- Implementing directed changes

VE consists of two parts: VE proposals (VEP) and VE change proposals (VECP). VEPs are developed and submitted by individual employees or contractors under contract to provide VE services or studies. VECPs are submitted under the VE clause of a contract.

FAR (Subpart 48.102, para (a)) requires the contracting activity to include VE provisions in appropriate supply, service, architect-engineer and construction contracts and the DoD to provide contractors a fair share of the savings on accepted VECPs.

PMs and Systems Engineers should encourage the development and submittal of VEPs and VECPs and consider applying VE in the development, procurement, production and life-cycle support of services, materiel and facilities for:

- Hardware, software and/or human components
- Development, production, test or manufacturing
- Specifications and standards
- Facilities design and construction
- Contract requirements
- Program documentation

Additional resources available to the PM and Systems Engineer to learn more about VE include the Defense Acquisition University (DAU) Continuous Learning Module, CLE001, "Value Engineering" and the VE initiatives webpage on the DASD(SE) website. For examples of potential areas in which the application of VEPs and VECPs may provide a benefit, see SD-24 Chapter 2, "Opportunities of VE Application," and Chapter 3, "VE over a System's Lifecycle."

CH 3–2.4.5 Lessons Learned, Best Practices and Case Studies

Most programs represent a new combination of existing capabilities or the insertion of incremental advances in technology. By reviewing the successes, failures, problems and solutions of similar programs, Program Managers (PMs) and Systems Engineers can gain insights into risks, uncertainties and opportunities that their programs may encounter.

Lessons learned and case studies generally describe areas of risk, pitfalls encountered in programs and strategies employed to mitigate or fix problems when they arise. Best practices are proven techniques and strategies that can prevent common problems and improve quality, cost or both.

Best practices and lessons learned are applicable to all aspects of a program -- technical, managerial and programmatic -- and at any point in the acquisition life cycle. However, they are not universal or "one-size-fits-all" solutions. The greatest benefits occur when PMs and Systems Engineers judiciously select and tailor successful practices or strategies from analogous programs/systems and tailor them to meet current program needs.

Standards, such as those for design, build, test and certification, are a compilation of lessons learned over time. PMs and Systems Engineers should be aware that Standards are not ad hoc requirements developed by a single engineer or program office. Standards result from years of execution knowledge gained across management, engineering, manufacturing or sustainment.

The Acquisition Streamlining and Standardization Information System (ASSIST) database is the official source for current DoD specifications and standards and identifies DoD-adopted non-government standards (NGS). In many cases, DoD uses NGS, as required in 15 USC 272 Notes "Utilization of Consensus Technical Standards by Federal Agencies" and implemented in Circular A-119, DoDI 4120.24 (3.b. – Page 1), and FAR (Subpart 11.101, para (b)) in preference to developing and maintaining Government specifications and standards, unless it is inconsistent with applicable law or otherwise impractical. PMs should consider the following sources when considering which specifications and standards to apply; the Global Information Grid (GIG) Technical Guidance Federation (previously known as the DoD Information Technology Standards Registry (DISR)), the Standardization Directory (SD) 21 (Listing of Specifications and Standards Mandated for use by the Department of Defense by Public Laws or Government Regulations), and U.S.-ratified materiel international standardization agreements (ISAs).

Various organizations in DoD, industry and academia produce and maintain online repositories of standards, lessons learned, best practices, and case studies. These resources can serve as a starting point for PMs and Systems Engineers to search for and find relevant data that can be applied to their current program. Knowledge-sharing resources include, but are not limited to:

- Service lessons learned repositories (including Service safety centers)
- Government Accountability Office reports
- DoD Systems Engineering community of practice websites
- Defense Standardization Program Office (DSPO)
- Other Departments and Agencies such as National Aeronautics and Space Administration (NASA), Department of Energy (DoE) or National Institute of Standards and Technology (NIST)
- Professional organizations such as the International Council on Systems Engineering (INCOSE) or the Institute of Electrical and Electronics Engineers (IEEE)
- Industry organizations such as National Defense Industrial Association (NDIA) or Aerospace Industries Association (AIA)
- Non-government standards development organizations such as Society of Automotive Engineers (SAE) International and International Organization for Standards (ISO)

PMs and Systems Engineers are encouraged to research current analogous programs, not just past programs, that may be experiencing similar challenges and have not yet formally documented what they have learned. In order to aid both internal program activities and in external collaborative information sharing, the PM and Systems Engineer should ensure that the program establishes and utilizes a robust process to identify and document best practices and lessons learned. This process should focus on ensuring accurate and timely documentation of all relevant information, and the Systems Engineer should monitor its use and products throughout the life cycle. Each best practice or lesson learned that is developed throughout the program execution should include enough contextual information about the program and surrounding circumstances so that future practitioners can discern the relevancy and usefulness of the best practice. PMs and Systems Engineers should consider using these data as a form of process improvement feedback, or as evidence for proposing policy and guidance changes.

CH 3–2.5 Engineering Resources

Organizing and staffing the systems engineering (SE) organization and providing supporting resources and tools are critical tasks that merit attention from both the Program Manager (PM) and Systems Engineer because these tasks influence the effective implementation and control of the SE approach. The PM is responsible for developing a tailored strategy that enables a cost-effective program to deliver a required capability within the needed delivery time. Program tailoring should include SE assessments of maturity and risk in order to determine the appropriate entry point into the acquisition life cycle and to identify opportunities to streamline the acquisition strategy. Therefore, the PM should create a program office structure ensuring the Systems Engineer is an integrated part of the program planning and execution activities. In accordance with DoDI 5000.66, this includes ensuring that program offices for MDAPs or MAIS programs will have a qualified Chief Engineer/Chief Systems Engineer with key leadership position criteria defined in the USD(AT&L) policy memorandum, "Key Leadership Positions and Qualification Criteria," November 8, 2013.

Building an integrated SE team with the expertise and knowledge to implement and execute an effective program is a key to success. Providing the SE team with the necessary SE tools and techniques to perform and manage SE activities and processes will increase productivity of the organization, reduce system cost and schedule, and improve capabilities and adaptability (see CH 3–2.4. Tools, Techniques, and Lessons Learned). The structure and size of the SE organization should reflect both the risk and complexity of the system under development and its life-cycle phase. The Systems Engineering Plan (SEP) describes the SE organizations of both the Government program office and, when available, the developer organization.

Roles and Responsibilities

To provide the required capabilities in the most efficient and effective manner, the PM should ensure completion of the following activities that affect the technical approach:

- Ensuring proper level of governance is applied
- Ensuring processes are followed and reporting is in compliance with plans
- Interfacing with the end users and developers to determine changes in operational requirements or concepts of operations that may affect the development of the desired capability
- Ensuring coordinated development and updating of acquisition strategy documents (e.g., Acquisition Strategy (AS)), program plans (e.g., SEP, Program Protection Plan (PPP), Test and Evaluation Master Plan (TEMP), Life Cycle Sustainment Plan (LCSP)), and cost and budget documents
- Establishing program office organization (roles, responsibilities, authorities accountabilities) and staffing the program office and Government technical team with qualified (trained and experienced) Systems Engineers and other relevant technical professionals
- Integrating all aspects of the program office, including business processes relating to program management, SE, test and program control
- Ensuring all necessary memoranda of understanding and agreement (MOU/MOAs) are in place and sufficiently detailed
- Resourcing the managers of all functional areas, such as administration, engineering, logistics, test, etc.
- Managing program risks and opportunities by developing, resourcing and implementing realistic mitigation and management strategies
- Approving the configuration management plan and ensuring adequate resources are allocated for implementing configuration management throughout the life cycle
- Reviewing/approving Engineering Change Proposal (ECP) requests and determining the path forward required by any baseline changes
- Ensuring contracting activities are coordinated with the program systems engineering team
- Approving the contractor systems engineering management plan (SEMP); ensuring consistency between the program SEP and SEMP

The Systems Engineer is responsible for planning and overseeing all technical activity within the program office and for managing effective SE processes. The Systems Engineer should ensure the PM has sufficient and clear information for scheduling and resource-allocation decisions. In addition, the Systems Engineer implements and controls the technical effort by:

- Implementing and maintaining disciplined SE processes
- Understanding the nature of the system under development, the needs of the end user, and the operating environment as described in the concept of operations
- Conducting activities in support of contract award and execution.
- Ensuring that no unauthorized changes or commitments are made with the contractor or developer
- Understanding how the system fits into a larger system of systems (SoS) context, and coordinating so the requisite mission analysis efforts are undertaken.
- Providing recommendations on the contract strategy

35

- Assisting in generating affordability goals and caps and should-cost goals by analyzing and verifying technical assumptions used in the cost analyses and related cost and budget documents
- Assessing process improvement activities in support of should-cost goals.
- Developing and maintaining the SEP in coordination with key stakeholders and other functional experts who participate in the program development activities.
- Tracking and managing the execution of the contract's SE-related tasks and activities in each acquisition phase as detailed in the SEP
- Working closely with developer's SE teams to ensure integrated and effective processes are executed and documented in the SEMP
- Planning and executing the formal technical reviews and audits
- Tracking and reporting baseline changes and recommending a path forward, as a part of configuration management
- Supporting the PM in configuration management activities
- Identifying and mitigating the program's technical risks which include
  - Integration risks
  - Engineering risks
  - Critical technology risks assessed in the Technology Readiness Assessment (TRA) (MDAPs only)
- Measuring and tracking program maturity using technical performance measures, requirements stability, and integrated schedules
- Updating the PPP
- Staffing the engineering team with qualified and appropriate engineers.
- Supporting updates to the TEMP and LCSP
- Supporting test and evaluation activities as documented in the TEMP (see Chief Developmental Tester responsibilities in CH 8–2.4.1.)
- Reviewing requirements traceability matrix and cross reference matrix (verification)
- Managing root cause and corrective action (RCCA) efforts along with supporting the risk and opportunity boards
- Supporting the selection of qualified vendors for parts, materiel, and processes (for hardware and software)
- Reviewing deliverables on the contract to ensure compliance and utility, and to ensure appropriate format and content

One of the key responsibilities of the Systems Engineer is to provide insight/oversight of the technical activities of the capability acquisition. To ensure the success of integrated processes the Systems Engineer should maintain continuous engagement with the developer responsible to build, deploy and sustain the system or capability being acquired. This continuous engagement is necessary to ensure a common understanding of program goals, objectives and activities. The program office and developer SE team should further maintain frequent, effective communication, in accordance with the contract, as they manage and execute program activities and trade-off decisions.

The PM and Systems Engineer focus on the transformation of required operational and sustainment needs into a system design capability. As the design solution evolves through the application of the eight technical processes, the verification component or test organization provides confidence that the design solution that evolved from the requirements analysis, functional allocation and design synthesis properly addresses the desired capabilities. The Chief Developmental Tester, working in tandem with the Systems Engineer, accomplishes the verification loop of the SE process. For programs on DASD(DT&E) oversight, Systems Engineers will be included on the Test and Evaluation (T&E) Working-Level Integrated Product Team (WIPT), as a test data stakeholder. Together the Systems Engineer and Chief Developmental Tester generate and analyze data from the integrated tests. The developer uses the test results to improve system performance, the SE team uses the test results for risk assessments and the acquisition community and operational evaluators use the test results for operational assessments of the evolving system. This strategy for test and evaluation should be consistent with and complementary to the SEP. The PM and the Systems Engineer work closely with the Chief Developmental Tester to facilitate coordinated verification and validation activities.

36

Stakeholders

The PM has the critical role of approving a systems engineering (SE) approach that includes all stakeholders. The Systems Engineer coordinates with all participants to translate the operational needs and capabilities into technically feasible, affordable, testable, measurable, sustainable, achievable (within scheduled need dates) and operationally effective and suitable system requirements. The Systems Engineer is responsible for planning and overseeing all technical activity within the program office and for managing stakeholder expectations. Early and frequent involvement with stakeholders by both the PM and the Systems Engineer facilitates the successful execution of SE activities throughout the acquisition life cycle.

Most program personnel are involved in one or more of the 16 SE processes. Personnel from non-SE organizations or from outside the program office (e.g., end users, requirements sponsors, maintainers, testers, planners) should be integrated within the program's technical management activities so they have the ability to actively participate throughout the life cycle in support of SE-related activities.

The following is a partial list of the stakeholders who contribute to and benefit from SE activities and processes:

- Warfighters and other end users
- Milestone Decision Authority (MDA)
- Resource sponsors
- Budget authority
- Developers
- Enabled or enabling systems in the system of systems (SoS)
- Security Manager or System Security Engineer
- Chief Developmental Tester
- Operational test organization
- Certification and accreditation authorities
- Maintainers and logisticians (materiel readiness and sustainment)
- Intelligence community
- Trainers
- Budget and cost analysts
- Contracting officers and associated staff
- Environment, safety and occupational health (ESOH) staff
- Contractors who build, test, deploy and/or support the capability under development
- Companion programs

Integrated Product Teams

An effective SE organization is typically structured as one or more integrated product teams (IPTs). An IPT is a multidisciplinary group of representatives from all appropriate functional disciplines who are collectively responsible for delivering a defined product or process. The purpose of an IPT is to conduct activities as an integrated, collaborative effort with a focus on delivering the required capability(ies) to the end user. In developing the program office and SE organizational structure, the PM and Systems Engineer should know and understand both the design and functions of the developer's technical organization along with the developer's business model (in-house vs. outsourced). This understanding is critical to ensuring effective coordination and oversight of developer activities and can affect how meetings are set up and conducted, how configuration management is executed, etc. In some cases, the PM and Systems Engineer may organize multiple IPTs to align with the major products in the program's Work Breakdown Structure. In smaller programs, the SE organization may be organized as a single IPT.

IPTs provide both the Government and developer stakeholders with the opportunity to maintain continuous engagement. This continuous engagement is necessary to ensure a common understanding of program goals, objectives, and activities. These Government/developer IPTs should further maintain effective communication as they manage and execute those activities and trade-off decisions. The program's SE processes should include all stakeholders in order to ensure the success of program efforts throughout the acquisition life cycle.

For Major Defense Acquisition Programs, the PM ensures that the program office is structured to interface with the SE WIPT (a multidisciplinary team responsible for the planning and execution of SE) to address DoD leadership concerns and interests. The SE WIPT is chartered by the PM and is usually chaired by the Systems Engineer. The SE WIPT includes representatives from the Office of the Under Secretary of Defense for Acquisition, Technology, and Logistics (OUSD(AT&L)) and the component acquisition executive's organization, both Government and developer IPT leads from the program, the Program Executive Office Systems Engineer, and the developer Systems Engineer. A generic SE WIPT charter is available on the ODASD(SE) Policy and Guidance website under "Guidance and Tools." Additional information about IPTs can be found in CH 1–3.3.5.

CH 3–2.6 Certifications
Certifications provide a formal acknowledgment by an approval authority that a system or program meets specific requirements. Certifications, in many cases, are based on statute or regulations and drive systems engineering (SE) planning (i.e., a program may not be able to test or deploy the capability without certain certifications). Used throughout the acquisition life cycle, certifications reduce program risk and increase understanding of the system. Certain specific certifications are required before additional design, integration, network access, or testing can take place. For example, airworthiness certifications need to be in place before an aircraft can begin flight testing. Often programs insufficiently plan for the number of required certifications. Insufficient planning for certifications can have a negative impact on program costs and schedule.

Obtaining the various certifications can be a lengthy process. As a result, the Program Manager (PM) should ensure that the time necessary to obtain any required certification is factored into technical planning. By planning for the activities required to achieve the necessary certifications, the PM and Systems Engineer can ensure that development of the system continues uninterrupted while the program meets all system certification requirements. Early planning allows the Systems Engineer and technical team to begin interacting with certification authorities, which sets the foundation for communication throughout the development of the system.

The Systems Engineering Plan (SEP) Outline requires programs to provide a certification matrix that identifies applicable technical certifications and when they are required during the acquisition life cycle. Programs should include certification activities and events in the Integrated Master Schedule (IMS) and the Integrated Master Plan (IMP).

A non-exhaustive list of certifications is available on the DASD(SE) website. Furthermore, PMs and Systems Engineers should consult both Joint and Service-specific domain experts to determine other certifications that may be required.

CH 3–2.7 Systems Engineering Role in Contracting
The Systems Engineer should actively participate in developing program contract tasks to ensure that the appropriate technical activities are contained and properly scoped in the contract. Proper scoping of the technical tasks in the Statement of Work (SOW), Statement of Objectives (SOO), or Performance Work Statement (PWS) is necessary to ensure that the final system meets end user's needs. Often contracting activities may appear to be primarily programmatic in nature (e.g., acquisition strategy development, writing requests for proposal, performing market research, developing the Contract Data Requirements List (CDRL)) but, in fact, they reflect technical planning and should be influenced by the desired technical content. For example, technical understanding of data rights can be a key element in planning for modularity and open systems design, or the decision to choose an incremental acquisition strategy depends on generic functionality groupings that may not be appropriate for every system.

The Systems Engineer should contribute to the development of contract incentives and/or incentive approaches that promote an understanding of the technical risks and opportunities inherent in the selected development approach. Incentives such as award fee may be tied to program performance and progress that may be evaluated during technical reviews, or more frequently the incentive is tied to the

38

completion of a technical review. If that is the case, the developer may have a strong incentive to call the review complete as soon as possible. The Systems Engineer and Program Manager (PM) exercise best judgment in an objective and informed manner to ensure the reviews are not prematurely declared completed in order for the developer to qualify for the contract incentive.

Another area to which incentives are tied is the Earned Value Management System (EVMS). The PM should ensure that the EVMS, tied to any incentive, measures the quality and technical maturity of technical work products instead of just the quantity of work. If contracts include earned value (EV) incentives, the criteria should be stated clearly and should be based on technical performance. EV incentives should be linked quantitatively with:

- Technical performance measurement (TPM)
- Progress against requirements
- Development maturity
- Exit criteria of life-cycle phases
- Significant work packages and work products

Additional information about EVMS can be found in CH 1–4.2.16. The PM should make it a priority to engage with industry to clarify Government expectations and ensure a common understanding of the capability desired, need dates, risks, complexity, and scope. Access to current market information is critical for the program office as it defines requirements for acquisition programs. It is equally important for the contracting officers as they develop acquisition strategies, seek opportunities for small businesses, and negotiate contract terms. The best source of this information is usually found within industry partners. OMB memo, "Myth-busting 3: Further Improving Industry Communication with Effective Debriefings" addresses productive interactions between federal agencies and industry partners. These interactions are strongly encouraged to ensure that the Government clearly understands the marketplace and can award a contract or order for an effective solution at a reasonable price. Early, frequent engagement with industry is especially important for complex, high-risk procurements, including (but not limited to) those for large information technology (IT) projects. PMs should develop ways to remove unnecessary barriers to reasonable communication and develop vendor communications plans, consistent with existing law and regulation, which promote responsible exchanges.

The program office uses a Request for Information (RFI) to communicate expectations and plans, including the expected business rhythm for contract execution. This communication ensures the offerors have an opportunity to provide a tight linkage across the Integrated Master Plan (IMP), Work Breakdown Structure (WBS), Integrated Master Schedule (IMS), risk and opportunity management, and cost in their proposals. Early industry engagement opportunities include pre-solicitation notices, industry days, and other market research venues.

Before releasing the RFP, the program office should develop and mature the performance and functional specifications that need to be included in the RFP. The RFP and supporting technical documentation clearly define the Government's expectations in terms of the performance and functional specifications, program planning, program process, risks, and assumptions. The RFP also should direct potential offerors to structure their approach to reflect the Government's expectations.

In support of the Program Manager, the Systems Engineer should ensure that technical documents accurately and clearly communicate the Government's requirements including mandatory design, build, test, certification, approval, and acceptance criteria. This ensures the developer is made aware of all required processes and objective quality evidence (OQE) to be produced, to include processes leading to certification, approval, and acceptance using predetermined OQE. In addition, the PM should consider providing all offerors with the Program Protection Plan (PPP), the IMP and top-level schedule (with internal and external dependencies), expected business rhythm, current risk assessments, and the SEP (either an approved or a draft SEP) as part of the RFP. Consistent with DoDI 5000.02, Enc 3, sec. 2, the SEP may be applied as guidance or as a compliance document depending on the maturity of the plan and the acquisition strategy. Before providing the SEP to the offerors, the PM and Systems Engineer should determine if the document contains sensitive information and, if so, remove this sensitive information from the SEP before attaching it to the RFP.

In an effort to promote a higher probability of mission success, Major Defense Acquisition Programs should review, tailor and implement applicable mission assurance concepts and principles when developing their contract requirements. Major Defense Acquisition Programs should use resources provided by their service (for example, the Aerospace/Air Force Mission Assurance Guide TOR-2007(8546)-6018).

Although there are many opportunities for contract-related interactions between the Government and potential offerors prior to contract award, the RFP remains the primary tool for shaping the contract, the program and ultimately the system. See the "Guide for Integrating Systems Engineering into DoD Acquisition Contracts, Version 1.0, 2006" for additional guidance on the content and format of RFPs.

Within the RFP development team, the Systems Engineer should be responsible for the technical aspects of the RFP and should perform the following actions:

- Referencing current required operational documentation and system performance specifications.
- Identifying SE process requirements (for example, requirements management, configuration management and risk management; see CH 3–4. Additional Planning Considerations).
- Providing available and appropriate architecture(s) characterizing the system's interoperability requirements.
- Identifying any design considerations including production; reliability and maintainability (R&M); environment, safety and occupational health (ESOH); human systems integration (HSI); and security.
- Identifying for delivery Government-required technical data rights produced by the developer.
- Listing and describing technical assessment evidence and events, including technical reviews, audits, and certifications and associated entrance/exit criteria
- Specifying data protection, SoS and system testing and verification requirements.
- Coordinating with Chief Developmental Tester with regard to the test and evaluation requirements.
- Providing a requirements verification traceability database (requirements and test method).
- Specifying meetings and technical documentation between the program office and the developer.
- Conducting a review of the deliverables (what data, level of detail, data rights and when needed) and buying only what is needed in concert with should-cost goals.
- Leading or supporting the technical evaluation during source selection, to include providing inputs to the development of source selection criteria.
- Performing schedule risk assessments as part of the source selection evaluation process.
- Supporting the Independent Management Review (Peer Review) of the RFP before release.
- Identifying external or SoS interfaces and ensuring the technical interface requirement and task scope are unambiguous to the offerors.
- Identifying requirements for the protection of critical program information (CPI) and mission-critical functions and components (see CH 9–3.1.)
- Providing a clear description of the minimum technical requirements used to determine the technical acceptability of a proposal.

Table 11 contains the typical technical contents of the RFP and the associated Systems Engineer's responsibilities, and should not be considered an exhaustive or mandatory list.

Table 11: Typical Technical Contents of a RFP

	Typical Technical Contents	SE Responsibilities
Section C	<ul><li>Statement of Work (SOW)</li><li>System Performance Specification</li></ul>	<ul><li>Provide program technical requirements and technical aspects in the SOW</li></ul>

	Typical Technical Contents	**SE Responsibilities**
Description of Work to Be Performed	• Operational Documents (CONOPS/OMS/MP, SoS, Requirements, etc.) • Available and applicable architecture(s) • Engineering processes	• Generate the system performance specification • Identify application of SE processes • Identify appropriate technical specifications and standards
Section H Special Contract Requirements	• Key personnel • Government-furnished equipment or information (GFE or GFI) • Obsolescence management • Warranties • Options for delivery of software • Award fees	• Include a clear statement of any special contract requirements that are not included in other sections of the uniform contract format
Section J Attachments	• Systems Engineering Plan (SEP) • Program Work Breakdown Structure (WBS) • Integrated Master Plan (IMP) • Top-level program schedule • Contract Data Requirements List (CDRL) • Contract security classification specification • Data rights attachment	• Support development of WBS, IMP, top-level program schedule, CDRL and Contract Security Specification • Ensure that sufficient time is allotted to develop high-quality specifications and plans prior to releasing the RFP
Section K Representations, Certifications, and Other Statements	• Data rights	• Identify provisions that require representations, certifications or the submission of other information by offerors • Consider including a provision requiring offerors to identify any technical data or computer software the offeror proposes to deliver to the Government after award with less than unlimited rights

41

	Typical Technical Contents	SE Responsibilities
Section L Instructions on Content and Structure of RFP Response	• Systems engineering solution • Systems engineering management processes • Technical baseline management • Technical reviews and audits • Risk management processes and known key risk areas • Mandatory (i.e., statute- and regulation-driven) and advised design considerations • Technical organization • Technical data required for a Streamlined Life Cycle Assessment (LCA)	• Adequately define the offeror's design • Provide technical background and context for the offeror's solution • Describe the offeror's SE technical and management processes • Provide consistency across the SOW and system performance specifications • Demonstrate alignment with Government processes
Section M Source Selection Evaluation Factors	• Technical: technical solution, supporting data, performance specification • Management: SOW, Contractor Systems Engineering Management Plan (SEMP), IMS, risks and opportunity management plans • Environmental objectives (when appropriate) • Quality or product assurance • Past performance • Price or cost to the Government • Extent offeror's rights in the data rights attachment meet Government's needs	• Define technical evaluation factors and provide SE specific evaluation criteria used to assess proposals • Participate on or lead the technical evaluation team • Provide technical personnel to participate on each evaluation factor team (e.g., management, past performance, cost) • Provide consistency across the SOW and system performance specifications • Evaluate RFP responses against technical requirements, threshold requirements, management (e.g., SEMP, WBS, and program schedule), and consistency across the proposal (e.g., link between WBS, program schedule, risks, and cost) • Identify and assess the technical risks and opportunities for each proposal, including

42

	Typical Technical Contents	SE Responsibilities
		schedule risks and related risk and opportunity handling plans • Define clearly, in both the Source Selection Plan and Section M, the minimum technical requirements that will be used to determine the technical acceptability of the proposal if using the Lowest Price Technically Acceptable (LPTA) source selection method (see FAR (Subpart 15.101-2)).

CH 3–3. Business Practice: Systems Engineering Activities in the Life Cycle

This section is split into three subsections:

- CH 3–3.1.: Life-Cycle Expectations provides introductory material and life-cycle context
- CH 3–3.2.: Systems Engineering Activities in Life-Cycle Phases describes the Systems Engineer's role in each phase of the weapon system acquisition life cycle. The notional technical reviews and audits in each phase are identified
- CH 3–3.3.: Technical Reviews and Audits provides an in-depth description of technical reviews and audits. This arrangement accommodates the planning and conducting of the technical reviews and audits in accordance with a program's specific needs. Some large and complex programs may require each technical review and audit; others may combine technical reviews and audits or get permission to not conduct certain reviews

CH 3–3.1 Life-Cycle Expectations

Systems engineering (SE) provides the technical foundation for all acquisition activities regardless of acquisition category (ACAT) or acquisition model (e.g., weapon system or information system). The SE framework described in this chapter spans the entire acquisition life cycle and is based on Department of Defense Directive (DoDD) 5000.01, Enc. 1 and Department of Defense Instruction (DoDI) 5000.02, para 5.d. Framework content should be tailored and structured to fit the technology maturity, risks, interdependencies, related characteristics and context for the program or the system of interest. The succeeding sections identify the SE activities, processes, inputs, outputs, and expectations during each acquisition phase and for each technical review and audit.

Acquisition milestones and SE technical reviews and audits serve as key points throughout the life cycle to evaluate significant achievements and assess technical maturity and risk. Table 12: Technical Maturity Points identifies the objectives of each SE assessment and the technical maturity point marked by each review. The Materiel Development Decision (MDD) review is the entry point into the acquisition process and is mandatory for all programs in accordance with DoDI 5000.02, para 5.d.1. Depending on the maturity of the preferred materiel solution, the Milestone Decision Authority (MDA) designates the initial review milestone. This would normally be the MDD, but it can be A, B, or C. In any case, the decision is documented in the Acquisition Decision Memorandum (ADM) published immediately after an MDD event.

43

Since the review milestone is chosen consistent with the maturity of the preferred materiel solution, entry at any milestone requires evidence of the associated solution maturity, as summarized in Table 12: Technical Maturity Points.

Department experience (e.g., Government Accountability Office (GAO) Report 12-400SP) has found that successful programs use knowledge-based product development practices that include steps to gather knowledge to confirm the program's technologies are mature, their designs are stable and their production processes are in control. Successful materiel developers ensure a high level of knowledge is achieved at key junctures in development. Table 12 summarizes the concept of technical maturity points.

Table 12: Technical Maturity Points

Technical Maturity Points			
DoD Acquisition Milestone/Decision Point & Technical Review/ Audit	Objective	Technical Maturity Point	Additional Information
Materiel Development Decision (MDD)	Decision to assess potential materiel solutions and appropriate phase for entry into acquisition life cycle.	Capability gap met by acquiring a materiel solution.	Technically feasible solutions have the potential to effectively address a validated capability need. Technical risks understood.
Alternative Systems Review (ASR)	Recommendation that the preferred materiel solution can affordably meet user needs with acceptable risk.	System parameters defined; balanced with cost, schedule and risk.	Initial system performance established and plan for further analyses (e.g., assessing technical maturity and associated risks) supports Milestone A criteria.
Milestone A	Decision to invest in technology maturation and preliminary design.	Affordable solution found for identified need with acceptable technology risk, scope, and complexity.	Affordability goals identified and technology development plans, time, funding, and other resources match customer needs. Prototyping and end-item development strategy for Technology Maturation and Risk Reduction (TMRR) phase focused on key technical risk areas.
System Requirements Review (SRR)	Recommendation to proceed into development with acceptable risk.	Level of understanding of top-level system/ performance requirements is adequate to support further requirements analysis and design activities.	Government and contractor mutually understand system /performance requirements including: (1) the preferred materiel solution (including its support concept) from the Materiel Solution Analysis (MSA) phase; (2) plan for technology maturation; and (3) maturity of interdependent systems.

Technical Maturity Points			
DoD Acquisition Milestone/Decision Point & Technical Review/ Audit	Objective	Technical Maturity Point	Additional Information
System Functional Review (SFR)	Recommendation that functional baseline satisfies performance requirements and to begin preliminary design with acceptable risk.	Functional baseline established and under formal configuration control. System functions in the system performance specification decomposed and defined in specifications for lower level elements, that is, system segments and major subsystems.	Functional requirements and verification methods support achievement of performance requirements. Acceptable technical risk of achieving allocated baseline. See CH 3–4.1.6. Configuration Management Process for a description of baselines.
Capability Development Document (CDD) Validation	Requirements validation authority action. Provides a basis for preliminary design activities and the PDR.	Major cost and performance trades have been completed and enough risk reduction has been completed to support a decision to commit to the set of requirements (i.e., CDD or equivalent)	Support preparation for CDD validation by performing systems engineering trade-off analysis addressing relationships of cost, requirements, design, and schedule. Once validated, a Configuration Steering Board assumes responsibility to review all requirements changes and any significant technical configuration changes for ACAT I and IA programs in development, production, and sustainment that have the potential to result in cost and schedule impacts to the program.
Preliminary Design Review (PDR)	Recommendation that allocated baseline satisfies user requirements and developer ready to begin detailed design with acceptable risk.	Allocated baseline established such that design provides sufficient confidence to proceed with detailed design. Baseline also supports 10 USC 2366b certification, if applicable.	Preliminary design and basic system architecture support capability need and affordability goals and/or caps achievement. See CH 3–4.1.6. Configuration Management Process for a description of baselines.

Technical Maturity Points			
DoD Acquisition Milestone/Decision Point & Technical Review/ Audit	Objective	Technical Maturity Point	Additional Information
Development Request for Proposal (RFP) Release Decision Point	Determination that program plans are affordable and executable and that the program is ready to release RFPs for EMD and/or for LRIP (or Limited Deployment options for MAIS programs).	Systems engineering trades completed and have informed program requirements. Competitive and risk reduction prototyping and the development of the preliminary design have influenced risk management plans and should-cost initiatives.	The Request for Proposal (RFP) reflects the program's plans articulated in the draft (as defined in DoDI 5000.02, para 5.d.6) Acquisition Strategy and other draft, key planning documents such as the Systems Engineering Plan (SEP), Program Protection Plan (PPP), Test and Evaluation Master Plan (TEMP), and Life-Cycle Sustainment Plan (LCSP).
Milestone B	Decision to invest in product development, integration, and verification as well as manufacturing process development; decision on LRIP quantity (or scope of Limited Deployments for MAIS programs).	Critical technologies assessed able to meet required performance and are ready for further development. Resources and requirements match.	Maturity, integration, and producibility of the preliminary design (including critical technologies) and availability of key resources (time, funding, other) match customer needs. Should-cost goals defined.
Critical Design Review (CDR)	Recommendation to start fabricating, integrating, and testing test articles with acceptable risk.	Product design is stable. Initial product baseline established.	Initial product baseline established by the system detailed design documentation; affordability/should-cost goals confirmed. Government assumes control of initial product baseline as appropriate. See CH 3–4.1.6. Configuration Management Process for a description of baselines.
System Verification Review (SVR)/Functional Configuration Audit (FCA)	Recommendation that the system as tested has been verified (i.e., product baseline is compliant with the functional baseline) and is ready for validation (operational assessment) with acceptable risk.	System design verified to conform to functional baseline.	Actual system (which represents the production configuration) has been verified through required analysis, demonstration, examination, and/or testing. Synonymous with system-level Functional Configuration Audit (FCA). See CH 3–4.1.6. Configuration Management Process for a description of baselines.

46

Technical Maturity Points			
DoD Acquisition Milestone/Decision Point & Technical Review/ Audit	**Objective**	**Technical Maturity Point**	**Additional Information**
Production Readiness Review (PRR)	Recommendation that production processes are mature enough to begin limited production with acceptable risk.	Design and manufacturing are ready to begin production.	Production engineering problems resolved and ready to enter production phase.
Milestone C and Limited Deployment Decision	Decision to produce production-representative units for operational test and evaluation (OT&E) and/or decision that increment of capability is ready for Limited Deployment.	Manufacturing processes are mature enough to support Low-Rate Initial Production (LRIP) (and / or Limited Deployment) and generate production-representative articles for OT&E. Increment of capability has stable design.	Production readiness meets cost, schedule, and quality targets. Begin initial deployment and/or deploy increment of capability.
Physical Configuration Audit (PCA)	Recommendation to start full-rate production and/or full deployment with acceptable risk.	Product baseline established. Verifies the design and manufacturing documentation, following update of the product baseline to account for resolved OT&E issues, matches the physical configuration.	Confirmation that the system to be deployed matches the product baseline. Product configuration finalized and system meets user's needs. Conducted after OT&E issues are resolved. See CH 3–4.1.6. Configuration Management Process for a description of baselines.
Full-Rate Production Decision Review (FRP DR) or Full Deployment Decision Review (FDDR)	Decision to begin full-rate production and/or decision to begin full deployment.	Manufacturing processes are mature and support full-rate production and/or capability demonstrated in operational environment supporting full deployment (i.e., system validated through OT&E).	Delivers fully funded quantity of systems and supporting materiel and services for the program or increment to the users.

Figure 7: Weapon System Development Life Cycle provides the end-to-end perspective and the integration of SE technical reviews and audits across the system life cycle.

The Systems Engineer supports the Program Manager in the development and implementation of a technical program strategy. SE processes help deliver capabilities that meet warfighter needs within cost and schedule by balancing end-user needs, design considerations, resource constraints and risk. The

47

Systems Engineer uses technical reviews and audits to assess whether preplanned technical maturity points are reached during the acquisition life cycle as the system and system elements mature. The identification and mitigation of technical risks leading up to reviews and audits facilitates achieving entrance criteria at each of these points (see the DoD Risk, Issue, and Opportunity Management Guide for Defense Acquisition Programs.) Special attention should be made to ensure the consistency of analysis that supports key decision and transition points throughout the program's life cycle. For instance, models, simulations, tools and data should be integrated into the SE activities and reused to the greatest extent possible (see CH 3–2.4.2. Modeling and Simulation). This knowledge forms the basis for the Systems Engineer's recommendations to the Program Manager (PM) on how to technically proceed with the program.

Figure 7: Weapon System Development Life Cycle

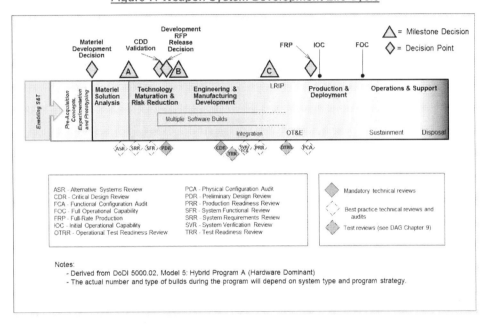

CH 3–3.1.1 Systems Engineering in Defense Acquisition Program Models

DoDI 5000.02, para 5.c. identifies several acquisition models for Program Managers (PMs) to use as a starting point in structuring a program to acquire a specific product. The PM selects and tailors the acquisition model based on the dominant characteristics of the product being acquired or the need for accelerated acquisition. This chapter contains information nominally based upon the Hybrid Model A (Hardware Dominant), since most weapon system programs include software development, hardware development and integration.

The PM and the Systems Engineer can use the descriptions of technical reviews and audits, phases, decision points and processes in this chapter to help select and tailor an acquisition strategy for a program. The resulting program structure is documented in the Acquisition Strategy and other plans, including the Systems Engineering Plan.

Table 13: Acquisition Models contains a summary of the set of acquisition models described in DoDI 5000.02, para 5.c. The second column contains the expected application for each model and highlights the relevant systems engineering activities identified in this chapter. This information can be used to guide the application of processes described in CH 3–4., as necessary.

Table 13: Acquisition Models

48

Acquisition Program Model	Key Characteristics and Systems Engineering Considerations
Model 1: **Hardware Intensive Program**	**Key Characteristics** • Products requiring development of DoD unique hardware **Systems Engineering Considerations** • Activities: See CH 3–3.2. • Reviews: See CH 3–3.3.; assumes minimal software development so Software Specification Review (SSR) may not be necessary • Products: See CH 3–3.2.
Model 2: **Defense Unique Software Intensive Program**	**Key Characteristics** • Products requiring complex, defense unique software where several software builds are developed, integrated and tested before a mature software product can be deployed. • Generally hosted on commercial off-the-shelf computing platforms or existing military computing platforms **Systems Engineering Considerations** • Activities: See CH 3–2.3.1. and CH 3–3.2.; assumes minimal hardware development so manufacturing aspects may not apply; some Commercial Off the Shelf (COTS) production planning may be necessary • Reviews: See CH 3–3.3.; SSR as precursor to Preliminary Design Review (PDR), System Verification Review/Functional Configuration Audit (SVR/FCA), minimal Physical Configuration Audit (PCA), no Low-Rate Initial Production (LRIP) and no Full Rate Production (FRP) decisions; include Full Deployment (FD) decision; multiple reviews may be necessary for each build, Post Implementation Review (PIR) may be appropriate. Development RFP Release decision point determines scope of limited deployment for MAIS programs. At Milestone B finalize scope of limited deployment. At Milestone C and/or Limited Deployment decision, the increment of capability is reviewed for limited deployment. • Products: See CH 3–3.2. and CH 6–3.3.

49

Acquisition Program Model	Key Characteristics and Systems Engineering Considerations
Model 3: Incrementally Deployed Software Intensive Program **(See also** DoDI 5000.02, Enc 11, DoDI 5000.75**, and** DAG Chapter 6**, "Acquiring IT & Business Systems)**	**Key Characteristics** • Products requiring the integration of existing software adapted for DoD • Distinguished from Model 2 by the fact of incremental deployment of a capability in relatively short intervals • Model sometimes adopted for Defense Business Systems (DBS) (See DoDI 5000.75) • Uses limited deployment decisions in lieu of MS C • Each incremental capability starts with a separate pre-Milestone B decision • Several increments necessary to achieve overall required capability; for DBS there are schedule constraints **Systems Engineering Considerations** • Activities: See CH 3–2.3.1. and CH 3–3.2.; assumes no hardware development so manufacturing aspects do not apply; may be some COTS production planning necessary • Reviews: See CH 3–3.3.; SSR as precursor to PDR, minimal PCA, no LRIP, and no FRP decisions; multiple reviews may be necessary for each build and/or increment including PIR; multiple pre-Milestone B decisions; include Limited Deployment Decisions (LDD) and Full Deployment Decisions (FDD); IOC occurs before FDD. Development RFP Release decision point determines scope of limited deployment for MAIS programs. At Milestone B finalize scope of limited deployment. At Milestone C and/or Limited Deployment decision, the increment of capability is reviewed for limited deployment • Products: See CH 3–3.2.
Model 4: Accelerated Acquisition Program	**Key Characteristics** • Products requiring development and deployment as quickly as possible, usually motivated by a potential adversary achieving technological surprise, and featuring a greater acceptance of program risk • For accelerated acquisition programs regardless of ACAT level. For programs to be deployed in less than 2 years and below the cost thresholds for ACAT I and IA programs see DoDI 5000.02, Enc 13 • Schedule considerations take precedence over cost and technical risk considerations • Compresses or eliminates phases of the process • May combine objectives of the nominal milestones and decision points into fewer decision events **Systems Engineering Considerations** • Activities: Close and frequent interaction with the operational sponsor to ensure operational objective and measurable desired operational effect is clearly understood. System trade studies weigh achieving operational objectives and effect more highly than long term sustainability or cost. Conduct safety assessment and address risks. Minimum development and test with some concurrency • Reviews: Tailored to program objectives; balance technical risks, operational needs, and timelines • Products: Only as necessary to support PM decisions, DAB decisions, statutory requirements, planned deployment and sustainment needs
Model 5:	**Key Characteristics** • Products requiring hardware development and/or integration as well as software development

Acquisition Program Model	Key Characteristics and Systems Engineering Considerations
Hybrid Program A (Hardware Dominant)	• Program structure combines the characteristics of Models 1 and 2 • Milestone B and C decisions should include criteria for software maturity • Many modern weapon systems contain substantial hardware and software development resulting in some form of this Model 5 **Systems Engineering Considerations** • Activities: See CH 3–2.3.1. and CH 3–3.2.; Hardware development may determine overall schedule, decision points and milestones, but software development requires tight integration and may dictate pace of program execution. • Reviews: See CH 3–3.3.; SSR may be appropriate • Products: See CH 3–3.2.
Model 6: Hybrid Program B (Software Dominant)	**Key Characteristics** • Products requiring software development and/or integration as well as limited hardware development • Each increment includes intermediate builds • Each incremental capability starts with a separate Milestone B decision • Several increments necessary to achieve overall required capability. **Systems Engineering Considerations** • Activities: See CH 3–2.3.1. and CH 3–3.2.; ; software development is tightly integrated and coordinated with limited hardware development; software development organized into series of builds • Reviews: See CH 3–3.3.; SSR as precursor to PDR, minimal PCA, multiple reviews may be necessary for each build and/or increment including PIR; multiple pre-Milestone B decisions; include LF and FD decisions; IOC occurs before FDD. Development RFP Release decision point determines scope of limited deployment for MAIS programs. At Milestone B finalize scope of limited deployment. At Milestone C and/or Limited Deployment decision, the increment of capability is reviewed for limited deployment. • Products: See CH 3–3.2. and CH 6–3.3.

As a subset of Model 4, products with less than ACAT I or IA cost thresholds, to be deployed in less than two years, and responding to Urgent Operational Needs (UONs) may fall within the procedures described in DoDI 5000.02, Enc 13 for Urgent Capability Acquisition.. (UONs are defined in CJCSI 3170.01.) The rapid acquisition life cycle has no Materiel Development Decision (MDD) and usually combines objectives of the generic milestones and decision points into fewer decision events. Since these products are usually non-developmental items (NDI) or near-NDI products, the primary systems engineering (SE) considerations are to ensure the capability is safe and secure, and meets warfighter needs and national security needs.

Life-cycle phase names may vary by acquisition model. For instance, some models are appropriate for incremental deliveries and have a subset of phases that are repeated, as identified in Table 14. The table provides a visual sense of the variation in phases between the DoDI 5000.02, para 5.c. acquisition models. This can help the PM and Systems Engineer select and tailor the acquisition model for the program. The transition from one phase to another is program-unique, documented in the Acquisition Strategy and approved by the Milestone Decision Authority (MDA).

Table 14: Variation in Phase Terminology for Each Acquisition Model

51

Acquisition Model	Phases				
Generic	MSA	TMRR	EMD	P&D	O&S
Model 1: Hardware Intensive Program	MSA	TMRR	EMD	P&D	O&S
Model 2: Defense Unique Software Intensive Program	MSA	TMRR	EMD	Deployment	O&S
Model 3: Incrementally Deployed Software Intensive Program	MSA	Risk Reduction*	Development & Deployment*		O&S
Model 4: Accelerated Acquisition Program	MSA	Concurrent TMRR and Development		Concurrent P&D	O&S
Model 5: Hybrid Program A (Hardware Dominant)	MSA	TMRR	EMD	P&D	O&S
Model 6: Hybrid Program B (Software Dominant)	MSA	TMRR*	EMD*	P&D*	O&S
Urgent Capability Acquisition	Pre-Development		Development & Assessment	P&D	O&S
Legend	EMD - Engineering and Manufacturing Development				
	MSA - Materiel Solution Analysis				
	O&S - Operations and Support				
	P&D - Production and Deployment				
	TMRR - Technology Maturation and Risk Reduction				

Note: * = repeated for each increment

The meaning of Limited Deployment, as used in Models 2, 3 and 6, is contextually dependent. The scope of deployments can be driven by deployment of the full capability to a limited number of sites (i.e., Model 2), or driven by deployment of software increments and therefore increments of capability (i.e., Model 3), or a combination of both (i.e., Model 6).

52

CH 3–3.1.2 Systems of Systems

Whether or not a system is formally acknowledged as a system of systems (SoS), nearly all DoD systems function as part of an SoS to deliver a necessary capability to the warfighter (see Systems Engineering Guide for Systems of Systems on the Deputy Assistant Secretary of Defense for Systems Engineering (DASD(SE) website). SoS systems engineering (SE) is an ongoing iterative process as shown in the SoS SE Implementers' View in Figure 8: SoS SE Implementers' View. The backbone of SoS SE implementation is a continuous analysis that considers changes from the broader operational mission environment as well as feedback from the ongoing engineering process.

Capability solutions to support a mission or set of missions are a challenge that may require a level of iterative analysis performed at the nexus between SoS SE and mission analysis. This iterative analysis is a multi-disciplinary activity called mission engineering. Mission Engineering (ME) is the deliberate planning, analyzing, organizing and integrating of current and emerging operational and system capabilities to achieve desired warfighting mission effects.

The ME results provide the basis for developing and evolving the SoS architecture, identifying or negotiating changes to the constituent systems that impact the SoS and working with the constituent systems to implement and integrate those changes. This view of SoS SE implementation provides structure to the evolution of the SoS through changes in constituent systems, which are typically on different life-cycle timelines, adapting as systems come in and move out and as Concept of Operations / Operational Mode Summary / Mission Profile (CONOPS/OMS/MP) adapt and change. Hence the need for continually updating the SoS analysis and adapting the architecture and updating systems on an ongoing basis.

Figure 8: SoS SE Implementers' View

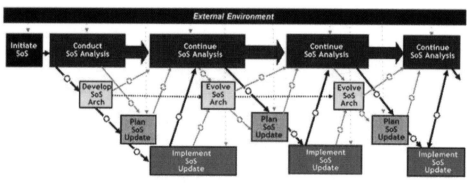

Therefore, SoS SE planning and implementation should consider and leverage the development plans of the individual systems in order to balance SoS needs with individual system needs. Finally, SoS SE should address the end-to-end behavior of the ensemble of systems, addressing the key issues that affect this end-to-end behavior with particular emphasis on integration and interoperability. Effective application of SoS SE addresses organizational as well as technical issues in making SE trades and decisions. The Systems Engineer has different roles and authorities at the system versus the SoS level. The SoS-level Systems Engineer can provide the technical foundation for effective user capabilities by conducting balanced technical management of the SoS, using an SoS architecture based on open systems and loose coupling and focusing on the design strategy and trades (both at establishment and through evolution). They should collaborate with multiple Systems Engineers across multiple systems. Each Systems Engineer has the authority for his or her system implementation. These waves of implementations and upgrades taken as a whole provide the SoS capability. For a more detailed discussion of Figure 8, see the paper, "An Implementers' View of Systems Engineering for Systems of Systems".

Consideration of SoS in SE for Individual Systems

Most acquisition programs address the development or major upgrade of individual systems (in contrast to SoS). Understanding the SoS context(s) of the system (including use in multiple operational environments) is critical to developing requirements for the system, so when delivered, it operates effectively in user operational environments. From the Joint Capabilities Integration and Development System (JCIDS) Capabilities-Based Assessment (CBA) through sustainment activities, it is important to recognize how the system context influences system requirements. An up-to-date CONOPS/OMS/MP for the system is basic to understanding the system context, notably, mission and task threads and data exchanges that have an impact on the system. Systems engineers of individual systems should ensure SoS considerations and risks are addressed throughout the acquisition life cycle by:

- Identifying system dependencies and interoperability needs (See CH 3–4.3.13. Interoperability and Dependencies)
- Factoring these into the development of system concepts, requirements and risks
- Addressing these through trade analysis, system architecture and design, interface development and management and verification and validation

Both from an individual system perspective and the SoS perspective, PMs and Systems Engineers have found it difficult to coordinate and balance the acquisition objectives and strategies for a given system with those of the SoS and other constituent systems. A senior governance body is useful to provide a forum for discussion and decision. This forum should address functional capabilities, technical plans, configuration management and strategies with respect to interfaces, interdependences, risks and risk mitigation. It is critical to address all equities and make collective decisions that can be implemented in changes to a system's configuration.

One SoS best practice is to monitor closely interdependent programs, with checkpoints at scheduled design reviews to assess program progress, assess related risks and determine actions to mitigate potentially negative impacts. Another best practice is to have the technical representatives from each system participate in each others' SFR, PDR, and CDR.

Table 15 lists SoS considerations for systems at each stage of acquisition. At each phase, the SE approach to addressing SoS-related dependencies should be addressed in the Systems Engineering Plan (SEP).

Table 15: Key SoS Considerations for Systems by Acquisition Phase

Acquisition Phase	Considerations
Pre-Materiel Development Decision (Pre-MDD)	**Focus** - Define role of the system in supporting a mission capability, including relationship to other systems in the SoS which support that capability **Evidence/Products** - End-to-end depiction (e.g., mission thread) of capability gap in context of systems currently supporting capability **Measure/Metrics** - Activities supported by the system in relationship to other systems and the context - Physical environment information needs Joint Doctrine, Organization, Training, materiel, Leadership and Education, Personnel, Facilities and Policy (DOTmLPF-P) for the system and the SoS - Identification of stakeholders **Responsibilities/ Interdependencies** - Provided by the JCIDS analysis and the evidence provided at MDD

54

Acquisition Phase	Considerations
Materiel Solution Analysis (MSA)	**Focus** • In the Analysis of Alternatives (AoA), consider the alternatives in the context of the larger SoS supporting the capability • In the operational analysis and concept engineering for the preferred materiel solution, consider the new system in the SoS context; identify dependencies and relationships with other systems, including key interfaces and technical risks based on SoS considerations to be addressed in Technology Maturation and Risk Reduction (TMRR) • Identify the nature of the dependencies and interfaces, including the parties involved, and an initial plan for addressing these including initial memoranda of agreement (MOAs) • Identify non-materiel changes needed to implement a specific materiel solution, e.g. changes to tools, techniques and procedures to enable the SoS capability. **Evidence/Products** • AoA criteria or results relevant to SoS dependencies or interfaces • Definition of key system dependencies or interfaces that influence system requirements • Initial management plans with supporting MOAs, including draft Interface Control Agreements (ICAs) for collaborations with other systems in a SoS • Risks associated with SoS dependencies (both programmatic and technical) and interoperability requirements, including environment, safety and occupational health (ESOH), and security risks to be accepted by Joint Authorities **Measure/Metrics** • SoS-related requirements in draft system performance specification and/or Pre-MS A Request for Proposal (RFP) • MOAs with key parties in SoS dependencies or relationships **Responsibilities/Interdependencies** • Systems engineers of the systems involved in the SoS or SoS SE if one exists • End users • Requirements Manager (s) for requirements per JCIDS Manual • PM(s) responsible for Memorandum of Agreements (MOA) • Contracting Officer(s) responsible for RFPs

55

Acquisition Phase	Considerations
Technology Maturation and Risk Reduction (TMRR)	**Focus** • Assess the technical approaches and risks for addressing system requirements including considerations for the system as a component operating in a SoS context (including dependencies, interoperability and interfaces) • Address considerations of changes needed in other systems for the systems in acquisition to meet capability objectives **Evidence/Products** • An interface management plan that is a part of a configuration management plan, including ICAs • Risks associated with SoS dependencies (both programmatic and technical) and interoperability requirements, including environment, safety and occupational health (ESOH), and security risks to be accepted by Joint Authorities. • Output of studies which validate the technical fit and operational suitability of the system under development within the SoS **Measure/Metrics** • Final interface specifications • MOAs and schedule for interface management plan • Progress with respect to schedule and plan milestones • Progress with respect to expected performance **Responsibilities/Interdependencies** • Developers of this system and the other systems involved with the dependencies of interface; shared configuration management (CM) • Interface Management Working Group (IMWG) • End users
Engineering Manufacturing Development (EMD)	**Focus** • Develop, verify and validate the detailed design that addresses system requirements, considering the SoS context including recognized dependencies and interfaces **Evidence/Products** • Interface documentation, test plans and test reports • Progress on MOAs with system's dependencies • Risks associated with SoS dependencies (both programmatic and technical) and interoperability requirements, including environment, safety and occupational health (ESOH), and security risks to be accepted by Joint Authorities. **Measure/Metrics** • Successful development and test of interfaces • Progress with respect to SoS schedule and plan milestones • Progress with respect to expected performance **Responsibilities/Interdependencies** • Materiel developers • IMWG • Testers • End users

Acquisition Phase	Considerations
Production & Deployment (P&D) and Operations and Support (O&S)	**Focus** • Verify the as-built interfaces meet specs and support operational needs. • Support effective system operation in a SoS context **Evidence/Products** • Test reports **Measure/Metrics** • Successful test results **Responsibilities/Interdependencies** • Materiel developers • Testers • End users

For a more detailed discussion of SE for SoS, including some useful information documented in 'Recommended Practices: System of Systems Considerations in the Engineering of Systems, August 2014, TR-JSA/TP4-1-2014'.

CH 3–3.2 Systems Engineering Activities in Life-Cycle Phases

This section describes, from several perspectives, the technical activities typically performed in each phase of the acquisition life cycle. First, the objectives and an overview of the phase are described to provide context. Then, a sequence of subsections address the roles and responsibilities of a System Engineer in a program office, along with the inputs normally required to constrain the technical activities. Each phase description ends with a table summarizing the expected technical outputs from the phase. While technical reviews and audits are mentioned in this section, the details are covered in CH 3–3.3. Technical Reviews and Audits.

CH 3–3.2.1 Pre-Materiel Development Decision

The objectives of the pre-Materiel Development Decision (MDD) efforts are to obtain a clear understanding of user needs, identify a range of technically feasible candidate materiel solution approaches, consider near-term opportunities to provide a more rapid interim response and develop a plan for the next acquisition phase, including the required resources. This knowledge supports the Milestone Decision Authority's (MDA) decision to authorize entry into the acquisition life cycle and pursue a materiel solution. An additional objective is to characterize trade space, risks and mission interdependencies to support the start of the Analysis of Alternatives (AoA).

Policy in this area comes from two perspectives: the Joint Capabilities Integration and Development System (JCIDS) defined in Chairman of the Joint Chiefs of Staff Instruction (CJCSI) 3170.01 and the Defense Acquisition System (DAS) defined in DoDD 5000.01.

Development planning (DP) encompasses the engineering analysis and technical planning activities that provide the foundation for informed investment decisions on the path a materiel development follows to meet operational needs effectively, affordably and sustainably. DP activities are initiated prior to the Materiel Development Decision, continue throughout the Materiel Solution Analysis phase, and eventually transition to the program environment.

Attention to critical systems engineering (SE) processes and functions, particularly during early phases in acquisition, is essential to ensuring that programs deliver capabilities on time and on budget. The effective execution of pre-MDD SE efforts provides the foundation for user-driven requirements and technically feasible solution options that ensure an executable program. At MDD, the MDA not only decides whether an investment is made to fill the capability gap but also determines the fundamental path the materiel development will follow. This decision should be based on effective development planning.

An important aspect of the pre-MDD effort is to narrow the field of possible solutions to a reasonable set that is analyzed in the AoA. Early recognition of constraints, combined with analysis of technical feasibility, can eliminate many initial ideas because they lack the potential to meet the need in a timely, sustainable and cost-effective manner. Conversely, the range of alternatives analyzed in the AoA are chosen from a sufficiently broad solution space. Whenever possible, the Systems Engineer should try to engage with the end user (e.g., Requirements Manager) before the Initial Capabilities Document (ICD) and associated operational architecture is validated by the Joint Requirements Oversight Council (JROC) (see CH 3–4.2.1. Stakeholder Requirements Definition Process).

Studies have found that "programs that considered a broad range of alternatives tended to have better cost and schedule outcomes than the programs that looked at a narrow scope of alternatives." (See GAO-09-665 Analysis of Alternatives, Page 6.)

The work performed in this time frame should be well documented and transitioned to be used in future phases of the Acquisition Life Cycle. This is so the Program Manager (PM) and Systems Engineer, when assigned, can benefit from the mutual understanding of the basis of need (requirements) and the art of the possible (concepts/materiel solutions). To achieve these benefits, the Systems Engineer should proactively collaborate with the Science and Technology (S&T) and user communities.

Roles and Responsibilities

Often there is no assigned PM or Systems Engineer at this point in the weapon system's life cycle. Instead, a designated Service representative (e.g., Requirements Manager) is orchestrating and leading the preparations for MDD. This leader is responsible for synthesizing the necessary information to support a favorable decision. See DoDI 5000.02, Enc 3, sec. 3 and MDD Development Planning Templates. As a best practice, consideration should be given to designating a Service engineering representative to support concept and requirements definition and associated decisions in preparation for the MDD.

The designated Service representative should make use of appropriate models and simulations (CH 3–2.4.2. Modeling and Simulation) to develop required MDD evidence. The designated Service representative also should consider issuing a Request for Information (RFI) to industry to help identify and characterize alternative solutions.

Inputs

Table 16 summarizes the primary inputs and technical outputs associated with this part of the life cycle. Unlike the sections that follow, this pre-MDD period is the bridge between JCIDS and the DAS.

Table 16: Inputs Associated with Pre-MDD

Inputs for Pre-MDD
Draft Initial Capabilities Document (ICD) (See CJCSI 3170.01) • Product of Capability-Based Assessment (CBA) or equivalent
Other analyses • Other prior analytic, experimental, prototyping and/or technology demonstration efforts may be provided by the S&T community • Results of Market Research: 1) to identify existing technologies and products; and, 2) to understand potential solutions, technologies and sources

The MDD review requires an ICD that represents an operational capability need validated in accordance with CJCSI 3170.01. The Joint Staff provides this document, which is generally the output of a Capability-Based Assessment (CBA) or other studies. The designated Service representative should have access to both the ICD and supporting studies. Other technical information (such as models and simulations) may

58

be useful for understanding both the need and its context. The S&T community can contribute pertinent data and information on relevant technologies, prototypes, experiments and/or analysis. The DASD(SE) web site provides an <u>example</u> of how a program may provide evidence at the MDD review to support the MDA decision.

Activities

Figure 9 provides the end-to-end perspective and the integration of SE technical reviews and audits across the acquisition life cycle.

Figure 9: Weapon System Development Life Cycle

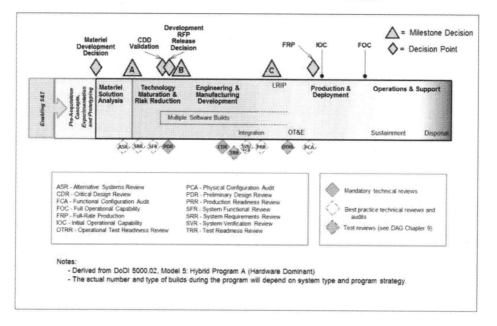

During pre-MDD, SE activities focus on:

- Achieving an in-depth understanding of the operational capability gaps defined in the ICD and identifying the sources of the gap(s), which, if addressed by a materiel solution, could achieve the needed capability
- Identifying an appropriate range of candidate materiel solutions from across the trade space to meet the need
- Identifying near-term opportunities to provide a more rapid interim response to the capability need
- Working with the S&T community (across Government, industry and academia) as well as other collaborators to build the technical knowledge base for each candidate materiel solution in the AoA Guidance to include experimentation and prototyping
- Analyzing trade space to determine performance versus cost benefits of potential solutions
- Planning for the technical efforts required during the next phase
- Performing an early evaluation of risks associated with the alternatives to be analyzed in the next phase
- Working with requirements developers to ensure the quality of all operational requirements from an SE perspective

59

Outputs and Products

This effort ends after a successful MDD review in which the MDA approves entry into the Defense Acquisition System. This decision is documented in a signed Acquisition Decision Memorandum (ADM), which specifies the approved entry point, typically the Materiel Solution Analysis (MSA) phase. Outputs of pre-MDD efforts provided in Table 17 also include approved AoA Guidance and an AoA Study Plan, which should be informed by SE.

Table 17: Technical Outputs Associated with Pre-MDD

Technical Outputs from Pre-MDD
Informed advice to the ICD
Informed advice to the AoA Guidance and Study Plan (See CH 2–2.3.)
Informed advice to the plan and budget for the next phase, including support to the AoA and non-AoA technical efforts required to prepare for the initial milestone review
Informed advice to the ADM

All potential materiel solutions pass through an MDD before entering the DAS. However, the MDA may authorize entry at any point in the acquisition life cycle based on the solution's technical maturity and risk. Technical risk has several elements: technology risk, engineering risk and integration risk. If the Service-recommended entry point is beyond the MSA phase, for example, part way through the Technology Maturation and Risk Reduction (TMRR) phase, the program provides evidence that all MSA and TMRR phase-specific entrance criteria and statutory requirements are met and that the solution's technical maturity supports entry at the point in the phase being proposed. Emphasis should be placed on the soundness of supporting technical information and plans in order to inform the MDA's decision, as opposed to which documents may or may not be complete.

As the next section explains, the MSA phase is made up of more than an AoA; it includes technical tasks to determine the preferred materiel solution based on the AoA results and technical tasks to prepare for the initial milestone review. Therefore, the technical plan and budget presented at the MDD should reflect the full range of activities required in the next phase.

CH 3–3.2.2 Materiel Solution Analysis Phase

The objective of the Materiel Solution Analysis (MSA) phase is to select and adequately describe a preferred materiel solution to satisfy the phase-specific entrance criteria for the next program milestone designated by the Milestone Decision Authority (MDA). Prior to completion of the MSA Phase, the Component Acquisition Executive (CAE) selects a Program Manager (PM) and establishes a Program Office to complete the necessary actions associated with planning the acquisition program. Usually, but not always, the next milestone is a decision to invest in technology maturation, risk reduction activities and preliminary design in the Technology Maturation and Risk Reduction (TMRR) phase. The systems engineering (SE) activities in the MSA phase result in several key products. First, a system model and/or architecture is developed that captures operational context and envisioned concepts, describes the system boundaries and interfaces, and addresses operational and functional requirements. Second, a preliminary system performance specification is developed that defines the performance of the preferred materiel solution. Third, the Systems Engineer advises the PM on what is to be prototyped, why and how.

During the MSA phase, the program team identifies a materiel solution to address user capability gaps partially based on an Analysis of Alternatives (AoA) (i.e., analysis of the set of candidate materiel solutions) led by the Director, Cost Analysis and Program Evaluation (CAPE) and conducted by a designated DoD Component. Once the Service sponsor selects a preferred materiel solution, the program team focuses engineering and technical analysis on this solution to ensure development plans, schedule, funding and other resources match customer needs and match the complexity of the preferred materiel

60

solution. SE activities should be integrated with MSA phase-specific test, evaluation, logistics and sustainment activities identified in CH 8–4.1. and CH 4–3.1.

This phase has two major blocks of activity: (1) the AoA; and (2) the post-AoA operational analysis and concept engineering to prepare for a next program milestone designated by the MDA (see Figure 10: Activities in Materiel Solution Analysis Phase).

The AoA team considers a range of alternatives and evaluates them from multiple perspectives as directed by the AoA Guidance and AoA Study Plan. Engineering considerations including technical risk should be a component of the AoA Guidance and be addressed in the AoA Study Plan.

Figure 10: Activities in Material Solution Analysis Phase

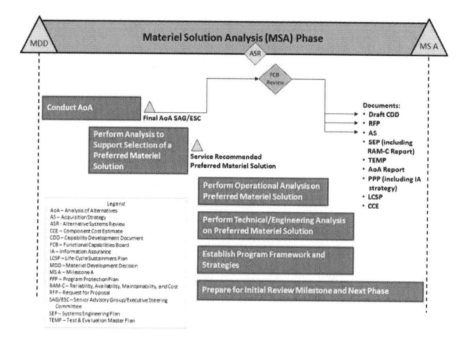

The objective of the AoA is to analyze and characterize each alternative (or alternative approach) relative to the others. The AoA does not result in a recommendation for a preferred alternative; it provides information that the Service sponsor uses to select which materiel solution to pursue. The Systems Engineer should participate in the AoA to help analyze performance and feasibility and to optimize alternatives. Using the AoA results, the Service sponsor may conduct additional engineering analysis to support the selection of a preferred materiel solution from the remaining trade space of candidate materiel solutions. After choosing the preferred materiel solution, the Service sponsor matures the solution in preparation for the next program milestone designated by the MDA.

After the AoA, program systems engineers establish the technical performance requirements consistent with the draft Capability Development Document (CDD), required at the next program milestone designated by the MDA, assuming it is Milestone A. These requirements form the basis for the system performance specification placed on contract for the TMRR phase; they also inform plans to mitigate risk in the TMRR phase.

In the MSA phase, the DoD Component combat developer (e.g., Requirements Manager) prepares a Concept of Operations/Operational Mode Summary/Mission Profile (CONOPS/OMS/MP), consistent with the validated/approved capability requirements document, typically an Initial Capabilities Document. The

61

CONOPS/OMS/MP includes the operational tasks, events, durations, frequency, operating conditions and environment in which the recommended materiel solution is to perform each mission and each phase of a mission. The CONOPS/OMS/MP informs the MSA phase activities and the development of plans for the next phase.

During MSA, several planning elements are addressed to frame the way forward for the MDA's decision at the next program milestone. SE is a primary source for addressing several of these planning elements. The planning elements include:

- Capability need, architecture
- System concept, architecture
- Key interfaces (including external interfaces and dependencies)
- Acquisition approach
- Engineering/technical approach
- Test and evaluation approach
- Program management approach
- External dependencies/agreements
- Schedule
- Resources
- Risks

See CH 3–4.1.1. Technical Planning Process. These planning elements are documented in various program plans such as the Acquisition Strategy (AS), Test and Evaluation Master Plan (TEMP), Program Protection Plan (PPP), next-phase Request for Proposal (RFP) and the Systems Engineering Plan (SEP). The SEP describes the SE efforts necessary to provide informed advice to these other planning artifacts (see the SEP Outline).

SE provides, for example, the technical basis for TMRR phase planning and execution, including identification of critical technologies, development of a competitive and risk reduction prototyping strategy and establishment of other plans that drive risk-reduction efforts. This early SE effort lays the foundation for the TMRR phase contract award(s) and preliminary designs, which confirm the system's basic architecture.

Roles and Responsibilities

In addition to the general responsibilities identified in CH 3–2.5. Engineering Resources, the PM focuses on the following MSA activities, which rely on and support SE efforts:

- Preparing for and supporting source selection activities for the upcoming phase solicitation and contract award
- Supporting the requirement community with the development of the draft CDD, assuming the next phase is TMRR
- Developing the AS, which incorporates necessary risk-reduction activities
- Staffing the program office with qualified (trained and experienced) systems engineers

In addition to the general roles and responsibilities described in CH 3–2.5. Engineering Resources, during this phase it is the Systems Engineer's responsibility to:

- Lead and manage the execution of the technical activities in this phase
- Measure and track the system's technical maturity
- Identify technologies that should be included in an assessment of technical risk.
- Perform trade studies
- Support preparations for the RFP package and assist in structuring the evaluation teams for technical aspects of the review

62

- Develop the system performance specification. See CH 3–4.1.6. Configuration Management Process. A particular program's naming convention for specifications should be captured in the SEP and other plans and processes tailored for the program
- Ensure integration of key design considerations into the system performance specification
- Develop technical approaches and plans, and document them in the SEP.
- Ensure the phase technical artifacts are consistent and support objectives of the next phase

Inputs

Table 18 summarizes the primary inputs associated with this part of the life cycle (see DoDI 5000.02, para 5.d.2). The table assumes the next phase is TMRR, but most of the technical outputs would be applicable going into any follow-on phase.

Table 18: Inputs Associated with MSA Phase

Inputs for MSA Phase
Initial Capabilities Document (ICD) (See CJCSI 3170.01) • Product of Capability Based Assessment (CBA) or equivalent
Validated On-Line Life-cycle Threat (VOLT) Report (See DoDI 5000.02 (Enc 1, Table 2) and CH 7–4.1.2.)
AoA Guidance and AoA Study Plan (See CH 2–2.3.)
Acquisition Decision Memorandum (ADM) (may contain additional direction)
Other analyses generated pre-MDD • Other prior analytic, prototyping and/or technology demonstration efforts conducted by the S&T community; technology insertion/transition can occur at any point in the life cycle • Results of Market Research: 1) to identify existing technologies and products; and 2) to understand potential solutions, technologies, and sources

The ICD, AoA Guidance, and AoA Study Plan should be available prior to the start of the MSA phase. Results of other related analyses may be available, for example, from the Capability Based Assessment (see CH 3–4.2.1. Stakeholder Requirements Definition Process) or other prior analytic and/or prototyping efforts conducted by the S&T community.

Activities

The MSA phase activities begin after a favorable MDD review has been held (see CH 3–3.2.1. Pre-Materiel Development Decision) and end when the phase-specific entrance criteria for the next program milestone, designated by the MDA, have been met. Figure 11 provides the end-to-end perspective and the integration of SE technical reviews and audits across the acquisition life cycle.

Figure 11: Weapon System Development Life Cycle

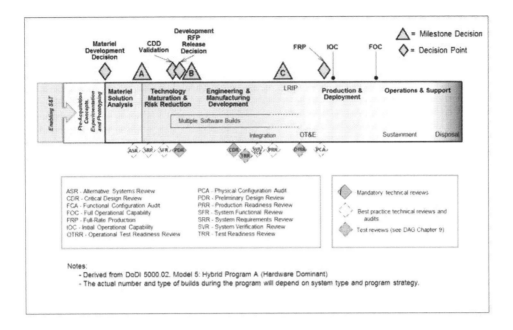

Notes:
- Derived from DoDI 5000.02, Model 5: Hybrid Program A (Hardware Dominant)
- The actual number and type of builds during the program will depend on system type and program strategy.

Referring back to Figure 10, which shows the major blocks of technical activities in the MSA phase:

- **Conduct AoA.** Includes all activities and analyses conducted by the AoA Study team under the direction of the Senior Advisory Group/Executive Steering Committee (SAG/ESC) and CAPE, or Service equivalent. Concludes with a final SAG/ESC and AoA Report. Systems Engineers should support this activity.
- **Perform Analysis to Support Selection of a Preferred Materiel Solution.** Includes all engineering activities and technical analysis performed to support Service selection of the preferred materiel solution by balancing cost, performance, schedule and risk.
- **Perform Operational Analysis on Preferred Materiel Solution**. Supports the definition of the performance requirements in the operational context, Functional Capabilities Board (FCB) review and the development of the draft CDD (see CJCSI 3170.01 Joint Capabilities Integration and Development System (JCIDS) and CH 3–4.2.1. Stakeholders Requirements Definition Process). The Systems Engineer should support the operational requirement/user/operational test community to ensure the Concept of Operations/Operational Mode Summary/Mission Profile (CONOPS/OMS/MP) is detailed enough to verify and validate system performance and operational capability. This activity could include the development of design reference missions/use cases that assist in the verification and validation process. Through analysis, the Systems Engineer also helps to identify key technology elements, determine external interfaces and establish interoperability requirements.
- **Perform Engineering and Technical Analysis on Preferred Materiel Solution.** This includes all engineering activities and technical analysis performed on the Service-selected preferred materiel solution in support of the development and maturation of a materiel solution concept, associated system performance specification and technical plans for the next phase.
- **Establish Program Framework and Strategies.** All activities to converge on the overarching strategies and plans for the acquisition of the system. Attention should be given to identifying and documenting agreements with external organizations. This documentation should include, for example, the contributions of S&T organizations and plans for transitioning technology into a program.

64

- **Prepare for Initial Review Milestone and Next Phase.** Includes all activities to compile technical and programmatic analysis and plans to meet the entrance criteria for the next program milestone designated by the MDA. See DoDI 5000.02, para 5.d.2 for phase objectives and exit criteria.

The technical review typically conducted in the MSA phase is the Alternative Systems Review (ASR) (see CH 3–3.3.1. Alternative Systems Review).

Outputs and Products

The knowledge gained during this phase, based on both the AoA and other analyses, should provide confidence that a technically feasible solution approach matches user needs and is affordable with reasonable risk (See Table 19. Technical outputs associated with technical reviews in this phase are addressed later in this chapter.)

Table 19: Technical Outputs Associated with MSA Phase

Technical Outputs from MSA Phase
Informed advice to the draft Capability Development Document (CDD)
Informed advice to Acquisition Decision Memorandum (ADM) and, when applicable, 10 USC 2366a certification
Informed advice to the AoA Report (See CH 2–2.3.)
Informed advice to the selection of the preferred materiel solution
• Selection of the preferred materiel solution is documented in the ADM
SEP (See DoDI 5000.02, Enc 3, sec. 2 and CH 3–2.2. Systems Engineering Plan)
Reliability, Availability, Maintainability, and Cost Rationale Report (RAM-C Report) (See DoDI 5000.02, Enc 3, sec. 12 and CH 3–4.3.19.)
• Attachment to SEP
Reliability Growth Curves (RGC) (See DoDI 5000.02, Enc 3, sec. 12 and CH 3–4.3.19.)
• Included in SEP
PPP (See DoDI 5000.02, Enc 3, sec. 13 and CH 9–3.4.2.2.)
Trade-off analysis results (See DoDI 5000.02, Enc 3, sec. 4)
• Results could include knees-in-the-curves sensitivity analyses, product selections, etc.
Assumptions and constraints
• Rationale for all assumptions, constraints and basis for trades
Environment, Safety and Occupational Health (ESOH) planning (See DoDI 5000.02, Enc 3, sec. 16 and CH 3–4.3.9.)
Assessment of technical risk and development of mitigation plans (See CH 3-4.1.5. and the DoD Risk, Issue, and Opportunity Management Guide for Defense Acquisition Programs.)
Consideration of technology issues
Initial identification of critical technologies
Interdependencies/interfaces/memoranda of agreement (MOAs)
• Understanding of the unique program interdependencies, interfaces, and associated MOAs
Life-Cycle Mission Data Plan for Intelligence Mission Data (IMD)-dependent programs (See CH 3–4.3.12. Intelligence (Life-Cycle Mission Data Plan) and CH 7–4.1.3.)
• Initial LMDP

Technical Outputs from MSA Phase
Draft system performance specification

Other technical information generated during the MSA phase:
  • Architectures, system models and simulations
  • Results of Market Research: 1) to identify existing technologies and products; and 2) to understand potential solutions, technologies, and sources appropriate for maturing the product in the next phase

Prototyping strategy (See DoDI 5000.02, para 5.d.4 and DoDI 5000.02, Enc 1, Table 2, Acquisition Strategy))
 	
  • Relationship between draft system performance specification and prototyping objectives is established and plans for next phase are consistent with it, both from a prototyping and preliminary system design perspective
 	
  • Includes identification of key system elements to be prototyped prior to Milestone B
 	
  • Documented in the AS

Informed advice to Affordability and Resource Estimates (See CH 3–2.4.4. Value Engineering, CH 3–4.3.2. Affordability – Systems Engineering Trade-Off Analyses, CH 1–4.2.15., and CH 2–2.1.)
 	
  • Affordability goals are established and treated as Key Performance Parameters (KPPs) at the next program milestone designated by the MDA
 	
  • Identify the likely design performance points where trade-off analyses occur during the next phase
 	
  • Value engineering results, as appropriate

Informed advice to the Life-Cycle Sustainment Plan (LCSP) (See CH 4–3.1.)
Informed advice to the Test and Evaluation Master Plan (TEMP) (See CH 8–4.1.)
Informed advice to the developmental test and evaluation (DT&E) planning including Early Operational Assessments (EOAs) (See CH 8–4.1.)
Informed advice to the Request for Proposal (RFP)   • Informed advice including system performance specification, SOW, CDRLs and source-selection criteria
Informed advice to the Acquisition Strategy (AS) (See CH 1–4.1.)   • Informed advice on engineering approaches and strategies, external dependencies, resource requirements, schedule and risks
Informed advice for the Spectrum Supportability Risk Assessment (See DoDI 4650.01 and CH 3–4.3.20.)

CH 3–3.2.3 Technology Maturation and Risk Reduction Phase

The primary objective of the Technology Maturation and Risk Reduction (TMRR) phase is to reduce technical risk and develop a sufficient understanding of the materiel solution to support sound investment decisions at the pre-Engineering and Manufacturing Development (EMD) Review and at Milestone B regarding whether to initiate a formal acquisition program. The Systems Engineer supports the production of a preliminary system design that achieves a suitable level of system maturity for low-risk entry into EMD (See Figure 12.) Usually the Systems Engineer implements a strategy of prototyping on a system element or subsystem level, balancing capability needs and design considerations to synthesize system requirements for a preliminary end-item design for the system. The prototyping objectives should focus on risk reduction and/or competition.

66

The major efforts associated with the TMRR phase are:

- Determining the appropriate set of technologies to integrate into a full system.
- Maturing the technologies, including demonstrating and assessing them in a relevant environment.
- Conducting prototyping of the system and/or system elements.
- Performing trade studies, refine requirements and revise designs.
- Developing the preliminary design, including functional and allocated baselines, specifications, interface control drawings/documents, architectures and system models.
- Performing developmental test activities as appropriate.

<u>**Figure 12: Systems Engineering Activities in the Technology Maturation and Risk Reduction Phase**</u>

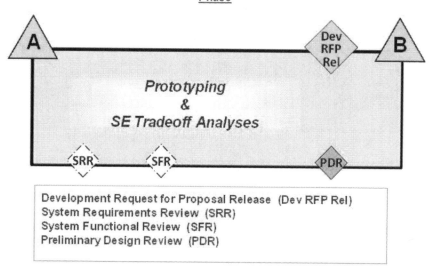

SE activities should be integrated with TMRR phase-specific test and evaluation and logistics and sustainment activities identified in <u>CH 8–4.2.</u> and <u>CH 4–3.2.</u>, respectively.

During the TMRR phase, the program develops and demonstrates prototype designs to reduce technical risk, validate design approaches, validate cost estimates and refine requirements. In addition, the TMRR phase efforts ensure the level of expertise required to operate and maintain the product is consistent with the force structure. Technology development is an iterative process of maturing technologies and refining user performance parameters to accommodate those technologies that do not sufficiently mature (requirements trades). The Initial Capabilities Document, the Acquisition Strategy (AS), Systems Engineering Plan (SEP) and Capability Development Document (CDD) guide the efforts of this phase. The CDD enters the TMRR phase as a draft (as described in <u>DoDI 5000.02, Enc 1, Table 2</u> and CJCSI 3170.01) and is validated during this phase to support preliminary design activities and the PDR.

There are two key technical objectives in the TMRR phase: technical risk reduction and initial system development activity, culminating in preliminary design. The Systems Engineer in the TMRR phase manages activities to evaluate prototyped solutions (competitive and risk reduction prototypes) against performance, cost and schedule constraints to balance the total system solution space. This information can then be used to inform the finalization of the system performance specification as a basis for functional analysis and preliminary design.

67

Effective systems engineering (SE), applied in accordance with the SEP and gated by technical reviews, reduces program risk, identifies potential management issues in a timely manner and supports key program decisions. The TMRR phase provides the Program Manager (PM) with a preliminary design and allocated baseline that are realistic and credible.

Roles and Responsibilities

The program office team provides technical management and may employ industry, Government laboratories, the Service science and technology (S&T) community or Federally Funded Research and Development Centers (FFRDCs)/universities to accomplish specific risk-reduction or prototype tasks as described in the SEP.

In addition to the general responsibilities identified in CH 3–2.5. Engineering Resources, the PM focuses on the following TMRR activities, which rely on and support SE efforts:

- Awarding TMRR phase contract(s).
- Providing resources for technical reviews.
- Planning and executing the Technology Readiness Assessment (TRA) (MDAPS only).
- Influencing development of the CDD.
- Developing the Acquisition Strategy (AS).
- Developing the strategy and objectives for use of prototypes; considering both contracted efforts and government sources.
- Supporting the Development RFP Release Decision Point.
- Ensuring the Government preserves the rights needed to be consistent with the life-cycle acquisition and support strategy. During TMRR, proprietary development and design can often lead to issues with intellectual property and associated data rights (see CH 3–4.1.7. Technical Data Management Process).
- Supporting the Configuration Steering Board in accordance with DoDI 5000.02, para 5.d.5b once the CDD has been validated. This board assumes responsibility to review all requirements changes and any significant technical configuration changes for ACAT I and IA programs in development, production and sustainment that have the potential to result in cost and schedule impacts to the program.

In addition to the general roles and responsibilities described in CH 3–2.5. Engineering Resources, during this phase it is the Systems Engineer's responsibility to:

- Lead and manage the execution of the technical activities as documented in the SEP.
- Plan and execute technical reviews, including the System Requirements Review (SRR), System Functional Review (SFR), and Preliminary Design Review (PDR)
- Measure and track program maturity using technical performance measures, requirements stability and integrated schedules.
- Support award of TMRR phase contract(s), as necessary.
- Balance and integrate key design considerations.
- Maintain the Systems Engineering Plan (SEP), including generating the update in support of Milestone B.
- Lead the initial development of the system to include functional analysis, definition of the functional and allocated baselines and preliminary design (see CH 3–4.2.2. Requirements Analysis Process and CH 3–4.2.3. Architecture Design Process).
- Support configuration management of the baselines, since they are required in later technical reviews, audits and test activities (e.g., functional baseline at the Functional Configuration Audits (FCAs)).
- Conduct technical activities in support of the Development RFP Release Decision Point.
- Conduct a rigorous and persistent assessment of technical risk, determine risk mitigation plans and work with the PM to resource the mitigation plans.
- Support the Technology Readiness Assessment (TRA) including creation of the plan, the pre-EMD preliminary TRA and the TRA final report (MDAPs only).

68

- Support requirements management, and monitor for unnecessary requirements growth (e.g., derived versus implied requirements).
- Manage interfaces and dependencies.
- Maintain oversight of the system (software and hardware) development processes, system testing, documentation updates and tracking of the system development efforts.
- Support the PM in his interactions with the Configuration Steering Board.

Inputs

Table 20 summarizes the primary inputs associated with this part of the life cycle.

Table 20: Inputs Associated with TMRR Phase

Inputs for TMRR Phase
DoD Component combat developer (e.g., Requirements Manager) provides: • Draft Capability Development Document (CDD) • Concept of Operations/Operational Mode Summary/Mission Profile (CONOPS/OMS/MP)
Analysis of Alternatives (AoA) Report and AoA Sufficiency Report (See CH 2–2.3.)
Preferred materiel solution • Selection of preferred materiel solution is documented in the ADM
Acquisition Decision Memorandum (ADM) (may contain additional direction)
SEP (See DoDI 5000.02, Enc 3, sec. 2 and CH 3–2.2. Systems Engineering Plan)
Reliability, Availability, Maintainability and Cost Rationale (RAM-C) Report (See DoDI 5000.02, Enc 3, sec. 12 and CH 3–4.3.19.) • Attachment to SEP
Reliability Growth Curves (RGC) (See DoDI 5000.02, Enc 3, sec. 12 and CH 3–4.3.19.) • Included in SEP
Program Protection Plan (PPP) (See DoDI 5000.02, Enc 3, sec. 13 and CH 9–3.4.2.2.)
Trade-off analysis results (See DoDI 5000.02, Enc 3, sec. 4) • Results could include knees-in-the-curves sensitivity analyses, product selections, results of automation trades, etc.
Assumptions and constraints • Rationale for all assumptions, constraints and basis for trades
Environment, safety and occupational health (ESOH) planning (See DoDI 5000.02, Enc 3, sec. 16 and CH 3–4.3.9.)
Risk assessment (See CH 3–4.1.5.) • Key risks identified at Milestone A guide TMRR phase activities
Consideration of technology issues
Initial identification of critical technologies • MSA phase may have identified an initial list of critical technologies
Interdependencies/interfaces/memoranda of agreements (MOAs)
Life-Cycle Mission Data Plan for Intelligence Mission Data (IMD)-dependent programs (See CH 3–4.3.12. Intelligence (Life-Cycle Mission Data Plan) and CH 7–4.1.3.)
Draft system performance specification
Other technical information generated during the MSA phase • Architectures, system models and simulations

Inputs for TMRR Phase
• Results of Market Research: 1) to identify existing technologies and products; and 2) to understand potential solutions, technologies, and sources appropriate for maturing the product in this phase
Prototyping strategy (See DoDI 5000.02, para 5.d.4 and DoDI 5000.02, Enc 1, Table 2, Acquisition Strategy)) • Includes identification of key system elements to be prototyped prior to Milestone B
Validated On-Line Life-cycle Threat (VOLT) Report (See DoDI 5000.02 (Enc 1, Table 2) and CH 7–4.1.2.)
Affordability Assessment (See CH 1–4.2.15. and CH 3–4.3.2.) • Affordability goals are established and treated as a Key Performance Parameters (KPPs) at Milestone A • Affordability goals drive engineering trade-offs and sensitivity analyses about capability priorities in the TMRR phase
AS (See CH 1–4.1.)
Life-Cycle Sustainment Plan (LCSP) (See CH 4–3.1.)
Test and Evaluation Master Plan (TEMP) (See CH 8–4.1.)
Informed advice to the developmental test and evaluation (DT&E) assessments (See CH 8–4.1.) • Includes Early Operational Assessments (EOAs)
Draft and final Request for Proposal (RFP)
Security Classification Guide (SCG)
Other analyses • Other prior analytic, prototyping and/or technology demonstration efforts done by the S&T community. Technology insertion/transition can occur at any point in the life cycle
Spectrum Supportability Risk Assessment (See DoDI 4650.01 and CH 3–4.3.20.)

Activities

The TMRR phase activities begin when a favorable Milestone A decision has been made (see CH 3–3.2.2. Materiel Solution Analysis Phase) and end with a successful Milestone B decision. Figure 13 provides the end-to-end perspective and the integration of SE technical reviews and audits across the acquisition life cycle.

Figure 13: Weapon System Development Life Cycle

70

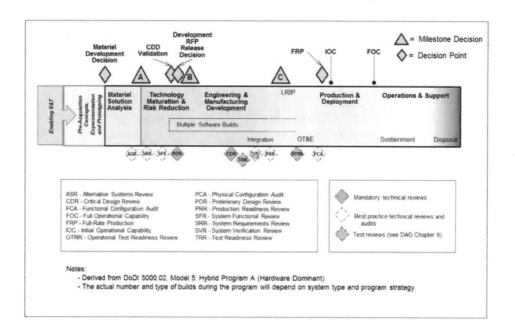

Notes:
- Derived from DoDI 5000.02, Model 5: Hybrid Program A (Hardware Dominant)
- The actual number and type of builds during the program will depend on system type and program strategy.

The TMRR phase addresses a set of critical activities leading to the decision to establish a program of record. The SE activities are aimed at reducing technical risk and providing the technical foundation for this decision. Depending on the nature of the technology development strategy, the order and characteristics of these activities may change. During the TMRR phase, systems engineers follow comprehensive, iterative processes to accomplish the following:

- **Perform Technology Maturation**. The AS identifies technologies requiring further maturation before they can be implemented within a solution. Technology maturation involves design, development, integration and testing. There could be one or more risk areas related to hardware, software or information technology, and there may be multiple industry contracts/Government efforts for maturing the technology. The TEMP should stipulate the test and evaluation approach for assessing the results of the technology maturation activities (see CH 8–4.2.). The Systems Engineer participates in the technology readiness assessment (TRA). The TRA focuses only on technology maturity as opposed to engineering and integration risk. DoDI 5000.02, para 5.d.4 and OSD TRA Guidance provide policy and guidance for TRAs.

- **Perform Prototyping**. Prototyping is an engineering technique employed for several reasons: to reduce risk, inform requirements and encourage competition. For example, the primary objective for competitive prototyping (CP) is acquiring more innovative solutions at better value by ensuring competition. CP are addressed in statute for MDAPs (see P.L. 114-92 (SEC. 822 para (c))). Other prototypes should be considered if they materially reduce engineering and manufacturing development risk at an acceptable cost. At this point in the life cycle, the CP strategy should focus on mitigating key technical risk areas. The program office should have a clear understanding of technical, engineering and integration risks at Milestone A. Current policy does not require full-up system prototypes; therefore, competitive prototyping may include prototyping critical technologies, system elements, integration of system elements or full-up prototypes. Because a primary objective of this type of prototyping is to support a follow-on award choice between developers, contract incentives should be aligned to CP strategy goals. These goals most often emphasize cost, schedule and performance realism and quantification. Contract goals should require the solutions demonstrated during CP be used in the subsequent PDR/CDR designs. The CP strategy should be identified in the SEP and AS, tasks specified in RFPs/Task Orders, technically managed by the program office and included in the TEMP with specific test

71

objectives. Risk reduction prototypes can be at the system level or can focus on technologies, sub-components or components, and may or may not include objectives associated with competitive contracts. And in nearly all cases, prototypes can be extremely useful in assessing technical performance, supporting trade studies and updating requirements.

- **Perform System Trade Analysis**. The Systems Engineer assesses alternatives with respect to performance, cost, schedule and risk, and makes a recommendation to the PM. The SE assessment should consider the full range of relevant factors, for example, affordability goals and caps, technology maturity, development and deployment constraints, modular open system approaches and user-identified needs and shortfalls. System trades should be used to inform and shape the CDD and cost and schedule objectives to be documented in the Acquisition Program Baseline (APB).
- **Develop System Architecture.** See CH 3–4.2.3. Architecture Design Process for additional information.
- **Develop Functional Baseline.** See CH 3–4.1.6. Configuration Management Process for additional information.
- **Develop Allocated Baseline.** See CH 3–4.1.6. Configuration Management Process for additional information.
- **Develop Preliminary Design(s).** May involve competitive, preliminary design activities up to and including PDRs. See CH 3–3.3.4. Preliminary Design Review for additional information.
- **Develop Allocated Technical Performance Measures (TPMs).** The allocated baseline establishes the first physical representation of the system as system elements with system-level capabilities allocated to system element-level technical performance measures.
- **Support CDD Validation.** The purpose of this support is to inform the MDA and requirements validation authority about the technical feasibility, affordability and testability of the proposed requirements. CDD (or an equivalent requirements document) forms a basis for the set of requirements used for design activities, development and production. Specific SE attention is given to trade-off analysis, showing how cost varies as a function of system requirements (including Key Performance Parameters), major design parameters and schedule. The results should identify major affordability drivers.
- **Support Development RFP Release Decision Point.** The purpose of the MDA-level review is to assess the AS, RFP and key related planning documents and determine whether program plans are affordable and executable and reflect sound business arrangements. Specific SE attention is given to engineering trades and their relationship to program requirements and risk management. Typically, this event occurs after PDR to allow for feedback from the PDR into the technical aspects of the RFP. The Development RFP Release event can come before the PDR if there is confidence the RFP will not need to be substantially changed.
- **Finalize Documents.** The Systems Engineer updates the SEP and PPP and provides inputs for updating the LCSP, TEMP and other program documents.

The Systems Engineer uses technical reviews and audits to assess whether preplanned technical maturity points are reached during the acquisition life cycle as the system and system elements mature. A key method for doing this is to identify technical risks associated with achieving entrance criteria at each of these points (See the DoD Risk, Issue, and Opportunity Management Guide for Defense Acquisition Programs.) Technical reviews typically conducted in the TMRR phase are:

- **System Requirements Review (SRR)** (see CH 3–3.3.2. System Requirements Review)
- **System Functional Review (SFR)** (see CH 3–3.3.3. System Functional Review)
- **Software Specification Review (SSR)** for programs with significant software development; a SSR is typically performed before, and in support of, a PDR. The SSR technical assessment establishes the software requirements baseline for the system elements under review (e.g., computer software configuration items (CSCI)) to ensure their preliminary design and, ultimately, the software solution has a reasonable expectation of being operationally effective and suitable.
- **Preliminary Design Review (PDR)** mandated (unless formally waived) to confirm the development of the allocated baseline (see CH 3–3.3.4. Preliminary Design Review)

Test activities during the TMRR phase that depend on SE support and involvement include developmental test and evaluation of system and/or system element prototypes and Early Operational Assessments (EOAs). Developmental Test and Evaluation (DT&E) activities, for example, should be closely coordinated between the engineering and test communities, since DT&E activities support:

- Technical risk identification, risk assessment and risk mitigation
- Providing empirical data to validate models and simulations and
- Assessing technical performance and system maturity (see CH 8–4.2.)

Outputs and Products

The technical outputs identified in Table 21 are some of the inputs necessary to support SE activities in the EMD phase. The outputs should support the technical recommendation at Milestone B that an affordable solution has been found for the identified need with acceptable risk, scope and complexity. Technical outputs associated with technical reviews in this phase are addressed later in this chapter.

Table 21: Technical Outputs Associated with TMRR Phase

Technical Outputs from TMRR Phase
Informed advice to Acquisition Decision Memorandum (ADM) and, when applicable, 10 USC 2366b certification
Preliminary system design • Updated functional and allocated baselines • Associated technical products including associated design and management decisions
SEP (updated) (See DoDI 5000.02, Enc 3, sec. 2 and CH 3–2.2. Systems Engineering Plan) • If programs enter the acquisition life cycle at Milestone B, this is their initial SEP
Updated Integrated Master Plan (IMP), Integrated Master Schedule (IMS) and memoranda of agreement (MOAs)/ memoranda of understanding (MOUs)
RAM-C Report (updated) (See DoDI 5000.02, Enc 3, sec. 12 and CH 3–4.3.19.) • Attachment to SEP • If programs enter the acquisition life cycle at Milestone B, this is their initial RAM-C Report
RGC (updated) (See DoDI 5000.02, Enc 3, sec. 12 and CH 3–4.3.19.) • Included in SEP and TEMP
PPP (updated) (See DoDI 5000.02, Enc 3, sec. 13 and CH 9–3.4.2.3.) • If programs enter the acquisition life cycle at Milestone B, this is their initial PPP
Trade-off analysis results (See DoDI 5000.02, Enc 3, sec. 4) • Updated results could include knees-in-the-curves sensitivity analyses, product selections, etc. • Updated results of automation trades: Informed advice for automation levels as related to system architecture or software and personnel cost trades • Informed advice for CDD validation; showing how cost varies as a function of system requirements (including Key Performance Parameters), major design parameters and schedule; identify major affordability drivers
Assumptions and constraints • Rationale for all assumptions, constraints and basis for trades • Interdependencies defined
Environment, safety and occupational health (ESOH) analyses (See DoDI 5000.02, Enc 3, sec. 16) • Programmatic Environment, Safety and Occupational Health Evaluation (PESHE) and NEPA/EO 12114 Compliance Schedule

73

Technical Outputs from TMRR Phase
Assessment of technical risk (See CH 3–4.1.5. and the DoD Risk, Issue, and Opportunity Management Guide for Defense Acquisition Programs.) • Ensure key risks are adequately mitigated before exiting the TMRR phase • Include SoS risks associated with governance, interdependencies and complexity
Consideration of technology issues
Technology Readiness Assessment (TRA) (MDAPs only) (See DoDI 5000.02, Enc 1, Table 2) • TRA Plan • Confirmation at the end of TMRR phase that critical technologies have been demonstrated in a relevant environment • Preliminary TRA required at Development RFP Release Decision Point • TRA final report
Interdependencies/interfaces/memoranda of agreement (MOAs) • Understanding of the unique program interdependencies, interfaces and associated MOAs
Life-Cycle Mission Data Plan for Intelligence Mission Data (IMD)-dependent programs (updated) (See CH 7–4.1.3. and CH 3–4.3.12. Intelligence (Life-Cycle Mission Data Plan))
Updated system performance specification
System preliminary design including functional baseline and allocated baseline
Other technical information generated during the TMRR phase • Architectures, system models and simulations • Results of Market Research: 1) to identify existing technologies and products; and 2) to understand potential solutions, technologies and sources appropriate for maturing the product in the next phase
Prototyping strategy and results of TMRR prototyping activities • Including identification of key system elements to be prototyped in EMD Phase and documented in the Acquisition Strategy (AS)
PDR assessment (See DoDI 5000.02, Enc 3, sec. 7, DoDI 5134.16, and CH 3–3.3.4.) • For ACAT ID and ACAT IAM programs, DASD(SE) performs the assessment to inform the MDA • For ACAT IC and ACAT IAC programs, the Component Acquisition Executive conducts the PDR assessment
Informed advice to Acquisition Program Baseline (APB) • APB inputs include the SE affordability assessments, schedule inputs and performance inputs
Establishes technical information that is the basis of the cost analysis requirements description (CARD) and manpower documentation (See CH 2–3.5. and CH 5–3.1.)
Informed advice to Affordability and Resource Estimates (See CH 3–2.4.4. Value Engineering, CH 3–4.3.2. Affordability – Systems Engineering Trade-Off Analyses, CH 1–4.2.15. and CH 2–2.1.) • Affordability caps continue to be treated as KPPs at Milestone B; results of engineering trade-off analyses showing how the program established a cost-effective design point for cost/affordability drivers • Should-cost goals defined at Milestone B to achieve efficiencies and control unproductive expenses without sacrificing sound investment in product affordability • Value engineering results, as appropriate
Informed advice to Acquisition Strategy (AS) (See CH 1–4.1.) • Informed advice on engineering approaches and strategies, external dependencies, resource requirements, schedule, and risks
Informed advice to LCSP (updated) (See CH 4–3.2.)

74

Technical Outputs from TMRR Phase
• System support and maintenance objectives and requirements established; updated will-cost values and affordability goals and caps as documented in the Life-Cycle Sustainment Plan (LCSP), including Informed advice to manpower documentation
Initial Information Support Plan (ISP) (See CH 6–3.8.)
Informed advice to Test and Evaluation Master Plan (TEMP) (See CH 8–4.2.)
Early developmental test and evaluation (DT&E) assessments, including Early Operational Assessments (EOAs) (See CH 8–4.2.)
Informed advice to draft and final Development Request for Proposal (RFP) • Informed advice including system performance specification, SOW, CDRLs and source selection criteria • Support preparation for Development RFP Release Decision Point
Informed advice for the Spectrum Supportability Risk Assessment (See DoDI 4650.01 and CH 3–4.3.20.)
Informed advice for Waveform Assessment Application (See DoDI 4630.09)

CH 3–3.2.4 Engineering and Manufacturing Development Phase

The primary objective of the Engineering and Manufacturing Development (EMD) phase is to develop the initial product baseline, verify it meets the functional and allocated baselines and transform the preliminary design into a producible design, all within the schedule and cost constraints of the program.

Figure 14: Systems Engineering Activities in the Engineering and Manufacturing Development Phase

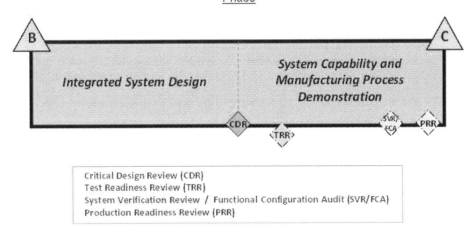

Systems engineering (SE) activities support development of the detailed design, verification that requirements are met, reduction in system-level risk and assessment of readiness to begin production and/or deployment (see Figure 14).

Primary SE focus areas in EMD include:

- Completing the detailed build-to design of the system.
- Establishing the initial product baseline.
- Conducting the integration and tests of system elements and the system (where feasible).
- Demonstrating system maturity and readiness to begin production for operational test and/or deployment and sustainment activities.

The EMD phase includes technical assessment and control efforts to effectively manage risks and increase confidence in meeting system performance, schedule and cost goals. SE activities should be integrated with EMD phase-specific test and evaluation, and logistics and sustainment activities identified in CH 8–4.3. and CH 4–3.3., respectively. The planning, scheduling and conduct of event-driven technical reviews (Critical Design Review (CDR), Functional Configuration Audit (FCA), System Verification Review (SVR), and Production Readiness Review (PRR)) are vital to provide key points for assessing system maturity and the effectiveness of risk-reduction strategies.

A well-planned EMD phase Systems Engineering Plan (SEP) builds on the results of previous activities and significantly increases the likelihood of a successful program compliant with the approved Acquisition Program Baseline (APB).

The Limited Deployment Decisions in program Model 3 (see CH 3–3.1.1. Systems Engineering in Defense Acquisition Program Models) are the points at which an increment of capability is reviewed for Limited Deployment. Approval depends in part on specific criteria defined at Milestone B and included in the Milestone B ADM. Implementing the technical planning as defined in the approved SEP guides the execution of the complex and myriad tasks associated with completing the detailed design and integration, and supports developmental test and evaluation activities. The SEP also highlights the linkage between Technical Performance Measures (TPM), risk management and earned-value

76

management activities to support tracking of cost growth trends. Achieving predefined EMD technical review criteria provides confidence that the system meets stated performance requirements (including interoperability and supportability requirements) and that design and development have matured to support the initiation of the Production and Deployment (P&D) phase.

Roles and Responsibilities

In addition to the general responsibilities identified in CH 3–2.5. Engineering Resources, the Program Manager (PM) focuses on the following EMD activities, which rely on and support SE efforts:

- Conducting activities in support of the EMD contract award.
- Resourcing and conducting event-driven CDR, FCA, SVR and PRR, and assess whether review criteria are met.
- Ensuring the Government preserves the rights they need, consistent with the life-cycle acquisition and support strategy.
- Establishing and manage the initial product baseline established at the CDR.
- Determining path forward on configuration changes to the initial product baseline after CDR, to the extent the competitive environment permits (see CH 3–4.1.6. Configuration Management Process).
- Accepting system deliveries (i.e., DD-250), as appropriate.
- Supporting the Configuration Steering Board in accordance with DoDI 5000.02, para 5.d.5.b.

In addition to the general roles and responsibilities described in CH 3–2.5. Engineering Resources, during this phase it is the Systems Engineer's responsibility for:

- Managing the system design to satisfy the operational requirements, within the constraints of cost and schedule, and to evaluate the system design, identify deficiencies and make recommendations for corrective action.
- Conducting or supporting the technical evaluation in support of source selection for the EMD contract award.
- Maintaining requirements traceability and linkage to the initial product baseline.
- Conducting event-driven technical reviews, advising the PM on review criteria readiness.
- Leading preparation and conduct of technical reviews.
- Tracking and reporting initial product baseline changes after CDR and recommend the path forward in accordance with the Configuration Management (CM) process, to the extent the competitive environment allows (see CH 3–4.1.6. Configuration Management Process).
- Supporting determination of production rates and delivery schedules.
- Supporting test and evaluation activities: identify system evaluation targets driving system development and support operational assessments as documented in the Test and Evaluation Master Plan (TEMP) (see CH 8–4.3.).
- Aligning the SEP with the TEMP on SE processes, methods and tools identified for use during test and evaluation.
- Analyzing deficiencies discovered from operational assessments and verification methods (developmental test and evaluation); develop and implement solutions to include, but not limited to, rebalancing of system requirements.
- Supporting logistics and sustainment activities as documented in the Life-Cycle Sustainment Plan (LCSP) (see CH 4–3.3.).
- Maintaining the SEP, including generating the update in support of Milestone C.
- Ensure manufacturing process development and maturation efforts.
- Developing approaches and plans to verify mature fabrication and manufacturing processes and determine manufacturing readiness (see the Manufacturing Readiness Level (MRL) Deskbook as one source for assessing manufacturing readiness).
- Conducting a rigorous production risk assessment and determine risk mitigation plans.

77

- Identifying system design features that enhance producibility (efforts usually focus on design simplification, fabrication tolerances and avoidance of hazardous materials).
- Applying value engineering techniques to system design features to ensure they achieve their essential functions at the lowest life-cycle cost consistent with required performance, reliability, quality and safety.
- Conducting producibility trade studies to determine the most cost-effective fabrication and manufacturing process.
- Assessing Low-Rate Initial Production (LRIP) feasibility within program constraints (may include assessing contractor and principal subcontractor production experience and capability, new fabrication technology, special tooling and production personnel training requirements).
- Identifying long-lead items and critical materials.
- Supporting update to production costs as a part of life-cycle cost management.
- Continuing to support the configuration management process to control changes to the product baseline during test and deployment.
- Maintaining oversight of the system (software and hardware) development processes, system testing, documentation updates and tracking of the system development efforts.
- Supporting the PM in his or her interactions with the Configuration Steering Board.

Inputs

Table 22 summarizes the primary inputs associated with this part of the life cycle.

Table 22: Inputs Associated with EMD Phase

Inputs for EMD Phase
Capability Development Document (CDD) and Concept of Operations/Operational Mode Summary/Mission Profile (CONOPS/OMS/MP)
Acquisition Decision Memorandum (ADM) (may contain additional direction)
Preliminary system design including functional and allocated baselines (see CH 3–4.1.6. Configuration Management Process)
SEP (See DoDI 5000.02, Enc 3, sec. 2 and CH 3–2.2. Systems Engineering Plan) • If programs enter the acquisition life cycle at Milestone B, this is their initial SEP
Reliability, Availability, Maintainability, and Cost Rationale (RAM-C) Report (See DoDI 5000.02, Enc 3, sec. 12 and CH 3–4.3.19.) • Attachment to SEP • If programs enter the acquisition life cycle at Milestone B, this is their initial RAM-C Report
Reliability Growth Curves (RGCs) (See DoDI 5000.02, Enc 3, sec. 12 and CH 3–4.3.19.) • Included in SEP and TEMP
Program Protection Plan (PPP) (See DoDI 5000.02, Enc 3, sec. 13 and CH 9–3.4.2.3.) • If programs enter the acquisition life cycle at Milestone B, this is the initial PPP
Trade-off analysis results (See DoDI 5000.02, Enc 3, sec. 4) • Results could include knees-in-the-curves sensitivity analyses, product selections, etc.
Assumptions and constraints • Rationale for all assumptions, constraints and basis for trades • Interdependencies defined
Environment, safety and occupational health (ESOH) analyses (See DoDI 5000.02, Enc 3, sec. 16 and CH 3–4.3.9.) • Programmatic Environment, Safety, and Occupational Health Evaluation (PESHE) and NEPA/EO 12114 Compliance Schedule
Assessment of technical risk (See CH 3–4.1.5.)
Consideration of technology issues

78

Inputs for EMD Phase
Technology Readiness Assessment (TRA) (MDAPs only) (See DoDI 5000.02, Enc 1, Table 2) • Confirmation that critical technologies have been demonstrated in a relevant environment
Interdependencies/interfaces/memoranda of agreement (MOAs)
Life-Cycle Mission Data Plan for Intelligence Mission Data (IMD)-dependent programs (See CH 3–4.3.12. Intelligence (Life-Cycle Mission Data Plan) and CH 7–4.1.3.)
System performance specification, including verification matrix
Other technical information, such as architectures, system models and simulations generated during the TMRR phase
Prototyping strategy (See DoDI 5000.02, para 5.d.4 and DoDI 5000.02, Enc 1, Table 2, Acquisition Strategy)
Validated On-Line Life-cycle Threat (VOLT) Report (See DoDI 5000.02 (Enc 1, Table 2) and CH 7–4.1.2.)
Acquisition Program Baseline (APB)
Affordability Assessment (See CH 1–4.2.15. and CH 3–4.3.2.) • Affordability caps treated as KPPs; results of engineering trade-off analyses show cost/schedule/performance trade space around affordability drivers • Should-cost goals designed to achieve efficiencies and control unproductive expenses without sacrificing sound investment in product affordability
Acquisition Strategy (AS) (See CH 1–4.1.)
Life-Cycle Sustainment Plan (LCSP) (updated) (See CH 4–3.2.)
Initial Information Support Plan (ISP) (See CH 6–3.8.)
Test and Evaluation Master Plan (TEMP) (See CH 8–4.2.) • System Test Objectives
Informed advice to the developmental test and evaluation (DT&E) planning, including Operational Assessments (OAs) (See CH 8–4.2.) • System test objectives
Draft and final Request for Proposal (RFP)
Security Classification Guide (SCG) (updated)
Other analyses • Other prior analytic, prototyping and/or technology demonstration efforts performed by the S&T community. Technology insertion/transition can occur at any point in the life cycle
Spectrum Supportability Risk Assessment (See DoDI 4650.01 and CH 3–4.3.20.)

Activities

The EMD phase activities begin when a favorable Milestone B decision has been made (see CH 3–3.2.3. Technology Maturation and Risk Reduction Phase) and end with a successful Milestone C decision. Figure 15 provides the end-to-end perspective and the integration of SE technical reviews and audits across the acquisition life cycle.

Figure 15: Weapon System Development Life Cycle

79

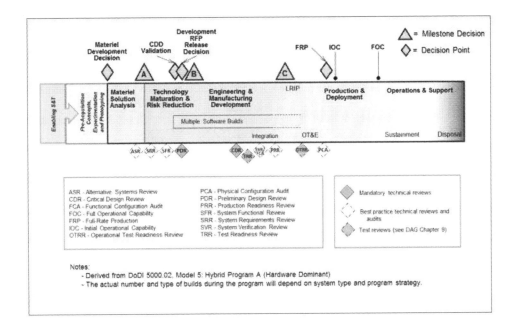

SE activities to support the EMD effort include:

- Realization of the system architecture.
- Performance of system element trade-offs.
- Use of prototypes to mature system designs and drawings. If the program strategy includes competitive development, this may include competitive prototyping during the EMD phase.
- Conduct Human Systems Integration analysis such as task and functional analysis, develop mission use and operational use scenarios and establish initial human performance thresholds.
- Development of the initial product baseline and a stable design that conforms to program cost, schedule and performance requirements (see CH 3–4.1.6. Configuration Management Process).
- Support for the establishment of the developmental test and evaluation environment and associated resources (e.g., people, equipment, test cases and test ranges).
- Support of materiel readiness and logistical support efforts.
- Preparation for production by identifying critical manufacturing processes, key product characteristics and any manufacturing risks.
- Build, integrate and test system elements.
- Fabricate and assemble the system elements and system to the initial product baseline.
- Manage changes of software requirements, projected changes to software size and integration of software components.
- Identify the process to proactively manage and mitigate Diminishing Manufacturing Sources and Material Shortages (DMSMS) issues in future life-cycle phases.
- Integrate the system and verify compliance with the functional and allocated baselines through developmental test and evaluation (DT&E) efforts (see CH 8–4.3. for more on DT&E).
- Update risk, issue and opportunity plans. Identify, analyze, mitigate and monitor risks and issues; and identify, analyze, manage and monitor opportunities. (See the DoD Risk, Issue, and Opportunity Management Guide for Defense Acquisition Programs.)
- Address problem/failure reports through the use of a comprehensive data-collection approach, such as Failure Reporting, Analysis, and Corrective Action System (FRACAS).
- Refine the initial product baseline and support the development of the Capability Production Document (CPD).

80

- Complete producibility activities supporting manufacturing readiness or implementation and initial deployment activities for information systems.
- Support initiation of materiel readiness and logistical support activities including deployment options and training development.
- Perform Environment, Safety and Occupational Health (ESOH) risk management analyses and ESOH risk acceptance.
- Produce NEPA/EO 12114 documentation.
- Perform corrosion risk assessment.
- Complete certifications as appropriate (see CH 3–2.6. Certifications).
- Evolve the system architecture to reflect EMD trade-off decisions and incorporate stakeholder feedback.

The Systems Engineer uses technical reviews and audits to assess whether preplanned technical maturity points are reached during the acquisition life cycle as the system and system elements mature. A key method for doing this is to identify technical risks associated with achieving entrance criteria at each of these points (see the DoD Risk, Issue and Opportunity Management Guide for Defense Acquisition Programs available on the DASD(SE) web site.) Technical reviews and audits typically conducted in EMD:

- Critical Design Review (CDR) (mandated, establishes initial product baseline, see CH 3–3.3.5. Critical Design Review)
- System Verification Review/Functional Configuration Audit (SVR/FCA) (See CH 3–3.3.6. System Verification Review/Functional Configuration Audit)
- Production Readiness Review (PRR) (CH 3–3.3.7. Production Readiness Review)

Test activities during the EMD phase that depend on SE support and involvement include Test Readiness Reviews (TRRs), Developmental Test and Evaluation (DT&E) and Operational Assessments (OAs). The Systems Engineer, in collaboration with the Chief Developmental Tester, should identify system evaluation targets driving system development and support operational assessments as documented in the Test and Evaluation Master Plan (TEMP). Associated SE activities and plans should be in the SEP (see CH 3–2.2. Systems Engineering Plan, 3.3. Technical Reviews and Audits, and CH 8–3.5.).

Outputs and Products

The technical outputs and products identified in Table 23 are some of the inputs necessary to support SE processes in the P&D phase. They should support the technical recommendation at Milestone C that manufacturing processes are mature enough to support Low-Rate Initial Production (LRIP) and generate production-representative articles for operational test and evaluation (OT&E). Technical outputs associated with technical reviews in this phase are addressed later in this chapter.

Table 23: Technical Outputs Associated with EMD Phase

Technical Outputs from EMD Phase
Informed advice to CPD
Informed advice to Acquisition Decision Memorandum (ADM) and 10 USC 2366b certification (if Milestone C is program initiation)
Verified system • Updated functional, allocated, and initial product baselines; verified production processes and verification results/ decisions • Associated technical products including associated design and management decisions
SEP (updated) (See DoDI 5000.02, Enc 3, sec. 2 and CH 3–2.2. Systems Engineering Plan)

Technical Outputs from EMD Phase
Updated IMP, IMS, and MOAs/MOUs
RAM-C Report (updated) (See DoDI 5000.02, Enc 3, sec. 12 and CH 3–4.3.19.) • Attachment to SEP
RGC (updated) (See DoDI 5000.02, Enc 3, sec. 12 and CH 3–4.3.19.) • Included in SEP and TEMP
PPP (updated) (See DoDI 5000.02, Enc 3, sec. 13 and CH 9–3.4.2.4.)
Trade-off analysis results (See DoDI 5000.02, Enc 3, sec. 4) • Results could include knees-in-the-curves sensitivity analyses, product selections, etc.
Assumptions and constraints • Rationale for all assumptions, constraints and basis for trades • Interdependencies updated
ESOH analyses (See DoDI 5000.02, Enc 3, sec. 16) • Updated Programmatic Environment, Safety, and Occupational Health Evaluation (PESHE) and NEPA/E.O. 12114 Compliance Schedule
Human Systems Integration Analysis results (See CH 5–3.2.) • Mapping of all tasks/functions to human and/or system, • Mission and Operational Use scenarios that support downstream testing and • Informed advice relative to crew/maintainer skill level and numbers of personnel required to support operations
Assessment of technical risk (See CH 3–4.1.5. and the DoD Risk, Issue, and Opportunity Management Guide for Defense Acquisition Programs.) • Risk assessment identifying mitigation plans for acceptable risks to allow the program to initiate production, deployment and operational test and evaluation activities • Update system of systems (SoS) risks associated with governance, interdependencies and complexity
Manufacturing readiness (See DoDI 5000.02, Enc 3, sec. 10 and CH 3–4.3.18.) • Assessment of manufacturing readiness supports Milestone C and initiation of production • Manufacturing processes have been effectively demonstrated and are under control
Interdependencies/interfaces/memoranda of agreement (MOAs) • Understanding of the unique program interdependencies, interfaces and associated MOAs
Life-Cycle Mission Data Plan for Intelligence Mission Data (IMD)-dependent programs (updated) (See CH 3–4.3.12. Intelligence (Life-Cycle Mission Data Plan) and CH 7–4.1.3.)
System performance specification (updated if necessary), including verification matrix • System element specifications, including verification matrix
Initial product baseline
Other technical information, such as architectures, system models and simulations generated during the EMD phase
Results of EMD prototyping activities
Manufacturing prototyping activities support P&D phase
Critical Design Review (CDR) Assessment (See DoDI 5000.02, Enc 3, sec. 7, DoDI 5134.16, and CH 3–3.3.5.) • For ACAT ID and ACAT IAM programs, DASD(SE) performs the assessment to inform the Milestone Decision Authority (MDA) • For ACAT IC and ACAT IAC programs, the Component Acquisition Executive conducts the CDR assessment

82

Technical Outputs from EMD Phase
Informed advice to APB • Updated will-cost values and affordability caps as documented in the Acquisition Program Baseline and Acquisition Strategy
Establishes technical information that is the basis of the updates to the Cost Analysis Requirements Description (CARD) and manpower documentation (See CH 2–3.5. and CH 5–3.1.)
Informed advice to Affordability and Resource Estimates (See CH 3–2.4.4. Value Engineering, CH 3–4.3.2. Affordability – Systems Engineering Trade-Off Analyses, CH 1–4.2.15. and CH 2–2.1.) • Should-cost goals updated to achieve efficiencies and control unproductive expenses without sacrificing sound investment in product affordability • Value engineering results, as appropriate
Manufacturing, performance and quality metrics critical to program success are identified and tracked • Manufacturing drawings are sufficiently complete
Production budget/cost model validated and resources considered sufficient to support LRIP and FRP • Inputs to Milestone C, LRIP, and FRP DR
Informed advice to Acquisition Strategy (AS) (See CH 1–4.1.) • Informed advice on engineering approaches and strategies, external dependencies, resource requirements, schedule and risks
Informed advice to LCSP (updated) (See CH 4–3.3.) • System Support and Maintenance Objectives and Requirements established • Updated will-cost values and affordability caps as documented in the LCSP, including Informed advice to manpower documentation • Confirmation of logistics and sustainment needs (i.e., facilities, training, support equipment) and implementation supporting initial deployment efforts
ISP of Record (See CH 6–3.8.)
Informed advice to TEMP (updated) (See CH 8–4.3.) • System test objectives
Informed advice to the DT&E assessments (See CH 8–4.3.) • System test objectives
Informed advice to draft & final RFP for LRIP • Informed advice, including system performance specification, Statement of Work (SOW), Contract Data Requirements List (CDRLs), and source selection criteria
Informed advice for the Spectrum Supportability Risk Assessment (See DoDI 4650.01 and CH 3–4.3.20.)
Informed advice for Waveform Assessment Application (See DoDI 4630.09)

CH 3–3.2.5 Production and Deployment Phase

The objective of the Production and Deployment (P&D) phase is to validate the product design and to deliver the quantity of systems required for full operating capability, including all enabling system elements and supporting material and services. Systems engineering (SE) in P&D delivers the product baseline as validated during operational testing, and supports deployment and transition of capability to all end users, the warfighters and supporting organizations. SE activities, for example, maintenance approach, training and technical manuals, should be integrated with P&D phase-specific test and evaluation and logistics and sustainment activities identified in CH 8–4.4. and CH 4–3.4., respectively. This phase typically has several major efforts as shown in Figure 16: Low-Rate Initial Production (LRIP), Operational Test and Evaluation (OT&E), Full-Rate Production (FRP) and Full Deployment (FD), and deployment of capability in support of the Initial and Full Operational Capabilities. The Full-Rate

Production Decision Review (FRP DR) and/or Full Deployment Decision Review (FD DR) serves as a key decision point between LRIP (and OT&E) and FRP/FD.

<u>Figure 16: Systems Engineering Activities in the Production and Deployment Phase</u>

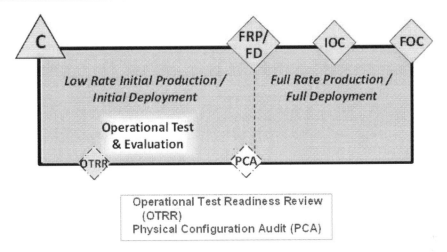

Manufacturing development should be complete at Milestone C, but improvements or redesigns may require unanticipated, additional manufacturing process development and additional testing (e.g., delta qualification or delta first article test). For example, it may be discovered that changing the product design may provide enhancements in manufacturing or other supporting processes. At the conclusion of LRIP, all manufacturing development should be completed, with no significant manufacturing risks carried into FRP. The dynamic nature of the varied production elements requires a proactive approach to mitigate emerging risks.

Readiness for OT&E is a significant assessment of a system's maturity (see <u>CH 8–3.9.2.</u>). The Systems Engineer plays a key role in ensuring systems are ready to enter OT&E. Scarce resources are wasted when an operational test is halted or terminated early because of technical problems, which should have been resolved before the start of OT&E.

During deployment, units attain Initial Operational Capability (IOC), then Full Operational Capability (FOC).

Besides ensuring a successful FOC, SE activities include:

- Maturing manufacturing, production and deployment procedures.
- Responding to deficiencies and develop corrective actions.
- Supporting validation of system performance associated with OT&E.
- Validating the production configuration prior to FRP / FD.

Roles and Responsibilities

In addition to the general responsibilities identified in <u>CH 3–2.5.</u> Engineering Resources, the Program Manager (PM) focuses on the following P&D activities, which rely on and support SE efforts:

- Conducting activities in support of the production contract award(s).
- Ensuring Government intellectual property and data rights information are captured in the technical baseline.

84

- Resourcing and conducting event-driven technical reviews (including the Physical Configuration Audit (PCA), Post Implementation Review (PIR), and FRP and/or FD DR) and ensure that criteria are met.
- Managing and controlling the product baseline.
- Managing risks, in particular the manufacturing, production and deployment risks.
- Accepting system deliveries (i.e., DD-250).
- Supporting the Configuration Steering Board in accordance with DoDI 5000.02, para 5.d.5.b.

In addition to the general responsibilities identified in CH 3–2.5. Engineering Resources, the Systems Engineer is responsible for:

- Analyzing deficiencies discovered from OT&E, acceptance tests, production reports and maintenance reports and provide correction actions.
- Conducting rigorous production risk assessments; plan and resource effective risk mitigation actions.
- Continuing conducting producibility trade studies to determine the most cost-effective fabrication/manufacturing process.
- Developing approaches and plans to validate fabrication/manufacturing processes.
- Assessing full-rate production feasibility within program constraints. This may include assessing contractor and principal subcontractor production experience and capability, new fabrication technology, special tooling and production personnel training requirements.
- Identifying long-lead items and critical materials; plan for obsolescence and implement DMSMS measures to mitigate impacts to production and sustainment.
- Updating production costs as a part of life-cycle cost management.
- Supporting updates to the production schedules.
- Supporting technical reviews and production decisions.
- Supporting materiel readiness and logistical activities, including deployment and training.
- Continuing to support the configuration management process to control changes to the product baseline during test and deployment.
- Updating and maintain system certifications and interfaces with external systems, as necessary.
- Maintaining oversight of the system (software and hardware) development processes, system testing, documentation updates and tracking of the system development efforts.
- Supporting the PM in his or her interactions with the Configuration Steering Board.

Inputs

Table 24 summarizes the primary inputs associated with this part of the life cycle.

Table 24: Inputs Associated with P&D Phase

Inputs for P&D Phase
Capability Production Document (CPD) and Concept of Operations/Operational Mode Summary/Mission Profile (CONOPS/OMS/MP)

Acquisition Decision Memorandums (ADM) associated with Milestone C, LRIP and FRP DR and FD DR
   • ADMs may contain additional direction
   • Milestone C may not coincide with LRIP
   • FRP DR and FD DR ADMs are issued during P&D phase

SEP (See DoDI 5000.02, Enc 3, sec. 2 and CH 3–2.2. Systems Engineering Plan)   • Updated functional, allocated and product baselines; verified and validated production processes and validation results/decisions

85

Inputs for P&D Phase
• Updated technical products including associated design and management decisions
Reliability, Availability, Maintainability, and Cost Rationale (RAM-C) Report (See DoDI 5000.02, Enc 3, sec. 12 and CH 3–4.3.19.) • Attachment to SEP
Reliability growth curves (RGCs) (See DoDI 5000.02, Enc 3, sec. 12 and CH 3–4.3.19.) • Included in SEP and TEMP
PPP (See DoDI 5000.02, Enc 3, sec. 13 and CH 9–3.4.2.4.) • Updated at FRP DR and/or FD DR
Trade-off analysis results (see DoDI 5000.02, Enc 3, sec. 4) • Results could include knees-in-the-curves sensitivity analyses, product selections, etc. • P&D phase trade studies may support manufacturing or other system mods (technology insertion, technology refresh, etc.)
Assumptions and constraints • Rationale for all assumptions, constraints, and basis for trades
Environment, Safety and Occupational Health (ESOH) analyses (See DoDI 5000.02, Enc 3, sec. 16 and CH 3–4.3.9.) • Programmatic Environment, Safety, and Occupational Health Evaluation (PESHE) and NEPA/EO 12114 Compliance Schedule
Risk assessment (See CH 3–4.1.5.) • Risk mitigation plans • Acceptable risks for achieving Initial Operational Capability (IOC) and Full Operational Capability (FOC) •
Manufacturing readiness (See DoDI 5000.02, Enc 3, sec. 10 and CH 3–4.3.18.) • Assessment of manufacturing readiness supports Milestone C and initiation of production
Interdependencies/interfaces/memoranda of agreement (MOAs) • Understanding of the unique program interdependencies, interfaces and associated MOA
Life-Cycle Mission Data Plan for Intelligence Mission Data (IMD)-dependent programs (See CH 3–4.3.12. Intelligence (Life-Cycle Mission Data Plan) and CH 7–4.1.3.)
System performance specification (updated if necessary) including verification matrix • System element specifications (updated if necessary) including verification matrix
Manufacturing, performance and quality metrics critical to program success are identified and tracked • Manufacturing drawings are sufficiently complete
Product baseline
Product acceptance test
Other technical information such as architectures, system models and simulations generated during the EMD phase
Results of EMD prototyping activities
Manufacturing prototyping activities supporting P&D phase
Validated On-Line Life-cycle Threat (VOLT) Report (See DoDI 5000.02 (Enc 1, Table 2) and CH 7-4.1.2.)
Acquisition Program Baseline (APB)
Affordability and Resource Estimates (See CH 3–2.4.4. Value Engineering, CH 3–4.3.2. Affordability – Systems Engineering Trade-Off Analyses, CH 1–4.2.15. and CH 2–2.1.) • Affordability goals treated as KPPs

86

Inputs for P&D Phase
• Should-cost goals to achieve efficiencies and control unproductive expenses • Updated will-cost values and affordability caps as documented in the Life-Cycle Sustainment Plan (LCSP), including informed advice to manpower documentation • Value engineering results, as appropriate
Supply chain sources
Updated Manufacturing processes
Production budget/cost model validated and resources considered sufficient to support LRIP and FRP
Acquisition Strategy (AS) (See CH 1–4.1.)
LCSP (See CH 4–3.3.)
Human Systems Integration (HSI) analyses (See CH 5–3.2.) • Manpower, personnel and training (MPT) requirement updates • Refinement of HSI inputs to specifications, human system interfaces design, multi-domain verification, testing and usability evaluations
TEMP (See CH 8–4.3.) • System test objectives
Developmental test and evaluation (DT&E) assessments (See CH 8–4.3.) • System test objectives
Draft and final RFP
Security Classification Guide (SCG)
Information Support Plan (ISP) of Record (See CH 6–3.8.)
Other analyses • Other prior analytic, prototyping and/or technology demonstration efforts completed by the science and technology (S&T) community; technology insertion/transition can occur at any point in the life cycle
Spectrum Supportability Risk Assessment (See DoDI 4650.01 and CH 3–4.3.20.)

Activities

The P&D phase SE activities begin when a favorable Milestone C decision has been made (see CH 3–3.2.4. Engineering and Manufacturing Development Phase) and end when FOC is achieved. Figure 17 provides the end-to-end perspective and the integration of SE technical reviews and audits across the acquisition life cycle.

Figure 17: Weapon System Development Life Cycle

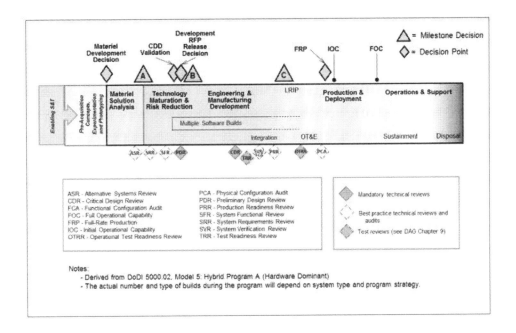

SE activities that occur throughout the P&D phase include:

- Providing technical support to prepare for the Operations and Support (O&S) phase, reviewing and providing inputs on the maintenance approach, acquisition strategy, training and technical manuals.
- Updating risk, issue and opportunity plans. Identifying, analyzing, mitigating and monitoring risks and issues; and identifying, analyzing, managing and monitoring opportunities. (See the DoD Risk, Issue, and Opportunity Management Guide for Defense Acquisition Programs.)
- Assessing the impact of system requirements changes resulting from evolving threats, changes to operational environment or in response to changes within the SoS or interfacing systems.
- Analyzing system deficiencies generated during OT&E, acceptance testing, production and deployment.
- Addressing problem/failure reports through the use of a comprehensive data collection approach like a Failure Reporting, Analysis and Corrective Action System (FRACAS).
- Managing and controlling configuration updates (hardware, software and specifications) to the product baseline.
- Re-verifying and validating production configuration.

SE provides inputs to OT&E readiness assessments including:

- Assessment of DT&E, coordinated with the Chief Developmental Tester, to support approval to enter OT&E.
- Analysis of the system's progress in achieving performance metrics (see CH 3–4.1.3. Technical Assessment Process).
- Assessment of technical risk.
- Assessment of software maturity and status of software trouble reports.
- Identification of any potential design constraints affecting the system's expected performance during OT&E.

88

In both the P&D and O&S phases the Systems Engineer should identify and plan for potential obsolescence impacts (i.e., Diminishing Manufacturing Sources and Material Shortages (DMSMS)). DMSMS problems are an increasing concern as the service lives of DoD weapon systems are extended and the product life cycle for high-technology system elements decreases.

The PCA is a SE audit typically conducted in the P&D phase (see CH 3–3.3.8. Physical Configuration Audit for additional information regarding the PCA). The Systems Engineer should identify technical risks associated with achieving entrance criteria for this audit (see the DoD Risk, Issue, and Opportunity Management Guide for Defense Acquisition Programs.)

Test activities during the P&D phase that depend on SE support and involvement include the DT&E Assessment, Operational Test Readiness Reviews (OTRRs), initial and follow-on OT&E (IOT&E and FOT&E) and live-fire test and evaluations (LFT&E), as appropriate (see CH 8–4.4.). In addition, any corrective actions or design changes implemented in response to test identified deficiencies require additional regression testing.

The Systems Engineer, in collaboration with the Chief Developmental Tester, should identify the technical support needed for operational assessments and document in the Test and Evaluation Master Plan (TEMP). Associated SE activities and plans should be in the SEP (see CH 3–2.2. Systems Engineering Plan, CH 3-3.3. Technical Reviews and Audits Overview, and CH 8–3.5.).

Outputs and Products

The technical outputs and products from the P&D phase identified in Table 25 are some of the inputs necessary to support SE processes in the O&S phase. They should support the program's transition into full operations and sustainment. Technical outputs associated with technical reviews in this phase are addressed later in this chapter.

Table 25: Technical Outputs Associated with P&D Phase

Technical Outputs from P&D Phase
Informed advice to CPD Update   • CPD may be updated to justify system enhancements and modifications from the P&D phase
Informed advice to ADM
Updated IMP, IMS, and MOAs/MOUs

Validated system
   • Updated functional, allocated and product baselines; verified and validated production processes and validation results/decisions
   • Associated technical products including associated design and management decisions

PPP (updated) (See DoDI 5000.02, Enc 3, sec. 13 and CH 9–3.4.2.5.) • Updated at FRP DR and/or FD DR
Trade-off analysis results (See DoDI 5000.02, Enc 3, sec. 4)   • P&D Phase trade studies may support manufacturing or other system mods (technology insertion, technology refresh, etc.)
Assumptions and constraints   • Rationale for all assumptions, constraints and basis for trades
ESOH analyses (See DoDI 5000.02, Enc 3, sec. 16 and CH 3–4.3.9.)   • Updated Programmatic Environment, Safety, and Occupational Health Evaluation (PESHE) and NEPA/EO 12114 Compliance Schedule
Assessment of technical risk (updated) (See CH 3–4.1.5. and the DoD Risk, Issue, and Opportunity Management Guide for Defense Acquisition Programs.)   • Risk assessment identifying mitigation plans, acceptable risks for achieving FOC
Interdependencies/interfaces/memoranda of agreement (MOAs)

89

Technical Outputs from P&D Phase
• Understanding of the unique program interdependencies, interfaces and associated MOA
Life-Cycle Mission Data Plan for Intelligence Mission Data (IMD)-dependent programs (updated) (See CH 3–4.3.12. Intelligence (Life-Cycle Mission Data Plan) and CH 7–4.1.3.)
System performance specification (updated if necessary) including verification matrix; system element specifications (updated if necessary) including verification matrix
Manufacturing and production metrics
PCA results and an updated product baseline (See CH 3–3.3.8.)
Acceptance test data to assess product conformance and to support DD250 of end items
Other technical information such as architectures, system models and simulations generated during the P&D phase
Technical information that is the basis of the updates to the Cost Analysis Requirements Description (CARD) and manpower documentation (See CH 2–3.5. and CH 5–3.1.)
Industrial base capabilities; updated manufacturing processes and supply chain sources
Informed advice to Life-Cycle Sustainment Plan (LCSP) (See CH 4–3.4.) • Updated at FRP DR and/or FDDR • Updated will-cost values and affordability caps as documented in the LCSP, including informed advice to manpower documentation • Value engineering results, as appropriate (see CH 3–2.4.4.) • Updated list of production tooling and facilities that need to be retained post-production to support continued operational and maintenance of the system.
Human Systems Integration (HSI) analyses (See CH 5–3.2.) • Final manpower and personnel requirements • Training program implementation • HSI participation in Engineering Change Proposal (ECP) process • Human performance results (includes workload, situation awareness, time to perform tasks, errors)
Informed advice to TEMP (updated) (See CH 8–4.4.) • System Test Objectives
Operational Test and Evaluation (OT&E) Assessments/Reports (See CH 8–4.4.) • System Test Objectives
Draft and final RFP(s) for production and SE support to O&S activities
Informed advice for the Spectrum Supportability Risk Assessment (See DoDI 4650.01 and CH 3–4.3.20.)

CH 3–3.2.6 Operations and Support Phase

The objective of the Operations and Support (O&S) phase is to execute a support program that meets operational support performance requirements and sustains the system in the most cost-effective manner over its total life cycle. Planning for this phase begins in the Materiel Solution Analysis (MSA) phase, matures through the Technology Maturation and Risk Reduction (TMRR) and Engineering and Manufacturing Development (EMD) phases, and is documented in the Life-Cycle Sustainment Plan (LCSP). Systems engineering (SE) in the O&S phase assesses whether the deployed system and enabling system elements continue to provide the needed capability in a safe, sustainable and cost-effective manner. SE efforts consist of data collection, assessment and corrective action cycles to maintain a system's operational suitability and operational effectiveness.

Sustainment activities supporting system operations begin in this phase and should address two major efforts: life-cycle sustainment and disposal. SE efforts during life-cycle sustainment include Environment, Safety and Occupational Health (ESOH) assessments, technology refresh, functionality modification and

90

life-extension modifications. (See CH 3–4.3. Design Considerations for other technical factors needing continued attention during this phase.)

When the system no longer provides an effective or efficient capability to the warfighter, the Department should make an informed decision to either modify or dispose of it. However, a related proactive aspect in the Production and Deployment and O&S phases is engineering analysis to identify potential obsolescence impacts (i.e., Diminishing Manufacturing Sources and Material Shortages (DMSMS)). DMSMS problems are an increasing concern as the service lives of DoD weapon systems are extended and the product life cycle for high-technology system elements decreases (see CH 3–4.3.8. Diminishing Manufacturing Sources and Material Shortages).

Roles and Responsibilities

In addition to the general responsibilities identified in CH 3–2.5. Engineering Resources, the Program Manager (PM) focuses on the following O&S activities, which rely on and support SE efforts include:

- Working with the user to document performance and sustainment requirements in performance agreements, specifying objective outcomes, measures, resource commitments and stakeholder responsibilities.
- Employing effective Performance-Based Life-Cycle Product Support implementation and management.
- Maintaining operational readiness.
- Following acquisition program practices for major modifications or Service Life Extension Program (SLEP).
- Supporting the Configuration Steering Board in accordance with DoDI 5000.02, para 5.d.5.b.

In addition to the general responsibilities identified in CH 3–2.5. Engineering Resources, the Systems Engineer is responsible for the following tasks:

- Refining the maintenance program to minimize total life-cycle cost while achieving readiness and sustainability objectives.
- Assessing end-user feedback and conducting engineering investigations as required.
- Leading teams to translate end-user feedback into corrective action plans and recommending technical changes.
- Developing and implementing approved system proposed changes to ensure end-user needs continue to be met.
- Conducting ESOH risk assessments and maintaining oversight of critical safety item supply chain management.
- Conducting analysis to identify and mitigate potential obsolescence impacts (i.e., Diminishing Manufacturing Sources and Material Shortages (DMSMS)).
- Supporting implementation of follow-on development efforts in response to formal decisions to extend the weapon system's service life (e.g., through a Service Life Extension Program (SLEP)) or to initiate a major modification (may be treated as a stand-alone acquisition program).
- Updating and maintaining system certifications and external SoS interfaces.
- Supporting the PM in his interactions with the Configuration Steering Board.

Inputs

Table 26 summarizes the primary inputs associated with this part of the life cycle.

Table 26: Inputs Associated with O&S Phase

Inputs for O&S Phase
Acquisition Decision Memoranda (ADMs) associated with Milestone C and Full Deployment (FD) decision review (DR) • ADMs may contain additional direction • O&S may start as early as Milestone C (e.g., software) and overlap P&D phase • FD DR would involve O&S
Trade-off analysis results (See DoDI 5000.02, Enc 3, sec. 4) • P&D phase trade studies may support manufacturing or other system modifications (technology insertion, technology refresh, etc.)
ESOH analyses (updated) (See DoDI 5000.02, Enc 3, sec. 16 and CH 3–4.3.9.) • ESOH analyses continue during O&S to include hazard analysis and supporting NEPA/EO 12114 compliance for modifications and disposal
Risk assessment (See CH 3–4.1.5.)
Interdependencies/interfaces/memoranda of agreement (MOAs)
System performance specification
Field failures
Other technical information, such as architectures, system models and simulations generated during the P&D phase
LCSP (See CH 4–3.4.)
Information Support Plan (ISP) of Record (See CH 6–3.8.)
Test and Evaluation Master Plan (TEMP) (See CH 8–4.4.)
Request for Proposal (RFP) for SE support to O&S activities
Program Protection Plan (PPP) (See DoDI 5000.02, Enc 3, sec. 13 and CH 9–3.4.2.5.)
Other analyses • End-user feedback and trouble reports • Other prior analytic, prototyping, and/or technology demonstration efforts conducted by the science and technology (S&T) community • Technology insertion/transition studies can occur at any point in the life cycle
Spectrum Supportability Risk Assessment (See DoDI 4650.01 and CH 3–4.3.20.)
Life-Cycle Mission Data Plan for Intelligence Mission Data (IMD)-dependent programs (See CH 3–4.3.12. Intelligence (Life-Cycle Mission Data Plan) and CH 7–4.1.3.)

Activities

The O&S phase overlaps with the Production and Deployment (P&D) phase, since O&S activities begin when the first system is deployed. O&S ends when a system is demilitarized and disposed of. Figure 18 provides the end-to-end perspective and the integration of SE technical reviews and audits across the acquisition life cycle.

Figure 18: Weapon System Development Life Cycle

92

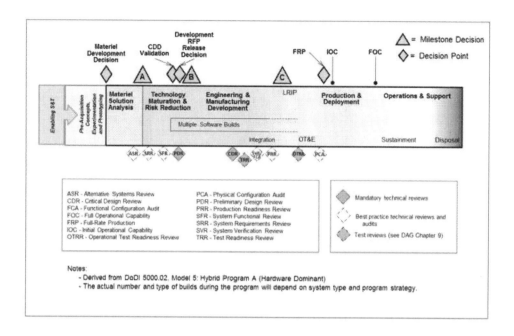

SE activities should be integrated with O&S phase-specific test and evaluation and logistics and sustainment activities identified in CH 8–4.5. and CH 4–3.5., respectively. The O&S activities in which the Systems Engineer should participate include:

- Updating risk, issue and opportunity plans. Identifying, analyzing, mitigating, and monitoring risks and issues; and identifying, analyzing managing and monitoring opportunities. (See the DoD Risk, Issue, and Opportunity Management Guide for Defense Acquisition Programs).
- Addressing problem/failure reports through the use of a comprehensive data collection approach such as a Failure Reporting, Analysis and Corrective Action System (FRACAS).
- Processing and analyzing mission data.
- Managing preplanned product improvements (P3I) and assessing the impact of system requirements changes resulting from evolving threats, changes to operational environment or in response to changes within the SoS or interfacing systems.
- Making changes to the system technical baseline to maintain it as the authoritative source; changes may be due to PCAs, ECPs or changes to interfaces to external systems.
- Developing and implementing technology refresh schedules.
- Conducting technology insertion efforts as needed to maintain or improve system performance.
- Updating system safety assessments.
- Performing engineering analysis to investigate the impact of DMSMS issues.
- Working with vendors and the general technical community to determine opportunities for technology insertion to improve reliability and affordability.

The disposal activities in which the Systems Engineer should participate include:

- Supporting demilitarizing and disposing of the system; in accordance with all legal and regulatory requirements and policy relating to safety (including explosives safety), security and the environment.
- Documenting lessons learned.
- Archiving data.

93

Outputs and Products

The technical outputs and products identified in Table 27 are necessary to support SE processes to   sustain the system, including modifications.

Table 27: Technical Outputs Associated with O&S Phase

Technical Outputs from O&S Phase
Safe, sustainable and reliable system that meets operational needs
Trade-off analysis results (See DoDI 5000.02, Enc 3, sec. 4) • O&S phase trade studies support system modifications and/or disposal efforts
Assessment of technical risk (See CH 3–4.1.5. and the DoD Risk, Issue, and Opportunity Management Guide for Defense Acquisition Programs.)
Interdependencies/interfaces/memoranda of agreement (MOAs)
Information Support Plan (ISP) of Record (See CH 6–3.8.)
In-service performance and failure data
Value engineering results, as appropriate (See CH 3–2.4.4. Value Engineering)
Engineering Change Proposal (ECP) packages

CH 3–3.3 Technical Reviews and Audits

For DoD weapon systems development, a properly tailored series of technical reviews and audits provide key points throughout the life cycle to evaluate significant achievements and assess technical maturity and risk. DoDI 5000.02, Enc 1 presents the statutory, regulatory and milestone requirements for acquisition programs. The Program Manager (PM) and Systems Engineer work to properly align the technical reviews to support knowledge-based milestone decisions that streamline the acquisition life cycle and save precious taxpayer dollars. Technical reviews and audits allow the PM and Systems Engineer to jointly define and control the program's technical effort by establishing the success criteria for each review and audit. A well-defined program facilitates effective monitoring and control through increasingly mature points (see Technical Maturity Point table in CH 3–3.1. Life Cycle Expectations).

Technical reviews of program progress should be event driven and conducted when the system under development meets the review entrance criteria as documented in the SEP. A key associated activity is to identify technical risks associated with achieving entrance criteria at each of these points (see the DoD Risk, Issue, and Opportunity Management Guide for Defense Acquisition Programs). Systems engineering (SE) is an event-driven process based on successful completion of key events as opposed to arbitrary calendar dates. As such, the SEP should clarify the timing of events in relation to other SE and program events. While the initial SEP and Integrated Master Schedule have the expected occurrence in the time of various milestones (such as overall system CDR), the plan should be updated to reflect changes to the actual timing of SE activities, reviews and decisions.

Figure 19 provides the end-to-end perspective and the integration of SE technical reviews and audits across the acquisition life cycle. Any program that is not initiated at Milestone C is required by DoDI 5000.02, Enc 3, sec. 7 to include a PDR and CDR.

Figure 19: Weapon System Development Life Cycle

94

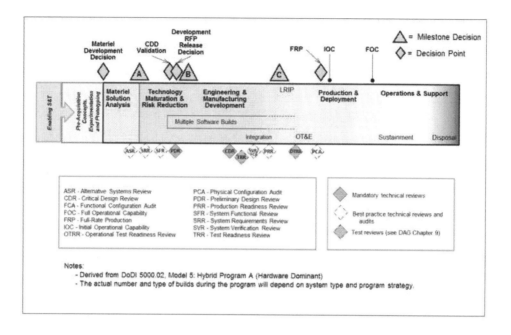

Properly structured, technical reviews and audits support the Defense Acquisition System by:

- Providing a disciplined sequence of activities to define, assess and control the maturity of the system's design and technical baseline, reducing risk over time
- Facilitating an accurate technical assessment of the system's ability to satisfy operational requirements established in capability requirements documents
- Providing a framework for interaction with the Joint Capabilities Integration and Development System (JCIDS) and Planning, Programming, Budgeting and Execution (PPBE) processes
- Providing a technical assessment and assurance that the end product fulfills the design and process requirements

Successful development of a complex weapon system requires a knowledge-based approach. Increasing levels of knowledge are a natural consequence of design maturation; however, successful programs establish a deliberate acquisition approach whereby major investment decision points are supported by requisite levels of knowledge. The Government Accountability Office's (GAO) study on Assessments of Selected Weapons Programs (GAO-12-400SP) provides quantitative evidence to affirm this best practice.

Figure 19 illustrates the notional sequence of technical reviews and audits. It also provides typical timing associated with the acquisition phases. Technical reviews should occur when the requisite knowledge is expected and required. This section provides guidance on entrance and exit criteria for the level of maturity expected at each technical review and audit. OSD established the expected reviews and audits for each acquisition phase in the outline for the Systems Engineering Plan (SEP). These policy and guidance documents provide a starting point for the PM and Systems Engineer to develop the program's unique set of technical reviews and audits. Tailoring is expected to best suit the program objectives (see CH 3–2. Background). The SEP captures the output of this tailoring and is reviewed and approved to solidify the program plan.

Programs that tailor the timing and scope of these technical reviews and audits to satisfy program objectives increase the probability of successfully delivering required capability to the warfighter. Technical reviews provide the forum to frame important issues and assumptions. They define options necessary to balance risk in support of continued development.

95

The technical baseline (including the functional, allocated and product baselines) established at the conclusion of certain technical reviews inform all other program activity. Accurate baselines and disciplined reviews serve to integrate and synchronize the system as it matures, which facilitates more effective milestone decisions and ultimately provides better warfighting capability for less money. The technical baseline provides an accurate and controlled basis for:

- Managing change.
- Cost estimates, which inform the PPBE process and the Acquisition Program Baseline (APB).
- Program technical plans and schedules, which also inform the APB.
- Contracting activity.
- Test and Evaluation efforts.
- Risk analysis and risk balancing.
- Reports to acquisition executives and Congress.

The PM and the Systems Engineer need to keep in mind that technical reviews and audits provide visibility into the quality and completeness of the developer's work products. These requirements should be captured in the contract specifications or SOW. The program office should consider providing the SEP with the Request for Proposal (RFP) and requiring the contractor deliver a SE Management Plan (SEMP) that is consistent with the SEP. As a best practice, the SEMP should include entrance criteria and associated design data requirements for each technical review and audit. The configuration and technical data management plans should clearly define the audit requirements.

For complex systems, reviews and audits may be conducted for one or more system elements, depending on the interdependencies involved. These incremental system element-level reviews lead to an overall system-level review or audit. After all incremental reviews are complete, an overall summary review is conducted to provide an integrated system analysis and capability assessment that could not be conducted by a single incremental review. Each incremental review should complete a functional or physical area of design. This completed area of design may need to be reopened if other system elements drive additional changes in this area. If the schedule is being preserved through parallel design and build decisions, any system deficiency that leads to reopening design may result in rework and possible material scrap.

While the Test Readiness Reviews (TRR) is a technical review, it is addressed in CH 8–3.9. The TRR is used to assess a contractor's readiness for testing configuration items, including hardware and software. They typically involve a review of earlier or lower-level test products and test results from completed tests and a look forward to verify the test resources, test cases, test scenarios, test scripts, environment and test data have been prepared for the next test activity. TRRs typically occur in the EMD and P&D phase of a program.

To design for security, the program protection planning and execution activities should be integrated into the systems engineering technical reviews and audits. See CH 9–3.4.3. for system security engineering (SSE) criteria for each systems engineering technical review and audit.

Roles and Responsibilities

For each technical review, a technical review chair is identified and is responsible for evaluating products and determining the criteria are met and that actions items are closed. The Service chooses the technical review chair, who could be the PM, Systems Engineer or other subject matter expert selected according to the Service's guidance. This guidance may identify roles and responsibilities associated with technical reviews and audits. It also may specify the types of design artifacts required for various technical reviews. In the absence of additional guidance, each program should develop and document its tailored design review plan in the SEP.

The following notional duties and responsibilities associated with the PM and Systems Engineer should be considered in the absence of specific Service or lower level (e.g., System Command or Program Executive Officer (PEO)) guidance:

96

The PM is typically responsible for:

- Co-developing with the Systems Engineer the technical objectives of the program that guide the technical reviews and audits
- Co-developing with the Systems Engineer the earned value credit derived from the review
- Approving, funding and staffing the planned technical reviews and audits; documenting this plan in the SEP and applicable contract documents
- Ensuring the plan for each review includes participants with sufficient objectivity with respect to satisfying the pre-established review criteria
- Ensuring the plan addresses the need for timely and sufficient data to satisfy the statutory and regulatory requirements of DoDI 5000.02, Enc 1.
- Controlling the configuration of each baseline and convening configuration steering boards when user requirement changes are warranted. This can lead to an unscheduled gateway into the Functional Capabilities Board (FCB) and JCIDS process not identified in Figure 19 above

The Systems Engineer is typically responsible for:

- Co-developing with the PM the technical objectives of the program that guide the technical reviews and audits
- Developing and documenting the technical review and audit plan in the SEP, carefully tailoring each event to satisfy program objectives and SEP outline guidance associated with the minimum technical reviews and audits
- Ensuring the plan is event based with pre-established review criteria for each event, informed by the knowledge point objectives in Table 12: Technical Maturity Points
- Identifying the resources required to support the plan; ensuring the activities leading up to the official review and audit are integrated. See Figure 20.
- Ensuring technical reviews and audits are incorporated into the IMP and IMS
- Coordinating with Chief Development Tester to provide at each technical review: DT&E activities to-date, planned activities, assessments to-date and risk areas
- Ensuring a status of applicable design considerations are provided at each technical review
- Establishing technical reviews and audits and their review criteria in the applicable contract documents (e.g., Statement of Work (SOW), IMP)
- Monitoring and controlling execution of the established plans
- Coordinating with the appointed technical review chairperson on the technical review plans and supporting execution of the technical reviews
- Assigning responsibilities for closure actions and recommend to the chairperson and PM when a system technical review should be considered complete, see Figure 20

Figure 20: Technical Review Process

97

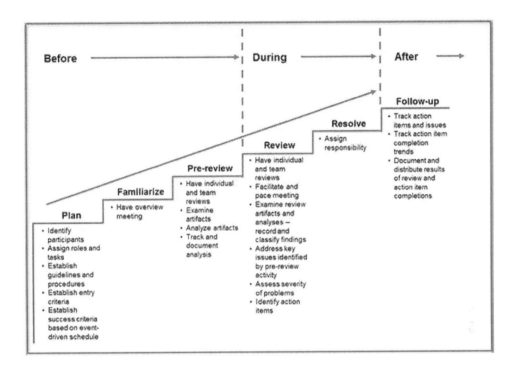

The PM and Systems Engineer should identify key stakeholders who have an interest or role in the review, which may include:

- Technical review chairperson
- Program Executive Office
- Contracting Officer
- Defense Contract Management Agency (DCMA) and Defense Contract Audit Agency (DCAA)
- Product Support Manager
- Product Improvement Manager/Requirements Officer
- End-user Community
- Chief Developmental Tester
- Interdependent Acquisition Programs
- Business Financial Manager
- Deputy Assistant Secretary of Defense for Systems Engineering (DASD(SE))
- Service Technical Leadership such as chief engineers
- Subject Matter Experts

Review Criteria

Specific review criteria are provided in each technical review and audit section below. These criteria should be achieved and all action items closed before a technical review is considered complete. The Systems Engineer may refer to IEEE 15288.2 "Standard for Technical Reviews and Audits on Defense Programs" as a resource. Instructions for how DoD military and civilian employees can access the IEEE 15288.2 via ASSIST are located on the DASD(SE) website. When comparing this section on technical reviews and audits to IEEE 15288.2 keep in mind:

98

- The Alternative Systems Review is focused on achieving a government-to-government understanding of the user's needs and the preferred materiel solution. It occurs in the Materiel Solution Analysis phase before a development contract is awarded.
- The Test Readiness Review (TRR) is addressed in CH 8–3.9.1.
- With the exception of TRR, this chapter addresses all technical reviews and audits in clauses 5 and 6 of IEEE 15288.2. The standard has annexes that address software-specific and other reviews that may be useful, depending on program needs.

Contract incentives are frequently tied to completion of technical reviews. Some stakeholders may have a strong incentive to call the review complete as soon as possible. The review chairperson and Systems Engineer should exercise best judgment in an objective, informed manner to ensure the reviews are not prematurely declared complete.

CH 3–3.3.1 Alternative Systems Review

The Alternative Systems Review (ASR) is held to support a dialogue between the end user and acquisition community and leads to a draft performance specification for the preferred materiel solution. The ASR typically occurs during the Materiel Solution Analysis (MSA) phase, after completion of the Analysis of Alternatives (AoA) and before Milestone A. It focuses technical efforts on requirements analysis.

The ASR should evaluate whether there is sufficient understanding of the technical maturity, feasibility and risk of the preferred materiel solution, in terms of addressing the operational capability needs in the Initial Capabilities Document (ICD) and meeting affordability, technology and operational effectiveness and suitability goals.

The ASR helps the Program Manager (PM) and Systems Engineer ensure that further engineering and technical analysis needed to draft the system performance specification is consistent with customer needs.

CJCSI 3170.01 calls for a Functional Capabilities Board (FCB) review prior to Milestone A. This FCB review should ensure compatibility between the operational capability needs in the ICD and the maturity, feasibility and risks of the preferred materiel solution.

Roles and Responsibilities

The unique PM responsibilities associated with an ASR include:

- Approving, funding and staffing the ASR.

The unique Systems Engineer responsibilities associated with an ASR include:

- Ensuring adequate plans are in place to complete the necessary technical activities for the ASR.
- Ensuring results of all technical trade studies are captured in documents that are carried through to the next phase.
- Ensuring technical risk items are identified and analyzed, and appropriate mitigation plans are in place. This activity should include, for example, the identification of critical technologies and identification of key interfaces with supporting or enabling systems.

Inputs and Review Criteria

The ASR typically occurs after the AoA is complete and after a preferred materiel solution is selected by the lead Service or Component but before the FCB review. Figure 21 provides the end-to-end perspective and the integration of SE technical reviews and audits across the acquisition life cycle.

This timing allows the focus of the ASR to be on the preferred materiel solution rather than on all the alternatives, and allows for some post-AoA technical analysis to be completed and inform the FCB deliberations.

Figure 21: Weapon System Development Life Cycle

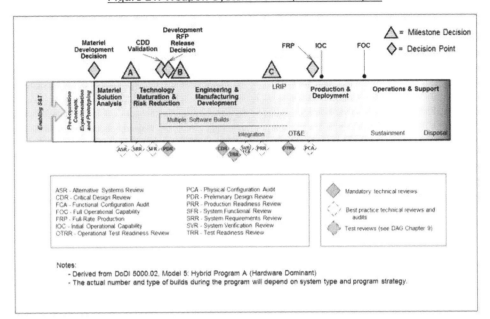

- The AoA results are an input to the ASR. The AoA should have evaluated a number of candidate materiel solutions and identified those alternatives that can meet the user requirements within the remaining trade space (including cost and affordability constraints).
- After the AoA is complete, the operational requirements community and the acquisition community collaboratively identify one or more preferred materiel solution(s) with the potential to be affordable, operationally effective and suitable, sustainable and technically and technologically achievable (i.e., able to provide a timely solution to the stated operational capability need at an acceptable level of risk). This preferred materiel solution is also an input to the ASR.
- The draft Concept of Operations/Operational Mode Summary/Mission Profile (CONOPS/OMS/MP) should be available as an input to the ASR. It should have been available for use in the AoA and can then be used to support development of missions and operational scenarios to evaluate the preferred materiel solution.

Table 28 identifies the products and associated review criteria normally seen as part of the ASR. The Chief Engineer should review this table and tailor the criteria for the program. The ASR should not begin until the criteria are met. A resource for ASR preparation is IEEE 15288.2 "Standard for Technical Reviews and Audits on Defense Programs". This is a best practice review.

Table 28: ASR Products and Criteria

Product	ASR Criteria
Refined Joint Requirements	- Joint context and initial CONOPS/OMS/MP updated to reflect current user position about capability gap(s), supported missions, interfacing/enabling systems in the operational architecture; overall system of systems (SoS) context - Required related solutions and supporting references (ICD and CDDs) identified

100

	• Joint refined thresholds and objectives initially stated as broad measures of effectiveness and suitability (e.g., KPPs, KSAs, need date)
Initial Architecture for the Preferred Materiel Solution(s)	• High-level description of the preferred materiel solution(s) is available and sufficiently detailed and understood to enable further technical analysis in preparation for Milestone A • SoS interfaces and external dependencies are adequately defined
System Performance Specification	• Clear understanding of the system requirements consistent with the ICD and draft CDD (if available) • System requirements are sufficiently understood to enable functional definition • Draft system performance specification has sufficiently conservative requirements to allow for design trade space • Relationship between draft system performance specification and risk reduction prototyping and competitive prototyping objectives is established
Preferred Materiel Solution(s) Documentation	• Comprehensive rationale is available for the preferred materiel solution(s), based on the AoA • Key assumptions and constraints associated with preferred materiel solution(s) are identified and support the conclusion that this solution can reasonably be expected to satisfy the ICD (or draft CDD if available) in terms of technical, operational, risk and schedule/cost (affordability) criteria • Results of trade studies/technical demonstrations for concept risk reduction, if available • Initial producibility assessments of solution concepts
Risk Assessment	• Technical risks are identified, and mitigation plans are in development • Initial hazard analysis/system safety analysis for preferred solution(s) complete

Outputs and Products

The Technical Review Chair determines when the review is complete. ASR technical outputs should include, but not be limited to, the following products, including supporting rationale and trade-off analysis results:

- Refined description of the preferred materiel solution to support further development
- Informed advice to the user-developed draft Capability Development Document (CDD) required at Milestone A

CH 3–3.3.2 System Requirements Review

The System Requirements Review (SRR) is a multi-disciplined technical review to ensure that the developer understands the system requirements and is ready to proceed with the initial system design. This review assesses whether the system requirements as captured in the system performance specification (sometimes referred to as the System Requirements Document (SRD)):

- Are consistent with the preferred materiel solution (including its support concept) from the Materiel Solution Analysis (MSA) phase.
- Are consistent with technology maturation plans.
- Adequately consider the maturity of interdependent systems.

All system requirements and performance requirements derived from the Initial Capabilities Document (ICD) or draft Capability Development Document (CDD) should be defined and consistent with cost, schedule, risk and other system constraints and with end-user expectations. Also important to this review

101

is a mutual understanding (between the program office and the developer) of the technical risk inherent in the system performance specification.

For Major Defense Acquisition Programs (MDAPs), DoDI 5000.02, para 5.d.3 requires a Milestone A before approving release of the final Request for Proposal (RFP) for the Technology Maturation and Risk Reduction (TMRR) phase; therefore, it is suggested that the program office perform a review similar to an SRR to assess readiness and risks of the technical content of the draft RFP(s) prior to Milestone A and ensure performance requirements are traceable to capability requirements. This program office review should occur after the selection of the preferred solution and after sufficient analysis has occurred to develop a draft system performance specification.

If the program's Acquisition Strategy (AS) includes competing contractual efforts during the TMRR phase, an SRR should be held with each participating developer to ensure the requirements are thoroughly and properly understood and they are ready to proceed into initial system design with acceptable risk. This review also ensures that system of systems (SoS) requirements, in the form of logical and physical interfaces and desired performance outcomes, have been levied on the system to be procured and are consistent with the ICD and/or draft CDD. These requirements are documented in the system performance specification and managed through external communication and technical interfaces in accordance with the Systems Engineering Plan (SEP).

Roles and Responsibilities

The unique Program Manager (PM) responsibilities associated with an SRR include:

- Approving, funding, and staffing the SRR as planned in the SEP developed by the Systems Engineer.
- Managing and approving changes to the system performance specification.
- Establishing the plan to System Functional Review (SFR) in applicable contract documents, including the SE Master Plan, Integrated Master Schedule (IMS) and Integrated Master Plan (IMP).
- Ensuring the plan includes subject matter experts to participate in each review.

The unique Systems Engineer responsibilities associated with an SRR include:

- Ensuring all performance requirements, both explicit and derived, are defined and traceable (both directions) between requirements in the draft CDD including Key Performance Parameters (KPPs), Key System Attributes (KSAs), other system attributes and the system performance specification (see JCIDS Manual (Enclosure D)) (requires Common Access Card (CAC) to access website).
- Ensuring verification methods are identified for all system requirements.
- Ensuring risk items associated with system requirements are identified and analyzed, and mitigation plans are in place.
- Ensuring adequate plans are in place to complete the technical activities to proceed from SRR to the SFR.
- Ensuring plans to proceed to SFR allow for contingencies.
- Ensuring all interface are documented for the SoS and included in the performance specification.

Inputs and Review Criteria

Figure 22 provides the end-to-end perspective and the integration of SE technical reviews and audits across the acquisition life cycle. The SRR criteria are developed to best support the program's technical scope and risk and are documented in the program's SEP at Milestone A.

Figure 22: Weapon System Development Life Cycle

102

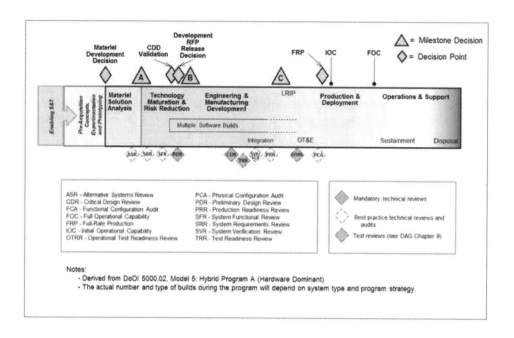

Notes:
- Derived from DoDI 5000.02, Model 5: Hybrid Program A (Hardware Dominant)
- The actual number and type of builds during the program will depend on system type and program strategy.

Table 29 identifies the products and associated review criteria normally seen as part of the SRR. The Chief Engineer should review this table and tailor the criteria for the program. The system-level SRR review should not begin until the criteria, identified by the Chief Engineer and documented in the SEP, are met and any prior technical reviews are complete and their action items closed. This is also an opportunity to assess whether technical requirements from all acquisition documentation (e.g., Program Protection Plan (PPP), Test and Evaluation Master Plan (TEMP), Reliability, Availability, Maintainability, and Cost Rationale (RAM-C) Report) are flowed to specifications. If the program's AS includes competing contractual efforts, an SRR should be held with each developer. A resource for SRR preparation is IEEE 15288.2 "Standard for Technical Reviews and Audits on Defense Programs". This is a best practice review.

Table 29: SRR Products and Criteria

Product	SRR Criteria
Cost Estimate	• Preliminary Cost Analysis Requirements Description (CARD) is consistent with the approved system performance specification • Preliminary software development estimates established with effort, schedule, and cost analysis • Updated cost estimate fits within the existing budget
Risk Assessment	• Technical risks are identified, and mitigation plans are in place
System Performance Specification	• Contractor clearly demonstrates an understanding of the system requirements consistent with the ICD and draft CDD • System requirements are sufficiently detailed and understood to enable functional definition and functional decomposition • System requirements are assessed to be verifiable (see Chief Developmental Tester in CH 8–4.2.)

103

Product	SRR Criteria
	• Requirements can be met given the plans for technology maturation • External interfaces to the system have been documented in interface control documents • SoS technical interfaces are adequately defined, including interdependences associated with schedule, test, and configuration changes • Preliminary identification of all software components (tactical, support, deliverable, non-deliverable, etc.) are completed • Human Systems Integration (HSI) and sustainment requirements have been reviewed and included in the overall system design (See CH 3–4.3.10. and CH 5–4.) • Contractor has adequately expanded the system performance specification to reflect tailored, derived and correlated design requirements • Bidirectional requirements traceability between the draft CDD, the Statement of Work (SOW) and the system performance specification has been documented • System performance specification is approved, including stakeholder concurrence, with sufficiently conservative requirements to allow for design trade space
Technical Plans	• Contractors Systems Engineering Management Plan (SEMP) is complete and adequate • Cost and critical path drivers have been identified • The program schedule is executable with an acceptable level of technical and cost risk • Adequate processes and metrics are in place for the program to succeed • SE is properly staffed • Program is executable within the existing budget • Software functionality in the system performance specification is consistent with the software-sizing estimates and the resource-loaded schedule • Programming languages and architectures, security requirements and operational and support concepts have been identified • Hazards have been reviewed and mitigating courses of action have been allocated within the overall system design • Key technology elements have been identified, readiness assessed and maturation plans developed • Software development strategy is complete and adequate • Program technical risks are adequately identified and documented such that there is a clear understanding regarding the contractor's ability to meet the specification requirements • Draft verification methodologies have been adequately defined for each specification requirement • Certifying agencies have been identified and certification requirements are understood • Draft test plans have been developed in support of the TMRR phase (See Chief Developmental Tester in CH 8–4.2.) • Government and contractor configuration management (CM) strategies are complete and adequate • Planning for creation and/or use of models and simulations has begun and is captured in appropriate program plans.

104

Product	SRR Criteria
	• The manufacturing and production strategy is complete and adequate • Integrated Master Schedule (IMS) adequately identifies the critical path and is resourced at reasonable levels, based on realistic performance/efficiency expectations • Unique work requirements for risk reduction prototyping and competitive prototyping have been identified • Product support plan and sustainment concepts have been defined with the corresponding metrics

Output and Products

The Technical Review Chair determines when the review is complete. Once the products have been reviewed and approved in SRR, they provide a sound technical basis for proceeding with the system's functional definition and preliminary design.

CH 3–3.3.3 System Functional Review

The System Functional Review (SFR) is held to evaluate whether the functional baseline satisfies the end-user requirements and capability needs and whether functional requirements and verification methods support achievement of performance requirements. At completion of the SFR, the functional baseline is normally taken under configuration control.

The functional baseline describes the system's performance (functional, interoperability and interface characteristics) and the verification required to demonstrate the achievement of those specified characteristics. The functional baseline is directly traceable to the operational requirements contained in the Initial Capabilities Document (ICD) and draft Capability Development Document (CDD). The Program Manager (PM) establishes Government control of the functional baseline at the SFR and verifies it through Functional Configuration Audits (FCA) leading up to the system level FCA or the System Verification Review (SVR). For additional information, see CH 3–4.1.6. Configuration Management Process.

A successful SFR, which typically occurs during the Technology Maturation and Risk Reduction (TMRR) phase, reduces the risk of continuing the technical effort toward the Preliminary Design Review (PDR). The SFR is used to:

- Assess whether a balanced definition of the system's major elements has been developed, including their functionality and performance requirements
- Assess whether the functional baseline is technically achievable with regard to cost, schedule and performance
- Confirm that the system performance specification (typically put on contract) is realistic and provides a sound technical foundation for preliminary design
- Establish functional baseline and verification criteria to be used during FCA

Roles and Responsibilities

The unique PM responsibilities associated with an SFR include:

- Approving, funding, and staffing the SFR as planned in the Systems Engineering Plan (SEP) developed by the Systems Engineer.
- Managing and approving changes to the system performance specification.
- Establishing the plan to PDR in applicable contract documents, including the SE Management Plan (SEMP), Integrated Master Schedule (IMS) and Integrated Master Plan (IMP).
- Ensuring the plan includes subject matter experts to participate in each review.

105

- Controlling the configuration of the Government-controlled subset of the functional baseline.
- Chairing the configuration control board (CCB) for the system performance specification and other documentation used to control the functional baseline.

The unique Systems Engineer responsibilities associated with an SFR include:

- Ensuring adequate plans are in place to complete the necessary technical activities to proceed from SFR to PDR.
- Ensuring plans to proceed to PDR allow for contingencies.
- Ensuring all performance requirements, both explicit and derived, are defined and traceable (both directions) between requirements in the draft CDD to include Key Performance Parameters (KPPs), Key System Attributes (KSAs) other system attributes, and the system performance specification (see CJCSI 3170.01 JCIDS).
- Ensuring verification methods are identified for all requirements.
- Ensuring risk items associated with functional requirements are identified and analyzed, and mitigation plans are in place.

Inputs and Review Criteria

The SFR criteria are developed to best support the program's technical scope and risk and are documented in the program's SEP at Milestone A. Figure 23 provides the end-to-end perspective and the integration of SE technical reviews and audits across the acquisition life cycle.

Figure 23: Weapon System Development Life Cycle

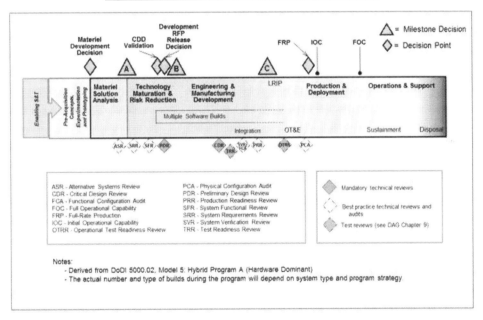

Table 30 identifies the products and associated review criteria normally seen as part of the SFR. The Chief Engineer should review this table and tailor the criteria for the program. The system-level SFR review should not begin until the criteria, identified by the Chief Engineer and documented in the SEP, are met and any prior technical reviews are complete and their action items closed. If the program's Acquisition Strategy (AS) includes competing contractual efforts, an SFR should be held with each

106

participating developer. A resource for SFR preparation is <u>IEEE 15288.2 "Standard for Technical Reviews and Audits on Defense Programs."</u> This is a best practice review.

Table 30: SFR Products and Criteria

Product	SFR Criteria
Functional Baseline Documentation	• Understood and assessed to be achievable within cost and schedule constraints • Established functional baseline by mapping system requirements in the system performance specification to lower level elements and their segment and major subsystem performance specifications • Documented performance requirements traced to (draft) CDD requirements and reflecting clear linkage to the system of system (SoS) context(s) (including use in multiple operational environments) • Documented performance requirements reflect design considerations • Documented verification requirements, including testing, for FCA/SVR
Major System Element Definition	• Documented allocated requirements optimized through analyses (including functional analysis and sensitivity analysis), trade studies and risk assessments
Risk Assessment	• Identified and documented risks, including ESOH mitigation measure requirements, at levels that warrant continued engineering development
Technical Plans	• Established detailed plan/schedule, sufficiently resourced to continue design and development

Outputs and Products

The Technical Review Chair determines when the review is complete. Once the products have been reviewed and approved in SFR, they provide a sound technical basis for proceeding into preliminary design.

CH 3–3.3.4 Preliminary Design Review

The Preliminary Design Review (PDR) should provide sufficient confidence to proceed with detailed design. The PDR ensures the preliminary design and basic system architecture are complete, that there is technical confidence the capability need can be satisfied within cost and schedule goals and that risks have been identified and mitigation plans established. It also provides the acquisition community, end user and other stakeholders with an opportunity to understand the trade studies conducted during the preliminary design, and thus confirm that design decisions are consistent with the user's performance and schedule needs and the validated Capability Development Document (CDD). The PDR also establishes the allocated baseline.

The allocated baseline describes the functional and interface requirements to a level in the system architecture sufficient to define hardware configuration item requirements distinct from software configuration item requirements, together with the verification required to demonstrate achievement of those requirements. The allocated baseline for each lower-level system element (hardware and software) is usually established and put under configuration control at the system element PDR. This process is repeated for each system element and culminates in the Program Manager (PM) establishing the complete allocated baseline at the system-level PDR. The PM then verifies the allocated baseline at the

107

Functional Configuration Audit (FCA) and/or System Verification Review (SVR) (see CH 3–4.1.6. Configuration Management Process).

The PDR is mandatory per DoDI 5000.02, Enc 3, sec. 7. The timing of the review should consider the following:

- PDR is conducted prior to Milestone B and prior to the contract award for Engineering and Manufacturing Development for all programs unless waived. (See DoDI 5000.02, para 5.d.4 and DoDI 5000.02, para 5.d.7.) Additionally, 10 U.S.C. 2366b requires the Milestone Decision Authority (MDA) certify all Major Defense Acquisition Programs (MDAPs) at Milestone B. This certification requires the conduct and assessment of a PDR, unless waived for national security reasons.
- The timing of PDR relative to the Development Request for Proposal (RFP) Release Decision Point is at the discretion of the DoD Component and should balance the need for more mature design information with the costs of extending the activities of multiple sources or having a gap in development. Regardless of this relationship, the PDR assessment is done after PDR and prior to Milestone B to support the MDA decision to enter detailed design. (See DoDI 5000.02, para 5.d.7.)

For MDAPs and MAIS programs, a PDR assessment is conducted and provided to the MDA. For ACAT ID and ACAT IAM programs, DASD(SE) conducts a PDR assessment to inform the MDA of technical risks and the program's readiness to proceed into detailed design. For ACAT IC and ACAT IAC programs, the Component Acquisition Executive conducts the PDR assessment.

Any tailoring with respect to establishing an allocated baseline at PDR prior to Milestone B should be consistent with the approved Acquisition Strategy (AS) and documented in the Systems Engineering Plan (SEP). In a competitive environment, each developer should establish an allocated baseline to meet the definition prescribed in the RFP and associated system performance specification, consistent with their individual design approach. Since the functional and allocated baselines are critical to providing the Engineering and Manufacturing Development (EMD) bidders with a complete technical package, best practices dictate that the PDR be completed prior to the Development RFP Release Decision Point. The tailoring strategy may also include conduct of a delta-PDR after Milestone B if the allocated baseline has changed significantly.

A successful PDR confirms that the system's preliminary design:

- Satisfies the operational and suitability requirements of the validated CDD, as documented in the system performance specification.
- Is affordable, producible, sustainable and carries an acceptable level of risk.
- Is composed of technologies demonstrated in a relevant environment that can be integrated into a system with acceptable levels of risk.
- Is complete and ready for detailed design.
- Provides the technical basis for the Milestone B investment decision and Acquisition Program Baseline (APB).
- Is fully captured and properly allocated in the specifications for each system element and all interface documentation (including system of systems (SoS) interdependencies).

The PDR establishes the allocated baseline, which is placed under formal configuration control at this point. The allocated baseline is complete when:

- All system-level functional and interface requirements have been decomposed and allocated to the lowest level of the specification tree for all system elements (i.e., configuration item level).
- All external interfaces to the system, as addressed at the System Requirements Review, have been documented in interface control documents.
- All internal interfaces of the system (system element to system element) have been documented in interface control documents.

108

- Verification requirements to demonstrate achievement of all specified allocated performance characteristics have been documented.
- Design constraints have been captured and incorporated into the requirements and design.

Some of the benefits realized from a PDR with the attributes identified above would be to:

- Establish the technical basis for the Cost Analysis Requirements Description (CARD), documenting all assumptions and rationale needed to support an accurate cost estimate for the APB; technically informed cost estimates enable better should-cost/will-cost management.
- Establish the technical requirements for the detailed design, EMD contract specifications and Statement of Work (SOW).
- Establish an accurate basis to quantify risk and identify opportunities.
- Provide the technical foundation for 10 USC 2366b certification required for all MDAPs.

Some design decisions leading up to PDR may precipitate discussions with the operational requirements community because they could have an impact on the CDD. Depending upon the nature/urgency of the capability required and the current state of the technology, incremental development might be required. In this case the Sponsor should document these increments in the CDD and the PM and Systems Engineer should update relevant program plans.

Roles and Responsibilities

The PM and Systems Engineer may hold incremental PDRs for lower-level system elements, culminating with a system-level PDR. The system PDR assesses the preliminary design as captured in system performance specifications for the lower-level system elements; it further ensures that documentation for the preliminary design correctly and completely captures each such specification. The PM and Systems Engineer evaluate the designs and associated logistics elements to determine whether they correctly and completely implemented all allocated system requirements, and whether they have maintained traceability to the CDD.

Though many Service systems commands or PEOs define the roles and responsibilities of the PM and Systems Engineer, the following notional duties and responsibilities should be considered:

The PM's responsibilities include the following:

- Approving, funding and staffing the system PDR as planned in the SEP developed by the Systems Engineer.
- Establishing the plan to CDR in applicable contract documents including the SE Management Plan (SEMP), Integrated Master Schedule (IMS) and Integrated Master Plan (IMP).
- Ensuring the SEP includes subject matter experts to participate in each review.
- Controlling the configuration of the Government-controlled subset of the functional and allocated baselines; convene Configuration Steering Boards when changes are warranted.

The Systems Engineer's responsibilities include the following:

- Developing and executing the system PDR plans with established quantifiable review criteria, carefully tailored to satisfy program objectives.
- Ensuring the pre-established PDR criteria have been met.
- Providing industry with an opportunity to participate in this PDR planning (pre-contract award is a best practice, where applicable).
- Ensuring assessments and risks associated with all design constraints and considerations are conducted, documented and provided (e.g., reliability and maintainability, corrosion and Environment, Safety and Occupational Health (ESOH) considerations).
- Updating risk, issue and opportunity plans. Identifying, analyzing, mitigating, and monitoring risks and issues; and identifying, analyzing, managing and monitoring opportunities. (See the DoD Risk, Issue, and Opportunity Management Guide for Defense Acquisition Programs.) Monitor and control the execution of the PDR closure plans.

109

- Documenting the plan to CDR in the SEP and elsewhere as appropriate.

Inputs and Review Criteria

Figure 24 provides the end-to-end perspective and the integration of SE technical reviews and audits across the acquisition life cycle.

Figure 24: Weapon System Development Life Cycle

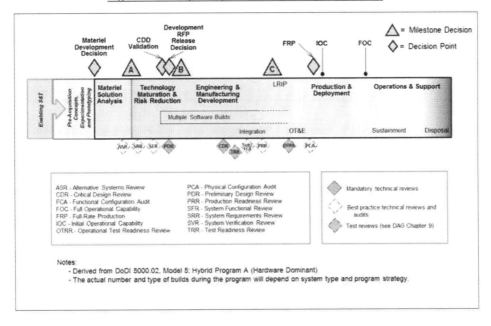

The PDR review criteria are developed to best support the program's technical scope and risk; they are documented in the program's SEP no later than Milestone A. Table 31 identifies the products and associated review criteria normally seen as part of the PDR. The Chief Engineer should review this table and tailor the criteria for the program. The system-level PDR review should not begin until the criteria, identified by the Chief Engineer and documented in the SEP, are met and any prior technical reviews are complete and their action items closed. A resource for PDR preparation is IEEE 15288.2 "Standard for Technical Reviews and Audits on Defense Programs". The PDR is a mandatory technical review.

Table 31: PDR Products and Criteria

Product	PDR Criteria
Cost Estimate	• System cost model has been updated, allocated to lower system element levels and tracked against targets; production cost model constructed • Updated CARD is consistent with the proposed allocated baseline
Risk Assessment	• All risk assessments and risk mitigation plans have been updated, documented, formally addressed and implemented • Approach/Strategy for test and evaluation defined in the Test and Evaluation Master Plan (TEMP) accounts for risks with a mitigation plan;

110

Product	PDR Criteria
	necessary integration and test resources are documented within the TEMP and current availability align with the program IMS (SE coordinates with the Chief Developmental Tester in this area; refer to CH 8–4.2.) • ESOH risks are known and being mitigated • Risks are at an acceptable level to continue with detailed design • Unique software risks identified/assessed and mitigation plans developed and implemented • Risks associated with intelligence mission data (IMD) dependencies have been identified and addressed; refer to CH 3–4.3.12. Intelligence (Life-Cycle Mission Data Plan)
Technical Baseline Documentation (Allocated)	• Capability Development Document (CDD) is validated per CJCSI 3170.01 • Analysis of system performance is complete and assessed to meet requirements • Preliminary design satisfies design considerations (see CH 3–4.2.2. Requirements Analysis Process) • Producibility assessments of key technologies are complete • Preliminary system-level design is producible and assessed to be within the production budget • Assessment of the technical effort and design indicates potential for operational test and evaluation success (operationally effective and operationally suitable) • All Critical Safety Items (CSIs) and Critical Application Items (CAIs) are identified • Functional failure mode, effects and criticality analysis (FMECA) is completed • Estimate of system reliability and maintainability updated, based on engineering analyses, initial test results, or other sources of demonstrated reliability and maintainability • Computer system and software architecture designs have been established; all Computer Software Configuration Items (CSCIs), Computer Software Components (CSCs), and Computer Software Units (CSUs) have been defined • Software Requirements Specifications (SRSs) and Interface Requirement Specifications (IRSs), including verification plans, are complete and baselined for all CSCs and satisfy the functional requirements • Interface control documents trace all software interface requirements to the CSCIs and CSUs • Preliminary software design has been defined and captured • All required software-related documents are baselined and delivered • Allocated baseline documentation is sufficiently complete and correct to enable detailed design to proceed with proper configuration management • Preliminary design (hardware and software), including interface descriptions, is complete and satisfies all requirements in the functional baseline • Requirements trace between functional and allocated baselines is complete and consistent
Technical Plans	• All entry criteria stated in the contract (e.g., Statement of Work (SOW), SEP, approved SEMP and system performance specification) have been satisfied

Product	PDR Criteria
	• Integrating activities of any lower-level PDRs have occurred; identified issues are documented in action plans • Plan to CDR is accurately documented in the SEP as well as the IMP and IMS • Program is properly staffed • Adequate processes and metrics are in place for the program to succeed • Program schedule, as depicted in the updated IMS (See CH 3–4.1.1.2. Integrated Master Plan and CH 3–4.1.1.3. Integrated Master Schedule) is executable within acceptable technical and cost risks • Program is executable with the existing budget and the approved product baseline • Trade studies and system producibility assessments are under way • Majority of manufacturing processes have been defined, characterized, and documented • Logistics (sustainment) and training systems planning and documentation are sufficiently complete to support the review • Life Cycle Sustainment Plan (LCSP) is approved, including updates on program sustainment development efforts and schedules based on current budgets and firm supportability design features • Information Support Plan (ISP) is drafted and scheduled for formal review prior to Milestone B • LCSP includes software support requirements • Long-lead and key supply chain elements are identified • Computer system and software design/development approach have been confirmed through analyses, demonstrations, and prototyping in a relevant environment • Software increments have been defined and capabilities allocated to specific increments • Software trade studies addressing commercial-off-the-shelf, reuse, and other software-related issues are completed • Software development process is defined in a baselined Software Development Plan and reflected in the IMP and IMS • Software development schedules reflect contractor software processes and IMP/IMS software events for current and future development phases • Software development environment and test/integration labs have been established with sufficient fidelity and capacity • Software metrics have been defined and a reporting process has been implemented; metrics are being actively tracked and assessed • The TEMP documents the overall structure and objectives of the Test and Evaluation program and articulates the necessary resources to accomplish each phase of test. It provides a framework within which to generate detailed T&E plans and documents schedule and resource implications associated with the T&E program • Software development estimates (i.e., size, effort (cost), and schedule) are updated

Outputs and Products

The Technical Review Chair determines when the review is complete. Completion of the PDR establishes that:

• The allocated baseline has been established and placed under configuration control.

112

- Technical data for the preliminary design are complete, satisfy the system performance specification and provide a sufficient foundation for detailed design to proceed.
- Risks have been assessed and are acceptable, with any risk mitigation plans approved and documented in the IMS.
- Feasibility, cost and schedule are determined to be within acceptable risk margins.
- IMS is updated (including systems and software critical path drivers) and includes all activities required to complete CDR (assuming same developer responsible for PDR and CDR).
- Corrective action plans for issues identified in the PDR have been completed.
- CARD is updated and reflects the design in the allocated baseline.
- LCSP is updated to reflect development efforts and schedules.

Preliminary Design Review (PDR) Assessment

A system-level PDR assessment is required for MDAPs and MAIS programs per DoDI 5000.02, Enc 3, sec. 7. This assessment informs the MDA of the technical risks and the program's readiness to proceed into detailed design, supporting the Milestone B decision point and, for MDAPS only, 10 USC 2366b Milestone B certification. In compliance with DoDI 5000.02, Enc 3, sec. 7, the Deputy Assistant Secretary of Defense for Systems Engineering (DASD(SE)) conducts PDR assessments on ACAT ID and ACAT IAM programs, and the Component Acquisition Executive (CAE) conducts the PDR assessments on ACAT IC and ACAT IAC programs. In support of this, MDAP and MAIS PMs are required to invite the DASD(SE) and the CAE to their PDRs and make the PDR artifacts available.

DASD(SE) reviews the conduct of the program's PDR, to include system element-level reviews as appropriate, and provides the MDA with an assessment of the following:

- The conduct and adequacy of the PDR to include the participation of stakeholders, technical authorities and subject matter experts; status of the PDR entrance and exit criteria; open Requests for Action/Information; and closure of the system element and system-level reviews.
- The program technical schedule and schedule risk assessments.
- The program's risks, issues and opportunities.
- The establishment and configuration control of the allocated baseline as demonstrated by the completion of the development specifications for each Configuration Item (CI); internal and external interface control documents; design constraints incorporated into the requirements and design; and system, system elements and CI verification plans.
- The conduct and results of any prototyping and trade studies conducted to reduce technical risk, validate design and assess integration.
- The preliminary design's ability to meet KPP, KSA and TPM thresholds and the proposed corrective actions to address any performance gaps, as appropriate.
- Key Systems Engineering design considerations.

CH 3–3.3.5 Critical Design Review

The Critical Design Review (CDR), which occurs during the EMD phase, confirms the system design is stable and is expected to meet system performance requirements, confirms the system is on track to achieve affordability and should-cost goals as evidenced by the detailed design documentation and establishes the initial product baseline.

The CDR provides the acquisition community with evidence that the system, down to the lowest system element level, has a reasonable expectation of satisfying the requirements of the system performance specification as derived from the Capability Development Document (CDD) within current cost and schedule constraints. At this point in the program, system performance expectations are based on analysis and any prototype testing/demonstration efforts conducted at the system element and/or system level. Demonstration of a complete system is not expected to be accomplished by this point.

The CDR establishes the initial product baseline for the system and its constituent system elements. It also establishes requirements and system interfaces for enabling system elements such as support equipment, training system, maintenance and data systems. The CDR should establish an accurate basis to assess remaining risk and identify new opportunities. At this point the system has reached the necessary level of maturity to start fabricating, integrating, and testing pre-production articles with acceptable risk.

The product baseline describes the detailed design for production, fielding/deployment and operations and support. The product baseline prescribes all necessary physical (form, fit and function) characteristics and selected functional characteristics designated for production acceptance testing and production test requirements. It is traceable to the system performance requirements contained in the CDD. The initial system element product baseline is established and placed under configuration control at the system element CDR and verified later at the Physical Configuration Audit (PCA). In accordance with DoDI 5000.02, Enc 3, sec. 8, the Program Manager (PM) assumes control of the initial product baseline at the completion of the system level CDR to the extent that the competitive environment permits. This does not necessarily mean that the PM takes delivery and acceptance of the Technical Data Package (TDP) (for more information, see CH 3–4.1.6. Configuration Management Process).

Roles and Responsibilities

The Systems Engineer documents the approach for the CDR in the Systems Engineering Plan (SEP). This includes identification of criteria and artifacts defining the product baseline.

The PM reviews and approves the approach, ensures the required resources are available and recommends review participants.

The PM and Systems Engineer may hold incremental CDRs for lower-level system elements, culminating with a system-level CDR. The system CDR assesses the final design as captured in system performance specifications for the lower-level system elements; it further ensures that documentation for the detailed design correctly and completely captures each such specification. The PM and Systems Engineer evaluate the detailed designs and associated logistics elements to determine whether they correctly and completely implement all allocated system requirements, and whether they have maintained traceability to the CDD.

The PM's responsibilities include:

- Approving, funding and staffing the system CDR as planned in the SEP developed by the Systems Engineer.
- Establishing the plan to the System Verification Review (SVR) in applicable contract documents including the SE Management Plan (SEMP), Integrated Master Schedule (IMS) and Integrated Master Plan (IMP).
- Ensuring the plan includes subject matter experts to participate in each review.
- Controlling the configuration of the Government-controlled subset of the functional, allocated and product baselines; convene Configuration Steering Boards (CSBs) when changes are warranted.

The Systems Engineer's responsibilities include:

- Developing and executing the system CDR plans with established quantifiable review criteria, carefully tailored to satisfy program objectives.
- Ensuring the pre-established review criteria have been met to ensure the design has been captured in the allocated baseline and initial product baseline.
- Ensuring assessments and risks associated with all design constraints and considerations are conducted, documented and provided (e.g., reliability and maintainability, corrosion, and Environment, Safety and Occupational Health (ESOH) considerations).
- Updating risk, issue and opportunity plans. Identifying, analyzing, mitigating, and monitoring risks and issues; and identifying, analyzing, managing and monitoring opportunities. (See the DoD Risk, Issue, and Opportunity Management Guide for Defense Acquisition Programs.) Monitor and control the execution of the CDR closure plans.
- Documenting the plan to SVR in the SEP and elsewhere as appropriate.

114

The CDR is mandatory for MDAP and MAIS programs per DoDI 5000.02, Enc 3, sec. 7. A CDR assessment will be conducted -- assessing the conduct of the review and the program technical risk -- and will be provided to the MDA. For ACAT ID and IAM programs, DASD(SE) conducts the CDR assessment. For ACAT IC and IAC programs, the Component Acquisition Executive conducts the CDR assessment.

Inputs and Review Criteria

Figure 25 provides the end-to-end perspective and the integration of SE technical reviews and audits across the acquisition life cycle.

Figure 25: Weapon System Development Life Cycle

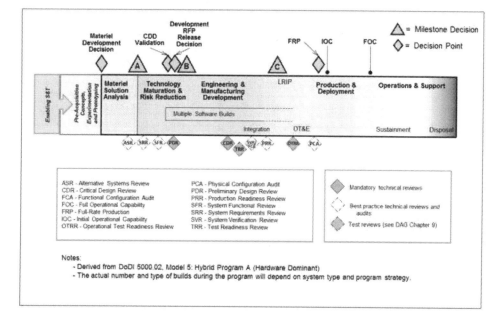

The March 2012 Government Accountability Office (GAO) report, "Assessments of Selected Weapon Programs," suggests a best practice is to achieve design stability at the system-level CDR. A general rule is that 75 to 90 percent of (manufacturing quality) product drawings, software design specification(s) and associated instructions (100 percent for all Critical Safety Items (CSIs) and Critical Application Items (CAIs) should be complete in order to provide tangible evidence of a stable product design. A prototype demonstration shows that the design is capable of meeting performance requirements.

The CDR review criteria are developed to best support the program's technical scope and risk and are documented in the program's SEP no later than Milestone B.

Table 32 identifies the products and associated review criteria normally seen as part of the CDR. The Chief Engineer should review this table and tailor the criteria for the program. The system-level CDR should not begin until the criteria, identified by the Chief Engineer and documented in the SEP, are met, any prior technical reviews are complete, and their action items closed. A resource for CDR preparation is IEEE 15288.2 "Standard for Technical Reviews and Audits on Defense Programs". The CDR is a mandatory technical review.

Table 32: CDR Products and Criteria

115

Product	CDR Criteria
Cost Estimate	• Updated Cost Analysis Requirements Description (CARD) is consistent with the approved initial product baseline • System production cost model has been updated, allocated to system-element level and tracked against targets
Technical Baseline Documentation (Initial Product)	• Detailed design (hardware and software), including interface descriptions, are complete and satisfy all requirements in the functional baseline • Requirements trace among functional, allocated and initial product baselines is complete and consistent • Key product characteristics having the most impact on system performance, assembly, cost, reliability and sustainment or ESOH have been identified to support production decisions • Initial product baseline documentation is sufficiently complete and correct to enable hardware fabrication and software coding to proceed with proper configuration management • Assessment of the technical effort and design indicates potential for operational test and evaluation success (operationally effective and operationally suitable) (See CH 8–4.3.) • 100% of Critical Safety Items and Critical Application Items have completed drawings, specifications and instructions • Failure mode, effects and criticality analysis (FMECA) is complete • Estimate of system reliability and maintainability based on engineering analyses, initial test results or other sources of demonstrated reliability and maintainability • Detailed design satisfies sustainment and Human Systems Integration (HSI) requirements (See CH 5–4.) • Software functionality in the approved initial product baseline is consistent with the updated software metrics and resource-loaded schedule • Software and interface documents are sufficiently complete to support the review • Detailed design is producible and assessed to be within the production budget • Process control plans have been developed for critical manufacturing processes • Critical manufacturing processes that affect the key product characteristics have been identified, and the capability to meet design tolerances has been determined • Verification (developmental test and evaluation (DT&E)) assessment to date is consistent with the initial product baseline and indicates the potential for test and evaluation success (See Test and Evaluation Master Plan (TEMP) and Chief Developmental Tester in CH 8–4.3.)
Risk Assessment	• All risk assessments and risk mitigation plans have been updated, documented, formally addressed and implemented • Approach/Strategy for test and evaluation defined in the TEMP accounts for risks with a mitigation plan; necessary integration and test resources are documented in the TEMP and current availabilities align with the Program's IMS (Systems Engineer coordinates with Chief Developmental Tester in this area; see CH 8–4.3.) • ESOH risks are known and being mitigated • Risks associated with intelligence mission data (IMD) dependencies have been identified and addressed; refer to CH 3–4.3.12. Intelligence (Life-Cycle Mission Data Plan)
Technical Plans	• PDR is successfully completed; all PDR actions are closed

116

Product	CDR Criteria
	• Integrating activities of any lower-level CDRs have occurred; identified issues are documented in action plans • All entry criteria stated in the contract (e.g., SOW, SEP, approved SEMP and system performance specification) have been satisfied • Adequate processes and metrics are in place for the program to succeed • Program schedule as depicted in the updated IMS (see CH 3–4.1.1.2. Integrated Master Plan and CH 3-4.1.1.3. Integrated Master Schedule) is executable (within acceptable technical/cost risks) • Program is properly staffed • Program is executable with the existing budget and the approved initial product baseline • Detailed trade studies and system producibility assessments are under way • Issues cited in the ISP are being satisfactorily addressed • Materials and tooling are available to meet the pilot line schedule • Logistics (sustainment) and training systems planning and documentation are sufficiently complete to support the review • Life-Cycle Sustainment Plan (LCSP), including updates on program sustainment development efforts and schedules based on current budgets, test and evaluation results and firm supportability design features, is approved • Long-lead procurement plans are in place; supply chain assessments are complete

Outputs and Products

The Technical Review Chair determines when the review is complete. Completion of the CDR should provide the following:

- An established initial product baseline.
- Acceptable risks with mitigation plans approved and documented in the IMS.
- Updated CARD (or CARD-like document) based on the initial product baseline.
- Updated program development schedule including fabrication, test and evaluation, software coding and critical path drivers.
- Corrective action plans for issues identified in the CDR.
- Updated LCSP, including program sustainment development efforts and schedules based on current budgets, test evaluation results, and firm supportability design features.

Note that baselines for some supporting items might not be at the detailed level and may lag the system-level CDR. Enabling systems may be on different life-cycle timelines. The CDR agenda should include a review of all this information, but any statement that all of the detailed design activity on these systems is complete may lead to misunderstandings. As an example, development of simulators and other training systems tends to lag behind weapon system development.

Critical Design Review (CDR) Assessment

A system-level CDR assessment is required for MDAPs and MAIS programs. This assessment informs the MDA of the technical risks and the program's readiness to proceed. In compliance with DoDI 5000.02, Enc 3, sec. 7, the Deputy Assistant Secretary of Defense for Systems Engineering (DASD(SE)) is directed to conduct CDR assessments on ACAT ID and ACAT IAM programs; and the Component Acquisition Executive (CAE) is to conduct CDR assessments on ACAT IC and ACAT IAC programs. In support of this policy direction, MDAP and MAIS PMs are required to invite DASD(SE) and CAE to their CDRs and make the CDR artifacts available.

DASD(SE) reviews the conduct of the program's CDR, to include system-element level reviews as appropriate, and provides the MDA with an assessment of the following:

- The conduct and adequacy of the CDR, including the participation of stakeholders, technical authorities and subject matter experts; status of the CDR entrance and exit criteria; open Requests for Action/Information; and closure of the system elements and system-level reviews.
- The program technical schedule and schedule risk assessments.
- The program's risks, issues and opportunities.
- The establishment and configuration control of the initial product baseline as demonstrated by the completion of build-to documentation for hardware and software configuration items, including production models, drawings, software design specifications, materials lists, manufacturing processes and qualification plans/procedures.
- The design's ability to meet KPP, KSA and TPM thresholds and the proposed corrective actions to address any performance gaps, as appropriate.
- Key Systems Engineering design considerations.

CH 3–3.3.6 System Verification Review/Functional Configuration Audit

The System Verification Review (SVR) is the technical assessment point at which the actual system performance is verified to meet the requirements in the system performance specification and is documented in the functional baseline. The Functional Configuration Audit (FCA) is the technical audit during which the actual performance of a system element is verified and documented to meet the requirements in the system element performance specification in the allocated baseline. Further information on FCA can be found in MIL-HDBK-61 (Configuration Management Guidance). SVR and FCA are sometimes used synonymously when the FCA is at the system level. The SVR/FCA typically occurs during the Engineering and Manufacturing Development (EMD) phase.

When a full-up system prototype is not part of the program's acquisition strategy, the FCA is used to validate system element functionality. Other system-level analysis is then used to ascertain whether the program risk warrants proceeding to system initial production for Operational Test and Evaluation (OT&E). Verification of system performance is later accomplished on a production system.

A successful SVR/FCA reduces the risk when proceeding into initial production for the system to be used in operational test and evaluation (OT&E). The SVR/FCA is used to:

- Assess whether system development is satisfactorily completed.
- Review the completed documentation of the Verification Process for completeness and adequacy.
- Determine that the system is ready to proceed to the next phase and OT&E with acceptable risk (see CH 8–4.3.)
- Confirm that the product baseline meets the requirements of the functional baseline and therefore has a high likelihood of meeting the warfighter requirements documented in the Capability Development Document (CDD) and/or Capability Production Document (CPD).

Roles and Responsibilities

The unique Program Manager (PM) responsibilities associated with an SVR/FCA include:

- Approving, funding and staffing the SVR/FCA as planned in the Systems Engineering Plan (SEP) developed by the Systems Engineer.
- Establishing the plan to the Production Readiness Review (PRR) in applicable contract documents, including the SE Management Plan (SEMP), Integrated Master Schedule (IMS) and Integrated Master Plan (IMP).
- Ensuring the SEP includes subject matter experts to participate in each technical review/audit.
- Continuing to control appropriate changes to the product baseline (see CH 3–4.1.6. Configuration Management Process).

The unique Systems Engineer responsibilities associated with an SVR/FCA include:

- Developing and executing the SVR/FCA plans with established quantifiable review criteria, carefully tailored to satisfy program objectives.
- Ensuring the pre-established technical review/audit criteria have been met.
- Ensuring all requirements in the system performance specification have been verified through the appropriate verification method and have been appropriately documented.
- Verifying configuration items (CIs) and software CIs have achieved the requirements in their specifications.
- Ensuring technical risk items associated with the verified product baseline are identified and analyzed, and mitigation plans are in place.
- Monitoring and controlling the execution of the SVR/FCA closure plans.
- Ensuring adequate plans and resources are in place to accomplish the necessary technical activities between SVR, PRR and Physical Configuration Audit (PCA); these plans should allow for contingencies.

Inputs and Review Criteria

Figure 26 provides the end-to-end perspective and the integration of SE technical reviews and audits across the acquisition life cycle.

<u>Figure 26:Weapon System Development Life Cycle</u>

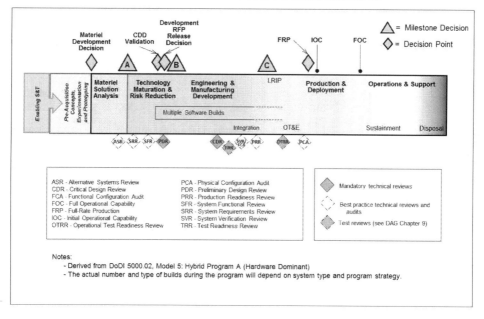

The SVR/FCA criteria are developed to best support the program's technical scope and risk and are documented in the program's SEP no later than Milestone B. Table 33 identifies the products and associated review criteria normally seen as part of the SVR/FCA. The Chief Engineer should review this table and tailor the criteria for the program. The system-level SVR/FCA review should not begin until the criteria, identified by the Chief Engineer and documented in the SEP, are met and any prior technical reviews are complete and their action items closed. A resource for SVR preparation is <u>IEEE 15288.2</u> <u>"Standard for Technical Reviews and Audits on Defense Programs"</u>. This is a best practice review.

Table 33: SVR/FCA Products and Criteria

119

Product	SVR/FCA Criteria
Technical Baseline Documentation (Functional and/or Allocated) Verification	• Documented achievement of functional and/or allocated baseline requirements through the appropriate documented verification method (analysis, demonstration, examination, testing or any combination thereof) are reviewed and verified (Note: verification testing may include developmental, operational (e.g., Early Operational Assessments (EOAs), Operational Assessments (OAs]) and/or live fire testing) • Assessment that the documented product baseline for the initial production system has an acceptable risk of operational test failure during OT&E
Risk Assessment	• Identified and documented risks (including ESOH) have been accepted at the appropriate management level prior to initial production for the system to be used in OT&E
Technical Plans	• Detailed plan/schedule has been established and sufficiently resourced to continue development

Outputs and Products

The Technical Review Chair determines when the review is complete. Once the products have been reviewed and approved in SVR/FCA, they provide a sound technical basis for proceeding into initial production for the system to be used in OT&E.

CH 3–3.3.7 Production Readiness Review

The Production Readiness Review (PRR) for the system determines whether the system design is ready for production, and whether the developer has accomplished adequate production planning for entering Low-Rate Initial Production (LRIP) and Full-Rate Production (FRP). Production readiness increases over time with incremental assessments accomplished at various points in the life cycle of a program.

In the early stages, production readiness assessments should focus on high-level manufacturing concerns such as the need for identifying high-risk and low-yield manufacturing processes or materials, or the requirement for manufacturing development efforts to satisfy design requirements. As the system design matures, the assessments should focus on adequate production planning, facilities allocation, producibility changes, identification and fabrication of tools and test equipment and long-lead items. The system PRR, held prior to Milestone C, should provide evidence that the system can be produced with acceptable risk and no breaches in cost, schedule or performance thresholds. The PRR should also consider what production systems should be retained after system deployment to sustain and maintain the system through its life cycle. See the EMD Phase production activities described in DoDI 5000.02, para 5.d.9.

For complex systems, a PRR may be conducted for one or more system elements. In addition, periodic production readiness assessments should be conducted during the Engineering and Manufacturing Development phase to identify and mitigate risks as the design progresses. The incremental reviews lead to an overall system PRR. See CH 3–3.3. Technical Reviews and Audits for more on this incremental approach.

Roles and Responsibilities

The unique Program Manager (PM) responsibilities associated with a system PRR include:

- Approving, funding and staffing the PRR as planned in the Systems Engineering Plan (SEP) developed by the Systems Engineer.

120

- Establishing the plan to Physical Configuration Audit (PCA) in applicable contract documents, including the SE Management Plan (SEMP), Integrated Master Schedule (IMS) and Integrated Master Plan (IMP).
- Ensuring the plan includes subject matter experts to participate in each review.
- Determining if the readiness of manufacturing processes, quality management system and production planning (i.e., facilities, tooling and test equipment capacity, personnel development and certification, process documentation, inventory management, supplier management, etc.) provide low-risk assurances for supporting LRIP and FRP.
- Continuing to control appropriate changes to the product baseline (see CH 3–4.1.6. Configuration Management Process).

The unique Systems Engineer responsibilities associated with a system PRR include:

- Developing and executing the PRR plans with established quantifiable review criteria, carefully tailored to satisfy program objectives.
- Ensuring the pre-established review criteria have been met to make sure the production capability forms a satisfactory, affordable and sustainable basis for proceeding into LRIP and FRP.
- Advising the PM on whether production capability forms a satisfactory, affordable and sustainable basis for proceeding into LRIP and FRP.
- Ensuring adequate plans and resources are in place to proceed from PRR to PCA and FRP Decision Review (DR).
- Ensuring plans to proceed to PCA and FRP DR allow for contingencies.
- Ensuring production implementation supports overall performance and maintainability requirements.
- Monitoring and controlling the execution of the PRR closure plans.

Inputs and Review Criteria

Figure 27 provides the end-to-end perspective and the integration of SE technical reviews and audits across the acquisition life cycle.

<u>Figure 27: Weapon System Development Life Cycle</u>

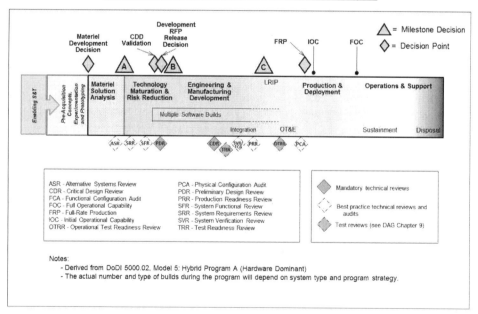

The PRR criteria are developed to best support the program's technical scope and risk and are documented in the program's SEP no later than Milestone B. Table 34 identifies the products and associated review criteria normally seen as part of the PRR. The Chief Engineer should review this table and tailor the criteria for the program. The system-level PRR review should not begin until the criteria, identified by the Chief Engineer and documented in the SEP, are met, any prior technical reviews are complete and their action items closed. A resource for PRR preparation is IEEE 15288.2 "Standard for Technical Reviews and Audits on Defense Programs". This is a best practice review.

Table 34: PRR Products and Criteria

Product	PRR Criteria
Cost Estimate	• System, as designed, is producible within the production budget • Production cost model is based on the stable detailed design and supply chain, and has been validated
Risk Assessment	• Producibility trade studies and risk assessments are completed • Manufacturing, production and quality risks are identified, and a mitigation plan exists to mitigate those risk(s) • Environment, Safety and Occupational Health (ESOH) risks are known and mitigated
Technical Baseline Documentation (Product)	• Product baseline is stable and under proper configuration control to enable hardware fabrication in low-rate production • Technologies are mature and proven in the final form, in operational environments • Manufacturing processes are stable and have been demonstrated in a pilot line environment • Adequate production line processes and metrics are in place for the delivery of on-time, quality products
Technical Plans	• Prior readiness reviews are completed and action items closed • Supply chain is stable and adequate to support planned LRIP and FRP • Program is properly staffed with qualified production, quality (engineering and assurance) and manufacturing personnel • Product acceptance system, including acceptance test procedures and associated equipment, has been validated and put under configuration control • Production facilities are ready and required personnel are trained • Delivery schedule is executable (technical/cost risks, long lead items) • Diminishing Manufacturing Sources and Material Shortages (DMSMS) plan is in place and mitigates the risk of obsolescence during LRIP and FRP

A follow-on PRR may be appropriate in the Production and Deployment (PD) phase for the prime contractor and major subcontractors if:

- Changes (from the Engineering and Manufacturing Development (EMD) phase system design) in materials and/or manufacturing processes are required when entering or during the Production and Deployment (P&D) phase.
- Production start-up or re-start occurs after a significant shutdown period.
- Production start-up is with a new contractor
- The manufacturing site is relocated

122

The PRR is designed as a system-level preparation tool and should be used for assessing risk as the system transitions from development to FRP. For more information, see the approaches described in CH 3–4.3.18. Producibility, Quality, and Manufacturing Readiness.

Outputs and Products

The Technical Review Chair determines when the review is complete. Results of the PRR and associated manufacturing readiness assessments are typically documented in a written report or out-brief. The results should be reported, based on the criteria documented in the SEP, using the PRR checklist. Another source of information is the Manufacturing Readiness Level Deskbook to be used as appropriate.

CH 3–3.3.8 Physical Configuration Audit

The Physical Configuration Audit (PCA) is a formal examination of the "as-built" configuration of the system or a configuration item against its technical documentation to establish or verify its product baseline. The objective of the PCA is to resolve any discrepancies between the production-representative item that has successfully passed Operational Test and Evaluation (OT&E) and the associated documentation currently under configuration control. A successful PCA provides the Milestone Decision Authority (MDA) with evidence that the product design is stable, the capability meets end-user needs and production risks are acceptably low. At the conclusion of the PCA, the final product baseline is established and all subsequent changes are processed by formal engineering change action. Further information can be found in MIL-HDBK-61 (Configuration Management Guidance).

The PCA is an event-driven technical assessment that typically occurs during the Production and Deployment (P&D) phase, after successful system validation but prior to the Full-Rate Production Decision Review (FRP DR). A PCA conducted during FRP may miss the opportunity to avoid costly defects built into production. While the system-level PCA typically occurs before the FRP DR, other system element PCAs may be conducted at various points in advance of the system-level PCA.

A properly conducted and documented PCA provides a major knowledge point in preparation for investment decisions at FRP DR. The PCA confirms:

- Any testing deficiencies have been resolved and appropriate changes implemented; changes to the product baseline have been incorporated into current design documentation.
- All production-related activities (tooling, acceptance/inspection equipment, instructions, molds, jigs and make-buy decisions) are focused on a validated and accurate design.
- Any system elements that were affected/redesigned after the completion of the Functional Configuration Audit (FCA) also meet contract requirements.
- All hardware CIs and software CIs are accurately represented by their product baseline information.
- The manufacturing processes, quality control system, measurement and test equipment and training are adequately planned, tracked, and controlled.

Roles and Responsibilities

The unique Program Manager (PM) responsibilities associated with a system PCA include:

- Determining the scope of the PCA, including which specific system elements will be audited and to what depth and any associated risk.
- Approving, funding and staffing the PCA as planned in the Systems Engineering Plan (SEP) developed by the Systems Engineer.
- Establishing the plan to FRP DR in applicable contract documents, including the SE Management Plan (SEMP), Integrated Master Schedule (IMS) and Integrated Master Plan (IMP).
- Ensuring the plan includes subject matter experts to participate in each review.
- Determining if the readiness of manufacturing processes, quality management system and production planning (i.e., facilities, tooling and test equipment capacity, personnel development

and certification, process documentation, inventory management, supplier management, etc.) provide low-risk assurances for supporting FRP.

- Continuing to control appropriate changes to the product baseline (see CH 3–4.1.6. Configuration Management Process).

The unique Systems Engineer responsibilities associated with a system PCA include:

- Developing and executing the PCA plans with established quantifiable review criteria, carefully tailored to satisfy program objectives.
- Coordinating with configuration management and manufacturing SMEs and the production contractor/production facility to develop an efficient approach to the PCA.
- Identifying method(s) of examining the production-representative item (e.g., disassembly, inspection and reassembly) and verifying the item against related design documentation.
- Ensuring the pre-established review criteria have been met to make sure the production capability forms a satisfactory, affordable and sustainable basis for proceeding with FRP.
- Ensuring that for software CIs a detailed audit of design documentation, listings and operations and support documents is completed.
- Advising the PM on whether production capability forms a satisfactory, affordable and sustainable basis for proceeding into FRP.
- Ensuring adequate plans and resources are in place to get from PCA to Full Operational Capability (FOC).
- Ensuring plans to get to FOC allow for contingencies.
- Ensuring production implementation supports overall performance and maintainability requirements.
- Ensuring Technical Data Packages (TDP) have been transferred to the government in accordance with the contract.
- Monitoring and controlling the execution of the PCA closure plans.
- Identifying risks associated with meeting program objectives, given the proposed PCA plans.

When the program does not plan to control the detailed design or purchase the item's technical data, the developer should conduct an internal PCA to define the starting point for controlling the detailed design of the item and establishing a product baseline.

Inputs and Audit Criteria

Figure 28 provides the end-to-end perspective and the integration of SE technical reviews and audits across the acquisition life cycle.

Figure 28: Weapon System Development Life Cycle

124

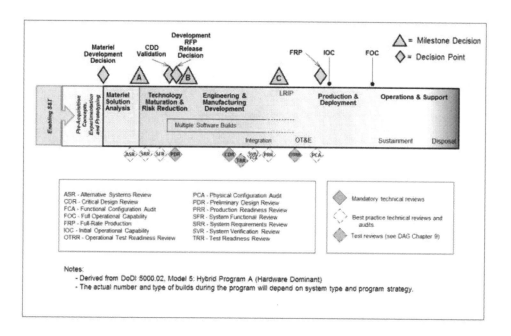

Notes:
- Derived from DoDI 5000.02, Model 5: Hybrid Program A (Hardware Dominant)
- The actual number and type of builds during the program will depend on system type and program strategy.

The PCA criteria are developed to best support the program's technical scope and risk and are documented in the program's SEP no later than Milestone C. The PCA is conducted when these criteria are considered to be met.

Table 35 identifies the products and associated review criteria normally seen as part of the PCA. The Chief Engineer should review this table and tailor the criteria for the program. The system-level PCA review should not begin until the criteria, identified by the Chief Engineer and documented in the SEP, are met and any prior technical reviews are complete and their action items closed. IEEE 15288.2 "Standard for Technical Reviews and Audits on Defense Programs" can be used as a resource for audit preparation. This is a best practice audit.

Table 35: PCA Products and Criteria

Product	PCA Criteria
Product Baseline Documentation	• Assessment that the product baseline is complete and accurately reflects the configuration of the representative production item that was inspected and validated through OT&E
Risk Assessment	• Risks are identified and documented at levels low enough to continue with full-rate production and deployment
Technical Plans	• A detailed plan and schedule are established and sufficiently resourced to proceed with full-rate production and deployment

Outputs and Products

125

The Technical Review Chair determines when the review is complete. The primary output of the PCA is a verified product baseline that accurately reflects the validated system and supports a favorable FRP DR.

CH 3–4. Additional Planning Considerations

The systems engineering (SE) processes are used by contractor and Government organizations to provide a framework and methodology to plan, manage and implement technical activities throughout the acquisition life cycle. SE planning and execution should focus on applying the processes and tools in a rigorous, integrated and disciplined manner to achieve a system solution that balances performance, cost, schedule and risk. The eight technical management processes provide a consistent framework for managing technical activities and identifying the technical information and events critical to the success of the program. The eight technical processes ensure the system design, and the delivered capability reflect the requirements that the stakeholders have expressed. All 16 SE processes are applicable to each of the six Defense Acquisition Program Models. As a whole, the SE processes provide a systematic approach focused on providing needed capability to the operational end user. Successful implementation of the SE processes results in an integrated capability solution that is:

- Responsive to the needs of the end user.
- Balanced among multiple requirements, design considerations and program costs and schedules.
- Able to operate in complex system-of-systems (SoS) environments as required.

All organizations performing SE should scale their application and use of these processes to the type of product or system being developed. This scaling should reflect the system's maturity and complexity, size and scope, life-cycle phase and other relevant considerations. Disciplined application of the SE processes provides a technical framework that enables sound decision making, increases product knowledge and helps reduce risk. The following subsections, as indicated in Table 36, discuss the SE processes in more detail.

Table 36: Systems Engineering Processes

Technical Management Processes	Technical Processes
Technical Planning (CH 3–4.1.1.)	Stakeholder Requirements Definition (CH 3–4.2.1.)
Decision Analysis (CH 3–4.1.2.)	Requirements Analysis (CH 3–4.2.2.)
Technical Assessment (CH 3–4.1.3.)	Architecture Design (CH 3–4.2.3.)
Requirements Management (CH 3–4.1.4.)	Implementation (CH 3–4.2.4.)
Risk Management (CH 3–4.1.5.)	Integration (CH 3–4.2.5.)
Configuration Management (CH 3–4.1.6.)	Verification (CH 3–4.2.6.)
Technical Data Management (CH 3–4.1.7.)	Validation (CH 3–4.2.7.)
Interface Management (CH 3–4.1.8.)	Transition (CH 3–4.2.8.)

Industry SE standards that describe best practices in accomplishing SE include, but are not limited to, the following:

- ISO/IEC/IEEE 15288, Systems and Software Engineering-System Life Cycle Processes
- IEEE 15288.1, Standard for Application of Systems Engineering on Defense Programs

ISO/IEC/IEEE 15288 is a non-Government standard (NGS), developed jointly by SE stakeholders in industry, Government and academia, that establishes a common process framework for describing the life cycle of man-made systems. It defines a set of SE processes and associated terminology for the full-system life cycle, including conception, development, production, utilization, support and retirement. It is supported by a Government-initiated NGS, IEEE 15288.1, which expands on the SE life cycle processes

126

of ISO/IEC/IEEE 15288 with additional detail specific to DoD acquisition projects. IEEE 15288.1 also adds requirements for SE outputs and the attributes (criteria) for each process.

Both ISO/IEC/IEEE 15288 and IEEE 15288.1 have been adopted for use by DoD. Adoption expresses formal acceptance of an NGS for use in direct procurement, as a reference in another document or as guidance in the design, manufacturing, testing or support of materiel. An adopted NGS is not a mandatory document; it is deemed appropriate for use by DoD organizations. Therefore, it is up to each Program Management Office (PMO) to determine if and how these standards should be used to support a particular project. Instructions for how DoD military and civilian employees can access the IEEE 15288.1 via ASSIST are located on the DASD(SE) website.

There is not a one-to-one mapping between the SE processes in the ISO/IEC/IEEE 15288 and the DAG, but the same information is conveyed in both documents. Figure 29 depicts how the DAG SE processes/activities map to the ISO/IEC/IEEE 15288 processes. The figure does not cover the ISO/IEC/IEEE 15288 Agreement and Organizational project-enabling processes because those apply to commercial system development and is outside the scope of DoD acquisition.

Figure 29: DAG SE Processes/Activities Mapped to ISO/IEC/IEEE 15288 SE Processes

	DoD SE Processes (DAG section)	ISO/IEC/IEEE 15288 Processes (Clause)
TECHNICAL MGMT PROCESSES	Technical Planning (4.1.1)	Project Planning (6.3.1)
	Decision Analysis (4.1.2)	Decision Management (6.3.3)
	Technical Assessment (4.1.3)	Project Assessment and Control (6.3.2)
		Measurement (6.3.7)
	Requirements Management (4.1.4)*	System Requirements Definition (6.4.3)
	Risk Management (4.1.5)	Risk Management (6.3.4)
	Configuration Management (4.1.6)	Configuration Management (6.3.5)
	Technical Data Management (4.1.7)	Information Management (6.3.6)
	Interface Management (4.1.8)	Architecture Definition (6.4.4)
	Covered by Section 4.3.18 PQM and DAG CH 1 Section 4.8 Encouraging a Quality Focus	Quality Assurance (6.3.8)
TECHNICAL PROCESSES	Covered by Sections 2.3 System Level Considerations and 3.1.2. SoS	Business or Mission Analysis (6.4.1)
	Stakeholder Requirements Definition (4.2.1)	Stakeholder Needs and Requirements Definition (6.4.2)
	Requirements Analysis (4.2.2)*	System Requirements Definition (6.4.3)
	Architecture Design (4.2.3)	Architecture Definition (6.4.4)
	Implementation (4.2.4)	Design Definition (6.4.5)
		Implementation (6.4.7)
	Covered throughout Sections 3.2 SE Activities in the Life-cycle and 4.3 Design Considerations	System Analysis (6.4.6)
	Integration (4.2.5)	Integration (6.4.8)
	Verification (4.2.6)	Verification (6.4.9)
	Validation (4.2.7)	Validation (6.4.11)
	Transition (4.2.8)	Transition (6.4.10)
	Covered by DAG CH 4 Life Cycle Sustainment	Operation (6.4.12)
	Covered by DAG CH 4 Life Cycle Sustainment	Maintenance (6.4.13)
	Covered by Section 4.3.7 Demilitarization and Disposal and DAG CH 4 Life Cycle Sustainment	Disposal (6.4.14)

*DAG Chapter 3 Requirements Management and Requirements Analysis processes are covered by ISO/IEC/IEEE 15288 – System Requirements Definition

Roles, Responsibilities, and Activities

The Program Manager (PM) and Systems Engineer use the technical management processes as insight and control functions for the overall technical development of the system throughout the acquisition life cycle. They use the technical processes to design, create and analyze the system, system elements and enabling system elements required for production, integration, test, deployment, support, operation, and disposal.

The SE processes, and their constituent activities and tasks, are not meant to be performed in a particular time-dependent or serial sequence. The PM and Systems Engineer apply the processes iteratively, recursively and in parallel (as applicable) throughout the life cycle to translate identified capability needs into balanced and integrated system solutions. The Systems Engineer is responsible for developing the

127

plan and applying the SE processes across the program, monitoring execution throughout the life cycle and taking necessary steps to improve process efficiency and effectiveness.

Figure 30 is a representation of how much effort is typically focused on each of the SE processes throughout the acquisition life cycle. The PM and Systems Engineer should apply appropriate resources with the requisite skill sets to ensure successful execution of each process.

Figure 30: Notional Emphasis of Systems Engineering Processes throughout the Defense Weapon System Acquisition Life Cycle

Legend: ● = Major Use, ◉ = Moderate Use, ○ = Minor Use

Process	Pre-MDD	MSA	TMRR	EMD	P&D	O&S
TECH MGMT PROCESSES						
Decision Analysis	●	●	●	●	●	●
Technical Planning	●	●	●	●	●	●
Technical Assessment	◉	●	●	●	●	●
Requirements Management	◉	●	●	●	●	●
Risk & Opportunity Management	◉	●	●	●	●	●
Configuration Management	○	◉	●	●	●	●
Technical Data Management	○	●	●	●	●	●
Interface Management	◉	●	●	●	●	●
TECHNICAL PROCESSES						
Stakeholder Requirements Definition	◉	●	●	◉	○	○
Requirements Analysis	◉	●	●	●	○	○
Architecture Design	◉	●	●	●	○	○
Implementation	○	◉	◉	●	◉	○
Integration	○	◉	◉	●	●	○
Verification	○	◉	◉	●	●	◉
Validation	○	◉	◉	●	●	●
Transition	○	○	◉	●	●	●

CH 3–4.1 Technical Management Processes

In DoD systems engineering, there are 8 technical management processes. The technical management processes are the foundational, enabling processes and are used consistently throughout the system life cycle to help manage the system development. The technical management processes are described in Sections 4.1.1 through 4.1.8.

CH 3–4.1.1 Technical Planning Process

The Technical Planning process provides a framework to define the scope of the technical effort required to develop, deploy and sustain the system, and provides critical quantitative inputs to program planning and life-cycle cost estimates. Technical planning provides the Program Manager (PM) and Systems Engineer with a framework to accomplish the technical activities that collectively increase product maturity and knowledge and reduce technical risks. Defining the scope of the technical effort provides:

- An accurate basis for program cost and schedule estimates, documented in the Independent Cost Estimate (ICE), Cost Analysis Requirements Description (CARD) and Acquisition Program Baseline (APB).

128

- A foundation for risk identification and management (see CH 3–4.1.5. Risk Management Process).
- Quantitative measures supporting the Technical Assessment process (see CH 3–4.1.3.) identifies system maturity.
- An accurately constructed and resourced IMS supporting the assignment of Earned Value.

The resulting program cost estimates and risk assessments are essential to support milestone decisions, establish the plan for accomplishing work against which contract performance is measured and enable mandatory program certifications (e.g., 10 USC 2366a or 10 USC 2366b).

Technical planning includes the program's plan for technical reviews and audits (see CH 3–3.3.). It should also account for resources (skilled workforce, support equipment/tools, facilities, etc.) necessary to develop, test, produce, deploy and sustain the system.

Technical planning should be performed in conjunction with, and address, key elements and products governing other SE processes to ensure the program's technical plan is comprehensive and coherent. For example, it should be used with the Technical Assessment process to evaluate the progress and achievements against requirements, plans and overall program objectives. If significant variances are detected, this process includes appropriate re-planning.

The PM and Systems Engineer should ensure technical planning remains current throughout the acquisition life cycle. They should initiate technical planning activities early in the life cycle before the Materiel Development Decision (see CH 3–3.2.1. Pre-Materiel Development Decision) and during the Materiel Solution Analysis (MSA) phase (see CH 3–3.2.2. Materiel Solution Analysis Phase). Beginning in MSA, programs begin to capture their technical planning in the Systems Engineering Plan (SEP) (see CH 3–2.2. Systems Engineering Plan), which is required at each milestone review from Milestone A to Milestone C. Technical planning leverages the Concept of Operations/Operational Mode Summary/Mission Profile (CONOPS/OMS/MP), which is available in the MSA phase. The CONOPS/OMS/MP is a document consistent with the validated/approved capability requirements document to include the operational tasks, events, durations, frequency, operating conditions and environments under which the recommended materiel solution is to perform each mission and each phase of a mission.

As the system matures and issues arise throughout the life cycle, the PM and Systems Engineer should consistently look for root cause(s) and implement corrective actions in order to enable programmatic and technical success. Modifications to the SE processes and SEP may be required because of root cause and corrective action analysis and implementation. .

Activities and Products

The PM is ultimately responsible for the development, management and execution of all program plans (See CH 1-3.4). The Systems Engineer is responsible for:

- Developing, maintaining and executing the program's SEP.
- Tracking alignment of the developer's Systems Engineering Management Plan (SEMP).
- Providing key technical inputs and ensuring SEP alignment to other program plans (Acquisition Strategy (AS), Test and Evaluation Master Plan (TEMP), Life-Cycle Sustainment Plan (LCSP) and Programmatic Environment, Safety and Occupational Health Evaluation (PESHE).

Technical Planning should reflect the context of the organization and comply with all applicable policies. The PM and Systems Engineer should consider all relevant constraints when identifying technical tasks, sequencing these tasks and estimating resources and budgets. Inputs to the technical planning process vary over time as the program evolves and the system matures. Technical Planning includes the following activities:

- Defining the scope and objectives of the technical effort.
- Identifying constraints and risks.

129

- Establishing roles and responsibilities.
- Dividing the program scope and objective into discrete elements.
- Identifying technical reviews and audits as well as their timing.
- Establishing schedules and costs.
- Preparing or updating planning documentation.
- Scaling SE processes based on the scope and complexity of the program/system.
- Identifying areas for potential tailoring (including rationale) for MDA approval.

Key factors that the Systems Engineer should consider when accomplishing technical planning include:

- Capability needs (requirements, gaps, threats, operational context, Concept of Operations/Operational Mode Summary/Mission Profile (CONOPS/OMS/MP))
- The system concept or materiel solution
- Key interfaces and interdependencies that exist or need to be developed
- The acquisition approach and strategy, from both a business and a contract perspective
- The chosen engineering approach and development strategy
- The strategy and approach for test and evaluation, for both developmental and operational testing (See CH 8–3.1. and CH 8–3.2. for additional information regarding interactions with the Chief Developmental Tester)
- Program management approach, including organization, processes and products
- External dependencies and agreements with other systems or organizations that may be in place
- Need date
- Availability of resources, including funds, personnel, facilities, etc.
- Program risks
- Risk management strategies

In addition to the SEP, the technical planning effort supports the development of the following documents:

- Work Breakdown Structure (see CH 3–4.1.1.1.) -- a framework for specifying program objectives
- Integrated Master Plan (see CH 3–4.1.1.2.) -- an event-based plan consisting of a hierarchy of program events that need to be accomplished
- Integrated Master Schedule (see CH 3–4.1.1.3.) -- an integrated, networked schedule that contains all lower-level tasks required to support program events

Other useful resources available to assist the PM and Systems Engineer in the Technical Planning process can be found in the "Guidance & Tools" section of the ODASD(SE) Policy and Guidance website.

CH 3–4.1.1.1 Work Breakdown Structure

The Work Breakdown Structure (WBS) represents the decomposition of both the scope of work and defines the hierarchically related product-oriented elements necessary to accomplish program objectives and develop required deliverables. It provides a product-oriented division of tasks by breaking down work scope for authorizing, tracking and reporting purposes. The WBS is defined, developed and maintained throughout the acquisition life cycle based on a disciplined application of the systems engineering (SE) process. The goal is to develop a structure that defines the logical relationship among all program elements to a specified level of indenture. Requirements for developing a WBS can be found in MIL-STD-881 (Work Breakdown Structures for Defense Materiel Items). MIL-STD-881 shall be used as required by the mandatory DI-MGMT-81861 (Integrated Program Management Report (IPMR)).

The WBS integrates technical, cost and schedule parameters, giving the Program Manager (PM) a tool to:

- Ensure the traceability of all program activities.
- Identify significant risk drivers.
- Forecast cost and schedule performance.
- Develop corrective action plans as needed.

130

An effective WBS takes into consideration several things. It should encompass the work defined by the project scope, and capture Government and contractor deliverables to provide adequate insight for effective program management. Keeping in mind that the definition of scope between elements should not overlap, a WBS dictionary should be created to clarify distinctions among all elements. These elements should also be defined in terms of outcomes, not actions, as decomposing planned outcomes to the desired end of the program provides a more accurate measure of cost, schedule and technical progress.

There are two types of WBS: (1) the Program WBS; and (2) the Contract WBS (including flow-down reporting requirements). The Program WBS provides a framework for specifying program objectives. Each WBS element provides logical summary levels for assessing technical accomplishments, supporting the required event-based technical reviews and measuring cost and schedule performance. It represents the entire program from the Government PM's responsibility, including elements such as program office operations, manpower, government furnished equipment and government testing. A Program WBS is typically defined to level 3 or level 4 of indenture to provide a summary level, or starting point, for the Contract WBS that does not constrain the contractor in developing the program. However, the Program WBS may be defined to a lower level of indenture if the Government considers certain elements as high-cost, high-risk, or high-interest.

The Contract WBS, of which there may be several for a single program, governs the elements of a specific contract. It is the Government-approved WBS for program reporting purposes that represents an agreement between the Government and contractor addressing the expected hierarchy of outcomes at a level that can be analyzed and assessed, and incorporates all program elements, such as hardware, software, services, data and facilities, which are the contractor's responsibility. This includes the contractor's discretionary extension to lower levels, in accordance with Government direction and the contract Statement of Work (SOW). The Contract WBS usually requires a contract modification before approved changes can be incorporated, and whenever it is revised, traceability to the previous version needs to be maintained.

The WBS displays and defines the program and product, or products, to be developed and/or produced and provides a common thread for the Earned Value Management System (EVMS), the Integrated Master Plan (IMP) and the Integrated Master Schedule (IMS) to better understand and communicate program cost and schedule performance. The PM, in conjunction with the Systems Engineer, should develop a comprehensive WBS early in the program to support planning, cost and schedule estimation and risk management activities. Additional information about EVMS can be found in CH 1–4.2.16.

Planning program tasks by WBS element serves as the basis for mapping development of the technical baseline and aids in estimating and scheduling resource requirements (people, facilities and equipment). By breaking the system into successively smaller pieces, the PM ensures system elements and enabling system elements are identified in terms of cost, schedule and performance goals, thereby reducing overall program risk in the process.

CH 3–4.1.1.2 Integrated Master Plan

The Integrated Master Plan (IMP) is a high-level, event-driven, schedule and planning document that outlines the events, significant accomplishments and accomplishment criteria needed for successful program completion. The IMP should document the tasks required to define, develop and deliver a system, and to facilitate operation and support of that system throughout its life cycle. As a top-level document, the IMP should encompass all Integrated Product Team (IPT) and Work Breakdown Structure (WBS) elements. It should also depict the hierarchy of program activities, and relate each major program event to supporting events.

In an environment of competitive contracts, the successful Offeror's IMP should be included in the resulting contract for use in execution of the program. As a result, the IMP becomes a contractual document and forms the basis for schedule execution.

CH 3–4.1.1.3 Integrated Master Schedule

The Integrated Master Schedule (IMS) is a low-level, event-driven, calendar-based schedule and planning document that describes the entire scope of work, including all government, contractor and sub-contractor activities, necessary for successful program execution, from start to finish. It is a logical extension of the IMP, depicting the scope of work as an integrated hierarchy of milestones, tasks, subtasks, activities and deliverables. It should also describe the work required to complete the effort in sufficient detail, to include start date, event duration and finish date for all activities, to organize the overall hierarchical flow of work. This assists the Program Manager (PM) in comprehending the links and relationships between various activities, including the resources supporting them.

Together, the PM and Systems Engineer should monitor development of the IMS to ensure that activity durations and resources are reasonable. This oversight aids analysis of program risks and development of mitigation plans in the event that any of those activities become delayed or over budget. As such, the IMS serves as a tool for time-phasing work, assessing technical performance, and once baselined, forms the framework for Earned Value Management System (EVMS). IMS activities should be directly traceable to the IMP and the WBS, and together allow integrated assessments of cost, schedule and technical performance, along with associated risks.

For effective program insight, management and control, an IMS should:

- Establish a schedule with baseline start and finish dates
- Identify critical path, milestones and activities
- Indicate significant constraints and relationships
- Provide current status and forecast completion dates of scheduled work to enable comparison of planned and actual program accomplishments
- Provide horizontal traceability of interrelationships among activities
- Provide interdependent sequencing of all work authorized on the contract in a manner compatible with SOW, WBS, IMP events and key acquisition milestones

Figure 31: IMP/IMS Hierarchy and Content

132

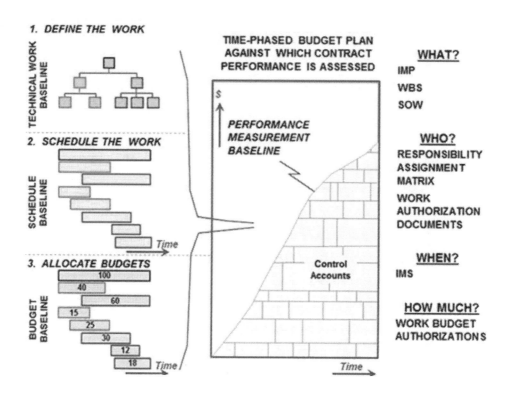

Figure 31 depicts a hierarchical approach to developing and populating the IMS. The PM should review the IMS for completeness, consistency and compatibility on a routine basis. During these reviews, the PM should evaluate logic relationships and event durations to ensure they align with program goals, identify and account for risk and plan for desired mitigation. The PM and Systems Engineer should ensure that the System Engineering Plan (SEP) and other technical planning documents capture technical review criteria, event-driven outcomes and mechanisms for assessing technical maturity and risk in a manner consistent with the tasks and schedules delineated in the IMS.

It may be helpful to view the IMS as a collection of subordinate, interrelated schedules. In alignment with the WBS, the IMS has both a higher-level component, focused on Government events and activities, and a lower-level component, detailing elements for contracted activities and tasks. Consistent and in alignment with the Government-approved IMP, the IMS is baselined after approval of the contractor(s)' schedules at the Integrated Baseline Review (IBR). For major acquisition programs, the IBR is typically conducted within 6 months after the contract award to facilitate an understanding and agreement of the detail needed to manage the effort. Once the IBR is complete and the baseline IMS is established, the change management process should be implemented to approve subsequent modifications to the IMS. Contractor IMS submissions to the Program Office should comply with DI-MGMT-81861 (Integrated Program Management Record (IPMR)), with each submission updated to reflect actual start and actual finish of activities, to date.

Early identification of, and adherence to, critical path tasks is essential to ensure the program remains on track toward achieving schedule and cost goals. The IMS provides linkages between tasks to capture the relationship of predecessor and successor tasks required to initiate or complete major tasks. It facilitates stakeholder communication by establishing expectations and dependencies, particularly for tasks performed by different organizations and identifies all risk mitigation activities. The IMS helps the PM and Systems Engineer:

133

- Identify a baseline for program monitoring, reporting and control.
- Plan, execute and track risk mitigation efforts.
- Support resource analysis and leveling, exploration of alternatives and cost/schedule trade-off studies.
- Provide a roadmap for stakeholders.

The Integrated Master Plan and Integrated Master Schedule Preparation and Use Guide provides additional guidance on developing and implementing these technical planning tools.

CH 3–4.1.1.4 Schedule Risk Assessments

A Schedule Risk Assessment (SRA) predicts the completion date of a target milestone or program event by assigning a best, worst and most likely outcome to each task for that event. By quantitatively assigning risk to each event in the baseline schedule and identifying the potential impact of uncertainty in meeting program completion, an SRA can help the Program Manager (PM) determine the likelihood of an acquisition program meeting its proposed deadlines by evaluating schedule risks and applying estimated duration ranges.

Monte Carlo is one technique used to generate multiple runs simulating project progress. It performs a schedule risk assessment against a baseline program plan for all non-summary, non-milestone tasks (see Figure 32). Each simulation run generates a duration for every project activity, given an uncertainty profile previously defined by the contractor. The quality of the assessment depends on the quality of the input data. Knowledge about the potential impact of these estimation errors should be tracked in the project risk register or within the IMS (see CH 3–4.1.5. Risk Management Process).

When part of the contract, the DI-MGMT-81861 (Integrated Program Management Report IPMR specifies when SRAs should be performed. Contractors and subcontractors should perform an SRA on their schedule prior to an IBR, before processing an Over Target Baseline/Over Target Schedule, or as required by the contract. The results from an SRA inform management decisions, support what-if scenarios and provide input for mitigating risk.

Figure 32: Schedule Risk Assessment Histogram

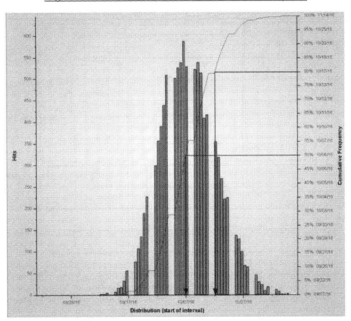

CH 3–4.1.2 Decision Analysis Process

The Decision Analysis process transforms a broadly stated decision opportunity into a traceable, defendable and actionable plan. It encompasses one or more discrete analyses at one or more lower (e.g., system element) levels and aggregates them into a higher-level view (e.g., system "scorecard" presentation) relevant to the decision maker and other stakeholders. Decision Analysis can be the central process for formulating, managing and executing an effective and efficient program at any point in the life cycle.

Decision Analysis and associated trade studies should be integrated with, and mutually supportive of, aspects of several SE processes in the early stages of the program, in particular:

- Technical Planning (see CH 3–4.1.1.)
- Technical Assessment (see CH 3–4.1.3.)
- Stakeholder Requirements Definition (see CH 3–4.2.1.)
- Requirements Analysis (see CH 3–4.2.2.)
- Architecture Design (see CH 3–4.2.3.)

A well-executed decision analysis or trade-off analysis helps the Program Manager (PM) and the Systems Engineer understand the impact of various uncertainties, identify one or more course(s) of action that balance competing objectives and objectively communicate the results to decision makers. As such, it provides the basis for selecting a viable and effective alternative from among many under consideration.

Decision Analysis applies to technical decisions at all levels, from evaluating top-level architectural concepts to sizing major system elements to selecting small design details. The breadth and depth of the analysis should be scaled to both the scope of the decision and the needs and expectations of the decision maker(s).

Activities and Products

Decision Analysis teams generally include a lead analyst with a suite of reasoning tools, subject matter experts with access to appropriate models and analytical tools and a representative set of end users and other stakeholders. A robust Decision Analysis process acknowledges that the decision maker has full responsibility, authority and accountability for the decision at hand.

Decision Analysis typically includes the following steps:

- Identifying the problem or issue.
- Reviewing requirements and assumptions to establish the overall decision context.
- Framing/structuring the decision in terms of supporting program/project objectives.
- Identifying methods and tools to be used in the analyses (see CH 3–2.4. Tools, Techniques and Lessons Learned).
- Developing decision criteria (objectives and measures), criteria weight and associated rationale.
- Identifying, recording and tracking assumptions.
- Identifying and defining alternatives to be evaluated (for high-level analyses, these are generally directed, although additional ones may arise during the course of the analysis).
- Analyzing and assessing alternatives against criteria.
- Synthesizing results.
- Analyzing sensitivities.
- Developing decision briefing with action/implementation plan(s).
- Making appropriate recommendation(s) to decision maker as expected/requested.

Sound recommendations and action plans are the principal output of a well-framed and well-executed Decision Analysis process. The ability to drill down quickly from overall trade-space visualizations to detailed analyses that support the synthesized views is particularly useful to decision makers in understanding the basis of observations and conclusions.

135

CH 3–4.1.3 Technical Assessment Process

The Technical Assessment process provides a fact-based understanding of the current level of product knowledge, technical maturity, program status and technical risk by comparing assessment results against defined criteria. These assessment results enable a better understanding of the health and maturity of the program, giving the Program Manager (PM) a sound technical basis upon which to make program decisions.

Disciplined technical assessment activities begin early in a system's life cycle. These activities begin by examining the status of development planning activities and efforts in the Materiel Solution Analysis (MSA) phase. During the Technology Maturation and Risk Reduction (TMRR) and Engineering and Manufacturing Development (EMD) phases, technical assessments provide a basis for tracking development of the system and lower-level system element designs. Disciplined technical assessments support the establishment of the various baselines and achievement of system verification. Technical assessment activities also include manufacturing and production activities during the Production and Deployment (P&D) phase and continue through the Operations and Support (O&S) phase to support reliability growth and sustainment engineering efforts.

The PM and Systems Engineer evaluate technical maturity in support of program decisions at the key event-driven technical reviews and audits (see CH 3–3.3. Technical Reviews and Audits) that occur throughout the acquisition life cycle. The PM and Systems Engineer use various measures and metrics, including Technical Performance Measures (TPM) and leading indicators, to gauge technical progress against planned goals, objectives and requirements. (See CH 3–4.1.3.1. Technical Performance Measures for more information.)

Technical assessments against agreed-upon measures enable data-driven decisions. Evidence-based evaluations that communicate progress and technical risk are essential for the PM to determine the need for revised program plans or technical risk mitigation actions throughout the acquisition life cycle.

Technical Assessment provides:

- An evaluation of the program's technical progress measured against the expected/planned performance for that period of time.
- An objective means of identifying, quantifying and monitoring a system's technical risks.
- A rigorous method to help define corrective actions that may be needed to address and resolve identified technical risks.

Activities and Products

The PM should ensure that technical assessments routinely occur throughout the life cycle on a reporting timeline that supports forecasting and timely resolution of risks -- informing decision makers of technical progress to plan and supporting EVMS. Some elements of technical assessments should be done on a monthly basis to inform programmatic attention, while other assessments may be quarterly or yearly. In all cases the assessment timelines should allow for tracking trends over time to show stability and impact of correction actions before major reviews and milestones. The PM should ensure that assessments are appropriately contracted, resourced and staffed, and include appropriate stakeholder and subject matter expert participation.

Technical assessment products should form the basis of both the input criteria as well as the output of event-driven criteria for Technical reviews and audits (see CH 3–3.3. Technical Reviews and Audits). For example, percentage completion of documents/drawings could be entrance criteria for the review, and the output is an objective assessment of technical progress, maturity and risk. Technical assessments need to be considered as part of all SE processes (see CH 3–4. Additional Planning Considerations); all SE processes support activities that contribute to the assessment of program status, technical maturity, and risk in various areas (e.g., schedule, technology, manufacturing, and/or threat).

The PM should approve the Technical Assessment products for the program as part of three documents: (1) the performance measurement baseline (PMB) (see CH 1–4.2.16.2.1.) to capture time-phased

136

measures against the Work Breakdown Structure (WBS) (see CH 3–4.1.3.1. Technical Performance Measures); (2) a resource-allocated Integrated Master Schedule (IMS) (see CH 3–4.1.1.3.); and (3) the Systems Engineering Plan (see CH 3–2.2.) to govern the overall measures and metrics to be collected, update cycle, tasking, control thresholds and expected analysis.

The Systems Engineer assists the PM in planning and conducting the Technical Assessment process. This assistance may include advising on technical reviews and audits, defining the technical documentation and artifacts that serve as review criteria for each review/audit, and identifying technical performance measures and metrics. Specific activities should include:

- Establishing event-driven technical planning.
- Identifying appropriate measures and metrics.
- Conducting analyses to assess risks and develop risk mitigation strategies.
- Conducting assessments of technical maturity, process health and stability and risk to communicate progress to stakeholders and authorities at key decision points.
- Proposing changes in the technical approach to reduce the program's technical risks.
- Advising the PM on the program's technical readiness to proceed to the next phase of effort.
- Including decision maker stakeholders and subject matter experts as appropriate for reviews and audits.

Inputs to the Technical Assessment process should include approved program plans (e.g., Systems Engineering Plan, Acquisition Strategy (AS), Acquisition Program Baseline (APB), engineering products (i.e., TPMs, drawings, specifications and reports, prototypes, system elements and engineering development modules), and current performance metrics. Outputs may include various reports and findings (e.g., technical review reports, corrective actions, Program Support Assessment (PSA) findings or test reports).

CH 3–4.1.3.1 Technical Performance Measures

Technical performance measures and metrics (TPMs) are the method of collecting and providing information to Program Managers (PM) and Systems Engineers at routine intervals for decision making. Metrics are measures collected over time for the purpose of seeing trends and forecasting program progress to plan. TPMs encompass the quantifiable attributes of both the system's development processes and status, as well as the system's product performance and maturity. Early in the life cycle the TPMs may be estimated based on numerous assumptions and modeling and simulation. As the life cycle proceeds, actual demonstrated data replaces estimates and adds to the fidelity of the information. The insight gained can be at any level: the entire system, sub- system elements, enabling system elements, and other contributing mission (e.g. SoS) elements, as well as all of the SE processes and SE disciplines in use across the program.

The goal of having a robust TPM process is the ability for the PM, Systems Engineer and senior decision makers to: (1) gain quantifiable insight to technical progress, trends and risks; (2) empirically forecast the impact on program cost, schedule, and performance; and (3) provide measurable feedback of changes made to program planning or execution to mitigate potentially unfavorable outcomes. Additionally, if sufficient level of margin exists, then TPMs help identify trade space and can be used by PMs to balance cost, schedule and performance throughout the life cycle. The PM and SE should use TPM data as the basis of evidence to support entrance/exit criteria, incentives and direction given at technical reviews or milestone decisions. TPMs provide leading indicators of performance deficiencies or system risk.

Activities and Products

TPMs should be identified, tailored and updated in the SEP to fit the acquisition phase of the program. As the program progresses through the acquisition cycle TPMs should be added, updated or deleted. TPMs should be chosen that will both confirm the performance of the program in the current phase, but also provide leading indicators to future risk and issues in the next phase. In early phases of a program (e.g., Pre-Milestone A), a program should document a strategy for identifying, prioritizing and selecting TPMs. As the program matures, the program should document in a SEP the actual TPMs to be used. Further TPM guidance is provided in the DASD(SE) SEP outline.

137

TPM Categories and Definitions

Although the specific TPMs used to monitor a program are unique to that program, there are 15 categories that are of concern within the Department across all DoD acquisition programs. Having TPMs in each of these core categories is considered best practice for effective technical management. For each of the categories in Table 37: Core TPM Category Definitions, the PM and System Engineer should consider at least one TPM to address product and process performance. For some categories, such as "System Performance," there should be multiple TPMs to monitor forecasted performance of each Key Performance Parameter (KPP) and each Key System Attribute (KSA). The traceability of the TPMs to the core categories should be documented in the SEP. The following two figures address the organization of the core TPM categories as well as their definitions.

Table 37: Core TPM Category Definitions

Core TPM Category	Description of TPM
Mission Integration Management (SoS Integration /Interoperability)	Metrics evaluate the stability, maturity and adequacy of external interfaces to understand the risks from/to other programs integrating with the program toward providing the required capability, on-time and within budget. Understand the growth, change and correctness of the definition of external and internal interfaces. Evaluate the integration risks based on the interface maturity. (See DAG CH 3–4.2.5. Integration and CH 3–4.3.13. Interoperability and Dependencies)
Mission (End-to-End) Performance	Measure of the overall ability of a system to accomplish a mission when used by representative personnel in the environment planned in conjunction with external systems. Metrics should provide an understanding of the projected performance regarding a mission thread achieving the intended mission capability.
Reliability, Availability and Maintainability (RAM)	Metrics should evaluate the requirements imposed on the system to ensure operationally ready for use when needed, will successfully perform assigned functions and can be economically operated and maintained within the scope of logistics concepts and policies. (See CH 3–4.3.19. Reliability and Maintainability Engineering)
System Performance	Metrics should evaluate the performance of the system or subsystem elements in achieving critical technical attributes (e.g., weight) that contribute to meeting system requirements. There should be multiple TPMs to monitor forecasted performance of KPPs and KSAs.
System (Information) Security	System assurance evaluates the safeguarding of the system and the technical data anywhere in the acquisition process, to include the technologies being developed, the support systems (e.g., test and simulation equipment) and research data with military applications. (See CH 9–3.2.)
Manufacturing Management	Metrics should evaluate the extent to which the product can be manufactured with relative ease at minimum cost and maximum reliability. (See CH 3–4.3.18. Producibility, Quality, and Manufacturing Readiness)
Manufacturing Quality	System manufacturing quality metrics should track both quality of conformance and quality of design. Quality of conformances is the effectiveness of the design and manufacturing functions in executing the product manufacturing requirements and process specifications while meeting tolerances, process control limits and target yields for a given product group (e.g., defects per quantity produced). (See CH 3–4.3.18. Producibility, Quality, and Manufacturing Readiness)
Schedule Management	Include metrics to assess both schedule health (e.g., the DCMA 14-point health check), associated completeness of the WBS and the risk register. A

138

Core TPM Category	Description of TPM
	healthy, complete and risk-enabled schedule forms the technical basis for EVMS. Strong schedule metrics are paramount for accurate EVMS data. (See CH 1–4.2.16.)
Staffing and Personnel Management	Metrics should evaluate the adequacy of the effort, skills, experience and quantity of personnel assigned to the program to meet management objectives throughout the acquisition life cycle.
Resource Management	Metrics should evaluate the adequacy of resources and/or tools (e.g. models, simulations, automated tools, synthetic environments) to support the schedule. Also see Table 49: Product Support Considerations.
Software Development Management	Metrics should evaluate software development progress against the software development plan. For example, the rate of code generation (lines of code per man-hour). (See CH 3–2.3.1. Software)
Software Quality	Metrics should address software technical performance and quality (e.g., defects, rework) evaluating the software's ability to meet user needs. (See CH 3–2.3.1. Software)
Requirements Management	Evaluate the stability and adequacy of the requirements to provide the required capability, on-time and within budget. Includes the growth, change, completeness and correctness of system requirements. (See CH 3–4.1.4. Requirements Management Process)
Risk Management	Metrics should include the number of risks open over time or an aggregate of risk exposure (the potential impact to the performance, cost and schedule). (See CH 3–4.1.5. Risk Management Process)
Test Management	Metrics should include measures of the stability of the verification and validation process (e.g., number of test points, development of test vignettes and test readiness). (See CH 8–3.5.5.)

TPM Hierarchy

As shown in Figure 33, TPMs at the Management Decisional level may be allocated or decomposed into supporting details associated with subsystem assemblies along the lines of the WBS and/or organizational management hierarchies. As examples: a system weight TPM may be allocated to separate subsystem assemblies or a software productivity TPM may be added to effectively manage a high-risk subcontractor's development efforts.

Figure 33: TPM Hierarchy

139

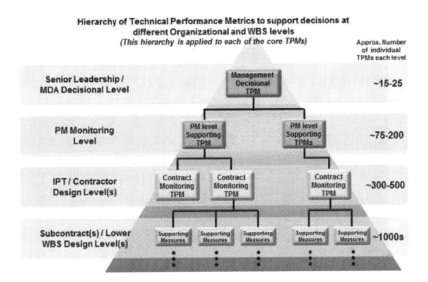

Hierarchy of Technical Performance Metrics to support decisions at
different Organizational and WBS levels
(This hierarchy is applied to each of the core TPMs)

TPM Characteristics

Figure 34 depicts the characteristics of a properly defined and monitored TPM to provide early detection or prediction of problems that require management. TPM reporting should be in terms of actual versus planned progress, plotted as a function of time and aligned with key points in the program schedule (e.g., technical reviews). A continuous (historical) plot of planned and actual values for each TPM, along with program planning information, enables assessment of performance trends (i.e., progress-to-plan relationships with respect to both objective and threshold values). As illustrated in the figure, there are four attributes of a good metric:

- The measure is quantifiable with defined criteria and consistent methods for determining a measurement point.
- The interval of measure collections is routine and on a cycle to support timely evaluation of corrective action and enable statistical forecasting and the overall condition by observing the change of the measured attribute over time.
- There is a curve of an expected plan, goal, control limits or threshold values over time for the appropriate phase to measure against as-to status, as well as to determine stability, and if the measure is in control. At a minimum, each review and assessment point should have a planned value.
- The attribute being measured should be strongly relevant to a program risk, a programmatic decision, a contractual incentive, a key developmental process or a predictor of required system performance. Strongly suggested are metrics that allow the forecasting of each KPP and KSA as well as known developmental process risks such as software development, schedule health, requirements stability and mission integration/interoperability.

Figure 34: Leading Indicators Influence Risk Mitigation Planning

140

Example of a well thought out TPM

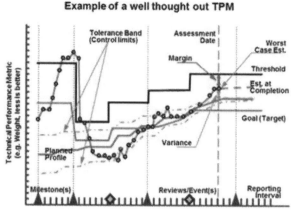

Worst Case Estimate	(WCE) Measured or estimated progress to be compared with planned progress. WCE accounts for contingency (see below)
Estimate at Completion	Forecasted WCE value of a TPM at designated completion
Planned profile	Time phased expected values (based on prior experience)
Tolerance Band	Management control limits representing projected level of error or control within the process
Goal (Target)	Desired objective profile values. Usually set to allow design trade space between Goal and Threshold
Threshold	Limiting acceptable profile values, usually the required or specified values
Variance	Difference between the Planned Profile and WCE
Margin	Difference between the WCE and Threshold value

To achieve an accurate status, TPM reporting should account for uncertainties such as measurement error and the immaturity of the item being measured. Allotted values for these uncertainties are termed "Contingency" and are used to adjust the Current Best Estimate to arrive at a Worst Case Estimate for purposes of comparison against the planned profile, Thresholds and Goals. For example, if a surrogate item is used to determine a measured value, it would warrant a greater contingency factored into the WCE than if the actual end item were used. Important to note is that Contingency is allocated as part of each WCE data point and typically decreases as the system and measurements mature, while Margin is not allocated. "Margin" is the amount of growth that can be accommodated while still remaining within the threshold (the remainder of Threshold minus WCE). Margin is potential trade space available to the PM to potentially offset under-achieving measures. Figure 35 depicts the relationship between Contingency, CBE, WCE, Threshold and Margin, as well as example criteria of how contingency changes as the system/testing matures.

Figure 35: TPM Contingency Definitions

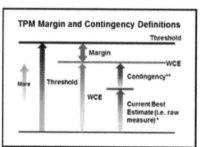

Example guidelines to allocate Contingency to each estimated measure to account for uncertainty

Basis for Current Best Estimate Value			Contingency
Maturity of item/process being measured	Estimating Technique	Estimating Technique (alternate)	Uncertainty to be included in the WCE
Paper Design	Analysis, legacy similarity	Guess	15%
Roll-up of Component-level items	Extrapolated tests, Bottom-up models	Analysis	10%
Integrated model/ prototype	Integration lab demo	Modeling	7%
Test article	Representative test	Demo	4%
Final article	End-to-end test in real environment (e.g., OT&E)	Test	0%

For a data collection point determine the worst case (largest contingency) associated with the applicable item maturity or estimating technique. Apply that contingency percentage to the current best estimate to arrive at the WCE for that collection interval. An example is highlighted: A representative test is done with a roll-up of components. This results in a worst case Contingency of 10%, resulting in: WCE = CBE +10%

* Current Best Estimate value is the raw estimate of the metric determined either by prediction, analysis, direct measurement, and/or bottoms-up estimation without consideration for error.
** Contingency accounts for the uncertainty in estimation and immaturity of the item being measured.

141

CH 3–4.1.3.2 Program Support Assessments

The Office of the Deputy Assistant Secretary of Defense for Systems Engineering (ODASD(SE)) conducts Program Support Assessments (PSAs) of Major Defense Acquisition Programs (MDAP) and Major Automated Information System (MAIS) programs and other programs as directed by the DAE to help shape the program's technical planning and management approaches. Like any independent review, the PSA prevents problems by early recognition of risks and identification of proposed mitigation activities. PSA requirements appear in DoDI 5000.02, Enc 3, sec. 20. The assessments are designed to help Program Managers (PMs) shape technical planning and improve execution by providing actionable recommendations and by identifying engineering and integration risks as well as mitigation activities.

DoD Components will provide access to all Major Defense Acquisition Programs (MDAPs) and Major Automated Information Systems (MAIS) program records and data, including technical review artifacts, classified, unclassified, competition sensitive, and proprietary information that the DASD(SE) considers necessary to carry out these assessments within the scope of DoD Instruction 5134.16. ODASD(SE) personnel conducting PSAs will possess proper identification, personnel security clearance (as required), Non-Disclosure Agreement (NDA) (as required), and need to know. Early conduct of PSAs should help the PM identify and resolve any program planning or execution issues well before major program decisions. Table 38 lists important PSA attributes.

Table 38: PSA Attributes

Cross-functional	<ul><li>No "stovepipes"</li><li>All reviewers look at multiple areas</li><li>All observations and comments are adjudicated with the entire team and program office</li></ul>
Multidisciplinary	<ul><li>Wide range of functional representation (internal ODASD(SE), AT&L, consultants)</li><li>Wide range of reviewer expertise</li><li>Multiple reviewers look at each area</li></ul>
Independent	<ul><li>Minimize "program expert" bias</li><li>No Government or contractor competitors</li><li>No program advocates or antagonists</li></ul>
Consistent	<ul><li>Application of common criteria derived from policy and guidance ensure all potential risks, issues, and opportunities are considered</li><li>Treat all programs equally and fairly</li></ul>
Tailorable	<ul><li>Adapt to type of review</li><li>Adapt focus on identified challenges</li></ul>

The Service (SAE, PEO, PMO) can request similar non-advocate reviews, which may serve as independent technical risk peer reviews. These assessments can be tailored for a specific request, and results are provided only to the requester.

Activities and Products

When practical, the initial PSA occurs nine to twelve months before a milestone decision review; follow-up engagements in concert with scheduled program activities and a final engagement (two to three months before the milestone), which assesses the implementation of key recommendations and the mitigation of risks in order to improve program planning and execution. The PSA typically consists of two- to three-day visits to the program office (and developer(s) as applicable).

PSAs focus on all SE processes appropriate to the life cycle phase but are broader in scope to consider all aspects of acquisition management, including resource planning, management methods and tools, earned value management, logistics and other areas. The Defense Acquisition Program Support (DAPS)

142

Methodology is a source for tailorable criteria and review questions and helps ensure consistency in reviews. The DAPS Methodology includes:

- Mission capabilities/requirements generation
- Resources
- Management
- Technical planning and process
- Program performance

Insights from PSAs aid the development of the Systems Engineering Plan (SEP) (see CH 3–2.2. Systems Engineering Plan) as well as the Request for Proposals (RFPs), and they ensure that the program has adequately addressed SE equities in these documents. After its engagement with the program in preparation for the pre-Milestone A PSA, the ODASD(SE) staff maintains continuous engagement with the program to monitor its execution of the planning reflected in the SEP. PSAs before Milestones B, C, and the Full-Rate Production decision can make use of information already vetted during SE WIPT meetings, various technical reviews (see CH 3–3.3. Technical Reviews and Audits), and program management reviews in order to help reduce the PSA burden on the program office and developer staff. PSA action items may be documented in the milestone review's Acquisition Decision Memorandum (ADM).

CH 3–4.1.4 Requirements Management Process
The Requirements Management process maintains a current and approved set of requirements over the entire acquisition life cycle. This helps ensure delivery of a capability that meets the intended mission performance, as stipulated by the operational user.

The end-user needs are usually identified in operational terms at the system level during implementation of the Stakeholder Requirements Definition and Requirements Analysis processes (see CH 3–4.2.1. Stakeholder Requirements Definition Process and 4.2.2. Requirements Analysis Process, respectively). Through the Requirements Management process, the Systems Engineer tracks requirement changes and maintains traceability of end-user needs to the system performance specification and, ultimately, the delivered capability. As the system design evolves to lower levels of detail, the Systems Engineer traces the high-level requirements down to the system elements through the lowest level of the design.

Requirements Management provides bottom-up traceability from any derived lower-level requirement up to the applicable source (system-level requirement) from which it originates. This bi-directional traceability is the key to effective management of system requirements. It enables the development of an analytical understanding of any system-wide effects of changes to requirements for a given system element, updating requirements documentation with rationale and impacts for approved changes. At the same time, bi-directional traceability ensures that approved changes do not create any "orphaned" lower-level requirements (i.e., that all bottom-up relationships to applicable system-level requirements remain valid after the change). Bi-directional traceability also ensures that higher-level requirements are properly flowed to lower-level requirements and system element designs so that there are no "childless parent" higher-level requirements (i.e., each high-level requirement is ultimately being addressed by lower-level requirements and system element designs).

Robust Requirements Management, implemented in synchronization with the program's Configuration Management process (see CH 3–4.1.6. Configuration Management Process), can help the program to avoid or mitigate unintended or unanticipated consequences of changes through rigorous documentation of the system performance specification. Thoughtful analysis and management of requirements can help lay the foundation for system affordability.

Activities and Products

The Program Manager (PM) should keep leadership and all stakeholders informed of cost, schedule and performance impacts associated with requirement changes and requirements growth.

The Systems Engineer establishes and maintains a Requirements Traceability Matrix (RTM), which captures all the requirements in the system performance specification, their decomposition/derivation and allocation history and rationale for all entries and changes. The requirements should be:

- Traceable to and from the stated end-user needs.
- Correctly allocated, with potential effects of proposed changes fully investigated, understood and communicated to the PM.
- Feasibly allocated, i.e., lower-level system elements cannot have the same or wider tolerance bands as those of the higher-level system elements into which they are incorporated.

All affected stakeholders and decision makers should fully understand the effects of proposed changes to requirements at the system or system element level before they accept any changes for incorporation into the design. The RTM provides significant benefits during trade-off analysis activities, since it captures the system-wide effects of proposed changes to established requirements.

In accordance with DoDI 5000.02, para 5.d.5.b, Component Acquisition Executives (CAE) establish Configuration Steering Boards (CSB), following Capability Development Document (CDD) validation, for Acquisition Category (ACAT) I and IA programs in development, production and sustainment. The CSB reviews all requirements changes and any significant technical configuration changes that have the potential to result in cost and schedule impacts to the program. In a continuous effort to reduce Total Ownership Cost (TOC), the PM, in consultation with the Program Executive Officer (PEO) and requirements sponsor, will identify and propose to the CSB recommended requirements changes, to include de-scoping options, that reduce the program cost and/or moderate requirements needed to respond to any threat developments. These recommended changes will be presented to the CSB with supporting rationale addressing operational implications.

CH 3–2.4. Tools, Techniques and Lessons Learned contains information about SE tools generally employed in the Requirements Management process. There are many commercial software packages specifically designed for the traceability aspect of Requirements Management, from top-level operational requirements down to the lowest-level system elements in the Work Breakdown Structure.

CH 3–4.1.5 Risk Management Process

The most important decisions to control risk are made early in a program life cycle. During the early phases, the program works with the requirements community to help shape the product concept and requirements. PMs and teams should understand the capabilities under development and perform a detailed analysis to identify the key risks. Where necessary, prioritizing requirements and making trade-offs should be accomplished to meet affordability objectives. Once the concept and requirements are in place, the team determines the basic program structure, the acquisition strategy and which acquisition phase to enter, based on the type and level of key risks.

Defense programs encounter risks and issues that should be anticipated and addressed on a continuing basis. Risk and issue management are closely related and use similar processes. Opportunity management is complementary to risk management and helps achieve should-cost objectives. Risks, Issues and Opportunities may be in areas including, but not limited to, technology, integration, quality, manufacturing, logistics, requirements, software, test and reliability. DoDI 5000.02, Enc 2, sec. 6.d requires the Program Manager (PM) to present top program risks and associated risk mitigation plans at all relevant decision points and milestones. DoDI 5000.02, Enc 2, sec. 6.d also specifies risk management techniques the PM is required to consider when developing the acquisition strategy. Technical risk management is addressed in DoDI 5000.02, Enc 3, sec. 5.

Technical, programmatic and business events can develop into risks, issues or opportunities, each with cost, schedule or performance consequences as shown in Figure 36.

Figure 36: Risk, Issues, and Opportunities

144

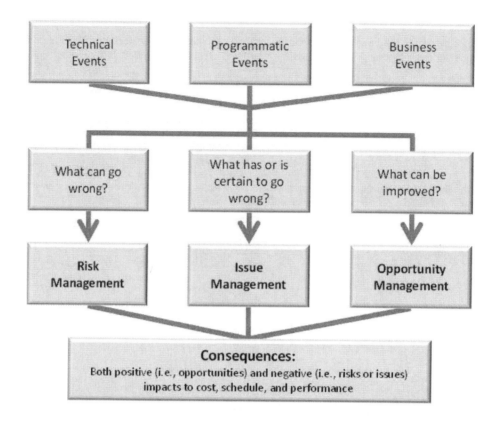

Statute requires PMs to document a comprehensive approach for managing and mitigating risk (including technical, cost and schedule risk) in the Acquisition Strategy (AS) for major defense acquisition programs and major systems. Per statute, the approach for major defense acquisition programs and major systems must identify the major sources of risk for each phase and must include consideration of risk mitigation techniques such as prototyping, modeling and simulation, technology demonstration and decision points, multiple design approaches and other considerations (P.L. 114-92 (SEC. 822 paras (a) and (b))).

The program's risk profile is the dominant consideration in deciding which contract type to pursue. The type of contract, cost-plus or fixed-price, fundamentally will affect the roles and actions of the government and industry in managing risk. Cost-plus contracts are best suited to situations in which the inherent technical risks are greater (typically during development). Fixed-price development is most appropriate when the requirements are stable and expected to remain unchanged, where technical and technology risks are understood and minimal and the contractor has demonstrated a capability to perform work of the type required.

Systems engineers support the PM in executing a risk management program. The systems engineer's primary concern is with technical risks, issues and opportunities. Programs are required to summarize the risk management approach and planning activities in the Systems Engineering Plan. The systems engineer should assess and describe cost and schedule implications of risks, issues and opportunities at technical reviews. Risk mitigation activities should be reflected in the program's Integrated Master Schedule and Integrated Master Plan.

The PM establishes and typically chairs the government Risk Management Board (RMB) as a senior group supporting risk management. The RMB usually includes the individuals who represent the various

145

functionalities of the program office, such as program control, the chief engineer, logistics, test, systems engineering, contracting officer as warranted, a user representative and others depending on the agenda.

The PM may document the risk management process in more detail in a Program Risk Process (PRP) -- a best practice. While the processes support risk management, the risk mitigation plans, which focus on risk reduction for individual risks (i.e., the output of the processes), are significantly more important. As a best practice, the programs may combine their Risk, Issue and Opportunity plans in a combined (RIO) document. A good PRP should:

- Explain the risk management working structure.
- Define an approach to identify, analyze, mitigate, and monitor risks, issues and opportunities across the program.
- Document the process to request and allocate resources (personnel, schedule and budget) to mitigate risks and issues.
- Define the means to monitor the effectiveness of the risk management process.
- Document the processes as they apply to contractors, subcontractors and teammates.

Separate from the PRP, as a best practice, the government and contractor should utilize a common or electronically compatible tool(s) to collectively identify, analyze, mitigate and monitor the program's risks, issues and opportunities. An example of a tool is the Risk Register. Other context for risk identification and management can be found in CH 3–4.3. Design Considerations. Two specific examples of risk context are Environment, Safety and Occupational Health (ESOH) and cybersecurity. CH 3–4.3.9. addresses ESOH and contains information regarding ESOH-related risk management. CH 3–4.3.24. addresses System Security Engineering and contains information on the Risk Management Framework for DoD Information Technology. The associated DoDI 8510.01 establishes processes for ensuring confidentiality, integrity and availability for DoD Information Technology programs. Programs should consider these specialized risk processes when creating their program risk process.

For additional information on managing risks, issues and opportunities, see the Department of Defense Risk, Issue, and Opportunity Management Guide for Defense Acquisition Programs available on the DASD(SE) web site.

CH 3–4.1.5.1 Risk Management

Risks are potential future events or conditions that may have a negative effect on achieving program objectives for cost, schedule, and performance. They are defined by:

- The undesired event and/or condition
- The probability of an undesired event or condition occurring
- The consequences, or impact, of the undesired event, should it occur

Risk planning identifies risks and develops a strategy to mitigate those risks. The risk assessment will help determine where to enter in the life cycle. The PM could recommend the program enter the life cycle at Milestone A, B, or C, depending on the maturity of the material solution and associated risks. Whatever the entry point, the solution has to be adequately matured as risks are retired throughout the program's acquisition life cycle.

If technology maturity or requirements stability risks exist, the PM should structure a program to enter the life cycle at Milestone A to conduct Technology Maturation and Risk Reduction (TMRR). Examples of TMRR phase risk reduction activities include:

- Building and testing competitive prototypes in order to validate achievability of the requirements and demonstrating the ability to integrate new technologies into mature architectures.
- Planning knowledge points to converge on results of systems engineering trade-off analysis, which balance cost (affordability), schedule and performance requirements.
- Proposing design to account for complexities of program interdependencies and interfaces.
- Identifying and assessing materials and manufacturing processes the program will require.

146

- Performing technical reviews through preliminary design to assess problematic requirements and risks that may prevent meeting operational requirements and cost/affordability targets.

If technologies are mature, the integration of components has been demonstrated, and the requirements are stable and achievable, the PM can consider entering directly at Milestone B to begin Engineering and Manufacturing Development (EMD) with acceptable risk. Examples of EMD phase risk reduction activities include:

- Performing technical reviews to finalize the design and verification testing to confirm it meets requirements.
- Performing manufacturing readiness assessments (MRA) to confirm the ability to produce the product.
- Performing development testing, which concentrates early testing on risks so there is adequate time for necessary re-design and re-test.
- Establishing and managing size, weight, power and cooling (SWAP-C) performance and R&M allocations for all subsystems.

If a materiel solution already exists and requires only military modification or orientation, the PM can structure the program to enter at Milestone C with a small research and development effort to militarize the product. Developmental testing should demonstrate the ability to meet requirements with a stable design. Example production phase risk reduction activities include:

- Conducting a thorough PCA and MRA to verify production does not introduce new risks.
- Identifying and assessing delivery schedule dependencies with external programs/users.
- Addressing risk associated with adapting the product to military needs, follow-on increments, or deferred activities.
- Identifying sustaining engineering needs and fund as appropriate.

Activities and Products

The Risk Management process encompasses five significant activities: planning, identification, analysis, mitigation and monitoring. PMs are encouraged to apply the fundamentals of the activities presented here to improve the management of their programs. Table 39 describes an overview of the focus of each activity and the products that are generally produced from the activity.

Table 39: Risk Management Process Activities

Activity	Answers the Question	Products
Risk Planning	*What is the program's risk management process?*	• Program Risk Process • Likelihood and consequence criteria • Risk tools • Tailored program risk training material
Risk Identification	*What can go wrong? Are there emerging risks based on TPM performance trends or updates?*	• List of potential risk statements in an "If…, then…" construct
Risk Analysis	*What is the likelihood of the undesirable event occurring and the severity of the consequences?*	• Quantified likelihood and consequence ratings, should the risk be realized • Approved risks entered and tracked in a risk register

147

Activity	Answers the Question	Products
Risk Mitigation	*Should the risk be accepted, avoided, transferred, or controlled? (Various terms are used to describe "Risk Mitigation" to include Risk Treatment or Risk Handling.)*	• Acquisition Strategy and SEP with mitigation activities • Activities entered into Integrated Master Schedule (IMS) • Burn-down plan with metrics identified to track progress
Risk Monitoring	*How has the risk changed?*	• Status updates of mitigation activities to burn-down plan • Risk register updates • Closure of mitigated risks

The planning process documents the activities to implement the risk management process. It should address the program's risk management organization (e.g., RMBs and working groups, frequency of meetings and members, etc.), assumptions and use of any risk management tools. The program should address risk training, culture, processes and tools.

Risk identification involves examining the program to identify risks and associated cause(s) that may have negative consequences. While various formal or informal methods can be used to identify risk, all personnel should be encouraged to do so.

Risk statements should contain two elements: the potential event and the associated consequences. If known, the risk statement should include a third element: an existing contributing circumstance (cause) of the risk. If not known, it is a best practice to conduct a root cause analysis. Risk statements should be written to define the potential event that could adversely affect the ability of the program to meet objectives. Using a structured approach for specifying and communicating risk precludes vague and/or inconsistent risk statements. An example method includes a two-part statement in the "if–then" format. See the Department of Defense Risk, Issue, and Opportunity Management Guide for Defense Acquisition Programs available on the DASD(SE) web site.

Risk analysis estimates the likelihood of the risk event occurring, coupled with the possible cost, schedule and performance consequences (if the risk is realized) in terms of impact to the program. Risk consequence is measured as a deviation against the program's performance, schedule or cost baseline and should be tailored for the program. PMs should consider the program's performance, schedule and cost thresholds and use these thresholds to set meaningful consequence criteria tailored to their program. Approved risks should then be entered into a risk register and a risk reporting matrix, as shown below in Figure 37.

Figure 37: Risk Reporting Matrix Example

148

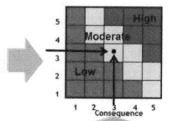

Level	Likelihood	Probability of Occurrence
5	Near Certainty	> 80% to ≤ 99%
4	Highly Likely	> 60% to ≤ 80%
3	Likely	> 40% to ≤ 60%
2	Low Likelihood	> 20% to ≤ 40%
1	Not Likely	> 1% to ≤ 20%

After conducting a risk analysis, the PM should decide whether the risk should be accepted (and monitored), avoided, transferred or controlled. PMs should alert the next level of management when the ability to mitigate a high risk exceeds their authority or resources. As an example, see concept of risk acceptance authority in the Military Handbook (MIL-HDBK) 882, para 4.3. Control seeks to actively reduce risk to an acceptable level in order to minimize potential program impacts. Risk control activities often reduce the likelihood of a risk event occurring, although consequences associated with a risk may be reduced if the program changes the design architecture or addresses binding constraints. Examples of top-level mitigation activities may include:

- System or subsystem competitive or risk reduction prototyping focused on burning down the most critical technical risks (e.g., technology, engineering, and integration).
- Deferring capability to a follow-on increment.
- Establishing events that increase knowledge of whether risks are successfully being abated.
- Limiting the number of critical technologies.
- Developing a realistic program schedule that is "event-" versus "schedule-" driven.
- Identifying off-ramps (i.e., a contingency plan to utilize mature technology in case technology is not developed successfully to meet critical program performance or schedule) for selected technologies in the IMS.
- Conducting systems engineering trade-off analyses leading up to preliminary design to support finalization of achievable requirements.

After the PM approves the mitigation strategy, the program should systematically track and evaluate the performance of risk mitigation plans against risk burndown plans as well as assess performance achievement through associated TPMs. The PM should update leaders with the current risk status at least quarterly, before major reviews and whenever there are significant changes.

Programs should integrate risk management with other program management tools. Risk mitigation activities should include assigned resources reflected in the IMP, IMS, and earned value management

149

(EVM) baselines. Programs should use appropriate Technical Performance Measures (TPM) and metrics to aid in monitoring the progress of mitigation plans.

Managing Cross Program Risks

Internal and external interfaces are significant sources of risk. Interdependent programs may have disconnects regarding resources; hardware and software development schedules; space, weight, power and cooling (SWAP-C) requirements; immature technologies; testing results; or other areas. Interdependent programs should have a process to manage interfaces and integration risks jointly, share information and foster a mutually supportive environment.

The following actions aid in managing activities when deploying a new system that depends on programs outside the Program Executive Officer's (PEO's) portfolio or from another Service:

- CAEs act as or appoint a technical authority within the Service(s) or OSD, who can influence critical interfaces with external programs.
- Develop Memorandums of Agreements (MOA) between PMs and PEOs to identify and manage critical interfaces.
- Set up an Interface Control Working Group to identify and resolve interface issues.
- Develop and maintain a synchronized schedule.
- Develop an integration plan that tracks interdependent program touch points, identifies risks and institutes a plan to mitigate them.

CH 3–4.1.5.2 Issue Management

Issues are unwanted events or conditions with negative effects that have occurred or are certain to occur (probability of one) in the future. Whereas risk management applies resources to lessen the likelihood and/or the consequence of a future event, issue management applies resources to mitigate consequences associated with a realized risk. As risks increase in probability, programs should anticipate their realization, as issues with early plans developed to limit the consequences.

The consequence of an issue should be addressed to prevent impeding program progress. Programs can take advantage of similar practices for identifying, analyzing, mitigating, and monitoring both risks and issues. Programs may evaluate whether a separate issue specific board is necessary or whether issue management may be executed more effectively and efficiently along with the RMB.

Issue Management encompasses five significant activities as outlined in Table 40.

Table 40: Issue Management Process Activities

Activity	Answers the Question	Products
Issue Planning	*What is the program's issue management process?*	• Issue management process • Issue management plan
Issue Identification	*What has or will go wrong?*	• Statements of the problems
Issue Analysis	*What is the consequence of the issue?*	• Cost, schedule and performance impacts on the program quantified • Issues entered and tracked in an issue register
Issue Mitigation	*Should the issue be ignored or controlled?*	• Approved courses of action (COA) to address the issue • Activities entered into IMS • Metrics identified to track progress

150

Activity	Answers the Question	Products
Issue Monitoring	*Has the issue changed?*	• Status updates of COA activities • Issue tracking sheet updated • Closure of issue

Approved issues should be analyzed using the program's risk management consequence criteria, and the results entered into an issue tracking register. Unlike risks, no evaluation of issue likelihood is necessary. Issues should be reported in a matrix as in Figure 38.

<u>Figure 38: Issue Reporting Matrix</u>

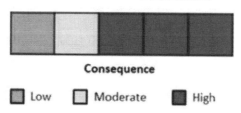

Consequence

☐ Low   ☐ Moderate   ■ High

The issue management approach should identify problems, assess the severity and urgency of their possible impact on the program and develop associated closure plans. PMs and Systems Engineers should develop a course of action, similar to that described in <u>CH 3–4.1.5.1.</u> Risk Management, to address and manage program issues with resourced action plans, as appropriate. Mitigation options include ignoring the issue, accepting the consequences without further action based on the results of a cost/schedule/performance business case analysis and controlling the issue by implementing a plan to reduce issue consequences. Issues should be reviewed during the program office and contractor's regularly scheduled meetings. As with risks, mitigation activities should be included in the program IMS and the tracking register.

CH 3–4.1.5.3 Opportunity Management
An opportunity is a potential future benefit to the program's cost, schedule, and/or performance baseline. Program Managers (PMs) and Systems Engineers should use opportunity management to identify, analyze, manage, and monitor initiatives that can capture these opportunities and achieve should-cost goals.

Opportunity management encompasses the activities as outlined in Table 41.

Table 41: Opportunity Management Process Activities

Activity	Answers the Question	Products
Opportunity Planning	*What is the program's opportunity management process?*	• Opportunity management process • Opportunity management plan
Opportunity Identification	*What can be improved?*	• Statements of the opportunity

151

Activity	Answers the Question	Products
Opportunity Analysis	*What is the business case analysis of the opportunity?*	• Benefits quantified in terms of cost, schedule and performance • Cost and likelihood to achieve benefit understood • Cost-benefit analysis report • Opportunity entered into register
Opportunity Management	*Should the opportunity be pursued, reevaluated or rejected?*	• Allocated resources to pursue opportunity • Activities entered into IMS • Metrics identified to track progress
Opportunity Monitoring	*How has the opportunity changed?*	• Status updates of management activities • Opportunity tracking sheet updated • Closure of opportunity

Once a capture plan is approved, the program should assign an owner and track it in an opportunity register. The engineering team usually leads or assists with a cost, schedule and performance business case analysis for each potential opportunity. Opportunities with sufficient potential should be evaluated relative to the potential management options of pursue, defer to reevaluate or reject. Programs can also plan parallel on-ramps for research and development activities that might provide opportunities.

The business case analysis should address the potential benefit as well as the resources required and likelihood of achieving the benefit. Management activities should be included in the register and inserted into the program Integrated Master Schedule in order to track progress to plan. Once in place, the program office should monitor the plan by collecting actual cost versus planned cost, schedule, performance and benefit information. The potential changes in the opportunity status are tracked, as in Figure 39 and management plans adjusted as required.

Figure 39: Opportunity Tracking Matrix Example

Opportunity	Likelihood	Cost to Implement	Return on Investment					Program Priority	Management Strategy	Owner	Expected Closure
			Monetary			Schedule	Performance				
			RDT&E	Procurement	O&M						
Opportunity 1: Procure Smith rotor blades instead of Jones rotor blades.	Mod	$3.2M			$4M	3 month margin	4% greater lift	#2	Reevaluate - Summarize the mitigation plan	Mr. Bill Smith	March 2017
Opportunity 2: Open Architecture Cockpit	Mod	$2.2M		$8.2M	$6M			#3	Defer	Ms Dana Jones	May 2017
Opportunity 3: Cheaper composite mounting plates	High	$211K		$0.4M	$3.6M	4 months less long-lead time needed	15 lbs less weight	#1	Summarize the mitigation plan to realize the opportunity	Ms. Kim Johnson	January 2017

CH 3–4.1.6 Configuration Management Process

The Configuration Management process establishes and maintains the consistency of a system's functional, performance and physical attributes with its requirements, design and operational information and allows technical insight into all levels of the system design throughout the system's life cycle.

152

Effective configuration management supports the establishment and maintenance of the functional, allocated and product baseline. Establishing rigorous configuration control enables the successful development, test, production, delivery and sustainment of the needed capability to the end user.

Configuration Management activities support:

- Traceability of designs to requirements.
- Proper identification and documentation of system elements, interfaces, and interdependencies.
- Timely and thorough vetting and disposition of change requests.
- Control and documentation of approved changes to baselines
- Proper and timely incorporation of verified changes in all affected items and documentation.
- Consistent and appropriate provisions in the Engineering Change Proposal (ECP) and related contract actions.
- Consistency between a product and its design requirements, supporting documentation and associated production and sustainment systems.
- A complete audit trail of design decisions and modifications.
- Continued assurance of system supportability and interoperability, consistent with the approved acquisition and life-cycle sustainment strategies.

Configuration Management facilitates the orderly development of a system through establishment of the technical baseline (including the functional, allocated and product baselines), and their assessment and approval at various technical reviews and audits. A baseline is an agreed-upon description of the attributes of a product at a point in time, which serves as a basis for change. Upon approval, the technical baseline documentation is placed under formal configuration control. Through Configuration Management, the program identifies, controls and tracks changes to the technical baseline, ensuring changes occur only after thorough assessments of performance, cost and schedule impacts, as well as associated risks.

The following baselines are critical to executing Configuration Management:

- Functional Baseline: Describes the system's performance (functional, interoperability and interface characteristics) and the verification required to demonstrate the achievement of those specified characteristics. It is directly traceable to the operational requirements contained in the Initial Capabilities Document (ICD). The Program Manager (PM) establishes Government control of the functional baseline at the System Functional Review (SFR) and verifies it through Functional Configuration Audits (FCA) leading up to the system-level FCA or the System Verification Review (SVR). Attributes of the functional baseline include:
  o Assessed to be achievable within cost and schedule constraints
  o Documentation of established interfaces between functional segments
  o Documented performance requirements traced to (draft) Capability Development Document (CDD) requirements
  o Reflects design considerations and clear linkage in the systems of systems (SoS) context
  o Documented verification requirements
- Allocated Baseline: Describes the functional and interface characteristics for all system elements (allocated and derived from the higher-level product structure hierarchy) and the verification required to demonstrate achievement of those specified characteristics. The allocated baseline for each lower-level system element (hardware and software) is usually established and put under configuration control at the system element Preliminary Design Review (PDR). This process is repeated for each system element and culminates in the complete allocated baseline at the system-level PDR. The PM then verifies the allocated baseline at the FCA and/or SVR. Attributes of the allocated baseline include:
  o All system-level functional performance requirements decomposed (or directly allocated) to lower-level specifications (configuration items (CI) for system elements)
  o Uniquely identified CIs for all system elements at the lowest level of the specification tree
  o All interfaces, both internal (between element CIs) and external (between the system under development and other systems), documented in interface control documents

- o Verification requirements to demonstrate achievement of all specified functional performance characteristics (element CI to element CI level and at the system level) documented
  - o Design constraints documented and incorporated into the design
- Product Baseline: Describes the detailed design for production, fielding/deployment and operations and support. The product baseline prescribes all necessary physical (form, fit and function) characteristics and selected functional characteristics designated for production acceptance testing and production test requirements. It is traceable to the system performance requirements contained in the CDD. The initial product baseline includes "build-to" specifications for hardware (product, process, material specifications, engineering drawings and other related data) and software (software module design - "code-to" specifications). The initial system element product baseline is established and placed under configuration control at the system element Critical Design Review (CDR) and verified later at the Physical Configuration Audit. In accordance with DoDI 5000.02, Enc 3, sec. 8, the PM assumes control of the initial product baseline at the completion of the system-level CDR to the extent that the competitive environment permits. This does not necessarily mean that the PM takes delivery and acceptance of the Technical Data Package. Attributes of the product baseline include:
  - o Requirements Traceability Matrix (RTM) is complete.
  - o The detailed design (hardware and software), including interface descriptions, satisfies the CDD or any available draft Capability Production Document (CPD) and pertinent design considerations.
  - o Hardware, software and interface documentation are complete.
  - o Key product characteristics having the most impact on system performance, assembly, cost, reliability, ESOH and sustainment have been identified.
  - o Traceability from design documentation to system and system element verification requirements and methods is complete.
  - o Manufacturing processes that affect the key characteristics have been identified, and capability to meet design tolerances has been determined.

Activities and Products

The program office and developer share responsibility for planning, implementing and overseeing the Configuration Management process and its supporting activities. The distribution of responsibilities between the program office and the developer varies, based on the acquisition strategy and the life-cycle phase.

The PM approves the Configuration Management Plan and should ensure adequate resources are allocated for implementing Configuration Management throughout the life cycle. The PM assesses the impact of proposed changes to a baseline, approves changes -- usually through a Configuration Control Board (CCB) (see MIL-HDBK-61 (Configuration Management Guidance) and SAE-GEIA-HB-649 (Configuration Management Standard Implementation Guide) for additional information), and ensures proper documentation of decisions, rationale and coordination of changes.

The Systems Engineer ensures Configuration Management planning is complete, and should document details and activities in the program's Systems Engineering Plan (SEP) and the supporting Configuration Management Plan (CMP) (as appropriate). In accordance with DoDI 5000.02, Enc 3, sec. 8, the PM, with the support of the Systems Engineer, ensures that the configuration management approach is consistent with the Intellectual Property Strategy (See CH 3–4.1.7. Technical Data Management Process). The CM process described in the DoD-adopted standard American National Standards Institute/Electronic Industry Association (ANSI/EIA)-649, Configuration Management Standard, consists of five interrelated functions that, when collectively applied, allow the program to maintain consistency between product configuration information and the product throughout its life cycle. The five CM functions are:

- Configuration Management Planning and Management
- Configuration Identification
- Configuration Change Management
- Configuration Status Accounting

154

- Configuration Verification and Audit

In addition, the DoD-adopted standard EIA-649-1, Configuration Management Requirements for Defense Contracts, implements the principles outlined in ANSI/EIA-649B for use by defense organizations and industry partners during all phases of the acquisition life cycle. It makes provisions for innovative implementation and tailoring of specific configuration management processes to be used by system suppliers, developers, integrators, maintainers and sustainers.

CH 3–4.1.7 Technical Data Management Process

The Technical Data Management process provides a framework to acquire, manage, maintain and ensure access to the technical data and computer software required to manage and support a system throughout the acquisition life cycle (see CH 3–4.3.24. System Security Engineering for information regarding protection of critical program information). Key Technical Data Management considerations include understanding and protecting Government intellectual property and data rights, achieving competition goals, maximizing options for product support and enabling performance of downstream life-cycle functions. DoDI 5000.02, Enc 2, sec. 6.a contains Technical Data Management requirements for Acquisition Category (ACAT) I and II programs.

Acquiring the necessary data and data rights, in accordance with Military Standard (MIL-STD)-31000, for acquisition, upgrades, and management of technical data provide:

- Information necessary to understand and evaluate system designs throughout the life cycle.
- Ability to operate and sustain weapon systems under a variety of changing technical, operational, and programmatic environments.
- Ability to re-compete item acquisition, upgrades, and sustainment activities in the interest of achieving cost savings; the lack of technical data and/or data rights often makes it difficult or impossible to award contracts to anyone other than the original manufacturer, thereby taking away much or all of the Government's ability to reduce total ownership costs (TOC).

Activities and Products

The Program Manager (PM) and Systems Engineer, in conjunction with the Product Support Manager, should ensure that life-cycle requirements for weapon system-related data products and data rights are identified early and appropriate contract provisions are put in place to enable deliveries of these products. Figure 40 shows the activities associated with Technical Data Management, including:

- Identify Data Requirements

- Formulate the program's Intellectual Property (IP) Strategy and technical data management approach, with an emphasis on technical and product data needed to provide support throughout the acquisition life cycle. (See CH 1–4.2.18. for more information about Data Rights).
- Ensure that data requirements are documented in the IP Strategy; summarized in the Acquisition Strategy (AS) and presented with the Life-Cycle Sustainment Plan (LCSP) during the Operations and Support Phase; and submitted at each milestone before award of the contract for the next life-cycle phase.
- Based on the technical baseline, identify assemblies, subassemblies, and parts that are candidates for Government ownership of data rights. Include this information in AoAs, trade studies and as input to RFPs.
- Consider not only the immediate, short-term costs of acquiring the needed technical data and data rights but also the long-term cost savings resulting from the ability to compete production and logistics support activities and reduce TOC. Understand that the Government can possess either Government Purpose or Unlimited Rights to use many types of technical data and data rights, at no additional cost, based on the type of technical data and the source of funding used to generate the data (see DoD Open Systems Architecture Contract Guidebook for Program Managers for more information about data rights).

155

- Consider any requirements to acquire rights to production and sustainment tooling and facilities, including processes required to use this equipment. Where the government has acquired rights to specific parts, these rights do not necessarily also convey rights to the equipment or processes used to produce the parts.

- Acquire Data

- Use explicit contract Statement of Work (SOW) tasks to require the developer to perform the work that generates the required data. The content, format and quality requirements should be specified in the contract.
- Use current, approved Data Item Descriptions (DID) and Contract Data Requirements Lists (CDRL) in each contract to order the delivery of the required technical data and computer software.
- Consider obtaining data through an open business model with emphasis on having open, modular system architectures that can be supported through multiple competitive alternatives. The model may include modular open systems approaches as a part of the design methodology supported by an IP strategy, which may be implemented over the life cycle of a product. (See CH 3–2.4.1. Modular Open Systems Approach.)

- Receive, Verify and Accept Data

- Ensure verification of content, format, and quality of all required product-related data received from originators.
- Inspect contractually ordered data deliverables to ensure markings are in accordance with the relevant data rights agreements and DFARS clauses and contain appropriate distribution statements and/or export control statements.

Caution: Acceptance of delivered data not marked consistent with the contract can result in the Government "losing" legitimate rights to technical data and can incur significant legal liability on the Government and the individual Government employees. Regaining those rights generally requires costly and time-consuming legal actions.

- Store, Maintain and Control Data

- Budget for and fund the maintenance and upkeep of product data throughout the life cycle.
- An Integrated Data Environment (IDE) or Product Life-cycle Management (PLM) system allows every activity involved with the program to create, store, access, manipulate and exchange digital data.
- To the greatest extent practical, programs should use existing IDE/PLM infrastructure such as repositories operated by Commodity Commands and other organizations. (Program-unique IDEs are discouraged because of the high infrastructure cost; furthermore, multiple IDEs inhibit access, sharing and reuse of data across programs.)
- Ensure all changes to the data are made in a timely manner and are documented in the program IDE or PLM system.

- Use and Exchange Data

Plan for and establish methods for access and reuse of product data by all personnel and organizations that perform life-cycle support activities.

Figure 40: Data Management Activities

156

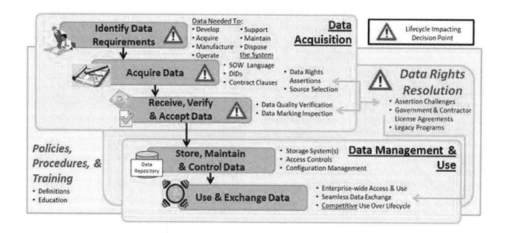

In support of the Government's requirement for a Technical Data Package (TDP), the PM should also consider all product-related data (e.g., technical manuals, repair instructions and design/analysis data) to:

- Allow logistics support activities.
- Better enable sustainment engineering.
- Apply, implement, and manage product upgrades.

Contractually deliverable data should be identified and ordered at the specific "data product" level, (e.g., two-dimensional drawings, three-dimensional Computer-Aided Design (CAD) models, technical manuals, etc.). Figure 41 provides a notional representation of different types of product-related data.

Caution: PMs and Systems Engineers should be aware that terms such as "technical data," "product data," and "TDP" are imprecise, not equivalent, and often incorrectly used interchangeably.

Resources for establishing and conducting Technical Data Management activities include but are not limited to:

- DoD 5010.12-M, Procedures for the Acquisition and Management of Technical Data
- Army Data and Data Right (D&DR) Guide
- Army Regulation 25-1 Army Information Technology
- Army Pamphlet 25-1-1 Army Information Technology Implementation Instructions
- Air Force Product Data Acquisition (PDAQ) guidance
- Air Force Technical Data and Computer Software Rights Handbook
- Navy Technical Manual SL150-AA-PRO-010/DMP - Data Management Program
- MIL-HDBK-245 (Preparation of Statement of Work (SOW))
- MIL-STD-963 (Data Item Descriptions)
- MIL-STD-31000 (Technical Data Packages)

Figure 41: Data Taxonomy

157

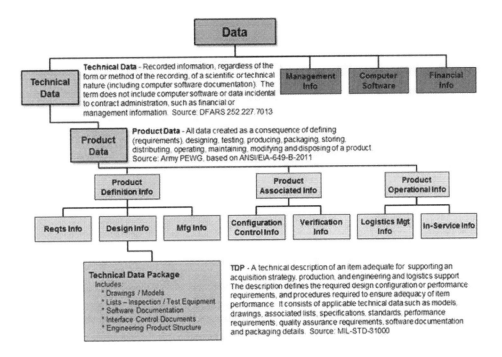

- Data Protection

The Program Manager is responsible for protecting system data, whether the data is stored and managed by the Government or by contractors. The DoD policy with regard to data protection, marking, and release can be found in:

- DoDD 5230.25
- DoDI 5230.24
- DoDM 5400.07
- DoDI 5200.01

Data containing information subject to restrictions are protected in accordance with the appropriate guidance, contract, or agreement. Guidance on distribution statements, restrictive markings and restrictions on use, release or disclosure of data can be found in the DFARS (Subpart 252.227-7013 and 7014), and DoDI 5230.24.

When digital data are used, the data should display applicable restriction markings, legends and distribution statements clearly and visibly when the data are first opened or accessed. These safeguards not only ensure Government compliance regarding the use of data but also guarantee and safeguard contractor data delivered to the Government and extend responsibilities of data handling and use to parties who subsequently use the data.

P.L. 107-347 (SEC 208 para (b)) and DoDI 5400.16, "DoD Privacy Impact Assessment (PIA) Guidance" requires that PIA be conducted before developing or purchasing any DoD information system that collects, maintains, uses or disseminates personally identifiable information about members of the public, federal personnel, DoD contractors and, in some cases, foreign nationals. Available PIA guidance provides procedures for completing and approving PIAs.

158

All data deliverables should include distribution statements. Processes should be established to protect all data that contain critical technology information, as well as ensure that limited distribution data, intellectual property data or proprietary data are properly handled throughout the life cycle, whether the data are in hard-copy or digital format.

CH 3–4.1.8 Interface Management Process

The Interface Management process provides a framework to identify, define, manage and ensure compliance with internal and external system interfaces. The Interface Management process helps ensure that developers capture all internal and external interface requirements and requirements changes in accordance with the program's Configuration Management Plan. Materiel developers also should communicate interface information to their counterparts responsible for affected systems and system elements, and should plan for coherent testing to verify expected performance and, ultimately, operational performance.

Systems are composed of system elements and may operate as part of larger systems of systems (SoS). The design, definition and management of the physical and logical interfaces, both internal (communications between system elements) and external (communications between the system and other systems), are critical to program success. Both types of interfaces have become increasingly important as system complexity has increased, along with the demands for systems to operate in highly interdependent SoS environments (see CH 3–3.1.2. Systems of Systems). Interfaces play a critical role in all systems and systems of systems that interact to deliver a collective capability. Complex systems consist of numerous interfaces of various types. When the circumstances reach a point that the number and complexity of interfaces can no longer be managed effectively, poor interface configuration control can result in degraded system performance, affordability, sustainability and maintainability.

The use of standard interface specifications enables a modular and open systems approach (see CH 3–2.4.1. Modular Open Systems Approach). Modular, open systems with standardized interfaces facilitate innovation and competition in future technology insertion and refresh efforts for the system. When necessary to use a non-standard interface specification, acquiring the rights to the design as part of the program's Intellectual Property Strategy may be an enabling option.

Explicit management of the definition, development, implementation and test of internal and external interfaces, including any associated dependencies, helps ensure that systems operate as designed and meet stakeholder expectations throughout the life cycle. The DoD Architecture Framework (DoDAF) provides guidance on how to generate operational and system views that describe interface relationships in a manner common across the DoD user community. Interface management should consider programmatic issues (e.g., roles and responsibilities, funding and scheduling) in addition to the technical aspects of systems engineering (SE) and integration.

Activities and Products

Interface management is an iterative process: as knowledge of the system and system elements increases during design activities, verifiable lower-level requirements and interfaces are defined and refined. Materiel developers should assess impacts of the originally defined capabilities and interfaces, performance parameter thresholds and objectives and the overall system when defining and modifying interfaces.

The Program Manager (PM) and Systems Engineer should ensure that the program's interface management plan:

- Documents the system's internal and external interfaces and their requirement specifications.
- Identifies preferred and discretionary interface standards and their profiles.
- Provides justification for the selection and procedure for upgrading interface standards.
- Describes the certifications and tests applicable to each interface or standard
- Is consistent with the program's configuration management plan.

159

The PM and Systems Engineer should ensure that the developer documents all system interface requirements (see CH 3–4.1.4. Requirements Management Process), places them under appropriate levels of configuration management and makes them available to the appropriate stakeholders. These documented interface requirements serve critical functions at all levels of the system throughout the life cycle, including:

- Developing functional and physical architectures.
- Facilitating competitive bids.
- Enabling integration of systems and lower-level system elements.
- Supporting system maintenance, future enhancements, and upgrades.
- Providing input data for continuous risk management efforts.

The Systems Engineer responsible for interface management has numerous key tasks throughout the life cycle, including:

- Defining and establishing interface specifications.
- Assessing compliance of interfaces among configuration items composing systems or SoS.
- Monitoring the viability and integrity of interfaces within a system.
- Establishing an interface management plan to assess existing and emerging interface standards and profiles, to update interfaces and to abandon obsolete architectures.

The PM should establish an Interface Control Working Group (ICWG) composed of appropriate technical representatives from the interfacing activities and other interested participating organizations. The ICWG serves as a forum to develop and provide interface requirements, as well as to focus on detail interface definition and timely resolution of issues. In the SoS environment, external program offices and developers collaborate as members of the ICWG.

CH 3–4.2 Technical Processes
Whereas the technical management processes provide insight of, and control over, the technical development of a system throughout its life cycle, the technical processes are used to design, develop and analyze the system, system elements and enabling system elements required for integration, test, production, deployment, support, operation and disposal. The eight technical processes discussed in sections 4.2.1 through 4.2.8 provide a framework for ensuring and maintaining traceability between stakeholder requirements, systems design and the eventual delivered capability.

CH 3–4.2.1 Stakeholder Requirements Definition Process
The Stakeholder Requirements Definition process translates stakeholder capability needs into a set of technical requirements. The process helps ensure each individual stakeholder's requirements, expectations and perceived constraints are understood from the acquisition perspective. Failing to perform an exhaustive Stakeholder Requirements Definition process could result in significant requirements creep, rework due to misunderstanding of end-user needs, unexpected contract modifications, cost growth and schedule slip. The objective of this process is to help ensure that stakeholder requirements are feasible, balanced and fully integrated as more information is learned through requirements analysis.

Stakeholder Requirements Definition bridges the gap between the identification of a materiel need, described in the Joint Capabilities Integration and Development System (JCIDS) CJCSI 3170.01, and the acquisition of a materiel solution, governed by the Defense Acquisition System, i.e., DoDD 5000.01 and DoDI 5000.02. Defense Business Systems (DBS) do not employ JCIDS procedures for the development and validation of capability requirements documents (See DoDI 5000.75).

The Stakeholder Requirements Definition process complements Requirements Analysis and Architecture Design (see CH 3–4.2.2. Requirements Analysis Process and CH 3–4.2.3. Architecture Design Process, respectively). These three processes are recursively applied at each level of the system's specifications and then iteratively within each level throughout development.

160

The DoD Architecture Framework (DoDAF) provides an approach for DoD architecture development, presentation and integration for both warfighting operations and business operations and processes. For the Net Ready Key Performance Parameter (NR-KPP), the JCIDS manual specifies the data needed to elaborate, communicate, verify and validate a system's interoperability requirements and design. System architectural descriptions contain three primary viewpoints: Capability, Operational, and Systems. In the case of the NR-KPP, these viewpoints contain essential architecture data that describe a system's interoperability requirements and design from multiple perspectives. DoDAF provides a standardized approach for capturing and presenting this architectural data. This standardization facilitates improved communication and sharing of technical information among various stakeholders and across organizational boundaries.

The Program Manager (PM) and Systems Engineer are responsible for supporting the Stakeholder Requirements Definition process and should work with the end user to establish and refine operational needs, attributes, performance parameters and constraints documented in JCIDS documents.

Stakeholder Requirements Definition activities are performed throughout the acquisition life cycle and include the following activities:

- Elicit stakeholder capability objectives
  o Identify stakeholders who have an interest in the system and maintain relationships with the stakeholders and their organizations throughout the system's entire life cycle.
  o Elicit capability objectives from the stakeholders about what the system will accomplish and how well.
- Define stakeholder requirements
  o Define the perceived constraints on a system solution.
  o Define the relevant environment (including threat target and critical intelligence parameters per JCIDS Manual Page B-28) and support scenarios that can be used to analyze the operation of the system.
  o Define potential requirements that may not have been formally specified by any of the stakeholders.
- Analyze and maintain stakeholder requirements
  o Analyze requirements for specificity, completeness, consistency, measurability, testability and feasibility.
  o Negotiate modifications with stakeholders to resolve requirement discrepancies.
  o Validate, record and maintain stakeholder requirements throughout the system life cycle.
  o Support the Requirements Analysis process to establish and maintain a traceability matrix to document how the system requirements are intended to meet the stakeholder objectives and achieve stakeholder agreements.

The authoritative source for stakeholder requirements are documents produced via the JCIDS such as the Initial Capabilities Document (ICD), Capability Development Document (CDD), and the Capability Production Document (CPD). JCIDS analyzes gaps in existing and/or future warfighting operations and provides a process that allows the Joint Requirements Oversight Council to balance joint equities and make informed decisions on validation and prioritization of capability needs. In preparation for, and presentation at the CDD Validation or Requirements Decision Point, DoDI 5000.02, para 5.d.4 requires the PM to conduct a systems engineering trade-off analysis showing how cost varies as a function of the major design parameters. (Also, see CH 3–4.3.2. Affordability – Systems Engineering Trade-Off Analyses.)

CH 3–4.2.2 Requirements Analysis Process
The Requirements Analysis process results in the decomposition of end-user needs (usually identified in operational terms at the system level during implementation of the Stakeholder Requirements Definition process; see CH 3–4.2.1. Stakeholder Requirements Definition Process) into clear, achievable and verifiable requirements. As the system design evolves, Requirements Analysis activities support

161

allocation and derivation of requirements down to the system elements representing the lowest level of the design. The allocated requirements form the basis of contracting language and the system performance specification. The resultant system requirements are addressed at technical reviews and audits throughout the acquisition life cycle and captured in applicable program and systems engineering (SE) technical documentation.

The Requirements Analysis process objectives include:

- Linking the needs of the end users to the system, system elements and enabling system elements to be designed and developed.
- Defining a system that meets end-users' operational mission requirements within specified cost and schedule constraints.
- Providing insight into the interactions among various functions to achieve a set of balanced requirements based on user objectives.

The Requirements Analysis process provides:

- Translation of end-user needs (usually stated in operational terms) to unambiguous, verifiable and feasible system performance specification requirements.
- Incorporation of design considerations, including statutory and regulatory constraints (see CH 3–4.3. Design Considerations).
- Allocation of requirements from the system-level specification to the lowest-level system elements and enabling system elements.
- Rationale for specification requirements and their decomposition/allocation.
- A mechanism to support trade-off analyses between related requirements to provide maximized mission assurance within cost and schedule constraints.
- A framework for accurate assessment of system performance throughout the life cycle.

The process of defining, deriving and refining requirements proceeds as follows:

- Analyze user requirements.
- Translate end-user needs into basic functions.
- Develop a quantifiable set of performance requirements by defining the functional boundaries of the system in terms of the behavior and properties to be provided.
- Define each function that the system is required to perform.
- Define implementation constraints (stakeholder requirements or solution limitations).
- Translate performance requirements into specific system technical design requirements and functions.

The Requirements Analysis process is an iterative activity whereby system requirements are identified, refined, analyzed and traded to remove deficiencies and minimize the impacts of potential cost drivers to establish an agreed-to set of requirements coordinated with the appropriate stakeholders. Poorly written requirements can lead to significant problems in the areas of schedule, cost or performance, and can thus increase program risk. A well-crafted set of functional/performance requirements can then be translated into design requirements for the total system over its life cycle and can allow stakeholders to assess system performance during execution of the Verification and Validation processes (see CH 3–4.2.6. Verification Process and CH 3–4.2.7. Validation Process, respectively). Good requirements have the following attributes:

- Necessary
- Unique
- Unambiguous -- clear and concise
- Complete
- Consistent
- Technically feasible/achievable/obtainable
- Traceable

- Measurable/quantifiable
- Verifiable (e.g., Testable)
- Able to be validated
- Operationally effective
- Singular

The Requirements Analysis process ensures that requirements derived from user-specified capability needs are analyzed, decomposed, and functionally detailed across the system design. Early development and definition of requirements using the attributes listed above reduces development time, enables achievement of cost and schedule objectives and increases the quality of the final system. Requirements Analysis encompasses the definition and refinement of the system, system elements, enabling system elements and associated functional and performance requirements. The development of the functional baseline is largely a product of the Requirements Analysis process. All requirements are placed under configuration control, tracked and managed as described in the Requirements Management process and Configuration Management process (see CH 3–4.1.4. Requirements Management Process and CH 3–4.1.6. Configuration Management Process, respectively).

CH 3–4.2.3 Architecture Design Process

The Architecture Design process is a trade and synthesis method to allow the Program Manager (PM) and Systems Engineer to translate the outputs of the Stakeholder Requirements Definition and Requirements Analysis processes into alternative design solutions and establishes the architectural design of candidate solutions that may be found in a system model. The alternative design solutions may include hardware, software and human elements; their enabling system elements; and related internal and external interfaces. The Architecture Design process, combined with Stakeholder Requirements Definition and Requirements Analysis, provides key insights into technical risks early in the acquisition life cycle, allowing for early development of mitigation strategies. Architecture Design is integral to ensuring that multiple well-supported solutions are considered. The Architecture Design process supports analysis of design considerations and enables reasoning about key system aspects and attributes such as reliability, maintainability, survivability, sustainability, performance and total ownership cost.

Architecture design synthesizes multiple potential solutions from system performance requirements, evaluates those solutions and eventually describes the system down to the individual system element for implementation. The Architecture Design process is iterative and strives to seek a balance among cost, schedule, performance, and risk that still meets stakeholder needs. The development of the system architecture should adhere to sound systems engineering (SE) and conform to industry standards as applicable. The functional architecture should be part of the functional baseline, and the physical architecture should be part of the allocated and product baselines. The system architecture should be placed under configuration control and maintained in a robust repository that maintains the architecture descriptions and its relationships to each of the baselines. This control provides the Systems Engineer with a means of ensuring consistency of the system architecture definition throughout the acquisition life cycle.

The functional architecture provides the foundation for defining the system architecture through the allocation of functions and sub-functions to hardware/software, databases, facilities and human operations to achieve its mission. The physical architecture consists of one or more product structures, or views, of the physical solution. The product structure may consist of conceptual design drawings, schematics and/or block diagrams that define the system's form and the arrangement of the system elements and associated interfaces. The DoD Architecture Framework (DoDAF) provides guidance on how to generate operational and system views that describe interface relationships in a manner common across the DoD user community (see the DoD CIO DoDAF page for additional information).

The development of the physical architecture is an iterative and recursive process and evolves together with the functional requirements and functional architecture. Development of the physical architecture is complete when the system has been decomposed to the lowest system element (usually the lowest replaceable unit of the support strategy). It is critical that this process identify the design drivers and driving requirements as early as possible.

163

The PM may oversee Architecture Design efforts to gain and maintain insights into program schedule and cost drivers for use in the evaluation of alternative architectures, excursions, mitigation approaches, etc.

Key activities in the Architecture Design process include:

- Analyzing and synthesizing the physical architecture and appropriate allocation.
- Analyzing constraint requirements.
- Identifying and defining physical interfaces and system elements.
- Identifying and defining critical attributes of the physical system elements, including design budgets (e.g., weight, reliability) and open system principles.

During this process, derived requirements come from solution decisions. It is essential to identify derived requirements and ensure that they are traceable and part of the allocated requirements. For each given solution alternative, the Decision Analysis process trades off requirements against given solution alternatives. For each solution alternative, based on programmatic decisions, certain performance requirements may be emphasized over others. The essence of this activity is to achieve a balanced and feasible design with acceptable risk; that falls within the program design constraints. An integral part of defining and refining the functional and physical architecture is to provide technical support to the market research, especially early in the acquisition life cycle. Systems engineers should analyze whether existing products (commercial or non-developmental items) can meet user performance requirements or whether technologies can realistically be matured within the required time frame. When possible, mature technologies should be used to satisfy end-user needs.

The output of this process is the allocated baseline, which includes the documentation that describes the physical architecture of the system and the specifications that describe the functional and performance requirements for each configuration item, along with the interfaces that compose the system. In addition, Work Breakdown Structures (WBS) and other technical planning documentation are updated. The system architecture and the resulting design documentation should be sufficiently detailed to:

- Confirm the upward and downward traceability of requirements.
- Confirm the interoperability and open system performance requirements.
- Sufficiently define products and processes to support implementation, verification and validation of the system.
- Establish achievable alternatives to allow key stakeholders to make informed decisions.

Confirmation of requirements traceability and the soundness of the selected physical architecture can be accomplished using a cost-effective combination of design modeling and analysis, as applicable.

The result of the Architecture Design process is an architectural design that meets the end-user capability needs shown in the Requirements Management process to have all stated and derived requirements allocated to lower-level system elements and to have the possibility of meeting cost, schedule and performance objectives. The architectural design should be able to be communicated to the customers and to the design engineers. The level of detail of the architectural design depends on the complexity of the system and the support strategy. It should be detailed enough to bound the cost and schedule of the delivered system, define the interfaces, assure customers that the requirements can be met and control the design process down to the lowest removable unit to support operations and sustainment. This architecture design may be documented and found in a program's system model. Once identified, the system architecture is placed under configuration management.

CH 3–4.2.4 Implementation Process

The Implementation process is comprised of two primary efforts: design and realization. The outputs of the Implementation process include the detailed design, down to the lowest level system elements in the system architecture, and the fabrication/production procedures of forming, joining and finishing, or coding for software. Depending on technology maturity, the Implementation process may develop, buy or reuse system elements to render the system. Implementation is integral to systematically increasing maturity, reducing risk and ensuring the system is ready for Integration, Verification, and Validation. The Implementation process provides a system that satisfies specified design and stakeholder performance

164

requirements. As a best practice, the Systems Engineer should develop an implementation plan that includes implementation procedures, fabrication processes, tools and equipment, implementation tolerances and verification uncertainties.

Design

Implementation begins in the Materiel Solution Analysis (MSA) phase, where the Analysis of Alternatives informs whether the preferred materiel solution can be developed, bought or reused. This analysis takes many forms, such as the use of models, simulations, experiments and prototypes through which competing systems can be assessed. Careful decisions regarding the design of system elements can enable the use of open (non-proprietary) standards and an open systems or modular approach that may allow for resiliency as well as reduce costs and promote competition during development, production, technology refresh and life-cycle extension. Design activities may include:

- Identifying and analyzing the constraints that the technology and design and realization techniques impose on the design solution.
- Developing design and implementation prototypes and solutions for the system elements.
- Analyzing candidate system element design and implementation solutions and conducting variability studies to identify conflicts and resolution alternatives to ensure system integrity.
- Identifying fabrication and quality procedures, and documenting design assumptions and decisions in the final system elements drawings or technical data package.
- Identifying any special tools or processes required to sustain custom, or non-COTS, parts.

Realization

Realization is the process of building the system elements using specified materials and fabrication and production tools/procedures identified during design. Early fabrication and production planning is critical for the successful realization and delivery of the needed capability. System elements are built to the product baseline and should meet quality standards. Realization activities may include:

- Obtaining or acquiring access to materials and tools required to build system elements.
- Obtaining external system elements as applicable.
- Building system elements in accordance with implementation procedures, tolerances and applicable ESOH, security, and privacy.
- Determining system elements functionality against specified product quality characteristics.
- Document fabrication and production issues and associated corrective actions.
- Delivering implemented system elements for integration and verification.

The output of the Implementation process is the physical system elements as identified in the product baseline, including fabrication and production methods.

CH 3–4.2.5 Integration Process
The Integration process provides a framework to systematically assemble lower-level system elements into successively higher-level system elements, iterative with verification until the system itself emerges. Integration is essential to increasing system maturity, reducing risk and preparing the system for transition to the warfighter.

The Program Manager (PM), with support from the Systems Engineer, is responsible for planning, managing and executing the Integration process. Experience has shown that programs that develop an integration plan are more successful. This plan defines the stages of integration during which system elements are successively integrated to form higher-level elements and eventually the finished product. Alternative integration paths should be considered. The integration plan should include a description of the required Systems Integration Laboratories or other facilities, personnel, test stands, harnesses, testing software and integration schedule.

The Interface Management process is critical to the success of the Integration process. Interface control specifications or interface control documents should be confirmed early on and placed under strict configuration control. All of the program's external interfaces and dependencies should be documented in the program's Systems Engineering Plan (SEP). The SEP Outline requires that all programs with external dependencies and/or interfaces establish Memoranda of Agreement (MOA) in order to formally establish commitments and management procedures. A current table showing the status of all MOAs is mandated as part of the program SEP, which is updated in each phase.

Integration activities support the Interface Management process by verifying that accurate and effective interface specifications are documented. In parallel, the verification methods for each integration level are developed and included in the allocated baseline. The successive integration phases follow the sequence defined in the program's integration plan and lead to the final product being ready for verification and validation.

CH 3–4.2.6 Verification Process

The Verification process provides the evidence that the system or system element performs its intended functions and meets all performance requirements listed in the system performance specification and functional and allocated baselines. Verification answers the question, "Did you build the system correctly?" Verification is a key risk-reduction activity in the implementation and integration of a system and enables the program to catch defects in system elements before integration at the next level, thereby preventing costly troubleshooting and rework.

The Program Manager (PM) and Systems Engineer, in coordination with the Chief Developmental Tester, manage verification activities and methods as defined in the functional and allocated baselines and review the results of verification. Guidance for managing and coordinating integrated testing activities can be found in CH 8–3.3. and in DoDI 5000.02, Enc 5, sec. 11.a.

Verification begins during Requirements Analysis, when top-level stakeholder performance requirements are decomposed and eventually allocated to system elements in the initial system performance specification and interface control specifications. During this process, the program determines how and when each requirement should be verified and the tasks required to do so, as well as the necessary resources (i.e., test equipment, range time, personnel, etc.). The resulting verification matrix and supporting documentation become part of the functional and allocated baselines.

Verification may be accomplished by any combination of the following methods:

- **Demonstration.** Demonstration is the performance of operations at the system or system element level where visual observations are the primary means of verification. Demonstration is used when quantitative assurance is not required for the verification of the requirements.
- **Examination.** Visual inspection of equipment and evaluation of drawings and other pertinent design data and processes should be used to verify conformance with characteristics such as physical, material, part and product marking and workmanship.
- **Analysis.** Analysis is the use of recognized analytic techniques (including computer models) to interpret or explain the behavior/performance of the system element. Analysis of test data or review and analysis of design data should be used as appropriate to verify requirements.
- **Test.** Test is an activity designed to provide data on functional features and equipment operation under fully controlled and traceable conditions. The data are subsequently used to evaluate quantitative characteristics.

Designs are verified at all levels of the physical architecture through a cost-effective combination of these methods, all of which can be aided by modeling and simulation.

Verification activities and results are documented among the artifacts for Functional Configuration Audits (FCA) and the System Verification Review (SVR) (see CH 3–3.3.6. System Verification Review/Functional Configuration Audit). When possible, verification should stress the system, or system elements, under realistic conditions representative of its intended use.

The individual system elements provided by the Implementation process are verified through developmental test and evaluation (DT&E), acceptance testing or qualification testing. During the

166

Integration process, the successively higher-level system elements may be verified before they move on to the next level of integration. Verification of the system as a whole occurs when integration is complete. As design changes occur, each change should be assessed for potential impact to the qualified baseline. This may include a need to repeat portions of verification in order to mitigate risk of performance degradation.

The output of the Verification process is a verified production-representative article with documentation to support Initial Operational Test and Evaluation (IOT&E). The SVR provides a determination of the extent to which the system meets the system performance specification.

CH 3–4.2.7 Validation Process

The Validation process provides the objective evidence that the capability provided by the system complies with stakeholder performance requirements, achieving its use in its intended operational environment. Validation answers the question, "Is it the right solution to the problem?" Validation consists of evaluating the operational effectiveness, operational suitability, sustainability and survivability (including cybersecurity) or lethality of the system or system elements under operationally realistic conditions.

The Program Manager (PM) and Systems Engineer support the Validation process. The Chief Developmental Tester is responsible for the execution of the Validation process, which is typically conducted by independent testers as documented in the Test and Evaluation Master Plan (TEMP) (See CH 8–3.6.). System end users and other stakeholders are typically involved in validation activities. Guidance for managing and coordinating integrated testing activities can be found in CH 8–3.3. and DoDI 5000.02, Enc 5, sec. 11.a. Using and engaging integrated test teams, composed of knowledgeable and experienced Government and industry developmental and operational testers bring different perspectives and allow for an efficient use of resources.

Validation activities can be conducted in the intended operational environment or on an approved simulated environment. Early program-validation activities assist in the production of validated Concept of Operations/Operational Mode Summary/Mission Profile (CONOPS/OMS/MP), system performance specifications, use cases, functional and physical system architectures and test cases. Validation is applied to the product baseline to ensure the emerging design meets the end-user needs. Models, simulations, mockups and prototypes may be used in these early activities. They are often combined with the verification activities (see CH 3–4.2.6. Verification Process). Aggressive early validation significantly mitigates the risk to the program by identifying operational issues up front when they are easier and less costly to fix. This ultimately improves system performance during the final validation activity (e.g., operational test and evaluation (OT&E)) (See CH 8–3.2.)

Final validation involves operational testing on a production-representative system in an operationally realistic environment (See CH 8–3.2.1.) The product of the Validation process is a validated system and enabling system elements, leading to approval for Full-Rate Production (FRP) and/or a Full Deployment (FD) Decision Review (DR).

CH 3–4.2.8 Transition Process

The Transition process moves any system element to the next level in the physical architecture. For the end-item system, it is the process to install and deploy the system to the user in the operational environment. The end-item system may need to be integrated with other systems in the operational environment, honoring the defined external interfaces. In this case, the Transition process needs to be performed in conjunction with the Integration process and Interface Management process for a smooth transition.

Early planning for system transition reduces risk and supports smooth delivery and rapid acceptance by the system's end user. Transition considerations should include, as appropriate, end-user and maintainer requirements, training, deployability, support tasks, support equipment and packaging, handling, storage and transportation (PHS&T). Part of the Transition process is ensuring that each site is properly prepared for the receipt, acceptance and/or installation of the system.

167

The Transition process includes maintenance and supportability activities for the deployed system and its enabling system elements, as well as a process for reporting and resolving deficiencies. The DoDI 5000.02, Enc 6, sec. 3 requires that sustainment and support planning be documented in the LCSP, which is required for all acquisition programs and reviewed before Milestones A, B, and C, as well as the Full-Rate Production Decision Review (FRP DR).

The Program Manager (PM), Systems Engineer, and Product Support Manager oversee all transition plans and activities required to install or deploy the end-item system, and associated enabling system elements, to the operational environment. The Systems Engineer leads engineering efforts to correct deficiencies found during transition and fielding. PMs should ensure all deliverables, particularly documentation (i.e., drawings, tech manuals, etc.), have been received from the contractor and made available to the activity responsible for sustaining the system through disposal.

CH 3–4.3 Design Considerations

The Program Manager (PM) and Systems Engineer should consider and document all statutory and regulatory requirements, as well as other design considerations, in order to:

- Translate the end-user desired capabilities into a structured system of interrelated design specifications that support delivery of required operational capability.
- Enable trade-offs among the design considerations in support of achieving desired mission effectiveness within cost and schedule constraints.
- Incorporate design considerations into the set of system requirements, as some are mandated by laws, regulations or treaties, while others are mandated by the domain or DoD Component or Agency; these mandates should be incorporated during the Requirements Analysis process to achieve balance across all system requirements.

Some design considerations are concepts that assist trade-offs and should be accommodated or applied to each system or program. Others are constraints, boundaries or limitations, with values that can sometimes be tailored or negotiated, but which generally represent immovable parts of the trade space. The PM and Systems Engineer should show evidence of critical thinking in addressing the design considerations, as documented in the program SEP. According to the SEP Outline, the SEP should include a table of design considerations that are critical to the program and are an integral part of the design process, including trade-off analyses.

With the understanding that each design consideration is a discrete item to investigate during the design process, the PM, Systems Engineer, and other stakeholders should also view design considerations as an integrated set of variables that can influence one another. The PM and Systems Engineer should consider them in conjunction with one another, as early as the Analysis of Alternatives, to achieve better mission performance and to preclude a stovepipe view during design.

The design considerations listed in Table 42 should be assessed for applicability to the system, as they may not all be appropriate. Table 42 lists the statutory requirements for the design considerations covered in this chapter, as well as applicable policy and guidance related to those design considerations. Note that MIL-STD-882 is included in the Policy and Guidance table as it is mandated by DoDI 5000.02, Enc 3, sec. 16. Other standards may be mandated by other DoD Directives and Instructions, but they are not listed in this table. Table 42 is not all inclusive; it does not include any additional design considerations levied by the Service, the Center, the platform, or the domain. Not all design considerations are equally important or critical to a given program, but all should be examined for relevancy.

Table 42: Design Considerations

168

Design Consideration	Section Number	Statutory Requirement	Policy & Guidance
Accessibility (Section 508 Compliance)	**4.3.1**	• Section 508 of the Rehabilitation Act (i.e., 29 U.S.C. 794d)	• DoDD 8000.01 • DoDI 5000.02, Enclosure 11 • DoD 8400.01-M • FAR 39.204
Affordability - SE Trade-Off Analysis	**4.3.2**		• DoDI 5000.02, Enclosures 1, 2, 3, and 8 • USD(AT&L) memorandum, "Implementation Directive for Better Buying Power 3.0: Achieving Dominant Capabilities through Technical Excellence and Innovation," April 9, 2015 • USD(AT&L) memorandum, "Better Buying Power 2.0: Continuing the Pursuit for Greater Efficiency and Productivity in Defense Spending," November 13, 2012 • USD(AT&L) memorandum, "Implementation Directive for Better Buying Power- Restoring Affordability and Productivity in Defense Spending," November 3, 2010 • USD(AT&L) memorandum, "Better Buying Power: Guidance for Obtaining Greater Efficiency and Productivity in Defense Spending," September 14, 2010
Anti-Counterfeiting	**4.3.3**	• P.L. 112-81 (SEC 818)	• DoDI 4140.67
Commercial-Off-the-Shelf (COTS)	**4.3.4**	• 41 USC 104 and 1907 • P.L. 103-355 (SEC 8104) • P.L. 104-106 (SEC 357)	• SD-2
Corrosion Prevention and Control (CPC)	**4.3.5**		• DoDD 5000.01, Enclosure 1, paragraph E1.1.17 • DoDI 5000.02, Enclosures 1 and 3 • DoDI 5000.67 • DoD Corrosion Prevention and Control Planning Guidebook • DFARS 223.73

169

Design Consideration	Section Number	Statutory Requirement	Policy & Guidance
Critical Safety Item (CSI)	4.3.6	• P.L. 108-136 (SEC 802) • P.L. 109-364 (SEC 130) • 10 USC 2319	• DoDM 4140.01, Encl. 11 • JACG Aviation CSI Management Handbook • SECNAVINST 4140.2 • AFI 20-106 • DA Pam 95-9 • DLAI 3200.4 • DCMA INST CSI (AV) Management of Aviation Critical Safety Items • DFARS 209.270, 246.407, 246.504, 246.371 and 252.246-7003
Demilitarization and Disposal	4.3.7		• DoDI 4160.28, Volume 1 • DoDI 5000.02 Procedures and Encl. 6 and 13 • DoDM 4140.01, Encl. 6 • DoD 4160.21-M • MIL-STD-882
Diminishing Manufacturing Sources and Material Shortages (DMSMS)	4.3.8		• SD-22
Environment, Safety and Occupational Health (ESOH)	4.3.9	• 42 USC 4321 • EO 12114	• DoDI 5000.02, Encl. 1, 3, 6, 7, and 13 • DoDD 4715.21 • MIL-STD-882 • DFARS 223.73 • FAR 23.2, 23.4, 23.7 and 23.8
Human Systems Integration (HSI)	4.3.10		• DoDD 5000.01, Encl. 1, para E1.1.29 • DoDI 5000.02, Encl. 7
Insensitive Munitions	4.3.11	• 10 USC 2389	• DoDD 6055.9 • Secretary of Defense Memorandum, "DoD Policy on Submunition Reliability," January 10, 2001 • USD(AT&L) Memorandum, "Joint Insensitive Munitions Test Standards and Compliance Assessment," February 10, 2010 • USD(AT&L) Memorandum, "Insensitive Munitions Strategic Plans," July 21, 2004 • DoD Acquisition Manager's Handbook for Insensitive Munitions, Revision 02, November 2008

170

Design Consideration	Section Number	Statutory Requirement	Policy & Guidance
Intelligence (Life-cycle Mission Data Plan (LMDP))	4.3.12		• DoDD 5250.01 • DoDI 5000.02, Encl. 1
Interoperability and Dependency (I&D)	4.3.13	• 44 USC 3506	• DoDD 4630.05 • DoDD 5000.01 • DoDI 2010.06 • DoDI 4630.8 • DoDI 5000.02 • CJCSI 3170.01 • JCIDS Manual
Item Unique Identification (IUID)	4.3.14		• DoDD 8320.03 • DoDI 4151.19 • DoDI 5000.02, Encl. 1 and 3 • DoDI 5000.64 • DoDI 8320.04 • DoD Guide to Uniquely Identifying Items, Version 2.5, September 15, 2012 • DoD Guidelines for Engineering, Manufacturing and Maintenance Documentation Requirements, April 20, 2007 • DFARS 211.274-2, 252.211-7003, 252.211-7007
Modular Design	4.3.15	• 10 USC 2430	• DoDI 5000.02, Encl. 1 and 3 • DoD 5010.12-M • USD(AT&L) memorandum, "Implementation Directive for Better Buying Power 3.0: Achieving Dominant Capabilities through Technical Excellence and Innovation," April 9, 2015 • USD(AT&L) Memorandum, "Better Buying Power 2.0: Continuing the Pursuit for Greater Efficiency and Productivity in Defense Spending," November 13, 2012
Operational Energy	4.3.16	• 10 USC 138c	• CJCSI 3170.01 • JCIDS Manual
Packaging, Handling, Storage and Transportation (PHS&T)	4.3.17	• 49 CFR Parts 171-180	• DoDI 4540.07 • DoD 4145.19-R • DoD 4140.27-M • DTR 4500.9-R
Producibility, Quality & Manufacturing (PQM)	4.3.18	• P.L. 111-383 (SEC 812)	• DoDI 5000.02, Encl. 3 • DFARS 207.105, 215.304

171

Design Consideration	Section Number	Statutory Requirement	Policy & Guidance
Reliability & Maintainability (R&M) Engineering	4.3.19	• P.L. 111-23 (SEC 102)	• DoDI 5000.02, Encl. 3 • DoD Reliability, Availability, Maintainability, and Cost Rationale (RAM-C) Report Manual
Spectrum Management	4.3.20	• 47 USC 305 • 47 USC 901 - 904 • P.L. 102-538 (SEC 104)	• DoDD 3222.3 • DoDI 4650.01 • DoDI 5000.02, Encl. 1 and 3 • AR 5-12 • AFI 33-118 • SECNAVINST 2400.1 and 2400.2 • OPNAVINST 2400.20
Standardization	4.3.21	• 10 USC 2451-2457 • P.L. 82-436	• DoDI 4120.24 • DoDM 4120.24 • SD-19
Supportability	4.3.22		• DoDD 5000.01, Encl. 1, paragraphs E1.1.17, E1.1.29 • DoDI 4151.22 • DoDI 5000.02, Enclosure 1 and 6 • DoD 4151.22-M • SD-19 • MIL-HDBK-502
Survivability (including CBRN) & Susceptibility	4.3.23	• P.L. 108-375 (SEC 1053)	• DoDI 3150.09 • DoDI 5000.02, Encl. 4, and 5
System Security Engineering (SSE)	4.3.24	• 10 USC 2358	• DoDI 5000.02, Encl. 1, 3, and 11 • DoDI 5200.39 • DoDI 5200.44 • DoDI O-5240.24 • DoDI 8500 Series • DoDI 8582.01 • Program Protection Plan Outline and Guidance, Version 1.0, July 2011

CH 3–4.3.1 Accessibility (Section 508 Compliance)

All Electronic and Information Technology (E&IT) systems comply with Section 508 of the Rehabilitation Act (i.e., 29 U.S.C. 794d), unless exempt under FAR (Subpart 39.204, para (b)) as a military system or National Security System. Compliance with Section 508 provides access by Federal employees with disabilities and the public to information and data that able-bodied persons can access through E&IT systems. Section 508 should be considered as a design requirement, addressed at each technical review and clearly stated in the Acquisition Strategy and Systems Engineering Plan.

Program Managers (PMs) should ensure Section 508 compliance, unless exempt, while Systems Engineers are responsible for implementation through use of standards and compliant tools and products.

172

Resources to aid programs in complying are in Table 43. Additional information on accessibility is found in DoDI 5000.02, Enc 11, sec. 14; DAG Chapter 5 Manpower Planning & Human Systems Integration; and Chapter 6 Acquiring Information Technology and Business Systems.

Table 43: Links to Section 508 Government Resources

Description of Link	Active Link
Section 508 technical standards	http://www.access-board.gov/508.htm
Federal rules for Section 508 implementation hosted by GSA has: • Roles and responsibilities of procurement officials and engineers • 508 best practices • Products and techniques	https://www.section508.gov/
The "Buy Accessible System" GSA site has free tools and guides for conduct of Section 508-compliant acquisitions as well as on-line training and help desk	https://www.buyaccessible.gov/
Department of Health and Human Services has: • Check lists • Code library • Test tools	http://www.hhs.gov/ found by searching on "section 508"
Department of Justice home page for ADA has federal laws and pending legislation	https://www.ada.gov/
Department of Veteran Affairs reports on Section 508 products and tools and tracks user comments	http://www.section508.va.gov/

CH 3–4.3.2 Affordability -- Systems Engineering Trade-Off Analyses

Affordability is the degree to which the capability benefits are worth the system's total life-cycle cost and support DoD strategic goals. Systems engineering (SE) trade-off analyses for affordability, a special application of the Decision Analysis process (see CH 3–4.1.2.) should:

- Support the establishment of realistic affordability caps as documented in the program's Acquisition Program Baseline (APB).
- Serve as inputs for the will-cost estimate and should-cost targets, including related should-cost initiatives.
- Enable continuous monitoring of program life-cycle costs with respect to affordability caps across the system life cycle.

DoDI 5000.02, Enc 8, sec. 3.e requires the Milestone Decision Authority (MDA) to establish tentative cost and inventory goals at Materiel Development Decision (MDD) and affordability goals at Milestone A to inform early requirements and design trade-offs. Affordability caps are set at the Development RFP Release Decision, Milestone B, and beyond for unit procurement and sustainment costs. According to DoDI 5000.02, Enc 8, sec. 3.e, affordability caps are established as fixed-cost requirements equivalent to Key Performance Parameters (KPP).

173

The affordability goal forms the basis for the SE trade-off and sensitivity analyses conducted to ensure that requirements are affordable and technically feasible, and to inform the validation of the Capability Development Document (or equivalent requirements document) from an affordability standpoint. SE trade-off analyses also support the establishment of affordability caps at the Development RFP Release Decision, Milestone B, and subsequent reviews. The affordability goal is nominally the average unit acquisition cost and average annual operations and support cost per unit. For indefinite quantity of production units, the affordability goal may be the total acquisition cost (see CH 1–4.2.15. and DoDI 5000.02, Enc 8, for more information regarding the affordability goal/cap).

The independently generated will-cost estimate is used to defend the program budget but does not account for potential efficiencies. The should-cost target is based on the efficient use of resources and effective implementation of processes identified as should-cost initiatives, and is the focus of SE activities and program management decisions across the life cycle. Should-cost management is implemented in all acquisition programs (all ACATs) regardless of the life-cycle phase in accordance with DoDI 5000.02, Enc 2, sec. 6.e.

The SE trade-offs are conducted among cost, schedule and performance objectives to ensure the program is affordable. The Program Manager (PM) should identify the design performance points that are the focus of trade-off analyses to establish cost and schedule trade space. The PM presents the results of the trade-off analyses at program milestone/technical reviews, showing how the system's life-cycle cost varies as a function of system requirements, major design parameters and schedule. The results are used to identify cost and affordability drivers and to demonstrate how the cost-effective design point is established for the system.

The PM and Systems Engineer use the results of SE trade-off analyses for affordability to inform system requirements and ensure that, when taken collectively, the requirements are compelling, affordable and achievable within the time frame available to the program.

The SE trade-off analyses are executed by a resourced team that consists of a decision maker with full responsibility, authority and accountability for the trade at hand; a trade-off analyst with a suite of reasoning tools; subject matter experts with performance models; and a representative set of end users and other stakeholders.

Throughout the system life cycle, the Systems Engineer continuously monitors affordability drivers, identifies opportunities to reduce life-cycle costs (should-cost initiatives), and conducts SE trade-off analyses as needed to meet program cost, schedule and performance requirements.

CH 3–4.3.3 Anti-Counterfeiting

An increasing threat of counterfeit (and fraudulent) parts in the global marketplace affects every component of the program from commercial-off-the-shelf (COTS) assemblies to military-unique systems. Preventing counterfeit parts from entering the supply chain reduces cost and negative impacts to program schedule and system performance. DoDI 4140.67 "DoD Counterfeit Prevention Policy" provides direction for anti-counterfeit measures for DoD weapon and information systems acquisition and sustainment to prevent the introduction of counterfeit materiel.

Counterfeit parts are becoming pervasive in various supply chains and therefore have become a significant threat to the Defense supply chain. Counterfeiters' motives are primarily greed (profit) and/or malicious intent. Counterfeits may appear at all phases of the life cycle, making it necessary for the Program Manager (PM), Systems Engineer, and Product Support Manager to plan for prevention, detection, remediation, reporting and restitution activities from the beginning of the life cycle to disposal and demilitarization.

In order to properly assess the risks of counterfeit products, the PM needs to be aware that anti-counterfeit activities have relationships, as described in Table 44, with many of the other design considerations outlined in CH 3–4.3. Design Considerations, such as:

Table 44: Anti-Counterfeit Design Considerations Relationships

174

Design Consideration	Relationship
Commercial-Off-the-Shelf (COTS)	The Government and its industry agents have little to no visibility into the supply chains that create COTS products. Implications of this lack of visibility into the supply chain include counterfeit vulnerabilities and counterfeit parts being more readily available.
Corrosion Prevention and Control (CPC)	Counterfeits, by their nature, may have been falsely certified. In addition, if the counterfeit is a compound/material or component (e.g., gaskets, ground wires) intended to prevent or reduce corrosion, then effects of wear may appear sooner than predicted and the impacts to the system may be worse than expected or catastrophic.
Critical Safety Items (CSI)	From an anti-counterfeiting risk-based approach, CSIs should be more carefully scrutinized to ensure no counterfeits infiltrate the supply chain.
Demilitarization and Disposal	An excellent source for counterfeiters to obtain parts that can be turned into "used sold as new" parts (fraudulently certified as new).
Diminishing Manufacturing Sources and Material Shortages (DMSMS)	As systems age and the trustworthy sources for the piece parts dry up, counterfeiters increasingly take advantage of the situation by offering a source for hard-to-find parts.
Environment, Safety and Occupational Health (ESOH)	Several examples of counterfeit materials that can increase ESOH risks include: false R-134, a refrigerant which produces explosive by-products; fire extinguishers compressed with air; and faulty smoke detectors. Furthermore, Restriction of Hazardous Substances (RoHS) (2002/95/EC) has led to increased numbers of counterfeits, where a lead-free (Pb-free) microcircuit is sold as having tin-lead (SnPb) leads.
Item Unique Identification (IUID)	Successful implementation of IUID could reduce the ability of counterfeiters to introduce parts into supply. Conversely, IUID may provide a false sense of security if it can be duplicated by counterfeiters.
Modular Open Systems Approach (MOSA)	MOSA could provide a means to quickly certify a newer, more available part for use in weapon systems, thus reducing the impact of DMSMS. Conversely, it could also result in more part numbers (equivalents) being introduced into supply, thus increasing the likelihood of counterfeit intrusion.
Producibility, Quality and Manufacturing (PQM)	PQM can be severely degraded if supply is contaminated with counterfeits.
Reliability and Maintainability Engineering	Counterfeits that somehow get past receipt inspection and test can have radically different reliability and failure modes than the "honest" part.
Supportability	Increased failure rates due to counterfeits can have a negative impact on supportability and might drive the wrong problem-resolution behaviors and increase sustainment costs.
System Security Engineering (SSE)	SSE implements anti-counterfeit protection measures as part of a comprehensive plan to protect CPI and mission-critical functions and components (See DAG Chapter 9).

During development of the Systems Engineering Plan (SEP) and Program Protection Plan (PPP), the PM,

Systems Engineer and Product Support Manager should consider these relationships and develop plans to address the threat.

175

CH 3–4.3.4 Commercial-Off-the-Shelf

The use of commercial-off-the-shelf (COTS) items, including Non-Developmental Items, can provide significant opportunities for efficiencies during system development but also can introduce certain issues that should be considered and mitigated if the program is to realize the expected benefits.

The primary benefits of using COTS components in system design are to:

- Reduce development time.
- Allow faster insertion of new technology.
- Lower life-cycle costs by taking advantage of the more readily available and up-to-date commercial industrial base.

However, regardless of the extent to which a system is made up of commercial items, the Program Manager (PM) and Systems Engineer still develop, integrate, test, evaluate, deliver, sustain and manage the overall system.

Among concerns with using COTS products are:

- Subtle differences in product use can significantly affect system effectiveness; Environment, Safety and Occupational Health (ESOH); reliability; and durability.
- If integration requires a "modified COTS product," meaning that a COTS product may not be designed for many military environments (which, by definition, is not a COTS product under 41 USC 104, but is allowed under 41 USC 1907), then the program may lose the ability to use the vendor's subsequent product upgrades or to find a suitable replacement for the product from other commercial sources.
- The vendors can embed proprietary functions into COTS products, limiting supply sources.
- Vendors do not have to provide design information and often restrict purchasers from reverse engineering their intellectual property.
- Licensing agreements vary and can be very restrictive while limiting the vendor's liability for merchantability for intended purposes.
- Supply chain risk management of COTS items is limited by the vendor, who is under no obligation to the purchaser to provide such information.
- Incorporating COTS products places constraints on the rest of the design and reduces trade space; functionality, interfaces and reliability and maintainability characteristics are embedded in the choice of a COTS system element.
- Difficulty in finding suitable replacements and/or alternate items if the COTS vendor stops manufacturing the product or changes the configuration drastically, requiring the need to maintain different configurations of a single product.
- The program needs to understand the "pedigree" of the qualified vendors for the COTS product.
- The graphical user interface (GUI) design may not completely support user tasks, which can cause inefficient workarounds and improper use of the system by the user.

The marketplace drives COTS product definition, application and evolution. COTS products presume a flexible architecture and often depend on product releases that are designed to be used "as is" to meet general business needs and not a specific organization's needs. The commercial product life cycle is usually much shorter than the equivalent military product life cycle. Programs should consider the potential availability of suitable replacement and/or alternative items throughout the longer, military life cycle, and should monitor the commercial marketplace through market research activities and ongoing alignment of business and technical processes. This necessary activity imposes additional cost, schedule, and performance risks for which the acquisition community should plan. COTS products should be evaluated to meet all performance and reliability requirements during all environmental conditions and service life requirements specified by the intended application requirements documents.

P.L. 103-355 (SEC 8104) and P.L. 104-106 (SEC 357), both endorse the use of COTS products by the Federal Government but have slightly different definitions, with the latter allowing for modifications to COTS products.

176

The Systems Engineer should ensure open system design, identification and mitigation of ESOH and security risks, survivable technology insertion, or refresh throughout the projected system life cycle.

The PM and Systems Engineer should consider the following when evaluating use of COTS products:

- The intended product-use environment and the extent to which this environment differs from (or is similar to) the commercial-use environment
- Integration, documentation, security, Human System Integration, ESOH, hardware/software integrity, reliability risk, program protection and corrosion susceptibility/risk
- Planning for life-cycle activities (including sustainment, supply chain risks, obsolescence, and disposal)
- Developing relationships with vendors, Foreign Ownership Control, and Influence (FOCI) (see Defense Security Service for the latest policy regarding COTS products from FOCI sources)
- Supportability, if product modifications are made or if vendor or marketplace changes occur
- Test and evaluation of COTS items (including early identification of screening, functionality testing and usability assessments) (See CH 8–2.1.)
- Protecting intellectual property rights by being aware of pertinent intellectual property rights issues associated with commercial items acquisitions, especially with the acquisition of commercial software products. When acquiring Intellectual Property (IP) license rights, the acquisition community should consider the core principles described in the DoD guide: "Intellectual Property: Navigating through Commercial Waters."
- Ability to modify or interface COTS software with other software even if Government-generated or owned
- Ability to have insight into configuration management, and the features and functions of upgrades and changes
- Ability to instrument and/or test aspects of COTS products

CH 3–4.3.5 Corrosion Prevention and Control
The corrosion of military equipment and facilities costs the DoD over $20 billion annually. In addition, corrosion degrades system availability; safety; and Environment, Safety and Occupational Health (ESOH) factors. Therefore, acquisition officials should fully consider corrosion prevention and mitigation as early as possible in the acquisition life cycle (even prior to Milestone A), and implement appropriate strategies to minimize the life-cycle impact.

Sound Corrosion Prevention and Control (CPC) planning reduces life-cycle costs, improves maintainability and availability and enhances ESOH compliance. The DoD Corrosion Prevention and Control Planning Guidebook for Military Systems and Equipment (MS&E) (i.e. CPC Planning Guidebook) helps Program Managers (PMs), Systems Engineers, Product Support Managers and other program staff develop and execute a comprehensive CPC approach.

DoDI 5000.02, DoDI 5000.67 and DoDD 4151.18 require CPC planning and execution for all acquisition programs across the life cycle. In accordance with DoDI 5000.02, Enc 3, sec. 15, the PM is responsible for identifying and evaluating corrosion considerations throughout the acquisition and sustainment phases to reduce, control or mitigate corrosion. The PM and Systems Engineer should conduct CPC planning, ensure corrosion control requirements are included in the system design and verified as part of test and acceptance programs and include CPC management and design considerations in the Systems Engineering Plan (SEP) and Life-Cycle Sustainment Plan (LCSP). DoDI 5000.02, Enc 6, sec. 2 further integrates CPC planning into sustainment. Product support planning should mitigate the appropriate CPC risks inherent in the system design to meet sustainment requirements.

Good CPC planning and execution includes, but is not limited to, the following elements:

- Engaging corrosion expertise relevant to the system and its operating environment throughout the life cycle.
- Examining legacy systems for possible corrosion-design improvements.

177

- Documenting alternative material and process assessments that offer increased corrosion protection.
- Including CPC as a consideration in trade studies involving cost, useful service life and effectiveness.
- Incorporating CPC requirements, plans, specification, standards and criteria into relevant contractual documentation for all equipment and facilities.
- Including CPC in integrated product support element (IPSE) development and evaluation, to include facilities (see DAG Chapter 4).
- Identifying planning, resourcing and acquisition of corrosion-related features for longevity, lowest total ownership cost (TOC) and sustained system effectiveness.
- Retaining access to CPC resources throughout the life cycle.

All designated Acquisition Category (ACAT) programs are required to conduct CPC planning across their life cycle. For Major Automated Information System (MAIS) programs, the extent of CPC planning and the breadth of documentation should consider the type of system and correlate the system's corrosion risk to mission criticality and the harshness of the operational environment. Refer to the *DoD Corrosion Prevention and Control Planning Guidebook for MS&E* for more information.

In addition to the SEP and LCSP, CPC planning and execution for all ACAT programs should be reflected in other program documents, including, but not limited to:

- Acquisition Strategy (AS)
- Test and Evaluation Master Plan (TEMP)
- Request for Proposal (RFP) and contract
- Program schedule -- Integrated Master Plan/Integrated Master Schedule (IMP/IMS)
- Funding/budget
- Programmatic ESOH Evaluation (i.e., DFARS (Subpart 223.73, Minimizing the Use of Hexavalent Chromium))
- System finish/process specification (add to the Statement of Work (SOW) and as a Data Item Description (DID) to the Contract Data Requirements List (CDRL))
- Contractor Corrosion Prevention and Control Plan (add to the SOW/Statement of Objectives (SOO)/ Performance Work Statement (PWS) and as a DID to the CDRL)
- System performance specifications

In the contract and RFP, CPC planning and execution should be addressed in the management and technical content of each contract/RFP section and subsection, including, but not limited to, the SOW, IMP/IMS, CDRL, DID, and system performance specifications (see CH 3–2.7. Systems Engineering Role in Contracting and the *DoD Corrosion Prevention and Control Planning Guidebook for MS&E*).

CH 3–4.3.6 Critical Safety Item

A Critical Safety Item (CSI) is a part, assembly or support equipment whose failure could cause loss of life, permanent disability or major injury, loss of a system or significant equipment damage. Special attention should be placed on CSIs to prevent the potential catastrophic or critical consequences of failure. Significant problems occurred when DoD purchased CSIs from suppliers with limited knowledge of the item's design intent, application, failure modes, failure effects or failure implications.

The purpose of CSI analysis is to ensure that Program Managers (PMs) for DoD acquisition programs who enter into contracts involving CSIs do so only with resources approved by the Design Control Activity (DCA). The DCA is defined by law as the systems command of a military department. The DCA is responsible for the airworthiness or seaworthiness certification of the system in which a CSI is used.

The intent of CSI laws, policies, regulations and guidance is to reduce the likelihood and consequence of failure by mitigating receipt of defective, suspect, improperly documented, unapproved and fraudulent parts having catastrophic potential. These statutory requirements are contained in P.L. 108-136 (SEC 802), enacted to address aviation CSIs, and P.L. 109-364 (SEC 130), enacted to address ship CSIs, embedded in 10 USC 2319. The statute addresses three specific areas:

- Establish that the DCA is responsible for processes concerning the management and identification of CSIs used in procurement, modification repair, and overhaul of aviation and ship systems.
- Require that DoD work only with sources approved by the DCA for contracts involving CSIs.
- Require that CSI deliveries and services performed meet all technical and quality requirements established by the DCA.

CSI policies and guidance ensure that items of supply that are most critical to operational safety are rigorously managed and controlled in terms of:

- Supplier capability
- Conformance to technical requirements
- Controls on changes or deviations
- Inspection, installation, maintenance and repair requirements

DoDM 4140.01, Volume 11 establishes top-level procedures for the management of aviation CSIs. The Joint Aeronautical Commanders Group issued the Aviation Critical Safety Items (CSIs) Management Handbook. This guidance establishes standard user-level operating practices for aviation CSIs across the Services, the Defense Logistics Agency (DLA), the Defense Contract Management Agency (DCMA), and other Federal agencies. Appendix I of the Aviation CSI Management Handbook is a joint Military Service/Defense Agency instruction on "Management of Aviation Critical Safety Items" issued on January 25, 2006. This instruction (SECNAVINST 4140.2, AFI 20-106, DA Pam 95-9, DLAI 3200.4, and DCMA INST CSI (AV)) addresses requirements for identifying, acquiring, ensuring quality of, managing and disposing of aviation CSIs. Similar policies and guidance are being developed and/or revised to address ship CSIs as defined by public law.

The Defense Federal Acquisition Regulation Supplement (DFARS) was amended to implement the contractual aspects regarding aviation CSIs. Comparable DFARS amendments are being developed to address ship CSIs. DFARS (Subpart 209.270) states that the DCA is responsible for:

- Identifying items that meet aviation CSI criteria.
- Approving qualification requirements.
- Qualifying suppliers.

This supplement states that the contracting activity contracts for aviation CSIs only with suppliers approved by the DCA. PMs should coordinate with the contracting activity to ensure that they contract for aviation CSIs only with suppliers approved by the DCA and that nonconforming aviation CSIs are to be accepted only with the DCA's approval, as required by DFARS (Subpart 246.407). DFARS (Subpart 246.407) was amended to state that DCA authority can be delegated for minor nonconformance. DFARS (Subpart 246.504) requires DCA concurrence before certificates of conformance are issued to accept aviation CSIs.

Because the developer may uncover problems with products after items are delivered, DFARS (Subpart 246.371) and DFARS (Subpart 252.246-7003) require the developer to notify the procuring and contracting officers within 72 hours after discovering or obtaining credible information that a delivered CSI may have discrepancies that affect safety. PMs should coordinate with the contracting authority to be kept aware of materiel recalls and shortfalls that may impact production rates and sustainment.

The CSI list evolves as the design, production processes and supportability analyses mature. PMs identify and document CSIs during design and development to influence critical downstream processes, such as initial provisioning, supply support and manufacturing planning to ensure adequate management of CSIs throughout a system's Operations and Support (O&S) phase. The PM should ensure that the allocated baseline established at the Preliminary Design Review (PDR) includes an initial list of proposed CSIs and a proposed process for selecting and approving CSIs, and that it addresses the critical characteristics of those items. Prior to the Critical Design Review (CDR), the program office, with support from the DCA and developer/OEM contractors, should ensure there is a clear understanding of CSI processes, terms and criteria. The initial product baseline, established at CDR, should have 100% of drawings completed for the CSIs. Throughout Low-Rate Initial Production (LRIP) (if applicable), conduct of the Physical Configuration Audit (PCA) and establishment of the product baseline, the program should update the CSI list and review it to ensure the list reflects the delivered system. Before the Full-Rate Production/Full Deployment Decision Review (FRP/FD DR), a final CSI list should be documented and approved by the DCA.

CH 3–4.3.7 Demilitarization and Disposal

The incorporation of demilitarization (DEMIL) and disposal requirements into the initial system design is critical to ensure compliance with:

- All DoD DEMIL and disposal policies
- All legal and regulatory requirements and policies relating to safety (including explosive safety), security, and the environment

Program Managers (PMs) and Product Support Managers should ensure, as an essential part of systems engineering, that DEMIL and disposal requirements are incorporated in system design to minimize DoD's liabilities, reduce costs and protect critical program information and technology. This includes integrating DEMIL and disposal into the allocated baseline approved at the Preliminary Design Review (PDR) and refining DEMIL and disposal requirements in the initial product baseline at the Critical Design Review (CDR). DEMIL and disposal requirements are included in the program's Systems Engineering Plan (SEP), Life-Cycle Sustainment Plan (LCSP) and contract(s). For munitions programs, DEMIL and disposal documentation need to be in place before the start of Developmental Test and Evaluation.

DEMIL eliminates functional capabilities and inherent military design features from both serviceable and unserviceable DoD materiel. It is the act of destroying the military offensive or defensive advantages inherent in certain types of equipment or material. DEMIL may include mutilation, scrapping, melting, burning or alteration designed to prevent the further use of this equipment and material for its originally intended military or lethal purpose. Systems Engineers integrate DEMIL considerations into system design to recover critical materials and protect assets, information and technologies from uncontrolled or unwanted release and disruption or reverse engineering. PMs should ensure the DEMIL of materiel is accomplished in accordance with DoDI 4160.28, DoD Demilitarization Program.

Disposal is the process of reusing, transferring, donating, selling or destroying excess surplus and foreign excess property. Disposal first ensures adequate screening is accomplished to satisfy all valid DoD and other U.S. Government agency needs. After assurances that Government needs for surplus DoD property are met, the materiel disposition process:

- Permits authorized transfer or donation to Government or non-Government entities.
- Obligates DoD to obtain the best-available monetary return to the Government for property sold.

PMs ensure disposal is accomplished in accordance with DoDM 4140.01, Volume 6 and DoDM 4160.21-M, Volume 1, Defense Materiel Disposition: Disposal Guidance and Procedures.

The program's plan for DEMIL and disposal of DoD excess and surplus property protects the environment and personnel and minimizes the need for abandonment or destruction. During system design, the Systems Engineer supports the PM's plans for the system's demilitarization and disposal, through the identification and documentation of hazards and hazardous materials related to the system, using MIL-STD-882 (System Safety). Early, balanced analyses of Environment, Safety and Occupational Health (ESOH) hazards relative to the system's design enable the PM to make informed decisions based on alternatives and provide a clear understanding of trade-offs and consequences, both near term and over the system's life cycle.

CH 3–4.3.8 Diminishing Manufacturing Sources and Material Shortages

Diminishing Manufacturing Sources and Material Shortages (DMSMS) is the loss, or impending loss, of manufacturers or suppliers of items, raw materials or software. DMSMS-generated shortages in the ongoing production capability or life-cycle support of a weapon system or shortages in any training,

180

support or test equipment already in the field can endanger mission effectiveness. While DMSMS issues can be caused by many factors, their occurrence is inevitable.

The Program Manager (PM) should incorporate a technology management strategy into design activities as a best practice to reduce DMSMS cost and readiness impacts throughout the life cycle. The PM and Systems Engineer should develop a technology management strategy for maintaining insight into technology trends and internal product changes by the manufacturer, and testing the effects of those changes on the system when necessary. This insight into technology trends could potentially:

- Result in seamless upgrade paths for technologies and system elements.
- Provide a timetable for replacing system elements even if they are not obsolete.

The Systems Engineer should be aware of and consider DMSMS management during system design. Following are several practices that the program should consider to minimize DMSMS risk throughout the life cycle of the system:

- Avoid selecting technology and components that are near the end of their functional life.
- During the design process, proactively assess the risk of parts obsolescence while selecting parts.
- When feasible, use an Modular Open Systems Approach (MOSA) to enable technology insertion/refreshment more easily than with design-specific approaches.
- Proactively monitor supplier bases to prevent designing in obsolescence; participate in cooperative reporting forums, such as the Government-Industry Data Exchange Program (GIDEP), to reduce or eliminate expenditures of resources by sharing technical information essential during research, design, development, production and operational phases of the life cycle of systems, facilities and equipment.
- Proactively monitor potential availability problems to resolve them before they cause an impact in performance readiness or spending.

In addition, by using MIL-STD-3018 (Parts Management), the program can enhance the reliability of the system and mitigate part obsolescence due to DMSMS.

A useful resource for additional guidance is SD-22 (Diminishing Manufacturing Sources and Material Shortages (DMSMS) Guidebook).

CH 3–4.3.9 Environment, Safety and Occupational Health

Environment, Safety and Occupational Health (ESOH) analyses are an integral, ongoing part of the systems engineering (SE) process throughout the life cycle. The benefits of early integration of ESOH considerations include:

- Mitigation of program cost and schedule risks from actions that cause damage to people, equipment or the environment.
- Reduction of Operations and Support and disposal costs to achieve system affordability.
- Provision of a safe, suitable, supportable and sustainable capability able to operate world-wide, including opportunities for Foreign Military Sales.

Throughout each acquisition phase, programs conduct their ESOH analyses to:

- Identify and mitigate potential risks to the system and its associated personnel.
- Manage ESOH design considerations from the beginning of the SE effort.
- Plan for compliance with 42 USC 4321, National Environmental Policy Act (NEPA), and Executive Order (EO) 12114, Environmental Effects Abroad of Major Federal Actions.
- Ensure compliance with statutory ESOH requirements.

ESOH in Systems Engineering

DoDI 5000.02, Enc 3, sec. 16 requires programs to use the system safety methodology in MIL-STD-882 to manage their ESOH considerations as an integral part of the program's overall SE process. This starts with including ESOH management planning in the Milestone A SEP to cover Technology Maturation and Risk Reduction (TMRR) activities and continues throughout the system's life cycle.

DoD defines ESOH in MIL-STD-882 (System Safety) as *"the combination of disciplines that encompass the processes and approaches for addressing laws, regulations, EOs, DoD policies, environmental compliance, and hazards associated with environmental impacts, system safety (e.g., platforms, systems, system-of-systems, weapons, explosives, software, ordnance, combat systems), occupational safety and health, hazardous materials management, and pollution prevention."*

The PM uses the system safety methodology for the identification, documentation and management of ESOH hazards and their associated risks during the system's development and sustainment. The Program Manager, with support from the Systems Engineer, eliminates hazards where possible, and manages ESOH risks where hazards cannot be eliminated. MIL-STD-882 provides a matrix and defines probability and severity criteria to categorize ESOH risks.

MIL-STD-882 provides a structured, yet flexible, framework for hazard analysis and risk assessment for a specific system application (including system hardware and software). As an example for software, Subject Matter Experts (SMEs) use the MIL-STD 882 process for assessing the software contribution to system risk, which considers the potential risk severity and degree of control the software exercises over the hardware, and dictates the analysis level of rigor needed to reduce the risk level. The Joint Services Software Safety Authorities' "Software System Safety Implementation Process and Tasks Supporting MIL-STD-882" is a concise "Implementation Guide" to assist in the implementation of the software system safety requirements and guidance contained in MIL-STD-882 and the Joint Software System Safety Engineering Handbook (JSSSEH) process descriptions complement MIL-STD-882 for these analyses.

The PM and Systems Engineer should also identify and integrate ESOH requirements into the SE process. Examples of this include, but are not limited to, the following:

- Complying with NEPA, EO 12114, and applicable environmental quality requirements, which will require assessing the system's operation and maintenance pollutant emissions.
- Obtaining required design certifications, such as Airworthiness for air systems.
- Prohibiting or strictly controlling the use of banned or restricted hazardous materials, such as hexavalent chrome and ozone-depleting substances.

The PM and the Systems Engineer ensure ESOH is addressed during the Technology Maturation and Risk Reduction (TMRR) phase by including their ESOH plans in the Milestone A SEP. This is critical because the program conducts most of their developmental testing and finalizes a significant portion of the system design during TMRR. During TMRR, the ESOH SME can provide the most cost-effective ESOH support to the program by identifying and then eliminating or mitigating ESOH hazards and ensuring ESOH compliance during system testing and design development.

At Milestone B, the Systems Engineer and their ESOH SMEs document the results of their TMRR ESOH activities in the Programmatic ESOH Evaluation (PESHE) and their NEPA/EO 12114 Compliance Schedule. The PESHE consists of the ESOH hazard data, hazardous materials management data and any additional ESOH compliance information required to support analyses at test, training, fielding and disposal sites.

Finally, properly integrating ESOH in SE requires addressing the following key areas:

- Programs should integrate ESOH and system safety activities by incorporating various functional disciplines such as system safety engineers, fire protection engineers, occupational health professionals and environmental engineers to identify hazards and mitigate risks through the SE process.
- Programs should document ESOH management planning in the SEP, not the PESHE. The PESHE should document data generated by ESOH analyses conducted in support of program execution.

182

- Programs should continue to conduct assessment of the system and its hazards throughout the system life cycle to address system changes for any potential to alter existing risk levels (even for accepted ESOH risks) or to add hazards.

ESOH System Design Requirements

The Systems Engineer identifies the ESOH requirements applicable to the system throughout its life cycle from statutes, regulations, policies, design standards and capability documents. From these requirements, the Systems Engineer should derive ESOH design requirements and include them in capability documents, technical specifications, solicitations and contracts.

ESOH in Program Documents

Together the Systems Engineer and their ESOH SMEs use the SEP to document the program's plan to integrate ESOH into the SE process, incorporating ESOH as a mandatory design, test, sustainment and disposal consideration. They use the Programmatic ESOH Evaluation (PESHE) and the NEPA/EO 12114 Compliance Schedule to document the results of the program's implementation of their ESOH planning. This approach segments required ESOH information across the SEP, PESHE and NEPA/EO 12114 Compliance Schedule to avoid duplication and enhance ESOH integration.

The SEP should include the ESOH management planning information listed in Table 45.

Table 45: ESOH Information in SEP

Column Heading in SEP Table 4.6-1	Expected Information (provided or attached)
Cognizant PMO Organization	Organizational structure for integrating ESOH (or refer to Table 3.4.4-2 if it includes the ESOH team details) and the Program Office ESOH point of contact
Certification	Required ESOH approvals, endorsements, releases, and the designated high and serious risk acceptance user representative(s)
Documentation	PESHE and NEPA/EO 12114 Compliance Schedule
Contractual Requirements (CDRL#)	ESOH contractual language, ESOH Contract Data Requirements List (CDRL) items, and ESOH DFARS clauses
Description / Comments	Description of how design minimizes ESOH risks by summarizing how the program has integrated ESOH considerations into SE processes including the method for tracking hazards and ESOH risks and mitigation plans throughout the life cycle of system

The Systems Engineer and ESOH SMEs also provide input to other program documentation such as the: Acquisition Strategy (AS), Test and Evaluation Master Plan (TEMP), Life-Cycle Sustainment Plan (LCSP), system performance specifications, solicitations, contracts and capability documents.

As the repository for ESOH data and information, the PESHE includes, but is not limited to:

- ESOH Risk Matrices (for hardware and software) used by the program with definitions for severity categories, probability levels, risk levels and risk acceptance and user representative concurrence authorities. (NOTE: If a program is using risk matrices other than those required by MIL-STD-882, the program documents the formal Component approval for those alternative matrices in the PESHE.)
- The following data for each hazard: Hazard Tracking System (HTS) identification number; identified hazards (to include descriptions); associated mishaps (potential mishaps resulting from the hazard); risk assessments (to include the initial, target, and event(s) Risk Assessment Codes (RACs) and risk levels); identified risk mitigation measures; selected (and funded) mitigation measures; hazard status (current RAC and risk level based on any mitigation actions that have been implemented, verified and validated); verification of risk reductions (i.e., status of assessments of mitigation effectiveness); and risk acceptances (records of each risk acceptance

183

decision to include the names of the risk acceptance authority and user representative(s); and dates of risk acceptance and user concurrence(s)). (NOTE: providing an electronic copy of the current data from the HTS would satisfy this requirement.)

- In addition to the applicable hazard and risk data, include the following data for each hazardous material, hazardous waste and pollutant associated with the system: the specific uses, locations, quantities and plans for their minimization and/or safe disposal. (NOTE: providing an electronic copy of the current data from either the HTS (if it includes this information) or the hazardous materials management data would satisfy this requirement.)
- Environmental impact information not included in the HTS or hazardous materials tracking system needed to support NEPA/EO 12114 compliance activities.

NOTE: Programs should use the results of the sustainability analysis (see CH 3–2.4.3. Sustainability Analysis) to inform the hazard analysis.

DoDI 5000.02, Enc 3, sec. 16 requires that each program maintain a NEPA/EO 12114 compliance schedule. This schedule includes, but is not limited to:

- Each proposed action (e.g., testing or fielding)
- Proponent for each action (i.e., the organization that exercises primary management responsibility for a proposed action or activity)
- Anticipated start date for each action at each specific location
- Anticipated NEPA/EO 12114 document type
- Anticipated start and completion dates for each document
- The document approval authority

The PM should incorporate the NEPA / EO 12114 Compliance Schedule into the Program Office's Integrated Master Schedule (IMS) and Integrated Master Plan (IMP).

Because actions occurring during the TMRR phase may require NEPA/EO 12114 compliance, the program should identify these compliance requirements in the Milestone A SEP. DoDI 5000.02, Enc 3, sec. 16 also requires programs to support other organizations NEPA/EO 12114 analyses involving their systems.

ESOH Activities by Phase

Table 46 aligns typical ESOH activities by phase.

Table 46: ESOH Activities by Phase

Acquisition Phase	Typical ESOH Activities
Materiel Solution Analysis (MSA)	<ul><li>Participate in Analysis of Alternatives (AoA)</li><li>Provide inputs to the SEP, draft Capability Development Document (CDD), Corrosion Prevention and Control (CPC) Planning, AS, Life-Cycle Sustainment Plan (LCSP) and draft Request for Proposal (RFP)</li></ul>
Technology Maturation and Risk Reduction (TMRR)	<ul><li>Participate in prototyping and design development through the Integrated Product Team (IPT) structure to identify and mitigate ESOH risks in the product to be developed in the next phase</li><li>Prepare initial PESHE and NEPA/EO 12114 Compliance Schedule</li><li>Ensure NEPA/EO 12114 compliance, ESOH risk acceptance, Preliminary Design Review (PDR) risk reporting, and safety releases</li><li>Inputs to SEP, CPC Planning, final CDD, Test and Evaluation Master Plan (TEMP), LCSP, and draft RFP</li></ul>

184

Acquisition Phase	Typical ESOH Activities
Engineering and Manufacturing Development (EMD)	• Participate in trades and design development activities through the IPT structure • Evaluate Test and Evaluation (T&E) results, to include assessment of ESOH risk mitigations • Update NEPA/EO 12114 Compliance Schedule and PESHE; support NEPA/EO 12114 compliance activities, ESOH risk acceptance • Obtain required ESOH approvals, endorsements and releases; provide inputs to the SEP, CPC Planning, LCSP, Capability Production Document (CPD) and draft RFP
Production and Deployment (P&D)	• Participate in initial Configuration Control Board (CCB) process • Evaluate T&E results, to include assessment of ESOH risk mitigations • Analyze deficiency reports • Review Physical Configuration Audit (PCA) • Update NEPA/EO 12114 Compliance Schedule and PESHE • Support NEPA/EO 12114 compliance activities and ESOH risk mitigations • Obtain required ESOH approvals, endorsements and releases • Support Initial Operational Capability (IOC) and Full Operational Capability (FOC) • Provide inputs to the LCSP, CPC Planning, and product support package
Operations and Support (O&S)	• Participate in mishap investigations and the CCB process • Analyze system use data such as deficiency reports, hazard reports, regulatory violations, etc. • Keep the PESHE data current; support NEPA/EO 12114 compliance activities and ESOH risk acceptance • Provide inputs to draft Joint Capabilities Integration and Development System (JCIDS) documents and CPC Planning

ESOH Risk Management

The PM is also responsible for ensuring the appropriate management level accepts ESOH risks prior to exposing people, equipment or the environment to those risks.

- High ESOH risks require Component Acquisition Executive (CAE) acceptance
- Serious ESOH risks require Program Executive Officer (PEO)-level acceptance
- Medium and Low ESOH risks require PM acceptance

Any time a risk level increases the PM should ensure the appropriate management level accepts the new risk level prior to exposing people, equipment or the environment to the new risk level. This means a given ESOH risk may require multiple risk acceptances as the risk level changes across the life of a system. For example:

- During development, the risk level will change as the program funds and implements identified mitigations.
- During testing, the risk level may change due to test configurations, which differ from the eventual system design.
- During sustainment of a fielded system, the risk level may change as the system ages and as more information about a given risk becomes available.

185

The Systems Engineer, in support of the PM, uses the MIL-STD-882 methodology to manage ESOH risks. DoDI 5000.02, Enc 3, sec. 16 identifies the appropriate management level authorized to accept ESOH risks. Before accepting a risk, the appropriate acceptance authority requires user representative concurrence from the DoD Component(s) responsible for the personnel, equipment or environment exposed to the risk.

For joint programs, the ESOH risk acceptance authorities reside within the lead DoD Component (unless the Milestone Decision Authority (MDA) approves an alternative) and each participating DoD Component provides an appropriate user representative. Joint programs should identify the specific risk acceptance authority and user representative offices in the PESHE. If a joint program uses a memorandum of agreement (MOA) to document risk acceptance authority and user representative offices, they should attach the MOA to the PESHE.

The program documents formal risk acceptances as part of the program record (e.g., Hazard Tracking System). If a risk level increases for a hazard, a new risk acceptance is required prior to exposing people, equipment or the environment to the increased risk. The program also participates in system-related mishap investigations to assess contributing hazards, risks and mitigations.

DoDI 5000.02, Enc 3, sec. 16 requires programs to report the status of current high and serious ESOH risks at program reviews and fielding decisions and the status of all ESOH risks at technical reviews. The purpose of this reporting is to inform the MDA, PEO, PM and end user about trades being made and ESOH risks that need to be accepted. Each ESOH risk report includes the following:

- The hazard, potential mishap, initial RAC and risk level
- Mitigation measure(s) and funding status
- Target RAC and risk level
- Current RAC and risk level
- Risk acceptance/user representative concurrence status

In accordance with MIL-STD-882, a risk is never closed nor is the term "residual" risk used. This enables programs to ensure, as their system changes occur over time; they assess those changes for any potential to alter existing risk levels or to add hazards. This also enables a program to determine the potential for eliminating hazards or reducing their risk levels as the program implements system design or operating and maintenance procedure changes.

Hazardous Materials Management

When Hazardous Materials (HAZMAT) and chemicals/materials of evolving regulatory concern are designed into the system or used for system operation and maintenance, the Program Manager and Systems Engineer assess and document the ESOH risks for each combination of HAZMAT and application. (NOTE: The use of certain HAZMATs in system design can increase life-cycle cost and create barriers to Foreign Military Sales.) The Systems Engineer can use the optional Task 108, Hazardous Materials Management Plan, in MIL-STD-882 and/or the Aerospace Industries Association (AIA) National Aerospace Standard (NAS) 411, Hazardous Materials Management Program, as the basis for a program's HAZMAT management. Both Task 108 and NAS 411 require a contractual listing of the HAZMAT, which the program intends to manage. The contractual listing categorizes each listed HAZMAT as Prohibited, Restricted or Tracked. NAS 411-1, Hazardous Material Target List, provides a DoD-AIA agreed-upon baseline listing of HAZMAT for each category to use as the starting point in defining the program's list of HAZMAT. When using either Task 108 or NAS 411, the Program Manager and Systems Engineer should document the following data elements for each listed HAZMAT:

- HAZMAT item or substance name (with Chemical Abstract Services (CAS) Number if available)
- HAZMAT Category (Prohibited, Restricted or Tracked)
- Special Material Content Code (SMCC) as designated in DoD 4100.39-M, Volume 10
- The locations, quantities, and usage of each HAZMAT embedded in the system or used during operations and support of the system, with traceability, as applicable, to version specific hardware designs

186

- ESOH requirements for demilitarization and disposal
- Energetic qualification information, as applicable
- Reasonably anticipated quantities of hazardous waste generated during normal operation and maintenance
- Reasonably anticipated HAZMAT (whether categorized or not) generated during the system's life cycle (e.g., installation, Government test and evaluation, normal use and maintenance or repair of the system)
- Hazardous emissions/discharges, including those reasonably anticipated in emergency situations
- Special control, training, handling, Personal Protective Equipment (PPE) and storage requirements, to include provision of required Safety Data Sheets (SDSs), previously called Material Safety Data Sheets (MSDSs)

The Systems Engineer manages hexavalent chromium usage in systems to balance the requirements for corrosion prevention and control and the procedures in DFARS (Subpart 223.73 - Minimizing the Use of Hexavalent Chromium). For more information on chemicals/materials of evolving regulatory concern, refer to the DENIX website.

Safety Release for Testing

The PM, in concert with the user and the T&E community, provides safety releases (to include formal ESOH risk acceptance in accordance with DoDI 5000.02, Enc 3, sec. 16), to the developmental and operational testers before any test exposing personnel to ESOH hazards. The safety release addresses each system hazard present during the test and includes formal risk acceptance for each hazard. The program's safety release is in addition to any test range safety release requirements, but it should support test range analyses required for a range-generated test release. Safety releases should be documented as part of the Program Record.

The PM should provide a transmittal letter to the involved test organization with a detailed listing of the system hazards germane to the test that includes the current risk level and documented risk acceptance along with information on all implemented mitigations.

Sustainable Procurement Program

In an effort to enhance and sustain mission readiness over the system life cycle, reduce reliance on resources and reduce the DoD footprint, programs should follow the policy and procedures identified in the DoD Sustainable Procurement Program (SPP). SPP benefits include:

- Improving mission performance by decreasing life cycle costs and reducing liabilities.
- Reducing impacts to human health and the environment.
- Ensuring availability of chemicals and materials.
- Enhancing installation and national security by reducing dependence on foreign energy sources.
- Contributing to regulatory compliance.
- Increasing potential for Foreign Military Sales.

PMs should implement the applicable SPP procedures in FAR (Subparts 23.2, 23.4, 23.7 and 23.8) to select materials and products that are energy-efficient, water conserving and environmentally preferable. More information on SPP is available on the DENIX website.

Climate Change

In an effort to continuously adapt current and future DoD operations to address the impacts of climate change, and to maintain an effective and efficient U.S. military, DoDD 4715.21 (para 1.2, 2.1, and 2.4) requires programs to integrate climate change considerations, including life-cycle analyses, into acquisitions.

Key Resources

- Acquisition Community Connection/ESOH

- Defense Acquisition University Continuous Learning Modules "CLE 009 -- ESOH in Systems Engineering" and "CLR 030 - ESOH in JCIDS"
- Defense Federal Acquisition Regulation Supplement (DFARS)
- Federal Acquisition Regulation (FAR)
- Joint Software System Safety Engineering Handbook, August 27, 2010
- MIL-STD-882 with 25 optional Tasks

CH 3–4.3.10 Human Systems Integration

Systems engineering (SE) addresses the three major elements of each system: hardware, software and human. SE integrates human capability considerations with the other specialty engineering disciplines to achieve total system performance requirements by factoring into the system design the capabilities and limitations of the human operators, maintainers and users.

Throughout the acquisition life cycle, the Systems Engineer should apply Human Systems Integration (HSI) design criteria, principles and practices described in MIL-STD-1472 (Human Engineering) and MIL-STD-46855 (Human Engineering Requirements for Military Systems, Equipment and Facilities).

The HSI effort assists the Systems Engineer to minimize ownership costs and ensure the system is built to accommodate the human performance characteristics of users who operate, maintain and support the total system. The total system includes not only the mission equipment but also the users, training and training devices and operational and support infrastructure.

The Program Manager (PM) has overall responsibility for integrating the HSI effort into the program. These responsibilities are described in DAG Chapter 5 Manpower Planning & Human Systems Integration.

The Systems Engineer supports the PM by leading HSI efforts. The Systems Engineer should work with the manpower, personnel, training, safety, health, habitability, personnel survivability and Human Factors Engineering (HFE) stakeholders to develop the HSI effort. The Systems Engineer translates and integrates those human capability considerations, as contained in the capabilities documents, into quantifiable system requirements. Requirements for conducting HSI efforts should be specified for inclusion in the Statement of Work and contract. HSI should also be addressed in the Systems Engineering Plan (SEP), specifications, Test and Evaluation Master Plan (TEMP), Software Development Plan (SDP), Life-Cycle Sustainment Plan (LCSP) and other appropriate program documentation. The SEP Outline requires that HSI be addressed as a design consideration.

Elements of an effective HSI effort, described in DAG Chapter 5 Manpower Planning & Human Systems Integration, should:

- Provide a better operational solution to the warfighters.
- Lead to the development or improvement of all human interfaces.
- Achieve required effectiveness of human performance during system testing, operation, maintenance, support, transport, demilitarization and disposal.
- Ensure the demands upon personnel resources, skills, training and costs are planned and accounted for at every stage in the system life cycle.
- Ensure that overall human performance is within the knowledge, skills and abilities of the designated operators, maintainers and users to support mission tasking.

CH 3–4.3.11 Insensitive Munitions

The term "Insensitive Munitions" (IM) implies that unanticipated stimuli will not produce an explosive yield, in accordance with MIL-STD-2105 (Hazard Assessment Tests for Non-Nuclear Munitions). IM minimizes the probability of inadvertent initiation and the severity of subsequent collateral damage to weapon platforms, logistic systems and personnel when munitions are subjected to unanticipated stimuli during manufacture, handling, storage, transport, deployment or disposal, or due to accidents or action by an adversary.

IM is a component of explosives ordnance safety described in 10 USC 2389, which specifies that it is the responsibility of DoD to ensure IM under development or procurement are safe, to the extent practicable, throughout development and fielding when subjected to unplanned stimuli, (e.g., electro-magnetic interference, vibration or shock). In accordance with DoDD 5000.01, Enc. 1 and DoDI 5000.02, Enc 3, sec. 17), the Program Manager (PM) and Systems Engineer for munitions programs and other energetic devices (such as ordnance, warheads, bombs and rocket motors) and munitions handling, storage and transport programs have an overriding responsibility to address safety aspects of their programs in trade studies, design reviews, milestone reviews and in JCIDS documents.

The PM and Systems Engineer for munitions programs, regardless of ACAT level, should have safety as a top consideration when performing trade studies or making program decisions. The PM and cognizant technical staff should coordinate harmonized IM/Hazard Classification (HC) test plans with the Service IM/HC testing review organizations. The Service organizations should coordinate the IM/HC with the Joint Services Insensitive Munitions Technical Panel (JSIMTP), Joint Service Hazard classifiers and the DoD Explosives Safety Board (DDESB), which is chartered by DoDD 6055.9E, Explosives Safety Management and the DDESB. Aspects of IM also apply to nuclear weapons but are not addressed here.

The primary document to address IM is the Insensitive Munitions Strategic Plan (IMSP), as required by USD(AT&L) memorandum, "Insensitive Munitions Strategic Plans," July 21, 2004, which establishes DoD policy for the annual submission of IMSPs to the Joint Requirements Oversight Council (JROC) and Office of the Under Secretary of Defense (Acquisition, Technology, and Logistics) (OUSD(AT&L)), by the Program Executive Officer (PEO) for munitions programs. USD(AT&L) memorandum, "Joint Insensitive Munitions Test Standards and Compliance Assessment." February 10, 2010, establishes policy for oversight and compliance assessment. The DoD Standard Operating Procedure (SOP) for IMSP and the Plan of Action and Milestones (POA&M), defined by Joint Business Rules, March 2011, define the content of the IMSP, which spans the Future Years Defense Plan (FYDP) and includes currently funded as well as unfunded requirements. The DoD Acquisition Manager's Handbook for Insensitive Munitions contains the above-referenced documents and appendices for each Service's policy and review board process.

The IMSP is the primary program output required by USD(AT&L) and the Joint Staff to provide evidence that the program is in compliance with all applicable laws and regulations. Both the Component-level and DoD-level IM review organizations can provide additional guidance and can assess the adequacy of the IMSP. In addition to the IMSP, the Analysis of Alternatives, Acquisition Strategy, Systems Engineering Plan, Test and Evaluation Master Plan, Risk Management Plan and other JCIDS documents called for in CJCSI 3170.01 and the JCIDS Manual (requires Common Access Card (CAC) to access website), address aspects of explosives ordnance safety, including IM.

CH 3–4.3.12 Intelligence (Life-Cycle Mission Data Plan)
In collaboration with the intelligence community and the operational sponsor(s), the Program Manager (PM), with support from the Systems Engineer and Chief Developmental Tester, is responsible for planning, identifying, documenting, communicating and programming for life-cycle intelligence mission data support (see Figure 42 and DoDD 5250.01.)

Modern weapon systems are inherently dependent on a variety of scientific and technical intelligence products throughout every stage of their life cycle. Hence, planning for intelligence Mission Data (IMD) support, which informs design and development trade-offs, risk assessments and decisions is essential to satisfying system requirements. Similarly, communicating IMD requirements to the DoD intelligence community that supplies the necessary intelligence data is critical to achieving system capabilities.

Modern weapon systems are often intended to operate in threat and target environments throughout the world in multiple domains. System design decisions, development trade-offs and advanced technology insertion may be optimized, thereby creating sensitivities to changes in adversary capabilities in the threat and target environments. Critical intelligence parameters (CIP) represent key performance thresholds of foreign threat systems, which, if exceeded, could compromise the mission effectiveness of the system in development. Therefore, these CIPs (for example, radar cross-section, armor type or thickness or

189

acoustic characteristics) should be identified and communicated to the intelligence community for tracking and immediate notification if breached. See CH 7–4.1.4. for more information on CIPs.

Intelligence life-cycle mission data planning is necessary to effectively:

- Derive functional baseline requirements and life-cycle IMD requirements necessary to identify, define, and refine sensors, algorithms and intelligence data needs and trade-offs.
- Design, develop, test and evaluate IMD-dependent sensors, algorithms, systems, processes and interfaces.
- Conduct effectiveness analyses and risk assessments.
- Identify and acquire threat and target parameters that support digital modeling and simulation (see CH 3–2.4.2. Modeling and Simulation).
- Develop technical performance measures to inform test and evaluation.
- Inform decision making and science and technology investments for identifying IMD production and collection requirements.
- Assess system capability and limitations.
- Ensure system flexibility and agility in response to a dynamic threat and target environment.

Figure 42: Intelligence Mission Data (IMD) Life Cycle Timeline

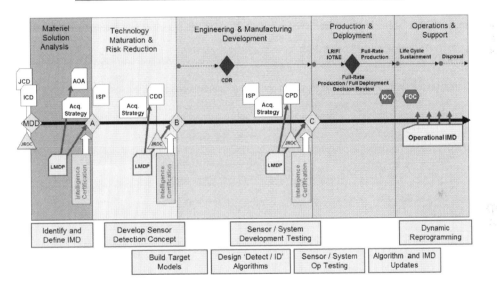

The initial Life-Cycle Mission Data Plan (LMDP) is due at Milestone A, with a draft update due at the Development RFP Release Decision Point and approval at Milestone B by the DoD Component (see DoDI 5000.02, Enc 1, Table 2). Additional updates to the LMDP are due at Milestone C and the Full Rate Production/Full Deployment Decision.

CH 7–4.1.3. provides key linkages to the system performance specification (sometimes called the System Requirements Document (SRD)), Systems Engineering Plan (SEP) and Test and Evaluation Master Plan (TEMP). These three products are directly affected by IMD requirements.

CH 3–4.3.13 Interoperability and Dependencies
Almost all DoD systems operate in a system of systems (SoS) context relying upon other systems to provide desired user capabilities -- making it vital that interoperability needs and external dependencies are identified early and incorporated into system requirements. When identifying system requirements, it is critical to consider the operational and SoS context (see CH 3–3.1.2. Systems of Systems). These

190

include, but are not limited to, physical requirements (e.g., size, power limits, etc.), electronic requirements (e.g., signature, interference, etc.) and information exchange/management (e.g., network, bandwidth, information needs, etc.). These system requirements also include interdependencies with other systems. For efficiency, systems often rely on either services provided by other systems during operations or reuse of system elements developed by other programs.

Interoperability is the requirement that the program's system interact with other systems through transport of information, energy or matter. For example, an air-launched missile is required to be interoperable with its delivery platform(s). Information is exchanged. A mechanical interface secures the missile until launch and so on. Usually, interoperability involves external interfaces (see CH 3–4.1.8. Interface Management Process) and is essential for the creation of systems of systems (SoS). Every system is required to be certified interoperable before it is fielded. The Joint Interoperability Test Command (JITC) is responsible for this certification.

Dependencies are relationships between different programs that cause one program to rely on another program's actions or products to successfully meet its requirements. As examples, a ship development program may require prototypes of mission modules being developed by another program in the course of developmental testing, or a weapon may depend on new sensor capabilities provided by another system. The program depends on the mission module or sensor program to enable it to meet its testing schedule. A schedule issue could occur if the needed prototypes are not available in time for the tests. A performance issue could occur if the designs of the two systems do not support the needed end-to-end capability.

The common element linking interoperability and dependencies (I&D) is the need for cooperation and/or coordination between separate programs. Two common ways to meet this need are memoranda of agreements (MOAs) and invited attendance at program technical reviews and other technical meetings. MOAs are agreements between programs that specify expectations as to performance, resources, management and schedules. Interchange between engineers and managers at technical meetings opens lines of communication, which permits risk identification and early mitigation.

The Program Manager (PM) is responsible for ensuring that the operational and SoS context for the system are well understood. The PM is also responsible for establishing required MOAs and managing relationships with other programs.

The Systems Engineer has the responsibility for ensuring all interoperability and dependency impacts are analyzed and collaborated with the appropriate internal/external stakeholders and translated into system requirements and design considerations.

Analysis conducted for the SoS contexts for the system -- where the system is dependent on other systems and where the system needs to interact with other systems -- enables translation of interoperability and dependencies (I&D) into system requirements. I&D requirements call for collaborative implementation approaches with external organizations, including identification, management and control of key interfaces. Areas of dependency and interoperability should be reviewed for risks to the program and plans made to manage and mitigate those risks. This review includes system interdependencies (e.g., a weapon may depend on new sensor capabilities provided by another system) and information exchanges with other systems required to support mission capabilities. For efficiency, systems may rely on system elements developed by others for key functionality, either through services (e.g., weather information) provided by other systems or through reuse of system elements (e.g., engines, radios) developed by other programs. These contexts are analyzed to identify system requirements and risks, including actions needed by external parties (e.g., other systems or infrastructure) for the system to meet user requirements.

Additional DoD policy and guidance regarding I&D, summarized below, are directed at ensuring that systems work effectively with other systems:

- Interoperability of information technology and National Security System (NSS) acquisition programs are required to comply with DoDI 8330.01, CJCSI 3170.01, the JCIDS Manual (requires Common Access Card (CAC) to access website), and 44 USC 3506.

- DoDD 5000.01, Enc. 1:
  - Ability of acquired systems to exchange information and services with other systems and to interoperate with other United States forces and coalition partners, and, as appropriate, with other United States Government departments and agencies.
  - Providing systems and systems of systems that are interoperable and able to communicate across a universal infrastructure that includes organizational interactions, other systems, networks and information-exchange capabilities.
- DoDI 5000.02: An integrated system design that defines system and system of systems functionality and interfaces, and reduces system-level risk.
- DoDI 2010.06: Pursuing opportunities throughout the acquisition life cycle that enhance international cooperation and improve interoperability.

CH 3–4.3.14 Item Unique Identification

Item Unique Identification (IUID) is a systematic process to globally and unambiguously distinguish one item from all the other items that DoD buys or owns. IUID-enabled Serialized Item Management (SIM) provides a capability that allows DoD to locate, control, value and manage its assets throughout the life cycle. A robust SIM program provides tools and processes to assist informed decision making to achieve both better weapon system reliability and readiness at reduced total ownership cost. IUID-enabled SIM provides DoD with a standard methodology to:

- Consistently capture the value of all individual items it buys/owns.
- Trace these items during their use.
- Combat counterfeiting of parts.
- Associate valuable business intelligence to an item throughout its life cycle via automatic identification technology and connections to automated information systems.

Program Managers (PMs) and Product Support Managers should budget, plan for and implement IUID-enabled SIM as an integral activity within MIL-STD-130 (Identification Marking of U.S. Military Property) requisite item identification processes to identify and track applicable major end items and configuration-controlled items. IUID implemented in accordance with DoDI 8320.04 and IUID Implementation Plans are required for all milestone decisions as directed by DoDI 5000.02, Enc 1, Table 2. IUID-specific design considerations are required in the Systems Engineering Plan (SEP) and SIM planning and implementation required by DoDI 4151.19 are addressed in the Life-Cycle Sustainment Plan (LCSP).

The Systems Engineer considers what to mark and how to incorporate the IUID mark within MIL-STD-130 item-marking requirements when formulating design decisions. In addition, the Systems Engineer considers where product and maintenance information reside and how the life-cycle data are used within the configuration management and product support systems -- including new and legacy information systems.

The DoD Guide to Uniquely Identifying Items provides guidance on implementing IUID intended for use by Department of Defense (DoD) contractors and their suppliers, who put unique item identifier (UII) marks on new items during production, as directed in the contract.

CH 3–4.3.15 Modular Design

Modular design allows for modifications to systems, recombination of existing capabilities and upgrade of system elements, to enable competition, innovation, rapidly responding to a changing environment, etc. Designing for modularity is a key technical principle for implementing a modular open systems approach (MOSA) and is a complementary piece to the open system practices in contracting. The major tenet of a modular design strategy is to develop loosely coupled systems, where modules can be decoupled, separated or even re-arranged. When designing for modularity, the system should be appropriately partitioned into discrete, scalable, self-contained functional elements by decomposing and decoupling the functions of a system. This functional partitioning results in elements that can now be composed into modules that can be reconfigured or even replaced.

Acquisition programs implementing a modular design provide flexible system designs, which allow for the replacement or recombination of subsystems and components. It is important for the program management to understand the expected benefit from modular design as part of implementing a MOSA strategy. This understanding provides guidance to the system realization, on which enabling elements (e.g., standards, contract clauses, engineering tools, etc.) to use. MOSA benefits are usually categorized into five individually useful areas, which often overlap: cost savings/cost avoidance; increased competition; enhanced interoperability; application of innovative elements; and ability to realize technology upgrade opportunities easily.

Program Managers (PMs) should understand both the positive and negative outcomes from implementing a modular design and determine if the realization of a particular benefit outweighs the potential negative consequence. When scoping where the system should implement modular design, the PM and Systems Engineer should consider multiple factors, such as anticipated obsolescence, technical innovation, preplanned product improvements to meet performance, etc. These circumstances will vary across systems. System engineers should conduct design trades to support the PM in deciding where to implement modularity into the system design, including how to organize system components, where to put interfaces and which interface specifications and standards to select. (For additional details see CH 3–2.4.1. Modular Open Systems Approach.)

CH 3–4.3.16 Operational Energy

Emerging threats to the logistic resupply of operational forces, the trend toward ever greater energy demand in the operational forces and increasing costs to operate and resupply energy-intensive systems have all put increasing focus on lowering system and unit energy demand. Reducing the force's dependence on energy logistics can improve the force's mobility and resilience and increase its control over the timing and conditions of the fight. Focusing on energy as an explicit design consideration and systems engineering (SE) category is a significant change in practice and thinking that will help manage emerging operational challenges.

The Program Manager (PM) and Systems Engineer can help lower operational energy by addressing issues associated with the system's energy logistics support and power resupply frequency.

This approach should generate informed choices based on the threshold and objective values of the Energy Key Performance Parameter (KPP) for the system. For liquid energy-consuming systems, the top-level units of measure for the Energy KPP might be gallons of fuel demanded (consumed) over a defined set of duty cycles or for accomplishing a specified mission goal such as a sortie. These measures may be further decomposed into weight, range, electric power demand and other relevant measures to inform the necessary SE trade-off analysis. The intended result is a comprehensive set of trade-space choices for industry to consider to deliver solutions that are not only energy efficient but also mission-effective and affordable. See the Joint Capabilities Integration and Development System (JCIDS) Manual linked at the end of this section for more information on the Operational Energy KPP.

Energy's relationship to performance arises from the operational context in which the system is used. Accordingly, the scenarios that illustrate how the system is used, as part of a unit of maneuver, are essential to understanding the energy supply and demand constraints to be managed. This is essentially the same approach as balancing survivability goals against lethality goals in the engineering trade space. Operational energy issues include:

- How the system and combat unit refuel/recharge in the battlespace scenarios, and how often.
- How this refueling/recharging requirement might constrain our forces (limit their freedom of action, on-station time, signature, etc.)
- How the adversary depicted in the defining scenarios might delay, disrupt and/or defeat our forces by interdicting this system's refueling/recharging logistics.
- How much force protection could be diverted from combat missions to protecting these refueling/recharging events when and where required.

Systems Engineers should consider incorporating energy demand in design, technology, materials, and related issues into the system trade space along with other performance issues, so that oppressive energy resupply needs are not inadvertently introduced in the attempt to achieve other performance goals (e.g., survivability, lethality). In practice, this means requirements managers should factor into the system design the necessity of refueling/recharging using the same scenarios used to illustrate other performance requirements, and allowing the adversary a realistic chance to interdict the refueling/recharging effort. Systems Engineers may find it necessary to have a continuing dialogue with the warfighter (the user and requirements manager) to help grasp the operational impact of these issues and depict them in trade-space decisions.

Energy-related engineering analysis should begin early enough to support initial Analysis of Alternatives (AoA) planning following the Materiel Development Decision, and should also be routinely updated to inform any AoA performed later in the life cycle (i.e., in support of block upgrades and modifications).

The following documents provide the PM and Systems Engineer with additional insight into the issue of Operational Energy in the acquisition life cycle:

- JCIDS Manual (for the Energy KPP; requires Common Access Card (CAC) to access website)
- Operational Energy Strategy
- Defense Science Board Task Force report on Operational Energy, February 2008
- Defense Science Board Task Force report on Operational Energy, May 2001

NOTE: The results of the sustainability analysis (see CH 3–2.4.3. Sustainability Analysis) can be used to inform energy analyses.

CH 3–4.3.17 Packaging, Handling, Storage and Transportation
The program team employs Packaging, Handling, Storage and Transportation (PHS&T) principles/methods to ensure the necessary equipment reaches the warfighter while minimizing risk of damage to the equipment during handling, storage and transportation -- frequently in highly challenging and corrosive operational environments.

Thorough PHS&T requirements promote supportability and sustainability of major end items, reparable system elements and supporting test equipment. PHS&T focuses on transportation, handling and storage (short- and long-term) constraints on performance resulting from driving size, weight, parts robustness and shelf life.

Program Managers (PMs) and Systems Engineers should ensure PHS&T is addressed during the requirements analysis process, and validated throughout each phase of the systems engineering (SE) development of the weapon system. All PHS&T requirements should be verified before entering the Production and Deployment phase, as this phase will require the implementation of PHS&T for a weapon system delivery to the warfighter during low rate initial production. DoDI 4540.07 identifies specifics regarding PHS&T as related to systems engineering of weapon systems acquisitions. In addition, the following documents address PHS&T:

- MIL-STD-2073-1 (Standard Practice for Military Packaging)
- MIL-STD-129 (Military Marking for Shipment and Storage)
- ASTM-D3951, Standard Practice for Commercial Packaging
- DoDM 4140.27, Volume 1
- DTR 4500.9-R, Defense Transportation Regulation
- 49 CFR Parts 171-180, Transportation

CH 3–4.3.18 Producibility, Quality and Manufacturing Readiness
Producibility

Producibility is a design accomplishment for the relative ease of manufacturing. Like manufacturing and other key system design functions, producibility is integral to delivering capability to the warfighter effectively and efficiently. Producible designs are lower risk, more cost-effective and repeatable, which enhances product reliability and supportability. Producibility should be assessed at both a product and

194

enterprise (i.e., organizational, prime contractor facility) level. The Program Manager(PM) should implement producibility engineering and planning efforts early and should continuously assess the integrated processes and resources needed to successfully achieve producibility.

To assess producibility on a product level, both the product and its manufacturing processes should be measured. Manufacturing processes should be monitored and controlled, through measurement, to ensure that they can repeatedly produce accurate, high-quality products, which helps the program meet objectives for limiting process variability to a tolerable range.

To assess producibility within a manufacturing enterprise level, the organization should evaluate producibility performance on a product-specific basis. This evaluation allows the organization to understand the strengths and weaknesses of its producibility approach better, so enhancements can be identified and measures of processes, products, and the producibility system (integrated processes and resources needed for achieving producibility) can be tailored to strive for continuous improvement.

The PM should ensure that the producibility program focuses on the following five elements to build and maintain a successful producibility system:

1. Establish a producibility infrastructure:
    * Organize for producibility
    * Integrate producibility into the program's risk management program
    * Incorporate producibility into the new product strategy
    * Employ producibility design guidelines
2. Determine Process Capability:
    * Determine Process Capability (Cpk)
    * Understand and document company and supplier processes
    * Plan for future process capabilities
3. Address producibility during initial design efforts:
    * Identify design objectives
    * Identify key characteristics of the design
    * Perform trade studies on alternative product and process designs
    * Develop a manufacturing plan
    * Perform complexity analysis
4. Address producibility during detailed design:
    * Address producibility measurements at Preliminary Design Review (PDR), Critical Design Review (CDR), Production Readiness Review (PRR) and Full-Rate Production Design Review (FRP DR)
    * Optimize manufacturing plans as the design matures
5. Measure producibility processes, products and systems.

Producibility should be a Technical Performance Measure (TPM) for the program, and the program's strategy for producibility should be contained in paragraph 3.6 of the program's Systems Engineering Plan (SEP). Planned producibility engineering activities for previous and subsequent phases also should be summarized in the SEP. As a key design accomplishment, producibility should be included in the SEP, mapping key design considerations into the Request for Proposal (RFP) and subsequently into the contract.

Quality in Design

Design engineering focuses on concurrent development of the total system, using capable manufacturing processes leading to a producible, testable, sustainable and affordable product that meets defined requirements. The design phase is critical because product life-cycle costs are committed at this point. The objectives of quality design efforts are to:

* Achieve effective and efficient manufacturing with necessary process controls to meet system requirements.
* Transition to production with no significant manufacturing process and reliability risks that could breach production thresholds for cost and performance.

195

To ensure consistency in applying quality planning and process control, the program should establish a Quality Management System (QMS) early, ideally at Milestone A (See CH 1–4.2.19. for more information on Quality Management.)The QMS should be defined and documented in the Acquisition Strategy (AS). The process should be integrated into these documents as a systems engineering (SE) practice that supports the successful transition of capability development to full-rate production and delivery of systems to support warfighter missions.

The primary focus of the QMS should be to ensure efficiency in processes, and should be integrated with Statistical Process Control (SPC) to eliminate defects and control variation in production. The QMS should aid the transition from system development to production by controlling life-cycle cost and reducing complexities that are often found when quality is not integrated as a function of the design. Therefore, to achieve high-quality (product characteristics meet specification requirements), an end product should be designed so that:

- Processes to produce the end product are in statistical control (uniformity in manufacturing and production).
- Design specifications are aligned with manufacturing process capabilities.
- Functional design integrates producibility requirements (measure of relative ease of manufacturing) with no significant compromises to quality and performance.

The PM and Systems Engineer should take into consideration that process capability goes beyond machine capability. The process should include the effects of change in workers, materials, fabrication methods, tooling and equipment, setup and other conditions. Process capability data should be collected throughout process and product development. Data collection efforts should be continuously refined, using test articles, through production.

In addition to QMS and SPC, understanding and improving processes may require common and/or new tools and techniques to eliminate defects and variation in processes.

Another quality management tool available to the PM is parts management. MIL-STD-3018 (Parts Management) provides requirements for the implementation of an effective Parts Management Program (PMP) on DoD acquisitions.

Quality should be a TPM for the program, and the program's strategy for managing quality should be included in the SEP. Planned quality engineering and management activities for previous and subsequent phases also should be summarized in the SEP. As a key design accomplishment, quality should be included in the SEP mapping key design considerations into contracts.

Two valuable tools to assist in creating quality in design are Six Sigma and Quality Function Deployment (QFD). Six Sigma techniques identify and reduce all sources of product variation -- machines, materials, methods, measurement system, the environment and the people in the process. QFD is a structured approach to understanding customer requirements and translating them into products that satisfy those needs.

Assessing Manufacturing Readiness and Risk

PMs of programs with a manufacturing component should ensure contractors have a robust manufacturing management system. Planned manufacturing management activities for previous and subsequent phases also should be summarized in the SEP. As a key design accomplishment, efficient and cost-effective manufacturing should be included in the SEP, mapping key design considerations into contracts. The SAE AS6500, Manufacturing Management Program, contains best practices for a manufacturing management system, has been adopted for use by DoD and may be placed on contract with tailoring appropriate to the program's needs.

Manufacturing feasibility, processes and risk should be assessed early in the Materiel Solution Analysis (MSA) phase, and continuously through the Production and Deployment (P&D) phase in all acquisition

196

programs. To ensure integration of manufacturing readiness and risk as part of design activities, the focus should be on system risk reduction, manufacturing process reliability and producibility.

PMs should use existing manufacturing processes whenever practical to support low-risk manufacturing. When the design requires new manufacturing capability, the PM may need to consider new manufacturing technologies or process flexibility (e.g., rate and configuration insensitivity), which introduces risk. DoDI 5000.02, Enc 3, sec. 10, defines the requirements for manufacturing processes and manufacturing risks. See DFARS (Subpart 207.105 – Contents of Written Acquisition Plans) for specific guidance on manufacturing actions planned by the PM to execute the approach established in the AS and to guide contractual implementation. These include:

- Consideration of requirements for efficient manufacture during the design and production of the system
- The availability of raw materials, special alloys, composite materials, components, tooling and production test equipment
- The use of advanced manufacturing technology, processes and systems
- The use of contract solicitations that encourage competing offerors to acquire modern technology, production equipment and production systems (including hardware and software)
- Methods to encourage investment in advanced manufacturing technology, production equipment and processes
- During source selection, increased emphasis on the efficiency of production.
- Expanded use of commercial manufacturing processes rather than processes specified by DoD

Low-risk manufacturing readiness includes early planning and investments in producibility requirements, manufacturing process capabilities and quality management to ensure effective and efficient manufacturing and transition to production. It also includes assessments of the industrial base. Manufacturing risk is evaluated through manufacturing readiness assessments, which are integrated with existing program assessments throughout the acquisition life cycle. The PM should assess manufacturing readiness in the program's earliest phase, and the assessment should be continuous. The PM should report on the program's manufacturing readiness progress/status during each technical review, Program Support Assessment, or its equivalent, and before each milestone decision.

Successful manufacturing has many dimensions. Industry and Government have identified best practices in the following nine manufacturing risk categories. PMs should use the best practices to assess their programs early and should report on these areas during technical reviews and before acquisition milestones. Implementation of these best practices should be tailored according to product domains, complexity and maturity of critical technologies, manufacturing processes and specific risks that have been identified throughout the assessment process. These categories should help frame the risk assessment and focus mitigation strategies:

- Technology and the Industrial Base: assess the capability of the national technology and industrial base to support the design, development, production, operation, uninterrupted maintenance support and eventual disposal (environmental impacts) of the system.
- Design: assess the maturity and stability of the evolving system design and evaluate any related impact on manufacturing readiness.
- Cost and Funding: examine the risk associated with reaching manufacturing cost targets.
- Materials: assess the risks associated with materials (including basic/raw materials, components, semi-finished parts and subassemblies).
- Process Capability and Control: assess the risks that the manufacturing processes are able to reflect the design intent (repeatability and affordability) of key characteristics.
- Quality Management: assess the risks and management efforts to control quality and foster continuous improvement.
- Manufacturing Workforce (Engineering and Production): assess the required skills, certification requirements, availability and required number of personnel to support the manufacturing effort.
- Facilities: assess the capabilities and capacity of key manufacturing facilities (prime, subcontractor, supplier, vendor and maintenance/repair)

197

- Manufacturing Management: assess the orchestration of all elements needed to translate the design into an integrated and fielded system (meeting program goals for affordability and availability).

As part of the manufacturing strategy development effort, the PM needs to understand the contractor/vendor business strategy and the impacts to Government risk identification and mitigation efforts, such as the Make/Buy decisions and supply chain risks assessments. Additional guidance on assessing manufacturing risks can be found in the Manufacturing Readiness Guide.

Assessment and mitigation of manufacturing risk should begin as early as possible in a program's acquisition life cycle -- including conducting a manufacturing feasibility assessment as part of the AoA.

The PM and Systems Engineer should consider the manufacturing readiness and manufacturing-readiness processes of potential contractors and subcontractors as a part of the source selection for major defense acquisition programs, see DFARS (Subpart 215.304).

The PM and Systems Engineer should assess manufacturing readiness during the acquisition life cycle, as described in Table 47.

Table 47: Manufacturing Readiness Assessment Points During the Acquisition Life Cycle

Manufacturing Readiness Assessment Points	Considerations
1. Post-AoA assessment during the Materiel Solution Analysis Phase. As part of the AoA, manufacturing risks should have been assessed for each of the competing alternatives (see the MRL Implementation Guide for one source of specific assessment factors). Risks for the preferred system concept should be assessed and identified at this point. The overall assessment should consider whether:	• Program critical technologies are ready for the Technology Maturation and Risk Reduction phase • Required investments in manufacturing technology development have been identified • Processes to ensure manufacturability, producibility and quality are in place and are sufficient to produce prototypes. Manufacturing risks and mitigation plans are in place for building prototypes • Cost objectives have been established and manufacturing cost drivers have been identified; draft Key Performance Parameters have been identified as well as any special tooling, facilities, material handling and skills required • Producibility assessment of the preferred system concept has been completed, and the industrial base capabilities, current state of critical manufacturing processes and potential supply chain sources have all been surveyed
2. Technology Maturation and Risk Reduction, Development RFP Release Decision. As the program approaches the Development RFP Release Decision and the Milestone B decision, critical technologies should have matured sufficiently for 2366b certification and demonstrated in a relevant environment and should consider:	• The program should be nearing acceptance of a preliminary system design • An initial manufacturing approach has been developed • Manufacturing processes have been defined and characterized, but there are still significant engineering and/or design changes in the system itself; manufacturing processes that have not been defined or that may change as the design matures should be identified

198

Manufacturing Readiness Assessment Points	Considerations
	• Preliminary design, producibility assessments, and trade studies of key technologies and components should have been completed • Prototype manufacturing processes and technologies, materials, tooling and test equipment, as well as personnel skills have been demonstrated on systems and/or subsystems in a production-relevant environment • Cost, yield and rate analyses have been performed to assess how prototype data compare with target objectives, and the program has in place appropriate risk reduction to achieve cost requirements or establish a new baseline, which should include design trades • Producibility considerations should have shaped system development plans, and the Industrial Base Capabilities assessment (in the AS for Milestone B) has confirmed the viability of the supplier base
3. Production Readiness Review. A production readiness review identifies the risks of transitioning from development to production. Manufacturing is a function of production; in order to transition to production without significant risk it is important that key processes have been considered and evaluated during the PRR, such as ensuring:	• The detailed system design is complete and stable to support low-rate initial production (LRIP) • Technologies are mature and proven in a production environment, and manufacturing and quality processes are capable, in control and ready for low-rate production • All materials, manpower, tooling, test equipment, and facilities have been proven on pilot lines and are available to meet the planned low-rate production schedule • Cost and yield and rate analyses are updated with pilot line results • Known producibility risks pose no significant challenges for low-rate production • Supplier qualification testing and first article inspections have been completed • Industrial base capabilities assessment for Milestone C has been completed and shows that the supply chain is adequate to support LRIP
4. Full Rate Production (FRP) Decision Review. To support FRP, there should be no significant manufacturing process and reliability risks remaining. Manufacturing and production readiness results should be presented that provide objective evidence of manufacturing readiness. The results should include recommendations for mitigating any remaining low (acceptable) risk, based on assessment of manufacturing readiness for FRP which should include (but not be limited to):	• LRIP learning curves that include tested and applied continuous improvements • Meeting all systems engineering and design requirements • Evidence of a stable system design demonstrated through successful test and evaluation • Evidence that materials, parts, manpower, tooling, test equipment and facilities are available to meet planned production rates • Evidence that manufacturing processes are capable, in control, and have achieved planned FRP objectives

199

Manufacturing Readiness Assessment Points	Considerations
	• Plans are in place for mitigating and monitoring production risks • LRIP cost targets data have been met; learning curves have been analyzed and used to develop the FRP cost model

CH 3–4.3.19 Reliability and Maintainability Engineering

The purpose of Reliability and Maintainability (R&M) engineering (Maintainability includes Built-In-Test (BIT)) is to influence system design in order to increase mission capability and availability and decrease logistics burden and cost over a system's life cycle. Properly planned, R&M engineering reduces cost and schedule risks by preventing or identifying R&M deficiencies early in development. This early action results in increased acquisition efficiency and higher success rates during operational testing, and can even occur in the development process as early as the Engineering and Manufacturing Development (EMD) phase.

DoDI 5000.02, Enc 3, sec. 12 requires Program Managers (PMs) to implement a comprehensive R&M engineering program as an integral part of the systems engineering (SE) process. The Systems Engineer should understand that R&M parameters have an impact on the system's performance, availability, logistics supportability, and total ownership cost. To ensure a successful R&M engineering program, the Systems Engineer should as a minimum integrate the following activities across the program's engineering organization and processes:

- Providing adequate R&M staffing.
- Ensuring R&M engineering is fully integrated into SE activities, Integrated Product Teams and other stakeholder organizations (i.e., Logistics, Test & Evaluation (T&E), and System Safety).
- Ensuring specifications contain realistic quantitative R&M requirements traceable to the Initial Capabilities Document (ICD), Capability Development Document (CDD) and Capability Production Document (CPD).
- Ensuring that R&M engineering activities and deliverables in the Request for Proposal (RFP) are appropriate for the program phase and product type.
- Ensuring that R&M Data Item Descriptions (DIDs) that will be placed on contract are appropriately tailored (see the Guidance for Tailoring R&M Engineering Data on the DASD(SE) website).
- Integrating R&M engineering activities and reliability growth planning curve(s) in the Systems Engineering Plan (SEP) at Milestones A and B and at the Development RFP Release Decision Point.
- Planning verification methods for each R&M requirement.
- Ensuring the verification methods for each R&M requirement are described in the Test and Evaluation Master Plan (TEMP), along with a reliability growth planning curve beginning at Milestone B.
- Planning for system and system element reliability growth (i.e. Highly Accelerated Life Test, Accelerated Life Test or conventional reliability growth tests for newly developed equipment).
- Ensuring data from R&M analyses, demonstrations and tests are properly used to influence life-cycle product support planning, availability assessments, cost estimating and other related program analyses.
- Identifying and tracking R&M risks and Technical Performance Measures.
- Assessing R&M status during program technical reviews.
- Including consideration of R&M in all configuration changes and trade-off analyses.

As part of the SE process, the R&M engineer should be responsible for the R&M activities by the acquisition phase outlined in Table 48.

200

Acquisition Phase	R&M Activities
Materiel Solution Analysis (MSA) Phase. During the MSA Phase, the R&M engineer, as part of the program SE team, should:	• Analyze conceptual design approaches and estimate the feasibility with respect to R&M ICD performance capabilities • Perform AoA trade-off studies among R&M, availability and other system performance parameters to arrive at a preferred system alternative. The studies should be performed in conjunction with product support, cost and design personnel, using the DoD RAM-C Rationale Report Manual • Conduct a Reliability, Availability, Maintainability and Cost (RAM-C) analysis. For Major Defense Acquisition Programs (MDAP), prepare a preliminary RAM-C Rationale Report and attach the report to the SEP for Milestone A • Translate ICD performance capabilities and draft CDD thresholds to R&M specification requirements based on the Concept of Operations/Operational Mode Summary/Mission Profile (CONOPS/OMS/MP), failure definitions and utilization rates • Develop a system reliability growth planning curve and include it in the SEP. Reliability growth curves should be stated in a series of intermediate goals and tracked through fully integrated, system-level test and evaluation events until the reliability threshold is achieved. If a single curve is not adequate to describe overall system reliability, curves for critical subsystems, with rationale for their selection, should be provided • Use data from the RAM-C Rationale Report to provide the following for logistics design support: a. The initial failure mode assessment, including effects of failure on system performance and the probable manner in which each failure mode would be detected to provide guidance to planning and the conceptual design of the diagnostics concept and maturation process b. Failure rate and removal rate estimates, for both corrective and preventive maintenance, to provide a realistic basis for equipment and replaceable unit spares provisioning planning • Define contractor R&M engineering activities in the RFP and contract Statement of Work for the TMRR phase, which should include: a. Allocations b. Block diagrams and modeling c. Predictions d. Failure Mode, Effects and Criticality Analysis (FMECA) e. Subsystem and system-level reliability growth planning activities f. R&M tests and demonstrations g. Failure Reporting, Analysis and Corrective Action System (FRACAS)
Technology Maturation and Risk Reduction (TMRR) Phase. During the TMRR phase, the R&M engineer, as part of the program SE team, should:	• Participate in trade studies during requirements analysis and architecture design • Review results of R&M engineering analyses, verification tests, design approach, availability assessments and maintenance concept

201

Acquisition Phase	R&M Activities
	optimization to verify conformance to requirements, and to identify potential R&M problem areas
	• Contribute to integrated test planning to avoid duplication and afford a more complete utilization of all test data for R&M assessment. Comprehensive test planning should include subsystem reliability growth and maintainability and BIT demonstrations as appropriate
	• Understand schedule and resource constraints, and adjust the reliability growth planning curve based on more mature knowledge points. Include updated reliability growth planning curve in the SEP at the Development RFP Release Decision Point and at Milestone B, and in the TEMP at Milestone B
	• Integrate R&M engineering analyses with logistics design support in the following areas: requirements and functional analysis; test planning; Reliability Centered Maintenance (RCM) and Condition Based Maintenance Plus (CBM+); and refinement of the maintenance concept, including the Level of Repair Analysis (LORA) and maintenance task analysis
	• Verify that plans have been established for the selection and application criteria of parts, materials and processes to limit reliability risks
	• Define contractor R&M engineering activities in the RFP and contract Statement of Work (SOW) for the EMD phase, during which R&M quantitative requirements and verification methods are incorporated
	• Update the RAM-C analysis to support the Development RFP Release Decision Point ensuring the JCIDS Sustainment Thresholds in the CDD are valid and feasible. For MDAPs, attach the updated RAM-C Rationale Report to the SEP for Milestone B
Engineering and Manufacturing Development (EMD) Phase. During the EMD phase, the R&M engineer, as part of the program SE team, should:	• Perform evaluations to assess R&M status and problems
	• Update the RAM-C analysis, ensuring the JCIDS Sustainment Thresholds in the CPD are valid. For MDAPs, attach the updated RAM-C Rationale Report to the SEP for Milestone C.
	• Ensure that the product baseline design and required testing can meet the R&M requirements
	• Ensure the final FMECA identifies failure modes, and their detection methods, that could result in personnel injury and/or mission loss, and ensure they are mitigated in the design
	• Ensure that the detailed R&M prediction to assess system potential to meet design requirements is complete
	• Verify through appropriate subsystem/equipment-level tests the readiness to enter system-level testing at or above the initial reliability established in the reliability growth planning curve in both the SEP and the TEMP
	• Verify system conformance to specified R&M requirements through appropriate demonstration and test
	• Implement a FRACAS to ensure feedback of failure data during test and to apply and track corrective actions
	• Coordinate with the Chief Developmental Tester (T&E Lead) and Operational Test Agencies (OTA) to ensure that the program office and OTA data collection agree on R&M monitoring and failure

202

Acquisition Phase	R&M Activities
	definitions, and that R&M and BIT scoring processes are consistent in verification of requirements through all levels of testing • Define contractor R&M engineering activities in the RFP and contract SOW for the P&D phase to ensure adequate R&M engineering activities take place during P&D and the RFP and contract SOW provide adequate consideration of R&M in re-procurements, spares and repair parts • Verify that parts, materials and processes meet system requirements through the use of a management plan detailing reliability risk considerations and evaluation strategies for the intended service life. Include flow of requirements to subcontractors and suppliers. See MIL-STD-1546 (Parts, Materials, and Processes Control Program for Space and Launch Vehicles) and MIL-STD-1547 (Electronic Parts, Materials, and Processes for Space and Launch Vehicles) and MIL-STD-11991 (General Standard for Parts, Materials, and Processes)
Production and Deployment (P&D) Phase. During the P&D phase, the R&M engineer, as part of the programs SE team should:	• Verify initial production control of R&M degradation factors by test and inspection, production data analysis, and supplemental tests • Verify R&M characteristics, maintenance concept, repair policies, Government technical evaluation and maintenance procedures by T&E • Identify R&M and production-related BIT improvement opportunities via FRACAS and field data assessment • Review Engineering Change Proposals (ECP), operational mission/deployment changes and variations for impact on R&M • Update R&M predictions and FMECAs based on production tests, demonstration tests, operational evaluation and field results and apply them to the models previously developed to assess impacts on maintenance procedures, spares, manpower, packaging design, test equipment, missions and availability • Verify that parts, materials and processes management requirements for limiting reliability risk and "lessons learned" are utilized during all design change efforts including change proposals, variations, substitutions, product improvement efforts or any other hardware change effort
Operations and Support (O&S) Phase. During the O&S phase, the R&M engineer, as part of the program SE team should:	• Assess operational data to determine the adequacy of R&M and BIT characteristics performance; maintenance planning, features and procedures; provisioning plans, test equipment design; and maintenance training • Identify problem areas for correction through ongoing closed-loop FRACAS and field data assessment • Monitor availability rates and respond to negative trends and data anomalies

CH 3–4.3.20 Spectrum Management

Warfighters use spectrum-dependent systems for communications, sensors (i.e., radar), navigation beacons, jammers, homing devices, anti-Improvised Explosive Devices (IED) and other purposes. Often emitters are in close physical proximity to each other and to civilian devices that should not be disrupted by military signals. Spectrum-dependent developers should be aware of the enemy electronic order of battle and countermeasures, and plan accordingly. Devices (including commercial items) that do not account for countermeasures may have vulnerabilities in hostile environments.

203

Spectrum management requirements are needed for all spectrum-dependent systems. Any system that uses an antenna or a platform that mounts such systems is a spectrum-dependent system. If a platform obtains a spectrum-dependent system as Government-furnished equipment (GFE), the platform Program Manager (PM) is responsible for ensuring that the GFE PM has obtained the needed permissions. Both programs are required to submit a Spectrum Supportability Risk Assessment (SSRA). The platform SSRA can reference the GFE SSRA, but may have to expand upon it regarding host-nation features or other information not contained in the GFE-level SSRA. The Systems Engineer should be aware of the worldwide rules for spectrum management and the need to obtain host-nation permission for each transmitter and frequency assignment.

PMs need to ensure that spectrum access is adequate and that it is granted in the Continental United States (CONUS) and wherever else the equipment is deployed. The Pre-Milestone A Analysis of Alternatives (AoA) should address spectrum needs as part of concept formulation. Both the SSRA and DD-1494 are required for each milestone (see DoDI 4650.01). The SSRA is used within the DoD as the basis for assessing the feasibility of building and fielding equipment that operate within assigned frequency bands and identifying potential de-confliction situations. The DD-1494, Application for Equipment Frequency Allocation, has four stages, which reflect the increasing maturity of available spectrum information during development. The DD-1494 form is submitted to National Telecommunications and Information Administration (NTIA) for approval of spectrum allocation, without which emitters cannot operate within CONUS, and to the International Telecommunications Union (ITU) for satellites. The NTIA Manual of Regulations and Procedures for Federal Radio Frequency Management (Redbook) chapter 3 addresses international treaty aspects of the spectrum, and chapter 4 addresses frequency allocations.

The Systems Engineer has a lead role in defining spectrum needs, throughput and power requirements and other attributes of the signals in space (outside the antenna -- not in the transmission device) and the antenna characteristics and platform mounting details, as well as the safety aspects of emitters with regard to the Hazards of Electromagnetic Radiation to Ordnance (HERO), Personnel (HERP) and Fuel (HERF). The Systems Engineer should be aware that portions of the spectrum previously assigned to DoD or other Federal users are being sold for commercial use. Thus, previously approved DD-1494 can be revoked, requiring modifications to designs and even to fielded equipment. Similarly, host nations can alter prior agreements, as commercial applications encroach upon previously available spectrum.

Each nation reserves the right to control emitters operating within its territory; thus, host- nation agreements are essential in support of deployment. PMs and Systems Engineers of platforms that mount multiple emitters and receivers need to obtain spectrum access for each emitter and ensure that those emitters and receivers do not produce mutual interference or interact with ordnance (see DoDD 3222.3, MIL-STD-461 (Requirements for the Control of Electromagnetic Interference Characteristics of Subsystems and Equipment), MIL-STD-464 (Electromagnetic Environmental Effects Requirements for Systems), MIL-HDBK-235-1 (Military Operational Electromagnetic Environment Profiles Part 1C General Guidance), MIL-HDBK-237 (Electromagnetic Environmental Effects and Spectrum Supportability Guidance for the Acquisition Process), MIL-HDBK-240 (Hazards of Electromagnetic Radiation to Ordnance Test Guide), and "Joint Services Guide for Development of a Spectrum Supportability Risk

Assessment"). The Defense Information Systems Agency (DISA), Defense Spectrum Organization provides spectrum support and planning for DoD. See Figure 43 for spectrum activities by acquisition phase. This figure summarizes the requirements of DoDI 4650.01.

Figure 43: Spectrum-Related Activities by Life-Cycle Phase

204

Defense Acquisition Life Cycle Phase	Materiel Solution Analysis	Technology Maturation & Risk Reduction	Engineering & Manufacturing Development	Production & Deployment	Operations & Support
Spectrum Supportability Risk Assessment (SSRA)	Prepare SSRA	Update SSRA	Update SSRA	Update SSRA	Update SSRA for mission & technical changes
DD-1494, Application for Equipment Frequency Allocation	Stage 1 (Conceptual)	Stage 2 (Experimental)	Stage 3 (Developmental) NTIA approval needed before transmission tests	Stage 4 (Operational) NTIA approval needed before deployment or when changes occur	
Program Management, Systems Engineering, and Testers Electromagnetic Environmental Effects (E3) Tasks	E3 assessment for SSRA	Update E3 assessment for SSRA	Update E3 assessment for SSRA	Update E3 assessment for SSRA	Resolve interference
	Define EME & E3 requirements (i.e., frequency bands, throughput, power, operational areas, etc.)	Update EME; Prepare E3 inputs to ISP, TEMP and acquisition documents. Address at PDR	E3 & EME inputs to TEMP & ISP; HERO, HERP, HERF, TEMPEST, & EMI address at CDR; DT&E transmission tests after Stage 3 approval	Conduct OT&E tests including E3 tests IAW TEMP; E3 assessment report	Deployed support
	Consider host nation (HN) constraints	Obtain HN comments via SMO	Begin HN discussions via SMO	Obtain HN approval before deployment	Maintain HN approval

CDR – Critical Design Review
DT&E – developmental test and evaluation
E3 – electromagnetic environmental effects
EME – electromagnetic environment
EMI – electromagnetic interference
ISP – Information Support Plan

HERF – hazard of electromagnetic radiation on fuel
HERO – hazard of electromagnetic radiation on ordnance
HERP – hazard of electromagnetic radiation on personnel
HN – host nation
IAW – in accordance with
NTIA – National Telecommunications and Information Administration

OT&E – operational test and evaluation
PDR – Preliminary Design Review
SMO – spectrum management office
SSRA – spectrum supportability risk assessment
T&E – test and evaluation
TEMP – Test and Evaluation Master Plan

CH 3–4.3.21 Standardization

Standardization supports the achievement of commonality and interoperability of parts and processes with United States forces and our allies, promotes safety, provides for life-cycle sustainment and allows for rapid, cost-effective technology insertion through use of standard interfaces and open systems. Standardization is an enabling tool to provide the warfighter with systems and equipment that are interoperable, reliable, sustainable and affordable. Standardization plays a key role in defining systems engineering (SE) best practices and processes.

The Program Manager (PM) balances the decision to use standardized agreements, practices, products, parts, processes, interfaces and methods with required capabilities, operational environment, technology feasibility and growth and cost-effectiveness.

DoDM 4120.24, Enclosure 4, Standardization in the Acquisition Process, provides policies on standardization considerations, how to document standardization decisions, and a discussion of the tailoring of standardization documents. It also provides references to key resources for the standardization process.

Parts management is a standardization design strategy available to PMs. Benefits of parts standardization include:

- Reducing the number of unique or specialized parts used in a system (or across systems).
- Reducing the logistics footprint.
- Lowering life-cycle costs.

In addition, parts management can enhance the reliability of the system and mitigate part obsolescence due to Diminishing Manufacturing Sources and Material Shortages (DMSMS). MIL-STD-3018 (Parts Management) dictates that program offices should apply standardization processes to:

205

- Improve parts commonality.
- Reduce total ownership costs.
- Reduce proliferation of parts.
- Promote the use of parts with acceptable performance, quality, and reliability.

The Systems Engineer is responsible for:

- Implementing parts management contractual requirements.
- Approving contractor submitted plans.
- Ensuring parts management objectives are met.

Additional guidance on parts management may be found in SD-19 (Parts Management Guide).

CH 3–4.3.22 Supportability

Supportability refers to the inherent characteristics of the system and the enabling system elements that allow effective and efficient sustainment (including maintenance and other support functions) throughout the system's life cycle. By addressing supportability as part of the system design, the Program Manager (PM), through the Systems Engineer and Product Support Manager, ensures the system reaches Initial Operational Capability (IOC) with the required enabling system elements in place. The benefits to the program are:

- Cost savings
- Fielding of a more affordable logistics infrastructure
- Improved Materiel and Operational Availability
- Reduced footprint

Supportability analysis is an iterative activity conducted during the system's development, and is used by the PM and Product Support Manager to develop and define the system's support strategy. It includes sustainment-related should-cost management and risk and opportunity management efforts across the life cycle. Supportability analysis begins in stakeholder requirements definition, as part of the Analysis of Alternatives (AoA), and continues through the design, test and evaluation, production and deployment activities/phases of the system. The supportability analysis and the resultant product support package mature in parallel with the evolution of the design, and should be documented in an integrated data/decision environment.

Early consideration of supportability needs during Requirements Analysis, Architecture Design and Implementation processes are critical to ensure the delivered capability is operationally suitable, effective, sustainable and affordable. The system baseline should incorporate inherent supportability characteristics and should include the design of the enabling support infrastructure. Details can be found in DoDI 5000.02, Enc 6 and DAG Chapter 4, but typical product support considerations are listed in Table 49.

Table 49: Product Support Considerations

Element	Typical Considerations
Manpower and Personnel	Specifically support personnel for installation, checkout sustaining support and maintenance
Training and Training Support	For the system operators and maintenance personnel
Supply Support	Including repairable and non-repairable spares, consumables and special supplies

206

Element	Typical Considerations
Support Equipment	Including tools, condition and state monitoring, diagnostic and checkout special test and calibration equipment
Computer Resources	Operating systems and software supporting logistics functions and associated infrastructure
Packaging, Handling, Storage and Transportation	Special provisions, containers and transportation needs
Facilities and Infrastructure	Including facilities to support logistics and sustainment actions at all levels
Technical Data	Including system installation and checkout procedures; operating and maintenance instructions and records; alteration and modification instructions, etc.
Usage and Maintenance Data	Including data acquisition, movement, storage and analytic capability to support life-cycle support decisions

The PM is responsible for approving life-cycle trades throughout the acquisition process. To ensure the design incorporates life-cycle supportability, the program should involve logisticians and end users early in the Stakeholder Requirements Definition process to develop a performance-based product support strategy (including maintenance, servicing and calibration requirements). Reliability Centered Maintenance (RCM) analysis and Conditioned Based Maintenance Plus (CBM+) (see DoD 4151.22-M and DoDI 4151.22) are important initiatives that enable the performance of maintenance based on evidence of need as provided by RCM analysis and other enabling processes and technologies.

RCM, as defined in DoD 4151.22-M, is a systematic approach for analyzing the system/system element functions and potential failures to identify and define preventive or scheduled maintenance tasks for an equipment end item. Tasks may be preventive, predictive or proactive in nature. RCM results provide operational availability with an acceptable level of risk in an efficient and cost-effective manner.

Additionally, the Product Support Manager and Systems Engineer should ensure that supportability analysis activities are documented in the Systems Engineering Plan (SEP) and the Life-Cycle Sustainment Plan (LCSP), and that the supportability design requirements are documented in the functional baseline. The results of the supportability analysis activities including the servicing, calibration, corrective and preventive maintenance requirements are also summarized in the LCSP. (The LCSP outline calls out specific supportability related phase and milestone expectations.)

The Systems Engineer, working with the Product Support Manager and PM, identifies and mitigates the supportability life-cycle cost drivers to ensure the system is affordable across the life cycle. This includes identifying factors that drive the program's life-cycle costs and Sustainment Key Performance Parameter/Key System Attributes (KPP/KSA) to establish affordable and achievable goals and caps (see CH 3–2. Background, CH 3–4.3.2. Affordability – Systems Engineering Trade-Off Analyses, and CH 1–4.2.15.). Once the goals are established the focus turns to the specific metrics driving the Operation and Support (O&S) cost and Sustainment KPP/KSAs that can be directly influenced by the design. These drivers are then decomposed into functional and allocated requirements that can be directly traced to the cost targets and the Operational Availability (A_O) and Materiel Availability (A_M) (see DAG Chapter 4). The cost-benefit analysis, jointly conducted by the Systems Engineer and Product Support Manager within the supportability analysis process, provides insight into supportability drivers and includes the impact of resources on readiness. Engineering analyses (i.e., Failure Mode, Effects and Criticality Analysis (FMECA); supportability analysis predictions; and diagnostics architecture) provide critical data to impact the design for supportability and to influence the product support package.

CH 3–4.3.23 Survivability and Susceptibility

A system with a balanced survivability and susceptibility approach ensures operational crew and personnel safety while satisfying mission effectiveness and operational readiness requirements.

Survivability is the capability of a system and its crew to avoid or withstand a hostile environment without suffering an abortive impairment of its ability to accomplish its designated mission. Susceptibility is the degree to which a device, piece of equipment or weapon system is open to effective attack as a result of one or more inherent weaknesses. Manmade and natural environmental conditions described in MIL-STD-810 (Environmental Engineering Considerations and Laboratory Tests) (e.g., sand, vibration, shock, immersion, fog, etc.), electromagnetic environment described in MIL-STD-461 (Requirements for the Control of Electromagnetic Interference Characteristics of Subsystems and Equipment) and MIL-STD-464 (Electromagnetic Environmental Effects Requirements for Systems), and cyber environment should also be considered in system design.

Susceptibility is a function of operational tactics, countermeasures, probability of an enemy threat, etc. Susceptibility is considered a subset of survivability. Vulnerability is the characteristics of a system that cause it to suffer a definite degradation (loss or reduction of capability to perform the designated mission) as a result of having been subjected to a certain (defined) level of effects in an unnatural (manmade) or natural (e.g., lightning, solar storms) hostile environment. Vulnerability is also considered a subset of survivability.

Design and testing ensure that the system and crew can withstand manmade hostile environments without the crew suffering acute chronic illness, disability or death. The Program Manager (PM), supported by the Systems Engineer, should fully assess system and crew survivability against all anticipated threats, at all levels of conflict, throughout the system life cycle. The goal of survivability and susceptibility is to:

- Provide mission assurance while maximizing warfighter safety (or minimizing their exposure to threats).
- Incorporate balanced survivability, with consideration to the use of signature reduction with countermeasures.
- Incorporate susceptibility reduction features that prevent or reduce engagement of threat weapons.
- Provide mission planning and dynamic situational awareness features.

The mandatory System Survivability Key Performance Parameter (KPP) is applicable to all Capability Development Documents (CDD) and Capability Production Documents (CPD). The System Survivability KPP may include:

- Reducing a system's likelihood of being engaged by hostile fire, through attributes such as speed, maneuverability, detectability and countermeasures.
- Reducing the system's vulnerability if hit by hostile fire, through attributes such as armor and redundancy of critical components.
- Enabling operation in degraded electromagnetic (EM), space or cyber environments.
- Allowing the system to survive and continue to operate in, or after exposure to, a chemical, biological, radiological and nuclear (CBRN) environment, if required.

If the system or program has been designated by the Director, Operational Test and Evaluation (DOT&E), for live-fire test and evaluation (LFT&E) oversight, the PM should integrate test and evaluation (T&E) to address crew survivability issues into the LFT&E program supporting the Secretary of Defense LFT&E Report to Congress.

If the system or program has been designated a CBRN mission-critical system, the PM should address CBRN survivability, in accordance with DoDI 3150.09, The Chemical, Biological, Radiological and Nuclear (CBRN) Survivability Policy. The PM should ensure that progress toward CBRN survivability requirements is documented in the applicable Service CBRN mission-critical report. More information on CBRN can be found on the CBRN Survivability DoDTechipedia page [CAC-enabled].

Unless waived by the Milestone Decision Authority (MDA), mission-critical systems, including crew, regardless of acquisition category, should be survivable to the threat levels anticipated in their projected operating environment as portrayed in their platform-specific Validated On-line Life-cycle Threat (VOLT) Report (see DoDI 5000.02 (Enc 1, Table 2) and CH 7-4.1.2.).

The Systems Engineer should describe in the Systems Engineering Plan:

- How the design incorporates susceptibility and vulnerability reduction and CBRN survivability requirements.
- How progress toward these are tracked over the acquisition life cycle.

Additional techniques include rapid reconstruction (reparability) to maximize wartime availability and sortie rates and incorporating damage tolerance in the system design.

CH 3–4.3.24 System Security Engineering

System Security Engineering (SSE) activities allow for identification and incorporation of security design and process requirements into risk identification and management in the requirements trade space.

SSE is an element of system engineering (SE) that applies scientific and engineering principles to identify security vulnerabilities and minimize or contain risks associated with these vulnerabilities. Program Protection is the Department's integrating process for mitigating and managing risks to advanced technology and mission-critical system functionality from foreign collection, design vulnerability or supply chain exploit/insertion, battlefield loss and unauthorized or inadvertent disclosure throughout the acquisition life cycle. The Program Protection processes capture SSE analysis in the system requirements and design documents and SSE verification in the test plans, procedures and results documents. The Program Protection Plan (PPP) (see CH 9–2.3.) documents the comprehensive approach to system security engineering analysis and the associated results.

SSE analysis results should be captured in the PPP, provided at each technical review and audit (see CH 9–3.4.) and incorporated into the technical review assessment criteria as well as the functional, allocated and product baselines. The PPP is approved by the Milestone Decision Authority (MDA) at each milestone decision review and at the Full-Rate Production/Full-Deployment (FRP/FD) decision, with a draft PPP (as defined in DoDI 5000.02, Enc 1, Table 2 and DoDI 5000.02, Enc 3, sec. 13.a) due at the Development Request for Proposals (RFP) Release Decision Point. The analysis should be used to update the technical baselines prior to each technical review and key knowledge point throughout the life cycle. It should also inform the development and release of each RFP (see CH 9–4.1.) by incorporating SSE process requirements and the system security requirements into the appropriate solicitation documentation.

The Program Manager (PM) is responsible for employing SSE practices and preparing a PPP to guide the program's efforts and the actions of others. The Systems Engineer and/or System Security Engineer is responsible for ensuring a balanced set of security requirements, designs, testing and risk management are incorporated and addressed in the their respective trade spaces. The Systems Engineer and/or System Security Engineer is responsible for leading and facilitating cross-discipline teams to conduct the SSE analysis necessary for development of the PPP. The cross-discipline interactions reach beyond the SSE community to the test and logistics communities. CH 9–2.5. further details the program protection roles and responsibilities.

To address SSE as a design consideration, the Systems Engineering and Systems Security Engineer should ensure the system architecture and design addresses how the system:

- Manages access to, and use of, the system and system resources.
- Is configured to minimize exposure of vulnerabilities that could impact the mission through techniques such as design choice, component choice, security technical implementation guides and patch management in the development environment (including integration and T&E), in production and throughout sustainment.
- Is structured to protect and preserve system functions or resources, e.g., through segmentation, separation, isolation or partitioning.
- Monitors, detects and responds to security anomalies.
- Maintains priority system functions under adverse conditions.
- Interfaces with DoD Information Network or other external security services.

The early and frequent consideration of SSE principles reduces re-work and expense resulting from late-to-need security requirements (e.g., anti-tamper, exportability features, supply chain risk management, secure design, defense-in-depth and cybersecurity implementation.)

CH 3–Version and Revision History

The table below tracks chapter changes. It indicates the current version number and date published, and provides a brief description of the content.

Version #	Revision Date	Reason
0	2/1/17	Chapter 3 initial upload
1	5/5/17	Minor updates to align with DoDI 5000.02 Change 2 and to address comments received from the user community.

210

CH 4–1. Purpose

The Defense Acquisition Guidebook (DAG), Chapter 4, provides guidance for Program Managers (PMs) and Program Support Managers (PSMs) to develop and execute successful sustainment strategies, and to document those strategies in a Life Cycle Sustainment Plan (LCSP) that aids program management, communication, and collaboration with critical stakeholders.

CH 4–2. Background

Life cycle sustainment comprises the range of planning, implementation and execution activities that support the sustainment of weapon systems. Best practice and guidance for ensuring that these systems meet sustainment objectives and satisfy user sustainment needs includes sustainment considerations in all phases of the program's life cycle. These acquisition lifecycle phases are formalized in DoDI 5000.02, and offer PMs and PSMs guidance on the development and execution of effective LCSPs and the collaboration and information exchanges needed between sustainment and systems engineering communities.

CH 4–2.1 Purpose of Life Cycle Sustainment Planning

The purpose of life cycle sustainment planning is to maximize readiness by delivering the best possible product support outcomes at the lowest Operating and Support (O&S) cost. Sustainment is a distributed and long-term activity that requires the alignment of the program office, requirements community, systems engineers, sustainment commands, logistics community, resource sponsors, and others. These disparate communities of interest place a high value on planning and documenting plans, as they are likely to be executed over the course of years or decades. Sustainment planning begins before a material solution exists, to ensure that sustainment can be effectively executed when the first production quantities are fielded; it continues to evolve until disposal. Programs that emphasize sustainment early in the system life cycle deliver designs with the highest likelihood of achieving operational performance requirements and reduced demand for sustainment.

CH 4–2.2 Life Cycle Sustainment Overview

Life cycle sustainment planning is a key function of the defense acquisition system for the development of military capabilities. The goal of life cycle sustainment planning is to maximize readiness by delivering the best possible product support outcomes at the lowest O&S Cost.

While weapon system sustainment does not actually begin until the first production units are fielded, sustainment planning begins at the earliest stages of the defense acquisition system. Successful post-fielding sustainment performance depends on critical thinking during requirements development and solution analysis.

Figure 1 shows the major sustainment planning activities within the defense acquisition system program structure.

Figure 1: Overview of Life Cycle Sustainment Activities

Sustainment Plan Content across milestones: Materiel Development · (A) · Developmental RFP Release · (B) · (C) · Full-Rate Production

Phases: Solution Analysis | Technology Maturation & Risk Reduction | Engineering Manufacturing & Development | Production & Deployment | Operations & Support

Sustainment Requirements
- Define > Decompose > Allocate; Performance Metrics (Ao, Am, Rm, O&S costs)
- Test Data > Performance Validation; Reliability Growth Progress

Product Support Strategy*
- Maintenance
- Supply
- Intellectual Property (IP)
- Manpower

- Core Applicability — Workload est. Level of Repair Source of Repair — Standup
- Options for Supply Chain Mgmt — Initial Spares DT/IOT&E Provisioning — Deliveries
- Options for Repair Data, Manufacturing Specs — Data Delivery
- O/I/D Maintenance and Supply Estimate

Arrangements
- Support options (AoA)
- Supportability Analysis & Design Trades, IP Options
- Interim Support | Performance-Based

Schedule
- Major Logistics Events Identified ** — Product Support Element Dev / Fielding — Site Activations / Operational Cap
- Design/Support Trades (Reviews)
- Sustainment integrated with Test & Eval Events
- Contracting Actions
- Commercial/Organic Transitions

- Cost
- Funding

- O&S Contribution to Life Cycle Cost Estimate > Sustainment Implications of ICE/SCP Variances
- Identification and mitigation of unfunded requirements

Management
- PSM Designated > Product Support Organization Staffed
- Product Support IPT Established > Integrated with External Stakeholders

LCSP Revision Areas
- O&S Affordability
- Should Cost

- Goal | Cap
- Pareto Cost Drivers > Identify Should Cost Initiatives > Schedule/Execute Initiatives

< *Note.* Ao/Am/Rm = Operational Availability/Materiel Availability/Materiel Reliability; AoA = Analysis of Alternatives; Dev = Development; DT = Developmental Testing; Est = Estimate; Eval = Evaluation; ICE = Independent Cost Estimate; IOT&E = Initial Operational Test & Evaluation; LCSP = Life-Cycle Sustainment Plan; Mgmt = Management; O&S = Operations & Support; O/I/D = Organizational-/Intermediate-/Depot (Levels of Maintenance); PSM = Product Support Manager; RFP = Request for Proposal; SCP = Service Cost Position; Specs = Specifications.

In this chapter, the terms "sustainment" and "product support" are used synonymously. The term "strategy" applies to the integration of the requirements, a product support package, and resources. The product support strategy should be developed as soon as possible in the life cycle of a program, preferably as soon as a materiel solution to a requirement is identified. The strategy is updated and refined throughout the product life cycle to disposal.

The execution of the strategy is outlined in an LCSP, which includes the array of product support functions required to sustain the product until the end of its useful life. The term "plan" applies to the elaboration of the strategy with the set of planning tasks and activities to stimulate critical thinking by managers and teams responsible for sustainment planning. The LCSP serves as the central management tool for all aspects of the strategy and is developed in parallel with other Milestone A decision documents. To develop a best value solution to a product's sustainment requirements, PMs ensure all aspects of logistics are covered.

The LCSP helps the PM develop a complete and detailed product support package, resulting in successful product support arrangements (PSAs). The product support package provides the detailed implementation approach for the product support strategy. A product support package consists of the combination of product support elements needed to achieve the sustainment requirements and the set of arrangements that programs establish with organic and commercial sustainment providers.

The backbone of the product support package is the Integrated Product Support (IPS) Elements. These 12 elements, described in detail in the IPS Element Guidebook, can be grouped into three buckets that cover the range of life cycle logistics functions. The three buckets and corresponding elements are:

- Life cycle management
  - Product Support Management
  - Supply Support
  - Packing, Handling, Storage, and Transportation (PHST)
  - Maintenance Planning and Management
- Technical management
  - Design Interface
  - Sustaining Engineering
  - Technical Data
  - Computer Resources
- Infrastructure management
  - Support Equipment
  - Training & Training Support
  - Manpower and Personnel
  - Facilities and Infrastructure.

These IPS elements are relatively immature in the Materiel Solution Analysis (MSA) Phase, as there is too little data about the materiel solution to build a complete plan. As the logistics, requirements, engineering, and resource communities mature the program and refine the product support strategy, the PM increases the detail of each IPS element in the product support package to inform the execution of the strategy and PSAs.

PSAs are the mechanisms for delivering the sustainment functions in the product support package. These arrangements are entered into with Product Support Providers (PSPs), who perform the required sustainment functions. These PSPs may be commercial industry, organic depot, or hybrid arrangements. Industry partner arrangements are governed under contract; service-level agreements govern work with organic depots. PMs and DoD Component-level stakeholders holistically evaluate the system (whether as a system, a system-of-systems, or components/sub-components) and the potential sustainment providers (industry, organic, or a partnership) through source or support/repair analyses to determine the best-value PSAs.

The strategy, as manifested in the product support package and documented in the LCSP, should grow with the development of the system. The product support package supports the Warfighter by maximizing reliability and availability, while also minimizing cost to the taxpayer.

CH 4–2.2.1 The Life Cycle Sustainment Plan

The Life Cycle Sustainment Plan (LCSP) is an evolutionary management document describing the program's approach to achieve a flexible, performance-oriented product support capability. This plan is the program's primary management tool to satisfy the Warfighter's sustainment requirements through the delivery of a product support package. The LCSP is expected to evolve throughout the acquisition process with the maturity of the system and provide clarity for the program's life cycle product support strategy. Additionally, it may be tailored based on varying entry points in the acquisition process.

The plan describes sustainment influences on system design, as well as the technical, business, and management activities to develop, implement, and deliver a product support package that maintains affordable system operational effectiveness over the system's life cycle. It also seeks to reduce cost without sacrificing necessary levels of program support. Development of a life cycle product support strategy and plan are critical steps in the delivery of the product support package. The LCSP remains an active management tool throughout the O&S phase and is continually updated to ensure sustainment performance satisfies the Warfighter's needs.

Program Managers (PMs) for all programs are responsible for developing and maintaining an LCSP consistent with the product support strategy, beginning at Milestone A. By Milestone B, the LCSP describes the actions for achieving sustainment requirements. By Milestone C, it describes the content and implementation status of the product support package (including any sustainment contracts) to achieve and maintain the sustainment requirements. After Milestone C, it describes the plans for sustaining materiel availability and for accommodating modifications, upgrades, and re-procurement.

CH 4–2.2.2 Principal Actors

The DoDI 5000.02 designates a PM as the individual with responsibility for, and authority, to accomplish program objectives. This guidance was written to support the PM in execution of this responsibility. As the PM's key leader for sustainment planning, the Product Support Manager (PSM) has primary responsibility for implementing many of the actions, processes, and procedures included in this chapter. The PSM provides subject matter expertise to the PM for product support, from concept through disposal. The responsibilities of the PSM are defined in 10 USC 2337 (see US Code), although the PSM roles and responsibilities in the post-production O&S phase vary by DoD Component.

While this guidance is directed at the PM (and by extension, the PSM), there may be instances where there is no designated person for the role, such as during early capability or concept development. When there is no assigned PSM, trained life cycle logisticians (LCLs) in headquarters organizations or Program Executive Offices (PEOs), or temporarily assigned PSMs, can complete necessary actions. For lower tier programs (Acquisition Category III/IV), a PSM or life cycle logistics (LCL) staff with a portfolio of programs performs the necessary activities. Early in the Materiel Solution Analysis phase, when there may be no program office, this guidance uses the acronym "LCL" interchangeably to refer not only to *life cycle logistics,* but also to the individual responsible for sustainment planning—the *life cycle logistician.*

CH 4–2.2.3 Statute, Policy, and Guidance

PMs and PSMs should know and understand the statutory and regulatory mandates for sustainment. The major sustainment policy and guidance derive from:

- US Code, Title 10, Section 2337, Life-cycle management and product support:

This is the governing statute requiring DoD to perform life-cycle management; it establishes and defines the role of the Product Support Manager (PSM).

- DoDI 5000.02, Operation of the Defense Acquisition System:

This instruction establishes policy for the management of all acquisition programs, including requirements for life-cycle sustainment planning. The policy describes the content and approval requirements for LCSPs throughout the acquisition life cycle and into the Operating and Support (O&S) phase. Its Enclosure 6, Life-cycle Sustainment, documents the application of sustainment planning policies and procedures.

CH 4–3. Business Practice

The Guidance section describes sustainment planning and execution across the program life cycle. It is organized by acquisition phase to support the DoD Component Life Cycle Logistician (LCL), Program Manager (PM), and Product Support Manager (PSM) as they shepherd a program through the defense acquisition system and into sustainment.

CH 4–3.1 Materiel Solution Analysis Phase

Sustainment planning begins at the earliest stages of the defense acquisition system. Successful post-fielding sustainment performance depends on thoughtful consideration during requirements development and solution analysis. The Materiel Solution Analysis (MSA) Phase provides the first opportunity to influence the supportability and affordability of weapon systems by balancing Warfighter requirements and operational capabilities with support capacity, capability, and cost.

An approved Materiel Development Decision (MDD) begins the MSA Phase and the Milestone A decision completes the phase. Prior to program office stand-up, which may be the case during the MDD and Analysis of Alternatives (AoA), the LCLs are responsible for initiating sustainment planning. Once the program office is initiated (usually before Milestone A), the PM and PSM assume primary responsibility for sustainment planning.

Figure 2: MSA Sustainment Planning Activities

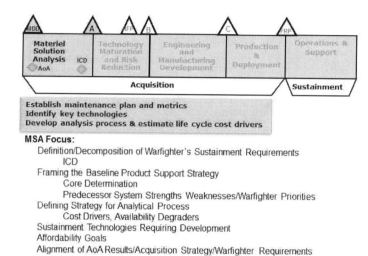

AoA = Analysis of Alternatives; FRP = Full Rate Production; ICD = Initial Capability Document; MDD = Materiel Development Decision; MSA = Materiel Solution Analysis RFP = Request for Proposal.

CH 4–3.1.1 Materiel Development Decision

The Materiel Development Decision (MDD) is the entry point into the acquisition process for many new weapon systems. The Initial Capability Document (ICD), or other validated requirements document, and the AoA Study Guidance are required at this decision point to guide the program's execution of MSA.

The LCL at MDD focuses on cost estimates and funding requirements necessary to conduct the range of logistics and sustainment studies and analyses. Supportability analysis may include AoA, affordability assessment, sustainment Concept of Operations (CONOPS), and market research. Each of these provides logistics and sustainment data for the materiel solution alternatives.

CH 4–3.1.1.1 Initial Capability Document

The Initial Capability Document (ICD) is the first of the three major requirements documents in the Joint Capabilities Integration and Development System (JCIDS) that generate sustainment requirements. The lessons learned from fielded systems and capability-based assessments may help define the sustainment content in the ICD. These analyses can be valuable in establishing sustainment constraints such as logistics footprint and weight, and human factors such as skill and education levels required for specific maintenance tasks.

Program offices should collaborate with requirements developers, sustainment commands, and DoD Component acquisition leadership (e.g., Assistant Secretary of the Army for Acquisition, Logistics and Technology; Deputy Assistant Secretary of the Navy for Expeditionary Programs and Logistics Management; Deputy Assistant Secretary of the Air Force for Logistics and Product Support) to continually enhance sustainment effectiveness by factoring the lessons from legacy platform sustainment issues into new programs. Specifying sustainment capability gaps in the ICD helps ensure the AoA considers the potential product's entire life cycle and forms the basis for effective contractual requirements. See CJCSI 3170.01I JCIDS Manual, Encl. D – Pages D-17 –28 for additional information on the ICD.

CH 4–3.1.2 Analysis of Alternatives

The Materiel Development Decision directs the execution of the Analysis of Alternatives (AoA) through the AoA Study Guidance and AoA Study Plan. This section focuses on the sustainment aspects of the AoA and defers to CH 2 for a more complete treatment of the AoA.

During the AoA, materiel alternatives are evaluated for operational suitability, ability to meet Warfighter KPPs and KSAs, and affordability. LCLs participate in the AoA to influence technology trade-offs and provide subject matter expertise to identify risks and opportunities in cost, maintainability, and readiness that may be driven by technology options and the operational environment.

The LCLs should ensure that the AoA Study Plan considers sustainment in the study's ground rules, alternatives, and cost analysis. The ground rules should include assumptions relative to the operating environment that may impact supportability and warrant explicit planning and execution consideration. To preserve a fair comparison when evaluating alternative materiel solutions, LCLs should ensure that the maintenance and support concept is consistent for all alternatives and employment concepts (peacetime, wartime, contingency).

In some AoAs, alternative support concepts (e.g., maintenance, training, supply chain) may also be evaluated to determine the most cost-effective support concept. The number of alternative support concepts that may be evaluated as part of the AoA is bound by the resources and schedule. It is critical that LCLs be included in the AoA study team to ensure the selected support concepts offer the greatest potential performance and cost benefits. An LCL's subject matter expertise can help the study better balance near-term design, procurement, and system performance decisions with long-term readiness and cost performance.

CH 4–3.1.2.1 Sustainment Criteria

Requirements trade-offs should balance performance characteristics (e.g., speed, payload and maneuverability) with sustainment (e.g., availability, reliability, and O&S Cost). These performance attributes may be included as criteria in the AoA to ensure study results retain a life cycle perspective.

CH 4–3.1.2.1.1 Materiel Availability

Materiel Availability (A_m) is a measure of the percentage of the total inventory of a system that is mission capable. More specifically, it is the share of end items operationally capable (ready for tasking) of performing an assigned mission at a given time, based on materiel condition. If the ICD identifies a gap in sustainment, this may be reflected in the selection of availability performance as an assessment factor in the AoA.

The AoA assumes specific scenarios and CONOPS to baseline an affordability parameter across alternatives. LCL communications with resource sponsors and the requirements community should include sustainment strategies and their ability to meet availability requirements in current operations plans. Issues to highlight include historical availability rates, organic versus contractor logistics support in forward areas, and funding priorities.

CH 4–3.1.2.1.2 O&S Cost

During development of the Study Plan, the LCL should ensure that Operating and Support Cost (O&S Cost) is a criterion in the AoA. O&S Cost may be a critical factor in selecting between multiple sustainment strategies. The cost estimators consider the specific sustainment differences between the AoA alternatives to be sustainment discriminators.

Cost estimates during the AoA often consider the life cycle cost (sum of acquisition, O&S, and disposal costs). The cost estimator focuses on the sustainment discriminators that yield relative cost differences among the alternatives. The LCL supports the AoA cost estimating team by identifying and specifying sustainment specific discriminators as assumptions in the AoA alternatives. Common sustainment discriminators in the AoA cost estimate may include but are not limited to:

- Maintenance strategy
- System/component weights
- Number of systems to be sustained
- Fuel usage/energy consumption
- System complexity
- Operational Tempo (OPTEMPO) constraints
- Required manning to operate/maintain/support
- Transportation requirements, including storage and environmental requirements
- Planned/required future upgrades
- Software refresh schedules/licensing agreements
- Hardware refresh cycles
- Projected service life

LCLs may also help identify legacy or analogous systems to use as sources of reference data. Legacy/analogous systems are those that perform the same (or similar) mission or share technical characteristics with the potential new system. Typically, little (if any) data is available on potential new systems considered as alternatives, but legacy/analogous system costs may offer useful insight as the basis of O&S Cost estimates during the AoA.

In the course of conducting the AoA, cost estimators identify and highlight areas of risk, the realization of which could lead to increased costs. These risk areas are often useful starting points for the LCL or PM to identify O&S Should Cost initiatives. While the O&S phase may be years or even decades in the future, the O&S Should Cost that influence system design typically yields the greatest long-term performance and cost benefits. Should Cost is covered more in Section 3.1.5.3.3.

CH 4–3.1.3 Sustainment Planning

DoD Components should begin product support planning as soon as the Milestone Decision Authority (MDA) determines that a materiel solution is needed to satisfy the capability requirement. This timing often precedes formal establishment of a program of record and staffing of a program office. PMs should use the insights and critical thinking embodied in such acquisition deliverables as the AoA; Reliability, Availability, Maintainability, and Cost (RAM-C) Rationale Report; and Concept of Operations/Operational Mode Summary/Mission Profile (CONOPS/OMS/MP); and in requirement documents such as the ICD and Capability Development Document (CDD) as the logical basis for the sustainment plan.

During the MSA Phase, the PM (or LCL if a program office has not yet been initiated), develops a sustainment strategy based on the results of the AoA and trade studies, and recommends refinements to Warfighter requirements and sustainment metrics. The PM coordinates with the requirements, operations, and systems engineering communities to analyze the intended use of the capability and identify design considerations that enhance the operational suitability, sustainability, and affordability. The PM identifies and quantifies O&S Cost and readiness drivers as an integral part of the AoA and MSA and pursues opportunities for improvement.

Sustainment planning during MSA includes determining the capabilities and major constraints (e.g., cost, schedule, available technologies) that inform the acquisition strategy and program structure for both the system design and its sustainment. PMs explore alternative sustainment strategies. Based on the early system concept, the program may investigate different options for sustainment strategies that consider how best to use the government's investment in existing support infrastructure, maintenance capacity, supply support, and unique support capabilities offered by industry.

The PM uses trade studies and analyses to compare alternative sustainment strategies. Then, the PM establishes a baseline sustainment strategy based on the legacy system, analogous systems, existing component/sub-component level repair, and Warfighter and DoD Component preferences. This strategy includes an outline of product support, levels of repair, manpower, schedule, etc. The sustainment strategy is articulated in a draft LCSP.

The PM uses the systems engineering process to assess technological risk that might result in failure to achieve performance requirements. As the PM considers system design alternative risk and opportunity analyses of candidate technologies, the PM should also consider the risks to achieving reliability goals, maintainability of the technology in its intended environment, and life cycle cost implications of the candidate technology. Risk considerations may include repair technologies that may need to be created and changes to the existing skill sets of maintenance personnel. The PM also identifies opportunities to apply new technologies and techniques that can enhance the maintainability of equipment and reduce life cycle cost.

CH 4–3.1.3.1 Analysis Process

The LCL/PM participates in trade studies, cost analyses, and business case analyses (BCAs) to evaluate the costs, benefits, and risks of different sustainment strategies. The depth of supportability evaluation may be constrained by available legacy data and analytical resources, but even high-level evaluation this early in system development can significantly reduce the risk of O&S Cost overruns and readiness shortfalls, post-fielding. The LCL/PM should also assess the timing of these analyses against the program development timeline.

The LCL/PM uses analytical techniques that enable comparisons of requirements, technologies, and systems against legacy/analogous systems to assess alternative sustainment strategies. Alternatives could include commercial and organic sources (when not constrained by law) of repair and supply, alternative levels of repair, or use of other DoD Components' or allied capabilities. The LCL/PM should analyze potential new sustainment technologies for inclusion in the sustainment strategy. The LCL/PM also conducts use studies to understand the impact to sustainment of the intended operational environment. The results of these analyses inform the program schedule, development of resource requirements, and the LCSP. Further guidance can be found in the Product Support BCA Guidebook.

The PM evaluates proposed maintenance technologies to understand reliability maturity, potential failure modes, and maintainability challenges. This allows the PM to identify potential sources of repair and further trade studies, and can help identify the need to develop new repair technologies or facilitate existing capabilities. The results of these evaluations feed Request for Proposal (RFP) development, data rights strategies, sustainment strategy, and LCSP development.

CH 4–3.1.3.2 Maintenance Planning

The PM uses the supportability analyses to develop a maintenance plan for the new system. This maintenance plan is part of the draft LCSP.

The PM drafts a maintenance plan by comparing the legacy system with the intended use/environment of the emerging system, along with knowledge of the developing technology. The PM identifies when maintenance is likely to be required and at which level of maintenance (organizational, intermediate, or depot). The PM, working with systems engineers, drafts scheduled and unscheduled maintenance tasks based on engineering assessments of failure modes and effects, wear-out rates, life limits, need for corrosion inspections, etc. The PM considers conceptual system design(s) and uses the initial removal rate estimates for each replaceable/repairable item to forecast likely requirements, including spares and repair parts.

CH 4–3.1.3.2.1 Core Determination

Core logistics capability (See US Code Title 10, 2464) is required to ensure a stable source of technical competence to ensure effective and timely response to mobilization, national defense contingency situations, or other emergency requirements. Programs undergo a core determination process to evaluate whether the statutory requirements apply and informs the program's 2366a certification submission.

The core depot determination is based on whether the legacy platform was deemed core or if the new system supports a Joint Chiefs of Staff tasking. The determination process is governed by DoDI 4151.20.

CH 4–3.1.3.2.2 Level of Maintenance

The maintenance plan identifies the planned levels of maintenance used to sustain the weapon system. The maintenance plan includes an outline of levels of repair, including core organic depot maintenance when applicable, as well as the supply support plan. Organizational-level maintenance may be decomposed into repair by organic personnel, interim contract support, or the contractor logistics support. The PM also assesses the duration of contractor logistics support necessary to support any planned transitions to organic support and identifies legacy secondary items already organically supported and the Depot Source of Repair. The PM considers software sustainment depot support (organic versus Original Equipment Manufacturer (OEM) contractor field service representatives to inform the development of the LCSP.

The PM highlights those new technologies that lack depot repair and may require further investment and development planning. This assessment of likely depots can help the PM identify expertise to evaluate facilitation requirements, schedules, and resources when depot-level maintenance is included in the maintenance plan.

Based on the proposed material solutions and technologies, the PM works with the DoD Component to identify potential sources of repair. Among the considerations in identifying sources of repair are capabilities to support similar system and subsystem hardware and software. Programs should investigate potential sources of repair both within a DoD Component and within other DoD Components.

The PM continually refines the maintenance plan in subsequent phases of the program. As the design matures, the maintenance plan serves as a key component of the LCSP, cost estimates, RFP requirements, Intellectual Property (IP) requirements, and budget development.

CH 4–3.1.3.3 Manpower Assessments
The PM conducts manpower assessments and trade studies to determine required skill levels and training, optimal workforce personnel mix (military/civilian/contractor) and constraints. This analysis provides the basis for resourcing the program office, field activity, contractor, and Warfighter personnel. The assessed skill levels informs the Cost Analysis Requirements Description (CARD) development to ensure accurate cost estimates and budget formulation. For more, see the manpower assessment section in the OSD CAPE's "Operating and Support Cost Estimating Guide."

CH 4–3.1.3.4 Interim Support Requirements
Based on materiel solution and technology maturity, the PM assesses whether a contractor interim support period is required and the scope of support needed. Interim support requirements refer to temporary contractor support in lieu of a permanent support solution (organic or commercial) for a predetermined time that allows a DoD Component to deliberately plan and program for investment in required support resources (spares, technical data, support equipment, training equipment, etc.), while a permanent support capability is put in place. Interim support is usually required for support of prototypes and early test and production assets during development and initial fielding. The PM first identifies those support activities that are required prior to fielding the permanent support solution and then develops a plan for implementing the interim support solution and transitioning to the permanent support solution.

CH 4–3.1.3.5 IPT Development
During this phase, the PM establishes multidisciplinary integrated product teams (IPTs) that achieve the performance outcomes by integrating individual logistics support elements or technical disciplines. Teams include representatives from stakeholder organizations, including DoD Component headquarters, operational and logistics commands, and industry. IPTs include expertise from disciplines such as engineering, cost estimation, resource management, contracting, information technology, supply, maintenance, corrosion control, and transportation. The PM should ensure that IPTs for systems engineering, testing, cost estimating, resource management, and contract development include logistics expertise and stakeholder participants.

CH 4–3.1.4 Design Interface
The design phase can best influence sustainment outcomes, as decisions made during this time can make it easier to maintain and reduce O&S Costs. The systems engineering process relies on balancing often conflicting requirements such as weight versus reliability. The design decisions rely on thorough trade studies that can accurately and completely provide the life cycle cost impact for each alternative being assessed. It is difficult and expensive to redesign to restore reliability or maintainability; close

interaction between the sustainment, engineering, and design communities throughout the design phase delivers required maintainability and reliability.

The PM should formulate design requirements to minimize support equipment, including testing, measurement, and diagnostic equipment. When the use of support equipment cannot be eliminated, the PM should standardize support equipment design for the broadest possible range of applications, consistent with maintenance concepts.

The PM should also consider the use of Condition Based Maintenance Plus when selecting maintenance concepts, technologies, and processes for all new weapon systems, equipment, and materiel programs. Readiness requirements, life cycle cost goals, and Reliability-Centered Maintenance (RCM) based functional analysis should be formulated in a comprehensive reliability and maintainability (R&M) engineering program.

CH 4–3.1.4.1 Reliability, Availability, Maintainability, and Cost Rationale Report

The Reliability, Availability, Maintainability, and Cost (RAM-C) Rationale Report provides a quantitative basis for reliability requirements and improves cost estimates and program planning. The PM participates in the RAM-C analysis, along with the R&M engineer and cost analyst, to ensure that the Sustainment KPPs and KSAs are valid and feasible and that appropriate trade studies have been conducted to illustrate the trade space between the sustainment parameters. This report is used throughout the system's life cycle as a baseline for how requirements are measured and tested. For more, see the RAM-C Rationale Report Manual and CH 3 Section 4.3.19 Table 48 R&M Activities by Acquisition Phase.

CH 4–3.1.4.2 System Performance Specification

The PM ensures the draft system performance specification to support the Technology Maturation and Risk Reduction (TMRR) RFP translates the R&M threshold values from the draft CDD. Once reliability allocations have been made to key subsystems, the PM should track design performance and report shortfalls (if any) at design reviews and acquisition decision points. The PM can leverage the Sustainment Command subject matter experts (e.g., PEO logisticians or legacy/analogous program logisticians) to help assess the new system R&M engineering requirements against legacy/analogous platform performance to identify risks.

The PM should ensure the draft design specification includes R&M requirements (e.g., Built-in-Test Detection). The ICD and subsequent draft CDD Sustainment KPPs and KSAs should be measurable so they support the system demonstration during Developmental Testing. The PM can leverage DoD Component test and evaluation subject matter experts to help guide the draft design specification language (value and definition) and the Test and Evaluation Master Plan (TEMP).

CH 4–3.1.4.3 Alternative Systems Review

As part of the Alternative Systems Review (ASR), the PM ensures that sustainment requirements for the alternatives are consistent with the RAM-C Rationale Report and are captured and reflected in the draft CDD. Additionally, the PM ensures that these capabilities and requirements are achievable in the preferred materiel solution and that the results of the MSA Phase (capabilities, requirements, preferred system concept and planning) indicate acceptable sustainment risk for moving into TMRR. See CH 3 Section 3.3.1 for additional information on the ASR.

CH 4–3.1.5 Milestone A

Milestone A is a risk reduction and investment decision. For product support planning, this decision establishes the product support strategy for the new capability. Table 1 lists key sustainment questions for the elements of the LCSP. This framework stimulates critical thinking but is not a complete listing of questions.

Table 1: Key Sustainment Questions at Milestone A

LCSP Section	Considerations
Introduction	Does the strategy require sustainment technology development?

Product Support Performance	Have the Warfighter requirements (including planned operational environment and availability) been included in the draft CDD and decomposed to affordable sustainment design-to requirements (both weapon system and support systems)?
Product Support Strategy	Have the plans for maintenance, supply, technical data, and manpower been defined such that cost and schedule estimates can be made? Are there alternatives? Are there planned sustainment trades?
Product Support Arrangements	Have the TMRR phase sustainment-related tasks been identified? Are legacy/analogous system PSAs applicable?
Product Support Package Status	Have the specific design features the PSM will assess in the TMRR phase design reviews been identified?
Regulatory/Statutory Requirements that Influence Sustainment	Has core depot applicability been addressed? Has the program included how and when the requirements will be met?
Integrated Schedule	Are logistics objectives linked to Program milestones? This includes Initial Operational Capability) (IOC), Initial Operational Test & Evaluation (IOT&E), Full Operational Capability (FOC), Material Support Date (MSD), etc.? Are major logistics events identified in sufficient detail for estimating sustainment costs? Are analyses phased to support milestones?
Cost / Funding / Affordability	Are O&S Cost affordability goals established? Has a program office Life Cycle Cost Estimate (LCCE) been developed? Are there Should Cost management targets for sustainment?
Management	Is the PSM in place? Are IPTs in place to address TMRR phase sustainment issues? Does the program/LCSP address competition across the system life cycle?
Supportability Analysis	What analyses ensure affordable logistics and readiness (Level of Repair Analysis [LORA], depot support, organizational manning, and use studies)? What alternatives have been identified as Should Cost initiatives?
Additional Sustainment Planning Factors	Are O&S Cost drivers for the legacy/analogous system and risk identified?
LCSP Annexes	Are sustainment Cost Estimates and their drivers identified?

CH 4–3.1.5.1 Draft Capability Development Document

Before Milestone A, the DoD Component's requirements developer formulates a draft Capability Development Document (CDD), informed by the ICD and the AoA. This document contains all requirements for the system. The mandatory sustainment requirement is broken involves three attributes that enable affordable logistics performance: the Availability KPP, the Reliability Key System Attribute (KSA), and the O&S Cost KSA.

The draft CDD reflects DoD Component requirements based on information documented in a system's Operational Mode Summary/Mission Profile (OMS/MP). The PM should ensure the development of the CDD remains synchronized with the OMS/MP. This synchronization prevents acquiring a design based on outdated missions or modes that under- or over-specify the system's utilization or operating environments. The PM's knowledge of operating modes and profiles facilitates integration of requirements from other function domains to achieve the CDD's sustainment metrics. Additionally, OMS/MP data is useful in other logistics planning efforts such as facilitating maintenance cycle planning (organizational, intermediate and depot), informing sustainment models and simulations, and determining infrastructure requirements. See CJCSI 3170.01I JCIDS Manual, Encl. D - Pages D-47-62 for CDD information.

Sustainment metrics are developed and measured together, as well as in concert with the other system KPP and KSAs. An unachievable value in any metric can have a ripple effect on the other sustainment or system performance metrics and may drive up development and O&S Costs. The LCL/PSM and the Chief Engineer collaborate on establishing and refining the sustainment metrics. The LCL/PSM should understand and influence the engineer's reliability and maintainability requirements, while the Chief Engineer should understand the support limitations of the planned sustainment strategy. This partnership ensures the overall system design supports realistic and suitable sustainment capabilities; it lays the foundation of cooperation through system development and production. Additionally, the sustainment metrics provide the linkage to integrate the product support elements.

The JCIDS Manual provides a useful reference of sustainment metric definitions across weapon system types in Table D-D-2, Recommended Sustainment Metrics, in the CJCSI 3170.01I JCIDS Manual, Appendix D, Encl. D - Page D-D-6.

CH 4–3.1.5.1.1 Key Performance Parameter: Availability

Availability defines the number of end items available for operational use as a share of the total number of end items in the inventory. Availability is central to determining the number of end items needed to fulfill the required number of operational units at any given time. The Availability KPP is divided into Materiel Availability (A_m) and Operational Availability (A_o), which are both important but focus on different aspects of availability. Figure 3 shows the calculations for each of the parameters.

Figure 3: Calculating Available Metrics

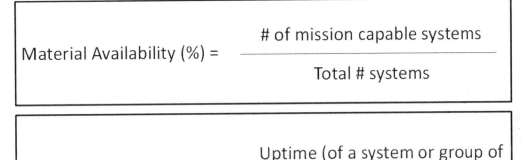

The A_m KPP applies to the entire fielded inventory of systems, including training, prepositioned, attrition reserve units, etc. By accounting for the entire inventory of fielded items, A_m ensures that items that are in depot or in transit to depot are accounted for as sources of non-mission capable status for the DoD's total inventory. By providing a holistic view of a population of end items, A_m can be linked to DoD's operations plans requirements and ability to meet missions.

The A_o KPP focuses on availability of operational end items that are assigned to a unit and expected to be available. A_o is expressed as the percentage of time that a system or group of systems within a unit are operationally capable of performing an assigned mission and can be expressed as (uptime/ (uptime +

downtime)). In this case, non-mission capable systems are driven by component failure rates and capabilities and capacity of the support infrastructure. Support factors that drive mean downtime include maintenance, supply, and administrative delays. This metric allows the Warfighter to understand how frequently a system should be expected to be unavailable.

While A_m and A_o cover different aspects of availability, their values should be mutually supportive, achievable, and built on the lower-level sustainment metrics discussed in Section 0.

CH 4–3.1.5.1.2 Key System Attribute: Reliability

Reliability measures the probability that a system will perform without failure over a specified interval under specified conditions. Reliability should be sufficient to support the warfighting capability needed in its expected operating environment. Considerations of reliability support both KPP availability metrics, A_m and A_o. Reliability may be expressed initially as a desired failure-free interval that can be converted to a failure frequency for use as a requirement.

The Reliability KSA provides a baseline measure to guide design engineers as the system is developed. The KSA enables analyses of the resulting configuration to include reliability modeling, reliability allocation, reliability prediction, and failure mode effects and criticality analysis. System reliability has a direct impact on maintenance time and manpower, spare parts usage and investments, A_o, logistics infrastructure, and life-cycle costs.

The Reliability KSA provides the basis for the eventual system design specification that will be placed on contract. Collaboration among the requirement authority, the PM and/or LCL, and the systems engineer at this point can facilitate a reliability definition and quantification that support follow on analyses such as the RAM-C, design trades, etc. For more on reliability, see CH 3 Section 4.3.19.

CH 4–3.1.5.1.3 Key System Attribute: Operating & Support (O&S) Cost

O&S Cost covers all Cost Assessment and Program Evaluation (CAPE) O&S Cost elements (as defined in Chapter 6 of the CAPE Operating & Support Cost-Estimating Guide) across the program's life cycle. Its inclusion as a mandatory sustainment metric ensures that sustainment performance is not considered in isolation from the associated sustainment costs. Modifying any of the sustainment parameters has a waterfall effect on the others, especially O&S Cost. The PM should seek balance between each metric that reflects realistic availability and reliability requirements and associated O&S Costs to achieve them. The DoD Component cost community can help frame the O&S Cost impacts of availability and reliability requirements to inform trade-off decisions. The O&S Cost KSA definitions are identical to those in the O&S Cost objective and threshold set in the Acquisition Program Baseline (APB).

CH 4–3.1.5.1.4 Other Metrics and Attributes

Other non-mandatory sustainment metrics are useful tools to include in a requirements document and subsequent systems specification and contracts. Maintainability metrics, including Mean Downtime and Mean Time To Repair, provide the foundation of the Availability KPP outcome. Maintainability metrics allow the requirements developer to understand how long it takes to restore available status. Including maintainability in a requirements document helps improve logistics readiness. Other subordinate metrics that offer greater maintainability and availability fidelity include corrective maintenance, mission maintainability, and maintenance burden. See CJCSI 3170.01I, Appendix A, Encl. D, Page D-A-19 for additional detail. The DoD RAM-C Manual, Table 2-1, Page 8-10 also has a helpful matrix of metrics.

The draft CDD ensures the other sustainment-critical metrics enable the mandatory Sustainment KPPs and KSAs. Examples of these metrics include logistics footprint, maintenance burden, transportability, and Built-In Test Equipment (BITE) fault isolation and detection rates with a false alarm rate. CJCSI 3170.0I JCIDS Manual, Appendix A, Encl. D, 7.f – Page D-A-18 contains a list of potential additional sustainment KSAs and additional performance attributes in the JCIDS.

Lessons learned from legacy and other current systems should inform the inclusion of maintainability, diagnostics, prognostics, tooling requirements, and other sustainment metrics early in the design process. The LCL/PM should use this information to drive explicit budget inputs for the development of new technologies to improve the reliability, maintainability, and supportability of DoD materiel, including the cost, schedule, and performance of the sustainment strategy.

CH 4–3.1.5.1.5 Affordability

The Affordability section in the draft CDD contains cost and funding data projections from the resource sponsor in support of the Milestone A decision. If the O&S Cost KSA exceeds the O&S Cost affordability constraint, the program's early development starts in an O&S Cost deficit. The PM uses this information to identify resource shortfalls and to align resource demand and logistics attributes. See Section 3.2.4.1.2 for more on O&S affordability.

At the Milestone A decision point, the DoD Component presents an affordability analysis and proposed affordability goals based on resources the resource sponsor projects to be available in the portfolio(s) of the program under consideration. From this analysis, the PM, with the resource sponsor, determines an affordability metric for these goals to be used throughout the program life. The PM tailors the O&S Cost metric to the type of program. Average annual O&S Cost per unit is the most common metric. Information systems programs with no production quantities frequently use average annual total O&S Cost over the first 10 years of fielding. Missile programs often use average annual O&S Cost per year, since most of the support costs on that type of system are not unit specific. The PM also ensures that the metric definition is clear about what it includes (i.e., the metric specifically identifies which CAPE O&S Cost Elements are included and whether or not disposal costs are included).

CH 4–3.1.5.2 Life Cycle Sustainment Plan in MSA

During the MSA Phase, the PM drafts the LCSP based on the baseline product support strategy. The LCSP draws on sustainment assumptions, analysis, and decisions determined in the AoA, requirements, technology development strategy, and acquisition strategy. The LCSP to support Milestone A includes a definition/decomposition of Warfighter sustainment requirements and contains the framing assumptions for product support strategy development.

The LCSP includes the plan to determine cost and availability drivers, the Core Depot Determination, the results of analysis of legacy/analogous system sustainment strengths and weaknesses, and Warfighter requirements. The LCSP also identifies key sustainment technologies and addresses affordability targets.

Additionally, the PM uses the LCSP to aid in developing the RFP requirements, including specifications, statements of objectives, statements of work, and proposed deliverable data items.

CH 4–3.1.5.2.1 Schedule of Product Support Activities

The PM synchronizes product support development activities and analyses with the program master schedule events, including design reviews, test activities, RFPs, and contract development activities. The results guide the integration of activities within the program and ensure efficient and timely product development.

CH 4–3.1.5.3 Resource Management

While PMs do not control resource management functions that are external to the program office, they play a key role in supporting those that do by supplying necessary data and justifications and by reviewing resource management products. The PM works with cost estimators, program/budget managers, and resource sponsors to inform affordability analysis, resource requirements, cost projections and savings initiatives.

CH 4–3.1.5.3.1 Cost Estimating

To prepare the program for the Milestone A decision, the PM is involved in two major efforts related to O&S Cost estimating: the development of the LCSP and the development of the Independent Cost Estimate (ICE), Service Cost Position (SCP), and/or Program Office Estimate (POE). The LCSP annotated outline contains a full description of the O&S Cost information required to support the Milestone A decision.

The CAPE ICE, SCP, and/or POE cost estimates at Milestone A cover the entire life cycle, focusing on major cost drivers. A cost driver is a factor that influences or contributes to the cost. Major cost drivers are those inputs that change the total O&S Cost the most in absolute value (e.g., fuel consumption, number of units, program life span). If the MDA decides to carry forward multiple alternatives from the AoA, the Milestone A estimate includes each alternative's LCCE.

It is important to include all O&S Cost elements (as defined in the CAPE O&S Cost Estimating Guide) since the ICE/SCP/POE becomes the basis for the budget after the Milestone A decision. For each CAPE O&S Cost element, the PM provides relevant requirements to the O&S Cost estimator.

Cost estimates at this phase rely on analogy to legacy/analogous systems. Cost estimators may ask the PM to identify legacy/analogous systems. Legacy/analogous systems are those that perform the same (or similar) mission or share technical characteristics with the system being estimated.

Cost estimators use the Cost Analysis Requirements Description (CARD) as the detailed description of the acquisition program to baseline the estimate. The CARD is a technical description of the program. The CAPE provides more information on the CARD in the DoDI 5000.73. In the CARD, the PM defines the sustainment and logistics technical baseline in enough detail that the cost estimator can develop a credible estimate that reflects the planned sustainment strategy. The PM uses the O&S, the Quantities and O&S Time Phased, and the Manpower Time Phased sections of the CARD template (available in the CAPE Cost Assessment Data Enterprise) to determine the data inputs required.

The sustainment assumptions in the LCSP are critical when developing the CARD. Once developed, the CARD will elaborate on sustainment assumptions such that the document offers cost estimating inputs that estimators can discretely price. The CARD likely references the LCSP for key assumptions and contains more technical detail and specific parameters useful in cost estimating. For example, the LCSP may report a system will use three levels of maintenance, while the CARD details six maintenance periods that last three months each and require 25,000 man-days of effort each period.

The MDA may direct the DoD Component to fund the program to either the ICE, SCP, or POE (or some combination thereof). The PM uses this decision in all future logistics funding submissions. As requirements change due to technical, programmatic, or planning changes in the program, the PM may need to highlight and explain discrepancies between the budgeted amount and the logistics requirements.

CH 4–3.1.5.3.2 Program Office Programming and Budgeting Activities

The PMs input at Milestone A focuses on funding requirements necessary to mature critical technology and reduce risks for the logistics and sustainment capabilities that comprise the materiel solution. Funding for important logistics and sustainment-related studies and analyses following Milestone A should support updates to the AoA and market research, as well as the Cost as an Independent Variable, Supportability, and Technology Risk Reduction assessments. Other funding considerations include those needed to establish the Supportability Integrated Product Team and the Integrated Logistics Support Management Program, as well as funds needed to initiate a Product Support BCA.

CH 4–3.1.5.3.3 Should Cost

Should Cost is an attempt to drive productivity improvement during contract negotiation and program execution by scrutinizing every element of program cost, assessing whether each element can be reduced relative to the year before, challenging learning curves, dissecting overheads and indirect costs, and targeting cost reduction with profit incentive. The Better Buying Power implementation memoranda and directives introduce the concept of Should Cost, which applies to both acquisition and O&S Costs.

Examining the O&S Cost drivers of legacy/analogous programs used in the Milestone A cost estimates points to likely targets for Should Cost initiatives in the new system. Section 4.2.1 of the O&S Cost Management Guidebook provides a full description of the types of analyses that help to identify O&S Cost drivers.

The Should Cost Portal provides examples of successful Should Cost initiatives across DoD Components, commodities, acquisition categories, and life cycle phases; it also provides Should Cost training, techniques, and tools. The PM documents O&S Should Cost initiatives in the LCSP.

CH 4–3.1.5.4 Sustainment Quad Chart

The Sustainment quad chart provides sustainment information in a standardized format that PMs use to report status at programmatic reviews. The quad chart helps the PM present the program's sustainment strategy, schedule, performance metrics, and cost during decision and in-progress reviews with milestone decision authorities. Reporting begins at program initiation and continues through each subsequent milestone and production decision, and at other reviews when directed. The chart is the PM's platform to demonstrate successes or communicate issues. It highlights and promotes innovative sustainment strategies, improved readiness outcomes, and reductions on O&S Costs. Completion of the quad chart is also an opportunity to capture sustainment issues and strategy, and ensure the sustainment metrics and costs are affordable.

The chart contains four broad areas. The Product Support Strategy quad (upper left) highlights the current and planned sustainment approach. The PM details the issues in meeting the strategy and planned steps for resolutions. The Schedule section (lower left) shows specific key logistics events. Dates for issue resolution events and support strategy are included here. Metrics data (upper right) compares current estimates and demonstrated performance against both program goals and thresholds in addition to the previous system (where applicable). The O&S Cost data quad (lower right) offers both an annual and total cost comparison between the new system and the previous one. Colors for both right-hand quads show positive and negative performance.

The template for the Sustainment Quad Chart is in Figure 4.

Figure 4: Sustainment Quad Chart Template

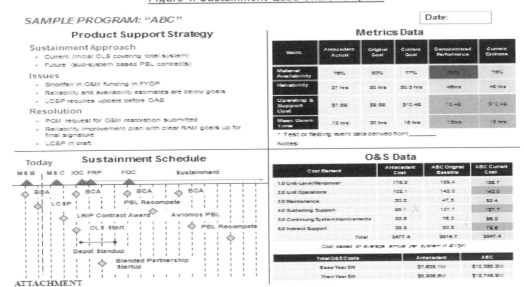

BCA = Business Case Analysis ; CLS = Contractor Logistics Support; DAB = Defense Acquisition Board; FOC = Full Operational Capability; FRP = Full Rate Production; FYDP = Future Years Defense Program; IOC = Initial Operational Capability; LCSP = Life-Cycle Sustainment Plan; LRIP = Low-Rate Initial Production; O&M = Operation and Maintenance; PBL = Performance-Based Logistics; POM = Program Objective Memorandum; RAM = Reliability, Availability, Maintainability

CH 4–3.2 Technology Maturation and Risk Reduction Phase

Planning for sustainment ramps up during the Technology Maturation and Risk Reduction (TMRR) phase. The PM evaluates the materiel solution for operational suitability, ability to meet KPPs and KSAs, and life cycle affordability. The PM defines risks and opportunities to sustainment and refines the sustainment strategy and requirements. Figure 5 outlines the major activities in TMRR, including development of the product support strategy and refinement of requirements and metrics.

Figure 5: TMRR Sustainment Activities

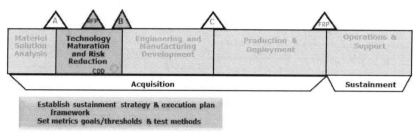

CH 4–3.2.1 Sustainment Planning and Analysis

Sustainment planning in TMRR refines sustainment requirements and the sustainment strategy. The resulting sustainment strategy in the LCSP shapes the Development RFPs for the next phase of the program, including specifications, objectives, tasks, and data.

CH 4–3.2.1.1 Sustainment Strategy

The PM revises the sustainment strategy during TMRR by conducting analyses that help identify risks and opportunities in O&S Cost, maintainability, availability, reliability, and readiness.

The PM uses the systems engineering process to assess and refine technological and programmatic risks to achieving performance requirements, including sustainment and affordability. The PM assesses risk and opportunities with maturing technologies to achieving reliability goals, maintainability of the technology in its intended environment, and life cycle cost implications of the technology. Considerations may include suitability for the intended operational environment, reliability and maintainability, manpower, impacts and repair technologies that may need to be created, skill sets of maintenance personnel, and producibility. The program also identifies opportunities to apply new technologies and techniques that will enhance the maintainability of equipment or reduce life cycle cost.

The PM considers planning factors that take intended use, climate, terrain, and operational tempo for the system into account. Using a ground vehicle, for example, with notional numeric values:

- Are systems engineering limitations based on hours, miles, rounds (should the system be capable of 200,000 miles of driving without any major repair)?
- Will it be operated in a moderately dry climate with no extensive corrosion anticipated for 40 years (including dry rot or deterioration of wire harnesses)?
- What is the planned operational tempo in annual miles driven and in what environments?
- How many miles will it be driven off road?
- Will it demand long idling periods of time?
- How might deployments (with or without reset), intended maintenance (field, sustainment, DOL and Depot) and environment may potentially extend or shorten estimate?

This analysis may also include limitations on weight logistics footprint, manpower availability, and skills. Based on analysis of the intended use of the system and the decomposition of the Warfighter's requirements, the PM ensures that the system specification includes supportability design requirements. Specifications include:

- Availability and reliability requirements, such as mean time between failures, mean time between maintenance actions;
- Maintainability requirements such as Mean Downtime and Mean Time to Repair; and
- Built-in-Test/diagnostic requirements such as mean time to fault isolate and ambiguity metrics.

Supportability design requirements may also include logistics footprint restrictions, maintenance personnel skill level restrictions, and transportability requirements, including size and weight restrictions.

CH 4–3.2.1.1.1 Framework and Plan for Analyses

The PM reviews the design maturity of the proposed materiel solution and support system in conjunction with other program disciplines, including systems engineering and testing to develop an initial plan to mature and verify the system design, including product support. The PM develops an analytical framework that ties specific product support analysis to design maturity activities. The PM should conduct initial planning for design reviews and test events and consider the sustainment inputs and outputs for these events. The resulting analytical plan is documented in the LCSP.

The PM identifies whether there are alternatives to the product support strategy or constituent elements of the strategy. The PM considers alternatives such as the current product support strategy for the legacy/analogous system and product support strategies used for similar systems currently in use by the U.S. military, foreign militaries, or commercially. The PM conducts an analysis of availability and O&S Cost drivers, which can reveal potential alternatives for support.

Once alternative product support strategies are identified, the PM determines the types of trade studies and BCAs that will identify the costs, investments, and risks associated with each alternative strategy. The analyses may need to be executed at a system level or may be specific to a sub-system or single product support element. The PM can use the Product Support BCA Guidebook to assist in scoping and tailoring analysis.

The DoD Component might also conduct an Independent Logistics Assessment (ILA) to review the product support strategy and assess how the strategy leads to successfully and affordably operating and sustaining the system. See more on ILAs in Section 4.1.2.2 and in the Logistics Assessment Guidebook.

The PM aligns the conduct of product support analyses, including BCAs, with the maturation of the system. These analyses are time phased and documented in the Integrated Master Schedule. For instance, when considering investments in depot level capabilities for sub-components, the PM might consider whether to wait until after Preliminary Design Review (PDR) or Critical Design Review (CDR) to conduct Level of Repair Analysis (LORA) to determine if components are economically repairable prior to completing Source of Repair Analysis.

CH 4–3.2.1.1.2 Product Support Package Development

The product support package is the collection of support elements required to field and maintain the readiness and operational capability of weapon systems, subsystems, and components. Development of the product support package during this phase starts with designing for supportability and technology trade-offs. The goal is affordable and technologically feasible design thresholds that satisfy Warfighter requirements. These design decisions will influence the support package, such as determining whether two- or three-level maintenance is appropriate, the range and depth of required provisioning, the need for unique support equipment, and technical manuals and training required to support the system.

Manpower, facilities, information systems, and the rest of the product support elements are also impacted by design and business decisions. The LCSP documents the product support package development status.

Some additional Product Support Package elements that warrant consideration include:

- Serialized Item Management techniques to effectively manage populations of select items throughout their life cycle. The PM should employ Item Unique Identification (IUID) (1) to enable life cycle management of assets; (2) to support asset valuation and accountability for audit readiness on the general property, plant, and equipment inventory and operating materials and supplies portions of DoD financial statements; (3) to identify unique items in financial, property accountability, acquisition, and logistics (including supply, maintenance, and distribution) automated information systems and business processes; and (4) to support counterfeit material risk reduction.
- Corrosion prevention and control programs and preservation techniques address corrosion throughout the system life cycle. Use of corrosion preventative and control methods may include effective design practices, material selection, protective finishes, production processes, packaging, storage environments, protection during shipment, and maintenance procedures.
- Opportunities to incorporate standardized (common) systems, components, spare parts, and support equipment, which preserve flexibility and options for competition in sustainment. The PM should consider RFP requirements that   promote standard and capable manufacturing processes that could be used or repurposed to support depot activities and promote structured, consistent processes for software development and sustainment activities based on standard maturity models.

CH 4–3.2.1.1.3 Product Support Integrators and Providers

The PM performs value analysis that is documented and objective and that explores costs, benefits, and risks to determine the best product support integrator and providers. These entities are either commercial or organic, but special consideration should be given to exploiting organic capabilities, as DoD has already expended resources to acquire those capabilities. The PM should also include economic and readiness considerations and the potential for diminishing manufacturing sources. Analysis includes considerations for small business, competition requirements, and obsolescence issues as part of determining the supply chain in developing the Product Support Strategy.

The PM determines interim support requirements and specific solutions for support of prototype assets during development. The PM should consider contractor field service representatives as part of the Courses of Action (CoAs) assessment and product support solution. Additionally, integrating DoD civilian logistics assistance representatives into the support solution during development may facilitate transition to logistics assistance representatives at Initial Operational Capability (IOC) if they are part of the interim support and permanent support solution.

CH 4–3.2.1.1.4 Core Workload and Estimate

If the core determination results in required organic depot support, the PM works with DoD Component-level organizations to determine what workload will be maintained in the depot (e.g., engine, airframe, chassis). Once the type of work to be completed in the depot is determined, the PM develops an estimate for that core depot workload. The core depot workload assessment is measured projected man-hours.

Because specific design details may not be known prior to a PDR, the PM may need to estimate the core workload man-hours based on data from legacy or analogous systems.

CH 4–3.2.1.1.5 Life Cycle Sustainment Plan Reviews

During the TMRR phase, the PM updates the LCSP to refine the activities that occur during subsequent phases of the program. The PM ensures that sufficient sustainment planning is in place to influence the RFP. Depending on the Acquisition Category level, the PM holds LCSP review meetings with key stakeholders, including sustainment commands; Warfighter organizations; Office of the Under Secretary of Defense for Acquisition, Technology and Logistics; and DoD Component oversight organizations to discuss the Product Support Strategy. Potential discussion points:

- Identification of LCSP annexes to include and rationale for excluded annexes.
- Sustainment metrics (requirements) and their incorporation into the draft RFP.
- O&S Cost & Affordability Goals/Caps.
- Portfolio level affordability.
- Planned core applicability or requirements.
- Planning for IP and data rights strategy.
- Legacy system versus future program cost drivers.
- Should Cost initiatives.
- Developmental testing/operational testing integration with the Sustainment Plan.
- Transportability testing timeline.
- Impact of final source selection (before or after Milestone B).

A key benefit of developing an LCSP is to facilitate coordination among stakeholders who provide inputs to the system's ultimate sustainment or who execute functions specified in the plan. The purpose of LCSP reviews is to reveal program risks and challenges early and to discuss and coordinate mitigating actions.

CH 4–3.2.1.2 Maintenance Plan

As part of the revision of the sustainment strategy during TMRR, the PM updates the maintenance plan based on design knowledge obtained during the TMRR phase and input from industry. Considerations may include whether the proposed material solutions are commercially available off-the-shelf (COTS) or government off-the-shelf (GOTS), require development of new repair capabilities, are deemed not economical to repair, or require intermediate/off-equipment field maintenance.

CH 4–3.2.1.2.1 Scheduled Maintenance

The PM considers how the system's service life will impact life cycle costs. As the design matures, the PM determines if scheduled maintenance may be required and how each maintenance event may vary depending on sub-component life. Other events to plan for could include recapitalization cycles, secondary item depot level repair, end item overhauls, and OEM-dependent depot repair (to include software sustainment).

Along with organizational and intermediate maintenance considerations, designing for supportability includes assessing the need for depot level overhaul. Analysis begins in this phase and is finalized as the design matures and fatigue and failure modes are better understood.

CH 4–3.2.1.2.2 Software Sustainment

The PM plans for software sustainment in two general categories: post-deployment software support and post-production software support.

The PM develops a sustainment strategy and potential source(s) of software support based on analyses of the system's operational and support requirements, as well as the operational concept. In developing the program's software sustainment strategy, the PM considers the extent of COTS and/or GOTS software; new software development; security classification; certification; and accreditation, including authorities to operate. The PM also considers test and integration needs, transition of operational software and support tools from the developer to the post-deployment support organizations, help-desk requirements, and safety critical requirements.

Properly phasing or programming for the software maintenance cost allows early budget planning for program support. Estimated costs for post-deployment software support include system patches, technology refresh, system help desk support, licenses, cybersecurity/information assurance vulnerability assessments, certification, initial field and depot software maintenance, and manning required for sustainment. Planning for technology refresh includes identifying the initial refresh year and the frequency of refresh.

CH 4–3.2.1.3 Resource Management
The PM's inputs during this phase focus on refining cost estimates and funding requirements necessary to mature critical technology and reduce risks for the logistics and sustainment-related capabilities that comprise the materiel solution.

CH 4–3.2.1.3.1 Program Office Programming and Budget Activities
Funding for important logistics and sustainment-related studies and analysis following Milestone B include that needed to update the AoA, market research, and CAIV assessments, as well as to refine the Product Support BCA. Other funding considerations include corrosion prevention, Item Unique Identification (IUID), maintenance, supply chain management, sustaining engineering, and other plans.

CH 4–3.2.1.3.2 Affordability
The O&S Cost affordability goals documented in the Acquisition Decision Memorandum at Milestone A guide the cost and engineering trade-offs during TMRR. As the design matures, the PM ensures that O&S Cost affordability remains a factor in engineering and sustainment trades.

If the O&S Cost estimate is at or near its O&S Cost affordability goal leading up to the Development RFP Release Decision Point, the PM actively manages known O&S Cost risks against that goal. At the Development RFP Release Decision Point, the MDA sets the O&S Cost affordability cap.

CH 4–3.2.1.3.3 Cost Estimating
Cost estimating during the TMRR phase supports the Development RFP Release and Milestone B decision through the update of the LCSP and the LCCE.

A DoD Component-approved draft LCSP is required to support this decision point (DoDI DoDI 5000.02, Encl. 1, Table 2) based on the PM's update to the program's Milestone A LCSP.

An updated O&S Cost estimate is not statutorily required for this decision point (DoDI DoDI 5000.02, Encl. 1, Table 2). The CAPE may provide an updated estimate to the MDA to support the release of the RFP. No formal CARD update is required for this estimate, although cost estimators may ask the PM to provide data and/or validate assumption changes if the CAPE plans to provide an updated O&S Cost estimate to the MDA.

CH 4–3.2.2 Design Interface
In the TMRR phase, the PM allocates reliability and maintainability requirements in the design. Once allocations have been made to key subsystems, the PM should track design performance and report shortfalls (if any) at design reviews and Defense Acquisition Boards. The PM monitors system reliability performance in early integration test results. DoD Component or software lab test failures may yield insight into system design capability to achieve R&M requirements.

The PM ensures logistics support and overall sustainment performance requirements in the design specification are decomposed into functions/segments in the functional baseline at the System Functional Review. The PM updates the logistics supportability analyses as the latest R&M engineering analyses (including updated failure rate and failure mode data) are performed. The engineering analysis also identifies strategic design opportunities for focused diagnostics, prognostics, and performance monitoring/fault localization. The PM is an active participant in the RAM-C analysis to support the development of the RAM-C Rationale Report needed for the Development RFP Release and Milestone B.

The PM should align the design of hardware intensive IPS elements, including support equipment and Packing, Handling, Storage, and Transportation (PHST) concurrently and in coordination with the system design to ensure R&M degradation factors are mitigated. This includes damage during maintenance, shock and vibration exposure in transportation and handling, exposure to extreme temperatures in transportation and storage, and relative humidity of the storage environment.

CH 4–3.2.2.1 Risk Reduction
The PM's focus throughout TMRR should be on mitigating the more challenging technical performance requirements (e.g., weight, power, etc.). If the program can emerge from TMRR with sufficient performance margin, the program design will be much lower risk to demonstrating all the design requirements (including R&M) in the Engineering and Manufacturing Development (EMD) phase. Conversely, with no margin in critical technologies entering EMD, R&M (and O&S Cost) may need reduced (traded away) to meet system weight or performance shortfalls as the design matures after CDR. The PM input to proposed design changes that reduce weight should include the estimated impact to reliability and the resulting increase in O&S Cost.

CH 4–3.2.2.2 System Requirements Review and System Functional Review
As part of the System Requirements Review, the PM ensures that the sustainment capabilities requirements captured in the CDD are aligned with sustainment requirements specified in the system performance specification. During the System Functional Review, the PM also ensures that the specified sustainment capabilities and requirements are achievable in the system design resulting from the technology maturation and demonstration activities. Additionally, the PM assesses the results of these risk reduction activities and identifies risks that may impact the upcoming system functional analysis and decomposition of sustainment requirements. For additional information, see CH 3 Section 3.3.2 on the System Requirements Review and CH 3 Section 3.3.3 on the System Functional Review.

CH 4–3.2.2.3 Preliminary Design Review
As part of the Preliminary Design Review (PDR), the PM ensures that all sustainment requirements have been analyzed, decomposed, allocated to Configuration Items, and captured in program documentation. Allocated sustainment requirements should have full traceability back to the system performance specification, the RAM-C Rationale, and the CDD. The PM also ensures that the specified sustainment capabilities and requirements are achievable in the system preliminary design as defined in the Configuration Items specifications. Additionally, the PM assesses the preliminary design from a sustainment perspective and identifies risks that may affect 10 USC 2366b (see US Code) certification, the program/system detail design in EMD, Product Support Package preliminary design, and the Milestone B decision.

The PM needs to ensure the PDR includes all R&M thresholds from the CDD. The design now includes derived requirements that support maintainability (such as Built-in-Test, capability fault detection, and false alarm rate). Throughout TMRR, the PM encourages design trades to support Condition Based Maintenance Plus. These prognostic and fault detection capabilities are justified by their contribution to meeting availability and maintainability. As part of the software development strategy requirements, the PM identifies documentation required for software sustainment (either commercial or organic).

See CH 3 Section 3.3.4 additional information on PDRs at both the subsystem and system levels.

CH 4–3.2.3 Development RFP Release
In the June 2011 Defense Acquisition Executive (DAE) memo, "Improving Milestone Process Effectiveness," the DAE states that the Development Request for Proposal (RFP) Release Decision Point (also known as the Pre-EMD or the Pre-Milestone B review) is the "most important single decision point in the entire life cycle."

This decision point is also critical to a program's product support planning, establishing in contracts and design specifications those elements that are critical to delivery of the capability and its attendant product support. Table 2 provides some TMRR phase product support considerations in preparation for this decision. As previously noted, this is not an all-inclusive list but provides a basic framework for critical thinking for product support planning.

Table 2: Key Sustainment Questions at Pre-Milestone B RFP Release

LCSP Section	Considerations
Introduction	Has the program identified the tasks required to integrate sustainment features into the weapon system and identified the required Product Support Package design requirements?
Product Support Performance	Are Warfighter requirements traceable to RFP specifications (availability, reliability, O&S Cost)? How will the requirements be tested and verified?
Product Support Strategy	Can the product support plan be traced to the RFP? Does the RFP reflect the IP/data rights strategy? Does the RFP include supportability trades for the Product Support Strategy?
Product Support Arrangements	Does the LCSP include process and timeline for determining PSAs, including support during IOT&E and any Low-Rate Initial Production (LRIP) options?
Product Support Package Status	Does the schedule include evaluation points to assess status of product support development?
Regulatory/Statutory Requirements that Influence Sustainment	Are core depot transition (contractor to organic) requirements addressed?
Integrated Schedule	Are program milestones (IOC IOT&E, FOC, MSD, etc.) linked to logistics objectives? Are support element delivery dates aligned with the TEMP?
Cost / Funding / Affordability	Have O&S Affordability goals been established? Has a program office LCCE been developed, and does it include disposal costs? Have O&S Should Cost initiatives been identified?
Management	Are the organizational structure and interfaces with key stakeholders identified? Is there sufficient expertise to conduct a source selection?
Supportability Analysis	Is the analytical framework traceable to the RFP, and are explicit provisions included for trade studies, LORA, depot support, organizational manning, and use studies?
Additional Sustainment Planning Factors	Can the O&S Cost drivers, assumptions and risks be addressed in RFP? Can they be mitigated? Does the RFP include assertions for Intellectual Property rights and provisions for data pricing and delivery where needed?
LCSP Annexes	Is Core Depot Applicability addressed?

CH 4–3.2.3.1 Capability Development Document

Required capabilities are refined in the TMRR phase. The sustainment strategy builds on the capability gaps and requirements highlighted in the MSA Phase and documents them as requirements in the validated Capability Development Document (CDD). The PSM partners with the systems engineer to refine the threshold and objective range value for each sustainment metric. Studies, trades, data models, and analyses executed in TMRR identify the technical capabilities, risks, and limitations of the alternative sustainment strategies and design alternatives. These results influence the final values assigned in the CDD, confirming or refining those identified in the draft CDD. Feedback from TMRR phase testing and modeling improves the realism, affordability, and testability of sustainment metrics.

The sustainment metrics identified in the CDD flow into the system specification and subsequent contract RFP. The specific values for Sustainment KPPs and KSAs in the CDD require vetting by Service and Office of the Secretary of Defense testing agencies. The PM should be aware if developmental testing, reliability modeling, or technology improvement efforts show outcomes not supporting requirements from the draft CDD. The approved CDD should reflect results from TMRR events to avoid unachievable or unaffordable capabilities. The CDD is the last opportunity to influence sustainment requirements without significant cost, schedule, or performance impacts later in program development. See CJCSI 3170.01I JCIDS Manual, Encl. D – Pages D-47-62 for additional information on the CDD.

CH 4–3.2.3.2 LCSP and Product Support Strategy

The PM participates in the Pre-Milestone B RFP development and the review of industry proposals prior to award. The PM's goal is to ensure that the RFP conveys the sustainment strategy, specified sustainment requirements, and required data and deliverables to industry. The RFP includes requirements for the contractor to propose data development and delivery, and sustainment metrics. The PM should consider sustainment outcomes in developing incentive or award fees.

The PM uses the LCSP to assist in the development of the RFP Statement of Work (SOW), which articulates product support requirements to the Contractor for the EMD phase that will allow a product support package to be delivered during production. The SOW includes the requirements for analyses, design interface, and product support development and test activities.

The LCSP articulates the decomposition of sustainment metrics that will be included in the RFP specifications, the proposed verification processes/test points, and the major analytical work that will be required from the contractor, and the data deliverables and IP that the government will require of the contractor to execute the product support strategy.

CH 4–3.2.3.3 Reliability and Maintainability in the EMD RFP

When the PM prepares the Engineering and Manufacturing Development (EMD) RFP package, it should include demonstrating R&M requirements. Any R&M requirements that remain medium or high risk after TMRR phase testing should be reflected in the incentive planning. The PM should consider an incentive for the contractor to remain within a set percentage boundary for the reliability growth curve throughout EMD. The PSM considers requesting production tooling be designed for subsequent use by the organic depot. The contract should require the design delivery data package include a complete bill of materials to support the PSM's obsolescence tracking and management responsibilities (see FY14 NDAA, Sec 803). The PM considers how anti-tamper and foreign military sales requirements will impact the design specification. The RFP for EMD should include a contractor sustainment support Contract Data Requirements List (CDRL) to provide all test failure data (to include vendor and sub-vendors) and report all repair work and repair cost data for each warranty (if applicable) repair. Contractor repair data will inform cost estimates and organic sustainment planning.

CH 4–3.2.3.4 Sustainment Planning

As early as the TMRR phase, the PM can use the LCSP to develop RFPs that provide potential vendors with sustainment requirements and insight into the operational and maintenance environments in which the materiel solution must perform. While preparing for the Milestone B source selection process, the PM considers the following evaluation criteria:

- Reliability risk based on each vendor's capability to meet potential reliability metrics and the threshold hours/miles.
- Successful transportability testing prior to source selection.
- O&S Cost estimates. The government could chose to provide an O&S Cost model/formula and assumptions of CONOPS and usage or could request specific data from each bidder independently to evaluate O&S Costs. The PM ensures that the O&S Cost evaluation include total government costs to operate and support the system, not just contractor costs.

The PM uses the LCSP to develop RFP requirements that consider sustainment and reliability outcomes during the Pre-Milestone B RFP process:

- The System Performance Specifications support the RFP and clearly identify sustainment and reliability requirements.
- The Program Office evaluates achieving reliability requirements as a condition for source selection.

In the Special Contract Requirements section of the RFP (Section H), the program provides a Milestone B evaluation guideline. The PM lists sustainment criteria that will be refined and updated during each successive phase, and outlines exact procedures and criteria that will evolve over the program life. The PM identifies criteria for the decision to exercise a Low-Rate Initial Production (LRIP) option upon source selection and informs vendors when the government intends to make final source selection. While not an all-inclusive list, the PM should consider these source selection criteria:

- Evaluate EMD performance against the Systems Performance Specification, including all aspects of reliability and sustainment requirements.
- Assess quality of the logistics management information data, provisioning planning, and technical manuals.
- Analyze price of LRIP/Full-Rate Production (FRP) ceiling price and not-to-exceed price for a specified number of end items.
- Evaluate the system reliability models and predictions that support the specification requirements. Including reliability metrics enables evaluation of offeror's approach and expected R&M performance. For example, define a specified mileage/hour mean time between operational mission failure through a combination of reliability growth testing and operational assessment per approved program reliability growth curve.

As early as the TMRR phase, the program can address O&S Cost management through a series of CDRL requirements. The Program Office could use reports required in the RFP and SOW to track part consumption trends, cost drivers, and failure causes to improve training, redesign when necessary, increase reliability, and decrease O&S Cost. Examples include (1) Class IX Service and Consumption Report(s) that outline and track sub-component replacement; (2) Parts Repair Report(s) to track when a line replaceable unit is removed, returned to service rates, scrap rates, and sub-component failures. The PM could use these and other reports called for in the RFP and SOW to track part consumption trends, cost drivers, and failure causes to improve training, redesign when necessary, increase reliability, and decrease O&S Cost.

CH 4–3.2.3.5 Software Sustainment
The RFP should require complete software documentation. Without documentation, the Product Support Provider (whether contractor or organic) has limited insight into how the software was designed and implemented. Incompleteness or omissions in documentation increase software maintenance costs because software engineers have to reverse engineer the code to determine how it works. In addition, this process increases the risk of inadvertently introducing errors into the code.

To support transition to the software Product Support Provider (PSP), the PM should determine what constitutes complete documentation for their system. At a minimum, it should address why the system was designed, how it was developed, what it consists of, where functions were allocated to different subsystems, and an overall architecture or blueprint. Plans on how the program office intended to handle COTS and configuration management issues are essential for sustainment and continued implementation. Interface definitions must be documented. Database designs and their documentation are essential to understanding their purpose within the system. Also, the development environment needs to be defined so the sustainment organization knows what tools were used to develop and support the system. This information is contained in the following documents:

- Initial Design Document
- System/Subsystem Design Document
- System and Software Architectures
- COTS Management Plan
- Configuration Management Plan
- Interface Control Document
- Database Design And Documentation
- Software Development Environment Documentation

developed, software sustainment tasks are not forgotten or removed from the development contr tasking. While the development contractor may not necessarily be selected as the sustainment organization, the development contractor is responsible for developing and maintaining document that the sustainment organization will need. The program office is responsible for ensuring that th contractor does not create documentation that is proprietary or undeliverable. (Note: Even though cancelled in 1998, the MIL-STD-498, Section 5.13, Preparing for Software Transition, contains go background and reference material in this area).

CH 4–3.2.3.6 Should Cost

The Development RFP provides an opportunity for implementing Should Cost initiatives by setting requirements for addressing system deficiencies and risks. For example, if the engineers and cos estimators identified repair time as an O&S Cost driver, the PM may develop a Should Cost initiat reduce repair time. The Development RFP may include language that provides an incentive for th to design the system in a way that reduces repair time.

The Should Cost portal provides examples of successful Should Cost initiatives across DoD Com commodities, acquisition categories, and life cycle phases; it also provides Should Cost training, techniques, and tools.

CH 4–3.2.4 Milestone B

Milestone B is the critical decision point in an acquisition program because it commits the organiz resources to a specific product, budget profile, choice of suppliers, contract term, schedule, and sequence of events leading to production and fielding. For product support planning, many of the activities affect the effectiveness and cost of sustainment. Table 3 provides some considerations necessary to implement effective and efficient product support.

Table 3: Key Sustainment Questions at Milestone B

LCSP Section	Considerations
Introduction	Has the sustainment program been adjusted to take into account the selection results? Does the program address support of development and any early operational capabilities or assessments?
Product Support Performance	Have metrics for availability, reliability, and cost been established? Ar requirements traceable to contractual design requirements? How will sustainment requirements be tested and verified? Is a reliability growt place?
Product Support Strategy	Are the product support requirements defined (organizational mainten depot level maintenance, training, support equipment, technical data)
Product Support Arrangements	Are PSAs to support IOT&E and contract options in place?
Product Support Package Status	Are the product support package requirements defined (organizationa maintenance, depot level maintenance, training, support equipment, t data)? How will the product support package be tested and verified? Milestone-B ILA been completed and risk mitigation planned?
Regulatory/Statutory Requirements that Influence Sustainment	Has core depot workload been estimated? Is preliminary Depot Sourc Repair complete?

LCSP Section	Considerations
Integrated Schedule	Does the schedule reflect detailed product support elements development and fielding plans aligned with program milestones? Does the schedule align supportability analysis to decision points?
Cost / Funding / Affordability	Have O&S affordability caps been established? Have CAPE ICE and SCP been reconciled? Do RDT&E and acquisition budgets include product support element development and delivery? Are O&S Should Cost initiatives initiated?
Management	Is the organizational structure in place (government and contractor)? Are projections of organizational structure and manpower to support fielding and operations identified?
Supportability Analysis	Is there a detailed plan for completing required analyses?
Additional Sustainment Planning Factors	Are mitigation plans in place for O&S Cost drivers and risks?
LCSP Annexes	Are Source of Repair Analysis results, a Depot Source of Repair decision, projected core depot workload, and BCA results documented?

CH 4–3.2.4.1 LCSP to Support Milestone B Review

The Life Cycle Sustainment Plan (LCSP) is formally approved by the acquisition executive or that person's designee prior to the Milestone B decision to enter into EMD. The PM updates the LCSP to reflect the results of the RFP and/or source selection to inform the activities during EMD. For competitive procurements, if the PM cannot update the LCSP to reflect the results of the source selection prior to Milestone B, the PM can propose a schedule to the acquisition executive to update the plan after source selection.

CH 4–3.2.4.1.1 Intellectual Property Strategy

By Milestone A, the PM will have developed an Intellectual Property (IP) Strategy that includes planning for the acquisition and delivery of data that will be required to execute the sustainment strategy. Planning for the IP Strategy should begin by the TMRR phase, although it is not required to be included in the LCSP until the FRP decision review (DR). While preparing for the source selection at Milestone B, the PM addresses:

- The cost of the Technical Data Package (TDP), both for the entire package and broken out by component/sub-component. TDP is an important selection criterion, as acquiring data rights may be needed to support future competition.
- Regardless of the government's decision to purchase the TDP, the Program Office normally includes an Operation, Maintenance, Installation, and Training (OMIT) clause that obligates the winning vendor to provide necessary repair instructions for government purposes (i.e., establishment of organic repair capabilities).
- Technical manual, national maintenance work requirements, depot maintenance work requirements, and troubleshooting and repair procedures could also be included in Integrated Product Support (IPS) Contract Line Item Numbers.

The PM may consider establishing a future decision point for choosing to buy or not to buy technical data, to support the LRIP decision. The PM should plan for the delivery of technical data and IP rights and should consider the following options for RFPs and contracts early in the program's life cycle:

- Priced contract options to address potential future delivery of technical data previously not acquired (for legacy systems, previous ships in the same class, or earlier contracts).

- Comprehensively establish program contracts to provide the government with all anticipated technical data requirements. If an unforeseen need for technical data emerges, the Deferred Ordering of Technical Data or Computer Software clause (DFARS 252.227-7027) allows the government to contractually require delivery of technical data developed under an existing contract for use in future procurements.
- If the Program Office identifies additional data not previously acquired or if additional license rights are required for previously contracted data, the PM can determine how to proceed, considering the costs, benefits and risks involved. Alternatives such as data escrow or an option for acquiring data at a later point in time may be considered.

The PM should plan to obtain unlimited rights for noncommercial technical data and computer software that is funded exclusively at government expense. The PM should negotiate for Government Purpose Rights, where practicable, for privately funded technical data required for the sustainment of critical systems. Provisions could include deliverables to the government for technical data that allows, where practicable, distribution to other industry organizations throughout the life cycle of the system.

The PM reviews the rights associated with each data in the contactor's proposal or identified during program supportability analyses. If the long-term needs of the government can be satisfied with the rights as offered, the Program Office may choose not to acquire additional rights. If the rights offered would not support the long-term needs of the program, the contractor may be directed to seek an alternate item to meet the design needs. If an alternate item is not available, the Program Office may consider the pursuit and cost of additional license rights. Alternatively, proactive planning may provide for the use and protection of the data subject to the limited rights license.

Table 4 provides FAR/DFARS clauses regarding technical data that may be included in all contracts and in future solicitations and contracts to account for and protect government data rights.

Table 4: Technical Data Clauses

Clause Number	Clause Title
252.227-7013	Rights in Technical Data-Noncommercial Items
252.227-7014	Rights in Noncommercial Computer Software and Noncommercial Computer Software Documentation
252.227-7015	Technical Data-Commercial Items
252.227-7017	Identification and Assertion of Use, Release, or Disclosure Restrictions
252.227-7019	Validation of Asserted Restrictions-Computer Software
252.227-7025	Limitations on the Use or Disclosure of Government-Furnished Information Marked with Restrictive Legends
252.227-7027	Deferred Ordering of Technical Data or Computer Software
252.227-7028	Technical Data or Computer Software Previously Delivered to the Government
252.227-7030	Technical Data-Withholding of Payment
252.227-7037	Validation of Restrictive Markings on Technical Data

CH 4–3.2.4.1.2 Cost Estimating

In preparation for Milestone B, the PM should ensure revisions to the LCSP are factored into updates to the O&S Cost estimate. The Office of the Under Secretary of Defense for Acquisition, Technology and Logistics LCSP annotated outline offers guidance on structuring O&S Cost information to support the program's transition to detailed design. Revisions to the CARD are the PM's mechanism for translating changes in the LCSP since Milestone A into an updated O&S Cost estimate. Knowledge gained through TMRR allowed the PM to add planning detail to the sustainment strategy. The PM should focus on these key sections of the CARD: O&S Quantities, O&S Time Phased, and Manpower Time Phased. The CAPE provides more information on the CARD in the DoDI 5000.73.

At Milestone B, the cost estimators update the LCCE, including O&S and disposal costs, by evaluating changes in sustainment assumptions since the Milestone A cost estimate. Changes to sustainment assumptions are likely due to key learning points resolved as part of the TMRR and reflected in the current programmatic and technical baseline of the system. Additionally, Milestone A cost estimate assumptions based on legacy and analogous systems may be updated to incorporate engineering and planning factors for the new system. Where O&S Should Cost initiatives identified in preparation for Milestone A and during TMRR have yielded results, cost estimators should adjust assumptions accordingly, and PMs should highlight such successes as part of the Milestone B preparation.

The program's Business Financial Manager (BFM) enters the MDA's funding direction in the APB. Specifically for O&S, the APB reflects the O&S Cost estimate as the objective O&S Cost value in both Base Year and Then Year dollars. The BFM sets the threshold value as the objective value plus 10 percent. An APB O&S Cost breach occurs when the current estimate is more than 10 percent greater than the objective. When a breach occurs, the PM, with the help of cost estimators and the BFM, explain the O&S Cost increase in a Program Deviation Report to the MDA.

The PM also monitors the O&S Cost estimate with respect to the O&S Cost affordability cap. Affordability puts the life cycle cost of a new system within the context of the DoD Component budget and/or a portfolio of systems. The DoD Component resource sponsor (for example, the Service "-8"), not the PM, is responsible for developing the O&S affordability analysis. The O&S Cost affordability goal is not a cost estimate. It is the amount of long-term DoD Component funding available for the system.

DoD Components have the flexibility to conduct affordability analyses differently. Enclosure 8 of DoDI 5000.02 establishes eight basic constructs that apply across any affordability analysis. The O&S Cost affordability analysis covers the entire planned service life of the system. An affordability cap, equivalent to a KPP, is established at Milestone B and documented in the program's APB.

CH 4–3.2.4.1.3 Should Cost

By the Milestone B decision, PMs should be investigating potential cost drivers based on design parameters for Should Cost Initiatives. For example, if the system designers expect that the repair time of a particular component is part of the critical path of the entire maintenance period, the PM may recommend a Should Cost initiative to reduce the repair time of that item.

PMs also begin to evaluate if previous O&S Should Cost initiatives are delivering expected savings. For example, if the PM created a Should Cost initiative to reduce how often a maintainer replaces a particular component, modeling may provide a count of how many times the component will need to be replaced in operation. Once the PM is confident that the Should Cost initiative will yield the expected results, the PM provides the technical parameters and expected savings associated to the O&S Cost estimator and reflects the changes in the CARD. The O&S Cost estimator incorporates the information into the updated O&S estimate.

The PM should consider steps the program might take to ensure the viability of future O&S Should Cost initiatives. For instance, the PM may anticipate establishing a post-fielding Should Cost initiative that involves multi-vendor competition for supply support. A key success factor in implementing such a Should Cost initiative is the program's access to and legal right to use part data in competitive procurements.

Establishing the appropriate data rights assertions and beginning the process of pricing and procuring the data may be most cost effectively done through the EMD contract.

The Should Cost portal provides examples of successful Should Cost initiatives across DoD Components, commodities, acquisition category, and life cycle phase; it also provides Should Cost training, techniques, and tools.

The PM should record all O&S Should Cost initiatives in the LCSP. The LCSP annotated outline contains a full description of the Should Cost initiative information required to support the Milestone B decision.

O&S Should Cost initiatives are a way for the program to meet established O&S Cost affordability constraints. However, the PM should not stop developing and implementing O&S Should Cost initiatives if/when the O&S Will Cost estimate is lower than the O&S Cost Affordability constraint. PMs use O&S Should Cost initiatives as an ongoing way to improve the O&S Cost and performance of the system.

CH 4–3.3 Engineering and Manufacturing Development Phase
The sustainment focus during the Engineering and Manufacturing Development (EMD) phase is to plan for development, testing, and delivery of the product support package. As the system design matures, the PM continues to influence the design to reduce risks in reliability, maintainability, availability and O&S Cost. The PM also conducts additional analyses to refine the Product Support Strategy and plans for the initial fielding of the weapon system and the transition to O&S. Figure 6 depicts the sustainment activates during EMD.

BCA = Business Case Analysis; EMD = Engineering and Manufacturing Development; FMECA = Failure Modes and Effects Criticality Analysis; FRP = Full-Rate Production; LORA = Level of Repair Analysis; O&S = Operations & Support; RCM = Reliability-Centered Maintenance; RFP = Request for Proposal; TMRR = Technology Maturation and Risk Reduction.

Figure 6: EMD Sustainment Activities

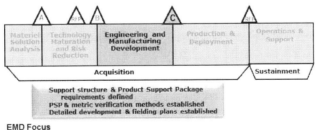

EMD Focus
Plan to define product support package & supply chain
    Detailed product support element requirements
    Detailed product support package development & implementation
Logistics Assessment/Sustainment Issues/Risks/Opportunities identification
Execution of analytical strategy (BCAs/FMECA/RCM/LORA)
    Trade Studies results/impacts
Performance verification methods
Fielding plans
Detailed Resource Requirements/Execution Plan
Supports O&S Estimates/Depot Workload Projections
Should Cost opportunities

CH 4–3.3.1 Sustainment Planning: Product Support Package Development

The PM's sustainment focus during EMD is the product support package. The product support package is further defined by assigning sustainment requirements to specific subsystems and equipment. Support plans for both the system and its logistic support system are developed as the system design matures. The PM ensures the program documentation, and planning, programming, and budgeting actions are put into place to develop, field, and sustain the product support package. Technical Performance Measures are established to monitor the linkage between design and supportability; they may be jointly developed by the systems engineering and product support teams at the start of the program and managed during EMD.

The PM ensures the elements of the product support package have been tested and demonstrated (organizational maintenance, training, support equipment, technical data), the reliability growth is on target, and the sustainment metrics are achievable by Full Operational Capability (FOC). The following key elements are included as part of the product support package development:

- Technical manuals
- Support equipment requirements, unique support equipment (organic, intermediate, depot), and provisioning for common and unique support equipment
- Spares and support equipment required to support testing and initial fielding, and to ensure sufficient funding and provisioning is in place
- Identifying field service representatives needed during Developmental Test and Operational Test, and at IOC, and sufficient funding and training in time to support development and fielding
- Interim support requirements and resources

CH 4–3.3.1.1 Trade Studies and Analyses

During EMD, the PM oversees the execution of planned technical and business analyses as the design develops and matures. Supportability analyses, modeling and simulation, and life cycle costing are applied and integrated with the systems engineering process in increasing levels of detail. These analyses help evaluate the relative costs and benefits of support and maintenance strategies, identify and mitigate sustainment risks, and create the data required to justify the support strategy. The Product Support BCA Guidebook provides analytical techniques for performing cost/benefit analyses. RCM analysis, LORA, and Depot Source of Repair Analysis should be considered.

CH 4–3.3.1.2 Product Support Element Requirements

Integrated Product Support (IPS) Element trades are made as part of ongoing negotiations between Warfighters and sustainers to finalize PSA requirements for Product Support Integrators (PSIs) and PSPs. From this, the PM updates the product support organization according to each IPS element, including the entities, required service levels, PSAs, information channels, and any other pertinent information.

CH 4–3.3.1.3 Product Support Package Validation

In the EMD phase, the PM ensures that testing validates that the design meets the sustainment requirements. The Systems Engineering Plan (SEP) includes the processes to validate the required product support package performance. The PM also ensures that sustainment metrics are estimated based on the latest configuration and test results. Finally, the PM ensures that the approved product support package's capabilities, including supply chain and other logistics processes and products, are demonstrated and validated.

CH 4–3.3.1.4 Maintenance Plan

The Product Support (PS) Integrated Product Team (IPT) updates the maintenance plan based on EMD analyses. Failure Modes and Effects Criticality Analysis (FMECA), Reliability-Centered Maintenance (RCM) and LORA results, as well as cost benefit analysis, may drive changes to the level of repair. The PS IPT should include maintenance experts, both military and depot-level civilian maintainers, to evaluate specific maintenance analyses as the system evolves, including:

- **Levels of Repair:** The LORA begun prior to the PDR is finalized after the CDR. The analysis provides recommendations as to whether subcomponents are economically repairable and at what maintenance level the task can be accomplished. The output from this analysis informs the final maintenance plan, provisioning requirements, manpower and training assessments, and technical manual and support equipment requirements.
- **Logistics Analysis:** During EMD, PMs supervise various logistics analyses such as LORA, task analysis, and RCM analysis, etc. Contractors may provide logistics data with deliverables previously outlined and formatted in the contract SOW and developed in training packages and technical manuals using the results. The Program Office reviews the analyses and logistics data to determine effectiveness and for use during source selection.

After source selection, contractors refine the system's design for LRIP and update their logistics analyses and support products.

CH 4–3.3.1.5 Core Workload and Depot Source of Repair
Prior to Milestone C, the PM refines core depot workload estimates based on the CDR. The PM also works with DoD Component stakeholders to identify potential depots for all components/sub-components of the program. The Depot Source of Repair analysis and decision process helps select the location for the depot workload and helps ensure effective use of commercial and organic depot maintenance resources that deliver best value to the program. The PM also projects the date and the funding for those depots to commence operation (IOC plus four years).

CH 4–3.3.1.6 Supply Chain Evaluation
The supply chain is finalized to reflect the product support strategy. Every aspect of the supply chain supports the Warfighter required performance and cost metrics. Processes are put in place to automatically and electronically share data and information between all Services, agencies, and commercial entities in the supply chain. The supply chain evaluation focus is on ensuring operational supportability and verifying performance. It includes a comprehensive description of the elements and fielding plan.

CH 4–3.3.1.7 Development of PSAs
Most product support strategies depend on product support arrangements (PSAs) with both organic and commercial industry. The PM determines the blend of public and private providers, and the relationship between them, to achieve an effective product support strategy that delivers Warfighter operational readiness. Programs should seek to effectively deliver the requirements of the product support package at best value to the government while attractive to commercial providers. Performance metrics used to measure achievement of the required outcomes and the solution (and associated product support package) are adjusted as required to effectively and affordably sustain the weapon system. Decisions made during the development phases impact the ability to execute performance solutions and arrangements after fielding.

The weapon system design should minimize the need for logistics resources, thus reducing O&S Costs. During development, the LCSP addresses supportability requirements and the technical and product support data needed to use competition and other sources of supply during sustainment. As the program transitions from development to fielding and sustainment, performance based arrangements may be used with product support integrators and/or providers to align the supply chain with Warfighter outcomes, or the PM may retain the responsibility and risk for performance at the program level.

CH 4–3.3.1.8 The Product Support Package and Metric Verification Methods
The Test and Evaluation Master Plan (TEMP) includes the means to verify that the product support elements that comprise the package (e.g., training, support equipment, maintenance and operator publications, spares, etc.) can achieve stated thresholds. Developmental and operational testing methods include parametric estimation, engineering analysis, modeling and simulation, and demonstration.

Supportability analysis is performed as design and other technical information on the equipment reaches maturity. This analysis is performed for the weapon system and support equipment as an integral part of the systems engineering processes and events. Data collection is via the SEP and TEMP. Examples of data collection and reporting are FRACAS (Failure Reporting, Analysis, and Corrective Action System) methods, and LORA using the collected failure and repair data to determine optimal maintenance levels. (See also CH 3 Section 4 for additional planning considerations.)

CH 4–3.3.1.9 Development of Fielding Plans
Each DoD Component develops a fielding plan that provides sufficient time and information to plan, program, and budget for the necessary materiel, personnel, skills, and facilities to receive, train, use, maintain, and support new weapon systems. Fielding plans should address and support the transfer of any displaced systems remaining in service. Fielding plans include all information required to track, stock, ship, and account for the new end items and any additional items associated with the new equipment (e.g., tools, support equipment, spares, manuals, etc.).

The PM plans fielding with the Service Materiel Command or Hardware Systems Commands. For joint programs, fielding plans are generally addressed in a Memorandum of Agreement between the DoD Components. When international partners are involved, the Joint Program Office may use a charter to outline general governance that allows for detailed fielding planning among DoD Components and international partners. Unless stated otherwise, DoD Components retain their fielding authority. For programs that support either joint or individual DoD Components, fielding plans identify variant type, quantity, number of lots, scheduled purchase plan, and location/agency/unit by date and quantity.

CH 4–3.3.1.10 Software Sustainment Transition Plan
During EMD, the program plans the transition of software support to sustainment. The PM, using output from design reviews, LORA, and Source of Repair Analysis processes, develops transition plans that may include transition of support databases, development and software support environment infrastructure, laboratory and test environments, and spares. The PM plans for licensing agreements and other arrangements that will allow access to COTS and proprietary software needed to sustain software capability. The PM develops draft release procedures with the Warfighter/end users so that the system can be periodically updated with minimal impact to operations. The program plans the transition of system documentation and the stand-up of help desk, server, and software maintenance functions in conjunction with the software developer and the designated software sustainment organizations.

During the transition to post-production software support (Milestone C), fielding occurs, the hardware production line ends, and software maintenance reaches steady state. For post-production software support, the PM should be sure to program funding for the cost of government labor to include field service engineers (government and contractor), certification and accreditation, lab operation, license updates, and the risk management process. (Office of the Secretary of Defense has replaced the information assurance process with updated cybersecurity requirements and the risk management process).

CH 4–3.3.1.11 Data Rights
By Milestone C, the Intellectual Property Strategy documents how much technical data is optimal for the government to purchase. For example, analysis may reveal the return on investment is much greater when purchasing only the technical data for 30 secondary items at $500M versus $4B for the entire vehicle's system technical data.

CH 4–3.3.2 Design Interface
During the EMD phase, the PM continues to assess and refine technological and programmatic risks to achieving performance requirements, including sustainment and affordability, and works with design engineers to demonstrate the R&M requirements during Developmental Test.

As technologies are integrated into the design, the PM assesses risk and opportunities with the system to achieving reliability thresholds, maintainability of the technology in its intended environment, and life cycle cost. The PM includes an analysis of sustainment risks at major program reviews such as CDRs and Production Readiness Reviews (PRRs). Risks may include operational environment suitability, reliability, and maintainability, manpower, and repair technologies. Producibility and required maintenance skills are also taken into account. Risks should be discussed and documented in the SEP; see CH 3 Section 2.2 and CH 3 Section 4.1.5

The PM then develops mitigation plans for identified risks and continues to identify opportunities to apply new technologies and techniques that will enhance the maintainability of equipment or reduce life cycle cost. These opportunities may be documented and tracked as Should Cost initiatives or incorporated into the program of record as part of the maturing design.

Entrance criteria for the CDR include design considerations impacting R&M thresholds. The PM addresses any shortfalls in meeting the sustainment requirements from the CDD and provides a plan to achieve a balanced design that considers all requirements, including BITE/Predictive Health Monitoring. The PM performs trade studies to determine which Predictive Health Monitoring capabilities demonstrate sufficient value for inclusion in the final design. The PM should monitor reliability growth, understand the impacts of trends, and identify and monitor critical technical performance parameters throughout EMD. Without margins in critical performance factors, the program design may not achieve R&M thresholds (which get traded off) and meet the O&S Cost cap. Additionally, the PM's program schedule and budget should include planning for obsolescence beginning in EMD.

CH 4–3.3.2.1 Software Sustainment
The PM should monitor the software developer's progress, including complete and current software documentation, which should include sufficient detail to support a system's successful transition to the sustainment organization. The PM should monitor the software developer's progress to ensure these documents stay on the development schedule.

Lack of appropriate documents limits insight into how the software was designed and implemented, and the software engineers may have to reverse engineer the code to determine its function. Reverse engineering increases the risk of inadvertently introducing errors into the code.

A software architecture feature to consider requiring is interchangeability of different COTS software products in the software architecture. System architecture should be designed such that the system, as a whole, is insulated from COTS internal product interfaces. When COTS products change, it should not drive changes to the system design interfaces. Consideration should also be given to COTS products that perform the same or similar functions so that alternative products may be options for future integration. For example, sometime during a system's life cycle, a COTS product may need replacement for fiscal or functional reasons. Programs should ensure that alternative products are available and functional within the architectural constraints. If the system depends on a specific COTS product that has no acceptable alternatives, performing future upgrades and sustainment could be difficult or impossible.

CH 4–3.3.2.2 Developmental Test and Evaluation
The PM monitors and analyzes Developmental Test and possibly early Operational Test event results to justify the required investments to address any R&M shortfalls. The PM needs to understand test results to identify any remaining high or medium risks to meeting R&M. The PM should request a deficiency correction plan to address these risks in the RFP for the LRIP contract incentive plan.

CH 4–3.3.2.3 Preliminary Design Review
The Preliminary Design Review (PDR) may occur after Milestone B for non-MDAP programs. For additional PDR discussion, see CH 3 Section 3.3.4.

CH 4–3.3.2.4 Critical Design Review
As part of the Critical Design Review (CDR), the PM assesses the sustainment capabilities and attributes of the system (and subsystem) design and assesses this capability against the CDD and the allocated sustainment requirements defined at PDR. The PM also considers how the sustainment attributes of the detailed design integrate with the capabilities of the product support package. Additionally, the PM assesses the detail design from a sustainment perspective and identifies risks that may impact the depot workloads and estimates of the 2366b certification, product support package development, maintenance demonstrations, and other sustainment-related test events. See CH 3 Section 3.3.5 for additional information on CDR purpose and the timing of CDRs at both the subsystem and system levels.

CH 4–3.3.2.5 Test Readiness Review

As part of any Test Readiness Reviews, the PM assesses the readiness for test (readiness of test planning, test article(s), and test environment) from a sustainment perspective and assesses how the test will verify and/or validate sustainment capabilities and requirements. Test results should inform the product support package development. See CH 8 Section 3.9.1 for additional information on TRRs.

CH 4–3.3.2.6 System Verification Review

As part of the System Verification Review, the PM should assess the collective results of system verifications to determine the extent to which sustainment requirements have been successfully verified and, more importantly, determine sustainment performance shortfalls. Of critical importance are the impacts of these shortfalls on the Capability Production Document (CPD), and the product support package as it readies for system deployment. The PM should ensure that all system verification and validation information is reflected in the Product Support Package. Deployment risks and impacts should be fully defined and appropriate mitigation actions included in the program's plan and budget. See CH 3 Section 3.3.6 for additional information on System Verification Review.

CH 4–3.3.2.7 Production Readiness Review

As part of the Production Readiness Review (PRR), the PM assesses the readiness of production processes and facilities to ramp to volume and meet the system's end item and sustainment demands. The PM assesses how the proposed production methods may affect sustainment and identifies the sustainment risks associated with increased levels of production rate (LRIP and FRP). Any sustainment risks should inform the product support package design and the program's planning for production and deployment. See CH 3 Section 3.3.7 for additional information on PRR.

CH 4–3.3.3 Milestone C

As noted in DoDI 5000.02, the activities undertaken by the PM to finalize designs for product support elements and integrate them into a comprehensive product support package are approved as part of the Milestone C decision. Table 5 shows a sample of the considerations taken by a PSM and staff to prepare for implementing a system's product support package.

Table 5: Key Sustainment Questions at Milestone C

LCSP Section	Considerations
Introduction	Does the program have an executable plan to deploying the Product support package based on the achieved design as reflected in the test results?
Product Support Performance	Are requirements included in the CPD? Has the product support package been tested and demonstrated (organizational maintenance, training, support equipment, technical data)? Is the reliability growth on target? Are sustainment metrics achievable by FOC)?
Product Support Strategy	Are product support elements defined and resources programmed? Is the Depot Source of Repair finalized?
Product Support Arrangements	Are PSAs to support IOT&E and contract options in place and ready for execution? Are future arrangements and alternatives defined?
Product Support Package Status	Are Product support elements defined and resources programmed? Has a Milestone-C ILA been completed and risk mitigation executed?
Regulatory/Statutory Requirements that Influence Sustainment	Has the Depot Source of Repair been finalized and workload estimate updated? Is the depot stand-up planned and funded?

Integrated Schedule	Are detailed site fielding plans, product support elements delivery tied to program milestones (IOC IOT&E, FOC, MSD, etc.)?
Cost / Funding / Affordability	Have O&S affordability caps been updated? Have updated CAPE ICE and SCP been reconciled? Have disposal costs been updated to the final production design? Do acquisition budgets include product support element delivery? Are O&S Should Cost initiatives implemented?
Management	Is the organizational structure in place (government and contractor)? Are projections of organizational structure and manpower to support fielding and operations identified?
Supportability Analysis	Are analyses complete and results implemented?
Additional Sustainment Planning Factors	Are detailed site fielding plans refined?
LCSP Annexes	Is the Depot Source of Repair documented as part of the CLA? Are supportability analyses results documented? Are depot workload projections updated?

CH 4–3.3.3.1 Capability Production Document

The PM refines the sustainment requirements from the CDD with engineering and test events into the CPD metrics. The CPD prepares a program for a production decision and verifies that all proposed requirements fill capability gaps. Sustainment KPP and KSA values are refined based on lessons learned in development, testing, and modeling in the EMD phase and through PM engagement with resource sponsors. These refinements in CPD capability requirements should also be integrated with engineering and testing plans.

During the EMD phase, the testing and engineering community conducts verification and validation of each sustainment technical parameter. The PM's engagement with both communities in the prior TMRR phase enables successful testing of sustainment capabilities in EMD.

See CJCSI 3170.01I JCIDS Manual, Encl. D – Pages D-67-81 for additional information.

CH 4–3.3.3.2 Life Cycle Sustainment Plan

The Life Cycle Sustainment Plan (LCSP) at Milestone C should lay out the plan to verify sustainment metrics and requirements, deliver product support to test and evaluation assets, and provide support for initial fielding. It should include addressing any interim contractor support requirements, identifying depot sources of repair and anticipated depot workload, and providing plans to implement the product support strategy over time. The LCSP is updated based on the results of engineering design reviews and should provide the findings of ILAs. Design decisions can impact the product support package by driving changes in failure rates, O&S Costs, maintenance plans, discard decisions, provisioning requirements, required support equipment, technical data, and training. The PM also should identify opportunities to reduce O&S Costs using Should Cost initiatives, address risks to sustainment, and identify mitigation strategies.

CH 4–3.3.3.2.1 Cost Estimating

During the EMD phase, the O&S Cost estimate can change to reflect updated testing data and O&S Should Cost initiative results. Cost estimating supports the Milestone C decision through the update of the LCSP and the LCCE. The Office of the Under Secretary of Defense for Acquisition, Technology and Logistics LCSP annotated outline offers guidance on structuring O&S Cost information to support the program's transition to production. The PM should continue to update and refine the CARD to ensure O&S Cost estimates align with the most up-to-date sustainment planning assumptions. The CAPE provides more information on the CARD in the DoDI 5000.73. Revised cost estimates may also be required if the program experiences a Critical Nunn-McCurdy Breach. The PM should monitor changes to the O&S Cost estimate in the context of the O&S Cost affordability cap.

At Milestone C, the cost estimators update the LCCE, including O&S and disposal costs, from Milestone B to reflect the current programmatic and technical baseline. An ICE is only required if the Milestone C decision authorizes LRIP. The PM provides actual testing data and results to the cost estimators for incorporation into the updated O&S estimate, as well as cost savings from any successful O&S Should Cost Initiatives.

CH 4–3.3.3.2.2 Should Cost

O&S Should Cost initiative opportunities continue after development, although PMs can expect these later Should Cost initiatives to yield lower savings since it is difficult to change design characteristics once the system is built. By the Milestone C decision, Should Cost Initiatives may reflect O&S Cost drivers highlighted during testing.

As the program's design is finalized, O&S Should Cost initiatives that were geared toward significant design influence should have achieved their desired effect. The PM should continue to identify design controllable O&S Should Cost options that may lend themselves to future engineering changes. Development and Operational Tests are likely to provide insights into possible design controllable O&S Should Cost initiatives. In addition, the program should collaborate with the respective materiel support providers—government and commercial—to identify sustainment productivity improvement opportunities that may be formalized in O&S Should Cost initiatives. Such opportunities are likely to exist in maintenance, supply support, facilities, support equipment, training, storage, transportation, and information systems, among other areas. This is a valuable point in the acquisition process for the PS IPT to actively seek input and subject matter expertise from materiel commands, the original equipment manufacturer, and third party logistics providers. The Should Cost portal provides examples of successful Should Cost initiatives across DoD Components, commodities, acquisition category, and life cycle phase; it also provides Should Cost training, techniques, and tools. The PM records the O&S Should Cost initiatives in the LCSP.

CH 4–3.3.3.2.3 Program Office Programming and Budget Activities

PMs inform cost estimates and develop funding requirements to support the Milestone C decision. The PM's input at Milestone C focuses on cost estimates and funding requirements necessary to procure and sustain logistics and sustainment-related capabilities to stand-up support for the operational test assets and initial production systems (initial spares, support equipment, information systems, initial training capability, etc.).

CH 4–3.4 FRP&D Phase

During the Production and Deployment (P&D) phase, the sustainment function in the program shifts from planning to execution and oversight. The PM, with support from the PS IPT, executes the planned delivery, verification, and deployment of the product support package to support the early production items. The PM refines and executes plans for initial fielding of the product support package for Operational Test events, IOC, interim support, and transition to FOC. Supply support and depot maintenance capabilities are put in place, and PSAs (such as Interim Contractor Support contracts, Public Private Partnerships, and Performance-Based Logistics [PBL] arrangements) are executed and monitored to ensure that providers are achieving required performance.

The P&D phase includes the FRP DR, which authorizes Full-Rate Production (or full deployment) of the system. Figure 7 depicts the sustainment activates during P&D.

Figure 7: P & D Sustainment Planning Activities

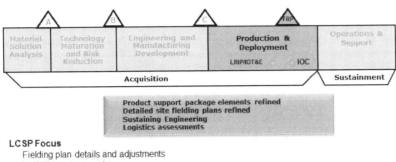

LCSP Focus

Fielding plan details and adjustments
Logistics assessments
    How sustainment performance requirements will be measured, managed, assessed
        and reported (Availability/Reliability/Maintainability/Affordability)
Identification of Sustainment Risks/Issues and Resolutions
    Design demonstrated/Early Fielding Issues
Analytical and management processes for :
    Refining product support package elements
    Fielded performance management and metrics
    Cost drivers and availability degraders
Refinement of Resource Requirements/Workload Estimates/Cost Estimates
Should Cost Initiatives

FRP = Full-Rate Production; IOC = Initial Operational Capability; IOT&E = Initial Operational Testing and Evaluation; LCSP = Life-Cycle Sustainment Plan; LRIP = Low-Rate Initial Production; O&S = Operations & Support; RFP = Request for Proposal

CH 4–3.4.1 Sustainment Planning & Execution

Sustainment planning during FRP&D centers on incorporating lessons learned from beginning phases of implementing the product support package, refining the fielding plan, and contracting for sustainment. The PM uses the LCSP during this phase to manage the program's fielding efforts and to execute the required product support infrastructure, including PSAs, maintenance and supply capabilities, and sustaining engineering and logistics functions. The PM updates the LCSP based on results from logistics evaluation reports on operating procedures, maintenance procedures, maintenance analysis reports, and Packing, Handling, Storage, and Transportation (PHST) verification reports.

CH 4–3.4.1.1 Delivery of Product Support Elements

The product support package is fielded at operational sites where sustainment and product support capabilities may be proven in an operational environment. Performance is measured against availability, reliability, and cost metrics. As testing is executed, the program identifies issues, establishes remediation plans, and executes appropriate mitigation steps. Finally, the product support organization is measured against its ability to meet planned A_m, reliability, O&S Cost, and other sustainment metrics required to support the Warfighter. The following are typically among the first elements that may be implemented as part of the product support package:

- Technical data delivery.

- Support equipment requirements, unique support equipment (Organization, Intermediate, and Depot), and provisioning for common and unique support equipment.
- Spares and PHST required to support fielding, funding and provisioning. The PM re-evaluates PHST and support equipment designs and design interfaces to ensure compatibility with production configuration and revalidates, by test and initial field data, the adequacy of design.
- Field service representatives, sufficient funding and training in sufficient time to support fielding.
- Interim support requirements and resources.

The PM also focuses on cost estimates and funding requirements necessary to fund delivery of the product support package, sustain fielded systems, and meet training and operational readiness requirements within affordability constraints. Other logistics and sustainment-related funding considerations include those needed to investigate Engineering Change Proposals (ECPs), develop Modification Work Orders (MWOs) and initiate pre-planned product improvements.

CH 4–3.4.1.2 Fielding Plan Details and Adjustments

The PM provides support required to sustain the system within the budget. The PM may need to tell senior management the consequences and impacts on the Sustainment KPPs/KSAs of budget constraints. The PM also coordinates with the contractors, supply chain elements, and operators to integrate their individual efforts in executing the LCSP. Additionally, the PM monitors changes to the design, operational environment, and supply chain to adjust the product support elements within the product support package. Finally, the PM looks for improvements to reduce the product support package cost.

The PM can use a program management dashboard that employs such tools as statistical process control charts or real-time performance meters to provide program updates. The PM monitors leading indicators that can aid in identifying and mitigating potential product support issues.

The PM uses continuous data collection to validate that availability, reliability, and cost performance is consistent with or diverges from the LCSP. If the analysis indicates a change in sustainment planning is warranted, the PM should update the LCSP as necessary. Changes in sustainment planning may include modifications to repair procedures, training, technical data/manuals, and inventory levels. The resulting changes to the product support package ensure effective and cost efficient readiness.

CH 4–3.4.1.3 Sustainment Contracting

As systems are fielded and logistics demand can be reasonably forecasted, the PM may begin implementing performance-based arrangements. Initially, such arrangements may be short-term cost-type incentive arrangements until sufficient cost data and technical data on failure modes and rates and field reliability data are collected. Cost-type incentive contracts share cost risk between the government and the PSP, allowing for incremental transfer of risk to the PSI and/or PSP. Later arrangements may use a combination of fixed-price contracts with incentives and other consideration as the design stabilizes. Long-term periods of performance may be used to incentivize industry investment, provide for continuous product improvement, and reduce cost. Public-Private Partnerships are an excellent way to leverage the best of government and commercial expertise. The commercial PSI or PSP provides lean repair processes, a responsive supply chain for bit/piece parts, and sustaining engineering. The public sector provides a skilled workforce at competitive labor rates and repair and transportation assets. Once fielded, the performance-based arrangements are measured against their ability to directly meet or support planned A_m, R_m, O&S Cost, and other sustainment metrics. For more, see the PBL Guidebook – Page 24.

CH 4–3.4.1.4 Transition of Software Support

During FRP&D, the program begins to transition software support to sustainment. The transition includes transition of support databases, development and software support environment infrastructure, laboratory and test environments, and spares. The program establishes release procedures with the Warfighter/end users so that the system can be updated (perhaps frequently) with minimal impact to operations. The program supports the transition of system documentation and the stand-up of help desk, server, and software maintenance functions in conjunction with the software developer and the designated software sustainment organizations.

CH 4–3.4.2 Design Interface

During this phase, the system design requirements are verified and validated for operational suitability. Feedback from initial operational testing may require re-analysis of product support elements within the product support package. Initial fielding may also reveal system design deficiencies, which may require engineering changes that affect product support.

The PM assesses ECPs for impact on the sustainment plan and O&S Cost. The PM can request that the FRP RFP include maintenance of the Logistics Supportability Analysis database (where applicable) or other support and supply data, to support future modifications and obsolescence re-designs. The PM can also request a CDRL in follow-on production RFPs for delivery of all contractor repair work data. The CDRL should include repair work scope and repair cost and recommended design improvements or value engineering proposals to further reduce O&S Costs.

The PM should update relevant supportability analyses and support planning based on results of the contractor's R&M analyses, failure diagnosis, problem investigation, functional and environmental qualification tests, and R&M demonstration tests.

The PM monitors the design factors for possible reliability degradation due to shock and vibration exposure in transportation and handling, exposure to extreme temperatures in transportation and storage, and expected relative humidity in the storage environment.

CH 4–3.4.2.1 Operational Test Readiness Review

As part of the Operational Test Readiness Review (OTRR), the PM assesses the system's sustainment readiness and capability to support operational test. Logistics support elements (e.g., spares, maintenance procedures, repair parts, and training) need to be in place with the operational testers. Additionally, the PM ensures that the sustainment performance of the system is sufficient to support operational test objectives and that the sustainment risks associated with the operational test have been analyzed and appropriate risk mitigation alternatives determined. See CH 8 Section 3.9.2 for additional information on OTRR purpose and timing.

CH 4–3.4.3 FRP Decision Review

The Full-Rate Production (FRP) Decision or Full Deployment Decision authorizes the program to proceed to FRP or Full Deployment. The LCSP at FRP focuses on measurement and assessment of sustainment performance, sustaining A_m, and adjustments to the product support package.

The purpose of FRP is to review manufacturing processes, acceptable performance and reliability, and the establishment of adequate sustainment and support systems. Table 6 provides some considerations for product support planning, implementation, and monitoring that correspond with this decision review.

Table 6: Key Sustainment Questions at FRP Decision Review

LCSP Section	Considerations
Introduction	Has the program demonstrated that the sustainment requirements have been met or will be achieved at FOC? Does the program have a correction plan for any problems?
Product Support Performance	Has the product support package been demonstrated in operations (organizational maintenance, training, support equipment, technical data)? Is the reliability growth on target? Are the sustainment metrics achievable by FOC? Are issues identified and mitigation plans in place?
Product Support Strategy	Are the product support elements in place? Are performance-based arrangements established or being executed as planned?
Product Support Arrangements	Are PSAs executed?

Product Support Package Status	Are all product support elements in place? Has the ILA been completed and risk mitigation executed?
Regulatory/Statutory Requirements that Influence Sustainment	Is the core depot stand-up on track to meet the required date?
Integrated Schedule	Will program meet MSD and core depot schedules? Have fielding plans been adjusted for mitigation plans and ECPs?
Cost / Funding / Affordability	Are O&S affordability caps being met or on track to be met? Have updated CAPE ICE and SCP been reconciled? Do Acquisition and/or Service O&M budgets include product support element delivery? Have O&S Should Cost initiatives been completed and/or additional initiatives been established?
Management	Does the Organizational structure support fielding schedule, operations and sustainment?
Supportability Analysis	Are results validated from operational data and additional analyses identified? Are should cost efforts underway to help reduce/control sustainment costs?
Additional Sustainment Planning Factors	How is feedback from fielding and operations incorporated into the program to drive should cost initiatives?
LCSP Annexes	Are sustainment costs & their drivers tracked in revalidating if the product support strategy needs to be updated?

Additionally, the PSM updates the LCSP to support the FRP decision based on satisfactory performance in IOT&E and other evaluations. The PSM documents any deficiencies in the product support package based on initial deployment and plans and resources to correct those deficiencies.

The LCSP details how fielded performance of the system is measured, how system level performance is sub-allocated to PSPs, and how PSI and/or PSP performance is measured, assessed, and reported. Metrics (e.g., availability rates, failure rates, repair rates, supply fill rates) may be established for each indenture of product support.

CH 4–3.4.3.1 Cost Estimating
The PM's main involvement in the FRP O&S Cost estimate is in the refinement of the CARD to reflect sustainment changes to the programmatic and technical baseline since Milestone C. For more on cost estimating, see Section 0.

CH 4–3.4.3.2 Should Cost
As the program nears FRP, operational test and fielding data provides insight into major cost drivers and areas in which O&S Should Cost initiatives are likely to yield the greatest benefit. While there still may be modest, incremental opportunity to influence O&S Costs through engineering changes, the program should dedicate increasing effort to identifying Should Cost initiatives that target active cost management among the organizations and infrastructure supporting what may be a rapidly growing inventory of fielded systems.

Where a program's sustainment planning includes interim contractor support, O&S Should Cost initiatives should seek contract incentives that align performance objectives with cost control objectives for the PSP or PSI. Should Cost initiatives may also yield benefits where they streamline or accelerate transition from contractor support to organic support. Additionally, shifting from a sole source commercial support provider to a competitive situation may constitute one or more O&S Should Cost initiatives as the program ramps to full fielding and steady state O&S. Where a program's sustainment plan calls for longer term commercial support and demand variability sufficiently predictable to support fixed price contracting,

O&S Should Cost initiatives may center on establishing longer term performance-based arrangements at component, sub-system or system levels (see the PBL Guidebook).

The PM should record all O&S Should Cost initiatives in the LCSP.

CH 4–3.5 Operating and Support Phase

The Operating and Support (O&S) phase is the culmination of the sustainment planning done in the previous phases. During this phase, the PM is focused on supporting the Warfighter's operations and training by executing the sustainment strategy, monitoring the performance of the system, assessing the effectiveness and affordability of the product support strategy, and making adjustments to the product support package. Figure 8 depicts the sustainment activates during O&S.

Figure 8: O & S Phase Sustainment Planning Activities

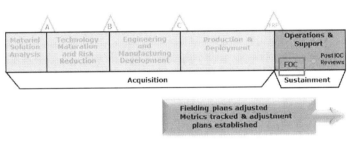

FOC = Full Operational Capability; FRP = Full-Rate Production; IOC = Initial Operational Capability; LCSP = Life-Cycle Sustainment Plan; O&S = Operations & Support

CH 4–3.5.1 Monitor System Performance

As the product support strategy is executed, the PM monitors the performance of the operating system and identifies risks and issues to continuing to achieve the Warfighter's sustainment goals affordably. The PM assesses risks and opportunities that may result from changes in CONOPS, ECPs, or the industrial base, or results of analyses of the maturing system.

As shortfalls in system performance operation are identified in O&S, the PM conducts analyses to determine the best Courses of Action (CoAs). Corrective actions may require maintenance plan changes, process changes, modification of agreements, changes to product support elements, or system design changes. The PS IPT may need to conduct BCAs, systems engineering trades, and logistics analyses to determine the most effective CoA. Potential CoAs may include changes to maintenance procedures, levels of repair, or product support elements, or system/component redesigns.

CH 4–3.5.2 Assessing Product Support Performance
In the O&S phase, the PM monitors product support performance against sustainment metrics and takes corrective action if needed. The product support package is refined and adjusted based on performance, evolving operational needs, and improvement initiatives. PMs ensure that support systems and services have been delivered and depot maintenance is being performed as outlined in the LCSP.

With the system operational, actual data is available as a basis for analysis and product support decision making. This data may reveal risks in operational usage, system reliability, demand rates, response times, funding requirements, and product support package performance, which require mitigation.

PMs should revalidate their program's product support strategy and ensure that it still meets suitability and affordability requirements. Indeed, 10 USC 2337(b)(2)(g) [see 10 USC 2337 (US Code)], requires a revalidated BCA when the product support strategy is changed, or every five years, whichever comes first. PMs should continually monitor and assess the sustainment strategy's suitability, particularly regarding changes in operating conditions or program assumptions. The PM also helps inform the life extension and disposal decisions, although the PM is not the decision authority. Additionally, incremental development of systems may require multiple configurations or blocks of a weapon system, and the product support strategy should reflect these requirements.

CH 4–3.5.2.1 Monitoring and Assessing the Supply Chain
The PM tracks and reports supply chain performance and its effectiveness. Tracking should include the sustainment metric drivers in the supply chain and the root cause of performance shortfalls. Special emphasis is placed on tracking the drivers for the key enabler technologies that most impact A_m.

PMs also work closely with their PSIs or supply support activities to monitor the health and efficiency of the supply chain. The risk of Diminishing Manufacturing Sources and Materiel Shortages (DMSMS) increases over time, and the PM should monitor this through annual assessments of the supplier base health.

As performance-based arrangements are implemented with industry, a balance should be reached between using increased competition to keep a downward pressure on prices and contract lengths that encourage investment in process and product improvement through innovation. The goal is to deliver reliable performance at reduced costs versus competing simply to drive cost down without regard to increasing the variability in performance experienced by the Warfighter. If the item is sole sourced to one manufacturer, emphasis should be placed on contractor reliability investments using an appropriate period of performance that allows a return on such investment.

CH 4–3.5.2.2 Software Sustainment
Software sustainment during O&S includes managing system obsolescence, technology refresh, source code escrow, vendor license management, and COTS-aggregate system architectures. Programs should ensure that Integrated Master Schedules for incorporating COTS products align different products and versions to minimize management complexity.

CH 4–3.5.2.3 Resource Management
During O&S, the PM works with cost estimators, program and budget managers, and resource sponsors to use actual sustainment cost data to align resource requirements, cost projections, and savings initiatives. The PMs input during this phase focuses on cost estimates and funding requirements necessary to sustain the fielded systems and meet training and operational readiness requirements within affordability constraints. Specific inputs include funding requirements related to replenishment spares and support equipment, hardware and software depot maintenance, modifications, system safety investigations, etc. Other logistics and sustainment-related funding considerations for the program include those needed to conduct post-fielding reviews, execute a technology refreshment program, ensure system security, and provide for resource sustainment contracts and service-level agreements.

CH 4–3.5.2.3.1 Should Cost

O&S Should Cost initiative opportunities do not end once the system is fielded, although PMs should expect later Should Cost initiatives to yield lower savings since it is difficult to change design characteristics once the system is built. After IOC, Should Cost Initiatives may reflect O&S Cost drivers highlighted during operation and use of the system.

This is also the time for the PM to evaluate whether the prior O&S Should Cost initiatives have produced the expected savings. For example, if the O&S Should Cost initiative was to reduce how often a particular component is replaced, operational data will confirm how many times the component actually needed replacement.

The Should Cost portal provides examples of successful Should Cost initiatives across DoD Components, commodities, acquisition category, and life cycle phase; it also provides Should Cost training, techniques, and tools.

CH 4–3.5.2.3.2 Cost and Software Data Reporting Requirements

Monitoring of sustainment contracts is also important for tracking and forecasting expenditures. The PM's role in the Cost and Software Data Reporting (CSDR) process is to work with the cost estimators and contracting professionals to ensure that the CDRLs are included in sustainment contracts beginning with the development of the RFP through the signing of the contract. The CAPE requires CSDR for sustainment contracts totaling greater than $50M, regardless of contract type. The OSD CAPE's Cost Assessment Data Enterprise (CADE) website provides more CSDR and related information at the CDSR Reporting Timeline webpage.

CH 4–3.5.2.4 Sustainment Review

As part of Sustainment Reviews during O&S, the PM ensures that sustainment performance of fielded units has been continually assessed and all service-use data (e.g., readiness degraders, changes in operational usage or environment, material failures, hazard reports, etc.) have been collected, analyzed, and assessed for operational and safety risks. The PM ensures that trend analysis is used to determine sustainment performance drivers and that planning is in place to address system modifications, ECPs, and other actions to resolve sustainment issues and improve sustainment performance over time. Monitoring the supply chain for obsolescence and diminishing manufacturing sources is part of this activity. FY17 NDAA Section 849(c) requires each military department to conduct major weapon system Sustainment Reviews not later than five years after achieving initial operational capability and throughout the life cycle. Additionally, DODI 5000.02, Encl 6, Para. 5 Product Support Reviews, requires PSMs to assess logistics during PSAs and technical reviews and to conduct ILAs throughout the acquisition process and every five years after IOC.

CH 4–3.5.2.5 Independent Logistics Assessment

The Independent Logistics Assessment (ILA) assesses the program office's product support strategy and how it will lead to the successful operation of a system at an affordable cost. The PM can refer to the LA Guidebook for details on how to plan, schedule, and execute periodic ILAs following FRP. Defense Acquisition University also has additional ILA resources, including links to individual DoD Component guidance.

CH 4–3.5.3 Adjusting the Product Support Package

The PM assesses the effectiveness of the sustainment plan to evaluate and revise the product support package due to changes in operational requirements (operational tempo, operational environment, mission changes), sustainment challenges (infrastructure and/or capabilities), or funding constraints. Changes to the sustainment strategy that ultimately lead to revisions of the product support package should involve an assessment of different courses of action such that relative costs, benefits, and risks are clearly understood. (See Product Support BCA Guidebook for additional guidance).

After fielding, a program and its product support package may undergo changes based on realities in the field. Operations may drive program changes through shifts in CONOPS, the threat environment, and the organization. Technology changes may also drive product support updates, including modernization to address obsolescence in the form of ECPs and the introduction of new technologies. The PM ensures there is sufficient logistics and sustaining engineering expertise to monitor the fielded performance of the system, conduct analysis, identify root causes of performance shortfalls, and make ECP recommendations. The PM collects and analyzes actual field data and justifies potential design modifications to achieve R&M requirements and/or further reduce O&S Cost.

CH 4–3.5.3.1 Capturing Program Changes

The LCSP remains the central document for sustainment planning throughout the programs life cycle and should reflect changes to the product support package. When changes in the product support package warrant, the PM updates the LCSP. Updates align the changing needs of the Warfighter and the DoD Component's evolving sustainment requirements with the product support strategy.

The LCSP annotated outline contains a full description of the items required in the LCSP update, but significant potential items to update may include:

- Scheduled events such as ECP incorporation, test events, etc., that impact sustainment;
- Maintenance plans for the system and components, including changes to the LORA;
- Results of any trade studies or BCAs, including changes to PSPs, sources of repair, and resource requirements;
- Design changes due to performance shortfalls, obsolescence issues, or modernization;
- O&S Cost estimates based on evolving programmatic assumptions, tracking of actual expenditures, and performance of Should Cost initiatives; and
- Funding and budgeting changes due to actuals from fielded systems, operational shortfalls, and budget environment.

Incorporating changes to sustainment plans ensures continued system performance and addresses Warfighter needs throughout the program life.

CH 4–4. Additional Planning Considerations

DoDI 5000.02 encourages the tailoring of acquisition approaches to most efficiently achieve program objectives. Section 4 identifies considerations specific to different system types.

- Section 4.1 provides guidance specific to Major Defense Acquisition Programs and Major Weapon Systems, as the rest of the guidebook is intended to be broadly applicable to all programs.
- Section 4.2 presents considerations specific to systems that are being rapidly acquired and/or fielded.
- Sections 4.3 through 4.8 offer considerations for tailoring sustainment plans to the unique design, development, and operational features of different system types, including vehicles, ships, aircraft, information systems, munitions, and space systems.

CH 4–4.1 MDAP Processes

This section offers guidance for tailoring and adapting sustainment planning for the unique needs of Major Defense Acquisition Programs (MDAPs).

CH 4–4.1.1 Milestone A

At Milestone A, MDAPs have one additional assessment requirement.

CH 4–4.1.1.1 10 USC 2366a Certification and Core Logistics Determination

In general, 10 USC 2366a (see US Code) requires that the Milestone Decision Authority (MDA) determine that an MDAP is sufficiently mature to enter technology development. Section (b)(5) of the statute requires a determination that sustainment planning has been done and that a core logistics determination has been made. In addition, 10 USC 2464 (see US Code) requires the Service to establish organic depot repair capabilities for core workload.

To meet the sustainment planning requirements in these statutes, prior to Milestone A, the DoD Component produces a core logistics determination to evaluate whether the statute applies to the proposed material solution. (Note: The Army is an exception and does not provide a Core Determination to PMs. The Army determination process for the PM is outlined in Army Regulation 700-127.)

CH 4–4.1.2 Milestone B
At Milestone B, MDAPs have two additional assessment requirements.

CH 4–4.1.2.1 10 USC 2366b Certification and Core Workload Assessment
In 10 USC 2366(b), provisions (3)(E) and (3)(F) require the MDA to certify to Congress that an MDAP has conducted sufficient logistics planning to inform an independent cost estimate and that the program has estimated core depot workload prior to approving entrance into EMD. The MDA-approved Milestone B LCSP, along with the approved Service Cost Estimate, meets the requirement. The Program Manager (PM) develops a projection of core depot workload (if any) in terms of projected man-hours, which will be required at Milestone B to satisfy the requirements for MDA certification that the program has met the requirements of 10 USC 2366b provision (3)(F) (see US Code). Because specific design details may not be known prior to a PDR, the PM may need to estimate the core workload man-hours based on data from predecessor or similar systems.

CH 4–4.1.2.2 Independent Logistics Assessment
An Independent Logistics Assessment (ILA) is an analysis of a program's supportability planning. Execution of the ILA is at the discretion of the DoD Components but preferably by a team independent of the program. For example, in the Army, the PEO assigns an ILA lead and team not associated with the program. The PM can refer to the LA Guidebook for details on how to plan, schedule, and execute an ILA to support the Milestone B decision. An ILA is an assessment of the product support strategy and an assessment of how this strategy leads to successfully operating a system affordably. Conducting the ILA early in the program phase where the design can be influenced is critical to fielding a sustainable system. The ILA should then be re-done at each milestone and periodically thereafter as the design matures.

The ILA provides the PM an independent assessment of the sustainment issues and risk with the program. The PM develops plans to resolve issues and mitigate risks. The PM documents the results of the ILA, as well plans for resolution in the LCSP. The PM incorporates risks into the program's risk management process.

An ILA is required for review by the MDA for MDAPs at Milestone B. The Logistics Assessment Guidebook is an important reference for understanding and conducting these reviews.

CH 4–4.1.3 Milestone C
At Milestone C, MDAPs have one additional assessment requirement.

CH 4–4.1.3.1 Independent Logistics Assessment
An Independent Logistics Assessment (ILA) is required for review by the MDA for MDAPs at Milestone C. At Milestone C, the ILA should verify that each product support element has been addressed and that the resources required for fielding have been programmed. The ILA should also help identify program risks to achieving availability, reliability, and maintainability of the system in its intended environment affordably. Refer to the DoD Component LA Guidebook for details on how to plan, schedule, and execute an ILA to support Milestone C decision reviews.

CH 4–4.1.4 Full-Rate Production Decision Review
At the Full-Rate Production Decision Review (FRP DR), MDAPs have one additional assessment requirement.

CH 4–4.1.4.1 Independent Logistics Assessment
Independent Logistics Assessments (ILAs) offer programs and their respective Services an opportunity to evaluate the effectiveness of sustainment plans once IOC has been achieved. Results of ILAs should be used to adjust the product support strategy as needed to ensure sustainment requirements can be met and O&S Costs remain affordable. For more on ILAs, see Section 4.1.2.2.

CH 4–4.2 Rapid Acquisition and Fielding

Rapid fielding activities support urgent operational needs field capabilities in less than two years. In contrast to a traditional program, sustainment of a rapid capability typically involves fewer assets. Contract line items in the development and procurement contract usually govern sustainment of these end items. While rapidly deploying and sustaining capability to the Warfighter are the most essential goals of rapid acquisitions, PMs should ensure contractors have in place processes and procedures to collect sustainment data for the capability, primarily focused on contractor actions, workload, and resources necessary to ensure asset availability. This requires the PM to apply critical thinking to determine what data collection is feasible given the mission, location, access, and operating environment. Collecting sustainment data for a carrier launched unmanned aerial vehicle differs greatly from collecting data for a short range unmanned aerial vehicle operating in a contested environment.

The collection of sustainment data is useful for the duration of the immediate mission, as it gives the PM insight into needed improvements in both system performance and supportability, such as for training, spares, technical data, operating software, support equipment, and maintenance (DoDI 5000.02, Encl. 13, 4d(3)(a))—Page 149). During the Disposition Analysis process, collected sustainment data informs the disposition options as determined by the designated disposition official and provides data for development of planning, programming, and budgeting data for all three disposition options: disposal, continuation in current contingency, and program of record (DoDI 5000.02, Encl. 13, 4e(5)—Page 150).

For capabilities that continue in the current contingency or transition to a program of record, operational sustainment data supports the product support strategy, including development of the Integrated Product Support elements. This data informs performance and sustainment metrics, requests for proposals, and contracts. It also helps identify critical reliability, availability, and maintainability improvements for the current configuration. Sustainment data also provides critical information for the sustainment analyses to determine the system's product support strategy through public, private, or hybrid PSAs.

CH 4–4.3 Ship Systems

Ships and other system-of-systems programs are some of the most complicated weapons the DoD buys and sustains. The complication arises from the interdependency of the systems in a single entity (like a ship) where multiple program offices (or commands or agencies) manage the individual systems. Each system may be its own MDAP or Acquisition Category program outside of the major ship program. The PM should communicate with all organizations within the program's sphere of influence and be able to articulate which systems are included in the sustainment planning/execution for the ship program. There may be systems that are not part of the acquisition of the ship but that become part of the sustainment planning once installed on the ship. The PM should maintain relationships with all stakeholders to ensure a smooth transition from designing to building to sustaining the system.

For ship programs, the sustainment metrics may need to exist at a lower level than the entire platform. While every sub-system on a ship has a role and is important, the PM should consider that a single failure or even the failure of a specific sub-system may not cause mission failure. The precise definition of the sustainment metrics is a way to reflect this. Some programs, particularly submarines, create a list of mission critical systems. Mission critical systems are those systems whose failure would prevent the ship from continuing its mission and force the ship to wait for repair. Once these mission critical systems are identified, the PM defines the sustainment metrics in a way that supports accomplishment of the mission. This can also focus sustainment planning and execution on the most important elements of the program. The availability metric can be shaped to reflect this. For example, a program may set an availability metric based on Mean Time Between Mission Critical System Failure.

CH 4–4.4 Aircraft

Aircraft sustainment cost is usually centered on a few key subsystems (e.g., engines, ejection seats, or auxiliary power units) that are generally not developed by the air system prime contractor. These subsystems are critical to the success of the program, but PMs should carefully manage the allocations to the sub-contractors for system performance, reliability, and sustainment cost. Program Management Reviews should include assessing performance of these sub-contractors to meet the requirements.

CH 4–4.4.1 GFE versus CFE and When to Break Out

Successful acquisition programs have procured key subsystems as Government-Furnished Equipment (GFE) to, for example, the airframe OEM. The GFE contracts give the PM greater control over the performance of the sub-system contracts. This avoids the risk that the airframe prime will sub-optimize the engine design (in this example). This could happen when the prime has the ability to require additional thrust from the engine to alleviate airframe weight increases. Increasing the engine thrust output may be the easier path for the prime but usually results in a decreased engine's life limits and significant increases in engine O&S during the system's life cycle. If the engine (or other cost-intensive subsystem) is to be procured through the prime during the development phase, the program office should perform BCAs to determine when and if those subsystems can be broken out to be procured and sustained as GFE. This may reduce the likelihood of future non-value added pass-through charges paid to the prime contractor.

CH 4–4.4.2 Sustaining Modified Common Commercial Aircraft Systems

The government will often buy a successful commercially operated civilian aircraft to be modified for military use. Examples are the Navy's P-8A based on the Boeing 737 and the U.S. Air Force KC-46 based on the Boeing 757. The core determination analysis should carefully discern between sustainment of the common commercial airframe and the mission-unique systems. Decisions on sources of repair for commercially derived military platforms should be supported by holistic assessments of the costs benefits and risks of commercial, government, or some mix of both.

CH 4–4.4.3 Cost Saving Initiatives for Common Commercial Aircraft Systems

Often, the common commercial airframe is flown from the final assembly plant to another facility for modification and installation of mission-unique systems. These aircraft can be on the ground for three years or more. Consider requiring only a temporary use of the engines and removing/returning them. Delaying purchase of the common commercial engines until the modified aircraft is ready to begin flight test avoids the cost of storage and cost of maintaining the engines to keep up with Federal Aviation Administration mandated engineering changes for the three-year (or longer) period. Also, consider requiring the aircraft system and components can be capable of being downgraded to Unclassified to support maintenance periods. Top Secret components have costly logistic burden in maintenance and the supply chain.

CH 4–4.5 Space Systems

Space system acquisitions generally have two major segments: the space segment and the ground segment. Sometimes, launch is considered an additional segment. The ground segment is further decomposed to ground or control (tracking, telemetry, and communication) systems, and user equipment and terminals, any of which may have mobile elements.

Due to the extreme nature of the space environment, the requirements and design of the space vehicle bus/satellite payload are extremely robust. Sustainment planning focuses on the support provided for the health of the space vehicle/satellite performing its mission (maintaining required orbit, anomaly resolution, etc.) via the tracking, telemetry, and command system and the necessary support to maintain the system's software resident in both segments.

Sustainment planning for the ground segment is similar to that of other terrestrial systems and the planning processes and elements as outlined in the Planning sections of this chapter. However, a space system's ground segment operating requirements are usually around the clock 365 days per year and primarily consist of COTS, or COTS-modified, hardware and software. These elements increase the criticality and importance for PMs to ensure a rigorous and disciplined examination of all aspects of the ground segments support strategy, including planning for organic depot support and determination of the minimum essential IP and data rights for sustainment.

COTS and COTS-modified hardware and software used in ground segments can be as much as 98 percent of the total system. As such, PMs should put in place processes and procedures to track upgrades in the commercial product that provide enhanced processing capability, capacity, and storage. Additionally, the PM should monitor and assess counterfeit and DMSMS risks across the system's life cycle. This process will require accelerated technology refresh cycles of 3-4 years, which are generally greater than that of other terrestrial COTS and COTS-modified systems and affects both the security certification and accreditation of the system and the system's operation and support costs.

On-orbit work or work to manage the satellites after launch is costly because the space vehicle/satellite cannot be off-line for repair, modification, or upgrade for extended periods. To address this, space systems acquire technical expertise services for the space segment as on-site operational support. Also acquired is a variety of ground equipment that mimics the satellite/space vehicle for testing of software changes (e.g., SILS). PMs ensure these test assets maintain configuration alignment with the primary ground control segment, The PM should ensure that IP provisions in the development and production contracts support the sustainment plan. These provisions should be explicit in terms of data delivery where the program plans to compete sustainment for the system. A system's support planning has to include the operational support technical services, maintenance and upkeep of the support systems, as well as the primary ground segment that communicates with the satellite (tracking, telemetry, and command).

Finally, space systems are completely net-centric and therefore have more robust program protection, cybersecurity, and computer network monitoring requirements than most terrestrial platforms. PMs should ensure the processes and procedures put in place for space systems (space and ground) to gain and maintain a system's authority to operate are maintained across the system life cycle. This may require both Red Team and Blue Team testing for major software releases and hardware interfacing with the Defense Information Systems Network.

CH 4–4.6 Munitions and One-Time Use Systems

Munitions and other one-time use systems have unique sustainment considerations, as they may be inactive for long periods of time between delivery and use, so stockpile reliability and monitoring strategies are important considerations to achieving required readiness and availability outcomes. These strategies support Serviceable in Service Times and other age limits (e.g., a 10-year wooden round concept) with stockpile sampling used to extend life intervals. PMs should plan for the resources in terms of budget, talent, and facilities necessary to conduct the stockpile reliability and age exploration programs.

Materiel Availability (A_m) requirements for munitions typically have high values, as most munitions are considered "up" while in storage or awaiting use, with only a small amount in depots or in the transportation pipeline. The A_m requirement directly supports Warfighter needs and includes quantities necessary for live fire testing, age exploration and destructive testing supporting stockpile reliability programs.

Sustainment strategies for munitions vary according to the testability and reparability of the end item. A key enabling technology for testable systems is BITE. The PM's advocacy for including diagnostic and prognostic capabilities in requirements documents allows testable and repairable systems to remain in the field rather than a time-based return for overhaul. Portable BITE sets enable a PM to conduct inspections outside of the organic or commercial depots and enhance stockpile reliability programs, saving transportation costs. While BITE helps collect the data on electronic components (guidance and control), other components (energetics and fuses) may need to be destructively tested or require physical inspection to determine if they are still serviceable.

Packing, Handling, Storage, and Transportation (PHST) requirements are a key O&S Cost driver for missiles and munitions, and reducing transportation requirements allows significant cost savings. Storage maintainability design factors include ensuring access to desiccant, self-reporting of impending battery failures, and ability to upload software and test while containers are stacked. PHST and Environment, Safety and Occupational Health requirements are important to address early in the LCSP, given their significant O&S Cost percentage for munitions programs and safety requirements for transporting all-up-rounds, live warheads, propulsion systems, and other sensitive munitions components. Munitions PMs also focus on incorporating sustainment requirements for training assets including captive air training missiles, missile round trainers, missile containers, empty round trainers, and ground/dummy training munitions—all of which require varying levels of maintenance, necessitating similar sustainment planning along with the all-up-rounds.

An additional consideration for munitions PMs is depot maintenance requirements while the system is still in production. If done at a government facility, complying with IOC plus four-year requirement is challenging, given likely small amounts of workload early in the life cycle. PMs should examine facility and Military Construction costs early in development to ensure legal compliance and adequate sustainment infrastructure. If a contractor facility is used for depot maintenance and the systems are still in production, consider whether the OEM is the vendor and has the capacity to do simultaneous depot maintenance alongside production. If not, maintenance and overhaul requirements may suffer in comparison to new production if using the same tooling and production line.

CH 4–4.7 Information Systems

Information system acquisitions are categorized as either business or non-business systems. Due to the rapid nature of technology changes, the requirements and design of information systems are extremely robust. Sustainment planning focuses on providing support so the system can perform its mission (accessing a variety of information for mission force calculations, compiling medical data for world-wide support between DoD agencies, assembling data for security access for mission support, etc.) and support to maintain the system's hardware and software.

Sustainment planning for information systems includes operating requirements that are usually around the clock 365 days per year, and consist of COTS, GOTS or COTS-modified, hardware and software. These elements increase the criticality and importance for PMs to ensure a rigorous and disciplined examination of all aspects of the system support strategy, including the requirement and planning for organic depot support and determination of the minimum essential IP and data rights for sustainment. PMs should put in place processes and procedures to monitor vendor products for enhanced or increased processing capability, capacity, and storage, as well as properly assessing risk management to the systems, such as DMSMS. PMs should also maintain good configuration control across a system's life cycle and assess impacts to any information system with interdependency and interoperability requirements. Due to the nature of information systems rapid technology changes, most technology refresh cycles occur every 3-4 years and affect both the system security certification and accreditation, and the system's operation and support costs.

Finally, information systems are completely net-centric and have more robust program protection, cybersecurity, and computer network monitoring requirements. PMs should ensure the processes and procedures put in place to gain and maintain a system's authority to operate are continued across the life cycle of the system. This may require both Red Team and Blue Team testing for major software releases and hardware interfacing with the Global Information Grid and the Defense Information Systems Network.

It is imperative that costs associated with the preceding activities are included in the system's Life Cycle Cost Estimate, affordability goals and caps, and the planning, programming, and budgeting process. The oversight, management, and updating of these costs are required across the system's life cycle until disposal.

CH 4–4.8 Modification Programs

During the O&S phase, a program may require modifications to meet emerging requirements, improve performance, address safety issues, reduce operating costs, or extend operational life. Additionally, modern acquisition programs are dependent on technology and thus may require technology refresh and insertion at a higher rate than legacy systems. Across DoD, the definition of modification varies from the replacement of a component to an MDAP-sized investment.

During the development of program modifications, the PM develops an acquisition strategy that considers whether a change will be implemented in remaining production units only, retrofitted into fielded units, or implemented on an attrition basis as supply is replenished. If the program is implemented in production without retrofit, the PM should analyze the potential impacts to readiness and cost of maintaining multiple configurations. In planning for the retrofit of modifications, the PM should consider urgency of the modification; impact to ongoing operations; manufacturing lead times, production rates, skill levels, and training and tooling required; and level of maintenance at which the change can be incorporated (i.e., organizational level, depot level, or return to the manufacturer).

The PM develops the product support package required to implement the change (e.g., installation instructions, training) and plans for changes needed to the original system's product support package to support the change once implemented. Depending on the scope of the modification, the PSM may need to update the LCSP depending on the impact to the product support elements. Examples of product support changes that drive an update to the LCSP include changes in reliability, significant increases or decreases in funding required to support the change, changes in level of repair, or major changes in CONOPS.

CH 4–Version and Revision History

The table below tracks chapter changes. It indicates the current version number and date published, and provides a brief description of the content.

Version #	Revision Date	Reason
0	2/1/2017	Chapter 4 initial upload

CH 5–1. Purpose

The Defense Acquisition Guidebook (DAG), Chapter 5, addresses Manpower Planning and Human Systems Integration (HSI) in the Defense Acquisition process. It provides guidance for including a total-systems approach; documenting manpower, personnel and training elements; and use of program manager tools that incorporate HSI considerations in the acquisition process appropriately. It also explains how HSI minimizes total ownership costs over the life cycle of a program.

CH 5–2. Background

Manpower Planning and HSI are integral parts of the Defense Acquisition Process. They focus on the role of the human in the Department of Defense (DoD) Acquisition process, and the significance manpower plays in the total ownership costs to operate, maintain, train, and support a system over the course of its life cycle. Without Manpower Planning, programs can miss pertinent key elements of HSI, suffer from millions of dollars in unnecessary costs, and result in harm to the warfighter. HSI's objective is to provide equal consideration of the human element along with the hardware and software processes for engineering a system that optimizes total system performance and minimizes total ownership costs. In addition, with the requirement for PMs to address supportability early in the early phases of the program, HSI is a key element of both engineering and supportability/logistics processes.

CH 5–2.1 Manpower Planning and Human Systems Integration

Manpower is typically the highest cost driver in the development and sustainment of acquisition programs, and can account for 67-70 percent of the program budget. When Manpower Planning is engaged along with HSI, PMs have the tools to effectively manage systems and to ensure that the human element of the system is included in the pros, cons, and risks of using a program.

CH 5–2.1.1 Manpower Planning Role in Human Systems Integration

The role of Manpower planning is to establish the right mix of personnel required for a program: military (Active, Guard, and Reserve), government civilians (U.S. and foreign nationals) and contract support manpower. Manpower analysts determine the number of people required, authorized, and available to operate, maintain, support and train for the system. Requirements are based on the range of operations during peacetime, low-intensity conflict and wartime, and should consider continuous, sustained operations, and required surge capability.

CH 5–2.2 Human Systems Integration Payoff

The payoff of utilizing HSI in all acquisition planning is enormous. Cost benefits include improved manpower utilization, reduced training costs, reduced maintenance time, and improved user acceptance decrease overall program costs. Improved operational performance can result in fewer errors, and improved design trade-off decisions can reduce life-cycle costs and decrease the need of redesigns and retrofits. Section 4.2 discusses the HSI domains, which should be considered for acquisition planning.

CH 5–3. Best Practice

DoD Instruction 5000.02 (Encl. 7) requires the PM to work with the manpower community to determine the most efficient and cost-effective mix of DoD manpower and contract support, and to identify any issues (e.g., resource shortfalls) that could impact the PM's ability to execute the program. This collaboration is conducted within the HSI framework to ensure integration with the other HSI domains.

The HSI lead for a program/project should be able to draw expertise from the manpower community to provide program assistance. For example, the decision to use Government civilians or contract labor where there is a high likelihood of hostile fire should be carefully considered. Additionally, the PM should consult with the manpower community in advance of planning for operational support services, to ensure that a sufficient workload is retained in-house to provide for career progression, sea-to-shore and overseas rotation, and combat augmentation adequately. The PM should also ensure that inherently governmental and exempted commercial functions are not contracted. These determinations should be based on current Workforce Mix Guidance (DoDI 1100.22 (Encl. 7).

The PM should evaluate the manpower required and/or available to support a new system, and consider manpower constraints when establishing contract specifications to ensure that the human resource demands of the system do not exceed the projected supply. This assessment shall determine whether the new system requires a higher, lower or equal number of personnel than the predecessor system, and whether the distribution of ranks/grade will change. Critical manpower constraints should be identified in the Departments' capability documents to ensure that manpower requirements remain within DoD Component end-strength constraints. If sufficient end strength is not available, a request for an increase in authorizations should be submitted and approved as part of the trade-off process.

When assessing manpower, the system designers should examine labor-intensive, "high-driver" tasks. Moreover, these high-driver tasks might result from hardware design or hardware/software interface design problems. These tasks can sometimes be eliminated during engineering design by increasing equipment or software performance. Based on a top-down functional analysis, an assessment should be conducted to determine which functions should be automated, eliminated, consolidated or simplified to keep the manpower numbers within constraints.

Manpower requirements should be based on task analyses, which consider all factors, including fatigue; cognitive, physical and sensory overload, and environmental conditions (e.g., heat/cold); and reduced visibility. Additionally, manpower requirements should be calculated in conjunction with personnel capabilities, training and human factors engineering trade-offs.

Tasks and workload for individual systems, systems-of-systems and families-of-systems should be reviewed together to identify commonalities, merge operations and avoid duplication. The cumulative effects of systems-of-systems, families-of-systems and related systems integration should be considered when developing manpower requirements.

When reviewing support activities, the PM should work with manpower and functional representatives to identify process improvements, design options or other initiatives to reduce manpower requirements, improve the efficiency or effectiveness of support services or enhance the cross-functional integration of support activities.

The support strategy should consider the approach used to provide for the most-efficient and cost-effective mix of manpower and contract support. The support strategy should also identify any cost, schedule, performance issues; or uncompleted analyses that could impact the PM's ability to execute the program.

CH 5–3.1 Manpower Planning

The requirements of manpower planning for MDAPS are included in Operating and Support Cost-Estimating Guide (para 3.10.1 – Page 3-20) for inclusion in the Cost Assessment and Program Evaluation (CAPE) Cost Analysis Requirements Description (CARD). Additionally, manpower-planning documentation is used by Service components to estimate the number and types of people needed for specific programs and by personnel and training communities to plan and forecast their program requirements.

DoD components should require manpower planning documentation for all Acquisition Category (ACAT) I through ACAT IV programs to support development of CARD and Life Cycle Sustainment Estimates.

At program initiation, the Service component manpower authority and PM, in consultation with the MDA, should agree to reporting requirements and assumptions for manpower planning based on ACAT level and on whether the program has significant manpower implications.

Required and recommended data elements of manpower planning should meet CARD and/or Life Cycle Cost Estimate content requirements. Lower level ACAT/AAP programs with little to no manpower implications/risks may not need extensive manpower planning documentation. PMs should agree upon required manpower planning with the component manpower authority. The component manpower authority should approve the manpower planning for MDAP and designated manpower-significant programs prior to submission of the program CARD at major milestones.

Additionally, USD (P&R) promulgates separate and specific guidance concerning acquisition-related Total Force manpower planning. This guidance addresses the enduring need to provide Total Force manpower projections -- active/reserve military, Government civilians, and contracted services for the ICE/CARD.

This ensures that manpower plans are feasible and affordable and result in desired operational and support capabilities.

CH 5–3.2 Total Systems Approach

The total systems approach includes equipment and software as well as people who operate, maintain and support the system; training requirements and training devices; and the operational and support infrastructure. HSI practitioners assist PMs by focusing attention on the human part of the system, and by integrating and inserting manpower, personnel, training, human factors engineering, environment, safety, occupational health hazards and personnel survivability considerations into the Defense Acquisition process. Consistent with DoDI 5000.02 (Encl.7), when addressing HSI, the PM should address each of the "domains" of HSI. A comprehensive integration within and across these domains is required, as outlined in Section 4.2 of this chapter. Chapter 1 Section 3.3.5 discusses Integrated Product and Process Development (IPPD) and Integrated Product Teams (IPTs) for acquisition planning activities.

IPPD is a management technique that integrates all acquisition activities, starting with a capabilities definition through systems engineering, production, fielding/deployment and operational support in order to optimize the design, manufacturing, business and supportability processes. At the core of the IPPD technique are IPTs. HSI should be a key consideration during the formation of IPTs. HSI representatives should be included as members of systems engineering and design teams and other IPTs that deal with human-oriented acquisition issues or topics. The various HSI domain experts should have the opportunity to work in an integrated structure to impact the system comprehensively. Domain experts working different IPT structures may make significant changes/inputs to the system without fully appreciating the effects their changes may have on other domains. Only by working closely together can the HSI practitioners bring an optimum set of human interfaces to the Systems Engineering and Systems Acquisition Processes.

HSI participants assist in IPPD as part of the IPTs by ensuring the HSI parameters/requirements in the Initial Capabilities Document (ICD), Capability Development Document, and Capability Production Document are based upon and consistent with the user representative's strategic goals and strategies. These parameters/requirements are addressed throughout the acquisition process, starting in the Capabilities-Based Assessment (CBA) and ICD and continuing throughout the engineering design, trade-off analysis, testing, fielding/deployment and operational support phases.

Performance and HSI domain issues, identified in legacy systems and by design capability risk reviews, are used to establish a preliminary list for risk management. These issues should be evaluated and managed throughout the system's life cycle at a management level consistent with the hazard.

The tools, methodologies, risk-assessment/mitigations, and set of assumptions used by the acquisition community to assess manpower and personnel and training requirements, measure human-in-the-loop system performance, and evaluate safety, occupational health hazards, survivability and habitability, need to be consistent with what the functional communities/user representatives use to evaluate performance and establish performance based metrics.

The HSI participants should ensure that the factors used by the acquisition community to develop cost estimates are consistent with:

- Manpower and personnel documentation requirements,
- Training requirements reported in the DoD Component training plans, and
- Assessments of safety and health hazards documented in the Programmatic Environment, Safety, and Occupational Health Evaluation documentation.

The HSI participants should also ensure that the Manpower Estimates and Training Strategies reported during the acquisition milestone reviews are reflected in the manning documents, training plans, personnel rosters, and budget submissions when the systems are fielded.

CH 5–3.3 Human Systems Integration References

Table 1 contains HSI-related policy and direction.

Table 1: Human Systems Integration Related Policy and Direction

Issuance Number	Title
DoD Directive 1100.4	Guidance for Manpower Programs
DoD Directive 1322.18	Military Training
DoD Instruction 1100.22	Guidance for Determining Workforce Mix
DoD Instruction 1322.26	Development, Management and Delivery of Distributed Learning" Training Transformation Implementation Plan
CJCS Instruction 3170.01	Joint Capabilities Integration and Development System
JCIDS Manual	Operation of the Joint Capabilities Integration and Development System
Joint Military Dictionary (JP 1-02)	Department of Defense Dictionary of Military and Associated Terms
AR 602-1	Human Factors Engineering Program
AR 602-2	Manpower and Personnel Integration (MANPRINT) in the Systems Acquisition Process

Table 2 contains military standards (MIL-STD), DoD handbooks (DOD-HDBK) and), military handbooks (MIL-HDBK); standard practices that may be used to support HSI analysis.

Table 2: HSI Discretionary Practices

Issuance Number	Title
MIL-STD-882D	Standard Practice for System Safety
MIL-STD-1472	DoD Design Criteria Standard: Human Engineering
MIL-STD-46855A	DoD Standard Practice, Human Engineering Requirements for Military Systems, Equipment and Facilities
DOD-HDBK-743	Anthropometry of U. S. Military Personnel
MIL-PRF-29612	Performance Specification, Training Data Products A Guide for Early Embedded Training Decisions
ASTM F1166-07	Standard Practice for Human Engineering Design for Marine Systems, Equipment and Facilities
ASTM F1337-10	Standard Practice for Human Systems Integration Program Requirements for Ships and Marine Systems, Equipment and Facilities

CH 5–4. Human Systems Integration

The key to a successful HSI strategy is comprehensive integration across the HSI domains, and also across other core acquisition and engineering processes. This integration is dependent on an accurate HSI plan that includes the comprehensive integration of requirements. The optimization of total system performance and determination of the most-effective, efficient and affordable design requires upfront requirements analyses. The HSI domains (manpower, personnel, training, environment, safety and occupational health, human factors engineering, survivability and habitability) can and should be used to help determine and work the science and technology gaps to address all aspects of the system (hardware, software and human).

The PM should integrate system requirements for the HSI domains with each other, and with the total system. As work is done to satisfy these requirements, it is vital that each HSI domain anticipate and respond to changes made by other domains or which may be made within other processes or imposed by other program constraints. These integration efforts should be reflected in updates to the requirements, objectives and thresholds in the Capability Development Documents.

In today's Joint environment, the integration across systems-of-systems is necessary to achieve a fully networked Joint warfighting capability. The warfighter requires a fully networked environment and must be able to operate efficiently and effectively across the continuum of systems -- from initial recognition of the opportunity to engage, through mission completion. To accomplish this, HSI domains and human capabilities and constraints should be considered in analytic assumptions and system-of-systems analysis, modeling and testing. This provides opportunities for integration, synchronization, collaboration and coordination of capabilities to meet human-centered requirements. A fully integrated investment strategy with joint sponsorship from the Materiel Development Decision on through the series of incremental developments may be required.

CH 5–4.1 Human Systems Integration Strategy, Risk and Risk Mitigation

Acquisition Systems designs have historically been overly complex; difficult to train, learn to use and operate, and maintain. Designs should enable mission/program success by being easier to train, operate, and maintain. Systems should also be safe and efficient, cost-effective, and less likely to require redesign. Inputs from the HSI domains (manpower, personnel, training, environment, safety and occupational health, human factors engineering, personnel survivability, and habitability) should be used to determine and address performance impacts to all aspects of the system (hardware, software, and human).

HSI goals are to ensure that these systems, programs, and missions incorporate effective human-systems interfaces; achieve the required level of human performance; demand economical personnel resources, skills, and training; minimize life-cycle costs; and manage risk of loss or injury to personnel, equipment, and the environment.

The ultimate goal is to ensure that HSI is considered, planned for, and implemented early in the acquisition process, and throughout the life cycle of the program. HSI planning includes the identification of HSI-related risks and the associated cost, schedule and performance impacts, as well as the associated mitigation plans to address risk. HSI-related risks should be clearly identified and included among the other risks managed and documented by the PM.

The development of an HSI strategy should be initiated early in the acquisition process, when the need for a new capability or improvements to an existing capability is first established. To satisfy the requirements of DoDI 5000.02 (Enclosure 7), the PM should have a plan for HSI in place prior to entering Engineering and Manufacturing Development. The PM should describe the technical and management approach for meeting HSI parameters in the capabilities documents, and identify and provide ways to manage any HSI-related cost, schedule or performance issues that could adversely affect program execution.

When a defense system has complex human-systems interfaces; significant manpower or training costs; personnel concerns; or safety, health hazard, habitability, survivability, or human factors engineering issues the PM should use the HSI plan to describe the process to identify solutions. HSI risks and risk mitigation should be addressed in the PM's risk-management program.

The HSI plan should address potential readiness or performance risks and how these risks should be identified and mitigated. For example, skill degradation can impact combat capability and readiness. The HSI plan should call for studies to identify operations that pose the highest risk of skill decay. When analysis indicates that the combat capability of the system is tied to the operator's ability to perform discrete tasks that are easily degraded (such as those contained in a set of procedures), solutions such as system design, procedural changes, or embedded training should be considered to address the problem. Information overload and requirements for the warfighter to integrate data from multiple sources dynamically can result in degradation of situational awareness and overall readiness. Careful consideration of common user interfaces, information sources, and system workload management should mitigate this risk. An on-board "performance measurements capability" can also be developed to support immediate feedback to the operators/maintainers and possibly serve as a readiness measure to the unit commander. The lack of available ranges and other training facilities, when deployed, are issues that should be addressed. The increased use of mission rehearsal, as part of mission planning, and the preparation process and alternatives supporting mission rehearsal should be addressed in the HSI plan. Team skills training and joint battle space integration training should also be considered in the HSI plan and tied to readiness. Additionally, HSI issues should be addressed at system technical reviews and milestone decision reviews.

The PM's Programmatic Environment, Safety and Occupational Health Evaluation (PESHE) describes the strategy for integrating Environment, Safety, and Occupational Health (ESOH) considerations into the systems engineering process and defines how PESHE is linked to the effort to integrate HSI considerations into systems engineering. The PESHE also describes how ESOH risks are managed and how ESOH and HSI efforts are integrated. It summarizes ESOH risk information (hazard identification, risk assessment, mitigation decisions, residual risk acceptance and evaluation of mitigation effectiveness). The HSI Strategy should address the linkage between HSI and ESOH and how the program has been structured to avoid duplication of effort.

PMs should establish a logistics support concept (e.g., two level, three level), training plans, and manpower and personnel concepts that when taken together, provide for cost-effective, total, life-cycle support. MIL-HDBK-29612-1A, -2A, -3A, & -4A (Development of Interactive Multimedia Instruction) may be used as a guide for Instructional Systems Development/Systems Approach to the training and education process for the development of instructional materials. Manpower, personnel and training analyses should be tied to supportability analyses and should be addressed in the HSI plan.

Program risks related to cost, schedule, performance, supportability, and/or technology can negatively impact program affordability and supportability. The PM should prepare a "fallback" position to mitigate any such negative effects on HSI objectives. For example, if the proposed system design relies heavily on new technology or software to reduce operational or support-manning requirements, the PM should be prepared with design alternatives to mitigate the impact of technology or software that is not available when expected.

CH 5–4.2 Human Systems Integration Domains

The goal of HSI is not to duplicate efforts that are owned by the Services and program stakeholders, but rather to integrate human concerns in balance with life-cycle objectives comprehensively and robustly. The effective practice of HSI requires assessing the impact of HSI domains to arrive at viable recommendations for decision makers. Combinations of the HSI domains and the additional factors of systems engineering form the trade-space for HSI inclusion in risk assessment tests and evaluations. All HSI domains should be addressed in acquisition planning efforts. HSI domains are inter-related; changes in system design or capabilities could improve one HSI domain and adversely affect another. For example, reducing manpower or increasing skill levels for a specific maintenance job could increase training demands because more is required of the people performing the job. Program trade-off decisions should include the impact on HSI domains/issues. All of the domains are defined and described in this section.

Manpower - The number of military, civilian, and contractor personnel required and available to operate, maintain, sustain and provide training for systems.

Personnel - The cognitive and physical capabilities required to train, operate, maintain, and sustain materiel and information systems.

Training - The instruction or education and on-the-job or unit training required to provide personnel and units with their essential job skills, knowledges, values, and attitudes.

Human Factors Engineering - The integration of human characteristics into system definition, design, development and evaluation to optimize human machine performance under operational conditions.

Environment, Safety and Occupational Health (ESOH) Hazards – The minimization of human or machine errors or failures that cause injurious accidents.

Survivability - The characteristics of a system that can reduce fratricide, detectability and probability of being attacked, and can minimize system damage and soldier injury.

Habitability - The consideration of the characteristics of systems focused on satisfying personnel needs that are dependent upon physical environment, such as berthing and hygiene.

CH 5–4.2.1 Manpower

Manpower factors are those job tasks, operation/maintenance rates, associated workload, and operational conditions (e.g., risk of hostile fire) that are used to determine the number and mix of military and Government civilian manpower and contract support necessary to operate, maintain, support and provide training for the system. Manpower officials contribute to the Defense acquisition process by ensuring that the PM pursues engineering designs that optimize manpower and keep human resource costs at affordable levels (i.e., consistent with strategic manpower documentation and plans). Technology-based approaches used to reduce manpower requirements and control life-cycle costs should be identified in the capabilities documents early in the process. For example, material-handling equipment can be used to reduce labor-intensive material-handling operations, and embedded training can be used to reduce the number of instructors.

CH 5–4.2.2 Personnel

Personnel factors are those human aptitudes (i.e., cognitive, physical and sensory capabilities), knowledge, skills, abilities and experience levels that are needed to properly perform job tasks. Personnel factors are used to develop the military occupational specialties (or equivalent DoD Component personnel system classifications) and civilian job series of system operators, maintainers, trainers and support personnel. Personnel officials contribute to the Defense acquisition process by ensuring that the PM pursues engineering designs that minimize personnel requirements, and keep the human aptitudes necessary for operation and maintenance of the equipment at levels consistent with what will be available in the user population at the time the system is fielded.

CH 5–4.2.2.1 Personnel Parameters/Requirements

DoDI 5000.02 (Enclosure 7) requires the PM to work with the personnel community to define the performance characteristics of the user population, or "target audience," early in the acquisition process. The PM should work with the personnel community to establish a Target Audience Description (TAD) that identifies the cognitive, physical and sensory abilities --i.e., capabilities and limitations, of the operators, maintainers and support personnel expected to be in place at the time the system is fielded. When establishing the TAD, Human Systems Integration (HSI) practitioners should verify whether there are any recruitment or retention trends that could significantly alter the characteristics of the user population over the life of the system. Additionally, HSI analysts should consult with the personnel community and verify whether there are new personnel policies that could significantly alter the scope of the user population (e.g., policy changes governing women in combat significantly changed the anthropometric requirements for occupational specialties).

Per DoDI 5000.02 (Enclosure 7), to the extent possible, systems should not be designed to require cognitive, physical or sensory skills beyond those found in the specified user population. During functional analysis and allocation, tasks should be allocated to the human component consistent with the human attributes (i.e., capabilities and limitations) of the user population to ensure compatibility, interoperability and integration of all functional and physical interfaces. Personnel requirements should be established that are consistent with the knowledge, skills and abilities (KSAs) of the user population expected to be in place at the time the system is fielded and over the life of the program. Personnel requirements are usually stated as a percentage of the population. For example, capability documents might require "physically accommodating the central 90% of the target audience." Setting specific, quantifiable personnel requirements in the Capability Documents assist the establishment of test criteria in the Test and Evaluation Master Plan.

CH 5–4.2.2.2 Personnel Planning

Personnel capabilities are normally reflected as KSAs, and other characteristics. The availability of personnel and their KSAs should be identified early in the acquisition process. The DoD Components have a limited inventory of personnel available, each with a finite set of cognitive, physical, and psychomotor abilities. This could affect specific system thresholds.

The PM should use the TAD as a baseline for personnel requirements assessment. The TAD should include information such as inventory, force structure, standards of grade authorizations, personnel classification (e.g., Military Occupational Code/Navy Enlisted Classification), description, biographical information, anthropometric data, physical qualifications, aptitude descriptions as measured by the Armed Services Vocational Aptitude Battery (ASVAB), task performance information, skill grade authorization, Military Physical Profile Serial System (PULHES), security clearance levels, and other related factors.

The PM should assess and compare the cognitive and physical demands of the projected system against the projected personnel supply. The PM should also determine the physical limitations of the target audience (e.g., color vision, acuity and hearing). The PM should identify any shortfalls highlighted by these studies.

The PM should determine if the new system contains any aptitude-sensitive critical tasks. If so, the PM should determine if it is likely that personnel in the target audience can perform the critical tasks of the job.

The PM should consider personnel factors, such as availability, recruitment, skill identifiers, promotion and assignment. The PM should consider the impact on recruiting, retention, promotions and career progression when establishing program costs, and should assess these factors during trade-off analyses.

The PM should use a truly representative sample of the target population during Test and Evaluation (T&E) to get an accurate measure of system performance. A representative sample during T&E helps identify aptitude constraints that affect system use.

Individual system and platform personnel requirements should be developed in close collaboration with related systems throughout the Department and in various phases of the acquisition process to identify commonalities, merge requirements and avoid duplication. The PM should consider the cumulative effects of system-of-systems, family-of-systems and related systems integration in the development of personnel requirements.

The PM should summarize major personnel initiatives that are necessary to achieve readiness or rotation objectives or to reduce manpower or training costs, when developing the acquisition strategy. The Life-Cycle Sustainment Plans should address modifications to the knowledge, skills and abilities of military occupational specialties for system operators, maintainers or support personnel and should highlight the modifications having cost or schedule issues that could adversely impact program execution. The PM should also address actions to combine, modify or establish new military occupational specialties or additional skill indicators, or issues relating to hard-to-fill occupations if they impact the PM's ability to execute the program.

CH 5–4.2.3 Training

Training gives users, operators, maintainers, leaders, and support personnel the opportunity to acquire, gain, or enhance knowledge and skills, and concurrently develop their cognitive, physical, sensory, team dynamics, and adaptive abilities to conduct joint operations and achieve maximized and fiscally sustainable system life cycles. The training of people as a component of material solutions delivers the intended capability to improve or fill capability gaps.

Cost-and mission-effective training facilitates DoD acquisition policy that requires optimized total system performance and minimizes the cost of ownership through a "total system approach" to acquisition management. The systems engineering concept of a purposely designed *total system* includes not only the mission system equipment, but, more critically, the people who operate, maintain, lead, and support these acquired systems -- including the training, training systems, and the operational and support infrastructure.

The Human Systems Integration (HSI) Training Domain assists PMs throughout the acquired system's life cycle by focusing attention on the human interface with the acquired system, and by integrating and inserting manpower, personnel, training, human factors engineering, environment, safety, occupational health, habitability and survivability as Systems Engineered elements into the Defense Acquisition process. The Systems Engineered practice of continuous application of human-centered methods and tools ensures maximum operational and training effectiveness of the newly acquired system throughout its life cycle. Systems Engineering in DoD Acquisition provides perspectives on the use of systems engineered/developed training approaches to translate user-defined capabilities into engineering specifications and outlines the role of the PM in integrated system design activities.

In all cases, the paramount goal of training for new systems is to develop and sustain a ready, well-trained individual/unit, while giving strong consideration to options that can reduce life-cycle costs, and provide positive contributions to the joint context of a system and provide a positive readiness outcome.

CH 5–4.2.3.1 Statutory and Regulatory Basis
Training of user, operator, maintainer, and leader personnel should be performed to achieve intended capabilities of new systems acquisition; enable joint integration, interoperability and testing; and ensure sustainment goals over the life cycle of weapon systems To facilitate timely, cost-effective and appropriate training, the content, development and planning of training should be performed during the earliest phases (e.g., Material Solution and Technology Development Phases) of the acquisition processes,". This is outlined within the AoA, System Training Plans (e.g. STRAPs, NTSPs, or STPs) Acquisition Strategies (AS) and Acquisition Program Baselines (APB).

To ensure appropriate training for new systems acquisition and traceability to life-cycle sustainment costs estimates, systems engineering processes should assess training impacts of materiel decision trades and appropriately documented. New Equipment Training (NET) plans (e.g., STRAPs, NTSPs and STPs) should identify service joint warfighting training requirements. Training planning and training-cost estimates should be incorporated within the Cost Analysis Requirements Description (CARD) and Life-Cycle Sustainment Plans (LCSPs).

CH 5–4.2.3.2 Training Planning
Training Planning helps the PM understand acquisition program (new or upgraded) systems training as a key performance parameter to successfully integrate DoD Decision Support Systems, e.g. the Acquisition System (DoD 5000 Series), the Joint Capabilities Integration and Development System (JCIDS) and the Planning, Programming, Budgeting & Execution (PPBE) Process, and to effectively translate joint capabilities into training system design features.

Initially, the JCIDS process should address joint training requirements for military (Active, Reserve and Guard) and civilian support personnel who will operate, maintain, lead, and support the acquired system.

Training programs should employ integrated cost-effective solutions, and may consist of a blend of capabilities that use existing training program insights and introduce new performance-based training innovations. These may include requirements for school and unit training, as well as new equipment training or sustainment training. They also may include requirements for instructor and key personnel training and new equipment training teams.

Training planning should be initiated early by the PM, in coordination with the training community within the capabilities-development process beginning with the Capabilities- Based Assessment and Analysis of Alternatives. These support the development of the Initial Capabilities Document, inform the Materiel Development Decision to support the Material Solutions Analysis phase, and continue the development of the Capability Development Document.

Training should also be considered in collaboration with the other HSI domains in order to capture the full range of human integration issues to be considered within the Systems Engineering process.

Early training planning informs the Capability Development Document and should characterize the specific system training requirements, and identify the training Key Performance Parameters:

- Allow for interactions between platforms or units (e.g., through advanced simulation and virtual exercises) and provide training realism to include threats (e.g., virtual and surrogate), a realistic electronic warfare environment, communications and weapons.
- Appropriately embedded training capabilities that do not degrade system performance below-threshold values nor degrade the maintainability or component life of the system are preferred
- Initial Operational Capability (IOC) is attained and training capabilities are met by the IOC.
- An embedded performance measurement capability to support immediate feedback to the operators/maintainers and possibly to serve as a readiness measure for the unit commander.
- Training logistics necessary to support the training concept (e.g., requirements for new or upgrades to existing training facilities).
- Provide concurrent capability with actual equipment, training devices, and systems.

The training community should be specific in translating capabilities into system requirements. They should also set training resource constraints. These capabilities and constraints can be facilitated and worked through system integration efforts in several of the other HSI domains. Examples are:

- The training community should consider whether the system should be designed with a mode of operation that allows operators to train interactively on a continuous basis, even when deployed in remote/austere locations.
- The training community should consider whether the system should be capable of exhibiting fault conditions for a specified set of failures to allow rehearsal of repair procedures for isolating faults, or require that the system be capable of interconnecting with other (specific) embedded trainers in both static and employed conditions.
- The training community should consider whether embedded training capabilities allow enhancements to live maneuvers such that a realistic spectrum of threats is encountered (e.g., synthetic radar warnings generated during flight).
- The training community should consider whether the integrated training system should be fully tested, validated, verified and ready for training at the training base as criteria for declaring IOC.

From the earliest stages of development and as the system matures, the PM should emphasize training requirements that enhance the user's capabilities, improve readiness, and reduce individual and collective training costs over the life of the system. These may include requirements for expert systems, intelligent tutors, embedded diagnostics, virtual environments and embedded training capabilities. Examples of training that enhances user's capabilities include:

- Interactive electronic technical manuals to provide a training forum that can significantly reduce schoolhouse training and may require lower skill levels for maintenance personnel while actually improving their capability to maintain an operational system.
- Requirements for an embedded just-in-time mission rehearsal capability supported by the latest intelligence information and an integrated global training system/network that allows team training and participation in large-scale mission rehearsal exercises can be used to improve readiness.
- In all cases, the paramount goal of the training/instructional system should be to develop and sustain a ready, well-trained individual/unit/theater/joint, while giving strong consideration to options that can reduce life-cycle costs and provide positive contributions to the joint context of a system, where appropriate.
- Training devices and simulators are systems that, in some cases, may qualify for their own set of HSI requirements. For instance, the training community may require the following attributes of a training simulator:
  - Accommodate "the central 90 percent of the male and female population on critical body dimensions."
  - Not increase manpower requirements and considerations of reductions in manpower requirements.
  - Consider reduced skill sets to maintain because of embedded instrumentation.
  - Be High Level Architecture compliant.

- o Be Sharable Content Object Reference Model (as in DoDI 1322.26 compliant).
- o Be Test and Training Enabling Architecture (overview) compliant.
- o Use reusable modeling and simulation devices and architectures.

The acquisition program should be specific in translating new system capabilities into the system and its inherent training requirements.

From the earliest stages of development and as the future system design matures, the PM should emphasize training requirements that enhance the user's capabilities, interoperability and improve readiness, and reduce individual and collective training costs over the life of the system. This may include requirements for expert systems, intelligent tutors, embedded diagnostics, virtual environments and embedded training capabilities.

CH 5–4.2.3.3 Development of Training Requirements

When developing the training system, the PM shall employ transformational training concepts, strategies and tools such as computer-based and interactive courseware, simulators and embedded training consistent with the program's acquisition strategy, goals, and objectives and reflect the tenants outlined in the next generation training strategy.

In addition, the program should address the requirement for a systems training key performance parameter, as described in the JCIDS Manual (Encl. D-G-1).

The USD (P&R), with the manpower, personnel and training communities, assesses the ability of the acquisition process to support the Military Departments, COCOMs and other DoD Components acquisition programs from a manpower, personnel and training readiness perspective.

The acquisition program characterizes training planning, development and execution within the (CARD). Life-Cycle Support Plans and Reports are tailored to each document type. These training summaries capture the support traceability of planned training across acquisition and capability documents, and includes logistics support planning for training, training equipment, and training device acquisitions and installations.

CH 5–4.2.3.3.1 Embedded Training

Both the sponsor and the PM provide analysis that demonstrates careful consideration to the use of embedded training as defined in DoDD 1322.18 (para 3.b.) "Military Training": The sponsor's decisions to use embedded training should be determined very early in the capabilities-assessment process. Analysis will be conducted to compare the embedded training with more-traditional training media (e.g., simulator-based training, traditional classroom instruction and/or maneuver training) for consideration of a system's Total Operating Cost. The analysis will compare the costs and the impact of embedded training (e.g., training operators and maintenance personnel on site, compared with off-station travel to a temporary duty location for training).

CH 5–4.2.4 Human Factors Engineering

The PM employs human factors engineering to design systems that require minimal manpower; provide effective training; can be operated, maintained, and supported by users; and are suitable (habitable and safe with minimal environmental and occupational health hazards) and survivable -- for both the crew and equipment in accordance with DoDI 5000.02 (Encl. 7).

The human factors that need to be considered in the integration are discussed below. Human factors are the end-user cognitive, physical, sensory and team dynamic abilities required to perform system operational, maintenance and support job tasks. Human factors engineers contribute to the acquisition process by ensuring that the PM provides for the effective utilization of personnel by designing systems that capitalize on and do not exceed the abilities (cognitive, physical, sensory and team dynamic) of the user population. The human factors engineering community works to integrate the human characteristics of the user population into the system definition, design, development and evaluation processes to optimize human-machine performance for operation, maintenance and sustainment of the system.

Human factors engineering is primarily concerned with designing human-system interfaces consistent with the physical, cognitive and sensory abilities of the user population. Human-system interfaces include:

- **Functional interfaces** - Functions and tasks, and allocation of functions to human performance or automation.
- **Informational interfaces** - Information and characteristics of information that provide the human with the knowledge, understanding and awareness of what is happening in the tactical environment and in the system.
- **Environmental interfaces** - The natural and artificial environments, environmental controls, and facility design.
- **Cooperational interfaces** - Provisions for team performance, cooperation, collaboration and communication among team members and with other personnel.
- **Organizational interfaces** - Job design, management structure, command authority, policies and regulations that impact behavior.
- **Operational interfaces** - Aspects of a system that support successful operation of the system such as procedures, documentation, workloads and job aids.
- **Cognitive interfaces** - Decision rules, decision support systems, provision for maintaining situational awareness, mental models of the tactical environment, provisions for knowledge generation, cognitive skills and attitudes and memory aids.
- **Physical interfaces** - Hardware and software elements designed to enable and facilitate effective and safe human performance such as controls, displays, workstations, worksites, accesses, labels and markings, structures, steps and ladders, handholds, maintenance provisions, etc..

CH 5–4.2.4.1 Parameters/Requirements

Human factors requirements, objectives and thresholds should be derived from each of the HSI domains and should provide for the effective utilization of personnel through the accommodation of the cognitive, physical and sensory characteristics that directly enhance or constrain system performance. In many cases, the interface design limitation may require trade-offs in several of the other domains and vice versa.

Cognitive requirements address the human capability to evaluate and process information. Requirements are typically stated in terms of response times and are typically established to avoid excessive cognitive workload. Operations that entail a high number of complex tasks in a short time period can result in cognitive overload and safety hazards. The capability documents should specify whether there are human-in-the-loop requirements. These could include requirements for "human in control," "manual override" or "completely autonomous operations." Knowledge, skills, and abilities for operators, maintainers, and other support personnel continuously change with the increasing complexity of emerging systems. These requirements should be cross-correlated with each of the HSI domains.

Physical requirements are typically stated as anthropometric (measurements of the human body), strength and weight factors. Physical requirements are often tied to human performance, safety and occupational health concerns. To ensure that the users can operate, maintain and support the system, requirements should be stated in terms of the user population. For instance, when the user requires a weapon that is "one-man portable," weight thresholds and objectives should be based on the strength limitations of the user population and other related factors (e.g., the weight of other gear and equipment and the operational environment). For example, it may be appropriate to require that "the system be capable of being physically maintained by 90% of both the male and female population, inclusive of battle dress or arctic and Mission Oriented Protective Postures-Level 4 protective garments inside the cab," or that "the crew station physically accommodate 90% of the female/male population, defined by current anthropometric data, for accomplishment of the full range of mission functions."

Sensory requirements are typically stated as visual, olfactory (smell) or hearing factors. The Capability Development Document should identify operational considerations that affect sensory processes. For example, systems may need to operate in noisy environments where weapons are being fired or on an overcast moonless night with no auxiliary illumination. Visual acuity or other sensory requirements may limit the target audience for certain specialties.

CH 5–4.2.4.2 Application of Human Factors Engineering

Human Factors Engineering (HFE) plays an important role in each phase of the acquisition cycle, to include requirements of development, system definition, design, development, evaluation and system support for reliability and maintainability in the field. To realize the potential of HFE contributions, HFE must be incorporated into the design process at the earliest stages of the acquisition process (i.e., during the Materiel Solution Analysis and Technology Development phases). It should be supported by inputs from the other HSI domains as well as the other Systems Engineering processes. The right decisions about the human-machine interfaces early in the design process optimize the human performance, and hence, the total systems performance. HFE participation continues to each succeeding acquisition phase, continuing to work trade-offs based on inputs from the other HSI domains and the hardware and software designs/adaptations. The HFE practitioners provide expertise that includes design criteria, analysis and modeling tools and measurement methods that help to ensure that program office design systems are operationally suitable, safe, survivable, effective, usable and cost-effective. In any system acquisition process, it is important to recognize the differences between the competencies (skills and knowledge) required for the various warfighters. Application of HFE processes leads to an understanding of the competencies needed for the job, and help identify if requirements for knowledge, skills and abilities (KSAs) exceed what the user can provide and whether the deficiency leads to a training or operational problem. HFE tools and techniques can be used to identify the KSAs of the target audience and account for different classes and levels of users and the need for various types of information products, training, training systems, and other aids. While it is critical to understand the information processing and net-centric requirements of the system, it is equally important to understand the factors affecting format and display of the data presented to the user to avoid cognitive overload. This applies equally to the system being designed as well as to the systems that interface with the system. The system should not place undue workload or other stress on systems with which it must interface.

CH 5–4.2.4.2.1 General Guidelines

HFE principles, guideline and criteria should be applied during development and acquisition of military systems, equipment and facilities to integrate personnel effectively into the design of the system. An HFE effort should be provided to develop or improve all human interfaces of the system; achieve required effectiveness of human performance during system operation, maintenance, support, control and transport; and, make economical demands upon personnel resources, skills, training and costs. The HFE effort should be well integrated with the other HSI domain participation, and should include, but not necessarily be limited to, active participation in the following three major interrelated areas of system development.

CH 5–4.2.4.2.2 Analysis

Identify the functions to be performed by the system in achieving its mission objectives and analyze them to determine the best allocation of personnel, equipment, software or combinations thereof. Allocated functions should be further dissected to define the specific tasks to be performed to accomplish the functions. Each task should be analyzed to determine the human performance parameters; the system, equipment and software capabilities; and the operational/environmental conditions under which the tasks are conducted. Task parameters should be quantified where possible, and should be expressed in a form that permits effective studies of the human-system interfaces in relation to the total system operation. HFE high-risk areas should be identified as part of the analysis. Task analysis should include maintenance and sustainment functions performed by crew and support facilities. Analyses should be updated as required to remain current with the design effort.

CH 5–4.2.4.2.3 Design and Development

HFE should be applied to the design and development of the system equipment, software, procedures, work environments and facilities associated with all functions requiring personnel interaction. This HFE effort should convert the mission, system and task analysis data into a detailed design and development plan to create human-system interface that will operate within human performance capabilities, facilitate/optimize human performance in meeting system functional requirements and accomplish the mission objectives.

CH 5–4.2.4.2.4 Test and Evaluation

Human Factors Engineering (HFE) and the evaluation of all human interfaces should be integrated into engineering design and development tests, contractor demonstrations, flight tests, acceptance tests, other development tests, and operational testing. Compliance with human interface requirements should be tested as early as possible. Test and Evaluation (T&E) should include evaluation of maintenance and sustainment activities and evaluation of the dimensions and configuration of the environment relative to criteria for HFE and each of the other HSI domains. Findings, analyses, evaluations, design reviews, modeling, simulations, demonstrations and other early engineering tests should be used in planning and conducting later tests. Test planning should be directed toward verifying that the system can be operated, maintained, supported and controlled by user personnel in its intended operational environment with the intended training. Test planning should also consider data needed or provided by operational test and evaluation. (See Chapter 8 – Test and Evaluation).

CH 5–4.2.5 Environment, Safety and Occupational Health Hazards

Environment, safety and occupational health hazards include design features and operating characteristics of a system that create significant risks of bodily injury or death, loud noise, chemical and biological substances, extreme temperatures and radiation energy. Each of the various military departments/services treat the three HSI domains of Environment, Safety and Occupational Health (ESOH) differently, based on oversight and reporting responsibility within each of the services. DoD ESOH Guidance for systems acquisition programs can be found in. What is important to the HSI practitioner and the systems engineer is that these three domains are of vital importance to the HSI effort, and are integrated within it. While the ESOH communities have unique reporting requirements that trace to National-level mandates, the importance of integrating these domains in the HSI construct cannot be overemphasized. The human aspect brings a host of issues to a system that should be accommodated in each of these three areas; each must be considered in consonance with the other HSI domains. How they are considered in an integrated manner is left to the PM and Systems Engineering.

Environment includes the natural and manmade conditions in and around the system and the operational context within which the system will be operated and supported. This "environment" affects the human ability to function as a part of the system.

Safety factors consist of those system design characteristics that serve to minimize the potential for mishaps -- causing death or injury to operators, maintainers, and supporters or threatening the survival and/or operation of the system. Prevalent issues encompass factors that threaten the safe operation and/or survival of the platform: walking and working surfaces, including work at heights; pressure extremes; and control of hazardous energy releases such as mechanical, electrical, fluids under pressure, ionizing or non-ionizing radiation (often referred to as "lock-out/tag-out"), fire and explosions.

Occupational health factors are those system design features that serve to minimize the risk of injury, acute or chronic illness or disability and/or reduce job performance of personnel who operate, maintain or support the system. Prevalent issues include noise, chemical safety, atmospheric hazards (including those associated with confined space entry and oxygen deficiency), vibration, ionizing and non-ionizing radiation and human factors issues that can create chronic disease and discomfort such as repetitive motion diseases. Many occupational health problems, particularly noise and chemical management, overlap with environmental impacts. Human factor stresses that create the risk of chronic disease and discomfort overlap with occupational health considerations.

CH 5–4.2.5.1 ESOH Hazard Parameters and Requirements

Environment, safety, and health hazard parameters should address all activities inherent to the life cycle of the system, including test activity, operations, support, maintenance and final demilitarization and disposal. Environment, safety, and health hazard requirements should be stated in measurable terms, whenever possible. For example, it may be appropriate to establish thresholds for the maximum level of acoustic noise, vibration, acceleration shock, blast, temperature or humidity or impact forces etc., or "safeguards against uncontrolled variability beyond specified safe limits," where the Capability Documents specify the "safe limits." Safety and health hazard requirements often stem from human factor issues and are typically based on lessons learned from comparable or predecessor systems. For example, both physical dimensions and weight are critical safety requirements for the accommodation of pilots in ejection-seat designs. Environment, safety, and health hazard thresholds are often justified in terms of human performance requirements, because, for example, extreme temperature and humidity can degrade job performance and lead to frequent or critical errors. Another methodology for specifying safety and health requirements is to specify the allowable level of residual risk as defined in MIL-STD-882D (DoD Standard Practice for System Safety), for example, "There shall be no high or serious residual risks present in the system."

CH 5–4.2.5.2 Programmatic ESOH Evaluation
The HSI Plan should recognize the appropriate timing for the Programmatic Environment, Safety, and Occupational Health Evaluation (PESHE) and define how the program intends to ensure the effective and efficient flow of information to and from the ESOH domain experts to work the integration of environment, safety, and health considerations into the systems engineering process and all its required products.

CH 5–4.2.5.2.1 Health Hazard Analysis
Health Hazards Analysis (HHA) should be conducted during each phase of the acquisition process, beginning with a review of issues related to predecessor systems. During early stages of the acquisition process, sufficient information may not always be available to develop a complete HHA. As additional information becomes available, the initial analyses are refined and updated to identify health hazards, assess the risks determine how to mitigate the risks, formally accept the residual risks and monitor the effectiveness of the mitigation measures. The health hazard risk information is documented in the PESHE. Health hazard assessments should include cost avoidance figures to support trade-off analysis. There are nine health hazard issues typically addressed in an HHA, defined below.

Acoustical Energy - The potential energy that transmits through the air and interacts with the body to cause hearing loss or damage to internal organs.

Biological Substances - An infectious substance generally capable of causing permanent disability or life-threatening or fatal disease in otherwise healthy humans.

Chemical Substances - The hazards from excessive airborne concentrations of toxic materials contracted through inhalation, ingestion and skin or eye contract.

Oxygen Deficiency - The displacement of atmospheric oxygen from enclosed spaces or at high altitudes.

Radiation Energy - Ionizing: The radiation causing ionization when interfacing with living or inanimate mater. Non-ionizing: The emissions from the electromagnetic spectrum with insufficient energy to produce ionizing of molecules.

Shock - The mechanical impulse or impact on an individual from the acceleration or deceleration of a medium.

Temperature Extremes and Humidity - The human health effects associated with high or low temperatures, sometimes exacerbated by the use of a materiel system.

Trauma - Physical: The impact to the eyes or body surface by a sharp or blunt object. Musculoskeletal: The effects to the system while lifting heavy objects.

Vibration - The contact of a mechanically oscillating surface with the human body.

CH 5–4.2.6 Survivability
Survivability factors consist of those system design features that reduce the risk of fratricide, detection and the probability of being attacked and that enable the crew to withstand natural and manmade hostile environments without aborting the mission or suffering acute chronic illness, disability or death. Survivability attributes, as described in the Joint Military Dictionary (JP 1-02), are those that contribute to

the survivability of manned systems. In the HSI construct, the human is considered integral to the system, and personnel survivability should be considered in the encompassing "system" context.

CH 5–4.2.6.1 Survivability Parameters/Requirements

A Survivability/Force Protection Key Performance Parameter should be considered for any "manned system or system designed to enhance personnel survivability" when the system may be employed in an asymmetric threat environment. The Capability Documents should include applicable survivability parameters, which may include requirements to eliminate significant risks of fratricide or detectability or to be survivable in adverse weather conditions and the nuclear, biological and chemical (NBC) battlefield. NBC survivability, by definition, encompasses the instantaneous, cumulative and residual effects of NBC weapons upon the system, including its personnel. It may be appropriate to require that the system "permit performance of mission-essential operations, communications, maintenance, re-supply, and decontamination tasks by suitably clothed, trained and acclimatized personnel for the survival periods and NBC environments required by the system."

The consideration of survivability should also include system requirements to ensure the integrity of the crew compartment and rapid egress when the system is damaged or destroyed. It may be appropriate to require that the system provide for adequate emergency systems for contingency management, escape, survival and rescue.

CH 5–4.2.6.2 Survivability Planning

The Joint Capabilities Integration and Development System capability documents define the program's combat performance and survivability needs. Consistent with those needs, the Program Manager (PM) should establish a survivability program. This program, overseen by the PM, should seek to minimize: the probability of encountering combat threats; the severity of potential wounds and injury incurred by personnel operating or maintaining the system; and, the risk of potential fratricidal incidents. To maximize effectiveness, the PM should assess survivability in close coordination with systems engineering and test and evaluation activities.

Survivability assessments assume the warfighter is integral to the system during combat. Damage to the equipment by enemy action, fratricide or an improperly functioning component of the system can endanger the warfighter. The survivability program should assess these events and their consequences. Once these initial determinations are made, the design of the equipment should be evaluated to determine if there are potential secondary effects on the personnel. Each management decision to accept a potential risk should be formally documented by the appropriate management level as defined in DoDI 5000.02 (Encl. 7).

During the early stages of the acquisition process, sufficient information may not always be available to develop a complete list of survivability issues. An initial report is prepared; listing those identified issues and any findings and conclusions. Classified data and findings are to be appropriately handled according to each DoD Component's guidelines. Survivability issues typically are divided into the following components:

- **Reduce Fratricide** - Fratricide is the unforeseen and unintentional death or injury of "friendly" personnel resulting from friendly forces employment of weapons and munitions. To avoid these types of survivability issues, personnel systems and weapon systems should include anti-fratricide systems, such as Identification of Friend or Foe and Situational Awareness systems.
- **Reduce Detectability** - Reduce detectability considers a number of issues to minimize signatures and reduce the ranges of detection of friendly personnel and equipment by confounding visual, acoustic, electromagnetic, infrared/thermal and radar signatures and methods that may be utilized by enemy equipment and personnel. Methods of reducing detectability could include camouflage, low-observable technology, smoke, countermeasures, signature distortion, training and/or doctrine.
- **Reduce Probability of Attack** - Analysts should seek to reduce the probability of attack by avoiding the appearance as a high-value target and by actively preventing or deterring attack by warning sensors and the use of active countermeasures.
- **Minimize Damage if Attacked** - Analysts should seek to minimize damage, if attacked, by:
  - Designing the system to protect the operators and crew members from enemy attacks.

- o   Improving tactics in the field so survivability is increased.
- o   Designing the system to protect the crew from on-board hazards in the event of an attack (e.g., fuel, munitions, etc.).
- o   Designing the system to minimize the risk to supporting personnel if the system is attacked. Subject matter experts in areas such as nuclear, biological and chemical warfare, ballistics, electronic warfare, directed energy, laser hardening, medical treatment, physiology, human factors and Information Operations can add additional issues.
- **Minimize Injury -** Analysts should seek to minimize:
- o   Combat, enemy weapon-caused injuries.
- o   The combat-damaged system's potential sources and types of injury to both its crew and supported troops as it is used and maintained in the field.
- o   The system's ability to prevent further injury to the fighter after being attacked.
- o   The system's ability to support treatment and evacuation of injured personnel. Combat-caused injuries or other possible injuries are addressed in this portion of personnel survivability, along with the different perspectives on potential mechanisms for reducing damage. Evacuation capability and personal equipment needs (e.g., uniform straps to pull a crew member through a small evacuation port) are addressed here.
- **Minimize Physical and Mental Fatigue -** Analysts should seek to minimize injuries that can be directly traced to physical or mental fatigue. These types of injuries can be traced to complex or repetitive tasks, physically taxing operations, sleep deprivation or high-stress environments.
- **Survive Extreme Environments -** This component addresses issues that may arise once the warfighter evacuates or is forced from a combat-affected system such as an aircraft or watercraft and should immediately survive extreme conditions encountered in the sea or air until rescued or an improved situation on land is reached. Dependent upon requirements, this may also include some extreme environmental conditions found on land, but generally this component is for sea and air, where the need is immediate for special consideration to maintain an individual's life. Survival issues for downed pilots behind enemy lines should be considered here.

The PM should summarize plans for survivability in the Life-Cycle Sustainment Plan, Section 3.1.5 under Other Sustainment Considerations. If the system or program has been designated by Director, Operational Test & Evaluation for live-fire test and evaluation (LFT&E) oversight, the PM should integrate T&E to address crew survivability issues into the LFT&E program to support Congressional requirements. The PM should address the special equipment or gear needed to sustain crew operations in an operational environment.

CH 5–4.2.7 Habitability
Habitability factors are those living and working conditions necessary to sustain the morale, safety, health and comfort of the user population. They directly contribute to personnel effectiveness and mission accomplishment, and often preclude recruitment and retention problems. Examples include: lighting, space, ventilation and sanitation; noise and temperature control (i.e., heating and air conditioning); religious, medical and food services availability; and berthing, bathing and personal hygiene.

Habitability consists of those characteristics of systems, facilities (temporary and permanent) and services necessary to satisfy personnel needs. Habitability factors are those living and working conditions that result in levels of personnel morale, safety, health and comfort adequate to sustain maximum personnel effectiveness, support mission performance and prevent personnel retention problems.

CH 5–4.2.7.1 Habitability Parameters/Requirements
Habitability is one of several important factors included in the overall consideration of unit mission readiness. Per DoDI 5000.02 (Encl.7), the PM shall work with habitability representatives to establish requirements for the physical environment (e.g., adequate light, space, ventilation and sanitation, and temperature and noise control). If appropriate, requirements for personal services (e.g., religious, medical and mess) and living conditions (e.g., berthing and personal hygiene) if the habitability factors have a direct impact on meeting or sustaining performance requirements, sustaining mission effectiveness or having such an adverse impact on quality of life or morale that recruitment or retention

rates could be degraded. Examples include requirements for heating and air-conditioning, noise filters, lavatories, showers, dry-cleaning, and laundry.

While a system, facility and/or service should not be designed solely around optimum habitability factors, these factors cannot be systematically traded-off in support of other readiness elements without eventually degrading mission performance.

CH 5–4.2.7.2 Habitability Planning

The PM should address habitability planning in the Life-Cycle Sustainment Plan Section 3.1.5 Other Sustainment Considerations and identify habitability issues that could impact personnel morale, safety, health or comfort or degrade personnel performance or unit readiness or result in recruitment or retention problems.

CH 5–Version and Revision History

The table below tracks chapter changes. It indicates the current version number and date published, and provides a brief description of the content.

Version #	Revision Date	Reason
0	2/1/16	Chapter 5 initial upload

CH 6–1. Purpose

The Defense Acquisition Guidebook (DAG), Chapter 6, provides guidance on where overarching policy may have unique application to the acquisition of Information Technology (IT) in the Department of Defense. The goal is to enable the functional and acquisition communities who are developing and deploying IT capabilities to deploy at the speed at which they become viable – and ensure those capabilities are secure, net-centric, and available to users.

CH 6–2. Background

CH 6–2.1 DoD Information Technology (IT)

The DoD provides the IT infrastructure for our nation's defenses and the 24/7/365 constant cybersecurity vigilance that is required to defend us from our determined cyber foes.

Historically, DoD's IT investments were made to meet the needs of individual projects, programs, organizations, and facilities. This decentralized approach resulted in large cumulative costs and a patchwork of capabilities that created cyber vulnerabilities and limited the ability to capitalize on the promise of new developments in IT. That picture is now changing as better enterprise capabilities are being developed and implemented.

"IT" is a large, umbrella term covering many capabilities embodied in computer hardware, software, networking and application hosting services that are essential to warfighting operations and efficient management of warfighting and the Department. Figure 1 depicts some of the types of IT operated in the Department, which are applicable to the topics discussed in Chapter 6. It is not exhaustive of all IT but describes the most common types in the Department.

Figure 1: DoD Information Technology (IT)

CH 6–2.1.1 Key DoD IT Categories

There are varying types of IT managed in the Department though not all are managed in a "traditional" manner through the acquisition process as outlined in the DoDI 5000.02. Table 1 explains the broad categories of IT which are acquired and managed under more traditional acquisition structures while Table 2 outlines some exceptions to these processes.

Table 1: IT Managed Under Standard DoD Acquisition Processes

Major Category	Description
Automated Information System (AIS)	As defined in Enclosure 1 Table 1 of DoDI 5000.02 (Footnote 4), an AIS is a system of computer hardware, software, data or telecommunications that performs functions such as collecting, processing, storing, transmitting, and displaying information. AISs exclude hardware and software embedded in a weapons system. Despite minor differences in the definitions, the term "AIS" is synonymous with "IS." While the word "automated" is historically part of the AIS term, the need for it has greatly diminished now that few people would contemplate an IS that does not take advantage of the automation offered by computer hardware and software. We have now taken to use the term "Information System (IS)," especially when needing to distinguish IS from weapons systems.
Defense Business System (DBS)	As defined in Title 10 U.S.C. section 2222, a DBS is an information system that is operated by, for, or on behalf of the Department of Defense, including any of the following: (i) a financial system; (ii) a financial data feeder system; (iii) a contracting system; (iv) a logistics system; (v) a planning and budgeting system; (vi) An installations management system; (vii) a human resources management system; (viii) a training and readiness system. DBS are not NSS, nor are they systems operated exclusively by the defense commissary system or the exchange system or conducted for the morale, welfare, and recreation of members of the armed forces using non-appropriated funds.
Information Systems (IS)	As defined in Title 44 U.S.C section 3502, an Information System is a discrete set of information resources organized for the collection, processing, maintenance, use, sharing, dissemination, or disposition of information.
Information Technology (IT)	As defined in Title 40 U.S.C section 11101, information technology is any equipment or interconnected system or subsystem of equipment, used in the automatic acquisition, storage, analysis, evaluation, manipulation, management, movement, control, display, switching, interchange, transmission, or reception of data or information; includes computers, ancillary equipment (including imaging peripherals, input, output, and storage devices necessary for security and surveillance), peripheral equipment designed to be controlled by the central processing unit of a computer, software, firmware and similar procedures, services (including support services, and related resources). IT is equipment used by the DoD directly or is used by a contractor under a contract with the DoD that requires the use of that equipment. This term does not include the definition of National Security Systems as defined in Title 44 U.S.C section 3552.
Major Automated Information System (MAIS)	Per 10 USC 2445a, a MAIS is an AIS that has been so designated by the Milestone Decision Authority (MDA), or meets one or more of the estimated cost magnitude criteria listed in Enclosure 1 Table 1 of DoDI 5000.02.
National Security Systems (NSS)	Defined by the Title 44 U.S.C. section 3552 NSS are telecommunications or information systems operated by or on behalf of the Federal Government, the function, operation, or use of which: • involves intelligence activities, cryptologic activities related to national security, command and control of military forces, equipment that is an integral part of a weapon or weapons system, or, is critical to the direct fulfillment of military or intelligence missions; **OR** • is protected at all times by procedures established for information that has been specifically authorized under criteria established by an Executive order or an Act

Major Category	Description
	of Congress to be kept classified in the interest of national defense or foreign policy. NSS do not include systems used for routine administrative and business applications (including payroll, finance, logistics, and personnel management applications), i.e., DBS.

Table 2: IT Exceptions to Standard DoD Acquisition Processes

Major Category	Description
IT Infrastructure	IT infrastructure is generally non-developmental, commercial-off-the-shelf hardware equipment, and not the subject of its own "acquisition program." Infrastructure is a critical factor to most if not all IT acquisition programs, however, and more and more is being managed as an integrated facet of the overall program. The cybersecurity posture of a program's infrastructure is critical. Sometimes, the extent of customization of connected components and integration prompts treatment as an acquisition program, putting it in the category of an Information System. Otherwise, IT infrastructure is acquired as a commodity.
Embedded IT	Embedded IT (refer to definition of "AIS" in Enclosure 1 Table 1 of DoDI 5000.02 Page 44) is described as computer resources, both hardware and software, that are an integral part of a weapon or weapon system; used for highly sensitive classified programs (as determined by the Secretary of Defense); used for other highly sensitive IT programs; or determined by the Defense Acquisition Executive or designee to be better overseen as a non-AIS program (e.g., a program with a low ratio of RDT&E funding to total program acquisition costs or that requires significant hardware development). This form of IT capability acquisition is usually better managed as a subsystem of the larger weapon system. The embedded IT subsystem PM usually reports to the weapon system PM and in these circumstances oversight of embedded IT programs or subprograms is not distinct from the parent weapon system program.
Services	Many aspects of IT can be acquired as a service: hardware, software, infrastructure services, and data can all be acquired on a subscription basis, and this form of acquisition is covered by (new) DoDI 5000.74 "Defense Acquisition of Services." DoDI 5000.74 applies to programs with "a total estimated acquisition value in current year dollars at or above the simplified acquisition threshold." If, however, the estimated costs exceed any of the MAIS definition thresholds of DoDI 5000.02, the program is treated in the nature of an Information System (MAIS) program.

CH 6–2.1.2 DoD Information Technology (IT) Acquisition

Acquisition programs are categorized based on the criteria in Enclosure 1 Table 1 of DoDI 5000.02 but are generally categorized based on the cost of the program. CH 1 includes a broader discussion of acquisition categories, or ACATs, and explains the thresholds. In terms of specific applicability to IT programs:

- ACAT I programs are either Major Defense Acquisition Programs (MDAPs) or Major Automated Information Systems (MAIS);
- Large IT programs are most often MAIS programs (i.e., they are typically not managed as MDAPs even if they meet the MDAP threshold); and
- AIS programs do not fall into the ACAT II category – they are either ACAT I or ACAT III.
- Regarding decision authority for IT programs:
- The Under Secretary of Defense for Acquisition, Technology and Logistics (USD(AT&L)) is the Defense Acquisition Executive (DAE) (or, Milestone Decision Authority (MDA)) and will typically review MAIS and MDAP programs as the MDA, unless this authority is delegated.
- The Component Acquisition Executive (CAE) or Service Acquisition Executive (SAE) reviews ACAT III programs as the MDA.

The term "Pre-MAIS" (program) used to refer to a MAIS program before it became baselined at Milestone B—a formality previously necessary before it would be recognized as a true "program." The acquisition community, however, commonly uses the term "program" for an acquisition effort well before it achieves its Milestone B decision. Congress became concerned that this formality was used to avoid some reporting requirements and amended the title 10 USC Chapter 144A MAIS reporting statute to capture "pre-MAIS". Further evolution in the MAIS oversight community yielded the current term "unbaselined MAIS" for a large AIS program until it achieves a signed (approved) Acquisition Program Baseline, or APB.

Programs may also be deemed special interest for any number of reasons and treated as an MDAP or MAIS – though often these programs are managed in a highly tailored way, and may only be managed as such temporarily.

Many aspects of IT can be acquired as a service; hardware, software, and data can all be acquired on a subscription basis, and this form of acquisition is covered by a recently published DoDI 5000.74 "Defense Acquisition of Services." This policy applies to programs with "a total estimated acquisition value in current year dollars at or above the simplified acquisition threshold." (See DoDI 5000.74 paragraph 2a(2).) If, however, the estimated costs exceed any of the MAIS definition thresholds of DoDI 5000.02 the program is treated in the nature of a program (of the MAIS variety) and not a service. (See DoDI 5000.74 paragraph 2b(1).)

Additional information on ACAT designations and on MDAP / MAIS categorizations is available from the following resources:

- Title 10 Section 2430 – MDAPs
- Title 10 Chapter 144A – MAIS Programs
- DoDI 5000.02 (Encl. 1, Table 1 Page 44).
- Defense Acquisition University (DAU) Course – Acquisition 101

CH 6–3. Business Practice
CH 6–3.1 Oversight and Tailoring
MDA designation and associated oversight is determined by DoDI 5000.02 (Enclosure 1 Table 1) and adjusted through consideration of estimated cost magnitude, risk assessment, third party interest, acquisition phase, subject matter, and system function. This generally applies to programs for acquiring IT, including Information Systems, IT embedded in weapon systems, IT infrastructure, and information services; however, each of those genera of IT acquisition requires a customized (if not unique) approach to structuring the program and providing for its oversight.

From a program structuring / process perspective, the goal should be to design and scope a program that will deliver capability rapidly, while tailoring out unneeded or non-value added steps. Tailoring must begin up-front, with key stakeholders involved to create buy-in to the approach. In general, tailoring should consider multiple factors including program size, scope, risk, urgency of need, and technical complexity. IT programs are often excellent candidates for tailoring as they necessitate more rapid deployments and more frequent upgrades of capability. CH 1 Section 4.2.3 includes additional discussion on tailoring.

Generally, the PM proposes and the MDA approves tailoring decisions in an ADM. Tailoring discussions should occur with program leadership, stakeholders, and the MDA (if possible) very early on in the program and should continue throughout. There are various methods of tailoring described throughout this Chapter.

CH 6–3.2 Program Structure

There is no one best way to structure or "tailor" an IT acquisition program. Consistent with applicable statutes and regulations, time constraints for delivery of the capability, solution characteristics, and performance criteria all will determine program strategies and oversight (to include documentation of program information, acquisition phases, timing and scope of decision reviews, and decision levels) to fit the particular conditions of any IT program, similar to weapons systems programs. Refer to CH 1 Section 3.3 for detailed discussions on organizing an acquisition program.

For an IT program, the hardware/software mix and the degree of customization at minimum will impact how that program is structured and managed – though many other factors ultimately impact these decisions (i.e., funding availability, requirements prioritization, risk, etc.).

In the DoD acquisition context, the terms "Program" and "Increment" refer to the management structure of the acquisition effort. The term "program," however, is used in confusingly similar ways by the acquisition community as well as other communities within DoD. An "Acquisition Program" is used by the acquisition community to refer to the basic unit of management for an acquisition effort. In the DoDI 5000.02 the terms "Acquisition Program" and "Increment" are often used interchangeably.

The basic unit of management for a Weapon System (WS) acquisition is a Program. WS acquisitions are often lengthy endeavors spanning decades. IS or IT acquisitions—in contrast—require a tighter acquisition cycle because technology must be developed or configured and deployed before it becomes obsolete. The pace of development and change in software is fast, and the general expectation is that software acquisitions can and should react at the same speed. Congress has recognized this too, and several statutes now encourage structuring IT acquisitions for shorter, more rapidly deployed Increments. The Increment, therefore, has quickly become the basic unit for management of an IT acquisition.

Program (WS) = acquisition program = Increment (IT)

An Increment is a militarily useful and supportable operational capability that can be developed, produced, deployed, and sustained. Each Increment must have an Acquisition Program Baseline (APB) with its own set of threshold and objective values set by the user. In the context of an IS acquisition, this means that both threshold and objective values for cost, schedule, and performance parameters must be established for each Increment.

The terms "generation" and "block" have been used for IS acquisitions, but they are more useful in the context of WS hardware acquisition. The Department generally discourages use of these terms for IT acquisitions in favor of consistent use of the term "Increment."

The term "Program" in the IT context refers to the summation of a succession of Increments, and is a consolidation of acquisition efforts that is useful for Planning, Programming, Budgeting, and Execution System (PPBE) purposes. An IT "Program" does not have its own APB, rather each Program Increment has its own APB and is a separate acquisition program as defined in DoDD 5000.01 (Para 3.2 – Page 4)

Program (IT) = Σ Increments (IT)

Some additional terms are useful in reference to the software itself. The terms "version," "release," and "iteration" all relate to the sequence and importance of a particular software application. For example, the hypothetical Application 2.3.4 is Iteration 4 of Release 3 of Version 2.

The term "version" is regularly used together with a hierarchically structured number such as 2.4.3 to refer to and track the series of improvements or progress of software development. These numbers are assigned in increasing order and correspond to new developments in the software. Logically, the initial number of a Version should reflect the Increment to which it belongs; Version 3.1.1 should be part of the Increment 3 effort.

CH 6–3.3 DoD Acquisition Models

The Department's six acquisition models are high level processes that encompass the acquisition of a system in the DoD; though not all are used for the acquisition of IT; models 1 and 4 have been omitted from the discussion. Descriptions of all models are available in DoDI 5000.02 (Page 9) as well as CH 1 of the DAG. Table 3 provides descriptions, example and drawbacks of those models that are typically used for acquiring IT in the Department.

Table 3: Models Used for the Acquisition of IT

Model	Description of Model	Examples	Challenges
MODEL 2 Defense Unique Software Intensive Program	• Used for complex, usually defense unique software programs that are deployed only after several software builds have been completed. • Subsequent software builds only proceed after successful completion of program milestones.	• Military unique command and control (C2) systems • Significant upgrades to the combat systems found on major weapons systems such as surface combatants and tactical aircraft.	• Can lead to long waits between deliveries that can cause product obsolescence • Slow delivery can cause customer dissatisfaction and push back
MODEL 3 Incrementally Deployed Software Intensive Program	• Most often referred to as the "Defense Business Systems" Model. • Used for software development programs where the deployment of the full capability will occur in multiple Increments as new capability is developed and delivered, nominally in 1- to 2-year cycles. • It is distinguished from model 2 by the rapid delivery of capability through multiple Increments. • Each Increment provides part of the overall required program capability. • There is some concurrency of development for each Increment. • Can be used for COTS software development with multiple modular capabilities.	• DBSs • Upgrades to some C2 system software • Upgrades to weapons systems software	• Problems in Increments may be difficult to fix in other concurrent Increments. • Concurrent Deliveries can be difficult to manage especially in complex systems. • The program can become overwhelmed with frequent milestone or deployment decision points and associated approval reviews.
MODEL 5 Hybrid Program A (Hardware Dominant)	• Used for developing systems where hardware and software development is occurring simultaneously. • The implementation of prototypes determine overall schedule, but software development and deployment must be tightly integrated and	• Aircraft, ship or land vehicle development where software is a critical component of weapon system delivery.	• Difficult to manage the timing for both HW and SW deliveries.

Model	Description of Model	Examples	Challenges
	coordinated with hardware development and delivery. • Software builds should lead up to the full capability needed to satisfy program requirements and Initial Operational Capability (IOC).		
MODEL 6 Hybrid Model B (Software Dominant),	• Used for software intensive product development with a mix of incrementally deployed software releases that includes intermediate software builds. • All of the characteristics of Model 3 also apply to this Model.	• DBSs • Upgrades to some C2 system software • Upgrades to weapons systems software	• It is a complex model to plan and execute successfully. • Highly integrated complex software and hardware development, poses special risks to program cost and schedule

CH 6–3.4 Common Software Development Methods

The DoD uses many different variations and combinations of software development methods, but they generally fall into three major categories: Waterfall, Incremental and Agile. These development methods are also used for other types of project implementation plans other than SW development. The DoD's most widely used development method for IT is Incremental, though more and more organizations are working to adopt Agile; or are incorporating principles of agile into their software development practices.

CH 6–3.4.1 Waterfall

The Waterfall method is a classical software development method where tasks are arranged to fall sequentially. One phase is completed before the next phase is started. Several software builds are completed before deployment. In its purest form, all requirements are known before IT is developed and the finished product is not delivered until all tasks are completed. For large and complex projects, this can mean that the underlying technology is obsolete before delivery. It also assumes an unrealistic view that organizations are static with the product's requirements remaining the same throughout the life of the project. If one task is not completed on time, the entire project can be halted. This method provides the greatest risk to user satisfaction; however, it also typically provides the lowest risk to meeting contractual requirements.

CH 6–3.4.2 Incremental

The Incremental method has been used to correct some of the problems associated with the Waterfall method. Note that "Spiral" and "Evolutionary Acquisition" are sometimes used synonymously with "Incremental". These terms actually vary slightly from one another and of the three, the preferred term, as used in the DoDI 5000.02, is Incremental. It has the goal of delivering additional improved capability in block Increments over time. This method allows tasks to be developed concurrently. If well managed, this method allows the product to be delivered earlier. In the DoD, you will generally see an initial deployment of 60%-80% of the product delivered; with the remaining capabilities delivered incrementally later.

A variant of Incremental is often used where an Increment is broken down into multiple manageable releases (i.e., Increment 1; Release 1.1; Release 1.2). This may enable both the Functional and the Program Manager to better manage requirements and deployments into smaller "chunks" of capability, getting capability into users' hands more quickly.

CH 6–3.4.3 Agile

In 2001 a group of software developers got together to develop a set of best practices for developing software earlier, with greater customer satisfaction, and higher quality. The group developed the Agile Manifesto:

- Individuals and interactions over processes and tools
- Working software over comprehensive documentation
- Customer collaboration over contract negotiation
- Responding to change over following a plan

The manifesto was further elaborated in the Agile Principles.

The best practices established through the Agile Manifesto and Principles are not necessarily new. However, they have been very difficult for the DoD to implement.

In Agile's purest form, end user(s) should sit with developers in order to make instant decisions on user functionality. High level requirements are initially prioritized and developed quickly by small teams in order to get a working product quickly to the customer. There are several Agile methods have been developed from the Agile Manifesto and Principles including eXtreme Programming (XP), Scrum, and Adaptive Software Development (ASD). An excellent description of the various Agile development methods is provided in a White Paper developed by the Software Engineering Institute titled, "Considerations for using Agile in DoD Acquisition."

Agile methods are typically used for small, low risk projects. However, some large DBS ERP programs have recently begun to incorporate agile principles to some degree of success, such as using Scrum or Sprints as part of their normal software development practices.

Table 4: A Comparison of Software Development Methods

Method	Description	Best Used For	Advantages	Disadvantages
Waterfall	• Uses independent development phases that are completed sequentially • Serial, "big-bang" solution with one long cycle times	• Programs where the requirements are very well understood at the onset of the project • Functionality to be delivered is mature and static • Best fits with Model 5, though also Model 1 (not described here)	• Typically low risk of not meeting contractual requirements if applied correctly • All functionality is delivered at the same time • Easiest delivery schedule management	• High risk of user dissatisfaction • Requires a complete set of requirements at the onset • Difficult to incorporate user feedback • Experimental code or prototypes are discarded after use

Method	Description	Best Used For	Advantages	Disadvantages
Incremental	• Development phases can be completed concurrently • Generally 60-80% of product is initially delivered with incremental deliveries delivered later	• Projects where all requirements are not known at beginning of project • Best fits with Models 2, 3, and 6	• Users can provide feedback earlier • Developers have opportunity to identify potential problems earlier • Does not require a complete set of requirements at onset of project • Overlapping deployments or tasks produce usable functionality earlier	• Schedule with concurrent tasks is difficult to manage • If well managed, project can be delivered earlier • Experimental code or prototypes are discarded after use
Agile	• Customer satisfaction is highest priority • Can be thought of as both a set of software development best practice as well as a software development method • Requirements are prioritized, multiple, rapidly executed Increments are developed and capabilities are released to the customer as soon as possible • Prototypes may be used as a starting place • It utilizes a modular, open-systems approach. • Documentation is kept to an absolute minimum	• Small- to mid-sized applications • Best fits with Models 3, 4, 6	• Customers get a workable product more quickly • Less documentation, more usable code • Continual involvement of the end user • Developers are able to easily course correct • Scope creep virtually eliminated	• Requires dedicated on site customer collaboration • Difficult to resolve Agile's lack of documentation required and the DoD's statutory and regulatory documentation requirements • Difficult to price because all requirements are not scoped at beginning of project

CH 6–3.4.4 Approach to IT Acquisition

The Department's six acquisition models are high level processes that encompass the acquisition of a system in the DoD. As described in Section 3.3, Models 2, 3, 5, and 6 are the most commonly used for IT acquisition. However, any one of the acquisition models could potentially be tailored and used to acquire IT. The following diagram breaks down a notional version of a DoD acquisition model and explains various activities that may occur throughout for not only a generic IT acquisition but points out some specialized activities that might occur on a Defense Business System (DBS), for example. These activities will be described in more detail throughout this chapter.

Figure 2: "Notional" DoD IT Acquisition Model

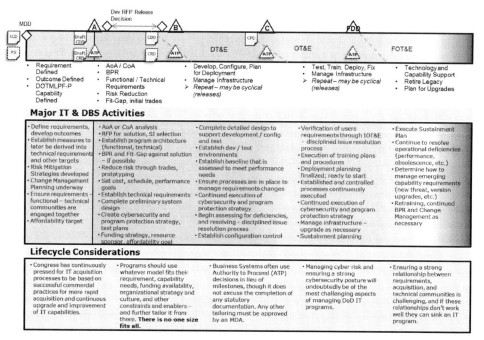

CH 6–3.5 DOTMLPF-P Capabilities

As described in the DoDI 5000.02 (Page 4), all acquisition programs respond to validated capability requirements. The Department defines capabilities from a holistic, end-to-end standpoint – these are referred to as Doctrine, Organization, Training, Materiel, Leadership, Personnel, Facilities and Policy (DOTMLPF-P) capabilities. A DOTMLPF-P capability is the ability to perform specific actions that, when taken as a whole, solve a requirement (need, business need, problem, gap, etc.). Capabilities should be forward looking; they describe the business or mission functions that must be executed in the future and they serve as the foundation from which the future requirements are derived from, and from which the future program is developed and executed.

In capability analysis, DOTMLPF-P capabilities are always centered on a business or mission function need as opposed to IT or materiel components. The capabilities are also prioritized based on their ability to solve the problem (operational effectiveness) as well as the anticipated benefits of the capability.

The requirements process for most non-IT programs is called the Joint Capabilities Integration and Development System (JCIDS) process. Non-DBS IT programs use the JCIDS IT-Box process, while DBS use the Problem Statement process under the authority of the Deputy Chief Management Officer (DCMO).

Figure 3 illustrates the general interaction between the requirements and acquisition processes. This interaction is also depicted in Figure 2, the Notional DoD IT Acquisition model.

Figure 3: Interaction between Capability Requirements and Acquisition Processes

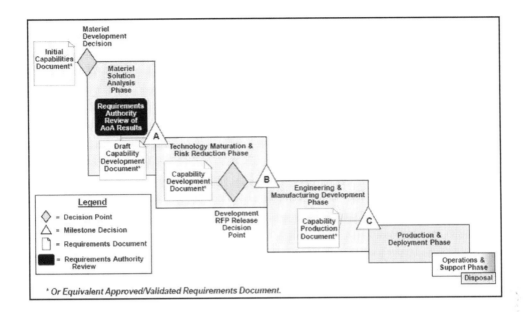

CH 6–3.5.1 JCIDS IT Box

The JCIDS process supports identifying, assessing, validating, and prioritizing joint military capability requirements. The JCIDS IT Box was created to provide agile and responsive capability requirements process to enable rapid development of IT capabilities. Similar to the DBS community, the IS acquisition and programming communities agree that IS development is different from major weapons systems, the processes for which are hardware-focused.

Figure 4: IT Box Process

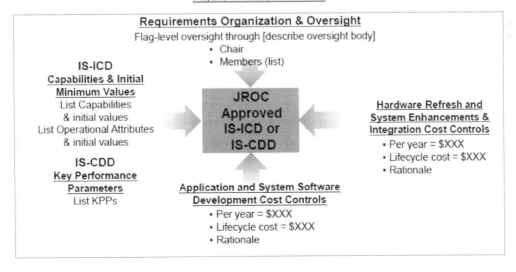

IT Box Applies To	IT Box Does Not Apply To
• Information Systems (IS) with software development only • Includes integration of COTS hardware • Program costs that exceed $15 million	• Defense Business Systems (DBS) • Systems that are an integral part of a weapon or weapon system • IS with a developmental cost less than $15 million

The Information System Initial Capabilities Document (IS-ICD) and the IS-Capabilities Development Document (IS-CDD) are used in implementation of the IT Box. These are variants of the standard ICD and CDD used in the JCIDS process and are designed to focus on facilitating more efficient and timely software development efforts. The major difference between the IS-ICD and the IS-CDD is that capabilities outlined get refined and presented as Key Performance Parameters (KPPs), Key System Attributes (KSAs) with specific threshold requirements and objective targets. CDDs are not required as successor documents for non-MDAP IS-ICDs and CPDs are not required as successor documents for IS-CDDs. CH 7 also discusses JCIDS documents from an intel perspective.

Detailed Guidance for the Information System ICD (IS-ICD) and the IS-CDD are provided in the JCIDS Manual. An IT Box Primer has also been developed by DAU.

Detailed guidance for both the IS-ICD and IS-CDD are provided in the JCIDS Manual which includes examples of potential IS ICD/CDD follow-on documents such as the following:

- Requirements Definition Package (RDP) – identifies KPPs and nonmaterial changes
- Capability Drop (CD) – lower level document that specifies the characteristics of a "widget" or "app" for partial deployment of the system

As the IS-ICD and IS-CDD only streamline the applicable requirements processes, the Sponsor must still ensure compliance with acquisition policy and processes in DoDI 5000.02.

CH 6–3.5.2 Defense Business Systems

Defense Business Systems (DBS) support DoD business activities such as acquisition, financial management, contracting, logistics, strategic planning and budgeting, installations and environment, and human resource management. DBS follow a process governed by Title 10, U.S.C. 2222 and the Defense Business Council (DBC) and have unique processes and procedures in both the requirements and acquisition aspects of the DoD Acquisition lifecycle. They do not follow the IT-Box and do not generally utilize IT-Box or traditional JCIDS process documentation.

Additional information about the DBC can be accessed from DCMO's DBC webpage. The DBC is the governing body who oversees defense business operations on behalf of the Secretary under the authority of Title 10, U.S.C. 2222 and the DBC Charter.

The DBC serves as the:

- Principal governance body for vetting issues related to management, improvement of defense business operations; and other issues to include performance management, pursuant to the Government Performance and Results Modernization Act (GPRMA) of 2010.
- Department's Investment Review Board (IRB) for business systems, pursuant to Title 10, U.S.C. 2222

The DBC is co-chaired by the Deputy Chief Management Officer (DCMO) and the DoD Chief Information Officer (CIO).

Defense Business System (DBS) capability requirements are defined beginning with the Problem Statement and other supporting documentation such as a System Requirements Document (SRD) or Capabilities Requirements Document (CRD), though the methods through which more detailed requirements are documented are not dictated by policy. Capability requirements are further defined throughout the lifecycle of the system. Configuration Control Boards (CCBs) are most often used to determine capability requirement veracity and priority.

DBS do not use the JCIDS process for defining requirements, generally, unless the requirement is deemed joint interest. At that point, the Joint Staff will provide guidance for any additional requirements or documentation that will be needed.

CH 6–3.5.2.1 Problem Statements

A Problem Statement identifies a business need and the Doctrine, Organization, Training, Materiel, Leadership, Personnel, Facilities and Policy (DOTMLPF-P) capabilities required to solve it. A Problem Statement is required for all expected DBS investments expected to cost $1M or more over the FYDP. Recent changes implemented by the FY2016 National Defense Authorization Act (NDAA) will affect not only the threshold for the Problem Statement Process but will likely drive changes to the overall process and templates used for it. Revised guidance from the Office of the DCMO is forthcoming – current and revised guidance is located on the DCMO website.

A Problem Statement should not be an IT solutions document. Rather, it should clearly define a need, why it exists, the context in which it exists, and the intended outcome that is desired from solving the need expressed as a comprehensive DOTMLPF-P capability. In addition, the Problem Statement includes measurable business outcomes, a rough order of magnitude cost estimate and projected/anticipated financial return measures such as net present value, payback or return on investment.

The Problem Statement is refined over time (i.e., decomposed into greater detail as more information is known). However, it is often approved only once unless a substantive scope change or fundamental change to the business need occurs. The Problem Statement must be validated by the prior to a Materiel Development Decision (MDD) or equivalent. It also serves as an input to the acquisition process and to the acquisition strategy, as well as any more detailed requirements planning.

Generally, all DBS follow processes defined by the DCMO for capability requirements review. However, the Joint Requirements Oversight Council (JROC) has the ability to review Problem Statements to determine if JROC interest exists. At that time, the JROC (or the applicable Functional Capabilities Board [FCB]) may levy additional requirements on the DBS for requirements review.

CH 6–3.5.2.2 Authority to Proceed (ATP) Decisions

DBS more and more frequently use event-based decision points called ATPs. An ATP is a method of tailoring for DBS in order to achieve more efficient and effective capability delivery, wherein regulatory requirements are "tailored in" rather than "tailored out". ATPs may be used to authorize entry into a new program phase, denote the authorization of program activity, or in lieu of a standard acquisition milestone such as an A or a B. There are three critical things to keep in mind when using ATPs:

- Use of an ATP should be based on the specific DBS product and overall approach to DOTMLPF-P capability delivery.
- The Program Manager should propose usage of ATPs and associated documentation requirements to the MDA as early as possible and document the MDA's tailored approach in the program acquisition strategy.
- Statutory requirements normally aligned to acquisition milestones must be completed and aligned with an analogous ATP; statutory requirements cannot be waived unless the statute permits.

CH 6–3.5.3 Business Process Reengineering (BPR)

Modifying the core code of a Commercial-Off-The-Shelf (COTS) product should be avoided. Importantly, business process reengineering is a function applicable to all IT that involves a process as its backbone to operate. BPR is most commonly thought of, however, as a companion activity to business system implementation. For DBS under Title 10, U.S.C section 2222 it is directed that "defense business processes are reviewed, and as appropriate revised, through business process reengineering to match best commercial practices, to the maximum extent practicable, so as to minimize customization of commercial business systems".

Adhering to the processes in a COTS product as much as possible is an industry best practice. A 2015 report by Panorama Consulting found that of the 562 companies they surveyed:

- The majority (66%) did little to no customization (defined as modifying one-quarter or less of the solution).
- 34% did "significant" (22%), "extreme" (7%), or "complete" (5%) customization to their ERP implementation.

In industry, customization is most often focused on processes that will give a company competitive advantage or make them unique – however; since the federal government is not profit-driven and rather is being mandated by Congress to specifically not customize its products, the push should be to utilize BPR and to adhere to the out of the box products as much as possible. Functional Sponsors and Program Managers should try to find ways to modify existing business processes rather than customizing commercial software products to meet their needs. Discussions on common standards (Section 3.7) and requirements and configuration management (Section 3.5.5) are important to being successful in this area.

While it is possible to add code in the form of Reports (R), Interfaces (I), Conversions (C), Enhancements (E), Forms (F) and Workflows (W) (RICE-FW), this practice significantly increases program costs and should be minimized as much as possible through BPR. In many cases there will only be a few instances where BPR is not possible. For example, due to policy or law, it may be necessary to build or acquire needed reports, interfaces, conversions, and extensions. In these cases, adding to the product must be done under strong configuration control.

The Functional Sponsor, representing the needs of the user, leads the BPR effort. BPR may include eliminating non-value added processes, consolidating separate functional tasks into end-to-end cross-functional processes, and integrating business functions as much as possible to improve business operations and to achieve the desired outcome(s). BPR is a continuous process and requires a rethinking of why the "As-Is" process came to be and how it can be improved to achieve efficiencies.

Ideally BPR will begin prior to the start of the Acquisition process to understand the picture of "what good looks like". However, BPR truly cannot be completed until a solution is selected to understand the underlying business processes of the product.

Major duties and responsibilities of BPR stakeholders:

- The Functional Sponsor (or Sponsor), informed by input from the corresponding DoD Military Component, is responsible for BPR.
- The PM is responsible for analyzing and considering the results of the BPR and using the goals of the reengineered process to shape the program.
- Technical SMEs (including test and engineering), to understand the impact of process changes vs. technical changes
- Cost SMEs, to understand the cost impacts of process changes vs. technical changes

CH 6–3.5.4 Developing Relevant Outcomes

Successful capability delivery in IT programs relies upon the ability to track progress toward completion. Generally, Performance Measures/Attributes are used to determine the degree to which a DOTMLPF-P capability has been successfully implemented. Measures and Attributes are tied to each Capability in order to answer the question: how will we know if this Capability has been fulfilled? The Performance Measures are defined at a mission or business level and can be broken down into process or system metrics later in the transformation effort. Outcomes define "what good looks like" to indicate when success has been achieved at varying levels (strategic, business, program, KPPs, KSAs, etc.) – and, to indicate when failure may be on the horizon.

Performance measures identify the performance-based metrics that provide visibility to the outcomes progress towards completion. IT programs should initiate a top-down decomposition process of outcomes and performance measures development, where high-level outcomes are developed early on and then decomposed further into business and program outcomes as more detail is learned throughout.

Any outcome should explicitly state the business value of the resources to be invested and to allow leadership to prioritize and weigh investments. The outcome provides strategic alignment and clear criterion against which to evaluate potential approaches. It always starts with the desired result and is used to focus behaviors and results by answering the "what's in it for me?" question. Corresponding measures must be specific, actionable, measureable, relevant, and timely operational capabilities that can be achieved against their corresponding outcomes.

It is important to note that the Functional Sponsor (who represents the needs of the user[s] that originally identified the problem, need, or requirement) is ultimately responsible for declaring whether the needed capability has been delivered.

Integrated teams should develop measures and metrics – while the exercise may be led by a Functional Sponsor or representative, it requires involvement from the Program Manager or key representatives from the program office, as well as SMEs from the test and engineering communities to ensure that measures are realistic, relevant, and testable from the beginning.

CH 6–3.5.5 Requirements Management

Documenting and managing requirements is one of the biggest challenges in DoD IT systems, and is critical to ensure effective delivery of a comprehensive DOTMLPF-P capability. For example: A 2009 GAO audit found that DoD and service officials responsible for conducting AoA's indicated that often proposed capability requirements are so specific that they effectively eliminate all but the service sponsor's preferred concepts instead of considering other alternatives (GAO-09-655, September 2009).

The process of requirements and configuration management is described in CH3, Systems Engineering and also in DoDI 5000.02 Encl. 3 Sec 8. The bottom line is that ensuring strong requirements and configuration management processes will ensure traceability and insight into all levels of development and design of the DOTMLPF-P solution. It is critical to establish and maintain consistency of a system's functional, performance, and physical attributes with its requirements, design, and operational information throughout a system's life cycle.

Effective control processes will allow a PM to better manage cost, schedule, and performance; and enable the PM to deliver a product that the Functional customer had envisioned:

- Configuration Control Boards (CCBs)
  - The use of CCBs is one of the most common (and effective) ways to control and manage requirements on IT programs. CCBs are most commonly partnerships between the functional and programmatic communities, involving tradeoffs of software requirements – depending on what level the CCB is held at in the organization. They may be referred to as Enterprise (or Executive) CCBs, Software CCBs, Requirements CCBs, or by other nomenclatures.
- Baseline Management
  - Depending on the type of IT implementation, many programs manage the implementation of the software baseline (and changes to it) separately from the modernization program. This can offer both challenges and benefits, but managing separately can become unwieldy on a large program if the efforts are not in sync with one another.
- Tools
  - Many DoD IT programs, most often due to the volume of requirements they must contend with, use automated tools to manage different parts of the requirements process – and some are customized for the type of software development process that is being followed. The scope of tools available include: Issue Management, Agile, Project Management, Product Management, Requirements Development, Requirements Management, Visual Modeling, Testing, User Interface/User Experience (UI/UX) Mockup, etc.

CH 6–3.6 Managing IT Program Investments

The overarching Planning, Programming, Budgeting, and Execution process is described in CH 1 Section 3.2.2 and Cost Estimation in CH 1 Section 3.4.3.5. Defense Budget Materials are available on the DoD Comptroller's website and are updated every Fiscal Year. Finally, DAU offers a continuous learning module, CLB 023 Software Cost Estimating. Annual IT Budget Submission guidance is published by the DoD CIO to adjust the submission process outlined in the FMR to ensure currency with OMB guidance. Contact DCIO-R&A or your Component budget office for the most current guidance.

More specifically, there are two major budget submission requirements for DoD IT investments: IT Budget Estimate Submission (BES) and the Congressional Justification submission or President's Budget (PB) Request. Instructions for submitting IT specific budgets can be found in DoD 7000.14-R Financial Management Regulation Volume 2B, Chapter 18 Information Technology (Including Cyberspace Operations) dated September 2015.

DoD utilizes several systems to capture and maintain IT investment information including Department of Defense Information Technology Investment Portal (DITIP) and the Select & Native Programming Data Input System for Information Technology (SNaP-IT).

During the first phase in the annual budget cycle, the Office of the Director, Cost Assessment and Program Evaluation (D, CAPE) and the Office of the Under Secretary of Defense (Comptroller) (USD(C)) are responsible for conducting an annual Program Budget Review PBR on all DoD resources and require a data submission from all DoD Components.

Components are also required to submit supplemental PBR data on their Major Defense Acquisition Programs (MDAPs) and Major Automated Information System (MAIS) programs. This supplemental submission of MDAP and MAIS data supports ongoing OUSD(AT&L) data transparency and data alignment efforts initially directed in the Fiscal Year 2011 Integrated Program Review Resource Management Directive 700 study.

Data submission is required for all current MDAPs and MAIS programs, as well as acquisition program concepts and Unbaselined MAIS programs that will achieve Milestone B prior to the end of the calendar year, or have been certified under the provisions of section 2366a of title 10 United States Code. The MDAP and MAIS program data must include all acquisition costs (RDT&E, Procurement, MILCON, Acquisition O&M, Working Capital Funds, or Other Financing with an explanation) and MDAP quantities (RDT&E and Procurement) for the full acquisition cycle of each MDAP and each MAIS program (by fiscal year and funding appropriation). For MAIS programs, the total life-cycle cost is the development cost plus ten years of Operation and Support (O&S) costs following Full Deployment declaration. For MDAP programs, the full acquisition lifecycle and associated funding is defined by the D, CAPE and USD(C) PBR Submission Guidance.

All MDAPs and MAIS programs submit annual PBR data that has been coordinated with and approved by the appropriate Component Acquisition Executive (CAE) into their Component's acquisition information system. For efficient information sharing, the CAE systems publish the data to Acquisition Visibility (AV) using the Defense Acquisition Management Information Retrieval (DAMIR) system Web Services. Components without access to one of the Component acquisition information systems use the DAMIR "Create or Edit a Budget Report" module. Notwithstanding the method of transmission, exposure, or publication, the CAE-approved PBR data is be available for consumption by AV and AV subscribers as determined by annual guidance.

CH 6–3.6.1 Federal IT Dashboard

The Federal IT Dashboard (ITDB) displays general information on over 7,000 Federal IT investments and detailed data for over 700 'major" investments. DOD's IT investments on the Federal IT Dashboard span the investment lifecycle (planning and budgeting, acquisition, management in-use). A general overview and tutorial of the Federal IT Dashboard can be accessed here. The DoD CIO ratings process is conducted semiannually and was designed in accordance with Office of Management and Budget (OMB) and internal DoD policies, processes, and procedures.

The Federal ITDB has high visibility with GAO, OMB, and now even Congress, who all use it as a tool to identify troubled investments. The Federal Information Technology Acquisition Reform Act (FITARA) now requires the DoD CIO to review any DoD investment on the ITDB that receives a high risk rating for four consecutive quarters and provide a report to relevant House and Senate committees, in addition to OMB.

The DoD CIO publishes guidance on how to assess investments that must be reported on the Federal IT dashboard and utilizes a CIO Ratings Recommendations submission page (CAC-enabled), which contains the latest reference documents, approved ratings, stakeholder ratings recommendations, and POCs for completing the ratings process. Guidance is provided in the "Department of Defense Chief Information Officer (DoD CIO) Ratings Process for the Federal Information Technology (IT) Dashboard," dated March 25, 2014 and available within the above linked site.

CH 6–3.6.2 IT Budget Estimate Submission (BES)

Guidance and formats for the preparation and submission of the Information Technology Budget Estimate Submission (BES) to the DoD CIO are provided in DITIP and through SNaP-IT.

CH 6–3.6.3 President's Budget (PB) Request

The President's Budget request for the DoD is submitted to Congress by the President. All DoD Components that require funding for IT programs and/or Cyberspace operations submit budget requests that are authorized by the DoD Component, OSD, the Office of Management and Budget (OMB), the President, and ultimately by Congress. Budget requests are prioritized based on the mission objectives of the Component, DoD and the President. General guidance for budget request submission requirements is presented in Volume 2A, Chapter 1 of the DoD Financial Management Regulation (FMR) and in the OSD Program/Budget guidance memos.

CH 6–3.6.4 MAIS Annual Report (MAR)

Title 10 U.S.C §2445b requires that the Secretary of Defense submit, to the Congress, annual reports on all MAIS, Unbaselined MAIS and pre-MAIS acquisition programs. This annual report, known as the MAIS Annual Report (MAR), is also a budget exhibit. The MAR is submitted through the Defense Acquisition Management Information Retrieval (DAMIR) system. MARs are delivered to Congress within 45 days after the President's Budget, as directed by statute.

CH 6–3.6.4.1 OMB Policy

OMB Circular A-11 provides guidance to Federal programs on how to prepare and submit materials required for OMB and Presidential review of agency budget requests. The guide to OMB Circular Number A–11 provides a description of the contents of the Circular. Section 25.5 of the Circular provides a table with the required contents of the Budget Request to be submitted to OMB.

Section 53 of Circular A-11 provides guidance pertaining to IT and E-Government. Specifically it provides instructions for submitting an Agency's IT Portfolio Summary (formally known as Exhibit 53A), an Agency's IT Security Portfolio (formally known as 53B) and an Agency's Cloud Spending Summary (formally known as 53C).

The policy and specific instructions on managing Federal information resources are provided in OMB Circular A-130, "Management of Federal Information Resources." The policies in the Circular apply to the information activities of all agencies of the executive branch of the Federal government. The Department of Defense Information Technology Information Portal (DITIP) and/or Select and Native Programming – Information Technology (SNaP-IT) systems are used to gather information requested by OMB.

CH 6–3.6.4.2 IT Business Case

The IT Business Case, formerly known as the Exhibit 300, pertains to reporting requirements for Section 55 of OMB Circular A-11. The Major IT Business Case Exhibit (see page 26) (formally known as Exhibit 300A) and the Major IT Business Case Detail Exhibit (see page 34) (formally known as Exhibit 300B) are companion pieces an Agency's IT Portfolio Summary, IT Security Portfolio and Cloud Spending Summary. These Exhibits, together with the agency's Enterprise Architecture program, define how to manage the IT Capital Planning and Control Process. The IT Portfolio Summary is a tool for reporting the funding of the portfolio of all IT investments within a Department while the Major IT Business Case Exhibit is a tool for detailed justifications of major "IT Investments". The Major IT Business Case Detail Exhibit is for the management of the execution of those investments through their project life cycle and into their useful life in production.

In a January 8, 2016 memorandum the Director, Acquisition Resources and Analysis and Deputy CIO for Resources and Analysis wrote that "starting with the FY 2017 President's Budget (PB) submission, the Department will singularly report to Congress and the Office of Management and Budget (OMB) utilizing the annual (MAIS Annual Report) and (Selected Acquisition Report) submissions", to eliminate duplicate reporting in the former Ex. 300. It is important to note that this is a rapidly changing process in the Department and applies only to active MDAP and MAIS programs currently using the MAR or SAR to accomplish the business case requirement. It is very likely that updated guidance on the business case requirement will be issued imminently. For example, beginning with the FY2018 PB, the Department is planning to utilize similar MAR-like data reporting and processes for all Major IT Investments – even if they currently do not report as part of a MAR or SAR process.

CH 6–3.6.5 Affordability
The purpose of conducting an Affordability Analysis is to avoid starting or continuing programs that cannot be produced and supported utilizing future budgets. Affordability is relatively straight forward when procuring tanks; however, it can be difficult to determine for some IT investments such as IT Services where there are no specific "units".

The best opportunity for determining affordability is through tailoring capability requirements before and during the development of an Analysis of Alternatives (AoA). Components should incorporate estimated funding streams for future programs within their affordability analyses at the earliest conceptual point and specify those estimates at the MDD and beyond to inform system design and alternative selection.

Prior to MS B (or the equivalent ATP), affordability goals are considered targets and are used to help scope the AoA and other required analyses in order to achieve an affordable program to be put on contract at RFP release and to be baselined at MS B. Once requirements and the product definition are firm, affordability caps are established to provide fixed cost requirements that are functionally equivalent to Key Performance Parameters (KPPs).

Additional policy regarding conducting affordability analysis is located in DoDI 5000.02 (Encl. 8) and DoDI 5000.02 (Encl. 10 – sec 2).

CH 6–3.6.6 Lifecycle Cost Estimating for IT
Developing a well thought out Lifecycle Cost Estimate (LCCE) with costs from inception to retirement is crucial for the following:

- Establishing fiscal feasibility of the program
- Informing Analyses of Alternatives (AoAs)
- Guiding capability requirements and engineering tradeoffs
- Setting realistic program baselines to control life-cycle costs, and
- Instill more cost-conscious management in the DoD.

Life-Cycle Cost (LCC) estimating represents the total cost to the Government for an IS, weapon system, program and/or investment over its full life. It includes all developmental costs, procurement costs, MILCON costs, operations and support costs, and disposal costs. LCC encompasses direct and indirect initial costs plus any periodic or continuing sustainment costs, and all contract and in-house costs, in all cost categories and all related appropriations/funds.

LCC may be broken down to describe the cost of delivering a certain capability or useful segment of an IT investment. LCC normally includes 10 years of sustainment funding following Full Operational Capability (FOC) or Full Deployment for Automated Information Systems. For investments with no known end date that are beyond FOC, LCC estimate should include 10 years of sustainment.

The Director of Cost Assessment and Program Evaluation (DCAPE) provides policies and procedures for developing LCCEs for all DoD acquisition programs. DCAPE also reviews cost estimates and cost analyses conducted in connection with Major Defense Acquisition Programs (MDAPs) and Major Automated Information System (MAIS) programs.

The DCAPE also conducts Independent Cost Estimates (ICE) and cost analyses for MAIS (if directed by the MDA, or if a program is in a critical change – otherwise an ICE is typically not required) and MDAP programs. The documentation of each MDAP or MAIS program cost estimate prepared by DCAPE and/or Service or Agency includes the elements of program cost risk identified and accounted for, how they were, evaluated and possible mitigation measures.

The DCAPE requires use of a Cost Analysis Requirements Description (CARD). The CARD is a complete description of the system at a level of detail appropriate for calculating costs. DCAPE provides CARD development guidance tailored to the specific review being conducted and the type of system being developed. However, all CARDs, no matter how tailored, will provide a program description that includes a summary of the acquisition approach, expected constraints, system characteristics, quantities, operational factors, operational support strategy, preliminary schedules, test programs, technology maturation and risk reduction plans, and appropriate system analogs. Additional content may be required as requested by DCAPE.

Should the contractor proposed solutions entering the Technology Maturation and Risk Reduction Phase differ significantly from the design reflected in the Milestone A CARD, the Program Manager will report any differences that might alter the basis for the MDA's Milestone A decision to DCAPE and the MDA. The MDA will determine whether an additional review is required prior to contract award.

At the Development RFP Release Decision Point, the program described in the final CARD will reflect the Program Manager's and PEO's best estimate of the materiel solution that will be pursued following Milestone B. The final CARD is updated to reflect all new program information prior to Milestone B.

For DBSs, a Cost Element Structure is required when developing a Business Case. An example of commonly used elements is provided in the DoD Enterprise IT Business Case Analysis Template Appendix B. The Cost Element Structure is the most critical element of the BCA process to ensure consistent, comparable cost estimates on IT.

DoD Components develop a DoD Component Cost Estimate that covers the entire life cycle of the program for all MAIS programs at any time an Economic Analysis is due.

Guidance for developing LCCEs is provided in the DoDI 5000.02 (Encl. 10 – sec 2). Additional information on LCCEs can be found in the DoD 7000.14-R Financial Management Regulation Volume 2B, Chapter 18 dated September 2015.

CH 6–3.6.6.1 Should-Cost and Will-Cost

The concept of "should-cost" is driven by the DoD culture of cost-consciousness. It is focused on controlling the cost of the actual work that we are doing and expect to do and to identify and eliminate inefficient and non-productive tasks from our programs. Should-cost is a tool to manage all costs throughout the lifecycle, and it operates in parallel with the effort to constrain requirements in order to costs all the way through to sustainment of the capability. In particular, should-cost estimates inform negotiations with industry over contract costs and incentives. The should-cost approach challenges us to do our best to find specific ways to beat the Independent Cost Estimate (ICE) or Program Estimate (which should already reflect the affordability requirements) and other cost projections funded in budgets (i.e., "will-cost"), when we find sensible opportunities to do so. For example, should-cost does not mean trading away the long-term value of sound design practices and disciplined engineering management for short-term gain.

In 2011, the USD(AT&L) and the Comptroller signed out a memo containing the "ingredients" to should-cost management. Another excellent resources is the April 2014 Issue of the Defense Acquisition Research Journal examined how programs have implemented should-cost, the types of savings identified and realized, and best practices and lessons learned that might be adopted by other programs in the Department.

Should-cost is reported through the DAES review process. For additional information on should-cost and will-cost, visit CH 1 Section 4.2.17.

CH 6–3.6.7 Program Funding Chart

The program funding chart is often referred to as the "Spruill Chart". The purpose of the Program Funding Chart is to capture the primary acquisition and sustainment program budgets relative to the previous President's Budget and latest estimate of funds required to execute the program. Instructions and links to the Spruill Chart are available here and are CAC-enabled. The template is updated as Programming, Planning, Budgeting, and Execution System (PPBE) events occur. The Spruill Chart features prominently throughout the DAB process.

The basic instructions for the Spruill Chart are to report all RDT&E, Procurement and MILCON investments supporting the baselined acquisition program, consistent with the Selected Acquisition Report (if applicable). Report all weapon system O&M associated with the program, consistent with the Operating and Support estimates reported in the SAR (if applicable). Other appropriations supporting O&S are not reported.

CH 6–3.6.8 IT Portfolio Management

Portfolios can be based on mission areas or commodity types, and will define a collection of products or capabilities that can be managed together for investment analysis and oversight purposes. Components will normally make tradeoffs within portfolios, but if necessary, can and should make tradeoffs across portfolios to provide adequate resources for high-priority programs

Component level affordability analysis examines all programs and portfolios together, extending over enough years to reveal the life-cycle cost and inventory implications of planned program for the Component. The same analysis is used as individual programs come up for review. Nominally, affordability analysis covers 30 to 40 years into the future.

Authority for portfolio management is found in many locations. For example:

- DoDI 5000.02
- DoDD 8115.01 "Information Technology Portfolio Management"
- DoDI 8115.02 "Information Technology Portfolio Management Implementation"
- DoDI 7045.28 "Capability Portfolio Management"

Guidance or best practices on how to conduct portfolio management is more difficult to come by.

- For DBS specifically: Guidance for Review and Certification of Defense Business Systems
- GAO 15-466, "Opportunities Exist to Improve the Department of Defense's Portfolio Management"

CH 6–3.6.8.1 Defense Business Systems Investment Review (Certification)

Certification of investments are required for covered defense business systems (i.e., those DBSs with funding >$1M over the period of the current Future Years Defense Program (FYDP)). All appropriations require certification. In addition, all funding including funds from another DoD Component must be certified. These rules have changed with the FY2016 NDAA and this guidance will be updated accordingly when the DCMO introduces updated policy.

As part of the DBS certification process, DoD Components (e.g., MILDEPS and Defense Agencies) annually develop Organizational Execution Plans (OEPs). Each OEP is comprised of three elements: the Portfolio Certification Request, the OEP briefing, and views of authoritative data from DoD Information Technology Portfolio Repository (DITPR) and Select & Native Programming Data Input System for Information Technology (SNaP-IT). DoD Defense Business Council (DBC) members assess Component OEPs and provide recommendations to the Chair on certification of funds. The DCMO approves OEP certifications and records the outcomes in investment decision memoranda (IDMs).

Current DBS certification instructions are provided in the DCMO's Guidance for Review and Certification of Defense Business Systems, Version 3.4 dated February 2015.

Specific instructions for utilizing the Defense Information Technology Investment Portal (DITIP) for DBS certification management can be accessed from the DITIP webpage. Select the link "DITIP Instruction-DBS Certification Management" in the Documents section.

CH 6–3.6.8.1.1 Integrated Business Framework

The Integrated Business Framework provides the overarching structure used to govern and manage the Department's business operations from the creation of aligned business strategies and investment plans, to the measurement of outcomes. A description of the framework is provided on Page 5 of the DCMO's Guidance for Review and Certification of Defense Business Systems, Version 3.4 dated February 2015. The framework is also designed to facilitate a cross-functional, enterprise-wide view for the governance of portfolios of DBSs investments over the FYDP for review and certification. The DoD's Strategic Management Plan (SMP) is as an enterprise plan for improving DoD's business operations. The Department is currently transitioning toward incorporating the business strategy into an Agency Strategic Plan (ASP) that will provide a more comprehensive plan and measures.

CH 6–3.6.8.2 Clinger-Cohen Act

The Clinger-Cohen Act, or Subtitle III of Title 40 of the United States Code (formerly known as Division E of the Clinger-Cohen Act (CCA) (hereinafter referred to as "Title 40/CCA") applies to all IT investments, including National Security Systems (NSS). Title 40/CCA requires Federal agencies to focus more on the results achieved through its IT investments, while streamlining the Federal IT procurement process. Specifically, this Act introduces much more rigor and structure into how agencies approach the selection and management of IT projects.

Title 40/CCA generated a number of significant changes in the roles and responsibilities of various Federal agencies in managing the acquisition of IT. It elevated oversight responsibility to the Director of the Office of Management and Budget (OMB) and established and gave oversight responsibilities to the departmental Chief Information Officer (CIO). Also, under this Act, the head of each agency is required to implement a process for maximizing the value and assessing and managing the risks of the agency's IT acquisitions.

In DoD, the DoD CIO has the primary responsibility of providing management and oversight of all Department IT to ensure the Department's IT systems are interoperable, secure, properly justified, and contribute to mission goals.

The basic requirements of the Title 40/CCA, relating to DoD's acquisition process, have been institutionalized in DoD Instruction 5000.02, in particular, Enclosure 5 (IT Considerations). The requirements delineated in this section must also be considered and applied to all IT investments, regardless of acquisition category, and tailored commensurate to size, complexity, scope, and risk levels.

Figure 5: Title 40 – Clinger Cohen Act Compliance

Category	Statutory Authority		Regulatory Authority
	40 U.S.C. Subtitle III ((aka Clinger-Cohen Act (CCA))	2001 NDAA §811 (P.L. 106-398)	DoDI 5000.02
MDAP	Comply	n/a	Confirm* Compliance by Component CIO
MAIS	Comply	Confirm Compliance	Confirm Compliance by Component CIO
All Other	Comply	n/a	Confirm Compliance by Component CIO or as delegated
* "Certifications" of CCA compliance are no longer required by any statute or regulation.			

PMs, program sponsors/domain owners, members of the joint staff, and DoD Component CIO responsibilities are further explained and detailed in the IT Community of Practice knowledge center which also contains a vast array of information pertinent to specific aspects of Title 40/CCA compliance.

A comprehensive compilation of Federal laws, OMB and Budget circulars, DoD directives and instructions, and OSD policy memorandums, relevant to all aspects of Title 40/CCA compliance, is available in the CCA Policy Folder of the Acquisition Community Connection. The Title 40/CCA Compliance Table details actions required to comply with Title 40/CCA regulatory requirements, mandatory DoD policy, and the applicable program documentation that can be used to fulfill the requirement.

The requirements in this table must be satisfied before Milestone approval of any Acquisition Category (ACAT) I (i.e., Major Defense Acquisition Program (MDAP)) and ACAT IA (i.e., MAIS Program) and prior to the award of any contract for the acquisition of a Mission-Critical or Mission-Essential IT system, at any level.

The requirements delineated in this table must also be considered and applied to all IT investments, regardless of acquisition category, and tailored commensurate to size, complexity, scope, and risk levels.

CH 6–3.6.9 Contracting - Special Circumstances and Best Practices
Fundamentally, there is no one "best fit" type of contract for the acquisition of information technology. Many program offices have found that having a contracting officer integrated into the program planning activities up-front to gain subject matter expertise into the IT capability enables more appropriate contracting vehicles to be applied.

When acquiring IT and developing requests for proposals (RFPs) and contract statements of work (SOWs), they should be reviewed as part of the acquisition process to ensure that IT standards established in a program's requirements document are translated into clear contractual requirements.

Various methodologies, toolsets, and information repositories have been developed to assist the Program Manager (PM) in the implementation of COTS software-based programs. The remainder of this section provides the PM descriptions of best practices, available tools and methods, and critical success factors for use in the acquisition of commercially-based solutions.

CH 6–3.6.9.1 Enterprise Software Initiative

The DoD Enterprise Software Initiative (DoD ESI) is a joint, Chief Information Officer (CIO)-sponsored project designed to: "Lead in the establishment and management of enterprise COTS information technology (IT) agreements, assets, and policies for the purpose of lowering total cost of ownership across the DoD, Coast Guard and Intelligence communities." DoD ESI is a key advisor to the DoD Strategic Sourcing Directors Board. With active working members from OSD, Department of the Army, Department of the Navy, Department of the Air Force, Defense Logistics Agency, Defense Information Systems Agency, National Geospatial-Intelligence Agency, Defense Intelligence Agency, Director of National Intelligence, and Defense Finance and Accounting Service, the DoD ESI team collaborates to create Enterprise Software Agreements (ESA) for use by DoD, the Intelligence Community, and U.S. Coast Guard IT buyers. ESA negotiations and management activities are performed by IT acquisition professionals within participating DoD Components, who are designated ESI "Software Product Managers (SPM)." SPMs are supported by experienced IT contracting experts.

The DoD ESI can use the Defense Working Capital Fund to provide "up-front money" for initial wholesale software buys and multi-year financing for DoD customers. This funding process assures maximum leverage of the combined buying power of the Department of Defense, producing large software cost discounts.

On-line resources include the DoD ESI website listing general products, services and procedures the Defense Federal Acquisition Regulation Supplement Subpart 208.74; and the DoDI 5000.02 (Encl. 11, Sec. 10).

CH 6–3.6.9.2 Defense Federal Acquisition Regulations
The Defense Federal Acquisition Regulations (DFARs) contains contractual requirements for IT. Some of the subsections of interest are subpart 239.71 regarding security and privacy for computer systems, subpart 208.74 on enterprise software agreements and subpart 227.72 for policy on the acquisition of commercial computer software and commercial computer software documentation.

CH 6–3.6.9.3 Defense Information Systems Agency (DISA) Support
Purchasing telecommunications and IT products and services for the military is one of DISA's key roles within the DoD. The DISA Contracts Guide (CAC Only) is provided by Defense Information Technology Contracting Organization (DITCO); it contains a list of Premier Contracts as well as ordering instructions. In addition:

- DISA provides Enterprise Acquisition Services (EAS) for purchasing telecommunications and information technology (IT) products and services from the worldwide commercial sector to meet Department of Defense (DoD) and authorized non-defense customers' needs. Services include acquisition planning, procurement, tariff surveillance, cost and price analyses, and contract administration. DISA is the mandated single source for procuring DoD long haul telecommunications requirements.
- DISA establishes large contract vehicles available to DoD for essential IT services such as engineering, hardware, equipment and maintenance, integration and support, information security, computer technology, satellite bandwidth, and Defense Information System Network (DISN) access.

CH 6–3.6.9.4 Strategic Sourcing

Strategic Sourcing is about buying smartly and collaboratively in an effort to reduce costs and maximize the use of available funds. While this concept is most often thought of in the context of supply chain management, it has strong applicability to information technology in terms of buying bulk software, licenses, and / or services. Resources for Strategic Sourcing assistance include:

- In an effort to enhance collaboration and integration, the OSD Office of Defense Procurement and Acquisition Policy (DPAP) provides multiple resources for Strategic Sourcing opportunities and best practices and sits on the government-wide Strategic Sourcing Leadership Council (SSLC), whose objective is to lead the government's efforts to increase the use of government-wide management and sourcing of goods and services.
- DPAP also has a DoD-Wide Strategic Sourcing (DWSS) CONOPS available to explain how to use the DWSS program.
- Finally the DAU Acquisition Community Connection has a Community of Practice for Strategic Sourcing available with many best practices.

CH 6–3.6.9.5 Data Rights

Data Rights is a shorthand way to refer to the Government's license rights in major categories of valuable intellectual property, and it factors critically into how a capability is contracted for and how data is managed for the life of a program. Data Rights are also discussed in CH 4 Section 3.3.1.11.

Data Rights for technical data and computer software fall into eight categories:

- **Unlimited Rights.** Developed exclusively at Government expense, and certain types of data (e.g., Form, Fit, and Function data [FFF]; Operation, Maintenance, Installation, and Training [OMIT]), these rights involve the right to use, modify, reproduce, display, release, or disclose technical data in whole or in part, in any manner, and for any purpose whatsoever, and to have or authorize others to do so.
- **Government Purpose Rights.** This right involves the right to use, duplicate, or disclose technical data for Government purposes only, and to have or permit others to do so for Government purposes only. Government purposes include competitive procurement, but do not include the right to permit others to use the data for commercial purposes.
- **Limited Rights.** A limited rights agreement permits the Government to use proprietary technical data in whole or in part. It also means that the Government has to obtain the expressed permission of the party providing the technical data to release it, or disclose it, outside the Government.
- **Restricted Rights.** Developed exclusively at private expense
- **Specifically Negotiated License Rights.** This right pertains whenever the standard license arrangements are modified to the mutual agreement of the contractor and the Government. In this case, the exact terms are spelled out in a specific license agreement unique to each application.
- **Small Business Innovative Research (SBIR) Data Rights.** All technical data or computer software generated under a SBIR contract. Government users cannot release or disclose outside the Government except to Government support contractors.
- **Commercial Technical Data License Rights.** Applies to technical data related to commercial items (developed at private expense). Managed in the same manner as Limited Rights.
- **Commercial Computer Software Licenses.** Applies to any commercial computer software or software documentation. Managed as specified in the commercial license offered to the public.

Only under very unique circumstances does the Government acquire title to or ownership of technical data or computer software developed under DoD contracts – even if the Government funded 100% of the development. Instead, the Government acquires a license to use, release, or disclose that technical data or computer software to persons who are not Government employees. Therefore, the DoD often negotiates over license rights and not ownership of technical data or computer software to be delivered under a contract. A Program Manager must ensure that all Technical Data and Computer Software and related license rights required for procurement and sustainment of a system are available throughout a system's life cycle.

The DFARS, subpart 227.71 (rights in technical data) prescribes policies and procedures for the acquisition of technical data and the rights to use, modify, reproduce, release, perform, display, or disclose technical data. Statutory references Title 10 U.S.C Section 2320 and Title 10, U.S. Code, Section 2321 also provide additional information. Other resources for learning about data rights include:

- DAU continuous learning module CLE 068 "Intellectual Property and Data Rights"
- 2013 Better Buying Power Trifold – "Understanding and Leveraging Data Rights in DoD Acquisitions"
- Army Data and Data Rights Guide (D&DR Guide), 2015

CH 6–3.7 Common IT Standards

The DoDI 8301.01, "Information Technology Standards in the DoD" is the overarching policy for IT standards in order to promote interoperability, information sharing, reuse, portability, and cybersecurity within the DoD. It is policy that DoD-approved and adopted standards are listed in the DoD IT Standards Registry (DISR), which enables centralization and transparency of available and applicable standards across the Department. To request an account, please fill out the form located here.

CH 6–3.7.1 Enterprise Architecture

All DoD architectures, including warfighter, intelligence, business, and component enterprise architectures, are part of the DoD Enterprise Architecture (EA). The DoD EA is defined as a federation of descriptions that provide context and rules for accomplishing the mission of the Department. These descriptions are developed and maintained at the Department, Capability Area, and Component levels and collectively define the people, processes, and technology required in the "current" and "target" environments, and the roadmap for transition to the target environment. As the Secretary of Defense's principal staff assistant for IT and information resources management, the DoD Chief Information Officer (DoD CIO) develops, maintains, and facilitates the use of the DoD EA to guide and oversee the evolution of the Department's IT-related investments to meet operational needs.

To comply with the enterprise architecture:

- Follow the DoD Architecture Framework (DoDAF) guidance in creating architectural views. This guidance is met by creating an architecture that captures the specific data needed to support decision making. The specific data is predicated by explicitly identifying the intended use and scope of the architecture in question. DODAF guidance can be accessed through the Office of the Deputy Chief Management Officer's DODAF webpage.
- Meet the DODAF Meta-model (DM2) Physical Exchange Specification (PES) requirements for sharing/reusing architecture data. DODAF Meta-model (DM2) guidance can be accessed from the DCMO's DODAF Meta-model webpage.
- When building systems, requests for proposals (RFPs) and contract statements of work (SOWs) should be reviewed as part of approved acquisition processes to ensure IT standards established in ICDs, CDDs, CPDs or Problem Statements are translated into clear contractual requirements.
- Meet the purpose and intent of the DoDD 8320.02 for securely sharing electronic data, information, and IT services and securely enabling the discovery of shared data.
- Mandatory Core Designated DoD Enterprise Services are common, globally-accessible services designated by the DoD CIO and mandated for use by all programs and initiatives. No capability comparable to the Mandatory Core Designated DoD ES is to be developed unless there is a waiver granted by the DoD CIO.

CH 6–3.7.1.1 Open Systems Architecture

PMs are responsible for applying open systems approaches in product designs where feasible and cost-effective. Open systems and modular architectures provide valuable mechanisms for continuing competition and incremental upgrades, and to facilitate reuse across the joint force. PMs should use open systems architecture design principles to support an open business model (see paragraph 6a(4) in Enclosure 2 of the DoDI 5000.02).

CH 6–3.7.1.2 Business Enterprise Architecture (BEA)

The Business Enterprise Architecture (BEA) is the enterprise architecture for the DoD Business Mission Area and reflects DoD business transformation priorities; the business capabilities required to support those priorities; and the combinations of enterprise systems and initiatives that enable those capabilities. It also supports use of this information within an End-to-End (E2E) framework.

The purpose of the BEA is to provide a blueprint for DoD business transformation that helps ensure the right capabilities, resources and materiel are rapidly delivered to our warfighters – what they need, when they need it, where they need it, anywhere in the world. The BEA guides and constrains implementation of interoperable defense business system solutions as required by Title 10 U.S.C section 2222. It also guides information technology investment management to align with strategic business capabilities as required by the Clinger-Cohen Act, and supports Office of Management and Budget (OMB) and Government Accountability Office (GAO) policies.

The Strategic Management Plan (SMP), Functional Strategies as developed by the appropriate DoD Principal Staff Assistants and the Organizational Execution Plans (OEP) as developed by DoD Components are the drivers of BEA release content.

CH 6–3.7.2 Audit Readiness and Audit Standards

DOD's financial management has been on GAO's High Risk List since 1995 because of pervasive deficiencies in financial and related business management systems, processes, and controls. Congress has mandated a full audit of DOD's FY2018 financial statements, the results of which must be submitted to Congress by March 31, 2019. A critical piece in aiding the Department to achieve financial auditability is the Comptroller's Financial Improvement and Audit Readiness (FIAR) Plan and the accompanying FIAR Guidance. The FIAR Guidance serves as a standard reference guide for existing and new users involved in all audit readiness initiatives across the Department. The DoD Comptroller's FIAR Directorate has also published an extensive and helpful resource of tools, templates and work products.

The FIAR Guidance contains discussion of common critical standards in order to aid the Department in achieving auditability, which ultimately impacts the requirements and configurations of IT systems as they are developed, deployed and managed:

- Federal Managers' Financial Integrity Act of 1982 (FMFIA), which established overall requirements for management's responsibilities with respect to internal controls.
- The Chief Financial Officers (CFO) Act of 1990 (Public Law 101-576), the purpose of which is to drive improvement of government financial management and creates standards of performance and disclosure.
- The Federal Financial Management Improvement Act of 1996 (FFMIA), which requires agencies to incorporate applicable federal accounting standards into their financial management systems, maintain A-123 compliant systems, and regularly and report on those systems.
- The Federal Information Security Modernization Act of 2014 (FISMA 2014) requires the head of each agency to implement policies and procedures to cost-effectively reduce information technology security risks to an acceptable level, and emphasize cybersecurity.
- The GAO's "Green Book" or Standards for Internal Control in the Federal Government sets the standards for an effective internal control system for federal agencies. An entity uses the Green Book to help achieve its objectives related to operations, reporting, and compliance.
- Federal Information System Controls Audit Manual (FISCAM) provides a methodology for performing IT / IS control audits of federal and other governmental entities in accordance with professional standards. The FISCAM is the basis on which DoD IT / IS are assessed in accordance with the FIAR Guidance.
- Defense Finance and Accounting Service – Financial Management Systems Requirements Manual General and Administrative Information (FFMIA) 7900.4-M "Blue Book" enables compliance with the FFMIA.

CH 6–3.7.3 Standard Financial Information Structure (SFIS)

The Standard Financial Information Structure (SFIS) is a comprehensive data structure that supports requirements for budgeting, financial accounting, cost/performance, and external reporting needs across the DoD enterprise. SFIS standardizes financial reporting across DoD and allows revenues and expenses to be reported by programs that align with major goals, rather than basing reporting primarily on appropriation categories. It also enables decision-makers to efficiently compare programs and their associated activities and costs across the department and provides a basis for common valuation of DoD programs, assets, and liabilities.

CH 6–3.7.4 Item Unique Identification

Item Unique Identification (IUID) is an international standards-based approach adopted by the DoD and its implementation is driven by and required by DoDD 8320.03. IUID makes the acquisition, repair, and deployment of items faster and more efficient through achievement of information sharing, visibility, assurance, and interoperability. IUID is required for all new DoD acquisitions; items the government already owns (i.e., legacy items); and government furnished property meeting any one of the following criteria:

- the item has a line item acquisition cost in its contract of $5,000 or more
- the item is or will be serially managed by the DoD
- the item is or will be controlled or mission essential
- permanent identification is or will be wanted for any other reason

IUID rules may apply differently for embedded systems. Items requiring IUID must be assigned a globally unique, permanent unique item identifier, or UII, and the UII registered, along with other item identifying information, in the DoD IUID Registry. Tools and guidance for implementing IUID are available in the IUID Toolbox.

CH 6–3.8 Interoperability

Interoperability, guided by the DoDI 8330.01, is the ability of systems, units, or forces to provide data, information, materiel, and services to, and accept the same from, other systems, units, or forces and to use the data, information, materiel, and services so exchanged to enable them to operate effectively together. Information Technology (IT) and NSS interoperability includes both the technical exchange of information and the end-to-end operational effectiveness of that exchange of information as required for mission accomplishment. Interoperability is more than just information exchange. It includes systems, processes, procedures, organizations and missions over the life cycle, and it should be balanced with IA.

Supportability for IT systems and NSS is the ability of systems and infrastructure components, external to a specific IT or NSS, to aid, protect, complement, or sustain the design, development, testing, training, or operations of the IT or NSS to achieve its required operational and functional capabilities.

IT and NSS interoperability and supportability needs, for a given capability, be identified through:

- The Defense Acquisition System (as defined in the DoD 5000 series issuances)
- The Joint Capabilities Integration and Development System process
- The DBS Problem Statement Process
- The Doctrine, Organization, Training, Materiel, Leadership and Education Personnel and Facilities (DOTMLPF) change recommendation process

CH 6–3.8.1 Interoperability Requirements and Verification

For all information technology, measurable interoperability requirements must be identified, formally validated through NR KPP certification, and then formally tested through an interoperability certification process. The Joint Interoperability Test Command (JITC) produces an Interoperability Process Guide which outlines the procedures and documentation required for Joint Interoperability Test and Certification, waiver processing, and associated processes and procedures. It also addresses interoperability test and certification based on the Net-Ready Key Performance Parameter (NR KPP). More on the role of JITC can be found in CH 8 Section 2.3.4.1.

Interoperability requirements must be documented in a succinct, measurable, and testable manner as an NR KPP. The NR KPP must describe a set of performance measures (MOEs and MOPs). The NR KPP must assess information requirements, information timeliness, and net-ready attributes required for both the technical exchange of information and the end-to-end operational effectiveness of that exchange.

The ISP is a key document in achieving interoperability certification. The ISP describes IT and information needs, dependencies, and interfaces for programs. It focuses on the efficient and effective exchange of information that, if not properly managed, could limit or restrict the operation of the program in accordance with its defined capability. Interoperability testing is further described in CH 8 Section 3.7.6.

CH 6–3.8.1.1 Net-Ready KPP

Net-ready attributes determine specific criteria for interoperability, and operationally effective end-to-end information exchanges which are traceable to their associated operational context, and are measurable, testable, and support efficient and effective T&E.

- The NR KPP identifies operational, net-centric requirements in terms of threshold and objective values for MOEs and MOPs. The NR KPP covers all communication, computing, and EM spectrum requirements involving information elements among producer, sender, receiver, and consumer. Information elements include the information, product, and service JCIDS Manual 12 February 2015 D-E-3 Appendix E Enclosure D exchanges. These exchanges enable successful completion of the warfighter mission or joint business processes.
- The NR KPP includes three attributes derived through a three step process of mission analysis, information analysis, and systems engineering. These attributes are then documented in solution architectures developed according to the current DODAF standard.
  - Attribute 1: Supports military operations
  - Attribute 2: Is entered and managed on the network
  - Attribute 3: Effectively exchanges information

The most recent JCIDS Manual dated 12 February 2015 added a Certification Guide for the Net-Ready KPP (NR KPP) and expanded the Content Guide for the NR KPP with the majority of the content from CJCSI 6212.01F. Remaining content from CJCSI 6212.01F related to roles and responsibilities is consolidated into CJCSI 5123.01G.

CH 6–3.8.2 Interface Design and Management

One of the most challenging aspect of IT system development in DoD deals with system interfaces. In a net-centric environment, the shift is to a "many-to-many" exchange of data, enabling many users and applications to leverage the same data-extending beyond the previous focus on standardized, predefined, point-to-point interfaces. Hence, the objectives are to ensure that all data are visible, available, and usable-when needed and where needed-to accelerate decision cycles. Many-to-many exchanges of data occur between systems, through interfaces that are sometimes predefined or sometimes unanticipated. Metadata is available to allow mediation or translation of data between interfaces, as needed.

PMs should have written agreements with any interface partners (i.e., such as between DFAS-DLA, or between the Air Force and DFAS) which indicate the agreement made and requirements documented for the subject program and those programs necessary for information support.

Typically, these interface dependencies will be documented in Information Support Plans (ISPs) for both System A (the information recipient) and System B (the information provider) though could be documented differently depending on the program's document tailoring strategy. More information on the interface management process is located in CH 4 Section 4.1.8.

CH 6–3.8.3 Modeling & Simulation

DoD Directive 8000.01 encourages pilots, modeling and simulation (M&S), experimentation, and prototype projects, appropriately sized to achieve desired objectives, and not be used in lieu of testing or acquisition processes to implement the production version of the information solution. This concept equally applies to IT systems, which may pilot and prototype differently than weapons systems but may find it just as beneficial.

M&S tools can be used by multiple functional area disciplines during all life-cycle phases. Modeling is essential to aid in understanding complex systems and system interdependencies, and to communicate among team members and stakeholders. Simulation provides a means to explore concepts, system characteristics, and alternatives; open up the trade space; facilitate informed decisions and assess overall system performance.

The Director, Systems Analysis within the Office of the Deputy Assistant Secretary of Defense for Systems Engineering guides the M&S community. More detailed M&S procedures are described in detail in CH 3 Section 2.4.2. Another resource is the DoD Modeling and Simulation Coordination Office, or M&SCO. M&S specific to test and evaluation is located in CH 8 Section 3.7.7.

CH 6–3.9 Enterprise Services
The Department of Defense is rapidly moving to a multi-provider Enterprise Cloud Environment to deliver the most innovative, efficient, and secure information and IT services in support of the Department's mission, anywhere, anytime, on any authorized device. The DoD CIO is accelerating and synchronizing efforts that create enterprise-wide capabilities and Enterprise Services while eliminating the unnecessary duplication of capabilities.

CH 6–3.9.1 Joint Information Environment
DoD, through the CIO's Strategy for Implementing the Joint Information Environment (JIE) is transitioning to a single, joint, secure, reliable and agile command, control, communications and computing (C4) enterprise information environment.

The JIE is a construct that facilitates the convergence of the DoD's multiple networks into one common and shared global network. The intent is to provide enterprise services such as email, Internet/Web access, common software applications, and cloud computing. Primary objectives behind this transition are increased operational efficiency, enhanced network security and cost savings through reduced infrastructure and manpower.

The JIE is a fundamental shift in the way the DoD will consolidate and manage IT infrastructure, services, and assets in order to realign, restructure, and modernize how the Department's IT networks and systems are constructed, operated, and defended. JIE will consolidate and standardize the design and architecture of the Department's networks. The JIE represents the DoD migration from military service-centric IT infrastructures and capabilities, with their mixture of disparate networks and applications, to enterprise capabilities based on common infrastructure and shared services to support Joint needs. These needs include networks, security services, cyber defenses, data centers, and operation management centers. Consolidation and standardization will result in a single, reliable, resilient, and agile information enterprise for use by the joint forces and mission partners. The key attributes of the JIE include:

- Shared JIE technology infrastructure: a network that is defendable and virtually accessible from any location globally, strategic to tactical locations; DoD level consolidation of data centers and network operations centers; a single security architecture; and the use of enterprise services.
- The JIE infrastructure will look, feel and operate by common standards regardless of service provider and/or use (i.e., mission specific utilization) and will apply common tactics, techniques and procedures developed at the enterprise level.
- Capabilities required across DoD to enable information sharing, collaboration and interoperability will be provisioned as enterprise services. Email, Web access, mass data storage and data analytics for decision support will be provided to any access point.
- The JIE effort does not preclude the Navy, for example, or any other Service from becoming a service provider for one or more designated enterprise services or infrastructure capabilities. As such, the Navy could be called upon to support the provisioning of enterprise service(s) for the entire DoD.
- Services and Agencies are beginning to adopt JIE standards for existing programs of record and adapt to JIE standards and requirements in future IT modernization.
- Services and Components that operate and maintain portions of the shared IT infrastructure (i.e., switches, servers, routers, etc.) will do so in accordance with the appropriate IT Technical

Authority through the Joint Information Environment Technical Synchronization Office (led by the Defense Information Systems Agency), and with operational direction provided by U.S. Cyber Command.

CH 6–3.9.1.1 Joint Regional Security Stacks (JRSS)

DISA's joint regional security stacks (JRSS) represents a single security architecture; it constitutes a suite of equipment that performs firewall functions, intrusion detection and prevention, enterprise management, virtual routing and forwarding (VRF), and provides a host of network security capabilities. JRSS is a cornerstone of JIE implementation and part of a larger modernization effort to upgrade the bandwidth capacity of the Defense Information Systems Network (DISN). Installation is in progress at ten of the eleven JRSS sites planned in the continental United States (CONUS) and five sites planned outside CONUS (OCONUS). JRSS familiarization training is available through DISA. The benefits for PMs and other implementers of IT are as follows:

- JRSS offers increased visualization into the network. Deploying JRSS enables the department to inspect data, retrieve threat and malware data on the network and troubleshoot, and then patch, protect, and defend the network.
- JRSS will improve the effectiveness and efficiency of the network by ensuring that there is sufficient capacity to support the transition of services and capabilities from being hosted locally by the military departments.
- JRSS will support the concepts of the JIE and specifically will reduce duplication of security standards.

CH 6–3.9.2 Cloud Computing

In its simplest sense, cloud computing is the delivery of IT as a service. Instead of purchasing an IT system and all its necessary peripherals that is maintained on premise, by utilizing cloud computing, an organization can acquire an IT capability or set of capabilities (aka Cloud Service Offerings (CSOs)) that are accessed from a network. The IT needed to create, store, and deliver the capability is maintained off-site by Cloud Service Providers (CSPs). Cloud computing services can deliver more efficient IT than traditional acquisition approaches. Organizations pay for the IT capability or service based on the amount of usage. A formal definition is provided in the National Institute of Standards and Technology (NIST) Definition of Cloud Computing Special Publication 800-145:

"Cloud computing is a model for enabling ubiquitous, convenient, on-demand network access to a shared pool of configurable computing resources (e.g., networks, servers, storage, applications, and services) that can be rapidly provisioned and released with minimal management effort or service provider interaction."

As applications and capabilities are moved to the Cloud, DoD PMs will select CSOs that are offered in one of three Service Models and four Deployment Models:

Service Models:

- Infrastructure as a Service (IaaS): Processing, storage, networks, and other fundamental computing resources. Purchaser generally still has control over operating systems, storage, and deployed applications; and possibly limited control of select networking components (e.g., host firewalls).
- Platform as a Service (PaaS): Applications created using programming languages, libraries, services, and tools supported by the CSP. (This capability does not necessarily preclude the use of compatible programming languages, libraries, services, and tools from other sources.) The purchaser does not manage or control the underlying cloud infrastructure including network, servers, operating systems, or storage, but has control over the deployed applications and possibly configuration settings for the application-hosting environment.
- Software as a Service (SaaS): Applications running on a cloud infrastructure. The applications are accessible from various client devices through either a thin client interface, such as a web browser (e.g., web-based email), or a program interface. The purchaser does

not manage or control the underlying cloud infrastructure including network, servers, operating systems, storage, or even individual application capabilities, with the possible exception of limited user-specific application configuration settings.

Deployment Models:

- Public cloud infrastructures operate in a multi-tenant environment whose resources are allocated for the general public. Public clouds tend to be large and provide economies of scale for their customers. However, security and privacy concerns are heightened because any individual or organization can potentially access the same cloud infrastructure.
- Private cloud infrastructures are operated only for an individual organization. The organization can leverage the scalability and performance aspects of cloud computing, but the infrastructure is isolated from that of other organizations, improving security and privacy. Because of their specialized nature, private clouds can be just as costly as dedicated data centers.
- Community cloud infrastructures are private clouds provisioned for a specific community of interest with shared concerns, such as a government-only cloud.
- Hybrid cloud infrastructures are combinations of any two or more of the other cloud infrastructures.

Figure 6 compares these three models to the traditional (on premise) data center model, where DoD provides all of the infrastructure components.

Figure 6: Cloud Computing Services Models Overview and Responsibilities

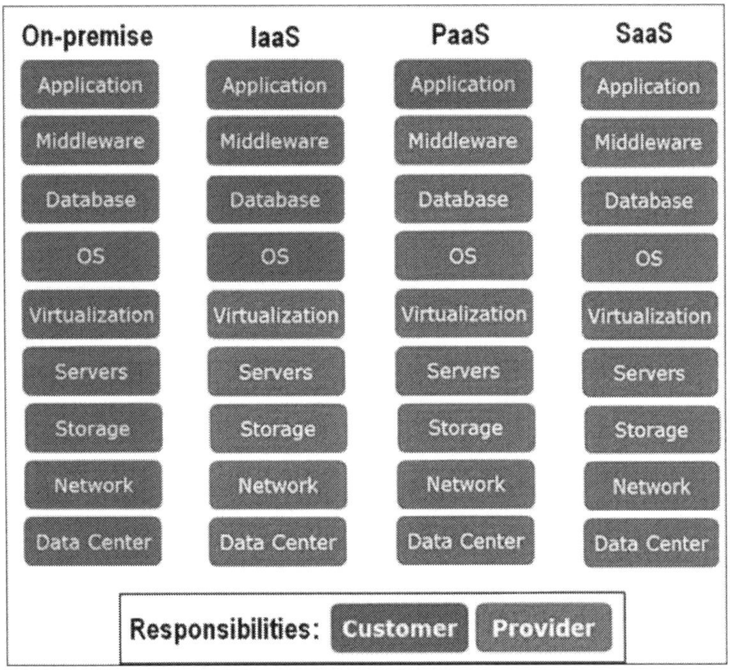

CH 6–3.9.2.1 Interpreting Cloud Policy and Guidance

The DoD CIO, through a December 15, 2014 memorandum, enumerates DoD Component responsibilities when acquiring commercial cloud services to include the following:

- Provide an analysis of the cloud services requested using the DoD CIO IT Business Case Analysis (BCA) template as a guide;
- Consider DISA provided cloud services as an alternative in the BCA; and
- Have the approval of the Component CIO; provide a copy of the BCA to the DoD CIO.

DoD PMs should make and document a "cloud-or-not-cloud" determination as part of the IT BCA process using the following information as a guide:

- On Demand Self-service: The CSP may provision the CSO without human interaction;
- Broad Network Access: The CSO is available to a variety of devices over a wide range of networks using standard protocols;
- Resource Pooling: The CSP's computing infrastructure may be provisioned and shared among multiple tenants without their knowledge;
- Rapid Elasticity: The CSO has the ability to expand and contract to meet the demands of the customer's application.
- Measured Service: The CSP has the ability to meter the resource usage with enough detail to support customer requirements.

Additional cloud policy and guidance that you must follow when acquiring and implementing cloud services include:

DoD Cloud Computing Security Requirements Guide (CC SRG): was built upon the DoD Instruction 8510.01, Risk Management Framework (RMF) for DoD Information Technology to integrate with the DoD RMF Authorization Process and Office of Management and Budget (OMB) policy regarding federal government use of cloud computing.

The CC SRG is an essential guide to identify the cybersecurity controls and information impact levels (IILs) for hosting DoD missions in CSOs up to and including SECRET, based on the type of data to be hosted in the CSO. The CC SRG establishes the baseline security requirements for DoD PMs and their Authorizing Officials (AOs) and must be followed when contracting for and implementing systems and applications using DoD and non-DoD CSOs regardless of service or deployment models. The CC SRG also identifies the roles and responsibilities that DoD Mission Owners, PMs, CSPs, and the DoD PM's Cybersecurity Service Provider (CSSP) play in operating and securing cloud hosted systems. DoD PMs that offer DoD owned and operated cloud services are subject to the same regulations as all DoD information systems, and must comply with the DoD CC SRG.

Defense Information Systems Agency (DISA) as the Department's Risk Management Executive, uses the CC SRG to oversee the required DoD cybersecurity assessment of a CSP's CSO that results in the issuance of a DoD Provisional Authorization (DoD PA). The DoD PA is an assessment indicating that the CSO is potentially suitable for use up to an indicated impact level as defined within the CC SRG. The latest version of the CC SRG can always be found here.

DFARS Subpart 239.7 – Cloud Computing implements policy developed within the DoD CIO and the CC SRG for the acquisition of cloud computing services. The provision, 252.239-7009, "Representation of Use of Cloud Computing," must be used in solicitations for information technology services. This allows the offeror to represent their intention to utilize cloud computing services in performance of the contract or not. The clause 252.239-7010, "Cloud Computing Services," must be used in solicitations and contracts for information technology services. This provides standard contract language for the acquisition of cloud computing services, including access, security, and reporting requirements.

The DFARS states, that the contracting officer should only award a contract to acquire cloud computing services from any CSP (e.g., contractor or subcontractor, regardless of tier) that has been granted a DoD PA with two exceptions: (a) DoD CIO waiver the requirement or (b) CSO is hosted in a DoD facility and has DoD PA prior to operational use.

DoD PMs must provide the Contracting Officer all detailed requirements associated with this clause and others that need to be included in the purchase request when contracting for CSOs.

CH 6–3.9.2.2 Cloud Service Acquisition Process Steps

There are four major inter-related steps to follow when acquiring cloud services for the DoD.

Step 1: Determine Appropriate Information Impact Levels and Categorize Mission and Data Risk.
When acquiring cloud services, DoD PMs need to consider both the impact of data loss/compromise (security) and the priority of the service relative to the primary mission of the DoD (Mission Impact). The focus is on the CSO not the provider of the service who may offer services that are eligible at different information impact levels. The following provides a summary of the four information impact levels defined in the CC Security Requirements Guide (SRG) coupled with some of the distinguishing requirements and characteristics:

- **Level 2**. The system processes DoD information that has been cleared for public release; information that has been released through the Freedom of Information Act (FOIA); and information available to the public even if it requires a login. Level 2 applies to non- NSS only.
- **Level 4**. The system processes DoD Controlled Unclassified Information (CUI) (i.e., For Official Use Only (FOUO), Moderate and Sensitive Personally Identifiable Information (PII) (i.e., social security numbers, alien ID and other immigration documents, passport numbers, driver's license numbers, vehicle identification numbers, and license plates), Non-Appropriated Fund (NAF) data, and other non-CUI mission critical systems that are not NSS systems.
- **Level 5.** The system processes CUI requiring higher protection, mission essential, critical infrastructure (military or civilian), deployment and troop movement, International Traffic in Arms Regulation (ITAR) data, or unclassified nuclear data. It also includes highly sensitive PII which could include Protected Health Information (PHI), law enforcement, and other data that contains sexual assault information.
- **Level 6.** Level 6 accommodates information that has been determined: (i) pursuant to Executive Order 12958 as amended by Executive Order 13292, or any predecessor Order, to be classified national security information; or (ii) pursuant to the Atomic Energy Act of 1954, as amended, to be Restricted Data (RD). Only information classified as SECRET, in accordance with the applicable executive orders, is applicable to this level.

Step 2: Identify Approved CSOs and Roles and Responsibilities.

Once the DoD PM and their AO determines what types of cloud services are to be acquired (IaaS, PaaS, or SaaS) and the Information Impact Level the CSP needs to support, the appropriate cloud service alternatives can be evaluated and the required IT BCA can be performed. DoD PMs then select CSOs based on their security posture and the risk tolerance of the PM and their AO. The PM should identify existing approved CSOs that have a current PA from DISA by referring to the DoD Cloud Catalog (CAC required to access) maintained by DISA.

Moving to the cloud underscores the need for PMs to understand the distinction between what is and is not provided and addressed by the CSP. DoD PMs need to clearly identify roles and responsibilities as they will vary depending on the service model as illustrated in Figure 6 above. Therefore, a fundamental consideration for DoD PMs should be determining the appropriate contractual relationships between all parties to ensure that mission capabilities can be met from a holistic systems view.

Step 3: Ensure Cyber Defense.

DoD PMs that acquire or use cloud services remain responsible for ensuring end-to-end security and protection of their system/application IAW the CC SRG. As the DoD strives to maximize the use of commercial cloud computing, the DoD Information Network (DODIN) perimeter must continue to be protected against cyber threats from external connections.

CSOs hosting IIL 4/5 must be connected to the DODIN through a CAP or other boundary defense mechanism that has been approved by DoD CIO. CSOs hosting IIL 2 will connect through the Internet. DoD PMs and their AOs must ensure that prior to transitioning to a CSO, a supporting Cyber Defense

Service Provider (CSSP) has been identified and confirmed; and the required monitoring capabilities must be functional prior to operational use.

Step 4: Cloud Service Registration and Reporting

DoD PMs must report their cloud computing activities as follows:

- **Registration in DISA System Network Approval Process (SNAP):** DoD PMs must register all CSOs that they plan on acquiring or are using, regardless of IIL or the network connection or CAP requirement, in the DISA's SNAP system in the Mission Owner (Cloud IT Project) Module. (NOTE: registration is required, see instructions on the SNAP website for details).
- **Registration in DITPR:** DoD PMs must register use of the CSP's CSO in the DoD Information Portfolio Registry (DITPR).
- **Investment Reporting via SNaP-IT:** Program Managers must analyze cloud computing options and report cloud service funding investments during the course of DoD budget and acquisition processes for each CSO as follows:
  - Ensure that an investment line item has been created in Select and Native Programming Data Input System – Information Technology (SNaP-IT) for each investment in a CSO;
  - Report all funding related to cloud computing by Deployment Model and Service Model for the Prior Year, Current Year and Budget Year.

CH 6–3.9.2.3 Contracting for Cloud Services

Contracting for commercial CSOs brings additional risks and concerns that could adversely affect the mission but may not be apparent and are not typically addressed in traditional contracting best practices. For example, typical vendor contract terms and conditions may not be detailed enough concerning items that are expected to be encountered once operations and services begin, i.e., operations, maintenance, and the cybersecurity of the DoD system residing in the CSO. Other concerns include ensuring that the Inspector General and Law Enforcement are able to perform their responsibilities. Each DoD PM should coordinate with their legal counsel, privacy, and procurement offices when they move IT services to the commercial cloud, and ensure compliance with Federal Records Management, and other OMB and DoD requirements.

Identifying and determining risk is an integral factor in cloud contracting decisions. Cybersecurity (relative to cloud) is concerned with risks to the DODIN (CSO/DODIN risks) and risks specific to a mission and its data (CSO/mission risk). The CC SRG is the primary source governing the selection, accreditation, and ongoing accreditation and use of cloud services within the DoD. Although the CC SRG is quite comprehensive, the DoD PM must take the time to comprehend it in order to determine if additional requirements need to be reflected in the SLA or contract.

Initial decisions regarding CSO/DODIN risk are normally made through the DoD PA assessment and authorization process. Ongoing adherence to the CC SRG is periodically reviewed and the CSO's network behavior is being continuously monitored in order to identify if there is an increase in CSO/DODIN risk; the DoD PA and/or access to the CSO may be terminated depending on the severity of risk.

Initial decisions regarding CSO/mission risk are made through the mission owner's agency ATO process. Remember, a CSO with a DoD PA does not eliminate the requirement for a given application using the CSO to have an ATO (or IATT) prior to commencing operations. For example, prior to contract award the AO should review DoD PA artifacts to understand the risks that the mission may inherit and request that compensating controls be implemented by the CSP prior to obtaining an ATO. The compensating controls must be reflected in the SLA/contract as well as processes to assure they remain valid.

Therefore, it is essential that DoD PMs determine exactly what they are responsible for as well as the roles and responsibilities of all other stakeholders that may include the CSP, the Contractor if not the CSP, Sub-contractor, an outsourced 3rd party integrator or CSP, cybersecurity personnel, or other entities. DoD PMs must fully understand, describe and negotiate their key expectations and ensure that they are specifically addressed in the contract/Task Order (TO), Acquisition Plan, Contract Performance Work Statement (PWS) or SLA for cloud computing contracts.

PMs and appropriate staff should become familiar with the DFARS Subpart 239.76 (Cloud Computing), and the associated DFARS 252.239-7009 Provision and DFARS 252.239-7010 Clause, the supporting Procedures, Guidance and Instructions (PGI) 239.76 – Cloud Computing and the CC SRG.

Table 5, "Information and/or actions required for DoD PMs" should be read in conjunction with the DFARS subpart, provision and clause, PGIs and the CC SRG. It identifies the specific information and/or requirements the PM needs to provide the Contracting Officer (CO) to enable the CO to execute a contract that protects DoD equities and minimizes risk. In addition, activities that require PM coordination and risk assessment decisions with the PM's AO or other DoD entities are identified.

Table 5: Information and/or actions required for DoD PMs

Description	Information and/or actions required for DoD PMs
General Procedures for Cloud Services	• Determine Information Impact Level (IIL) as detailed in the CC SRG. • Provide written justification as needed by CO.
Government Data & Government-Related Data	• Identify, document, and provide CO with unambiguous descriptions and formats of Government data and Government-related data need to enforce all terms in clause where, "Government data and Government-related data" are referenced in DFARS 252.239-7010. • These descriptions and formats of Government data and Government-related will be required by CO.
Security Requirements – Change in Representation DFARS 252.239-7010 (b) (1)	• Post contract award; if the contractor notifies the CO of a change in DFARS Provision 252.239-7009 then, it is likely that the entire approach will require reevaluation. • In collaboration with AO, reevaluate the proposed approach and determine if the change is acceptable. • Provide written notice and/or justification to support approval or disapproval decision to CO.
Security Requirements – Waiver DFARS 252.239-7010 (b) (2)	• Collaborate with AO and DoD CIO to determine and document what specific requirements of the CC SRG may/have been waived. • Provide CO with necessary documentation needed to specify extent and conditions of the DoD CIO waiver.
Location of Data – DFARS 252.239-7010 (b) (3)	• Collaborate with AO to determine (only for Level 2 or Level 4 data) if it is permitted to maintain Government data at a location outside the 50 States, the District of Columbia, and outlying areas of the United States. • Provide written justification as needed by CO.
Limitations on Access, Use and Disclosure DFARS 252.239-7010 (c) (1)	• Collaborate with AO to review and determine and unambiguously document if any access to or use of Government Data or Government-related Data requested or specified by contractor is permissible and if so under what limitations and/or conditions. • Provide CO with documentation authorizing access.

Description	Information and/or actions required for DoD PMs
Cyber Incident Reporting DFARS 252.239-7010 (d)	• Identify a Government point of contract (POC) for CO to contact if a cyber-incident occurs in connection with the cloud computing services being provided. **If a cyber-incident occurs:** • Procedures should be developed (to include, Mission Owner, Cybersecurity Service Provider (CSSP), and Contractor) to collect, preserve and protect Incident Information; these processes will vary depending on service model (IaaS, PaaS and SaaS). • With the AO, CSSP, and the Contractor, assess and determine the potential impact of the cyber incident and response.
Malicious Software DFARS 252.239-7010 (e)	• Collaborate with AO and other DoD entities to produce detailed instructions on submitting malicious software that was/may-have-been discovered in connection with a reportable cyber incident. • Provide the CO with the specific instructions produced.
Cyber Incident – **Requesting Media and Data** DFARS 252.239-7010 (f)	• Collaborate with AO and other DoD entities to determine if the media that was preserved and/or the data that was collected (when a cyber-incident was discovered) are required by the DoD. • If required, instruct CO to request media and data from the contactor
Cyber Incident – **Access to Information or** **Equipment** DFARS 252.239-7010 (g)	• Collaborate with AO and other DoD entities to determine if access to additional information or equipment is needed to conduct forensic analysis. • If needed, instruct CO to request access to additional information and/or equipment.
Cyber Incident – **Damage Assessment** DFARS 252.239-7010 (h)	• Collaborate with AO and other DoD entities to determine if damage assessment is required. • If damage assessment is required, inform CO to request damage assessment information from contractor. • Upon completion of damage assessment activities, provide the CO with a report documenting all findings that will be included in the contract files.
Records Management and **Facility Access** DFARS 252.239-7010 (i)	• When acquiring SaaS, provide a records retention schedule to the CO to be incorporated in the contract that includes, but is not limited to, secure storage, ability to retrieve, and proper disposition of all federal records. • When acquiring IaaS/PaaS, maintain a copy of the Contractor's and/or CSP's records retention policies for Government related data.
Records Management – **Format of Data** DFARS 252.239-7010 (i) (1)	• Collaborate with AO and all other related DoD stakeholders to provide the CO with unambiguous description of formats of Government data and Government-related data needed to enforce the terms in clause.
Records Management – **Contract Closeout** DFARS 252.239-7010 (i) (2)	• Collaborate with AO and, if necessary, the Component Records Management Officer (CMRO), to determine how Government Data and Government-related data is to be handled during contract closeout. • Provide CO with unambiguous description of how contractor is to transfer, retain, or dispose and confirm disposal of Government Data and Government-related data as part of contract closeout needed to enforce the terms in clause.

Description	Information and/or actions required for DoD PMs
Records Management – **Required Accesses to …** DFARS 252.239-7010 (i) (3)	• Collaborate with AO and all other stakeholder DoD entities to identify and ensure that all Government or its authorized representatives have determined and documented what physical, system, and/or system-wide accesses and response timeframes the contractor will need to provide in order to support their lawful activities. • Provide CO with unambiguous description of all accesses and timeframes required in the contract/SLA.
Notification Of Third Party **Access Requests** DFARS 252.239-7010 (j)	• Identify the government point of contact (POC) responsible for coordinating the response to any subpoena or other third party access received by the contractor providing the cloud service. • Provide CO with the government POC. **If third party access request is received:** • Coordinate the response with the DoD mission or data owner.
Spillage DFARS 252.239-7010 (k)	• Identify the contractor POC and government POC to contact if any spillage occurs regarding the cloud service being provided. • Provide CO with the POCs and procedures needed to enforce the terms in clause. • Ensure that agency procedures for addressing a spillage are documented. **If spillage occurs:** • Follow agency procedures.
Subcontracts DFARS 252.239-7010 (l)	• Provide CO with requirements related to flow down when contracting for PaaS or SaaS which leverages an IaaS or PaaS from a third party CSP
Contractor Terms And **Conditions - Terms Of** **Service (ToS)** Subpart 239.7601-1 (a)	• Collaborate with AO to review contractor's Terms of Service and produce document detailing where they may be found to impede or conflict with mission and cyber security requirements. • Provide CO with the document to ensure conflicts are resolved as part of the other processes the CO needs to perform in order to meet the intent of this Subpart.
Inspection, Audit, **Investigation Support** Subpart 239.7601-1 (c) (3)	• Provide CO with requirements to support authorized activities regarding Government Data or Government-related Data, or CSO service model.
Inspection, Audit, **Investigation Search &** **Access** Subpart 239.7601-1 (c) (4)	• Provide CO with requirements to support and cooperate with authorized activities' system-wide search and access.

Description	Information and/or actions required for DoD PMs
Other Consideration – Cybersecurity Compliance CC – SRG	<ul><li>Collaborate with AO to ensure that cybersecurity requirements or processes not otherwise addressed in the CC SRG and DoD PA assessment are documented. DoD PMs must ensure that issues identified throughout the life of the contract that may adversely impact CSO/mission risk, and thereby jeopardize the validity of the ATO, are addressed in the contract/SLA. For example, if DISA discovers that the CSP is not meeting on-going security requirements they will notify affected Mission Owners/PMs and work with the CSP to develop a corrective Plan of Actions and Milestones (POA& M).</li><li>Review DISA's assessment of the Contractor's corrective POA&M.</li><li>Collaborate with AO to make a risk determination with regard to their specific usage of the CSO and ATO.</li><li>Collaborate with AO and CO to determine if contracting action to incorporate the CSP's POA&M is needed; annotate contract files as needed.</li></ul>
Change In CSP Ownership CC – SRG	<ul><li>Collaborate with AO to determine how to address the impact of a change of ownership of the CSP. If such change necessitates off-boarding and retrieval of information/data, produce document that describes how the Contractor is to transfer, retain, or dispose and confirm disposal of Government Data and Government-related data.</li><li>Provide CO with the document so that off-boarding processes can be reflected in the contract/SLA.</li></ul>
Disaster recovery (DR) and Continuity of Operations (COOP)	<ul><li>As a best business practice, require that the Contractor (CSP or third party) plans for Disaster Recovery (DR) and Continuity of Operations (COOP) and implement their infrastructures to support it</li></ul>
Exit Process	<ul><li>Provide CO with unambiguous document describing how contractor is to transfer, retain, or dispose and confirm disposal of Government Data and Government-related data and/or migrate applications upon completion or termination of the contract.</li><li>Provide CO with the document so that close-out processes can be reflected in the contract/SLA.</li></ul>

In addition to the specific information and/or activities previously identified that DoD PMs need to provide, there are other considerations that could adversely affect the mission. Table 6, "Contracting Considerations for DoD PMs" details areas that should be included in any risk calculus, as well as the cost/benefit tradeoffs and risk analysis that have been identified by developing the business case analysis.

Table 6: Contracting Considerations for DoD PMs

Description	Contracting Considerations for DoD PMs
Banner	<ul><li>Banner language provides consent for the Department to view any content on the system without a warrant</li><li>When acquiring software as a service, consider requiring the CSP to display DoD's approved banner language prior to allowing a user access to the system</li></ul>

Description	Contracting Considerations for DoD PMs
Direct Contractual Relationship	• Contractual liability to the government only exists with the prime contractor. When the DoD PM acquires a commercial service through an intermediary (e.g., system integrator, value added reseller), only the intermediary is accountable to the government. This reduces the contractual liability to the CSP acting as the subcontractor, but increases the risks to the government.
Exit Strategy and Plan	• Consider developing an interoperable strategy to move systems/applications from one CSP to another
Indemnification	• Consider requiring the CSP to indemnify the government against lawsuits; this protects the government when third parties sue the government for a tort when the CSP, not the government, was liable.
Insurance	• Consider requiring a CSP to use insurance services to pay for any costs stemming from a breach of DoD data (e.g., PII or PHI) or to replace any damages to the DoD system, including credit monitoring
Ownership Rights	• Consider if any third party will own any aspects of assets that are applied for service provisioning
Training	• Consider whether a training and change management program might be needed to optimize implementation of security and cyber defense changes

SLAs

DoD PMs should negotiate required service levels and expected performance with a key objective to reduce areas of potential conflict. Responsibilities and the appropriate support levels to meet requirements related to operations and maintenance of the environment, system management and administration services, logistics, performance, reliability/back-ups and disaster recovery functions should be clearly defined. DoD PMs should identify appropriate specific service level requirements and performance expected from a provider, how that performance will be measured, and what enforcement mechanisms will be used to ensure the specified performance levels are achieved in a SLA.

Table 7, "Requirements to be incorporated into SLAs" identifies the key requirements to be incorporated in DoD Cloud Contract SLAs, to help ensure the Contractor (and the CSP) meet the DoD's contract objectives and CSOs perform effectively, efficiently, and securely:

Table 7: Requirements to be incorporated in SLAs

DESCRIPTION	Requirements to be incorporated in SLAs
Roles And Responsibilities	Define roles and responsibilities for the DoD, CSP, Contractor, Sub-contractor, 3rd party integrator or others to include: • PMs, PM's System Administrators • NetOPS/Tier 2 & 3 support • PM's Cybersecurity (CS) entities, Cybersecurity Service Providers (CSSPs- Mission & Boundary CS) • CSPs CS entities, Trusted Internet Connection (TIC) support • CSP's or Contractor Audit or Forensic support • Contractor's Operations and Maintenance support

DESCRIPTION	Requirements to be incorporated in SLAs
Definitions/Terms	Provide a glossary of the key terms to supplement DFARS and CC SRG definitions to include continuity, outage, emergency, planned outage, unplanned outage, high availability, recovery, breach of service agreement, and other terms related to service performance and service reliability
Dates	Identify the dates when the contract/SLA is active or when measurement of the SLA will begin
Accessibility	Provide a list of the accessibility standards, policies and regulations that must be met by the service
Availability	Identify availability requirements, e.g. percentage of time that the system or data will be available and usable
Data Location	Data location – list the geographic locations that data may be processed and stored, and if the Government can specify location requests
Data Examination	If the Government data is co-located with non-Government data, identify: • how the Contractor, and the CSP if not the Prime Contractor, will isolate the Government data into an environment where it may be reviewed, scanned, or forensically evaluated in a secure space • How access will be limited to authorized Government personnel identified by the CO, and without the Contractor's involvement
Records Management	Records management – How and when the Contractor will retain or dispose of DoD records in the format specified as directed by the Contracting Officer
Protection Of Personally Identifiable Information (PII) And Personal Health Information (PHI)	• Protection of Personally Identifiable Information (PII) is covered in the CC SRG. However, the table, *"Privacy Overlay C/CE Not Included in FedRAMP M or FedRAMP+"* identifies PII/PHI requirements that are not covered in the current DoD PA assessment. • In collaboration with the AO, define and produce document with requirements for the identified PII/PHI controls associated with: Access Control, Audit and Accountability, Security Assessment and Authorization; System Interconnections – Enhancement, Configuration Management, Incident Response, Media Protection, Personnel Screening, Risk Evaluations, System and Communications Protection, etc. • Provide CO with the document so that additional requirements can be reflected in the SLAs or contracts.
Information Security; Security Performance To Include: Data Protection, Continuous Monitoring / Vulnerability Management, Incidence Response	The DoD PA does not assess certain security controls/control enhancements (C/CEs) that are identified in the CC SRG (e.g. availability of information related to continuous monitoring, incident response, vulnerability management, etc.). • Define and produce document describing responsibilities associated with the identified C/CEs for Access Control, Audit and Accountability, Device Identification and Authentication Enhancement and System and Communications Protection. • Provide CO with the document so that identified responsibilities can be reflected in the SLAs or contracts.

DESCRIPTION	Requirements to be incorporated in SLAs
Service Performance **To include: Capacity, Elasticity, Service Monitoring, Exception Criteria, Response Time**	Identify Service performance measures with all responsible parties including those that are responsible for measuring performance. These should include capacity and capability of the CSO, elasticity, service monitoring, exception criteria, response time Additional system quality measures for service performance include accuracy, portability, interoperability, standards compliance, reliability, scalability, agility, fault tolerance, serviceability, usability, durability, etc.
Service Reliability **To include: Resilience / Fault Tolerance, Backup & Restoration, Continuity of Ops**	How Service reliability measures with all responsible parties are performed differs between IaaS, PaaS and SaaS services provided. As appropriate to the cloud service model, specify requirements for service resilience, preservation, protection, and secure back up of all audit trails and transaction logs of the system/network operations For SaaS providers, specify requirements for continuity of operations, and management of outages
Attestation, Certification, & Audits	Identify attestation and certification requirements to include FedRAMP Authorizations, DoD PA, and all requirements to comply with DoD policies
Exit Strategy	Identify exit details/procedures for ensuring continuity with minimal disruption in the case of exit/termination of service when catastrophe or failure to perform/early termination, or completion of contract occur to include: • The level of Contractor assistance in the exit process and any associated fees • How and when the DoD data and networks will transition back to the DoD • How the data will be transmitted and completely removed from the Contractor's environment once the exit process is complete.
Penalties	Identify a range of enforceable penalties and remedies, such as termination, for non-compliance with SLA performance measures. These penalties may be already included in FAR and DFAR standard clauses (i.e., Charge back approaches for unexcused performance failures)

CH 6–3.10 Protecting Information Technology

The Department released its Cybersecurity Strategy on April 17, 2015. It identifies the DoD's three primary cyber missions.

- The DoD must defend its own networks, systems, and information
- DoD must be prepared to defend the United States and its interests against cyberattacks of significant consequence.
- Third, if directed by the President or the Secretary of Defense, DoD must be able to provide integrated cyber capabilities to support military operations and contingency plans.

The DoD's networks and systems are vulnerable to intrusions and attacks, and it is critical to develop and implement strong cybersecurity and program protection strategies and plans.

CH 6–3.10.1 Cybersecurity

Cybersecurity risk management tasks should begin early in the system development life cycle and are important in shaping the security capabilities of the system. If not effectively performed early, the tasks, undertaken later in the lifecycle, will be more costly and time consuming to implement, and could negatively impact the performance of the system and its overall cybersecurity.

There are two general categories of cybersecurity operations – defensive and offensive.

- Defensive Cybersecurity. The protection of information against unauthorized disclosure, transfer, modification, or destruction, whether accidental or intentional.
- Offensive Cyber Operations. Joint Publication 3-12 (R) defines Offensive Cyberspace Operations as "Cyberspace operations intended to project power by the application of force in or through cyberspace. However, for SNaP-IT and OMB taxonomy purpose, Offensive Cyberspace Operations are activities that actively gather information, manipulate, disrupt, deny, degrade, or destroy adversary computer information systems, information, or networks through cyberspace.

All acquisitions of systems containing IT, including NSS, must produce a Cybersecurity Strategy. Beginning at Milestone A, PMs will submit the Cybersecurity Strategy to the cognizant CIO for review and approval prior to milestone decisions or RFP release per Enclosure 1, Table 2 of the DoDI 5000.02. The Cybersecurity Strategy is attached as an appendix to the Program Protection Plan (PPP) for submittal. More information on the Cybersecurity Strategy is located in CH 8 Section 3.5.7.

CH 6–3.10.1.1 Responsibility

Cybersecurity is both a functional and acquisition responsibility due to its criticality. Both PMs and Functional Sponsors or Managers should be familiar with statutory and regulatory requirements governing cybersecurity, and understand the major tasks involved in developing an cybersecurity organization, defining cybersecurity requirements, incorporating cybersecurity in a program's architecture, developing a Cybersecurity Strategy, conducting appropriate cybersecurity testing, and achieving cybersecurity certification and accreditation for the program.

DoD recently revised several of its policies to more explicitly address the integration of cybersecurity into acquisition processes:

- Department of Defense Instruction (DoDI) 8510.01, Risk Management Framework (RMF) for DoD Information Technology (IT), March 12, 2014; cancels the previous DoD Information Assurance Certification and Accreditation Process (DIACAP) and institutes a new, risk-based approach to cybersecurity through the Risk Management Framework
- DoDI 5000.02, Operation of the Defense Acquisition System, January 7, 2015; includes regulatory cybersecurity requirements such as the Cybersecurity Strategy artifact and risk management activities involving Authorizing Officials (AO)
- DoDI 8500.01, Cybersecurity, March 14, 2014; establishes that cybersecurity must be fully integrated into system life cycles

CH 6–3.10.2 Program Protection Planning

For the acquisition of software-intensive IT, especially IT used in National Security Systems, PMs should consider the significant operational threat posed by the intentional or inadvertent insertion of malicious code. The risks associated with these supply chain risk management (SCRM) issues are being managed within the context of program protection planning. CH 9 Section 2.3 regarding Program Protection Plan requirements as well as key practices and intelligence support from the Defense Intelligence Agency SCRM Treat Assessment Center (TAC).

For IT systems, areas of particular interest are protection and assurance activities undertaken during the integration and development of commercial off-the-shelf (COTS) components activities designed to mitigate attacks against the operational system (the fielded system); and activities that address threats to the development environment.

Additional information on program protection planning is provided in:

- The template and guide for the Program Protection Plan
- Guidance on Software Assurance Countermeasures
- CH 9 Section 2.2 Program Protection Policy and Guidance

CH 6–3.10.3 Risk Management Framework for IT

The RMF informs the entire acquisition process, beginning with requirements development and programs should be converting from the DoD Information Assurance Certification and Accreditation Process (DIACAP). A DIACAP and RMF knowledge portal (CAC required) is available in addition to a number of other resources:

- RMF Training Documents, April 4, 2014
- RMF Implementation, April 4, 2014
- Cybersecurity and RMF Implementation Training Video, May 8, 2014
- National Institute of Standards and Technology Special Publication 800-37, "Guide for Applying the Risk Management Framework to Federal Information Systems: A Security Life Cycle Approach," February 2010
- Program Manager's Guidebook for Integrating the Cybersecurity RMF into the System Lifecycle, September 2015
- CH 9 Section 3.2.2 Risk Management Framework for DoD IT

While the RMF and requirements and acquisition hierarchies are distinct, they share a common baseline of security system engineering documentation and coordination among decision authorities. Engagement between the cybersecurity and acquisition communities is critical to management of cybersecurity-related risks to system performance.

CH 6–3.10.3.1 Categorizing Information Technology for Security

DoD Instruction 8510.01, Risk Management Framework (RMF) for DoD Information Technology (IT) Enclosure 6 establishes the process to categorize IT, select security controls, implement those controls, assess the controls, achieve authorization of the system and monitor the security controls. In the categorization process, the PMs/ ISO identifies the potential impact (low, moderate, or high) resulting from loss of confidentiality, integrity, and availability if a security breach occurs. For acquisition programs, this categorization will be documented as a required capability in the initial capabilities document, the capability development document, the capabilities production document, and the cybersecurity strategy within the program protection plan (PPP).

CH 6–3.11 Test and Evaluation for Information Technology

On September 14, 2010, the Director, Operational Test and Evaluation, signed a memorandum entitled "Guidelines for Conducting Operational Test and Evaluation of Information and Business Systems." The guidelines help streamline and simplify COTS software testing procedures. They assist in tailoring pre-deployment test events to the operational risk of a specific system increment acquired under OSD oversight. For increments that are of insignificant to moderate risk, these guidelines streamline the operational test and evaluation process by potentially reducing the degree of testing. Simple questions characterize the risk and environment upon which to base test decisions, for example, "If the increment is primarily COTS, or government off-the-shelf items, what is the past performance and reliability?"

CH 8 describes various testing policies and practices.

CH 6–3.11.1 Prototyping and Piloting

Risk reduction prototypes will be included if they will materially reduce engineering and manufacturing development risk at an acceptable cost. Risk reduction prototypes can be at the system level or can focus on sub-systems or components.

The OSD office of Emerging Capability and Prototyping may be able to assist in guiding your prototyping activities.

- Proof-of-principle prototyping validates the technical feasibility of a capability and explores its operational value.
- Pre–engineering and manufacturing development prototyping advances capabilities that have already demonstrated some technical and operational promise.

Typically this type of activity is done on items that are not COTS; however, prototyping and piloting may still hold value in a tailored manner for information technology in the risk reduction phase in order to see real-time application of technology to down-select.

CH 6–3.11.2 Developmental Testing

Developmental Test & Evaluation (DT&E) is used to verify that the system under test meets all technical requirements. MDAP and MAIS ACAT I and IA programs are supported by a chief developmental tester and a governmental test agency that serves as the lead DT&E organization. The PM, who is ultimately responsible for all aspects of system development, selects a Chief Developmental Tester. The Chief Development Tester is a highly experienced T&E professional, authorized by the PM to conduct all duties in the area of T&E for the program. Inputs from the Chief Developmental Tester to the contract, engineering specifications, systems engineering efforts, budget, program schedule, etc., are essential if the PM is to manage T&E aspects of the program efficiently.

For IT programs, one of the most critical aspects of developmental test is to ensure an operationally-representative DT environment.

Additional guidance on developmental testing is available in the DoDI 5000.02 Enclosure 4 as well as CH 4 Section 3.3.2.2.

CH 6–3.11.3 Operational Testing

The appropriate operational test organization will conduct operational testing in a realistic threat environment. The threat environment will be based on the program's System Threat Assessment Report and appropriate scenarios. For MDAPs, MAIS programs, and other programs on the DOT&E Oversight List, the DOT&E will provide a report providing the opinion of the DOT&E as to whether the program is operationally effective, suitable, and survivable before the MDA makes a decision to proceed beyond LRIP. For programs on the DOT&E Oversight List, operational testing will be conducted in accordance with the approved TEMP and operational test plan. The Department's independent operational test agencies likely have guides or other training available on how to conduct operational testing, especially tailored to Service requirements. The Air Force Operational Test and Evaluation Center (AFOTEC), for example, has a detailed operational test guide available.

Additional guidance on operational testing is available in the DoDI 5000.02 Encl. 5 Sec 7 as well as CH 8 Section 3.2.

CH 6–3.11.4 Cybersecurity Test and Evaluation

Per the DOT&E Cybersecurity T&E Guidebook, "Potential cyber vulnerabilities, when combined with a determined and capable threat, pose a significant security problem for the DoD and its warfighters. Cybersecurity test and evaluation (T&E) assists in the development and fielding of more secure, resilient systems to address this problem." The Guidebook outlines steps for planning, analysis, and implementation of cybersecurity T&E. Fundamentally, cybersecurity T&E consists of iterative processes, starting at the initiation of an acquisition and continuing throughout the entire life cycle.

The critical piece of documentation is the Test and Evaluation Master Plan (TEMP). The RMF may also drive cybersecurity testing requirements.

Process

Develop a strategy and budget resources for cybersecurity testing. The test program will include, as much as possible, activities to test and evaluate a system in a mission environment with a representative cyber-threat capability. CH 8 Section 3.2.4 discusses survivability and cybersecurity testing as well.

- Beginning at Milestone A, the TEMP will document a strategy and resources for cybersecurity T&E. At a minimum, software in all systems will be assessed for vulnerabilities. Mission critical systems or mission critical functions and components will also require penetration testing from an emulated threat in an operationally realistic environment during OT&E.
- Beginning at Milestone B, appropriate measures will be included in the TEMP and used to evaluate operational capability to protect, detect, react, and restore to sustain continuity of operation. The TEMP will document the threats to be used, which should be selected based on the best current information available from the intelligence community.
- The Program Manager, T&E subject matter experts, and applicable certification stakeholders will assist the user in writing testable measures for cybersecurity and interoperability.
- The Program Manager and Operational Test Authority will conduct periodic cybersecurity risk assessments to determine the appropriate Blue/Green/Red Team, and operational impact test events in alignment with the overall test strategy for evaluating the program for real world effects. Defense business systems will undergo Theft/Fraud operational impact testing.

CH 6–3.12 Sustaining Information Technology

CH 6–3.12.1 Post Implementation Reviews

The requirement for a PIR is outlined in the DoDI 5000.02 Enclosure 11 (Page 120) and is directed by Title 40 U.S.C. 11313.

The Functional Sponsor, in coordination with the Component CIO and Program Manager, is responsible for developing a plan and conducting a PIR for all fully deployed IT, including NSS. PIRs are intended report the degree to which DOTMLPF-P changes have achieved the established measures of effectiveness for the desired capability; evaluate systems to ensure positive return on investment and decide whether continuation, modification, or termination of the systems is necessary to meet mission requirements; and document lessons learned from the PIR. If the PIR overlaps with Follow-on Operational Test and Evaluation, the sponsor should coordinate planning of both events for efficiency. The basic high-level process for conducting a PIR is:

- Plan for the PIR and document in a PIR Plan
- Conduct the PIR, ensuring discussion of items such as ROI, measures met / not met, lessons learned, benefits achieved, etc.
- Conduct analysis based on the PIR findings
- Document the results in a PIR Report for feedback into the sustainment program

CH 6–3.12.2 Operations and Sustainment of IT

The purpose of O&S for IT is to execute the product support strategy, satisfy materiel readiness and operational support performance requirements, and sustain the system over its life cycle (to include disposal). The O&S Phase begins after the production or deployment decision and is based on an MDA-approved Lifecycle Sustainment Plan (LCSP). DoDI 5000.02 Encl. 6 includes a broader discussion of sustainment planning to include LCSPs and metrics. Sustainment planning is discussed throughout CH 4 beginning in Section 2.1. LCSPs are also discussed in CH 8 Section 3.5.12.

The phase has two major efforts, Sustainment and Disposal. The LCSP, prepared by the Program Manager and approved by the MDA, is the basis for the activities conducted during this phase.

Sustainment

During this phase, the Program Manager will deploy the product support package and monitor its performance according to the LCSP. The LCSP may include time-phased transitions between commercial, organic, and partnered product support providers. The Program Manager will ensure resources are programmed and necessary IP deliverables and associated license rights, tools, equipment, and facilities are acquired to support each of the levels of maintenance that will provide product support; and will establish necessary organic depot maintenance capability in compliance with statute and the LCSP.

Disposal

At the end of its useful life, a system will be demilitarized and disposed of in accordance with all legal and regulatory requirements and policy relating to safety (including explosives safety), security, and the environment.

CH 6–3.12.3 Upgrades

Upgrades on business capabilities and system occur on a relatively regular basis and throughout the lifecycle. This includes:

- Ongoing maintenance to correct existing processing, performance and implementation defects.
- Regular enhancements based on user feedback
- Preventive maintenance for software efficiency and to prevent corruption (e.g., anti-virus tools).
- Identification of new requirements or upgrades to improve performance, maintainability, and add functionality. If the changes are major in terms of cost, schedule, and or / performance, it may require the instantiation of a new program increment.

CH 6–4. Additional Planning Considerations

Additional best practices or other unique process requirements for the development and implementation of IT programs are discussed throughout this section.

CH 6–4.1 Best Practice and Lessons Learned

The following best practices for IT acquisition were originally introduced in 2010 through the Better Buying Power (BBP) initiative and built upon through successive BBP iterations. The principles of BBP apply to all acquisitions, and are being adopted through the IT acquisition community to improve affordability and delivery outcomes in IT acquisition. Many of the BBP principles that have translated throughout programs are:

- affordability constraints;
  - view resources: affordability
- should-cost management,
  - view resources: cost control
- elimination of unproductive processes and bureaucracy (i.e., tailoring);
  - view resources: eliminate unproductive processes
- strong incentives to industry,
  - view resources: incentives and communication with industry
- promoting competition,
  - view resources: promoting competition
- improving innovation, and product quality;
  - view resources: improving innovation
- In addition to
  - promoting technical excellence;
  - use of data to inform policy, and
  - a focus on cybersecurity to secure sensitive and classified data

Furthermore, the USD(AT&L) has solicited feedback from those individuals actually acquiring and implementing systems in the Department – and published it for others to read and learn from. For example, in 2015 the USD asked Program Managers of various ACAT I programs to submit assessments to him. With permission, he compiled some of them into a report which is available for viewing here. Taking this theme even a step further, the USD(AT&L) solicited feedback from Program Executive Officers (PEOs) regarding their portfolios and any suggestions they might have for improving results. Those results, which are mostly unedited, were published in the July-August 2016 Issue of DAU's Defense AT&L Magazine.

Finally, the Government Accountability Office (GAO) has identified a set of essential and complementary management disciplines that provide a sound foundation for information technology (IT) management.

These include: IT strategic planning, Enterprise architecture, IT investment management and Information Security; additional information is available through the GAO's website on the issue summary.

CH 6–4.2 Root Cause Analysis

One of the issues the Department faces with successfully fielding IT capabilities is making the leap from problem to solution too quickly, resulting in a solution that doesn't meet the fundamental need but rather provides temporary "band-aids" for its symptoms. The tendency to "do something now!" must be appropriately balanced with a process that mitigates the risk of fixing a symptom vs. its root cause(s). Root Cause Analysis is a structured approach to determining a problem's causal factors and identifying what behaviors, actions, inactions, or conditions need to be changed in order to eliminate the problem.

There is no single methodology for performing Root Cause Analysis and various approaches can yield satisfactory results. Different approaches to identify potential root causes include:

- Affinity Diagram
- Fishbone Diagram
- Five Whys Analysis
- Pareto Diagram
- Value Analysis

Your Service / Component may have a specific preference toward root cause analysis methodology. The results of a root cause analysis will eventually lead to the definition of a requirement, which will be documented in a Problem Statement or an ICD, depending on the type of requirement.

CH 6–4.3 General Management Practices for IT Programs

The following are best practices for management of IT programs. Some are controllable at the individual Program Management level, while some are more strategic in nature and will require involvement of a PEO-type leader to ensure the right level of strategy and management oversight of a program:

- Ensure linkage to an IT strategic planning process, which typically occurs at the agency level (but may be derived and managed at lower levels in an agency or Service).
- Document a process to integrate IT management operations and decisions with organizational planning, budget, financial management, human resources management, and program decisions.
- Require that cyber security management processes be integrated with strategic and operational planning processes.
- Institute a process to account for all IT-related expenses and results.
- Prepare an enterprise wide strategic information resources management plan. At a minimum, an information resources management plan should (1) describe how IT activities will be used to help accomplish agency missions and operations, including related resources; and (2) identify a major IT acquisition program(s) or any phase or increment of that program that has significantly deviated from cost, performance, or schedule goals established for the program.
- Ensure its performance plan required under the Government Performance and Results Act of 1993 (GPRA), as amended by the GPRA Modernization Act of 2010 (1) describes how IT supports strategic and program goals; (2) identifies the resources and time periods required to implement the information security program plan required by FISMA; and (3) describes major IT acquisitions contained in the capital asset plan that will bear significantly on the achievement of a performance goal.
- Have a documented process to (1) develop IT goals in support of agency needs; (2) measure progress against these goals; and (3) assign roles and responsibilities for achieving these goals.
- Establish goals that, at a minimum, address how IT contributes to (1) program productivity, (2) efficiency, (3) effectiveness, and (4) service delivery to the public (if applicable).
- Establish IT performance measures to monitor actual-versus-expected performance. Measures should align with the GPRA performance plan.
- In an annual report, to be included in the budget submission, describe progress in using IT to improve the efficiency and effectiveness of agency operations and, as appropriate, deliver services to the public.

- Benchmark IT management processes against appropriate public and private sector organizations and/or processes in terms of costs, speed, productivity, and quality of outputs and outcomes.

CH 6–4.3.1 Risk Management and Mitigation

Successful risk management requires thoughtful planning and resourcing, and should be implemented as early as possible in the life cycle beginning with the Materiel Solution Analysis phase. The goal is to identify risks to inform decisions and handling strategies before the risks become issues. DAU has a risk management course available for basic training as well.

Risk management needs to be both top-down (embraced by the PM and others) and bottom-up (from working-level engineers) to be successful. PMs should encourage everyone on their program to take ownership of the risk management program and should be careful not to cultivate a "shoot the messenger" culture. All personnel should be encouraged to identify risks, issues, and opportunities and, as appropriate, to support analysis, handling, and monitoring activities.

Organizational implementation and process quality are equally important in determining a program's risk management effectiveness. A poorly implemented risk management process will not contribute to program success and may lead to program inefficiency. It is essential that programs define, implement, and document an appropriate risk management approach that is organized, comprehensive, and iterative, by addressing the following questions:

1. Risk Planning: What is the program's risk management process?
2. Risk Identification: What can go wrong?
3. Risk Analysis: What are the likelihood and consequence of the risk?
4. Risk Handling: Should the risk be accepted, avoided, transferred, or mitigated?
5. Risk Monitoring: How has the risk changed?

Figure 7: Risk Management Process

CH 6–4.4 Process Support Tools

Table 8: Process Support Tools - Examples

Tool	Description
DITPR DoD Information Technology Portfolio Repository	The unclassified authoritative inventory of IT systems. It contains information on DoD's mission critical and mission essential information technology systems and their interfaces including the following: system names, acronyms, descriptions, sponsoring component, approval authority, points of contact, and other basic information. The information stored in DITPR provides DoD decision makers an over-arching view of DoD's IT capabilities for making resource decisions. It is the responsibility of the Program Manager (PM) to ensure that IT is registered and follows all applicable DoD Component Chief Information Officer (CIO) procedures and guidance. Additional information about DITPR can be accessed from here. DITPR can be accessed here. A DITPR account can be requested here.
DITIP DoD Information Technology Investment Portal	DITIP provides a centralized location for IT investment portfolio data, is the authoritative data source for DoD IT Header information, and aligns IT systems information in the Defense IT Portfolio Registry (DITPR) with budget information in the Select and Native Programming Data Input System for IT (SNaP-IT). A DITIP account can be requested here. For additional guidance on managing DBS using DITIP, access the DITIP website and select "DITIP Instructions – DBS Certification Management".
SNaP-IT Select & Native Programming Data Input System for Information Technology	SNAP-IT the is the authoritative Department of Defense (DoD) database used for publishing the DoD Information Technology (IT) Budget Estimates to Congress, the Circular A-11 Section 53 and Section 300 exhibits to the Office of Management and Budget (OMB), and for monthly IT performance reporting to the IT Dashboard. you can access SNaP-IT guidance for these work products within the DoD Financial Management Regulation (7000.14-R, Volume 2B, Chapter 18) or within annual budget guidance issued by OUSD(C), D,CAPE, and DoD CIO. SNAP-IT can be accessed here.
PRCP Program Resources Collection Process	DoD web-based application designed to prepare and manage direct program budget details. All MDAPs shall submit PBR data at the sub-program level and all MAIS programs shall submit at the Increment level as appropriate, consistent with the Track-to-Budget rules established for the data submission to PRCP, per the program/budget transparency requirements of the Fiscal Year Integrated Program/Budget Submission Guidance. PRCP is available on the SIPRnet.
DAMIR Defense Acquisition Management Information Retrieval	Provides enterprise visibility to Acquisition program information. DAMIR streamlines acquisition management and oversight by leveraging web services, authoritative data sources, data collection, and data repository capabilities. DAMIR identifies various data sources that the Acquisition community uses to manage Major Defense Acquisition Programs (MDAP) and Major Automated Information Systems (MAIS) programs and provides a unified web-based interface through which to present that information. DAMIR is the authoritative source for Selected Acquisition Reports (SAR), SAR Baseline, Acquisition Program Baselines (APB), MAIS Annual Reports (MAR), MAIS Original Estimates (MAIS OE), and Assessments. It is a powerful reporting and analysis tool with robust data checks, validation, standardization and workflow leveling. It has extensive security capabilities as well as both classified and unclassified versions. One component of DAMIR, Purview, is an executive information system that displays program information such as mission and description, cost & funding, schedule, and performance. The DAMIR site, with directions for obtaining an account, can be accessed here.

Tool	Description
AIR Acquisition Information Repository	A searchable document repository for final milestone documents for Pre-Major Defense Acquisition Programs, Unbaselined Major Automated Information Systems, Acquisition Category (ACAT) ID, ACAT IAM, and Special Interest Programs. PMs are not responsible for uploading reports directly, but programmatic reports, such as an Analysis of Alternatives (AoA) or Clinger Cohen Act (CCA) compliance confirmation will be uploaded by the responsible agency. A list of these reports with the corresponding Office of Primary Responsibility (OPR), as well as the rationale behind AIR can be found at in the Acquisition Information Repository Implementation Guidance Memorandum signed by the USD(AT&L) dated September 25, 2012. To access the AIR site, with directions for obtaining an account, go here.
DAT DAE Action Tracker	DAT is a System that tracks action items from Acquisition Decision Memorandums (ADMs) and their status. The decisions and direction resulting from each acquisition milestone and other major decision point reviews are documented in an ADM. ADMs are ultimately signed by the MDA. The status of all ADM-directed actions for MAIS, MDAP, and Special Interest programs are tracked in DAT. As a PM it is important to pay close attention and work to quickly rectify any ADM actions because of their high visibility. DAT can be accessed here.
EMASS Enterprise Mission Assurance Support Service	A web-based tool that automates and integrates services for cybersecurity managements and maintains an enterprise baseline for security controls. It manages several services including scorecard measurement, dashboard reporting, generation of Risk Management Framework (RMF) for the DoD and DOD Information Assurance Certification and Accreditation Process (DIACAP) Package Reports, and reporting of applicable Federal Information Security Management Act (FISMA) reports. eMass also manages all cybersecurity compliance activities from system registration through system decommissioning. PMs are responsible for following the RMF process for the selection and specification of security controls for an information system. eMass can be accessed at https://disa.deps.mil/ext/cop/mae/netops/eMASS/SitePages/Home.aspx. Directions for obtaining an eMASS account can be found at http://www.disa.mil/~/media/Files/DISA/Services/EMASS/eMASS_user_account.pdf.

CH 6–4.5 Data Sharing Tools

This section addresses those tools, technology standards and specifications that are key enablers in driving data and information sharing. The section attempts to be comprehensive; yet, acknowledges the difficulty in keeping pace with rapidly evolving technologies. All of these enablers are recommended for use, as applicable. PMs should recognize that some are mandated in different policies and guidance documents and use as required.

The following table provides a brief description of some sample tools that can be used when implementing the sharing of data, information, and IT services.

Table 9: Data Sharing Tools - Examples

Tool	Purpose
Access Controls	Provides the mechanism to validate the rights or privileges (authorization) and claims of identity (authentication) for a user and matches those user credentials to defined access policies in order to make the grant or deny decision that is enforced through the policy enforcement point.

Tool	Purpose
Adapter Services	Provides transformation or mediation of data assets and exchange formats. To be used for legacy system or data integration and federated domain transportation.
Cryptographic Binding	Creates a relationship between data objects and metadata tags by hashing the data object(s) and metadata and signing over the hashes with a signature using cryptography as a technique to ensure the integrity and authentication of data (i.e., no modifications, deletions or insertions by unauthorized sources).
Data Services Environment (DSE)	Provides an on-line repository enabling developers to reuse, understand, and share existing data assets. It addresses structural and semantic metadata such as schemas, web service description language, stylesheets, and taxonomies; descriptive metadata about proposed and approved ADSs, including their relationships and their responsible governance authorities; and descriptive, semantic, and structural metadata about services and other functional capabilities, including service definitions and specifications that can be discovered for subsequent use.
Data Tagging User Interface (UI)	Adds metadata tags to a data asset on the backend via a general Web UI, portal or local tagging tool. It is primarily used in a thin client or cloud environment.
DoD Information Technology (IT) Standards Registry (DISR)	The DISR is an online repository of IT standards. It defines the service areas, interfaces, standards (registry elements), and standards profiles applicable to all DoD systems. Use of the registry is mandated for the development and acquisition of new or modified fielded IT systems throughout the DoD.
DoD Storefront	Provides an access point for end-users to discover data assets.
Enterprise Authoritative Data Source (EADS)	Provides a registry of DoD data needs, data sources authoritative bodies (ABs) and AB-approved assertions on the context upon which a given data source is authoritative. EADS is part of the Data Services Environment (DSE).
Enterprise Catalog	Provides a repository for data providers to publish DDMS-compliant discovery metacards.
Enhanced Information Support Plan (EISP)	The Enhanced Information Support Plan (EISP) tool is used to fulfill the requirements for creating an ISP. For more information, see section 7.3.6 of this Guidebook.
Enterprise Messaging	Allows applications to publish and receive information such as special reports, alerts, briefs or section-specific information over specialized logical messaging channels.
Federated Search	Provides the ability to find information across multiple sources without guesswork to use as part of Content Discovery. No special expertise in a complex query language or interface is required.
Forge.mil	Enables the collaborative development and use of open source and DoD community source software.
Global Information Grid (GIG) Technical Guidance – Federation (GTG-F)	The GTG-F is a suite of software applications that provides technical guidance. The GTG-F content consists of and is based on GIG net-centric IT standards, associated profiles, engineering best practices and reference implementation specifications.
Metadata Registry (MDR)	Collects, stores, and disseminates structural and semantic metadata artifacts critical to successful development, operation and maintenance of existing and future DoD capabilities. MDR is part of the DSE.

Tool	Purpose
Metadata Tagging Tools (e.g., AMTT)	Tools that extract information from data assets in order to generate metacards or documents with imbedded metadata.
Net-Centric Publisher (NCP)	Automatically publishes data assets to the Metadata Registry, Service Registry and Enterprise Catalog. NCP is part of the DSE.
Search Widgets and Applications	Leverages services for search and discovery of metadata cards and assets for various widgets and applications, primarily during the development and design phases.
Secure Data Tagging Tool (SDTT) Suite	NSA data tagging toolset. It includes reusable components that allow analysts and stakeholders to create metadata tags, validate them for conformance and reasonability to Controlled Access Program Coordination Office (CAPCO) or other standards, and perform cryptographic binding of the metadata to the data asset(s).
Security Mechanisms	Provides security implementations, configurations and protocols aimed at mitigating or stopping security threats throughout the enterprise. Includes mechanisms such as IdAM, XML Gateways, PKI, etc.
Service Discovery (SD)	Searches the Enterprise Service Registry for service providers and services. SD is part of the DSE.
Service Registry (SR) (Universal Description Discovery and Integration [UDDI])	Provides the information required for an application developer to locate an appropriate service, determine the features and functions provided by that service, identify how to invoke the service, and determine where the service resides.
Smart Data	Tags all the data so users can track it, know the sensitivity, and apply access control values, provenance and smart routing.
Transport Protocols	Provide a standardized means for routing and transportation across a net-centric environment. Can be any of the technical protocols used for transportation and routing such as Hyper Text Protocol (HTTP), SOAP/HTTP, SOAP/Java Message Service (JMS), FTP, etc.
User Authentication and Authorization Services	Provides dynamic and account based access control to support the automated provision of web services and attribute-based access to data and resources using policy decision points and policy enforcement points. This is the foundation for access control throughout the Joint Information Environment (JIE).

CH 6–Version and Revision History

The table below tracks chapter changes. It indicates the current version number and date published, and provides a brief description of the content.

Version #	Revision Date	Reason
0	11/2/16	Chapter 6 initial upload
0	02/01/17	CH 6–3.9.2 Cloud Computing – links validation

CH 7–1. Purpose

The Defense Acquisition Guidebook (DAG), Chapter 7, provides guidance to Program Managers (PMs) on how to use intelligence information and data to ensure maximum warfighting capability at a minimum risk to cost and schedule.

CH 7–2. Background

Intelligence is a key factor in understanding the current and future threat posed by foreign weapon and information technology system capabilities, and should therefore affect United States (U.S.) weapons and information technology system acquisition decisions. For systems to achieve their intended capabilities, consideration of the threat must be constantly reviewed and considered throughout the life cycle of each system. Threat and intelligence support considerations should affect all decisions from defining requirements and capabilities, through initial concept phases, planning, research, full-scale development, production, test and evaluation, deployment, and system upgrade, all the way through disposal: cradle to grave. Threat analysis and intelligence support requirements inform and enable program capabilities and minimize costs to the government throughout the entire acquisition process.

While the dialogue between the Defense Intelligence Enterprise (DIE) and acquisition community bridges the cultural divide or stovepipes, that same dialogue is no less important between the requirements and intelligence communities. The requirements developer should call on the supporting intelligence SME at the earliest stages of development for assistance in determining if the requirements being developed will involve intelligence support, especially IMD. The determination and statement of the intelligence support requirements, or lack thereof, are recorded and transmitted to the acquisition program manager in each capability document.

CH 7–2.1 Expected Benefits

The integration of intelligence has become increasingly critical to DoD acquisition programs. Threat intelligence analysis and/or intelligence supportability requirements inform the acquisition community and enable weapon system capabilities. They also minimize risk and cost to the government throughout the entire acquisition process.

Early determination of intelligence supportability requirements increases the likelihood that the delivered system will be fully capable and more survivable against the relevant adversary threats. It also reduces risk to acquisition cost, schedule, and performance through the early identification of threat capabilities and the work to be performed by the DIE; it also reduces risk to proper tasking of the DIE at the appropriate acquisition milestone through production requirements, identification of capability gaps, risk considerations, mitigation steps, and negotiated delivery dates for products.

CH 7–3. Business Practice

The importance of determining at the earliest possible time that an acquisition program has intelligence supportability requirements cannot be overstated. As stated earlier, the engagement to determine intelligence support starts with the Sponsor and the supporting intelligence SME.

CH 7–3.1 Intelligence and Requirements

The JCIDS Manual (Appendix I to Encl. D) provides a general description of the nine intelligence support requirement categories to assist the Sponsor and stakeholders in identifying intelligence support requirements and sufficiency or risk of shortfalls in the DIE needed to support a materiel capability solution.

CH 7–3.1.1 Early Intelligence and Requirements Engagement

The JCIDS Manual (paragraph 1.a.(2)) states that it is crucial for the Sponsor to identify intelligence support requirements, particularly IMD dependency, in all capability requirement documents or state there are no such requirements, Therefore, the Sponsor should engage the supporting intelligence SME to assist in determining whether or not a materiel capability solution is IMD-dependent and/or involve other intelligence supportability requirements. The acquisition PM is the beneficiary of this determination and is not responsible for making the determination. If the capability requirement documents identify intelligence supportability requirements, the Sponsor should establish a line of communications among the Sponsor, acquisition PM, and operator, and their respective supporting intelligence SMEs.

CH 7–3.1.2 Advantages of Early Intelligence and Requirements Engagement

The communication between these communities, especially with the supporting intelligence SMEs, should improve efficiency and effectiveness and minimize errors in identifying and requesting adequate intelligence support to acquisition. For example, without greater integration of threat and intelligence within the program structure, the program runs the risk of being out of sync with changes in the threat of record or of a new threat materializing, increases risk during Developmental Operational Test and Evaluation, and ultimately risks system failure when operationally deployed.

CH 7–3.2 Capability Requirements and Intelligence

The Joint Staff provides review, coordination, and certification/endorsement functions in support of the JCIDS process. These functions include intelligence supportability requirements for intelligence certification, and threat validation. All acquisition programs that are expected to operate in a threat environment should be developed in accordance with the most current threat information. The applicable threat information should be continually updated to account for threats throughout the acquisition program's life cycle. The supporting intelligence SMEs to the Sponsor should be invaluable in incorporating adversarial threat capabilities throughout the JCIDS review process, and will review and validate the threat input within the JCIDS documents.

CH 7–3.2.1 Documents and Intelligence Collaboration

This section addresses the capabilities documents that identify intelligence supportability requirements. It also describes the intelligence certification process regarding intelligence support within an acquisition program.

CH 7–3.2.1.1 JCIDS Documentation

The Sponsor's supporting intelligence SME should help drive the threat(s) of record in support of JCIDS document development. The supporting intelligence SME should also review all ICDs, CDDs, and CPDs -- as well as Joint ICDs, CDDs, and CPDs, which involve their service equities -- during the JCIDS document-staffing process to ensure that the threat information and the addressing of the nine JCIDS intelligence support categories meet JCIDS requirements.

Initial Capabilities Document (ICD). The initiating DoD Component prepares a concise threat summary and threat rationale, working with Defense Intelligence Agency's (DIA's) Defense Technology and Long-Range Analysis Office (TLA-3) as needed. If validated Threat Modules or Validated Online Lifecycle Threat (VOLT) Reports (see Sections 4.1.1 and 4.1.2) are available and address the threat areas affecting U.S. capability, these documents should be used as the primary sources for the threat statements. The ICDs reference the threat documents used to support the analysis.

Capability Development Document (CDD). The initiating DoD Component prepares a concise threat summary and threat rationale, working with DIA/TLA-3, as needed. If validated Threat Modules or VOLT Reports are available and address the threat areas affecting U.S. capability, these documents should be used as the primary sources for the threat statements.

Capability Production Document (CPD). The initiating DoD Component prepares a concise threat summary and threat rationale, working with DIA/TLA-3, as needed. If validated Threat Modules or VOLT Reports are available and address the threat areas affecting U.S. capability, these documents should be used as the primary sources for the threat statements.

CH 7–3.2.1.2 Validated Online Lifecycle Threat (VOLT) and Threat Modules

Deleted.

CH 7–3.2.1.3 Intelligence Certification Process

The Intelligence Certification Process involves the evaluation of threat documentation and the nine JCIDS intelligence support categories with respect to system architecture, security, and intelligence interoperability standards.

The J28 Intelligence Requirements Certification Office (IRCO) acts on behalf of the DJ-2 and the J-2/DDJ28 as the lead intelligence entity within the Joint Staff for intelligence certification of capability requirement documents. It provides intelligence certification of capability requirement documents. See CJCSI 5123.01G (para 2.c.(5), Encl. B) for details on IRCO. The IRCO engages members of the DIE during intelligence certification. The IRCO can be contacted for assistance at (757) 836-7030 or through SIPRNet channels (https://intelshare.intelink.sgov.gov/ sites/IRCO/SitePages/Home.aspx).

CH 7–3.2.2 Advantages of Capability Requirements and Intelligence Collaboration

The early identification of IMD dependency and/or other intelligence supportability needs in the requirements process will inform identification of potential gaps or shortfalls in intelligence support to an Acquisition Category (ACAT) program, particularly, IMD. This early identification should allow the DIE, PM, and eventually the operator time and flexibility in addressing any recognized gap or shortfall in intelligence support.

CH 7–4. Additional Planning Considerations

Threat support and the nine JCIDS intelligence support categories play an increasingly significant role in the successful development of the U.S. capabilities that provide an advantage on the battlefield. This section addresses the capabilities and intelligence documents required by DoDI 5000.02, Encl 1, sec. 3 (Table 2) and their linkages to the Acquisition, Intelligence, and Requirements communities.

CH 7–4.1 Threat Support

Threat Intelligence support to the acquisition process provides an understanding of foreign threat capabilities. It should be continually updated to account for upgrades to adversarial capabilities throughout the program to ensure that the technological advantage over adversarial capabilities is maintained. See the graphic in Figure 1.

Figure 1 illustrates the range of support provided by the threat intelligence community over the life of a particular capability shortfall identification process and the resulting system acquisition program. The Defense Intelligence Threat Library (DITL) informs the capability shortfall identification process as well as during the early phases of system acquisition prior to the generation of the VOLT. The Threat Modules in the DITL project foreign capabilities in particular threat areas looking out 20 years.

Figure 1: Life-Cycle Intelligence Analysis Requirements

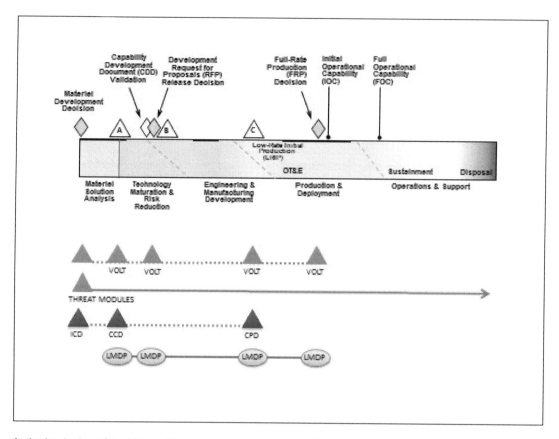

At the beginning of the Material Solution Analysis phase, the Sponsor should contact the supporting intelligence production center (IPC) to support the integration of validated threat information into the technology development approach in the Analysis of Alternatives. Threat information may come from DIA-validated Threat Modules or other DIA/Service-validated VOLTs that align with the capability mission, concept of operations (CONOPs), and employment timeline.

Once the Sponsor, PM, or other appropriate enabler identifies concepts or prototypes for the materiel solution, the program office or Sponsor should task the supporting IPC for the lead Service to produce a VOLT report. The program office should work closely with the supporting IPC to provide system-specific characteristics, employment CONOPS, and employment timeline as they evolve. The program office should also work with the Sponsor and VOLT validation authority to identify Critical Intelligence Parameters (CIPs) and ensure that DoD IC production requirements are levied against those CIPs.

CH 7–4.1.1 Threat Modules

DoDI 5000.02, Encl 1, sec. 3 (DITL (Threat Modules) row, Table 2) describes the Threat Modules as regulatory documents that are produced by the DIE and are required to be updated every 2 years, independent of acquisition decision events. Threat Modules serve as the analytical foundation for VOLT Reports and maintain projections of technology and adversary capability trends over the next 20 years.

The Threat Modules are defined as comprehensive, authoritative, and validated assessments of foreign threats, relative to MDAP and MAIS programs. Modules project the threat environment in a given threat topic out 20 years and constitute the DIE position with respect to those topics. Threat module types include counter sensor; cyberspace; employment/tactic, techniques or procedures; platform/target; sensor; technology warning; and weapons.

CH 7–4.1.2 VOLT

DoDI 5000.02, Encl 1, sec. 3 (VOLT row, Table 2) lists the VOLT as a regulatory document for MDAP and MAIS programs. These programs require a unique, system-specific VOLT Report to support capability development and PM assessments of mission needs and capability gaps against likely threat capabilities at initial operational capability (IOC).

VOLT Reports are required for all other programs unless waived by the Milestone Decision Authority (MDA). Programs on the Director, Operational Test, and Evaluation (DOT&E) Oversight List require a unique, system-specific VOLT, unless waived by both the MDA and the DOT&E. DoD Components produce a VOLT. DIA validates the VOLT for ACAT ID or IAM programs; the DoD Component validates the VOLT for ACAT IC or IAC programs and below.

The VOLT is defined as the authoritative threat assessment tailored for and normally focused on one specific MDAP and authorized for use in the Defense Acquisition Management process. The VOLT reports involve the application of threat modules, and are to be written to articulate the relevance of each module to a specific acquisition program or planned capability. At the discretion of the responsible MDA, VOLTs can be used in the future to support multiple programs that address like performance attributes, share an employment CONOPs, and have a similar employment timeline.

CH 7–4.1.3 Life-Cycle Mission Data Plan

DoDI 5000.02, Encl 1, sec. 3 (LMDP row, Table 2, Encl. 1) lists the LMDP as a regulatory requirement for all ACAT programs if the system is dependent on IMD. The LMDP is a Milestone A requirement and a Program Executive Officer and Component Acquisition Executive-approved draft update is due for a Development Request for Proposal Release. The DoD Component approves the draft update at Milestone B.

CH 7–4.1.3.1 "V" Process

Figure 2 depicts the five phases of the LMDP process, called the "V" process. In Phase I, the PM, in collaboration with the Sponsor, identifies all known IMD requirements. Phases II-IV involve the DIE lead; the description of these phases is in Section 4.1.3.2 below. In Phase V, the Sponsor determines which shortfalls should be addressed, the appropriate course(s) of action to mitigate risk, and the risk associated with the remaining IMD shortfalls. Supplemental 001, Life-Cycle Mission Data Plan (LMDP) and Intelligence Mission Data (IMD) planning, of this chapter provides details of the LMDP process.

Figure 2: Five Phases of the LMDP Process

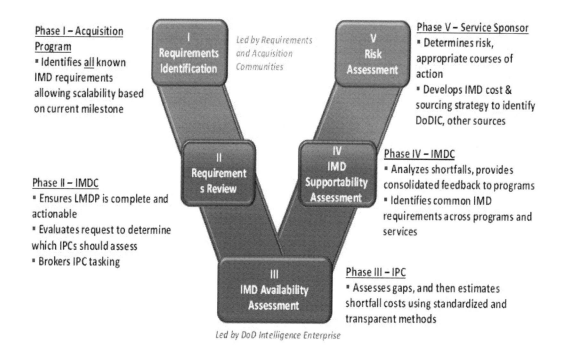

Phase I – Acquisition Program
▪ Identifies all known IMD requirements allowing scalability based on current milestone

Led by Requirements and Acquisition Communities

Phase V – Service Sponsor
▪ Determines risk, appropriate courses of action
▪ Develops IMD cost & sourcing strategy to identify DoDIC, other sources

Phase II – IMDC
▪ Ensures LMDP is complete and actionable
▪ Evaluates request to determine which IPCs should assess
▪ Brokers IPC tasking

Phase IV – IMDC
▪ Analyzes shortfalls, provides consolidated feedback to programs
▪ Identifies common IMD requirements across programs and services

Phase III – IPC
▪ Assesses gaps, and then estimates shortfall costs using standardized and transparent methods

Led by DoD Intelligence Enterprise

Process is scalable...iterative...repeatable

CH 7–4.1.3.2 Intelligence input to the "V" Process

Phases II-IV involve intelligence input from the IMD Center (IMDC) and Service IPCs. In Phase II, the IMDC evaluates the submitted LMDP IMD requirements list for sufficiency and determines which IPCs should assess each IMD request. In Phase III, the IPC assesses any gaps associated with each IMD request and estimates the shortfall costs. In Phase IV, the IMDC identifies common IMD requirements across ACAT Programs and Services. The IMDC also analyzes the shortfalls and provides consolidated feedback to the appropriate PM.

CH 7–4.1.4 System Threat Assessment Report (STAR)

Deleted.

CH 7–4.1.5 Support to Operational Test and Evaluation

The Test and Evaluation Master Plan should define specific intelligence requirements to support program operational test and evaluation. When requested by the appropriate authority in the offices of the DOT&E or the Under Secretary of Defense for Acquisition, Technology and Logistics (USD(AT&L)), DIA, working with the DIE, should provide additional intelligence support to the operational testing of programs on the annual DOT&E Oversight List. DIA support should include certification that the threat information in the test plan is correct and consistent with existing assessments.

Per DoDI 5000 02, para 5.d.11, programs on the DOT&E Oversight List should be considered as MDAPs for testing and evaluation purposes and should require a VOI T regardless of ACAT designation. Details on the VOLT are available at paragraph 4.1.2.of this chapter.

CH 7–4.2 Intelligence Mission Data Support

DoDI 5000.02 (LMDP row, Table 2) lists the LMDP as a regulatory document and is required only if the system is dependent on IMD. DoDD 5250.01 (glossary) defines IMD as DoD intelligence used for programming platform mission systems in development, testing, operations, and sustainment, including, but not limited to, the functional areas of signatures, electronic warfare integrated reprogramming (EWIR), order of battle (OOB), characteristics and performance (C&P), and geospatial intelligence (GEOINT).

CH 7–4.2.1 IMD Functional Areas

The JCIDS Manual (para 2.e., Appendix I, Encl. D) addresses these functional areas as follows:

CH 7–4.2.1.1 Signatures

Signatures are defined as the distinctive characteristics, or sets of characteristics, that consistently recur and identify a piece of equipment, materiel, activity, or event. Signature support is the provision of such data to capability solutions that use signatures in their design, development, testing, training, or operations of sensors, models, or algorithms for the purpose of: combat identification; blue force tracking; targeting; or detecting or identifying activities, events, persons, materiel, or equipment.

CH 7–4.2.1.2 EWIR

EWIR involves assessed, all-source intelligence data on adversary and non-adversary commercial systems, to include technical parametric and performance data, observed electronic intelligence data on foreign emitters from the National Security Agency, and engineering-value/measured data on domestic emitters.

CH 7–4.2.1.3 OOB

OOB is the identification, command structure, strength, and disposition of personnel, equipment, and units of an armed force.

CH 7–4.2.1.4 C&P

C&P refers to all-source derived assessments of foreign military system capabilities and physical attributes.

CH 7–4.2.1.5 GEOINT

GEOINT provides programs with mapping, charting and geodesy, geospatial information, imagery intelligence, and other GEOINT data, data products, and services to support operations, navigation, terrain visualization, targeting, and the characterization of the physical and manmade environments.

CH 7–4.2.2 Consideration of IMD

The JCIDS Manual (para 2.e.(2), Appendix I, Encl. D) further states that IMD requirements "must be considered" as early as the AoA when one or more of the alternatives under consideration are likely to be dependent on IMD to ensure mission effectiveness. Consideration is to be given for alternatives that are not IMD-dependent or those that can be satisfied by IMD already produced by the DIE. Alternatives requiring additional IMD production by the DIE should only be considered where the value of the additional mission effectiveness exceeds the cost associated with generating and maintaining the additional IMD

CH 7–4.2.3 Reference Sources on IMD

DoDD 5250.01 and the DIA Intelligence Mission Data SharePoint Site (SIPRNet – http://intelshare.intelink.sgov.gov/sites/imdc/lmdppublicshare/default. aspx) provide details on IMD.

CH 7–4.3 Counterintelligence Support

Counterintelligence (CI) support involves the gathering of information and conduct of activities to identify, deceive, exploit, disrupt, or protect against espionage, other intelligence activities, sabotage, or assassinations conducted for or on behalf of foreign powers, organizations or persons or their agents, or international terrorist organizations or activities.

Military Department Counterintelligence Organizations (MDCOs) include the Army's 902nd Military Intelligence Group, Navy Criminal Investigative Service and Air Force Office of Special Investigations.

These MDCOs produce Multi-Discipline CI Threat Assessments (MDCITAs), which focus on the foreign collection threat to critical program information (CPI) in Joint and Service ACAT programs and feed into the process for the identification and selection of measures for the protection of CPI. The MDCITA is a key element of the Program Protection Plan (PPP). These MDCOs also address the Targeting Technology Risk Assessment (TTRA), which is another CI threat assessment focusing on CPI and a milestone requirement. See Section 4.3.2.for details on the TTRA.

The other principle CI product the MDCOs provides to acquisition is the Counterintelligence Support Plan (CISP). The CISP describes the planning for the execution of CI activities for acquisition programs with CPI, to include Cleared Defense Contractors considered essential by an acquisition program manager where CPI is present. An acquisition PM could also request, with justification, a CISP for a program that does not identify CPI. Details on the CISP are available in Chapter 9.

CH 7–4.3.1 Program Protection Plan

DoDI 5000.02, Encl 1, sec. 3 (PPP row, Table 2, Encl. 1) lists the PPP as a regulatory requirement at Milestones A through C. It is a risk -based, comprehensive, living plan to guide efforts to manage the risks to CPI and mission-critical functions and critical components. The full range of security functions and counterintelligence traditionally dominate program protection planning for the protection of CPI and critical components. Details on the PPP are available in Chapter 9.

CH 7–4.3.2 Technology Targeting Risk Assessment (TTRA)

The TTRA is a Milestone A requirement document for all ACATs I-III programs. It is a country-by-country assessment conducted by the DoD entities within DIE that quantifies risks to CPI and related enabling technologies for weapons systems; advanced technologies or programs; facilities such as laboratories, factories, research and development sites (e.g., test ranges); and military installations. The TTRA evaluates five independent risk factors, each of which contributes to an overall risk factor. The five areas evaluated are: 1) technology competence; 2) national level of interest; 3) risk of technology diversion; 4) ability to assimilate; and, 5) technology protection risk.

The MDCITA, or CI Threat Assessment, is a comprehensive analysis or study that focuses on the foreign intelligence collection threat to the CPI of a DoD ACAT program. It is a key required element of the PPP, which is the comprehensive plan that describes the integration and synchronization of all measures selected for the protection of CPI.

Since the TTRA and MDCITA both focus on the foreign intelligence collection threat to CPI, the CI community encourages the merger of all-source intelligence supporting the analysis for these two analytical products into a sole-source CI product. Since the MDCITA is a key element of the PPP, the CI component that produces the MDCITA should incorporate the objectives of the TTRA into its CI analytical product to avoid redundancy and to tie a single CI threat assessment product directly to the PPP.

CH 7–4.4 Intelligence Manpower Support

The JCIDS Manual (para 2 a., Appendix I, Encl. D) states that, if the capability solution is IMD-dependent and/or has intelligence supportability requirements for development, testing, training, and/or operation, then the PM should consider including intelligence personnel in the manning structure of the Program Management Office. Details on the manpower estimate are available in Chapter 5.

CH 7–4.5 Intelligence Resource Support

The JCIDS Manual (para 2.b., Appendix I, Encl. D) states that the intelligence resource support category should address whether intelligence funding should be a consideration driven by the IMD dependency and/or the intelligence supportability requirements of the capability solution. Sponsor and PM should devote special attention to the requirement for IMD early in the capability life cycle, including the consideration of resourcing for IMD production prior to Milestone A.

In the event that the Sponsor and/or PM identifies unique or specialized intelligence supportability requirements for the ACAT program, the Sponsor and/or PM should collaborate with their respective supporting intelligence SMEs to determine or negotiate the source of the funding for such requirements.

CH 7–4.6 Intelligence Planning and Operations Support

The JCIDS Manual (para 2.c., Appendix I, Encl. D) states that intelligence planning and operations support requirements involve six interrelated elements in the Joint Intelligence Process, or what is traditionally termed the "intelligence cycle." These six elements are planning and direction, collection, processing and exploitation, analysis and production, dissemination and integration, and evaluation and feedback. While not specifically an intelligence requirement, adequate consideration should be given to the requirements of data transport, especially of airborne intelligence and reconnaissance and surveillance platforms -- an area that has experienced tremendous growth over the past decade.

CH 7–4.6.1 Planning and Direction

This category includes the receipt, identification, and prioritization of intelligence requirements; the development of concepts of intelligence operations and architectures; tasking appropriate intelligence elements for the collection of information or the production of finished intelligence; and submitting requests for collection, exploitation, or all-source production support to external, supporting intelligence entities.

Sponsors must address whether mission-planning requirements have been considered and identified, to include manpower, systems, tools, mission-planning data (Red, Gray, Blue, and White), or other non-materiel requirements of intelligence units, personnel training on systems architecture, and compatibility with current and future Defense Intelligence Information Enterprise architecture

Joint Publication (JP) 2-01 (Section A) provides additional information on planning and direction.

CH 7–4.6.2 Collection

Collection includes those activities related to the acquisition of data needed to satisfy specified requirements. This is managed by collection managers, whose duties include selecting the most-appropriate, available asset(s) and associated processing, exploitation, and dissemination (PED) and then tasking selected asset(s) and associated PED to conduct collection missions.

Collection-management support refers to the personnel, expertise, training, and systems required to ensure that intelligence information requests are submitted through the appropriate channels; that intelligence-collection assets (e.g., Service, national, joint, coalition, and multinational) are effectively employed to collect the required information; and that the collected information is disseminated to the entity that made the original request and to all other end users requiring this information.

The JCIDS Manual (para 2.c.(2), Appendix I to Encl. D), and JP 2-01 (Section B) provide additional details on collection.

CH 7–4.6.3 Processing and Exploitation

Data initially received from the sensor arrives in various forms, depending on the nature of the sensing device. Depending on the source, the raw input may be in the form of digitized data, unintelligible voice transmissions, or large digital files containing un-rectified images of the Earth. This collection output is converted by sensor-specific processing measures into visual, auditory, or textual information that is intelligible to humans, and can then be used by intelligence analysts and other consumers. The data conversion may be automated using algorithmic fusion, cuing, data analytics, and automated exploitation. Exploitation entails the further translation and contextualizing of information resulting from collection and initial processing into a product the planner, decision-maker, or intelligence analyst can assimilate cognitively.

The Sponsor should address whether sufficient personnel and resources will be in place for effective processing and exploitation. Whenever possible, the Sponsor should also address required data, coverage, scale, timeliness, formats, accuracy, and resolution level. The Sponsor should then consider whether the intelligence architecture will support the volume of data requiring processing and ensure data is in standard formats to support interoperability. Depending on the specific requirements of Sponsor's capability solution being supported, you will consider the types of delivery/communications systems required and the volume of information that will be delivered.

The JCIDS Manual (para 2.c.(3), Appendix I to Encl. D), and JP 2-01 (Section C) provide additional information on processing and exploitation.

CH 7–4.6.4 Analysis and Production

During analysis and production, intelligence is produced from the information gathered by collection capabilities, and from the refinement and compilation of intelligence received from external organizations. All available processed information is integrated, evaluated, analyzed, and interpreted to create products that will satisfy requesters or users.

Intelligence products are generally placed in one of eight production categories: 1) warning; 2) current; 3) general military; 4) target 5) science and technology 6) CI; 7) identity intelligence and, 8) estimative intelligence. The categories are distinguished from each other primarily by the purpose for which the intelligence was produced.

The Sponsor should address the necessary or desired product format, production timeline; and necessary update requirements that will be available and have been requested to support their capability solutions. Consider whether sufficient personnel and resources will be in place for effective analysis and production.

The JCIDS Manual (para 2.c.(4), Appendix I to Encl. D), and JP 2-01 (Section C) provide additional information on analysis and production.

CH 7–4.6.5 Dissemination and Integration

This category involves the timely distribution of critical information and finished intelligence, readily accessible by the user, to the appropriate consumer. The movement toward a net-centric environment has reduced the technical challenges related to information dissemination. Nevertheless, intelligence infrastructure (such as intelligence networks, systems, and software) and intelligence resources -- such as funded programs or manpower -- remain critical (and necessary) components of information delivery.

This category should encompass the specific requirements of the capability solution being supported, which may include: timeliness and means of delivery; interoperability of delivery/communications systems; format of information delivered; and information/ product storage location, capacity, and accessibility.

The JCIDS Manual (para 2.c.(5), Appendix I to Encl. D), and JP 2-01 (Section C) provide additional information on dissemination and integration.

CH 7–4.6.6 Evaluation and Feedback

Evaluation and feedback occur continuously throughout the intelligence process, and as an assessment of the intelligence process as a whole. Intelligence personnel at all levels, as well as users of intelligence, should assess the execution of the intelligence tasks being performed to identify deficiencies within the intelligence process and to determine if intelligence requirements are being satisfied. The goal of evaluation and feedback is to identify issues as early as possible to minimize information gaps and to mitigate capability shortfalls.

When possible, this category should address capability solution requirements for means, formats, information needs, and periodicity of assessments to support decisions about reprioritization of intelligence requirements, shifts in collection emphasis, changes to analytic levels of effort, reallocation of available intelligence assets, training of intelligence personnel, and the development of new intelligence capabilities.

The JCIDS Manual (para 2.c.(6), Appendix I to Encl. D), and JP 2-01 (Section C) provides additional information on evaluation and feedback.

CH 7–4.7 Targeting Support

The JCIDS Manual (para 2.d., Appendix I, Encl. D) describes targeting as the process of selecting and prioritizing targets and matching the appropriate response to them, considering commander's guidance and objectives, planning requirements at all warfare levels, and operational requirements and capabilities. Intelligence targeting support shortfalls may detrimentally affect the capability solution's successful development, on-time delivery schedule, and, ultimately, its operational status.

This targeting support category should address requirements for support to target development, mission planning, precise positioning, bomb damage assessment, munitions effects assessment, weaponeering, the anticipated volume of targets to be managed and the numbers of target folders to be produced, and associated targets or aim points to plan for during mission planning.

CH 7–4.8 Warning Support

The JCIDS Manual (para 2.f., Appendix I, Encl. D) characterizes warning support as a traditional intelligence mission of "Indications and Warning" – identifying and defining a potential threat and then monitoring it. However, in terms of intelligence support to acquisition, warning support should focus on the information that enables that system capability to remain scientifically and technologically superior to developing or projected adversary capabilities. This support depends on the identification of CIPs by the Requirements Developer and PM, in collaboration with their support intelligence SME. A CIP represents a threat capability or threshold and changes to which could critically impact the effectiveness and survivability of a proposed system (CIP breach).

DIA Instruction 5000.002 (para 4.2.4.2.2) states that the IPC producing the VOLT "will monitor the CIP thresholds and determine when the CIP has been breached." When a CIP threshold is breached for a program requiring DIA validation, the responsible IPC will notify DIA/TLA-3, the appropriate intelligence element supporting the program office, and the program office of the breach. For ACAT ID and IAM programs, DIA should provide breach notification to the offices of the USD(AT&L) and Under Secretary of Defense (Intelligence), the Services, Joint Staff, and the DOT&E, at a minimum. For ACAT IC, II, III, and IV programs, the Defense Intelligence Analysis Program producer and/or DIA should notify the PM of the affected program, as well as the Service acquisition, intelligence, requirements, and T&E organizations. However, the matrix support intelligence SME should establish a continuous line of communications with the respective Service IPC to ensure that the program receives appropriate notification of a CIP breach affecting its system capability.

CH 7–4.9 Space Intelligence Support

The JCIDS Manual (para 2.g., Appendix I, Encl. D) states that space intelligence support involves requirements for space-based capability solutions; other capability solutions relying on space-derived capabilities; and platforms that perform space control or space support. This category also includes intelligence information, infrastructure, or resources that provide space-specific intelligence analysis on foreign space capabilities.

The space intelligence support category should also address requirements for space intelligence coverage, whether periodic or persistent; timeliness; security; form of support necessary; and accuracy.

CH 7–4.10 Intelligence Training Support

Historically, some acquisition programs have required specific support in terms of specialized training conducted by intelligence SMEs during part or all of an ACAT program's life cycle.

Such specialized training requirements may include training additional personnel in existing training programs and/or in a new, unique training program that will be developed to support the ACAT program. In either case, the requirement for specific training to support part or all of an ACAT program's life cycle should be identified as early as possible in the acquisition process. For non-MDAPs, the PM should ensure that a close coordination relationship exists with the program matrix support intelligence SME, as well as with the requirements developer and requirements support intelligence expert. This close relationship should foster the early identification of any unique or specialized intelligence training requirement throughout the ACAT program's life cycle.

Chapter 7 Supplement—Life-Cycle Mission Data Plan
CH 7-S–1. Overview

Modern weapon systems are inherently dependent on a variety of scientific and technical intelligence products throughout every stage of their life-cycle. Intelligence Mission Data (IMD) provides essential data for building system models, developing algorithms, optimizing sensor design, system testing and evaluation (T&E), and validating sensor functionality. Therefore, it is important for systems to consider IMD as a potential cost, schedule or performance risk and initiate IMD planning as early as possible in the acquisition process. Ideally, IMD considerations will inform technology transition decisions and development planning efforts in advance of entrance into the Joint Capabilities Integration and Development System process and Defense Acquisition System.

The Defense Intelligence Enterprise (DIE) resources are known to be limited in ability to support the full range of existing IMD requirements; therefore, programs will gain greater insight into their potential IMD risk if they define their requirements with sufficient detail to receive a DIE assessment of availability and data cost. Systems that are designed to fully leverage what is already available or is planned to be available from the DIE will carry less risk from IMD shortfalls.

DoDD 5250.01 establishes direction for life-cycle IMD planning to include, but not limited to, the following functional areas: Signatures, Electronic Warfare Integrated Reprogramming (EWIR), Order of Battle (OOB), Characteristics and Performance (C&P), and Geospatial Intelligence (GEOINT). Notably, it creates the Intelligence Mission Data Center (IMDC) as a resource to support IMD efforts DoD-wide.

DoDD 5250.01 and DoDI 5000.02, Encl 1, sec. 3 (LMDP row, Table 2, Enclosure 1) require all IMD-dependent technology and acquisition programs and efforts to submit an LMDP throughout their respective life-cycle. The LMDP facilitates collaboration and coordination between the acquisition, requirements and intelligence communities for how the system will be supported with IMD across its life-cycle. Supporting intelligence offices assist programs with the development of LMDPs, coordination with IMD producers and resolving issues associated with IMD. They also facilitate assistance from the IMDC.

CH 7-S–1.1. Purpose

The purpose of this supplement is to describe the process for the development of the LMDP.

CH 7-S–1.2. Summary of the Supplement

This supplement depicts the step-by-step process related to the addressing of the IMD requirements in support of the development of the LMDP. Since the LMDP is IMD dependent, this supplement provides questions to be addressed and actions to be taken at each milestone and at various phases of the life cycle of the acquisition program.

CH 7-S–2. LMDP Process

The life-cycle mission data planning process follows the systems engineering "V" process to define, assess and manage IMD needs, timelines, gaps and risks. This collaborative planning process enables programs along with the requirements community to identify how the system will be supported by the DIE with IMD necessary to meet acquisition program development and test timelines as well as the full range of support necessary to conduct operations and sustainment. The results of this planning process are captured in the system's LMDP.

Supporting intelligence offices guide programs in specific formats/processes for LMDP development, coordination and approval within each Service. Additionally, IMDC recommended formats for the LMDP can be found on the IMDC SharePoint sites and Defense Acquisition University's website. The IMDC has developed a tool, the "IMD Management, Analysis and Reporting System (IMARS)" to facilitate the identification, assessment and analysis of IMD requirements.

The following steps and acquisition phase aligned questions can assist a program with identifying IMD requirements and incorporating IMD planning into program execution:

- The first step in the LMDP development process is the systems engineering level analysis of system attributes to derive of IMD requirements. This analysis should be conducted by program office systems engineers in collaboration with intelligence personnel who can trace attributes to relevant intelligence products and services. Once IMD data dependencies are identified, supporting intelligence offices can facilitate their submission to the Service Intelligence Production Centers (IPCs) and IMDC for review and feedback.
- Once these organizations have received a system's list of IMD requirements, Service IPCs review their IMD holdings against the required IMD based upon specific data accuracy/fidelity needs. Where gaps are found, the IPCs use a Cost Assessment and Program Evaluation or CAPE (Office of the Secretary of Defense - Director, CAPE) compliant costing methodology to articulate costs for closing data gaps.
- The IMDC facilitates provision of Service IPC costing and availability assessments to the supporting intelligence office and the program along with insights into other programs with similar gaps.

Programs, along with requirements sponsors can then apply acquisition and operational risk assessment methodologies and determine appropriate courses of action that address identified IMD gaps and aid in prioritization of their IMD requirements. This supports identification of relative IMD priorities and risk mitigation for use in IMD planning.

CH 7-S–2.1. Materiel Solution Analysis Phase to Milestone (MS) A

A program's strategy document (Acquisition Strategy (AS)) is an appropriate place to identify the (a) systems and subsystems of the program that require IMD necessary to deliver the intended capabilities; and (b) IMD funding requirements as appropriate.

Since final material solutions are yet to be approved prior to MS A, specific system configuration and detailed IMD requirements are generally not known. However, based on the intended operational mission, the program should identify the likely IMD type(s) (e.g. Radar, Thermal, Acoustic, Electronic Warfare Integrated Reprogramming (EWIR), Geospatial Intelligence (GEOINT), etc.) the domain (e.g. Space, Air, Land, Naval, Missile Defense, etc.), data fidelity (e.g. queuing quality), and possibly sub-categories within a domain (e.g. for Air: Fighter Aircraft) for each subsystem that requires the data can be identified.

IMD requirements and related implications to design, performance, and T&E, are best accounted for and considered throughout the Materiel Solution Analysis Phase.
Relevant questions to consider and actions to take during this phase include:

Questions:

- Has the program been identified for Foreign Military Sales (FMS)? If yes, then how will this affect design, development, testing, disclosure and releasability of IMD-dependent components?
- For each proposed material solution identified during the Analysis of Alternatives (AoA) process, will the solution require the detection and identification of an activity, event, person, material, or equipment? If yes, then for each proposed detection or identification method (radar, electro-optical/infrared (EO/IR), acoustic, chemical, etc.), assess the technical feasibility of acquiring IMD within cost and schedule constraints. Consider the quality of available IMD, the capability of the DIE to deliver IMD and whether the IMD needs to be collected, processed and/or developed.

Actions:

- Consider IMD during development of the preliminary system specification, system functions that will likely drive the need for IMD, either directly or through derived requirements.
- Consider potential IMD requirements during development of mission and functional threads.

Consider IMD requirements during development of T&E strategies and plans based on the need to verify and validate detection and identification functionality. Characterize associated technical risk in the T&E Strategy. Estimate IMD delivery requirements to meet projected test schedules so that the program can articulate to the DIE their need dates for specified IMD.

CH 7-S–2.2. Technology Development Phase to MS B

As a program approaches MS B, the LMDP can be expanded to include mission or capability specific details to support program development. For example, as the design matures, additional details should emerge about the design of the sensors and the algorithms. The LMDP might also identify any IMD-based models and earlier submissions for IMD submitted to a Service IPC (National Air and Space Intelligence Center, National Ground Intelligence Center, Office of Naval Intelligence, Missile and Space Intelligence Center, etc.), other IMD production efforts (e.g. lab, warfare research center, or other agency, organization, etc.), and planned IMD collection events that the program will conduct.

Based on initial IMD requirements defined for MS A, refine and add details for the MS B LMDP during development of the Systems Performance Specification and the Allocated Baseline. Submit any new or refined IMD requirements to the Service IPCs and IMDC for costing and availability assessment and then update the LMDP with results of that assessment. Relative questions to consider and actions to take during this phase include:

Questions:

- Has the program been identified for FMS? If yes, then how will this affect design, development, testing, disclosure and releasability of IMD-dependent components?
- For each proposed detection/identification method (radar, EO/IR, acoustic, chemical, etc.), does the required IMD (signature, EWIR, GEOINT, OOB, C&P) already exist (at the estimated quality needed) or will it need to be processed, produced, or collected?

- Is the required detection/identification technology sufficiently mature (Technology Readiness Level 6 or higher) to proceed into end-item design or MS B?
- Which IMD-dependent performance requirements need to be verified through T&E?
- Does the program have IMD requirements derived from Modeling and Simulation activities?
- Can the estimated IMD processing, production, collection be completed within required cost and schedule?
- Do the detection/identification algorithms or processes need to be designed to accommodate IMD updates?
- Is there potential for the detection/identification hardware and software to perform IMD collection and provide updates to IMD databases? If yes, has a design study been conducted to assess feasibility and cost/benefit analysis?
- Have significant IMD-dependent functions been included in the proposed exit criteria for the Engineering & Manufacturing Development (EMD) Phase?
- Has the program's spectrum requirements taken into account bandwidth needed for IMD updates during system operations and sustainment?
- Should any IMD data sets be considered as Government Furnished Equipment for the EMD Contract?

Actions:

- During the functional allocation process, conduct sensitivity analyses on IMD level of quality (e.g. resolution, frequency range, etc.) to assess quality of available data versus required quality to meet performance key performance parameters/key system attributes.
- Define system level functional and performance requirements derived from items such as: Concept of Operations (CONOPS), system-level performance metrics, mission threads/use cases, and usage environment. Document results and requirements in the System Requirements Document, LMDP, and Systems Engineering Plan (SEP) as appropriate.

Assess IMD requirements and schedule relative to Director, Operational T&E needs. Document results in the LMDP and by reference in the T&E Master Plan.

CH 7-S–2.3. Engineering and Manufacturing Phase to MS C

This LMDP will be an update to the previous LMDP. The purpose is to add any new IMD considerations resulting from design maturity or changes in the CONOPS. It should include expected IMD data flows for system employment in an operational environment. The LMDP should include information on IMD data existing within the program (modeling and simulation or measured physical parameters) for sensor or algorithm development or for testing purposes, and; information on the existence of any blue IMD collected to support the program. Additionally, the IMD production concept must be defined and coordinated with the DIE. At a minimum this should include the identification of organizations for the production of IMD, addressing responsible entities for adversary commercial systems, and US systems (blue). This information is required to ensure that this form of IMD is available through the DoD data sources.

Based on IMD requirements defined at MS B, refine and add details for the MS C LMDP during development of the System Functional Specifications and the Initial Product Baseline. Relevant questions to consider and actions to take during this phase include:

Questions:

- Has the program been identified for FMS? If yes, then how will this affect design, development, testing, disclosure and releasability of IMD-dependent components?
- For each proposed detection/identification method (radar, EO/IR, acoustic, chemical, etc.), has IMD (signature, EWIR, GEOINT, OOB, C&P) required for system operations and sustainment been planned for in the LMDP and AS, at the level of quality needed?
- Which IMD requirements need to be verified in Follow-on T&E (FOT&E)?

Actions:

- Determine IMD-related schedule events (need date from Intelligence Production Center, algorithm or sensor critical test-related dates, etc.) for inclusion in the System Technical Schedule within the SEP.
- Assess IMD-related functions for inclusion in Risk Management assessments in the SEP.

Assess IMD requirements and schedule relative to FOT&E needs. Document results in the LMDP and by reference in the updated TEMP.

CH 7-S-2.4. Low-Rate Initial Production to Full-Rate Production/Full Deployment Decision Review to Disposal

In preparation for initial operational capability, an LMDP update is required to ensure congruence with the Final Production Baseline and to fully account for required operational signatures based on the latest threat assessments and CONOPS for the system. This LMDP also needs to fully account for IMD sustainment plans including identification of processes and data sources which are essential for system operations, such as: IMD production processes; IMD databases; IMD verification and validation for operational use; processes and systems which support development and dissemination of IMD data for operational missions.

This LMDP should take into consideration relevant Combatant Command or operating unit processes for updating and fulfilling IMD requirements during operation and sustainment of the system. Relevant questions to consider and actions to take during this phase include:

Questions

- For FMS versions of the system, have IMD-dependent components been verified for release and authorized by the Designated Disclosure Authority?
- Have IMD support requirements been addressed in the Operations and Support Phase?
- Does the current CONOPS for the system drive new or updated IMD requirements? Have these new/updated IMD requirements been handed off to the operational requirements prioritization processes?
- If the operational system has an IMD reprogramming process, is the reprogramming system and organization ready for operations?

Actions

- Coordinate the LMDP with the requirements sponsor.
- Confirm operations of the IMD reprogramming process.

CH 7-Version and Revision History

The table below tracks chapter changes. It indicates the current version number and date published, and provides a brief description of the content.

Version #	Revision Date	Reason
0	2/1/17	Chapter 7 administrative changes
1	4/27/17	Chapter 7 administratively updated to coincide with DoDI 5000.02, CH 2, primarily establishing the VOLT and Threat Modules, and replacing the ITEA, CTA and STAR.

| 2 | 6/8/17 | Chapter 7 link in paragraph 7-3.2.1.3 corrected and administrative changes made for clarification. |

CH 8-1. Purpose

The Defense Acquisition Guidebook (DAG), Chapter 8, provides guidance on the process and procedures for managing risks through planning and executing an effective and affordable test and evaluation (T&E) program that enables the Department of Defense (DoD) to acquire systems that work. With a robust and rigorous T&E program, engineers and decision-makers have the knowledge and support they need to manage risks, measure progress, and characterize operational effectiveness, operational suitability and survivability (including cybersecurity), or lethality.

The fundamental purpose of test and evaluation (T&E) is to enable the DoD to acquire systems that work. To that end, T&E provides engineers and decision-makers with knowledge to assist in managing risks, to measure technical progress, and to characterize operational effectiveness, operational suitability and survivability (including cybersecurity), or lethality. This is done by planning and executing a robust and rigorous T&E program. The objective of a T&E program is to characterize system capabilities across the intended operational conditions, verify that testable requirements are met or not met, and inform decision-makers, in accordance with DoDI 5000.02 (Encl. 4, para 2(a) – page 90). To that end, T&E enables the DoD to: acquire systems that work, provide engineers and decision-makers with knowledge to assist in managing risks, measure technical progress, and characterize operational effectiveness, operational suitability, and survivability (including cybersecurity), or lethality of the system in the intended operational environment. This is done by planning and executing a robust and rigorous T&E program.

CH 8–2. Background

The determination of how much and what kind of testing is sufficient for a program is a core challenge to the development of any T&E strategy. A new technical effort or a significant improvement in capability over a current system may require a significant amount of effort in developing the system. Therefore, programs need a comprehensive T&E strategy to inform acquisition decisions. In assessing the level of evaluations necessary, consider the maturity of the technologies used, the complexity of integration, and the operational environment of the system.

CH 8–2.1 T&E Strategy

The strategy for T&E begins with a review and understanding of the threat and the requirements. Program managers devise a T&E strategy generating the knowledge necessary for the acquisition, programmatic, operational, technical, and life-cycle support decisions of a program. Forming an effective T&E strategy requires careful analysis to determine the appropriate scope and depth of evaluations to be completed. This approach to T&E strategy development is to plan for the evaluation before testing, execute the test program, and conduct the evaluation as test data become available. This creates an environment where the evaluation guides the formulation of test objectives, configurations, conditions, data requirements, and analysis to develop information in support of the decision-making process.

Scientific Test & Analysis Techniques (STAT) should be used in designing an effective and efficient T&E program, in accordance with DoDI 5000.02 (Encl. 5, para 5(e) – page 101), in order to balance risk and the level of knowledge required for evaluations.

A non-developmental item (i.e., Commercial-Off-The-Shelf (COTS) or Government-Off-The-Shelf (GOTS)) still requires evaluation to assess capability. This may not involve much testing, but needs to ensure the item meets advertised capability, maturity, integration, and interoperability requirements. Therefore, developmental testing may be limited in scope, with operational testing focusing on the operational effectiveness, operational suitability, and survivability (including cybersecurity) or lethality of the system in the intended operational environment.

Evaluation assessments also address key risks or issues associated with sustaining the system capability in operational use, as well as the overall logistics effort, maintenance (both corrective and preventative), servicing, calibration, and support aspects.

CH 8–2.2 DoD T&E Organizations

The Deputy Assistant Secretary of Defense for Developmental Test and Evaluation (DASD(DT&E)) develops policy and guidance for developmental test and evaluation (DT&E) within the Department of Defense (DoD). The DASD(DT&E) also serves as the Director, Test Resource Management Center (TRMC) for oversight of DoD T&E resources and infrastructure. The DASD(DT&E) closely coordinates with the Deputy Assistant Secretary of Defense for Systems Engineering (DASD(SE)), and routinely coordinates with other Office of the Secretary of Defense (OSD) organizations.

The Director, Operational Test and Evaluation (DOT&E) provides oversight of operational test and evaluation (OT&E), and live fire test and evaluation (LFT&E), for programs on the DOT&E Oversight List, in accordance with DoDI 5000.02 (Encl. 5, para 3(a) – page 99). The DOT&E is responsible for generating OT&E and LFT&E policy for all programs within the DoD.

In accordance with 10 USC 139 (para e(2)), and 10 USC 139b (para a(6)), the Secretary of Defense (SecDef) ensures both DASD(DT&E) and DOT&E have access to all records and data of the DoD (including the records and data of each Military Department and including classified and proprietary information, as appropriate) that they consider necessary in order to carry out their respective duties.

The DASD(DT&E) and DOT&E share or coordinate on the following responsibilities:

- Prescribe policies and procedures for T&E within the DoD.
- Provide advice, assessments, and recommendations to the SecDef, DepSecDef, and USD(AT&L), as well as support Overarching Integrated Product Teams (OIPTs) and Defense Acquisition Boards (DABs)/Information Technology Acquisition Boards for programs.
- Assess the adequacy of T&E strategies and plans for programs on the major defense acquisition program (MDAP), major automated information system (MAIS), AT&L Special Interest list, and DOT&E Oversight Lists by approving or disapproving Test and Evaluation Master Plans (TEMPs).
- Monitor and review DT&E, OT&E, and LFT&E events to assess adequacy of test planning, identify test execution issues, assess progress of T&E efforts, and obtain data for separate evaluations.
- Participate in the Developmental Test Readiness Review (TRR) and Operational Test Readiness Review (OTRR) process by providing assessments and recommendations concerning a system's readiness for operational testing.
- Provide assessments of system performance, T&E, and interoperability/information security for the Defense Acquisition Executive Summary (DAES) process.
- Assist program managers (PMs) in developing, assessing, and updating their T&E strategy, schedule and resources, and evaluating system performance.

CH 8–2.2.1 DASD(DT&E)

The Deputy Assistant Secretary of Defense for Developmental Test and Evaluation (DASD(DT&E)) serves as the principal advisor to the SecDef and the USD(AT&L) for DT&E in the DoD; and, as such, has responsibilities and duties as prescribed in 10 USC 139b (Para a(5)), as well as DoDI 5134.17 (1(b) – page 3), Deputy Assistant Secretary of Defense for Developmental Test and Evaluation (DASD(DT&E)). Refer to DASD(DT&E) for additional information. In this capacity, the DASD(DT&E) shall:

- Develop policies and guidance for:
  - The planning, execution, and reporting of DT&E in the DoD, including integration and DT&E of software.
  - The integration of developmental and operational tests in coordination with the Director, Operational Test & Evaluation.
  - The planning, execution, and reporting of DT&E executed jointly by more than one Military Department or Defense Agency.
  - The use of DT&E planning principles and best practices.

- o Development of TEMPs in conjunction with the DOT&E.
- o Inclusion of provisions in Requests for Proposals (RFPs) that relate to DT&E.
- o The use of DT&E approaches to effectively support reliability growth programs.
- o The reporting of DT&E results to the DASD(DT&E) and USD(AT&L).
- Provide advice and make recommendations to the Secretary of Defense and the USD(AT&L) regarding DT&E and the execution of these activities within and across defense acquisition programs.
- Provide guidance to defense acquisition programs for developing and documenting the program's evaluation strategy and management approach in the TEMP throughout the program's life cycle.
- Act as an advisory member of the Defense Acquisition Board (DAB) and other key acquisition bodies; provide independent assessments of program DT&E, execution, and risk.
- Provide a recommendation to approve or disapprove the MDAP DT&E plans as well as advise the relevant technical authorities for these programs on the incorporation of best practices for developmental test from across the Department.
- Beginning with the Materiel Development Decision, monitor the development test and evaluation program activities of Major Defense Acquisition Programs (MDAPs) and review the DT&E plans for those programs in the TEMP.
- Serve as the T&E Functional Leader for the T&E acquisition career field within the DoD, providing advocacy, oversight, and guidance to elements of the acquisition workforce responsible for test and evaluation.
- Inform the Joint Capabilities Integration and Development System (JCIDS) process to ensure key technical requirements are measurable, testable, and achievable.
- Inform the DAES process.
- Submit, not later than March 31 of each year, to the congressional defense committees, an annual report as outlined in 10 USC 139b (Para d).
- Consult with the Assistant Secretary of Defense for Research and Engineering (ASD(R&E)) on technological maturity and integration risk of critical technologies of MDAPs.
- Periodically review the organizations and capabilities of the Military Departments with respect to DT&E and identify needed changes or improvements to such organizations and capabilities.

CH 8–2.2.2 Office of the D,OT&E

The Office of the Director, Operational Test and Evaluation (D,OT&E), a principal staff assistant and advisor to the Secretary of Defense, has specific responsibilities assigned by 10 USC 139 and 2399 for OT&E and 10 USC 2366 for LFT&E. Additional responsibilities are identified in DoD Directive (DoDD) 5141.02, Director of Operational Test and Evaluation.

For purposes here, DOT&E:

- Prescribes policies and procedures for the conduct of OT&E and LFT&E for DoD.
- Monitors and reviews OT&E and LFT&E activities in the DoD.
- Exercises oversight responsibility for ACAT I or other programs in which the SecDef has special interest or for which DOT&E determines oversight is required, in accordance with DoDI 5000.02 (Encl. 5, para 3(a) – page 99).
- Publishes the DOT&E Oversight List, which identifies all programs under oversight for OT&E and/or LFT&E.
- Assesses the adequacy of OT&E and LFT&E performed by the Services and Operational Test Agencies (OTAs) for programs under DOT&E oversight.
- Approves the TEMP for oversight programs.
- Approves, in writing, the adequacy of operational test plans for those programs under DOT&E oversight prior to the commencement of operational testing.

- Approves, in writing, the use of data collected outside an approved operational test plan for use in operational evaluation.
- Approves LFT&E strategies and waivers prior to commencement of LFT&E activities.
- Approves the quantity of test articles required for operational testing of MDAPs; to include what is production representative for purposes of adequate and realistic OT&E, for programs on DOT&E oversight.
- Independently assesses the adequacy of testing and the operational effectiveness, operational suitability, and survivability (including cybersecurity) or lethality of programs under oversight.
- Provides independent reports to the SecDef, Congress, and USD(AT&L), among others, to support acquisition and operational decisions.
- Submits a report to the SecDef and Congress before systems on OSD DOT&E Oversight may proceed Beyond Low Rate Initial Production (BLRIP).
- Advises the DoD Executive Agent for Space and the acquiring Military Department on T&E of DoD Space MDAPs and other space programs designated for T&E oversight, in support of DoDD 3100.10, Space Policy (Encl. 2, para 3(a) –page 8).
- Provides support to the Director, Joint Improvised-Threat Defeat Agency (JIDA), consistent with DoDD 2000.19E, Joint Improvised Explosive Device Defeat Organization (JIEDDO) (Para 6.12 – page 8).
- Oversees and assesses operational capability demonstrations conducted by the Missile Defense Agency (MDA), consistent with DoDD 5134.09, Missile Defense Agency (MDA) (Para 6(c)(18)(b) – page 5).
- Establishes policy on the verification, validation, and accreditation (VV&A) of models and simulations used in support of OT&E and LFT&E.
- Oversees the International T&E (IT&E) program for the SecDef.
- Oversees and prescribes policy, as appropriate, to ensure adequate usage and verification of protection of human subjects and adherence to ethical standards in OT&E and LFT&E, in support of DoDD 3216.02, Protection of Human Subjects and Adherence to Ethical Standards in DoD-Supported Research (Part II – page 36).
- Assists and advises the Chairman of the Joint Chiefs of Staff (CJCS) in efforts to ensure the JCIDS documents, in terms verifiable through testing or analysis in support of Chairman of the Joint Chiefs of Staff Instruction (CJCSI) 3170.01I, (Para 4(f)(7) – page 4), Joint Capabilities Integration and Development System, provides the expected joint operational mission environment, mission level measures of effectiveness (MOEs), and key performance parameters (KPPs).
- Manages:
  - Efforts to improve interoperability and cybersecurity in the department through the operational evaluation of the systems under oversight and major exercises conducted by the combatant commands and the Military Departments.
  - Joint Test and Evaluation (JT&E) program (DoD Common Access Card (CAC) required).
  - Joint Live Fire program.
  - Center for Countermeasures.
  - Activities of the Joint Aircraft Survivability program.
  - Activities of the Joint Technical Coordinating Group for Munitions Effectiveness and producing the Joint Munitions Effectiveness Manual.
  - Activities of the T&E Threat Resource Activity.

The DOT&E prescribes policies and procedures for the conduct of OT&E and LFT&E in the DoD, in accordance with 10 USC 139 and 2366, respectively. For programs under DOT&E oversight, DOT&E

serves as the final approval authority for OT&E and LFT&E planning, including approval of the TEMP. DOT&E staff representatives provide advice to, and actively participate in, acquisition program T&E Working-Level Integrated Product Teams (WIPTs). DOT&E is a member/advisor of both the Joint Requirements Oversight Council (JROC) and the OIPT, providing advice and recommendations at DAB reviews; and has direct access to both USD(AT&L) and the SecDef, on all matters relating to OT&E.

PMs initiate early engagement with DOT&E through the Service and Defense Agency T&E Executives and independent Operational Test Agencies (OTAs). PMs also charter a T&E WIPT to aid in development of strategies for T&E and the TEMP. Since OT&E acts as a validation process for Systems Engineering, early engagement of the OTA and DOT&E is essential. Also, an early comprehensive assessment of the Analysis of Alternatives and any emerging requirements documents helps clarify and ensure the rationale, measurability, and testability of requirements, and clarify the associated implications to cost and schedule. These actions require close and continuous coordination with users, sponsors, developers, and all potential test organizations to ensure correct understanding and articulation of end-game expectations during program planning and documentation.

DOT&E approves all OT&E plans for all programs on the DOT&E Oversight List (DoD CAC required), including, but not limited to, early operational assessments (EOAs), operational assessments (OAs), Limited User Tests (LUTs), IOT&E, and Follow-on Operational Test & Evaluation (FOT&E). In accordance with 10 USC 139, OTAs provide DOT&E plans to assess adequacy of data collection and analysis planning to support DOT&E's independent assessment of a system's operational effectiveness, operational suitability, and survivability (including cybersecurity) or lethality. Additionally, OTAs schedule a test concept briefing at least 180 days prior to the anticipated start of an operational test. OTAs provide OT&E plans for DOT&E approval at least 60 days prior to the start of test events.

In accordance with 10 USC 139, the D,OT&E approves the number of low-rate initial production (LRIP) systems required for adequate operational testing of programs on the DOT&E Oversight List. For programs not on DOT&E oversight for operational testing, the Service OTA determines the number of LRIP systems required for OT&E. DOT&E and the OTAs routinely engage the PM in those decisions. For programs not on the DOT&E Oversight List, the Service or Defense Agency OTA works with the PMs for OT&E, including planning, applicable oversight, and execution and reporting; in accordance with DoDI 5000.02 (Encl. 5, para 3(a) – page 99).

In accordance with 10 USC 2399 (Para a), an MDAP must complete IOT&E before proceeding beyond LRIP.

In accordance with DoDD 5141.02 (Para 6(c) – page 5), in addition to OT&E oversight, the SecDef charges DOT&E with approving waivers to Full-Up, System-Level (FUSL) LFT&E and approval of required alternative LFT&E plans prior to Milestone B. For more detailed information on the waiver process, see DAG CH 8.3.2.5.5., Full-up, System-Level Testing Waiver Process.

Refer to DOT&E for additional information.

CH 8–2.2.3 Test Resource Management Center

In accordance with 10 USC 139b (Para a(7)), the DASD(DT&E) serves concurrently as Director, Test Resource Management Center (TRMC), a field activity reporting directly to the USD(AT&L). 10 USC 196 (Para c) and DoDD 5105.71, Department of Defense Test Resource Management Center (TRMC), define the specific responsibilities of the TRMC, including the planning for, and assessment of, the adequacy of the Major Range and Test Facility Base (MRTFB). TRMC maintains awareness of other T&E facilities and resources, within and outside the DoD, and their impacts on DoD test capability in support of development, acquisition, fielding, and sustainment of defense systems. Within TRMC, the T&E Range Oversight (TERO) staff provides expertise on the MRTFB and assists DASD(DT&E) staff specialists in the review of TEMPs for adequacy of test infrastructure supporting a program's T&E. Bi-annually, TRMC produces the DoD T&E Resources Strategic Plan to inform DoD and Congress about the projected future of the T&E infrastructure's capability, to fulfill the T&E needs of the department. DoDI 3150.09, The

Chemical, Biological, Radiological, and Nuclear (CBRN) Survivability Policy, (Encl. 2, para 8(c) – page 14), states that TRMC assesses T&E infrastructure to ensure CBRN survivability test capabilities and resources are adequate or gaps are identified for investments.

TRMC oversees the MRTFB in accordance with responsibilities found in DoDD 3200.11, Major Range and Test Facility Base (MRTFB).

CH 8–2.2.3.1 Major Range & Test Facility Base

The Major Range and Test Facility Base (MRTFB) is the designated core set of DoD T&E infrastructure (open-air ranges, test facilities, instrumentation data processing, and other test resources) and associated workforce to provide T&E capabilities in support of the DoD acquisition system. The DoD, through the TRMC, oversees sustainment of all MRTFB T&E organizations or activities with a skilled workforce, and T&E technical capabilities and processes. MRTFB capabilities are available to all components under a common charge policy defined in DoD 7000.14-R, FMR Volume 11A, CH 12. Funding of MRTFB activities is designed to:

- Assure the most cost effective development and testing of materiel.
- Provide for inter-Service compatibility, efficiency, and equity without influencing technical testing decisions or inhibiting legitimate and valid testing.

The MRTFB is described in DoDD 3200.11, Major Range and Test Facility Base (MRTFB), and operates in accordance with DoDI 3200.18, Management and Operation of the Major Range and Test Facility Base (MRTFB). The Director, TRMC publishes for the SecDef the composition of the MRTFB activities, which can be found in DoDD 3200.11 (Para 5.1.2. – page 3). The TRMC TERO staff can assist in assessing MRTFB capabilities for programs through the DASD(DT&E) staff specialist participating in the T&E WIPT, or program managers can query TRMC directly through the TERO mailbox at: osd.pentagon.ousd-atl.mbx.trmc-tero@mail.mil.

CH 8–2.2.3.2 Non-Major Range & Test Facility Base Capabilities

DoDI 5000.02 (Encl. 4, para 5(b) – page 95), instructs programs to use government T&E facilities, unless an exception can be justified as cost-effective to the government. When programs consider locations to best accomplish T&E within budget and schedule, they start with MRTFB activities. MDAPs and MAIS rely on T&E facilities and other infrastructure owned and managed by the Services for a majority of their T&E infrastructure needs, and for the Lead DT&E Organization to determine and arrange for participating test organizations (MRTFB and non-MRTFB), as needed, to complement their capabilities to fully execute the T&E program. Reimbursement rates for use of all DoD or government T&E capabilities are subject to DoD 7000.14-R, FMR Vol.11A, CH 12. Use of or investment in commercial test capabilities requires a Cost Benefit Analysis (CBA) before incorporating or scheduling test plans. The TEMP articulates a concise summary of the CBA for the use of any commercial test facilities.

DoD does not provide a single source catalog of DoD T&E capabilities. For MDAPs, the Lead DT&E Organization should have knowledge of all government test resources for testing similar technologies and commodities, and should be able to advise the Chief Developmental Tester and the T&E WIPT of their recommendations. The Lead DT&E Organization can, if needed, query TRMC or contact TRMC directly for assistance in assessing potential test facilities and ranges via e-mail at: osd.pentagon.ousd-atl.mbx.trmc-tero@mail.mil with the subject line: "Test Capabilities Directory Assistance Request." In the e-mail, provide program or organization name, short description of T&E capability needed, and an e-mail and phone number for the point of contact requesting information. A TERO staff support agent will assist in your T&E capabilities query.

Table 1 provides a list of T&E capability links, by DoD Component.

Table 1: DoD T&E Capability Links

| ARMY | Army Test and Evaluation Command (ATEC) |
| | This site links to Army MRTFB sites as well as some non-MRTFB sites. |

NAVY	Naval Air Systems Command (NAVAIR)
	Request contact information for NAVAIR 5.0 Test and Evaluation.
	Naval Sea Systems Command (NAVSEA)
	Reference the "Pocket Guide" for Warranted Technical Authorities listing or request contact information for the SEA 05B R&SE T&E office.
	Marine Corps Systems Command (MARCORSYSCOM)
	Request the Command Officer of the Day provide contact information for T&E in Deputy Commander Systems Engineering, Interoperability, Architectures & Technology (DC SIAT) office.
	SPAWAR
	Request contact information from Navy N84.

| AIR FORCE | AFOTEC |

| OTHER | Range Commanders Council (RCC) |
| | Links to various DoD range facilities. The Secretariat may be able to provide contact information for various RCC members or Standing Groups. |

CH 8–2.2.3.3 Joint Mission Environment Test Capability

The Joint Mission Environment Test Capability (JMETC) program's mission is to provide a DoD-wide capability for distributed T&E of warfighter capabilities in a Joint context for interoperability, cybersecurity, KPP compliance testing, developmental testing (DT) and operational testing (OT), as well as Joint Mission Capability Portfolio testing, in accordance with DoDI 5000.02 (Encl. 4, para 3(f) – page 92). The program provides a test infrastructure necessary to conduct distributed test events integrating live, virtual, and constructive (LVC) test resources configured to support the users' needs. Distributed testing provides for near real-time "Test-Fix-Test" and integrated DT and OT methods that can provide early discovery of system problems. JMETC provides a dedicated help desk, common integration software for linking sites, accredited test tools, and distributed testing subject matter experts (SMEs) to support users with requirements development, test planning, cybersecurity, network troubleshooting, and use of test tools.

In the fall of 2012, TRMC assumed responsibility and funding for the National Cyber Range (NCR). The NCR provides a high-fidelity, realistic cyber environment to conduct sophisticated cyber training and support for cyber testing during all phases of the system life cycle as well as testing of complex system-of-systems. The NCR supports the ability to design, deploy, and sanitize large-scale, high-fidelity test and training environments in which malicious threats can be released on operationally representative systems and networks to assess their impact. The NCR provides the capability to emulate military and adversary networks at a relevant level of sophistication needed to execute realistic cyber tests, as well as cyber mission rehearsals. An integrated tool suite provides automation and the ability to support multiple concurrent events, executed in isolated test beds at different levels of classification. NCR SMEs are available, at the discretion of the user, to support the planning, execution, and analysis of test and training events. The NCR has the capability to collaborate/integrate with other cyber ranges using secure networks when test events require special capabilities, additional scale, or connectivity to remote sites or assets.

For contact information and a map of JMETC distributed capabilities, locate the "Interoperability & Cyber Test" link on the DASD(DT&E)/Director, TRMC website, or directly from the JMETC website (Requires JMETC account).

CH 8–2.3 Component T&E Organizations

This section provides information on the varying DoD and Service T&E organizations, as highlighted in DoDI 5000.02 (Encl. 4 – page 90) and DoDI 5000.02 & Encl. 5 – page 98), and provides information on their functions and responsibilities.

CH 8–2.3.1 Army T&E Executive

The Army T&E Executive is the Director, T&E Office under the authority, direction, and control of the Deputy Under Secretary of the Army. Army Regulation (AR) 73-1 (CH 2 (2-1) – page 2) [NOTE: due to authentication controls, you must start from Army ePubs page and search in Publications/Administrative/Army Regulations for AR 73-1.] lists key Army T&E Executive duties and responsibilities include:

- Serving as the senior advisor to the Secretary of the Army and the Chief of Staff, Army, on all Army T&E matters.
- Advising the Army Systems Acquisition Review Council (ASARC), the Army Requirements Oversight Council (AROC), and OIPTs on T&E matters.
- Approving test-related documentation for the Secretary of the Army and forwarding, as appropriate, to OSD.
- Coordinating T&E matters with the Joint Staff and OSD, including serving as the principal Army interface on matters of T&E with the USD(AT&L) and DOT&E.
- Overseeing all Army T&E missions and functions, to include formulating overarching Army T&E strategy, policy, and program direction; providing policy oversight, and management of resources.
- Providing Headquarters, Department of the Army oversight on the funding of the Army Threat Simulator program, Army Targets program, and Army Instrumentation program.
- Overseeing Army responsibilities in Joint T&E, Foreign Comparative Testing (FCT), and multi-Service and multi-national T&E acquisition programs.
- Serving as the Army T&E functional chief for the T&E acquisition workforce career field.

CH 8–2.3.2 Air Force T&E Executive

The Air Force T&E Executive serves as the Director, Air Force Test and Evaluation (AF/TE), who serves under the authority and direction of the Secretary of the Air Force (SECAF) and the Chief of Staff of the Air Force (CSAF), in accordance with Headquarters Air Force Mission Directive 1-52 (HAF MD 1-52). In this capacity, the AF/TE:

- Functions as the sole focal point for Air Force T&E policy, guidance, direction, and oversight for the formulation, review, and execution of T&E plans, programs, and budgets.
- Functions as the chief T&E advisor to senior Air Force leadership on T&E processes; including contractor testing, DT&E, OT&E, LFT&E, and the use of modeling and simulation in T&E.

- Functions as the final T&E review authority and signatory for TEMPs prior to Component Acquisition Executive (CAE) and OSD approval and signature.
- Collaborates with requirements sponsors and system developers to improve operational requirements, system development, and the fielding of operationally effective, operationally suitable, safe, and survivable systems.
- Reviews and/or prepares T&E information for timely release to OSD, Congress, and decision-makers.
- Oversees the Air Force T&E infrastructure by determining the adequacy of T&E resources required to support system acquisition activities. Administers various T&E resource processes and chairs or serves on various committees, boards, and groups supporting T&E activities.
- Acts as the single point of entry for the Air Force Foreign Materiel program.
- Manages the Air Force Joint Test & Evaluation program according to DoDI 5010.41, Joint Test and Evaluation (JT&E) program.
- Functions as the certifying authority for T&E personnel in the Acquisition Professional Development Program (APDP) when not delegated to the Major Commands (MAJCOMs).

CH 8–2.3.3 Navy T&E Executive

The Director, Innovation, Test and Evaluation, and Technology Requirements (Office of the Chief of Naval Operations ((OPNAV) N84) serves as the Department of Navy (DON) T&E Executive, as outlined in Secretary of the Navy Instruction (SECNAVINST) 5000.2E (Para 7(g) – page 7). The DON T&E Executive reports to the Chief of Naval Operations (CNO), the Commandant of the Marine Corps (CMC), and the Principal Military Deputy to the Assistant Secretary of the Navy for Research, Development, and Acquisition (PMD ASN(RDA)), on all matters pertaining to T&E.

The DON T&E Executive supports and advises the Vice Chief of Naval Operations (VCNO) regarding the VCNO's role on the T&E Executive Board of Directors and serves as the Navy representative on the T&E Executive Board of Directors (Executive Secretariat).

The Director, Test and Evaluation and Technology Requirements (N84):

- Approves all Navy TEMPs for the CNO.
- Establishes Navy T&E requirements and promulgates policy, regulation, and procedures governing Navy T&E.
- Acts for CNO in resolving T&E requirements.

CH 8–2.3.4 Operational Test Agencies

This section provides information on the Defense Information Systems Agency (DISA) and the Service's Operational Test Agencies (OTAs). In accordance with DoDD 5000.01 (Encl. 1, para E1.1.8. – page 6), each Military Department shall establish an independent OTA reporting directly to the Service Chief to plan and conduct operational tests, report results, and provide evaluations of operational effectiveness, operational suitability, and survivability (including cybersecurity) or lethality.

CH 8–2.3.4.1 DISA Joint Interoperability Test Command

The Defense Information Systems Agency (DISA) Joint Interoperability Test Command (JITC) conducts operational testing of information technology and National Security Systems acquired by DISA, other DoD organizations, and non-DoD entities to ensure operational effectiveness, operational suitability, and survivability (including cybersecurity) or lethality, and security, in accordance with DoDD 5105.19 (Para 6.1.8.4. – page 6). JITC assists in the preparation of critical operational issues and develops, defines, and publishes measures of operational effectiveness, operational suitability, and survivability (including cybersecurity) or lethality, and measures of performance. The division also directs and approves OT&E methods for data collection, reduction, and analysis.

As part of the overall OT&E mission, JITC executes these specific methodologies for determining levels of operational testing appropriate to the risk posed by specific system increments:

- Prepare a risk assessment.
- Determine appropriate level of OT&E.
- Develop an OT&E plan appropriate for the level of test.
- Conduct test activities and prepare a report.
- Provide operational effectiveness, operational suitability, and survivability (including cybersecurity) or lethality and security recommendations.

CH 8–2.3.4.2 Army T&E Command

The U.S. Army Test and Evaluation Command (ATEC) is the Army's OTA and consists of the U.S. Army Evaluation Center (AEC), U.S. Army Operational Test Command (OTC), and Test Centers. AEC produces independent comprehensive evaluations and assessments by consolidating all DT, OT, and other credible data so as to provide essential information to decision-makers. Additionally, AEC produces system safety documentation. OTC plans, conducts, and reports on operational tests in order to provide essential information to AEC. ATEC's Test Centers plan, conduct, and report on developmental tests in order to provide essential information to AEC. Army Regulation 73-1 (Para 2 (2-2(d)(7) – page 3) [NOTE: due to authentication controls, you must start from Army ePubs page and search in Publications/Administrative/Army Regulations for AR 73-1.] provides additional information on ATEC responsibilities.

CH 8–2.3.4.3 Air Force Operational T&E Center

The Air Force Operational Test and Evaluation Center (AFOTEC) tests and evaluates new Air Force warfighting capabilities in operationally realistic environments, influencing and informing national resource decisions, in accordance with Air Force Mission Directive 14 (AFMD-14) and Air Force Instruction 99-103 (AFI 99-103) (CH 3.11 – page 28).

CH 8–2.3.4.4 Navy Commander of Operational T&E

The Navy Commander of Operational Test and Evaluation (COMOPTEVFOR) provides an independent and objective evaluation for the operational effectiveness, operational suitability, and survivability (including cybersecurity) or lethality of naval aviation; surface; subsurface; command, control, communications, computers, and intelligence (C4I); cryptologic; and space systems in support of DoD and Navy acquisition and fleet introduction decisions, in accordance with SECNAVINST 5000.2E (Para 7(i) – page 8).

CH 8–2.3.4.5 Marine Corps Operational T&E Activity

The Marine Corps Operational Test and Evaluation Activity (MCOTEA) provides operational testing and evaluation for the Marine Corps, and conducts additional testing and evaluation, as required, supporting the Marine Corps mission to man, train, equip, and sustain a force in readiness, in accordance with SECNAVINST 5000.2E (Para 7(i) – page 8).

CH 8–2.3.5 T&E Executive Board of Directors

The Test and Evaluation Executive Board of Directors (BOD) leads development of corporate OSD guidance for T&E infrastructure and configuration management, standards and policy, and investments. The BOD acts as the agent for the Service Vice Chiefs and equivalent Office of the Under Secretary of Defense (OUSD) and Defense Agency representatives with T&E management responsibilities. It consists of the Service T&E executives and equivalent OUSD and Defense Agency representatives with T&E infrastructure management responsibilities.

For more information on the T&E Executive Board of Directors, see the T&E Executive Board of Directors Charter.

CH 8–2.4 Program Office T&E Personnel & Support

Management responsibility for an acquisition program's T&E ultimately resides with the PMs. However, the planning, executing, and reporting of T&E involves interactions, support, and engagement from other organizations within OSD, the Services, Defense Agencies, and in some cases, other government agencies, as well as the system contractor(s). In accordance with DoDI 5000.02 (Encl. 4, para 3(e) – page 91, program managers will designate a T&E WIPT (also known as an Integrated Test Team), as soon as practicable after the Materiel Development Decision to support development of T&E strategies and estimates of resource requirements. An early charter for a T&E WIPT proves essential to the success of a T&E program. The Chief Developmental Tester chairs the T&E WIPT. For additional information, consult "Rules of the Road – A Guide for Leading a Successful Integrated Product Team" (October, 1999).

The PM, in concert with the user and the T&E community, coordinates DT&E, OT&E, LFT&E, system-of-systems (SoS) performance testing, interoperability testing, cybersecurity testing, reliability growth testing, safety testing, modeling and simulation (M&S), and CBRN survivability activities into an efficient continuum, closely integrated with requirements definition and systems design and development. The PM has responsibility for developing and obtaining final approval of the TEMP, which describes the overall strategy for T&E supporting the program's Acquisition Strategy (AS) and Systems Engineering Plan (SEP); the validated ICD, CDD, or CPD; the Concept of Operations/Operational Mode Summary/Mission Profile (CONOPS/OMS/MP); mandatory Enterprise Architecture views; as well as the resources necessary to execute the test program.

For additional information on PM duties and responsibilities, see DoDI 5000.02 (Encl. 2 – page 73).

CH 8–2.4.1 Chief Developmental Tester

As outlined in 10 USC 1706 (para a), DoDI 5000.02 (Encl. 4, para 3(a) – page 91), and the AT&L Memorandum, "Key Leadership Positions and Qualification Criteria," PMs will designate a Chief Developmental Tester for each MDAP and MAIS program. PMs for MDAP programs shall designate a government test agency as the Lead DT&E Organization, in accordance with 10 USC 139b (Para (c)(1)(a)). Further, PMs are to designate a Chief Developmental Tester and Lead DT&E Organization as soon as practicable after program office establishment.

For MDAP and MAIS programs, the Chief Developmental Tester position is filled by a properly qualified member of the Armed Forces or full-time employee of the DoD in a Key Leadership Position (KLP). The Chief Developmental Tester is to occupy a Defense Acquisition Workforce Improvement Act (DAWIA) T&E acquisition-coded position designated as a KLP, and be assigned or matrixed to a single ACAT program. A Chief Developmental Tester is to be designated for all ACAT II programs and below. ACAT II and below Chief Developmental Testers are to occupy a DAWIA T&E Coded position, but are not required to be designated as a KLP.

The Chief Developmental Tester has responsibility for:

- Coordinating the planning, management, and oversight of all DT&E activities for the program.
- Maintaining insight into contractor activities under the program.
- Overseeing the T&E activities of other participating government activities under the program.
- Helping program managers make technically informed, objective judgments about contractor developmental test and evaluation results under the program.
- Chairing the T&E WIPT.

CH 8–2.4.2 Key Leadership Positions

The USD(AT&L) memorandum, "Key Leadership Positions and Qualification Criteria," ensures KLPs are assigned to all MDAP and MAIS (ACAT I and ACAT IA) programs. Mandatory KI Ps include the Chief Developmental Tester who, in compliance with the memorandum, is to be designated in the position category associated with the lead function (T&E), and designated to a single ACAT program.

Positions are to be filled by properly qualified members of the Armed Forces or full-time employees of the DoD. KLPs require a significant level of authority commensurate with the responsibility and accountability for acquisition program success. The five factors identified as essential requirements for selection are education, experience, cross-functional competencies, tenure, and currency. Additional functional-specific requirements and preferences for KLPs are located at the DAU iCatalog. These requirements are updated annually by the functional leader for each career field.

CH 8–2.4.3 T&E Working-Level Integrated Product Team

Integrated Product Teams (IPTs) (also known as Integrated Test Teams) serve as an integral part of the DoD acquisition oversight and review process. DoD adopted the use of IPTs as an approach for the review and oversight of the acquisition process. IPTs take advantage of all members' expertise, produce an acceptable product, and facilitate decision-making.

In accordance with DoDI 5000.02 (Encl. 4, para 3(e) – page 91 & Encl. 5, para 4(a) – page 99), the T&E WIPT serves as a defined forum supporting the PM and other program working-level integrated product planning groups on all aspects of a program's T&E efforts and tracks the T&E program in all phases. This effort includes T&E program strategy, design, development, oversight; and the analysis, assessment, and reporting of test results. T&E WIPTs meet, as required, to help the PM resolve test issues. The Chief Developmental Tester ensures the PM establishes and charters a T&E WIPT as soon as practicable after the Materiel Development Decision, thus ensuring involvement in program strategy discussions and plans.

The T&E WIPT will include empowered representatives of test data stakeholders such as systems engineering, DT&E, OT&E, LFT&E, product support, the user, the intelligence community, and applicable certification authorities. The T&E WIPT is chaired by the Chief Developmental Tester and the membership includes, as a minimum, the following representative membership:

- The designated government Lead DT&E Organization.
- The designated Operational Test Agency (OTA).
- Proponent/User.
- Oversight organizations (OSD or Service/Defense Agency Headquarters, depending on whether the program is on oversight).
- Organizations issuing certifications and accreditations based on test data (e.g., Security Control Assessor (SCA), JITC, etc.).
- All evaluating and reporting organizations for the program.
- Organizations that generate test data for the program.
- Organizations requiring T&E data for the program.
- Other supporting or participating test organizations, when appropriate.
- Logistics and training organizations, when appropriate.
- The system contractor, when the contract has been awarded.
- Intelligence/Threat organization.

The T&E WIPT:

- Provides a forum for involvement by all key organizations in the T&E effort.
- Supports the development and tracking of an integrated test program for DT, OT, live fire, and modeling and simulation to support evaluations.
- Supports the development and maintenance of the integrated test schedule.
- Identifies and resolves test issues.
- Documents a TEMP development and coordination schedule as quickly as possible to ensure all interested parties are afforded an opportunity to contribute to TEMP development.
- Explores and facilitates opportunities to conduct Integrated Testing to meet DT/OT objectives.

The PM may form lower level functional working groups that report to the WIPT. These groups focus on specific areas such as integrated test planning; cybersecurity; software T&E; reliability; modeling and simulation development and use; verification, validation, and accreditation (VV&A); and threat support.

CH 8–2.4.4 Lead Developmental T&E Organization

In accordance with 10 USC 139b (Para (c)) and DoDI 5000.02 (Encl. 4, para 3(b) – page 91), each MDAP is to be supported by a Lead DT&E Organization. The Lead DT&E Organization is a government test organization and should be independent from the program office, when feasible. The Lead DT&E Organization has responsibility for:

- Providing technical expertise on T&E issues to the Chief Developmental Tester for the program.
- Conducting DT&E activities for the program, as directed by the Chief Developmental Tester.
- Assisting the Chief Developmental Tester in providing oversight of contractors under the program and in reaching technically informed, objective judgments about contractor DT&E results under the program.

For all other programs, a Lead DT&E Organization is used, when feasible, and identified in the CH 8–3.6 Test & Evaluation Master Plan.

CH 8–2.5 Program Engagement

This section provides information on DASD(DT&E) and DOT&E program engagement efforts.

CH 8–2.5.1 DT&E Engagement List

DASD(DT&E) monitors the activities of MDAP and MAIS programs, as well as USD(AT&L) designated special interest programs. In accordance with DoDI 5000.02 (Encl. 4, para 2(e) – page 91), DASD(DT&E) uses the MDAP, MAIS, and AT&L designated special interest lists (active programs and select inactive programs) to identify programs for DT&E oversight.

Access to the USD(AT&L) designated special interest list requires a Defense Acquisition Management Information Retrieval (DAMIR) account (DoD CAC required). Once inside DAMIR, find the "Business Intelligence" link and select Standard Data Queries, then select Program Information, and then select Special Interest Program List, which can then be exported into one of several formats.

For MDAP and MAIS definitions, see DoDI 5000.02 (Encl. 1, Table 1 – page 44).

CH 8–2.5.2 DOT&E Oversight List

Based on DoDI 5000.02 (Encl. 5, para 3 – page 99), the Director, Operational Test and Evaluation (DOT&E) designates programs for OT&E and/or LFT&E oversight, and publishes a DOT&E Oversight List. DOT&E considers all programs for inclusion, regardless of ACAT level, and can add to or delete from the list at any time. DOT&E considerations for inclusion on formal T&E oversight include:

- ACAT level.
- Potential for Joint designation.
- Potential for establishment as an acquisition program (such as Technology Projects identified in DoDI 5000.02 (Encl. 13, para 4(a)(3)(h) – page 147) or a pre-Major Defense Acquisition Program (MDAP)).
- Stage of development or production.
- Potential for DAES reporting.
- Congressional and/or DoD interest.

- Programmatic risk (cost, schedule, or performance).
- Past programmatic history of the developmental command.
- Relationship with other systems as part of a system-of-systems (SoS).
- Technical complexity of system.
- CBRN mission-critical systems.

CH 8–2.6 Program Reporting

This section provides information on the various DASD(DT&E) and DOT&E program reporting requirements.

CH 8–2.6.1 DT&E Program Reporting

DoDI 5000.02 (Encl. 1, Tables 2 – 8), summarizes statutory and regulatory reporting requirements, as well as specifying report requirements. The program reports that follow can be found in Table 5, and exceptions to reporting can be found in Table 6 of DoDI 5000.02 (Encl. 1).

CH 8–2.6.1.1 Congressional Notification of Conducting DT&E without an Approved TEMP

In accordance with P.L. 112-239, (SEC. 904 para h(3)), the USD(AT&L) notifies Congress not later than 30 days after any decision to conduct DT&E on an MDAP without an approved TEMP in place. The PM prepares and submits the notification to the USD(AT&L). The notification must include:

- A written explanation of the basis for the decision.
- A timeline for getting an approved plan in place.

A copy of the notification is provided to the DOT&E.

CH 8–2.6.1.2 DT&E Exception Reporting

Table 2 identifies the two cases for which Developmental Test and Evaluation (DT&E) submits an annual report to Congress.

Table 2: DT & E Exception Reporting

In accordance with P.L. 112-239 (SEC. 904 para (h(1)(A)) & (B)), the USD(AT&L) submits an annual Report to Congress (from fiscal year 2013 through fiscal year 2018) for the following conditions:	
Case 1	When an MDAP proceeds with implementing a TEMP that includes a developmental test plan disapproved by the DASD(DT&E).
	The Chief Developmental Tester needs to assist the PM to provide DASD(DT&E) the essential information for inclusion in the report. The report includes: ○ A description of the specific aspects of the DT&E plan determined to be inadequate. ○ An explanation of why the program disregarded the DASD(DT&E)'s recommendations. ○ A description of the steps taken to address the concerns of the DASD(DT&E).

	In accordance with P.L. 112-239 (SEC. 904 para (h(1)(A)) & (B)), the USD(AT&L) submits an annual Report to Congress (from fiscal year 2013 through fiscal year 2018) for the following conditions:
Case 2	When an MDAP proceeds to IOT&E following an assessment by DASD(DT&E) that the program is not ready for operational testing.
	The Chief Developmental Tester needs to assist the PM in providing the essential information to the DASD(DT&E) for inclusion in the report. The report includes: ○ An explanation of why the program proceeded to IOT&E despite the DASD(DT&E) findings. ○ A description of the aspects of the TEMP that had to be set aside to enable the program to proceed to IOT&E. ○ A description of how the program addressed the specific areas of concern raised in the assessment of operational test readiness. ○ A statement of whether IOT&E identified any significant shortcomings in the program.

CH 8–2.6.2 DOT&E Reporting

In accordance with 10 USC 2399 (Para a), the Director, Operational Test and Evaluation (DOT&E) provides a Beyond Low-Rate Initial Production (BLRIP) report to the SecDef, USD(AT&L), and congressional defense committees on the adequacy of OT&E conducted for each MDAP), and whether the results of such T&E confirm that the items or components actually tested are operationally effective, operationally suitable, and survivable (including cybersecurity) for combat. Additionally, in accordance with DoDI 5000.02 (Table 2 – pages 47-58), DOT&E completes the LFT&E report requirement for submission to the congressional defense committees, SecDef, and USD(AT&L) before the system may proceed to Full-Rate Production (FRP). For purposes of compliance with completion of IOT&E, the PM ensures the system under test reflects production-configuration or production-representative systems, preferably LRIP articles.

CH 8–2.7 TEMP Overview

The Test and Evaluation Master Plan (TEMP) is a signed contract among DOT&E, the DASD(DT&E), senior DoD Component leadership, the lead OTA, and the PM describing an acquisition program's T&E strategy and planned T&E activities over a program's life cycle, in accordance with DoDI 5000.02 (Encl. 5, para 5(a) – page 100). It serves as an executive summary and provides a developmental and operational evaluation framework to identify key data that will contribute to assessing the system's progress toward achieving requirements. It also is used as a guide when developing detailed T&E plans and documents, as well as schedule and resource implications associated with the T&E program. The program manager will use the TEMP as the primary planning and management tool for all test activities starting at Milestone A.

The TEMP includes a strategy for T&E and begins with a review and understanding of the threat and the requirements. The purpose of a T&E program is to characterize system capabilities across the intended operational conditions, verify that testable requirements are met or not met, and inform decision-makers. Program managers devise a T&E strategy generating the knowledge necessary for the acquisition, programmatic, operational, technical, and life-cycle support decisions of a program. Forming an effective T&E strategy requires careful analysis to determine the appropriate scope and depth of evaluations to be completed. This approach to T&E strategy development is to plan for the evaluation before testing, execute the test program, and conduct the evaluation as test data become available. This creates an environment where the evaluation guides the formulation of test objectives, configurations, conditions, data requirements, and analysis to develop information in support of the decision-making process.

For more information, go to DAG CH 8.3.6., Test & Evaluation Master Plan.

CH 8–3. Guidance

In accordance with 10 USC 139b, 139, 2399, 2400, and 2366 as well as DoDI 5134.17 and DoDD 5141.02, DoD employs three formal types of T&E (DT, OT, and LFT&E). Within these broad categories, the Military Departments and Defense Agencies have their own directives, guidance, organizations, T&E resources, ranges, and facilities specific to their needs.

This section provides the responsibilities and distinguishing features of each type of T&E. In addition, this section provides information on Integrated Testing and which programs should conduct such testing whenever feasible, to permit all stakeholders to use the same data in support of their respective evaluations.

The TRMC, in accordance with 10 USC 196 (Para c(1)(A)(i)), oversees the Major Range and Test Facility Base (MRTFB), and ensures availability of capabilities to support T&E.

Although the words *test* and *evaluation* are sometimes used interchangeably, they are two different concepts:

- Testing is a program or procedure designed to measure characteristics of an entity under identified conditions.
- Evaluation is the determination and substantiated judgment of risk associated with the significance, worth, or quality of capabilities or limitations of an entity, components, integrated system, or participant in a system-of-systems, using criteria established by systems engineers or users.

CH 8–3.1 Developmental T&E

Developmental Test and Evaluation (DT&E) is the disciplined process of generating substantiated knowledge on the capabilities and limitations of systems, subsystems, components, software, and materiel. This knowledge is used to inform decision-makers on risks in acquisition, programmatic, technical, and operational decisions throughout the acquisition life cycle. DT&E assesses maturity of technologies, system design, readiness for production, acceptance of government ownership of systems, readiness to participate in distributed and operational T&E, and sustainment in accordance with DoDI 5000.02 (Encl. 4, para 2(e) – page 90).

Both test and evaluation are necessary to gain value from a DT&E effort. In the context of DT&E, an entity can be a technology, process, materiel, software modules, components, subsystems, systems, and system-of-systems. Identified conditions refer to test conditions that are controlled, uncontrolled, measured, or not measured. Developmental evaluations are accomplished using criteria derived from various sources. The most common sources are the mission sets from the Concept of Operations/Operational Mode Summary/Mission Profile (CONOPS/OMS/MP), the capability gaps, user requirements specified in the capabilities documents (Initial Capabilities Document (ICD), Capability Development Document (CDD), Capability Production Document (CPD)), Critical Operational Issues (COIs), and Critical Operational Issues and Criteria (COIC), the design measures contained in the technical requirements documents (TRD), and contractual performance specifications. One set of tests can result in multiple developmental evaluations.

A DT&E program will:

- Verify achievement of critical technical parameters and the ability to achieve key performance parameters, and assess progress toward achievement of critical operational issues.
- Assess the system's ability to achieve the thresholds prescribed in the capabilities documents.

- Provide data to the program manager to enable root cause determination and to identify corrective actions.
- Validate system functionality.
- Provide information for cost, performance, and schedule tradeoffs.
- Assess system specification compliance.
- Report on program progress to plan for reliability growth and to assess reliability and maintainability to performance for use during key reviews.
- Identify system capabilities, limitations, and deficiencies.
- Include T&E activities to detect cyber vulnerabilities within custom and commodity hardware and software.
- Assess system safety.
- Assess compatibility with legacy systems.
- Stress the system within the intended operationally relevant mission environment.
- Support cybersecurity assessments and authorization, including Risk Management Framework security controls.
- Support the interoperability certification process.
- Document achievement of contractual technical performance, and verify incremental improvements and system corrective actions.
- Assess entry criteria for Initial Operational Test and Evaluation (IOT&E) and Follow-On Operational Test and Evaluation.
- Provide DT&E data to validate parameters in models and simulations.
- Assess the maturity of the chosen integrated technologies.

Other areas DT&E contributes to include:

- Data collection, migration, management, and archiving.
- Software functionality validation.
- Cybersecurity.
- Interoperability.
- Interface design and management.
- Integration.
- Modeling and simulation verification, validation, and accreditation.
- Environmental compliance and impact.
- Reliability.
- Logistics Demonstration.

CH 8–3.1.1 Program Planning

The Test and Evaluation Master Plan (TEMP) is the primary planning and management tool for the integrated test program, in accordance with DoDI 5000.02 (Encl. 4, para 5 – page 93). At a minimum, the following documents (unless MDA waiver is obtained) are used to support development of the TEMP:

- JCIDS documents (ICD, CDD, CPD).
- Critical Operational Issues (COIs) and Critical Operational Issue Criteria (COIC).
- Analysis of Alternatives (AoA).
- System Threat Assessment Report (STAR) (Note: The Validated Online Life-cycle Threat (VOLT) is being developed to replace the STAR.).
- Acquisition Strategy (AS).
- Systems Engineering Plan (SEP).
- Program Protection Plan (PPP).
- Cybersecurity Strategy.

- Security Plan.
- Security Assessment Plan.
- Information Support Plan (ISP).
- Acquisition Program Baseline (APB).
- Cost Analysis Requirements Description (CARD).
- Concept of Operations/Operational Mode Summary/Mission Profile (CONOPS/OMS/MP).

CH 8–3.1.2 Evaluation of Developmental Test Adequacy

DT&E provides feedback to the PMs and decision-makers to inform decision-making throughout the acquisition cycle. The PM uses the TEMP as the primary planning and management tool for the integrated test program. The TEMP should describe a logical DT&E strategy, including: (1) decisions to be informed by the DT&E information, (2) evaluations to inform those decisions, (3) test and modeling and simulation events to be conducted to generate the data for the evaluation, and (4) resources to be used and schedules to be followed to execute T&E events. A comprehensive DT&E program generates the key data used to evaluate technologies, components, subsystems, interoperability, cybersecurity, and reliability capabilities. In accordance with DoDI 5000.02 (Encl. 4, para 5(a)(6) – page 94), the TEMP includes a developmental evaluation framework that shows the correlation/mapping between decisions, capabilities to be evaluated, measures to be used to quantify the capabilities, and test and modeling and simulation events.

CH 8–3.2 Operational T&E

Service and Defense Agency OTAs have the responsibility for planning, conducting, and assessing the results of OT&E. OT&E is used to determine the operational effectiveness, operational suitability, and survivability (including cybersecurity) or lethality of a system when operated under realistic operational conditions, including Joint combat operations and system-of-systems concept of employment; evaluates whether threshold requirements in the approved JCIDS documents and critical operational issues have been satisfied; assesses impacts to combat operations; and provides additional information on the system's operational capabilities, limitations, and deficiencies.

The OTAs and DOT&E have a requirement to address operational effectiveness, operational suitability, and survivability (including cybersecurity) or lethality in their evaluations. This evaluation is a mission capability assessment influenced more by the combatant commander/force commander's operational plans and concept of operations than specific system requirements and takes into account all associated systems (an end to end, system-of-systems evaluation) involved in the kill chain. In some instances, programs have successfully demonstrated their Key Performance Parameters (KPPs), Key System Attributes (KSAs), and Critical Technical Parameters (CTPs), but were not evaluated as Operationally Effective and/or Operationally Suitable by DOT&E. Conversely, some programs were evaluated as Operationally Effective and/or Operationally Suitable by DOT&E even though they did not successfully achieve one or more KPPs/KSAs/CTPs. Program managers work closely with the OTA and DOT&E to help determine the assessment of mission capabilities in OT; evaluations include both an assessment of KPPs/KSAs/CTPs, and an assessment of mission effectiveness with a focus on the intended operating environments, threats, concept of operations, critical operational issues, and the concept of employment across the operational envelope. In the memorandum, "Reporting of Operational Test and Evaluation (OT&E) Results," the DOT&E states:

- The data used for evaluation are appropriately called measures of effectiveness, because they measure the military effect (mission accomplishment) that comes from the use of the system in its expected environment. This statement of policy precludes measuring operational effectiveness, operational suitability, and survivability (including cybersecurity), or lethality solely on the basis of system-particular performance parameters.
- ". . . "performance attributes" (sic) are often what the program manager is required to deliver....they are not the military effect or measure of operational effectiveness required for achieving the primary purpose" of a mission capability.

- "It is therefore unacceptable in evaluating and reporting operational effectiveness, operational suitability, and survivability (including cybersecurity), or lethality, to parse requirements and narrow the definition of mission accomplishment so that MOP are confused with MOE."

OTAs have a responsibility for early and continued involvement in a system's test program. OTAs conduct EOAs during the Technology Maturation and Risk Reduction (TMRR) phase and OAs during Engineering and Manufacturing Development (EMD) phase. OTAs are also involved in reviewing Capabilities Documents to assess measurability, testability, and operational relevancy of requirements in the JCIDS documents (i.e., Capability Development Document (CDD) and Capability Production Document (CPD)). OTAs' primary responsibilities include the assessment of test adequacy and the evaluation of a system's operational effectiveness, operational suitability, and survivability (including cybersecurity) or lethality, or operational security completed in IOT&E and, when necessary, Follow-on Operational Test and Evaluation (FOT&E).

General guidelines for the conduct of OT&E include:

- For dedicated IOT&E, typical users operate and maintain the system under test conditions simulating combat and peacetime operations.
- OT&E uses the most current threats or threat representations to simulate actual threat performance and assess operational effectiveness, operational suitability, and survivability (including cybersecurity) or lethality of the system in expected operating environments. Threat representations are validated by the DoD Components using Defense Intelligence Agency (DIA) or the DoD Component intelligence agency approved and validated threat data that describe threat characteristics and performance. DOT&E approves validation reports for threat surrogate systems planned to be used to support OT&E for OSD oversight programs.
- Conducting cybersecurity T&E for all weapon, information, and Command, Control, Communications, Computers, Intelligence, Surveillance, and Reconnaissance (C4ISR) systems depending on external information sources, or providing information to other DoD (or non-DoD) systems. Cybersecurity assessments will include both IP and non-IP (1553 bus, data links, etc.).
- Persons employed by the contractor for the system under development may only participate in the OT&E of systems to the extent the PM planned for their involvement in the operation, maintenance, and other support of the system in peacetime or when deployed in combat.
- Testing production representative systems includes any system accurately representing its final configuration, using mature and stable hardware and software that accurately mirrors the production configuration, but not necessarily produced on a final production line.
- OTAs assume configuration control of test articles (hardware, software, and firmware) prior to OT&E.

CH 8–3.2.1 Evaluation of Operational Test Adequacy

Operational Test adequacy encompasses both test planning and test execution. Operational testing requires the testing of systems under test conditions simulating combat and peacetime operations. In addition, the system must be production-representative, and typical operators must operate and maintain the system. An adequate evaluation requires sufficient testing in this environment to draw conclusions. Considerations include:

- Realistic combat-like conditions
  - o Equipment and personnel under realistic stress and operations tempo.
  - o Threat representative forces.
  - o End-to-end mission testing.
  - o Realistic combat tactics for friendly and enemy.

- o Operationally realistic environment, targets, countermeasures.
- o Includes all interfacing systems.
- Production representative system for IOT&E
  - o Articles off production line preferred.
  - o Production representative materials and process.
  - o Representative hardware and software.
  - o Representative logistics, maintenance, and training manuals.
- Adequate resources
  - o Sample size and test duration.
  - o Size of test unit for friendly and threat surrogate forces, including unique threat equipment.
  - o Threat portrayal.
  - o Data collection systems and personnel.
- Representative typical users
  - o Properly trained personnel, crews, and unit.
  - o Typical support personnel and support package.
  - o Missions given to units (friendly and hostile).
- System is substantially used to support the mission.
- Collected data are sufficiently complete and accurate.

For more information, see the TEMP Guide.

CH 8–3.2.2 Evaluation of Operational Effectiveness

DoD defines operational effectiveness as the overall degree of mission accomplishment of a system when used by representative personnel in the environment(s) planned or expected for operational employment of the system as well as against or in the presence of realistic and representative threats, including cyber threats. Effectiveness determinations are made considering organization, training, doctrine, tactics, survivability or operational security, vulnerability, and threat.

The evaluation of operational effectiveness is linked to mission accomplishment within the context of the Concept of Operations/Operational Mode Summary/Mission Profile (CONOPS/OMS/MP)/Employment. Effectiveness determinations are not limited solely to the evaluation of KPPs, but should also consider how the system's performance varies over the variety of operational conditions and against the variety of threats that the user would encounter when employing the system. Effectiveness determinations might also include a comparison of mission capability to legacy systems, if appropriate, and necessary data are available or are collected to enable such assessments. Early planning for the evaluation considers any special test requirements, such as the need for large test areas or ranges or supporting forces, requirements for threat systems or simulators, modeling test beds, new instrumentation, or other unique support requirements.

For weapon systems, integrate LFT&E of system lethality into the evaluation of weapon system effectiveness. For example, operational testing could identify likely shot lines, hit points, burst points, or miss distances, providing a context for LFT&E lethality assessments. Fuse performance, as determined under DT&E, can provide information for both OT&E and LFT&E.

CH 8–3.2.3 Evaluation of Operational Suitability

Operational suitability defines the degree to which a system is satisfactorily placed and operated in field use, with consideration given to reliability, availability, compatibility, transportability, interoperability, wartime usage rates, maintainability, safety, human factors, manpower supportability, logistics supportability, documentation, environmental effects, and training infrastructure requirements.

Early planning for the operational suitability evaluation includes any special needs for the number of operating hours, environmental testing, maintenance demonstrations, testing profiles, usability of DT&E data, or other unique test requirements.

Operational suitability is evaluated in a mission context to provide meaningful results. Determinations of reliability and availability must be based on data from system use under operationally realistic system loading while conducting mission operations by field users in all environments and planned operating conditions. Similarly, maintaining a required operational tempo over an extended period while conducting realistic missions gives insight into the interactions of various suitability factors.

Suitability determinations consider how system reliability and availability are affected by different operating environments and conditions and, if appropriate, assess wear-out effects. The ability of the user to set up and employ the system, as well as the complexity of user interfaces and the adequacy of training, are components of the suitability determination. Logistics supply chains and the impacts to operational availability are assessed to the extent possible during OT&E.

Software-intensive systems and hybrid systems' suitability assessment includes the availability, representativeness, and adequacy of their maintenance test environments and regression testing procedures. The ability to reproduce failures observed in the actual system and patching process of the maintenance environment are components of the system's suitability determination.

CH 8–3.2.4 Evaluation of Survivability & Cybersecurity

Survivability defines the degree to which a system can operate in the presence of threats, avoid detection by threats, the extent of damage and ability to maintain operations following engagement by threat weapons, and recover from threat weapon effects. These threats are to include both the kinetic and cyber domains. Survivability and cybersecurity include the elements of susceptibility, vulnerability, and recoverability. As such, survivability and cybersecurity act as an important contributor to operational effectiveness, operational suitability, and survivability (including cybersecurity) or lethality. All systems under OT&E oversight receive a survivability and cybersecurity assessment if exposed to cyber or kinetic threat weapons in a combat environment or to combat-induced conditions that may degrade capabilities, regardless of designation for LFT&E oversight. For example, unmanned vehicles may not have a requirement to undergo survivability LFT&E under 10 USC 2366, but receive an assessment for survivability. The assessment may identify issues needing to be addressed through testing.

The purpose of cybersecurity operational test and evaluation is to evaluate the ability of a unit equipped with a system to support assigned missions in the expected operational environment. The system is considered to encompass hardware, software, user operators, maintainers, and the training of Tactics, Techniques, and Procedures used to carry out the Concept of Operations. The operational environment includes other systems that exchange information with the system under test (system-of-systems, including the network environment), end users, administrators and cyber defenders, as well as representative cyber threats. For more information on cybersecurity testing, see DAG CH 8.3.7.5., Cybersecurity.

Integrate DT&E, OT&E, and LFT&E strategies to ensure the consistent assessment of the full spectrum of system survivability and cybersecurity. The Critical Operational Issue (COIs) include any issues that need to be addressed in the OT&E evaluation of survivability and cybersecurity. In accordance with 10 USC 2366, systems under LFT&E oversight must address personnel survivability and integrate it into the overall system evaluation of survivability and cybersecurity conducted under OT&E.

Generally, LFT&E addresses vulnerability and recoverability while OT&E addresses susceptibility, but areas of overlap exist. The evaluation of LFT&E results require realistic hit distributions. The OT&E evaluation of susceptibility might identify realistic hit distributions of likely threats, hit/burst points, and representative shot lines providing a context for LFT&E vulnerability assessments. DT&E and OT&E testing of susceptibility may provide other LFT&E insights, such as information on signatures, employment of countermeasures, and tactics used for evasion of threat weapons. Similarly, LFT&E tests, such as Total Ship Survivability trials, may provide OT&E evaluators with demonstrations of operability and suitability in a combat environment.

Recoverability addresses the consequences of system damage. Following combat damage, recoverability is the ability to take emergency action to prevent loss of the system, to reduce personnel casualties, or to regain weapon system combat mission capabilities. LFT&E typically addresses recoverability; however, both OT&E and LFT&E have an interest in tests relating to recoverability from combat damage or from peacetime accidents.

LFT&E conducts Real Time Casualty Assessment (RTCA) during IOT&E to ensure assumptions supporting the RTCA remain consistent with LFT&E results.

CH 8–3.2.5 Live Fire Test & Evaluation

This section provides information on Live Fire Test and Evaluation (LFT&E) objectives, evaluation of covered systems, early LFT&E, the waiver process, and personnel survivability, in accordance with DoDI 5000.02 (Encl. 5, para 11 – page 107).

CH 8–3.2.5.1 Live Fire Test & Evaluation Objectives

PMs plan and execute an LFT&E program if DOT&E designates their program for LFT&E oversight, in accordance with DoDI 5000.02 (Encl. 5, para 9 – page 105). LFT&E program objectives provide a timely evaluation of the vulnerability/lethality of a system as it progresses through design and development prior to full-rate production. In particular, LFT&E programs:

- Provide information to decision-makers on potential user casualties, vulnerabilities, and lethality, taking into equal consideration susceptibility to attack and combat performance of the system.
- Ensure testing of the system under realistic combat conditions includes knowledge of user casualties and system vulnerabilities or lethality.
- Allow for correction in design or employment of any design deficiency identified by T&E before proceeding beyond LRIP.
- Assess recoverability from battle damage and battle damage repair capabilities and issues.

The PM includes planning factors in the structure and schedule for the LFT&E Strategy to accommodate and incorporate any design changes resulting from testing and analysis before proceeding beyond LRIP.

CH 8–3.2.5.2 Covered Systems

A covered system defines a system that DOT&E, acting for the SecDef, designates for LFT&E oversight, in accordance with DoDI 5000.02 (Encl. 5, para 9 – page 105). These systems include, but are not limited to, the following categories:

- Any major system within the meaning of that term in 10 USC 2302 (Para 5), including user-occupied systems, and designed to provide some degree of protection to its occupants in combat.
- A conventional munitions program or missile program; or a conventional munitions program planning to acquire more than 1,000,000 rounds (regardless of major system status).
- A modification to a covered system likely to significantly affect the survivability or lethality of such a system.

CH 8–3.2.5.3 Early Live Fire Test & Evaluation

In accordance with DoDI 5000.02 (Encl. 5, para 11(a)(2) – page 107), conducting LFT&E events early in a program's life cycle allows time to correct any design deficiency demonstrated by T&E when impacts to program costs and schedule are least. Where appropriate, the PM may correct the design or recommend adjusting the employment of the covered system before proceeding beyond LRIP. LFT&E typically includes testing at the component, subassembly, and subsystem level; and may also draw upon design analyses, modeling and simulation, combat data, and related sources such as analyses of safety and mishap data. As a standard practice, this occurs regardless of whether the LFT&E program culminates with Full-Up, System-Level (FUSL) testing or not.

CH 8–3.2.5.4 Full-Up, System-Level Testing

10 USC 2366 (Para b) defines Full-Up, System-Level Testing as testing that fully satisfies the statutory requirement for "realistic survivability" or "realistic lethality testing." The criteria for FUSL testing differ somewhat based on the type of testing: survivability, operational security, or lethality. The following are types of FUSL testing:

- Vulnerability testing is conducted using munitions likely to be encountered in combat on a complete system loaded or equipped with all the dangerous materials that normally would be on board in combat (including flammables and explosives), and with all critical subsystems operating that could make a difference in determining the test outcome.
- Lethality testing of production-representative munitions or missiles, for which the target is representative of the class of systems that includes the threat; and the target and test conditions are sufficiently realistic to demonstrate the lethality effects the weapon is designed to produce.

CH 8–3.2.5.5 Full-Up, System-Level Testing Waiver Process

In accordance with 10 USC 2366 (Para c), an LFT&E program includes FUSL testing unless granted a waiver. When required, a waiver package is submitted to the appropriate congressional defense committees prior to Milestone B; or, in the case of a system or program initiated at Milestone B, as soon as practicable after Milestone B; or, if initiated at Milestone C, as soon as practicable after Milestone C. Typically, this occurs at the time of TEMP approval.

The waiver package includes certification by the Defense Acquisition Executive (DAE) to Congress that FUSL testing would prove unreasonably expensive and impractical. In accordance with DoDI 5000.02 (Encl. 1, Table 6), it also includes a DOT&E-approved alternative plan for conducting LFT&E in the absence of FUSL testing. Typically, the alternative plan reflects the LFT&E strategy in the TEMP. This alternative plan includes LFT&E of components, subassemblies, or subsystems and, as appropriate, additional design analyses, modeling and simulation, and combat data analyses.

CH 8–3.2.5.6 Personnel Survivability

LFT&E has a statutory requirement to address personnel survivability (i.e., force protection) for covered systems as part of "realistic survivability testing." In 10 USC 2366 (Para e(3)), the term realistic survivability testing means "testing for vulnerability of the system in combat by firing munitions likely to be encountered in combat (or munitions with a capability similar to such munitions" at the system configured for combat. The primary emphasis is on testing vulnerability with respect to potential user casualties and taking into equal consideration the system's susceptibility to attack as well as the combat performance of the system. Personnel survivability should be addressed through dedicated measures of evaluation, such as "expected casualties" supported by specific details on the type and severity of injury, as well as the potential operational impact of such casualties on the ability of the platform to accomplish its mission after a threat engagement, when appropriate. Personnel survivability must also be addressed even in cases where the platform cannot survive.

CH 8–3.3 Integrated Testing

Integrated testing is a concept that capitalizes on the idea that test events can be planned and executed to provide data for both developmental and operational evaluations from the same events. DoDI 5000.02 (Encl. 5, para 11(a)(4) – page 107) defines Integrated Testing as the collaborative planning and collaborative execution of test phases and events to provide shared data in support of independent analysis, evaluation, and reporting by all stakeholders, particularly developmental (both contractor and government), and operational T&E communities. It requires the active participation of the lead OTA in planning the integrated tests with the program office so that the operational objectives are understood, the testing is conducted in an operationally realistic manner, and the resultant data are relevant for use in operational evaluations. The integrated testing approach is documented in the program TEMP. The data pedigree (test conditions and methodologies) are coordinated with the stakeholders prior to execution of the test event.

Integrated testing goals include:

- Conducting a seamless test program producing credible qualitative and quantitative data useful to all evaluators.
- Allowing for the sharing of test events where a single test point or mission can provide data to satisfy multiple objectives without compromising either the developmental or operational test objectives.
- Attaining synergy of effort among all T&E stakeholders including contractor, government developmental and operational representatives, interoperability, cybersecurity, and certification testing in order to maximize use of available test resources and infrastructure.

Integrated testing serves as an implementation concept for test design, not as a new type of T&E. Programs intentionally design integrated testing into the earliest program strategies, plans, documentation, and test plans, preferably starting before Milestone A. Developing and adopting integrated testing strategies early in the process increases the opportunities and benefits. If done correctly, integrated testing provides greater opportunity for early identification of system design improvements, and may even change the course of system development during EMD. Integrated testing is generally more appropriate once the system design has stabilized and the concept of operations is understood. Integrated testing may reduce the scope and number of T&E resources needed in OT&E, if no deficiencies are uncovered and no further design changes are made. However, integrated testing does not replace or eliminate the need for dedicated IOT&E, as required by 10 USC 2399 and DoDI 5000.02 (Encl. 5, para 5(c)(2) – page 101).

Integrated Testing Principles

- While the idea of integrated testing may be well understood *in theory*, critical implementation requires an understanding of a few basic principles:
  - The integrated testing approach is documented within the TEMP.
  - Data pedigrees are coordinated with stakeholders prior to the start of the test event.
  - Integrated testing is intentionally designed into a program's strategy for T&E.
  - Common T&E parameters, methodologies, and terminology are agreed upon early within the T&E planning.
  - Integrated testing does not replace a dedicated IOT&E.
  - The T&E data are tailored to evaluation requirements.

It is critical that all stakeholders understand the scope of the evaluations required to assess development, design, risks, maturity of the system, the operational effectiveness, operational suitability, and survivability (including cybersecurity) or lethality. Up front, define the end state for evaluations, and then develop an integrated test approach that generates the data required to conduct separate evaluations.

For successful integrated testing, understanding and maintaining the pedigree of the data proves vital. The pedigree of the data refers to accurately documenting the configuration of the test asset and the actual test conditions under which each element of test data was obtained. The pedigree of the data indicates whether the test configuration represented operationally realistic or representative conditions.

The T&E WIPT plays an important role in maintaining the data pedigree within the integrated test process for a program.

For integrated test results to count for operational testing on DOT&E Oversight List programs, the lead OTA must develop a plan for the integrated test to be approved by DOT&E before the start of testing that, at a minimum, details the required test realism and conditions, operational test objectives, operational test metrics, production representative test articles, and data collection requirements, in accordance with DoDI 5000.02 (Encl. 5, para 11(a)(4)(b) – page 90). Data collected outside an approved operational test plan or major live-fire test plan can be used for a DOT&E operational or live fire evaluation if the data are approved by DOT&E. Depending on circumstances, DOT&E approval will not necessarily be possible in the TEMP and may require some other documentation. Data approval will be based on understanding the realism of the test scenario(s) used and the pedigree of the data. The data in question typically come from operational exercises, certification events, and developmental test events in operationally relevant environments. Data approval is coordinated with the Lead DT&E Organization and DOT&E prior to the start of testing. When advanced coordination is not possible, the Lead DT&E Organization facilitates data reuse (in a DOT&E assessment or evaluation) through independent documentation of the test data pedigree (test conditions and methodologies). For non-oversight programs, the OTA will determine what integrated test results will count for operational testing.

In accordance with DoDI 5000.02 (Encl. 4, para 2(c) – page 90), integrated testing provides shared data in support of independent analyses for all T&E stakeholders. Integrated testing must allow for and support separate and independent OT&E, in accordance with 10 USC 2399 and DoDI 5000.02 (Encl. 5, para 11(a)(4)(b)) – page 107).

CH 8–3.4 Test Risk Management & Mitigation

Risk management and mitigation is an important part of every acquisition program. The *Defense Acquisition Guide,* Chapters 1 and 3, address program risk management. The Risk Management Guide for DoD Acquisition provides more detailed information.

In accordance with DoDI 5000.02 (Encl. 5, para 6(c)(2)(a) – page 103), potential test-related risks include, but are not limited to:

- Program delays that may compress available test execution time.
- Test assets that may arrive late or have unresolved deficiencies.
- Availability of any other planned resources (facilities, personnel, etc.).
- An overly optimistic test schedule that prevents timely delivery of information.
- Environment, Safety, and Occupational Health (ESOH) risk management.

Nearly any assumption the PM makes regarding the test program may constitute a potential risk. Test limitations and constraints also pose potential risks. Early T&E WIPT meetings include discussions on risk identification and mitigation.

The T&E WIPT also assesses the severity of the risk according to the program's risk management plan. Normally, medium and high-risk items are elevated to the program's risk management board for action, while low risks remain with the Chief Developmental Tester and the T&E WIPT for management. A formal risk mitigation plan is developed for medium and high risks, and the mitigation steps are included in the program integrated master schedule. Again, following the program's risk management plan for guidance is the best course of action.

Medium and high test risks known at the time of TEMP development are included in the TEMP, rather than a generic description of a risk management process. Risks may change over time, and the T&E WIPT regularly reviews test risks and actively works with the program's risk management board to keep test risks current.

For more information, DAG CH 8.3.24, Safety Reviews, serves as a reference source.

CH 8–3.5 Documentation Used in T&E

T&E personnel advise and engage in the development, review, and use of the following documentation from the outset of each development and acquisition program to ensure expectations and risk assessments remain realistic. These documents are used in development of the TEMP. In accordance with DoDI 5000.02 (Encl. 4, para 6(c) – page 96), the acquisition chain of command will have full and prompt access to all relevant documentation.

To assist in that effort, DASD(DT&E) and DOT&E coordinated with Defense Acquisition University (DAU) to provide a location to house relevant T&E Guidance Documents in one place. The DAU Acquisition Community Connection Test & Evaluation Community of Practice (T&E CoP) (DoD CAC login required) houses the relevant documents. T&E definitions in this chapter are found in the Glossary of Defense Acquisition Acronyms and Terms.

For more information on specific documents, refer to the Milestone Document Identification (MDID) website. The MDID provides a definition of the document, any notes on statutory and/or regulatory requirements, source documents for the specific document, and (if applicable) the approval authority. The MDID allows users to filter by program type, life-cycle event, source, and keyword.

CH 8–3.5.1 Joint Capabilities Integration & Development System

Chairman, Joint Chiefs of Staff Instruction (CJCSI) 3170.01I, Joint Capabilities Integration and Development System, establishes the Joint Capabilities Integration and Development System (JCIDS) process. The JCIDS process is a capabilities-based approach to requirements generation. The process is used by the Joint Requirements Oversight Council (JROC) to fulfill its advisory responsibilities outlined in 10 USC 181 (Para b) to the Chairman of the Joint Chiefs of Staff in identifying, assessing, validating, and prioritizing Joint military capability requirements.

The JCIDS provides a transparent process, allowing the JROC to balance Joint equities and make informed decisions on validation and prioritization of capability requirements. Outputs of the JCIDS process drive the Defense Acquisition System because all acquisition programs respond to validated Capability requirements.

The JCIDS process is tailorable and operates in an iterative manner. The initial capability requirements documents drive the early acquisition process, and the early acquisition process drives updates to capability requirements documents related to specific materiel and non-materiel capability solutions to be pursued. The updated capability requirements documents then drive the development, procurement, and fielding of materiel and non-materiel solutions, satisfying the capability requirements and closing associated capability gaps.

The JCIDS documents serve as a means for sponsors to submit capability requirements and capability gaps identified via established processes, along with other relevant information, for review and validation. The three Capability Requirements documents interacting with the acquisition process are typically called the Initial Capabilities Document (ICD), Capability Development Document (CDD), and Capability Production Document (CPD).

The JCIDS Manual complements CJCSI 3170.01I. It serves as a "living" document with updates incorporated as directed by the JROC. In accordance with the JCIDS Manual, Enclosure B:

- An ICD specifies one or more new capability requirements and associated capability gaps, which represent unacceptable operational risk if left unmitigated. The ICD also documents the intent to partially or wholly address identified capability gap(s) with a non-materiel solution, materiel solution, or some combination of the two. The ICD is the most common starting point for new capability requirements. The validated ICD is a critical entry criterion for the MDD, and guides the sponsor activities during the Materiel Solution Analysis (MSA) phase of acquisition, assessment of potential materiel solutions through an AoA, or similar studies, identifies associated Doctrine, Organization, Training, materiel, Leadership and Education, Personnel, Facilities-Policy (DOTmLPF-P) changes, and guides development of other acquisition information required for the Milestone (MS) A review.

- A validated CDD is a critical entry criterion for the development RFP release decision and MS B decision points, and guides the Sponsor in activities during the Engineering and Manufacturing Development (EMD) phase of acquisition. The validated CDD is a key factor in the MDA decision to initiate an acquisition program at MS B. In cases where MS B is not required, but an EMD phase of acquisition will be conducted, the CDD shall be validated ahead of the release of the RFP for the EMD phase of acquisition or the beginning of the EMD phase of acquisition, whichever comes first.

- A CPD provides authoritative, testable capability requirements, in terms of KPPs, KSAs, and additional performance attributes, for the Production and Deployment (P&D) phase of an acquisition program, and is an entrance criteria item necessary for each MS C acquisition decision. The CPD describes the actual performance of a capability solution delivering the required capability, if the system does not meet the threshold levels for the KPPs, or if the cost, schedule, or procurement quantities proposed have been changed since the CDD, the validation authority assesses whether or not the capability solution remains operationally acceptable. The validated CPD is a critical entry criterion for the MS C, and guides the Sponsor in activities during the P&D phase of acquisition. The validated CPD is a key factor in the MDA decision to initiate production of the capability solution at MS C. In cases where MS C is not required, the CPD shall be validated ahead of the release of the RFP for the P&D phase of acquisition or the beginning of the P&D phase of acquisition, whichever comes first.

The CDD and CPD identify the attributes contributing most significantly to the desired operational capability in threshold/objective format. These documents should present each attribute in terms of parameters that are traceable to their associated operational context, and are measurable, testable, and support efficient and effective T&E.

- When appropriate, the attribute includes any unique operating environments for the system. If the capability in a CDD/CPD is part of a system-of-system (SoS) solution, the attributes for the SoS level of performance are described and any unique attributes for each of the constituent systems.
- Other compatibility and interoperability attributes (e.g., databases, fuel, transportability, and ammunition) might need identification to ensure a capability's effectiveness.

The JCIDS process derives and documents performance attributes from analysis supporting the Capabilities-Based Assessment (CBA) and the Analysis of Alternatives (AoA). The CBA, AoA, Measures of Performance (MOPs), Measures of Effectiveness (MOEs), and Measures of Suitability (MOS) remain essential analyses and measures needed for evaluation of those performance attributes.

Test and evaluation personnel primarily assess the testability, measurability, and achievability, clarity of the capabilities required in the documents and provide that assessment to the PM and Chief Engineer. The basic assessment determines the measurability of the capability. Words such as "enhanced," "full spectrum," "unprecedented," "commander's intent," etc., are difficult to measure.

The tester also considers the cost of testing the requirements. The test organization works with the lead system engineer to identify extremely high cost requirements and with the cost estimators to develop alternatives, with modest changes to the requirements, which might yield substantial cost savings. Together, they request the applicable capability requirements validation authority to reevaluate these original requirements. KPPs and KSAs deserve special attention since they are included in the TEMP.

In accordance with DoDD 5141.02 (Para 4(o) – page 3), the D,OT&E assists the Chairman of the Joint Chiefs of Staff in efforts to ensure the expected Joint operational mission environment, mission-level MOEs, and KPPs are specified in JCIDS documents in verifiable terms through testing or analysis.

Refer to the JCIDS Manual for more information on JCIDS.

CH 8–3.5.2 Analysis of Alternatives

The Analysis of Alternatives (AoA) is an analysis that assesses potential materiel solutions that could satisfy validated capability requirement(s) documented in the ICD, and supports a decision on the most cost-effective solution to meeting the validated capability requirement(s). In developing feasible alternatives, the AoA identifies a wide range of solutions having a reasonable likelihood of providing the needed capability.

AoAs provide a foundation for the development of documents at the milestones, starting at Milestone A. The AoA is used when developing the T&E strategy for the preferred solution(s). The following are some areas in the AoA for the Chief Developmental Tester to consider when developing the T&E strategy:

- Scenarios, threats, environment, constraints and assumptions, timeframe, and excursions.
- Description of alternatives, non-viable alternatives, operations concepts, and support concepts.
- Mission tasks, MOE, MOP, effectiveness analysis, effective methodology, and effectiveness sensitivity analysis.
- Operational risk assessment.
- Technology/manufacturing risk assessment.
- Current/proposed schedules, designs, suppliers, operational employments, resources, dependencies, etc.
- Critical Technology Elements (CTEs).

For potential and designated ACAT I and ACAT IA programs, and for each Joint military or business requirement for which the Chairman of the JROC or the Investment Review Board is the validation authority, the Director of Cost Assessment and Program Evaluation (CAPE) develops and approves study guidance for the AoA.

The CAPE provides the AoA Study Guidance to the DoD Component or organization designated by the MDA or, for ACAT IA programs, to the office of the principal staff assistant responsible for the mission area, prior to the Materiel Development Decision and in sufficient time to permit preparation of the AoA Study Plan prior to the decision event. Per DoDI 5000.02 (Para 5(d)(1)(a) – page 16), programs coordinate the study plan with the MDA and gain approval from CAPE prior to the Materiel Development Decision. The designated DoD Component or other organization, or the principal staff assistant designates responsibility for completion of the study plan and the AoA.

At the Materiel Development Decision, the CAPE (or DoD Component equivalent) presents the AoA Study Guidance, and the AoA lead organization presents the AoA Study Plan. In addition, the Component provides the plan to staff and fund the actions preceding the next decision point (usually Milestone A) including, where appropriate, competitive concept definition studies by industry. If the Materiel Development Decision is approved, the MDA designates the lead DoD Component; determines the acquisition phase of entry; and identifies the initial review milestone, usually, but not always, a specific milestone as described in one of the program models.

In accordance with DoDI 5000.02 (Encl. 1, Table 2 – page 49), the PM provides the final AoA to CAPE not later than 60 calendar days prior to the Milestone A review (or the next decision point or milestone, as designated by the MDA). Not later than 15 business days prior to the Milestone A review, CAPE evaluates the AoA and provides a memorandum to the MDA, with copies to the head of the DoD Component or other organization or principal staff assistant assessing whether the analysis was completed consistent with CAPE study guidance and the CAPE-approved study plan.

Within the memorandum, CAPE assesses:

- The extent to which the AoA:
  o Examines sufficient feasible alternatives.

- o Considers trade-offs among cost, schedule, sustainment, and required capabilities for each alternative considered.
  - o Achieves the affordability goals established at Materiel Development Decision and with what risks.
  - o Uses sound methodology.
  - o Discusses key assumptions and variables, and sensitivity to changes in these.
  - o Bases conclusions or recommendations, if any, on the results of the analysis.
  - o Considers the fully burdened cost of energy (FBCE), where FBCE is a discriminator among alternatives.
- Whether additional analysis is required.
- How the AoA results are used to influence the direction of the program.

For more information on AoAs, see the DAG, CH 2.2.3.

CH 8–3.5.3 System Threat Assessment Report

Note: The Validated Online Life Cycle Threat (VOLT) is being developed to replace the STAR. Once approved, this section will be updated.

The System Threat Assessment Report (STAR) is the authoritative, system-specific threat capabilities document. The STAR describes the threat to be countered and the projected threat environment.

Based on DoDI 5000.02 (Encl. 4, para 5(c) – page 95), T&E personnel use the STAR as a reference for developing T&E plans, T&E resources and capability requirements, test scenarios, other T&E planning documents, as well as a guide for defining the threat environment for a mission-oriented context.

MDAP and MAIS programs require a unique, system-specific STAR, which is prepared by the appropriate Service Intelligence support, and the process is validated by the Defense Intelligence Agency (DIA). In accordance with DoDI 5000.02 (Encl 1, Table 2 – page 57), the assessment is required to be updated and validated at every acquisition milestone, although Services can update the document more frequently. All programs, unless waived by the MDA, must have a validated STAR in place at milestones beginning at Milestone A through Full Rate Production/Full Development (FRP/FD) at major decision points (and at program initiation for shipbuilding programs) unless waived by MDA. MDAP and MAIS programs require a unique, system-specific STAR. The assessment is system-specific to the degree that the system definition is available at the time the assessment is being prepared, and addresses projected adversary capabilities and maintains projections of technology and adversary capability trends over the next 20 years. DIA co-chairs the Threat Steering Group (TSG) for ACAT ID STARs with the producing command or center. STARs for ACAT IC MDAPs and System Threat Assessments (STAs) for ACAT II non-MDAPs are prepared and validated by the lead Service in accordance with Service regulations.

The T&E WIPT leverages the STAR (understand the threat) with other acquisition documents (e.g., CDD, SEP, PPP, etc.) when developing the T&E Strategy (Part III of the TEMP). The T&E WIPT refines the threat information found in the STAR to establish threat requirements for T&E. Since threats continue to evolve and mature with time, the T&E WIPT ensures the latest DIA-validated threat assessments are considered for T&E-specific threat requirements and incorporated into all threat-related acquisition documentation.

The T&E WIPT ensures adequate threat resources, such as Modeling and Simulation, threat surrogates, and targets are documented in the TEMP resource section (Part IV, 4.2.8.), and adequate validation and accreditation processes are completed in time to support required testing.

Refer to the DAG, CH 7.4.1.4. for more information on the STAR.

CH 8–3.5.4 Acquisition Strategy

The Acquisition Strategy (AS) is the PM's plan for program execution across the entire program life cycle. It is a comprehensive, integrated plan identifying the acquisition approach, and describes the business, technical, and support strategies the PM plans to employ to manage program risks and meet program objectives. The strategy evolves over time and continuously reflects the current status and desired goals of the program.

The AS defines the relationship between the acquisition phases and work efforts, and key program events such as decision points, reviews, contract awards, incentive structure, test activities, production lot or delivery quantities, operational deployment objectives, and any planned international cooperation and exportability. The strategy must reflect the PM's understanding of the business environment; technical alternatives; small business strategy; costs, risks, and risk mitigation approach; opportunities in the domestic and international markets; and the plan to support successful delivery of the capability at an affordable life-cycle price, on a realistic schedule.

A central element of all acquisition strategies is an executable plan to use developmental and operational testing to assess design, development, performance, operational effectiveness, operational suitability, and survivability (including cybersecurity) or lethality. DoDI 5000.02 (Encl. 1, Table 2 – page 47) requires an approved AS at Milestone A. Once approved by the MDA, the AS provides a basis for more detailed planning.

The PM includes the Chief Developmental Tester and the T&E WIPT in the development of the AS so the strategy for T&E fully supports the program's approach. The AS includes a description of the test program for both the contractor and the government. It also includes a description of the test program for each major phase of a major system acquisition and a discussion of the extent of testing accomplished before LRIP.

Refer to the DAG, CH 1.4.1. for more information on acquisition strategies.

CH 8–3.5.5 Systems Engineering Plan

The Systems Engineering Plan (SEP) documents key technical risks, processes, resources, metrics (Technical Performance Measurement (TPMs) and other metrics), SE products, quality control, and completed or scheduled SE activities. The SEP is a living document updated as needed to reflect the program's evolving SE approach and/or plans and current status. The purpose of the SEP is to help PMs develop, communicate, and manage the overall systems engineering (SE) approach guiding all technical activities of the program.

T&E personnel use the SEP as a reference for developing their strategy for T&E, evaluation framework (Developmental Evaluation Framework (DEF) and Operational Evaluation Framework (OEF)), TEMPs, test plans, and other planning documents. In compliance with DoDI 5000.02 (Para 5(a)(4)(f) – page 57), PMs will prepare a SEP as a management tool to guide the SE activities on the program. The SEP Outline identifies the minimum expected content to be addressed in the SEP. The SEP should be consistent with and complementary to the Acquisition Program Baseline (APB), Acquisition Strategy (AS), Test and Evaluation Master Plan (TEMP), Program Protection Plan (PPP), Life Cycle Sustainment Plan (LCSP), and other program plans as appropriate. The SEP is written in a common language to clearly communicate what the program plans to do in each phase of the acquisition life cycle and is written to avoid redundancy and maintain consistency with other planning documents.

Test and evaluation personnel focus on the areas listed in Table 3, based on the SEP Outline.

Table 3: T & E Focus Areas in System Engineering Plan

Chapter	Relevant Content
2.1.	Architectures and Interface control: Look for architecture products that may support test planning such as physical and functional interfaces.
2.2.	Technical Certifications: Include test activities to obtain certifications in Table 2.2.-1
3.1.	Technical Schedule and Schedule Risk Assessment: Ensure test activities are included in the schedule (Figure 3.1.-1). Discuss with the systems engineer, potential schedule risks that may impact testing.
3.4.4.	Engineering Team Organization and Staffing: Check if T&E WIPT is correctly described.
3.6.	Technical Performance Measures and Metrics: TPMs enable program managers, systems engineers, and senior decision-makers to: (1) gain quantifiable insight to technical progress, trends, and risks; (2) empirically forecast the impact on program cost, schedule, and performance; and (3) provide measurable feedback of changes made to program planning or execution to mitigate potentially unfavorable outcomes. TPMs can be traced to KPPs/KSAs, Critical Technology Elements (CTE), or key technical risks, which should be verified and/or validated by test. Determine intermediate testing and data required to support this. The TEMP reliability growth curve should be consistent with the reliability growth curve in the SEP. Critical Technical Parameters described in the TEMP can be traced to the TPMs in the SEP.
4.4.	Technical reviews: Discuss test data that may be required to support engineering reviews such as the Critical Design Review (CDR), System Verification Review (SVR), and Functional Configuration Audit (FCA).
Table 4.6.-2	Reliability, Availability, and Maintainability (RAM) Activity Planning and Timing: Ensure RAM test events are included. Discuss with the system engineer how test supports Failure Reporting, Analysis and Corrective Action System (FRACAS) activities.
4.7.	Engineering Tools: Determine interfaces between the systems engineering requirements tools in the SEP and the common T&E database in the TEMP.

Refer to the DAG, CH 3.2.2. for more information on the SEP.

CH 8–3.5.6 Program Protection Plan

In accordance with DoDI 5000.02 (Encl. 1, Table 2 – page 56), T&E personnel use the Program Protection Plan (PPP) as a reference for developing test plans, test resource and capability requirements, and other planning documents; and identifying how T&E processes protect critical information about the program from being revealed to unauthorized personnel. Program Protection is the department's holistic approach for delivering trusted, secure systems and is used to ensure programs adequately protect their technology, components, and information throughout the acquisition process.

The PPP, written by the program office, officially documents the protection plan for a given acquisition program. The PPP protects the system from foreign collection, design vulnerabilities, supply chain exploitation, tampering, and battlefield loss. The program office takes an end-to-end system view when developing and executing the PPP (external, interdependent, or government furnished components that may be outside the PM's control must be considered). The PPP provides a usable reference within the program for understanding and managing the full spectrum of program and system security activities. Programs update the PPP as threats and vulnerabilities change or are better understood.

The Chief Developmental Tester, in coordination with the T&E WIPT, uses the PPP (and the appended Acquisition Cybersecurity Strategy) as an input when developing a program's T&E strategy and individual test plans. The PPP provides information on a program's critical missions, critical functions, critical components, threats, vulnerabilities, and threat countermeasures. This information can be used to guide and focus testing. Testing may reveal vulnerabilities that, when exploited, may have an impact on mission completion.

Refer to the DAG, CH 9.2.3. for more information on the Program Protection Plan.

CH 8–3.5.7 Cybersecurity Strategy

In accordance with DoDI 8500.01, Cybersecurity, (Encl. 3, para 2(c)(2) – page 29), a Cybersecurity Strategy (formerly known as the Information Assurance (IA) strategy) describes the program's planned cybersecurity risk management. All acquisition of qualifying information technology (IT) must have an adequate and appropriate cybersecurity strategy that will be reviewed prior to acquisition milestone decisions and acquisition contract awards in accordance with P.L. 106-398 SEC. 811 (reference e(3)(G)), and must plan for developmental test oversight by DASD(DT&E) and operational test oversight by DOT&E.

In accordance with DoDI 5000.02 (Encl. 11, para 6(b) – page 136), all acquisition of systems containing IT, including National Security Systems (NSS), will have a Cybersecurity Strategy. Beginning at Milestone A, the program manager will submit the Cybersecurity Strategy to the DoD Component Chief Information Officer (CIO) for review and approval prior to milestone decisions or contract awards. For ACAT ID and all ACAT IA, the DoD CIO reviews and approves the strategy; for all other IT and NSS programs, the DoD Component CIO reviews and approves the strategy.

The Chief Developmental Tester, in coordination with the T&E WIPT, will review the Cybersecurity Strategy and leverage it in the development of the TEMP. Test organizations review the cybersecurity strategy for test data and test events needed to support certification. The Chief Developmental Tester, in coordination with the Lead DT&E Organization, ensures test events (including Cooperative Vulnerability Identification and Adversarial Cybersecurity DT&E activities) are planned early during developmental testing to avoid late identification of cyber weaknesses during operational testing.

Refer to the DAG, CH 8.3.5.7. for more information on cybersecurity.

CH 8–3.5.8 Security Plan

In accordance with DoDI 8510.01 (Encl. 6, para 1(d) – page 27), Risk Management Framework (RMF) for DoD Information Technology (IT), the Security Plan provides an overview of the security requirements for the system, system boundary description, the system identification, common controls identification, security control selections, subsystems security documentation (as required), and external services security documentation (as required). The plan can also contain, as supporting appendices or as references, other key security-related documents such as a risk assessment, privacy impact assessment, system interconnection agreements, contingency plan, security configurations, configuration management plan, and incident response plan.

The Information System Security Manger (ISSM) typically prepares the Security Plan. The Chief Developmental Tester, in coordination with the T&E WIPT, will review the Security Plan and leverage the plan in the development of the TEMP. The Chief Developmental Tester invites the ISSM to participate in the T&E WIPT, thus allowing a cross pollination of knowledge in TEMP development.

CH 8–3.5.9 Security Assessment Plan

The Security Assessment Plan contains selected controls and their corresponding security control assessment with a detailed roadmap of how to conduct such an assessment.

In accordance with DoDI 8510.01 (Encl. 6, para 2(d)(1) – page 32), Security Assessment Plans apply to those systems required to follow the Risk Management Framework. This plan is reviewed and approved by the Component Authorization Official (CAO).

As this plan contains the systems roadmap for selected control assessment, it is recommended that the Chief Developmental Tester include the Security Control Assessor (SCA) as part of T&E WIPT during TEMP development. In this way, there can be a collaboration of efforts between the Security Assessment Plan and TEMP for better alignment and synergy of effort. Of note, the Security Assessment Plan does not include such areas as schedule (when selected controls are assessed) and required recourses (to assess the selected controls). The T&E WIPT references the program Security Assessment Plan with the TEMP and depicts the schedule of control assessment in Part II and required resources in Part IV. This allows the PM to visualize the holistic assessment effort.

CH 8–3.5.10 Acquisition Program Baseline

The Acquisition Program Baseline (APB) is the agreement between the MDA and the PM, and his or her acquisition chain of command, used for tracking and reporting the life of the program or program increment. T&E personnel use the APB as a reference for developing test plans and schedules, test resource and capability requirements, and other planning documents, in an effort to ensure the strategy for test and evaluation remains consistent with the program's goals and objectives. DoDI 5000.02 (Encl. 1, Table 2 – page 47) requires every PM to propose and document program goals prior to, and for approval at, program initiation for all ACAT programs. For Major Defense Acquisition Programs (MDAPs), the APB satisfies the requirements in 10 USC 2435 and 2220. DoDI 5000.02 (Encl. 1, Table 3 – page 60) mandates the use of an APB for all other ACAT programs.

A separate APB is required for each increment of an MDAP or MAIS program, and each sub-program of an MDAP. Increments can be used to plan concurrent or sequential efforts to deliver capability more quickly and in line with the technological maturity of each increment. When an MDAP requires the delivery of two or more categories of end items that differ significantly in form and function, subprograms may be established.

Program goals consist of an objective value and a threshold value for each Key Performance Parameter (KPP) and Key System Attribute (KSA) parameter. Cost, schedule, and performance are intrinsically linked, and the objective and threshold values of all program goals are developed with these relationships in mind. The PM has responsibility for managing the trade space between program objectives and thresholds within the bounds of cost, schedule, and performance. The APB includes affordability caps for unit production and sustainment costs. Affordability caps are established as fixed cost requirements equivalent to KPPs.

The PM derives the APB from the users' performance requirements, schedule planning and requirements, and best estimates of total program cost consistent with projected funding. The sponsor of a capability needs document (i.e., Capability Development Document (CDD) or Capability Production Document (CPD)) provides an objective and threshold for each attribute that describes an aspect of a system or capability to be developed or acquired. The PM uses this information to develop an optimal product within the available trade space. APB parameter values represent the program as it is expected to be developed, produced and/or deployed, sustained, and funded.

Refer to the DAG, CH 8.3.5.10. for more information on APBs.

CH 8–3.5.11 Cost Analysis Requirements Description

For Acquisition Category (ACAT) I and ACAT IA programs, the Cost Analysis Requirements Description (CARD) is used to formally describe the acquisition program for purposes of preparing both the DoD Component Cost Estimate and the Cost Assessment Independent Cost Estimate. DoDI 5000.02 (Encl. 1, Table 2 – page 50) specifies that MDAPs and MAIS provide a CARD in support of major milestone decision points (Milestone A and Milestone B, with updates at the Development Request for Proposal (RFP) Release Decision, Milestone C Decision, and FRP/FD Decision).

The Chief Developmental Tester ensures the test portion of the program definition is sufficiently defined for an adequate estimate. The tester also reviews the cost estimates resulting from the CARD to ensure reasonable funding and that the funding is included in the Resources section of the TEMP. Finally, cost estimates for testing eventually appear in the Research, Development, Test & Evaluation (RDT&E) Exhibits (specifically R-2 and R-3 for test), which go to the President and Congress, and the T&E Budget Submissions (T&E-1), which go to the DoD.

Refer to the DAG, CH 2.3.5. for more information on the CARD.

CH 8–3.5.12 Life-Cycle Sustainment Plan

The Life Cycle Sustainment Plan (LCSP) describes sustainment influences on system design and the technical, business, and management activities to develop, implement, and deliver a product support package that maintains affordable system operational effectiveness, operational suitability, and survivability (including cybersecurity) or lethality over the system life cycle, and seeks to reduce cost without sacrificing necessary levels of program support. In accordance with DoDI 5000.02 (Encl. 6, para 4(b) – page 116), during the Engineering and Manufacturing Development (EMD) phase it is critical to have robust testing to ensure reliability requirements are met. As the design matures, the trade space for sustainment solutions narrows and the sustainment strategy becomes more refined.

CH 8–3.5.13 Information Support Plan

The Information Support Plan (ISP) serves as a key document in achieving interoperability certification. The ISP describes Information Technology (IT) and information needs, dependencies, and interfaces for programs in all acquisition categories. It focuses on the efficient and effective exchange of information that, if not properly managed, could limit or restrict the operation of the program from delivering its defined capability. The Net-Ready Key Performance Parameter (NR-KPP) identified in the CDD or CPD will also be used in the ISP to identify support required from external information systems. Bandwidth requirements data will also be documented in the ISP.

A draft ISP is due at the Development RFP Release Decision. An approved ISP is required at Milestone B and Milestone C, in accordance with DoDI 5000.02 (Encl. 1, Table 2 – page 53). T&E personnel use the NR-KPP and the ISP to identify how the system (key interfaces, components, and dependencies) needs to be tested and evaluated for the following abilities: users can enter and manage on a network; users can effectively exchange information; and the system supports military operations. The ISP and a CONOPS/OMS/MP can be used to develop good test scenarios for evaluating key information/data exchanges that have an impact on mission success. The TEMP should include the testing of critical interfaces in as close to a mission environment (including a cyber-contested environment) as possible. Include DT&E Interoperability events (contractor and government) that focus on key information/data exchanges as part of the overall T&E program. When feasible, plan interoperability testing as part of other test events (such as cybersecurity testing, Risk Management Frame (RMF) security controls assessment activities, functional testing, etc.). Document the test resources for interoperability events (e.g. Facilities, People, Test Environment, Funding, etc.) in the TEMP. Specific criteria defined at Milestone B, and included in the Milestone B Acquisition Decision Memorandum (ADM), may require the system to demonstrate interoperability prior to Milestone C. Programs should plan to obtain an Interim Authorization To Test (IATT) prior to demonstrating interoperability, in accordance with DoDI 5000.02 (Encl. 13, para 4(c)(2) – page 149).

CH 8–3.5.14 Life Cycle Mission Data Plans

In accordance with DoDD 5250.01 (Para 4(c) – page 2) and DoDI 5000.02 (Encl. 1, Table 2 – page 54), Life Cycle Mission Data Plans (LMDPs) are required for Intelligence Mission Data (IMD)-dependent programs. Intelligence Mission Data are defined as DoD intelligence-derived information used for programming platform mission systems in development, testing, operations and sustainment, including, but not limited to, the following functional areas: intelligence signatures, electronic warfare integrated reprogramming (EWIR), order of battle (OOB), characteristics and performance (C&P), and geospatial intelligence (GEOINT).

The LMDP defines specific IMD requirements for a program, and becomes more detailed as the system progresses toward IOC. During development of T&E strategies and plans, IMD requirements are identified based on the need to verify and validate detection and identification functionality for DT&E, and for operational effectiveness and operational survivability for OT&E. The TEMP should define specific intelligence requirements to support program developmental and operational test and evaluation. The LMDP should include information on IMD data existing within the program (modeling and simulation or measured physical parameters) for sensor or algorithm development, or for testing purposes.

Refer to the DAG, CH 7.4.1.3., for more information on Life Cycle Mission Data Plans (LMDPs) and DAG, CH 7.4.2., Intelligence Mission Data (IMD).

CH 8–3.6 Test & Evaluation Master Plan

The Test and Evaluation Master Plan (TEMP) is a document that describes the overall structure and objectives of the T&E program and articulates the necessary resources to accomplish each phase, in accordance with DoDI 5000.02 (Para 5(a)(4)(f) – page 4). It provides a framework within which to generate detailed T&E plans and documents schedule and resource implications associated with the T&E program. The TEMP serves as the overarching document for managing a T&E program.

In accordance with DoDI 5000.02 (Encl. 4, para 2(c) – page 90) and DoDI 5000.02 (Encl. 5, para 1(b) – page 98), the TEMP identifies the necessary DT&E, OT&E, and LFT&E activities. It relates program schedule, test management strategy and structure, and required resources to: KPPs and KSAs, as identified within the Capability Development Document (CDD); Critical Operational Issues (COIs); and Critical Technical Parameters (CTPs) developed by the Chief Developmental Tester, in collaboration with the Chief Engineer/Lead System Engineer, and coordinated with the T&E WIPT.

The TEMP includes objectives and thresholds documented in the CDD, CPD, evaluation criteria, and milestone decision points. For multi-Service or Joint programs, a single integrated TEMP is required. Component-unique content requirements, particularly evaluation criteria associated with COIs, can be addressed in a Component-prepared annex to the basic TEMP.

In accordance with DoDI 5000.02 (Encl. 4, para 3(d) – page 91), the PM uses the TEMP as the primary planning and management tool for all test activities starting at Milestone A. The PM will prepare and update the TEMP at Milestone B and to support the Development RFP Release Decision and FRP/FD decision points. Additionally, the TEMP will have to be updated prior to Milestone C based on the CPD, and any remaining DT&E prior to IOT&E, and updates to IOT&E.

Program Management Offices (PMOs) develop a TEMP (and subsequent updates) to document the following:

- Roles and responsibilities, including Chief Developmental Tester and Lead DT&E Organization.
- Certification requirements necessary for the conduct of T&E.
- An event-driven T&E schedule.
- The T&E strategy aligned with and supporting the approved acquisition strategy to provide early identification of design and integration issues and adequate, risk-reducing T&E information to support decisions.

- The integration of developmental and operational tests into an efficient test continuum.
- The strategy for T&E.
- Starting at Milestone A, a developmental evaluation methodology.
- Starting at Milestone B, a developmental evaluation framework.
- The T&E resources, which should be in alignment with the CARD and T&E budget exhibits (ACAT I programs).
- The test and evaluation strategies to efficiently identify technology and functionality limitations and capabilities of alternative concepts to support early cost performance trade-off decisions.
- Adequate measures to support the program's reliability growth plan and requirements for a Reliability, Availability, Maintainability Cost (RAM-C) Rationale Report defined in DoD RAM Cost Rationale Manual, for Milestones B and C.
- The modeling and simulation approach and where it is used in the test events, including the resources required and methodology for their verification, validation, and accreditation (VV&A); and how the PM and OTA plan to accredit M&S for OT use.
- A T&E approach that stresses the system under test to at least the limits of the Operational Mode Summary/Mission Profile, and for some systems, beyond the normal operating limits to ensure the robustness of the design.
- The plan for demonstration of maturity of the production process through production qualification testing (PQT) of low-rate initial production (LRIP) assets prior to full-rate production (FRP).
- The plan for using the System Threat Assessment (STA) or System Threat Assessment Report (STAR) as a basis for scoping a realistic test environment.
- The approach for demonstrating performance against threats and their countermeasures as identified in the Defense Intelligence Agency (DIA) or component-validated threat document.
- The cybersecurity test and evaluation approach. Additionally, the approach should coordinate development of the Security Assessment Plan with the development of the TEMP in support of the Risk Management Framework (RMF) process. (The RMF process and certification can be a useful entrance criterion for cybersecurity T&E, but it does not obviate the need for T&E.)
- The plan for Joint interoperability assessments required to certify system-of-systems interoperability.
- For business systems, the identification of the certification requirements needed to support the compliance factors established by the Office of the Under Secretary of Defense (Comptroller) (USD(C)) for financial management, enterprise resource planning, and mixed financial management systems.
- A system-of-systems network architecture diagram, including removable media and laptops, etc., for cybersecurity assessment.

The following contains a basic TEMP outline, which highlights the key TEMP topics needing addressed. Go to T&E Guidance Documents for an editable TEMP Format and additional TEMP information.

Refer to the TEMP Guidebook for more detail regarding TEMP content.

TEMP FORMAT	
PART I – Introduction	
1.1.	Purpose
1.2.	Mission Description
1.2.1.	Mission Overview
1.2.2.	Concept of Operations
1.2.3.	Operational Users
1.3.	System Description
1.3.1.	Program Background

4.2.7.	Operational Force Test Support
4.2.8.	Models, Simulations, and Test Beds
4.2.9.	Joint Operational Test Environment
4.2.10.	Special Requirements
4.3.	Federal, State, and Local Requirements
4.4.	Manpower / Personnel and Training
4.5.	Test Funding Summary

	APPENDICES

Appendix A	Bibliography
Appendix B	Acronyms
Appendix C	Points of Contact

The following appendices provide a location for additional information, as necessary

Appendix D	Scientific Test and Analysis Techniques
Appendix E	Cybersecurity
Appendix F	Reliability Growth Plan
Appendix G	Requirements Rationale

Additional Appendices, as needed

CH 8–3.6.1 T&E Resources

The PM, in coordination with the T&E WIPT, must identify and plan for all T&E resources (including Cybersecurity) needed to adequately support DT&E, OT&E, and LFT&E, in accordance with DoDI 5000.02 (Encl. 4, para 2(d) – page 90).

"Test and Evaluation Resources" refers to the elements necessary to plan, execute, and evaluate a test event or test campaign. These elements include funding, manpower for test conduct and support (e.g., cybersecurity teams, subject matter experts, additional testers, data collectors, trusted agents, etc.), test articles (e.g. system under test, accompanying assets, targets, threats, and expendables), models, simulations, test facilities, special instrumentation, frequency management and control, and base or facility support services. Programs identify one-of-a-kind T&E resources and long-lead items early in the acquisition process in order to allot adequate funding for development and use. In accordance with DoDI 5000.02 (Encl. 4, para 5(b) – page 95), programs must use existing DoD government T&E infrastructure unless an exception can be justified as cost-effective to the government.

In accordance with DoDI 5000.02 (Encl. 5, para 10 – page 106), all TEMPs will specify the T&E resources necessary to execute the T&E program, the organization responsible for providing each element, and when the elements are needed. Additionally, T&E funds are also stated in budgeting documents, such as the program's budget and T&E-1 exhibits.

T&E resources provided by the contractor must be identified in either the development or production contract.

CH 8–3.6.2 Requirements Rationale

In accordance with DoDI 5000.02 (Encl. 5, para 5(d)(2) – page 101), the TEMP provides a working link to the Component's operational rationale for the requirements in the Capability Development Document (CDD) or equivalent requirements document. If the rationale documented in the requirements document is adequate to support test planning and evaluation, then no further clarification is necessary. DoDI

5000.02 (Encl. 4, para 4(a) – page 92) states that DT&E activities will start when requirements are being developed to ensure that key technical requirements are measurable, testable, and achievable. In cases where the requirement is derived or transformed for testability or the operational rationale is unclear, this annex explains the operational rationale and/or the derivation of the metric as well as the chosen numerical thresholds. For example, requirements documents often specify the reliability requirement in terms of the probability of completing a reference mission; for testability, this is often translated to a mean time between failures. In this case, the assumptions supporting the derivation of the mean time between failures should be documented in the requirements rationale annex as well as the original justification for the probability of mission completion.

CH 8–3.6.3 Critical Technical Parameters

Acquisition programs have hundreds or thousands of technical parameters that need to be addressed during development.

CTPs are used in developmental test and evaluation to identify critical system characteristics that, when measured and achieved, allow the attainment of a desired user capability, In accordance with DoDI 5000.02 (Encl. 4, para 4(b)(1) – page 92). CTPs are measures derived from desired user capabilities and are focused on critical design features or risk areas (e.g., technical maturity, Critical Technology Elements (CTEs), physical characteristics, technical measures, or reliability, availability, and maintainability (RAM) issues). If CTPs are not achieved during development, they will indicate a significant risk in the delivery of required user capabilities. CTPs link to high risk areas having an impact on program success. CTPs are tracked during EMD and may need to evolve/change as the system matures. It may also be necessary to resolve existing CTPs and identify new CTPs as the system progresses during development. The status of achieving CTPs is provided to the Milestone Decision Authority as part of the DT&E Program Assessment at Milestone C or Limited Deployment. Any CTP not resolved prior to entering the LRIP decision should be documented and action plans provided that resolve the unresolved CTPs prior to the FRP Decision Review.

Technical Performance Measures (TPMs) are metrics and measures evaluating technical progress (i.e., product maturity) as part of the systems engineering process. Some TPMs can be CTPs; however, every TPM is not a CTP. TPMs are measured through inspection, demonstration, test, and analysis. Systems Engineering (SE) uses TPMs to balance cost, schedule, and performance throughout the life cycle when integrated with other management methods such as the Work Breakdown Structure (WBS) and Earned Value Management System (EVMS). Examples of TPMs include measures such as weight, speed, volume, cross-section, power, cooling, bandwidth, throughput, lines of code, reliability, maintainability, etc.

CTPs measure the critical system characteristics that, when achieved, enable the attainment of desired operational performance capabilities (in the mission context). CTPs do not simply restate the KPPs and/or KSAs. Each CTP has a direct or significant indirect correlation to a KPP and/or KSA that measures a physical characteristic essential to the evaluation of the KPP or KSA, In accordance with DoDI 5000.02 (Encl. 5, para 5(e)(2)(c) – page 102). CTPs are directly measurable during developmental testing and included as part of the developmental evaluation plans included in the TEMP. Examples of CTPs include fuel consumption, engine thrust, data upload time, latency, bore sight accuracy, etc.

The Chief Developmental Tester has responsibility for collaborating with the program's Chief or Lead Systems Engineer on the identification of CTPs. The Lead DT&E Organization can assist in the development of CTPs as well as the developmental evaluation plans for the CTPs. The evaluation of CTPs is important in assessing the maturity of the system and to inform the PM as to whether the system is on (or behind) the planned development schedule or is likely (or not likely) to achieve an operational capability, but is not the only component of projecting mission capability. The projection of mission capability requires an evaluation of other areas such as interoperability of systems and subsystems in the mission context, when used by a typical operator. CTPs associated with the systems/subsystems can provide a basis for selecting entry or exit criteria that needs to be demonstrated to make a decision to continue with the next major developmental test or test phase. CTPs are a driver in the scope/magnitude of the T&E program.

CH 8–3.6.4 T&E Plans

This section provides information on detailed test and evaluation planning for test or data collection events or test series identified in the TEMP, in accordance with DoDI 5000.02 (Encl. 4, para 6(a) – page 96) and DoDI 5000.02 (Encl. 5, para 1(b) – page 98).

CH 8–3.6.4.1 Evaluation Plans

Planning for a specific test or data collection event or test series is preceded by an evaluation plan. Evaluation plans are to be directly traceable to the evaluation framework for the program, include expected results, and are informed by WIPTs to ensure the meeting of all data needs, in accordance with DoDI 5000.02 (Encl. 4, para 5(a)(2)(d) – page 93).

CH 8–3.6.4.2 Test or Data Collection Plans

Test or data collection plans come in a variety of formats and styles but contain the following content:

- Objectives.
- Test schedule.
- Test resource (facilities, instrumentation requirements, personnel, test articles, test support equipment, etc.).
- Data collection plan.
- Test techniques.
- Test points.
- Evaluation criteria.
- Limitations.
- Test management structure and information.
- Safety considerations.

In accordance with DoDI 5000.02 (Encl. 4, para 3(d) – page 91), test plans document why tests are accomplished and what the goal(s) of the test are (the objectives), how tests are conducted (the test techniques, test points, and execution plan), what conditions and factors are controlled and varied in the test, what data are acquired (including the instrumentation requirements), how data are used to answer the objectives (the data analysis plan), and when and what types of reports are needed (management information). Test plans are the vehicles that translate test concepts and statistical/analytical test design into concrete resources, procedures, actions, and responsibilities. The size and complexity of a test program and its associated test plan are determined by the nature of the system being tested and the type of testing that is accomplished. Some major weapon systems may require large numbers of separate tests to satisfy test objectives, and thus require a multi-volume test plan; other testing may be well-defined by a relatively brief test plan. Modeling and simulation may be used for the realization of proposed test scenarios (including test plans), instrumentation set-up, distribution and adequacy of resources, and schedules. Schedules allow for system-under-test set-up, instrumentation calibrations, weather conditions, availability of test support personnel, and other support.

Government Developmental Test Plans. The government test plan provides explicit instructions for the conduct of tests and sub-tests. It governs test control, test configurations, data collection, data analysis, and administrative aspects of the tester's operations. The Lead DT&E Organization and or test officer prepares a test plan in accordance with the directions provided by the Chief Developmental Tester, TEMP, and test directive, and determines the best plan for the testing of the system for the area(s) assigned.

Contractor Developmental Test Plans. If the data from the contractor DT&E are to be used by the Chief Developmental Tester, the test plan should reflect all the requirements to support the systems evaluation. When the system contractor is conducting DT&E, whether at the contractor's facilities or government test site, a test plan is provided to the Chief Developmental Tester for review and approval, in accordance with DoDI 5000.02 (Encl. 4, para 5(a)(2)(d) – page 93).

Operational Test Plans. The Operational Test Agency (OTA) plans, develops, and executes the Operational Test Plan (OTP), in accordance with DoDI 5000.02 (Encl. 5, para 11(a)(3) – page 107). An OTP is prepared for an operational assessment (OA), an Initial Operational Test and Evaluation (IOT&E), a Follow-on Operational Test and Evaluation (FOT&E), and other operational test events identified in the TEMP. The OTP documents adequate testing to assess whether the system under test is operationally effective and operationally suitable when used by representative, properly trained personnel in an operationally realistic environment. In the case of OA, the OTP documents testing that supports progress towards the assessment of operational effectiveness, operational suitability, and survivability (including cybersecurity) or lethality. The OTP documents the test design, supporting methodology, and analytic details required for the specific operational test. Additionally, the cybersecurity Cooperative Vulnerability and Penetration Assessment (CVPA) and Adversarial Assessment (AA) test plans must be approved by DOT&E in order to get the credit for these tests.

CH 8–3.7 Key Considerations in T&E Strategy Development

The following are key considerations in developing the TEMP, in accordance with DoDI 5000.02 (Encl. 4, para 2(c) – page 90).

CH 8–3.7.1 Use of Government Test Facilities for T&E

In accordance with DoDI 5000.02 (Encl. 4, para 5(b) – page 95), programs will use DoD government T&E capabilities and invest in government T&E infrastructure unless a program can justify the exception as cost-effective to the government. In addition, PMs will conduct a Cost Benefit Analysis (CBA) for exceptions to this policy and obtain approval through the TEMP approval process before acquiring or using non-government, program-unique test facilities or resources.

In accordance with DoDI 5000.02 (Encl. 4, para 3(f) – page 92), the PM must take full advantage of DoD ranges, laboratories, and other resources and programs; and consult with their Lead DT&E Organization to determine availability and adequacy of DoD or other government-owned test capabilities and resources to execute proposed T&E strategies. Approaches to resolving test capability and resource gaps are to be identified in the strategy for T&E.

The Test Resource Management Center (TRMC) can provide assistance in identifying available government test facilities. T&E WIPTs utilize their DASD(DT&E) representative to engage TRMC supporting staff experts on test ranges and facilities.

CH 8–3.7.2 Evaluation Methodology & Framework

This section describes both the developmental and operational evaluation approaches. Each approach consists of an evaluation methodology and an evaluation framework.

Part 3 of the TEMP Format includes the program's evaluation implementation plans. Parts 3.2 and 3.3 include the developmental evaluation methodology and framework, and parts 3.5 and 3.6 include the operational evaluation methodology and framework. In accordance with DoDI 5000.02 (Encl. 4, para 5(a)(10) – page 95), programs update both evaluation approaches with each TEMP update to account for system maturity, changes to source documents (e.g. CDD/CPD, AS, STAR, SEP, ISP, etc.), or contractor down select.

CH 8–3.7.2.1 Developmental Evaluation Methodology

As the system design matures, data or evaluations are needed to inform the program manager and other decision-makers on the progress the system is making towards meeting system requirements and achieving desired performance. To ensure information is available to inform decisions in a timely manner, evaluation planning must precede test planning. The Developmental Evaluation Methodology identifies the essential information needed to inform major programmatic decisions.

In accordance with DoDI 5000.02 (Encl. 4, para 5(a)(11) – page 95), starting at Milestone A the TEMP will include a developmental evaluation methodology providing essential information on programmatic and technical risks as well as information for major programmatic decisions. Starting at Milestone B, the developmental evaluation methodology will become the Developmental Evaluation Framework (DEF), identifying key data that will contribute to assessing progress toward achieving system requirements. However, from the onset of the program's evaluation planning, it is recommended that programs use a DEF to logically organize the DT&E strategy.

To ensure T&E focuses on informing the program's decision-making process throughout the acquisition life cycle, Part 3.1 of the TEMP includes the key program decision points and the information needed to support them (see "Decision Support Key" example). Answers to the Decision Support Questions (DSQ) from the DEF and the Critical Operational Issues (COIs) from the Operational Evaluation Framework (OEF) provide the T&E information used to inform decisions throughout the program acquisition.

Once evaluation planning is complete, the DEF and OEF identify opportunities for integrated testing where shared test events can provide data for both the developmental and operational evaluations. A conscious effort is required by the DT&E and OT&E communities to leverage opportunities suited for integrated testing, whenever feasible.

A separate summary of decision points and the information needed to support them is included in a table (see "Decision Support Key" example) to serve as a quick reference for evaluations in Part 3.1 of the TEMP Format.

CH 8–3.7.2.2 Developmental Evaluation Framework

In accordance with DoDI 5000.02 (Encl. 4, para 5(a)(11) – page 95), starting at Milestone B, the DEF identifies key data contributing to assessment progress towards achieving: key performance parameters (KPPs), key system attributes (KSAs), critical technical parameters (CTPs), interoperability requirements, cybersecurity requirements, reliability growth, maintainability attributes, developmental test objectives, and others, as needed. In addition, it shows the correlation/mapping between test events, key resources, and the decision(s) supported.

The DEF guides development of the DT&E strategy by focusing the thought process on logically identifying the critical program decisions and defining the information needed to inform them, and finally the test and modeling and simulation (M&S) events needed to generate the data for the evaluation. Once complete, the DEF format, identified in TEMP Section 3.2, articulates the results.

The DT&E strategy is built by defining its components (decisions, Decision Support Questions (DSQ), capabilities, technical measures, and test/modeling and simulation events) and articulating them in the DEF. The components of the DT&E strategy and the DEF are:

- Decisions: Decision points throughout the acquisition life cycle, made by decision-makers ranging from the program manager (PM) to the Milestone Decision Authority (MDA), to be informed by DT&E-gained knowledge.
  - Decisions are listed in the first row of the DEF, forming the matrix's columns.
  - Decisions reflected in the DEF should represent major turning/decision points in the acquisition strategy needing DT&E information in order to make an informed decision.

Examples may include milestone decisions, key integration points, technical readiness decisions, etc.

- Decision Support Questions (DSQ): Questions capturing the essence of the information needed to make informed decisions.
  - Each DSQ to be used to inform a decision is listed in the second row of the DEF, forming sub-columns under each decision. For example, the answers to DSQ#1 through DSQ#3 will be used to inform Decision #1.
  - The DSQ phrases the question the decision-maker needs to have answered based upon the system evaluation during DT&E, to make an informed decision. For example, the decision to move forward with system integration may be informed with DSQ such as: (1) Are the components to be integrated performing as required? (2) Are the basic platform capabilities performing as required?
- Developmental Evaluation Objectives (DEO): The system's performance, interoperability, cybersecurity, and reliability capabilities to be evaluated.
  - The system's technical capabilities, or DEO, are those areas that must be evaluated to answer the DSQ to inform the program's decisions.
  - The DEO, divided into the functional areas of performance, interoperability, cybersecurity, and reliability, are listed in the first column of the DEF, forming the category rows of the matrix.
  - The DEO are derived from the major categories of technical capabilities listed in the system's Technical Requirements Document or top-level System Specification. For example, an aircraft's technical performance capabilities may include flight performance and mission communication.
- Technical Measures (TM): The top-level measures, or capability sub-categories that quantify the capabilities.
  - The TM and their reference within the technical requirements document are listed in the second and third columns of the DEF, adjacent to the capability they quantify, forming the individual rows of the matrix.
  - The TM or capability sub-categories are the means for quantifying system performance at a strategic level of detail. Each capability should have a few TM listed to capture, at a strategic level of detail (or "inch-deep/mile-wide"), how the capability will be quantified during the system's evaluation. The TM should not be all the requirements listed in the technical requirements document, nor should the DEF replicate the program's Verification Cross Reference Matrix (VCRM). For example, the aircraft's flight performance could be quantified by measuring Range/Payload, Take-off/Landing, Airfield Ops, Instrument Approach, and Emergency Ops.
- Data Sources: The test, modeling and simulation, or other events generating the data needed for system evaluation.
  - Where a DSQ needs information about a system capability in order to inform the decision point, the DEF identifies the data source for the evaluation.
  - The test, modeling and simulation events, or other data sources used for the evaluation of the TM/system capabilities are listed at the DEF cells at the intersection between the DSQ needing information and the capability/TM. For example, Decision #1 is informed by answering DSQ#1 through DSQ#3. DSQ#1 is answered by evaluating system performance capability #1 by measuring TM#1 through TM#3 using data gathered during DT#1 and M&S#1.

Upon program office request, DASD(DT&E) will deploy a DEF Core Team to assist the program in tailoring the DEF concept to the specifics of the program's information needs, by facilitating the discussion and building a draft DEF product for the program's TEMP.

Table 4: Development Evaluation Framework Essential Information

Functional Evaluation Area	Categorical groupings of functional areas brought forward or derived from baseline documentation (Performance, Reliability, Cybersecurity, or Interoperability).
Decision supported	The significant program decision points where data and information gathered during testing are used to make decisions or give program direction. Not limited to major acquisition milestones.
Decision Support Question	Key question related to Performance, Reliability, Cybersecurity, or Interoperability that, when answered, determines the outcome of an evaluation for the decision supported.
Key system requirements (KPPs, KSAs, CTPs, etc.) and T&E measures	One or more fields of requirements identification and performance measurement: • **Technical requirements document reference**. Provides references to sources of technical requirements about which information is sought for a decision supported. Performance or Detailed Specifications are the preferred sources. JCIDS documents may be used prior to the development of government specifications. • **Description** (of technical requirements). Short plain text description of the requirement or technical measurement. • **Technical measures**. CTP, applicable TPMs, metrics, benchmarks. These have units and values. May include intermediate levels of performance associated with decision supported.
Method (technique, process, or verification method)	Method/methodology by which the data and information are gathered. Could be a test, model, simulation, observation, inspection, etc.
Test Event	Name of the test event(s) or other verification event(s) providing data for the technical measures and information to answer the decision support question.
Resources	Brief reference may appear here. Detailed in TEMP Part IV.
Cross Reference	Used to refer to related requirements, capabilities, and line items to aid in requirements traceability, precedence, interdependency, and causality.

The TEMP Guidebook provides Developmental Evaluation Framework examples.

CH 8–3.7.2.3 Operational Evaluation Framework

In accordance with DoDI 5000.02 (Encl. 5, para 6(d) – page 103), the Operational Evaluation Framework summarizes the mission-focused evaluation methodology and supporting test strategy, including the essential mission and system capabilities that contribute to operational effectiveness, operational suitability, and survivability (including cybersecurity) or lethality. The framework identifies the goal of the test within a mission context, mission-oriented response variables, factors that affect those variables, and test designs for strategically varying the factors across the operational envelope, test period, and test resources. The Operational Evaluation Framework may also include standard measures of program progress including: Critical Operational Issue Criteria (COIC), KPPs, KSAs, CTPs, interoperability requirements, cybersecurity requirements, reliability growth, maintainability attributes, and others as needed. The Operational Evaluation Framework focuses on:

- The subset of mission-oriented measures critical for assessing operational effectiveness, operational suitability, and survivability (including cybersecurity) or lethality.
- Resource, schedule, and cost drivers of the test program.

The Operational Evaluation Framework shows how the major test events and test phases link together to form a systematic, rigorous, and structured approach to quantitatively evaluate system capability across the operational envelope. When structured this way, the framework also becomes a tool for synthesizing and justifying the resources necessary for an adequate test.

Error! Reference source not found. identifies information for inclusion in the Operational Evaluation Framework.

Table 5: Operational Evaluation Framework Essential Information

Goal of the Test	Typically, the goal is to characterize operational missions and/or capabilities across the operational envelope. • Describe the operational missions and/or capabilities assessed. • Link each mission/capability to at least one mission-oriented response variable. • Address the associated COI(s) or COIC, where applicable.
Mission-oriented Response Variables (T&E Measures)	Quantitative T&E measures provide criteria for mission accomplishment (not technical performance for a single subsystem) and comprehensively cover the reasons for procuring the system (the need).
	Also include the resource, schedule, and cost drivers of the test program.
Test Design	Factors affecting the mission-oriented response variables during operational employment of the system.
	Scientific and statistical method for strategically varying the factors across the operational envelope.
	Statistical measures of merit (power and confidence), where appropriate. • Provide power calculations for determining the effect of factors on the response variables. • When an experimental design includes multiple statistical measures

	of merit (e.g., separate power values for several factors (and their interactions).
	Effect sizes for observing identified factors and their interactions, where appropriate.
	Provide a brief justification and description of the test, when not utilizing a scientific approach to test planning.
	Only provide a summary in the Operational Evaluation Framework; the body of the TEMP includes detailed test design information or a STAT appendix and is referenced in the Operational Evaluation Framework.
Test Period	Include all operational test periods when collecting data (e.g., LUT, OA, IOT&E, FOT&E, etc.).
Resources	High-level summary of the resources (time, people, places, and things) needed to execute an adequate test.

The Operational Evaluation Framework also aids Integrated Testing by identifying opportunities for using DT data for OT evaluation. In cases where OT evaluation leverages DT, the Operational Evaluation Framework links to the supporting Developmental Evaluation Framework and summarizes procedures for ensuring data collected in DT are both appropriate and adequate for OT evaluation.

The Operational Evaluation Framework matures as the system matures. Insert the Operational Evaluation Framework in Section 3 of the TEMP if short (less than 2 pages), embedded as an Excel table/database, or provided as an annex.

The TEMP Guidebook provides an Operational Evaluation Framework Example, showing ways the Operational Evaluation Framework could be organized and constructed. Each program remains unique and requires thoughtful trade-offs in applying this guidance. Programs can also use equivalent Service-specific formats identifying the same relationships and information.

CH 8–3.7.3 Reliability T&E

Initial reliability DT&E supports contractor design for reliability and assessment of design margins intended to provide system, subsystem, and component robustness, in accordance with DoDI 5000.02 (Encl. 4, para 5(a)(2)(e) – page 93) and DoDI 5000.02 (Encl. 5, para 6(c) – page 103). Even so, initial prototypes of complex systems will almost always have inherent reliability and performance deficiencies that generally could not have been foreseen and eliminated in the early design stages. To uncover and eliminate these deficiencies, T&E activities start early with prototypes and continue as the system hardware and software mature. Developmental tests are specifically planned and conducted to stress the system components to predetermined realistic levels at which inadequate design features will surface as system failures. These failures are analyzed, design modifications incorporated, and then the modified system is tested to verify the validity of the design change. This testing philosophy utilizes the test-analyze-fix-test (TAFT) procedure as the basic catalyst in achieving system reliability growth.

The ultimate goal of a reliability growth program is to increase system reliability to a stated requirement level by eliminating a sufficient number of inherent system failure modes. A successful system reliability growth program is dependent on several factors. First, an accurate determination must be made of the current system reliability status. Second, a test program must be planned that subjects the system to stress conditions that are adequate to uncover inherent failure models and to verify design modifications. Third, the Chief Developmental Tester must plan and resource the T&E activities required to support the

"TAFT" procedure as part of the TEMP. To adequately control these as well as other factors inherent in the reliability growth process, it is important to track reliability growth throughout the testing program. This is accomplished by periodically assessing system reliability at specified points in time during the development and comparing the current reliability to the planned level of achievement for that point in time. These assessments provide the necessary data and visibility to support the necessary corrective action activities.

Reliability assessment testing estimates the reliability of a component, subsystem, or production-representative system within operationally relevant conditions. The resulting reliability estimate can be compared to the reliability requirement and assessed in the context of the operational mission. Operational test organizations examine the implications of the achieved reliability in the context of the operational mission, which may lead to different conclusions than a simple comparison to the reliability requirement.

CH 8–3.7.3.1 Reliability Growth Testing

Reliability growth is achieved by eliminating initial design or manufacturing weaknesses in a system via failure mode discovery, analysis, and effective correction. Systems with comprehensive reliability growth programs are more likely to meet their development goals than systems without such programs. Activities of a comprehensive reliability growth program include:

- Initiating the reliability growth program from the beginning, as part of system design.
- Having a clear understanding of the intended mission(s) for the system, including the stresses associated with each mission, mission durations, and configuration control.
- Developing adequate requirements that are quantitative, mission-oriented, testable, achievable, reflect the desired reliability of the system, and cover the system's operational mission envelope.
- Establishing a reliability goal that supports being able to demonstrate the reliability requirement during developmental testing (DT) and operational testing (OT) with acceptable risk.
- Ensuring that the contract, and contracting and funding decisions support reliability growth efforts.
- Developing a reliability growth curve based on realistic assumptions that can be used as a tool to track progress during testing.
- Establishing intermediate reliability goals or entrance criteria and meeting these goals before proceeding to OT.
- Conducting testing that is of sufficient length and is representative of the system's operational mission profile.
- Supporting growth testing with reliability analyses that include Failure Modes and Effects Criticality Analysis (FMECA), Level of Repair analysis, reliability predictions.
- Establishing a Failure Reporting, Analysis, and Corrective Action System (FRACAS), Failure Review Board, and a RAM working group.
- Ensuring that reliability expectations during each phase of development are supported by realistic assumptions that are linked with systems engineering activities.
- Programs developing a path forward to address shortfalls when sufficient evidence exists that the demonstrated reliability is significantly below the growth curve.
- Ensuring the program is adequately resourced for engineering support to conduct failure analysis and corrective action solutions.

An effective Reliability Growth Program includes elements of planning, tracking, and projection that are part of an overall Reliability Growth Management strategy. MIL-HDBK-189C, Reliability Growth Management, provides more detail on all elements of reliability growth management. The goal of reliability growth planning is to optimize testing resources, quantify potential risks, and plan for successful achievement of reliability objectives. A well-thought-out reliability growth plan can serve as a significant management tool in identifying resources required to enhance system reliability and improve the likelihood of demonstrating the system reliability requirement.

In accordance with DoDI 5000.02 (Encl. 4, para 5(a)(2)(f) – page 94) and DoDI 5000.02 (Encl. 5, para 6(c)(2)(a) – page 103), as part of reliability growth planning, programs construct reliability growth planning curves (RGPC) to illustrate how reliability increases over time. The RGPC is a target; the curve does not imply that inherent system reliability automatically grows to achieve these values. On the contrary, attainment of these values is feasible only with the incorporation of an adequate number of effective designs and/or process fixes. RGPCs for hardware and hybrid (hardware and software) systems are typically based on the U.S. Army Materiel Systems Analysis Activity (AMSAA) Planning Model based on Projection Methodology (PM2) or the Crow-Extended Planning Model. MIL-HDBK-189C provides more detail on RGPCs.

The reliability growth tracking curve (RGTC) provides a gauge to track the progress of the reliability efforts. This is done by determining whether system reliability is increasing with time (i.e., growth is occurring) and to what degree (i.e., growth rate), and estimating the demonstrated reliability during testing. Both the Duane Model and the AMSAA Reliability Growth Tracking Model (RGTM) may be used to model growth. MIL-HDBK-189C, Reliability Growth Management, provides more detail on RGTCs.

Reliability projection is an assessment of the reliability that can be anticipated at some future point in the development program given corrective action. Projection is based on the reliability achievement to date and engineering assessments of future program characteristics. It is a particularly valuable analysis tool when a program is experiencing difficulties, because it enables investigation of program alternatives.

Guidance for documentation of reliability growth in TEMPs is discussed in the TEMP Guidebook.

Reliability is measured, monitored, and reported throughout the acquisition process. Reliability measurements and estimates are recorded on the RGTC and compared to the RGPC. Reliability growth strategies for systems not meeting entrance and exit criteria are revised, at a minimum, at each Milestone to reflect current system reliability. When necessary, reliability growth continues after the full-rate production (FRP) decision.

Refer to the DAG, CH 3.4.3.19., Reliability and Maintainability Engineering, for more information on Reliability.

CH 8–3.7.3.2 Reliability Assessment Testing

Reliability assessments primarily estimate the reliability of a production-representative system under operationally realistic conditions, In accordance with DoDI 5000.02 (Encl. 4, para 5(a)(2)(e) – page 93). Test personnel conduct reliability assessments on systems with fixed-design configurations. Operational testing is commonly used to reach statistically valid decisions regarding whether an item has achieved its specified reliability under the realistic conditions in which the user is expected to operate the system. Operational test organizations examine the implications of the achieved reliability in the context of the operational mission, which may lead to different conclusions than a simple comparison to the reliability requirement. Therefore, testing is long enough to demonstrate both the reliability requirement and an operationally meaningful reliability. If the program successfully executes a Reliability Growth Program through DT and prior to the OT, the chance of demonstrating the required reliability during OT is high.

The most common test methodology for a reliability assessment is a fixed duration test; other methods include two-stage and sequential test plans. A fixed duration test provides the exact test duration during the test planning process, whereas other methods have variable test lengths, depending on the observed failures in testing. The length of a fixed duration test is determined by balancing the expected system reliability, test duration, and the statistical risks (producer's risk versus consumer's risk). Operating characteristic (OC) curves are used to determine either the minimally acceptable reliability or the test duration as a function of the statistical risks. The risks are related to the reliability growth goal. DOT&E does not require any specific values for producer's and consumer's risk in OT. The rationale for the selection of test risks derives from the specifics of each program.

OC curves are constructed assuming any statistical distribution. It is common for time- or distance-based reliability requirements to assume a constant failure rate (exponential distribution). For equipment that operates only once (a one-shot device) or cyclically (such as pyrotechnic devices, missiles, fire warning systems, and switchgear), testing based on operating time is inappropriate. For these pass/fail systems, the binomial distribution is used to construct the OC curve.

Refer to the TEMP Guidebook for more information on using operating characteristic curves to determine the length of a demonstration test.

CH 8–3.7.3.3 Reliability T&E Tracking

The reliability process weaves reliability engineering across the design, testing, tracking, and assessment activities during total development cycle of an acquisition program. The purpose of reliability T&E tracking is to assess the reliability improvement of a system during development. Reliability growth tracking provides decision-makers the opportunity to gauge the progress of the reliability effort for a system. The choice of a reliability tracking model is dependent on the management strategy for incorporating corrective actions in the system. The management strategy for some programs may require a corrective action for specific failures while other management strategies may not.

CH 8–3.7.3.4 Reliability T&E Tools

The purpose of reliability engineering is to influence system design in order to increase mission capability, decrease logistics burden, and decrease life-cycle cost of the product. Reliability engineering includes a set of design and test activities that start early during the Materiel Solution Analysis phase and continue through the Operations and Support phase. A comprehensive T&E program includes the use of reliability T&E tools to discover and mitigate failure modes throughout the development and production process. Accelerated test methods such as HALT and HASS are well-recognized industry reliability test and screening methods.

Highly Accelerated Life Testing (HALT)/Highly Accelerated Stress Screening (HASS). The most common application of accelerated testing such as HALT and HASS occurs with electronic equipment. HALT is used during development to determine the operating and destruct limits. HASS is used during production to screen components to detect latent flaws. Although general guidelines exist for implementing HALT and HASS, tailoring is needed on each item and application. HALT and HASS are focused on detecting and eliminating failure modes at the component and sub-component level so that corrective actions can be implemented before the start of system-level testing.

A comprehensive T&E program includes practices such as HALT and HASS to discover and mitigate failure modes throughout the development and production process. Although general guidelines exist for implementing HALT and HASS, tailoring is needed on each item and application. HALT and HASS are focused on detecting and eliminating failure modes at the component and sub-component level so that corrective action can be taken.

Highly Accelerated Life Testing (HALT). HALT is an activity implemented along with design verification tests that are planned and conducted during the design and development process. HALT is not a compliance test and does not replace qualification testing requirements. HALT, which is part of an overall comprehensive T&E program, will quickly reveal failure modes that would/could occur during the life of the product under normal operating conditions.

HALT is a form of accelerated testing used to determine whether the item (e.g., components, sub-components) can withstand environmental stresses. Early in the design and development processes, HALT is conducted in a specialized environmental chamber to expose items to a full range of operating conditions. During HALT, environmental stresses are controlled and incrementally applied until they eventually reach a level beyond that which is expected during operational use. Stresses applied during HALT are typically temperature and/or vibration; however, other stresses, such as electrical or mechanical, are also considered. HALT, utilizing combinations of these stresses, is recommended to emulate real-world conditions.

Exposing items to environmental stresses forces failures in order to understand operational margins and identify weaknesses in the design that need corrective actions. If the item (component or sub-component) survives HALT, it passes the test. Any deficiencies identified during HALT are inspected and analyzed to guide refinement of the design and elimination of the cause(s) of failure.

Reliability growth testing (RGT) is conducted in parallel with HALT to provide engineering confirmation and feedback. Information captured from previous testing and analysis is used to ensure that any areas of concern are properly instrumented and tracked for future tests. Corrective actions are taken to mitigate the reliability deficiencies that arise during testing. Examples of corrective actions include engineering redesign of mechanical components, software recoding, and adjustments to training practices.

After the corrective actions are in place, accelerated tests can also be used to quickly verify the corrective actions. Dynamic M&S, finite element stress and heat transfer analysis, and component fatigue analysis toolsets are some of the methods utilized to predict failure mechanisms and support reliability assessments of the proposed design and any subsequent design revisions.

Highly Accelerated Stress Screening (HASS). HASS is discovery testing as compared to compliance testing. HASS identifies inferior/defective items by exposing the production item to accelerated stresses to identify defects early, before a large number of items with similar flaws are produced. HASS is implemented to ensure the reliability of production line products. HASS is one of several screening approaches used by the DoD/industry to provide the opportunity to substantially improve fielded product reliability and reduce overall cost of ownership.

HASS uses accelerated stresses (beyond the product specifications) on production items to identify latent and intermittent defects that are a result of a problem in the manufacturing process. The stresses applied during HASS are based on operational and destructive stress limits established during HALT. HASS is usually not recommended unless a comprehensive HALT has been performed.

CH 8–3.7.4 Scientific Test & Analysis Techniques

In accordance with DoDI 5000.02 (Encl. 4, para 5(a)(3) – page 94) and DoDI 5000.02 (Encl. 5, para 5(e) – page 101), T&E planning includes the use of Scientific Test and Analysis Techniques (STAT) to produce statistically defensible test results and effectively support decision-makers. STAT is defined as the scientific and statistical methods, with associated processes, used to enable the development of efficient, rigorous test strategies so as to yield defensible test results. STAT encompasses techniques such as design of experiments, observational studies, and survey design. The specific objective(s) of the test determines the suitability and specific application of each method.

STAT is applied to test design and analysis throughout all phases of the acquisition life cycle. Various types of test events (e.g., contractor, developmental, live fire, operational, cybersecurity, interoperability, and modeling and simulation) can utilize STAT to achieve defensible results. STAT enables estimation of technical performance requirements as well as the mission-oriented metrics of operational effectiveness, operational suitability, and survivability (including cybersecurity) or lethality over the entire operational envelope. Depending on the test goal, different STAT methods may apply. **Error! Reference source not found.**, provides some examples of what methods might apply at different test phases in a program's development, depending on the goal of the test.

Table 6: Linkage between STAT & Test Goals

Test Objective	Likely Applicable Test Phase	Potentially Useful Experimental Designs

Characterize performance across an operational envelope Determine whether a system meets requirements across a variety of operational conditions	DT and OT	Response surface designs, optimal designs, factorial designs, fractional factorial designs
Compare two or more systems across a variety of conditions	DT and OT	Factorial or fractional factorial designs, matched pairs optimal designs
Screen for important factors driving performance	CT and DT	Factorial or fractional factorial designs
Test for problem cases that degrade system performance	Primarily DT, OT for Business Systems	Combinatorial designs, Orthogonal Arrays, Space filling designs
Optimize system performance with respect to a set of conditions	CT and early DT	Response surface designs, optimal designs
Predict performance, reliability, or material properties at use conditions	CT and early DT	Response Surface Designs, Optimal Designs, Accelerated life tests
Improve system reliability or performance by determining robust system configurations	CT and early DT	Response surface designs, Taguchi designs (Robust Parameter Designs), Orthogonal Arrays

Note. DT = Developmental Test   OT = Operational Test   CT = Contractor Test.

The proper and early use of STAT produces tests yielding defensible results as well as answering the test objectives, identifying risks of making inaccurate conclusions, and reducing uncontrolled experimental error. A sequential testing approach allows test organizations to accumulate evidence of system performance across its operational envelope, thus leveraging information from previous tests. A statistical, scientifically based approach to testing also informs the systems engineering process, and enables a better understanding of the true state of technology and system performance throughout the acquisition life cycle.

A program applying STAT starts early in the acquisition process and assembles a team of subject matter experts to identify the primary evaluation metrics of interest against both the technical performance requirements, as well as the mission-oriented metrics that characterize the performance of the system and its capabilities in the context of a mission-oriented evaluation. The team identifies the factors, as well as the levels of these factors (i.e., the various conditions or settings that the factors can take), expected to drive the technical and operational performance of the system. The anticipated effects of each of the factors on the evaluation metrics are determined to aid in test planning. To maximize test efficiency, the team uses experimental design techniques to strategically vary factors across the various developmental, operational, and live fire test activities. The test design balances limited test resources with adequate coverage of the operational envelope, while minimizing test risks.

The TEMP outlines a brief overview of the test design philosophy and use of STAT. While the information content varies depending on which milestone the TEMP supports, the test design plan(s) reflect the complexity of the system. Often multiple test design plans are necessary to fully characterize the performance of the system under test. Besides factors and their levels, design details also include statistical measures of merit (including but not limited to power and confidence) on the relevant evaluation metrics. These statistical measures are important to understand "how much testing is enough," and they provide the decision-makers the quantitative basis to conduct trade-off analyses, and provide defensible measures of the test scope and needed resources. The merit of a test design is based not only on the number of test points, but also their placement within the operational envelope. The statistical measures of merit used to evaluate the statistical adequacy of the test design are consistent with the test goal. For example, if characterization of system performance across a variety of conditions is a test goal, then the power calculations provide a measure of the ability of the test to detect differences in performance amongst the conditions of the test. A supporting appendix to the TEMP provides the details of each of the test designs.

The analysis of test data and reporting of test results employ STAT as well. If advanced experimental design methods are used to develop the most efficient test design and execution plan, but the analysis of the data does not take advantage of the principles that drive that design, then the benefits are lost. STAT enables the data from testing to provide the most information from the data for the fewest resources. The reporting of average performance across all conditions varied in the test, for example, is dissuaded; as such, analysis methods can miss identifying important performance shortfalls. Comprehensive statistical analyses are employed to take advantage of the efficiencies and increased information provided by a rigorous experimental design.

For more information on STAT, visit the STAT in T&E Center of Excellence (STAT COE).

CH 8–3.7.5 Cybersecurity T&E
This section supports CH 8–3.19 Cyber Ranges

DoD missions increasingly depend upon complex, interconnected information technology (IT) environments. These environments are inherently vulnerable, providing opportunities for adversaries to negatively impact DoD missions. Addressing cybersecurity early in the acquisition process requires a comprehensive T&E program, which provides early discovery and allows for correction of developmental and operational issues, in support of the warfighter. The policy for Cybersecurity is defined in DoDI 5000.02 (Encl. 14), Cybersecurity in the Defense Acquisition System.

This section provides an overview to assist the Chief Developmental Testers and the entire test community in developing an approach to cybersecurity T&E. Per DoDI 8500.01 (Para 3(h)(3) – page 4), Cybersecurity remains an integral part of developmental and operational T&E. Cybersecurity T&E planning, analysis, and implementation develops an iterative process starting at the beginning of the acquisition life cycle and continuing through maintenance of the system.

Error! Reference source not found., depicts the Cybersecurity T&E Process phases, occurring from pre-Milestone A test planning, through developmental test, to cybersecurity OT&E after Milestone C.

Figure 1: Cybersecurity T & E Process Mapped to the Acquisition Lifecycle

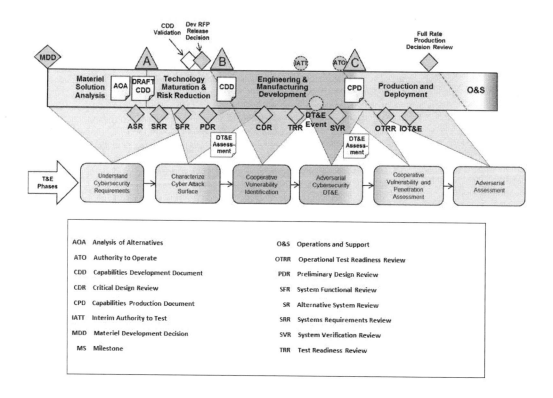

AOA	Analysis of Alternatives	O&S Operations and Support
ATO	Authority to Operate	OTRR Operational Test Readiness Review
CDD	Capabilities Development Document	PDR Preliminary Design Review
CDR	Critical Design Review	SFR System Functional Review
CPD	Capabilities Production Document	SR Alternative System Review
IATT	Interim Authority to Test	SRR Systems Requirements Review
MDD	Materiel Development Decision	SVR System Verification Review
MS	Milestone	TRR Test Readiness Review

This figure presents a baseline mapping of Cybersecurity T&E process phases to the acquisition life cycle; the mapping of process phases may be tailored to the acquisition model used by the program, as defined in DoDI 5000.02 (Encl. 5, para 8 – page 105). The process should translate cybersecurity requirements, host environments, threats, and other considerations into testing. Early developmental T&E involvement in acquisition planning and execution remains a key feature of the cybersecurity T&E Process (Note. Planning plays an important part of each phase in the acquisition process.) Additionally, programs can plan some phases to occur concurrently, depending upon when in the acquisition life cycle the program begins the process.

The Cybersecurity T&E process has six phases and is iterative (i.e., programs may repeat phases several times throughout the acquisition life cycle, due to changes in system architecture, new or emerging threats, and changes to the system environment). For example, the first two phases, which involve analysis to understand requirements and define the cyber-attack surface, may be iterated with a major change to the system architecture. These activities would be coincident with updates to the TEMP and with systems engineering activities to update requirements, architecture, and design.

The six phases of developmental and operational test preparation and execution are described in the following subsections.

CH 8–3.7.5.1 Understand Cybersecurity Requirements

As early as possible in the acquisition process, the Chief Developmental Tester, in collaboration with the T&E WIPT, should examine program documents (i.e., Acquisition Strategy, Cybersecurity Strategy, and other system requirements documents) to gain an understanding of system cybersecurity requirements. In accordance with DoDI 5000.02 (Encl. 11, para 6(a) – page 136), the Chief Developmental Tester and T&E WIPT ensure system cybersecurity requirements are complete and testable. Based on the requirements review, the T&E WIPT constructs a T&E strategy to address the cybersecurity requirements and threat profiles. This phase is performed iteratively, as system development proceeds.

CH 8–3.7.5.2 Characterize the Cyber Attack Surface

The attack surface defines the system's exposure to reachable and exploitable vulnerabilities, including any hardware, software, connection, data exchange, service, removable media, wireless or Radio Frequency (RF) communications, etc., that might expose the system to potential threat access. The T&E WIPT should update the Milestone B (or relevant milestone) TEMP with plans for testing and evaluating the elements and interfaces of the system deemed susceptible to cyber threats, in accordance with DoDI 5000.02 (Encl. 4, para 5(a)(9) – page 95).

CH 8–3.7.5.3 Cooperative Vulnerability Identification

In this phase, the Chief Developmental Tester defines vulnerability-type testing for contractor and government cybersecurity testing at the component and subsystem level. This testing assists in refining the scope and objectives for subsequent cybersecurity T&E and is integrated to the greatest extent possible into the T&E program as a whole. Preparation for vulnerability identification is performed, in part, by understanding the cybersecurity kill chain (i.e., by considering how an adversary might exploit vulnerabilities). The vulnerabilities identified in this and previous phases should be resolved or mitigated prior to proceeding to a full end-to-end DT&E assessment defined in the next activity.

CH 8–3.7.5.4 Adversarial Cybersecurity Developmental T&E

This phase serves as an end-to-end assessment in a representative mission context for the system under test in order to evaluate the readiness for limited procurement/deployment and operational testing. The cybersecurity DT&E assessment typically occurs before Milestone C. This activity focuses on conducting a rigorous cybersecurity test in an environment as realistic as available, and requires the use of a threat-representative test team that tests the potential and actual impacts to the system. Results of this testing are included as part of the DT&E assessment. Programs should resolve any shortfalls identified in this and previous phases prior to proceeding to operational test and evaluation, and programs should plan sufficient time and resources for these resolutions.

CH 8–3.7.5.5 Cooperative Vulnerability & Penetration Assessment

The following two sections discuss cybersecurity operational testing, which consists of two components: a Cooperative Vulnerability and Penetration Assessment, which is conducted in cooperation with the program manager, and an Adversarial Assessment, which emulates an actual adversary attack on the system and its associated network(s). Cybersecurity operational testing guidelines are provided in DOT&E's memorandum, "Procedures for Operational Test and Evaluation of Cybersecurity in Acquisition Programs," dated August 1, 2014. This phase consists of an overt, cooperative, and comprehensive examination of the system to identify vulnerabilities and characterize the system's operational cybersecurity status. A vulnerability assessment and penetration testing team should conduct this test event through document reviews, physical inspection, personnel interviews, and the use of automated scanning, password tests, and applicable exploitation tools. The assessment should be conducted in the intended operational environment, with representative operators to the greatest extent possible. In accordance with DoDI 8500.01 (Encl. 2, para 3(c) – page 18), this testing event may be integrated with DT&E activities (or earlier in the acquisition cycle) if conducted in a realistic operational environment; and if approved by the Director of Operational Test and Evaluation for programs on DOT&E Oversight.

CH 8–3.7.5.6 Adversarial Assessment

This phase assesses the ability of a system to support its missions while withstanding validated and representative cyber threat activity. In addition to assessing the effect on mission execution, the test should evaluate the ability of the system to detect threat activity, react to threat activity, and restore mission effectiveness degraded or lost due to threat activity. This test event should be conducted by an operational test agency employing a certified adversarial team to act as a cyber-aggressor, in accordance with DoDI 5000.02 (Encl. 5, para 8 – page 105). The adversarial assessment should include representative operators and users, local and non-local cyber network defenders (including upper tier computer network defense providers), an operational network configuration, and a representative mission with expected network traffic.

CH 8–3.7.5.7 Cybersecurity T&E Overarching Guidelines

Cybersecurity T&E overarching guidelines include:

- Test activities integrate Risk Management Framework (RMF) security controls assessments with tests of commonly exploited and emerging vulnerabilities early in the acquisition life cycle, in accordance with DoDI 8500.01 (Encl. 2, para 3(c) – page 18). Refer to the DoD RMF Knowledge Service (DoD CAC required) for more information on RMF security controls, in accordance with DoDI 5000.02 (Encl. 4, para 4(b)(13) – page 92).
- The TEMP details the ways testing provides the information needed to assess cybersecurity and inform acquisition decisions, in accordance with DoDI 5000.02 (Encl. 5, para 8(a) – page 105). Historically, TEMPs and associated test plans have not adequately addressed cybersecurity measures or resources. The process described here facilitates development and integration of cybersecurity T&E, including the use of specialized resources; and facilitates the documentation of cybersecurity T&E in the TEMP.
- Cybersecurity DT&E identifies issues related to resilience of military capabilities before Milestone C. Early discovery of system vulnerabilities can facilitate remediation to reduce impact on cost, schedule, and performance. DASD(DT&E) includes an evaluation of cybersecurity in Defense Acquisition Executive Summary (DAES) reviews and DT&E Program Assessments, provided at major decision points.
- Cybersecurity OT&E ensures the system under test can withstand realistic threat representative cyber-attacks and return to normal operations in the event of a cyber-attack. See the DOT&E memorandum, "Procedures for OT&E of Cybersecurity in Acquisition Programs," dated August 2014.
- The Cybersecurity T&E Process represents a "shift left" on the acquisition timeline because it requires earlier developmental T&E involvement.
- The Cybersecurity T&E process recommends the development and testing of mission-driven cybersecurity requirements, which may require specialized systems engineering and T&E expertise. The Chief Developmental Tester and/or operational test agency may request assistance from subject matter experts to implement this process.

Error! Reference source not found., provides some example issues programs may consider for inclusion in the Evaluation Framework:

Table 7: Cybersecurity Example Issues

Overarching Cybersecurity Developmental Issue	Does the system satisfy the specified and derived cybersecurity technical requirements for confidentiality, availability, and integrity; is the system able to sustain critical mission tasks in a cyber-contested environment?
Example Issue 1, Systems and Software Assurance	Are the system and the software developed securely?

Example Issue 2, RMF Requirements	Does the system satisfy baseline cybersecurity technical standards?
Example Issue 3, Vulnerability Assessment	Do exposed vulnerabilities adversely affect system resiliency?
Example Issue 4, System interoperability and functionality in response to exploited cyber vulnerabilities	Is the system sufficiently interoperable and able to sustain critical missions in response to exploited cyber vulnerabilities?

Refer to the Cybersecurity T&E Guidebook for additional information on cybersecurity T&E resources and an in-depth overview of the Cybersecurity T&E Process.

CH 8–3.7.6 Interoperability Testing of IT & NSS

All information technology (IT) and National Security Systems (NSS) must undergo interoperability T&E for certification prior to fielding, in accordance with:

- 10 USC 2223, Information Technology.
- DoDI 5000.02 (Encl. 4, para 4(b)(14) – page 93), Operation of the Defense Acquisition System.
- DoDI 8330.01, Interoperability of Information Technology (IT), Including National Security Systems (NSS).
- CJCSI 3170.01I, Joint Capabilities Integration and Development System.

This includes IT and NSS compliance with technical standards, Net-Ready Key Performance Parameters (NR-KPP), Enterprise Architectures, and spectrum supportability requirements.

For IT/NSS with *Joint, multinational,* or *interagency* interoperability requirements: the Joint Staff certifies the NR-KPP and Joint Interoperability Test Command (JITC) tests and certifies the system against the NR-KPP.

For all other IT/NSS: the individual DoD Components certify the NR-KPP and test, and certify the system against the NR-KPP.

Compliance with interoperability certification requirements must be maintained throughout a system's life cycle. In accordance with DoDI 8330.01 (Encl. 3, para 6(d)(2) – page 33), each system must be re-evaluated every four years to determine if it needs to be recertified. Independent of the four-year requirement, if system interoperability functionality or requirements change at any time, the system must be recertified.

Interoperability test certification is based on T&E results from system-of-systems events featuring execution of Joint mission threads in operationally realistic test configurations (including the cyber threat). Enterprise architectures are used to identify system interfaces and build operationally realistic environments. System-of-systems test events verify the system meets its interoperability requirements, including the three elements of the NR-KPP:

- Support military operations.

- Enter and be managed on the network.
- Effectively pass information.

NR-KPP attributes determine specific measurable and testable criteria for interoperability and operationally effective end-to-end information exchanges.

JITC establishes processes to ensure operational tests include operationally mission-oriented interoperability assessments and evaluations using common outcome-based assessment methodologies to test, assess, and report on the impact interoperability and information exchanges have on a system's effectiveness and mission accomplishment. JITC does this for all acquisitions with Joint, multinational, or interagency interoperability requirements, regardless of ACAT level. The DoD Components are expected to establish similar processes for systems without Joint, multinational, or interagency interoperability requirements.

Prior to executing comprehensive system-of-systems events, which frequently occur during the operational testing conducted after Milestone C, programs can address the latter two aspects of the Net-Ready KPP (NR-KPP) with subcomponent or simple connection test activities. These activities can take place earlier in the development process and can pinpoint issues at a time when they can be fixed more readily and less expensively. If possible, more comprehensive interoperability testing (with more systems) should take place in the later stages of developmental testing. For IT/NSS with Joint, multinational, or interagency interoperability requirements, JITC is directed to leverage previous, planned, and executed DT&E and OT&E test events, and their results to support Joint interoperability test certification and eliminate test duplication.

Programs should plan and execute interoperability test events during development. In order to plan and execute these tests during development, the Chief Developmental Tester should look for the NR-KPP and Enterprise architectures to be available (at least in draft version) prior to or at Milestone B.

The Chief Developmental Tester plans and programs (budget and resources) interoperability T&E activities and documents these activities in the TEMP. The plans included in the TEMP must describe the strategy for evaluating the NR-KPP and meeting interoperability certification requirements included in the Developmental Evaluation Framework. For programs with Joint, multinational, or interagency interoperability requirements, Chief Developmental Testers should include JITC as a member of the T&E WIPT and ensure they participate in TEMP development (this helps ensure that JITC can leverage the data collected during DT).

The appropriate DT&E authority approves TEMPs, or equivalent documents, for each ACAT program after verifying that adequate levels of DT&E to achieve interoperability certification are planned, resourced, and can be executed in a timely manner. For MDAPs, MAIS, and AT&L-designated special interest programs, the approval authority is DASD(DT&E). For all other programs, the DoD Component would designate an organization to approve the interoperability test plans within the TEMP. The JITC role, for those programs with Joint, multinational, or interagency interoperability requirements, is to advise DASD(DT&E) regarding the adequacy of test planning in support of joint interoperability test certification.

At Milestone C, the DT&E authority will provide the Milestone Decision Authority (MDA) with a DT&E Program Assessment that includes interoperability. The DT&E Program Assessment will include any unresolved interoperability-related problems that could cause death or injury, loss, or major damage to weapon systems, or decreases in the combat readiness of the using organization. For those programs with Joint, multinational, or interagency interoperability requirements, JITC will provide input for the fielding decision to the MDA and PM after test and certification activities have been completed in OT (post-Milestone C).

JITC Interoperability Process Guide (IPG)—For those programs with Joint, multinational, or interagency interoperability requirements, JITC has developed and published an Interoperability Process

Guide (IPG), in coordination with the DoD CIO, to document procedures and data requirements for interoperability testing and certification, waiver processing, and associated processes and procedures.

Interoperability Test Resources—The TRMC's JMETC Program provides a DoD-wide capability for distributed T&E. (See DAG, CH 2.2.3.3., Joint Mission Environment Test Capability for more information.)

Refer to the DAG, CH 6.3.8. for more information on Interoperability.

CH 8–3.7.7 Modeling & Simulation in T&E

This section provides information on the use of modeling and simulations in test and evaluation. Programs should identify the appropriate use of modeling and simulation for each test phase or event, in accordance with DoDI 5000.02 (Encl. 4, para 5(a)(10) – page 95) and (Encl. 5, para 6(d) – page 103).

CH 8–3.7.7.1 Modeling & Simulation Purpose & Application

Models and simulations are valuable in determining how to apply scarce test resources to high-payoff areas, help identify cost-effective test scenarios, and reduce risk of failure. During the conduct of tests, models, simulations, and digital artifacts can create realistic developmental and operational test scenarios and objectives; provide virtual environments to dry run test events; and provide testers the ability to conduct tests where the use of real-world assets is deemed impractical or costly. This may occur as part of system-of-systems tests, under hazardous/dangerous conditions, or in extreme environments. Programs can use models, simulations, and digital artifacts in post-test analysis to help provide insight and for interpolation or extrapolation of results to untested conditions.

Models and simulations provide programs with different tools as follows:

> Model: A physical, mathematical, or otherwise logical representation of a system, entity, phenomenon, or process.

> Simulation: A method for implementing a model over time.

The use of models, simulations, and digital artifacts provides a means to understand the risks associated with technical development and operational employment of a system. The PM must balance programmatic needs to better understand these risks with the cost and time required to obtain credible and trusted models, simulations, and digital artifacts to support the necessary capability. T&E often reveals "unknown unknowns" in system development and planned use, especially in live fire and operational environments. Whenever feasible, observation of system performance and the use of empirical data from testing are the most credible means to evaluate system performance.

Similarly, the Chief Developmental Tester and operational testers balance their needs to address the risks encountered in DT&E, OT&E, and LFT&E with the cost and time required to acquire and use adequate and credible model and simulation capabilities. Models, simulations, and digital artifacts can be used to support test planning, execution, and evaluation of test results. When models, simulations, and digital artifacts are needed to support T&E, the program plans for and funds the development for this capability. Validation efforts typically involve the collection of live data to provide the necessary information upon which to base the VV&A; and those efforts are planned and funded.

Programs plan for models, simulations, and digital artifacts for utility across a program's life cycle, modified and updated as required, to ensure use in and applicability to all increments of an evolutionary acquisition strategy. A program's T&E strategy leverages the advantages of models and simulations. Models, simulations, and digital artifacts planning addresses which of many possible uses of models, simulations, and digital artifacts the program plans to execute in support of T&E, in accordance with DoDI 5000.02 (Encl. 4, para 5(a)(5) – page 94).

Evaluators use a model-test-fix-model approach for interaction of T&E and modeling and simulation. This iterative process provides a cost-effective method for overcoming limitations and constraints upon T&E.

Refer to the M&S Supplemental Application List for an expanded list of applications of models, simulations, and digital artifacts considerations.

CH 8–3.7.7.2 Modeling & Simulation Processes & Implementation

All models and simulations used in T&E come from an authoritative source and are accredited by the intended user (PM or OTA). Programs can only receive accreditation through a rigorous VV&A process as well as an acknowledged acceptance by the user of their application requirements and documented in the TEMP, in accordance with DoDI 5000.02 (Encl. 4, para 5(a)(5) – page 94). Therefore, PMs identify the intended use of models and simulations early so they can make resources available to support development and VV&A of these tools. PMs also include the OTA early in their processes to gain confidence in the use of authoritative models and simulations, and possibly use of them in support of OT, in accordance with DoDI 5000.02 (Encl. 5, para 6(d) – page 103). When modeling and simulation tools are used as part of operational testing, the OTA independently accredits the tool.

T&E WIPT planning incorporates modeling and simulation into the overall T&E strategy (e.g., the employment of models and simulations in early designs, the use of models and simulations to demonstrate system integration risks, and the use of models and simulations to assist in planning the scope of live tests).

DT&E, OT&E, and LFT&E commonly integrate and use Live, Virtual, Constructive (LVC) capabilities and environments in T&E facilities and resources at open air ranges, system integration laboratories, installed system test facilities, and hardware-in-the-loop facilities. Credible modeling and simulation capabilities help to inform decision-making on system functionality, operational effectiveness, operational suitability, and survivability (including cybersecurity) or lethality, and operational security.

CH 8–3.7.7.3 Modeling & Simulation Policy & Guidance

Guidelines and instructions for the development and use of modeling and simulation (M&S) in acquisition are available from a variety of sources. Each program develops a modeling and simulation strategy to support overall program investments in modeling and simulation.

The Modeling and Simulation Coordination Office (M&SCO) Modeling and Simulation Catalog (DoD CAC required) is a user-friendly, web-based tool to collect M&S summary information and data, and provides a search capability to discover M&S resources for potential reuse and cost savings. The M&S Catalog is analogous to a "card catalog" (e.g., it assists in the discovery of resources, but does not generally contain the model or simulation code). For more information on the Modeling and Simulation Community of Interest Discovery Metadata Specification (MSC-DMS) and the M&S Community of Interest, see the M&SCO website.

Modeling and simulation products, and the manner of VV&A and other processes, conform to standards—both government and commercial. For example:

- IT standards identified in the DoD IT Standards Registry (DISR) (DoD CAC required).
- Standards identified in the DoD Architecture Framework Technical Standards Profile (TV-1) and Technical Standards Forecast (TV-2).
- ASSIST (DoD CAC required) is the official source for specifications and standards used by the DoD.
- Data standards.
- DoDI 5000.61, DoD Modeling and Simulation (M&S) Verification, Validation, and Accreditation (VV&A), provides further guidance on VV&A.
- VV&A standards:

- o   IEEE Std 1516.4-2007, IEEE Recommended Practice for VV&A of a Federation—An Overlay to the High Level Architecture Federation Development and Execution Process
- o   IEEE Std 1278.4-2003, IEEE Recommended Practice for Distributed Interactive Simulation - VV&A.
- o   DoD VV&A Recommended Practices Guide (RPG).
- o   MIL-STD-3022, Documentation of Verification, Validation, and Accreditation (VV&A) for Models and Simulations.

Refer to the DAG, CH 3.2.4.2., DOT&E's Guidance on the Validation of Models and Simulation used in Operational Test and Live Fire Assessments, and DoDD 5000.59, DoD Modeling and Simulation (M&S) Management, for more information and guidance on modeling and simulation.

CH 8–3.8 Technical Reviews Supported by T&E

This section provides information on additional technical reviews supported by the test community, in accordance with DoDI 5000.02 (Encl. 3, para 7 – page 83). The test community also supports engineering reviews as described in DAG CH 3.3.3., such as System Requirements Review (SRR), Preliminary Design Review (PDR), Critical Design Review (CDR), etc.

CH 8–3.8.1 Technology Readiness Assessments

A Technology Readiness Assessment (TRA) is a systematic, metrics-based process assessing the maturity of, and the risk associated with, critical technologies to be used in MDAPs. The PM conducts the TRA with the assistance of an independent team of subject matter experts (SMEs). TRAs are a statutory requirement for MDAPs and a regulatory information requirement for all other acquisition programs, in accordance with DoDI 5000.02 (Encl. 1, Table 2 – page 57). The program may conduct a TRA concurrently with other technical reviews (see DAG, CH 3, Systems Engineering).

A preliminary assessment is due for the Development RFP Release Decision. The Assistant Secretary of Defense (Research and Engineering) (ASD(R&E)) conducts an independent review and assessment of the TRA conducted by the PM and other factors to determine whether the technology in the program has been demonstrated in a relevant environment.

Public Law 113-291 requires that the ASD(R&E), in consultation with the DASD(DT&E), shall submit to the Secretary of Defense and to the congressional defense committees by March 1 of each year, a report on the technological maturity and integration risk of critical technologies of the major defense acquisition programs of the DoD. DASD(DT&E), in consultation with ASD(R&E), assesses the technologies at key stages in the acquisition process in accordance with 10 USC 139b.

The Chief Developmental Tester, upon consultation with the Lead DT&E Organization and the T&E WIPT, participates and assists in the assessment of the technologies.

Refer to 10 USC 2366b for more information.

CH 8–3.8.2 Preliminary Design Review

The PDR should provide sufficient confidence to proceed with detailed design. It ensures the preliminary design and basic system architecture are complete, that there is technical confidence the capability need can be satisfied within cost and schedule goals, and that risks have been identified and mitigation plans established. The PDR provides the acquisition community, end user, and other stakeholders with an opportunity to understand the trade studies conducted during the preliminary design, and thus confirm that design decisions are consistent with the user's performance and schedule needs prior to formal validation of the Capability Development Document (CDD). The PDR also establishes the allocated baseline.

In accordance with DoDI 5000.02 (Para 5(d)(4)(g)(1)(b) – page 21), the PM supports T&E planning by finalizing sustainment requirements to support the PDR. The Chief Developmental Tester and the Lead DT&E Organization participate in the PDR and provide any analysis and assessments to date, as needed. During the TMRR Phase, and unless waived by the MDA, a PDR is conducted so it occurs before Milestone B and prior to contract award for EMD. The results from the PDR are used to help define entrance criteria for Milestone B and support the Development RFP Release Decision.

Refer to the DAG, CH 3.3.4. for more information.

CH 8–3.8.3 Critical Design Review

The Critical Design Review (CDR) assesses design maturity, design build-to or code-to documentation, and remaining risks, and establishes the initial product baseline, in accordance with DoDI 5000.02 (Encl. 3, para 7(b)(2) – page 83). The CDR serves as the decision point identifying the system design is ready to begin developmental prototype hardware fabrication and/or software coding with acceptable risk. The system CDR occurs during the EMD phase.

Besides establishing the initial product baseline for the system and its constituent system elements, the CDR also establishes requirements and system interfaces for enabling system elements such as support equipment, training system, maintenance, and data systems. The CDR should establish an accurate basis to assess remaining risk and identify new opportunities.

The Chief Developmental Tester and the Lead DT&E Organization participate in the CDR and provide any analysis and assessments to date.

Refer to the DAG, CH 3.3.5 for more information.

CH 8–3.9 Test Reviews

Test reviews are required prior to the execution of test events (whether by phase or key test event, etc.), as appropriate for the program, and documented within the TEMP. DoDI 5000.02 (Encl. 4, para 5(a)(4) – page 94), states that "each major developmental test phase or event will have test entrance and exit criteria." Although there are numerous and different types of test events, there are basic tenets that apply.

CH 8–3.9.1 Test Readiness Reviews

A Test Readiness Review (TRR) provides the formal approval authority with a review showing that the system is ready to enter the test and that the funding and execution of a test executes the test and gathers the required information. TRRs assess test objectives, test methods and procedures, test scope, safety, and whether test resources have been properly identified and coordinated. TRRs are also intended to determine if any changes are required in planning, resources, training, equipment, or timing to successfully proceed with the test. If any of these items are not ready, senior leadership may decide to proceed with the test and accept the risk, or mitigate the risk in some manner. A TRR is conducted for those events identified in the TEMP, in accordance with DoDI 5000.02 (Encl. 4, para 6(a) – page 96).

Documentation. TRRs are annotated within the TEMP on the integrated test program schedule. For more information, see Part 2.5 of the DAG, CH 8.3.6., Test & Evaluation Master Plan. TRRs need to include entry/exit criteria, which the Chief Developmental Tester, with the T&E WIPT, proposes to the PM for approval.

Composition. The PM or Chief Developmental Tester chairs the TRR, which generally consists of the following subject matter experts:

- Program Manager
- Chief Developmental Tester
- Program Systems Engineer
- Logistician

- Safety
- Lead DT&E Organization representative
- OTA Representative (as required)
- Test Facility/Range Representative (as required)
- DoD Component T&E Representative (as required)
- DASD(DT&E) Representative (as required)
- DOT&E Representative (if on oversight)
- Other SMEs (e.g., cybersecurity, Trainer, etc.)
- Combat Developer/Tactics Developer/Fleet User.

CH 8–3.9.2 Operational Test Readiness Reviews

The OTRR is the formal approval process for deciding if a system is ready to enter operational testing, In accordance with DoDI 5000.02 (Encl. 5, para 12 – page 111). OTRRs are conducted to:

- Verify required contractor and/or developmental testing is complete with satisfactory system performance.
- Ensure OT test plans are approved and OT preparations are complete.
- Ensure other requirements supporting OT—such as threat representation validation reports and OTA accreditation of threat representations, models, simulations, and other test instrumentation—are complete.
- Verify that T&E and system under test resources and capabilities are available and ready to proceed with the OT&E.
- Verify system-under-test is production representative.
- Determine if any changes are required in planning, resources, training, equipment, or schedule in order to successfully execute the test.
- Identify any problems that impact on the start or adequate execution of the test and subsequent evaluation or assessment of the system.
- Make decisions as appropriate to resolve problems or to change or confirm scheduled requirements.
- Safety planning.

Schedule. DoD Components have internal processes for completing OTRRs. In general, the T&E WIPT initiates the process several months prior to convening the OTRR and oversees OT preparations and resolution of issues.

Composition. The OTA or responsible test organization chairs the OTRR. OTRR participants include:

- Program Manager
- Chief Developmental Tester
- Program Systems Engineer
- Sponsor
- Combat Developer/Capability Developer/Tactics Developer/Fleet User
- Logistician
- Safety
- Lead DT&E Organization Representative
- OTA Representative
- Test Facility/Range Representative (as required)
- DoD Component T&E Representative (as required)
- DASD(DT&E) Representative (as required)
- DOT&E Representative (if on oversight)

- Other SMEs (e.g., cybersecurity, trainer, etc.).

CH 8–3.10 Certifications

Certifications provide a formal acknowledgment by an approval authority that a system or program meets specific requirements. Certifications, in many cases, are based on statute or regulations and drive systems engineering (SE) planning (i.e., a program may not be able to test or field the capability without certain certifications). Used throughout the acquisition life cycle, certifications reduce program risk and increase understanding of the system. Certain specific certifications are required before additional design, integration, network access, or testing can take place (e.g., Airworthiness certifications need to be in place before an aircraft can begin operations). Often programs insufficiently plan for the number of required certifications. Insufficient planning for certifications can have a negative impact on program costs and schedule.

Refer to the DAG, CH 3.2.6. for more information on certifications.

The system under development may require certifications, and the Chief Developmental Tester, in collaboration with the T&E WIPT needs to review the CDD to better ascertain the types of certifications required. Once identified, the TEMP includes the appropriate T&E and reporting to support the requisite certifications.

Examples of Certifications include:

- 2366a/2366b Certification Memorandum, in accordance with DoDI 5000.02 (Encl.1, Table 2 – page 47).
- Interim Authority to Test (IATT)
- Authorization to Operate (ATO)
- Safety (either for government/military test organizations or operational users)
- Interoperability
- Airworthiness
- Seaworthiness
- Food and Drug Administration (FDA)
- National Institute for Occupational Safety and Health (NIOSH)
- Environmental Compliance.

CH 8–3.10.1 Unified Capabilities Testing & Certification

DoDI 8100.04 (Glossary – page 26) defines Unified Capabilities (UC) as the integration of voice, video, and data services delivered ubiquitously across a secure and highly available network infrastructure, independent of technology, to provide increased mission effectiveness to the warfighter and business communities. UC integrates standards-based communication and collaboration services including, but not limited to: messaging; voice, video, and web conferencing; unified communication; and collaboration applications or clients. These standards-based UC services must integrate with available enterprise applications, both business and warfighting.

The Unified Capabilities Certification Office (UCCO) manages the DoD UC-approved products list, providing guidance, coordination, and information to vendors and government sponsors throughout the entire process. The Unified Capabilities Requirements 2013 (UCR 2013) specifies the technical requirements for certification of approved products to be used in DoD networks to provide end-to-end UC. The UCR 2013 is the governing requirements document for all DoD network infrastructures and services that provide or support UC end-to-end; it takes precedence over subordinate documents, DoD standards, and commercial standards addressing UC. The UCR 2013 can be accessed via the DISA Approved Product List (APL) Process Guide page.

To achieve affordable, responsive, and efficient testing and certification of UC products for DoD Components, a distributed test concept was implemented. In accordance with DoDI 8100.04 (Encl. 2, para 2 – page 9), DISA/JITC serves as the primary test lab for the Defense Information Systems Network (DISN) and serves as the interoperability certification authority for all UC core products. Additionally, the Military Department (MILDEP) labs shall serve as the primary test labs for UC products that MILDEPs acquire and deploy at Base/Camp/Post/Stations and within tactical systems. UC Distributed Testing facilities include:

- DISA Joint Interoperability Test Command (JITC), Fort Huachuca, AZ
- DISA Joint Interoperability Test Command (JITC), Fort Meade, MD
- USAF Telecommunication Systems Security Assessment Program (TSSAP), San Antonio, TX
- Navy Space and Naval Warfare Systems Command (SPAWAR) Systems Center Atlantic, Portsmouth, VA
- Army Information Systems Engineering Command Technology Integration Center (TIC), Fort Huachuca, AZ

JITC develops UC test plans and formats for reporting results for all labs. The MILDEPs provide the results of UC testing to JITC for interoperability certification. The MILDEPs and JITC provide the results of UC Cybersecurity testing to DISA for Cybersecurity recommendations. The MILDEP Authorizing Official (AO) provides product and site accreditation for the installed UC products. In accordance with DoDI 8100.04 (Encl. 3, para 5(c)(5) – page 20), the DoD sponsor or the vendor shall be responsible for funding the testing and certification of UC products.

CH 8–3.10.2 Unified Capabilities Approved Products List

The Interoperability Certification and Cybersecurity Accreditation processes are applied to all UC product categories identified in the UCR 2013. The UCR 2013 defines the requirements that must be met for those products to be placed on the UC APL. The UC APL Process Guide defines the process by which UC and technology insertion products gain APL status.

For more information on UC and the APL, refer to the UC APL Process Guide and the UC APL (DoD CAC required).

CH 8–3.11 Developmental T&E Program Assessment

The DASD(DT&E) conducts DT&E Program Assessments for all MDAPs, MAIS, and programs designated as AT&L Special Interest programs, in accordance with DoDI 5000.02 (Encl. 4, para 6(b) – page 96). DT&E Program Assessments are completed at the Development RFP Release Decision Point, Milestones B and C, and updated to support the Operational Test Readiness Review (OTRR) or as requested by the MDA or PM. The MDA considers the results of the DT&E Program Assessment prior to making the Milestone Decision.

For MDAPs, MAIS programs, and USD(AT&L)-designated special interest programs, the DASD(DT&E) will provide the MDA with a program assessment at the Development RFP Release Decision Point, Milestones B and C, and updates thereafter to support the OTRR or as requested by the MDA or program manager. The program assessment will be based on the completed DT&E and any Operational T&E activities completed to date, and will address the adequacy of the program planning, the implications of testing results to date, and the risks to successfully meeting the goals of the remaining T&E events in the program.

For those programs not on DASD(DT&E) program engagement, the DoD Component assessment process includes a review of DT&E results, an assessment of the system's progress against the KPPs, KSAs, and CTPs in the TEMP; an analysis of identified technical risks to verify that those risks have been retired or mitigated to the extent possible during developmental testing; and a review of system certifications.

The DT&E Program Assessment for Development RFP Release Decision Point and Milestone B concentrates on:

- Plans
- Schedules
- Resources
- Additional Items (e.g., competitive prototyping, etc.)
- Recommendations.

The DT&E Program Assessment for Milestone C concentrates on:

- Adequacy of DT&E Planning
- Performance
- Reliability
- Interoperability
- Cybersecurity
- Recommendations.

DT&E Program Assessments are updated prior to IOT&E, as needed. DT&E Program Assessments can be performed at any time during the acquisition life cycle, if requested by the MDA or PM.

CH 8–3.12 Incorporating T&E into DoD Acquisition Contracts

Programs involve T&E personnel early and keep them involved with the PM, the KO, the SE, and the other program office leads throughout the contracting process, to ensure they understand, accept, and include T&E policies, practices, procedures, and requirements in the contract as necessary for program success, in accordance with DoDI 5000.02 (Encl. 4, para 4(b)(15) – page 93). Inputs from the Chief Developmental Tester, advised by the Lead DT&E Organization and the T&E WIPT, inform the contracting process on:

- The quantities, configurations, and types of deliverable test articles (expendable and non-expendable) and prototypes (if applicable) required for government T&E.
- Required contractor investments, expenditures, and developments required to support government T&E; e.g., threat simulators, targets, instrumentation, logistics and transportation for test preparation and set-ups, training, documentation, and personnel to support test events.
- Personnel and other support to T&E WIPT, integrated test teams.
- Contractor generated data and test reports for inclusion in the Contract Data Requirements List (CDRL).

In the early phases of development, the contractor plans and executes the majority of design testing that transitions technology from science and technology efforts into functional capabilities desired by the military, as well as qualification testing of sub-component parts and products from vendors that makes up the system delivered to the military. The Lead DT&E Organization and Participating Test Organizations need to understand the contractor testing capabilities, processes, data collection, and analysis methods to assess the appropriate amount of visibility into those test activities as well as determine data collection and transfer benefiting government test organizations to avoid redundant or unnecessary testing. Government test organizations determine cost/benefit ratios with visibility into proprietary activity and data transfer to the government. In addition, consideration is given to near- and end-state evaluations during operational testing (OT).

The PM, combat developer, and appropriate T&E personnel collaboratively develop the acquisition and T&E strategies so that users' capability-based operational requirements (i.e., CDD, Concept of Operations/Operational Mode Summary/Mission Profile (CONOPS/OMS/MP) are correctly translated into accurate contractual terms; and actions that give the highest probability of successful outcome for the government-contracted events provide for sufficient time to execute all regulatory and statutory T&E activities and reporting.

Incorporating T&E into DoD acquisition contracts is the test focus for the pre-RFP Review. It is essential that a good draft TEMP be available for the review and that the RFP adequately addresses the TEMP.

One key issue to remember: if the contract does not include a T&E item or requirement, *do not expect it!*

Refer to "Incorporating T&E into DoD Acquisition Contracts" for more information.

CH 8–3.13 Embedded Instrumentation

Embedded instrumentation is used to facilitate T&E data collection needs for measuring performance attributes and system diagnostics for debugging and failure analyses in an operational configuration (i.e., without having to change intended operational configuration to install additional instrumentation for testing). Operational Test Agencies (OTAs) should consider embedded instrumentation as their first choice for instrumented data collection. Embedded instrumentation requires independent accreditation and certification prior to use in OT&E. Also, embedded instrumentation could be optimized for facilitating training, logistics, and post-operational mission analysis and debrief.

Embedded instrumentation reduces the cost and complexity of adding additional instrumentation for the sole purpose of testing. While there is a cost for embedding instrumentation, the Chief Developmental Tester works with the logistician and trainer to share the costs and benefits of embedded instrumentation, as described above.

Sometimes, the developer has undocumented logs, ports, or tap points used during development for taking measurements. The Chief Developmental Tester looks for data products and rights to utilize this already planned instrumentation. Embedded instrumentation may include on-board data sensing and collection, storage, and/or real-time data transmission.

In accordance with DoDI 5000.02 (Encl. 4, para 5(a)(2)(d) – page 93), the PM, in coordination with the Chief Developmental Tester, ensures the program RFP includes any proposed use/application of embedded instrumentation, contractor involvement, and government oversight.

CH 8–3.14 Distributed Testing

Many of the capabilities used in, or to support, T&E are discussed in this chapter. These include land- or sea-based test facilities, legacy systems, new developments, threat systems, prototypes, etc. Also, the use of modeling and simulation is commonplace, which can be Live, Virtual, or Constructive (LVC). LVC capabilities can be integrated to provide Hardware-in-the-Loop (HITL or HWIL) or Systems Integration Laboratories, which can be used to support a T&E event. The majority of these T&E capabilities can be connected or linked.

In many cases, this is done with systems and capabilities that are not co-located so a distributed environment is developed to support the T&E event, in accordance with DoDI 5000.02 (Encl. 4, para 5(a)(6) – page 94). By sharing information through a Wide-Area Network (WAN) infrastructure, T&E capabilities can be linked across a test facility, across a T&E range, or around the world to form a distributed environment. Distributed Testing can be considered a process for linking various geographically separated LVC sites and capabilities together in a distributed environment; for use across the acquisition life cycle, to support and conduct the T&E of a subsystem, system, or system-of-systems (SoS) in a Joint or cyberspace environment.

Distributed Testing can be used to integrate systems and subsystems still under development as well as mature systems that already exist, but are located at geographically separated facilities. It can also be used to complement, or in some cases in lieu of, large-scale open air tests using actual operational hardware for the systems involved. Conducting Distributed Testing complements live-only testing and provides the means for rapid integration of components and systems early in a product's developmental life cycle. It also provides an efficient means of adding realism to T&E by providing systems and capabilities not otherwise available, or by including separate but interrelated systems and subsystems. Conducting T&E by integrating components and capabilities early in a product's developmental life cycle reduces the technical risk of components not working together. Complementing the risk reduction inherent in early Distributed Testing, is the cost savings of correcting technical deficiencies before they become part of the operational design.

While Distributed Testing is particularly suited for many T&E activities, such as assessing a data exchange between components, subsystems, systems, or within a SoS, distributed methodologies are not appropriate for all T&E. For example, Distributed Testing would not be appropriate for system performance testing, reliability testing, and other tests that do not include other systems or systems-of-systems. However, PMs and Operational Test Agencies may consider Distributed Testing in situations where necessary systems, components, or capabilities are not co-located in a central test site. Also, Distributed Testing methodologies are considered when a system is required to demonstrate interoperability, which is the capability to work effectively with other systems. PMs tasked with conducting cybersecurity T&E consider the benefits of Distributed Testing methodologies, which provide the needed infrastructure and capabilities.

The advantages realized by Distributed Testing include, but are not limited to:

- Integrated T&E – Allows test events to share a single test point or mission that can provide data to satisfy multiple objectives, without compromising the test objectives of either the DT or OT. Early identification of system and mission elements enables the development and execution of an efficient and effective DT/OT integration in the strategy for T&E. This allows an early "Operational Influence" into the developmental cycle, in accordance with DoDI 5000.02 (Encl. 5, para 11(a)(4) – page 107). If done correctly, the enhanced operational realism in DT&E provides greater opportunity for early identification of system design improvements, and may even change the course of system development. While Integrated T&E does not replace or eliminate the need for dedicated Initial Operational Test and Evaluation, as required by 10 USC 2399, Operational Test and Evaluation of Defense Acquisition Programs. The goal is to conduct a seamless test program producing credible data to all evaluators that address developmental, operational, and sustainment issues early in the acquisition process—when the issues are easier and cheaper to correct.
- A near real-time Test-Fix-Test capability –That is, as a test event uncovers flaws in a system, the designers can make a correction and then immediately conduct a re-test to ensure the flaw has been fixed. This is especially true of software and information exchanges used in Command and Control systems.
- The ability of T&E Programs to "move data—not people" – The distributed nature of the event means that large teams of data collectors and analysts need not be deployed locally for the test event. Data collection and most analysis can be conducted from the home station with near real-time access to the needed test data.
- A collaborative, virtual workplace – Enables a connective relationship between geographically dispersed Subject Matter Experts (SMEs) and entities in the system-of-systems environment that they wouldn't have otherwise. This relationship can foster communication and feedback that can provide significant improvements to the systems under evaluation and across the spectrum of the mission area.

In recent years, the DoD has stood up a capability to provide a department-wide capability that makes Distributed Testing more accessible. The Joint Mission Environment Test Capability (JMETC) Program

Office mission is to provide a DoD-wide capability for the T&E of warfighter capabilities in a Joint context for Interoperability, Key Performance Parameter (KPP) compliance testing, Developmental Testing (DT) and Operational Testing (OT), as well as Joint Mission Capability Portfolio testing.

Refer to JMETC for information on distributed testing.

CH 8–3.15 Threat Representation Evaluation

Beginning early in the acquisition life cycle, programs understand and monitor needs and requirements for threat representations to support testing since acquisition of intelligence information and physical assets can take significant time and resources, in accordance with DoDI 5000.02 (Encl. 4, para 5(a)(6) – page 94). For example, the identification of the need for surrogates in testing starts prior to Milestone A to ensure any needed changes or developments are understood early in the program. Validation and accreditation efforts of all surrogates used in operational testing begin no later than Milestone B, are ideally complete by Milestone B, and are documented in the TEMP, in accordance with DoDI 5000.02 (Encl. 5, para 10(c) – page 106). Regardless, threat representative validation and accreditation are completed prior to using any threat surrogate in operational and live fire tests.

"Threat representation" includes targets, models, simulations, simulators, emulators, stimulators, foreign materiel (that is, actual systems), U.S. equipment, and aerial, ground, sea-based, or other types of surrogates that portray specific foreign military weapon systems or civilian devices used in an adversarial military role. Scientific or technical equipment used to measure, sense, record, transmit, process, or display data during test or examination of materiel are not considered threat representative devices.

Threat Representation Validation. In order for the surrogate to be usable in a developmental or operational test, the surrogate is sufficiently representative of the threat(s) of interest to the fidelity necessary to accomplish the goals of the test. Threat representation validation is the process by which the users compare the key characteristics of the threat that are important to the performance of the system under test to those same key characteristics of the threat itself using DIA-approved threat data. Validation includes quantifying the variations, and assessing the likely impact of those differences on the potential use of the threat representation for testing. The validation is a substantive and quantitative analysis conducted by a group of subject matter experts knowledgeable of the threat, as well as the system being tested, to select appropriate parameters and characterize the effects of any difference between the threat and surrogate parameters and operating characteristics and assess the impacts due to differences from the perspective of its intended use(s).

For target development, threat representation validation normally is conducted around two events in a threat representation's life cycle:

- Prior to initial operational capability (IOC) for the target.
- Whenever major modifications are made to the target or significant changes occur in the threat or its operational use.

Threat Representation Accreditation. Threat representation accreditation is the process used to determine whether threat representations are suitable for a specific test. Threat representation accreditation examines any parametric differences to determine their impacts on the test application and extend general information obtained during the validation process to a specific test application by analyzing and assessing its use and noting specific test limitations. The threat representation validation analysis provides sufficient evidence of the threat representation's operational status, permitting analysts to quickly understand its performance or contribution to an operational test event. Also, the data requirements are compared to the latest intelligence and the capabilities of threat representations as characterized by current validation efforts.

Accreditation decisions must be based on current assessments of the performance of the surrogate system for the following reasons:

- Any differences between a threat representation and the corresponding actual threat system can distort representation of the threat and affect the subsequent analysis of the system's effectiveness. Even the differences accepted during development and validation can make the simulator/simulation or surrogate incapable of adequately representing the threat for a specific test application.
- The intelligence concerning threats is time-sensitive and dynamic. New intelligence can make a threat representation inappropriate for a given test application.
- Physical threat surrogates experience deterioration and failures that can render them no longer threat representative. Models and simulations often require updates due to intelligence data, operating system, or compiler changes.

The accreditation process establishes sufficient criteria and provides sufficient grounds for use of the threat representation in testing. Threat representation accreditation reflects all the relevant information available from validation testing and provides test organizations adequate information to determine whether or not it is credible and adequate capability for its intended test application. A current, complete validation analysis prior to accreditation for operational testing provides evidence of the threat representation realism to permit the operational analysts to assess the threat representation's contribution to an operational or live fire test event. If the threat representation is sufficient, the OTA (accreditation authority) certifies it for a specific test application.

For programs under DOT&E oversight, the Director, OT&E concurs on the use of any threat surrogate for operational or live-fire testing prior to the initiation of threat accreditation activities. In support of obtaining this concurrence, validation results and the underlying data are provided to DOT&E.

CH 8–3.16 T&E of Defense Business Systems

The majority of programs implementing Defense Business Systems (DBS) pursue commercial off-the-shelf (COTS) product solutions, and many DBS (especially large DBS) are based on well-established commercial Enterprise Resource Planning (ERP) systems. This results in several T&E considerations unique to DBS.

A summary of the T&E planning for developmental and operational test, jointly developed by the program manager, the functional sponsor, and the T&E community are included in acquisition strategies, TEMPs, etc. Early on in requirements development, DBS programs should perform a risk-based assessment to determine the level of testing needed to provide information to the decision-maker and validate requirements. Generally, the risk increases as the amount of modifications to the commercial product increases.

DBS normally do not employ the JCIDS process for development and validation of capability requirements. PMs document requirements in their Problem Statement, defining requirements as business needs supported by measurable business outcomes. The tester must work closely with the system engineer to ensure these business measurements are translated into functional requirements of the software solution.

The strategy for testing DBS considers data collected from both external sources and independent government testing to verify vendor's claims related to a product's functionality, reliability, maintainability, and compatibility.

DBS with Federal financial management capabilities meet auditability and financial compliance requirements as required by current statute and DoD policies. T&E planning includes a comprehensive process of auditability/financial compliance testing, including penetration testing focused on financial fraud/denial of service information.

For more information on Defense Business Systems, refer to DoDI 5000.02 (Encl. 12).

CH 8–3.17 Software T&E

The DoD acquisition process delivers systems providing secure, resilient capabilities in the expected operational environment. Software is a major driver of the functionality of components of DoD systems. Software T&E, particularly for business and communication systems, is distinct from traditional T&E, predominantly because there is no manufacturing involved. Software is developed and deployed, as opposed to being developed, manufactured, and deployed, in accordance with DoDI 5000.02 (Encl. 3, para 11 – page 84). Software T&E examines system performance from the perspectives of functionality, sustainability, and cybersecurity.

CH 8–3.17.1 Software T&E Overview

In accordance with DoDI 5000.02 (Encl. 5, para 7 – page 104), T&E of software considers the following principles:

- Are the software requirements documented and specified well enough to support T&E? Test planning requires engagement among managers, designers, testers, and users early in the development process, beginning as soon as practical after the Materiel Development Decision (MDD). Bi-directional traceability is established early for individual requirements with the software components implementing them (i.e., which components fulfill each requirement and what requirements do each component contribute to fulfilling). Early bi-directional traceability between components and test cases that test the correctness of their implementation is also needed. The Materiel Developer should work with the software developer to minimize the complexity of the software design and prepare the correct number of test cases for T&E purposes. During testing, performance monitoring relies on operational metrics derived from well-documented software requirements.
- What are the risks? Although software can be relatively inexpensive to change compared to hardware, some risks demand robust software testing and assurance prior to deployment. Mission critical functionality, operational dependability, and cybersecurity are usually high risks for software. All systems capable of sending or receiving digital information are required to conduct some level of cybersecurity testing. Software reliability and security are measured according to the latest available standards.
- Can the software be sustained? Is it reliable and maintainable? We can take advantage of zero-cost manufacturing and transport if we can assure ourselves that new software versions won't destroy previously functioning capabilities. Software developed consistent with good architectural and coding practices is cheaper to maintain and quicker to modify and release to operations, contributing to mission agility. Certain defects in non-critical software functionality that can be fixed later may be acceptable from the perspective of Office of the Secretary of Defense (OSD) oversight during test, provided the software is being managed well enough. Software maintainability is measured to the latest available standards.
- Can we make efficient use of tests and test tools to satisfy certification and other needs (and other standard T&E planning concerns)? For example, an operationally realistic maintenance environment during testing is developed and sustained to enable full capabilities for software patching and upgrades, software modification rollback, and automated regression testing.

CH 8–3.17.2 Software T&E Planning

Software test planning and test design are started in the early stages of functional baseline definition and iteratively refined with T&E execution throughout the phases of development, integration, system qualification, and in-service maintenance, in accordance with DoDI 5000.02 (Encl. 3, para 11 – page 84).

PMs involved with software acquisition need to understand at Milestone B how system logs and system status records interface with operational command and control. Automated collection and parsing of performance data are incorporated, as much as possible, into the system design, in accordance with DoDI 5000.02 (Encl. 4, para 5(a)(12) – page 95).

Software design and testing is greatly improved through in-depth reviews of selected aspects of the acquisition. These include:

- Architectural Review. Systems engineers and operational maintainers review the information architecture to ensure compliance with established standards.
- Cybersecurity Review. Operational network attackers and defenders engage with system designers in a table-top exercise to articulate expected cyber threats and defenses. For business systems, this includes the threat of financial fraud. The goal of the exercise is to validate and improve the system design for security.
- Development and Maintenance Review. The operational sustainment activity and developing activity jointly discuss and plan the software sustainment environment(s). This environment includes configuration control, defect tracking, and prioritization using the definitions contained in Annex J of IEEE Standard 12207.2, a high-fidelity simulation of the production environment for pre-production test, and automated testing within that environment that meets the statutory and regulatory test automation requirements. This review also includes metrics of reliability, performance efficiency, security, and maintainability.
- User Interface Review. Operational testers assist the Chief Developmental Tester and the developing activity in designing and executing an event that enables the developers to observe operational and administrative users interacting with prototype system interfaces in operationally realistic system use cases.
- Workflow Review. Operational testers and the developing activity participate in a table-top exercise that solicits feedback from operational and administrative users on the planned system workflows.
- Quality Assurance Plan Review. Operational testers, program managers, and other affected staff review the overall quality assurance plan incorporating all reviews, testing, and other quality assurance activities including those described above; ensuring they are incorporated into and are consistent with the development and delivery plans and requirements, and staff and necessary resources are available as needed to ensure completion of all quality assurance activities according to schedule.

All programs on DOT&E oversight require an Initial Operational Test and Evaluation (IOT&E). For software programs not on DOT&E oversight, the OTA determines whether an IOT&E is required. For software, early OT&E events normally support acquisition milestones, which incorporate substantial operational realism, in accordance with DoDI 5000.02 (Encl. 5, para 7 – page 104). Primarily, these events determine a system's potential for operational effectiveness, operational suitability, and survivability (including cybersecurity) or lethality before more extensive deployment. IOT&E can also be used to support system certification and training requirements. As feasible, testing is supported by a model (or emulated hardware or virtual machine) of the digital device(s) on which the software runs.

At IOT&E (or at a prior test event), PMs plan to demonstrate within a realistic environment:

- Performance monitoring of operational metrics to manage and operate each system capability (or the whole system, as appropriate).
- Operational suitability, including a demonstrated capability to maintain the software and a measurement of software maintainability.
- Software maintenance sustainment, including patch deployment, software upgrades, and rollbacks. (PMs need to sustain an operationally realistic maintenance test environment in which software patches can be developed and upgrades of all kinds (developed or commercial) can be tested), in accordance with DoDI 5000.02 (Encl. 5, para 7(a)(4) – page 104).

- End-to-end regression testing and defect tracing with such testing automated to the extent feasible in the maintenance test environment.

IOT&E for Incrementally Fielded Software Intensive programs normally consists of a full IOT&E event prior to the Full Deployment Decision (FDD), and are often conducted in a live mission environment so that little or no injection of specific mission threads is possible. Thus, the IOT&E events are guided by an updated assessment of the operational risks in the capabilities and system interactions that have not been successfully evaluated in previous operational testing. Nevertheless, developmental testing strives to investigate as much of the operational envelope as possible, including system response to anomalous inputs (so-called "negative testing").

CH 8–3.17.3 Risk-based Operational T&E of Software

In accordance with DoDI 5000.02 (Encl. 5, para 7(d)(1) – page 104), OT&E for software is guided by the assessment of operational risks of mission failure. A significant operational risk of mission failure is a risk at least moderately likely to occur, and if the risk does occur, then the impact causes a degradation or elimination of one or more mission-critical operational capabilities. The T&E strategy includes an evaluation by the T&E WIPT (or ITT) of the highest risk technologies in system design as well as any areas of excessive complexity in the system software architecture. Programs use standard metrics of the reliability, performance, and security risk of software to assess software risk. Cybersecurity is usually a high risk in software, and it is almost always necessary that a vulnerability and penetration assessment and a cyber-adversary assessment be conducted—the results of which are provided to DOT&E.

DOT&E Memorandum, Guidelines for Operational Test and Evaluation of Information and Business Systems, allows for three levels of software OT&E approval and execution for programs on DOT&E oversight:

- At higher risk, DOT&E approves, observes, and reports on the test.
- At middle risk, DOT&E approves the plan, but does not observe or report.
- At low risk, the OTA can approve the plan, and observe and report on results.

This policy does not have to apply all-or-nothing to the whole plan. Some aspects of OT can be designated as low risk while others have higher risk. Those parts identified as low risk can be managed internally by the OTA. The risk-based policy is the OTA's tool for flexible test design. OTAs can segment tests into risk-appropriate sub-tests.

Refer to DAG, CH 8.3.17.6., Software T&E in an Agile Environment for more information.

At any level of risk, the lead OTA is responsible for observing testing. At the lowest risk level, the lead OTA reviews plans, and observes developmental testing or integrated testing. At the highest risk level, the lead OTA executes a full OT&E in accordance with the DOT&E-approved test plan. For intermediate risks, the lead OTA coordinates with the responsible developmental testing organization to observe and execute integrated developmental testing/operational testing in accordance with a DOT&E-approved test plan. In all cases, the lead OTA informs DOT&E of the outcome of the OT&E. DOT&E then determines the requirement for a formal report.

All systems capable of sending or receiving digital information have to conduct some level of cybersecurity testing. OTAs conduct a risk assessment, identify all threat vectors, and propose an appropriate level of cybersecurity testing to DOT&E. The test plan contains details of how the operational test agency executes the vulnerability and adversarial assessments, including resources, schedule, expected tools, and data for collection. At a minimum, the software is thoroughly analyzed to detect any instances of the Common Vulnerabilities and Exposures (CVE) "Most Dangerous Software Errors." The plan identifies the environment used for both phases of testing and known test limitations due to anticipated deviations from the intended operational environment. The test plan also identifies the specific cyber threat(s) that the adversarial team is meant to portray, the data to be collected during the assessments, and how mission effects are to be determined.

CH 8–3.17.4 Software Support

For software in any system, the evaluation of operational suitability includes a demonstrated capability to use and maintain the software throughout the system's life cycle. In accordance with DoDI 5000.02 (Encl. 5, para 7(a)(4) – page 104), OT&E looks at the program's ability to sustain an operationally realistic maintenance test environment in which software patches and upgrades can be tested. This includes examining:

- Methods available to support software testing and evaluation in unit, integration, and system test phases across the life cycle.
- Data and configuration management methods and tools.
- The extent to which software T&E is embedded with and complementary to software code production as essential activities in actual software component construction (in contrast to T&E that is planned and executed as follow-on actions after software unit completion).
- Formal software T&E when considering selection and integration of new components with existing system elements.
- Formal, standards-based measurement of software maintainability.

CH 8–3.17.5 Software Test Tools & Environment

Test tools include software products that support test activities such as planning and controlling tests, creating test specifications, maintaining requirements, building initial test files and data, executing tests, maintaining configurations necessary to reproduce faults and failures, analyzing/evaluating test results, and maintaining data regarding test results and processes, in accordance with DoDI 5000.02 (Encl. 5, para 7(b) – page 104).

Test tools can provide benefits to the testing program both in the short and long term. A good testing tool potentially:

- Reduces time and effort for repetitive work; a static analysis tool can check coding standards much faster than a manual effort would.
- Provides more predictable and consistent results; eliminates some of the human elements, such as forgetfulness, incorrect assumptions, and mistakes.
- Provides access to and presents accurate test management information. Some test tools can retrieve test results from a database and display them as a chart.
- Ensures reports or findings are assessed objectively; eliminates potential bias.
- Automated testing tools have virtual users that can simulate user actions for many real users, which save the time and expense of using many real users for testing.

However, purchasing a test tool has some potential risks. These include:

- Underestimating the time, cost, and effort when introducing the tool. There could be difficulties in deploying the tool, or there could be resistance from experienced manual testers.
- Expecting more from the tool than it can deliver.
- Underestimating the time and effort needed to derive benefits from the test tool.
- The tool may be complicated, taking time to learn and requiring user training.
- Over-reliance on the tool. For example, tools can't necessarily analyze, suggest improvements, or evaluate future uses.
- Underestimating the effort required to maintain test assets generated by the tool.

- Failure to maintain data and records regarding tool use and results.

The types of tools for testing include tools for:

- Software Source Code Analysis and Measurement
- Unit and Integration Testing
- Data Collection for Performance Testing
- Software Functional and Regression Testing
- Software Load Testing
- Test Management.

The types of tools for related functions include tools for:

- Requirements Management
- Incident Management and Recording
- Configuration Management
- Continuous Integration and Build Management.

CH 8–3.17.6 Software T&E in an Agile Environment

Testing in an agile environment places more T&E focus at the unit level. Compared with non-agile methods, T&E:

- Occurs earlier in the development cycle.
- Occurs in closer cooperation with the developers.
- Occurs more frequently in shorter cycles.

CH 8–3.17.7 Other Software T&E Planning Concerns

Within the DoD acquisition domain, essential considerations for success in testing software include a structural quality and security-focused code audit/analysis as part of the Software Development Life Cycle (SDLC), in accordance with the most current Application Security and Development Security Technical Implementation Guide (STIG) and other relevant guidance documents for Java Run Time Environments and for the .NET Framework.

The following links provide additional information:

- Handbook of Software Reliability Engineering, published by IEEE Computer Society Press and McGraw-Hill Book Company (specifically, CH 13).
- The Consortium for IT Software Quality (CISQ), Specifications for Quality Characteristic Measures.

Medical devices and systems must comply with the SEP, in terms of the Health Insurance Portability and Accountability Act of 1996 (HIPAA) (P.L. 104.191) and Risk Management Framework (RMF) information protection procedures and measures. These procedures and measures ensure the software complies with the security standards specified in HIPAA as well as Subtitle D of the Health Information Technology for Economic and Clinical Health (HITECH) Act, Title VIII of Division A and Title IV of Division B of the American Recovery and Reinvestment Act of 2009 (P.L. 111.5). Most medical devices require Information Management/Information Technology (IM/IT) testing and validation of information security protocols.

Given that requirement, programs start test planning as early as possible. Programs also validate U.S. Food and Drug Administration (FDA) clearance prior to any medical software implementation.

This strategy identifies and describes:

- Required schedule, materiel, and expertise.
- Software evaluation metrics for Resource Management, Technical Requirements, and Product Quality, including Reliability, Security, Performance, and Maintainability.
- Models and simulations supporting software T&E, including accreditation status.

A defined T&E process is consistent with and complements software and system development, maintenance, and system engineering processes, is committed to continuous process improvement, and is aligned to support project phases and reviews, including an organizational and information flow hierarchy.

CH 8–3.18 Network-Centric Operations

Implementation of the DoD's transformation strategy as well as calls for shifting to an Information Age military, results in fewer platform-centric and more net-centric military forces. This requires increased information sharing across networks. The net-centric concept applies to a DoD enterprise-wide information management strategy that includes not only military force operations, but also all defense business processes, such as personnel actions, fuel purchases and delivery, commodity buying, deployment and sustainment activities, and acquisition and development. Key tenets of the strategy include:

- Handling information only once.
- Posting data before processing it.
- Users accessing data when needed.
- Collaborating to make sense of data.
- Diversifying network paths to provide reliable and secure network capabilities.

The shift away from point-to-point system interfaces to net-centric interfaces brings implications for the T&E community. The T&E community's challenge includes representing the integrated architecture in the intended operational environment for test. Furthermore, the shift to net-centric capabilities evolves gradually, no doubt with legacy point-to-point interfaces included in the architectures. PMs, with Program Executive Officer (PEO) support, work with the operating forces to integrate operational testing with training exercises, thereby bringing more resources to bear for the mutual benefit of both communities. It remains imperative that the T&E community engages the user community to assure that test strategies reflect the intended operational and sustainment/support architectures as well as interfaces where they test and evaluate intended capabilities, in accordance with DoDI 5000.02 (Encl. 4, para 5(a)(6) – page 94).

CH 8–3.19 Cyber Ranges

This section supports DAG CH 3.7.5., Cybersecurity T&E.

Cyber ranges provide capabilities and environments, which can be integrated at the appropriate classification levels to conduct research, development, experimentation, and testing of military capabilities within a cyberspace environment. They also can support training of military personnel in conducting cyber operations; development of tactics, techniques, and procedures (TTPs); and demonstrating the sustainment of critical missions in cyber-contested environments. Use of cyber ranges can provide a more realistic environment while minimizing risk to operational networks, particularly where the employment of cyber effects is impractical or high-risk. Other applications of cyber ranges include:

- An assessment of the scope and duration of advanced cyber effects.
- Component-level system interoperability testing.
- Combinations of developmental, operational, and integrated testing.
- Assessment and Authorization (Risk Management Framework) processes, in accordance with DoDI 8510.01, Risk Management Framework (RMF) for DoD Information Technology (IT).
- Immersive training with rapid experience building.

Adequate DT&E, OT&E, and assessments might include testing on cyber ranges due to one or more of the following reasons:

- Testing cannot occur on open operational networks.
- Representation of advanced cyber adversarial TTPs are not suitable for operational networks.
- Scaling requirements (e.g., number of users, hosts, or interconnected systems, amount of network traffic, etc.) cannot be otherwise achieved.
- Operational complexity and associated mission risk are such that the impact to operational networks is avoided.

The program office/Chief Developmental Tester works with the Lead DT&E Organization, cybersecurity dedicated professionals, Operational Test Agencies, DASD(DT&E), and DOT&E to incorporate cyber ranges into the overall test, evaluation, and assessment strategy. (Note: cyber ranges have not been used in lieu of OT&E, and they must be validated and accredited prior to their use for OT&E. In general, the Chief Developmental Tester, Security Control Assessor (SCA), OTA, and PM complete the following actions as early as possible in the acquisition life cycle:

- Identify all testing that will occur on a Cyber Range.
- Identify cyber events for integration with DT&E, OT&E, and assessment activities.
- Support development of linkages between the cyber range and developmental and operational networks.
- Plan for integration of system operators, network defenders, and threat emulations on the cyber range.
- Coordinate with cyber range staffs to ensure they understand the system under test (SUT), operational environment, user space, threat, test objectives, and planned test scenarios.
- Ensure intelligence community support to accurately represent adversarial threats and targets.
- Take measures to verify targets and offensive capabilities emulated on the range are realistic and representative.
- Ensure the entire emulated environment is of adequate fidelity to accomplish test objectives, support technical assessment, and demonstrate impact on operational mission. Emulated environments include:
  - Red – Any capability or environment attributed to adversary forces.
  - Blue – Any capability or environment attributed to own forces.
  - Gray – Cyber environment not owned by any military force, but leveraged by all cyber forces to obfuscate their actions.
- Coordinate with cyber range staffs to investigate any automated data collection capabilities that could support the test.

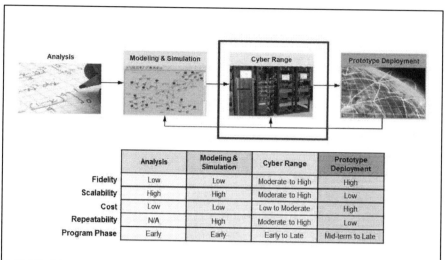

provides some guidance for choosing a cyber-event environment.

Figure 2: Cyber Event Environment

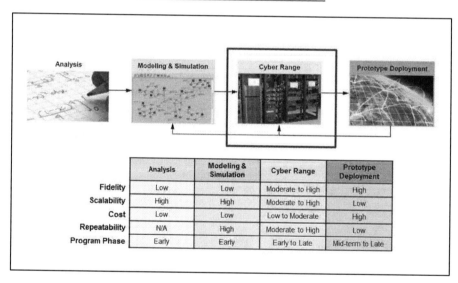

Table 8: Cyber Ranges provide an overview and contact information for the four DoD cyber ranges.

Table 8: Cyber Ranges

Cyber Ranges

Cyber Ranges			
R a n g e	**Command, Control, Communications, and Computers Assessment Division (C4AD)** Suffolk, VA Contact E-Mail: JS.DSC.J6.MBX.C4 AD-operations@mail.mil	**DoD Cybersecurity Range** Quantico, VA Contact E-Mail: IARangeCMT@ITSFAC. com	**Joint Information Operations Range (JIOR)** Norfolk, VA Contact Phone Numbers: (757)836-9787 or (757)836-9848	**National Cyber Range (NCR)** Orlando, FL Contact E-Mail: osd.pentagon.ousd-atl.mbx.trmc@mail.mil
M i s s i o n	C4AD conducts assessments of existing and emerging Command, Control, Communications, and Computers (C4) capabilities in a persistent C4 environment to achieve interoperable and integrated solutions that satisfy Joint operational requirements. Replicates Joint Warfighter C4 systems and addresses the interoperability of those systems.	Provides a persistent environment to support test and evaluation, exercise support, training, and education. A simulated representation of the Global Information Grid (GIG) Tier 1 environment, complete with network services for realistic system/network evaluation.	Creates a flexible, seamless, and persistent environment (infrastructure) that enables Combatant and Component Commanders to achieve the same level of confidence and expertise in employing information operations (IO) weapons that they have in kinetic weapons.	Provides a high-fidelity, realistic cyber environment to conduct sophisticated cyber training and support cyber testing during all phases of the system life cycle as well as testing of complex system-of-systems. The NCR enables a revolution in national cyber capabilities and accelerates technology transition. Includes agile setup of Multiple Independent Levels of Security (MILS) – sanitized Unclassified, Secret, or SCI environments for cyber training. and Program of Record testing.

Cyber Ranges				

C a p a b i l i t i e s	• C4AD can connect to the Joint Information Operations Range (JIOR) or operate in stand-alone mode.
	• Replicates operational Command and Control (C2) environments with actual hardware and software, enabling assessments of system and system-of-systems interoperability, operational capability, procedural compliance, and technical suitability to confirm readiness for deployment.
	• C4AD has demonstrated experience combining training exercises and test events to accomplish both test and training, and certification objectives.
		• The DoD Cybersecurity Range can operate in stand-alone mode or the Combatant Commanders/Services /Agencies (CC/S/A) with their individual cyber environments, can connect into the range through:
		  ○ The Joint Information Operations Range (JIOR)
		  ○ A Virtual Private Network (VPN) over the Internet and Defense Research and Engineering Network (DREN).
		• Persistent environment focused on cybersecurity and computer network defense.
		• Representation of the GIG Tier 1 Environment, complete with network services, for realistic system/network evaluation.
		• Provides generic DoD Tier II and Tier III capabilities.
		• Services include traffic generation, configurable user emulation. Malware, spyware, and BOTnets can be emulated and employed in the environment to stimulate training.
			• Closed, multi-level security (Top Secret/ Sensitive Compartmented Information (TS/SCI) environment built to conduct cyber and other non-kinetic activities.
			• Distributed network with service nodes at approximately 68 locations.
			• Forms a realistic and relevant live fire cyberspace environment supporting Combat Commands, Service, Agency, and test community training, testing, and experimentation across the IO and Cyberspace mission areas.
			• Can provide secure connectivity and transport for Coalition Partners.
			• Multiple simultaneous events at multiple levels of security.
			• Meets Capstone Concept for Joint Operations intent and provides a critical Joint Force cyberspace training and testing environment. It is the only "live fire" range supporting cyberspace and IO-related objectives in the Joint Training Enterprise.
				• NCR can connect to the JIOR, JMETC Multiple Independent Levels of Security (MILS) Network (JMN), or operate in stand-alone mode.
				• Specialized software facilitates rapid network design, reconfiguration, and sanitization, as well as network scaling.
				• Security architecture that enables a common infrastructure to be partitioned into MILS and leverage real malware.
				• End-to-end toolkit that automates the lengthy process of creating high-fidelity test environments.
				• Unique combination of subject matter expertise in cyber domain, cyber testing, cyber range management, and cyber testing tools.

Error! Reference source not found. provides a list of additional cyber resources and facilities accessible to DoD organizations.

Table 9: Other Cyber Resources & Facilities

Resource/Facility	Mission	Capabilities

Joint Mission Test Environment Test Capability (JMETC)
 	
Test Resource Management Center (TRMC)
 	
Alexandria, VA
 	
Contact Email:
 	
osd.pentagon.ousd-atl.mbx.trmc@mail.mil
 	
Contact Phone Number(s):
 	
571-372-2697
 	
571-372-2701
 	
571-372-2702
	JMETC provides the persistent, robust infrastructure (network integration software, tools, re-use repository) and technical expertise to integrate Live, Virtual, and Constructive systems for test and evaluation in Joint System-of-Systems and Cyber environments.	• JMETC SECRET Network (JSN) provides a distributed network infrastructure with 76 geographically separated nodes connecting live systems, Hardware-in-the-Loop (HWIL), Installed Systems Test Facilities (ISTF), and Virtual/Constructive simulations representing the system under test on range and laboratory facilities.
		• JMETC Multiple Independent Levels of Security (MILS) Network (JMN) provides closed connectivity between and among Cyber Ranges and Live, Virtual, and Constructive (LVC) test assets at multiple levels of classification Secret, Top Secret, Top Secret/Sensitive Compartmented Information, Special Access Program/Special Access Required (S, TS, TS/SCI, SAP/SAR). JMN provides the ability to peer with JIOR.
		• JMETC also maintains and provides access to Regional Service Delivery Points (RSDP), which provides the ability to create virtualized cyber environments for cybersecurity testing. RSDPs are:
		   ○ Extensible to cyber ranges to create more complex, higher scale environments.
		   ○ Provide enterprise computer storage as well as hosting common tools and services for the Cyber T&E, training, and experimentation communities.
		   ○ Geographically distributed to minimize latency and accessed through the JMN. There are currently two deployed RSDPs, with others planned for deployment.
		• Capabilities typically provided at no additional cost to the customer.

CH 8–3.20 Rapid Fielding Testing

One of DoD's highest priorities is to provide warfighters involved in conflict or preparing for imminent contingency operations with the capabilities urgently needed to overcome unforeseen threats, achieve mission success, and reduce risk of casualties. Joint Urgent Operational Needs (JUONs), Joint Emergent Operational Needs (JEONs) and related rapid acquisition activities are intended to support these efforts. In accordance with DoDI 5000.02 (Encl. 4, para 5(e) – page 96), required testing to verify safety, capabilities, and limitations is performed consistent with the urgency of fielding the capability. In collaboration with the supporting operational test organization, the PM for a rapid acquisition activity develops a highly tailored and abbreviated TEMP, which is consistent with the Acquisition Strategy (AS), in accordance with DoDI 5000.02 (Encl. 5, para 5(c)(1) – page 100). The TEMP describes a performance assessment plan that includes a program and test schedule, metrics, test methodologies, and test assets required. While the operational testing described is tailored and abbreviated, as much as possible, it follows the basic tenets of operational testing described in DAG CH 8.3.2.1., Evaluation of Operational Test Adequacy. If the program has been placed on DOT&E oversight, the PM has the TEMP approved by the DOT&E. The MDA, in consultation with the supporting operational test organization, and with the approval of DOT&E for programs on DOT&E oversight, determines the requirement for post-fielding assessments, whether the urgent need solution has been adequately reviewed, performs satisfactorily, is supportable, and is ready for production and deployment. DOT&E reports the results of required testing to the Secretary of Defense and provides copies to Congress and the MDA.

CH 8–3.21 T&E of Unmanned & Autonomous Systems

Test and evaluation programs involving Unmanned and Autonomous Systems (UAASs), as either a stand-alone system or as part of a system-of-systems, consider the increased technical complexity for testing, as well as challenges for range safety approval. The TEMP addresses the approach and T&E resources required to verify the performance of autonomous and semi-autonomous systems in making decisions for achieving the objectives of unmanned platforms such as aircraft, ground vehicles, or sea vehicles. The TEMP complies with DoDD 3000.09, Autonomy in Weapon Systems, to assess the risk of failures that could lead to unintended engagements or to loss of control of the system. Added to this complexity are the cybersecurity and interoperability requirements with companion platforms.

Test and evaluation of autonomous decision-making processes involves a new form of testing that allows for not knowing all input conditions being used by an algorithm, which in and of itself may be constantly changing its form. All that a tester may know for certain is the "statement of the success criteria" that the autonomous decision-making process is trying to satisfy. Significantly, this suggests that not only the tester tests the ability of the decision-making process to deliver a solution that enables successful mission completion; the tester may also now be testing the adequacy of the statement of the success criteria itself. While T&E of platforms and automated software are well-established disciplines, the emerging challenge confronting T&E involves how to adequately test a system's decision-making processes in which all inputs cannot be predicted, the algorithm may be changing, and repeatability is unlikely. Discovery of functionality, design, or integration issues after a system has been approved to enter production, or even worse, IOT&E, can adversely affect acquisition program cost and schedule; and most such issues result from lack of consideration of aspects on how a system is used or the environment in which it is intended to operate.

CH 8–3.22 Competitive Prototyping

Competitive prototyping is one of the areas the T&E WIPT (Chief Developmental Tester, Lead DT&E Organization, empowered representatives of test data producers and consumers) considers during development of the Milestone A TEMP. Competitive prototypes are part of the TMRR Phase unless specifically waived by the MDA at or prior to Milestone A.

A competitive prototype, or if this is not feasible, a single prototype or prototyping of critical subsystems prior to Milestone B is statutorily required to be part of the Acquisition Strategy for MDAPs, and is a regulatory requirement for all other programs, in accordance with P.L. 111-23, SEC. 203, Weapon Systems Acquisition Reform Act of 2009 and DoDI 5000.02 (Para 5(d)(4)(b)(2)(b) – page 19).

CH 8–3.23 EOD Validation & Verification Testing

DoDD 5160.62, Single Manager Responsibility for Military Explosive Ordnance Disposal Technology and Training (EODT&T), ensures that Military Department programs for the acquisition of explosive ordnance materiel and activities (including applicable weapon delivery systems) provide technical data and make available hardware for Explosive Ordnance Disposal (EOD) validation and verification testing, and recommend any unique tools necessary for EOD procedures.

This Directive requires:

- Testing and transportation of developmental explosive ordnance, including foreign ordnance being evaluated for possible U.S. acquisition, and does not begin until sufficient data on its hazards and functioning are available for EOD response to incidents or accidents during transportation and testing.
- EOD procedures, tools, and equipment to be developed, tested, jointly verified, and fielded before fielding of new explosive ordnance.
- Secretaries of the Military Departments to establish management controls to ensure that all programs for acquisition of explosive ordnance and applicable weapon delivery systems provide for the development of EOD technical source data in accordance with the specifications of the Single Manager for EODT&T, the availability of hardware for Joint EOD validation and verification testing, and the recommendation of tools necessary for EOD render-safe and disposal operations. All developers of explosive ordnance and applicable weapons delivery systems (except nuclear systems) provide sufficient quantities of inert and live explosive ordnance items for Joint validation and verification of EOD procedures and EOD training.

MIL-STD-882E (Para 4.3.2. – page 10), DoD Standard Practice for System Safety, identifies the DoD approach for identifying hazards and assessing and mitigating associated risks encountered in the development, test, production, use, and disposal of defense systems.

MIL-STD-882E (Task 101, para 101.2.5. – page 22) recommends reporting on the assessment and status of hazards at system, subsystem, and component technical reviews, such as the System Requirements Review (SRR), Preliminary Design Review (PDR), Critical Design Review (CDR), Test Readiness Review (TRR), and Production Readiness Review (PRR). The Standard identifies the requirements for certifications, independent review board evaluations, and special testing (e.g., insensitive munitions tests, Hazards of Electromagnetic Radiation to Ordnance (HERO), Electrostatic Discharge (ESD), and render-safe/emergency disposal procedures).

In accordance with MIL-STD-882E (Task 303 – page 82), T&E planning includes the following:

- Participation in the preparation and updating of the TEMP, including hazard considerations and identification of when hazard analyses, risk assessments, and risk acceptances shall be completed in order to support T&E schedules.
- Participation in the development of test plans and procedures, including hazard considerations that support:
  - Identification of mitigation measures to be verified and validated during a given test event with recommended evaluation criteria.
  - Identification of known system hazards present in a given test event, recommended test-unique mitigations, and test event risks.
  - Preparation of the Safety Release.
  - Analysis of hazards associated with test equipment and procedures.
  - Government completion of applicable environmental analysis and documentation pursuant to DoD Service-specific National Environmental Policy Act (NEPA) and Executive Order (EO) 12114 requirements in test and evaluation planning schedules.
  - Documentation of procedures for advising operators, maintainers, and test organizations involved in the test event of known hazards, their associated risks, test-unique mitigation measures, and risk acceptance status.
- Conduct of post-test event actions such as:
  - Analyze test results to assess effectiveness of mitigation measures as tested.

- o Analyze test results to identify and assess new system hazards and to potentially update risk assessments for known hazards. MIL-STD-882E provides more information.
- o Analyze incident, discrepancy, and mishap reports generated during test events for information on hazards and mitigation measures. Ensure mitigation measures are incorporated in future test plans as appropriate.
- o Document new or updated system-related hazard information in the Hazard Tracking System (HTS), as appropriate.

CH 8–3.24 Safety Reviews

DoD is committed to protecting personnel from accidental death, injury, or occupational illness and safeguarding defense systems, infrastructure, and property from accidental destruction or damage while executing its mission requirements of national defense.

Integral to these efforts is the use of a system safety approach to identify hazards and manage the associated risks. A key DoD objective is to expand the use of this system safety methodology to integrate risk management into the overall Systems Engineering (SE) process rather than addressing hazards as operational considerations.

MIL-STD-882E (Para 1.1.1. – page 1) identifies the DoD SE approach to eliminating hazards, where possible, and minimizing risks where those hazards cannot be eliminated. DoDI 5000.02 (Encl. 3, para 16(b) – page 87) identifies risk acceptance authorities for Environment, Safety and Occupational Health (ESOH). MIL-STD-882E covers hazards as they apply to systems/products/equipment/infrastructure (including both hardware and software) throughout design, development, test, production, use, and disposal.

The Chief Developmental Tester coordinates with the Program Lead System Engineer to identify the required safety reviews in support of T&E efforts and provide the required information. In-addition, the Chief Developmental Tester needs to coordinate with the program engineer for development and safety releases in support of T&E events in accordance with Component direction and guidance.

For more information, see MIL-STD 882E, DoD Standard Practice for System Safety.

CH 8–3.25 Medical Materiel T&E

The acquisition and management of medical materiel presents distinct challenges to the design and execution of an effective test and evaluation (T&E) program within the DoD acquisition framework.

Medical materiel acquisition is subject to the same laws and regulations as those governing other defense systems and has similar requirements for T&E. Frequently, the products considered for acquisition are commercial off-the-shelf (COTS), government off-the-shelf (GOTS), non-developmental items (NDI), and similar items adapted or repackaged for military use. For pharmaceuticals, medical devices, and monitoring systems, the minimum standard for use is certification or approval by federal regulating agencies, typically the U.S. Food and Drug Administration (FDA) or the Environmental Protection Agency (EPA). Appropriately constructed requirements documentation includes such certification or approval as a specified system key performance parameter (KPP). Planning for T&E of medical materiel systems begins with the development of user needs and continues throughout the acquisition process. FDA approval or Environmental Protection Agency (EPA) certification of a product, and the data provided from associated testing and clinical trials may provide a significant body of information useful to reduce the scope and cost of testing within DoD acquisition programs.

Additional considerations for medical systems may include requirements related to compliance with the Health Insurance Portability and Accountability Act (HIPAA), human subject research protections, human factors concerns, environmental testing, air-worthiness certifications (fixed and rotary wing) for systems employed on air evacuation platforms, and cybersecurity. Medical systems and devices that capture, store, process, or transmit data over information networks are also subject to the extensive requirements related to cybersecurity, as outlined in DoDI 8500.01 (Encl. 3, para 9(a)(2)(b) – page 39), Cybersecurity.

Use of the T&E WIPT structure is an effective mechanism to coordinate and organize the various entities for execution of the T&E program. Coordination of these activities across the Services in T&E of medical materiel is encouraged; consistent with DoDI 6430.02 (Encl. 4, para 6(d)(6) – page 11), Defense Medical Materiel Program, to promote uniformity, efficiency, and Joint interoperability in acquisition and life-cycle management of medical materiel required for military healthcare delivery in both military treatment facilities and in support of operations.

Refer to the Defense Health Agency, Defense Medical Materiel Standardization Program for additional information.

CH 8–3.26 CBRN T&E

In accordance with DoDI 3150.09 (Encl. 2, para 2(h)(i)(J) – page 10), the Assistant Secretary of Defense for Nuclear, Chemical, and Biological Defense Programs (DASD(NCB)) shall:

- Oversee Chemical, Biological, Radiological, and Nuclear (CBRN) Defense RDT&E.
- Establish CBRN Defense T&E standards in support of CBRN survivability in conjunction with the DASD(DT&E).
- Lead the process to develop Chemical, Biological, Radiological (CBR) contamination survivability test methodologies and standards through the Chemical Biological Defense Program (CBDP).
- Assess the T&E infrastructure and identify essential requirements to support DoD CBRN Survivability Policy initiatives in conjunction with the DASD(DT&E).

CBRN defense consists of several categories. Within the context of CBRN Defense T&E, CBRN survivability is the principal area and is explained in more detail in the following paragraphs.

In accordance with DoDI 3150.09 (Encl. 2, para 5 – page 12), the DASD(DT&E):

- Monitors DoD CBRN survivability policy for impact on current and future T&E policy and guidance, and T&E workforce training and education.
- Ensures that CBRN survivability is assessed for CBRN Medical Countermeasure Systems (MCS) on the USD(AT&L) MDAP, MAIS, and AT&L Special Interest lists.
- Helps the DASD(NCB) develop and review test protocols in support of CBRN survivability requirements.
- Provides representation to the CBRN Survivability Oversight Group (CSOG) and supporting working groups.

Materiel developers work with the operational test agencies, the DASD(DT&E), Office of the CBDP T&E Executive, Defense Threat Reduction Agency (DTRA), and the Military Services to develop strategies and TEMPs that realistically assess the CBRN survivability capabilities and requirements validated in the ICD, CDD, and CPD. Materiel developers will provide all T&E data to the DASD(DT&E) and DOT&E for programs on OSD T&E oversight. Additionally, the Military Departments will ensure that the TEMP describes how the T&E strategy will meet validated CBRN survivability requirements stated in the CDD and CDP for all CBRN MCS, in accordance with DoDI 3150.09 (Encl. 3, para 8(a) & (b) – page 24).

CH 8–3.26.1 CBRN Survivability

DoDI 3150.09 provides policy, assigns responsibilities, and establishes procedures for the execution of DoD Chemical, Biological, Radiological, and Nuclear (CBRN) Survivability Policy. It establishes how to identify mission-critical systems and specifies the subsets that must survive and operate in CBR environments, nuclear environments, or combined CBRN environments.

CBRN survivability is divided into two categories: CBR survivability, which is concerned with CBR contamination, including fallout and nuclear survivability, which covers initial nuclear weapons effects, including blast, electromagnetic pulse (EMP), and other initial radiation and shockwave effects. CBRN survivability is defined as:

> The capability of a system to avoid, withstand, or operate during and/or after exposure to a CBR environment (and relevant decontamination) or a nuclear environment, without losing the ability to accomplish the assigned mission.

Mission-critical systems are the primary focus of CBRN survivability. In accordance with DoDI 3150.09 (Glossary – page 37), a mission-critical system is a system whose operational effectiveness and operational suitability are essential to successful mission completion or to aggregate residual combat capability. If the system fails, the mission likely will not be completed. Such a system can be an auxiliary or supporting system, as well as a primary mission system. A CBRN mission-critical system is a system that is required to be employable and survivable in a CBR or nuclear environment. In accordance with DoDI 3150.09 (Para 3(b) – page 2), all ACAT I programs expected to operate in CBR or nuclear environments are designated as CBRN mission-critical systems. DoD Components are responsible for identifying mission-critical systems and specifying which must survive in CBR, Nuclear, or combined CBRN environments.

DoDI 3150.09 (Para 3c – page 2) directs that CBRN mission-critical systems must be survivable in accordance with the CBRN survivability requirements identified in their requirements documents (e.g., initial capabilities document (ICD), capability development document (CDD), capability production document (CPD)). All CBRN mission-critical systems under development, as a part of a DoD Acquisition System, are required to address CBRN survivability at each milestone, in accordance with DoDI 3150.09 (Para 3(c)(2) – page 2).

A subset of CBRN survivability involves the CBD program (CBDP). The CBDP falls under the auspices of the Joint Program Executive Office for Chemical and Biological Defense (JPEO CBD), which is responsible for providing research, development, fielding, and life-cycle support of CBRN defense equipment, medical countermeasures, and installation and force protection integration. DoDD 5160.05E (Para 7 – page 8) designates and defines the role of the Secretary of the Army as the DoD Executive Agent for CBD programs. As such, the Secretary of the Army is responsible for designating a CBD program T&E Executive, which for CBD programs is the Deputy Under Secretary of the Army for Test and Evaluation (DUSA-TE). The DUSA-TE serves as the T&E Executive for CBRN Defense. As such, the DUSA-TE Office provides CBRN Defense and CBDP T&E Enterprise oversight and coordinates all CBRN Defense T&E issues with the Joint Staff and OSD—specifically, the USD(AT&L), the DOT&E, and the DASD(DT&E).

For additional information and guidance regarding CBRN survivability, contact the JPEO CBD.

CH 8–3.26.2 CBRN Defense T&E

A Chemical, Biological, Radiological, and Nuclear (CBRN) mission-critical system T&E program can involve exposure of the system-under-test (SUT) to chemical and biological warfare agents, toxic industrial chemicals (TICs), toxic industrial materials (TIMs, including radionuclides), and nuclear effects such as radiation, thermal, EMP, shock, etc. Test and evaluation of such systems for vulnerabilities to any of these environments likely entails the use of multiple and geographically dispersed test facilities and associated logistics, stringent safety and security considerations, and risk of destruction of the SUT. These considerations are taken into account when planning and executing a T&E program involving a mission-critical system. It is also necessary to design a T&E program that leverages data from multiple test approaches, including system or component testing in chemical or biological safety chambers, full-system open air testing with simulants that represent the threat, or with stimulants that trigger end-to-end operational scenarios, and modeling and simulation.

Where CBD programs are concerned, the DUSA-TE employs the T&E Capabilities and Methodologies Integrated Process Team, or TECMIPT (requires registration), to oversee and manage their T&E programs. Through its Commodity Area Process Action Teams (CAPAT), the TECMIPT is responsible for identifying CBRN T&E infrastructure gaps, and developing and reviewing CBRN T&E standards.

JPEO-CBD has established a team of CBRN survivability subject matter experts to assist Service Acquisition Programs designated as CBRN MCS. These CBRN experts assist with the integration of CBD program systems and equipment into weapon's systems. The CBRN Survivability Trail Boss initiative offers weapon system program offices a single point of contact to help facilitate the research, development, T&E, procurement, delivery, and life cycle sustainment of CBRN defense materiel solutions that meet the program's documented requirements.

Figure 3: CBRN Trail Boss Overview

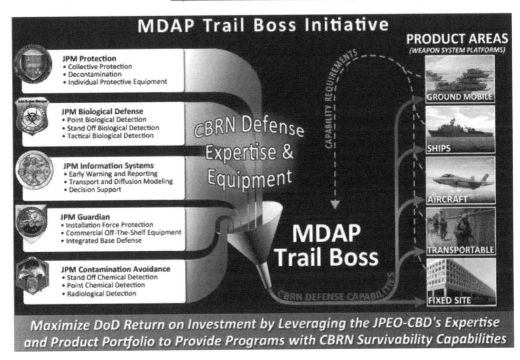

The MDAP Trail Boss initiative supports all ACAT level programs with CBRN survivability requirements. A program office should engage the Trail Boss team early in the requirements development process to leverage their expertise relative to trade space and test capabilities available to measure thresholds and objective CBRN survivability requirements.

For additional information and guidance regarding CBRN survivability, contact the JPEO CBD.

CH 8–3.27 Interoperability Testing of Geospatial Intelligence Systems

Geospatial Intelligence (GEOINT) is a specialized discipline within the defense and intelligence communities. GEOINT is made up of three key elements: geospatial information, imagery, and imagery intelligence. It is defined in 10 USC 467 as "the exploitation and analysis of imagery and geospatial information to describe, assess, and visually depict physical features and geographically referenced activities on the earth."

Due to the proliferation of GEOINT across DoD, compliance with GEOINT interoperability criteria is critical for systems that use, produce, or enable GEOINT. To assure systems collect and/or interact with GEOINT in compliance with mandated standards, the Director, National Geospatial-Intelligence Agency (NGA) is implementing a new process—the GEOINT Functional Manager Standards Assessment (GFMSA) (requires DoD CAC and Intelink Account). The GFMSA serves as recognition that a component of Information Technology (IT) or National Security System (NSS) has been tested and/or evaluated in a credible manner and found to meet the standards conformance and interoperability criteria set by the National System for Geospatial Intelligence (NSG) community. GFMSA is an authoritative means to confirm that interoperable GEOINT capabilities are delivered. Successful completion of the GFMSA T&E process optimizes potential for a system to meet its GEOINT-related operational performance objectives.

GFMSA fulfills the NGA responsibilities identified in DoDI 8330.01 (Encl. 2, para 12(a) – page 17), prescribing, mandating, and enforcing standards and architectures related to GEOINT. NGA, in coordination with the Joint Interoperability Test Command (JITC), the Responsible Test Organizations (RTOs), the Operational Test Agencies (OTAs), and the appropriate intelligence functional managers, develops interoperability T&E criteria, measures, and requirements related to GEOINT. GFMSA Qualifications infuse GEOINT awareness into the generalized net-centric data requirement. Each GFMSA Qualification has a set of GEOINT-aware 'Criteria' for measuring qualification success.

Generally, the GFMSA process consists of five basic steps, noting that the steps can be a repetitive/regressive process as conditions change. The steps, as depicted in **Error! Reference source not found.**, are:

Step 1. Identify mission capability requirements and associated MOE and MOP.

Step 2. Identify data, service, and technical requirements; and establish system and data content design in conformance with applicable GEOINT standards.

Step 3. Verify through T&E that data and services conform to both the GEOINT standards and the system design.

Step 4. Validate through T&E that the performance of the conforming design, data, and services fulfills the mission capability requirements established in step 1.

Step 5. GFMSA test results contribute to an interoperability certification determination. Submit test reports, certifications, and statuses substantiating GFMSA qualification to the Design for Manufacturability (DFM) for Architecture and Standards.

Figure 4: GEOINT Functional Manager Standards Assessment Qualification Cycle

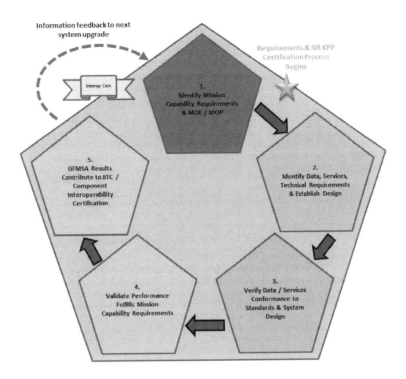

The GFMSA initiative is focused on ensuring consistent conformance to GEOINT standards by systems using, producing, or enabling GEOINT. Conformance to adopted GEOINT standards is critical to the ability of the NSG enterprise to efficiently collect, store, discover, retrieve, and utilize GEOINT data, products, and services in an interoperable manner.

Integrating GFMSA qualification objectives into TEMPs permits DT&E and OT&E testing and test results to support GEOINT-aware Joint interoperability test certification and eliminate test duplication. T&E events used to substantiate GFMSA qualification often span DT&E, OT&E, Interoperability, and other test activities, relying on multiple test events conducted by various test organizations. While conformance with applicable GEOINT standards is an essential step toward GFMSA qualification, the amount and type of testing varies based on characteristics of the component/system being evaluated. Developmental testing performed under government supervision that generates reliable and valid data can be used to determine technical capabilities and standards conformance status, and may supplement operational data for a GEOINT-aware interoperability evaluation. Each potential data collection opportunity is used in the overall T&E process to get the best GEOINT-aware, performance-based picture of the component/system in the most efficient manner possible to substantiate GFMSA qualification.

Refer to the GFMSA Resource Site (requires DoD CAC and Intelink Account) for more information and references.

CH 8–3.28 Testing in a Joint Environment

The phrase "testing in a Joint environment" originated in the U.S. Department of Defense final report, Testing in a Joint Environment Roadmap, Strategic Planning Guidance, Fiscal Years 2006-2011,

November 12, 2004. It refers to testing military systems as participating elements in overarching Joint SoS. This testing in a joint operational environment initiative supports the department's long-term strategy to test as it fights. Joint operations have become the mainstay of warfighting. Force transformation requires the T&E community to place a greater emphasis on testing Joint warfighting capabilities developed in response to the JCIDS process. Future T&E must ensure combatant commanders can rely on equipment to operate together effectively without introducing problems to warfighters. For a detailed discussion of changes needed to bring about this vision of T&E, see the final report cited above.

The Joint Mission Environment (JME) is defined as, "a subset of the Joint operational environment composed of force and non-force entities; conditions, circumstances, and influences within which forces employ capabilities to execute Joint tasks to meet a specific mission objective." It describes the expected operating environment of the system (or system-of-systems) under test, and includes all of the elements influencing the required performance the new "capability" demonstrates. These include the particular mission requirements in which the system is being employed; physical factors such as the blue and opposing force structures; geographic and demographic aspects of the Joint operating area, etc.; as well as the interactions between these elements.

To be successful, testing in the JME cannot be a new step added at the end of operational T&E, nor can it replace current DT or OT. It does, however, represent a departure from the way DoD acquisition professionals plan and execute systems engineering, DT&E, and OT&E—indeed, the entire acquisition process. Testing in a JME involves the appropriate combination of representative systems, forces, threats, and environmental conditions to support evaluations. These representations can be LVC, or distributed combinations thereof.

Testing in a JME applies throughout the life cycle of the system. Identification of a Joint issue/problem early in a system's life (including as early as the conceptual phase) reduces costs and issues. In accordance with DoDI 5000.02 (Encl. 5, para 5(d)(4) – page 101), this applies to evaluating system performance, or how well the system does what it is designed to do, as well as the system's contribution to the Joint mission, or how DoD employs the system to achieve the mission. A system's interaction with the JME is evaluated along an evaluation continuum using constructive and virtual representations and live systems in various combinations.

The JME and associated Joint capability requirements are defined in the ICD, CDD, and the CPD. The evaluation plans for assessing these requirements are articulated in the SEP and the TEMP at Milestone A. At the pre-EMD Review, evaluation plans for assessing these requirements are articulated in the pre-EMD draft documents (SEP, TEMP, and ISP). At Milestones B and C, they are articulated in the SEP, TEMP, and ISP. For each case, the selection of LVC systems used to recreate the JME to support testing depends on the purpose of the assessment and on the interactions the SUT has with other elements in the JME.

SoS testing can result in unexpected interactions and unintended consequences. T&E of SoS not only assesses performance to desired capability objectives, but also characterizes the additional capabilities or limitations due to unexpected interactions. The SoS concept includes the system in the broadest sense, from mission planning to sustainment. SoS is a new and evolving area for development, acquisition, and T&E.

This section also briefly addresses some additional areas as outlined in the "Testing in a Joint Environment Methods and Processes (M&P) Implementation Plan," originally produced by the M&P Working Group that was formed during the summer of 2004 to address testing in a Joint environment. The following are areas of concern:

- Description of Joint Mission Environments
- How to use the Joint Mission Environment
- Testing in a Joint Mission Environment Program Management Office Support
- Important Acquisition Program Responsibilities.

Refer to the Systems Engineering Guide for Systems-of-Systems for more information on testing in a Joint environment.

CH 8–3.28.1 Description of Joint Mission Environment

The JCIDS process creates requirements for effects and capabilities at the Joint mission level. This means JCIDS identifies desired mission-level effects that are shortfalls. Shortfalls are addressed by materiel and non-materiel solutions. Materiel or possible system (for a new/modified system or SoS) KPPs are then proposed to provide the desired mission level effect(s). Because of this, systems development should not begin and testing cannot occur without definition(s) of the JME and a defined Joint mission associated with a shortfall to be addressed by a system or systems.

With respect to obtaining information for selected Joint missions, users of the Joint environment can start with the universal Joint planning process to break down missions, but it is a process that starts at the Universal Joint Task List (UJTL) level and extends down to the Combatant Command (COCOM) level to plan Joint task force operations and/or training events. However, this level of "fidelity" may not be available at the JCIDS ICD/CDD/CPD level because it is mission-specific at the COCOM or Joint Task Force level.

The Joint mission descriptions set the stage for evaluation of a system(s) within a Joint mission area and provide testers what they need to plan the test. There are essential elements of the Joint mission description necessary to plan, execute, and analyze assessments and T&E throughout a system's acquisition process.

Additionally, users of the Joint environment determine and obtain representations for the threat, threat composition and disposition, and threat scheme of maneuver appropriate for the selected Joint mission/task. The currently approved "Guidance for the Development of the Force (GDF)" scenarios and/or the maturing "Defense Planning Scenarios" provide the source of this information. Coordination with the Service intelligence agencies and the Defense Intelligence Agency (DIA) is critical. The threat should be system-specific (specific to the platform under examination) and also mission-specific (specific to the Joint mission examined). The next step (after identification of the threat scenarios) is to determine what is used to represent the threat, which can be an LVC representation.

Different Services are referred to depending on the type of model needed for test, as the Services have generally focused their modeling efforts based on their usual area of operations. DoD M&S responsibilities are outlined in DoDD 5000.59, DoD Modeling and Simulation (M&S) Management. Additionally, the Modeling and Simulation Coordination Office (MSCO) defines the responsibilities of M&S Executive Agents. There should also be a standard set of environment/background models established for the JME.

CH 8–3.28.2 How to Use the Joint Mission Environment

Systems engineering and testing require insertion of concepts and systems into the JME as a standard part of the acquisition process.

The ultimate goal for systems engineering and testing in a Joint environment is the ability to insert any system into the applicable JME at any time during the life of a system. Two basic items are examined through insertion into the JME. The first item is to ensure the systems to be acquired are interoperable with other systems. This includes not only how they interact and communicate as expected and required, but also understanding SoS dependencies. The second item goes beyond the system interaction and communications to examine what value the systems add to Joint military capabilities. In other words, the second item is to assess the contribution of the system to the mission success.

Interoperability and contribution are examined each time a system is inserted into the JME, including times when substantive changes or upgrades are made to an individual system. Users can determine which Joint mission/task(s) to test for a system with a role in multiple missions.

Selection of the most stressing mission(s) and/or the mission(s) with the most interactions appears to be the most defensible approach. Test authorities must ensure that if another required mission involves a system interaction not included in the "most stressing" mission, the interaction is tested separately. Examining different Joint missions as the system progresses through the acquisition process is also a good approach, especially if there appear to be multiple stressing missions. Another option is to consult with the intended Joint users (COCOM & Service Combatant) and have them define representative mission tasks.

With respect to the criteria/process to determine the appropriate representation (live, virtual, or constructive) of players in each engineering (DT or OT) event, the supporting players that constitute the system-of-systems for the Joint mission are determined on a case-by-case basis. The goal is for the system being inserted into the JME to be the most mature representation available. However, it is always a live system for IOT&E.

CH 8–3.28.3 Joint Mission Environment Lead Developmental T&E Organization

Scheduling all of the assets in the JME, especially live assets participating in exercises, proves a complex undertaking. A management and scheduling capability exists, and it is assumed the PM establishes a Lead DT&E Organization (or equivalent) for this purpose. The Lead DT&E Organization coordinates all LVC assets and the script of events, which is the plan for the specific JME missions incorporating acquisition systems under test in accordance with their schedules. Note that acquisition systems tend to have fixed decision points where unplanned delays could severely impact production. Finally, with a complex facsimile of a mission environment in place and acquisition systems scheduled to perform missions within it, additional programs may ask to "join in" the scheduled events for testing, training exercises, or other special events. This is encouraged, but the testing needs of the sponsoring program take precedence over the needs of other participants, and their participation should not interfere with the core purpose of the JME events.

CH 8–3.29 Testing of Corrosion Prevention & Control

Corrosion is defined as the deterioration of a material or its properties due to a reaction of that material with its chemical environment, based on DoDI 5000.67 (Para 3(b) – page 1). Corrosion of military equipment and facilities costs the DoD over $20 billion annually, and approximately 25 percent of all weapon systems maintenance is corrosion-related. Corrosion degrades system availability and safety. Based on safety and cost factors, it is beneficial to demonstrate the performance of corrosion prevention and control (CPC) on DoD systems. Therefore, DoDI 5000.67 (Para 4(b) – page 2) states that CPC programs and preservation techniques shall be implemented throughout the life cycle of all military equipment and infrastructure. Not only does CPC testing provide verification of system availability in meeting stated requirements, it can also validate and suggest improvements of repairs for corrosion events. If excessive corrosion is experienced, performance feedback can lead to corrective actions or better corrosion risk-mitigation activities.

In accordance with DoDI 5000.02 (Encl. 4, para 5(a)(6) – page 94), programs must identify the resource requirements for CPC developmental testing. Programs need to identify and provide the assets (e.g., test articles, test facilities, Manpower, Personnel and Training, funding) necessary to verify CPC performance. Conducting DT and OT concurrently helps with the cost and schedule of accomplishing CPC testing. System CPC testing is mostly covered during suitability testing for availability, maintainability, safety and environmental effects. As system or subsystem material modifications occur or the operating environment changes, programs should consider updating CPC testing.

In accordance with DoDI 5000.02 (Encl. 3, Para 15 – page 87), verification and acceptance tests are required for the corrosion prevention and control design. Since corrosion is a time-dependent problem, creativity is required in developing test methods. Assessing past test methods and results to identify best practices and testing improvements for CPC is encouraged. The inclusion of corrosion subject matter expertise during T&E planning will ensure system corrosion test requirements are incorporated into system test plans. Conducting corrosion testing as early as practicable (starting with subassemblies and building up to full-scale articles) and potentially accelerating corrosion effects is critical, as the full effect of corrosion may not be seen until full-scale article testing or beyond.

At a minimum, CPC test requirements should be reflected in the Request for Proposal, Systems Engineering Plan (SEP), Life Cycle Sustainment Plan (LCSP), and Test and Evaluation Master Plan (TEMP), based on DoDI 5000.67 (Encl. 2, para 2(d)(1 & 2) – page 5).

For more information on corrosion prevention control, visit the DoD Corrosion and Prevention Control office at CorrDefense.org.

CH 8–4. Process Integration

This section describes how T&E supports the acquisition life cycle by phases, in accordance with DoDI 5000.02 (Encl. 4, para 2(b) – page 90). Involvement of T&E experts early in program planning better integrates T&E activities with the overall program planning and identifies the resources needed for the T&E program.

CH 8–4.1 Materiel Solution Analysis Phase

The purpose of this phase is to:

- Conduct the analysis and other activities needed to choose the concept for the product acquired.
- Translate validated capability gaps into system-specific requirements.
- Conduct planning to support a decision on the acquisition strategy for the product.

Key activities in this phase include:

- Designation of a Chief Developmental Tester and Lead DT&E Organization. in accordance with DoDI 5000.02 (Encl. 4, para 3(c) – page 91).
- Chartering a T&E WIPT and RAM IPT.
- Analysis of Alternative solutions.
- Key trades between cost and performance.
- Affordability analysis.
- Risk analysis.
- Planning for risk mitigation.
- Developing T&E strategy and plans.
- Review of threats and Intelligence Mission Data (IMD) identified or implied in the Integrated Threat Environment Assessment (ITEA) (NOTE: Soon to be replaced by the Validated Online Life-cycle Threat (VOLT)).

This phase ends when a Component has completed the necessary analysis and the activities necessary to support a decision to proceed to the next decision point and desired phase in the acquisition process. System testing does not occur before Milestone A.

CH 8–4.1.1 T&E Planning for Milestone A

Prior to completion of the Materiel Solution Analysis (MSA) Phase, the CAE selects a PM and establishes a program office to complete the necessary actions associated with planning the acquisition program. Additionally, a Chief Developmental Tester is identified as early as possible since the TMRR phase includes testing to support Milestone B, in accordance with DoDI 5000.02 (Encl. 4, para 3(c) – page 91).

The PM charters a T&E WIPT to assist in the T&E activities supporting a Milestone A decision (see CH 8–2.4.3 T&E Working-Level Integrated Product Team), in accordance with DoDI 5000.02 (Encl. 4, para 3(e) – page 91). The Chief Developmental Tester serves as chair of the T&E WIPT.

The Chief Developmental Tester is responsible for development of the Milestone A TEMP and participates in development of the Milestone A Acquisition Strategy. At Milestone A, an approved Acquisition Strategy and TEMP inform development of the final RFPs for the next phase of the program.

Milestone A TEMP. Projects that undergo a Milestone A decision have a T&E strategy documented in the TEMP, in accordance with DoDI 5000.02 (Encl. 4, para 5(a)(11) – page 95). Programs develop the initial TEMP during the Material Solution Analysis Phase in support of entry into Milestone A. The TEMP includes a description of the most promising system concepts, broad objectives, and an overall T&E strategy (including, DT&E, OT&E, and, if applicable, LFT&E). The Milestone A TEMP describes an evaluation methodology that provides essential information on programmatic and technical risks to inform the decision-maker. The evaluation methodology (and a framework, if needed) identify key data that contribute to assessing TMRR test assets (e.g., competitive prototypes, technology, etc.).

Programs derive the Milestone A TEMP and Evaluation Methodology from the Acquisition Strategy (AS), ICD, and draft CDD, including Enterprise architecture views, System Engineering Plan (SEP), Program Protection Plan (PPP), Critical Technical Parameters (CTP), and Analysis of Alternatives (AoA), and develop it in a collaborative environment utilizing the T&E WIPT. The WIPT assists in developing a T&E strategy describing how the capabilities in the ICD and draft CDD are tested and evaluated during system development. The TEMP leverages the ICD, draft CDD, and CONOPS/OMS/MP in order to have a firm understanding of the user requirements. The TEMP also takes into account the Systems Threat Assessment Report (STAR) and other acquisition products (e.g., SEP, PPP, etc.).

The Milestone A TEMP strategy evaluates system concepts against mission requirements. The T&E strategy in the TEMP includes the identification and management of associated risk, the use of modeling and simulation, and the identification of key resources.

The Milestone A TEMP includes sufficient information to describe in detail the T&E approach, focusing on the TMRR Phase, but also as far into the acquisition life cycle as feasible, based on information needs. The TEMP should consider the following information:

- Description of the developmental evaluation methodology that provides essential information on programmatic, technical risks, and major programmatic decisions, in accordance with DoDI 5000.02 (Encl. 4, para 5(a)(11) – page 95).
- Documentation of the T&E for phase completion that includes major test events required for milestone exit and entrance criteria.
- Description of each test phase or event.
- Identification of independent variables of significance affecting development, design, or operations.
- Assessment of the AoA assumptions and findings.
- Plan for evaluating prototypes, technology, etc.
- Documentation of the strategy and resources for cybersecurity T&E.
- Identification of the resources required to execute the planned T&E activities.
- Identification of the appropriate lessons learned concerning interoperability, test infrastructure, tools, and VV&A strategy.
- Documentation of the T&E program and master schedule for major T&E events.
- For MDAPs and MAIS, identification of the Chief Developmental Tester.
- For MDAPs, identification of the Lead DT&E Organization.

- Review of threats and Intelligence Mission Data (IMD) identified or implied in the STAR (soon to be replaced by the Validated Online Lifecycle Threat (VOLT)).

Refer to the TEMP Guidebook for more information.

T&E Role in Milestone A RFP. The evaluation strategy and an approved Acquisition Strategy inform development of the RFPs for any planned TMRR Phase contracts. A Chief Developmental Tester ensures the RFP adequately describes T&E management, evaluation requirements, T&E data management (including data rights), modeling and simulations, cybersecurity, T&E resources, and software management (during T&E execution). The RFP also includes reliability, availability, and maintainability (RAM) program requirements, including contractual design-for-reliability requirements. The Contract Data Requirements List (CDRL) identifies required contractor-generated test data, planned contractor T&E objectives and schedules, modeling and simulation to be used by contractor, verification and validation procedures, and planned contractor test facility acquisition.

Refer to Incorporating T&E into DoD Acquisition Contracts for more information.

CH 8–4.1.2 T&E Role in Milestone A Decision

The Milestone A decision approves program entry into the TMRR Phase. Prior to Milestone A approval, the Chief Developmental Tester ensures approval of the initial TEMP developed during the Materiel Solution Analysis (MSA) Phase, in accordance with DoDI 5000.02 (Encl. 4, para 3(a) – page 91). The RFP informs the Milestone A TEMP.

The responsible DoD Component may decide to perform technology maturation and risk reduction work in-house and/or award contracts associated with the conduct of this phase.

CH 8–4.1.2.1 Milestone A DT&E Program Assessment

For MDAPs, MAIS programs, and USD(AT&L)-designated special interest programs, the DASD(DT&E) will provide the MDA with a DT&E program assessment at the Milestone A Decision Point, in accordance with DoDI 5000.02 (Encl. 4, para 6(b) – page 96). The DT&E program assessment will be based on any DT&E activities completed to date as well as address the adequacy of the DT&E planning, DT&E strategy, DT&E schedule, developmental evaluation methodology, DT&E resources, and the risks to successfully meeting the goals of the DT&E activities in the Milestone A TEMP, in accordance with DoDI 5134.17 (Para 1(j) – page 4).

CH 8–4.1.3 Operational T&E Implications of CONOPS/OMS/MP

The Milestone A TEMP includes a discussion of the OT&E implications of the Concept of Operations/Operational Mode Summary/Mission Profile (CONOPS/OMS/MP). The OT&E implications discuss the missions and capabilities that the new system is intended to provide to using units, and how those new capabilities are assessed in OT&E. Any aspects of the CONOPS/OMS/MP that may require significant test assets, such as specialized units, target sets, ranges, threat emulators—threat models and simulations, threat actuals, intelligence mission data, or long production lead times—should be highlighted, in accordance with DoDI 5000.02 (Encl. 5, para 5(d) – page 101). The number of system units employed by the user in the context of an operational scenario (e.g., number of systems in a company), are identified to help scope the test program's resources. If the new system capability is intended to be applicable to a Joint force, the Joint aspects of the test program are considered here. If intended capabilities are to be fielded incrementally, the TEMP specifies which capabilities are tested in which test events. If applicable, the baseline against which the new system is judged is specified in the Milestone A TEMP, and resources allocated for the baseline testing as well as the new system testing.

Refer to the JCIDS Manual, Appendix B, Enclosure C, for more information on CONOPS.

CH 8–4.2 Technology Maturation & Risk Reduction Phase

In accordance with DoDI 5000.02 (Para 5(d)(4) – page 21), the TMRR phase mandates T&E support to help reduce technology, engineering, integration, and life-cycle cost risk of a program leading to three related decision points: CDD Validation Decision, Development RFP Release Decision, and the Milestone B Decision. The CDD Validation Decision informs decision-makers whether sufficient trades have been completed to support a decision to commit to the set of requirements for use in preliminary design activities, development, and production (subject to reconsideration and refinement as knowledge increases). The Development RFP Release Decision informs decision-makers whether planning for development is complete and a decision can be made to release an RFP for development (and possibly initial production) to industry. The Milestone B Decision is the decision that commits the resources (authorizes proceeding to award of the contract(s)) needed to conduct development leading to production and fielding of the product.

CH 8–4.2.1 T&E Execution during Technology Maturation & Risk Reduction

The Acquisition Strategy and the Milestone A TEMP guide this acquisition phase. The Chief Developmental Tester, in collaboration with the T&E WIPT, monitors the execution of the T&E events and reviews T&E reports, in accordance with DoDI 5000.02 (Encl. 4, para 3(a) & 3(b) – page 91). Multiple technology development demonstrations/evaluations, defined in the Acquisition Strategy (AS) and the TEMP, may prove necessary before the user and developer can substantiate a preferred solution is feasible, affordable, and supportable; satisfies validated capability requirements; and has acceptable technical risk. Programs identify critical program information during this phase as well as implement program protection measures to prevent disclosure of critical information.

Contractor DT&E. During early DT&E, the contractor approach includes tests and evaluations for optimizing designs and functionalities. The contractor may also use modeling and simulation, laboratory, test bench, and system mock-ups or prototypes to gain knowledge of integrated system performance. Government T&E organizations may observe the critical contractor testing, conduct additional T&E, and, when practical, facilitate early user involvement. The government may be able to utilize contractor data to enhance or replace planned government testing, and to enable T&E efficiencies to be realized if testing is observed by a government T&E organization. The TMRR contract with industry should support open communication between government and contractor test organizations.

Government DT&E. During early DT&E, the Chief Developmental Tester uses government testing to evaluate competitive prototypes, competing technologies, technology maturity of critical technology elements, etc. The Lead DT&E Organization conducts developmental testing and evaluation activities for the program, as directed by the Chief Developmental Tester. The Lead DT&E Organization also ensures the AoA assumptions and findings are validated.

Early Operational Assessments. Early Operational Assessments (EOAs) provide a means to evaluate a program's progress early in the process towards developing an operationally effective, suitable, and survivable system, in accordance with DoDI 5000.02 (Encl. 5, para 6(a)(1) – page 102). EOAs are typically an analysis, based on a review of current program plans and documentation, as well as data from early developmental testing, technology assessments, modeling and simulation, and program reviews. EOAs enable the OTA to provide early input on key issues that, if not corrected, could have a detrimental effect to the determination of operational effectiveness, operational suitability, and survivability (including cybersecurity) or lethality. EOAs provide a means to examine the links and consistency between the concept of operations, requirements, and technology limitations to provide recommendations to the program and the requirements authority.

EOA reports are provided to support one or more of the design phase life-cycle events (namely, the CDD Validation Decision, the Development RFP Release Decision, or Milestone B). For programs entering development at Milestone B, the lead OTA (as appropriate) prepares and reports EOA results after program initiation and prior to the Critical Design Review (CDR).

CH 8–4.2.2 T&E Support during Technology Maturation & Risk Reduction

The TMRR phase includes activities intended to reduce the specific risks associated with the functions, technologies, environments, and developed products. This includes additional design trades and requirements necessary to ensure an affordable product and an executable development, production, and sustainment program.

Logistics Risk Assessment. During the TMRR phase, programs conduct a logistics risk assessment as part of life-cycle considerations. The PM finalizes sustainment requirements for approval at the CDD Validation Decision, and decomposes sustainment requirements into more detailed requirements to support the Preliminary Design Review (PDR) and for use during the logistics risk assessment. The T&E WIPT leverages the logistics risk assessment during development of the Milestone B TEMP.

Refer to the DAG, CH 4, Life Cycle Logistics for more information.

Technology Readiness Assessment (TRA). The TRA is a systemic, metric-based process that establishes the maturity of critical technologies. The TRA may be conducted concurrently with other technical reviews. The Chief Developmental Tester assists the chief engineer/lead systems engineer when assessing the technological maturity and integration risk of critical technologies.

Refer to the DAG, CH 3.4.1.3., Technical Assessment Process, for more information.

Preliminary Design Review (PDR). Conducted after preliminary design efforts, but before the start of detail design, the PDR provides the first opportunity for the DoD to closely observe the contractor's hardware and software design. The contractor describes all design changes made with respect to trade studies, design considerations, and design decisions that provide a rationale for the system's preliminary design. The contractor also provides a hardware or hands-on demonstration of some of the preliminary designs to better illustrate important aspects. The Chief Developmental Tester provides developmental test data collected to date to support the PDR. Test organizations attend technical reviews to provide current assessments, keep abreast of program progress, and provide insight into design direction. Unless waived by the MDA, the Preliminary Design Review occurs prior to Milestone B.

Refer to the DAG, CH 3.3.3.4., Preliminary Design Review, for more information.

Capability Development Document (CDD) Validation. In accordance with DoDI 5000.02 (Para 5(d)(4)(b) – page 20), the Technology Maturation and Risk Reduction (TMRR) Phase requires continuous and close collaboration between the program office and the requirements validation authority. During this phase, the Requirements Authority for the program validates the final CDD in order to provide a basis for preliminary design activities and the Preliminary Design Review, which normally occurs prior to Milestone B unless waived by the MDA. Prior to validation, the program coordinates the Capability Development Document (or other draft requirements document) with the MDA to ensure requirements remain technically achievable and affordable. The T&E WIPT reviews the draft CDD and coordinates the input with the PM. This effort provides the T&E WIPT a key opportunity to review requirements, to determine if they are clear, testable, measurable, and technically achievable.

Refer to the DAG, CH 4.3.2.3.1., Capability Development Document, for more information.

CH 8–4.2.3 Development RFP Release Decision

Prior to the Development Request for Proposal (RFP) Release Decision, and prior to release of a request for proposal (RFP) for the Engineering and Manufacturing Development (EMD) phase, the PM submits the Acquisition Strategy (AS) and obtains MDA approval. The approved Acquisition Strategy informs development of the RFPs for Engineering and Manufacturing Development contracts.

The Chief Developmental Tester, in collaboration with the T&E WIPT, provides a draft Milestone B TEMP ("draft" means a DoD Component-approved draft) at the Development RFP Release Decision, in accordance with DoDI 5000.02 (Encl. 1, Table 2 – page 58).

The Development RFP Release Decision ensures, prior to the release of the solicitation for Engineering and Manufacturing Development, an executable and affordable program has been planned using a sound business approach. The goal is to avoid any major program delays at Milestone B, when source selection is already complete and award is imminent. Prior to release of the final RFP(s):

- There needs to be confidence that the program requirements to be bid against are firm and clearly stated.
- The risk of committing to development and presumably production has been or is adequately reduced prior to contract award and/or option exercise.
- The program structure, content, schedule, and funding are executable and the business approach and incentives are structured to both provide maximum value to the government and treat industry fairly and reasonably.

The T&E WIPT assists in RFP development to ensure it addresses key T&E requirements identified in the TEMP.

The Development RFP Release Decision authorizes the cognizant DoD Component to release an RFP to industry.

The RFP for EMD needs to address the contractor T&E activities across the programs that are critical for program success.

RFPs should address T&E-related needs, such as:

- Evaluation strategy
- Test articles
- T&E data rights
- Government access to:
  - Contractor test and evaluation data on system performance, interoperability, reliability, and cybersecurity, and, (if mission critical), nuclear effects survivability
  - Failure Reporting, Analysis, and Corrective Action System
  - Other test-related data/results or repositories
- Built-in test and embedded instrumentation (including software log files)
- Government use of contractor-conducted T&E
- Government review and approval of contractor T&E plans
- Government witness of contractor test events
- Government review of contractor evaluations
- Verification, validation, and accreditation of modeling and simulation to be used, including threats and threat environments
- Investment in contractor-owned test facilities
- Adjudication process for reliability, availability, and maintainability data
- Contractor participation in the T&E WIPT
- An Industry Test Lead, included in the key personnel clause, to participate and interact with the Chief Developmental Tester and Lead DT&E Organization
- Meta-data, formats, and specific data requirements are included in the Contract Data Requirements List (CDRL).

Refer to "Incorporating T&E into DoD Acquisition Contracts" for more information.

CH 8–4.2.4 T&E Master Plan at Milestone B

The TEMP at Milestone B focuses on the overall structure, major elements, and objectives of the T&E program. If applicable, the TEMP contains a mature strategy that commits to full-up, system-level, live fire testing, or a waiver request is submitted and approved for the LFT&E plan. The T&E WIPT plans and executes system modeling, simulation, and T&E activities into an integrated and efficient continuum. Per DoDI 5000.02 (Encl. 4, para 5(a)(11) – page 95), the TEMP at Milestone B will include a developmental evaluation framework.

Typical T&E planning activities supporting a Milestone B TEMP include:

- Determining types and quantities of data for collection and evaluation.
- Estimating the anticipated test risks/results through simulation and modeling.
- Establishing safe test procedures.
- Ensuring adequate environmental protections.
- Projecting resource and schedule requirements, including simulated threat environments and targets.
- Other planning activities, as identified in the TEMP Format.

The program must update the TEMP prior to each subsequent milestone decision.

A program may create the Milestone B TEMP based on an updated Milestone A TEMP. In accordance with DoDI 5000.02 (Encl. 4, para 5(c) – page 93), a program submits a DoD Component-approved draft not later than 45 days prior to the milestone decision. For Information Systems Acquisition, the Milestone B TEMP serves as a planning document for the IOT&E of limited fieldings.

CH 8–4.2.5 T&E Planning for Milestone B

The TEMP at Milestone B includes T&E information informing a variety of decisions, including:

- Planning Decisions: What T&E is performed and how to phase it to support system development and design?
- Management Decisions: Is the system ready to transition to the next development phase with associated exit criteria achieved and entrance criteria identified?
- Design Decisions: Is technical performance as planned, including assessment of design margin? If not, how can we improve performance?
- Contractual Decisions: How is performance best verified and does it work as specified?
- Logistical Decisions: What T&E must be performed to ensure the system, subsystems, and components are designed for reliability, maintainability, and supportability, and remain reliable, maintainable, and supportable?
- Acquisition Decisions: What T&E data are needed to support the decision?
- Intelligence Mission Data: What data are available?

The PM identifies DT&E phases or events in the TEMP as contractor or government DT&E. Contractor and government DT&E should provide a continuum that provides confidence in the system, subsystem, and component design solutions. Major DT&E phases and events are planned with a test readiness review (TRR) that includes entrance and exit criteria. Integrated testing can also provide confidence in the system, subsystem, and component design solutions.

In accordance with DoDI 5000.02 (Encl. 4, para 5(b) – page 93), programs will utilize government T&E capabilities, unless the program can identify a cost-effective exception. Additionally, programs must conduct a Cost Benefit Analysis (CBA) for exceptions to this policy, and document the assumptions and results of the CBA in the TEMP before acquiring non-government program-unique test facilities or resources.

The TEMP includes one or more reliability growth curves for reliability risk capabilities, components, and subcomponents, as appropriate. Growth program plans also include identification of contractor design for reliability activities.

CH 8–4.2.6 T&E Reporting in Milestone B Decision

The risk associated with a Milestone B decision is based on evaluations of any available test data and test reports. In accordance with DoDI 5000.02 (Encl. 4, para 6(c)(1) – page 96), DASD(DT&E) will have full and prompt access to all ongoing developmental testing, developmental test records, and test reports for all MDAP/MAIS programs. Prompt access allows DASD(DT&E) to conduct assessments in the TMRR phase for:

- Technology maturity
- Performance of Critical Technology Element (CTEs) to meet CTPs or other performance parameter thresholds
- Adequacy of executing the test plan submitted for the TMRR phase
- Risk reduction
- Request for Proposal (RFP)
- Adequacy of test plan for EMD phase.

CH 8–4.2.7 T&E Role in Milestone B Decision

Milestone B serves as the point at which a program is reviewed for entrance into the Engineering & Manufacturing Development (EMD) phase. In accordance with DoDI 5000.02 (Para 5(c)(2)(b)(4)(a) – page 8), the role of T&E at Milestone B is to inform the Milestone Decision Authority (MDA) as to whether the:

- Risks (technology, engineering, integration, safety, etc.) are understood and have been adequately mitigated.
- System has met or exceeds all T&E-related TMRR phase exit criteria.

CH 8–4.2.7.1 Milestone B DT&E Program Assessment

DASD(DT&E) conducts a DT&E Program Assessment for all MDAPs, MAIS, and programs designated as AT&L Special Interest, in accordance with DoDI 5000.02 (Encl. 4, para 6(b) – page 96). The DT&E Program Assessment bases its findings and recommendations on the results of all program T&E to date, including contractor and government DT&E, integrated tests, certifications, and prior operational assessments(s). The DT&E Program Assessment at Milestone B focuses on evaluating critical technology performance and maturity, risk reduction, and whether a program's planning, schedule, and resources are adequate to support future DT&E.

CH 8–4.2.7.2 Operational Test Agency Report of Operational Test and Evaluation Results

The program may include Early Operational Assessments (EOAs), as appropriate, in accordance with DoDI 5000.02 (Para 5(c)(2)(b)(4)(a) – page 8). The appropriate operational test activity reports the results to the Service Chief, and the MDA can also use the results in support of decisions.

CH 8–4.3 Engineering & Manufacturing Development Phase

The purpose of the EMD phase is to develop, build, and test a product to verify all operational and derived requirements have been met, and to support production or deployment decisions, in accordance with DoDI 5000.02 (Para 5(c)(2)(b)(3) – page 7).

CH 8–4.3.1 T&E Execution during Engineering & Manufacturing Development

In accordance with DoDI 5000.02 (Encl. 4, para 4(b) – page 92), DT&E activities include assessing the ability of the system, subsystem, and components to meet their stated, derived, and allocated requirements in a mission-oriented context. This includes assessment of design margin, technical parameters, and the approved KPPs in support of development, system production, and fielding. The effort requires completion of DT&E activities consistent with the TEMP, and may include operational assessments. Successful completion of adequate DT&E with production or fielding representative prototype test articles normally provides the basis for entering LRIP or Limited Fielding.

Contractor DT&E. Programs continue to utilize contractor-conducted DT&E and contractor-owned test facilities during EMD, as specified in the contract and Contract Data Requirements List (CDRL). The PM uses the TEMP as a source document when developing the request for proposal (RFP).

Government DT&E. In accordance with DoDI 5000.02 (Encl. 4, para 4(b) – page 92), the program executes government DT&E in order to validate the system to date in such areas as:

- Achievement of critical technical parameters and the ability to achieve key performance parameters.
- Assessment of the system's ability to achieve the thresholds.
- Assessment of the system's capabilities, limitations and deficiencies.
- Assessment of the system's safety.
- Assessment of the system's cybersecurity.
- Assessment of the system's ability to achieve interoperability certification.

Government DT&E not only verifies that the system meets the specification requirements, but also identifies the system's capabilities and limitations. If users are not available to support contractor human factors engineering tests, it is even more important that they participate in government DT&E. The TEMP describes a mission-oriented approach to DT&E that utilizes actual users in a mission context. The users are made available during DT&E to identify, early on, any deficiencies. The earlier deficiencies are found, the less cost and negative impact they have on the program. The mission-oriented approach also supports integrated testing to share test data among many stakeholders.

Development delays pose a schedule risk for DT&E. The Chief Developmental Tester should remain alert to the compression of test schedules and characterize the risk based on the information contained in the DEF. Test planning and execution may also generate schedule risks. The Chief Developmental Tester develops a detailed test schedule starting with the Test Readiness Review (TRR) immediately prior to test execution and works backward to capture all the tasks and resources for multiple internal and external sources needed to have a successful TRR decision, in accordance with DoDI 5000.02 (Encl. 4, para 6(a) – page 96). One or more senior-level intermediate TRRs are scheduled prior to the final TRR to assess progress and focus efforts on resolving issues. A schedule is developed from the last TRR forward to capture all the test execution and reporting tasks necessary to support the EMD and Milestone C decisions.

MDAP programs utilize their designated Lead DT&E Organization to support the Chief Developmental Tester in the planning, execution, and assessment of DT&E.

Operational Assessment (OA). An operational assessment is a test event conducted before initial production units are available and which incorporates substantial operational realism. An OA is conducted by the lead operational test agency (OTA) in accordance with a test plan approved by the Director, Operational Test and Evaluation (DOT&E) for programs subject to Office of the Secretary of Defense (OSD) operational test and evaluation (OT&E) oversight. As a general criterion for proceeding through Milestone C, the lead OTA will conduct and report results of at least one OA. An OA is usually required in support of the first limited fielding for acquisition models employing limited fieldings. An operational test, usually an OA, is required prior to deployment of Accelerated Acquisition Programs that are subject to OSD OT&E or Live Fire Test and Evaluation (LFT&E) oversight. An OA may be combined with training events. An OA is not required for programs that enter the acquisition system at Milestone C.

Low-Rate Initial Production (LRIP). Successful completion of adequate developmental testing with production or fielding representative prototype test articles normally serves as the basis for entering LRIP or Limited Fielding. DoDI 5000.02 (Encl. 4, para 6(a) – page 96) includes more detailed discussions of T&E requirements.

CH 8–4.3.2 Operational Test Agency Report of Results of Operational Assessment

Operational Assessments (OAs) provide a means to evaluate early in a program's life cycle, progress towards developing an operationally effective, suitable, and survivable system. OAs are based on a review of current program progress and documentation as well as data from test events that incorporate substantial operational realism to provide an assessment of mission capability under operationally realistic conditions. OAs can include dedicated early operational testing, and/or Limited User Testing as well as developmental test results, provided they are conducted with operational realism. OAs are developed to support Milestone C and Low-Rate Initial Production (LRIP) decisions, in accordance with DoDI 5000.02 (Encl. 5, para 4(b) – page 92). OAs serve to identify system deficiencies early that, if not corrected, could have a detrimental effect on the future determination of operational effectiveness, operational suitability, and survivability (including cybersecurity) or lethality, and/or survivability. In addition to identifying operationally critical system capabilities, risks to program success, and system limitations and deficiencies, OAs provide recommendations to the program on system improvements, suggested updates to requirements and concept of operations, and needed changes to the test program to ensure adequate testing prior to full-rate production decision or full-deployment decision.

CH 8–4.3.3 Live Fire Test & Evaluation

Live Fire Test and Evaluation (LFT&E) encompasses testing and evaluation over the course of a program, beginning with component-level testing during the initial design stage. T&E continues as the system matures from assemblies to subsystems, and finally to a full-up, system-level configuration. At the full-up, system-level, the weapon system is fully equipped for combat with all subsystems operational and powered. Early identification of deficiencies through LFT&E allows time to impact design trades and make design changes before finalizing production configurations, thereby reducing costs. Survivability and lethality testing conducted under the auspices of the LFT&E program generate information that directly supports the DOT&E mission of evaluating the operational effectiveness, operational suitability, and survivability (including cybersecurity) or lethality of major defense acquisition programs, in accordance with DoDI 5000.02 (Encl. 5, para 9 – page 105).

The test organization responsible for LFT&E events prepares a detailed test plan. The DoD Component and the Director, Operational Test and Evaluation (DOT&E) approve TEMPs, operational test plans, and live fire test plans. For programs under DOT&E oversight, the DOT&E provides the MDA with LFT&E assessments, in accordance with DoDI 5000.02 (Encl. 1, Table 2 – page 51).

Refer to DAG CH 8.3.2.5., Live Fire Test & Evaluation for more information.

CH 8–4.3.4 T&E Support during Engineering & Manufacturing Development

Entrance into the Engineering and Manufacturing Development (EMD) phase depends on technology maturity demonstrated during the TMRR phase, approved requirements, and full funding. The EMD phase effectively integrates T&E with the acquisition, engineering, and manufacturing processes. Developmental (government and contractor) and operational test agencies integrate seamlessly during this phase. The Chief Developmental Tester ensures the T&E program depth, breadth, and phasing remain adequate to uncover risks throughout the performance envelope to manage risks at the Milestone C LRIP decision, in accordance with DoDI 5000.02 (Encl. 4, para 3(a) – page 91).

Critical Design Review (CDR). The Critical Design Review assesses design maturity, design build-to documentation, and remaining risks, as well as establishing the initial product baseline. The CDR serves as the decision point signifying the system design has matured so that hardware fabrication can begin, with acceptable risk. The Chief Developmental Tester and the Lead DT&E Organization should attend the CDR and provide an up-to-date assessment of the system. During the development of the TEMP, the Chief Developmental Tester discusses the assessments needed for the CDR with the System Engineer.

Refer to CH 3.3.3.5., Critical Design Review, for more information on the CDR.

Long Lead Items. The milestone decision authority (MDA) may authorize the production of long lead items for LRIP or full production during Engineering and Manufacturing Development (EMD), subject to the availability of appropriations. Procurement of long lead items in advance of a Milestone C production decision provides items for T&E purposes and a more efficient transition to production. The amount of long lead items appropriate for a given program depends on the type of product acquired. The product's content dictates the need for early purchase of selected components or subsystems to affect a smooth production process. The MDA may authorize long lead items at any point during EMD, including at Milestone B. An authorized Acquisition Decision Memorandum (ADM) documents long lead items, along with any limits in content (i.e., listed items) and/or dollar value.

DOT&E approves the quantity of items for programs on oversight and the MDA authorizes the minimum LRIP quantities needed to provide production representative test articles for OT&E and to maintain continuity in production pending OT&E completion, in accordance with DoDI 5000.02 (Encl. 5, para 10(d) – page 106). For systems not on the DOT&E Oversight List for OT purposes, the OTA, following consultation with the PM, determines the number of test articles required for IOT&E. In accordance with 10 USC 2400. The program includes the LRIP quantity for an MDAP (with rationale for quantities exceeding 10 percent of the total production quantity documented in the acquisition strategy) in the first Selected Acquisition Report (SAR) submitted to Congress after its determination.

CH 8–4.3.5 T&E Planning for Milestone C

Milestone C is the point at which a program is reviewed for entrance into the Production and Deployment (P&D) phase. Approval depends on specific criteria defined at Milestone B and included in the Milestone B ADM. In accordance with DoDI 5000.02 (Para 5(d)(10)(a) – page 27) for Milestone C approval, the following general criteria apply:

- An approved Acquisition Strategy (AS).
- Demonstration that the production design is stable and meets stated and derived requirements based on acceptable performance in developmental test.
- An operational assessment.
- Mature software capability consistent with the software development schedule.
- No significant manufacturing risks.
- A validated final requirements document (normally a Capability Production Document (CPD)).
- Demonstrated cybersecurity.
- Demonstrated interoperability.
- Demonstrated operational supportability.
- Costs within affordability caps.
- Full funding in the Future Years Defense Program (FYDP).
- Properly phased production ramp up and/or fielding support.

TEMP at Milestone C. The Milestone C TEMP is an update of the Milestone B TEMP, including the developmental evaluation framework, in accordance with DoDI 5000.02 (Encl. 1, Table 2 – page 58). The Milestone C TEMP contains an updated T&E strategy for IOT&E. The program demonstrates the stability of production design and meets stated and derived requirements based on acceptable performance in developmental test, in accordance with DoDI 5000.02 (Encl. 5, para 5(c)(2) – page 101). Updated reliability growth curves at Milestone C reflect test results to date and any updates to the reliability growth plan.

Incremental Software Capability programs (and other acquisition models that do not have a Milestone C) are, in some cases, asked to provide an operational test plan for IOT&E.

RFP at Milestone C. Given the maturity of the program at this stage in the acquisition cycle, programs may need to update the RFP accordingly. The updated RFP may include changes to T&E requirements. The RFP is consistent with the Milestone C TEMP, CPD, Acquisition Strategy (AS), etc.

CH 8–4.3.6 T&E Reporting in Milestone C Decision

Development of the MDA position on the risk of a Milestone C approval for initiating Production is based on:

- Evaluations of DT and OT (if applicable) results from the preceding EMD phase, including consideration of how thoroughly the system was stressed during EMD (mission-oriented context and operationally realistic environments).
- Assessment of the risk of a design change affecting production.
- Adequacy of the DT&E planning (e.g., requirements that can be evaluated, TEMP adequacy and currency, developmental evaluation framework, DT&E schedule, test resources availability, and modeling and simulation evaluated for mission capabilities) for the remaining P&D phase.

In accordance with DoDI 5000.02 (Para 5(d)(10)(a) – page 27), T&E support of Milestone C entrance criteria includes:

- Evaluations of DT results.
- OA results.
- Security Assessment Report provided by the SCA.
- Any applicable certifications required (e.g., airworthiness, safety, etc.).

Based on the DT&E and OA results of EMD, reporting substantiates:

- Performance in DT&E.
- Test results that demonstrate a readiness for production.
- Mature software capability.
- Interoperability.
- Operational supportability.
- Cybersecurity.

CH 8–4.3.7 T&E Role in Milestone C Decision

Milestone C serves as the point at which a program is reviewed for entrance into the Production and Deployment Phase. In accordance with DoDI 5000.02 (Para 5(d)(10)(a) – page 27), the role of T&E at Milestone C is to inform the MDA as to whether the:

- Design is stable.
- System meets validated capability requirements.
- System has met or exceeds all directed EMD phase exit criteria.
- DT&E results support an initial production decision.
- OT&E results support an initial production decision

DT&E activities may continue past the initial production or fielding decision until requirements have been tested and verified.

CH 8–4.3.7.1 Milestone C DT&E Program Assessment

DASD(DT&E) conducts a DT&E Program Assessment at Milestone C for all MDAPs, MAIS, and programs designated as AT&L Special Interest, in accordance with DoDI 5000.02 (Encl. 4, para 6(b) – page 96). The MDA considers the results of the DT&E Program Assessment when making a determination of materiel system readiness for production. The DT&E Program Assessment bases its findings and recommendations on the results of testing to date, including: full-up system level DT&E, integrated tests, certifications, and prior operational assessments(s). The DT&E Program Assessment at Milestone C evaluates system performance (against key performance measures (e.g., KPPs, KSAs, CTPs, etc.)), reliability and/or availability, interoperability, and cybersecurity. DASD(DT&E) provides an updated DT&E Program Assessment prior to proceeding to IOT&E.

CH 8–4.3.7.2 Operational Test Agency Report of OT&E Results

In accordance with DoDI 5000.02 (Encl. 5, para 6(a)(2) – page 102), the Operational Test Agency (OTA) provides an OTA Report of OT&E results, based on OT conducted to date, in support of the Milestone C Decision. The OTA Report focuses on:

- Progress toward operational effectiveness, operational suitability, and survivability (including cybersecurity) or lethality.
- Significant trends noted in development efforts.
- Programmatic voids.
- Risk areas.
- Adequacy of requirements.
- The ability of the program to support adequate operational testing.

CH 8–4.4 Production & Deployment Phase

The Production and Deployment (P&D) phase produces and delivers requirements-compliant products to receiving military organizations.

The P&D phase begins with an LRIP or production/procurement decision by the MDA. LRIP initiates the manufacturing capability and also provides the production-representative systems for IOT&E, in accordance with DoDI 5000.02 (Para 5(d)(11)(b)(2) – page 28). LRIP efforts end when the MDA either terminates the program or approves FRP after determining the program demonstrates sufficient control of the manufacturing process along with acceptable system characteristics.

The P&D phase focuses on achieving an operational capability satisfying mission needs. Except as specifically approved by the MDA, programs have resolved or identified a funded resolution plan before proceeding beyond LRIP. Earlier DT&E has had the system operating in mission-oriented environments with sufficient operational realism ensuring the identification and correction of deficiencies prior to IOT&E.

Production Representative Test Articles. Operational test and evaluation (OT&E) requires production representative test articles. The TEMP lists the number of production representative test articles available for OT&E, which serves as part or all of the authorized LRIP quantity.

CH 8–4.4.1 T&E Execution during Production & Deployment

Test organizations are involved in the preparation for, and conduct of, DT&E during the P&D phase preceding IOT&E. If the DT&E during the preceding phases was designed to introduce the system under development to mission-oriented scenarios in operationally realistic environments, system capabilities and limitations are evident by now. The last DT&E preceding IOT&E includes the demonstration and verification of any corrections of deficiencies evidenced during earlier DT work, in accordance with DoDI 5000.02 (Encl. 4, para 4(b)(16) – page 93). The focus on mission analysis and the system's contribution to the mission imply that evaluations are not based solely on the extent to which a system meets KPPs and criteria accompanying critical issues. In addition to assessing how well system performance meets standards, test organizations also assess the system's contribution to accomplishing the overall mission.

DT&E. The Chief Developmental Tester plans for and ensures execution of DT events deemed necessary to address any remaining DT&E issues in order to assess entry into IOT&E and FRP.

IOT&E. The Service OTA conducts the IOT&E, executing the planned events based on the approved test plan, in accordance with DoDI 5000.02 (Encl. 5, para 11(a)(8) – page 108) and DoDI 5000.02 (Encl. 1, Table 2 – page 52).

LFT&E. The Service OTA or assigned test activity conducts the LFT&E, executing the planned events based on the approved LFT&E Plan, in accordance with DoDI 5000.02 (Encl. 5, para 11(b)(1) – page 109).

First Article Testing (FAT) and Acceptance Testing (AT). FAT and AT are two important test execution events during P&D. They are normally conducted by the contractor, using government-approved test plans and under the oversight of government personnel resident at the contractor facility (e.g., Defense Contract Management Agency (DCMA)) or project management office (PMO) personnel. As part of FAT, which tests the production processes, environmental stress screening (ESS), such as highly accelerated life testing (HALT), is conducted to identify and eliminate production flaws, such as bad soldering/welding, poor seal installation, etc. FAT may also test selected performance measures to ensure the production process does not degrade performance from earlier test findings. FAT is conducted expeditiously because the production line may continue to flow while FAT results are determined. AT is conducted on every delivered system and may be a limited functional test to ensure each system is properly working. It is important because it is the point where the government accepts ownership and responsibility of the system. It may also serve as the start point for the warranty coverage. The Chief Developmental Tester reviews and understands the contract details regarding FAT and AT.

FOT&E. FOT&E is conducted to complete unfinished IOT&E activity and evaluate major technical changes made to the system to correct identified deficiencies in the IOT&E. FOT&E evaluates whether or not the system continues to meet operational needs and retains operational effectiveness in a substantially new environment, as appropriate. It also provides a venue to address any DOT&E and/or OTA recommendations provided in the IOT&E report.

CH 8–4.4.2 T&E Support during Production & Deployment

Except as specifically approved by the MDA, critical deficiencies identified in EMD testing are resolved prior to proceeding beyond LRIP or Limited Deployment. Any remaining DT&E included in the Milestone C TEMP is conducted prior to proceeding to IOT&E. The Chief Developmental Tester and Lead DT&E Organization are involved in the preparation for, and conduct of, any remaining DT&E that precedes IOT&E, in accordance with DoDI 5000.02 (Encl. 4, para 4(b)(16) – page 93). Over the system life cycle, operational needs, technology advances, evolving threats, plans for system upgrades/improvements (e.g. engineering change proposals (ECPs), etc.), or a combination of these items may require a TEMP to describe the associated test program.

CH 8–4.4.3 T&E Planning during Production & Deployment

T&E activities include:

- Reviewing and updating TEMPs, as required.
- Updating VV&A plans.
- Updating and coordinating DT&E test plans, if necessary.
- Updating and coordinating OTA test plans.
- Reviewing intelligence, threat, and CONOPS/OMS/MP documents for changes.
- Preparing DT&E Program Assessment and OT reports.
- Supporting OTRRs.

Updated TEMP. After the full rate production decision or the full deployment decision and thereafter, DOT&E and/or DASD(DT&E) may direct the DoD Component Acquisition Executive (CAE) to provide TEMP updates or addenda to articulate additional testing (e.g., FOT&E, Verification of Correction of Deficiencies periods, test program for future increments). The OTA may also request TEMP updates or addenda to articulate additional testing. DoDI 5000.02 (Encl. 1, Table 2 – page 58) provides additional information.

Test Articles for FOT&E (if required). DOT&E approves the quantity of test articles required for all OT&E test events for any system under OSD OT&E oversight, in accordance with DoDI 5000.02 (Encl. 5, para 9 – page 105). For programs not on DOT&E oversight, the OTA determines the quantity of test articles required for all OT&E events, in accordance with 10 USC 2400.

T&E planning is also concerned with determining the mix of T&E best suited for a system's production qualification, production acceptance, and sustainment. The DCMA or government-equivalent representatives and procedures may encompass the production evaluations at the contractor's manufacturing site, or may require the T&E effort to establish and mature the processes. Therefore, the appropriate level of evaluation could range from none, for normal DCMA practices, to minimal for first article qualification checks, to more extensive evaluations based upon production qualification test (PQT) results for new or unique manufacturing techniques, especially with new technologies.

Refer to the DAG, CH 10.3.2.1.2.2., Quality Assurance Surveillance Plan, for information on Government Contract Quality Assurance (GCQA).

CH 8–4.4.4 T&E Role during Production & Deployment

Operational Test Agency Report of OTA Results. The appropriate operational test agency conducts operational testing with LRIP units. After test completion, the Service OTA provides an independent report assessing the operational effectiveness, operational suitability, and survivability (including cybersecurity) or lethality of the system. For oversight programs, the Service OTA provides the report to DOT&E.

Beyond LRIP Report. The Director, DOT&E provides the MDA, Secretary of Defense, and Congress with a Beyond LRIP Report documenting the results of OT&E and providing the Director's determination of whether the program proves operationally effective, operationally suitable, and survivable, in accordance with DoDI 5000.02 (Encl. 5, para 1(c) – page 98). For programs on the DOT&E Oversight List, operational testing occurs in accordance with the DOT&E-approved TEMP.

Refer to DoDI 5000.02, Encl. 5 for more information.

Full Rate Production (FRP). The MDA conducts a review to assess the results of initial OT&E, initial manufacturing, and initial deployment, and then determines whether or not to approve the program's proceeding to Full-Rate Production and/or Full Deployment, in accordance with DoDI 5000.02 (Encl. 5, para 5(b) – page 100). Continuing to Full-Rate Production and Deployment requires demonstrated control of the manufacturing process, acceptable performance and reliability, and the establishment of adequate sustainment and support systems.

CH 8–4.5 Operations & Support Phase

The operations and support (O&S) phase focuses on executing the product support strategy, satisfying materiel readiness and operational performance requirements, and sustaining the system in the most cost-effective manner over its total life cycle (including disposal).

O&S has two major efforts: life cycle sustainment and disposal, in accordance with DoDI 5000.02 (Para 5(d)(14)(b) – page 29). Effective sustainment of systems results from the design and development of supportable, reliable, and maintainable systems. Sustainment strategies can evolve throughout the system's life cycle. The PM works with system users to document performance and sustainment requirements in agreements specifying objective outcomes, measures, resource commitments, and stakeholder responsibilities. The Services, with system users, conduct continuing reviews of sustainment strategies to compare performance expectations against actual performance measures. The program disposes of the system in an appropriate manner when it reaches the end of its useful life.

CH 8–4.5.1 T&E Support during Operations & Support

During the support phase, the Chief Developmental Tester focuses on:

- Regression testing and evaluation of test articles that incorporate operationally significant improvements, modifications, and corrective actions prior to fielding improvements and modifications.
- Routine T&E of routine technical changes to all components and subcomponents.
- Demonstration of the maturity of the production process through production qualification testing (PQT) and production readiness review (PRR).
- Demonstration of the maturity of the software maintenance processes (if not completed in IOT&E or FOT&E).
- Surveillance testing.
- Shelf-life extension testing.

The PM may initiate system modifications, as necessary, to improve performance and reduce ownership costs. Test organizations remain aware of system modifications, review TEMP updates, and ensure PMs consider disposal during the design process, in accordance with DoDI 5000.02 (Encl. 5, para 5(b) – page 100). PMs document hazardous materials contained in the system in the programmatic environment, safety, and occupational health evaluation (PESHE) as well as estimate and plan for the system's demilitarization and safe disposal. The PM also considers the demilitarization of conventional ammunition during system design.

DOT&E determines when to remove a program from DOT&E oversight. Some of the typical reasons for removal include:

- A program is no longer in production.
- No additional follow-on operational testing.
- The program office is disbanded.
- Significant upgrades are no longer considered.

CH-8 Version and Revision History

Use the table below to provide the version number, the date that the particular version was approved and a brief description of the reason for and content changes contained in the revised version.

Version #	Revision Date	Reason
0	1 February 2017	DAG Chapter 8 Initial Upload.
1	6 April 2017	Section 8-3.7.4. Last sentence, removed hyperlink for "STAT" and corrected the URL for STAT COE.

CH 9–1. Purpose

The Defense Acquisition Guidebook (DAG), Chapter 9, provides guidance for the system security engineering (SSE) discipline and Department of Defense (DoD) program protection for defense acquisition programs. The program manager (PM) and the systems engineer (SE) should use DAG Chapters 3 and 9 to effectively plan and execute program protection activities across the acquisition life cycle.

CH 9–2. Background

Program protection provides the processes, methodologies, and techniques to enable program offices to identify information, components, and technologies, as well as determine the most appropriate mix of measures to protect the information, components, and technologies from known security threats and attacks. These protection measures impact the development of the system being acquired, the operations of the program office, and the means by which the items are acquired.

CH 9–2.1 Purpose of Program Protection

The purpose of program protection is to give PMs an effective way to understand, assess, and prioritize the broad spectrum of security threats and attacks to the acquisition program, and to identify the right, cost-effective mixture of measures to protect against such attacks. Since the scope of the acquisition program can include all program and system information, organization and personnel, enabling networks, and relevant systems (i.e., systems in acquisition, enabling systems, and support systems), PMs should consider security threats and attacks to the following program elements that can be exposed to targeting:

- Government program organization
- Contractor organizations and environments
- Software and hardware
- System interfaces
- Enabling and support equipment, systems, and facilities
- Fielded systems.

To address threats and vulnerabilities associated with these program elements, program protection focuses on (as shown in Figure 1):

- Information (including program and system information)
- Technology (critical program information (CPI))
- Components (mission-critical functionality).

Figure 1: Program Protection Focus Areas

Information	Technology	Components
What to Protect : Information on the system and about the program **How to Protect:** • Classification • Export Controls • Information Security • RMF for DoD IT **Goal:** Ensure key system and program data are protected from adversary collection	**What to Protect**: A capability element that contributes to the warfighters' technical advantage (CPI) **How to Protect:** • Anti-Tamper • Exportability Features **Goal:** Prevent the compromise and loss of CPI	**What to Protect** : Mission-critical functions and components **How to Protect:** • Software Assurance • Hardware Assurance/Trusted Microelectronics • Supply Chain Risk Management • Anti-Counterfeits **Goal:** Protect key mission-critical components from malicious activity

Trade-offs to establish an integrated, comprehensive protection scheme

CH 9–2.2 Program Protection Policy and Guidance

PMs and Systems Engineers (SEs) should know and understand the statutory and regulatory Systems Engineering (SE) mandates. Table 1 identifies top-level Program Protection-related policy.

Table 1: Key Program Protection Related Policies

Program Protection Policies
DoDI 5000.02, Operation of the Defense Acquisition System
DODI 5000.02, ENCL 14, Cybersecurity in the Defense Acquisition System
DoDI 5200.01, DoD Information Security Program and Protection of Sensitive Compartmented Information (SCI) and associated manuals (DoDM 5200.01 Vol 1-4)
DoDI 5200.39, Critical Program Information (CPI) Identification and Protection Within Research, Development, Test, and Evaluation (RDT&E)
DoDI 5200.44, Protection of Mission Critical Functions to Achieve Trusted Systems and Networks (TSN)
DoDM 5200.45, Instructions for Developing Security Classification Guides
DoDI 5230.24, Distribution Statements on Technical Documents
DoDD 5200.47E, Anti-Tamper (AT)
DoDI 8500.01, Cybersecurity
DoDI 8510.01, Risk Management Framework (RMF) for DoD Information Technology (IT)

DoDI 5000.02, Operation of the Defense Acquisition System establishes policy for the management of all acquisition programs, including requirements for program protection. For program protection, the policy describes the content, submission, and approval requirements for PPPs throughout the acquisition life cycle (Milestones A, B, C, plus Full Rate Production [FRP] or Full Deployment Decision [FDD]), including operations and maintenance. It also apprises management of the risks to program and system information and critical program information, as well as mission-critical functions and components associated with the program

DODD 5000.02, ENCL 14, Cybersecurity in the Defense Acquisition System prescribes procedures for acquisition responsibilities related to cybersecurity (CS) in the Defense Acquisition System.

DoDI 5200.01, DoD Information Security Program and Protection of Sensitive Compartmented Information (SCI) provides policy and responsibilities for collateral, special access programs, SCI, and controlled unclassified information (CUI) within an overarching DoD Information Security Program. The associated manuals provide procedures for the designation, marking, protection, and dissemination of CUI and classified information, including information categorized as collateral, SCI, and Special Access Program (SAP). For program protection, this issuance provides guidance for classification and declassification of DoD information that requires protection in the interest of national security.

DoDI 5200.39, Critical Program Information (CPI) Identification and Protection within Research, Development, Test, and Evaluation establishes policy that requires the identification and protection of CPI and defines CPI and its protections. Key activities include:

- Horizontal identification and protection analysis
- Anti-tamper analysis and protection
- Counterintelligence, intelligence, and security assessments and support
- International Cooperative Program CPI protection considerations.

DoDI 5200.44, Protection of Mission Critical Functions to Achieve Trusted Systems and Networks (TSN) establishes policy and responsibilities to minimize the risk that warfighting capability will be impaired due to vulnerabilities in system design or subversion of mission-critical functions or components (e.g., software, microelectronics). Key activities include:

- Identification of mission-critical functions and components
- Use of all-source intelligence analysis of suppliers of critical components
- Use of enhanced software and hardware vulnerability detection and mitigation
- Use of tailored acquisition and procurement strategies.

DoDM 5200.45, Instructions for Developing Security Classification Guides provide guidance for the development of security classification guidance.

DoDI 5230.24, Distribution Statements on Technical Documents establish policy for the marking and distribution of DoD technical information/documents.

DoDD 5200.47E, Anti-Tamper (AT) establishes policy and assigns responsibilities for AT protection of critical program information (CPI). It also designates the Under Secretary of Defense for Acquisition, Technology, and Logistics (USD(AT&L)) as the Principal Staff Assistant (PSA) responsible for oversight of the DoD AT program and policy, and designates the Secretary of the Air Force (SECAF) as the DoD Executive Agent (EA) for AT.

DoDI 8500.01, Cybersecurity establishes responsibility to protect and defend DoD information and information technology, and explicitly provides the Under Secretary of Defense for Acquisition, Technology and Logistics (USD) (AT&L) the responsibility to integrate policies established in the 8500.01 and its supporting guidance into acquisition policy, regulations, and guidance consistent with DoDD 5134.01.

DoDI 8510.01, Risk Management Framework (RMF) for DoD Information Technology (IT) establishes the requirement for DoD to implement the RMF to manage life cycle cybersecurity risk to DoD IT. For program protection, it establishes the following:

- The system categorization is to be documented in the cybersecurity strategy within the PPP.
- The security engineering of tailoring security control requirements and cybersecurity-testing considerations is integrated into the program's overall systems engineering process and then documented and updated in the Systems Engineering Plan (SEP) and PPP throughout the system life cycle.

Program protection guidance, in addition to the DAG, is provided on the Deputy Assistant Secretary of Defense for Systems Engineering (DASD [SE]) website, http://www.acq.osd.mil/se/initiatives/init_pp-sse.html.

CH 9–2.3 Program Protection Plan

The Program Protection Plan (PPP) is a living plan to guide efforts to manage the risks to CPI and mission-critical functions and components, as well as program and system information. This milestone acquisition document captures both systems security engineering (SSE) and security activities and the results of the analyses as the program and system become more defined.

PMs should employ SSE and security practices to prepare a PPP, using the Program Protection Plan Outline and Guidance. The PM should tailor the PPP as necessary to meet the characteristics of the system being acquired. The PM should also ensure that security considerations are incorporated into the system requirements, design, integration, and supply chain activities. The level of detail contained in the PPP should be commensurate with the maturity of the system design. The PPP should be updated for each of the technical reviews, and the security risks and mitigations should be assessed at each technical review.

The PPP is submitted for Milestone Decision Authority (MDA) approval at each Milestone review and the Full Rate Production or Full Deployment Decision Review. For programs with the Defense Acquisition Executive such as the MDA, PPPs are submitted to the DASD(SE) not less than 45 calendar days before the relevant review. Also, a DoD Component-approved draft PPP must be provided to the DASD(SE) 45 days before the Development Request for Proposal Release Decision Point.

After the Full Rate Production or Full Deployment Decision, the PPP should transition to the PM responsible for system sustainment and disposal.

CH 9–2.4 Program Protection Activities and Relationships

The goal of program protection is to help programs identify and implement the most appropriate mix of measures to protect the program and system information, components, and technologies from the known security threats and attacks across the acquisition life cycle.

With that goal in mind, the program management office should execute the following program protection activities. Program protection activities and their relationships to each other and to other defense acquisition functions are captured in Figure 2, which also includes the Chapter 9 sections that describe each activity and relationship.

Figure 2: Overview of Program Protection Activities and Relationships

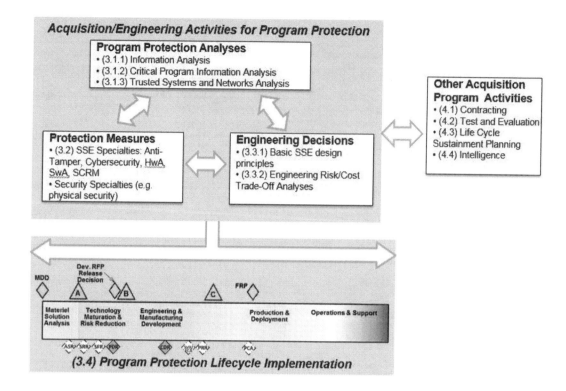

Acquisition/Engineering Activities for Program Protection

Program Protection Analyses
- (3.1.1) Information Analysis
- (3.1.2) Critical Program Information Analysis
- (3.1.3) Trusted Systems and Networks Analysis

Other Acquisition Program Activities
- (4.1) Contracting
- (4.2) Test and Evaluation
- (4.3) Life Cycle Sustainment Planning
- (4.4) Intelligence

Protection Measures
- (3.2) SSE Specialties: Anti-Tamper, Cybersecurity, HwA, SwA, SCRM
- Security Specialties (e.g. physical security)

Engineering Decisions
- (3.3.1) Basic SSE design principles
- (3.3.2) Engineering Risk/Cost Trade-Off Analyses

(3.4) Program Protection Lifecycle Implementation

- *Program Protection Analyses:* Activities to help programs understand the risks to a program's technology, components, and information.
- *Protection Measures:* Activities to derive protection measures from the specialties within system security engineering (i.e., anti-tamper, RMF for DoD IT, exportability features, hardware assurance, software assurance, and supply chain risk management) and general security specialties to address security threats and attacks. Each specialty has a set of analyses, approaches, and protections that programs can utilize.
- *Engineering Decisions:* Activities, primarily trade-offs, to determine the most appropriate set of requirements given the program constraints. For program protection, this means conducting trades among protection measures. There is also a basic set of security principles that should be incorporated into the system design.

All of the above activities are executed iteratively across the acquisition life cycle in order to refine protection measures as the system design matures. Additionally, throughout the life cycle, program protection informs and is informed by other aspects of defense acquisition, including contracting, test and evaluation, life-cycle sustainment planning, and intelligence.

The Program Protection activities are further described in Sections 3 and 4.

CH 9–2.5 Roles, Responsibilities, and Resources

Security, including cybersecurity, of DoD programs and systems is the collective responsibility of the entire acquisition workforce. However, the primary roles supporting program protection are the PM, systems engineer (SE), system security engineer, system security engineering specialists, security specialists, and chief developmental tester. The Program Management Office (PMO) is responsible for including the appropriate requirements in the solicitation in order to transition into the development effort.

Typical responsibilities for each of these roles are detailed below. Note that these roles are described functionally. Not every program will have an individual associated with each role; some programs will have individuals who fulfill multiple roles.

PMs have the overall responsibility for program protection planning throughout the acquisition life cycle as well as documenting the plans and results of the program protection analyses in a PPP, as required in DoDI 5000.02 encl. 1, Table 2 – Page 56. Specific responsibilities for the PM include:

- Managing the program protection risks
- Adequately resourcing program protection efforts (i.e., staff, budget)
- Initiating program protection efforts early and ensuring analyses are iteratively conducted throughout the acquisition life cycle
- Considering international acquisition and exportability early, along with their impact on program protection
- Incorporating program protection sufficiently into solicitations and contracts
- Completing and submitting the PPP for approval in accordance with DoDI 5000.02
- Support for activities to achieve protection consistency across programs.

SEs are responsible for ensuring the development and delivery of capability through the implementation of an approach with respect to cost, schedule, performance, and risk. This is accomplished using integrated and consistent systems engineering (SE) activities and processes, regardless of when a program enters the acquisition life cycle. The SE conducts trade-off analyses and integrates contributions from each engineering specialty and design consideration. Each plays a role in the design of the system, and it is the SE who works to synthesize and balance the requirements. One of these design considerations is system security engineering (SSE), which addresses program protection. As system security engineering relates to program protection, the SE is specifically responsible for:

- Integrating program protection/SSE into the program's systems engineering processes
- Conducting trade-off analyses with respect to system security and other design considerations
- Collaborating with the system security engineer on any system security requirements adjustments
- Incorporating system security requirements into the system performance specification, technical baselines, and solicitation documents
- Ensuring the PPP is informed by the systems engineering constraints and decisions
- Leading the development of the PPP.

System security engineers integrate contributions from system security engineering disciplines such as anti-tamper, RMF for DoD IT, exportability features, hardware assurance, software assurance, and supply chain risk management; and security specialties such as personnel security, industrial security, physical security, and information security. The outcome is a comprehensive program and system protection within the constraints of cost, schedule, and performance while maintaining an acceptable level of risk. To integrate all aspects of system security, the system security engineer leads the evaluation and balancing of security contributions to produce a coherent security capability across the system and the program. As it relates to program protection, the system security engineer is specifically responsible for:

- Conducting/leading program protection analyses for program and system information, CPI, and trusted systems and networks (TSN)
- Collaborating with system security engineering specialists and security specialists to assess vulnerabilities and identify protection measures
- Conducting trade-off analyses to integrate protection measures from across security engineering specialties and security specialties in order to reduce security risks to meet acceptable levels based on performance, cost, and schedule
- Translating protection measures into system security requirements, and adjusting them, based upon constraints and decisions relayed from the SE
- Collaborating with the SE to integrate the system security requirements into appropriate systems-engineering artifacts
- Ensure security approaches are documented in the PPP appropriately.

System security engineering specialists identify the system security threats and vulnerabilities and the appropriate system security protection measures within the scope of their system security engineering specialty. Specifically, these specialists are responsible for:

- Assisting the system security engineer with program protection analyses
- Identifying protection measures within their specialty
- Collaborating with the system security engineer to adjust protection measures based on constraints and decisions relayed from the SE
- Communicating resource needs to the SSE and SE.

As program protection integrates system security engineering specialties and security specialties, there is also a key role played by security specialists. Security specialists identify the security vulnerabilities and needed security protection measures within the scope of their security specialty. These specialists are specifically responsible for:

- Defining, implementing, and monitoring security protection measures
- Collaborating with the system security engineer in order to inform the program protection analyses and modifying the security protection measures to meet program needs.

The chief developmental tester ensures program protection is incorporated into the program's test and evaluation (T&E) efforts. The chief developmental tester is specifically responsible for:

- Planning of developmental test and evaluation (DT&E), which includes cooperative vulnerability testing
- Conducting verification and validation (V&V), with respect to system security requirements
- Ensuring required verifications against representative attack scenarios are performed, where applicable, to address system security requirements
- Planning for operational test and evaluation (OT&E), which should include adversarial testing—adversarial tests typically subject a system to a series of attacks, simulating the tactics of an actual threat exploiting the system's vulnerabilities; this may exclude testing from a hands-on reverse engineering perspective.

Contractors also play a key role in program protection. Contractors have the responsibility to conduct program protection planning and execution as contractually agreed upon (details on contracting for program protection can be found in Section 4.2). The Contractor's specific responsibilities for system security vary by contract, but typically include:

- Implementing security-related Federal Acquisition Regulations (FAR) and Defense Federal Acquisition Regulation Supplements (DFARS)
- Integrating system security as part of its systems engineering activities
- Supporting program protection analysis and contributing to government updates of the PPP for each of the systems engineering technical reviews
- Assessing and mitigating system security risks as part of the technical assessment.

There are also other resources outside of the program office that can play a key role to ensure that comprehensive program protection is implemented. These resources include:

- Intelligence and Counterintelligence: Threat information is a key resource to help inform PM decisions related to program protection across the acquisition life cycle. Various intelligence and counterintelligence activities are available to PMs through their DoD Component. More information on how intelligence and counterintelligence support informs program protection can be found in Section 4.5.
- Joint Acquisition Protection and Exploitation Cell (JAPEC): The JAPEC facilitates collaboration of PMs with the intelligence and counterintelligence communities on system security protection, and analysis of unclassified controlled technical information (CTI) losses. This analysis enables PMs

to determine if any necessary courses of action must be taken to mitigate the risks associated with losing technical information. More information about the JAPEC can be found in Section 4.4.1.

- Joint Federated Assurance Center (JFAC): The JFAC is a federation of DoD organizations that provides a variety of software (SwA) and hardware assurance (HwA) capabilities to support programs in mitigating their vulnerabilities. More information about how a program can utilize the services provided by the JFAC can be found in Section 4.5.
- DoD Executive Agent for Anti-Tamper (AT) and DoD Component Office of Primary Responsibility for AT: Confirms that AT requirements have been met before deployment and / or export of DoD systems with CPI.

PMs may use the above resources to support their program protection planning decisions.

CH 9–3. Best Practice

This Section describes the necessary program protection activities and how those activities are executed across the life cycle.

- Section 3.1 provides a description of analyses for each program protection consideration (i.e., information, technology, and components).
- Section 3.2 provides a description of each system security engineering (SSE) specialty and associated activities.
- Section 3.3 provides a description of key engineering design activities related to program protection, including key secure design principles and the execution of engineering trade-offs among protection measures.
- Section 3.4 provides guidance for executing the program protection activities described in Section 3.1 through 3.3 across the lifecycle, addressing each phase and relevant technical reviews and audits. These include the level of detail for the processes described in Section 3.2, as well as special considerations or areas of focus for specific points in the life cycle.

CH 9–3.1 Program Protection Analyses

There are three sets of interrelated analyses that are performed during program- protection planning, correlating to the three-program protection considerations listed in Section 2.1. Information Analysis (Section 3.1.1). Critical Program information (CPI) Analysis (Section 3.1.2), and Trusted Systems and Networks (TSN) Analysis (Section 3.1.3) encapsulate the methods and processes for protecting the program and system (information, technology, and components). These analyses are the primary activities for identifying and prioritizing what needs to be protected in the program and system.

The program protection processes, and their constituent activities and tasks, are not meant to be performed in a particular time-dependent or serial sequence. The Program Manager and Systems Engineer apply the processes iteratively, recursively, and in parallel (as applicable) throughout the life cycle to translate identified capability needs into balanced and integrated system-security solutions.

CH 9–3.1.1 Information Analysis

Information analysis is the set of activities that a program executes in order to identify, understand, and protect the information about the program and the information residing in the system being acquired. There are three information analysis activities:

- Identify information to be protected (Section 3.1.1.1): This includes the identification, classification, and marking of program and system information. It also provides the basis for a program to understand what information is associated with the program and system, as well as the importance of that information. Information identified provides the basis for decisions on protections (or other requirements) that must be implemented for the program and the system.
- Protect program information (Section 3.1.1.2): This includes activities related to selecting and implementing protections for information about the program. Information about the program

includes organizations and personnel supporting the program, logistics and test documentation, key technologies, applications, processes, capabilities, suppliers, and end items.

- Protect system information (Section 3.1.1.3): These are the activities related to selecting and implementing protections for information on the system being acquired, which is defined as information residing on, processed by, or transiting through the system being acquired. These protections aim to ensure the confidentiality, integrity, and availability of information to preserve the assurance of the system being acquired.

Information analysis and related protections cover classified information and unclassified covered defense information (with a particular emphasis on technical information), as well as information that alone might not be damaging and might be unclassified, but which, in combination with other information could allow an adversary to compromise, counter, clone, or defeat warfighting capability.

When conducting information analysis, programs should pay particular attention to the identification and protection of technical information because technical information includes much of the research and engineering associated with DoD's programs; the majority of it resides on unclassified systems. If stolen, this information provides adversaries with insight into U.S. defense and industrial capabilities and allows them to save time and expense in developing similar capabilities. Therefore, protecting this information is critical to preserving the intellectual property and competitive capabilities of the defense industrial base and the technological superiority of our fielded military systems.

The output associated with information analysis can inform other program protection analyses:

- Critical Program Information (CPI) Analysis: Classification of information may be used as an input to CPI analysis. Classified information related to a system capability may indicate that the capability is advanced enough to be considered CPI and the severity of consequence of CPI compromise. Inversely, CPI identification can feed information analysis. If an item is identified as CPI, then the information associated with that item may be classified or warrant additional protections if the information is unclassified.
- Trusted Systems and Networks (TSN) Analysis: When assessing the risk to a mission-critical function/component (which accounts for risk to the design documents, supply chains, software, etc.), consider the security protection measures triggered by classification and marking of the information associated with that function/component. These protections should be accounted for in the determination of the likelihood of compromise or effort required by the adversary to compromise the function or component.

CH 9–3.1.1.1 Foundational Activities
Activities related to the identification, classification, and marking of information associated with a program are driven by DoD information security policies. These activities provide the foundation for a program to understand the information associated with the program and the system, as well as the importance of that information. The results of these foundational activities drive decisions about protections (or other requirements), which must be implemented for the program and the system.

In accordance with the information security policies listed in the Introduction, the program will conduct the following activities as they relate to the program circumstances. Note that these activities are not unique to acquisition programs and should not represent a separate effort from those currently being executed by information security activities programs.

- Classification and marking of all program information. The policies for classification and marking are found in DoDI 5200.01, and associated guidelines are available in DoDM 5200.01 Volumes 1 through 4.
- Development of a Security Classification Guide (if necessary). DoDM 5200.45 provides guidelines for developing security classification guides.
- Application of distribution statements for technical information. Distribution statements are applied to all technical information (both classified and unclassified). Policy and guidelines for applying these statements are available in DoDI 5230.24, DoDM 5200.01 Volume 2, and DoDM 5200.01

Volume 4. It is important for programs to consider the secondary distribution necessary for technical documents, given the importance and vulnerability of DoD technical information.

Some additional key points related to these foundational activities include:

- For programs containing classified information, the program office will coordinate with the Original Classification Authority (OCA) to set information security levels for each element of the program including unclassified, controlled classified, or classified (Confidential through Top Secret), and direct the classification and marking of any technical information in accordance with DoDM 5200.01, Volumes 1 through 4, and DoDI 5230.24.
- The program office is responsible for establishing and promulgating the security classification guidance consistent with the requirements in DoDM 5200.45. The PM is responsible for ensuring the promulgation of program-applicable security classification guides to the Government and contractor teams.
- Programs that contain classified information, generally, also contain unclassified CTI.
- For programs that contain only unclassified information, the PM may want to develop a document similar to the format of the Security Classification Guide (SCG) as a mechanism to identify and protect unclassified CTI. This will assist in implementation of DFARS requirements for safeguarding covered defense information.

Programs use the results of these activities to apply appropriate information security protections for the program and the system (which are addressed in more detail in Sections 3.1.1.2 and 3.1.1.3).

CH 9–3.1.1.2 Implementing Program Information Protections

Within the program office, personnel handle information in accordance with DoD policies and procedures. Government information systems that store, process, or transmit program information are also operated in accordance with DoD policies and procedures. Additional protections, such as increased limits on the distribution of controlled technical information, may choose to be implemented by a program.

Beyond how the program office handles its information internally, the program office must also relay requirements for handling and marking information to contractors through solicitations and contracts. Key aspects of this include the following:

- Processes, procedures, and protection for government and contractors to address a compromise of classified information are described in DoDM 5200.01 Volume 1 through 4, DoDI 5220.22, National Industrial Security Program (NISP), DoDM 5220.22, National Industrial Security Program Operating Manual (NISPOM). Defense Security Service administers the NISP and provides appropriate security education, training, and awareness to industry and government personnel. The NISPOM is implemented through Federal Acquisition Regulation (FAR) Clause 52.204-2 for contracts handling classified information.
- Identification and marking of unclassified Covered Defense Information (CDI) triggers protection requirements in DoDI 8582.01 and the mandatory DFARS Clause 252.204-7012, "Safeguarding Covered Defense Information and Cyber Incident Reporting." Under DFARS Clause 252.204-7012, contractors are required to safeguard CDI NIST Special Publication 800-171, report cyber incidents of CDI and within 90 days of reporting the incident, provide media relevant to the incident to DoD when requested. Programmatic, strategic, and operational mitigations should be considered in determining an appropriate response to risks as the result of a cyber intrusion. Additionally, PMs are encouraged to engage eligible industry counterparts and recommend they participate in the Defense Industrial Base Cyber Security/Information Assurance Program, established in Part 236 of Title 32 of the Code of Federal Regulations.
- Instructions for handling and marking are typically incorporated through Contracts Data Requirements List (DD Form 1423, Block 9), which are included as part of solicitations and contracts.

Programs can determine what program information is released through a contract. To mitigate some risk of losing technical information, programs need to limit the technical information released to a contractor to only what is necessary to perform the work of the specific contract.

CH 9–3.1.1.3 Implementing System Information Protections

Protection of information residing on or transiting through DoD systems is driven by the need for availability, integrity, and confidentiality. The foundational activities related to identifying, classifying, and marking information provide the basis for understanding what information will be residing on or transiting through the system being acquired, and what the availability, integrity, and confidentiality needs are for each type of information. For instance, classified information has different availability, integrity, and confidentiality needs than unclassified information.

The program will then select protection measures to meet the availability, integrity, and confidentiality needs for the types of information residing on the system. While the program has flexibility in selecting protection measures, there are specific situations in which DoD policy drives the implementation more specifically. Some of these situations include:

- Cross-domain solutions: When there is information in the system of more than one classification level, there may be a need to implement a cross-domain solution (if the information needs to be moved between classification levels). Programs should use validated security solutions when available and appropriate, such as those managed by the Unified Cross Domain Services Management Office described in DoDI 8540.01.
- Encryption: Based on the level of encryption required, a program may need to incorporate Federal Information Processing Standards (FIPS) or National Security Agency (NSA) certified cryptographic products and technologies into systems in order to protect information types at rest and in transit. Programs with certain cryptographic requirements, as determined by the information type or other protection considerations, should coordinate development efforts with the NSA Information Assurance Directorate.

These protection measures are captured in NIST 800-53r4, which is Step 2 of the Risk Management Framework (RMF) for DoD IT policy.

CH 9–3.1.2 Critical Program Information Analysis

CPI is the U.S. capability elements that contribute to the warfighters' technical advantage, which if compromised, undermine U.S. military preeminence. U.S. capability elements may include, but are not limited to, software algorithms and specific hardware residing on the system, training equipment, and/or maintenance support equipment, as defined in DoDI 5200.39 (Glossary Page 11).

Simply, CPI are often DoD-unique capabilities, those that are developed and owned by the U.S., that are necessary for U.S. technological superiority.

CPI compromise (when an exploiter acquires the CPI) may:

- Reduce U.S. technological superiority and shorten the combat-effective life of the system as the adversary develops and fields comparable capabilities and/or countermeasures
- Require research, development, and acquisition resources to counter the impact of compromise and regain or maintain the advantage
- Protection measures should be put in place to deter, delay, detect, and respond to attempts to compromise CPI.

CPI analysis is the means by which programs identify, protect, and monitor CPI. This analysis should be conducted early and throughout the life cycle of the program. Additionally, because CPI is critical to U.S. technological superiority, its value extends beyond any one program. As a result, CPI analysis should consider the broader impact of CPI identification and protection on national security.

CH 9–3.1.2.1 Critical Program Information Identification

CPI identification is conducted to determine if organic CPI (CPI owned by your program) and/or inherited CPI (CPI owned by another program but incorporated into your program/system) exists in the currently-known system or will exist in the operational, deployed system. CPI identification is also conducted to identify CPI that is no longer considered to provide a U.S. technical advantage to the warfighter and may no longer require its current level of protection.

CPI should be identified early and reassessed throughout the life cycle of the program, to include: prior to each acquisition milestone; prior to each system's engineering technical review; throughout operations and sustainment, and specifically during software/hardware technology updates.

To identify CPI, programs should:

- Use DoD, DoD Component, and program resources (e.g., intelligence products, security classification guides, the Acquisition Security Database [ASDB], DoD policy, provisos within license agreements) to identify technology areas and performance/capability thresholds associated with an advanced, new, or unique warfighting capability.
- Decompose the system to the lowest level possible to identify system attributes that exceed a threshold, and thus may indicate the presence of CPI.A threshold is a boundary associated with a capability or level of performance that exceeds what is available commercially or exists in adversary inventories.
- Produce an initial or updated list of CPI, or documentation stating that the operational, deployed system does not or will not contain CPI. Obtain PM approval of the CPI, incorporate the CPI into the PPP, and obtain Milestone Decision Authority approval of the CPI as part of the PPP.

Identification of CPI within a program typically involves collaboration among and input from the PM, SE, systems security engineer, science and technology representative, security representative, anti-tamper, and intelligence/counter-intelligence representative, as well as other program offices (if CPI is being inherited).

Please refer to the Acquisition Security Database (ASDB) for examples of CPI. CPI is not:

- Personally Identifiable Information
- Individually Identifiable Health Information
- Financial Information
- Logistics Information
- Operational Information (waypoints and target location data)
- System Performance
- Designs
- Manufacturing Details
- Vulnerabilities and Weaknesses
- Unmodified Commercial-Off-The-Shelf
- Multi-Level Security Solutions (defined in Committee on National Security Systems Instruction (CNSSI) Number 4009)
- Cross Domain Solutions (defined in CNSSI Number 4009)
- Cryptographic Solutions (defined in CNSSI Number 4009)

While the above may be classified and thus protected accordingly, they are not CPI because one or more of the following apply:

- It is not a capability,
- Its compromise does not result in technology transferred that can be used by the adversary to bolster their warfighting capability by leveraging the transferred technology,
- Its compromise does not result in technology transferred that can be used by the adversary to counter U.S. capabilities based on weaknesses or patterns identified within the transferred technology, or

- It does not live on the weapons system, training equipment, maintenance support equipment, or other supporting end-item.

CH 9–3.1.2.2 Critical Program Information Protection Measure Selection

CPI protection should commence soon after the CPI has been identified, and, like CPI identification, CPI protection should also continue throughout the life cycle of the program.

CPI protection measures seek to deter, delay, detect, and react to attempts to compromise CPI on the end item as a result of hands-on, reverse engineering attacks. Protections triggered by the identification of CPI include anti-tamper and defense exportability features. Other protection measures, listed under other system security engineering specialties, may also contribute to the protection of CPI; however, these protections are not triggered by the identification of CPI. For example, information about CPI, including design and manufacturing know how, is typically classified and would be protected in accordance with a Security Classification Guide and through NIST 800-53r4 protections on a government program office and NIST 800-171 protections on contractor-owned information systems. An adversary may target the supply chain to obtain that design and manufacturing know how, and, if compromised, would have the same consequence as if the CPI were acquired by reverse engineering the end-item.

In order to select the appropriate protection measures, programs should consider the:

- Consequence of CPI compromise--the impact on U.S. technological superiority if the CPI is compromised
- Exposure of the system--the likelihood that an adversary will be able to obtain the end item through battlefield loss or export,
- Assessed threat--foreign adversary interest and skill in obtaining CPI
- Known vulnerabilities of the system.

For more information on consequence of CPI compromise, system exposure and vulnerabilities, please refer to the Anti-Tamper Technical Implementation Guide. For threat information, programs should request a Counterintelligence Threat Assessment from the supporting Defense Counterintelligence Component in accordance with DoDI O-5240.24. For more information on the assessed threat, please refer to DAG Chapter 7, Section 4.3.

To initiate and coordinate counterintelligence activities supporting your program, follow the instructions in DoDI O-5240.24, Enclosure 4. The results of this coordination should be documented in a formal and living plan describing the activities to be conducted by a Defense Counterintelligence Component in support of your program; this plan is known as the Counterintelligence Support Plan (CISP) and is an annex to the PPP. The CISP should be reviewed and updated annually.

For organic CPI, identify all appropriate protections. For inherited CPI, confirm that the inherited protections protect the CPI at a level appropriate to the inheriting system's circumstances; adjust or add protections as needed, given any change to consequence of CPI compromise, exposure of the system, the assessed threat, and known vulnerabilities.

CH 9–3.1.2.3 Critical Program Information Monitoring

CPI monitoring should commence soon after the CPI has been identified, and should continue throughout the life cycle of the program.

CPI monitoring is the process for determining if an event has occurred that requires the program to reassess CPI or its associated protections. Events may include, but are not limited to, the following:

- Operational Environment: A change in the physical location of the system with CPI other than that for which it was originally designed
- Protection Effectiveness: A change in the ability of the CPI protections to deter, delay, detect, and respond to attempts to compromise CPI
- Security Classification: A change to a relevant SCG, and thus the classification thresholds
- System Modification: A change to the system architecture and/or designs

- Capability Maturation: A change in the state-of-the-art for a particular capability and thus the thresholds used for CPI identification
- Threat: A change in foreign adversary interest and skill in obtaining CPI.

If these events occur, the program should reassess CPI and associated protection measures.

CH 9–3.1.2.4 Horizontal Protection of Critical Program Information

Because CPI is not always unique to one program (i.e., two programs may contain similar CPI, or one program may inherit CPI from another), there is a risk of not protecting CPI similarly across all programs. In doing so, programs may:

- Expose similar or the same CPI to greater risk
- Undermine or diminish the protection investment made by another program
- Apply an inconsistent level of resources to protect CPI.

To prevent this from happening, programs are required to ensure horizontal protection; they should apply a consistent level of protection to similar CPI.

To meet this requirement, programs should first understand that horizontal protection starts with horizontal identification. Horizontal identification, a consistent determination of CPI across two or more programs, is challenging, given that historically, this decision has been program-centric. However, given the importance of CPI to U.S. technological superiority, the Office of the Secretary of Defense (OSD) and the DoD Components provide tools and resources to assist programs in making consistent and aligned decisions.

In support of horizontal identification, programs should make use of CPI identification subject matter experts and technologists within their DoD Component, security classification guidance, and DoD policy (e.g., DoDI S-5230.28). Additionally, programs should consult the ASDB, including the list of example CPI, to help identify the same or similar CPI associated with other programs. For more information about the ASDB, please contact your DoD Component ASDB representative or email OSD.ASDBHelpdesk@mail.mil.

In support of horizontal protection, programs are encouraged to work with the DoD Office of the Executive Agent for Anti-Tamper (ATEA) and its DoD Component Office of Primary Responsibility for Anti-Tamper early and often for guidance.

Where horizontal protection disagreements arise, affected programs should discuss, negotiate, and agree upon the level of protection required to ensure that an equivalent level of risk is achieved across the affected systems, considering potential differences in system exposure. If programs cannot reach agreement, the ATEA may inform the Low Observable/Counter-Low Observable (LO/CLO) Tri-Service Committee and the Milestone Decision Authority of any AT-related horizontal protection issues per DoDD 5200.47E (Encl. 2, para 7.b. – Page 5).

CH 9–3.1.3 Trusted Systems and Networks Analysis

The goal of TSN Analysis is to protect those functions and components that are critical to conducting the system's intended mission(s) from intentional malicious insertion-related threats and attacks. TSN planning and execution activities include the following:

- Identification of the mission-critical functions and critical components of the system, commensurate with the system requirements decomposition
- Assessment and analysis of threats, vulnerabilities, and risk for identified mission-critical functions and critical components
- Risk mitigation and protection measures for planning and implementation
- Proactive planning and implementation of TSN key practices
- Trade-space considerations for protection measure selection
- Risk identification after protection measures are implemented, including follow-up mitigation plans and actions as well as assessments of residual risk.

TSN Analysis is completed by a program through conduct of a Criticality Analysis (CA), Threat Assessment (TA), Vulnerability Assessment (VA), Risk Assessment (RA), and Protection Measure Selection, all of which will be covered in greater detail in subsequent sections. The relationships between these activities are described in Figure 3. The TSN Analysis process is applied throughout the acquisition life cycle and should take into consideration the system security risks for the program. As the system evolves, the program should reconsider the criticality of the functions and components as well as the vulnerabilities and threats. By periodically repeating the risk management process, the program may identify additional threats and vulnerabilities that were not identified in previous iterations because the level of detail of the design was not sufficient to identify them. This continuous risk management process informs the system design trade-offs. Discovery of a potentially malicious source from the threat assessment may warrant additional checks for vulnerabilities in other (less critical) products procured from that source. For each program protection risk that is assessed as "high" or "very high," a risk cube and mitigation plans are needed.

Figure 3: TSN Analysis Methodology

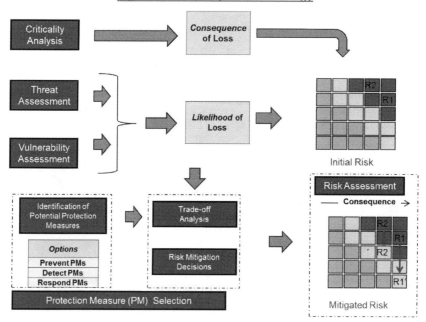

Efforts to identify mission-critical functions and critical components and their protection begin early in the life cycle and should be revised as system designs evolve and mature. Iterative application of TSN Analysis, reinforced by tools such as threat design sensitivity analysis, misuse scenario evaluation, fault isolation trees, and system response analysis, will yield incremental refinements in the determination of what to protect and how to protect it. The analysis should be updated at each of the systems engineering technical reviews to take into account the latest design and implementation decisions, as well as additional threat and vulnerability information.

Table 2 describes the level of detail required for TSN Analysis as it progresses through the life cycle, commensurate with its system specification level. In the Production and Deployment and the Operations and Support phases, it is expected that the analysis will be updated periodically to the level of detail of the Product Baseline (the same level of detail described in the column of the table labeled 'System Verification Review [SVR]/Functional Configuration Audit [FCA], Production and Deployment [P&D], and Operation & Sustainment (O & S) Phases A periodic analysis should be conducted to support the development of an updated PPP for the FRP/FDD Decision Review. For a system upgrade, a program may have to conduct the analyses at all levels of detail described in the Alternative Systems Review (ASR) through SVR/FCA, as the system upgrade goes through development and is delivered in the system. Sections 3.1.3.1 through 3.1.3.5 summarize the analyses and techniques that comprise the TSN Analysis. Additional guidance for the TSN Analysis can be found in the *Trusted Systems and Networks (TSN) Analysis* white paper found at the http://www.acq.osd.mil/se/initiatives/init_pp-sse.html website.

Table 2: TSN Analysis Level of Detail Throughout the Life Cycle

Life Cycle Event	Criticality Analysis (CA)	Vulnerability Assessment (VA)	Risk Assessment (RA)	Protection-Measure (PM)
ASR	• Mission-based functions	• Response to Milestone A Vulnerability Questionnaire	• Objective risk criteria established • Applied at function level	• Risk-based supply chain, design and software PM selected via trade-off study
SRR	• System requirements level functions	• Vulnerability Questionnaire and Vulnerability Database DB assessment	• Risk criteria updated applied at system level	• Risk-based system function level PM selection
SFR	• Subsystem level subfunctions	• Vulnerability Questionnaire and DB assessment to critical subsystem level	• Risk criteria updated and applied at subsystem level	• Risk based subsystem function level PM refinement and selection
PDR	• Assembly/ component	• Vulnerability Questionnaire and DB assessment to critical Assembly/Component	• Risk criteria updated and applied at assembly level	• Risk based assembly level PM selection
CDR	• Component/ part	• Vulnerability DB, static analysis and diversity assessment to critical component level	• Risk criteria updated and applied at component level	• Risk-based component level PM selection
SVR/FCA, P&D and O&S Phases	• Part (preliminary)	• Vulnerability DB, static analysis and diversity assessment to critical part level	• Risk criteria updated and applied at prelim part level of critical components	• Risk-based part level PM selection

All selected protection measures should be incorporated into relevant solicitations, system specifications, and statements of work. The Request for Proposal (RFP) should incorporate the results and decisions from the systems engineering technical review immediately preceding the RFP release. In the generic life cycle, the Technology Maturation and Risk Reduction (TMRR) phase RFP would be based on the ASR analysis results; the Engineering and Manufacturing Development (EMD) phase RFP would be based on the System Functional Review (SFR) analysis results; and the Production RFP would be based upon the Critical Design Review (CDR) analysis results.

CH 9–3.1.3.1 Criticality Analysis

The criticality analysis allows a program to focus attention and resources on the system capabilities, mission-critical functions, and critical components that matter most. Mission-critical functions are those functions of the system that, if corrupted or disabled, would likely lead to mission failure or degradation. Mission-critical components are primarily the elements of the system (hardware, software, and firmware) that implement mission-critical functions. It can include components that perform defensive functions that protect critical components, and components that have unobstructed access to critical components.

Criticality analysis includes the following iterative steps:

- Identify and group the mission capabilities the system will perform

- Identify the system's mission-critical functions based on mission capabilities, and assign criticality levels to those functions
- Map the mission-critical functions to the system architecture and identify the defined system components (hardware, software, and firmware) that implement those functions (i.e., components that are critical to the mission effectiveness of the system or an interfaced network)
- Allocate criticality levels to those components that have been defined
- Identify suppliers of critical components.

The identified functions and components are assigned levels of criticality commensurate with the consequence of their failure of the system's ability to perform its mission, as shown in Table 3.

Table 3: Protection Failure Criticality Levels

Criticality Level	Description
Level I Total Mission Failure	Failure that results in total compromise of mission capability
Level II Significant/Unacceptable Degradation	Failure that results in unacceptable compromise of mission capability or significant mission degradation
Level III Partial/Acceptable	Failure that results in partial compromise of mission capability or partial mission degradation
Level IV Negligible	Failure that results in little or no compromise of mission capability

The criticality analysis is an iterative process. The first iteration identifies the primary critical functions. The second iteration should be completed in conjunction with the vulnerability assessment to identify functions that have unobstructed access to the critical functions. These functions have the same level of criticality as the functions they access. The third iteration identifies components which enable the critical functions (e.g., if a critical function depends on a particular software library, that library is also critical).

When identifying critical functions, associated components, and their criticality levels, programs should consider the following:

- Microelectronics and software components are especially susceptible to malicious alteration throughout the program life cycle.
- Dependency analysis should be used to identify those functions on which critical functions depend, which themselves become critical functions (e.g., defensive functions and initialization functions).
- The program should identify all access points to protect unobstructed access to critical components (e.g., implement least-privilege restrictions).

When critical functions and components have been identified through the criticality analysis, the program may use the results along with the vulnerability assessment and threat assessment to determine the security risk.

The program office should perform a criticality analysis throughout the acquisition life cycle - at a minimum, before each systems engineering technical review.

CH 9–3.1.3.2 TSN Threat Analysis

All-source intelligence is available to the PM to understand the threats to the system and the threats posed by specific suppliers. Multiple sources of intelligence can be used to feed into this analysis.

One specific source for supplier threat information is DIA's DoD Supply Chain Risk Management (SCRM) Threat Analysis Center (TAC). DoD has designated the DIA to be the DoD enterprise focal point for threat assessments needed by the PM to inform and assess supplier risks.

DIA supplier threat assessments provide threat characterization of the identified suppliers to inform risk-mitigation activities. The PM and the engineering team should use these threats assessments to assist in developing appropriate mitigations for supply chain risks. TAC requests should be submitted for all Level I and Level II critical functions and components, as identified by a criticality analysis. At a minimum, a list of suppliers of critical components should be created. TAC requests may be submitted as soon as sources of critical functions and components are identified.

The PM should request threat analysis of supply chain risk through their respective DoD Component TSN Focal Points. For the policy and procedures regarding the request, receipts, and handling of TAC reports, refer to DoDI O-5240.24. It is expected that the number of supplier threat assessment requests will grow as the criticality analysis becomes more specific and the system architecture and boundaries are more fully specified. As a result, programs should expect to submit a greater number of TAC requests between Milestones B and C (i.e., Preliminary Design Review [PDR] and Critical Design Review [CDR]).

In addition, the Technology Targeting Risk Assessment (TTRA) is a MS A requirement for all ACAT programs. For further information, refer to DAG chapter 7, section 4.3.2.

In the absence of threat information, a program should assume a medium threat for Level I and Level II critical components, in order to avoid missing an opportunity for implementing cost-effective protection measures. If a threat is not assumed for critical components, and the threat report is returned indicating a high threat, the cost to mitigate the risk posed by the threat may be prohibitive.

CH 9–3.1.3.3 TSN Vulnerability Assessment

Vulnerability is any weakness in system design, development, production, or operation that can be exploited by a threat to defeat the system's mission objectives or significantly degrade its performance. Decisions about which vulnerabilities need to be addressed and which protection measures or mitigation approaches should be applied are based on an overall understanding of risks and program priorities. The search for vulnerabilities begins with these mission-critical functions and associated critical components. The vulnerability assessment is one step in the overall TSN Analysis process and interacts with other analyses in the following ways:

- Investigation of vulnerabilities may indicate the need to raise or at least reconsider the criticality levels of functions and components identified in earlier criticality analyses.
- Investigation of vulnerabilities may also identify additional threats, or opportunities for threats, that were not considered risks in earlier vulnerability assessments.
- Vulnerabilities inform the risk assessment and the protection measure risk cost-benefit trade-off.
- Discovery of a potentially malicious source from the threat assessment may warrant additional checks for vulnerabilities in other (less-critical) products procured from that source. Therefore, threat assessments can inform vulnerability assessments.

Potential malicious activities that could interfere with a system's operation should be considered throughout a system's design, development testing, production, and maintenance. Vulnerabilities identified early in a system's design can often be eliminated with simple design changes at lower cost than if implemented later. Vulnerabilities found later may require add-on protection measures or operating constraints that may be less effective and more expensive.

Common types of vulnerabilities that can be identified by a review of system design and engineering processes are:

- Access paths within the supply chain that allow threats to introduce components that could cause the system to fail at some later time (components here include hardware, software, and firmware)
- Access paths that allow threats to trigger a component malfunction or failure at a time of their choosing
- Existence of malicious code, counterfeit hardware, or other evidence of non-genuine information and communications technology (ICT)
- Vulnerabilities within the development environment and development processes.

The supply chain here includes any point in a system's design, engineering and manufacturing development, production, configuration in the field, updates, and maintenance. Access opportunities may be for extended or brief periods. The need to protect the supply chain extends the vulnerability assessment beyond the system to the program processes and tools used to obtain and maintain the hardware, software, and firmware components used in the system.

Six techniques and tools available for identifying vulnerabilities are:

- Milestone A vulnerability assessment questionnaire: A set of 'yes' or 'no' questions that a program answers to identify vulnerabilities in the Statement of Work (SOW) and system performance specification prior to RFP release.
- Vulnerability Database Assessment: Includes the Common Attack Pattern Enumeration and Classification database (CAPEC), used for the analysis of common destructive attack patterns; the Common Weakness Enumeration database (CWE), used to examine software architecture/design and source code for weaknesses; and the Common Vulnerability Enumeration database (CVE), used to identify software vulnerabilities that enable various types of attacks.
- Static analyzers: Identify software vulnerabilities and relate the vulnerabilities to the CWE and CVE entries. Some static and dynamic analyzer tools are available that will identify specific CVE- and CWE-listed vulnerabilities. These static and dynamic analyzers from different vendors apply different criteria and often find different vulnerabilities, meaning a program should determine which analyzer(s) is best suited for its specific program needs.
- Component diversity analysis: Examines the critical function designs for common components to assess the impact of malicious insertion to a component that is used to implement multiple critical functions or sub-functions.
- Fault Tree Analysis (FTA): FTA assumes a top-down analysis that uses Boolean logic to identify system failures. An important twist in applying FTA to SSE is that the potential sources of failures are malicious actors, not random device failures. Malicious actors invalidate many assumptions made about randomness and event independence in reliability analysis. FTA assumes hypothetical system or mission failures have occurred, and traces back through the system to determine the contributing component malfunctions or failures. For a vulnerability assessment, the possible access paths and opportunities that a threat would have to exercise to introduce the vulnerability or trigger the failure should also be considered.
- Red team penetration testing: Red teams typically subject a system and the development environment under test to a series of attacks, simulating the tactics of an actual threat, to test access controls and software vulnerabilities.

Vulnerability assessment techniques are further described in the *Trusted Systems and Networks (TSN)* white paper found at the http://www.acq.osd.mil/se/initiatives/init_pp-sse.html website.

CH 9–3.1.3.4 TSN Risk Assessment

A program must perform a risk assessment (RA), at a minimum, for each Level I and Level II critical function or component identified in its criticality analysis. The criticality level generated through the criticality analysis is used to determine the risk consequence. The risk likelihood is based upon the results of the vulnerability assessment and threat assessment, or the knowledge or suspicion of threats within the supply chain and of potential vulnerabilities within supplied hardware, software, and firmware products. A simple way to translate multiple vulnerabilities into likelihood is to use an equal weighting of a number of common vulnerabilities to create vulnerability likelihood. A similar approach is used to combine multiple threats into threat likelihood. Consider the difficulty in carrying out various cyber activities that are harmful, commensurate with threat information and potential vulnerabilities. Additional information on RAs is described in the *Trusted Systems and Networks (TSN) Analysis* white paper found at the http://www.acq.osd.mil/se/initiatives/init_pp-sse.html website.

CH 9–3.1.3.5 TSN Protection Measure Selection

TSN protection measures are cost-effective activities and attributes that manage risks to critical functions and components. They vary from process activities (e.g., using a blind buying strategy to obscure end use of a critical component) to design attributes and should be selected to mitigate a particular risk. For each protection measure being implemented, the program should identify someone responsible for its execution and a time- or event-phased plan for implementation.

A program typically selects protection measures after conducting a TSN risk assessment, although protection measures may be applied against other parts of the system, not just those identified as criticality Level I and Level II. There are "good hygiene" activities within each of the specialties described in Section 3.2 that may reduce TSN risk more broadly but may not occur as a direct result of a full TSN Analysis. The program should prepare a list of mitigations and protection measures to inform and provide options for analysis of trade-offs between cost and risk. No one set of mitigations is appropriate for all systems. The best set of mitigations and protection measures depends on a particular system--its environment, mission, and threats. Each mitigation or protection measure may have a phased implementation plan.

CH 9–3.2 SSE Specialties

This section provides an overview of the SSE specialties and how each contributes to program protection. The SSE specialties include anti-tamper, Risk Management Framework (RMF) for DoD IT, defense exportability features, hardware assurance/trusted microelectronics, software assurance, and supply chain risk management. Each specialty brings a unique perspective, methods, skills, and protections that contribute to an overall protection scheme.

In order to achieve the intended objectives of program protection, a program must select the most appropriate set of protection measures within program's cost, schedule, performance, and other constraints.

Beyond the SSE specialties described in this section, program protection also considers protections that are implemented through security specialties. The security specialties include all the traditional aspects of security, which are usually under the responsibility of the program's security manager. These include physical security, information security, industrial security, personnel security, and any unique security associated with certain DoD activities. These activities are typically driven by policies that aren't directly associated with program protection. However, when selecting protection measures from the SSE specialties, a program also considers the protections resulting from implementation of these traditional security specialties.

CH 9–3.2.1 Anti-Tamper

Anti-tamper (AT) is intended to deter, prevent, delay, or react to attempts to compromise CPI in order to impede adversary countermeasure development, unintended technology transfer, or alteration of a system due to reverse engineering. Consequently, AT is driven by the CPI that is identified via the process described in Section 3.1.2. Properly implemented AT should reduce the likelihood of CPI compromise resulting from reverse engineering attacks for systems in the hands of an adversary (i.e., those lost or left on the battlefield, or exported).

Upon the identification of CPI, program management offices should contact their DoD Component Office of Primary Responsibility (OPR) for AT for guidance. Programs should expect to conduct the activities in Table 4 below to support the identification and implementation of AT requirements and delivery of AT protections. Programs should repeat this analysis when events occur that trigger a reassessment of CPI protection measures (See section 3.1.2.3).

Table 4: AT Activities Throughout the Life Cycle

Life Cycle Event	Anti-Tamper Activities
ASR	• AT requirements for the preliminary system performance specification • AT implementation costs, vulnerabilities, and its impact on system performance or maintenance • Preliminary AT requirements incorporated into TMRR System Requirement Document SRD • AT requirements and design activities in TMRR SOW
SRR	• Updated AT requirements for the system performance specification
SFR	• Updated AT requirements addressed via the System Functional Baseline • Draft AT requirements incorporated into EMD SRD

Life Cycle Event	Anti-Tamper Activities
	• Address AT design and AT implementation activities in EMD SOW
PDR	• Updated AT requirements addressed via the Allocated Baseline
CDR	• Final AT requirements addressed via the Initial Product Baseline • AT implementation costs and residual vulnerabilities • AT Evaluation plan and execution • Final AT requirements incorporated into Production SRD • Final AT implementation activities in Production SOW
SVR/FCA, P&D and O&S Phases	• AT evaluation and associated evaluation results

To help meet these Systems Engineering and Technical Review objectives, programs must develop the AT products in Table 5 for review and concurrence by the DoD Executive Agent for AT (typically submitted as Appendix D of the PPP) or to the DoD Component OPR for Anti-Tamper (as delegated by the DoD Executive Agent for Anti-Tamper).

Table 5: Products and Timeline

AT Product:	AT Concept	Initial AT Plan	Final AT Plan	AT Evaluation Plan	AT Evaluation Report
Domestic Cases	Milestone A (105 days prior to)	PDR (60 days prior to)	CDR (60 days prior to)	CDR (60 days after)	Milestone C (60 days prior to)
Foreign Military Sales (FMS)	Letter of Offer and Acceptance Signature (105 days prior to)	PDR (60 days prior to) or 60 days post contract award	CDR (60 days prior to)	CDR (60 days after)	System Export (60 days prior to)
Direct Commercial Sales (DCS) and International Cooperative Program (IC)	Delivery of Sale Proposal or International Agreement Signature (105 days prior to)	PDR (60 days prior to)	CDR (60 days prior to)	CDR (60 days after)	System Export (60 days prior to)

Exemptions or exceptions for AT requirements must be documented, reviewed by the DoD Executive Agent for Anti-Tamper, and approved in the PPP by the MDA for the program.

The following AT reference documents are available via the DoD AT website or can be obtained through your DoD Component OPR for AT:

- AT Desk Reference: Provides programmatic guidance on AT Plan deliverables, evaluation points, schedules, and stakeholders
- AT Guidelines: Provides technical guidance on processes and methodologies for determining AT protection level requirements
- AT Security Classification Guide: Provides classification requirements for AT deliverables
- AT Plan Template: Provides the outline and guidance to assist with AT work product development

CH 9–3.2.2 Risk Management Framework for DoD IT

The Risk Management Framework for DoD IT replaces the DoD Information Assurance Certification and Accreditation Process (DIACAP) and manages the life cycle cybersecurity risk to DoD IT in accordance with the National Institute of Standards and Technology (NIST) Federal Information System and Organization information system policies, DoDI 8500.01 and DoDI 8510.01

Table 6 lists activities for PMs and SEs to incorporate the RMF for DoD IT activities into the system life cycle. For any system upgrades, a program may have to repeat analyses at all levels of detail described (ASR through SVR/FCA), at least informally, as the upgrade process progresses from requirements through production.

Table 6: RMF for DoD IT Activities Throughout the Life Cycle

Life Cycle Event	RMF for DoD IT Activities
ASR	• Categorize the information types • Select security control (SC) baseline • SC trace to the preliminary system performance specification • Incorporate SC requirements into the TMRR system performance specification and SOW
SRR	• Refine derived SC system-level requirements • Incorporate into specifications for the technical solution
SFR	• Tailor the security controls • Allocate tailored SC into system requirements • Ensure the updated tailored SC requirements are included in the system functional baseline • Incorporate CS functional requirements and verification methods into the initial Development RFP
PDR	• Tailor and Allocate SC requirements to the hardware and software design • Incorporate tailored SC requirements into system performance specification, SOW, and other contract documents for Development RFP • Align the security assessment plan with the T&E master plan to ensure inclusion of CS testing
CDR	• Tailor and Allocate SC requirements to the hardware and software design • Incorporate tailored SC requirements into system performance specification, SOW, and other contract documents for Development RFP • Align the security assessment plan with the T&E master plan to ensure inclusion of CS testing
SVR/FCA, P&D and O&S Phases	• Tailor and Allocate SC requirements to the hardware and software design • Incorporate tailored SC requirements into system performance specification, SOW, and other contract documents for Development RFP • Align the security assessment plan with the T&E master plan to ensure inclusion of CS testing

For more guidance on RMF, refer to:

- Department of the Air Force: Air Force Instruction 33-200
- Department of the Army: Guidance under development
- Department of the Navy: Secretary of the Navy Instruction 5239.3C

CH 9–3.2.3 Exportability Features

Defense exportability features include AT protection measures suitable for export and differential capability modifications, to include removal of technologies and/or capabilities that are prohibited for export. In support of program protection, defense exportability features are a means of protecting CPI in export configurations.

As early as possible, DoD program managers are encouraged to assess both: (1) the feasibility of designing and developing defense exportability features in initial designs, and, (2) the potential international demand for the system and expected benefits of foreign sales to the United States.

Early planning for defense exportability makes systems available to allies more rapidly, and at a lower cost per unit. This supports DoD's larger goal of enabling foreign sales in order to enhance coalition interoperability, decrease costs to DoD and international partners through economies of scale, and improve international competitiveness of U.S. defense systems.

For more information on defense exportability features and the associated DEF Pilot Program, refer to:

- DAG CH 1, Sections CH 1–3.4.3.7. and CH 1–4.2.8.
- USD(AT&L) Memorandum for DoD Component Acquisition Executives (CAEs), "Defense Exportability Features Policy Implementation Memorandum and Guidelines," dated April 9, 2015
- Director, International Cooperation, OUSD (AT&L) Memorandum for DoD CAEs, "Supplemental Guidance for Review and Submission of Industry Requests for an Adjusted DEF Pilot Program Cost-Sharing Portion," dated February 23, 2016.

CH 9–3.2.4 Hardware Assurance

Hardware Assurance (HwA) refers to the level of confidence that microelectronics (also known as microcircuits, semiconductors, and integrated circuits, including its embedded software and/or intellectual property) function as intended and are free of known vulnerabilities, either intentionally or unintentionally designed or inserted as part of the system's hardware and/or its embedded software and/or intellectual property, throughout the life cycle.

HwA protection measures reduce the likelihood an adversary will successfully: (1) exploit vulnerabilities built into microelectronics, their embedded software and/or intellectual property; (2) insert malicious logic in microelectronics during development, fabrication, and programming; or (3) introduce counterfeit microelectronics or unauthorized or tainted embedded software, intellectual property, or tools, into the supply chain –ultimately impacting the functionality of a microelectronics critical component.

The Program Management Office's TSN Analysis should identify if any of the following microelectronic types will be used in its program:

- Application-specific integrated circuits (ASICs) designed for a particular DoD end use
- Government-off-the-shelf (GOTS) components, designed for general military applications such as radiation hardened components or general purpose applications,
- Commercial-off-the-shelf (COTS) components, to include programmable logic devices (PLDs), field-programmable gate arrays (FPGAs), memory, and microprocessors, as well as analog to digital (A/D) and digital to analog (D/A) converters—this includes subassemblies such as cards, as well as fully assembled components. For example, FPGAs are COTS components, and the intellectual property used to program them are often COTS components as well. The intellectual property that is used can also be GOTS or custom developed.

Each type of microelectronics has a corresponding set of HwA protection measures that can be applied.

ASICs with a DoD-military end use must be acquired from a Defense Microelectronics Activity (DMEA)-accredited supplier. To ensure a trusted process flow, the PM should include a requirement in the solicitation, which directs the use of a DMEA-accredited Trusted Supplier as well as a fully trusted flow that flows down to the Trusted Supplier's subcontracted services.

Additionally, for ASICs and GOTS, the PM, during source selection, should require that the Original Component Manufacturer (OCM) has a process for independent verification, validation, and protection of intellectual property at each phase of the design process. Opportunities to insert malicious functionality start in the design process. To guard against unintentional defects as well as malicious acts during design and fabrication, the prudent OCM will conduct inspections, tests, and independent peer reviews. Beyond that, independent verification and validation options can be pursued based on perceived residual risk. The Joint Federation Assurance Center (JFAC) can advise programs on available options to ensure hardware.

COTS microelectronics, when DoD end use is apparent, should be handled by security cleared personnel and in cleared facilities as they move through the supply chain, especially where the printed circuit board population occurs and where FPGA or other COTS microelectronics programming and software assurance are performed. The use of security keys and verification of FPGA hardware and programming are also risk mitigations for avoiding malicious reprogramming. The program office should consult with the JFAC to determine if the JFAC has assessed the COTS microelectronics that are critical components of the system, as well as any embedded software or intellectual property used for their programming. If no previous assessment has been performed, the program office should determine if the JFAC recommends that the COTS microelectronics be assessed based on use within the system. If available, program offices should consider procuring their critical components that are COTS microelectronics from the Defense Logistics Agency's Qualified Manufacturers List (QML) or Qualified Supplier List of Distributors (QSLD). For all other COTS microelectronics, programs should use OCMs or their authorized distributors to the greatest extent possible.

When practical, the SOW should include the selective use of testing techniques to test for malicious functionality. It should also require the contractor to use its configuration management, parts management, and purchasing systems to manage their sourcing decisions and custody controls for microelectronics to reduce the likelihood of them being targeted for malicious attack.

The system's design and its critical functions and components are mapped during Criticality Analysis to the contractor Bills of Material (BOM) for the system.

The contractor and component suppliers use configuration and parts management processes and purchasing systems to establish and control product attributes and the technical baseline. These processes, in combination with the critical components identified on the BOM, provide the PM with a disciplined way of coordinating Supply Chain Risk Management (SCRM) considerations, to include HwA, during microcircuit selection, acquisition, and, later on, sustainment. They also facilitate the monitoring of the supply chain for possible product or source changes requiring the reassessment of HwA risk and convey special sourcing and handling considerations, e.g., chain of custody recording and bonded storage, for critical components to the logistics and purchasing communities.

Table 7 provides an overview of HwA life-cycle activities. Used in concert with Table 9, it provides a phased list of activities/products for PMs and SEs to manage microelectronic vulnerabilities, implement procurement process activities and constraints, and systematically establish requirements to increase hardware assurance. In the Production and Deployment phase and in the Operations and Support phases, it is expected that the analysis will be updated periodically to the level of detail of the Product Baseline (the same level of detail described in the column of the table labeled 'SVR/FCA, P&D and O&S Phases'). For any system upgrades, a program may have to repeat analyses at all levels of detail described (ASR through SVR/FCA), at least informally, as the upgrade process progresses from requirements through production.

Table 7: Hardware Assurance Activities Throughout the Life Cycle

Life Cycle Event	Hardware Assurance Activities
ASR	<ul><li>Identify notional critical functions to be implemented with microelectronics</li><li>Establish notional HwA protection measures</li><li>Incorporate HwA protections / acceptance criteria in the SOW</li><li>Establish microelectronics component manufacturer and distributor qualification criteria and/or sources e.g., Trusted Supplier, QML, QSLD, OCM, etc.</li></ul>
SRR	<ul><li>Ensure sources qualifications meet microelectronics criteria</li><li>For microelectronics purchases, establish HwA-related procurement practices e.g., life time buys, secured storage, selective testing of parts, etc., and criteria for manufacturers as well as the intellectual property, tools, etc., that are required to program critical components</li></ul>
SFR	<ul><li>Identify all microelectronic critical components as well as the embedded software, intellectual property, tools, etc. used to program them</li></ul>

Life Cycle Event	Hardware Assurance Activities
	• Select protection measures to include selective testing, vetting of intellectual property and tools • Update SOW for EMD phase with critical microelectronics supplier and verification and validation acceptance criteria
PDR	• Confirm use of DMEA-accredited Trusted Suppliers and trusted service flow for ASICs designed for DoD custom-end use • Confirm use of Defense Logistics Agency DLA, QML, Original Equipment Manufacturer OEM, or authorized distributor as appropriate for COTS and GOTS components • Confirm plan for use of life-time buys, secure storage and handling, and selective testing for parts where practicable; particularly for critical components • Ensure anti-counterfeit procedures, inspections, and traceability in place • Identify all microelectronic critical components as well as the embedded software, IP, tools, etc., used to program them • Confirm and revise protection measures, to include selective testing, vetting of IP and tools, etc., to be used as needed
CDR	• Update list of microelectronic critical components, to include the embedded software, Intellectual Property (IP), tools, etc., used to program them • Revise protection measures as needed • Initiate selective testing for malicious insertions where practicable, to included vetting and V&V of embedded software, IP, and tools
SVR/FCA, P&D and O&S Phases	• Update list of microelectronics critical components • Revise protection measures as needed • Continue selective testing for malicious insertions

CH 9–3.2.5 Software Assurance

Software assurance (SwA) is the level of confidence that software functions as intended and is free of known vulnerabilities, either intentionally or unintentionally designed or inserted as part of the software, throughout the life cycle Public Law 112-239-Jan 2013 see Section 933.

Malicious code and coding defects make systems vulnerable to attacks that may cause software to fail and thus pose a significant risk to DoD warfighting missions and national security interests. These vulnerabilities in software may be difficult and even impossible to detect; adversaries actively seek to identify and use these vulnerabilities as a means of attack. Adversaries may: (1) exploit vulnerabilities inadvertently built into software; (2) exploit flaws in the architecture and design that render the system more vulnerable; (3) insert malicious logic during development, test, and operation: or (4) introduce malicious inserts into the software supply chain. Any software, most importantly those that perform mission critical functions, can be targeted.

DoD systems incorporate an extensive amount of software; therefore, defense programs must conduct early planning to integrate software assurance protection measures to counter adversarial threats that may target that software. Of particular interest are software assurance protection measures:

- Undertaken during development, integration, and test
- Designed to mitigate attacks against the operational system (the fielded system)
- Address threats to the development environment.

A plan and statement of requirements for software assurance should be developed for the program early in the acquisition life cycle, and incorporate these requirements into the request for proposal (RFP) at each milestone. That plan should then be used by the program to track and measure SwA activities throughout the acquisition life cycle. The progress toward achieving the plan should be measured by actual accomplishments/results that are reported at each of the Systems Engineering Technical Reviews and recorded as part of the PPP.

Table 8 illustrates a sequence of acquisition activities across the life cycle for SwA. In the Production and Deployment phase, and the Operations and Support phase, it is expected that the analysis will be updated periodically to the level of detail of the Product Baseline (the same level of detail described in the column of the table labeled 'SVR/FCA, P&D and O&S Phases'). For any system upgrades, a program may have to repeat analyses at all levels of detail described (ASR through SVR/FCA), at least informally, as the upgrade process progresses from requirements through production. The SwA activities outlined in this table should be tailored to the program's specific characteristics and needs. For example, some programs may use agile and rapid development models, while other programs are structured around waterfall milestone technical/gate reviews. Automated software vulnerability analysis tools and remediation techniques should be incorporated throughout the life cycle, as required in DoDI 5000.02.

Table 8: Software Assurance Activities Throughout the Life Cycle

Life Cycle Event	Software Assurance Activities
ASR	• Identify SwA roles and responsibilities needs for the program • Contribute to selection of secure design and coding standards for the program • Identify critical functions that use software • Identify SwA activities across the system life cycle • Establish requirements to mitigate software vulnerabilities, defects, or failures based on mission risks • Incorporate SwA requirements into solicitations • Plan for SwA training and education • Develop and document an understanding of how your system may be attacked via software (i.e., attack patterns) • Plan for static analysis and other automated verification procedures and/or identify SwA service providers to assist with SwA services and when they will be performed (i.e. JFAC portal for more information)
SRR	• Select automated tools for design, vulnerability scan/analysis, etc. • Determine security requirements for programming languages, architectures, development environment, and operational environment • Develop plan for addressing SwA in legacy code • Establish assurance requirements for software to deter, detect, react, and recover from faults and attacks • Perform initial SwA reviews and inspections, and establish tracking processes for completion of assurance requirements
SFR	• Assess system requirements for inclusion of SwA • Establish baseline architecture and review for weaknesses (CWEs) and susceptibility to attack (CAPEC); refine potential attack surfaces and mission impacts
PDR	• Review architecture and design against secure design principles, which include system element isolation, least-common mechanism, least privilege, fault isolation, input checking, and validation • Determine if initial SwA Reviews and Inspections received from assurance testing activities are documented • Confirm that SwA requirements are mapped to module test cases and to the final acceptance test cases • Establish automated regression testing procedures and tools as a core process

Life Cycle Event	Software Assurance Activities
CDR	• Enforce secure coding practices through Code Inspection augmented by automated Static Analysis Tools
	• Detect vulnerabilities, weaknesses, and defects in the software; prioritize; and remediate
	• Assure chain-of-custody from development through sustainment for any known vulnerabilities and weaknesses remaining and mitigations planned
	• Assure hash checking for delivered products
	• Establish processes for timely remediation of known vulnerabilities (e.g., CVEs) in fielded COTS components
	• Ensure planned SwA testing provides variation in testing parameters, e.g., through application of Test Coverage Analyzers
	• Ensure program critical function software and Critical Components receive rigorous test coverage
SVR/FCA, P&D and O&S Phases	• Verify test resources and test cases, test scenarios and test data
	• Continue to enforce secure design and coding practices through inspections and automated scans for vulnerabilities and weaknesses
	• Maintain automated code vulnerability scans, reporting, prioritization, and execute defect remediation plans
	• Maintain and enhance automated regression tests and employ Test Coverage Analyzers to increase test coverage
	• Conduct periodic penetration tests using the enhanced automated test coverage
	• Monitor evolving threats and attacks, respond to incidents and defects, identify and fix vulnerabilities, and incorporate SwA enhancing upgrades. PMO should provide plan for updates, replacements, maintenance, or disposal of CPI, critical components, and critical functions software
	• Ensure chain-of-custody across development, from development to sustainment, and during sustainment for the record of weaknesses and vulnerabilities remaining and mitigations planned

Additional references and resources for developing a SwA strategy for DoD systems and technologies include:

- Joint Federated Assurance Center (JFAC), April 2016: The JFAC website, https://jfac.army.mil contains a growing body of knowledge, service-providing activities, tools, contracts, and help supporting the Department's use of SwA (DoD CAC required).
- State of the Art Resource (SOAR) for Software Vulnerability Detection, Test, and Evaluation, July 2014: Discusses families of tools available for use in the implementation of SwA across the life cycle.
- Software State of the Art Matrix, July 2014: Outlines the intended uses of various families of tools and the vulnerabilities they detect.
- DoD SwA Countermeasures White Paper, March 2014: The purpose of the software assurance protection measures section of the Program Protection Plan (PPP) is to help programs develop a plan and statement of requirements for SwA early in the acquisition life cycle and to incorporate the requirements into the request for proposals.
- Defense Information Agency (DISA) Security Technical Implementation Guides (STIGs), May 2015: The STIGs contain technical guidance to "lock down" information systems/software that might otherwise be vulnerable to malicious attack.
- Open Web Application Security Project (OWASP): The OWASP is an open community dedicated to enabling organizations to conceive, develop, acquire, operate, and maintain trustworthy applications.

- Build Security In Security Model (BSIMM), 2015: The BSIMM is designed to help you understand, measure, and plan a software security initiative.
- Common Weaknesses and Enumeration (CWE) Portal, A community-developed dictionary of software weaknesses and types. (CVE, CAPEC)
- DoD Risk, Issue, and Opportunity Management Guide for Defense Acquisition Programs, June 2015

CH 9–3.2.6 Supply Chain Risk Management

DoD systems and networks rely extensively on commercial, globally interconnected, and sourced components, which, while providing numerous benefits, also create opportunities for adversaries to intentionally affect mission-critical components while they are in the supply chain. Supply Chain Risk Management (SCRM) is a means for understanding and managing these supplier risks, and for identifying practices that reduce the risk of malicious or subversive exploitation of mission-critical components intended to affect component performance, as well as the risks posed by inherent vulnerabilities in the supply chain.

To effectively manage supply chain risks, programs should develop a set of SCRM practices and protection measures to minimize intentional malicious activities as well as to detect and respond to supply chain attacks. These practices and protections are procurement activities as well as HwA and SwA activities for critical components in the system.

PMs should implement practices and protection measures to the contractor in the solicitation through requirements in the Statement of Work (SOW) – during every phase of the lifecycle. Example protection measures include use of secure shipping practices, limiting component access to cleared personnel, and hiding the intended end use of the component.

Table 9 provides activities for PMs and SEs to assess supply chain vulnerabilities and implement processes to increase the security of the supply chain. In the Production and Deployment and in the Operations and Support phases, it is expected that the analysis will be updated periodically to the level of detail of the Product Baseline (the same level of detail described in the column of the table labeled 'SVR/FCA, P&D and O&S Phases'). For any system upgrades, a program may have to repeat analyses at all levels of detail described (ASR through SVR/FCA), at least informally, as the upgrade process progresses from requirements through production.

Table 9: SCRM Activities Throughout the Life Cycle

Life Cycle Event	SCRM Activities
ASR	• Identify supply chain threat mitigation practices for system critical functions • Incorporate SCRM practices into the SOW
SRR	• Refine supply chain practices • Update supply chain vulnerabilities • Update SCRM practices within the SOW • Update and elaborate System SCRM requirements
SFR	• Identify SCRM requirements for identified critical functions. • Include SCRM-related design requirements into system functional baseline
PDR	• Identify SCRM requirements for specific components implementing critical functions • Incorporate SCRM process and system requirements into system performance specification, SOW, and other contract documents for Development RFP
CDR	• Reassess supply chain vulnerabilities

Life Cycle Event	SCRM Activities
	• Update SCRM requirements for components based on the maturation of the system design
	• Update system performance specification and relevant documents for future contract releases to reflect updated SCRM requirements
SVR/FCA, P&D and O&S Phases	• Analyze component changes and assess supply chain risks associated with any tech refreshes
	• Update SCRM-related procurement, process, and system requirements in necessary contract documents

For more guidance on SCRM practices, see NIST Special Publication 800-161, Supply Chain Risk Management Practices for Federal Information Systems and Organizations.

CH 9–3.3 Engineering Design Activities

The program protection analyses and effort within each SSE specialty provide the requisite knowledge for identifying risks and selecting protections. These analyses have to be translated into an effective set of engineering requirements and reflected in the design. One way of ensuring that security is properly incorporated into the system is through secure design principles, as discussed in Section 3.3.1. Additionally, decisions related to protection-measure selection should be driven by trade-off analyses (Section 3.3.2), just as it is for any other design considerations.

CH 9–3.3.1 Secure Design Principles

Sufficiently mitigating program protection related risks is more successful and cost-effective if security is thoughtfully considered throughout the design process. One means of ensuring this is adhering to a set of secure design principles. As a design consideration, system security engineering's best practices include ensuring the system architecture and design address how the system:

- Manages access to, and use of the system and system resources
- Is configured to minimize exposure of vulnerabilities that could impact the mission, including techniques such as design choice, component choice, security technical implementation guides, and patch management in the development environment (including integration and T&E), in production, and throughout sustainment;
- Is structured to protect and preserve system functions or resources, e.g., through segmentation, separation, isolation, or partitioning;
- Monitors, detects, and responds to security anomalies;
- Maintains priority system functions under adverse conditions;
- Interfaces with DoD Information Network or other external security services.

CH 9–3.3.2 SSE Trade-off Analyses

Program protection provides the means for analyzing and integrating the protections offered by each system security engineering (SSE) specialty (see Section 3.2 for more on SSE specialties) to determine the most appropriate set of protection measures within the given constraints.

The typical method used for performing this analysis and integration is trade-off analyses. Trade-off analysis can help engineers make tough choices among competing system requirements in order to design an end solution within the constraints of cost, schedule, and performance while still maintaining an acceptable level of risk.

There are two levels of trade-off analyses that include system security (as shown in Figure 4):

- At the SSE-level, the system security engineer performs trade-off analyses to integrate the proposed protection measures from each SSE specialty into a single set of protection measures that most cost-effectively addresses the risks identified through program protection. This set becomes the SSE input to the SE's analysis.

- At the system-level, the SE performs trade-off analyses to balance overall system performance, system attributes/design considerations (which includes SSE as one consideration), cost, and schedule.

Figure 4: SSE Trade-off Analysis

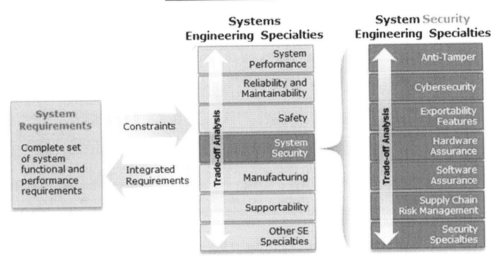

There may be multiple iterations of these analyses, as the initial SSE input (or portions of it) to the SE's analysis may be deemed unacceptable. This places a new constraint on the system security engineer, and means that the SSE-level analysis must be adjusted for this new constraint. This integration occurs regularly across the life cycle, as protection measures decisions will be affected as the design matures.

CH 9–3.4 SSE Activities in the Life Cycle

SSE activities analyze the threats, vulnerabilities, risks, and risk mitigations to CPI, mission-critical functions and critical components, and program and system information, with the results of these activities documented in the Program Protection Plan. The level of detail expected is commensurate with the level of the system specification, design, and implementation.

- Section 3.4.1 provides an overview of life-cycle expectations for program protection and system security engineering (SSE).
- Section 3.4.2 provides overviews of Program Protection and SSE expectations for each of the phases leading up to a major program Milestone. This security-specific material builds on the systems engineering activities, processes, input/output, and expectations described in DAG CH 3, Sections 3.2.1 to 3.2.6.
- Section 3.4.3 focuses on specific SSE objectives that should be met at technical reviews and audits, in which the protections are applicable.

CH 9–3.4.1 Life Cycle Expectations

The Program Protection Plan (PPP) is a living document, required at Milestones A, B, C, the Development RFP Decision Point, and the Full-Rate Production Decision Review or Full Deployment Decision Review as described in DoDI 5000.02 It is a best practice to update the PPP after any contract award to reflect the contractor's approved technical approach, before export decisions, through operations and sustainment; and to report progress at each technical review event.

Key SSE criteria can be specified for each of the phases leading up to a major program milestone, and it is important to establish these criteria across the full life cycle in order to build security into the system. Life cycle considerations, in general, include the following:

- Iteratively perform program protection analyses described in Sections 3.1 through 3.3 to assess and manage system and program security risks.
    - Determine mitigation approaches to address process vulnerabilities and design weaknesses.
    - Identify and implement protection measures.
    - Perform cost/benefit trade-offs where necessary.
- Integrate security into requirements and SE processes.
    - Integrate security requirements into the evolving system designs and baselines.
    - Use secure design considerations to inform life cycle trade-space decisions.
- Incorporate security requirements, processes, and protection measures into each contract throughout the acquisition life cycle. This includes relevant content in statements of work and the system performance specification, as described in Section 4.2.
- Identify life cycle resources needed to ensure sustainability of protection measures in operations.

CH 9–3.4.2 Activities in Life Cycle Phases
Within each phase of the acquisition life cycle, program protection activities and outcomes are driven by the maturity of the system. As the system matures, program protection analyses are iteratively updated and support the development of Program Protection Plans for each milestone and the appropriate milestone decisions.

CH 9–3.4.2.1 Pre-Materiel Development Decision
Based on the technical maturity of the system, the focus of program protections to begin to identify system security risks is based on the range of candidate materiel solution approaches. This program protection information supports the Milestone Decision Authority's (MDA) decision to authorize entry into the acquisition life cycle and pursue a materiel solution. A program protection plan is not required for the Materiel Development Decision.

CH 9–3.4.2.2 Materiel Solution Analysis Phase
Based on the technical maturity of the system, the focus of the program protection plan is to describe and document the plan, repeatable processes and methodologies, and resources to identify and mitigate system security risks. This key program protection information supports the Milestone A decision by providing evidence that the program has adequately addressed system security risks, given the technical maturity point.

During this phase, the program is required to develop an MDA-approved PPP for the Milestone A decision, which meets the SSE objectives described in the Alternative Systems Review section, Section 3.4.3.1. Additionally, the program office should incorporate generic program protection language into system performance specification and Statement of Work (SOW) during the development of draft Request for Proposal (RFP) in support of Technology Maturity and Risk Reduction phase (see Section 4.2)

CH 9–3.4.2.3 Technology Maturation and Risk Reduction Phase
Based on the technical maturity of the system, the focus of the program protection plan is to describe and document the plan, repeatable processes and methodologies, analyses performed, and resources to identify and mitigate system security risks. This is key program protection information to support the Milestone B decision by providing evidence that the program has adequately addressed system security risks, given the technical maturity point.

During this phase, the program is required to develop an updated DoD Component-approved draft PPP for the Development RFP Release Decision Point that meets the SSE objectives described in the System Requirements Review section, Section 3.4.3.2, as well as the System Functional Review section, Section 3.4.3.3. The program is also required to develop an updated MDA-approved PPP for the Milestone B decision, which meets the SSE objectives described in the Preliminary Design Review (PDR) section, Section 3.4.3.4, even if the program did not conduct a formal system-level PDR prior to the milestone.

Additionally, the program office should incorporate program protection language into the system performance specification and SOW during development of the RFP in support of the Engineering and Manufacturing Development phase and Low Rate Initial Production (if applicable) (see Section 4.2)

CH 9–3.4.2.4 Engineering and Manufacturing Development Phase

Based on the technical maturity of the system, the focus of the program protection plan is to describe and document the plan, repeatable processes and methodologies, analyses performed, and resources to identify and mitigate system security risks. This key program protection information supports the Milestone C decision by providing evidence that the program has adequately addressed system security risks, given the technical maturity point.

During this phase, the program is required to develop an updated MDA-approved PPP for the Milestone C decision that meets the SSE objectives described in the Critical Design Review (CDR) section, Section 3.4.3.5, even if the program did not conduct a formal CDR. It is also required to develop a System Verification Review/Functional Configuration Audit section, Section 3.4.3.6. In addition to the PPP, other deliverables that require updated system security material include the SEP, TEMP, System Threat Assessment, and Risk Assessment. Intermediate products, such as the product requirements and architecture, should be delivered and maintained as part of the products of system development, so they can be used in later system maintenance. This helps provide the traceability to maintain the system's security.

Additionally, the program office should incorporate program protection language into the system performance specification and SOW during development of the RFP in support of the Production and Deployment phase (see Section 4.2)

CH 9–3.4.2.5 Production and Deployment Phase

Based on the technical maturity of the system, the focus of the program protection plan is to describe and document the plan, repeatable processes and methodologies, analyses performed, and resources to identify and mitigate system security risks. This is key program protection information to support the FRP or FDD decision by providing evidence that the program has adequately addressed system security risks given the technical maturity point.

During the Production and Deployment phase, the program is required to develop an updated PPP for the Full Rate Production Decision Review (FRP DR) or Full Deployment Decision Review (FD DR) that reflects the Physical Configuration Audit (PCA)-verified Product Baseline. This update to the PPP should include content to the level of detail provided in the Bill of Material (BOM) as well as the SSE objectives described in the Physical Configuration Audit section, Section 3.4.3.8. The PPP should describe plans to phase in any needed system security risk mitigation. Further updates to the PPP should be incorporated, based upon updated threat, vulnerability, and BOM changes prior to Initial Operational Capability (IOC) and Full Operational Capability (FOC).

Additionally, the program office should incorporate program protection language into the system performance specification and SOW during the development of the RFP in support of the FRP DR or FD DR (see Section 4.2)

CH 9–3.4.2.6 Operations and Support Phase

While the primary emphasis of program protection is on the design and acquisition phases of a system life cycle, sustainment considerations should be addressed for the protection profile to secure the system throughout operations. Repair depots, for example, should be aware of CPI, mission-critical functions and components, as well as program and system information on systems they are maintaining so that the depots can appropriately protect these items from compromise and unauthorized disclosure.

Sustainment planning and execution seamlessly span a system's entire life cycle, from Materiel Solution Analysis to disposal. Sustainment planning should be flexible, using a criticality analysis focus, and reflect an evolutionary approach; it should accommodate modifications, upgrades, and re-procurement. The sustainment plan should be a part of the program's Acquisition Strategy and integrated with other key program planning documents as appropriate (e.g. PPP and Life Cycle Sustainment Plan).

CH 9–3.4.3 Technical Review and Audits

To design for security, the program incorporates program protection planning and execution activities in systems engineering technical reviews and audits.

Systems Engineering technical reviews and audits provide a key Systems Engineering health and risk assessment tool that is discussed in detail in CH 3 Section 3.3.

The following subparagraphs provide system security engineering (SSE) criteria, recommended as systems engineering technical review and audit entrance/exit criteria, in order to assess and ensure that an appropriate level and discipline of SSE activities are conducted across the full system context.

CH 9–3.4.3.1 Alternative Systems Review

The objectives for the Alternative Systems Review (ASR) are defined in Table 10 (from Chapter [CH] 3, Table 12). For a full description of ASR responsibilities, inputs and outputs, see CH 3 Section 3.3.1.

Table 10: ASR Objective (From CH 3-3.1. Table 12)

DoD Acquisition Technical Review	Objective	Technical Maturity Point	Additional Information
Alternative Systems Review (ASR)	Recommendation that the preferred materiel solution can affordably meet user needs with acceptable risk	System parameters defined; balanced with cost, schedule, and risk	Initial system performance established and plan for further analyses supports Milestone A criteria

At the technical maturity point associated with the ASR a program should have accomplished the following SSE objectives:

- Completed initial identification of program information classification and marking requirements (more information available in DAG Section 3.2.1).
- Completed an initial assessment of potential classified information and an initial CPI Analysis.
- Completed an initial Trusted Systems and Networks (TSN) Analysis, including the following:
  - An initial criticality analysis, threat assessment, and vulnerability assessment, performed with a focus on malicious insertion to the level of detail commensurate with mission-level functional requirements
  - An initial risk assessment and set of risk mitigations (protection measures) based upon the criticality analysis, threat assessment, and vulnerability assessment; these assessments include a focus on supply chain risk management (SCRM) and software assurance.
- Identified an initial set of risk mitigations (protection measures) for CPI and critical functions and incorporated the mitigations into the system requirements and into the system processes (e.g., procurement, configuration management, design, maintenance, and sustainment)
- Established plans to protect processes, tools, information elements, data, potential CPI and critical functions.

CH 9–3.4.3.2 System Requirements Review

The objectives for the System Requirements Review (SRR) are defined in the Table 12. For a full description of SRR responsibilities, inputs and outputs, see CH 3 Section CH 3–3.3.2.

Table 11: SRR Objective (From CH3-3.1. Table 12)

DoD Acquisition Technical Review	Objective	Technical Maturity Point	Additional Information
System Requirements Review (SRR)	Recommendation to proceed into development with acceptable risk	Level of understanding of top-level system/ performance requirements is adequate to support further requirements analysis and design activities.	Government and contractor mutually understand system /performance requirements including: (1) the preferred materiel solution (including its support concept) from the Materiel Solution Analysis (MSA) phase; (2) plan for technology maturation; and (3) maturity of interdependent systems.

At the technical maturity point associated with the SRR, a program should have accomplished the following SSE objectives:

- Addressed plans to protect CPI, critical functions/components, processes, tools, information elements, and data as part of the system requirements, Statement of Work (SOW), and solicitation.
- Completed a CPI Analysis, including as a minimum:
  - Identification of CPI
  - An assessment of the risk of CPI compromise, loss, or alteration
  - Determination of risk mitigations (protection measures)
- Completed a Trusted Systems and Networks (TSN) Analysis, including all the steps of the SSE risk management process:
  - Updated the criticality analysis, threat assessment, and vulnerability assessment with a focus on malicious insertion to the level of detail commensurate with the system performance specification.
  - Updated the risk assessment, a set of risk mitigations (protection measures), and a trade-off analysis to determine which risk mitigations are to be implemented in the system requirements.
  - Implemented relevant SCRM key practices on critical microelectronic components identified during criticality analysis.
- Completed an integrated security risk assessment including the risk of information exposure, technology and CPI compromise, and supply chain risk management (includes HwA and SwA).
- Considered security requirements in the development of the system performance requirements and non-tailorable design requirements.

CH 9–3.4.3.3 System Functional Review
The objectives for the System Functional Review (SFR) are defined in Table 12. For a full description of SFR responsibilities, inputs and outputs, see CH 3 Section 3.3.3.

Table 12: SFR Objective (From CH3-3.1. Table 12)

DoD Acquisition Technical Review	Objective	Technical Maturity Point	Additional Information
System Functional Review (SFR)	Recommendation that functional baseline satisfies performance requirements and to begin preliminary design with acceptable risk.	Functional baseline established and under formal configuration control. System functions in the system performance specification decomposed and defined in specifications for lower	Functional requirements and verification methods support achievement of performance requirements. Acceptable technical risk of achieving

DoD Acquisition Technical Review	Objective	Technical Maturity Point	Additional Information
		level elements, that is, system segments and major subsystems.	allocated baseline. See Ch 3 Section 4.1.6 Configuration Management Process for a description of baselines.

At the technical maturity point associated with the SFR, a program should have accomplished the following SSE objectives:

- Addressed plans to protect CPI, critical functions/components, processes, tools, information elements, and data as part of the system requirements.
- Completed an updated CPI Analysis, including as a minimum:
  - o Identification of CPI
  - o An assessment of the risk of CPI compromise, loss, or alteration
  - o Determination of risk mitigations (protection measures)
- Completed an updated TSN Analysis, including all the steps of the TSN risk management process:
  - o Updated the criticality analysis, threat assessment, and vulnerability assessment with a focus on malicious insertion to the level of detail commensurate with the SFR system specification and design.
  - o Updated the risk assessment, a set of risk mitigations (protection measures) and a trade-off analysis to determine which risk mitigations are to be implemented in the system requirements and processes.
- Implemented relevant SCRM key practices on critical microelectronic components identified during criticality analysis.
- Identified an updated set of risk mitigations (protection measures) for CPI and critical functions and has incorporated them into the subsystem and component requirements and into the system processes (e.g., procurement, configuration management, design, maintenance, and sustainment).
- Traced system security requirements to lower-level elements for all risk mitigations, to include requirements for classified information elements and applicable security controls.
- Established secure design and coding standards.
- Established an inter-organizational agreement for suppliers to notify entities affected by supply chain compromises.

CH 9–3.4.3.4 Preliminary Design Review

The objectives for the Preliminary Design Review (PDR) are defined in Table 13. For a full description of PDR responsibilities, inputs and outputs, see CH 3 Section 3.3.4.

Table 13: PDR Objective (From CH3-3.1. Table 12)

DoD Acquisition Technical Review	Objective	Technical Maturity Point	Additional Information
Preliminary Design Review (PDR)	Recommendation that allocated baseline satisfies user requirements and developer ready to begin detailed design with acceptable risk.	Allocated baseline established such that design provides sufficient confidence to proceed with detailed design. Baseline also supports 10 USC 2366b certification, if applicable.	Preliminary design and basic system architecture support capability need and affordability goals and/or caps achievement. See Ch 3 Section 4.1.6 Configuration

DoD Acquisition Technical Review	Objective	Technical Maturity Point	Additional Information
			Management Process for a description of baselines.

At the technical maturity point associated with the PDR, a program should have accomplished the following SSE objectives:

- Addressed plans to protect CPI, critical functions/components, processes, tools, information elements, and data as part of the system requirements, SOW, and solicitation
- Completed an updated CPI Analysis, including as a minimum:
  - Identification of CPI
  - Assessment of the risk of CPI compromise, loss, or alteration
  - Determination of risk mitigations (protection measures)
- Completed an updated TSN Analysis, including all the steps of the SSE risk management process:
  - Updated the criticality analysis, threat assessment, and vulnerability assessment with a focus on malicious insertion to the level of detail commensurate with the PDR system specification and design.
  - Updated the risk assessment, a set of risk mitigations (protection measures), and a trade-off analysis to determine which risk mitigations are to be implemented in the system requirements and processes.
- Implemented relevant SCRM key practices on critical microelectronic components identified during criticality analysis.
- System security requirements (including all protection measures/mitigations) have been traced to lower-level elements in the preliminary design (hardware – verifiable component characteristics; software – computer software components (CSC); computer software units (CSU); and the required security controls).
- Incorporated secure design and coding standards.
- Identified an updated set of risk mitigations (protection measures) for CPI and critical functions and incorporated these into preliminary design.
- Verified that there is an inter-organizational agreement for suppliers to notify entities affected by supply chain compromises

CH 9–3.4.3.5 Critical Design Review
The objectives for the Critical Design Review (CDR) are defined in Table 14. For a full description of CDR responsibilities, inputs, and outputs, see CH 3 Section 3.3.5.

Table 14: CDR Objective (From CH3-3.1, Table 12)

DoD Acquisition Technical Review	Objective	Technical Maturity Point	Additional Information
Critical Design Review (CDR)	Recommendation to start fabricating, integrating, and testing test articles with acceptable risk.	Product design is stable. Initial product baseline established.	Initial product baseline established by the system detailed design documentation; affordability/should-cost goals confirmed. Government assumes control of initial product baseline as appropriate. See Ch 3 Section 4.1.6 Configuration Management Process for

DoD Acquisition Technical Review	Objective	Technical Maturity Point	Additional Information
			a description of baselines.

At the technical maturity point associated with the CDR, a program should have accomplished the following SSE objectives:

- All system security requirements traced among the Functional, Allocated, and the Initial Product Baseline are complete, consistent, and incorporate measures to protect CPI, mission-critical functions and critical components, processes, tools, information elements, and data.
- Completed an updated CPI Analysis.
- Completed an updated Trusted Systems and Networks (TSN) Analysis.
- Implemented relevant SCRM key practices on critical microelectronic components identified during criticality analysis.
- Completed an updated risk assessment that reflects system security risks and status and updated these in the program's Risk Register/Database, reviewed to include the risks identified in the RMF Security Assessment Report (SAR), where applicable.
- Updated the Cost Analysis Requirements Description (CARD) based on the system product baseline, which reflects system security-related components.
- Updated the program schedule and critical path drivers to reflect all system security events
- Reviewed security-related test criteria for completion status.
- Reviewed DT&E assessments of cybersecurity T&E status, where applicable.
- Reviewed a draft Security Assessment Plan for needed remediation actions as input to the Security Assessment report to achieve Authorization to Operate (ATO).

CH 9–3.4.3.6 System Verification Review/ Functional Configuration Audit

The objectives for the System Verification Review (SVR) are defined in Table 15. For a full description of SVR responsibilities, inputs, and outputs, see CH 3–3.3.6.

Table 15: SVR Objective (From CH 3-3.1. Table 12)

DoD Acquisition Technical Review	Objective	Technical Maturity Point	Additional Information
System Verification Review (SVR)/Functional Configuration Audit (FCA)	Recommendation that the system as tested has been verified (i.e., product baseline is compliant with the functional baseline) and is ready for validation (operational assessment) with acceptable risk.	System design verified to conform to functional baseline.	Actual system (which represents the production configuration) has been verified through required analysis, demonstration, examination, and/or testing. Synonymous with system-level Functional Configuration Audit (FCA). See Ch 3 Section 4.1.6 Configuration Management Process for a description of baselines.

At the technical maturity point associated with the SVR, a program should have accomplished the following SSE objectives:

- Completed an updated CPI Analysis.

- Completed an updated Trusted Systems and Networks (TSN) Analysis, including all the steps of the SSE risk management process based on the system as tested and associated documentation. Include other specialized analysis such as fault tree analysis (FTA) and AT to identify derived system architecture and behavior changes.
- Established review criteria to specifically examine functionality of program protection requirements implemented in the system as tested.
- Assigned that audit personnel fully reflect the security disciplines necessary to assess all program protection measures implemented in the system as tested.
- Ensured that the program's non-recurring SSE requirements are executable with the existing budget.
- Program protection risks are known and being appropriately managed to an acceptable level of risk and residual risks identified.
- Verified the system through required analysis, demonstration, and testing (including blue/red team and penetration testing where applicable) after fully implementing all protection measures with results that indicate readiness for operational test and evaluation success (operationally effective and suitable).
- Fully documented, funded, and staffed life cycle sustainment protection measures for CPI and its critical function/component, including but not limited to software and cybersecurity vulnerability management, incident response, SCRM, and AT protections.

CH 9–3.4.3.7 Production Readiness Review

The objectives for the Production Readiness Review (PRR) are defined in Table 16. For a full description of PRR responsibilities, inputs, and outputs, see CH 3–3.3.7.

Table 16: PRR Objective (From DAG CH3-3.1. Table 12)

DoD Acquisition Technical Review	Objective	Technical Maturity Point	Additional Information
Production Readiness Review (PRR)	Recommendation that production processes are mature enough to begin limited production with acceptable risk.	Design and manufacturing are ready to begin production.	Production engineering problems resolved and ready to enter production phase.

At the technical maturity point associated with the PRR, a program should ensure that the same set of objectives as described in the SVR/FCA is appropriately updated.

CH 9–3.4.3.8 Physical Configuration Audit

The objective for the Physical Configuration Audit (PCA) is defined in Table 17. For a full description of PCA responsibilities, inputs, and outputs, see CH 3–3.3.8.

Table 17: PCA Objective (From CH3-3.1. Table 12)

DoD Acquisition Technical Review	Objective	Technical Maturity Point	Additional Information
Physical Configuration Audit (PCA)	Recommendation to start full-rate production and/or full deployment with acceptable risk.	Product baseline established. Verifies the design and manufacturing documentation, following update of the product baseline to account for resolved OT&E issues, matches the physical configuration.	Confirmation that the system to be deployed matches the product baseline. Product configuration finalized and system meets user's needs. Conducted after OT&E issues are resolved. See Ch 3 Section 4.1.6

DoD Acquisition Technical Review	Objective	Technical Maturity Point	Additional Information
			Configuration Management Process for a description of baselines.

At the technical maturity point associated with the PCA, a program should have accomplished the following SSE objectives:

- Ensured that counterfeit/substandard hardware/software components for CPI and critical components are not incorporated into the final system
- Ensured that any assurance-specific audits have been completed and documented
- Ensured that any source code delivered is actually the source code used by the system (where it is claimed to be)
- Ensured that packaging includes relevant seals to verify authenticity and impede tampering.

CH 9–4. Additional Planning Considerations

As a systems engineering design consideration, the activities to execute system security engineering and program protection are closely coupled with the systems engineering efforts. As with systems engineering, there are links between program protection and other key aspects of defense acquisition. This Section provides information on how program protection informs or is informed by other aspects of defense acquisition. It also provides additional program protection considerations that are unique to specific acquisition models or system domains.

- Section 4.1 addresses how program protection is incorporated into solicitations and contracts.
- Section 4.2 discusses the complementary relationship between program protection and test and evaluation (T&E).
- Section 4.3 addresses the influence of program protection on lifecycle sustainment planning.
- Section 4.4 addresses how intelligence and counterintelligence activities support program protection decisions.
- Section 4.5 addresses the Joint Federated Assurance Center (JFAC) and the ways programs can utilize the JFAC as part of their program protection activities.

CH 9–4.1 Contracting for Program Protection

The Systems Engineering (SE) role in contracting is described in CH 3–2.7. As part of this comprehensive SE role, the system security engineer has a key role in ensuring that program protection-related requirements (i.e., features in the system design, methods and processes used to develop the system) are included in contracts and solicitations. The content of the most current Program Protection Plan (PPP) and related analysis is used to drive the content of the Request for Proposal (RFP).

The results of each analysis are used to create the system performance specification protection measure requirements and the SOW protection measure requirements for the RFP. It is a best practice to include these requirements in the program/project's initial RFP issued for the system and then provide updates for subsequent RFPs. In cases where the design is not yet defined, the program protection requirements will mostly be in the form of Statement of Work (SOW) tasks that require the contractor to perform program protection methods to determine the needed system protection features.

Contents to be incorporated into the RFP include:

- Requirements derived from protection measures need to be incorporated into the System Requirements Document (SRD) and the SOW.
- PPP analysis activities, performed in parallel with the contractor's design and development, need to be incorporated as contractor activities into the SOW.

- When program protection needs to be a factor in source selection, add the necessary program protection topics to Section L and the associated evaluation criteria to Section M of the RFP.

RFPs may be issued for each phase of the Acquisition Life Cycle. The SE and system security engineering (SSE) technical content of the RFP is aligned to the SE baselines established at the most recent SE technical review. The RFP for each phase is often developed during the preceding phase.

Section C: Description/Specification/Work Statement. The following is a list of the ways in which protection measures are incorporated into Section C of the RFP:

- Protection measures that specify what the system will do are added to the SRD in the form of system requirements.
- Protection measures that describe how the contractor will develop the system (i.e., supply chain protections or software development standards) are added to the SOW in the form of SOW statements.
- Protection measures that describe program protection analysis (CPI and TSN) to be performed during the contract to identify additional protection measures are also added to the SOW as SOW statements.
- Protection measures that require supporting documentation to be provided to the government become a Contract Data Requirements List (CDRL), with a Data Item Description (DID) to explain the expected content. (The CDRL and DID are included in Section J, Exhibit A.)

Section I: Contract Clauses. Include the relevant DFARS clauses in Section I of the RFP. One particular clause is DFARS 252.204-7012, Safeguarding Covered Defense Information and Cyber Incident Reporting, which requires that:

- DoD and its contractors and subcontractors protect unclassified covered defense information, which includes unclassified controlled technical information, residing on their unclassified information systems
- Contractors report cyber incidents (e.g., unauthorized access and disclosure, lost media, denial of service) that affect unclassified covered defense information resident on or transiting the contactor's information system.

Per DFARS Subpart 204.73, all DoD solicitations and contracts are to include DFARS 252.204-7012, which sets forth the reporting criteria and requirements for safeguarding certain types of unclassified information, collectively referred to in the clause as Covered Defense Information (CDI).

Section I may also include DFARS clause 252.246-7007 Contractor Counterfeit Electronic Part Detection and Avoidance System, which addresses contractor responsibilities for detecting and avoiding the use or inclusion of counterfeit electronic parts, the use of trusted suppliers, and the requirements for contractors to report counterfeit electronic parts and suspect counterfeit electronic parts.

This section may also include FAR 52.204-21 Basic Safeguarding of Covered Contractor Information Systems, which requires contractors to limit information system access to authorized users and to control information posted or processed on publicly accessible information systems.

This section may also include FAR Clause 52.204-2 for contracts handling classified information.

Section J: List of Documents, Exhibits, and Other Attachments. Section J will list the attachments for the RFP and Exhibit A (CDRLs) for the entire contract. In each CDRL, the government indicates the distribution statement with which the contractor's deliverable is to be marked. Specifically for system security, the National Industrial Security Program Operating Manual (NISPOM) requires the government to include DD Form 254 (included as an exhibit and listed in Section J: List of Attachments), which defines to the contractor (or subcontractor) the security requirements and classification guidance that are necessary to perform on a classified contract. DD Form 254 requires that the contractor:

- Protect all classified information to which they have access or custody. A contractor performing work within the confines of a federal installation should safeguard classified information according to the procedures of the host installation or agency.
- Appoint a U.S. citizen employee, who is cleared as part of the facility clearance to be the facility security officer (FSO). The FSO will supervise and direct security measures necessary for implementing the applicable requirements from this manual, and related federal requirements for classified information.

Section L: Instructions, Conditions, and Notices to Offerors. Section L may request descriptions of the offeror's approach to program protection or to a specific aspect of program protection. For example, the following statement will allow the government to assess each competitor's approach to program protection and factor it into the source selection:

- For level I and level II critical functions and components the offeror should describe the approach to implementing protection measures and secure designs.

Alternatively, a narrower focus may be used in order for the government to assess each offeror's approach more comprehensively for areas of particular concern (e.g., SwA). The offeror should describe their approach to software assurance. At a minimum, the contract should describe its approach to:

- Secure design and coding standards
- Secure design and code inspections
- Static analysis tools
- Attack definition, weaknesses, and vulnerabilities
- Penetration testing
- Security monitoring and response

A set of generic RFP language is contained in the white paper titled "Suggested Language to Incorporate System Security Engineering for Trusted Systems and Networks into Department of Defense Requests for Proposals."

CH 9–4.2 T&E for Program Protection

The results of program protection analyses, which are documented in the PPP, may generate requirements that should be addressed by T&E. T&E personnel, led by the chief developmental tester (or equivalent), use the PPP and other system artifacts (such as the system design, system performance specifications, or statement of work activities) as references for developing test plans and test resource and capability requirements, and other information relating to testing and evaluation of the system. This information should be detailed in the Test and Evaluation Master Plan (TEMP).

One key aspect of T&E documentation in this area is the Developmental Evaluation Framework. The Developmental Evaluation Framework has four major areas. One of these areas is titled Cybersecurity. The categories underneath the Cybersecurity area are flexible and can be defined in any way necessary to meet program needs.

The system security engineer and DT&E test lead cooperate throughout the Acquisition Life Cycle to refine requirements and test plans, beginning before Milestone A. The system security engineer provides input to the DT&E test lead as system requirements are defined. The DT&E test lead uses those requirements to define needed testing and resources. The PPP informs the DT&E test lead's understanding of system requirements, including critical functions, and components and software vulnerabilities. When developmental testing begins, the DT&E test lead provides the system security engineer with test results, which should be analyzed to determine if the products work as specified. Analysis may suggest the need to refine requirements or make engineering changes to improve program protection.

CH 9–4.3 Life-Cycle Sustainment Planning for Program Protection

Addressing the security of a program and system does not stop once development ends. The threat environment, vulnerabilities, supply chains, and other components are constantly changing, impacting the security risk to the warfighter. Although there is no requirement to develop a Program Protection Plan (PPP) after the FRP or FD Decision Review point, all PPPs up to that point should have included plans for maintaining and updating protection measures throughout the life cycle. It is also best practice for a program to maintain and update the PPP as necessary to account for changes in the program and system (e.g., changes to a supplier of a critical component) or changes to the operational/threat environment (e.g., new attack vectors or vulnerabilities that impact the program protection risks).

CH 9–4.4 Intelligence Support for Program Protection

Program protection processes and analyses rely on intelligence inputs to better understand adversary warfighting capabilities, technological maturity, and counterintelligence inputs for more-complete comprehension of:

- Threats to program information, mission-critical functions and components, and CPI, including foreign collection methods,
- Successful attacks (compromise or loss events) as well as unsuccessful attacks.

Programs should request and analyze intelligence and counterintelligence products/reports (see CH 7–4.1. and CH 7–4.3. for specifics on the products/reports) to inform:

- CPI, TSN, and Information Analysis – What measures are most effective against a perceived threat or actual threat (attacks)?
- CPI Analysis – What capabilities are above and beyond those of our adversaries? What capabilities have been compromised? Are there threats to facilities with CPI, and are these facilities adequately protecting CPI?
- Information Analysis – What information has been compromised and lost?

These products/reports should be requested throughout the acquisition life cycle in order to inform program protection analysis during each stage of system development and to capture the evolving threat (i.e., more-advanced attacks and new threats based on the changing system environment).

CH 9–4.4.1 Joint Acquisition Protection and Exploitation Cell

The Joint Acquisition Protection and Exploitation Cell (JAPEC) integrates and coordinates analyses regarding unclassified Controlled Technical Information (CTI) losses. The JAPEC enables increased efforts across the DoD to proactively mitigate future losses and exploit opportunities to deter, deny, and disrupt adversaries that may threaten US military advantage. Key responsibilities of the JAPEC from a program's perspective include:

- Integrating all-source information in order to improve protection of CTI, which is common across programs and capabilities, and provide scalable options for analyzing the increasing threat to technologies that reside in or transit the Defense contractor-owned and contractor-operated networks
- Facilitating the identification of CTI, which is common across programs and technologies
- Providing referrals to the Military Departments' Counterintelligence Organizations (MDCO) or other defense agencies providing CI support for incidents involving compromised CTI
- Best practices for CTI protection.

Programs will utilize the expertise of the JAPEC as part of analyses of any compromised controlled technical information. The JAPEC will assist in the analysis and provide recommendations to the PM to address risks associated with compromised CTI. These recommendations may include, but are not limited to, such suggestions as:

- Program adjustments, including accelerating alternative technologies
- Warfighting changes, such as updating tactics, techniques, and procedures
- Capability requirements adjustments to address a change in threat
- Education and training in threat or counterintelligence
- Increasing protective features (e.g., use of isolated networks or increased use of classification guidance).

CH 9–4.5 Joint Federated Assurance Center

The Joint Federated Assurance Center (JFAC) is a federation of DoD organizations that have a variety of software (SwA) and hardware assurance (HwA) capabilities to support programs.

The JFAC develops, maintains, and offers vulnerability detection, analysis, and remediation capabilities through a federation of organizations and facilities from the Military Departments, Defense Agencies, other DoD activities, and other federal departments, agencies, and activities. The JFAC also facilitates collaboration with Science and Technology (S&T) acquisition, Test and Evaluation (T&E), and sustainment efforts to ensure that assurance capabilities and investments are effectively planned, executed, and coordinated to support program office needs.

Program offices are encouraged to visit the JFAC Portal for more information and guidance on how the JFAC can assist your program(s). A DoD CAC is required to open.

Additional details on the JFAC organization's capabilities and responsibilities can be found in Deputy Secretary of Defense Policy Memorandum 15-001 "Joint Federated Assurance Center (JFAC) Charter," dated February 9, 2015.

CH 9–Version and Revision History

The table below tracks chapter changes. It indicates the current version number and date published, and provides a brief description of the content.

Version #	Revision Date	Reason
0	02/02/2017	Chapter 9 Initial Upload
1	05/31/2017	Edited Section 9-3.1.3.2

CH 10–1. Purpose

The Defense Acquisition Guidebook (DAG), Chapter 10, provides guidance for executing a proven, repeatable process and set of procedures that contribute to successful services acquisition based on the Seven Steps to the Service Acquisition Process included in Department of Defense Instruction (DoDI) 5000.74, Defense Acquisition of Services (DoDI 5000.74). It is highly recommended that readers familiarize themselves with the DoDI and its seven enclosures prior to reading this chapter.

CH 10–2. Background

Congress, under 10 USC 2330, required the Secretary of Defense to establish a management structure; develop and maintain policies, procedures, and best practices guidelines for acquisition planning; requirements development; and other aspects involved with the procurement of contract services. DoDI 5000.74, Defense Acquisition of Services, dated January 5, 2016, defines the Services Category (S-CAT) levels, policies, responsibilities, and procedures for acquiring services. It provides a repeatable requirements process that is designed to produce a successful services acquisition.

CH 10–2.1 What is a Service?
CH 10–2.1.1 Acquisition of Services

DoD broadly divides procurements into two categories – products and services.

- Products are tangible assets or hardware, wholly owned and, often, inventoried by the Department or a responsible component. A product can range from a pencil to an aircraft carrier.
- Services encompass all non-product procurements and involve the performance of specific activities in support of DoD missions. Most importantly, services are rendered without the Department assuming full ownership of the assets performing that support. Services, in some instances, can be harder to identify, because they may include "product-like" acquisitions such as hardware leased to support IT needs or the professional services of a consulting firm leveraging its knowledge to produce a report of model for the Department's use.

One major way to identify service acquisition requirements is via the product and service code (PSC) that is entered into Federal Procurement Data System – Next Generation (FPDS-NG). The PSC begins with a letter for the service category. For example, Category R is for Professional, Administrative, and Management Support Services, and distinguishes whether an acquisition is a service or not.

Information Technology (IT) Services: These include providing the operation, support, and maintenance of IT, including long-haul communications and commercial satellite communications services, and may include providing commercial or military unique IT equipment with the services. IT services also include any IT or operation of IT such as the National Security Systems which are required for daily work performance. This includes outsourced IT-based business processes, outsourced IT, and outsourced information functions sometimes referred to as Cloud services, Infrastructure-as-a-Service, Platform-as-a-Service, Software-as-a-Service, and other "as-a-Service" terms referenced in the National Institute of Standards and Technology Special Publication 800-145.

CH 10–2.1.2 Service Contract

A service contract is a contract for performance that directly engages the time and effort of a contractor whose primary purpose is to perform an identifiable task rather than to furnish an end item or supply. A service may be either a non-personal or personal contract. It can also cover services performed by either professional or nonprofessional personnel, whether on an individual or organizational basis. Some of the areas in which service requirements are found include the following:

- Maintenance, overhaul, repair, servicing, rehabilitation, salvage, modernization, or modification of supplies, systems, or equipment
- Routine recurring maintenance of real property
- Housekeeping and base services
- Advisory and assistance services (A&AS)
- Operation of government-owned equipment, facilities, and systems

- Communication services, including Information Technology services
- Architect-engineering
- Transportation and related services
- Research and development

CH 10–2.1.3 Portfolio Management

Portfolio management is the grouping of DoD services into core portfolio categories, with each category then managed to achieve optimal acquisition, supply, and demand solutions. Portfolio management also enables a framework for oversight by the OUSD(AT&L), coupled with decentralized execution by the DoD Components.

The Program Manager/Functional Service Manager (PM/FSM) should understand how the services portfolios map to the Product Service Codes (PSC). PSCs are used universally across the federal government within FPDS-NG. Choosing the appropriate PSC allows the portfolio managers to run reports in FPDS-NG to see approximately how much is being spent on services. See CH 10–3.2.1. of this chapter for additional PSC guidance. The DoD portfolio management structure includes nine services portfolio groups, illustrated in Figure 1.

Figure 1: Nine Services Portfolio Groups

CH 10–2.2 Roles and Responsibilities

The DoDI 5000.74 discusses the different players and their duties within services acquisitions. Table 1 highlights only those unique responsibilities associated with each role; for a complete list go to the DoDI under Enclosure 2 (DoDI 5000.74, Enc. 2) and 3 (DoDI 5000.74, Enc. 3).

Table 1: Services Acquisition Oversight Roles and Responsibilities

Role	Responsibilities
Office of the Under Secretary of Defense for Acquisition, Technology, and Logistics (OUSD(AT&L))	<ul><li>Serve as or designates the senior DoD decision authority</li><li>Serve as the senior DoD decision authority for any special interest acquisition</li><li>Delegate the decision authority to DoD Component heads or the heads of other appropriate oversight entities</li><li>Appoint DoD Functional Domain Experts (FDEs) as the DoD-level leads for each service portfolio group</li></ul>

Role	Responsibilities
Director, Defense Procurement and Acquisition Policy (DPAP)	• Serve as the staff-level lead for Services Acquisition • Coordinate with the FDE regarding the specific portfolio or portfolio group and with the Office of Small Business Programs (OSBP) • Coordinate with the DoD Chief Information Officer (CIO) on proposed acquisitions of IT services • DPAP Services Acquisition (SA) Directorate is responsible for implementing and overseeing the execution of the DoDI 5000.74 to all of the DoD Components including the Military Departments.
DoD Components	• Use management controls and business intelligence systems to establish oversight and sustain situational awareness • Ensure services acquisitions use performance-based requirements and identify and measure cost, schedule, and performance outcomes • Enhance services acquisition planning and coordination by using multifunctional teams
DoD Functional Domain Experts (FDEs)	• Designated by the USD(AT&L), who are assigned to one or more of seven of the nine portfolio groups • Provide strategic leadership of the domain to improve planning, execution, and collaboration to achieve greater efficiency and reduce costs • Ensure processes are in place to monitor post-award performance • Develop appropriate metrics to track cost and performance within the portfolio groups, reduce redundant business arrangements, identify trends, and develop year-to-year comparisons to improve the efficiency and effectiveness of contracted services • Identify opportunities for strategic sourcing across the services portfolio group or portfolio category

Table 2 highlights only those unique responsibilities associated with each role; for a complete list go to the DoDI under Enclosure 4 (DoDI 5000.74, Enc. 4) and 5 (DoDI 5000.74, Enc. 5). The acquisition authority chain of command runs upward from the Program Manager (PM) or Functional Service Manager (FSM) to the designated decision authority for the Service Category (S-CAT) and ends with the Service or Component Acquisition Executive. See Table 1 (Page 3) of the DoDI 5000.74 for the S-CAT decision authority threshold, USD(AT&L) Decision Authority Memorandum, and your agency's policy to find the decision authority for S-CAT II through V.

Table 2: Services Acquisition Management

Role	Responsibilities
Senior Service Managers (SSMs)	• Planning, strategic sourcing, execution, and management of acquisitions of contracted services • Identify, forecast, and track pending requirements, along with their designated decision authority, across the service categories • Develop processes to implement the Services Requirements Review Boards (SRRBs) • Review, develop, and use data and metrics to support strategic management decisions and documenting business trends and costs, as needed
Program Manager (PM)/ Functional Service Manager (FSM) (For additional PM responsibilities or guidance, go to Chapter 1 of this DAG)	• Lead the multifunctional team (MFT) through the Service Acquisition Process • Lead developing, coordinating, and resourcing the requirement and overseeing it throughout the acquisition process • Understand the costs related to the services that their respective component is acquiring and establish "should-cost" expectations • Ensure selecting the best source to meet mission needs and that an effective performance management process is in place to guarantee the effective and timely delivery of services and achievement of "should-cost" goals
Multifunctional Team (MFT)	• Participate in a services acquisition workshop (SAW) • Apply an accurate IGCE outlining discrete costs within the overall services requirement, coupled with market research • Consider costs of labor skill mix and categories, service levels, frequency of performance, and dictated quality levels when developing a requirement to meet mission needs

CH 10–3. Business Practice

The acquisition of services is based on the Seven Steps to the Service Acquisition Process as laid out in DoDI 5000.74 and the DAU Service Acquisition Mall (SAM). The steps are further broken down into three phases: Planning, Development, and Execution. The Service Acquisition Process is broken down in Figure 2, which can also be found at the DAU SAM website.

Figure 2: Seven Steps to Services Acquisition Process

CH 10–3.1 Plan

The planning phase includes steps one, two, and three of the seven-step process. During the planning phase, the PM/ FSM should lead and form the MFT and get leadership support, in accordance with agency procedures. The PM/ FSM should establish a baseline and analyze the current service strategies; identify problem areas and projected mission changes; and request the MFT and the requirements owner define their key performance outcomes for this requirement. The amount of work to be done is based on complexity and funding. Market research should be performed to assess current technology and business practices, competition and small business opportunities, existing and potential new sources providing the service, and to determine if commercial buying practices can be adapted.

CH 10–3.1.1 Step One – Form the Team

The PM/ FSM, as designated by the Decision Authority or designee, is the lead responsible for bringing together the appropriate cross functional individuals for the MFT. The team members will understand the requirement, understand how the requirement relates to the mission, and be able to put an executable strategy together in support of the mission. Although not inclusive, the following individuals should be MFT members:

- PM/ FSM

- Contracting Officer
- Finance/Budget Officer
- Procurement Analyst
- Legal Advisor

- Customer/Requirements Owner (this person may be the same as the PM/ FSM)
- Contracting Officer Representative
- Cost and Price Analyst
- Small Business Specialist
- Quality Assurance Specialist
- Any other stakeholders who have a vested interest in the requirement

MFT members will participate in a services acquisition workshop (SAW). The SAWs are considered to be a best practice resource for services acquisitions. SAWs are required in some situations, but it is a preferred workshop for services acquisitions. The primary objectives of the SAW are to:

- Understand the services acquisition process;
- Apply and use the Acquisition Requirements Roadmap Tool (ARRT) to define and refine service requirements in order to create an initial draft of the Performance Work Statement (PWS) and Quality Assurance Surveillance Plan (QASP); and
- Develop specific acquisition-related documents (i.e., team charter, project plan, stakeholder analysis, PWS, QASP and an acquisition approach.)

To request a SAW, the PM/ FSM can visit the Skill Development Center at the Service Acquisition Mall and click on "Request a Service Acquisition Workshop (SAW) or send an email to SAW@dau.mil.

For the team to be successful, the team will achieve the following outcomes:

- Find the right people, with the appropriate expertise and skill set, for the team;
- Identify senior leadership and stakeholders who are impacted by the outcomes to ensure their involvement and support;
- Develop a Communication Plan to keep stakeholders and others informed of the program's status and direction;
- Create a project library to maintain the knowledge base; and,
- Identify and plan for needed training as the team moves through this acquisition.

The Decision Authority or designee determines the need for a certified PM or FSM based on the risk or complexity of the acquisition. The MFT members will have the required certifications for their specialty and the complexity of experience needed to support the requirement. A certified PM or FSM is required for service requirements valued at $100 million or more. The FSMs are required to take DAU training courses based on the S-CAT level of their services acquisition. (Refer to Table 1 (Page 3) of the DoDI 5000.74.) In accordance with DoD policy, the PM, Contracting Officer, and the COR must meet the certification and/or training requirements based on the complexity of the requirement.

FSMs are vital to the effective management and execution of service requirements below $100 million. FSMs have in-depth knowledge of the requirement being considered for contractor support, and have at least two years of experience managing, supporting, or leading contractor or government performance of work of similar scope and nature as the proposed requirement. The FSMs are required to take DAU training courses based on the S-CAT level of their service acquisition. (Refer to Table 1 (Page 3) of the DoDI 5000.74.)

SAM has additional information on the process and provides templates that can be used for Step One of the Seven Step process.

CH 10–3.1.2 Step Two – Review Current Strategy

The MFT is responsible for assessing the health of the current service acquisition, if one exists. If this is a new service acquisition, move to Step Three and use the questions below to formulate the strategy. To accomplish this assessment, the MFT will interview the stakeholders and key customers and capture their concerns, priorities, and projected requirements which will impact how the acquisition is developed. Some questions for the MFT to consider are:

- Have the needs of the current acquisition been met?
- Are the requirements under the current awarded contract still valid?
- What risks have developed under the current acquisition?
- What risks are acceptable as status quo?
- Can improvements be achieved? If not, what is the maximum loss of service that is acceptable?
- What metrics will be tracked and reported?
- Are there challenges with the current performance? If so, what are they?
- What are the issues associated with resolving problems?
- What is the current small business strategy for the prime contracts and subcontracts?
- How will staying with the status quo affect the mission over time?
- How will the improvements affect the mission over time?
- How is performance captured, if not being captured via metrics?

Based on the stakeholders' consolidated input, the MFT categorizes the input into performance results (outcomes). The performance results are reviewed and validated by all stakeholders, including key customers, to ensure the mission needs have been captured accurately. The MFT addresses any gaps between the current performance and his or her understanding of what the stakeholders are asking. The MFT discusses the funding impact if desired results are significantly beyond current budget levels. The feedback obtained is vital to ensuring the actions taken in subsequent steps are aligned with stakeholder outcomes and results. Based on the feedback, the MFT refines the desired results the team has developed. The MFT validates the refined results with stakeholders to ensure the acquisition is moving in the right direction.

The MFT also reviews the current contract terms and conditions and ensures the most current regulatory and statutory requirements are applied to the new services acquisition contract. For IT services acquisition, the MFT shall be familiar with Enclosure 7 (CH 10–3.5.) of the DoDI 5000.74 and with DAG Chapter 6 of this guidebook.

Taking time to invest in the above pays large dividends later in the acquisition process. Prior to moving forward with a follow-on or new service acquisition, the PM/ FSM is required to obtain approval from the SRRB chair. According to statue, a SRRB approval is required for all services acquisition at or above $10 million. As directed by the DoD Components Decision Authority policies, a SRRB approval is required for all services acquisitions above the SAT but less than $10 million. (Refer to Section 4 for a more detailed description of the SRRB process.)

SAM has additional information on the process and provides templates that can be used for <u>Step Two of the Seven-Step process</u>.

CH 10–3.1.3 Step Three – Perform Market Research

The purpose of Step Three is to gather and analyze information about the capabilities within the market to satisfy the agency needs. This step is vital for accomplishing the next two steps, Define Requirements and Develop Acquisition Strategy. The requirements owner within the MFT is responsible for conducting the initial market research. Market Research is conducted in accordance with <u>Federal Acquisition Regulation (FAR) Part 10</u>. The purpose of conducting market research is to discover if the services required for an acquisition are available in the marketplace, how the market place is implementing the capabilities needed, and whether or not any existing contract vehicles are available to execute the requirement. The key outcomes of the market research document are:

- Identifying market trends that affect the requirement;
- Determining how other activities are acquiring services similar to the requirement;
- Identifying leverage you may have in the market
- Determining the extent of competition and small business opportunities
- Identifying whether this service can be obtained through commercial practices

The MFT captures the analysis in a market research report which will support the requirements packaging and acquisition strategy.

SAM has additional information on the process and provides templates that can be used for <u>Step Three of the Seven-Step process</u>.

CH 10–3.1.3.1 Conduct Market Research

Market research is conducted before:

- Developing new requirements documents.
- Soliciting any offers over the simplified acquisition threshold (SAT).
- Soliciting offers for acquisitions that could lead to a bundled contract (15 U.S.C. 644(e)(2)(A)).
- Awarding a task or delivery order under an indefinite-delivery-indefinite-quantity (ID/IQ) contract over the SAT (10 U.S.C 2377(c)).
- Soliciting offers for acquisitions that could lead to a consolidation of contract requirements.
- Issuing a solicitation with tiered evaluation of offers in accordance with <u>Defense Federal Acquisition Regulation Supplement (DFARS) Subpart 210.001</u>.

The <u>Market Research Report Guide for Improving the Tradecraft in Services Acquisition</u> provides guidance for conducting market research.

To determine and identify the scope and extent of additional research needed; consider the following:

- Information already in hand, including personal knowledge of the market from prior requirements and the findings of recent research on similar requirements)
- Interviewing the customer(s) about the current contract
- Identifying information deficiencies
- One-on-one Meetings with industry
- Submit a Request for Information(RFI) or Sources Sought to FedBizOps
- Plan to collect additional market information (i.e., when and how) during the acquisition planning, pre-solicitation, solicitation, and evaluation phases

CH 10–3.1.3.2 Analyze and Document Market Research

Once all data is collected, analyze the information received. Categorizing the information received is recommended, i.e., past performance, requirements, competition, etc. Identify the following during the analysis:

- How will the requirement align to the market?
- What are the opportunities for competition and/or small business considerations?
- Did your market research reveal any new emerging technologies?
- What market trends (supply/demand) did the market research reveal and how can the information leverage the trend through requirements building or negotiations?

After the analysis of the data is complete, the findings and proposed strategy for acquiring the services needed are documented. The document describing the results of the market research is a Market Research Report. The amount of detail in the report is dependent upon the complexity, criticality, and size of the acquisition. The team follows its agency's policy on how to complete the market research report. The Market Research Report Guide for Improving the Tradecraft in Services Acquisition has a sample Market Research Report to assist with writing and creating a report.

Market Research is not finalized until Step Four – Define Requirements. The information from the market research is used to formulate the requirements document.

CH 10–3.2 Develop

The development phase includes steps four and five of the seven-step process. Step Four is Define Requirement and Step Five is Develop Acquisition Strategy. At this point, the three steps in the Planning Phase are completed: Form the Team, Review the Current Strategy, and Perform Market Research, in accordance with DoDI 5000.74 and agency policies. The Development Phase uses information acquired during the Planning Phase to develop the requirements document, Step Four, and acquisition strategy, Step Five.

CH 10–3.2.1 Step Four – Define Requirements

Requirements definition is the most important and most difficult part of services acquisitions. A good quality requirements document makes procuring and managing the service easier. With a properly developed requirements document, the team determines:

- What is important about the service
- If an industry day or contractor one-on-one's are necessary
- How the Quality Assurance Surveillance Plan (QASP) will be developed
- Whether more than one Contracting Officer's Representative is required
- What is the best contract type to utilize

During this phase, the team, with the PM or FSM as the lead, may produce the following:

- A risk analysis
- Performance objectives and standards through the use of a requirements road map concept
- Methods and means of inspection
- The PWS, SOW, or SOO
- Preliminary QASP
- The independent government cost estimate
- Stakeholder consensus

The team determines the best North American Industry Classification System Code (NAICS) and the Product and Service Code (PSC). The NAICS and Size Standards are established by the Small Business Administration (SBA), which establishes small business size standards on an industry-by-industry basis.

The PSC indicates "what" products and services are being purchased by the Federal Government and each contract action is reported in the FPDS-NG. The code is chosen based on the predominant product or service that is being purchased. It is very important the most accurate PSC is chosen for services acquisitions. The PSC is the basis by which many legally-mandated and agency reports provide the necessary data to effect Government and mission decisions. DoD has a PSC Selection Tool to assist the team in choosing the appropriate code for the requirement. The tool uses DoD's taxonomy to divide the PSCs into portfolio groups. The tool webpage also provides PSC to Object Classification Code (OCC) crosswalk and provides recommended NAICS codes for many PSCs. Additional Guidelines and PSC Code descriptions are in the Federal Procurement Data System Product and Service Codes Manual

The document templates can be found in the DAU Service Acquisition Mall, Service Acquisition Process.

CH 10–3.2.1.1 Risk Analysis

Risk is a measure of future uncertainties in achieving successful program performance goals. Risk is associated with all aspects of a requirement. It includes identifying events that are reasonably predicted that may threaten a mission. Risk addresses the potential variation from the planned approach and its expected outcome. Risk analysis includes all risk events and their relationships to each other. The risk assessment consists of two components: (1) probability (or likelihood) of that risk occurring in the future; and, (2) the consequence (or impact) of that future occurrence. Risk management requires a top-level assessment of the impact on the requirement when all risk events are considered, including those at the lower levels.

The PM/ FSM focuses on the critical areas that may impact the requirement/program and thus impact the performance results. Risk events may be determined by examining each required performance element and process in terms of sources or areas of risk. These areas are generally grouped as cost, schedule, and performance, with the latter including technical risk. There could be significant consequences if early risk assessment isn't accomplished. The following are some typical risk areas:

- Business/Programmatic Risk
    - Scheduling issues that may impact success
    - Contractors performing inherently governmental functions or unauthorized personal services
    - Stakeholders engagement
- Technical Risk
    - Maturity and relevancy of technology
    - Personnel turnover
    - Procurement fraud
- Funding Risk
    - Are funds identified for which availability is reliant on pending events or approvals?
    - Have adequate funds been identified?
- Process Risk
    - Are new processes required to be implemented?
    - Will the best contractors have time to propose?
- Organizational Risk
    - Implementing change in an organization
    - Organizational conflicts of interest
- Risk Summary
    - Overview of the risk associated with implementing the initiative e.g., is there adequate service life remaining to justify this change?
- Additional Areas
    - Environmental impact
    - Security (i.e., government property, control and oversight of facility access, clearances, etc.)
    - Safety
    - Occupational Health

Identifying risk areas requires the MFT to consider relationships among all the risks and to identify potential areas of concern that would have otherwise been overlooked. This is a continuous process, which examines each identified risk (that may change as circumstances change), isolates the cause, determines the effects, and then determines the appropriate risk mitigation plan. The MFT may consider requesting a risk mitigation plan be submitted as part of the offeror's proposal if there is a risk that needs to be addressed immediately. Figure 3 can assist with identifying what risks are considered high risk and need to be addressed within the offeror's proposal.

Additional guidance about Risk can be found in the Risk Management Guide, Balancing Incentives and Risks in Performance-Based Contracts and a DAU continuous learning course entitled CLM 017 Risk Management.

CH 10–3.2.1.2 Requirements Road Map

Figure 3: Risk Analysis Model – Tying It Together

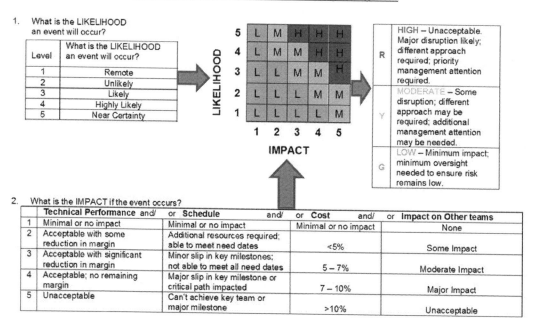

Requirements analysis is a systematic review of a requirement, given the data, information, and research gathered during the Planning Phase. This analysis is the basis for establishing high-level objectives, developing performance tasks and standards, writing the performance work statement, and developing the QASP. The preferred requirements document for acquiring services is a performance work statement or statement of objectives. The MFT is familiar with the Performance-Based Services Acquisition Guidebook when acquiring services.

The MFT will review Step Four under the Services Acquisition Mall. In this section of the mall, tools are provided to assist the team in creating a requirements road map, a performance work statement and statement of objectives, and a QASP. Another available tool is the Acquisition Requirements Roadmap Tool (ARRT) Suite. The Suite is a collection of tools that helps build strategic elements of acquisition documents by utilizing structured processes which help the team ask and answer the right questions related to the acquisition. The ARRT Suite includes a Requirements Definition tool, an Evaluation Factors tool, a Performance Assessment tool, and a Cost Estimation tool.

CH 10–3.2.1.2.1 Performance Work Statement (PWS) and Statement of Objectives (SOO)

There is no mandatory format for the PWS or the SOO. Follow your agency's procedures for the proper format required for these two documents. A sample format is provided under the Services Acquisition Mall. Some PWS or SOOs may require that acceptable quality levels be defined in the document.

When developing the PWS, the MFT may consider the following best practices and lessons learned:

- The purpose of defining your requirement at high level objectives and tasks is to encourage innovative solutions for your requirement. Don't specify the requirement so tightly that you get

the same solution from each offeror. If all offerors provide the same solution, there will be no creativity or innovation in the proposals.
- Remember that the way the PWS is written will either empower the private sector to craft innovative solutions, or stifle that ability.

After the MFT has completed the draft of the PWS, the team will review the PWS and answer the following questions to ensure it covers the required need:

- Does the PWS avoid specifying the number of contractor employees required to perform the work (except when absolutely necessary)?
- Does the PWS describe the outcomes (or results) rather than how to do the work?
- What constraints are placed in the PWS that restrict the contractor's ability to perform? Are they essential? Do they support the vision?
- Does the PWS avoid specifying the educational or skill level of the contract workers (except when absolutely necessary)?
- Can the contractor implement new technology to improve performance or to lower cost?
- Are commercial performance standards used?
- Do the performance standards address quantity, quality, and/or timeliness?
- Are the performance standards objectives easy to measure and timely?
- Are there incentives to motivate the contractor to improve performance or to reduce costs?
- Are there disincentives to handle poor performance?
- Will the contractor focus on continuous improvement?
- Is the assessment of quality a quantitative or qualitative assessment?
- Would two different CORs come to the same conclusion about the contractor's performance based on the performance standards objectives?
- Are AQLs clearly defined?
- Are the AQL levels realistic and achievable?
- Will the customer be satisfied if the AQL levels are exactly met? (Or will they only be satisfied at a higher quality level, or a lower level?)
- Are the individuals who will perform the evaluations identified?

CH 10–3.2.1.2.2 Quality Assurance Surveillance Plan (QASP)

The MFT will be familiar with the Quality Assurance provisions in the Federal Acquisition Regulation Part 46 and Defense Federal Acquisition Regulation Supplement Part 246, including its Procedures, Guidance and Information (PGI) Part 246, prior to developing the QASP that will be supporting the PWS or SOO.

The QASP is used to manage contractor performance by ensuring that systematic quality assurance methods validate that the contractor's quality control efforts are timely and effective and are delivering the required results. The QASP is intended to be a "living" document that should be reviewed and modified whenever necessary. The method and degree of performance assessment may change over time, depending on the level of confidence in the contractor. The premise is that the contractor, not the Government, is responsible for managing the QASP quality controls and ensuring that the performance meets the terms of the contract.

A few ways to assess a contractor's performance that can properly monitor performance and quality include:

- Methods of Surveillance: metrics, random sampling, periodic inspection, 100% inspection, customer feedback, and third party audits.
- Sampling Guide: a written procedure that states what will be checked, the AQL, and how the checking will be done.
- Decision Tables: identify different examples of unsatisfactory performance, probable cause factors, and the resulting consequences. When a service has failed to meet performance standards, a decision must be made as to who is at fault. A decision table is used for this purpose.

- Checklists: Used to record what has been checked by a sampling guide and to record information on contract items not covered by sampling.

Additional QASP information, such as the recommended document format, template, and training courses, is available on the Services Acquisition Mall Phase Four and the ACQuipedia QASP.

After the MFT completes the draft of the QASP, the team reviews the QASP and answers the following questions to ensure the required need is covered:

- Is the value of evaluating the contractor's performance on a certain task worth the cost of surveillance?
- Has customer feedback been incorporated into the QASP?
- Have assessment tools, i.e., methods of surveillance, sampling guide, etc., been provided in the QASP?

CH 10–3.2.1.2.3 Finalize Market Research Report and Develop Independent Government Cost Estimate (IGCE)

After the MFT completes the PWS and the QASP, the team compares the market research report to the actual requirements to determine if the needs to complete the mission are realistic or if changes to the market research report or requirements should be recommended. Once the analysis is complete, the market research report is finalized in accordance with agency procedures. Based on the market research results, the MFT develops the IGCE which supports the requirement.

The IGCE is the Government's independent estimate of the resources and projected cost of the resources a contractor will incur in the performance of the contract. The IGCE is very important to the acquisition strategy of the requirement. The IGCE helps determine what other policy, statue, and regulation requirements are necessary in order for this requirement to be released as a Request for Proposal. For example, the IGCE determines which Service Category Level applies and the Decision Authority.

Additional information on IGCEs is available in the Defense COR Handbook Appendix B.

CH 10–3.2.1.2.4 Services Requirements Review Board (SRRB)

Prior to moving onto Step 5 – Acquisition Strategy, the PM/ FSM is required to obtain approval from the SRRB chair as stated in Step 2 – Review Current Strategy. (Refer to Section 4 for a detailed description of the SRRB process.)

CH 10–3.2.2 Step Five – Develop Acquisition Strategy

The acquisition strategy describes the PM/ FSM's plan to achieve the execution of goals set within the service acquisition life cycle. The MFT summarizes the overall approach to acquiring services (to include the schedule, structure, risks, funding, and business strategy). The acquisition strategy document contains sufficient detail to allow senior leadership and the Service Category Decision Authority to assess whether the strategy makes good business sense, effectively implements laws and policies, and reflects management's priorities, including affordability. The strategy could evolve over time and should always reflect the current status and desired mission outcome.

The MFT will review Step Five under the Services Acquisition Mall.

The following are key outcomes of the Acquisition Strategy:

- Competition
- Small Business
- Select the appropriate contract type
- Determine a performance incentive approach
- Determine a method for selecting a contractor (Source selection approach)
- Develop appropriate planning documents

- Contracting Officer
- PM/ FSM
- Source Selection Official
- End Users, who have the technical background and investment in the requirement
- Cost/Price Analyst
- Technical Specialty such as Security, Quality Assurance

The evaluation team needs to be committed through the entire evaluation process. The DoD Source Selection Procedures, along with your agency's source selection procedures, help guide the source selection evaluation team. The Contracting Officer uses these procedures to complete Section L Instructions, conditions, and notices to offerors or respondents and M Evaluation factors for award, of the solicitation and develops the source selection plan.

CH 10–3.3.1.2 After Receipt of Proposals/Responses
The Contracting Officer gives the evaluation team complete instructions regarding the evaluation process. The Contracting Officer finalizes the award documentation, including the contract, price negotiation memorandum, and any other documents required by the FAR, DFARS and agency policy. Once the award documentation is reviewed, approved, and signed by the interested parties, the Contracting Officer announces the award within the GFE portal that was used to post the solicitation, such as FedBizOpps.

After the award is announced, the Contracting Officer may receive debrief requests within the time limit set forth in FAR Subpart 15.506, and the countdown protest period begins based on the time lines in the FAR. If there is a protest, the Contracting Officer will work with Legal, but the PM/ FSM and Evaluation Chairpersons may be asked to assist.

Once the award has been made and the protest period is over, it is time to execute the management of the services acquisition.

CH 10–3.3.2 Step Seven – Manage Performance
Once the contract is awarded, managing the performance becomes the number one duty of the PM/ FSM, COR, and the Contracting Officer, collectively known as the "administrative team." Other individuals needed to appropriately manage the performance are:

- Quality Assurance Specialist
- Contractor
- Legal
- Small Business Specialist, if a small business award

The administration performance team will review Step Seven under the Services Acquisition Mall.

CH 10–3.3.2.1 Contract Management
The Government administrative team finalizes the management plan discussed during the strategy phase. The following are finalized:

- Roles and Responsibilities of Each Team Member
- Go over and get the appropriate signatures on the COR Delegation Letter
- Conduct a post-award review, if required
- Communication plan between the team members and the SSM

The administrative team participates in the post-award conference, or kick-off meeting, which includes the awardee and all the stakeholders. During this conference, all the participating parties:

- Review the PM/ FSM performance management process
- Review each individual requirement stated in the PWS, SOW, and any attachments, update the QASP
- Ensure the incentive plan is introduced and understood by everyone
- Provide COR introductions

- Explain the Contractor Performance Assessment Reporting System (CPARS) and how it will be used to document the contractor's performance.

During the COR introductions, it is explained that the COR has administrative responsibility for the contract, but only the Contracting Officer can obligate government or change the contract terms and conditions. The COR is required to be certified for the complexity level needed for a services acquisition requirement in accordance with DoDI 5000.72, DoD Standard for Contracting Officer's Representative (COR) Certification, and the COR should perform their duties in accordance with their COR Designation Letter, the DoD COR Handbook, and any agency specific procedures.

In order to complete the transition from acquisition to performance, the contractor is incorporated into the performance management team. An essential element of performance management is open and frequent communication between the government and the contractor. Ensure the contractor clearly understands how performance is being measured to ensure there are no surprises. Characteristics of strong relationships include the following:

- Trust and open communication
- Strong leadership on both sides
- Ongoing, honest self-assessment
- Ongoing interaction via daily engagement, meetings, reports, or CPARS
- Ensuring mutual benefit or value throughout the relationship

CH 10–3.3.2.2 Performance Management

The PM/ FSM executes the performance management process discussed during the post-award conference and reviews the communication plan. Performance management includes a process for how data is collected annually, reported, and the inventory of contracted services requirements (DoDI 5000.74, Enc. 6 and CH 10–3.4. of this Chapter).

The performance management process also assesses the effectiveness of the contractor's performance against the strategy originally developed to determine if it is still achieving the required mission results. It will also identify what should be changed or modified during the next acquisition cycle to improve mission results. A record is kept identifying what improvements could be made the next time because, before you know it, it will be time to start the acquisition process all over again.

Service contracts may have performance periods lasting several years. Continuous improvement should be one of the acquisition team's goals. For example, regular meetings are planned with the contractor to identify actions both parties can take to improve efficiency. These might include the identification of significant cost drivers and what improvement actions could be taken, i.e., "should cost." Sometimes agencies require management reporting based on policy, without considering the cost of the requirement. For example, in one contract, an agency required certain reports to be delivered regularly each Friday. When asked to recommend changes, the contractor suggested the report due date be shifted to Monday because weekend processing time costs less. This type of collaborative action will set the stage for the contractor and government to work together to identify more effective and efficient ways to measure and manage the performance results over the life of the contract.

The PM/ FSM coordinates with the SSM to schedule an annual requirements review with the SRRB, and the Contracting Officer coordinates the post-award peer reviews. The post-award peer review criteria are designed to guide the administrative team focus on OUSD(AT&L) requirements.

CH 10–3.3.2.2.1 "Should Cost" Determination

"Should Cost" is a PM/ FSM's cost goal for an acquisition program, or particular activity or product within an acquisition program, developed by analyzing all the elements of the program's independent cost estimate ("will-cost estimate") and planning reasonable measures to reduce them. These specific, discrete "should-cost" initiatives are developed with prudent, cost-benefit-based considerations of associated risks, but without unacceptable reductions in the value received. A program's "should-cost" target represents what the PM/ FSM believes the program will cost if identified cost- saving initiatives are achieved.

The Acquisition of Services (DoDI 5000.74) definition of "should cost" differs from the DoDI 5000.02 "should cost" requirement.

Under an IDIQ contract, "Should cost" determinations are calculated at the task order level.

CH 10–3.3.2.3 Communications

Following the contract award, the communication plan is reviewed and a determination made for how and to whom contractor performance information is reported. It's vital to keep communication links open with both the contractor and stakeholders throughout the performance period of the contract. Establish regularly scheduled meetings with the contractor to keep everyone informed of pending actions which could impact performance. Discuss any issues the contractor may have, such as invoicing or payment problems. Identifying potential problems early is a key way to keep from having negative performance impacts. Implement the performance-reporting structure developed in Step Four.

Capturing and reporting performance information is critical for two reasons. First, it keeps your stakeholders well informed, based on actual performance results as measured by your CORs. Second, it provides documented performance trends and results to enable an open and honest discussion with the contractor concerning the results achieved. Performance reviews are held on a regular basis with both the stakeholders and contractor. The frequency of stakeholder reviews is often dictated by the importance or complexity of the service under contract. Quarterly performance reviews with stakeholders are a minimum. More complex acquisitions may require monthly reviews.

For most contracts, monthly contractor performance reviews is appropriate. For contracts of extreme importance or contracts in performance trouble, more frequent meetings may be required. During this review, the acquisition team should be asking these questions:

- Is the contractor performance meeting or exceeding the contract's performance standards?
- Are there problems or issues that we can address to mitigate risk?

There should be a time in each meeting when the agency asks, "Is there anything we are requiring that is extremely affecting your performance in terms of quality, cost, or schedule?" Actions discussed should be recorded for the convenience of all parties, with responsibilities and due dates assigned. At each review point, the QASP should be reviewed to determine if the approach to the inspection should be changed or revamped. If an objective or standard needs to be changed, it is necessary that both parties agree to any modification, however, the change may have a cost impact.

CH 10–3.4 Data Collection and Reporting

The PM/ FSM will provide input to the annual data collection requirements and reporting requirements in support of the DoD Services Acquisition Report and the annual reporting requirement under the Inventory of Services Contracts (ISC) to the senior officials and FDEs.

The PM/ FSM ensures within the performance management process that the process ensures that the required data elements needed for ISC reporting are collected. Additional information is available on the DPAP/CPIC Inventory of Services Contracts webpage.

CH 10–3.5 Information Technology

DoDI 5000.74 Enclosure 7 (DoDI 5000.74, Enc. 7, sec. 5) addresses IT Services. Services that are managed and reviewed as part of major and non-major defense acquisition programs and major and non-major IT acquisition programs; services that meet the Major Automated Information Systems thresholds (to include software as a service); or non-major programs whose primary purpose is to provide capabilities, goods, or systems in accordance with DoDI 5000.02 are exempt from DoDI 5000.74.

For more detailed guidance on to manage the IT acquisitions, refer to DAG Chapter 6, Acquisition Information Technology and Business Systems of this guidebook.

CH 10–4. Services Acquisition Reviews

CH 10–4.1 Acquisition Strategy and Peer Review

The acquisition strategy developed under Step Five shall be sent to the appropriate decision authority shown in Table 1 of the DoDI 5000.74. The guidance for the peer review is found under PGI 237.102.-76.

The decision authority is based on Acquisition of Services Categories (S-CATs). Contact the SSM to find out the decision authority for a particular service acquisition.

DFARS Subpart 201.170(a)(1) (i - iii) and (b)(1 - 3), requires peer reviews for all contracts, including services acquisitions at different dollar thresholds. DFARS Subpart and your agency policy and procedures are followed to complete this process.

CH 10–4.2 Services Requirements Review Boards (SRRBs)

Enclosure 5 (DoDI 5000.74, Enc. 5, sec. 3) of the DoDI 5000.74 addresses the critical role of requirements development, validation, and oversight in achieving a detailed understanding of where services dollars are spent and determining the appropriate investment to most efficiently meet the needs of the Warfighter. As stated in the DoDI, annual SRRBs are an important tool in the validation, optimization, and prioritization of current and future services acquisition requirements. At their core, SRRBs serve as a structured review process chaired by senior leaders to inform, assess, and support trade-off decisions regarding the cost, schedule, and performance for the acquisition of services. While SRRBs typically focus on contractor-provided services, a services requirements review also helps inform the decision to use organic capabilities (government civilians or military) vs. contracting for the required service.

There is no specific format for SRRBs, but there are, however, specific focus areas listed in the DoDI 5000.74 (DoDI 5000.74, Enc. 5, sec. 3) that allow each organization to tailor the process to meet unique missions and needs. A robust SRRB process includes, but is not limited to, the following common characteristics:

- Active leadership from both acquisition and operational chains of command
- Focus on the requirements (the need) as opposed to the contract (the means of fulfillment)
- Led by the requiring activity
- Executed at least annually; more often as needed
- Leverages multifunctional teams
- Identifies efficiencies, cost savings, and best practices

Additionally, SRRBs are most effective when the entire leadership team is present during all presentations and discussions. This provides an opportunity to hear and understand the connectivity and relative prioritization of all organizational requirements, which often leads to improved outcomes from the SRRB.

In executing SRRBs, organizations may achieve the following outcomes:

- Elimination of partial or entire non-value-added (or limited-marginal-value) contracted services capabilities
- Identification and elimination of redundant contracted capabilities
- Restructured work allocation
- Re-competing new requirements that better align to mission and marketplace
- Improved alignment of labor categories to work provided
- Opportunities for strategic sourcing of services capabilities
- Identification of inherently governmental activities not suitable for contracted services.

A major outcome of every SRRB should be a prioritized list of existing and anticipated requirements (both funded and unfunded). While every organization will have different specifics and orders of importance, all should include assessments of: